Fundamentals of Financial Institutions Management

The Irwin/McGraw-Hill Series in Finance, Insurance, and Real Estate

Stephen A. Ross
*Franco Modigliani Professor of
Financial Economics
Sloan School of Management
Massachusetts Institute of Technology
Consulting Editor*

FINANCIAL MANAGEMENT

Benninga and Sarig
Corporate Finance: A Valuation Approach

Block and Hirt
Foundations of Financial Management
Eighth Edition

Brealey and Myers
Principles of Corporate Finance
Fifth Edition

Brealey, Myers and Marcus
Fundamentals of Corporate Finance
Second Edition

Brooks
PC FinGame: The Financial Management Decision Game
Version 2.0 - DOS and Windows

Bruner
Case Studies in Finance: Managing for Corporate Value Creation
Third Edition

Chew
The New Corporate Finance: Where Theory Meets Practice
Second Edition

Grinblatt and Titman
Financial Markets and Corporate Strategy

Helfert
Techniques of Financial Analysis: A Modern Approach
Ninth Edition

Higgins
Analysis for Financial Management
Fifth Edition

Hite
A Programmed Learning Guide to Finance

Kester, Fruhan, Piper and Ruback
Case Problems in Finance
Eleventh Edition

Nunnally and Plath
Cases in Finance
Second Edition

Parker and Beaver
Risk Management: Challenges and Solutions

Ross, Westerfield and Jaffe
Corporate Finance
Fifth Edition

Ross, Westerfield and Jordan
Essentials of Corporate Finance
Second Edition

Ross, Westerfield and Jordan
Fundamentals of Corporate Finance
Fourth Edition

Schall and Haley
Introduction to Financial Management
Sixth Edition

Smith
The Modern Theory of Corporate Finance
Second Edition

White
Financial Analysis with an Electronic Calculator
Third Edition

INVESTMENTS

Ball and Kothari
Financial Statement Analysis

Bodie, Kane and Marcus
Essentials of Investments
Third Edition

Bodie, Kane and Marcus
Investments
Fourth Edition

Cohen, Zinbarg and Zeikel
Investment Analysis and Portfolio Management
Fifth Edition

Farrell
Portfolio Management: Theory and Applications
Second Edition

Hirt and Block
Fundamentals of Investment Management
Sixth Edition

Jarrow
Modeling Fixed Income Securities and Interest Rate Options

Morningstar, Inc. and Remaley
U.S. Equities OnFloppy Educational Version
Annual Edition

Shimko
The Innovative Investor
Excel Version

FINANCIAL INSTITUTIONS AND MARKETS

Cornett and Saunders
Fundamentals of Financial Institutions Management

Flannery and Flood
Flannery and Flood's ProBanker: A Financial Services Simulation

Johnson
Financial Institutions and Markets: A Global Perspective

Rose
Commercial Bank Management
Fourth Edition

Rose
Money and Capital Markets: Financial Institutions and Instruments in a Global Marketplace
Sixth Edition

Rose and Kolari
Financial Institutions: Understanding and Managing Financial Services
Fifth Edition

Santomero and Babbel
Financial Markets, Instruments, and Institutions

Saunders
Financial Institutions Management: A Modern Perspective
Second Edition

INTERNATIONAL FINANCE

Eun and Resnick
International Financial Management

Kester and Luehrman
Case Problems in International Finance
Second Edition

Levi
International Finance
Third Edition

Levich
International Financial Markets: Prices and Policies

Stonehill and Eiteman
Finance: An International Perspective

REAL ESTATE

Berston
California Real Estate Principles
Seventh Edition

Fundamentals of Financial Institutions Management

Marcia Millon Cornett

Southern Illinois University

Anthony Saunders

New York University

Boston Burr Ridge, IL Dubuque, IA Madison, WI New York San Francisco
St. Louis Bankok Bogotá Caracas Lisbon London Madrid Mexico City
Milan New Delhi Seoul Singapore Sydney Taipei Toronto

Irwin/McGraw-Hill

*A Division of The **McGraw-Hill** Companies*

FUNDAMENTALS OF FINANCIAL INSTITUTIONS MANAGEMENT

This book is printed on acid-free paper

1 2 3 4 5 6 7 8 9 0 VNH/VNH 9 3 2 1 0 9 8

ISBN 0-256-25367-6
ISBN 0-07-365511-2 (*Wall Street Journal* edition)

Vice president and editorial director: *Michael W. Junior*

Publisher: *Craig S. Beytien*

Senior sponsoring editor: *Randall Adams*

Developmental editor: *Martin D. Quinn*

Editorial assistant: *Paula M. Krauza*

Senior marketing manager: *Katie Rose-Matthews*

Project manager: *Amy Hill*

Production supervisor: *Michael R. McCormick*

Senior designer: *Crispin Prebys*

Supplement coordinator: *Cathy L. Tepper*

Compositor: *GAC Shepard Poorman Communications*

Typeface: *10/12 Times Roman*

Printer: *Von Hoffmann Press, Inc.*

LIBRARY OF CONGRESS CATALOGING-IN-PUBLICATION DATA

Cornett, Marcia.
    Fundamentals of financial institutions management/Marcia
Cornett, Anthony Saunders.
      p. cm.—(The Irwin/McGraw-Hill series in finance,
insurance, and real estate)
    Includes index.
    ISBN 0-256-25367-6
    1. Financial institutions.   I. Saunders, Anthony. II. Title.
III. Series.
HG1811.C66   1999   98-23631
332.1—dc21

http://www.mhhe.com

To the Millons and the Cornetts, especially Galen
Marcia Millon Cornett

To my father, Myer Saunders (1919–1998)
Tony Saunders

About the Authors

MARCIA MILLON CORNETT

Marcia Millon Cornett is a professor of finance at Southern Illinois University at Carbondale. She received her B.S. degree in economics from Knox College in Galesburg, Illinois, and her M.B.A. and Ph.D. in finance from Indiana University in Bloomington, Indiana. Dr. Cornett has written and published several articles in the areas of bank regulation, corporate finance, and investments. Articles authored by Dr. Cornett have appeared in such academic journals as the *Journal of Finance,* the *Journal of Money, Credit and Banking,* the *Journal of Financial Economics, Financial Management,* and the *Journal of Banking and Finance.* She is a member of the Financial Management Association, for which she currently serves as vice president for membership services; the American Finance Association, and the Western Finance Association. She also serves as an associate editor of *Financial Management* and is a member of the finance committee of the Southern Illinois University Credit Union. Dr. Cornett has also taught at the University of Colorado, Boston College, and Southern Methodist University.

ANTHONY SAUNDERS

Anthony Saunders is the John M. Schiff Professor of Finance and chair of the Department of Finance at the Stern School of Business at New York University. Professor Saunders received his Ph.D. from the London School of Economics and has taught both undergraduate and graduate level courses at NYU since 1978. Throughout his academic career, his teaching and research have specialized in financial institutions and international banking. He has served as a visiting professor all over the world, including INSEAD, the Stockholm School of Economics, and the University of Melbourne. He is currently on the executive committee of the Salomon Center for the Study of Financial Institutions, NYU.

Professor Saunders holds positions on the Board of Academic Consultants of the Federal Reserve Board of Governors and the Council of Research Advisors for the Federal National Mortgage Association. In addition, Dr. Saunders has acted as a visiting scholar at the Comptroller of the Currency and at the Federal Reserve Bank of Philadelphia. He also held a visiting position in the research department of the International Monetary Fund. He is the editor of the *Journal of Banking and Finance* and the *Journal of Financial Markets, Instruments and Institutions,* as well as the associate editor of eight other journals, including *Financial Management* and the *Journal of Money, Credit and Banking.* His research has been published in all of the major money and banking journals and in several books. In addition, he has authored or coauthored several professional books.

Contents in Brief

Table of Contents

Preface

The financial services industry is approaching full historical cycle. Originally the banking industry operated as a full service industry, performing directly or indirectly all financial services (commercial banking, investment banking, stock investing services, insurance providers, etc.). In the early 1930s the economic and industrial collapse resulted in the separation of some of these activities. In the 1970s and 1980s new, relatively unregulated financial services industries sprang up (i.e., mutual funds, brokerage funds, etc.) that separated the financial service functions even further. As we approach the turn of the century, regulatory barriers, technology, and financial innovation are changing such that a full set of financial services may again be offered by a single financial services firm. Not only are the boundaries between traditional industry sectors weakening, but competition is becoming global in nature as well.

Financial institutions are regularly in the news. We have seen a decade of mergers and acquisitions both within the commercial banking industry and between different types of financial institutions. Small community banks have more and more frequently been acquired by large national banks, and megamergers of the country's largest financial institutions are becoming commonplace. Two of the most recent examples of this are the merger of Travelers Group (an insurance company) with Citicorp (a commercial bank) for $83 billion dollars (the biggest merger of two financial institutions ever) and the merger of two commercial banks: BankAmerica and NationsBank for $60 billion (the first truly national commercial bank in the United States).

As the competitive environment changes, attention to profit and, more than ever, risk becomes increasingly important. This book offers a unique analysis of the risks faced by financial institutions (FIs) and the strategies for controlling and managing these risks. Special emphasis is also put on new areas of operations for FIs such as asset securitization, off-balance-sheet activities, and globalization of financial services.

While maintaining a risk measurement and management framework, *Fundamentals of Financial Institutions Management* provides a broader application of this important perspective. This book recognizes that financial service firms within the financial intermediation sector are evolving towards a single industry. Therefore, examining important decisions for all types of FIs is a significant focus of the coverage and examples within this book. The analytical rigor is mathematically accessible for all levels of students and balanced with a comprehensive discussion of the unique environment within which FIs operate. Important practical tools such as financial statement analysis and loan analysis will arm students with skills necessary to understand and manage a financial institution's risks in this dynamic environment. While descriptive concepts, so important to financial management (i.e., regulation, industry trends, industry characteristics, etc.) are included in the book, ample analytical techniques are included as practical tools in helping to manage a modern financial institution.

Intended Audience

Fundamentals of Financial Institutions Management is aimed at the first course in financial institutions or commercial bank management at both the undergraduate and MBA levels. While topics covered in this book are found in more sophisticated textbooks on financial institutions, the explanations and illustrations are aimed toward those with little or no practical or academic experience beyond the undergraduate level.

Main Features

Throughout the text, special features have been integrated to encourage student interaction with the text and to aid them in absorbing the material. Some of these features include:

- **Chapter-opening outlines** that offer students a snapshot view of what they can expect to learn from each chapter's discussion.
- **Bold key terms and marginal glossary** terms that emphasize the main vocabulary and concepts throughout the chapter. They emphasize the most important items and aid in studying.
- **In-chapter examples** that provide numerical demonstrations of the analytical material described in many chapters.
- **Concept questions** that allow students to test themselves on the main concepts within each major chapter section.
- **Contemporary Perspectives boxes** that demonstrate the application of chapter material to real, current events.
- **Integrative problem material** that covers all the main topics within the chapter.
- **End of Chapter Problems** that are written for varied levels of difficulty.

Organization

Since our focus is on return and risk and the sources of that return and risk in financial institutions, this book relates ways in which the managers of modern FIs can expand return with a managed level of risk to achieve the best, or most favorable, return-risk outcome for FI owners.

Chapter 1 introduces the special functions of FIs and takes an analytical look at how financial intermediation benefits today's economy. Chapter 2 presents an overview of the domestic and foreign financial markets. We describe the different financial markets, the securities traded in them, and how changes in interest rates, inflation, and foreign exchange rates impact the FI managers' decisions to hedge risk in the various markets.

Chapters 3 through 7 provide an overview describing the key characteristics and regulatory features of the major sectors of the U.S. financial services industry. We discuss depository institutions in Chapter 3, insurance institutions in Chapter 4, securities firms and investment banks in Chapter 5, finance companies in Chapter 6, and mutual fund firms in Chapter 7.

Chapter 8 describes the financial statements of a typical financial institution and the ratios used to analyze those statements. This chapter also goes through the financial analysis of actual financial statements for representative financial institutions.

In Chapter 9, we preview the risk-measurement and management sections with an overview of the risks facing a modern FI. We divide the chapters on risk measurement and management into two sections: measuring and managing risk on the balance sheet, and managing risk off the balance sheet.

In Chapter 10, we begin the on-balance-sheet risk measurement and management section by looking at the measurement of credit risk on individual loans and bonds and how this risk adversely impacts an FI's profits through losses and provisions against the loan and debt security portfolio. This chapter includes a detailed analysis of the lending process, including a description of differences in the process for various types of loan customers from small households to large corporations. In Chapter 11, we look at the risk of loan (asset) portfolios and the effects of loan concentrations on risk exposure. Chapter 12 explores two ways of removing credit risk from the loan portfolio: loan sales and asset securitization.

In Chapters 13 and 14, we look at ways in which FIs can insulate themselves from liquidity risk. In Chapter 15, we look at the key role deposit insurance and other guaranty schemes play in reducing liquidity risk. At the core of FI risk insulation is the size and adequacy of the owner's capital stake, which is the focus of Chapter 16.

In Chapters 17 and 18, we investigate the net interest margin as a source of profitability and risk, with a focus on the effects of interest rate volatility and the mismatching of asset and liability maturities on FI risk exposure. In Chapter 19, we finish off the section of on-balance-sheet risk management by analyzing market risk, a risk that results when FIs actively trade bonds, equities, and foreign exchange.

The management of risk off the balance sheet is examined in Chapters 20 through 23. Chapter 20 first provides an overview of the off-balance-sheet activities of the modern FI. These chapters highlight various new markets and instruments that have been innovated or engineered to allow FIs to better manage three important types of risk: interest rate risk, foreign exchange risk, and credit risk. These markets and instruments and their strategic use by FIs include futures and forwards (Chapter 21); options, caps, floors, and collars (Chapter 22); and swaps (Chapter 23).

Modern FIs do more than generate returns and bear risk through traditional maturity mismatching and credit extensions. They also are increasingly engaging in making technological investments to reduce costs (Chapter 24), pursuing both product and geographic diversification opportunities (Chapters 25 and 26), pursuing foreign exchange activities and overseas financial investments (Chapter 27), and engaging in sovereign lending and securities activities (Chapter 28). Each of these has implications for the size and variability of an FI's profits. These issues are examined in the final section of the book.

Ancillaries

To assist in course preparation, the following ancillaries are offered:

- The **Instructor's Manual** includes detailed chapter contents, additional examples for use in the classroom, and complete solutions to end-of-chapter question and problem materials.
- The **Test Bank** includes over 850 additional problems to be used for test material.
- The **Study Guide** provides a chapter summary, conceptual outline, and an applications section that includes definitional, conceptual, and quantitative problems for each chapter. Detailed solutions explain how answers were derived.

ACKNOWLEDGMENTS

We would like to thank Professor Hugh A. Thomas for allowing us to incorporate his material on Credit Analysis in Chapter 10 of the textbook. We would also like to thank Linda K. Frasier who prepared the draft manuscript of the textbook. Finally, we would like to thank a number of colleagues who assisted with the first edition of this textbook, as well as editions of Anthony Saunders' graduate level book, from which this textbook was conceived. These colleagues include:

Samuel Bulmash, *University of South Florida*

Paul Bursik, *St. Norbert's College*

Bruce Cochran, *San Jose State University*

Steve Cole, *University of North Texas*

Ken Cyree, *Bryant College*

Gayle DeLong, *New York University*

Anne Gleason, *University of Central Oklahoma*

Alan Grunewald, *Michigan State University*

John Hall, *University of Arkansas at Little Rock*

John Hall, *University of Missouri–Columbia*

John Halloran, *University of Notre Dame*

Sylvia Hudgins, *Old Dominion University*

Mel Jameson, *University of Nevada–Las Vegas*

Thomas Liaw, *St. John's University*

James McNulty, *Florida Atlantic University*

Roger Stover, *Iowa State University*

Ernest Swift, *Georgia State University*

Lankford Walker, *Eastern Illinois University*

John Wagster, *Wayne State University*

Jill Wetmore, *Saginaw Valley State University*

who reviewed this textbook. Victor Abraham of the University of California at Los Angeles served as error checker. Ray Gorman of Miami University wrote the testbank and end-of-chapter materials. Ken Cyree of Bryant College prepared the instructor's manual, and Sylvia Hudgins of Old Dominion University prepared the study guide.

We would also like to acknowledge our book team at McGraw-Hill: Shelly Kronzek, Associate Editor; Marty Quinn, Development Editor; Paula Krauza, Editorial Assistant; Craig Beytien, Publisher; Amy Hill, Project Manager; Cathy Tepper, Supplements Coordinator; Crispin Prebys, Designer; and Katie Rose-Matthews, Senior Marketing Manager.

Marcia Millon Cornett
Anthony Saunders

Section One

Introduction

Chapter One

Why Are Financial Intermediaries Special?

The major themes of this book are the measurement and management of the risks of financial intermediaries (FIs). In particular, although we might categorize or group FIs as life insurance companies, banks, finance companies, and so on, they face common risks. Specifically, all FIs described in this chapter and Chapters 3 through 7 (1) hold some assets that are potentially subject to default or credit risk and (2) tend to mismatch the maturities of their balance sheets' assets and liabilities to a greater or lesser extent and are thus exposed to interest rate risk. Moreover, all are exposed to some degree of saver withdrawal or liquidity risk, depending on the type of claims they have sold to liability holders. In addition, most FIs are exposed to some type of underwriting risk, whether through the sale of securities or the issue of various types of credit guarantees on or off the balance sheet. Finally, all FIs are exposed to operating cost risks because the production of financial services requires the

---

Table 1–1

AREAS OF FINANCIAL INTERMEDIARIES' SPECIALNESS IN THE PROVISION OF SERVICES

Information Costs   The aggregation of funds in an FI provides greater incentive to collect a firm's information and monitor its actions. The relatively large size of the FI allows this collection of information to be accomplished at a lower average cost (so-called economies of scale).

Liquidity and Price Risk   FIs provide financial claims to household savers with superior liquidity attributes and with lower price risk.

Transaction Cost Services   Similar to economies of scale in information production costs, an FI's size can result in economies of scale in transaction costs.

Maturity Intermediation   FIs can better bear the risk of mismatching the maturities of their assets and liabilities.

Money Supply Transmission   Depository institutions are the conduit through which monetary policy actions impact the rest of the financial system and the economy in general.

Credit Allocation   FIs are often viewed as the major, and sometimes only, source of financing for a particular sector of the economy, such as farming and residential real estate.

Intergenerational Wealth Transfers   FIs, especially life insurance companies and pension funds, provide savers the ability to transfer wealth from one generation to the next.

Payment Services   The efficiency with which depository institutions provide payment services directly benefits the economy.

Denomination Intermediation   FIs, such as mutual funds, allow small investors to overcome constraints to buying assets imposed by large minimum denomination size.

---

use of real resources and back-office support systems (labor and technology combined to provide services).

Because of these risks and the special role that FIs play in the financial system, FIs are singled out for special regulatory attention.[1] In this chapter, we first examine questions related to this specialness in general: What are the special functions that FIs—both depository institutions (banks, savings and loans, and credit unions) and nondepository institutions (insurance companies, securities firms, investment banks, finance companies, and mutual funds)—provide? How do these functions benefit the economy? These areas of specialness are summarized in Table 1–1. Second, we investigate what makes some FIs more special than others. Third, we look at how unique and long-lived the special functions of FIs really are.

---

[1] Some public utility suppliers such as gas, electric, telephone, and water companies are also singled out for regulation because of the special nature of their services and the costs imposed on society if they fail.

FINANCIAL INTERMEDIARIES'
SPECIALNESS

To understand the important economic function that FIs play, imagine a simple world in which they do not exist. In such a world, households generating excess savings by consuming less than they earn would have a basic choice: They could hold cash as an asset or invest it in the securities issued by corporations. In general, corporations issue securities to finance their investments in real assets and to cover the gap between their investment plans and their internally generated savings such as retained earnings. As shown in Figure 1–1, in such a world savings would flow from households to corporations; in return, financial claims (equity and debt securities) would flow from corporations to household savers. The same argument can be made to explain how FIs are essential in accommodating households and small businesses in need of funds.

In an economy without FIs, the level of fund flows between the household saver and the corporate sectors is likely to be quite low. There are several reasons for this. Once they have lent money to a firm by buying its financial claims, households need to monitor or check the firm's actions. They must be sure that its management neither absconds with nor wastes the funds on any projects that have low or negative net present values. Such monitoring actions are extremely costly for any given household because they require considerable time and expense to collect sufficiently high-quality information relative to the size of the average household saver's investment. Given this, each household likely would prefer to leave the monitoring to others; in the end, each household would do little or no monitoring. The resulting lack of monitoring would reduce the attractiveness and increase the risk of investing in corporate debt and equity.

covenants

Legal clauses in a bond contract that require the issuer of bonds to take or avoid certain actions.

In the real world, bondholders partially alleviate these problems by requiring restrictive clauses or **covenants** in bond contracts. Such covenants restrict the risk level of projects that a firm's management can undertake. Bondholders also hire bond trustees to oversee compliance with these covenants. However, the enforcement and monitoring of covenants are still quite costly, especially if the debt is long term and renewed infrequently.

The relatively long-term nature of corporate equity and debt creates a second disincentive for household investors to hold the direct financial claims issued by corporations. Specifically, given the choice between holding cash and long-term securities, the households may well choose to hold cash for **liquidity** reasons, especially if they plan to use savings to finance consumption expenditures in the near future.

liquidity

The ease with which an asset can be converted into cash.

price risk

The risk that an asset's sale price will be lower than its purchase price.

Finally, even though real-world financial markets provide some liquidity services by allowing households to trade corporate debt and equity securities among themselves, investors face a **price risk** upon the sale of securities, and the secondary market trading of securities involves various transaction costs. That is, the price at which household investors can sell securities on secondary markets such as the New York Stock Exchange (NYSE) may well differ from the price they initially paid for the securities.

Figure **1–1** *Flow of Funds in a World Without FIs*

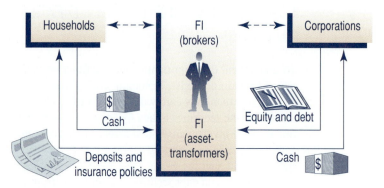

F i g u r e **1–2**   *Flow of Funds in a World with FIs*

Because of (1) monitoring costs, (2) liquidity costs, and (3) price risk, the average household saver may view direct investment in corporate securities as an unattractive proposition and prefer either not to save or to save in the form of cash.

However, the economy has developed an alternative and indirect way to channel household savings to the corporate sector. This is to channel savings via FIs. Due to the costs of monitoring, liquidity, and price risk, as well as for some other reasons explained later, savers often prefer to hold the financial claims issued by FIs rather than those issued by corporations. Consider Figure 1–2, which is a closer representation than Figure 1–1 of the world in which we live and the way funds flow in our economy. Notice how financial intermediaries or institutions are standing, or intermediating, between the household and corporate sectors. We discuss the technical details of the markets in which this occurs in Chapter 2.

These intermediaries fulfill two functions; any given FI might specialize in one or the other or both. The first function is brokerage. When acting as a pure broker, an FI acts as an agent for the saver in providing information and transaction services. For example, full-service securities firms (e.g., Merrill Lynch) carry out investment research and make investment recommendations for their retail (or household) clients as well as conduct the purchase or sale of securities for commission fees. Discount brokers (e.g., Charles Schwab) purchase or sell securities at better prices and with greater efficiency than household savers could achieve by trading on their own. This efficiency results in reduced costs of trading, or **economies of scale** (see Chapter 25 for a detailed discussion). Independent insurance brokers identify the best types of insurance policies that household savers can buy to fit their retirement plans. In fulfilling a brokerage function, the FI plays an extremely important role by reducing transaction and information costs or imperfections between households and corporations. Thus, the FI encourages a higher rate of savings than would exist otherwise.

The second function is asset transformation. In acting as an **asset transformer,** the FI issues financial claims far more attractive to household savers than the claims that corporations issue directly. That is, for many households, the financial claims issued by FIs dominate those issued directly by corporations due to lower monitoring costs, lower liquidity costs, and lower price risk (i.e., economies of scale). In acting as asset transformers, FIs purchase the financial claims issued by corporations—equities, bonds, and other debt claims called **primary securities** issued directly by the corporation in exchange for funds—and finance these purchases by selling financial claims to household investors and

economies of scale

The concept that cost reduction in trading and other transaction services results from increased efficiency when FIs perform these services.

asset transformer

Financial claims issued by an FI that are more attractive to household savers than are the claims directly issued by corporations.

primary securities

Financial obligations issued by corporations and backed by the real assets of those corporations.

Table **1–2**

SIMPLIFIED COMMERCIAL FIRM AND FI BALANCE SHEETS

Commercial Firm		Financial Intermediary	
Assets	**Liabilities**	**Assets**	**Liabilities**
Real assets (plant, machinery)	Primary securities (debt, equity)	Primary securities (debt, equity)	Secondary securities (deposits and insurance policies)

secondary securities

Financial obligations issued by FIs and backed by primary securities.

other sectors in the form of deposits, insurance policies, and so on. The financial claims of FIs may be considered **secondary securities** because these assets are backed by the primary securities issued by commercial corporations that in turn invest in real assets. Thus, these financial claims serve as indirect investments in the issuing corporation.

Simplified balance sheets of a commercial firm and an FI are shown in Table 1–2. Note that in the real world, FIs hold a small proportion of their assets in the form of real assets such as bank branch buildings. These simplified balance sheets reflect a reasonably accurate characterization of the operational differences between commercial firms and FIs.

How can FIs purchase the direct or primary securities issued by corporations and profitably transform them into secondary securities more attractive to household savers? This question strikes at the very heart of what makes FIs special and important to the economy. The answer lies in FIs' ability to reduce the three costs facing the saver who chooses to invest directly in corporate securities.

Information Costs

agency costs

The risk that owners and managers of firms receiving savers' funds will take actions with those funds contrary to the best interests of the savers.

delegated monitor

An economic agent appointed to act on behalf of smaller agents in collecting information and/or investing funds on their behalf.

One problem that an average saver directly investing in a commercial firm's financial claims faces is the high cost of information collection. Household savers must monitor firms' actions in a timely and complete fashion after purchasing securities. Failure to monitor exposes investors to **agency costs,** that is, the risk that the firm's owners or managers would take actions with the saver's money that are contrary to the promises contained in the covenants of its securities contracts. One solution to this problem is for a large number of small savers to place their funds with a single FI. This FI groups these funds together and invests them in the direct or primary financial claims issued by firms. This aggregation of funds resolves a number of problems. First, the large FI now has a much greater incentive to collect information and monitor the firm's actions because the FI has far more at stake than any small individual household. This alleviates the free-rider problem that exists when small household savers leave it to each other to collect information and monitor firms' actions. In a sense, small savers have appointed the FI as a **delegated monitor** to act on their behalf. Not only does the FI have a greater incentive to collect information, but also the average cost of collecting information is lower (i.e., information collection enjoys economies of scale). For example, a small investor's cost of buying a $100 broker's report may seem inordinately high for a $10,000 investment. For an FI with $10 million under management, however, the cost seems trivial. Such economies of scale of information production and collection tend to enhance the advantages to savers of using FIs rather than directly investing themselves.

Second, associated with the greater incentive to monitor and the costs involved in failing to monitor appropriately, FIs may develop new secondary securities that enable them to monitor more effectively. Thus, a richer menu of contracts may improve FIs' monitoring abilities. Perhaps the classic example of this is the bank loan. Bank loans are generally shorter-term debt contracts than bond contracts. This short-term nature allows the FI to exercise more monitoring power and control over the borrower. In particular, the information the FI generates regarding the firm is frequently updated as it makes its loan renewal decisions. When bank loan contracts are sufficiently short term, the banker becomes almost like an insider to the firm regarding informational familiarity with its operations and financial conditions. Indeed, this more frequent monitoring often replaces the need for the relatively inflexible and hard-to-enforce covenants found in bond contracts. Contemporary Perspectives Box 1–1, in fact, points out that not only do borrowing firms' stock prices generally react favorably around new loan and loan renewal announcements but also that the magnitude of the reaction is significantly related to the reputation of the lender. Moreover, by acting as partial corporate insiders and sending favorable information signals regarding the firm and its performance through bank loan renewals, the holders of outside debt and equity (such as traditional corporate securities) also benefit by acting on this information, as can firms that are then able to issue their securities at a lower cost. Thus, by acting as a delegated monitor and producing better and more timely information,

Contemporary Perspectives 1–1

The Effect of Lender Identity on a Borrowing Firm's Equity Return

Previous studies show that certain types of loan announcements generate significantly positive abnormal returns to the average borrower's equity. . . . Mikkelson and Partch (1986) first discovered that bank credit line announcements generate positive abnormal borrower returns. . . . James (1987) focuses directly on the announcement effects of bank loans and private placements, comparing them to public debt financing. For a sample of 80 bank loans, James reports a significant . . . average borrower abnormal return of 1.93 percent. . . . Preece and Mullineaux (1994) also test whether lender identity matters. Examining a sample of 439 short-term loan contracts, they find significantly positive borrower returns for loans from commercial banks, independent finance companies, and nonbank subsidiaries of bank holding companies. Lummer and McConnell (1989) distinguish

new bank loans from renewals that occurred within an existing bank relationship. Their sample's new loans generate a zero average abnormal return, while their renewals exhibit a strong and significant positive return. . . .

Why might the lender's identity matter? A lender's identity may convey information to outside equity investors in two ways. First, the lender might be known to prefer certain risk classes of private debt. If lenders obtain *private information* in the process of underwriting loans, their lending decisions would then convey valuable information about a borrower's true risk. This perspective resembles the notion that credit rating agencies can provide valuable information to outside investors, via their access to inside information or their unique ability to evaluate publicly available information. . . . Second, lenders may have different

monitoring abilities, which enhance a borrower's value by assuring that appropriate investment and spending decisions are implemented. . . .

Our analysis reconfirms that, unlike public debt issuances, private loan announcements are associated with positive borrower returns. Both bank and nonbank loans generate positive borrower abnormal returns, although we cannot reject the hypothesis that the means of these returns are identical. We do, however, find strong evidence that higher quality lenders are associated with significantly higher abnormal returns to the borrower's stock, even after controlling for borrower characteristics. This is consistent with the notion that an announced loan from a "good" banking firm conveys more positive information about the borrower's prospects than would a loan from a "mediocre" bank.

SOURCE: Matthew T. Billett, Mark J. Flannery, and Jon A. Garfinkel, *Journal of Finance*, June 1995, p. 699.

FIs reduce the degree of information imperfection and asymmetry between the ultimate sources and users of funds in the economy.

Liquidity and Price Risk

In addition to improving the flow and quality of information, FIs provide financial or secondary claims to household savers. Often these claims have liquidity attributes that are superior to those of primary securities such as corporate equity and bonds. For example, banks and thrift institutions (e.g., savings and loans) issue transaction account deposit contracts with a fixed principal value (and often a guaranteed interest rate) that can be withdrawn immediately on demand by household savers. Money market mutual funds issue shares to household savers that allow them to enjoy almost fixed principal (depositlike) contracts while often earning higher interest rates than bank deposits. Even life insurance companies allow policyholders to borrow against their policies held with the company at very short notice. The real puzzle is how FIs such as depository institutions can offer highly liquid and low price-risk contracts to savers on the liability side of their balance sheets while investing in relatively illiquid and higher price-risk securities issued by corporations on the asset side. Furthermore, how can FIs be confident enough to guarantee that they can provide liquidity services to investors and savers when they themselves invest in risky asset portfolios? Why should savers and investors believe FIs' promises regarding the liquidity of their investments?

diversify

The ability of an economic agent to reduce risk by holding a number of securities in a portfolio.

The answers to these questions lie in FIs' ability to **diversify** away some but not all of their portfolio risks. The concept of diversification is familiar to all students of finance. Basically, as long as the returns on different investments are not perfectly *positively* correlated, by exploiting the benefits of size, FIs diversify away significant amounts of portfolio risk—especially the risk specific to the individual firm issuing any given security. (We discuss the mechanics of diversification in the loan portfolio in Chapter 11.) Indeed, experiments in the United States and the United Kingdom have shown that diversifying across just 15 securities can bring significant diversification benefits to FIs and portfolio managers.[2] Further, as the number of securities in an FI's asset portfolio increases, portfolio risk falls, albeit at a diminishing rate. What is really going on here is that FIs exploit the law of large numbers in their investments, whereas due to their small size, many household savers are constrained to holding relatively undiversified portfolios. This risk diversification allows an FI to predict more accurately its expected return on its asset portfolio. A domestically and globally diversified FI may be able to generate an almost risk-free return on its assets. As a result, it can credibly fulfill its promise to households to supply highly liquid claims with little price or capital value risk. A good example of this is a bank's ability to offer highly liquid demand deposits—with a fixed principal value—as liabilities while investing in risky loans as assets. As long as an FI is sufficiently large to gain from diversification and monitoring, its financial claims are likely to be viewed as liquid and attractive to small savers when compared to direct investments in the capital market. The smaller and the less diversified an FI becomes, the less able it is to credibly promise household savers that its financial claims are highly liquid and of low capital risk. Specifically, the less diversified the FI, the higher the probability that it will default on its liability

---

[2] For a review of such studies, see E. J. Elton and M. J. Gruber, *Modern Portfolio Theory and Investment Analysis*, 5th ed. (New York: John Wiley, 1995), chapter 2.

obligations and the riskier and more illiquid its claims will be. In reality, small FIs that are relatively undiversified productwise and geographically experience the majority of financial institution failures. For example, widespread failures of small US banks, thrifts, and insurance companies occurred in the Southwest during the slump in oil and gas prices in the 1980s.[3]

Other Special Services

The preceding discussion has concentrated on three general or special services provided by FIs: reducing household savers' monitoring costs, increasing their liquidity, and reducing their price-risk exposure. Next we discuss two other special services provided by FIs: reduced transaction costs and maturity intermediation or asset transformation.

Reduced Transaction Cost.   FIs provide potential economies of scale in information collection and in transaction costs. For example, since May 1, 1975, fixed commissions for equity trades on the NYSE have been abolished. As a result, small retail buyers face higher commission charges or transaction costs than do large wholesale buyers. By grouping their assets in FIs that purchase assets in bulk—such as in mutual funds and pension funds—household savers can reduce the transaction costs of their asset purchases. In addition, bid-ask (buy-sell) spreads are normally lower for assets bought and sold in large numbers.

Maturity Intermediation.   An additional dimension of FIs' ability to reduce risk by diversification is that they are more able to bear the risk of mismatching the maturities of their assets and liabilities than are small household savers. Thus, FIs offer maturity intermediation services to the rest of the economy. Specifically, by maturity mismatching, FIs can produce new types of contracts, such as long-term mortgage loans to households, while still raising funds with short-term liability contracts. In addition, although such mismatches can subject an FI to interest rate risk (see Chapters 17 and 18), a large FI is better able than a small one to manage this risk through its superior access to markets and instruments for hedging such as loan sales and securitization (Chapter 12), futures (Chapter 21), swaps (Chapter 23), and options (Chapter 22).

Concept Questions

1. What are the three major risks to household savers from direct security purchases?
2. What is the asset transformation function of FIs?
3. What are primary securities and secondary securities?
4. What is the delegated monitor function that FIs perform?
5. What is the link between asset diversification and the liquidity of deposit contracts?
6. What is maturity intermediation?

---

[3] Nevertheless, in the 1980s, 9 of the 10 largest banking organizations in Texas also had to be closed, merged, or reorganized, in large part because of their undiversified exposures to the heavily oil- and gas-dependent Texas economy.

OTHER ASPECTS
OF SPECIALNESS

The theory of the flow of funds discussed in the previous section points to three principal reasons for believing that FIs are special (reduced monitoring costs, increased liquidity, and reduced price-risk exposure), along with two other associated reasons (reduced transaction costs and maturity intermediation). In reality, academics, policymakers, and regulators identify other areas of specialness relating to certain specific functions of FIs or groups of FIs. We discuss these next.

The Transmission of Monetary Policy

The highly liquid nature of bank and thrift deposits has resulted in their acceptance by the public as the most widely used medium of exchange in the economy. As the notes to Table 1–3 indicate, at the core of the three most commonly used definitions of the money supply—M1, M2, and M3—lie bank and/or thrift deposit contracts. Because the liabilities of depository institutions are a significant component of the money supply that impacts the rate of inflation, depository institutions—particularly commercial banks—play a key role in the *transmission of monetary policy* from the central bank to the rest of the economy. That is, depository institutions are the conduit through which monetary policy actions impact the rest of the financial sector and the economy in general.

Credit Allocation

An additional reason for viewing FIs as special is that they are the major, and sometimes only, source of financing for a particular sector of the economy preidentified as being in special need of financing. Policymakers in the United States and a number of other countries such as the United Kingdom have identified *residential real estate* as needing special subsidies. This has enhanced the specialness of FIs that most commonly service the needs of that sector. In the United States, savings and loans (S&Ls) and savings banks have traditionally served the credit needs of the residential real estate sector. In a similar fashion, farming is an especially important area of the economy in terms of the overall social welfare of the population. The US government has even directly encouraged financial institutions to specialize in financing this area of activity through the creation of Federal Farm Credit Banks.

Intergenerational Wealth Transfers or Time Intermediation

The ability of savers to transfer wealth from their youth to their old age and across generations is also of great importance to a country's social well-being. Because of this, special taxation relief and other subsidy mechanisms often encourage life insurance and pension funds to service and accommodate these needs.

Payment Services

Depository institutions such as banks and thrifts are special in that the efficiency with which they provide payment services directly benefits the economy. Two important payment services are check-clearing and wire transfer services. For example, on any given

Table **1-3**

MONEY STOCK, LIQUID ASSETS, AND DEBT MEASURES

(billions of dollars, averages of daily figures, seasonally adjusted)

| Measures | December | | | | | | July |
	1991	1992	1993	1994	1995	1996	1997
M1	897.7	1,024.8	1,128.4	1,148.7	1,124.8	1,081.1	1,062.1
M2	3,455.2	3,509.0	3,567.9	3,509.0	3,657.4	3,834.5	3,931.7
M3	4,180.4	4,183.0	4,232.0	4,319.4	4,572.4	4,933.2	5,145.5
L	4,992.9	5,057.1	5,135.0	5,303.4	5,681.9	6,098.8	6,342.2
Debt	11,171.1	11,706.1	12,335.4	13,153.2	13,866.9	14,485.7	14,840.0

NOTES: Composition of the money stock measures and debt is as follows:

M1: (1) currency outside the US Treasury, Federal Reserve Banks, and the vaults of depository institutions, (2) travelers checks of nonbank issuers, (3) demand deposits at all commercial banks other than those owed to depository institutions, the US government, and foreign banks and official institutions, less cash items in the process of collection and Federal Reserve float, and (4) other checkable deposits (OCDs), consisting of negotiable order of withdrawal (NOW) and automatic transfer service (ATS) accounts at depository institutions, credit union share draft accounts, and demand deposits at thrift institutions.

M2: M1 plus (1) overnight (and continuing contract) repurchase agreements (RPs) issued by all depository institutions and overnight Eurodollars issued to US residents by foreign branches of US banks worldwide, (2) savings (including money market deposit accounts [MMDAs]) and small time deposits (time deposits—including retail RPs—in amounts of less than $100,000), and (3) balances in both taxable and tax-exempt general-purpose and broker-dealer money market funds. Excludes individual retirement accounts (IRAs) and Keogh balances at depository institutions and money market funds.

M3: M2 plus (1) large time deposits and term RP liabilities (in amounts of $100,000 or more) issued by all depository institutions, (2) term Eurodollars held by US residents at foreign branches of US banks worldwide and at all banking offices in the United Kingdom and Canada, and (3) balances in both taxable and tax-exempt, institution-only money market funds.

L: M3 plus the nonbank public holdings of US savings bonds, short-term Treasury securities, commercial paper, and bankers acceptances, net of money market fund holdings of these assets.

Debt: The debt aggregate is the outstanding credit market debt of the domestic nonfinancial sectors—the federal sector (US government, not including government-sponsored enterprises or federally related mortgage pools) and the nonfederal sectors (state and local governments, households and nonprofit organizations, nonfinancial corporate and nonfarm noncorporate businesses, and farms).

SOURCE: *Federal Reserve Bulletin,* November 1997, Table A12, (Washington D.C.: Publication Services.)

day, approximately $2 trillion of payments is effected through Fedwire and CHIPS, the two large wholesale payment wire networks in the United States. Any breakdowns in these systems would likely produce gridlock to the payment system with resulting harmful effects to the economy.

Denomination Intermediation

Both money market and debt-equity mutual funds are special because they provide services relating to denomination intermediation. Because they are sold in very large denominations, many assets are either out of reach of individual savers or would result in savers holding highly undiversified asset portfolios. For example, the minimum size of a negotiable CD is $100,000; commercial paper (short-term corporate debt) is often sold in minimum packages of $250,000 or more. Individual savers may be unable to purchase such instruments. However, by buying shares in a money market mutual fund with other small investors, household savers overcome the constraints to buying assets imposed by large minimum denomination sizes. Such indirect access to these markets may allow small savers to generate higher returns on their portfolios as well.

Concept Questions

1. Why does the need for denomination intermediation arise?
2. What are the two major sectors that society has identified as deserving special attention in credit allocation?
3. Why is monetary policy transmitted through the banking system?
4. What payment services do FIs perform?

SPECIALNESS AND REGULATION

The preceding section showed that FIs are special because they provided various services to sectors of the economy. The general areas of FI specialness include the following:

- Information services.
- Liquidity services.
- Price-risk reduction services.
- Transaction cost services.
- Maturity intermediation services.

Areas of institution-specific specialness are as follows:

- Money supply transmission (banks).
- Credit allocation (thrifts, farm banks).
- Intergenerational transfers (pension funds, life insurance companies).
- Payment services (banks, thrifts).
- Denomination intermediation (mutual funds, pension funds).

negative externality

An action by an economic agent that imposes costs on other economic agents.

redlining

The procedure by which a banker refuses to make loans to residents living inside given geographic boundaries.

Failure to provide these services or a breakdown in their efficient provision can be costly to both the ultimate sources (households) and users (firms) of savings. The **negative externalities**[4] affecting firms and households when something goes wrong in the FI sector of the economy make a case for regulation. For example, bank failures may destroy household savings and at the same time restrict a firm's access to credit. Insurance company failures may leave households totally exposed in old age to catastrophic illnesses and sudden drops in income on retirement. In addition, individual FI failures may create doubts in savers' minds regarding the stability and solvency of FIs in general and cause panics and even runs on sound institutions. In addition, racial, sexual, age, or other discrimination—such as mortgage **redlining**—may unfairly exclude some potential financial service consumers from the marketplace. This type of market failure needs to be corrected by regulation.

[4] A good example of a negative externality is the cost to small businesses in a one-bank town should the local bank fail. These businesses could find it difficult to obtain financing elsewhere, and their customers may be similarly disadvantaged. As a result, the failure of the bank may have a negative or contagious effect on the economic prospects of the whole community, resulting in lower sales, production, and employment.

T a b l e **1-4**

AREAS OF FI SPECIALNESS IN REGULATION

Safety and Soundness Regulation   Layers of regulation have been imposed on FIs to protect depositors and borrowers against the risk of failure.

Monetary Policy Regulation   Regulators control and implement monetary policy by requiring minimum levels of cash reserves to be held against depository institution deposits.

Credit Allocation Regulation   Regulations support the FI's lending to socially important sectors, such as housing and farming.

Consumer Protection Regulation   Regulations are imposed to prevent the FI's ability to discriminate unfairly in lending.

Investor Protection Regulation   Laws protect investors who directly purchase securities and/or indirectly purchase securities by investing in mutual or pension funds.

Entry and Chartering Regulation   Entry and activity regulations limit the number of FIs in any given financial services sector, thus impacting the charter values of FIs operating in that sector.

Six types of regulation seek to enhance the net social welfare benefits of financial intermediaries' services. These are (1) safety and soundness regulation, (2) monetary policy regulation, (3) credit allocation regulation, (4) consumer protection regulation, (5) investor protection regulation, and (6) entry and chartering regulation. These regulations are summarized in Table 1–4. Regulation can be imposed at the federal or the state level and occasionally at the international level, as in the case of bank capital requirements (see Chapter 16).

Safety and Soundness Regulation

To protect depositors and borrowers against the risk of FI failure due, for example, to a lack of diversification in asset portfolios, regulators have developed layers of protective mechanisms, illustrated in Figure 1–3. Requirements encouraging FIs to diversify their assets are in the first layer of protection. Thus, banks are prohibited from making loans exceeding more than 15 percent of their own equity capital funds to any one company or borrower. A bank that has 6 percent of its assets funded by its own capital (and therefore 94 percent by deposits) can lend no more than 0.9 percent of its assets to any one party (i.e., 15 percent of 6 percent).

   The second layer of protection concerns the minimum level of capital or equity funds that the owners of an FI need to contribute to the funding of its operations. For example, bank, thrift, and insurance regulators are concerned with the minimum ratio of capital to (risk) assets. The higher the proportion of capital contributed by owners, the greater is the protection against insolvency risk to outside liability claimholders such as depositors and insurance policyholders. This occurs because losses on the asset portfolio due, for example, to the lack of diversification are legally borne by the equity holder first and then only after equity is totally wiped out by outside liability holders.[5] Consequently, by varying the required degree of equity capital, FI regulators can directly affect the degree of risk exposure faced by nonequity claimholders in FIs. (See Chapter 16 for more discussion on the role of capital in FIs.)

---

[5] Thus, equity holders are junior claimants and debt holders senior claimants to an FI's assets.

Diversify Assets

Loans   Investments   Cash

Guarantee Funds

Hold Sufficient Capital

Regulate by
Monitoring and Surveillance

F i g u r e **1–3**   *Layers of Regulation*

The third layer of protection is the provision of guaranty funds such as the Bank Insurance Fund (BIF) for banks, the Savings Association Insurance Fund (SAIF) for savings and loans, the Security Investors Protection Corporation (SIPC) for securities firms, and the state guaranty funds established (with regulator encouragement) to meet insolvency losses to small claimholders in the life and property-casualty insurance industries. By protecting FI claimholders when an FI collapses and owners' equity or net worth is wiped out, these funds create a demand for regulation of the insured institutions to protect the funds' resources (see Chapter 15 for more discussion). For example, the Federal Deposit Insurance Corporation (FDIC) monitors and regulates participants in both BIF and SAIF.

The fourth layer of regulation involves monitoring and surveillance. Regulators subject all FIs—whether banks, securities firms, or insurance companies—to varying degrees of monitoring and surveillance. This involves on-site examination of the FI by regulators as well as the FI's production of accounting statements and reports on a timely basis for off-site evaluation. Just as savers appoint FIs as delegated monitors to evaluate the behavior and actions of ultimate borrowers, society appoints regulators to monitor the behavior and performance of FIs.

Finally, note that regulation is not without costs for those regulated. For example, society's regulators may require FIs to have more equity capital than private owners believe is in their own best interests. Similarly, producing the information requested by regulators is costly for FIs because it involves the time of managers, lawyers, and accountants. Again, the socially optimal amount of information may differ from an FI's privately optimal amount.

net regulatory burden

The difference between the private costs of regulations and the private benefits for the producers of financial services.

Although regulation may be socially beneficial, it imposes private costs, or a regulatory burden, on individual FI owners and managers. Consequently, regulation attempts to enhance the social welfare benefits and mitigate the social costs of providing FI services. The difference between the private benefits to an FI from being regulated—such as insurance fund guarantees—and the private costs it faces from adhering to regulation—such as examinations—is called the **net regulatory burden**.[6] The higher the net regulatory burden on FIs, the more inefficiently they produce any given set of financial services from a private (FI) owner's perspective.

---

[6] Other regulated firms such as gas and electric utilities also face a complex set of regulations imposing a net regulatory burden on their operations.

Monetary Policy Regulation

outside money

That part of the money supply directly produced by the government or central bank, such as notes and coin.

inside money

That part of the money supply produced by the private banking system.

Another motivation for regulation concerns the special role that banks play in the transmission of monetary policy from the Federal Reserve (the central bank) to the rest of the economy. The central bank directly controls only the quantity of notes and coin in the economy—called **outside money**—whereas the bulk of the money supply is bank deposits—called **inside money.** In theory, a central bank can vary the amount of cash or outside money and directly affect a bank's reserve position as well as the amount of loans and deposits it can create without formally regulating the bank's portfolio. In practice, regulators have chosen to impose formal controls.[7] In most countries, regulators commonly impose a minimum level of required cash reserves to be held against deposits. Some argue that imposing such reserve requirements makes the control of the money supply and its transmission more predictable. Such reserves add to an FI's net regulatory burden if they are more than the institution believes are necessary for its own liquidity purposes. In general all FIs—whether banks or insurance companies—would choose to hold some cash reserves—even noninterest bearing—to meet the liquidity and transaction needs of their customers directly. For well-managed FIs, however, this optimal level is normally low, especially if the central bank (or other regulatory body) does not pay interest on required reserves. As a result, FIs often view required reserves as similar to a tax and as a positive cost of undertaking intermediation.[8]

Credit Allocation Regulation

Credit allocation regulation supports the FI's lending to socially important sectors such as housing and farming. These regulations may require an FI to hold a minimum amount of assets in one particular sector of the economy or to set maximum interest rates, prices, or fees to subsidize certain sectors. Examples of asset restrictions include the qualified thrift lender (QTL) test, which requires thrifts to hold 65 percent of their assets in residential mortgage-related assets to retain a thrift charter, and insurance regulations, such as those in New York state that set maximums on the amount of foreign or international assets in which insurance companies can invest. Examples of interest rate restrictions are the usury laws that many states set on the maximum rates that can be charged on mortgages and/or consumer loans, and regulations (now abolished) such as the Federal Reserve Bank's Regulation Q maximums on time and savings deposit interest rates.

Such price and quantity restrictions may be justified for social welfare reasons—especially if society prefers strong (and subsidized) housing and farming sectors. However, they can also be harmful to FIs that must bear the private costs of meeting many of these regulations. To the extent that the net private costs of such restrictions benefit society, they add to the costs and reduce the efficiency with which FIs undertake intermediation.

---

[7] In classic central banking theory, the amount of bank deposits (D) is determined as the product of 1 over the banking system's required (or desired) ratio of cash reserves to deposits (r) times the amount of bank reserves (R) outstanding, where R is composed of notes and coin plus bank deposits held on reserve at the central bank, $D = (1/r)R$. Thus, by varying R, given a relatively stable reserve ratio (r), the central bank can directly affect D, the amount of deposits or inside money that, as just noted, is a large component of the money supply. Even if not required to do so by regulation, banks would still tend to hold some cash reserves as a liquidity precaution against the sudden withdrawal of deposits or sudden arrival of new loan demand.

[8] In the United States, bank reserves held with the Central Bank (the Federal Reserve Bank, or the Fed) are non-interest bearing. In some other countries, interest is paid on bank reserves, thereby lowering the "regulatory tax" effect.

Consumer Protection Regulation

Congress passed the Community Reinvestment Act (CRA) and the Home Mortgage Disclosure Act (HMDA) to prevent discrimination by lending institutions. For example, since 1975, the HMDA has assisted the public in determining whether banks and other mortgage-lending institutions were meeting the needs of their local communities. HMDA is especially concerned about discrimination on the basis of age, race, sex, or income. Since 1990, depository institutions have used a standardized form to report to their chief federal regulator the reasons that they granted or denied credit. To get some idea of the information production cost of regulatory compliance in this area, the Federal Financial Institutions Examination Council processes information on as many as 6 million mortgage transactions from more than 9,300 institutions each quarter. (The council is a federal supervisory body comprising the members of the Federal Reserve, the Federal Deposit Insurance Corporation, and the Office of the Comptroller of the Currency.) Many analysts believe that community and consumer protection laws are imposing a considerable net regulatory burden on FIs without offsetting social benefits that enhance equal access to mortgage and lending markets.

Investor Protection Regulation

A considerable number of laws protect investors who use investment banks directly to purchase securities and/or indirectly to access securities markets through investing in mutual or pension funds. Various laws protect investors against abuses such as insider trading, lack of disclosure, outright malfeasance, and breach of fiduciary responsibilities. Important legislation affecting investment banks and mutual funds includes the Securities Acts of 1933 and 1934 and the Investment Company Act of 1940. As with consumer protection legislation, compliance with these acts can impose a net regulatory burden on FIs.

Entry and Chartering Regulation

The entry of FIs are regulated, as are their activities once they have been established. Increasing or decreasing the cost of entry into a financial sector affects the profitability of firms already competing in that industry. Thus, the industries heavily protected against new entrants by high direct costs (e.g., through capital contribution) and high indirect costs (e.g., by restricting individuals who can establish FIs) of entry produce larger profits for existing firms than those in which entry is relatively easy. In addition, regulations define the scope of permitted activities under a given charter. The broader the set of financial service activities permitted under a charter, the more valuable that charter is likely to be. Thus, barriers to entry and regulations pertaining to the scope of permitted activities affect an FI's *charter value* and the size of its net regulatory burden.

Concept Questions

1. Why should more regulation be imposed on FIs than on other types of private corporations?
2. What is an example of a negative externality?
3. What does the concept of net regulatory burden mean?
4. What six major types of regulation do FIs face?
5. What are the layers of protection provided by safety and soundness regulations? Describe each.
6. What is the difference between inside and outside money?

THE CHANGING DYNAMICS OF SPECIALNESS

At any moment in time, each FI supplies a set of financial services (brokerage related, asset transformation related, or both) and is subject to a given net regulatory burden. As the demands for the special features of financial services change due to changing preferences and technology, one or more areas of the financial services industry become less profitable. Similarly, changing regulations can increase or decrease the net regulatory burden faced in supplying financial services in any given area. These demand, cost, and regulatory pressures are reflected in changing market shares in different financial service areas as some contract and others expand. Clearly, an FI seeking to survive and prosper must be flexible enough to move toward growing financial service areas and from those that are contracting. If regulatory activity restrictions inhibit or reduce the flexibility with which FIs can alter their product mix, this would reduce their competitive ability and the efficiency with which they deliver financial services. That is, activity barriers within the financial services industry may reduce FIs' ability to diversify and potentially add to their net regulatory burden.

Historical Trends

In Table 1–5, we show the changing shares of total assets in the US financial services industry from 1860 to 1997. A number of important trends are clearly evident; most apparent is the decline in the total share of depository institutions since World War II. Specifically, the share of commercial banks declined from 55.9 to 36.1 percent between 1948 and 1997, while the share of thrifts (mutual savings banks, savings and loans, and credit unions) fell from 12.3 to 10.8 percent over the same period.[9] Similarly, insurance companies also witnessed a secular decline in their share, from 24.3 to 19.3 percent.

The most dramatic trends involve the increasing number of shares of pension funds and investment companies. Pension funds (private plus state and local) increased their asset share from 3.1 to 11.6 percent, while investment companies (mutual funds and money market mutual funds) increased their share from 1.3 to 14.3 percent.

Pension funds and investment companies differ from banks and insurance companies in that they give savers cheaper access to the direct securities markets. They do so by exploiting the comparative advantages of size and diversification, with the transformation of financial claims, such as maturity transformation, a lesser concern. Thus, open-ended mutual funds buy stocks and bonds directly in financial markets and issue to savers shares whose value is linked in a direct pro rata fashion to the value of the mutual fund's asset portfolio. Similarly, money market mutual funds invest in short-term financial assets such as commercial paper, CDs, and Treasury bills and issue shares linked directly to the value of their underlying portfolio. To the extent that these funds efficiently diversify, they also offer price-risk protection and liquidity services.

---

[9] Although bank assets as a percentage of total assets in the financial sector may have declined in recent years, this does not necessarily mean that banking activity has decreased. Boyd and Gertler show that banking activity has risen, albeit moderately, when measured against the growth of gross domestic product (GDP). (See J. H. Boyd and M. Gertler, "Are Banks Dead? Or, Are the Reports Greatly Exaggerated?" Federal Reserve Bank of Minneapolis, Research Department, Working Paper, May 1994). In addition, off-balance-sheet activity has replaced some of the traditional activities of commercial banks (see Chapter 20).

Table 1-5

PERCENTAGE SHARES OF ASSETS OF FINANCIAL INSTITUTIONS IN THE UNITED STATES, 1860–1997

	1860	1880	1900	1912	1922	1929	1939	1948	1960	1970	1980	1997*
Commercial banks	71.4%	60.6%	62.9%	64.5%	63.3%	53.7%	51.2%	55.9%	38.2%	37.9%	34.8%	36.1%
Thrift institutions	17.8	22.8	18.2	14.8	13.9	14.0	13.6	12.3	19.7	20.4	21.4	10.8
Insurance companies	10.7	13.9	13.8	16.6	16.7	18.6	27.2	24.3	23.8	18.9	16.1	19.3
Investment companies	—	—	—	—	0.0	2.4	1.9	1.3	2.9	3.5	3.6	14.3
Pension funds	—	—	0.0	0.0	0.0	0.7	2.1	3.1	9.7	13.0	17.4	11.6
Finance companies	—	0.0	0.0	0.0	0.0	2.0	2.2	2.0	4.6	4.8	5.1	5.9
Securities brokers and dealers	0.0	0.0	3.8	3.0	5.3	8.1	1.5	1.0	1.1	1.2	1.1	1.5
Mortgage companies	0.0	2.7	1.3	1.2	0.8	0.6	0.3	0.1	†	†	0.4	0.3
Real estate investment trusts	—	—	—	—	—	—	—	—	0.0	0.3	0.1	0.2
Total (percent)	100.0%	100.0%	100.0%	100.0%	100.0%	100.0%	100.0%	100.0%	100.0%	100.0%	100.0%	100.0%
Total (trillion dollars)	.001	.005	.016	.034	.075	.123	.129	.281	.596	1.328	4.025	11.38

Columns may not add to 100% due to rounding.

*As of June 30, 1997.

†Data not available.

SOURCE: Randall Kroszner, "The Evolution of Universal Banking and Its Regulation in Twentieth Century America," in Anthony Saunders and Ingo Walter, eds., *Universal Banking Financial System Design Reconsidered* (Burr Ridge, IL: Irwin, 1996), and *Federal Reserve Bulletin,* September 1997, Table 1.60.

The maturity and return characteristics of the financial claims issued by pension and mutual funds closely reflect the maturities of the direct equity and debt securities portfolios in which they invest. In contrast, for banks, thrifts, and insurance companies, the correlation between their asset portfolio maturities and the promised maturity of their liabilities is lower. Thus, banks may partially fund a 10-year commercial loan with demand deposits, a thrift may fund 30-year conventional mortgages with three-month time deposits, and a life insurance company may fund the purchase of 30-year junk bonds with a 7-year fixed-interest guaranteed investment contract (GIC).

To the extent that the financial services market is efficient and these trends reflect the forces of demand and supply, they indicate a current trend: Savers increasingly prefer investments that closely mimic diversified investments in the *direct* securities markets over the transformed financial claims offered by traditional FIs. This trend may also indicate that the net regulatory burden on traditional FIs—such as banks and insurance companies—is higher than that on pension funds and investment companies. As a result, traditional FIs are unable to produce their services as cost efficiently as they previously could.

Future Trends

The growth of mutual and pension funds coupled with investors' recent focus on direct investments in primary securities may be the beginning of a trend away from intermediation as the most efficient mechanism for savers to channel funds to borrowers. This trend may reflect changed investors' preferences toward risk and return; it may also reflect a decline in the relative costs of direct securities investment versus investment via FIs.

Table 1-6

US PRIVATE PLACEMENT MARKET ($ BILLIONS)

	1990	1991	1992	1993	1994	1995	1996	1997
144A placements	3.7	20.9	41.7	91.3	65.8	71.3	132.1	113.5
Total private placements	128.6	110.4	109.5	174.0	133.8	132.6	200.8	145.0

SOURCE: *Investment Dealer's Digest*, various issues. 1997 data are through June.

Certainly, the net regulatory burden that traditional FIs in the United States face has been high. For example, until recently, the ability of traditional FIs to diversify into areas such as mutual funds was relatively limited.[10]

Recent regulatory changes in the United States are partially alleviating the net regulatory burden by allowing FIs to move across traditional product boundaries and lines. For example, banks are now allowed to freely operate branches across state lines (see Chapter 26). More dramatically, barriers separating the operations of different types of FIs are being removed (see Chapter 25). As a result, bank profitability in the mid- to late 1990s has been better than it was for much of the 1980s (see Chapter 3).

Nevertheless, the direct financial markets are evolving even faster; due to technological advances, the costs of direct access by savers is ever falling. A good example of this is the private placement market, in which corporations sell securities directly to investors without underwriters and with a minimum of public disclosure about the issuing firm (see Contemporary Perspectives Box 1–2). Privately placed bonds and equity have traditionally been the most illiquid securities with only the very largest FIs or institutional investors being able or willing to buy and hold them in the absence of a secondary market. In April 1990, the Securities and Exchange Commission (SEC) amended its Regulation 144A. This allowed large investors to begin trading these privately placed securities among themselves even though, in general, privately placed securities do not satisfy the stringent disclosure and informational requirements that the SEC imposes on approved publicly registered issues. Although the SEC defined large investors able to trade privately placed securities as those with assets of $100 million or more—which excludes all but the very wealthiest household savers—it is reasonable to ask how long this size restriction will remain. As they become more sophisticated and the costs of information acquisition fall, savers will increasingly demand access to the private placement market. In such a world, savers would have a choice not only between the secondary securities from FIs and the primary securities publicly offered by corporations but also between publicly offered (registered) securities and privately offered (unregistered) securities. The recent growth of the 144A private placement market is shown in Table 1–6.

To some extent, this choice set is already available to the smaller investor willing to consider investing in bonds issued by corporations and foreign governments. Specifically, Eurodollar bonds are dollar-denominated bonds issued mainly in London and other

---

[10]However, banks have started buying mutual fund companies. For example, in 1994 Mellon Bank acquired Dreyfus Corporation, making Mellon the largest bank provider of mutual funds in the country.

Contemporary Perspectives 1–2

IBM to Let You Buy Stock Directly

The number of companies that allow investors to buy their stock directly without using a broker has grown to 228, with some major names, including IBM and Walt Disney Co., scheduled to join the ranks.

Among well-known companies that have instituted new plans are Bell Atlantic, BellSouth, Royal Dutch Petroleum, Warner-Lambert and Tribune Co., a Chicago-based entertainment and media company and the parent of the Sun-Sentinel. . . .

Direct-purchase plans allow investors to buy and sell stock without using a broker or paying the usual brokerage commissions. But most of the plans—and almost all of the new ones—charge fees to buy and sell.

While typically lower than what most brokers would charge, the fees would significantly bite into the returns of small investors planning to put in only a few dollars a month.

Tribune's fees and plan features are typical of many of the new plans. The minimum investment is $500, or $50 if the investor commits to have the $50 debited electronically from his checking account for at least 10 months. The minimum subsequent investment is $50, and the maximum is $120,000 a year.

The fees include $10, plus 10 cents a share, to make the initial investment, and $5, plus 10 cents a share, for subsequent investments (or $2 plus 10 cents a share if purchases are made by electronic debit). The fee to reinvest dividends is the lower of $3 or 5 percent of the amount reinvested, plus 10 cents a share.

SOURCE: Humberto Cruz, *Sun-Sentinel*, March 11,1997, p. 1D. Reprinted with permission of the *Sun-Sentinel*, Fort Lauderdale, Florida.

European centers such as Luxembourg. Since they are issued outside US territory, they are not required to be registered with the SEC. Only the highest-grade corporations issue these bonds because the problems of monitoring them and enforcing their covenant exclude riskier firms. Eurodollar bonds can even be resold in the United States 90 days after issue. In addition, they are available in small denominations of $1,000, pay coupon interest gross (i.e., do not deduct taxes at the source), and guarantee owners anonymity because they are issued in bearer form. Secondary trading is quite deep and facilitated by two clearing systems, Euroclear operated by Morgan Guaranty and CEDEL operated by a consortium of banks. As international barriers to investing fall and global financial service firms and markets become more available to small investors, the charter values, franchise, or specialness of traditional FIs is likely to become of less and less value.

Concept Questions

1. Is the share of bank and thrift assets growing as a proportion of total FI assets in the United States?
2. What are the fastest growing FIs in the United States?
3. What factors may be driving the trend away from intermediation as the most efficient mechanism for savers to channel funds to borrowers?
4. What are privately placed securities and Eurobonds?

S U M M A R Y

This chapter discussed the various factors and forces impacting financial intermediaries and the specialness of the services they provide. These forces may be such in the future that FIs, which have historically relied on making profits by performing traditional special functions such as asset transformation and providing liquidity services, will need to expand into selling financial services that interface with direct security market transactions such as asset management, clearance, settlement, and underwriting services. This is not to say that specialized or niche FIs cannot survive but that only the most efficient FIs will prosper as the competitive value of a specialized FI charter declines.

In the remainder of this textbook, we investigate the ways in which managers of FIs are measuring and managing this inventory of risks to produce the best return-risk trade-off for shareholders in an increasingly competitive and contestable market environment.

P E R T I N E N T   W E B   S I T E S

Board of Governors of the Federal Reserve   http://www. bog.frb.fed.us/
Federal Deposit Insurance Corp   http://www.fdic.gov/

Office of the Comptroller of Currency   http://www.occ. treas.gov/
US Treasury   http://www.ustreas.gov/

Why Are FIs Special?

1. How would economic transactions between savers (or households) and users of funds (or corporations) differ in a world without financial intermediaries (FIs)?
2. What risks are faced by investors who wish to purchase securities issued by corporations directly (i.e., without the intermediary functions offered by an FI)?
3. Financial intermediaries function as conduits between households and corporations in two ways. Explain.
4. Explain how financial institutions act as delegated monitors.
5. Explain the concept of *negative externality* and how it can be used to justify the extra regulatory attention received by financial institutions.
6. How do FIs solve the information and related agency costs when small savers invest directly in securities issued by corporations?
7. How do FIs alleviate the problem of liquidity risk faced by investors wishing to invest in securities of corporations?
8. How do financial institutions help individuals to diversify their portfolio risks? Which financial institution is best able to achieve this goal?
9. What does *maturity intermediation* mean?
10. Which intermediaries best fulfill the intergenerational wealth transfer function?
11. What does *credit allocation regulation* mean? What social benefit is this type of regulation intended to provide?
12. If financial markets operated perfectly and costlessly, financial intermediaries would not exist. Do you agree or disagree? Explain.
13. In what ways do commercial banks play an important role in the implementation and transmission of monetary policy?
14. Why are FIs among the most regulated sectors in the world? When is net regulatory burden positive for FIs?
15. What forms of protection and regulation do regulators of FIs impose to ensure their safety and soundness?
16. Distinguish between inside money and outside money. How does the Federal Reserve Board try to control the amount of inside money?
17. What are the differences between the different definitions of the money supply, M1, M2, and M3? Why is it important to track the level of the money supply?
18. Why do you think pension funds and investment companies have been growing rapidly in recent years at the expense of "traditional" banks and insurance companies?
19. What are some examples of the costs and benefits from regulation inherent in the definition of net regulatory burden?
20. How does the amended Regulation 144A of the Securities and Exchange Commission help in the process of financial disintermediation (i.e., enable savers to access users of funds directly)?
21. Go to the Federal Reserve Board's web site and find the latest figures for M1, M2, and M3. By what percentage rates have these measures of the money supply grown since July 1997?

Chapter Two

Financial Markets: The Fundamentals

Chapter 1 discussed the functioning of the financial system and the special role that financial intermediaries (FIs) play in the financial markets. Given their key role in the operations of the financial system FI managers must understand the operations of financial markets within which they participate. Making investment and financing decisions requires FI managers to understand the flow of funds throughout the economy as well as the technical details of the domestic and international financial markets in which these managers interact. This chapter examines the fundamental details and operations of various financial markets. It pays particular attention to the effect of interest rates on operations in the financial markets, both domestic and international.

FINANCIAL MARKETS

Financial markets can be distinguished along two major dimensions: (1) primary versus secondary markets and (2) money versus capital markets. This chapter discusses both dimensions.

Primary Markets versus Secondary Markets

primary markets

Markets in which corporations raise funds through new issues of securities.

Primary Markets.   **Primary markets** are markets in which corporations raise funds through *new* issues of securities, such as stocks and bonds. The new securities are sold to the initial buyers in exchange for funds that the issuer needs. Most primary market transactions go through investment banks (e.g., Morgan Stanley or Lehman Brothers), which serve as the intermediary between the lender and borrower of funds (see Chapter 5). The security issuer sells the securities to the investment bank, which then sells them to the initial lenders. Thus, funds pass from the lenders through the investment bank to the security issuer. The investment bank accomplishes the transfer by underwriting the securities. That is, the investment bank guarantees a price to the security issuer for the securities and then seeks to sell them to buyers (investors) at a higher price. As a result, the investment bank takes the risk that it may not be able to sell the securities to the public at the guaranteed or higher price. If this occurs, the investment bank takes a loss on its underwriting of the security.

initial public offering (IPO)

The first public issue of securities by a firm.

Primary market issues may be first-time issues by firms initially going public (e.g., allowing their equity to be publicly traded). These first-time issues are also referred to as **initial public offerings (IPOs).** For example, on December 1, 1997, NovaStar Financial Inc. announced a $3.75 million IPO of its common stock at $18 per share. It used the proceeds of the offering to fund the acquisition of the wholesale loan production affiliate, NovaStar Mortgage Inc. It sold the stock with the help of several investment banks, including Stifel, Nicolaus & Co. Inc., and NationsBank Montgomery Securities Inc. as the lead managers. Similarly, Franchise Mortgage Acceptance Co. raised $180 million (10 million shares at $18 per share) in its November 1997 IPO through NationsBank Montgomery Securities, Inc., Credit Suisse First Boston, and PaineWebber Inc. as the lead underwriters.

Primary markets sales also include the sale of additional or new shares of an already publicly traded firm. For example, in December 1997, Focal Inc. announced the sale of an additional 2.5 million shares of common stock (at $10 per share) through investment banks such as Lehman Brothers, Piper Jaffray Inc., and Pacific Growth Equities, Inc., as lead underwriters. Similarly, Furman Selz, NationsBank Montgomery Securities, Inc., and Dain Bosworth were the lead underwriters for Transcrypt International's October 1997 sale of an additional 5.175 million shares of common stock at $21 per share. The **tombstone** (the public announcement of the issue in the financial press) for this primary market sale is presented in Figure 2–1. Other investment banks (such as Chatsworth Securities; Cruttenden Roth; and Kirkpatrick, Pettis, Smith, Polian) were involved in the sale and distribution of the new issue but did not act as lead underwriters.

tombstone

A public announcement of a new issue of securities in the financial press.

secondary market

A market that trades existing securities.

Secondary Markets.   **Secondary markets** are the markets in which existing securities are traded. The New York Stock Exchange (NYSE) and the American Stock Exchange (ASE) are two well-known examples of secondary markets in equities.[1] Buyers of secondary market securities are economic units (consumers, businesses, and governments) with excess funds. Sellers of secondary market securities are economic units in need of funds (see Chapter 1). When a trader buys a security in a secondary market, funds are exchanged (with the help of a broker) between the buyer and the seller of the security. The original

---

[1] Most bonds are not traded on exchanges. Rather, FIs trade them over the counter (OTC) using telephone and computer networks. For example, less than 1 percent of corporate bonds outstanding are traded on organized exchanges such as the NYSE.

This announcement is neither an offer nor a solicitation of any offer to buy these securities. The offering is made only by the Prospectus

October 27 1997

5,175,000 Shares

Common Stock

Price $21 Per Share

Copies of the Prospectus may be obtained from such of the undersigned as may legally offer these securities in States in which the Prospectus may legally be distributed.

Furman Selz

NationsBanc Montgomery Securities, Inc.

Dain Bosworth
Incorporated

Chatsworth Securities LLC   **Cruttenden Roth**   **Kirkpatrick, Pettis, Smith, Polian Inc.**
Incorporated

F i g u r e **2–1**   *Tombstone Announcing the Primary Issue of Common Stock*

Table **2–1**

TOP NYSE VOLUME DAYS

Date	Volume (in thousands)
October 28, 1997	1,202,550
October 29, 1997	777,660
October 30, 1997	712,230
January 23, 1997	684,588
October 27, 1997	684,571
July 16, 1996	680,913
October 24, 1997	677,241
October 23, 1997	672,506
December 20, 1996	654,110
June 20, 1997	652,945
July 16, 1997	652,848
December 15, 1995	652,829

SOURCE: The New York Stock Exchange web page, Data Library, December, 1997.

issuer of the security is not involved in this transfer. In addition to stocks and bonds, secondary markets also exist for mortgages, some types of loans, foreign exchange, futures, and options.

Secondary markets offer benefits to both lenders (buyers of securities) and borrowers (sellers of securities). Even though the security issuer is not directly involved in the transfer of funds in the secondary market, the issuer does obtain information about the current market value of its securities. Secondary market trading reveals the consensus price of a security to the issuer. This information allows issuers to evaluate how well they are using the funds generated from securities issuance and provides information on how well their subsequent offerings might do in terms of raising new money and at what cost (e.g., the coupon interest rate that needs to be paid on a corporate bond issue).

Trading volume in most secondary markets is generally active. Some of the top volume trading days on the NYSE are listed in Table 2–1; on October 28, 1997, NYSE trading volume exceeded 1.2 billion shares.

Thus, secondary markets offer buyers and sellers liquidity as well as information about the fair market values of their investments. Increased liquidity then makes securities more desirable and easier for the issuing firm to sell initially in the primary market. Further, the existence of centralized markets for buying and selling securities allows buyers and sellers to trade at low transaction costs.

Money Markets versus Capital Markets

money markets

Markets that trade debt instruments with maturities of less than one year.

Money Markets.   **Money markets** are markets that trade debt instruments with maturities of one year or less. In the money markets, economic units with excess funds in the short term (consumers, businesses, and governments) can lend these funds (or buy money market securities) to economic units in need of funds for the short term (sellers of money market securities). The short-term nature of securities that trade in these markets means that price fluctuations and thus the risk of capital gains or losses on these securities are relatively small (see Chapters 17 and 18 on interest rate risk). Unlike capital markets (such as the

Table **2–2**

MONEY MARKET INSTRUMENTS OUTSTANDING, 1990–1997
(in billions of dollars)

	1990	1995	1996	1997
Commercial paper	$557.8	$677.7	$779.4	$836.8
Federal funds and repurchase agreements	372.3	660.1	698.7	717.1
U.S. Treasury bills	527.4	760.7	777.4	704.1
Negotiable CDs	546.9	476.9	590.8	605.4
Banker's acceptances	52.1	22.6	23.6	24.3

SOURCE: Federal Reserve Board, *Statistical Releases, Flow of Fund Accounts*, various issues.

equity markets), money markets do not operate in specific locations. Rather, money market transactions occur via telephones, wire transfers, and computer trading.

FIs frequently transact in money markets. Depository institutions are required to hold noninterest bearing deposits at Federal Reserve banks to satisfy reserve requirements (see Chapter 15). To keep the level of these noninterest bearing deposits to a minimum, these FIs invest any excess reserves in short-term money market instruments for periods as short as one day. Mutual funds, especially money market mutual funds (see Chapter 7), also invest heavily in money market instruments. The following section briefly describes the major money market instruments.

Money Market Instruments.   Table 2–2 lists outstanding amounts of the major money market instruments in the United States in 1990, 1995, 1996, and 1997. Notice that in 1997 commercial paper dominates the money market instruments outstanding, followed by federal funds and repurchase agreements and Treasury bills. As recently as 1990, however, commercial paper, negotiable CDs, and Treasury bills were nearly equal in amounts outstanding, and federal funds and repurchase agreements lagged behind. In recent years, federal funds and repurchase agreements have increased in importance, and Treasury bills and negotiable CDs have decreased in relative importance in the money markets.

U.S. Treasury Bills.   Treasury bills are obligations of the U.S. government issued to cover government budget deficits and to refinance maturing government debt. Treasury bills are issued in 3-, 6-, and 12-month maturities and pay a set amount at maturity with no intervening coupon interest payments. Even though Treasury bills are not the largest money market instrument measured by amount outstanding, they are the most actively traded money market instruments and consequently are the most liquid. Treasury bills are backed by the full faith and credit of the U.S. government and as a result are credit risk or default risk free (see Chapter 10).

Commercial Paper.   Commercial paper issues are short-term debt securities issued by large and medium-size corporations. It has been estimated that as many as 20,000 companies now have actual or potential access to the commercial paper market. Commercial paper is a popular way to raise short-term funds because, if the maturity is set at 270 days or less, the issuer does not have to file a registration with the Securities and Exchange Commission (SEC).

The commercial paper market has grown substantially (from $33 billion in 1970 to $836.8 billion in 1997). One reason for this growth is the increased use of technology to analyze the credit quality of potential commercial paper issuers. The increased ability to identify good quality companies has made issuing commercial paper easier for these companies. In addition, as the commercial paper market has grown, the relative importance of FI commercial loans has declined. This suggests that firms are increasingly using commercial paper as an alternative to borrowing funds from FIs such as banks.

Negotiable Certificates of Deposits.   A certificate of deposit (CD) is a debt instrument issued by a bank or thrift indicating that a customer has deposited an amount of money at the institution. The interest rate and maturity of the CD are specified at the time of issue. If the CD is negotiable, the holder of the CD may sell it in the open market prior to maturity. Negotiable CDs were introduced in the early 1960s when the Federal Reserve imposed deposit rate ceilings.[2] The negotiability gave CD holders the ability to earn a market rate of interest without loss of liquidity and was thus instrumental in helping FIs increase the amount of funds raised in money markets.

Federal Funds.   Federal (fed) funds are primarily one-day loans that banks make by loaning out excess deposits (cash reserves) that the banks hold at the central bank (the Federal Reserve) to banks and thrifts with deficient cash reserves or funds. Fed fund loans are unsecured. Lending banks transfer their excess deposits to the account of the deficient bank using the Federal Reserve's wire transfer system called *Fedwire* (see Chapter 24). The interest rate on these loans is called the *fed funds rate*. Regulators use this rate as a guide to monetary policy stringency.

Repurchase Agreements.   Repurchase agreements (repos or RPs) are agreements to sell securities and later repurchase them. Repos are essentially collateralized federal fund loans with a maturity of generally less than two weeks (although most have maturities of one day). Repos typically involve Treasury securities as collateral. For example, an FI with a large portfolio of Treasury securities can enter into a repo, selling a portion of its Treasury securities for a designated period to a firm with excess funds, promising to repurchase ("repo") the Treasury securities at the end of an agreed period (e.g., one-day, one-week).

Banker's Acceptances.   Letters of credit are used frequently to assist in commercial trade transactions; a letter of credit guarantees payment by a purchasing agent. For example, if Firm X ships goods to Firm Y, it may be concerned whether Firm Y will pay for those goods in 90 days. In this situation, an FI may act as a guarantor by issuing a letter of credit indicating its willingness to pay Firm X for the goods should Firm Y default on its 90-day payment obligation. Further, the FI involved usually accepts the responsibility to discount the letter of credit it has issued if the holder—in this case Firm Y—presents it for acceptance. That is, should Firm Y wish to obtain its funds early, it can present the letter of credit to the FI before the 90 days are up and receive the discounted value of those funds. In this case, the letter of credit converts into a *banker's acceptance*. The FI may then resell

---

[2] These ceilings were imposed under the Federal Reserve's Regulation Q on deposits under $100,000. To avoid this ceiling, negotiable CDs were issued with denominations exceeding $100,000. Interest rate ceilings on small denomination CDs (i.e., under $100,000) were discontinued in 1986. However, only large denomination CDs are traded.

Table **2-3**

CAPITAL MARKET INSTRUMENTS OUTSTANDING, 1990–1997

(in billions of dollars)

	1990	1995	1996	1997
Corporate stocks	$3,524.8	$8,389.9	$10,090.0	$10,099.2
Residential mortgages	2,966.5	3,921.6	4,225.8	4,280.1
Commercial and farm mortgages	837.7	787.8	826.4	833.0
Corporate bonds	1,703.1	2,776.0	3,049.6	3,081.6
Treasury securities	1,653.4	2,531.5	2,667.3	2,698.0
State and local government bonds	1,184.4	1,304.0	1,305.5	1,314.2
U.S. government-owned agencies	1,043.5	1,570.3	1,711.4	1,740.0
U.S. government-sponsored agencies	393.7	806.7	896.9	899.6
Bank and consumer loans	1,626.1	2,075.8	2,262.8	2,272.9

SOURCE: Federal Reserve Board, *Statistical Releases, Flow of Funds Accounts*, various issues.

the banker's acceptance to money market investors. Thus, the sale of a banker's acceptance provides an additional funding source for an FI.

capital markets

Markets that trade debt and equity instruments with maturities of more than one year.

Capital Markets.   **Capital markets** are markets that trade equity and debt instruments with maturities of more than one year. Given their longer maturity, these instruments experience wider price fluctuations and, therefore, higher interest rate risk than do money market instruments.[3]

Capital Market Instruments. Table 2–3 lists the major capital market instruments and their outstanding values in 1990, 1995, 1996, and 1997. Notice that corporate stocks represent the largest capital market instrument, followed by residential mortgages, and corporate bonds. It should be noted that the relative size of capital market instruments outstanding depends on two factors: number issued and price. One reason for the sharp increase in the size of equities is the post-1980 (and particularly the mid- to late 1990s) bull market.

Stock.   Common stock is an equity claim on a firm's net income and assets. Returns are in the form of dividend payments and capital appreciation in the price and value of the stock. Common stockholders are residual claimants because in the event of the bankruptcy of a firm, they are the last to be paid after debt holders and other claimants are compensated. Preferred stock is a hybrid instrument representing an equity interest in the firm but generally paying a fixed dividend.

Figure 2–2 shows the distribution of stock ownership in the United States in 1990 and 1997. Notice that in 1990, the household sector owned the majority of corporate stocks (50.6 percent) followed by financial institutions (42.4 percent), but the two sectors have switched in ownership rank in 1997. Financial institutions now dominate (owning 48.6 percent in 1997).

---

[3] In addition, their longer maturities subject these instruments to higher credit or default risk than money market instruments are subject to.

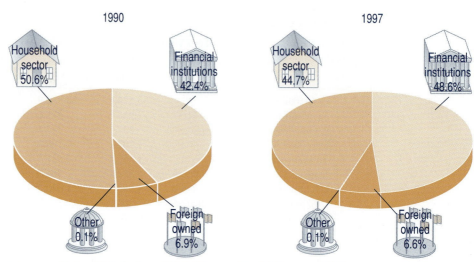

F i g u r e **2–2** *Distribution of Stock Ownership, 1990 versus 1997*

SOURCE: Federal Reserve Board, *Statistical Releases, Flow of Funds Accounts,* March 1998.

T a b l e **2–4**

MORTGAGE LOANS OUTSTANDING, 1990–1997
(in billions of dollars)

	1990	**1995**	**1996**	**1997**
1 to 4 family dwelling	$2,676.7	$3,633.8	$3,915.4	$3,966.8
Multifamily dwellings	289.8	287.8	310.4	313.3
Commercial property	758.8	703.2	738.3	744.6
Farms	78.9	84.6	88.1	88.4

SOURCE: Federal Reserve Board, *Statistical Releases, Flow of Funds Accounts,* various issues.

Mortgages. Mortgages are loans to individuals or businesses to purchase a home, land, or other real property. The mortgage market is the largest of the debt markets. Table 2–4 lists the major categories of mortgages. Home mortgages (1 to 4 families) are the largest loan category (77.6 percent of all mortgages in 1997), followed by multifamily dwellings (6.1 percent), commercial mortgages (used to finance real estate used for business purposes— 14.6 percent), and farms (1.7 percent).

asset securitization

The packaging and selling of loans and other assets backed by securities issued by an FI.

Many mortgages (particularly residential mortgages) are subsequently **securitized** by the mortgage issuer (i.e., they are packaged and sold as assets backing a publicly traded or privately held debt instrument). Securitization allows FIs' asset portfolios to become more liquid, provides a source of fee income, and helps reduce the effects of regulatory taxes such as capital requirements (see Chapter 16), reserve requirements (see Chapter 14), and deposit insurance premiums (see Chapter 15). We discuss later the agencies owned or sponsored by the U.S. government that securitize mortgage pools. We describe the major forms of securitization and discuss the process of securitization in more detail in Chapter 12.

Treasury Notes and Bonds. The U.S. government also issues Treasury notes and bonds, which are similar to Treasury bills. The original maturity on these longer term instruments

Contemporary Perspectives 2–1

US Debt Going into "Unchartered Territory"—Experts

The U.S. debt crisis has moved into "uncharted territory" as the protracted political impasse over the budget put in doubt the credit quality of the world's richest nation, experts said. "This is a completely uncharted territory," said Stanford University Professor of Economics John Taylor, commenting on the credit rating agency Moody's Investors Service's announcement it may cut the AAA— or top quality—rating of $387 billion worth of U.S. Treasury debt maturing on or with interest payments due on February 29 and onward.

The Republicans who control Congress are refusing to raise the U.S. $4.9 trillion debt limit unless President Clinton agrees to their terms to balance the budget. Treasury Secretary Robert Rubin said he would take extraordinary measures that would allow the United States to meet its financial obligations on February 15—but not past that date. Rubin forecast a U.S. default—which

financial markets have dubbed "the unthinkable"—on Feb. 29 or March 1. "Until they [rating agencies] actually do something, this is only an indication of what might happen," Taylor stressed. "This should not have too much of an effect on markets yet."

Moody's announcement came just 24 hours after Standard and Poor's Corp. told Reuters it would down-grade the U.S. debt to D—for default and, thus, below junk bond quality— from an impeccable AAA track record. "Until the nature of the situation is clarified, until we know what their [Treasury's] plans are in dealing with interest payments, this will have some effects on market rates," Taylor added.

Gregory Mankiw, Professor of Economics at Harvard University, questioned the actual magnitude of the impact an eventual U.S. default would have on U.S. assets. "It will be the perception versus the reality. . . .

Even if they default for five minutes, it would be hard for me to believe dealers would view this as a real type of default," Mankiw said. "I'm not sure this would have the same doomsday effect." Mankiw agreed with Taylor that Washington politics have drawn the U.S. debt rating into an unusual territory. "It has never been done that a country as credit-worthy as the United States has tried to default on its debt," he added.

"A few days of default would not affect the creditworthiness of the United States," Mankiw further said. "But to tie the debt limit [to the budget negotiations] is a risky strategy, it's going down a route where we cannot predict the conse-quences." Mankiw, however, stressed that many investors would be able to realize the temporary nature of a politically engineered default and buy cheaper U.S. Treasuries in hopes for solid profits—once the budget storm has passed.

SOURCE: Isabelle Clary, *Reuters Financial Service*, January 24, 1996. Reprinted by permission of Reuters.

---

ranges from 1 to 10 years for Treasury notes and up to 30 years for Treasury bonds. Also similar to T-bills, the trading volume in T-note and bond markets is extremely heavy, making these investments very liquid. Backed by the full faith and credit of the U.S. government, T-notes and bonds are essentially default risk free. However, in 1996 there was a concern that the U.S. government would default on its obligations (see Contemporary Perspectives Box 2–1).

investment-grade bond

Bond rated BBB or better by bond-rating agencies such as Moody's.

junk bond

Bond rated less than investment grade by bond-rating agencies.

Corporate Bonds.   Corporate bonds are long-term promissory notes issued by a company. For example, in December 1997, Texas Petrochemical Holdings, Inc., issued $57.65 million in new senior debt due to be paid in 2007. The new $57.65 million was in addition to $350.1 million in corporate debt that it already had outstanding. The coupon (or interest) rate on the new debt issue was 13.5 percent.

Issues are categorized as **investment-grade bonds** (corporate bonds rated as BBB or better by rating agencies) and **junk bonds** (corporate bonds rated as less than investment grade by rating agencies). Additionally, corporate bonds may be held and traded in public

Table **2–5**

CORPORATE BONDS OUTSTANDING, 1990–1997
(in billions of dollars)

	1990	1995	1996	1997
Nonfinancial corporate bonds	$1,008.2	$1,326.3	$1,398.8	$1,418.7
Banks and savings institutions	121.6	164.2	171.6	174.9
Nondepository financial institutions	457.9	994.9	1,141.9	1,146.3
Foreign	115.4	290.6	337.3	341.7

SOURCE: Federal Reserve Board, *Statistical Releases, Flow of Funds Accounts*, various issues.

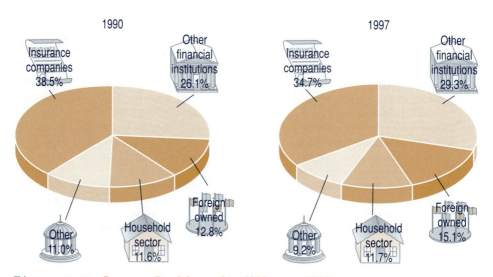

Figure **2–3** *Corporate Bond Ownership, 1990 versus 1997*

SOURCE: Federal Reserve Board, *Statistical Releases, Flow of Funds Accounts,* March 1998.

markets (i.e., the New York Exchange Bond Market) or may be traded over the counter (OTC).[4] The corporate bond issuer promises to pay interest (normally semiannually) and principal (on maturity) to the bond holder. Table 2–5 lists the distribution of corporate debt by issuer. Nonfinancial corporations are the major issuers of debt (46.0 percent of the total outstanding in 1997), followed by nondepository financial institutions (37.2 percent). Corporate debt is held as assets mainly by insurance companies (34.7 percent in 1997) and other financial institutions (29.3 percent); see Figure 2–3.

State and Government Bonds. State and local governments issue bonds (municipals), which are long-term promissory notes. Municipalities use municipals to finance expenditures on major projects, such as schools, roads, and public utility construction. Under

---

[4] As noted earlier, most corporate bonds are traded OTC.

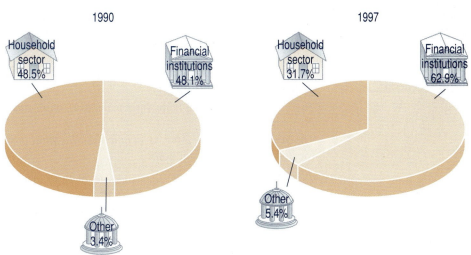

Figure **2-4**   *Municipal Security Ownership, 1990 versus 1997*

SOURCE: Federal Reserve Board, *Statistical Releases, Flow of Funds Accounts,* March 1998.

current U.S. tax laws, interest payments to holders of municipal bonds are not subject to federal, state, and local taxes.

general obligation bonds

Municipal bonds backed by the full faith and credit of the municipality that issued the debt.

revenue bonds

Municipal bonds backed by cash flows from the specific asset being financed.

Municipals can be either **general obligation bonds** (backed by the full faith and credit of the municipal issuer) or **revenue bonds** (backed by the cash flows of the specific asset—or project—being financed, for example, tolls from a bridge whose construction was financed by a revenue bond issue). In December 1997, Rhode Island Housing and Mortgage Finance Corp. approved $2.7 million in revenue bonds whose proceeds were to be used to convert old offices into loft space and apartments in downtown Providence, Rhode Island. Repayment of the revenue bonds is expected to come from the lease income from the offices and apartments.

Financial institutions have recently become the main investors in municipals (62.9 percent of the total outstanding in 1997), taking the lead from the household sector (31.7 percent of total); see Figure 2–4.

U.S. Government Agencies.   Agencies of the U.S. government issue *agency securities,* which are promissory notes. One U.S. government agency, the Government National Mortgage Association (Ginnie Mae or GNMA) is a directly owned government agency. Payments on these agency securities are backed by the full faith and credit of the U.S. government. The U.S. government sponsors other agencies. As a result, their securities are not completely backed by the government's full faith and credit. Thus, these agency securities are not 100 percent default risk free. Sponsorship provides agencies with a line of credit with the U.S. Treasury Department, however. Some of the major federal agencies (government owned and sponsored) and the amount of their mortgage pools outstanding in 1997 include the following:

1. The *Government National Mortgage Association (Ginnie Mae or GNMA)* acts as a guarantor to investors in mortgage-backed securities insured by the Federal Housing Authority (FHA), the Veterans Administration (VA), and the Farmers Housing Administration (FHA) ($520.9 billion).

2. The *Federal National Mortgage Association (Fannie Mae or FNMA)* purchases and sells federally insured and noninsured residential mortgages mainly issued by commercial banks ($637.9 billion).

3. The *Federal Home Loan Mortgage Corporation (Freddie Mac or FHLMC)* operates a secondary market for residential mortgages issued by savings and loans and other savings banks ($567.2 billion).

4. The *Farm Credit System* helps fund loans to farmers and other agricultural entities ($41.4 billion).

5. The *Student Loan Marketing Association (Sallie Mae)* provides a secondary market for student loans ($12.1 billion).

GNMA, FNMA, and FHLMC securities are directly involved in creating mortgage-backed pass-through securities (see Chapter 12). As noted earlier, $4,280.1 billion in residential mortgages was outstanding in 1997. GNMA, FNMA, and FHLMC, with $1,762.0 billion in securities represent 41.2 percent of all residential mortgages now securitized.

Consumer and Bank Commercial Loans.   The final two categories of capital market instruments include loans with maturities longer than one year made to consumers and businesses by depository institutions and finance companies. Until recently, the lack of an organized secondary market for these instruments had made them one of the least liquid of the capital market instruments outstanding. Over the last 10 years, however, a secondary market in large, long-term loans made by FIs to corporations has developed (see Chapter 12 on the loan sales market).

Concept Questions

1. What is the difference between primary and secondary markets?
2. What is the major distinction between money markets and capital markets?
3. What are the major instruments traded in the capital markets?

FOREIGN
EXCHANGE MARKETS

In addition to understanding domestic financial markets, the FI manager must understand the operations of the foreign exchange markets and foreign capital markets. FIs are increasingly operating globally. It is therefore essential that FI managers understand how events in other countries affect the returns and risks of the portfolios they manage. For example, events in Southeast Asia in 1997 impacted U.S. markets, resulting in the largest one-day drop in stock price values in the history of U.S. stock markets (see Contemporary Perspectives Box 2–2). The next section presents the basics of foreign exchange markets and prices.

Foreign Exchange Markets and Prices

Cash flows from assets denominated in a foreign currency expose U.S. investors to risk regarding the conversion of these cash flows into U.S. dollars. The actual amount of U.S.

Contemporary Perspectives 2–2

The Globe Shudders: The Asian Contagion Spreads, Sending the World's Markets on a Wild Ride

It was just hours after a second, tumultuous day in the U.S. stock market had come to an end. To the relief of investors around the world, the market last Tuesday had risen sharply, the first blessed evidence in three trading days that stocks weren't headed for the abyss. The day before, the Dow Jones industrial average had plunged 554 points before the New York Stock Exchange, like a referee finally stepping in a bloody and brutally one-sided fight, had for the second time that day called a halt to trading. Since the close of business on Wednesday, October 22, the Dow had plummeted 863 points—a response, in part, to increasing fears

that the unfolding economic debacle in East Asia would inevitably damage many American companies. . . .

It was not the week's only important lesson. The other was an indelible reminder—delivered with the subtlety of a wrecking ball—of just how interlinked global markets have become. Market signals whip around the world instantaneously, and for an economy as large as the United States', with its globally integrated corporations earning more and more overseas, that means there is hardly a place on the planet completely irrelevant to its economic health. At the end of the 20th century,

the business of America is business everywhere. Monday's Dow sell-off was triggered by yet another stunning rout in the troubled Hong Kong stock market; by Thursday, what just two weeks ago most analysts thought was a localized event (the Asia meltdown) had suddenly become the "Asian contagion"—a virus that had spread violently to South America's largest economy. Brazil, with large current account deficits and a flagging currency (just like some of East Asia's emerging economies), watched its stock market decline nearly 10 percent on Thursday.

SOURCE: Bill Powell, *Newsweek,* November 10, 1997, p. 32. From Newsweek, 1998 © 1997, Newsweek, Inc. All rights reserved. Reprinted by permission.

---

dollars received on a foreign investment depends on the exchange rate between the U.S. dollar and the foreign currency when the nondollar cash flow is received (and exchanged for U.S. dollars) at a future time. If the foreign currency depreciates (or declines in value) relative to the U.S. dollar over the investment period (i.e., the period between the time a foreign investment is made and the time it is liquidated), the dollar value of the cash flows received falls. If the foreign currency appreciates (or rises in value) relative to the U.S. dollar, the dollar value of cash flows received increases. This risk is referred to as *foreign exchange risk* and is discussed in more detail in Chapter 27 as are techniques for hedging foreign exchange risk, such as using FX futures, options, and swaps.

spot foreign exchange transaction

A transaction that involves the immediate exchange of currencies at the current (or spot) exchange rate.

Two major types of foreign exchange rate transactions are spot transactions and forward transactions. **Spot transactions** involve the immediate exchange of currencies at the current (or spot) exchange rate. Spot transactions can be conducted through the foreign exchange division of commercial banks or a nonbank foreign currency dealer. For example, a U.S. investor wanting to buy Italian lira through a local bank essentially has the dollars transferred from his or her bank account to the dollar account of a lira seller. Simultaneously, lira are transferred from the seller's account into an account designated by the U.S. investor. Moreover, many large FIs trade foreign currencies among themselves, seeking to profit on movements in spot exchange rates. As a result, foreign exchange markets, like corporate bond markets, trade mainly over the counter (i.e., without an organized or centralized exchange).

EXAMPLE 2–1

• • • • • • •   *Exchange Rate Risk*

On October 24, 1997, a U.S. FI plans to purchase 3 million French francs' (Ff) worth of French bonds from a French FI in one month's time. The French FI wants payment in French francs. Thus, the U.S. FI must convert dollars into French francs. The currency exchange rates on October 24, 1997 are reported in Table 2–6. The spot exchange rate of U.S. dollars to French francs is reported as .1679, or the U.S. FI must convert

$$\text{U.S.\$/Ff exchange rate} \times \text{Ff3 million} =$$
$$.1679 \times \text{Ff3 million} = \$503,700$$

into French francs today.

Table **2–6**

FOREIGN CURRENCY EXCHANGE RATES, OCTOBER 24, 1997

CURRENCY TRADING

EXCHANGE RATES

Friday, October 24, 1997

The New York foreign exchange selling rates below apply to trading among banks in amounts of $1 million and more, as quoted at 4 p.m. Eastern time by Dow Jones and other sources. Retail transactions provide fewer units of foreign currency per dollar.

Country	U.S. $ equiv. Fri	U.S. $ equiv. Thu	Currency per U.S. $ Fri	Currency per U.S. $ Thu
Argentina (Peso)	1.0014	1.0014	.9986	.9986
Australia (Dollar)	.6913	.7044	1.4466	1.4197
Austria (Schilling)	.07968	.07954	12.550	12.572
Bahrain (Dinar)	2.6525	2.6525	.3770	.3770
Belgium (Franc)	.02733	.02745	36.586	36.425
Brazil (Real)	.9083	.9086	1.1010	1.1006
Britain (Pound)	1.6340	1.6327	.6120	.6125
1-month forward	1.6318	1.6305	.6128	.6133
3-months forward	1.6278	1.6266	.6143	.6148
6-months forward	1.6222	1.6209	.6164	.6169
Canada (Dollar)	.7185	.7190	1.3918	1.3908
1-month forward	.7197	.7202	1.3894	1.3885
3-months forward	.7220	.7226	1.3851	1.3839
6-months forward	.7250	.7255	1.3794	1.3783
Chile (Peso)	.002413	.002426	414.35	412.25
China (Renminbi)	.1203	.1203	8.3133	8.3136
Colombia (Peso)	.0007892	.0007887	1267.10	1267.87
Czech. Rep. (Koruna)	....	....	....	....
Commercial rate	.03007	.03011	33.251	33.214
Denmark (Krone)	.1480	.1486	6.7590	6.7276
Ecuador (Sucre)	....	....	....	....
Floating rate	.0002417	.0002417	4138.00	4138.00
Finland (Markka)	.1883	.1894	5.3105	5.2801
France (Franc)	.1679	.1689	5.9545	5.9223
1-month forward	.1682	.1692	5.9438	5.9112
3-months forward	.1688	.1698	5.9225	5.8907
6-months forward	.1696	.1705	5.8951	5.8638
Germany (Mark)	.5628	.5658	1.7768	1.7675
1-month forward	.5638	.5668	1.7736	1.7642
3-months forward	.5658	.5688	1.7675	1.7582
6-months forward	.5685	.5714	1.7591	1.7501
Greece (Drachma)	.003584	.003601	278.98	277.69
Hong Kong (Dollar)	.1293	.1285	7.7337	7.7838
Hungary (Forint)	.005032	.005032	198.74	198.74
India (Rupee)	.02759	.02759	36.240	36.240
Indonesia (Rupiah)	.0002797	.0002786	3575.00	3590.00
Ireland (Punt)	1.4646	1.4706	.6828	.6800
Israel (Shekel)	.2808	.2831	3.5616	3.5325
Italy (Lira)	.0005760	.0005787	1736.00	1728.00
Japan (Yen)	.008201	.008197	121.94	122.00
1-month forward	.008237	.008233	121.40	121.47

Country	U.S. $ equiv. Fri	U.S. $ equiv. Thu	Currency per U.S. $ Fri	Currency per U.S. $ Thu
3-months forward	.008312	.008307	120.32	120.38
6-months forward	.008422	.008418	118.74	118.80
Jordan (Dinar)	1.4094	1.4094	.7095	.7095
Kuwait (Dinar)	3.2862	3.2862	.3043	.3043
Lebanon (Pound)	.0006530	.0006530	1531.50	1531.50
Malaysia (Ringgit)	.2948	.2979	3.3920	3.3570
Malta (Lira)	2.5316	2.5284	.3950	.3955
Mexico (Peso)	....	....	....	....
Floating rate	.1269	.1283	7.8800	7.7950
Netherland (Guilder)	.4996	.5024	2.0015	1.9906
New Zealand (Dollar)	.6188	.6243	1.6160	1.6018
Norway (Krone)	.1400	.1405	7.1418	7.1151
Pakistan (Rupee)	.02296	.02296	43.560	43.560
Peru (new Sol)	.3767	.3773	2.6547	2.6507
Philippines (Peso)	.02874	.02886	34.800	34.650
Poland (Zloty)	.2912	.2931	3.4345	3.4115
Portugal (Escudo)	.005533	.005561	180.72	179.83
Russia (Ruble) (a)	.0001700	.0001701	5881.00	5880.00
Saudi Arabia (Riyal)	.2666	.2666	3.7512	3.7505
Singapore (Dollar)	.6331	.6386	1.5795	1.5660
Slovak Rep. (Koruna)	.02958	.02959	33.811	33.792
South Africa (Rand)	.2115	.2115	4.7280	4.7285
South Korea (Won)	.001076	.001086	929.40	921.20
Spain (Peseta)	.006677	.006710	149.77	149.04
Sweden (Krona)	.1318	.1318	7.5878	7.5893
Switzerland (Franc)	.6826	.6831	1.4650	1.4640
1-month forward	.6848	.6853	1.4603	1.4592
3-months forward	.6890	.6895	1.4513	1.4503
6-months forward	.6952	.6957	1.4384	1.4375
Taiwan (Dollar)	.03293	.03308	30.365	30.230
Thailand (Baht)	.02591	.02632	38.600	38.000
Turkey (Lira)	.00000549	.00000551	182080.00	181505.00
United Arab (Dirham)	.2723	.2723	3.6725	3.6725
Uruguay (New Peso)	....	....	....	....
Financial	.1020	.1024	9.8050	9.7700
Venezuela (Bolivar)	.002006	.002007	498.62	498.38
SDR	1.3637	1.3644	.7333	.7329
ECU	1.1084	1.1151	....	....

Special Drawing Rights (SDR) are based on exchange rates for the U.S., German, British, French, and Japanese currencies. Source: International Monetary Fund.

European Currency Unit (ECU) is based on a basket of community currencies.

a-fixing, Moscow Interbank Currency Exchange.

The Wall Street Journal daily foreign exchange data for 1996 and 1997 may be purchased through the Readers' Reference Service (413) 592-3600.

SOURCE: The *Wall Street Journal*, October 27, 1997, p. C24. Reprinted by permission of The Wall Street Journal. © 1997 Dow Jones & Company, Inc. All Rights Reserved Worldwide.

Suppose that one month after the conversion of dollars to French francs, the French bond purchase deal falls through and the U.S. FI no longer needs the French francs it purchased at $.1679 per franc. The spot exchange rate of U.S. dollars to French francs has changed over the month to .155. The U.S. dollar value of 3 million French francs is now only

$$.155 \times \text{Ff3 million} = \$465,000$$

The depreciation of the French franc relative to the dollar over the month has caused the U.S. FI to suffer a $38,700 ($503,700 − $465,000) loss due to exchange rate fluctuations. • • •

forward foreign exchange transaction

A transaction that involves the exchange of currencies at a specified time in the future and at a specified rate (or forward exchange rate).

To avoid such a loss in the spot markets, the U.S. FI could have entered into a second type of transaction, a **forward transaction,** which is the exchange of currencies at a specified future date and a specified exchange rate (or forward exchange rate). Forward exchange rates for October 24, 1997 are also listed in Table 2–6. Forward contracts are typically written for a one-, three-, or six-month period from the date the contract is written, but in practice they can be written for any time period. For example, if the U.S. investor had entered into a one-month forward contract on the French franc on October 24, 1997, at the same time it purchased the spot francs, the U.S. investor would have been guaranteed an exchange rate of .1682 U.S. dollars per French franc or 5.9438 French francs per U.S. dollar from selling francs in one month's time. If the U.S. FI had sold francs one month forward at .1682 on October 24, 1997, it would have largely avoided the loss of $38,700 described in Example 2–1. Essentially, by using the one-month forward contract, the FI hedges its foreign currency risk in the spot market.[5] Chapter 27 examines foreign exchange risk in detail and discusses ways that FIs can use foreign exchange markets to protect themselves against such risk.

Concept Questions

1. What is the difference between a spot transaction and a forward transaction in foreign currency markets?
2. A U.S. investor is holding British pounds. What happens to the dollar value of the holdings if the pound appreciates in value?

INTEREST RATE FUNDAMENTALS

Interest rates determine the value (price) of transactions in money and capital markets, both in the U.S. and abroad and, as will be discussed later, affect the relationship between spot and forward foreign exchange rates. Given that the vast majority of the assets and liabilities of financial institutions are financial securities whose values are immediately affected by

---

[5] In this case, instead of selling the francs on the spot market at the end of the month (i.e., November 24) at the spot rate of .155 times Ff3 million, or $465,000, it receives (from the buyer of the one-month forward contract) .1682 times Ff3 million, or $504,600. In this case, the FI actually makes a small profit on the transaction equal to $504,600 minus $503,700, or $900.

T a b l e **2-7**

FACTORS AFFECTING INTEREST RATES

Inflation   The continual increase in the price level of a basket of goods and services.

Real Interest Rate   The interest rate that would exist on a default-free security if no inflation were expected.

Default Risk   The risk that a security's issuer will default on the security by missing an interest or principal payment.

Liquidity Risk   The risk that a security cannot be sold at a predictable price with low transaction costs at short notice.

Special Provisions   Provisions (e.g., taxability, convertibility, and callability) that impact the security holder beneficially or adversely and as such are reflected in the interest rates on securities that contain such provisions.

Time to Maturity   The length of time a security has until maturity.

---

interest rate changes, FI managers are intensely interested in estimating changes in interest rates. Many factors affect interest rates. These factors include inflation, the real interest rate in the economy, default risk, liquidity risk, special provisions, and term to maturity. We discuss each of these in this section and summarize them in Table 2–7.

Inflation

The first factor to affect interest rates is *actual or expected inflation*. Specifically, higher levels of actual or expected inflation are associated with higher levels of interest rates, and interest rates decline as inflation declines. The intuition behind the positive relationship between interest rates and inflation is that an investor who buys a financial asset must earn a higher interest rate when inflation increases to compensate for the increased opportunity cost of forgone consumption of real goods and services. **Inflation** is defined as the continual increase in the price level of a basket of goods and services. In the United States, inflation is measured by numerous indexes such as the Consumer Price Index (CPI) and the Producer Price Index (PPI).

inflation

The continual increase in the price level of a basket of goods and services.

Real Interest Rates

real interest rate

The interest rate that would exist on a default-free security if no inflation were expected.

A **real interest rate** is the interest rate that would exist on a default-free security if no inflation were expected. As such, it measures society's relative preferences for consuming today rather than tomorrow. The higher its preference to consume today (i.e., the higher its time value of money or rate of time preference), the higher is the real interest rate.

Default or Credit Risk

default risk

The risk that a security's issuer will default on that security by missing an interest or principal payment.

Default risk is the risk that a security's issuer will default on that security by missing an interest or principal payment. The higher the default risk, the higher the interest rate on the security. Not all securities exhibit the same default risk. For example, Treasury securities have no default risk and therefore carry the lowest interest rates. Some borrowers, such as corporations or individuals, have less predictable cash flows, and therefore lenders charge them an interest rate premium reflecting their probability of default (see Chapter 10). The difference between a quoted interest rate on a security and a Treasury security with similar maturity, liquidity, and other features is called a *default* or *credit risk premium*.

Liquidity Risk

liquidity risk

The risk that a security can be sold at a predictable price with low transaction costs on short notice.

A highly liquid asset is one that can be sold at a predictable price with low transaction costs and thus can be converted into its full cash value at short notice. The interest rate on a security reflects its relative liquidity with highly liquid assets carrying the lowest interest rates (all other characteristics being the same). Likewise, if a security is not liquid, investors add a **liquidity risk** premium to the market interest rate on the security. Liquid markets exist for government securities and stocks and bonds of large corporations. Securities such as real estate and those issued by small companies are relatively illiquid.

Special Provisions or Covenants

Numerous special provisions or covenants that may be written into the legal description of a security also affect interest rates. Some of these special provisions include taxability, convertibility, and callability.

For example, interest payments on municipal securities are tax free to the holder at the federal or state and local levels. Thus, the required interest rate demanded by a municipal bond holder is smaller than that on a comparable taxable bond, such as a Treasury bond (which is taxable at the federal level but not at the state or local levels) and a corporate bond (whose interest payments are taxable at the state and local levels as well as the federal levels).

Similarly, a convertible security offers the holder the opportunity to exchange one security for another type of the issuer's security at a preset price. Because of the value of this conversion "option," the convertible security holder requires a lower interest rate than a comparable nonconvertible security holder requires. In general, special provisions that provide benefits to the security holder (e.g., tax free status and convertibility) are associated with lower interest rates, and special provisions that provide benefits to the security issuer (e.g., callability, by which an issuer can retire—call—a security prior to maturity at a preset price) are associated with higher interest rates.

Term to Maturity

term structure of interest rates

A comparison of market yields on securities, assuming all characteristics except maturity are the same.

FIs analyze a fundamental relationship between interest rates and term to maturity, or the **term structure of interest rates**. The term structure of interest rates compares the market yields or interest rates on securities, assuming that all characteristics (i.e., default risk, liquidity risk) *except maturity* are the same. The yield curve for Treasury securities is the most commonly reported and analyzed yield curve. The shape of the yield curve on Treasury securities has taken many forms over the years, but the four most common shapes are shown in Figure 2–5. In (a), yields rise steadily with maturity when the yield curve is upward sloping. This is the most common yield curve. Part (b) shows an inverted or downward-sloping yield curve for which yields decline as maturity increases. Inverted yield curves were prevalent just before interest rates dropped in early 1992. Part (c) shows a humped yield curve, one most recently seen in mid- to late 1991. Finally, part (d) shows a flat yield curve in which term to maturity does not affect yield to maturity. This shape of the yield curve was last seen in the fall of 1989. Explanations for the shape of the yield curve fall predominantly into three theories: the unbiased expectations theory, the liquidity premium theory, and the market segmentation theory. Figure 2–6 presents the Treasury yield curve as of January 20, 1998.

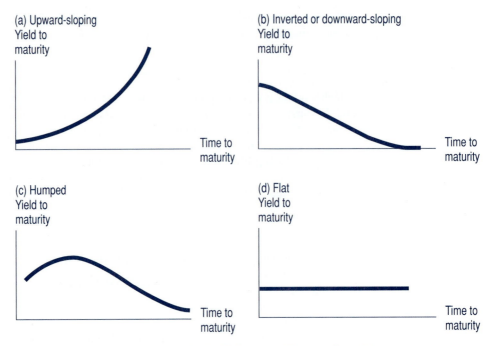

Figure **2-5**   *Common Shapes for Yield Curves on Treasury Securities*

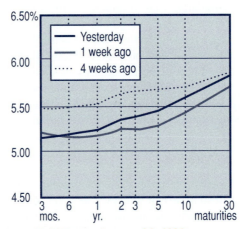

Figure **2-6**   *Treasury Yield Curve, January 20, 1998*

SOURCE: The *Wall Street Journal*, January 21, 1998, p. C24. Reprinted by permission of The Wall Street Journal. © 1998 Dow Jones & Company, Inc. All Rights Reserved Worldwide.

Unbiased Expectations Theory.   According to the unbiased expectations theory for the term structure of interest rates, at a given point in time the yield curve reflects the market's current expectations of future short-term rates. Thus, an upward-sloping yield curve reflects the market's expectation that short-term rates will rise throughout the relevant time period. Similarly, a flat yield curve reflects the expectation that short-term rates will remain constant over the relevant time period. The unbiased expectation theory posits that long-term rates are a geometric average of current and expected *future* short-term interest rates. The mathematical equation representing this relationship is

$$\bar{R}_N = [(1 + \bar{R}_1)(1 + E(\tilde{r}_2)) \ldots (1 + E(\tilde{r}_N))]^{1/N} - 1$$

where

$\bar{R}_N$ = actual N-period rate today
N = term to maturity
$\bar{R}_1$ = 1-year rate today and
$E(\tilde{r}_i)$ = expected one-year rates for years 2, 3, 4, ..., N in the future.

E X A M P L E   2 – 2

Construction of Yield Curve Using the Unbiased Expectations Theory of the Term Structure of Interest Rates

Suppose that the current and expected one-year T-bill rates over the next four years are as follows:

$$\bar{R}_1 = 6\%, \qquad E(\tilde{r}_2) = 7\%, \qquad E(\tilde{r}_3) = 7.5\%, \qquad E(\tilde{r}_4) = 8.5\%$$

Using the unbiased expectations theory, current (long-term) rates for one-, two-, three-, and four-year maturity Treasury securities is

$\bar{R}_1 = 6\%$
$\bar{R}_2 = [(1 + .06)(1 + .07)]^{1/2} - 1 = 6.499\%$
$\bar{R}_3 = [(1 + .06)(1 + .07)(1 + .075)]^{1/3} - 1 = 6.832\%$
$\bar{R}_4 = [(1 + .06)(1 + .07)(1 + .075)(1 + .085)]^{1/4} - 1 = 7.246\%$

and the yield curve should look like

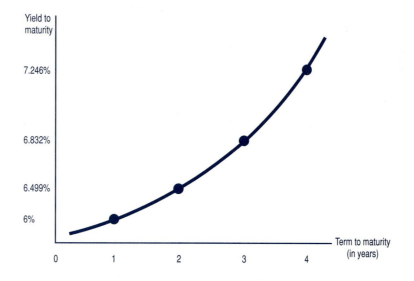

Thus, the yield curve reflects the market's expectations of persistently rising one-year, short-term interest rates in the future.[6]   •   •   •

---

[6] That is, $E(\tilde{r}_4) > E(\tilde{r}_3) > E(\tilde{r}_2) > \bar{R}_1$.

Liquidity Premium Theory.   The liquidity premium theory of the term structure of interest rates is based on the idea that investors will hold long-term maturities only if they are offered a premium to compensate for future uncertainty, which increases with an asset's maturity. In other words, the liquidity premium theory states that long-term rates are the geometric averages of current and expected short-term rates (as under the unbiased expectations theory) plus "liquidity" or risk premiums, which increase with the maturity of the security. For example, according to the liquidity premium theory, an upward-sloping yield curve may reflect the market's expectation that future short-term rates will be flat, but because liquidity premiums increase with maturity, the yield curve will nevertheless be upward sloping. The liquidity premium theory may be mathematically represented as

$$\bar{R}_N = [(1 + \bar{R}_1)(1 + E(\tilde{r}_2) + L_2) \ldots (1 + E(\tilde{r}_N) + L_N)]^{1/N} - 1$$

where

$$L_t = \text{liquidity premium for a period } t \text{ and } L_2 < L_3 < \ldots < L_N$$

Market Segmentation Theory.   The market segmentation theory argues that individual investors and FIs have specific maturity needs. Accordingly, the market segmentation theory does not consider securities with different maturities as perfect substitutes. Rather, individual investors and FIs have investment horizons dictated by the nature of the assets and liabilities they hold. Accordingly, interest rates are determined by distinct supply and demand conditions within a particular maturity need or market segment (e.g., the short end and long end of the market). The market segmentation theory assumes that neither investors nor borrowers are willing to shift from one maturity sector to another to take advantage of opportunities arising from relative changes in yields or interest rates (e.g., insurance companies generally prefer long-term securities, and banks generally prefer short-term securities). Figure 2–7 demonstrates how changes in the supply curve for short-versus long-term bonds result in changes in the shape of the yield to maturity curve. Specifically in Figure 2–7 the higher the yield on securities is (the lower the price), the higher is the demand for them.[7] Thus, as the supply of securities decreases in the short-term market and increases in the long-term market, the slope of the yield curve becomes steeper. If the supply of short-term securities had increased while the supply of long-term securities had decreased, the yield curve would have a flatter slope (and might even slope downward).

Concept Questions

1. What does *term structure of interest rates* mean?
2. What are the three explanations for the shape of the yield curve? Discuss and compare them.

· ·

---

[7] In general, the price and yield on a bond are inversely related. Thus, as the price of a bond falls (becomes cheaper), the demand for the bond will rise. This is the same as saying that as the yield on a bond rises, it becomes cheaper and the demand for it increases.

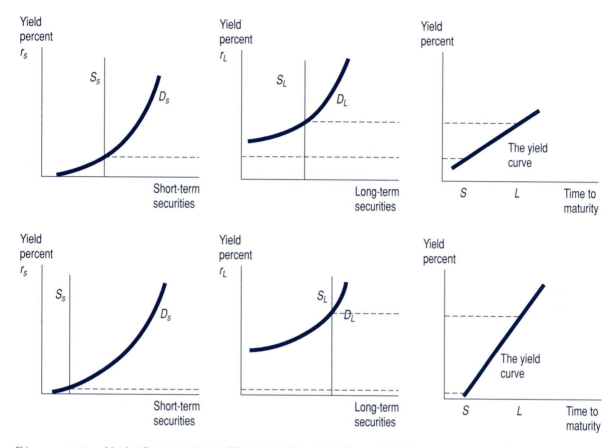

F i g u r e **2–7** *Market Segmentation and Determination of the Slope of Yield Curve*

INTERACTION OF INTEREST RATES, INFLATION, AND EXCHANGE RATES

As global financial markets become increasingly interlinked, so do interest rates, inflation, and foreign exchange rates. For example, higher domestic interest rates may attract foreign financial investment and impact the value of the domestic currency. In this section, we look at the effect that inflation (or change in the price level of a given set of goods and services) in one country has on its foreign currency exchange rates (purchasing power parity). We also examine the links between interest rates (domestic and foreign) and spot and forward foreign exchange rates (interest rate parity).

Purchasing Power Parity

purchasing power parity

The theory explaining the change in foreign currency exchange rates as inflation rates in the countries change.

One factor affecting a country's foreign currency exchange rate with another country is the relative inflation rate in each country. As inflation changes, foreign currency exchange rates adjust to account for relative differences in the price levels (inflation rates) in the two countries. One theory that explains how the adjustment takes place is the theory of **purchasing power parity (PPP)**. According to PPP, foreign currency exchange rates between two countries adjust to reflect changes in the countries' relative price levels (or inflation rates).

EXAMPLE 2–3

• • • • • •   *Application of Purchasing Power Parity*

Suppose that the price of a bundle of Russian-produced goods is 1,000 rubles,[8] and the same bundle of goods produced in the United States sells for $170. That is, the current spot exchange rate of Russian rubles for U.S. dollars, $S_{R/US}$, is .17. Let the price of the Russian-produced goods increase by 10 percent (i.e., inflation in Russia, i_R, is 10 percent) to 1,100 rubles and the U.S. price of the bundle of goods increase by 4 percent to $176.8 (i.e., inflation in the United States, i_{US}, is 4 percent). According to PPP, the 10 percent rise in the price of Russian goods combined with the 4 percent rise in the price of U.S. goods results in a depreciation of the Russian ruble and a relative appreciation of the U.S. dollar. Specifically, the exchange rate of Russian rubles to U.S. dollars should fall so that

$$\text{U.S. inflation rate} - \text{Russian inflation rate} = \frac{\text{Change in spot exchange rate of Russian rubles for U.S. dollars}}{\text{Initial spot exchange rate of Russian rubles for U.S. dollars}}$$

or

$$i_{US} - i_R = \Delta S_{R/US}/S_{R/US}$$

Plugging in the inflation and exchange rates, we get

$$.04 - .10 = \Delta S_{R/US}/.17$$

Rearranging to solve for the change in the spot rate of rubles for dollars ($\Delta S_{R/US}$), we have

$$\Delta S_{R/US} = (.04 - .10) \times .17 = -.0102 = -1.02\%$$

That is, the Russian ruble depreciates in value by 1.02 percent against the U.S. dollar. According to PPP, therefore, the new exchange rate of Russian rubles for U.S. dollars, $S^*_{R/US}$, is

$$S^*_{R/US} = .17 + (-.0102) = .1598 \qquad • \quad • \quad •$$

Interest Rate Parity

We discussed earlier that foreign exchange spot market risk can be reduced by entering into forward foreign exchange contracts. Look again at Table 2–6; spot rates and forward rates differ. For example, the spot exchange rate between the Canadian dollar and U.S. dollar was .7185 on October 24, 1997, meaning that one Canadian dollar could be exchanged today for .7185 U.S. dollar. The three-month forward rate between the two currencies, however, was .7220 on October 24, 1997. This forward exchange rate is determined by the spot exchange rate and the interest rates in the two countries.

The relationship between spot exchange rates, interest rates, and forward exchange rates is described as the **interest rate parity theorem (IRPT)**. Intuitively, the IRPT implies that, by hedging in the forward exchange rate market, an investor realizes the same returns on investments whether investing domestically or in a foreign country. This is a so-called no-arbitrage relationship in the sense that the investor cannot make a risk free return by taking offsetting positions in the domestic and foreign markets. The hedged dollar return on

interest rate parity theorem (IRPT)

The theory that the domestic interest rate should equal the foreign interest rate minus the expected appreciation of the domestic currency.

---

[8] As of January 1, 1998, Russian rubles were revalued by 1/1000th, so that 1,000 old rubles is now equal to 1 new ruble.

foreign investments just equals the return on domestic investments. Mathematically, the IRPT between the currencies of two countries (e.g., the United States and United Kingdom) can be expressed as

$$1 + r_{USt} = (1/S_t) \times (1 + r_{UKt}) \times F_t$$

Return on U.S. investment = Hedged return on foreign (U.K.) investment

where

$$1 + r_{USt} = 1 \text{ plus the interest rate on a U.S. investment maturing at time } t$$
$$1 + r_{UKt} = 1 \text{ plus the interest rate on a U.K. investment maturing at time } t$$
$$S_t = \$/\pounds \text{ spot exchange rate at time } t$$
$$F_t = \$/\pounds \text{ forward exchange rate at time } t$$

Rearranging, the IRPT can be expressed as

$$\frac{r_{USt} - r_{UKt}}{1 + r_{UKt}} = \frac{F_t - S_t}{S_t}$$

E X A M P L E   2 – 4

Application of Interest Rate Parity Theorem

Suppose that on October 24, 1997, a U.S. citizen has excess funds available to invest in either U.S. or U.K. time deposits. The investment horizon is one month. The interest rate available on British pound time deposits, r_{UK}, is 4.5 percent annually. The spot exchange rate of U.S. dollars for British pounds on October 24, 1997 (from Table 2–6) is \$1.634/\pounds, and the one-month forward rate is \$1.6318/\pounds. According to the IRPT, the interest rate on comparable U.S. time deposits should be

$$1 + r_{US} = (1/1.634) \times (1 + .045) \times 1.6318 = 1.0436$$

or the rate on U.S. time deposits should be 4.36 percent. We can rearrange this relationship as follows

$$\left(\frac{.0436 - .045}{1 + .045} \right) = \left(\frac{1.6318 - 1.634}{1.634} \right)$$
$$-.00134 \quad = \quad -.00134$$

Thus, the discounted spread between domestic and foreign interest rates is, in equilibrium, equal to the percentage spread between forward and spot exchange rates.   • • •

Suppose that in the preceding example, the annual rate on U.S. time deposits was 4.4 percent (rather than 4.36 percent). In this case, it would be profitable for the investor to put excess funds in the U.S. rather than the U.K. deposits. In fact, the arbitrage opportunity that exists results in a flow of funds out of U.K. time deposits into U.S. time deposits. According to the IRPT, this flow of funds would quickly drive up the U.S. dollar for British pound exchange rate until the potential profit opportunities from U.S. deposits are eliminated. Thus, any arbitrage opportunity should be small and fleeting.[9] That is, any long-term violations of

---

[9] In addition, as funds flowed out of U.K. time deposits, banks in the United Kingdom would have an incentive to raise rates. By comparison, as funds flowed into U.S. banks, the banks would have the incentive to lower rates. These two effects, combined with the effect on the spot rate of \$/\pounds, would once again equate the returns on domestic and foreign investments.

this relationship are likely to occur only if major imperfections exist in international deposit markets, including barriers to cross-border financial flows (see Chapter 26).

Concept Questions

1. What does the term *purchasing power parity* mean?
2. What is the interest rate parity condition? How does it relate to the existence or nonexistence of arbitrage opportunities?

SUMMARY

This chapter reviewed the basic operations of domestic and foreign financial markets. It described the way that funds flow through an economic system from lenders to borrowers and outlined the markets and instruments that lenders and borrowers employ. The chapter also discussed the exchange of U.S. dollars for foreign currencies and the way that changes in the exchange rates can affect an FI's returns. The chapter also introduced the determination of the term structure of interest rates as well as other factors that affect interest rates, such as credit risk, taxation, and liquidity. The chapter concluded with an examination of the interaction between interest rates and exchange rates. As international financial markets expand and become more integrated, FI managers must understand the markets in which FIs operate to be able to evaluate the potential return-risk trade-offs available to them.

PERTINENT WEB SITES

American Stock Exchange   http://www.amex.com/

Board of Governors of the Federal Reserve   http://www.bog.frb.fed.us/

Farm Credit Administration   http://www.fca.gov/

Federal Home Loan Bank   http://www.fhlbanks.com/

Federal Home Loan Mortgage Corp.   http://www.freddiemac.com/

Federal National Mortgage Association   http://www.fanniemae.com/

Federal Reserve Bank of St. Louis   http://www.stls.frb.org/

Government National Mortgage Assc.   http://www.ginniemae.gov/

National Association of Securities Dealers Automatic Quotations (NASDAQ)   http://www.nasdaq.com/

New York Stock Exchange   http://www.nyse.com/

Securities and Exchange Commission   http://www.sec.com/

Student Loan Marketing Association   http://www.salliemae.com/

U.S. Treasury   http://www.ustreas.gov/

Financial Markets: The Fundamentals

1. Classify the following transactions as taking place in a primary or secondary market:
   a. IBM issues $200 million of new common stock.
   b. New Company issues $50 million of common stock in an IPO.
   c. IBM sells $5 million of GM preferred stock from its marketable securities portfolio.
   d. Magellan Fund buys $100 million of previously issued IBM bonds.
   e. Prudential Insurance Co. sells $10 million of GM common stock.

2. Classify the following financial instruments as money market securities or capital market securities:
   a. Banker's acceptances.
   b. Commercial paper.
   c. Common stock.
   d. Corporate bonds.
   e. Mortgages.
   f. Negotiable certificates of deposit.
   g. Repurchase agreements.
   h. U.S. Treasury bills.
   i. U.S. Treasury notes.
   j. Federal funds.

3. How do the secondary markets benefit the original issuers of securities?

4. How does the location of the money market differ from that of the capital market?

5. Which of the money market instruments has grown fastest since 1990?

6. What is the difference between investment-grade bonds and junk bonds?

7. How do U.S. government agencies' securities differ from Treasury securities?

8. Go to the Ginnie Mae web site and look up the process for the issuance of Ginnie Mae securities.

9. Go to the *Wall Street Journal* and look up the following rates: federal funds, commercial paper, banker's acceptances, and certificates of deposit. How do the rates compare given approximately equal securities?

10. Classify the following transactions as occurring in the spot or forward markets:
    a. A U.S. bank sells $2 million of deutsche marks.
    b. A U.S. bank agrees to sell $4 million of Japanese yen in two months at a price agreed on today.
    c. A German bank buys $50 million.
    d. An Italian bank agrees to buy $100 million in 6 months at a price agreed on today.

11. If a U.S. bank is holding Japanese yen in its portfolio, what type of exchange rate movement most concerns the bank?

12. If a U.S. bank has entered a forward contract agreeing to sell Japanese yen in 60 days at a prespecified price, what type of exchange rate concerns the bank?

13. Last month, a U.S. investor purchased a forward contract to purchase Mexican pesos in 60 days. Since then, the peso/dollar exchange rate has increased. Has this increased exchange rate made the investor better off or worse off?

14. If we observe that a one-year Treasury security rate is higher than the two-year Treasury security rate, what can we infer about the one-year rate expected one year from now?

15. Suppose that we observe the following rates: $\bar{R}_1 = 8\%$, $\bar{R}_2 = 10\%$. If the unbiased expectations theory of the term structure of interest rates holds, what is the one-year interest rate expected one year from now, $E(\bar{r}_2)$?

16. Suppose that we observe the three-year Treasury security rate $(\bar{R}_3)$ to be 12 percent, the expected one-year rate next year—$E(\bar{r}_2)$—to be 8 percent, and the expected one-year rate the following year—$E(\bar{r}_3)$—to be 10 percent. If the unbiased expectations theory of the term structure of interest rates holds, what is the one-year Treasury security rate?

17. Suppose that we observe the following rates: $\bar{R}_1 = .10$, $\bar{R}_2 = .14$, and $E(\bar{r}_2) = .10$. If the liquidity premium theory of the term structure of interest rates holds, what is the liquidity premium for year 2?

18. If the interest rate in the United Kingdom is 8 percent, the interest rate in the United States is 10 percent, the spot exchange rate is $1.75/£, and interest rate parity holds, what must be the one-year forward exchange rate?

19. Suppose that all of the conditions in problem 18 hold except that the forward rate of exchange is also $1.75/£. How could an investor take advantage of this situation?

20. If a bundle of goods in Japan costs 4,000,000 yen while the same goods and services costs $40,000 in the U.S., what is the current exchange rate? If over the next year, inflation is 6 percent in Japan and 10 percent in the United States, what will the goods cost next year? Will the dollar devalue or appreciate relative to the yen over this time period?

21. What is the implication for cross-border trades if it can be shown that interest rate parity is maintained consistently across different markets and different currencies?

22. What are some reasons that interest rate parity may not hold in spite of the economic forces that should ensure the equilibrium relationship?

23. One form of the interest rate parity equation appears as $1 + r_{USt} = (1/S_t) \times (1 + r_{UKt}) \times F_t$ when both the spot and forward rates are in terms of dollars per pound or direct exchange rates. How would the equation be written if the exchanges rates were indirect, that is, pounds per dollar?

24. Assume that annual interest rates are 8 percent in the United States and 4 percent in Germany. An FI can borrow (by issuing CDs) or lend (by purchasing CDs) at these rates. The spot rate is $0.60/DM.
    a. If the forward rate is $0.64/DM, how could the bank arbitrage using a sum of $1 million? What is the spread earned?
    b. At what forward rate is this arbitrage eliminated?

Chapter Three

The Financial Services Industry: Depository Institutions

The theme of this book is that the products that modern financial intermediaries (FIs) sell and risks they face are becoming increasingly similar, as are the techniques they use to measure and manage these risks. The two panels in Table 3–1 indicate the products sold by the financial services industry in 1950 and in 1998. This chapter begins by describing three major FI groups, commercial banks, savings institutions, and credit unions, which are also called *depository institutions* because a significant proportion of their funds comes from customer deposits. Chapters 4 through 7 describe other (nondepository) FIs. Our attention focuses on three major characteristics of each group: (1) size, structure, and composition of the industry group, (2) balance sheets and recent trends, and (3) regulation.

As we examine the structure of depository institutions and their financial statements, notice a distinguishing feature between them and nonfinancial firms

Table **3–1**

PRODUCTS SOLD BY THE U.S. FINANCIAL SERVICES INDUSTRY

Institution	Payment Services	Savings Products	Fiduciary Services	Lending Business	Lending Consumer	Underwriting Issuance of Equity	Underwriting Issuance of Debt	Insurance and Risk Management Products
1950								
Depository institutions	X	X	X	X	X			
Insurance companies		X		*				X
Finance companies				*	X			
Securities firms		X	X			X	X	
Pension funds		X						
Mutual funds		X						
1998								
Depository institutions	X	X	X	X	X	†	†	X
Insurance companies	X	X	X	X	X	†	†	X
Finance companies	X	X	X	X	X	†	†	X
Securities firms	X	X	X	X	X	X	X	X
Pension funds		X	X	X				X
Mutual funds	X	X	X					X

*Minor involvement.

†Selective involvement via affiliates.

	Depository Institutions		Nonfinancial Firms	
	Assets	Liabilities and Equity	Assets	Liabilities and Equity
	Loans	Deposits	Deposits	Loans
	Other assets	Other liabilities and equity	Other assets	Other liabilities and equity

F i g u r e **3–1**   *Differences in Balance Sheets of Depository Institutions and Nonfinancial Firms*

illustrated in Figure 3–1. Specifically, depository institutions' major assets are loans and their major liabilities are deposits. Just the opposite is true for nonfinancial firms, whose deposits are listed as assets on the balance sheet and loans are listed as liabilities.

COMMERCIAL BANKS

Commercial Banks versus Savings Institutions and Credit Unions

Commercial banks represent the largest group of depository institutions in size. They perform functions similar to those of savings institutions (or thrifts) and credit unions; that

Table **3–2**

SUMMARY STATISTICS FOR U.S. COMMERCIAL BANKS, 1997

	Asset Size			
Year	$0–$100 million	$100 million –$1 billion	$1 billion– $10 billion	$10 billion+
Number of banks	6,047	2,888	306	67
Percent of U.S. banks	65.0	31.0	3.4	0.7
Total assets ($ billions)	$273.4	$711.0	$916.0	$2,870.8
Percent of U.S. banks' total assets	5.7	14.9	19.2	60.2

SOURCE: Federal Deposit Insurance Corporation, *Statistics on Banking*, Fourth Quarter, 1997.

is, they accept deposits (liabilities) and make loans (assets). The composition of assets and liabilities of commercial banks and savings institutions and credit unions differ; they vary much more for commercial banks. Commercial bank liabilities usually include several types of nondeposit sources of funds, and their loans are broader in range, including consumer, commercial, and real estate loans. Commercial banking activity is regulated separately from savings institutions and credit unions. Within the banking industry, the structure and composition of assets and liabilities also vary significantly for banks of different asset size.

Size, Structure, and Composition of the Industry

community bank

A bank that specializes in retail or consumer banking.

regional or superregional bank

A bank that engages in a complete array of wholesale commercial banking activities.

federal funds market

An interbank market for short-term borrowing and lending of bank reserves.

money center bank

A bank that relies heavily on nondeposit or borrowed sources of funds.

As of 1997, the United States had 9,308 commercial banks. Even though this may seem to be a large number, in fact the number of banks has been decreasing. For example, in 1985, the number of banks was 14,416; in 1989, it was 12,744. Subsequent chapters explore reasons for the drop in numbers (e.g., technology, Chapter 24; regulatory changes, Chapter 25; and competition,[1] Chapter 26).

Note the size distribution of the commercial banking industry (Table 3–2). Many banks are small; in fact, 8,935 banks, or 96.0 percent, accounted for approximately 20.6 percent of the assets of the industry in 1997. These small or **community banks**—with less than $1 billion in asset size—tend to specialize in retail or consumer banking, such as providing residential mortgages and consumer loans and accessing the local deposit base. The majority of banks in the largest two size classes ($1 billion or more in assets) are often either **regional or superregional banks.** They engage in a more complete array of wholesale commercial banking activities, encompassing consumer and residential lending as well as commercial and industrial lending (so-called C and I loans) both regionally and nationally. In addition, the big banks access markets for purchased funds, such as the interbank or **federal funds market,** to finance their lending and investment activities. Some of the very biggest banks often have the separate title **money center banks**, however; for example, in 1998, Salomon Brothers equity research department identified seven banking organizations in its money center bank group: Bank of New York, Bankers Trust, Chase Manhattan, Citicorp, J. P. Morgan, Republic NY Corporation, and First

---

[1] In particular, Chapter 26 provides a detailed discussion of the merger wave sweeping the commercial banking industry in the 1990s.

Contemporary Perspectives 3–1

Chase, Chemical Form America's Largest Bank

Chemical Bank Corp. and Chase Manhattan Corp. announced a $10 billion merger that will create North America's largest bank surpassing Citicorp. The merger is the latest in a string of merger and acquisition activity in the U.S. banking industry as banks look to expand their markets and reduce costs with the introduction of new federal interstate banking rules.

The two banks are expected to be a good fit as their commercial and retail businesses complement each other and opportunities for heavy cost cutting exist to the tune of about $1.5 billion out of the banks' combined $9.5 billion in annual costs.

The merged bank will have $300 billion in combined assets and will operate under the name Chase Manhattan. The deal will give the two companies increased critical mass to grab a bigger share of consumer and corporate banking as the big banks are now facing stiff competition from a large group of financial service providers such as brokerage firms, insurance companies and mutual funds.

SOURCE: Crosbie & Company Inc., *Mergers & Acquisitions in Canada,* September 1, 1995.

Chicago NBD.[2] This number has been declining because of mega-mergers (see Chapter 26). For example, in 1995, Chase Manhattan and Chemical Bank merged (see Contemporary Perspectives Box 3–1).

It is important to note that asset or lending size does not necessarily make a bank a money center bank. Thus, BankAmerica Corporation, with $258 billion in assets in 1997 (the fifth largest U.S. bank organization), is not a money center bank, but Republic NY Corporation (with only $58 billion in assets) is a money center bank. The distinction as a money center bank is partly location and partly its heavy reliance on nondeposit or borrowed sources of funds.[3] In fact, because of its extensive retail branch network, Bank of America, the subsidiary bank of BankAmerica Corporation, tends to be a net supplier of funds on the interbank market (federal funds market). By contrast, money center banks such as J. P. Morgan and Bankers Trust have no retail branches and rely almost entirely on wholesale and borrowed funds as sources of funds or liabilities. Money center banks are also major participants in foreign currency markets and are therefore subject to foreign exchange risk (see Chapter 27).

spread

The difference between lending and deposit rates.

The larger banks tend to fund themselves in national markets and to lend to large corporations. This means that the **spreads** (i.e., the difference between lending and deposit rates) in the past often have been narrower than those of smaller regional banks, which were more sheltered from competition in highly localized markets. As the barriers to interstate competition and expansion in banking have fallen in recent years, however, the largest banks' return on equity (ROE) have generally outperformed those of the smallest banks,

---

[2] These banking organizations are mostly holding companies that own and control the shares of a bank or banks. Thus, Citicorp is the bank organization (holding company) that owns and controls Citibank (the bank subsidiary).

[3] A money center bank is normally headquartered in New York or Chicago. These are the traditional national and regional centers for correspondent banking services offered to smaller community banks.

Table 3-3

ROA AND ROE OF DIFFERENT-SIZE BANKS, 1990–1997

Percentage Return on Assets (insured commercial banks by consolidated assets)

Year	All Banks	$0–$100 million	$100 million–$1 billion	$1 billion–$10 billion	$10 billion+
1990	0.49%	0.79%	0.78%	0.76%	0.38%
1991	0.54	0.83	0.83	0.54	0.44
1992	0.95	1.08	1.05	0.95	0.92
1993	1.22	1.16	1.19	1.33	1.24
1994	1.17	1.16	1.22	1.19	1.17
1995	1.17	1.18	1.25	1.28	1.10
1996	1.19	1.23	1.29	1.31	1.10
1997	1.24	1.25	1.39	1.30	1.18

Percentage Return on Equity (insured commercial banks by consolidated assets)

Year	All Banks	$0–$100 million	$100 million–$1 billion	$1 billion–$10 billion	$10 billion+
1990	7.64%	9.02%	9.95%	10.25%	6.68%
1991	8.05	9.40	10.51	7.50	7.35
1992	13.24	11.93	12.60	12.52	13.86
1993	15.67	12.29	13.61	14.02	16.81
1994	14.90	12.01	13.49	14.19	15.73
1995	14.68	11.37	13.48	15.04	15.60
1996	14.40	11.69	13.63	14.82	14.93
1997	14.71	11.57	14.50	14.30	15.32

SOURCE: Federal Deposit Insurance Corporation, *Quarterly Banking Profile*, various issues.

especially those with assets under $100 million (see Table 3–3).[4] The reverse has been true for return on assets (ROA); small banks (assets of less than $10 billion) have outperformed bigger banks. Notice too that all banks experienced record profit in the 1990s after record losses and numerous failures in the 1980s. (Chapter 8 discusses this trend in more detail.)

Balance Sheet and Trends

Assets.   Figure 3–2 shows the broad trends over the 1951–1998 period in the four principal earning asset areas of commercial banks: business loans (or commercial and industrial loans), securities, mortgages, and consumer loans. Although business loans were the major asset in bank balance sheets between 1965 and 1990, they have dropped in importance (as a proportion of the balance sheet) since 1990. At the same time, securities holdings and mortgages have increased in importance. These trends reflect a number of

---

[4] Arguably, the improved performance of larger banks also reflects improvements in the macroeconomy since the end of the 1989–1992 recession. That is, the improvement in big bank profitability may be temporary rather than permanent. Chapter 8 discusses ROE and ROA calculations in more detail.

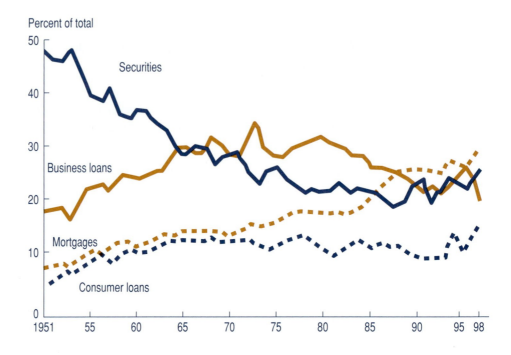

Figure **3-2** *Portfolio Shift: U.S. Commercial Banks' Financial Assets*

SOURCE: Federal Deposit Insurance Corporation, *Statistics on Banking,* various issues.

long-term and temporary influences. One important long-term influence has been the growth of the commercial paper market, which has become an alternative funding source to commercial bank loans for major corporations. Another has been the securitization of mortgages, the pooling and packaging of mortgage loans for sale in the form of bonds. A more temporary influence has been the so-called credit crunch and the decline in the demand for business loans as a result of the economic downturn and recession of the 1989–1992 period.

Consider the detailed balance sheet for all U.S. commercial banks as of August 27, 1997 (Table 3–4). Total loans amount to $3,083.4 billion and fall into four broad classes: business or commercial and industrial; commercial and residential real estate; individual, such as consumer loans for auto purchases and credit card debt; and all other loans, such as loans to less-developed countries. In the investment security portfolio of $1,027.7 billion, U.S. government securities, such as Treasury bonds, totaled $721.2 billion, with other securities (in particular, municipal securities and investment grade corporate bonds) making up the rest.[5]

A major inference we can draw from this asset structure is that modern commercial bank managers face a major risk in credit or default exposure (see Chapters 10 and 11).

---

[5] The footnotes to commercial bank balance sheets also distinguish between those securities held by banks for trading purposes, normally for less than one year, and those held for longer-term investment purposes. The large money center banks are often active in the secondary market trading of government securities, reflecting their important role as primary dealers in government securities at the time of Treasury security auctions.

Table **3-4**

BALANCE SHEET (ALL U.S. COMMERCIAL BANKS, AS OF AUGUST 27, 1997, IN BILLIONS OF DOLLARS)

Assets			Liabilities		
Loans and securities		$4,111.1	Total deposits		$3,029.0
Investment securities	1,027.7		Transaction accounts	711.8	
U.S. government securities	721.2		Nontransaction accounts	2,317.2	
Other	306.5		Large time deposits	608.8	
Total loans	3,083.4		Other	1,708.4	
Interbank loans	198.7		Borrowings		750.4
Loans excluding interbank	2,884.7		From banks in United States	276.5	
Commercial and industrial	830.4		From nonbanks in United States	473.9	
Real Estate	1,197.0		Other liabilities		487.4
Revolving home equity	94.2		Total liabilities		4,266.8
Other	1,102.8		Residual (assets less liabilities)		411.5
Individual	520.7				
All other	393.8				
Less: Reserve for loan losses	57.2				
Total cash assets		281.6			
Other assets		285.6			
Total assets		4,678.3			

SOURCE: *Federal Reserve Bulletin*, November 1997, p. A15 (seasonally adjusted).

Liabilities.   Commercial banks have two major sources of funds other than the equity provided by owners: deposits and borrowed or other liability funds. A major difference between banks and other firms is their high leverage. For example, banks had an average ratio of equity to assets of 8.80 percent in 1997; this implies that 91.20 percent of assets were funded by debt, either deposits or borrowed funds.

Note that in Table 3–4, which shows the aggregate balance sheet of U.S. banks, deposits amounted to $3,029.0 billion and borrowings and other liabilities were $750.4 and $487.4 billion, respectively. Of the total stock of deposits, transaction accounts represented 23.5 percent, or $711.8 billion. **Transaction accounts** are checkable deposits that either bear no interest (so-called demand deposits) or are interest bearing (most commonly called negotiable order of withdrawal accounts or **NOW accounts**). Since their introduction in 1980, interest-bearing checking accounts, especially NOW accounts, have dominated the transaction accounts of banks. Since limitations are imposed on the ability of corporations to hold such accounts and NOW accounts have minimum balance requirements, however, noninterest-bearing demand deposits are still held. The second major segment of deposits is retail or household savings and time deposits, normally individual account holdings of less than $100,000. Important components of bank retail savings accounts are small nontransaction accounts, which include passbook savings accounts and retail time deposits. Small nontransaction accounts compose 56.4 percent of total deposits. However, this disguises an important trend in the supply of these deposits to banks. Specifically, the amount

transaction accounts

The sum of noninterest-bearing demand deposits and interest-bearing checking accounts.

NOW account

An interest-bearing checking account.

money market mutual fund

A specialized mutual fund that offers depositlike interest-bearing claims to savers.

negotiable CDs

Fixed-maturity interest-bearing deposits with face values over $100,000 that can be resold in the secondary market.

in retail savings and time deposits has been falling in recent years, largely as a result of competition from **money market mutual funds**.[6] These funds pay a competitive rate of interest based on wholesale money market rates by pooling and investing funds (see Chapter 5) while requiring relatively small-denomination investments.

The third major source of deposit funds is the large time deposit (over $100,000)[7]; these deposits amounted to $608.8 billion, or approximately 20.1 percent of the stock of deposits, in August 1997. These are primarily **negotiable certificates of deposit** (deposit claims with promised interest rates and fixed maturities of at least 14 days) that can be resold to outside investors in an organized secondary market. As such, they are usually distinguished from retail time deposits by their negotiability and secondary market liquidity.

Nondeposit liabilities comprise borrowings and other liabilities that total 29 percent of all bank liabilities, or $1,237.8 billion. These categories include a broad array of instruments such as purchases of federal funds (bank reserves) on the interbank market and repurchase agreements (temporary swaps of securities for federal funds) at the short end of the maturity spectrum to the issuance of notes and bonds at the longer end.[8]

Overall, the liability structure of bank balance sheets tends to reflect a shorter maturity structure than the asset portfolio with relatively more liquid instruments such as deposits and interbank borrowings used to fund less liquid assets such as loans. Thus, maturity mismatch or interest rate risk and liquidity risk are key exposure concerns for bank managers (see Chapters 13, 17, and 18).

Off-Balance-Sheet Activities.   The balance sheet does not reflect many fee-related activities that banks conduct off the balance sheet. These activities include issuing various types of guarantees (such as letters of credit), which often have a strong insurance underwriting element, and making commitments to lend in the future for a fee. They also involve engaging in futures, forwards, options, and swap derivative transactions that are not reflected in the current balance sheet. As Chapter 20 discusses, off-balance-sheet activities are increasing in importance compared to the on-balance-sheet activities of many of the nation's largest banks. This is due to increased competition from other FIs and financial instruments in traditional areas of activity—commercial lending and deposit taking—as well as to fee, maturity interest rate risk management, and regulatory incentives to move off balance sheet. As will be discussed, these activities expose banks to new and important credit and other risks.

Regulation

The Regulators.   Unlike other countries that have one or sometimes two regulators, U.S. banks may be subject to the supervision and regulations of as many as four separate regulators. The key regulators are the Federal Deposit Insurance Corporation (FDIC), the Office of the Comptroller of the Currency (OCC), the Federal Reserve System (FRS), and state bank regulators. The next sections discuss the principal roles that each plays. The Appendix to this chapter lists the regulators that oversee the various activities of depository institutions.

---

[6] See U.S. General Accounting Office, "Mutual Funds: Impact on Bank Deposits and Credit Availability," GAO/GGD-95-230 (Washington, D.C.: Government Printing Office, 1995).

[7] $100,000 is the cap for explicit coverage under bank deposit insurance. We discuss this in more detail in Chapter 15.

[8] These instruments are explained in greater detail in later chapters, especially Chapter 14.

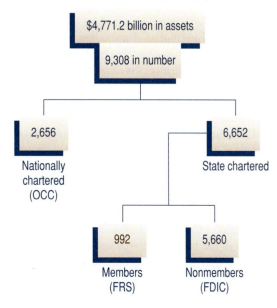

Figure **3-3**   *Bank Regulators*

SOURCE: FDIC, *Statistics on Banking*, Fourth Quarter, 1997.

The FDIC.   Established in 1933, the Federal Deposit Insurance Corporation insures the deposits of member banks. In so doing, it levies insurance premiums on member banks, manages the deposit insurance fund, and conducts bank examinations. In addition, when an insured bank is closed, the FDIC acts as the receiver and liquidator, although the closure decision itself is technically made by the bank chartering or licensing agency such as the OCC. Because of the problems in the thrift industry and the insolvency of the savings and loan (S&L) insurance fund (FSLIC) in 1989, the FDIC now manages both the commercial bank insurance fund and the S&L insurance fund. The Bank Insurance fund is called *BIF* and the S&L fund is the Savings Association Insurance Fund, or *SAIF*. The number of FDIC–BIF insured banks and the division between nationally and state-chartered banks is shown in Figure 3–3.

Office of the Comptroller of the Currency (OCC).   The OCC is the oldest bank regulatory agency; established in 1863, it is a subagency of the U.S. Treasury. Its primary function is to charter so-called national banks as well as to close them. In addition, OCC examines national banks and has the power to approve or disapprove their merger applications. Instead of seeking a national charter, however, banks can seek to be chartered by 1 of 50 individual state bank regulatory agencies. The choice of being a nationally chartered or state-chartered bank lies at the foundation of the **dual banking system** in the United States. Most large banks, such as Citibank, choose national charters, but others have state charters. For example, Morgan Guaranty, the money center bank subsidiary of J. P. Morgan, is chartered as a state bank under State of New York law. In September 1997, 2,656 banks were *nationally* chartered and 6,652 were *state* chartered, representing approximately 56 percent and 44 percent of total commercial bank assets, respectively.

dual banking system

The coexistence of both nationally and state-chartered banks as in the United States.

Federal Reserve System.   In addition to being concerned with the conduct of monetary policy, the Federal Reserve, as this country's central bank, also has regulatory power over some banks and, when relevant, their holding company parents. All nationally chartered banks shown in Figure 3–3 are automatically members of the Federal Reserve System (FRS); 992 of the state-chartered banks have also chosen to become members. Since 1980, all banks have had to meet the same noninterest-bearing reserve requirements whether they are members of the FRS or not. The primary advantages of FRS membership are direct access to the federal funds wire transfer network for nationwide interbank borrowing and lending of reserves and to the discount window for lender of last resort borrowing of funds. Finally, many banks are often owned and controlled by parent **holding companies**; for example, Citicorp is the parent holding company of Citibank (a national bank). Because the holding company's management can influence decisions taken by a bank subsidiary and thus influence its risk exposure, the FRS regulates and examines bank holding companies as well as the banks themselves.[9]

holding company

A parent company that owns a controlling interest in a subsidiary bank or other FI.

Regulations.   Commercial banks are among the most regulated firms in the U.S. economy. Because of the inherent special nature of banking and banking contracts, regulators have imposed numerous restrictions on their products and geographic activities. Table 3–5 lists the major laws beginning with the McFadden Act of 1927 to the Riegle-Neal Interstate Banking and Efficiency Act of 1994 and briefly describes the key features of each.

Table **3-5**

MAJOR FEATURES OF MAJOR BANK LAWS

1927 The McFadden Act

1. Subjected branching of nationally chartered banks to the same branching regulations as state-chartered banks.
2. Liberalized national banks' securities underwriting activities, which previously had to be conducted through state-chartered affiliates.

1933 The Banking Acts of 1933 (The Glass-Steagall Act)

1. Generally prohibited commercial banks from underwriting securities with four exceptions:
   a. Municipal general obligation bonds.
   b. U.S. government bonds.
   c. Private placements.
   d. Real estate loans.
2. In addition, established the FDIC to insure bank deposits.

1956 The Bank Holding Company Act

1. Restricted the banking and nonbanking acquisition activities of multibank holding companies.
2. Empowered the Federal Reserve to regulate multibank holding companies by
   a. Determining permissible activities.
   b. Exercising supervisory authority.
   c. Exercising chartering authority.
   d. Conducting bank examinations.

---

[9] The SEC has power to regulate the specialized securities subsidiaries of bank holding companies (so-called Section 20 subsidiaries).

Table **3–5** continued

1970 Amendments to the Bank Holding Company Act of 1956

1. Extended the BHC Act of 1956 to one-bank holding companies.
2. Restricted permissible BHC activities to those "closely related to banking."

1978 International Banking Act

1. Regulated foreign bank branches and agencies in the United States.
2. Subjected foreign banks to the McFadden and Glass-Steagall Acts.
3. Gave foreign banks access to Fedwire, the discount window, and deposit insurance.

1980 Depository Institutions Deregulation and Monetary Control Act (DIDMCA)

1. Set a six-year phaseout for Regulation Q interest rate ceilings on small time and savings deposits.
2. Authorized NOW accounts nationwide.
3. Introduced uniform reserve requirements for state and nationally chartered banks.
4. Increased the ceiling on deposit insurance coverage from $40,000 to $100,000.
5. Allowed federally chartered thrifts to make consumer and commercial loans (subject to size restrictions).

1982 Garn–St. Germain Depository Institutions Act (DIA)

1. Introduced money market deposit accounts (MMDAs) and super NOW accounts as interest rate-bearing savings accounts with limited check-writing features.
2. Allowed federally chartered thrifts more extensive lending powers and demand deposit-taking powers.
3. Allowed sound commercial banks to acquire failed savings banks.
4. Reaffirmed limitations on banks' ability to underwrite and distribute insurance.

1987 Competitive Equality in Banking Act (CEBA)

1. Redefined the definition of *bank* to limit the growth of nonbank banks.
2. Sought to recapitalize the Federal Savings and Loan Insurance Corporation (FSLIC).

1989 Financial Institutions Reform, Recovery, and Enforcement Act (FIRREA)

1. Limited savings banks' investments in nonresidential real estate, required divestiture of junk bond holdings (by 1994), and imposed a restrictive asset test to qualify as a savings bank (the qualified thrift lender test, or QTL).
2. Equalized the capital requirements of thrifts and banks.
3. Replaced FSLIC with FDIC-SAIF.
4. Replaced the Federal Home Loan Bank Board as the charterer of federal savings and loans with the Office of Thrift Supervision (OTS), an agency of the Treasury.
5. Created the Resolution Trust Corporation (RTC) to resolve failed and failing savings banks.

1991 Federal Deposit Insurance Corporation Improvement Act (FDICIA)

1. Introduced prompt corrective action (PCA), requiring mandatory interventions by regulators whenever a bank's capital falls.
2. Introduced risk-based deposit insurance premiums beginning in 1993.
3. Limited the use of "too big to fail" bailouts by federal regulators for large banks.
4. Extended federal regulation over foreign bank branches and agencies in the Foreign Bank Supervision and Enhancement Act (FBSEA).

1994 Riegle-Neal Interstate Banking and Branching Efficiency Act

1. Permitted bank holding companies to acquire banks in other states, starting September 1995.
2. Invalidated the laws of states that allow interstate banking only on a regional or reciprocal basis.
3. Beginning June 1997, permitted bank holding companies to convert out-of-state subsidiary banks into branches of a single interstate bank.
4. Also permitted newly chartered branches within a state if state law allows.

Even though later chapters will discuss these regulations, we now note the major objectives of each of these laws. The 1927 McFadden Act sought to restrict interstate bank branching; the 1933 Glass-Steagall Act sought to separate commercial banking from investment banking by limiting the powers of commercial banks to engage in securities activities. The Bank Holding Company Act of 1956 and its 1970 amendments strengthened restrictions on the nonbank activities of commercial banks by limiting the ability of a bank's parent holding company to engage in commercial, insurance, and other nonbank financial service activities. The 1978 International Banking Act extended federal regulation, such as the McFadden and Glass-Steagall Acts, to branches and agencies of foreign banks located in the United States for the first time, thereby seeking to level the competitive playing field between domestic and foreign banks. The 1980 Depository Institutions Deregulation and Monetary Control Act (DIDMCA) and the 1982 Garn-St. Germain Depository Institutions Act (DIA) are mainly deregulation acts in that they eliminated interest ceilings on deposits and allowed banks (and thrifts) new liability and asset powers.[10] As the next section on thrifts discusses, this deregulation is blamed, in part, for the thrift crisis that resulted in widespread failures and the insolvency of the FSLIC in 1989.

nonbank bank

A financial intermediary that undertakes many of the activities of a commercial bank without meeting the legal definition of a bank.

The Competitive Equality in Banking Act (CEBA) 1987 sought to impose controls over a growing number of **nonbank banks** that were established to avoid interstate banking restrictions and restrictions on nonbank ownership of banks imposed under the 1927 McFadden and the 1956 Bank Holding Company Acts. In 1989, Congress responded to the problems of thrifts and the collapse of the FSLIC with the passage of the Financial Institutions Reform, Recovery, and Enforcement Act (FIRREA). In 1991, Congress enacted the Federal Deposit Insurance Corporation Improvement Act (FDICIA) to deal with the large number of bank failures and the threatened insolvency of the FDIC, the insurance fund for commercial banks. Both the FIRREA and the FDICIA sought to pull back from some of the deregulatory elements of the 1980 DIDMCA and 1982 DIA. In 1994, the Riegle-Neal Act rolled back many of the restrictions on interstate banking imposed by the 1927 McFadden and 1956 Bank Holding Company Acts. In particular, in June 1997, bank holding companies were permitted to convert their bank subsidiaries in various states into branches, thus making interstate branching possible for the first time in 70 years.

Concept Questions

1. What are the major assets that commercial banks hold?
2. What are the major sources of funding for commercial banks?
3. What are the responsibilities of the three federal regulatory agencies in the United States?
4. What major regulations have affected the operations of U.S. commercial banks?

---

[10]In particular, Regulation Q ceilings on bank deposit rates were phased out in stages between March 1980 and March 1986.

SAVINGS
INSTITUTIONS

Savings institutions (or thrifts) comprise two different groups of FIs: savings and loan associations (S&Ls) and savings banks (SBs). They are usually grouped together because they not only provide important mortgage and/or lending services to households but also are important recipients of household savings. Historically, S&Ls have concentrated primarily on residential mortgages while savings banks have been operated as more diversified S&Ls having a large concentration of residential mortgage assets but holding commercial loans, corporate bonds, and corporate stock as well. The next sections review these two types of savings institutions.

Savings and Loans

Size, Structure, and Composition of the Industry.   The S&L industry prospered throughout most of the 20th century. The specialized institutions in this industry made long-term residential mortgages backed by short-term savings deposits. This was possible largely because of the Federal Reserve's policy of smoothing or targeting interest rates, especially in the 1960s and 1970s until October 1979, and the generally upward-sloping shape of the yield curve or the term structure of interest rates (see Chapter 2). During some periods, such as the early 1960s, the yield curve sloped downward, but for most of the post-World War II period, the upward-sloping yield curve meant that the interest rates on 30-year residential mortgage assets exceeded rates on short-term savings and time deposit liabilities. Moreover, significant shocks to interest rates were generally absent due to the Fed's policy of interest rate smoothing.

At the end of the 1970s, slightly fewer than 4,000 S&Ls had assets of approximately $0.6 trillion. During the October 1979 to October 1982 period, however, the Federal Reserve radically changed its monetary policy strategy by targeting bank reserves rather than interest rates in an attempt to lower the underlying rate of inflation (see Chapter 17 for more details). The Fed's restrictive monetary policy action led to a sudden and dramatic surge in interest rates, with rates on T-bills rising as high as 16 percent. This increase in short-term rates and the cost of funds had two effects. First, S&Ls faced negative interest spreads or **net interest margins** (i.e., interest income minus interest expense divided by earning assets) in funding much of their fixed-rate long-term residential mortgage portfolios over this period. Second, they had to pay more competitive interest rates on savings deposits to prevent **disintermediation** and the reinvestment of these funds in money market mutual fund accounts. Their ability to do this was constrained by the Federal Reserve's **Regulation Q ceilings**, which limited the rates that S&Ls could pay on traditional passbook savings account and retail time deposits.[11]

In part, to overcome the effects of rising rates and disintermediation on the S&L industry, Congress passed the DIDMCA and DIA (see Table 3–5); these expanded S&Ls' deposit-taking and asset investment powers. On the liability side, S&Ls were allowed to offer NOW accounts and more market rate–sensitive liabilities such as money market deposit accounts to limit disintermediation and to compete for funds. On the asset side, they were allowed to offer floating or adjustable-rate mortgages and to a limited extent expand into consumer and commercial lending. In addition, many state-chartered thrifts,

net interest margin

Interest income minus interest expense divided by earning assets.

disintermediation

Withdrawal of deposits from S&Ls and other depository institutions to be reinvested elsewhere.

Regulation Q ceiling

An interest ceiling imposed on small savings and time deposits at banks and thrifts until 1986.

---

[11]These Regulation Q ceilings were usually set at rates of 5¼ or 5½ percent.

Table 3-6

BALANCE SHEETS OF SAVINGS AND LOANS (PERCENTAGE OF TOTAL ASSETS AND LIABILITIES)

Item	1977	1982
Liabilities		
Fixed ceiling liabilities	87.3%	22.0%
Passbook and NOW accounts	33.9	15.6
Fixed ceiling time deposits	53.4	6.4
Market ceiling small time deposits	0.0	52.8
Money market certificates	0.0	28.6
Small saver certificates	0.0	19.3
Other small time deposits	0.0	4.9
Discretionary liabilities	8.6	23.2
Large time deposits	2.1	8.1
FHLB advances	4.7	10.3
Other borrowings	1.8	4.6
Other liabilities	4.0	2.0
Assets		
Mortgage assets	86.0	81.1
Fixed rate	86.0	74.9
Adjustable rate	0.0	6.2
Nonmortgage loans	2.3	2.6
Cash and investments	9.2	11.2
Other assets	2.5	5.1

SOURCE: *Federal Reserve Bulletin*, December 1982.

especially in California, Texas, and Florida, received wider investment powers that included real estate development loans often made through special-purpose subsidiaries. Note the structural shifts in S&L balance sheets between 1977 and 1982 in Table 3–6 and the effects on thrift industry profits in Table 3–7.

For many S&Ls, the new powers created safer and more diversified institutions. For a small but significant group whose earnings and shareholders' capital was being eroded in traditional lines of business, however, it meant the opportunity to take more risks in an attempt to return to profitability. This risk-taking or moral hazard behavior was accentuated by the policies of the S&L insurer, FSLIC. It chose not to close capital-depleted, economically insolvent S&Ls (a policy of **regulator forbearance**) and to maintain deposit insurance premium assessments independent of the risk of the S&L institution (see Chapter 15).[12] As a result, an alarming number of failures occurred in the 1982–1989 period along with rapid asset growth of the industry. Thus, although S&Ls decreased in number from 4,000 in 1980 to 2,600 in 1989 (or by 35 percent), their assets actually doubled from $600 billion to $1.2 trillion over the same period.

regulator forbearance

A policy not to close economically insolvent FIs but allowing them to continue in operation.

---

[12]We discuss moral hazard behavior and the empirical evidence regarding such behavior in more detail in Chapter 15.

Table 3-7

NET INCOME AT THRIFT INSTITUTIONS (AMOUNTS IN BILLIONS OF DOLLARS; PERCENTAGES AT ANNUAL RATES)

Year	FSLIC-Insured Savings and Loan Associations		All Operating Mutual Savings Banks	
	Amount	Percentage of Average Assets	Amount	Percentage of Average Assets
1970	0.9	0.57	0.2	0.27
1971	1.3	0.71	0.4	0.48
1972	1.7	0.77	0.6	0.60
1973	1.9	0.76	0.6	0.54
1974	1.5	0.54	0.4	0.35
1975	1.4	0.47	0.4	0.38
1976	2.3	0.63	0.6	0.45
1977	3.2	0.77	0.8	0.55
1978	3.9	0.82	0.9	0.58
1979	3.6	0.67	0.7	0.46
1980	0.8	0.14	–0.2	–0.12
1981	–4.6	–0.73	–1.4	–0.83
H1	–1.5	–0.49	–0.5	–0.56
H2	–3.1	–0.97	–0.9	–1.10
1982–H1	–3.3	–1.01	–0.8	–0.92

H = Half–year.

SOURCE: *Federal Reserve Bulletin,* December 1982.

The large number of S&L failures, especially in 1988 and 1989, depleted the resources of the FSLIC to such an extent that by 1989 it was massively insolvent. The resulting legislation, the FIRREA of 1989, abolished the FSLIC and created a new insurance fund (SAIF) under the management of the FDIC. In addition, the act created the Resolution Trust Corporation (RTC) to close the most insolvent S&Ls.[13] The FIRREA also strengthened the capital requirements of S&Ls and constrained their nonmortgage-related asset-holding powers under a newly imposed qualified thrift lender test, or **QTL test**.

QTL test

Qualified thrift lender test that sets a floor on the mortgage-related assets that thrifts can hold (currently, 65 percent).

As a result of closing weak S&Ls and strengthening capital requirements, the industry is significantly smaller both in terms of numbers and asset size in the 1990s. Thus, the number of S&Ls has decreased from 2,600 in 1989 to 1,481 in 1997 (by 43 percent) and assets have decreased from $1.2 trillion to $708 billion (by 41 percent) over the same period.

Balance Sheet and Recent Trends.   Even in its new smaller state, the future viability of the S&L industry in traditional mortgage lending areas is a matter of concern. This is due partly to intense competition for mortgages from other financial institutions such as commercial banks and specialized mortgage bankers. It is due also to the securitization of mortgages into mortgage-backed security pools by government-sponsored enterprises, which we discuss further in Chapter 12.[14] In addition, long-term mortgage lending exposes an FI to significant credit, interest rate, and liquidity risks.

---

[13]At the time of its dissolution in 1995, the RTC had resolved or closed more than 700 savings banks.

[14]The major enterprises are GNMA, FNMA, and FHLMC.

A 1992 study found that surviving thrifts improved their profit margin (6.93 percent in 1992 compared to 4.51 percent in 1987) and reduced their leverage while maintaining a relatively stable level of asset turnover.[15] Nevertheless, this improved performance was aided by the relatively low interest rate levels in the early 1990s, which helped S&Ls to expand their net interest margins (NIMs). The unresolved question is whether S&Ls can survive another period of sharply rising interest rates as in the early 1980s, given their restrained powers of asset diversification and heavy reliance on mortgage assets required by the QTL test for these institutions.[16] Indeed, S&L profitability weakened in 1997 due to higher short-term rates (which impact the interest expense or cost of funds to S&Ls) and lower long-term rates (which impact their interest income). While the **profit margin** (i.e., net income divided by total operating income) stood at 10.30 percent in 1997, the net interest margins of S&Ls narrowed from 3.48 percent in 1992 to 3.24 percent in 1997.

profit margin

Net profit divided by total operating income.

Table 3–8, the SAIF-Insured Institutions column shows the balance sheet of SAIF-insured S&Ls in 1997. On this balance sheet, mortgages and mortgage-backed securities (securitized pools of mortgages) represent 80.93 percent of total assets. As noted earlier, the FDICIA uses the QTL test to establish a minimum holding of 65 percent in mortgage-related assets for S&Ls. Reflecting the enhanced lending powers established under the 1980 DIDMCA and 1982 DIA, commercial loans and consumer loans amounted to 1.28 and 4.40 percent of assets, respectively. Finally, S&Ls are required to hold cash and investment securities for liquidity purposes and to meet regulator-imposed reserve requirements. In June 1997, cash and U.S. Treasury securities holdings amounted to 5.89 percent of total assets.

On the liability side of the balance sheet, small time and savings deposits are still the predominant source of funds, with total deposits accounting for 68.61 percent of total liabilities and net worth. The second most important source of funds is borrowing from the 12 Federal Home Loan Banks (FHLBs), which the S&Ls themselves own. Because of their size and government-sponsored status, FHLBs have access to wholesale money markets for notes and bonds and can relend the funds borrowed on these markets to S&Ls at a small markup over wholesale cost. Other borrowed funds include repurchase agreements and direct federal fund borrowings. Finally, net worth is the book value of the equity holders' capital contribution; it amounted to 8.43 percent in 1997.

Regulation.   The two main regulators of S&Ls are the Office of Thrift Supervision (OTS) and the FDIC-SAIF Fund.

The Office of Thrift Supervision.   Established in 1989 under the FIRREA, this office charters and examines all federal S&Ls. It also supervises the holding companies of S&Ls. State-chartered S&Ls are regulated by state agencies rather than the OTS.

The FDIC-SAIF Fund.   Also established in 1989 under the FIRREA and in the wake of FSLIC insolvency, the FDIC oversees and manages the Savings Association Insurance Fund (SAIF).

---

[15]C. Rossi, "The Viability of the Thrift Industry" (Washington, DC: Office of Thrift Supervision, December 1992).
[16]The FIRREA required 70 percent of S&L's assets to be mortgage related. The FDICIA reduced this to 65 percent.

Table **3–8**

ASSETS AND LIABILITIES OF SAVINGS BANKS AND S&LS, JUNE 30, 1997

	(1) BIF-Insured Savings Banks		(2) SAIF-Insured Institutions (S&Ls)*	
	($ Millions)	(Percent)	($ Millions)	(Percent)
Cash and due from	$ 5,279	1.64%	$ 16,962	2.40%
U.S. treasury and federal agency obligations	11,464	3.56	24,726	3.49
Mortgage loans	187,554	58.25	441,875	62.41
MBS (includes CMOs, POs, IOs)	59,490	18.48	131,166	18.52
Bonds, notes, debentures, and other securities	17,526	5.44	16,174	2.28
Corporate stock	5,568	1.73	3,662	0.52
Commercial loans	6,220	1.93	9,092	1.28
Consumer loans	15,652	4.86	31,169	4.40
Other loans and financing leases	768	0.24	1,393	0.20
Less: Allowance for loan losses and unearned income	2,515	0.78	4,333	0.61
Other assets	14,985	4.65	36,197	5.11
Total assets	$ 321,991	100.00	$ 708,083	100.00
Total deposits	234,233	72.75	485,806	68.61
Borrowings and mortgages warehousing	40,122	12.46	113,077	15.97
Federal fund, repository, and FHLB advances	16,205	5.03	41,289	5.83
Other liabilities	3,341	1.04	8,184	1.16
Total liabilities	293,901	91.28	648,356	91.57
Net worth†	28,090	8.72	59,727	8.43
Total liabilities and net worth	$ 321,991	100.00	$ 708,083	100.00
Number of banks	371		1,481	

*Excludes institutions in RTC conservatorship.

†Includes limited life preferred stock for BIF–insured state charter savings banks and redeemable preferred stock and minority interest for SAIF–insured institutions and BIF–insured FSBs.

SOURCE: FDIC, *Statistics on Banking*, Second Quarter, 1997.

Concept Questions

1. Are S&Ls likely to be more or less exposed to interest rate risk than banks? Explain your answer.
2. How do adjustable-rate mortgages help S&Ls?
3. Why should S&Ls with little or no equity capital seek to take more risk than well-capitalized S&Ls do?
4. Why could it be argued that the QTL test makes S&Ls more rather than less risky?

Savings Banks

Size, Structure, and Composition of the Industry.   Traditionally, savings banks were established as **mutual organizations** (in which the depositors are also legally the owners of the bank) in those states that permitted such organizations. These states are largely confined to the East Coast, for example, New York, New Jersey, and the New England states. In recent years, many of these institutions—similar to S&Ls—have switched from mutual to stock charters. In addition, fewer than 20 have switched to federal charters. In June 1997, 371 state-chartered mutual savings banks had $322 billion in assets; their deposits are insured by the FDIC under the BIF. This distinguishes savings banks from S&Ls, whose deposits are insured under the FDIC-SAIF.

mutual organization

Savings bank in which the depositors also own the bank.

Balance Sheet and Recent Trends.   Notice the major similarities and differences between S&Ls and savings banks in Table 3–8, which shows their respective assets and liabilities as of June 1997. Savings banks (in the first column of Table 3–8) have a heavy concentration (76.73 percent) of mortgage loans and mortgage-backed securities (MBSs), but this is less than the S&Ls' 80.93 percent in these assets. Over the years, savings banks have been allowed to diversify more into corporate bonds and stocks; their holdings are 7.17 percent compared to 2.80 percent for S&Ls. On the liability side, the major difference is that savings banks rely more on deposits than S&Ls do, and therefore savings banks have less borrowings. Finally, the ratio of the book value of net worth to total liabilities and net worth for savings banks stood at 8.72 percent (compared to 8.43 percent for S&Ls) in 1997.

Regulation.   Savings banks may be regulated at both the federal and state levels.

The FDIC-BIF.   Savings banks are insured under the FDIC's BIF and are thus subject to supervision and examination by the FDIC.

Other Regulators.   State-chartered savings banks (the vast majority) are regulated by state agencies. Those savings banks adopting federal charters are subject to the regulations of the OTS (the same as S&Ls).

Concept Questions

1.   What are four characteristics that differentiate savings banks from S&Ls?
2.   How are savings banks regulated?

CREDIT

UNIONS

Credit unions (CUs) are nonprofit depository institutions owned by their members (depositors) with a common bond (e.g., university students and employees, police associations, military bases) whose objective is to satisfy the depository and lending needs of their members. CU member deposits (shares) are used to provide loans to other members in need of funds. Any earnings from these loans are used to pay higher rates on member deposits, charge lower rates on member loans, or attract new members to the CU. Because credit unions do not issue common stock, the members technically own them. Also, because credit unions are nonprofit organizations, their net income is not taxed. This tax-exempt status allows CUs to offer higher rates on deposits and charge lower rates on some types of loans than banks and S&Ls.

Size, Structure, and Composition of the Industry and Recent Trends

Credit unions are the most numerous of the institutions (11,328 in 1997) that compose the depository institutions segment of the FI industry. Moreover, CUs were less affected by the crisis that affected commercial banks and savings institutions in the 1980s. This happened because more than 43 percent of their assets are small consumer loans, often for amounts less than $10,000. In addition, CUs tend to hold large amounts of government securities (almost 20 percent of their assets in 1997) and relatively small amounts of residential mortgages. CUs' lending activities are funded mainly by deposits contributed by their 70 million (in 1997) members who share some common thread or bond of association, usually geographical or occupational in nature.

To attract and keep customers, CUs have had to expand their services to compete with banks and S&Ls. For example, CUs now offer products and services from mortgages and auto loans (their traditional services) to credit lines and automated teller machines. Some credit unions now offer business and commercial loans to their employer groups. Because of their tax-exempt status, CUs can charge lower rates on these loans, a cost advantage over banks and S&Ls that customers have found very attractive. An example of the success of one military base–related credit union is presented in Contemporary Perspectives Box 3–2.

As CUs have expanded in number, size, and services, bankers claim that CUs unfairly compete with small banks that have historically been the major lender in small towns. For example, the American Bankers Association has made claims that the tax exemption for CUs gives them the equivalent of a $1 billion a year subsidy. The response of the Credit Union National Association (CUNA) is that any cost to taxpayers from CUs' tax exempt status is more than offset by benefits to members and, therefore, the social good they create. The CUNA estimates that the benefits of CU membership can range from $200 to $500 a year per member or, with almost 70 million members, a benefit of $14 billion to $35 billion per year.

In 1997, the banking industry filed two lawsuits in its push to narrow the widening membership rules governing credit unions. The first lawsuit challenged an occupation-based credit union's ability to accept members from companies unrelated to the firm that originally sponsored the credit union. In the second lawsuit, the American Bankers Association asked the courts to bar the federal government from allowing occupation-based credit unions to convert to community-based charters. Bankers argued in both lawsuits that such actions, broadening the membership of credit unions along other than occupation-based guidelines, would further exploit an unfair advantage allowed through the credit union tax-exempt status. In February 1998, the Supreme Court sided with banks in its decision that credit unions could no longer accept members that were not a part of the common bond of membership. In April 1998, however, the U.S. House of Representatives overwhelmingly passed a bill that allowed all existing members to keep their credit union accounts.

Table 3–9 shows the assets and liabilities for credit unions as of September 30, 1997. As of 1997, more than 11,300 credit unions had assets of $349.2 billion. This compares to $155 billion in assets in 1987, or a growth rate of 125 percent in that 10-year period. Individually, credit unions tend to be very small, with an average size of $28.3 million in 1997 compared to $465.1 million for banks. The total assets of all credit unions are approximately the same size as the largest U.S. banking organizations. For example, Chase Manhattan had $367 billion in assets in 1997.

Contemporary Perspectives 3–2

Piggy Banks with Muscles: As Credit Unions Boom, Financial Rivals Cry Foul

As the Carswell Air Force Base shrank to the vanishing point, its credit union, set up in 1956 with $35 in assets and seven members, was growing into one of the biggest financial service providers in the Dallas–Fort Worth metropolitan area.

Nearly six years ago, the announcement that Carswell was going to be shut, a victim of the end of the cold war, stunned the community and sent shock waves through the economy. But the announcement did not faze the Carswell Federal Credit Union. It simply changed its name to OmniAmerican and kept expanding.

Today, it counts 137,000 members employed at 1,300 businesses and organizations, ranging from the Boy Scouts of America to Pier One Imports. At the end of 1996, assets totaled $517 million, and OmniAmerican currently boasts 12 branches, from the original office at what is now the Fort Worth Joint Reserve Base to a spiffy $3 million office, complete with a baby grand player piano, abutting one of the city's toniest residential neighborhoods. . . .

Credit unions like OmniAmerican promote themselves as friends of the consumer, grass–roots organizations that offer higher interest on deposits and lower rates on loans than commercial banks. . . . OmniAmerican is one of the biggest and most efficiently managed of the nation's 11,900 credit unions. . . . To attract and hold customers, institutions like OmniAmerican are offering an increasingly diverse array of products and services, from mortgages and auto loans to credit lines to automated teller machines. Two years ago, OmniAmerican began making business and commercial loans to its employer groups. In a promotional book, the list of products and services it offers is nine pages long.

OmniAmerican has shown itself to be a master of marketing. In its literature, it says its potential membership exceeds 500,000 "locally, nationally and worldwide." At a number of its branches dotted throughout the Dallas–Fort Worth metropolitan area an electronic message flashes across outdoor screens 24 hours a day: "For the Truth . . . Ask About . . . Financial Freedom of Choice . . . Come Inside for Details . . . Join OmniAmerican."

Converts to credit unions sometimes have more than numbers on their minds, of course. Wendell Geiger, a former Air Force physician who now teaches at Texas Christian University, said bureaucratic intransigence at Bank One drove him and his wife into the arms of OmniAmerican a few years ago. "My wife had an account at Bank One, and was charged all the fees and what not," he said inside an OmniAmerican branch on a recent morning. "But when she went for a loan, they needed me to co-sign it. That's when we said forget it. It's not like she works at McDonald's."

SOURCE: Kenneth N. Gilpin, The *New York Times,* February 26, 1997, p. D1. Copyright © 1997 by The New York Times Co. Reprinted by Permission.

Regulation

Like savings banks and S&Ls, credit unions can be federally or state chartered. Approximately two-thirds of credit unions are federally chartered and subject to National Credit Union Administration (NCUA) regulation. In addition, through its insurance fund (NCUIF), the NCUA provides deposit insurance guarantees of up to $100,000 for insured credit unions. Currently, the NCUIF covers 98 percent of all credit union deposits.

Concept Questions

1. Why have credit unions prospered in recent years in comparison to S&Ls and savings banks?
2. What major assets do credit unions hold?

Table **3–9**

ASSETS AND LIABILITIES OF CREDIT UNIONS, SEPTEMBER 30, 1997

Assets	Billions of Dollars	Percentage	Liabilities and Equity	Billions of Dollars	Percentage
Checkable deposits and currency	$ 7.0	2.0	Checkable	$ 36.8	10.5
Time and savings deposits	16.8	4.8	Small time and savings	258.9	74.2
Federal funds and security RPs	3.8	1.1	Large time	13.4	3.8
			Shares/deposits	$ 309.1	88.5
Open market paper	0.2	0.1			
U.S. government securities	68.3	19.5	Other loans and advances	0.5	0.2
Treasury	15.8	4.5	Miscellaneous liabilities	7.0	2.0
Agency	52.5	15.0	Total liabilities	$ 316.6	90.7
Home mortgages	84.4	24.2	Total ownership shares	32.6	9.3
Consumer credit	150.7	43.1			
Credit market instruments	$ 303.6	86.9			
Mutual fund shares	2.5	0.7			
Miscellaneous assets	15.5	4.5			
Total assets	$ 349.2	100.0			

SOURCE: *Federal Reserve Bulletin,* December 1997, p. 74.

S U M M A R Y

This chapter provided an overview of the major activities of commercial banks, savings institutions, and credit unions as well as the agencies that regulate these depository institutions. The FRS, the FDIC, the OTS, and the OCC, in conjunction with state regulators, are the agencies that oversee the activities of these institutions. Each of these institutions relies heavily on deposits to fund its activities, although borrowed funds are becoming increasingly important for the largest institutions. Historically, commercial banks have concentrated on commercial or business lending and on investing in securities while savings institutions have concentrated on mortgage lending and credit unions on consumer lending. These differences are being eroded due to competitive forces, regulation, and changing financial and business technology. Indeed, in the late 1990s, the largest group of assets in commercial bank portfolios are mortgage related. This reliance on long-term lending (such as mortgages) and short-term funding means that the interest rate, credit, liquidity, and other risks faced by commercial banks, savings banks, and credit unions are becoming more similar than different. The measurement and management of such exposures are major themes of Chapters 9 through 28 of this book.

PERTINENT WEB SITES

American Bankers Association   http://www.aba.com/aba/

Bank Web Site Addresses   http://www.mybank.com/

Board of Governors of the Federal Reserve   http://www.bog.frb.fed.us/

Credit Union National Association   http://www.cuna.org/

Federal Deposit Insurance Corp   http://www.fdic.gov/

Federal Financial Institutions Examination Council   http://www.ffiec.gov/

Federal Trade Commission   http://www.ftc.gov/

General Accounting Office   http://www.gao.gov/

National Credit Union Administration   http://www.ncua.gov/

Office of the Comptroller of Currency   http://www.occ.treas.gov/

Office of Thrift Supervision   http://www.ots.treas.gov/

Securities and Exchange Commission   http://www.sec.gov/

APPENDIX: DEPOSITORY INSTITUTIONS AND THEIR REGULATORS

A. National banks	Federal Reserve, FDIC, OCC
B. State member banks	State authority, Federal Reserve, FDIC
C. State nonmember banks insured	State authority, Federal Reserve, FDIC
D. Noninsured state banks	State authority, Federal Reserve, FTC
E. Insured savings associations, federal*	OTS, Federal Reserve, FDIC
Insured savings associations, state†	State authority, OTS, Federal Reserve, FDIC
F. Uninsured savings associations, state	State authority, Federal Reserve, FTC
G. Credit unions, federal	NCUA, Federal Reserve, state authority
Credit unions, state	State authority, NCUA, Federal Reserve, FTC
H. Bank holding companies	Federal Reserve, state authority, FTC
I. Savings association holding companies	OTS, state authority, Federal Reserve, FTC
J. Foreign branches of U.S. banks, national and state members	Federal Reserve, state authority, OCC
Foreign branches of U.S. banks, insured state nonmembers	State authority, FDIC
K. Edge Act corporations	Federal Reserve
Agreement corporations	State authority, Federal Reserve
L. U.S. branches and agencies of foreign banks, federal	OCC, Federal Reserve, FDIC, FTC, state authority
U.S. branches and agencies of foreign banks, state	State authority, Federal Reserve, FDIC, OCC, FTC

The matrix provides an overview of primary regulators of depository institutions as of April 1998. It is not intended to cover each area of regulatory responsibility in detail. Further, the matrix and accompanying footnotes should not be considered either a substitute for or an interpretation of the regulations. Regulatory agencies should be consulted for answers to specific questions.

Legend

FDIC	Federal Deposit Insurance Corporation	NCUA	National Credit Union Administration
FTC	Federal Trade Commission	OCC	Office of the Comptroller of Currency
Federal Reserve	Board of Governors of the Federal Reserve System/Federal Reserve Banks	OTS	Office of Thrift Supervision

*Federal savings associations include any thrift institution such as federal savings banks, federally chartered under Section 5 of the Home Owners' Act.

†State savings associations include any state chartered savings bank, savings and loan association, building and loan association, homestead association, or cooperative bank.

SOURCE: Public Information Department, Federal Reserve Bank of New York, 33 Liberty Street, New York, NY 10045.

The Financial Services Industry: Depository Institutions

1. What does the term *depository institution* mean? How does a depository institution differ from an industrial corporation?

2. What are the major sources of funds for commercial banks in the United States? What are the major uses of funds for commercial banks in the United States? For each answer, specify where the item appears on the balance sheet of a typical commercial bank.

3. What has been the recent trend in the number of commercial banks in the United States? What factors account for this trend?

4. What is the difference between money center banks and regional banks? Contrast their activities with those of small commercial banks.

5. What are the principal types of financial assets for commercial banks? How has the relative importance of these assets changed for the past five decades? What are some of the forces that have caused these changes? What are the primary types of risk associated with these types of assets?

6. What are the principal liabilities for commercial banks? What does this liability structure tell us about the maturity of the liabilities of banks? What types of risks does this liability structure entail for commercial banks?

7. Compare and contrast the profitability ratios (ROE and ROA) of banks with assets below and above $100 million in Table 3–3 from 1993 through 1997. What conclusions can you derive from those numbers?

8. What does the term *off-balance-sheet* activity mean? What are some examples of them? What are some of the forces responsible for them?

9. How do the balance sheets of S&Ls and savings banks differ from those of commercial banks? How do their sizes compare?

10. What were the reasons for the crisis in the thrift industry in the late 1970s and early 1980s?

11. What two major pieces of legislation were adopted in the early 1980s to ameliorate the thrift crisis? Explain.

12. What shortcoming in the Depository Institutions Deregulation and Monetary Control Act of 1980 (DIDMCA) and the Garn-St. Germain Depository Institutions Act of 1982 (DIA) contributed to the failure of the thrift industry?

13. How did the Financial Institutions Reform, Recovery, and Enforcement Act (FIRREA) of 1989 and the Federal Deposit Insurance Corporation Improvement Act of 1991 reverse some of the key features of earlier legislation?

14. What are the main features of the Riegle-Neal Interstate Banking and Branching Efficiency Act of 1994? What major impact on commercial banking activity is expected from this legislation?

15. What are the similarities and differences among savings institutions (i.e., S&Ls and savings banks)?

16. What regulatory agencies oversee deposit insurance services to S&Ls and saving banks? How is the risk-based deposit insurance premium introduced in 1993 expected to reduce the number of failures in the future?

17. What happened to the value of the savings institutions in the period of time since October 1979? How did this shift contribute to the S&L crisis?

18. How can the recent decline in the size of the savings institution industry be explained?

19. Why were credit unions less affected by the S&L crisis than the savings institution industry?

20. How does a national bank differ from a state-chartered bank?

21. Go to the Federal Reserve Board's web site and find the latest figure for the total assets of all U.S. commercial banks. How does this compare with the figure from Table 3–4?

Chapter Four

The Financial Services Industry: Insurance Companies

T he primary function of insurance companies is to protect individuals and corporations (policyholders) from adverse events. By accepting premiums, insurance companies promise to compensate policyholders if certain prespecified events occur to them. The insurance industry is classified into two major groups, life and property-casualty. Life insurance provides protection in the event of untimely death, illnesses, and retirement. Property insurance protects against personal injury and liability such as accidents, theft, and fire.

This chapter discusses the main features of insurance companies by concentrating on (1) the size, structure, and composition of the industry in which they operate; (2) balance sheets and recent trends; and (3) regulations.

LIFE INSURANCE COMPANIES

Size, Structure, and Composition of the Industry

In 1997, the United States had 1,563 life insurance companies compared to 1,758 in 1980. The aggregate assets of life insurance companies were $2.30 trillion at the end of 1997 compared to $.48 trillion in 1980. The life insurance industry has experienced some major mergers in recent years as competition within the industry and with other FIs has increased (see Contemporary Perspectives Box 4–1).

Contemporary Perspectives 4–1

Insurer Grows, Equating Size and Survival

American General's $4.4 billion shopping spree to gain size and strengthen its position in the fiercely competitive insurance industry reached its culmination yesterday with an announcement by the company that it would acquire the USLife Corporation for $1.8 billion in stock.

The combined company would rank among the top four life insurers in the country with $300 billion of life insurance in force, 10 million customers, a network of 25,000 sales representatives and revenue of $9 billion.

USLife is only the latest and largest of five major acquisitions by American General over the last two years. The company said it was not finished searching for increased earnings and market share in an insurance industry that has become crowded with securities firms, banks and foreign companies, as well as insurers.

American General should be able to easily integrate USLife into its existing businesses, allowing it to expand the number of customers while cutting overlapping operations and lowering expenses. "Our near-

term, as well as our long-term strategy involves internal growth as well as external growth through acquisitions," said Rover M. Devlin, president and chief executive of American General. "We will continue to look at potential acquisitions. . . ."

"It's a good match, " said Andrew Kligerman, an analyst with Schroder, Wertheim & Company. "There is a need to generate critical mass in order to overcome declining profit margins and new entrants to the growing annuities market. For many companies, sales remain sluggish and expense ratios continue to be high. A quick and obvious solution is consolidation. I suspect that we're at the beginning of a more rapid consolidation of the industry. . . ."

The American General deal is but the latest in a wave of mergers and acquisitions that are beginning to swamp the insurance industry. The combined value of merger activity jumped to $31.8 billion in 1995, according to Houlihan Lokey's Mergerstat. The number of deals rose to 193 last year from 80 in 1993, and analysts expect the pace to quicken.

In December, a Dutch insurance giant, Aegon, acquired the insurance

operations of the Providian Corporation of Louisville for $2.6 billion. GE Capital has snapped up Life of Virginia and First Colony in transactions valued at $2.76 billion. Two years ago, the Massachusetts Mutual Life Insurance merged with Connecticut Mutual Life, and Metropolitan Life merged with New England Mutual Life. Some analysts expect many of the largest mutual life companies to transform themselves into publicly traded companies.

And if companies like American General are gaining heft, insurers with several lines of business are shedding some operations. Both the Chubb Corporation and USF&G are selling their life insurance operations and focusing on property and casualty insurance.

About 1,700 companies make up the insurance industry, Mr. Devlin said, but quickly added that when the dust settled from the latest round of deals, he expected that there would be only 25 to 30 significant firms and that they would control as much as 90 percent of the market.

Life insurance allows individuals to protect themselves and their beneficiaries against losses in income through premature death or retirement. By pooling risks, life insurance transfers income-related uncertainties from the insured individual to a group. Although life insurance may be their core activity area, modern life insurance companies also sell annuity contracts, manage pension plans, and provide accident and health insurance. We discuss these different activity lines in the following sections.

Life Insurance.   The four basic classes or lines of insurance are distinguished by the manner in which they are sold or marketed to purchasers. These classes are (1) ordinary life, (2) group life, (3) industrial life, and (4) credit life. Of the life insurance policies in force in the United States in the 1990s, ordinary life accounted for approximately 60 percent, group life for less than 40 percent, industrial life for less than 1 percent, and credit life for less than 2 percent of the almost $20 trillion contract value in force.

Ordinary Life.   Ordinary life insurance policies are marketed on an individual basis, usually in units of $1,000; policymakers make periodic premium payments. Despite the enormous variety of contractual forms, there are essentially five basic contractual types. The first three are traditional forms of ordinary life insurance, and the last two are newer contracts that originated in the 1970s and 1980s due to increased competition for savings from other segments of the financial services industry. The three traditional contractual forms are term life, whole life, and endowment life. The two newer forms are variable life and universal life. The key features of each of these contractual forms are identified as follows:

- *Term life.*   This policy is the closest to pure life insurance; it has no savings element attached. Essentially, an individual's beneficiary receives a payout at the time of the individual's death during the coverage period. The term of coverage can vary from as little as 1 year to 40 years or more.
- *Whole life.*   This policy protects the individual over an entire lifetime rather than for a specified coverage period. In return for periodic or level premiums, the individual's beneficiaries receive the face value of the life insurance contract on death. Thus, if the policyholder continues premium payments, the insurance company is certain to make a payment—unlike term insurance where a payment is made only if death occurs during the coverage period. As a result, whole life has a savings element as well as a pure insurance element.
- *Endowment life.*   This type of policy combines both a pure (term) insurance element with a savings element. It guarantees a payout to the beneficiaries of the policy if death occurs during some endowment period (e.g., prior to reaching retirement age). An insured person who lives to the endowment date receives the face amount of the policy.
- *Variable life.*   Unlike traditional policies that promise to pay the insured the fixed or face amount of a policy should a contingency arise, variable life insurance invests fixed premium payments in mutual funds of stocks, bonds, and money market instruments. Usually, policyholders can choose mutual fund investments to reflect their risk preferences. Thus, variable life provides an alternative way to build savings compared to the more traditional policies such as whole life because the value of the policy increases (or decreases) with the asset returns of the mutual fund in which premiums are invested.
- *Universal life and variable universal life.*   This policy allows the insured to change both the premium amounts and the maturity of the life contract, unlike traditional policies that maintain premiums at a given level over a fixed contract period. In addition, for some contracts, insurers invest premiums in money, equity, or bond mutual funds— as in variable life insurance—so that the savings or investment component of the contract reflects market returns. In this case, the policy is called *variable universal life*.

Group Life Insurance. This insurance covers a large number of insured persons under a single policy. Usually issued to corporate employers, these policies may be either *contributory* (where the employer covers a share of the cost of the insurance) or *noncontributory* (where the employer does not contribute to the cost of the insurance) for the employees themselves. The principal advantage of group life over ordinary life policies involves cost economies. These occur as the result of mass administration of plans, lower costs for evaluating individuals through medical screening and other rating systems, and reduced selling and commission costs.

Industrial Life. This type of life insurance currently represents a very small area of coverage. Industrial life usually involves weekly payments collected directly by representatives of the companies. To a large extent, the growth of group life insurance has led to the demise of industrial life as a major activity class.

Credit Life. This insurance protects lenders against a borrower's death prior to the repayment of a debt contract such as a mortgage or car loan. Usually, the face amount of the insurance policy reflects the outstanding principal and interest on the loan.

Other Life Insurer Activities. Three other major activities of life insurance companies are related to the sale of annuities, private pension plans, and accident and health insurance.

Annuities. Annuities represent the reverse of life insurance activities. Life insurance involves different contractual methods to *build up* a fund; annuities involve different methods of *liquidating* a fund, such as paying out a fund's proceeds. As with life insurance contracts, many different types of annuity contracts have been developed. Specifically, they can be sold to an individual or group and on either a fixed or variable basis by being linked to the return on some underlying investment portfolio. Individuals can purchase annuities with a single payment or payments spread over a number of years. Payments may be structured to begin immediately, or they can be deferred. These payments may cease at death or continue to be paid to beneficiaries for a number of years after death. Annuity sales in 1997 were $110 billion ($85 billion of which were variable annuities), topping the $100 billion mark for the second year in a row.[1]

E X A M P L E   4 – 1

Calculation of Fair Value on an Annuity Policy

Suppose that a person wants to purchase an annuity today that would pay $15,000 per year until the end of the person's life. The insurance company expects the person to live for 25 more years and can invest the amount received for the annuity at an assumed rate of 5 percent. The fair price for the annuity policy can be calculated as follows:

$$\text{Fair Value} = \frac{15,000}{1+r} + \frac{15,000}{(1+r)^2} + ... + \frac{15,000}{(1+r)^{25}}$$

$$= 15,000 \left[\frac{1}{1+r} + \frac{1}{(1+r)^2} + ... + \frac{1}{(1+r)^{25}} \right]$$

---

[1] As discussed in Chapter 25, life insurers are facing increasingly intense competition from banks in the annuity product market.

$$= 15,000\ [PVAF_{r=5\%,n=25}]$$
$$= 15,000\ [14.0939]$$
$$= \$211,409$$

where $PVAF_{r=5\%,n=25}$ is the present value annuity factor reflecting the present value of $1 invested at 5 percent over 25 years. Thus, the cost of purchasing this annuity today would be $211,409.[2] • • •

Private Pension Funds.   Insurance companies offer many alternative pension plans to private employers in an effort to attract this business away from other financial service companies such as commercial banks and securities firms. Some of their innovative pension plans are based on guaranteed investment contracts (GICs). With such plans the insurer guarantees not only the rate of interest credited to a pension plan over some given period—for example, five years—but also the annuity rates on beneficiaries' contracts. Other plans include immediate participation and separate account plans that follow more aggressive investment strategies than does traditional life insurance, such as investing premiums in special-purpose equity mutual funds. At the end of 1997, life insurance companies were managing $1.24 trillion in pension fund assets, equal to 35 percent of all private pension plans.

Accident and Health Insurance.   While life insurance protects against mortality risk, accident and health insurance protect against morbidity or ill health risk. More than $100 billion in premiums was written by life and health companies in the accident-health area in 1997. The major activity line is group insurance, which provides health insurance coverage to corporate employees. Other coverages included credit health plans, whereby individuals have their debt repayments insured against unexpected health contingencies and various types of renewable, nonrenewable, and guaranteed health and accident plans for individuals. In many respects, insurers in accident and health lines face loss exposures that are more similar to those that property-casualty insurers face than those that traditional insurers face (see the section on property-casualty insurance, which follows shortly).

Balance Sheet and Recent Trends

Assets.   Because of the long-term nature of their liabilities (resulting from the long-term nature of life insurance policyholders' claims) and the need to generate competitive returns on the savings elements of life insurance products, life insurance companies concentrate their asset investments at the longer end of the maturity spectrum (e.g., bond, equities, and government securities). Table 4–1 shows the distribution of life insurance assets. As you can see, in 1997 15.9 percent of assets were invested in government securities, 65.3 percent in corporate bonds and stocks, and 8.3 percent in mortgages, with other loans—including **policy loans** (i.e., loans made to policyholders using their policies as collateral)—composing the balance. The major trends have been a long-term increase in the proportion of bonds and equities[3] and a decline in the proportion of mortgages on the balance sheet.

policy loans

Loans made by an insurance company to its policyholders using their policies as collateral.

---

[2] Tables listing $PVAF_{r,n}$ are provided in the Appendix in the back of the text.
[3] The bull market of the 1980s and 1990s is likely a major reason for the large percentage of assets invested in equities.

Table **4–1**

LIFE INSURANCE COMPANY ASSETS

(distribution of assets of U.S. life insurance companies)

Year	Total Assets (in millions)	Government Securities	Corporate Securities		Mortgages	Real Estate	Policy Loans	Misc. Assets
			Bonds	Stocks				
1917	$ 5,941	9.6%	33.2%	1.4%	34.0%	3.0%	13.6%	5.2%
1920	7,320	18.4	26.7	1.0	33.4	2.3	11.7	6.5
1925	11,538	11.3	26.2	0.7	41.7	2.3	12.5	5.3
1930	18,880	8.0	26.0	2.8	40.2	2.9	14.9	5.2
1935	23,216	20.4	22.9	2.5	23.1	8.6	15.2	7.3
1940	30,802	27.5	28.1	2.0	19.4	6.7	10.0	6.3
1945	44,797	50.3	22.5	2.2	14.8	1.9	4.4	3.9
1950	64,020	25.2	36.3	3.3	25.1	2.2	3.8	4.1
1955	90,432	13.1	39.7	4.0	32.6	2.9	3.6	4.1
1960	119,576	9.9	39.1	4.2	34.9	3.1	4.4	4.4
1965	158,884	7.5	36.7	5.7	37.8	3.0	4.8	4.5
1970	207,254	5.3	35.3	7.4	35.9	3.0	7.8	5.3
1975	289,304	5.2	36.6	9.7	30.8	3.3	8.5	5.9
1980	479,210	6.9	37.5	9.9	27.4	3.1	8.6	6.6
1985	825,901	15.0	36.0	9.4	20.8	3.5	6.6	8.7
1986	937,551	15.4	36.5	9.7	20.6	3.4	5.8	8.6
1987	1,044,459	14.5	38.8	9.3	20.4	3.3	5.1	8.6
1988	1,166,870	13.7	41.2	8.9	20.0	3.2	4.6	8.4
1989	1,299,756	13.7	41.4	9.7	19.5	3.1	4.4	8.2
1990	1,408,208	15.0	41.4	9.1	19.2	3.1	4.4	7.8
1991	1,551,201	17.4	40.2	10.6	17.1	3.0	4.3	7.4
1992	1,664,531	19.2	40.3	11.5	14.8	3.1	4.3	6.8
1993	1,839,127	20.9	39.7	13.7	12.5	2.9	4.2	6.1
1994	1,930,500	20.4	41.0	14.6	11.2	2.2	4.4	6.2
1995	2,131,900	18.6	41.4	17.4	9.9	1.9	4.5	6.3
1996	2,271,700	17.0	42.4	21.0	9.0	1.7	4.4	4.5
1997	2,510,400	15.9	41.5	23.8	8.3	1.6	4.2	4.7

NOTE: Beginning with 1962, these data include the assets of separate accounts.

SOURCE: *Best's Review*, (Oldwick, NJ: A.M. Best Company), various issues; and *Federal Reserve Bulletin*, various issues.

policy reserves

A liability item for insurers that reflects their expected payment commitments on existing policy contracts.

surrender value of a policy

The cash value of a policy received from the insurer if a policyholder surrenders the policy prior to maturity; normally only a portion of the contract's face value.

Liabilities. The aggregate balance sheet for the life insurance industry at the end of 1996 is presented in Table 4–2. Looking at the liability side of the balance sheet, we see that $1.218 trillion, or 52.9 percent, of total liabilities and capital reflect the net **policy reserves** (i.e., the expected payment commitments on existing policy contracts). These reserves are based on actuarial assumptions regarding the insurers' expected future liability commitments to pay out on present contracts, including death benefits, matured endowments (lump sum or otherwise), and the cash **surrender value of policies** (i.e., the cash value paid to the policyholder if the policy is surrendered before it matures). Even though the actuarial assumptions underlying policy reserves are normally very conservative, unexpected fluctuations in future required payouts can occur; that is, underwriting life insurance is risky. For example, mortality rates—and life insurance payouts—might unexpectedly

Table 4–2

LIFE INSURANCE INDUSTRY BALANCE SHEET AS OF DECEMBER 31, 1996

(in thousands of dollars)

Assets		Percent of Total	Liabilities and Capital/Surplus		Percent of Total
Bonds	$1,197,999,008	52.0%	Net policy reserves	$1,217,958,797	52.9
Preferred stock	10,431,334	0.5	Policy claims	24,572,051	1.1
Common stock	54,340,911	2.4	Policy dividend		
Mortgage loans	204,018,925	8.9	accumulations	20,048,648	0.9
Real estate	37,645,179	1.6	Dividend reserve	13,805,878	0.6
Policy loans	98,254,683	4.3	Premium and		
Cash and deposits	3,490,208	0.1	deposit funds	201,701,005	8.7
Short-term investments	38,381,262	1.7	Commissions, taxes,		
Other invested assets	23,183,948	1.0	expenses	16,585,666	0.7
Life and annuity			Securities valuation		
premium due	12,869,630	0.6	reserve	32,684,136	1.4
Accident and health			Other liabilities	68,479,141	3.0
premium due	5,219,878	0.2	Separate account		
Accrued investment			business	569,461,870	24.7
income	23,799,912	1.0	Total capital and		
Separate account			surplus	137,716,655	6.0
assets	572,368,902	24.8	Capital	3,822,710	0.2
Other assets	21,010,068	0.9	Treasury stock	(359,666)	0.0
Total assets	$2,303,013,848	100.0	Paid-in and		
			contributed surplus	55,638,348	2.4
			Surplus notes	10,756,976	0.5
			Unassigned surplus	55,100,944	2.4
			Other surplus	2,034,149	0.1
			Other reserves	10,723,194	0.4
			Total liabilities and		
			capital/surplus	$2,303,013,848	100.0

SOURCE: *Best's Aggregates & Averages,* Life-Health, (Oldwick, NJ: A.M. Best Company, 1997) p.3.

separate account

Annuity program sponsored by life insurance companies in which the payoff on the policy is linked to the assets in which policy premiums are invested.

increase over those defined by historically based mortality tables due to a catastrophic epidemic such as AIDS. To meet unexpected future losses, the life insurer holds a capital and surplus reserve fund with which to meet such losses. The capital and surplus reserves of life insurers in 1996 totaled $138 billion, or 6.0 percent of total assets.[4] **Separate account** business was 24.7 percent of total assets in 1996. A separate account is a fund established and held separately from the insurance company's other assets. These funds may be invested without regard to the usual restrictions (i.e., they may be invested in all stocks, or all bonds, etc.). The payoff on the life insurance policy depends, then, on the return on the funds in the separate account. Another important life insurer liability, GICs (8.7 percent of total assets) are short- and medium-term debt instruments sold by insurance companies to fund their pension plan business (see premium and deposit funds in Table 4–2).

---

[4] An additional line of defense against unexpected underwriting losses is the insurer's investment income from its asset portfolio plus any new premium income flows.

Regulation

McCarran-Ferguson
Act of 1945

Regulation confirming
the primacy of state over
federal regulation of
insurance companies.

The most important legislation affecting the regulation of life insurance companies is the **McCarran-Ferguson Act of 1945**, which confirms the primacy of state over federal regulation of insurance companies. Thus, unlike the depository institutions we discussed in Chapter 3, which can be chartered at either federal or state levels, a life insurer is chartered entirely at the state level. In addition to chartering, state insurance commissions supervise and examine insurance companies using a coordinated examination system developed by the National Association of Insurance Commissioners (NAIC). An example of state insurance regulatory actions is the 1997 case of Prudential Insurance Company. Prudential's policyholders filed and settled (for $410 million) a class action lawsuit claiming that Prudential's sales representatives defrauded customers (talking them into using built-up cash value of older life insurance coverages to buy new, costlier policies). A task force of state insurance regulators from 45 states conducted an 18-month deceptive sales practices investigation. The report resulting from this investigation was instrumental in determining the legal settlement.

insurance guaranty
funds

A fund of required con-
tributions from within-
state insurance companies
to compensate insurance
company policyholders in
the event of a failure.

Other than supervision and examination, states also promote life **insurance guaranty funds.** In most cases, such funds are not permanent (as is the FDIC) but involve required contributions from surviving within-state insurance companies to compensate the policyholders of an insurer after a failure has occurred.

In recent years, life insurance companies have been under pressure to generate higher returns for savers and to invest on a long-term basis to better match their relatively long-term liability exposures. This has led a small but significant number of life insurance companies to expand their holdings of low-quality junk bonds and to invest heavily in long-term mortgage loans for commercial property development. In particular, the sharp decline in property values in Texas, the Northeast, and California has raised concerns about the credit, interest rate, and liquidity risk exposures of some large life insurance companies. As a result, insurance company regulators have imposed constraints on life insurers' holdings of low-quality junk bonds and have established a model investment law that restricts investment concentrations in low-credit-quality assets as well as holding concentrations in assets of individual issuers (see Chapter 11).

Concept Questions

1. What is the difference between a life insurance contract and an annuity contract?
2. What are the different forms of ordinary life insurance?
3. Why do life insurance companies invest in long-term assets?
4. What is the major source of life insurance underwriting risk?
5. Who are the main regulators for the life insurance industry?

PROPERTY-CASUALTY
INSURANCE

Size, Structure, and Composition of the Industry

Currently, some 2,300 companies sell property-casualty (PC) insurance, and approximately 700 firms write PC business in all or most of the United States. The U.S. PC insurance industry is quite concentrated. Collectively, the top 10 firms have a 42 percent share of the

Table 4-3

TWO-FIRM INSURANCE SELLER PREMIUM CONCENTRATIONS FOR 18 PROPERTY-CASUALTY LINES, 1986–1996

	Two Firm (seller) Concentration Ratio	
	1986	**1996**
Fire	13.5%	12.1%
Allied lines	11.6	12.3
Farm owners multiple peril	9.8	12.0
Homeowners multiple peril	27.9	35.1
Commercial multiple peril	14.1	12.4
Ocean marine	20.0	22.7
Inland marine	15.7	17.6
Medical malpractice	24.4	14.3
Workers' compensation	16.8	13.8
Other liability	18.4	25.5
Aircraft	23.0	25.0
Private passenger auto liability	29.9	33.2
Commercial auto liability	11.9	10.9
Private passenger auto physical damage	29.3	34.8
Commercial auto physical damage	7.6	10.4
Fidelity	34.5	32.1
Surety	13.5	14.9
Boiler and machinery	40.0	30.0
Total	13.9	19.2

SOURCE: *Best's Review*, (Oldwick, NJ: A.M. Best Company), August 1987 and 1997.

overall PC market measured by premiums written.[5] Table 4–3 shows the average two-firm concentration ratios for 18 property-casualty lines over the 1986–1996 period. In 1986, these concentration ratios varied from a low of 7.6 percent in commercial auto physical damage to a high of 40.0 percent in boiler and machinery, and the top two PC insurance sellers (State Farm and Allstate) wrote 13.9 percent of all insurance premiums. In 1996, concentration ratios ranged from 10.4 percent in commercial auto physical damage to 35.1 percent in homeowners multiple peril, and the top two firms (again, State Farm and Allstate) wrote 19.2 percent of all PC insurance premiums. Thus, the industry leaders appear to be increasing their domination of this financial service sector. In terms of the worldwide volume of PC insurance, U.S. firms wrote some 42 percent of premiums.[6] The total assets of the PC industry as of December 1996 were $802 billion, or approximately 35 percent of the life insurance industry's assets.

PC Insurance.   Property insurance involves insurance coverages related to the loss of real and personal property. Casualty—or perhaps more accurately, liability—insurance offers protection against legal liability exposures. However, distinctions between the two broad

---

[5] *Best Review*, August, 1997, p.32.
[6] Ibid., p. 56.

areas of property and liability insurance are becoming increasingly blurred. This is due to the tendency of PC insurers to offer multiple activity line coverages combining features of property and liability insurance into single policy packages—for example, homeowners multiple peril insurance. The following describes the key features of the main PC lines. Note, however, that some PC activity lines (e.g., auto insurance) are marketed as one product to individuals and another to commercial firms while other lines (e.g., boiler and machinery insurance targeted at commercial purchasers) are marketed to one specific group. To understand the importance of each line in premium income and losses incurred in 1996, review Table 4–4. The changing composition in **net premiums written** (NPW)

net premiums written

The entire amount of premiums on insurance contracts written.

Table **4–4**

PROPERTY AND CASUALTY INSURANCE
(industry underwriting by lines, 1996)

	Premiums Written*	Losses Incurred†
Fire	4,881,916	54.2
Allied lines	4,116,993	75.1
Multiple peril (MP) crop	1,394,777	106.0
Farm owners MP	1,392,079	83.8
Homeowners MP	27,201,471	76.6
Commercial MP—nonliability	11,235,307	68.4
Commercial MP—liability	9,611,270	56.1
Mortgage guaranty	1,825,333	55.5
Ocean marine	1,782,286	61.5
Inland marine	6,785,562	45.8
Financial guaranty	972,490	−0.6
Medical malpractice	5,912,266	60.8
Earthquake	1,349,542	4.8
Group accident and health	3,325,366	74.6
Other accident and health	2,180,999	46.5
Workers' compensation	27,098,363	65.0
Other liability	22,142,908	67.0
Products liability	2,051,763	126.4
Private passenger auto liability	69,001,161	65.3
Commercial auto liability	13,478,433	68.8
Private passenger auto PD	40,155,430	69.8
Commercial auto PD	4,804,689	64.9
Aircraft	1,164,052	73.2
Fidelity	909,606	40.3
Surety	2,737,035	26.6
Glass	13,902	18.9
Burglary and theft	126,976	16.2
Boiler and machinery	763,308	47.0
Credit	406,139	45.2
Other lines	2,103,027	90.2
Totals	270,924,449	66.3

*In thousands

†To premiums earned.

SOURCE: *Best's Review* (Oldwick, NJ: A.M. Best Company), August 1997, p. 32.

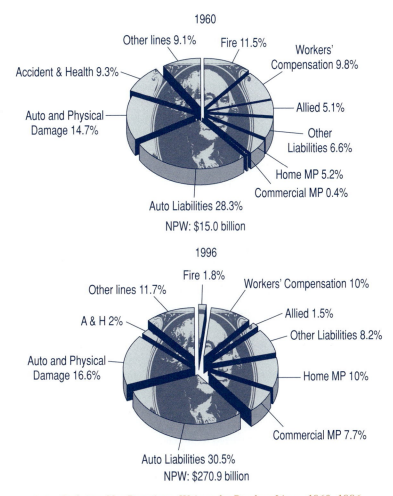

F i g u r e **4-1** *Industry Net Premiums Written by Product Lines, 1960–1996*

SOURCE: *Best's Aggregates & Averages, Property-Casualty* (Oldwick, NJ: A. M. Best Company, 1994), p. 183; and *Best's Review*, August 1997, p. 32.

(the entire amount of premiums on insurance contracts written) for major PC lines during the 1960–1996 period is shown in Figure 4–1. Important PC lines include the following:

Fire insurance and allied lines protect against the perils of fire, lightning, and removal of property damaged in a fire (3.3 percent of all premiums written in 1996; 16.6 percent in 1960).

Homeowners multiple peril (MP) insurance protects against multiple perils of damage to a personal dwelling and personal property as well as liability coverage against the financial consequences of legal liability resulting from injury to others. Thus, it combines features of both property and liability insurance (10.0 percent of all premiums written in 1996; 5.2 percent in 1960).

Commercial multiple peril insurance protects commercial firms against perils similar to homeowners multiple peril insurance (7.7 percent of all premiums written in 1996; 0.4 percent in 1960).

Automobile liability and physical damage (PD) insurance provides protection against (1) losses resulting from legal liability due to the ownership or use of the vehicle (auto liability) and (2) theft or damage to vehicles (auto physical damage) (47.1 percent of all premiums written in 1996; 43.0 percent in 1960).

Liability insurance (other than auto) provides protection to either individuals or commercial firms against nonautomobile-related legal liability. For commercial firms, this includes protection against liabilities relating to their business operations (other than personal injury to employees covered by workers' compensation insurance) and product liability hazards (8.2 percent of all premiums written in 1996; 6.6 percent in 1960).

Balance Sheet and Recent Trends

The Balance Sheet and Underwriting Risk.   The balance sheet of PC firms at the end of 1996 is shown in Table 4–5. Similar to life insurance companies, PC insurers invest the majority of their assets in long-term securities. Bonds ($486.6 billion), preferred stock ($11.5 billion), and common stock ($104.2 billion) represented 75.1 percent of total assets in 1996. Looking at their liabilities, we can see that major components are the loss reserves set aside to meet expected losses ($301.8 billion) from *underwriting* the PC lines just described and the loss adjustment expense ($63.5 billion) item which relates to expected administrative and related costs of adjusting (settling) these claims. The two items combined represent 45.5 percent of total liabilities and capital. **Unearned premiums** (a set-aside reserve that contains the portion of a premium that has been paid before insurance coverage has been provided) are also a major liability (13.5 percent of total liabilities and capital).

unearned premiums

Reserves set aside that contain the portion of a premium that has been paid before insurance coverage has been provided.

To understand how and why this loss reserve on the liability side of the balance sheet is established, we need to understand the risks of underwriting PC insurance. In particular, PC underwriting risk results when the premiums generated on a given insurance line are insufficient to cover (1) the claims (losses) incurred insuring the peril and (2) the administrative expenses of providing that insurance (legal expenses, commissions, taxes, etc.) after taking into account (3) the investment income generated between the time when the premiums are received and the time when they are paid. Thus, underwriting risk may result from (1) unexpected increases in loss rates, (2) unexpected increases in expenses, and/or (3) unexpected decreases in investment yields or returns. Next we look more carefully at each of these three areas of PC underwriting risk.

Loss Risk.   The key feature of claims loss exposure is the actuarial *predictability* of losses relative to premiums earned. This predictability depends on a number of characteristics or features of the perils insured, specifically

- *Property versus liability.* In general, the maximum levels of losses are more predictable for property lines than for liability lines. For example, the monetary value of the loss or damage to an auto is relatively easy to calculate, but the upper limit to the losses to which an insurer might be exposed in a product liability line—for example, asbestos damage to workers' health under other liability insurance—might be difficult if not impossible to estimate.
- *Severity versus frequency.* In general, loss rates are more predictable on low-severity, high-frequency lines than on high-severity, low-frequency lines. For example, losses in fire, auto, and homeowners peril lines tend to be expected to occur with high frequency

Table **4-5**

**BALANCE SHEET PROPERTY-CASUALTY INDUSTRY
AS OF DECEMBER 31, 1996**

(in thousands of dollars)

Assets		Percent of Total	Liabilities and Capital/Surplus		Percent of Total
Unaffiliated investments	$700,806,046	87.3%	Losses	301,795,151	37.6
Bonds	488,575,994	60.7	Loss adjustment expenses	63,523,411	7.9
Preferred stocks	11,492,176	1.4	Reinsurance payable on		
Common stocks	104,215,858	13.0	paid losses	2,049,871	0.3
Mortgage loans	2,312,336	0.3	Commissions, taxes,		
Real estate investment	1,683,626	0.2	expenses	12,244,889	1.5
Collateral loans	25,423	0.0	Federal income taxes	2,394,884	0.3
Cash and short-term			Borrowed money	459,801	0.1
investments	38,769,653	4.8	Interest on borrowed		
Other invested assets	13,220,260	1.7	money	20,514	0.0
Investments in affiliates	34,974,473	4.4	Unearned premiums	108,535,560	13.5
Real Estate, office	7,536,246	0.9	Dividends to stockholders	379,113	0.0
Premium Balance	57,521,904	7.2	Dividends to policyholders	1,693,746	0.2
Reinsurance funds	4,144,388	0.5	Reinsurance funds	8,833,614	1.1
Reinsurance recoverable	10,625,248	1.3	Loss portfolio		
Federal income taxes			transfer (assumed)	1,024,222	0.1
recoverable	1,393,750	0.2	Loss portfolio		
Electronic data processing			transfer (ceded)	(1,638,186)	−0.2
equipment	2,147,875	0.3	Amounts retained		
Accrued interest	8,631,287	1.1	for others	4,745,314	0.6
Receivables from affiliates	5,828,213	0.7	Foreign exchange rate		
Association accounts	2,617,529	0.3	adjustments	603,855	0.1
Receivable uninsured accident			Drafts outstanding	5,884,879	0.7
and health plans	53,422	0.0	Payable to affiliates	4,147,101	0.5
Future investment income			Payable for securities	1,445,923	0.2
on loss reserves	217,845	0.0	Amounts held for uninsured		
Other assets	8,320,453	1.1	accident and health plans	15,484	0.0
Total assets	802,307,961	100.0	Discount on loss reserve	(321,720)	−0.0
			Other liabilities	19,828,399	2.5
			Conditional reserves	9,114,739	1.1
			Policyholders' surplus	255,527,396	31.9
			Capital paid-up	$7,626,170	1.0
			Guaranty funds	264,404	0.0
			Surplus notes	4,065,629	0.5
			Assigned funds	115,162,334	14.4
			Unassigned funds	128,408,858	16.0
			Total liabilities and		
			capital/surplus	$802,307,961	100.0

SOURCE: *Best's Aggregates & Averages, Property-Casualty* (Oldwick, NJ: A. M. Best Company 1997), p. 2.

frequency of loss

The probability that a loss
will occur.

severity of loss

The size of a loss.

long-tail loss

A loss for which a claim
is made some time after a
policy was written.

and to be independently distributed across any pool of insured. Furthermore, the dollar loss of each event in the insured pool tends to be relatively small. Applying the law of large numbers, the expected loss potential of such lines—the **frequency of loss** times the extent of the damage (**severity of loss**)—may be estimable within quite small probability bounds. Other lines, such as earthquake, hurricane, and financial guaranty insurance, tend to insure very low-probability (frequency) events. Here, the probabilities are not always stationary, the individual risks in the insured pool are not independent, and the severity of the loss could be potentially enormous. This means that estimating expected loss rates (frequency times severity) is extremely difficult in these coverage areas. This higher uncertainty of losses forces PC firms to invest in more short-term assets and hold a larger percentage of capital and reserves than life insurance firms do.

- *Long tail versus short tail.* Some liability lines suffer from a long-tail risk exposure phenomenon that makes estimation of expected losses difficult. This **long-tail loss** arises in policies for which the peril occurs during a coverage period but a claim is not made or reported until many years later. Losses incurred but not reported have caused insurers significant problems in lines such as medical malpractice and other liability insurance where product damage suits (e.g., the Dalkon shield case and asbestos cases) have been filed many years after the event occurred and the coverage period expired.[7]

- *Product inflation versus social inflation.* Loss rates on all PC property policies are adversely affected by unexpected increases in inflation. Such increases were triggered, for example, by the oil price shocks of 1973 and 1978. However, in addition to a systematic unexpected inflation risk in each line, line-specific inflation risks may also exist. The inflation risk of property lines is likely to reflect the approximate underlying inflation risk of the economy. Liability lines may be subject to social inflation, as reflected in juries' willingness to award punitive and other liability damages at rates far above the underlying rate of inflation. Such social inflation has been particularly prevalent in commercial liability and medical malpractice insurance and has been directly attributed by some analysts to faults in the U.S. civil litigation system.

loss ratio

A measure of pure losses
incurred to premiums
earned.

premiums earned

Premiums received and
earned on insurance
contracts because time
has passed with no claim
filed.

The **loss ratio** measures the actual losses incurred on a specific policy line. It measures the ratio of losses incurred to **premiums earned** (premiums received and earned on insurance contracts because time has passed without a claim being filed). Thus, a loss ratio of less than 100 means that premiums earned were sufficient to cover losses incurred on that line. Aggregate loss ratios for the period 1951–1996 are shown in Table 4–6. Notice the steady increase in industry loss ratios over the period, increasing from the 60 percent range in the 1950s to the 70 and 80 percent range in the 1980s and 1990s. For example, in 1996 the aggregate loss ratio on all PC lines was 79.7. This includes, however, loss adjustment expenses (LAE) as well as losses. The pure loss ratio, net of LAE, in 1996 was 66.3 (see Table 4–4).

Expense Risk. The two major sources of expense risk to PC insurers are (1) loss adjustment expenses and (2) commissions and other expenses. LAEs relate to the costs surrounding the loss settlement process; for example, many PC insurers employ adjusters who determine the liability of an insurer and the size of an adjustment or settlement to make. The other major area of expense involves the commission costs paid to insurance brokers

---

[7] In some product liability cases, such as those involving asbestos, the nature of the risk being covered was not fully understood at the time many of the policies were written.

Table **4-6**

INDUSTRY UNDERWRITING RATIOS

Year	Loss Ratio*	Expense Ratio†	Combined Ratio	Dividends to Policyholders‡	Combined Ratio after Dividends
1951	60.3	34.0	94.3	2.6	96.9
1952	59.0	33.2	92.2	2.4	94.6
1953	57.9	32.9	90.9	2.6	93.4
1954	57.5	33.7	91.2	2.7	93.9
1955	58.9	33.9	92.9	2.7	95.6
1956	63.8	34.2	98.0	2.7	100.7
1957	66.1	33.7	99.8	2.4	102.3
1958	64.0	33.3	97.3	2.3	99.6
1959	63.0	32.5	95.5	2.2	97.7
1960	63.8	32.2	96.0	2.2	98.1
1961	64.2	32.3	96.5	2.1	98.6
1962	65.1	32.1	97.2	1.9	99.0
1963	67.7	32.2	99.9	2.1	102.0
1964	69.5	31.5	101.0	2.0	103.0
1965	70.3	30.4	100.7	1.9	102.6
1966	67.5	29.6	97.1	1.9	99.0
1967	68.7	29.5	98.2	2.0	100.2
1968	70.4	29.1	99.5	2.0	101.5
1969	72.2	28.4	100.6	1.9	102.5
1970	70.8	27.6	98.4	1.7	100.1
1971	67.5	27.2	94.7	1.7	96.4
1972	66.6	27.7	94.3	1.9	96.2
1973	69.3	28.0	97.3	1.9	99.2
1974	75.5	28.2	103.7	1.7	105.4
1975	79.3	27.3	106.6	1.3	107.9
1976	75.4	25.9	101.3	1.1	102.4
1977	70.7	25.3	96.0	1.2	97.2
1978	70.1	25.8	95.9	1.6	97.5
1979	73.1	26.0	99.1	1.5	100.6
1980	74.9	26.5	101.4	1.7	103.1
1981	76.8	27.4	104.1	1.9	106.0
1982	79.8	27.9	107.7	1.9	109.6
1983	81.5	28.4	109.9	2.1	112.0
1984	88.2	27.9	116.1	1.8	118.0
1985	88.7	25.9	114.6	1.6	116.3
1986	81.6	25.1	106.7	1.3	108.0
1987	77.9	25.3	103.3	1.3	104.6
1988	78.3	25.7	104.0	1.4	105.4
1989	82.0	26.0	107.9	1.3	109.2
1990	82.3	26.0	108.3	1.2	109.6
1991	81.1	26.4	107.6	1.3	108.8
1992	88.1	26.5	114.6	1.2	115.7
1993	79.5	26.2	105.7	1.1	106.9
1994	81.1	26.0	107.1	1.3	108.4
1995	78.8	26.2	105.0	1.4	106.4
1996	79.7	26.2	105.9	1.1	107.0

*Losses and adjustment expenses incurred to premiums earned.

†Expenses incurred (before federal income taxes) to premiums written.

‡Dividends to policyholders to premiums earned.

SOURCE: *Best's Aggregates & Averages, Property-Casualty,* (Oldwick, NJ: A. M. Best Company 1994), p. 158; and *Best's Review,* May 1997.

and sales agents and other expenses related to the acquisition of business. Table 4–6 also shows the expense ratio (excluding LAE) for PC insurers during the 1951–1996 period. In contrast to the increasing trend in the loss ratio, the expense ratio decreased over the period shown. These two sources of expense can account for significant portions of premiums. In 1996, for example, expenses other than LAE amounted to 26.2 percent of premiums written. Clearly, sharp rises in commissions and other operating costs can rapidly render an insurance line unprofitable.

combined ratio

A measure of the overall underwriting profitability of a line; equals the loss ratio plus the ratios of loss adjustment expenses to premiums earned as well as commission and other acquisition costs to premiums written minus any dividends paid to policyholders as a proportion of premiums earned.

A common measure of the overall underwriting profitability of a line, which includes both loss and expense experience, is the **combined ratio**. Technically, the combined ratio is equal to the loss ratio plus the ratios of LAE to premiums earned, commissions, and other acquisition costs and general expense costs to premiums written, minus any dividends paid to policyholders as a proportion of premiums earned. The combined ratio after dividends adds any dividends paid to policyholders as a portion of premiums earned to the combined ratio. If the combined ratio is less than 100, premiums alone are sufficient to cover both losses and expenses related to the line.

If premiums are insufficient and the combined ratio exceeds 100, the PC insurer must rely on investment income on premiums for overall profitability. For example, in 1996, the combined ratio before dividend payments was 105.9, indicating that premiums alone were insufficient to cover the costs of both losses and expenses related to writing PC insurance. Table 4–6 presents the combined ratio and its components for the PC industry for the years 1951–1996. We see that the trend over this period is toward decreased profitability. The industry's premiums generally covered losses and expenses until the 1980s. Since then, premiums have been unable to cover losses and expense (i.e., combined ratios have been consistently higher than 100).

Investment Yield/Return Risk. As discussed, when the combined ratio is higher than 100, overall profitability can be ensured only by a sufficient investment return on premiums earned. That is, PC firms invest premiums in assets between the time they receive the premiums and make payments to meet claims. For example, in 1996, net investment income to premiums earned (or the PC insurers' investment yield) was 10.0 percent. As a result, the overall average profitability (or **operating ratio**) of PC insurers was 97.0. It was equal to the combined ratio after dividends (107.0) minus the investment yield (10.0). Since the operating ratio was less than 100, PC insurers were profitable in 1996. However, lower net returns on investments (e.g., 6.9 percent rather than 10.0 percent) would have meant that underwriting PC insurance would have been marginally unprofitable. Thus, the behavior of interest rates and default rates on PC insurers' investments is crucial to the PC insurers' overall profitability. That is, measuring and managing credit and interest rate risk are key concerns of PC managers.

operating ratio

A measure of the overall profitability of a PC insurer; equals the combined ratio minus the investment yield.

EXAMPLE 4 – 2

• • • • • • •   *Calculation of PC Company Profitability*

Suppose that an insurance company's projected loss ratio is 79.8 percent, its expense ratio is 27.9 percent, and the company pays 2 percent of its premiums earned to policyholders as dividends. The combined ratio (after dividends) for this insurance company is equal to

Loss ratio + Expense ratio + Dividend ratio = Combined ratio after dividends
79.8   +   27.9   +   2.0   =   109.7

Thus, expected losses on all PC lines, expenses, and dividends exceeded premiums earned by 9.7 percent.

Suppose, however, that the company's investment portfolio yielded 12 percent; the operating ratio and overall profitability of the PC insurer are, respectively

$$\text{Operating ratio} = \text{Combined ratio after dividends} - \text{Investment yield}$$
$$= \qquad 109.7 \text{ percent} \qquad - \quad 12.0 \text{ percent}$$
$$= \qquad 97.7 \text{ percent}$$

and

$$\text{Overall profitability} = 100 - \text{Operating ratio}$$
$$= 100 - 97.7 \text{ percent}$$
$$= 2.3 \text{ percent.} \quad \bullet \quad \bullet \quad \bullet$$

Given the importance of investment returns to PC insurers' profitability, the balance sheet in Table 4–5 indicates that bonds—both treasury and corporate—dominated the asset portfolios of PC insurers. Bonds represented 60.7 percent of total assets and 69.4 percent of financial assets (so-called unaffiliated investments) in 1996.

Finally, if pure losses, LAE, and other costs are higher and investment yields are lower than expected, resulting in operating losses, PC insurers carry a significant amount of surplus reserves (policyholder surplus) to reduce the risk of insolvency. In 1996, the ratio of policyholder surplus to assets was 31.9 percent.

Recent Trends.   The period 1987–1996 was not very profitable for the PC industry. In particular, the combined ratio (the measure of loss plus expense risk) increased from 104.6 in 1987 to 115.7 in 1992 (see Figure 4–2), which was the highest ratio since 1985. (Remember that a combined ratio of 100 means that the premiums received cover all losses, expenses, and dividends; a combined ratio higher than 100 means that losses, expenses, and dividends totaled more than premiums earned.) The major reason for this rise was a succession of catastrophes from Hurricane Hugo in 1989, the San Francisco earthquake in 1991, the Oakland fires of 1991, to the losses (more than $15 billion) incurred in Florida as a result of Hurricane Andrew in 1991. In the terminology of PC insurers, the industry was in the trough of an **underwriting cycle**, that is, conditions were difficult. As an example of how bad things were in this industry, after 20 years of profits, Lloyd's of London (arguably one of the world's most well-known and respected insurers) posted a £510 million loss in 1991.[8]

In 1993, the industry showed signs of improvement, with the combined ratio falling to 106.9. In 1994, however, the ratio rose again to 108.4, partly as a result of the Northridge earthquake with estimated losses of $7 billion to $10 billion. The industry ratio fell back to 107.0 in 1996. Despite the $7.35 billion in catastrophe costs incurred, 1996 was considered to be a good year (see Contemporary Perspectives Box 4–2). A number of catastrophes of historically high severity impacted the period 1984–1996. This is shown in Figure 4–3.

The traditional reaction to losses or poor profit results has been the exit from the industry—through failure or otherwise—by less profitable firms and a rapid increase in premiums among the remaining ones. Historically, this has resulted in a fall in the combined ratio as premiums rise and an improvement occurs in the operating ratio and PC industry profitability. As the underwriting profitability cycle approaches its peak, however,

underwriting cycle

A pattern that the profits in the PC industry tend to follow.

---

[8] As Lloyd's management explained, the loss was a result of four years of unprecedented disaster claims. As a result of their losses, a group of Lloyd's investors sued the company for negligence in their business operations (some of which in the late 1990s were still working their way through the legal system).

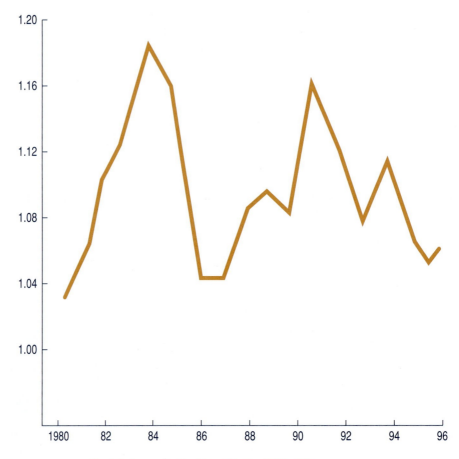

Figure **4–2** *The PC Insurers' Combined Ratio, 1980–1996*

SOURCE: *The Economist,* March 20, 1993, p. 86; S&P *Industry Survey: Insurance* (New York: The McGraw-Hill Companies, 1994), pp. 1–3; and *Best's Review*, May 1997.

new entrants to the industry emerge. These new entrants compete by cutting premiums and lowering underwriting quality standards, thus setting the stage for a downturn in the cycle again. On average, underwriting cycles measured from peak to peak can last anywhere from 6 to 10 years.

Regulation

Similar to life insurance companies, PC insurers are chartered by states and regulated by state commissions. In addition, state guaranty funds provide some protection to policy-holders should an insurance company fail. The National Association of Insurance Commissioners (NAIC) provides various services to state regulatory commissions. These include a standardized examination system, the Insurance Regulatory Information System (IRIS), to identify insurers with loss, combined, and other ratios operating outside normal ranges.

Catastrophe	Year	I.A. Amount* U.S. $(millions)
Hurricane Andrew	1992	15,900
Northridge earthquake	1994	7,200
Hurricane Hugo	1989	4,939
Hurricane Betsy	1965	2,346
Hurricane Opal	1995	2,100
Blizzard of '96	1996	2,000
Hurricane Iniki	1992	1,646
Blizzard of '93	1993	1,625
Hurricane Fran	1995	1,600
Hurricane Frederic	1979	1,575
Wind; hail; tornadoes	1974	1,395
Freeze	1983	1,280
Oakland fire	1991	1,273
Hurricane Cecelia	1970	1,169
Wind	1950	1,136
California earthquake	1989	1,130
Texas hailstorm	1995	1,100
Hurricane Alicia	1983	983
L.A. riots	1992	797

Mean = $90,929,977
1,163 catastrophes
Average 25.3 catastrophes per year
Average 6.3 catastrophes per quarter

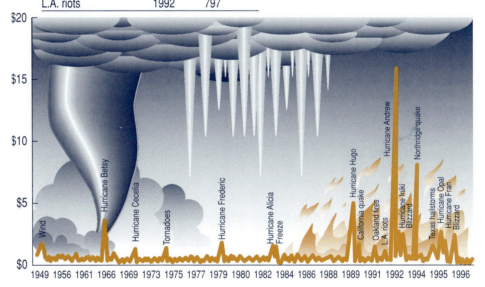

Figure **4–3**   *U.S. Catastrophes, 1949–1996*

*Adjusted for inflation.

SOURCE: Richard L. Sandor, Centre Financial Products, 1949–1994; authors' research, 1995–1996.

An additional burden that PC insurers face in some activity lines—especially auto insurance and workers' compensation insurance—is rate regulation. That is, given the public utility nature of some insurance lines, state commissioners set ceilings on premiums and premium increases, usually based on specific cost of capital and line risk exposure formulas for the insurance supplier. This has led some insurers to leave states such as New Jersey, Florida, and California, which have the most restrictive regulations.

Contemporary Perspectives 4–2

Catastrophes in 1996 Cost Insurance Firms Total of $7.35 Billion

Blizzards, hurricanes, tornadoes and other major catastrophes cost the insurance industry $7.35 billion last year, the third-lowest total since 1989, when Property Claim Services, a division of American Insurance Services Group Inc., began tracking such data.

The 41 catastrophes in 1996, however, resulted in 3.8 million insurance claims, the highest number since the industry trade group began compiling such data in 1989. The previous high was set in 1995, when 2.7 million claims were made. A disaster is counted as a catastrophe if it costs insurers more than $5 million.

"People are saying it wasn't a bad year in dollar losses. But more claims were handled than ever before," said Gary R. Kerney, chief of the property claim division. "More and more people are moving into catastrophe-prone areas in Florida, Texas and along the coast."

Last year opened with blizzards that blanketed the Northeast with snow in January and February, causing $2 billion in insured damage. Several spring and summer storms brought severe winds, hail and tornadoes. Five hurricanes made landfall, including Hurricane Fran in September, which resulted in $1.6 billion of insured damage.

Hurricane Fran was the worst single catastrophe in 1996, and North Carolina was the worst-affected state, with $1.5 billion in damage.

SOURCE: The *Wall Street Journal,* January 15, 1997, p. A4. Reprinted by permission of The Wall Street Journal. © 1997 Dow Jones & Company, Inc. All Rights Reserved Worldwide.

Concept Questions

1. Why do PC insurers hold more capital and reserves than life insurers do?
2. Why are life insurers' assets on average, longer in maturity than PC insurers' assets?
3. What are the main lines of insurance offered by PC insurers?
4. What are the components of the combined ratio?
5. How does the operating ratio differ from the combined ratio?
6. Why does the combined ratio tend to behave cyclically?

SUMMARY

This chapter examined the activities and regulation of insurance companies. The first part of the chapter described the various classes of life insurance and recent trends. The second part discussed property-casualty companies. The various lines that compose property-casualty insurance are becoming increasingly blurred as multiple activity line coverage's are offered. Both life and property-casualty insurance companies are regulated at the state rather than the federal level.

PERTINENT WEB SITES

National Association of Insurance Commissioners (NAIC)
http://www.naic.org/

New York State Insurance Department   http://www.ins.
state.ny.us/

The Financial Services Industry: Insurance Companies

1. How does the primary function of an insurance company compare with that of a depository institution?

2. Contrast the balance sheet of depository institutions with those of life insurance firms.

3. How has the composition of the assets of U.S. life insurance companies changed over time?

4. What are the similarities and differences among the four basic lines of life insurance products?

5. Explain how annuity activities represent the reverse of life insurance activities.

6. How can life insurance and annuity products be used to create a steady stream of cash disbursements and payments to avoid either paying or receiving a single lump-sum cash amount?

7. If an insurance company decides to offer another company a private pension fund, how would this change the insurance company's balance sheet?

8. How does the regulation of insurance companies compare with that of depository institutions?

9. a. Calculate the annual cash flows of a $1 million, 20-year fixed payment annuity earning a guaranteed 10 percent per annum if payments are to begin at the end of the current year.

   b. Calculate the annual cash flows of a $1 million, 20-year fixed payment annuity earning a guaranteed 10 percent per annum if payments are to begin at the end of five years.

10. You deposit $10,000 annually into a life insurance fund for the next 10 years at which time you plan to retire. Instead of a lump sum, you wish to receive annuities for the next 20 years. What is the annual payment you expect to receive beginning in year 11 if you assume an interest rate of 8 percent for the whole time period?

11. Suppose that a 65-year-old person wants to purchase an annuity from an insurance company that would pay $20,000 until the end of that person's life. The insurance company expects this person to live for 15 more years and would be willing to pay 6 percent on the annuity. How much should the insurance company ask this person to pay for

the annuity? A second 65-year-old person wants the same $20,000 annuity, but this person is much healthier and is expected to live for 20 years. If the same 6 percent interest rate applies, how much should this healthier person be charged for the annuity?

12. How do life insurance companies earn profits? How does investment in junk bonds increase their returns and what are the drawbacks?

13. How have the product lines based on net premiums written by insurance companies changed over time?

14. What are the two major lines of property-casualty (PC) insurance firms?

15. What are the three sources of underwriting risk in the PC industry?

16. How do increases in unexpected inflation affect PC insurers?

17. a. Is a line of property insurance profitable if its simple loss ratio is 73 percent, its loss adjustment expense is 12.5 percent, and its ratio of commissions and other acquisitions expenses is 18 percent?

    b. How does your answer to part (a) change if investment yields of 8 percent are added?

18. An insurance company's projected loss ratio is 77.5 percent and its loss adjustment expense ratio is 12.9 percent. It estimates that commission payments and dividends to policyholders will add another 16 percent. What is the minimum yield on investments required to maintain a positive operating ratio?

19. Which of the insurance lines listed here will be charged a higher premium by insurance companies and why?

    a. Low-severity, high-frequency lines versus high-severity, low-frequency lines.

    b. Long-tail versus short-tail lines.

20. An insurance company collected $3.6 million in premiums and disbursed $1.96 million in losses. Loss adjustment expenses amounted to 6.6 percent and dividends paid to policyholders totaled 1.2 percent. The total income generated from their investments were $170,000 after all expenses were paid. What is the net profitability in dollars?

Chapter Five

The Financial Services Industry: Securities Firms and Investment Banks

Securities firms and investment banks underwrite securities and engage in related activities such as trading and market making. Figure 5–1 shows activities that generate revenues for some of the largest firms in the industry. The largest companies in this industry perform multiple services; many other firms concentrate their services in one area only (either securities dealing trading or securities underwriting). Specifically, securities firms specialize primarily in the purchase, sale, and brokerage of securities (i.e., the retail side of the business); investment banks primarily engage in originating, underwriting, and distributing issues of securities (i.e., the commercial side of the business). Investment banks also undertake corporate finance activities such as advising on mergers, acquisitions, and corporate restructurings. Figure 5–2 reports merger activity for the period 1990–1997, a boom period for this line of business. Total volume of domestic mergers and acquisitions has increased from less than $200 billion in 1990 to $919 billion

Chapter Outline

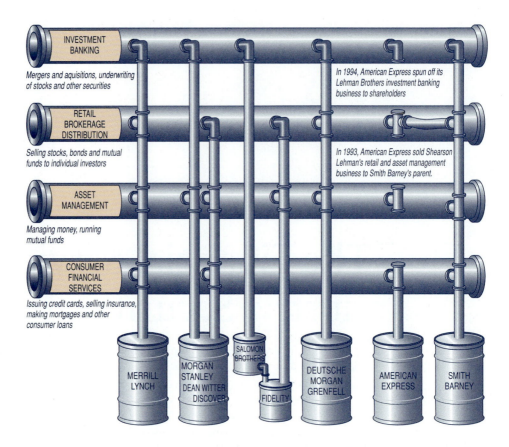

INVESTMENT BANKING

Mergers and aquisitions, underwriting of stocks and other securities

RETAIL BROKERAGE DISTRIBUTION

Selling stocks, bonds and mutual funds to individual investors

ASSET MANAGEMENT

Managing money, running mutual funds

CONSUMER FINANCIAL SERVICES

Issuing credit cards, selling insurance, making mortgages and other consumer loans

In 1994, American Express spun off its Lehman Brothers investment banking business to shareholders

In 1993, American Express sold Shearson Lehman's retail and asset management business to Smith Barney's parent.

MERRILL LYNCH   MORGAN STANLEY DEAN WITTER DISCOVER   SALOMON BROTHERS   FIDELITY   DEUTSCHE MORGAN GRENFELL   AMERICAN EXPRESS   SMITH BARNEY

F i g u r e **5–1**   *Tapping Revenue; Revenue Sources for Some of the Largest Investment Firms*

SOURCE: The *New York Times*, February 6, 1997, p. D1. Copyright © 1997 by The New York Times Co. Reprinted by Permission.

in 1997. The investment bank Morgan Stanley, Dean Witter, Discover alone managed $322.5 billion worth of these mergers. This chapter presents an overview of (1) the size, structure, and composition of the industry, (2) the key activities of securities firms, (3) the industry's balance sheet and recent trends, and (4) its regulation.

SIZE, STRUCTURE, AND COMPOSITION OF THE INDUSTRY

Because of the emphasis on securities trading and underwriting, the size of the industry is usually measured by the equity capital of the firms participating in the industry. This amounted to $65.6 billion at the end of 1996, supporting total assets of $1.75 trillion.

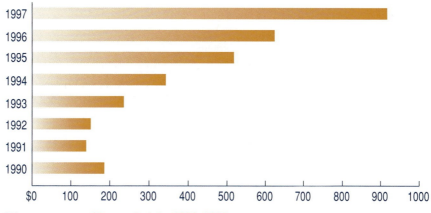

Merger Activity

Total volume of domestic mergers and acquisitions in billions of dollars.

F i g u r e **5–2**   *Merger Activity 1990–1997*

SOURCE: Securities Data Company, 1997.

Beginning in 1980 and until the stock market crash of October 19, 1987, the number of firms in the industry expanded dramatically from 5,248 in 1980 to 9,515 in 1987. The aftermath of the crash included a major shakeout, with the number of firms declining to 7,776 by 1996, or 18 percent since 1987. Concentration of business among the largest firms over this period has increased dramatically. According to data in Table 5–1, the largest investment bank in 1987, Salomon Brothers, held capital of $3.21 billion. By 1997 the largest investment bank, Merrill Lynch, held capital of $33.0 billion. Some of the significant growth in size has come through merger and acquisition by the top-ranked firms. Table 5–2 lists major U.S. securities industry merger and acquisition transactions, many of which involve repeated ownership changes of a company. Notice from this table that 7 of the largest 16 mergers occurred in 1997 and early 1998. Notice, too, how many recent mergers and acquisitions are interindustry mergers (i.e., insurance companies and investment banks). Figure 5–3 illustrates, for example, the many inter- and intraindustry transactions undertaken by Travelers Group and its subsidiaries prior to its merger with Citicorp in 1998. Recent regulatory changes (discussed briefly here and in detail in Chapter 25) are the cause for such mergers.

broker-dealers

Firms that assist in the trading of existing securities.

underwriting

Assisting in the issue of new securities.

The firms in the industry can be categorized along a number of dimensions. The first dimension includes the largest firms, the so-called national full-line firms that service both retail customers (especially by acting as **broker-dealers**, thus assisting in the trading of existing securities) and corporate customers (by **underwriting**, thus assisting in the issue of new securities). The major national full-line firms (ranked by capital) are Merrill Lynch[1] and Morgan Stanley, Dean Witter, Discover. In 1997, Morgan Stanley, ranked sixth in size of capital, and Dean Witter, Discover, ranked fifth in capital size, merged to create the largest investment bank in the world. Contemporary Perspectives Box 5–1 discusses this merger

---

[1] Merrill Lynch has been the largest firm in the industry for several years. Initial reports estimated that the Morgan Stanley, Dean Witter merger would boost it into the number 1 spot. These expectations, however, did not materialize.

Table **5-1**

LARGEST INVESTMENT COMPANIES RANKED
BY CAPITAL, 1987–1997

1997			1987		
Rank	Company	Capital (in billions of dollars)	Rank	Company	Capital (in billions of dollars)
1.	Merrill Lynch	$33.00	1.	Salomon Brothers	$3.21
2.	Morgan Stanley, Dean Witter	23.70	2.	Shearson Lehman Brothers *	3.12
3.	Smith Barney/Salomon	22.40	3.	Merrill Lynch	2.88
4.	Lehman Brothers Holdings	19.80	4.	Goldman Sachs	1.95
5.	Goldman Sachs Group	17.70	5.	Drexel Burnham Lambert†	1.85
6.	Bear Stearns	9.50	6.	First Boston Corp.	1.36
7.	Paine Webber Group	4.90	7.	Prudential-Bache Securities	1.29
8.	Donaldson, Lufkin & Jenrette	3.40	8.	Dean Witter Reynolds ‡	1.21
			9.	Bear Stearns	1.06
			10.	E.F. Hutton*	0.99
			11.	Morgan Stanley ‡	0.99

* Shearson Lehman Brothers and E. F. Hutton merged in 1988.

† Now defunct.

‡ Morgan Stanley and Dean Witter merged in 1997.

SOURCE: Securities Industry Association annual yearbooks, 1987 and 1997.

Table **5-2**

MAJOR U.S. SECURITIES INDUSTRY MERGER AND
ACQUISITION TRANSACTIONS

Rank	Deal	Price* (in billions of dollars)	Year
1.	**Travelers Group** merges with **Citicorp**	$83.0	1998
2.	**Dean Witter** merges with **Morgan Stanley**	10.2	1997
3.	**Travelers Group** acquires **Salomon Inc.**	9.0	1997
4.	**Sears** spins off **Dean Witter, Discover**	5.0	1993
5.	**Mellon Bank** acquires **Dreyfus**	1.8	1993
6.	**American Express** spins off **Lehman Bros. Holdings**	1.6	1994
7.	**Fleet Financial** acquires **Quick and Reilly**	1.6	1997
8.	**Primerica** acquires **Shearson**	1.2	1993
9.	**NationsBank** acquires **Montgomery Securities**	1.2	1997
10.	**Credit Suisse** acquires **First Boston**	1.1	1988
11.	**Shearson Lehman** acquires **E.F. Hutton**	1.0	1987
12.	**American Express** acquires **Shearson**	0.9	1981
13.	**Primerica** acquires **Smith Barney**	0.8	1987
14.	**Paine Webber** acquires **Kidder Peabody**	0.7	1994
15.	**U.S. Bancorp** acquires **Piper Jaffray**	0.7	1997
16.	**ING Group** acquires **Furman Selz**	0.6	1997

* Value of Dean Witter, Discover shares to be exchanged for Morgan Stanley stock, based on closing price of $40.625 on February 5, 1997.

SOURCE: Securities Data Company and *The Wall Street Journal,* various issues.

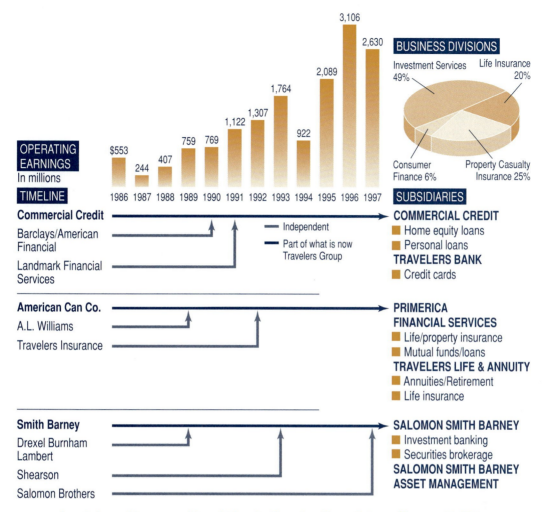

Figure **5-3**   *Interindustry Mergers and Acquisitions by Travelers Group Prior to Merger with Citicorp*

SOURCE: The *New York Times,* January 2, 1998, p. D5. Copyright © 1998 by The New York Times Co. Reprinted by Permission.

and the way that it revolutionized this industry's provision of investment banking services. The second dimension includes the national full-line firms that specialize more in corporate finance and are highly active in trading securities. Examples are Goldman Sachs, Salomon Brothers/Smith Barney. The third dimension includes the remainder of the industry:

1. Specialized investment bank subsidiaries of commercial bank holding companies (such as J. P. Morgan).

discount broker

A stockbroker that conducts trades for customers but does not offer investment advice.

2. Specialized **discount brokers** (such as Charles Schwab)[2] that effect trades for customers without offering investment advice or tips.

3. Regional securities firms that are often classified as large, medium, and small and concentrate on servicing customers in a particular region such as New York or California.

---

[2] Discount brokers usually charge lower commissions than do full-service brokers such as Merrill Lynch.

Contemporary Perspectives 5–1

Morgan Stanley Group and Dean Witter Plan an $8.8 Billion Merger:
They Face Challenge Melding Elite Institutional Firm with Large Retail Broker

For years, most Wall Street franchises were cleanly divided into blue-chip investment banks catering to institutional clients and brokerage houses serving individual investors. That landscape will soon change profoundly with the marriage of two Wall Street firms that personify those two cultural camps. Morgan Stanley Group Inc. and Dean Witter, Discover & Co. plan to announce a merger as early as today. It would create the largest securities firm in the world, people familiar with the transaction say.

With Morgan Stanley's market capitalization of $8.8 billion and Dean Witter valued in the market at $13 billion, the new firm would have a market capitalization topping $20 billion. The $8.8 billion merger—the biggest combination ever in the securities business—promises to usher in a new round of consolidation as securities firms scramble to find partners to compete with the new Wall Street giant.

Morgan Stanley and Dean Witter are making a bold bet that the future of the business lies in melding two camps that are called the "brains" and "brawn." The brains are blue-chip investment banks such as Morgan Stanley and Goldman, Sachs & Co. that provide strategic advice and underwrite stocks and bonds for corporate clients. The brawn encompasses big brokerage houses selling stocks, bonds and mutual funds to millions of small investors nationwide. These primarily "retail" operations include Dean Witter, which boasts the nation's third largest army of brokers, with more than 8,500. The merger is directly aimed at competing more effectively with Merrill Lynch & Co., the only Wall Street firm ever to successfully bridge the two camps. But Merrill has accomplished this through internal growth; no Wall Street firm has been able to pull it off through a merger. By becoming the nation's biggest securities firm in terms of capital, the combination of Morgan and Dean Witter will eclipse Merrill, which in 1996 led all other securities firms. It had 1996 net income of $1.6 billion. Morgan Stanley had 1996 net of $1 billion; Dean Witter posted net of $951.4 million.

The stunning move marks a remarkable change in strategy for white-shoe Morgan Stanley. Unlike Dean Witter, which serves small investors, Morgan Stanley has long catered to Wall Street's biggest blue-chip clients. It dates back to when the firm was the investment-banking arm of J.P. Morgan & Co., before the two giant institutions were split up during the Depression. After the stock-market crash of 1929, the Glass-Steagall act mandated the separation of commercial banks and securities firms. . . . The merger would give Morgan Stanley, with its risky investment-banking and trading businesses, a portfolio of stable franchises such as asset management and credit card. Many Wall Street firms have been trying to smooth out earnings bumps through more recurring streams of revenue. As of the end of last year, Dean Witter had $90 billion in assets under management and administration while Morgan Stanley had $171 billion in assets under management as of Nov. 30. The merger would make Morgan Stanley–Dean Witter the biggest asset-management company on Wall Street, after Merrill's $234 billion.

Meanwhile, Dean Witter's credit-card business has been the real cash cow over the past decade. Discover Card was one of the great success stories of the 1980s in the card business. . . . For Dean Witter, the merger would give it access to a vast array of investment-banking products, including hot initial public offerings and bond deals to hawk to small investors.

SOURCE: Anita Raghavan and Steven Lipin, *Wall Street Journal,* February 5, 1997, p. A1. Reprinted by permission of The Wall Street Journal. © 1997 Dow Jones & Company, Inc. All Rights Reserved.

Concept Questions

1. What trends have occurred in the number of securities firms since 1980?
2. What dimensions categorize firms in the securities industry?
3. What is the difference between brokerage services and underwriting services?

SECURITIES FIRMS'
ACTIVITY AREAS

Securities firms engage in seven key activity areas.[3]

Investing

Investing involves managing pools of assets such as closed- and open-ended mutual funds and, in competition with life insurance companies, pension funds. Securities firms can manage such funds either as agents for other investors or as principals for themselves. The objective in funds management is to choose asset allocations to beat some return-risk performance benchmark.[4]

Investment Banking

Investment banking refers to activities related to underwriting and distributing new issues of debt and equity. New issues can be either primary—the first-time issues of companies (sometimes called **IPOs** for initial public offerings)—or secondary issues—the new issues of seasoned firms whose debt or equity is already trading. Table 5–3 lists the top 10 underwriters based on total issues and by type of issue (i.e., common stock, debt, and IPOs) as of September 1997. The top 10 common stock underwriters represented 73 percent of the industry total. The top 10 debt underwriters represented 88 percent of the industry total. Obviously the industry is dominated by just a handful of top-tier underwriting firms.

Securities underwritings can be undertaken through either public or private offerings. In a private offering, an investment banker acts as a **private placement** agent for a fee, placing the securities with one or a few large institutional investors such as life insurance companies.[5] In a public offering, the securities may be underwritten either on a best-efforts or a firm commitment basis and offered to the public at large. With best-efforts underwriting, investment bankers act as *agents* on a fee basis related to their success in placing the issue. In firm commitment underwriting, the investment banker acts as a *principal,* purchasing the securities from the issuer at one price and seeking to place them with public investors at a slightly higher price. Finally, in addition to investment banking operations in the corporate securities markets, the investment banker may participate as an underwriter (primary dealer) in government, municipal, and mortgage-backed securities.

The Risk of Securities Underwriting.   An understanding of the risk of securities underwriting must include an understanding of the mechanics of firm commitment securities offerings. Some corporate securities are offered on a **best efforts** basis in which the underwriter does not guarantee a price to the issuer and acts more as a placing or distribution agent. The dominant form of underwriting in the United States, however, is a firm commitment offering. A **firm commitment offering** involves securities purchased by an underwriter directly from an issuing firm (say, at $99 per share), who then reoffers them to

IPO

A corporation's initial or first-time public offering of debt or equity.

private placement

A securities issue placed with one or a few large institutional investors.

best efforts underwriting

An underwriting in which the investment banker acts as an agent rather than as a principal that bears risk.

firm commitment offering

Securities offered from the issuing firm, purchased by an underwriter.

---

[3] See Ernest Bloch, *Inside Investment Banking,* 2nd ed. (Chicago: Irwin, 1989) for a similar list.

[4] Benchmarks include the securities market line given the fund's beta.

[5] See *Federal Reserve Bulletin,* February 1993, for an excellent description of the private placement market. Issuers of privately placed securities are not required to register with the SEC since the placements are made only to large sophisticated investors.

Table **5-3**

TEN LARGEST UNDERWRITING FIRMS RANKED BY ALL ISSUES AND TYPE OF ISSUE, 1997 (THROUGH SEPTEMBER)
(in billions of dollars)

Rank	All Issues	Value	Number of Issues	Rank	Common Stock Issues	Value	Number of Issues
1.	Merrill Lynch	$148.2	1,162	1.	Morgan Stanley, Dean Witter	$11.1	62
2.	Salomon Brothers	105.6	607	2.	Goldman Sachs	10.4	65
3.	Morgan Stanley, Dean Witter	104.9	1,002	3.	Merrill Lynch	9.6	67
4.	Goldman Sachs	100.9	844	4.	Donaldson, Lufkin & Jenrette	4.7	38
5.	Lehman Brothers	93.3	689	5.	Salomon Brothers	4.3	28
6.	J.P. Morgan	82.3	664	6.	Bankers Trust	4.3	46
7.	Credit Suisse First Boston	46.6	368	7.	Lehman Brothers	3.9	46
8.	Bear, Stearns	44.8	338	8.	Credit Suisse First Boston	3.4	23
9.	Donaldson, Lufkin & Jenrette	30.6	221	9.	Smith Barney	3.2	50
10.	Chase Manhattan	21.9	250	10.	Montgomery Securities	2.4	48
	Industry Total	$947.0	8,715		Industry Total	78.1	911

Rank	Investment Grade Debt Issues	Value	Number of Issues	Rank	Initial Public Offerings	Value	Number of Issues
1.	Merrill Lynch	$101.6	938	1.	Goldman Sachs	$4.3	23
2.	Morgan Stanley, Dean Witter	72.6	840	2.	Morgan Stanley, Dean Witter	3.4	25
3.	J.P. Morgan	68.6	621	3.	Merrill Lynch	2.8	20
4.	Salomon Brothers	64.7	454	4.	J.P. Morgan	1.4	6
5.	Goldman Sachs	64.1	685	5.	Credit Suisse First Boston	1.4	14
6.	Lehman Brothers	52.5	493	6.	Bear Stearns	1.1	9
7.	Credit Suisse First Boston	26.6	248	7.	Lehman Brothers	1.0	15
8.	Bear, Stearns	14.2	215	8.	Donaldson, Lufkin & Jenrette	0.9	12
9.	Chase Manhattan	12.9	224	9.	Montgomery Securities	0.8	24
10.	Smith Barney	10.5	171	10.	Salomon Brothers	0.7	7
	Industry Total	$553.4	6,374		Industry Total	$26.7	429

SOURCE: Securities Data Company, 1997.

the public or the market at large at a slightly higher price, say, $99.50. The difference between the underwriter's buy price ($99) and the public offer price ($99.50) is the spread that compensates the underwriter for accepting the principal risk of placing the securities with outside investors as well as any administrative and distribution costs associated with the underwriting. In our simple example of a $0.50 spread, the maximum revenue the underwriter can gain from underwriting the issue is $0.50 times the number of shares issued. Thus, if 1 million shares were offered, the maximum gross revenue for the underwriting would be $0.50 times 1,000,000 = $500,000. Note that once the public offering has been made and the price specified in the prospectus, the underwriter cannot raise the price during the offering period. In this example, the underwriter could not raise the price above $99.50, even after determining that the market valued the shares more highly.[6]

---

[6] The offering period is usually a maximum of 10 business days.

The upside return from underwriting is normally capped, but the downside risk is not and can be very large. The downside risk arises if the underwriter overprices the public offering, setting the public offer price higher than outside investors' valuations. As a result, the underwriter would be unable to sell the shares during the public offering period and would have to lower the price to get rid of the inventory of unsold shares, especially because this inventory is often financed by issuing commercial paper or repurchase (RP) agreements. In our example, if the underwriter has to lower the offering price to $99, the gross revenue from the underwriting would be zero since this is the price paid to the issuing firm. Any price less than $99 generates a loss. For example, suppose that the issue could be placed only at $97, the underwriter's losses would be $2 times 1,000,000 shares = $2 million.

An underwriter may take a big loss or big hit on an underwriting for a number of reasons. The first is simply overestimating the market's demand for the shares. The second is that in the short period between setting the public offering price and seeking to sell the securities to the public, security values may experience a major drop.

EXAMPLE 5–1

* * * * * *   *Calculation of Losses from Underwriting an Issue*

The classic example of this second type of underwriting risk is the sale of British Petroleum (BP) shares in October 1987 in the period surrounding the October 19, 1987 stock market crash. Underwriters set the bid price of the shares at £3.265 and the offer price at £3.30 on October 15, 1987, four days before the crash, and four large U.S. investment banks (including Goldman Sachs) agreed to underwrite 22 percent of the issue, or 505,800,000 shares. In the week following the October 19, 1987 crash, however, BP's share price fell to a low of £2.65 so that the underwriters faced a loss of as much as £0.615 per share (£3.265 – £2.65), or a total loss of £311 million. Note that the maximum gross revenue that U.S. underwriters could have made, if they had sold all shares at the originally planned offer price of £3.30, was [(£3.30 – £3.265) × 505.8 million] or £17,703,000. We show this profit

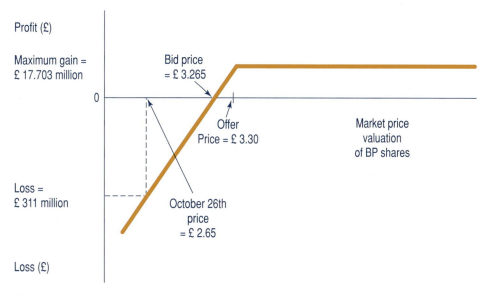

F i g u r e **5-4**   *Profit-Loss Function for British Petroleum Share Underwriting*

and loss trade-off in Figure 5–4. As you can see, firm commitment underwriting involves a potential payoff with a limited upside gain (£17,703,000) and a very large downside loss.

Of course, the big hit described in the BP case is unusual for three reasons. First, most new issues are underpriced rather than overpriced. Second, in the United States, the offer period is usually much shorter than in the BP examples, and third, stock market crashes are fortunately rare. • • •

Market Making

Market making involves creating a secondary market in an asset. Thus, in addition to being primary dealers in government securities and underwriters of corporate bonds and equities, investment bankers make a secondary market in these instruments. Market making can involve either agency or principal transactions. *Agency transactions* are two-way transactions on behalf of *customers*—for example, acting as a *stockbroker* or dealer for a fee or commission. In *principal transactions*, the market maker seeks to profit on the price movements of securities and takes either long or short inventory positions for its own account. (Or the market maker may take an inventory position to stabilize the market in the securities.[7])

Trading

Trading is closely related to the market-making activities just described; a trader takes an active net position in an underlying instrument or asset. There are at least four types of trading activities:

1. *Position trading* involves purchases of large blocks of securities to facilitate smooth functioning of the secondary markets in such securities.
2. *Pure arbitrage* entails buying an asset in one market at one price and selling it immediately in another market at a higher price.
3. *Risk arbitrage* involves buying blocks of securities in anticipation of some information release—such as a merger or takeover announcement or a Federal Reserve interest rate announcement.[8]
4. *Program trading* is associated with seeking a risk arbitrage between a cash market price (e.g., the Standard & Poor's 500 Stock Market Index) and the *futures* market price of that instrument, often with the aid of high-powered computers.[9]

As with many activities of securities firms, such trading can be conducted on behalf of a customer as an agent or on behalf of the firm as a principal. Many brokers are also starting to offer on-line trading services to their customers. Thus, customers may now conduct trading activities from their homes and offices (see Chapter 24).

---

[7] In general, full-service investment banks can become market makers in stocks on the National Association of Securities Dealers Automated Quotation (NASDAQ), but they have been prevented until recently from acting as market-making specialists on the NYSE.

[8] It is termed *risk arbitrage* because if the event does not actually occur—for example, if a merger does not take place or the Federal Reserve does not change interest rates—the trader stands to lose money.

[9] An example is investing cash in the S&P index and selling futures contracts on the S&P index. Since stocks and futures contracts trade in different markets, their prices are not always equal. Moreover, program trading can occur between cash markets in other assets, for example, commodities.

Cash Management

cash management account

Money market mutual fund sold by investment banks that offer check-writing privileges.

Investment banks offer bank depositlike **cash management accounts** (CMAs) to individual investors. Most of these accounts allow customers the ability to write checks against some type of mutual fund account (e.g., money market mutual fund). These accounts, when issued in association with commercial banks and thrifts, can even be covered by federal deposit insurance from the FDIC. CMAs have been instrumental in the securities industries' efforts to provide commercial banking services.

Mergers and Acquisitions

Investment banks frequently provide advice on and assistance in mergers and acquisitions. For example, they assist in finding merger partners, underwriting new securities to be issued by the merged firms, assessing the value of target firms, recommending terms of the merger agreement, and even assisting target firms in preventing a merger (for example, writing poison-pill provisions into a potential target firm's securities contracts).

Other Service Functions

These functions include custody and escrow services, clearance and settlement services, and research and advisory services, for example, giving advice on mergers and acquisitions (M&As). In performing these functions, the securities firm normally acts as an agent for a fee.

Concept Questions

1. What are the key areas of activities for securities firms?
2. What is the difference between a best-efforts and a firm commitment offering?
3. What are the four trading activities performed by securities firms?

BALANCE SHEET AND RECENT TRENDS

A major effect of the 1987 stock market crash was a sharp decline in stock market trading volume and, thus, in brokerage commissions earned by securities firms over the 1987–1991 period. These commissions began to recover only in 1992, with record trading volumes being achieved in 1995 through 1998 (when the Dow Jones and S&P Indexes hit new highs).[10] The decline in brokerage commissions actually began in 1977, however; it reflects an overall long-term fall in the importance of commission income as a percentage of revenues for securities firms as a result of the abolition of fixed commissions on securities

---

[10]The Dow Jones Industrial Average crossed the 5000 mark on November 21, 1995, when it closed at 5023.55. Less than 18 months later, the Dow topped 7000 when it closed at 7022.44 on February 14, 1997; in another five months, on July 17, 1997, it topped 8000, closing at 8038.88; and just nine months later, on April 6, 1998, it topped 9000, closing at 9033.23.

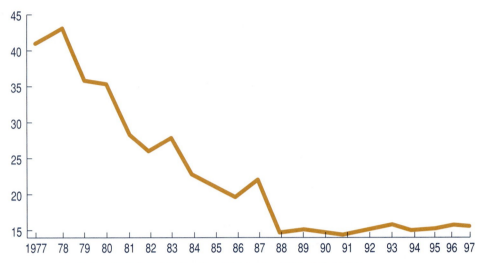

F i g u r e **5–5**   *Commission Income as a Percentage of Total Revenues*

SOURCE: Securities and Exchange Commission and Standard & Poor's *Industry Surveys,* various issues.

trades by the Securities and Exchange Commission (SEC) in May 1975 and the fierce competition for wholesale commissions and trades that followed (see Figure 5–5).[11]

Also affecting the profitability of the securities industry was the decline in new equity issues during the 1987–1990 period and in bond and equity underwriting in general. This was a result partly of the stock market crash, partly of a decline in mergers and acquisitions, and partly of investor concerns about junk bonds following the Michael Milken/Ivan Boesky-Drexel Burnham Lambert scandal, which resulted in that firm's failure. Drexel was once the most influential firm on Wall Street because of its pioneering work under Michael Milken in the junk bond market. Drexel went bankrupt, however, after officials pleaded guilty to six felony counts of federal securities fraud. Drexel and Milken were found to have "plundered" the S&L industry by manipulating financial markets. The essence of the legal action involved the fact that Milken, working for Drexel, used S&Ls to create a web of buyers that helped give the appearance of a market for junk bonds. The fraudulent market allowed Drexel to sell junk bonds at prices above their fair market values; S&Ls held almost 20 percent of junk bonds outstanding and when the junk bond market collapsed, many S&Ls, especially those in California, suffered large losses.

Between 1991 and 1997, however, the securities industry showed a resurgence in activity and profitability.[12] In fact, in 1997 underwriting topped the $1 trillion mark for only the second time ever; see Contemporary Perspectives Box 5–2. The two principal reasons for this (other than the resurgence of stock market volumes) were enhanced fixed income trading profits and increased growth in new issue underwritings. Between 1987 and 1997, securities firms in the aggregate nearly tripled their holdings of fixed income securities (corporate, foreign, mortgage-backed, and Treasury bonds) in a successful strategic

---

[11]Although a sharply increased volume of equities trading in 1992 returned commissions to 1987 levels, this may be a temporary phenomenon.

[12]Pretax return on equity for broker-dealers rose from 2.2 percent in 1990 to 23.6, 22, 26.7, and 29.1 percent in 1991, 1992, 1993, and 1996, respectively.

Contemporary Perspectives 5–2

No Signs of Slowing

The underwriting locomotive on Wall Street worked up such a head of steam in the first nine months of 1997 that full-year domestic issuance seems sure to top $1 trillion for only the second time in history. Total volume on all U.S. debt and equity issues reached $947 billion on 8,715 deals for the nine months, up 34 percent from $707.6 billion on 6,918 deals in the same period last year.

While the equity side has had its fair share of ups and downs in the period—and indeed finished the period down 8.5 percent from last year's first nine months—the fixed-income sector thus far in '97 has had a dream year. Investment-grade debt volume for the first three quarters had already topped the 1996 full-year total. Even if activity slows in the fourth quarter (and it looks like it may well do just the opposite), the public markets as a whole should easily surpass the $1.09 trillion record set in 1993. And some market sources, encouraged by what looks to be a solid October calendar, say that even equities—the market laggard—should turn in an improved performance in the last months of 1997. "The fourth quarter will be a lot stronger than people anticipated," one Wall Street underwriting executive says.

Extreme volatility marked the third quarter in stocks, as hundred-point losses or gains in the Dow became commonplace. . . . But the period is ending on a high note, as market sources note that the pipeline of new deals is bulging, and continuing trends bode well for fourth quarter and beyond. For example, follow-on stock deals led by selling shareholders continue to be a large contributor to equity volume, as does the still-strong mergers and acquisitions environment. The largest stock deal of the quarter highlighted both trends. On September 18, First Union Corp. sold $2.5 billion in stock globally through lead underwriter Morgan Stanley, Dean Witter, Discover & Co. . . .

The redemption cloud hanging over the convertible market dissipated a bit as convertible issuance grew in the third quarter, making it unlikely that redemptions will outpace new issuances this year as it has the past two years. . . . The investment-grade sector rocked the public markets through the first three quarters of this year, compiling an astounding $553.4 billion in proceeds raised in 6,347 deals. That not only surpasses last year's third quarter mark of $386.5 billion by 43 percent, it already tops the $511.4 billion raised for all of 1996.

The third quarter saw several other trends continue from earlier in the year. Deal size grew in both volume and complexity, and cross-border deals became even more acceptable to bond buyers. . . . For the fourth quarter, more of the same is expected in investment grade, market pros agree, with the very likely possibility that 1997 could be the strongest year ever for capital raising in the domestic debt markets.

SOURCE: Gregg Wirth and Erica Copulsky, *Investment Dealers' Digest,* October 6, 1997, p. 14. Reprinted with permission from Investment Dealers' Digest, October 6, 1997. Copyright 1997 by Securities Data Publishing, Inc. All Rights Reserved.

move to enhance trading profits. A heavy reliance on fixed income trading, however, can also produce losses if interest rates (and other asset prices) move in a direction other than expected. For example, Salomon Brothers and a number of other securities firms announced record trading losses on their bond trading activities in 1994. Thus, interest rate risk is now a focal area of investment bank risk exposure.

The growth in underwriting activity during the 1990–1997 period is evident from the fact that the total dollar value of underwriting activity increased from $314 billion in 1990 to $954 billion in 1996 and $947 billion through the first nine months of 1997 (with a peak at $1.087 trillion in 1993). New issue activity trebled over this period (Table 5–4). In particular, the booming financial markets of 1996 and 1997 sparked a large increase in underwriting activity; total corporate underwritings increased 33.8 percent from $713.1 billion in 1995 to $954.2 billion in 1996; through the first nine months of 1997, underwriting topped $947.0 billion. Additionally, pretax net income for securities firms reached $11.27 billion

Table 5-4

U.S. CORPORATE UNDERWRITING ACTIVITY

(in billions of dollars)

	Straight Corporate Debt	Con- vertible Debt	Asset- Backed Debt	Total Debt	High- Yield Bonds	Common Stock	Preferred Stock	Total Equity	All IPOs	Total Under- writing
1990	106.9	4.8	178.9	290.6	1.4	19.2	4.7	23.9	10.2	314.4
1991	200.6	7.5	299.0	507.1	10.0	56.0	20.0	76.0	25.1	583.1
1992	315.6	11.8	425.3	752.7	52.0	83.6	35.3	118.9	39.9	871.6
1993	439.2	20.1	474.5	933.8	89.0	116.3	36.7	153.0	57.5	1086.8
1994	374.3	9.6	255.7	639.6	49.4	85.5	20.4	105.9	33.8	745.5
1995	443.3	17.4	155.9	616.6	43.1	82.0	14.5	96.5	30.2	713.1
1996	511.4	38.5	248.7	798.6	73.8	115.1	40.5	155.6	50.0	954.2
1997*	524.9	32.9	259.6	817.4	93.0	78.1	51.5	129.6	26.7	947.0
% Change (1996 to 1997)	2.6%	−14.5%	4.4%	2.4%	26.0%	−32.1%	27.2%	−16.7%	−46.6%	0.8%

NOTE: High-yield bonds represent a subset of straight corporate debt. IPOs is a subset of common stock; true and closed-end fund IPOs are subsets of all IPOs.

*As of September 1997.

SOURCE: Securities Data Company and Securities Industry Association; *Security Trends,* October 19, 1992, and *Federal Reserve Bulletin,* various issues.

in 1996, 31 percent over the 1993 record of $8.6 billion, and the industry averaged a 29.1 percent return on equity.[13]

Despite the resurgence in underwriting business, the 1990s presented a new challenge for underwriters. Specifically, in 1987 the Federal Reserve allowed bank holding companies to expand their activities in securities underwriting (activities that had been prohibited since the Glass-Steagal Act was passed in 1933). By 1997, the special investment bank subsidiaries (so-called Section 20 subsidiaries) of commercial banks had captured 10 percent of the corporate debt underwriting market.

Note the current importance of securities trading and underwriting in the 1996 consolidated balance sheet of all securities firms in Table 5–5. Looking at the asset portfolio, long positions in securities and commodities accounted for 26.6 percent of assets, reverse repurchase agreements—securities purchased under agreements to resell (i.e., the broker gives a short-term loan to the repurchase agreement seller—see Chapter 2)—accounted for 35.8 percent of assets.

With respect to liabilities, repurchase agreements—securities sold under agreements to repurchase—were the major source of funds; these are securities temporarily lent in exchange for cash received. Repurchase agreements amounted to 47.7 percent of total liabilities and equity. The other major sources of funds were securities and commodities sold short for future delivery and broker-call bank loans. Equity capital amounted to only 3.8 percent of total assets, and total capital (equity capital plus subordinate liabilities) represented 5.8 percent of total assets. These levels are well below the level for depository

---

[13]This information is from the Securities Industry Association.

Table **5-5**

ASSETS AND LIABILITIES OF BROKER-DEALERS AS OF YEAR-END 1996

(in millions of dollars)

Assets		Liabilities	
Cash	$ 17,188.2	Bank loans payable	$ 58,698.5
Receivables from other broker-dealers	501,213.3	Payables to other broker-dealers	229,368.5
Receivables from customers	87,144.2	Payables to noncustomers	19,172.6
Receivables from noncustomers	7,440.1	Payables to customers	143,775.4
Long positions in securities and commodities	466,044.4	Short positions in securities and commodities	252,221.6
Securities and investments not readily		Securities sold under repurchase agreements	834,579.0
marketable	5,488.6	Other nonsubordinated liabilities	108,742.1
Securities purchased under agreements		Subordinated liabilities	36,631.7
to resell	625,978.3	Total liabilities	$1,683,189.4
Exchange membership	756.3		
Other assets	37,527.0	Capital	
Total assets	$1,748,780.4	Equity capital	$ 65,591.0
		Total capital	$ 102,222.7
		Number of firms	7,776

SOURCE: *Focus Report,* Office of Economic Analysis, U.S. Securities and Exchange Commission, (Washington, D.C.), 1997.

institutions presented in Chapter 3. One reason for lower capital levels is that securities firms' balance sheets contain mostly tradable (liquid) securities compared to the relatively illiquid loans that represent a significant portion of banks' asset portfolios. Securities firms are required to maintain a net worth (capital) to assets ratio in excess of 2 percent (see Chapter 16).

Concept Questions

1. What has been the trend in profitability in the securities industry over the last 10 years?
2. What are the major assets held by broker-dealers?
3. Why do broker-dealers tend to hold less equity capital than do commercial banks and thrifts?

REGULATION

The primary regulator of the securities industry is the Securities and Exchange Commission (SEC), established in 1934. The National Securities Markets Improvement Act (NSMIA) of 1996 reiterated the significance of the SEC in this capacity. Prior to NSMIA, most securities firms were subject to regulation from the SEC and each state in which they operated. NSMIA provides that states may still require securities firms to pay fees and file documents submitted to the SEC, but most of the regulatory burden imposed by states has been removed. States are also now prohibited from requiring registration of securities firms' transactions and from imposing substantive requirements on private placements. Thus, NSMIA effectively gives the SEC the exclusive regulatory jurisdiction over securities firms.

Two self-regulatory organizations are also involved in the day-to-day regulation of trading practices on the exchanges. They are the New York Stock Exchange (NYSE) and the National Association of Securities Dealers (NASD), the latter responsible for trading in the over-the-counter markets such as NASDAQ. They monitor trading abuses (such as insider trading) and securities firms' capital (solvency positions). The SEC also sets rules governing securities firms' underwriting and trading activities. For example, SEC Rule 415 on *shelf-offerings* allows large corporations to register their new issues with the SEC up to two years in advance.[14] SEC Rule 144A defines the boundaries between public offerings of securities and private placements of securities.

Finally, the Securities Investor Protection Corporation (SIPC) protects investors against losses of up to $500,000 on securities firm failures. This guaranty fund was created following the passage of the Securities Investor Protection Act in 1970 and is financed by premium contributions from member firms. The fund protects investor accounts in the event that a member broker-dealer can not meet its financial obligations to customers. The fund does not, however, protect against losses on a customer's account due to poor investment choices that reduce the value of their portfolio.

Concept Questions

1. What is the major result of NSMIA?
2. What two organizations monitor trading abuses?

• •

---

[14]They are called *shelf-offerings* because after registering the issue with the SEC, the firm can take the issue "off the shelf" and sell it to the market when conditions are the most favorable, for example, in the case of debt issues, when interest rates are low.

SUMMARY

This chapter presented an overview of security firms, which primarily offer retail services to investors, and investment banking firms, which primarily offer commercial activities to corporate customers. Firms in this industry assist in getting new issues of debt and equity to the markets. Additionally, this industry facilitates trading and market making of securities after they are issued. The chapter discussed the structure of the industry and changes in the degree of concentration in firm size in the industry over the last decade. Balance sheet information that highlighted the major assets and liabilities of firms in the industry was analyzed.

PERTINENT WEB SITES

National Association of Securities Dealers
    http://www.nasd.com/
Securities Data Company   http://www.
    securitiesdata.com/home.html

Securities and Exchange Commission   http://
    www.sec.gov/
Securities Investor Protection Corp.   http://
    www.sipc.org/

The Financial Services Industry: Securities Firms and Investment Banks

1. In what ways are securities firms and investment banks financial intermediaries?
2. How does the size of the securities and investment banking industry compare with the size of the commercial banking industry?
3. What are the different firms in the securities industry and how does each differ from the others?
4. Contrast the activities of securities firms with the activities of depository institutions and insurance firms.
5. What are the seven key activity areas of security firms and how were they impacted by the stock market crash of 1987?
6. What is the difference between pure arbitrage and risk arbitrage? If an investor observes the price of a stock trading in one exchange to be different from the price in another exchange, what form of arbitrage is applicable and how could the investor participate in that arbitrage?
7. What two factors accounted for the resurgence in profits for securities firms in the period 1991–1997? Are firms that trade in fixed income securities more or less likely to have volatile profits? Why or why not?
8. Explain the difference between an IPO and a secondary offering.
9. How does a public offering differ from a private placement?
10. How does a best-efforts underwriting differ from firm commitment underwriting? If you operated a company issuing stock for the first time, which type of underwriting would you prefer? Why might you still choose the alternative?
11. How do agency transactions differ from principal transactions for market makers?
12. Why have brokerage commissions earned by securities firms fallen since 1977?
13. What was the largest single asset and largest single liability of securities firms in 1996?
14. What benefits could a commercial banker obtain by getting into the investment banking business?
15. An investor notices that an ounce of gold is priced at $318 in London and $325 in New York. What action could the investor take to try to profit from the price discrepancy? Which of the four trading activities would this be? What might be some impediments to the success of the transaction?
16. An investment banker agrees to underwrite a $5,000,000 bond issue for JCN corporation on a firm commitment basis. The investment banker pays JCN on Thursday and plans to begin a public sale on Friday. What type of interest rate movement does the investment bank fear while holding these securities?
17. An investment banker pays $23.50 per share for 3,000,000 shares of KDO company. It then sells these shares to the public for $25. How much money does KDO receive? What is the investment banker's profit? What is the stock price of KDO?
18. MEP company has issued 5,000,000 new shares. Its investment banker agrees to underwrite these shares on a best-efforts basis. The investment banker is able to sell 4,200,000 shares for $54 per share. It charges MEP $1.25 per share sold. How much money does MEP receive? What is the investment banker's profit? What is the stock price of MEP?
19. Which type of security accounts for most underwriting in the United States?
20. Which is likely to be more costly to underwrite, corporate debt or equity? Explain.

Chapter Six

The Financial Services Industry: Finance Companies

he primary function of finance companies is to make loans to both individuals and businesses. Finance companies provide services including consumer lending, business lending, and mortgage financing. Some of finance companies' loans are similar to commercial bank loans, such as consumer and auto loans, but others are more specialized. As is the case for Jayhawk Acceptance Corp. described in Contemporary Perspectives Box 6–1, finance companies are always looking to expand into new and profitable consumer lending areas. Unlike banks, finance companies do not accept deposits but instead rely on short- and long-term debt. Additionally, finance companies often lend to customers that commercial banks consider too risky. This chapter discusses the size, structure, and composition of this industry, the services it provides, its competitive and financial situation, and its regulation.

Contemporary Perspectives 6–1

Jayhawk Sets Its Sights on Market for Vanity Loans

A unit of Jayhawk Acceptance Corp., one of a group of finance companies that lends money to used-car buyers with poor or no credit, has begun marketing loans in the Chicago area for tummy tucks, hair transplants and other procedures that usually aren't covered by health insurance. . . .

For Jayhawk, a Dallas-based firm that filed for bankruptcy protection last month after its prime lender declared it was in violation of its loan agreement, the medical loan program holds the promise of reaping large profits by capitalizing on America's vanity.

"Capitalism is getting a little bizarre," said Dr. Quentin Young, national coordinator for Physicians for a National Health Program. "I don't know what's crazier—the public's willingness to pay usurious interest rates for vanity purposes or the ingenuity of capitalists willing to break the bank," he said.

Jayhawk in August began issuing contracts with doctors to lend to their patients who are seeking cosmetic surgery or some dental procedures. "This is a big market," said Virginia Cleveland, a company spokeswoman, noting that some infertility doctors recently had joined the program.

Borrowers who pay the loans within a year pay an interest rate of 9.9 percent, while those who repay within the maximum of two years pay a rate of 13.9 percent.

Left unanswered, however, is what Jayhawk can repossess if a borrower defaults on the loan. "I guess they get the fat that's sucked out," said Young. Cleveland said: "It's no different than a credit card. You can't repossess a tank of gas."

SOURCE: John Schmeltzer, The *Chicago Tribune*, March 10, 1997, p.5, Zone: C. © Copyrighted Chicago Tribune Company. All rights reserved. Used with permission.

SIZE, STRUCTURE, AND COMPOSITION OF THE INDUSTRY

The finance company was originated during the Depression when General Electric Corp. created General Electric Capital Corp. (GECC) to finance appliance sales to cash-strapped customers unable to obtain installment credit from banks. By the late 1950s, banks had become more willing to make installment loans, so finance companies began looking outside their parent companies for business. For example, GECC's loan and lease portfolio today includes leases for more than 65,000 rail cars, 160 commercial airlines, and more than $1 billion in leveraged buyout financing and $20 billion in mortgage insurance premiums, along with more than $350 million in loans to General Electric customers.[1]

Finance companies have been among the fastest growing financial intermediary (FI) groups in recent years. As of the third quarter of 1997, their assets stood at $895.6 billion (see Table 6–1). Comparing this to assets of $104.3 billion at the end of 1977 (Table 6–2), this industry has experienced growth of more than 759 percent in the last 20 years. GMAC Commercial Mortgage Corp. (GMACCM), a subsidiary of General Motors Acceptance Corp. (GMAC), is in fact the largest commercial mortgage lender in the United States, with a mortgage portfolio of more than $40 billion in place. The company announced in 1997 that it had plans to expand its product mix to create one of the world's leading one-stop commercial finance companies.

---

[1] See GECC's 1997 annual report.

Table 6-1

ASSETS AND LIABILITIES OF U.S. FINANCE COMPANIES
(September 30, 1997)

Assets	Billions of Dollars	Percent of Total Assets	Liabilities and Capital	Billions of Dollars	Percent of Total Assets
Accounts receivable gross	$656.8	73.3	Bank loans	$19.3	2.2
Consumer	$255.0	28.5	Commercial paper	190.2	21.2
Business	313.1	34.9	Debt due to parent	61.7	6.9
Real estate	88.7	9.9	Debt not elsewhere classified	348.5	38.9
Less reserves for unearned income	(58.0)	(6.5)	All other liabilities	177.2	19.8
Less reserves for losses	(13.7)	(1.5)	Capital, surplus, and undivided profits	98.7	11.0
Accounts receivable net	585.1	65.3	Total liabilities and capital	895.6	100.0
All other	310.5	34.7			
Total assets	895.6	100.0			

SOURCE: *Federal Reserve Bulletin,* December 1997, p. A33.

Table 6-2

ASSETS AND LIABILITIES OF U.S. FINANCE COMPANIES
(December 31, 1977)

Assets	Billions of Dollars	Percent of Total Assets	Liabilities and Capital	Billions of Dollars	Percent of Total Assets
Accounts receivable gross	$99.2	95.1	Bank loans	5.9	5.7
Consumer	$44.0	42.2	Commercial paper	29.6	28.4
Business	55.2	52.9	Debt:		
Less reserves for unearned income and losses	(12.7)	(12.2)	Short term	6.2	5.9
Accounts receivable net	86.5	82.9	Long term	36.0	34.5
Cash and bank deposit	2.6	2.5	Other	11.5	11.0
Securities	0.9	0.9	Capital, surplus, and undivided profits	15.1	14.5
All others	14.3	13.7	Total liabilities and capital	104.3	100.0
Total assets	104.3	100.0			

SOURCE: *Federal Reserve Bulletin,* June 1978, p. A39.

sales finance institutions

Finance companies specializing in loans to customers of a particular retailer or manufacturer.

personal credit institutions

Finance companies specializing in installment and other loans to consumers.

business credit institutions

Finance companies specializing in business loans.

factoring

The process of purchasing accounts receivable from corporations (often at a discount) usually with no recourse to the seller should the receivables go bad.

Three major types of finance companies are (1) sales finance institutions, (2) personal credit institutions, and (3) business credit institutions. **Sales finance institutions** (e.g., Ford Motor Credit and Sears Roebuck Acceptance Corp.) specialize in making loans to customers of a specific retailer or manufacturer. **Personal credit institutions** (e.g., Household Finance Corp. and American General Finance) specialize in making installment and other loans to consumers. **Business credit institutions** (e.g., CIT Group and Heller Financial) provide financing to corporations, especially through equipment leasing and **factoring,** in which the finance company purchases accounts receivable from corporate customers. These accounts are purchased at a discount from their face value and the finance company assumes the responsibility for collecting the accounts receivable. Many finance companies (e.g., GMAC) perform more than one of these services.

The industry is quite concentrated; the 20 largest firms account for more than 80 percent of its assets. In addition, many of the largest finance companies such as GMAC tend to be wholly owned or captive subsidiaries of major manufacturing companies. A major role of a **captive finance company** is to provide financing for the purchase of products manufactured by the parent, as GMAC does for GM cars. Table 6–3 presents information for six of the largest finance companies.

Table 6–3

INFORMATION ON SIX LARGE FINANCE COMPANIES

AT&T Capital

Total assets, $9.5 billion; ROE, 12.1%. AT&T Capital, a recent spin-off of AT&T, is the largest publicly owned equipment leasing and finance company in the U.S. AT&T Capital has assisted more than 500,000 small and medium-size business customers. Although AT&T began its financial services as a leasing company, AT&T Capital has moved into lending, added SBA loans, and is expanding into asset-based lending. In their own words, AT&T Capital targets the underserved small business market because it is an area where we are well experienced given our vendor financing heritage. We realize a successful lender to small businesses must have customer intimacy—a relationship that enables us to anticipate customer needs. Entrepreneurs and small business managers frequently face limited operational and financial resources. We work hard to understand their businesses and accommodate their special needs. As a result, AT&T Capital focuses on improving its operational performance, turnaround time on loan processing, and overall responsiveness.

Their Web site stresses their business finance division that provides leasing and financing solutions to qualified small and medium-size businesses throughout the continental U.S. The site specifies transaction sizes of $3,000 to $2 million and the types of financing provided.

GE Capital Services

Total assets, $186 billion; ROE, 22%. GE Capital's parent company is the largest corporation in the world, based on the market value. GE Capital purchased ITT's small business finance corporation in 1995, thereby expanding its leasing base to SBA lending. Their Web site states, GE Capital Small Business Finance is a premier financing source for small business. The site focuses on SBA loans and highlights flexibility, experience, expertise, and the ability to help customers through the application process. Small Business Finance plans for 1996 included doubling GE's sales offices to 80 and being a preferred SBA lender in 40 markets.

Advanta

Total assets, $4.5 billion; ROE, 26%. A major provider of financial services to consumers and small businesses as well as a major credit provider, Advanta is partnering with American Express to offer a line of credit for office equipment leases. Their small business equipment leasing increased 42% in 1995. An indication that they're adding new products is the small business unit name change, from Advanta Leasing Services to Advanta Business Services.

Advanta has state-of-the-art credit-scoring and rapid application processing systems. The company, using target marketing and direct mail for a number of years, has experienced an outstanding response to its new business card.

Advanta's Web site states that the firm is specifically targeted to businesses looking for solutions on how to manage cash flow and equipment acquisitions easily. Advanta characterizes its Web site as "an information center that addresses the hows and whys of equipment financing and business credit." It also provides information about Advanta on sales and marketing and financial strategies and contacts for the customers.

Heller

Total assets, $9.6 billion; ROE, 9%. One of the largest commercial finance companies in the country, Heller's mission statement, contained in the company's 1995 annual report, is . . . to provide high-quality financial services and capital that help small and medium-size enterprises succeed. Our primary responsibility is to meet client needs.

Heller characterizes itself as hassle free, providing innovative solutions, and having an open dialogue with customers. "Hassle free" means simplified closings and investing in technology to respond quickly. "Innovative solutions" means providing flexible ways to meet customers' funding needs. "Open dialogue" refers to Heller's periodic client satisfaction surveys, formal relationship reviews, and ongoing research to gauge how well the company measures up to customer expectations.

Heller First Capital provides long-term financing to small businesses and franchises and SBA loans. Heller First Capital's small business finance unit provides traditional working capital to smaller firms and to turn-around companies. One of Heller's Web sites states, Heller First Capital provides long-term financing to independent small businesses and franchises using the U.S. SBA loan guarantee programs; another states, Heller Small Business Finance provides traditional working capital financing and receivables management to smaller firms as well as to turnaround companies. Both Web pages provide specific information on products and services offered, markets served, names and telephone numbers of contacts, and stress quick turnaround.

CIT Group

Total assets, $17.4 billion; ROE, 12.1%. A major commercial and consumer finance company, CIT Group is owned 80% by Dai-ichi Kangyo Bank and 20% by Chase Manhattan. The firm portrays itself as having industry expertise and technology, and CIT Group has cutting-edge technology that makes a huge volume of business possible. CIT's credit philosophy, included in its 1995 annual report, is "When we can't exactly give the customer what they're looking for, we find another way to make the transaction work." Their credit finance group has created a small loan division that provides collateralized financing and works with special situation.

CIT's Web site states, The working capital you need is closer than you think. The information on the site focuses on the specialized needs of high-tech industries and promotes CIT's flexibility, intelligence, and responsive and innovative solutions. Other information includes who they are, what they do, how they can help, and how to contact them.

American Express

Total assets, $107 billion; ROE, 22%. The largest issuer of corporate and business cards, American Express serves 1.5 million small businesses with corporate charge cards. The firm is preparing to sell prequalified lines of credit to small business customers in conjunction with Bank One and Wells Fargo, combining American Express's marketing expertise and the banks' underwriting skills. The lines of credit, accessible by check, will be $5,000 to $50,000 to preapproved American Express business charge card customers. American Express also offers small-ticket leases with Advanta, a new small business credit card with a $20,000 limit, new credit options, lease financing, and financial management services. American Express has a huge customer base and more than 10 years' experience with small business customers. American Express's Web site states, American Express Financial Advisors provide a wide range of products and services designed to meet the needs of small business owners.

SOURCE: *The Journal of Lending & Credit Risk Management*, December, 1996. *The Journal of Lending & Credit Risk Management* © 1996 by Robert Morris Associates, an association of lending professionals headquartered in Philadelphia. Written by Cynthia A. Glassman, a member of the Risk Management and Regulatory Practice Department at Ernst & Young, LLP, Washington, D.C.

Concept Questions

1. What are the three major types of finance companies? What types of customers does each serve?
2. What is a captive finance company?

• •

BALANCE SHEET
AND RECENT TRENDS

As mentioned earlier, finance companies provide three basic lending services: real estate, consumer, and business. The assets and liabilities of finance companies as of the third quarter of 1997 are presented in Table 6–1. Business and consumer loans (called *accounts receivable*) are the major assets held by finance companies; they represent 63.4 percent of total assets. In 1977, 95.1 percent of total assets were consumer and business loans. Over the last 20 years, however, finance companies have replaced consumer and business loans with increasing amounts of real estate loans and other assets.

Table 6–4 presents information concerning the industry's loans from 1994 through August 1997 for consumer, real estate, and business areas. In recent years, the fastest growing areas of asset business have been in the nonconsumer finance areas, especially leasing and business lending. In August 1997, consumer loans constituted 41.1 percent of all finance company loans, mortgages represented 15.7 percent, and business loans composed 43.1 percent. The increased leasing was encouraged by tax incentives provided under the 1981 Economic Recovery Act.

Consumer Loans

Consumer loans include motor vehicle loans and leases, other consumer loans, and securitized loans from each category. Motor vehicle loans and leases are traditionally the major type of consumer loan (72.5 percent of the consumer loan portfolio in August 1997). Table 6–5 data indicate that finance companies generally charge higher rates for automobile loans than do commercial banks. From 1994 to 1996, auto finance companies charged interest rates that were from 0.79 to 1.67 percent higher than those of commercial banks. The finance companies' generally higher rates on new car loans relative to those of commercial banks proved to be an anomaly in 1997. Because of economic problems in emerging market countries (see Chapter 28), new car sales by U.S. firms in 1997 were lower than normal. As an incentive to clear the expanding stock of new cars, auto finance companies owned by the major auto manufacturers slashed interest rates on new car loans (some as low as 3.9 percent). This type of low rate offered by finance companies is rare, however.

subprime lender

A finance company that lends to high-risk customers.

loan sharks

Subprime lenders that charge unfairly exorbitant rates to desperate, subprime borrowers.

The difference in rates that banks and finance companies generally charge for consumer loans is due to the fact that finance companies generally attract riskier customers than commercial banks do. In fact, customers that seek individual (or business) loans from finance companies are often those judged too risky to obtain loans from commercial banks or thrifts. It is, in fact, possible for individuals to obtain a mortgage from a **subprime lender** finance company even with a bankruptcy on their records. Banks rarely make such loans. Most finance companies that offer these mortgages, however, charge rates commensurate with the higher risk, and a few **loan shark** companies prey on desperate consumers,

Table **6-4**

FINANCE COMPANY LOANS OUTSTANDING FROM 1994 THROUGH AUGUST 1997

(in billions of dollars)

	1994	1995	1996	August 1997
Consumer	248.0	285.8	310.6	323.1
Motor vehicle loans	70.2	81.1	86.7	88.4
Motor vehicle leases	67.5	80.8	92.5	98.8
Revolving *	25.9	28.5	32.5	33.6
Other †	38.4	42.6	33.2	35.4
Securitized assets				
Motor vehicle loans	32.8	34.8	36.8	38.2
Motor vehicle leases	2.2	3.5	8.7	8.9
Revolving	n.a.	n.a.	0.0	0.0
Other	11.2	14.7	20.1	19.7
Real estate	66.9	72.4	111.9	123.5
One- to four-family	n.a.	n.a.	52.1	58.9
Other	n.a.	n.a.	30.5	30.4
Securitized real estate assets ‡				
One- to four-family	n.a.	n.a.	28.9	33.9
Other	n.a.	n.a.	0.4	0.3
Business	298.6	331.2	347.2	339.3
Motor vehicles	62.0	66.5	67.1	65.2
Retail loans	18.5	21.8	25.1	25.3
Wholesale loans §	35.2	36.6	33.0	30.5
Leases	8.3	8.0	9.0	9.4
Equipment	8.3	8.0	9.0	189.0
Loans	8.3	8.0	9.0	51.3
Leases	8.3	8.0	9.0	137.6
Other business receivables# . .	8.3	8.0	9.0	52.5
Securitized assets‡				
Motor Vehicles	8.3	8.0	9.0	19.8
Retail loans	8.3	8.0	9.0	2.3
Wholesale loans	8.3	8.0	9.0	17.5**
Leases	8.3	8.0	9.0	0.0
Equipment	8.3	8.0	9.0	10.3
Loans	8.3	8.0	9.0	4.1
Leases	8.3	8.0	9.0	6.2
Other business receivables #	8.3	8.0	9.0	2.4
Total	613.5	689.5	769.7	785.9

* Excludes revolving credit reported as held by depository institutions that are subsidiaries of finance companies.

† Includes personal cash loans, mobile home loans, and loans to purchase other types of consumer goods such as appliances, apparel, boats, and recreation vehicles.

‡ Outstanding balances of pools on which securities have been issued; these balances are no longer carried on the balance sheets of the loan originator.

§ Credit arising from transactions between manufacturers and dealers; that is, floor plan financing.

Includes loans on commercial accounts receivable, factored commercial accounts, and receivable dealer capital; small loans used primarily for business or farm purposes; and wholesale and lease paper for mobile homes, campers, and travel trailers.

** *Owned receivables* are those carried on the balance sheet of the institution. *Managed receivables* are outstanding balances of pools on which securities have been issued; these balances are no longer carried on the balance sheets of the loan originator.

SOURCE: *Federal Reserve Bulletin,* December, 1997, p. A33.

Contemporary Perspectives 6–2

A Risky Business Gets Even Riskier: Big Losses and Bad Accounting Leave
"Subprime" Lenders Reeling

The business of lending money to the millions of Americans with tarnished credit ratings—or none at all—has always been a walk on capitalism's wild side.

"Subprime" lending, as the business is known, is a volatile world of big risks, staggering profit potential and almost no barriers to entry. Its clients vary from swindlers with no intention of paying off their loans to hard-working immigrants and victims of personal tragedies like layoffs or debilitating illness. And the hardball tactics some lenders use to encourage borrowing or to collect on loans breed both lawsuits and criticism from consumer groups. . . .

In a business where the line between exploiting risk and drowning in it is thin, some players have gone "too close to the edge," said William A. Brandt, Jr., a corporate turnaround specialist, shortly after he was brought in late last

month to stabilize the Mercury Finance Company in the wake of disclosures that its earnings reports had been falsified from 1993 on.

The turmoil is rooted in the relentless growth in the number of Americans with blemishes on their credit records, ranging from repeated late payments to outright bankruptcy, making them a market far too large to ignore. Now with everyone from the biggest banks and giant credit companies like GE Capital to ambitious entrepreneurs piling in, the competitive pressures are exposing the cracks caused by ill-conceived growth strategies, poor management of operations and outright greed.

There had been periodic reminders that not everyone would be successful. In early 1995, Search Capital Group Inc., a rapidly expanding Dallas lender in the used-car market, was forced to put its eight operating units into bankruptcy. And

the attempt that year by TFC Enterprise to expand into civilian subprime auto loans from its core business of loans to soldiers generated huge losses through "a mixture of ineptitude and undue optimism," according to David Karsten, the chief financial officer since a new team of managers took over at TFC last year.

But it took the news of the padding of Mercury's books to really stun Wall Street. The company, based in the Chicago suburb of Lake Forest, Ill., is a relative giant in the $70 billion subprime auto loan sector, with some $1.5 billion in loans outstanding and a carefully cultivated reputation for sound, penny-pinching management. . . .

It is not just Mercury's fans who have been surprised. "I never dreamed this would happen," said Matthew Lindenbaum, a principal at Basswood Partners, a Paramus, N.J.,

charging exorbitant rates as high as 30 percent or more. Contemporary Perspectives Box 6–2 points out that such subprime lending by finance companies has landed some industry participants in less than a prime position themselves.

Other consumer loans include personal cash loans, mobile home loans, and loans to purchase other types of consumer goods such as appliances, apparel, general merchandise, and

Table **6–5**

CONSUMER CREDIT INTEREST RATES FOR 1994 THROUGH AUGUST 1997

Type	1994	1995	1996	August 1997
Commercial bank new car	8.12%	9.57%	9.05%	8.99%
Auto finance company new car	9.79	11.19	9.84	5.93

SOURCE: *Federal Reserve Bulletin*, November 1997, p. A36.

money manager that concentrates on financial stocks. Mr. Lindenbaum had been one of the few analysts warning that the kind of explosive growth Mercury and others had been reporting often led to problems that investors detected too late to save themselves.

Any impulse investors had to write off Mercury's woes as an aberration took a severe hit on Thursday. Reports from the industry trenches included a bankruptcy filing by the Jayhawk Acceptance Corporation, which finances car loans to some of the nation's riskiest buyers; the delay until Monday of an earnings report from First Enterprise Financial because of unexpected loan losses, and the downgrading of securities issued by Olympic Financial Ltd.

So far, the bad news has been heavily concentrated in the volatile auto-lending sector, but analysts say that investors are bound to be more cautious about the entire subprime world, at least for a while.

"It's going to have an effect on mortgages and credit cards," said Jewel Bickford managing director of Rothschild Capital Markets in New York, which helps finance companies assemble packages of auto loans, mortgages, credit card receivable and other assets that are sold as securities to investors. . . .

The success stories have been even more striking in other subprime markets. Investors in the Green Tree Financial Company of St. Paul, the leading subprime lender in mobile homes, enjoyed a return of 83.2 percent annually from 1991 through 1995, assuming they reinvested dividends—one of the best performances ever on Wall Street.

Borrowing money cheaply and lending it at sky-high rates is not the only way subprime lenders turbocharge profit margins. Many pay discounted prices for the loans that auto dealers send them, which provides an added cushion against losses. And, in a tactic often criticized by consumer advocates, car buyers are cajoled into buying insurance policies that would appear to pay off the loans in the event of death or disability but are much more expensive and limited in their coverage than many purchasers realize. It is easy to see why Wall Street fell in love with the finance companies. . . .

Lately, though, meeting expectations is becoming tougher as competition forces growth-driven finance companies to make riskier loans and share more of the pie with auto dealers. At the same time, as Olympic's debt downgrade highlighted, many finance companies will have to offer sweeter terms to their creditors to calm nerves after the recent bad news from Mercury and Jayhawk. . . .

"Subprime is an incredible business if you can manage it," said Mr. Mack, who is now chief executive of the Pinnacle Finance Company, a privately held Minneapolis provider of home improvement loans to people with credit problems.

SOURCE: Barnaby J. Feder. The *New York Times,* February 12, 1997, p. 1. Copyright © 1997 by The New York Times Co. Reprinted by Permission.

recreation vehicles. In August 1997, other consumer loans made up 27.5 percent of the consumer loan portfolio of finance companies.

Mortgages

securitized mortgage assets

Mortgages packaged and used as assets backing secondary market securities.

Residential and commercial mortgages have become a major component in finance company portfolios, although finance companies did not deal in mortgages in 1977 (Table 6–2). Mortgages include all loans secured by liens on any type of real estate. Mortgages can be made either directly or as **securitized mortgage assets** (e.g., mortgages packaged and used as assets backing secondary market securities).[2] The mortgages in the loan portfolio can be first or second mortgages in the form of home equity loans. Home equity loans have become very profitable for finance companies since the passage of the Tax Reform Act of 1986, which disallowed the tax deductibility of consumer interest payments other than those on home mortgages. Also, the bad debt expense and administrative costs on home equity loans are lower than on other finance company loans.

---

[2] Chapter 12 discusses the securitization of mortgages in more detail.

Business Loans

Business loans represent the largest portion of the loan portfolio of finance companies. Finance companies have several advantages over commercial banks in offering services to small business customers. First, they are not subject to regulations that restrict the type of products and services they can offer (discussed later). Second, because finance companies do not accept deposits, they have no bank-type regulators looking directly over their shoulders.[3] Third, being (in many cases) subsidiaries of holding companies, finance companies often have substantial industry and product expertise. Fourth—as mentioned with consumer loans—finance companies are more willing to accept risky customers than are commercial banks. Fifth, finance companies generally have lower overheads than banks (e.g., they do not need tellers/branches for deposit taking).

The major subcategories of business loans are retail and wholesale motor vehicle loans and leases (19.2 percent of all business loans in August 1997), equipment loans (55.7 percent), other business loans (15.5 percent), and securitized business assets (9.6 percent). Motor vehicle loans consist of retail loans that assist in transactions between the retail seller of the good and the ultimate consumer (ie., passenger car fleets and commercial land vehicles for which licenses are required). Wholesale loans are loan agreements between parties other than the companies' consumers. For example, GMAC provides wholesale financing to GM dealers for inventory floor plans. These activities extend to retail and wholesale leasing of motor vehicles as well. Business lending activities of finance companies also include equipment loans, with the finance company either owning or leasing the equipment directly to its industrial customer or providing the financial backing for a working capital loan or a loan to purchase or remodel the customer's facility. Indeed, equipment loans are currently the major category of business loans for finance companies. Other business loans include loans to businesses to finance accounts receivable, small farm loans, and wholesale loans and leases for mobile homes, campers, and trailers.

To finance asset growth, finance companies have relied primarily on short-term commercial paper and other debt (longer-term notes and bonds). As data in Table 6–1 indicate, in September 1997 commercial paper amounted to $190.2 billion (21.2 percent of total assets); other debt (due to parents and not elsewhere classified) totaled $410.2 billion (45.8 percent). Total capital comprised $98.7 billion (11.0 percent of total assets), and bank loans totaled $19.3 billion (2.2 percent of total assets). A comparison of these figures with those for 1977 (in Table 6–2) indicates that commercial paper was used more in 1977 (28.4 percent of total assets) while other debt (short and long term) was less significant as a source of financing (40.4 percent). Finance companies also now rely less heavily on bank loans for financing and hold less capital. In 1977, bank loans were 5.7 percent of total assets, and capital was 14.5 percent of the total.

As mentioned earlier, unlike banks and thrifts, finance companies cannot accept deposits. Rather, to finance assets, finance companies issue short-term commercial paper, with many having direct sale programs in which they sell commercial paper directly to mutual funds and other institutional investors on a continuous day-by-day basis. Finance companies are now the largest issuers in the short-term commercial paper market. Most commercial paper issues have maturities of 30 days or less, although they can be issued with maturities of up to 270 days.[4]

---

[3] Finance companies do, of course, have market participants observing their work and monitoring their activities.

[4] Commercial paper issued with a maturity longer than 270 days must be registered with the SEC (i.e., it is treated the same as publicly placed bonds).

The outlook for the industry as a whole is currently quite bright. Loan demand among lower- and middle-income consumers is strong. Because many of these potential borrowers have little savings, no slowdown in demand for finance company services is expected. The largest finance companies, those that lend to less risky individual and business customers, as well as to subprime borrowers (e.g., Household International, Associates First Capital, and Beneficial) are experiencing strong profits and loan growth. The industry's assets as a whole grew at a rate of 15.7 percent in 1997.

Some problems for industry participants specializing in loans to relatively lower-quality customers have been well publicized. For example, in 1997 Mercury Finance was discovered to be accumulating a reported $90 million in imaginary profits. Upon discovery of the irregularities, banks that had been competing to provide Mercury with financing pulled out so quickly that Mercury was pushed to the brink of insolvency. Similarly, Jayhawk Acceptance Corporation, which finances car loans to some of the nation's riskiest buyers, filed for bankruptcy in 1997. Indeed, some analysts predicted a shakeout in the market for subprime mortgages. For example, Cityscape Financial Corp. of Elmsford, New York, stated in 1997 that it could soon run out of cash to meet its obligations. This sector's biggest firms (e.g., Money Store, Inc., Aames Financial Corp., and FirstPlus Financial Group) were even at risk. The problem stemmed from accounting practices that result in recording fees and profits on mortgages up front when, in fact, earnings actually come in gradually.

Concept Questions

1. How have the major assets held by finance companies changed in the last 20 years?
2. How do subprime lender finance company customers differ from consumer loan customers at banks?
3. What advantages do finance companies offer over commercial banks to small business customers?

REGULATION

The Federal Reserve defines *finance company* as a firm (other than a depository institution) whose primary assets are loans to individuals and businesses. Finance companies, like depository institutions, are financial intermediaries that borrow funds for relending and make a profit on the difference between the interest rate on borrowed funds and the rate charged on the loans. Also like depository institutions, finance companies are subject to ceilings on the maximum loan size and loan rate assigned to any individual customer. Because finance companies do not accept deposits, however, they are not subject to extensive oversight of any specific federal or state regulators—they are much less regulated than banks or thrifts. Some of the largest finance companies offer services that compete directly with depository institutions (i.e., consumer installment loans and mortgage financing); see Table 6–3. The lack of regulatory oversight for these companies enables them to offer a wide scope of services and avoid the expense of regulatory compliance (e.g., that imposed on banks and thrifts by the Community Reinvestment Act of 1977, which requires these institutions to keep and file extensive reports that they are not discriminating in their lending practices; see Chapter 1).

Since finance companies are heavy borrowers in the capital markets, they need to signal their solvency and safety to investors. Such signals are usually sent by holding much higher equity or capital-asset ratios—and therefore, lower leverage ratios—than banks do. For example, the aggregate balance sheet for the third quarter of 1997 (Table 6–1) shows a capital-asset ratio of 11.0 percent for finance companies. This is compared to the capital-asset ratio of 8.80 percent reported in Table 3–4 for commercial banks. Some finance companies use default protection guarantees from their parent companies and/or guarantees such as letters of credit or lines of credit purchased for a fee from high-quality commercial or investment banks.

Concept Questions

1. Since finance companies seem to compete in the same lending markets as banks, why aren't they subject to the same regulations as banks?
2. How do finance companies signal solvency and safety to investors?

S U M M A R Y

This chapter presented an overview of the finance company industry. This industry competes directly with depository institutions for high-quality (prime) loan customers by specializing in consumer, real estate, and business loans. The industry also services subprime borrowers deemed too risky for depository institutions. Because firms in this industry do not accept deposits, however, they are not regulated to the same extent as depository institutions. Because they do not have access to deposits for their funding, finance companies rely instead on short- and long-term debt, especially commercial paper. The industry is generally growing and profitable, but some sectors of the industry are experiencing financial problems.

P E R T I N E N T   W E B   S I T E S

Advanta   http://www.advanta.com/
American Express   http://www.americanexpress.com/
AT&T Capital   http://www.attcap.com/
Board of Governors of the Federal Reserve http://www. bog.frb.fed.us/

CIT Group   http://www.citgroup.com/
GE Capital Services   http://www.ge.com/gec/
GMAC   http://www.gmacfs.com/
Heller First Capital   http://www.hellercap.com/
The Money Store   http://www.themoneystore.com/

The Financial Services Industry: Finance Companies

1. What are the three types of finance companies and how do they differ from commercial banks?
2. Why do you think finance companies have been among the fastest growing FI groups in recent years?
3. What are the three types of lending services offered by finance companies?
4. Compare Tables 5–5 and 6–1. Which firms have higher capital ratios (as a percentage of total assets), securities firms or finance companies? What does this indicate about the relative strengths of these two types of firms?
5. How does the amount of equity as a percentage of assets compare for finance companies and commercial banks? What accounts for the difference?
6. How does a finance company make money?
7. What has been the fastest growing area of asset business for finance companies?
8. Why do finance companies charge higher rates on motor vehicle loans than commercial banks do?
9. What advantages do finance companies have over banks in offering services to small business customers?

10. Why are finance companies less regulated than commercial banks?

11. Why have finance companies begun to offer more mortgage and home equity loans?

12. What is a wholesale motor vehicle loan?

13. What signal does a low debt-to-asset ratio for a finance company send to the capital markets?

14. Go to the GMAC web site (http://www.gmacfs.com/) and use the calculator function to find out how much the monthly payment would be on a $25,000 car with a $2,000 trade-in, a $1,500 down payment, and a 12% annual financing rate payable monthly for 36 months.

Chapter Seven

The Financial Services Industry: Mutual Funds

Mutual funds are financial intermediaries that pool the financial resources of individuals and companies and invest those resources in diversified portfolios of assets. Open-end mutual funds (the majority of mutual funds) sell new shares to investors and redeem outstanding shares on demand at their fair market value. Thus, they provide opportunities for small investors to invest in financial securities and diversify risk. Mutual funds are also able to enjoy economies of scale by incurring lower transaction costs and commissions. The tremendous increase in the market value of financial assets, such as equities, in the 1990s[1] and the relatively low-cost opportunity that mutual funds provide to investors (particularly small investors) who want to hold such assets, have caused the mutual fund industry to boom. At the end of 1997, more than 5,300 different companies held total assets of $3.7 trillion in mutual funds. This chapter presents an overview of the services offered by mutual funds and highlights their rapid growth in the last decade.

Chapter Outline

---

[1] For example the S&P index reported a return of more than 31 percent in 1997.

Contemporary Perspectives 7–1

Mutual Funds Rake in a Record $29.39 Billion

For mutual-fund investors, the rallying cry is clearly: "Greenspan? Who's he?"

A record-smashing $29.39 billion poured into stock mutual funds in January, suggesting that investors don't much care what the Federal Reserve chairman, who has been warning about investors' "exuberance," thinks about their appetite for stocks. The tremendous fund investing in January far surpassed the $24 billion that the mutual-fund industry's trade group had predicted would hit the market in the first month of the new year and handily beat the record $28.9 billion monthly inflow set in January a year ago.

"It really is incredible," marvels Melissa Brown, director of quantitative research at Prudential Securities, "Where is the money coming from?"

Ms. Brown, like some other analysts, worries about how much longer the flood of money can continue. "I think it's great that people are putting money into the equity market and saving for retirement," she says, "My concern is that if you do get a downturn, we might get flows out as rapid as we're getting flows in. It's an issue of the bigger they come, the harder they fall." And Mr. Greenspan has twice warned now that the stock market may be rising too fast.

But there's no evidence the deluge will ease soon. Fund executives say February is turning out to be a massive month, too, though it likely won't match the rate of inflow during January. Large company funds, growth-and-income funds and in particular index funds are taking in lots of cash, as investors pursue soaring big company stocks. . . .

Not all the money is going into stock funds investing in the United States. Funds investing in foreign stocks, and "global" funds that invest in both the United States and abroad, took in $6 billion in January, about 20 percent of the total. Several fund groups say international funds are taking in even more money this month than last.

Nevertheless, the $29.4 billion that poured into U.S. stock funds in January was a record, according to the Investment Company Institute, a Washington trade group for the fund industry. The second biggest month for U.S. stock funds was last May, when such funds took in a bit more than $21 billion.

SOURCE: Robert McGough, The *Wall Street Journal*, February 28, 1997, p. C1. Reprinted by permission of The *Wall Street Journal*, © Dow Jones & Company, Inc. All Rights Reserved Worldwide.

SIZE, STRUCTURE, AND COMPOSITION OF THE INDUSTRY

Historical Trends

The first mutual fund was begun in Boston in 1924. The industry grew very slowly at first; by 1970, 360 funds held about $50 billion in assets. This growth is attributed to the advent of money market mutual funds in 1972 (as investors looked for ways to earn market rates on short-term funds when regulatory ceilings constrained bank deposit rates), to tax-exempt money market mutual funds in 1979, and to an explosion of special-purpose equity, bond, and derivative funds (as capital market values soared in the 1990s). The number of funds and the asset size of the industry have increased dramatically. Table 7–1 documents this tremendous increase in mutual funds for various years from 1940 through 1996. For example, total assets invested in mutual funds (other than money market mutual funds) increased from $0.4 billion in 1940 to $2,637.4 billion in 1996. The majority of this increase occurred during the bull market run in the 1990s; total assets in 1990 were $568.5 billion. The growth continues despite warnings that the stock market is overvalued (see Contemporary Perspectives Box 7–1). As Figure 7–1 illustrates, in terms of asset size, the

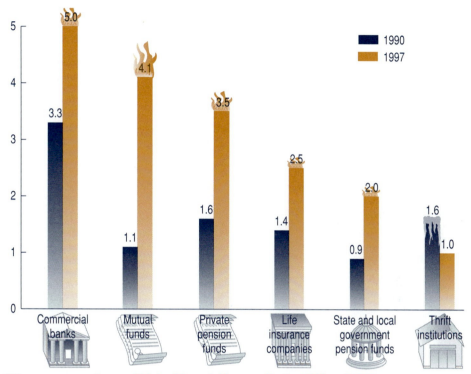

Figure **7-1**   *Assets of Major Financial Intermediaries, 1990 and 1997 (in trillions of dollars)*

NOTE: Data for 1990 are at year-end; data for 1997 are at the end of the third quarter. Commercial banks include U.S.–chartered commercial banks, foreign banking offices in the United States, bank holding companies, and banks in U.S.–affiliated areas.

SOURCE: Federal Reserve Board, *Statistical Releases, Flow of Fund Accounts,* March 1990 and December 1997.

Table **7-1**

GROWTH OF MUTUAL FUNDS FOR VARIOUS YEARS FROM 1940 TO 1996*

Year	Total Net Assets (in billions)	Gross Sales (in billions)	Redemptions (in billions)	Net Sales (in billions)	Shareholders (in thousands)	Number of Companies
1996	$2,637.4	$684.8	$398.7	$286.1	118,752	5,305
1995	2,070.5	477.2	313.6	168.7	101,597	4,764
1994	1,550.5	474.0	329.7	144.2	89,484	4,394
1993	1,510.0	511.6	231.4	280.2	70,049	3,638
1992	1,100.1	364.4	165.5	198.9	53,975	2,985
1991	853.1	236.6	116.3	120.3	45,030	2,606
1990	568.5	149.5	98.3	51.3	39,614	2,362
1980	58.4	10.0	8.2	1.8	7,325	458
1970	47.6	4.6	3.0	1.6	10,690	356
1960	17.0	2.1	0.8	1.3	4,898	161
1950	2.5	0.5	0.3	0.2	939	98
1940	0.4	N/A	N/A	N/A	296	68

*Data pertain to conventional fund members of the Investment Company Institute; money market funds not included. Institute "gross sales" figures include the proceeds of initial fund underwritings prior to 1970.

SOURCE: *Perspective,* Volume 3, No. 1, Investment Company Institute, Washington, D.C.

Table 7–2

TOP COMMERCIAL BANK INVOLVEMENT IN MUTUAL FUND BUSINESS

Rank	Company	Assets (in billions)	Rank among Mutual Fund Managers
1	Dreyfus Corp. (Mellon Bank)	$90.2	7
2	PNC Asset Management Group	36.6	23
3	Evergreen Keystone Investment Sec. (First Union)	33.7	27
4	NationsBanc Advisors	33.0	28
5	Chase Manhattan Bank	32.6	29
6	Wells Fargo	22.5	30
7	Bank One Investment	22.0	33
8	First Bank	19.2	36
9	Norwest Bank	17.7	41
10	Northern Trust	16.6	43

SOURCE: Lipper Analytical Services, Inc., press release, December 1997, Summit, N.J.

mutual fund (money market and long-term mutual funds) industry is larger than the life insurance industry but smaller than the commercial banking industry. This makes mutual funds the second most important FI group in the United States as measured by asset size.

Commercial banks have noticed tremendous growth in this area of FI services. Banks' share of all mutual fund assets managed was about 14 percent in 1997. See Table 7–2 for a list of the mutual fund assets managed by the top 10 banks and bank-owned companies participating in the industry. The rank of each, relative to the entire mutual fund industry, is also listed. Dreyfus (owned by Mellon bank) is the only bank in the top 10 list of all mutual fund managers, and most banks are still relatively small players (top 30s and 40s) in this industry.

Different Types of Mutual Funds

bond and income funds

Funds consisting of fixed-income capital market debt securities.

equity funds

Funds consisting of common and preferred stock securities.

money market mutual funds

Funds consisting of various mixtures of money market securities.

The mutual fund industry is usually considered to have two sectors: short-term funds and long-term funds. Long-term funds comprise **bond and income funds** (composed of fixed-income securities) and **equity funds** (composed of common and preferred stock securities). Short-term funds comprise taxable **money market mutual funds** (MMMFs) and tax-exempt money market mutual funds (containing various mixes of the money market securities discussed in Chapter 2). Tables 7–3 and 7–4 report the growth of bond and income as well as equity mutual funds relative to money market mutual funds. Table 7–3 presents the dollar values invested in various funds from 1991 through September 1997.

As of September 1997, 74.8 percent of all mutual fund assets were in long-term funds; the remaining funds, or 25.2 percent, were in money market mutual funds. According to data in Table 7–3, the percentage invested in long-term versus short-term funds can vary quite considerably over time. For example, the share of money market funds was 41.0 percent in 1991 compared to 25.2 percent in 1997. Money market mutual funds provide an alternative investment opportunity to interest-bearing deposits at commercial banks, which may explain the increase in MMMFs in the 1980s. That is, both investments are relatively safe and earn short-term returns. The major difference between the two is that interest-bearing deposits (below $100,000) are fully insured but, because of bank regulatory costs (such as reserve requirements, capital requirements, and deposit insurance premiums),

Table 7-3

GROWTH IN LONG-TERM VERSUS SHORT-TERM MUTUAL FUNDS FROM 1991 THROUGH SEPTEMBER 1997
(in billions of dollars)

	1991	1992	1993	1994	1995	1996	1997(Q3)
A. Bond and Income, and Equity Mutual Funds							
Holdings at market value	769.5	992.5	1,375.4	1,477.3	1,852.8	2,342.4	2,981.1
Household sector	586.6	727.9	990.9	1,047.4	1,247.8	1,582.9	1,990.9
Nonfinancial corporate business	14.8	21.1	29.8	31.1	45.7	58.6	80.0
State and local governments	9.4	14.9	21.3	29.1	35.0	37.0	38.9
Commercial banking	3.7	3.4	3.9	2.0	2.3	2.6	7.9
Credit unions	2.6	4.1	4.2	2.6	2.8	2.6	2.5
Bank personal trusts and estates	93.6	128.1	183.5	202.4	256.0	322.8	420.9
Life insurance companies	8.6	18.2	25.9	9.6	27.7	40.0	42.7
Private pension funds	50.2	74.9	16.0	55.1	237.9	295.9	397.3
B. Money Market Mutual Funds							
Total assets	535.0	539.5	559.6	602.9	745.3	891.1	1,005.1
Household sector	379.5	338.6	338.9	351.3	451.6	530.8	598.0
Nonfinancial corporate business	31.5	47.3	44.8	52.2	83.0	84.2	94.0
Nonfarm noncorporate business	3.6	3.6	3.9	4.0	4.1	4.3	4.6
Bank personal trusts and estates	29.6	29.2	29.3	29.9	32.0	41.4	49.1
Life insurance companies	19.6	25.0	31.5	16.2	22.8	40.7	54.0
Private pension funds	18.8	19.8	26.3	31.6	37.5	42.2	44.2
Funding corporations	52.4	75.9	86.0	117.8	120.2	147.5	161.2

SOURCE: *Federal Reserve Bulletin,* December, 1997, pp. 85 and 90.

Table 7-4

NUMBER OF MUTUAL FUNDS, 1980, 1990, AND 1996

Year	Equity	Bond and Income	Taxable Money Market	Tax-Exempt Money Market	Total
1980	288	170	96	10	564
1990	1,127	1,235	508	235	3,105
1996	2,626	2,679	665	323	6,293

SOURCE: *Perspective,* Volume 3, No. 1, Investment Company Institute, Washington, D.C.

offer lower returns than noninsured MMMFs. Thus, the net gain in switching to MMMFs is higher return in exchange for the loss of deposit insurance coverage. Many investors appear willing to give up insurance coverage to obtain additional returns.

The decline in the growth rate of short-term funds and increase in the growth rate of long-term funds in 1997 reflects the increase in equity returns during the period 1992–1997 and the generally low level of short-term interest rates over the period. However, this trend may be changing (see Contemporary Perspectives Box 7–2).

Contemporary Perspectives 7–2

A Low-Key Fund Group Nears a Limelight Level: Money Markets Approach $1 Trillion

Coming off one of its best years ever, the mutual fund industry is approaching yet another milestone, this one in a nook of the business that has attracted far less attention than stock funds and their persistent waves of cash.

Total assets in money market funds, now at $933 billion, are expected to top $1 trillion within a few weeks. The $1 trillion mark itself has little significance beyond its ability to satisfy humans' fascination with a figure that ends in a string of zeros. But the money market fund often thought of as the runt of the mutual fund litter is probably more responsible for the industry's success than either its stock or bond siblings.

"Money market funds were the launching pad for the whole mutual fund business," said Bruce R. Bent, president of the Reserve Fund, introduced in October 1971 and the first money market mutual fund. "They sensitized investors to the fact that they could do something with their money other than put it in a bank account."

Indeed, the growth of money market funds has been spectacular. While mutual funds that invest in stocks took at least 55 years—from the Investment Company Act of 1940 until 1995—to reach $1 trillion in assets, money market funds will do it in less than half that time.

Stock fund assets, which totaled $1.75 trillion at the end of 1996, still are much bigger than those in money market funds. But late last year, for the first time since 1991 the amount of assets in money funds surpassed the amount in bond funds. Just over one dollar of every four in mutual funds was in a money market fund at the end of the year.

Also last year, and again for the first time, American households had more of their financial assets in money market funds than in checking accounts. While savings accounts and bank time deposits still exceed household investments in money market funds by five to one, savings assets have been relatively flat for five years. Money funds, meanwhile, have grown.

They probably will continue to do so, and for several reasons, industry analysts say. Short-term interest rates have remained stubbornly high, "well above the psychologically important level of 5 percent," said Peter Crane, managing editor of IBC Money Fund Report, a newsletter.

The level is significant, Mr. Crane said, because "it makes investors feel like they're earning something substantial, and it leaves too small of a spread between the yields on bonds and money market funds to attract many people to bonds."

Many investors have not forgotten the pain inflicted on their bond fund investments in 1994, when the Federal Reserve Board began a series of interest rate increases that sent the value of bond funds tumbling down. And with Alan Greenspan, the Federal Reserve chairman, apparently intent on nipping in the bud any resurgence of inflation, it appears unlikely that short-term rates, and, therefore, money fund yields, will fall sharply anytime soon.

SOURCE: Edward Wyatt, The *New York Times,* February 2, 1997, p. F4. Copyright © 1997 by The New York Times Co. Reprinted by Permission.

Table 7–4 reports the growth in this industry based on the number of mutual funds in 1980, 1990, and 1996. All categories of funds have increased in number in the 1980s and 1990s; from a total of 564 in 1980 to 6,293 in 1996. Tax-exempt money market funds first became available in 1980. This is the major reason for their relatively small number (10 funds) in 1980. Also, the number of bond and income funds has surpassed equity funds: bond funds number 2,679 in 1996, up from 170 in 1980; equity funds number 2,626, up from 288.

Notice that in Table 7–3 households (i.e., small investors) own the majority of both long- and short-term funds, 66.8 percent for long-term mutual funds and 59.5 percent for short-term mutual funds. This is natural given that the rationale for the existence of mutual funds is to achieve superior diversification through fund and risk pooling than individual small investors could achieve on their own. Consider that wholesale CDs sell in minimum denominations of $100,000 each and often pay higher interest rates than passbook savings accounts or small time deposits offered by depository institutions. By pooling funds in a money market mutual fund, small investors can gain access to wholesale money markets and instruments and, therefore, to potentially higher returns.

Indeed, 37 million households (37 percent of all households) have been estimated to have owned mutual funds in 1996. Most are long-term owners with 64 percent making their first purchase after 1991. See Table 7–5 for the characteristics of household mutual fund owners. Compared with those who made their first purchase in 1990 or earlier, notice that individuals who made their first purchase of mutual fund shares after 1990 are younger (37 versus 46 years old), earn less ($50,000 versus $60,000), invest smaller amounts ($7,000 versus $25,000), and are fully aware of the risk involved with mutual fund investments (100 percent versus 96 percent). Most household owners are using mutual funds as vehicles for retirement savings (77 percent); 27 percent are using them to save for their children's education. Interestingly, the number of families with less than a college degree investing in mutual funds is increasing (40 percent for first purchasers before 1991, 45 percent for first purchasers in 1991 or later). The bull markets of the 1990s, the transaction cost reduction, and the diversification benefits achievable through mutual funds are again the likely reasons for these changes.

Mutual Fund Prospectus and Objectives

Regulations require that mutual fund managers specify the investment objectives of their funds in a prospectus sent to potential investors. The prospectus also includes a list of the securities that the fund holds. Despite this requirement, many large company funds, aiming to diversify across company size, held stocks of small companies in the late 1990s, contrary to the stated objective of investing in large companies. Fund managers justified the inclusion of seemingly small companies by fitting the smaller companies into their prospectus definition of "large" companies. For example, one fund manager stated that the definition of a small company is one that has less than $1 billion in equity capital versus a large company that has more than $1 billion (the median size of capital in Vanguard's Index 500 fund, which mimics the S&P 500 index, is $28 billion). Another fund manager explained small company inclusion in his prospectus's definition that up to 6 percent of the fund may be invested in small companies and up to 20 percent in mid-sized companies. The point here is that investors should read the prospectus carefully before making an investment.

The aggregate figures for long-term bond, income, and equity funds tend to obscure the fact that many different funds fall into these groups of funds. Table 7–6 classifies 18 major categories of investment objectives for mutual funds. These objectives and the assets allocated to each major category in 1997 are shown. The fund objective provides general information about the types of securities the mutual fund holds as assets. For example, aggressive growth funds hold securities (mainly equities) of the highest growth and highest-risk firms; growth funds also hold high growth and high-risk securities, but neither the growth nor the risk of these funds is as high as that of the aggressive growth funds.

See Table 7–7 for the largest (in total assets held) 20 mutual funds available at the end of 1997, including the fund objective, 12-month and five-year returns, and net asset value (discussed later). Fidelity's Magellan Fund was the largest fund at 1997 year-end (despite being closed to new investors; see the following). Fidelity and Vanguard offered 11 of the top 20 funds. Many of the top funds list either growth or growth and income as the fund objective, and all of the top 20 funds performed well in the bull market of the 1990s. Five-year returns ranged from a low of 95.9 percent for American Fund's European/Pacific to 151.8 percent for Fidelity's Growth and Income Fund. Thus, investors in these funds

Table 7-5

SELECTED CHARACTERISTICS OF HOUSEHOLD OWNERS OF MUTUAL FUNDS*

	First purchase in 1990 or earlier	First purchase in 1991 or later
Demographic characteristics		
Median age	46	37
Percent of households		
Married	73	63
Employed, full or part-time	79	88
Minor children[†]	41	48
Four-year college degree or more	60	55
Financial characteristics		
Median household income	$60,000	$50,000
Median household financial assets[‡]	$70,000	$25,000
Percent of households owning		
Individual stocks	57	48
Individual bonds	27	19
Annuities	29	18
IRA	75	60
401 (k)	51	50
Mutual fund ownership characteristics[§]		
Median mutual fund assets	$25,000	$7,000
Medium number of fund owned	3	2
Percent		
Household assets in mutual funds[#]	36	28
Fund types owned		
Equity	75	71
Bond and income	50	38
Money market	54	45
Investment goal[**]		
Retirement	81	77
Education	24	27
Risk tolerance to profile[††]		
Willing to take		
Substantial risk with expectation of substantial gain	8	10
Above-average risk with expectation of above-average gain	36	38
Average-risk with expectation of average gain	41	36
Below-average risk with expectation of below-average gain	10	13
No risk	6	3
Awareness: Agreed that investing in stock and bond funds involves risk	96	100
Evaluations: Assessed risk of most recent stock or bond fund purchase	67	71
Horizon: Assess mutual fund risk in time frame exceeding five years	65	62

* Characteristics of primary financial decision maker in the household.

[†] Percent of married households.

[‡] Excludes assets in employer-sponsored retirement plans.

[§] Excludes mutual funds in employer-sponsored retirement plans.

[#] Excludes any mutual fund assets held in employer-sponsored retirement plans.

[**] Multiple responses included.

[††] Responses of households with an investment goal.

SOURCE: *Perspective*, Volume 3, No. 1, Investment Company Institute, Washington, D.C.

Table **7-6**

TOTAL NET ASSET VALUE OF EQUITY AND BOND AND INCOME FUNDS BY INVESTMENT OBJECTIVE, DECEMBER 31, 1997

Objective of Fund	Combined Assets (in millions of dollars)	Percent of Total
Total net assets	**$2,637,398.0**	**100.0**
Aggressive growth	274,802.1	10.4
Growth	482,082.2	18.3
Growth & income	589,104.2	22.3
Precious metals	4,949.1	0.2
International	177,414.4	6.7
Global equity	106,554.1	4.0
Income—equity	116,022.8	4.4
Flexible portfolio	63,360.2	2.4
Balanced	99,202.0	3.8
Income—mixed	88,324.6	3.4
Income—bond	100,889.4	3.8
U.S. government income	79,507.9	3.0
Ginnie Mae	51,331.6	2.0
Global bond	37,458.4	1.4
Corporate bond	35,573.7	1.4
High-yield bond	78,260.3	3.0
National municipal bond—long-term	135,631.4	5.1
State municipal bond—long-term	116,929.6	4.4

SOURCE: *Perspective*, Volume 3, No. 1, Investment Company Institute, Washington, D.C.

consistently doubled their money and more. It should be noted, however, that prospectuses rarely mention the risk of returns (e.g., the fund's total return risk or even its "beta," or systematic risk). Currently, the SEC is proposing an initiative to require mutual funds to disclose more information about their return risk as well as the returns themselves. The results of the SEC's proposal would enable investors to be better able to compare return-risk trade-offs from investing in different mutual funds. Morningstar Mutual Funds is an excellent source of information on mutual funds, performance, prices, and so on.

Size and Mutual Fund Performance: The Case of the Magellan Fund

Fidelity's Magellan Fund has been a unique fund in the industry. Trading in the Magellan Fund began in the 1970s. Under the management of Peter Lynch from 1977 through May 1990 and Jeffrey Vinik into the mid-1990s, Magellan became the country's largest mutual fund. In the 13 years that Peter Lynch managed the fund, Magellan reported average returns of 29.2 percent per year (almost double the 15.9 percent average return on the S&P 500 Index). From July 1992 to August 1995, when Vinik managed the fund, Magellan returned a total of 78.85 percent (the average growth fund earned 52.86 percent over this period). Obviously, these tremendous returns resulted in a large increase in investor interest. The fund grew from $20 million when Lynch took control to more than $56 billion when Vinik left. In 1996 the Magellan Fund alone was larger in asset size than the whole industry had

Table 7-7

THE LARGEST MUTUAL FUNDS IN ASSETS HELD

Name of Fund	Objective	Total Assets (in millions)	Total Return 12 month	5 year	NAV
Fidelity Magellan	Growth	$63,035	20.4%	128.3%	91.53
Vanguard Index: 500	Growth/Income	48,264	26.0	139.0	86.86
American Funds: InvCoA	Growth/Income	39,235	24.4	119.5	27.47
American Funds: WshMut	Growth/Income	37,179	27.6	148.9	29.55
Fidelity Invest: Grw/Inc	Growth/Income	35,485	24.5	151.8	36.84
Fidelity Invest: Contra	Growth	30,263	17.7	138.1	44.89
Vanguard: WndsII	Growth/Income	23,545	25.6	146.7	27.62
Fidelity Invest: Puritan	Balanced	22,377	18.6	108.0	18.98
American Century: Ultra	Growth	22,204	15.2	122.0	26.20
Vanguard: Welltn	Balanced	21,340	19.6	111.0	28.92
Vanguard:Wndsr	Growth/Income	20,833	17.3	135.5	16.45
Fidelity Invest: Eq/Inc	Equity/Income	20,545	24.8	145.3	50.68
Fidelity Advisor: Grw Opp	Growth	20,408	22.7	146.4	41.08
American Funds: Income	Equity/Income	19,708	20.0	99.7	17.50
Janus: Fund	Capital appreciation	19,179	16.5	98.4	28.61
American Funds: Eupac	International	18,733	8.7	95.9	25.47
Putnam Funds A: Grw/Inc	Growth/Income	17,044	19.0	129.4	18.95
Fidelity Invest: Equity II	Equity/Income	16,651	21.9	127.0	26.11
American Funds: NewPer	Growth/Income	16,096	12.7	106.0	18.87
Dean Witter: Div/Grw	Growth/Income	15,400	20.3	115.6	52.68

SOURCE: Associated Press, December 28, 1997.

been in 1978; it was also twice as large as the second largest fund and larger than the third, fourth, and fifth largest funds combined. But with size comes problems. The fund became too large to exploit profitably many investment opportunities; any major changes in the portfolio had to be so large that they alone affected equity and asset prices. In late 1995, expecting a slowdown in technology earnings, Vinik switched from equity in technology companies to long-term bonds, but his expectations did not materialize. From September 1995 through April 1996, the fund earned only 2.78 percent while the average growth fund earned 15.02 percent. Vinik resigned in May 1996, and Bob Stansky assumed fund management. Taking an approach more similar to Lynch's and following strategies that mimicked indexes such as the S&P 500, Stanksy brought Magellan back to 20 percent returns, but they were still not comparable to other growth funds (the 23 percent return in 1997 ranked 272 of 661 funds tracked by Bloomberg Fund Performance). Despite this, Magellan's assets continued to grow to more than $63 billion, and, citing the inability to produce big profits with such a large fund, Magellan closed its doors to new investors in September 1997.

Investor Returns from Mutual Fund Ownership

The return for the investor from investing in mutual fund shares reflects three aspects of the underlying portfolio of mutual fund assets: first, the portfolio earns income and dividends on those assets; second, it experiences capital gains when the mutual fund sells the assets at prices higher than the purchase price; and third, capital appreciation in the underlying values of its assets adds to the value of mutual fund shares. With respect to capital appreciation, mutual fund assets are normally **marked-to-market** daily. This means that the managers of the fund calculate the current value of each mutual fund share by computing the daily market value of the fund's total asset portfolio and then divide this amount by the number of mutual fund shares outstanding. The resulting value is called the net asset value (**NAV**) of the fund. This is the price that investors obtain when they sell shares back to the fund that day or pay to buy any new shares in the fund on that day.

marked-to-market

Asset and balance sheet values adjusted to reflect current market prices.

E X A M P L E   7 – 1

* * * * * *

Calculation of NAV on an Open-End Mutual Fund

Today, a mutual fund contains 1,000 shares of Sears, Roebuck currently trading at $56.00, 2,000 shares of Mobil Oil currently trading at $70.25, and 1,500 shares of Household International currently trading at $120.50. The fund has 15,000 shares outstanding held by investors. Thus, today, the fund's NAV is calculated as

$$NAV = (1,000 \times \$56.00 + 2,000 \times \$70.25 + 1,500 \times \$120.50) \div 15,000 = \$25.15$$

NAV

The net asset value of a mutual fund which is equal to the market value of the assets in the mutual fund portfolio divided by the number of shares outstanding.

If next month Sears' shares increase to $62, Mobil shares increase to $78, and Household International's shares increase to $150, the NAV (assuming the same number of investors) would increase to

$$NAV = (1,000 \times \$62 + 2,000 \times \$78 + 1,500 \times \$150) \div 15,000 = \$29.53 \quad \bullet \quad \bullet \quad \bullet$$

open-end mutual fund

A fund for which the supply of shares is not fixed but can increase or decrease daily with purchases and redemptions of shares.

Most mutual funds are **open-end** in that the number of shares outstanding fluctuates daily with the amount of share redemptions and new purchases. With open-end funds, investors buy and sell shares from and to the mutual fund company. Thus, the demand for shares determines the number outstanding, and the market value of the underlying securities held in the mutual fund divided by the number of shareholders outstanding solely determines the NAV of shares.

E X A M P L E   7 – 2

* * * * * *

Calculation of NAV of an Open-End Mutual Fund When the Number of Investors Increases

Consider the facts in Example 7–1, but suppose that today 1,000 additional investors bought into the mutual fund at the current NAV of $25.15. This means that the fund manager has $25,150 additional funds to invest. Suppose that the fund manager decides to use these additional funds to buy additional shares in Sears. At today's market price, the manager can buy 449 additional shares ($25,150/$56) of Sears. Thus, its new portfolio of shares has 1,449 in Sears, 2,000 in Mobil, and 1,500 in Household International. At the end of the month, the NAV of the portfolio is

$$NAV = (1,499 \times \$62 + 2,000 \times \$78 + 1,500 \times \$150) \div 16,000 = \$29.62$$

Note that the fund's value increased over the month because of both capital appreciation and larger investment size and that the number of investors also increased from 15,000 to 16,000. Overall, however, the effect of the new investors on the fund's NAV was positive; it increased from $25.15 to $29.62 over a one-month period. A comparison of the NAV in Example 7–1 with the one in this example indicates that the additional investors enabled the fund to gain a higher NAV at the end of the month than had the number of investors remained static (i.e., $29.62 versus $29.53).   •   •   •

closed-end investment companies

Specialized investment companies that have a fixed supply of outstanding shares but invest in the securities and assets of other firms.

REIT

A real estate investment trust; a closed-end investment company that specializes in investing in mortgages, property, or real estate company shares.

load fund

A mutual fund with an up-front sales or commission charge that the investor must pay.

no-load fund

A mutual fund that does not charge up-front sales or commission charges on the sale of mutual fund shares to investors.

12b-1 fees

Fees relating to the distribution costs of mutual fund shares.

Open-end mutual funds can be compared with most regular corporations traded on stock exchanges and to **closed-end investment companies**, which have a fixed number of shares outstanding at any given time. For example, real estate investment trusts (**REITs**) are closed-end investment companies that specialize in investment in real estate company shares and/or in buying mortgages.[2] With closed-end funds investors must buy and sell the investment company's shares on a stock exchange as they do corporate stock. Since the number of shares available for purchase, at any moment in time, is fixed, the NAV of the fund's shares is determined not only by the value of the underlying shares but also by the demand for the investment company's shares themselves. When demand is high, the shares can trade for more than the NAV of the securities held in the fund. In this case, the fund is said to be *trading at a premium* (i.e., more than the fair market value of the securities held). When the value of the closed-end fund's shares are less than the NAV of its assets, its shares are said to be *trading at a discount* (i.e., less than the fair market value of the securities held).

Load versus No-Load Funds

An investor who buys a mutual fund share may be subject to a sales charge, sometimes as high as 8.5 percent. In this case, the fund is called a **load fund**. Funds that market shares directly to investors and do not use sales agents working for commissions and have no up-front commission charges are **no-load funds**. In general, no-load funds retain a small percentage (or fee) of investable funds to meet distribution costs and other operating costs. Such annual fees are known as **12b-1 fees** after the SEC rule covering such charges.[3]

The argument in favor of load funds is that they are more closely managed and therefore better managed. The cost of this increased attention may not be worthwhile, however; for example, see Table 7–8 for a list of the top 10 performing U.S. stock funds over the five years from September 1992 through September 1997 before and after adjusting returns for any up-front "load" fees. Notice that the ranking of every fund is reduced by at least one position and as many as seven positions when the return is adjusted for these sale charges. As Figure 7–2 indicates, investors are increasingly recognizing that this cost disadvantage outweighs the benefits of more management attention. In 1985, load funds represented almost 70 percent of mutual fund sales, and no-load funds represented just over 30 percent. By 1997, however, no-load fund sales led load fund sales by 57 to 43 percent.

Mutual fund quotes for Vanguard Index Funds from the *Wall Street Journal* on Friday, February 27, 1998 are presented in Table 7–9. The quote includes information on each fund's NAV; the change in its NAV from the previous day; the fund name and its objective; its year-to-date return; its four-week return; its one- through five-year return and rating (A through D); and its maximum initial (sales) charge. The maximum initial charge is listed as 0.00 for each of the Vanguard Index Funds, meaning that they are all no-load funds.

---

[2] Many closed-end funds are specialized funds investing in shares in countries such as Argentina, Brazil, or Mexico. The shares of these closed-end funds are traded on the NYSE or in the over-the-counter market. The total market value of funds invested in closed-end funds was $137.1 billion at the end of the third quarter of 1996. This compares to $3,059.8 billion invested in open-end funds at that time.

[3] 12b-1 fees are limited to a maximum of 0.25 percent.

Table **7–8**

IMPACT OF LOAD CHARGES ON MUTUAL FUND RETURNS

Fund	Total Return	Load	Adjusted Return	Adjusted Rank
AIM Aggressive Growth	31.6%	5.50%	30.1%	2
PBHG Growth	30.7	None	30.7	1
Franklin California Growth I	30.0	4.50	28.8	4
Spectra	29.9	None	29.9	3
FPA Capital	29.3	6.50	27.5	10
Franklin Small Cap Growth I	29.2	4.50	28.0	7
Robertson Stephens Value&Growth A	28.6	None	28.6	5
RSI Retirement Emerging Growth	28.3	None	28.3	6
Vanguard Primecap	27.9	None	27.9	8
Putnam New Opportunities A	27.9	5.75	26.4	17

SOURCE: *Perspective*, Volume 3, No. 1, Investment Company Institute, Washington, D.C.

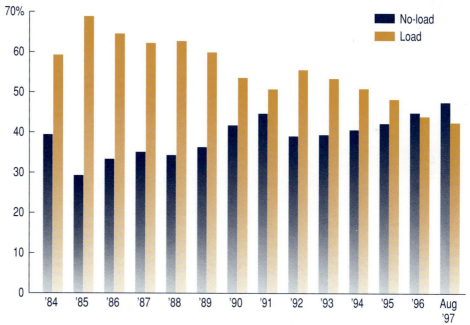

Figure **7–2**   *Load versus No-Load Sales*

SOURCE: *Perspective,* Volume 3, No. 1, Investment Company Institute, Washington, D.C.

Concept Questions

1. Where do mutual funds rank in terms of asset size of all FI industries?
2. What is the difference between short-term and long-term mutual funds?
3. What have been the trends as to the number of mutual funds since 1980?

Table **7-9**

MUTUAL FUND QUOTE

NAV	Net Chg	Fund Name	Inv Obj	YTD %ret	4Wk %ret	Total Return			Max Init Chrg
						1Yr	3Yr-R	5Yr-R	
		Vanguard Index Fds:							
97.56	+0.55	500	GI	+8.3	+7.5	+32.3 A	+31.6 A	+21.5 A	0.00
17.11	+0.05	Balanced	BL	+5.0	+4.7	+22.9 A	+21.4 B	+14.8 B	0.00
10.14	+0.10	EmerMkt r	EM	+1.5	+11.9	−22.9 E	+3.1 C	NS ..	0.00
22.54	+0.12	Europe	EU	+12.0	+7.8	+36.2 A	+26.5 A	+21.9 A	0.00
32.61	+0.25	Exten	MC	+6.0	+8.1	+30.2 B	+26.3 B	+18.8 B	0.00
32.61	+0.24	ExtenIst	...	NA	NA	NA ..	NA ..	NA ..	0.00
24.93	+0.10	Growth	GR	+10.7	+7.4	+35.8 A	+34.2 A	+22.4 A	0.00
97.03	+0.55	InstIdx	GI	+8.3	+7.5	+32.5 A	+31.8 A	+21.7 A	0.00
97.03	+0.54	InstPlus	GI	+8.3	+7.5	NS ..	NS ..	NS ..	0.00
10.22	−0.01	ITBond	IG	+1.2	+0.4	+10.3 A	+9.7 A	NS ..	0.00
10.76	−0.03	LTBond	LG	+0.8	+0.7	+15.8 A	NA ..	NS ..	0.00
8.20	+0.11	Pacific	PR	+6.2	−1.2	−16.1 B	−6.4 C	+1.9 B	0.00
25.11	+0.17	SmCap	SC	+5.7	+7.8	+30.6 B	+25.0 C	+18.4 C	0.00
25.12	+0.17	SmCapIst	SC	+5.8	+7.8	NS ..	NS ..	NS ..	0.00
10.02	−0.01	STBond	SG	+1.1	+0.2	+7.5 A	+7.4 A	NS ..	0.00
10.10	−0.01	TotBd	IG	+1.1	+0.5	+10.1 A	+9.3 A	+6.9 A	0.00
10.10	−0.01	TotBdIst	IG	+1.1	+0.5	+10.3 A	NS ..	NS ..	0.00
10.76	+0.08	TotIntl	IL	+9.0	+5.6	+8.1 D	NS ..	NS ..	0.00
24.40	+0.14	TotSt	GR	+7.8	+7.7	+31.7 B	+29.6 B	+20.3 B	0.00
24.40	+0.14	TotStIst	GR	+7.8	+7.7	NS ..	NS ..	NS ..	0.00
22.08	+0.16	Value	GI	+5.9	+7.6	+28.4 C	+28.9 C	+20.5 B	0.00

*GI = growth & income fund; BL = balanced fund; EM = emerging market fund; EU = European region fund; MC = middle–sized company fund; GR = growth fund; IG = intermediate maturity Treasury and government agency bond fund; LG = long-term Treasury and government agency bond fund; PR = Pacific region fund; and SC = small company fund.

SOURCE: The *Wall Street Journal,* February 27, 1998, p. C25. Reprinted by permission of The Wall Street Journal, © 1998 Dow Jones & Company, Inc. All Rights Reserved Worldwide.

4.   What are the two largest mutual fund companies? How have their funds performed in recent years?
5.   What is the difference between open-end and closed-end mutual funds?

BALANCE SHEET AND

RECENT TRENDS

Money Market Funds

Consider the distribution of assets of money market mutual funds from 1991 through September 1997 in Table 7–10. In the third quarter of 1997, $674.4 billion (75.7 percent of total assets) was invested in short-term financial securities—such as foreign deposits, domestic checkable deposits and currency, time and savings deposits, repurchase agreements (RPs or repos), open-market paper (mostly commercial paper), and U.S. government securities. Short-maturity asset holdings are an objective of these funds to retain their depositlike nature. In fact, most money market mutual fund shares have their values fixed at $1. Asset value fluctuations due to interest rate changes and any small default risk and capital gains or losses on assets are adjusted for by increasing or reducing the number of $1 shares owned by the investor.

Table 7-10

DISTRIBUTION OF ASSETS IN MONEY MARKET MUTUAL FUNDS FROM 1991 THROUGH SEPTEMBER 30, 1997

(in billions of dollars)

	1991	1992	1993	1994	1995	1996	1997
Total financial assets	**$535.0**	**$539.5**	**$559.6**	**$602.9**	**$745.3**	**$891.1**	**$1,005.1**
Foreign deposits	21.4	20.3	10.0	15.7	19.7	23.1	23.0
Checkable deposits and currency	−0.2	−2.7	−1.2	−2.5	−3.5	−1.1	−2.2
Time and savings deposits	35.1	34.6	31.9	31.4	52.3	82.7	115.0
Security RPs	67.0	65.9	66.4	68.8	87.8	103.8	124.7
Credit market instruments	403.9	408.6	429.0	459.0	545.5	634.3	678.7
Open–market paper	190.6	173.6	164.4	187.2	235.5	273.9	323.6
U.S. government securities	118.9	132.7	147.2	143.3	160.8	192.0	163.5
Treasury	78.3	78.4	79.4	66.1	70.0	90.2	75.0
Agency	40.6	54.3	67.8	77.2	90.8	101.8	88.5
Municipal securities	90.6	96.0	105.6	113.4	127.7	144.5	158.9
Corporate and foreign bonds	3.8	6.3	11.7	15.2	21.5	23.9	32.7
Miscellaneous assets	7.7	12.7	23.7	30.6	43.4	48.3	65.9

SOURCE: *Federal Reserve Bulletin*, December 11, 1997, p. 77.

Table 7-11

DISTRIBUTION OF ASSETS IN LONG-TERM BOND, INCOME, AND EQUITY MUTUAL FUNDS FROM 1991 THROUGH SEPTEMBER 30, 1997

(in billions of dollars)

	1991	1992	1993	1994	1995	1996	1997
Total financial assets	**$769.5**	**$992.5**	**$1,375.4**	**$1,477.3**	**$1,852.8**	**$2,342.4**	**$2,981.1**
Security RPs	12.2	21.9	38.7	43.1	50.2	47.5	60.2
Credit market instruments	440.2	566.4	725.9	718.8	771.3	820.2	891.7
Open-market paper	12.2	21.9	38.7	43.1	50.2	47.2	60.2
U.S. government securities	200.6	257.4	306.6	296.2	315.1	330.2	350.5
Treasury	133.5	169.5	200.9	194.1	205.3	214.1	226.1
Agency	67.1	87.9	105.7	102.1	109.9	116.1	124.4
Municipal securities	139.7	168.4	211.3	207.0	210.2	213.3	219.2
Corporate and foreign bonds	87.7	118.7	169.3	172.4	195.7	229.5	261.8
Corporate equities	308.9	401.3	607.4	709.6	1,024.9	1,470.0	2,021.7
Miscellaneous assets	8.2	3.0	3.3	5.9	6.3	4.7	7.5
Total shares outstanding	**769.5**	**992.5**	**1,375.4**	**1,477.3**	**1,852.8**	**2,342.4**	**2,981.1**

SOURCE: *Federal Reserve Bulletin*, December 11, 1997, p. 77.

Long-Term Funds

Note the asset distribution of long-term mutual funds in Table 7–11. As might be expected, it reflects the popularity of different types of bond and equity funds at various times. Underscoring the attractiveness of equity funds as of September 30, 1997, was the fact that corporate equities represented more than 67.8 percent of total long-term mutual fund asset portfolios. U.S. government securities and municipal securities were the next most popular assets (19.1 percent of the asset portfolio). In contrast, consider the distribution of assets in 1991 when the equity markets were not doing well. Corporate equities made up only 40.1 percent of the long-term mutual fund portfolios. U.S. government securities and municipals were the largest asset group at 44.2 percent of total assets.

Concept Questions

1. What have been the major assets held by mutual funds in the 1990s?
2. How does the asset distribution for money market mutual funds and long-term mutual funds differ?

REGULATION

Because mutual funds accept funds from small investors, this industry is one of the most closely regulated of the nondepository financial institution groups. Regulations have been enacted to protect investors against possible abuses by managers of mutual funds. The SEC is the primary regulator of mutual funds. Specifically, the Securities Act of 1933 requires a mutual fund to file a registration statement with the SEC and to set rules and procedures regarding the fund's prospectus sent to investors. In addition, the Securities Exchange Act of 1934 makes the purchase and sale of mutual fund shares subject to various antifraud provisions. This regulation requires the mutual fund to furnish full and accurate information on all financial and corporate matters to prospective fund purchasers. The 1934 act also appointed the National Association of Securities Dealers (NASD) to supervise mutual fund share distributions.

In 1940, Congress passed the Investment Advisers Act and Investment Company Act. The Investment Advisers Act regulates the activities of mutual fund advisers. The Investment Company Act established rules to prevent conflicts of interest, fraud, and excessive fees or charges for fund shares.

In recent years, the Insider Trading and Securities Fraud Enforcement Act passed in 1988 has required mutual funds to develop mechanisms and procedures to avoid insider trading abuses. In addition, the Market Reform Act of 1990 passed in the wake of the 1987 stock market crash affects the ability of mutual funds to conduct their business. This act allows the SEC to introduce circuit breakers to halt trading on exchanges and to restrict program trading when it deems necessary. Finally, the National Securities Markets Improvement Act (NSMIA) of 1996 (discussed in Chapter 5) also applies to mutual fund companies. Specifically, the NSMIA exempts mutual fund sellers from oversight by state securities regulators, thus reducing their regulatory burden.

Concept Questions

1. What is the primary regulator of mutual fund companies?
2. How did the NSMIA affect mutual funds?

SUMMARY

This chapter presented an overview of the mutual fund industry. Mutual funds pool funds from individuals and corporations and invest in diversified asset portfolios. Due to the tremendous increase in the value of financial assets—such as equities—in the 1990s and the cost-effective opportunity that mutual funds offer for small investors to participate in these markets, mutual funds have increased tremendously in size, number of funds, and number of shareholders. The chapter also discussed the two major categories of mutual funds—short-term and long-term open-end funds—highlighting the differences in their growth rates and the composition of their assets. The chapter also illustrated the calculation of the net asset values (NAV) of mutual fund shares.

PERTINENT WEB SITES

Bloomberg Fund Performance   http://www.bloomberg.com/ welcome.html

Fidelity Investments   http://www32.fidelity.com/

Morningstar, Inc.   http://www.morningstar.net/

National Association of Securities Dealers   http://www.nasd. com/

Securities and Exchange Commission   http://www.sec.gov/

Vanguard Group   http://www.vanguard.com/

The Financial Services Industry: Mutual Funds

1. What is a *mutual fund*? In what sense is it a financial intermediary?
2. What is the NAV of a mutual fund? What three sources of gains and losses affect the NAV?
3. What benefits do mutual funds have for individual investors?
4. What are the economic reasons for the existence of mutual funds?
5. What is the difference between open-end and closed-end mutual funds? Which of them tend to be more specialized?
6. How do the composition and size of short-term funds differ from those of long-term funds?
7. What appears to be the reason for the change in the composition of mutual funds over time?
8. How does the risk of short-term funds differ from that of long-term funds?
9. Why are most mutual funds held by individuals rather than corporations?
10. What are the three components of the return that an investor receives from a mutual fund?
11. Open-end Fund A has 100 shares of ATT valued at $100 each and 50 shares of Toro valued at $50 each. Closed-end Fund B has 75 shares of ATT and 100 shares of Toro.
    a. What are the NAVs of both funds using these prices?
    b. Assume that another 100 shares of ATT are added to Fund A. What is the effect on A's NAV if the prices remain unchanged?
    c. If the price of ATT stock increases to $105 and the price of Toro stock declines to $45, how does that impact the NAV of both funds? Assume that Fund A has only 100 shares of ATT.
12. A mutual fund has 200 shares of Fiat, Inc., currently trading at $14, and 200 shares of Microsoft, Inc., currently trading at $140. The fund has 100 shares outstanding.
    a. What is the NAV of the fund?
    b. If investors expect the price of Fiat shares to increase to $18 and the price of Microsoft to decline to $110 by the end of the year, what is the expected NAV at the end of the year?
    c. What is the maximum that the price of Microsoft can decline to maintain the NAV as estimated in (a)?
13. How does the regulation of mutual funds differ from that of other financial institutions?
14. Why do mutual funds require regulations?
15. How might an individual's preference for a mutual fund's objective change over time?
16. An investor purchases a mutual fund for $100. The fund pays dividends of $3, distributes a capital gain of $4, and charges a fee of $2 when the fund is sold one year later for $105. What is the net rate of return from this investment?

17. Suppose that you have a choice between two mutual funds, one a load fund with no annual 12b-1 fees and the other a no-load fund with a maximum 12b-1 fee. How would the length of your expected holding period influence your choice between these two funds?

18. How has the growth in mutual funds affected the growth in other types of financial intermediaries?

19. What is a REIT? What type of interest rate risks would it face?

20. Go the Fidelity Investments web site and look up the annual 1, 5, and 10 year returns for the Fidelity Select Biotechnology Fund.

Chapter Eight

Evaluating the Performance of Financial Intermediaries

U nlike other private corporations, financial intermediaries (FI's) are unique in the level of regulatory attention they receive. Like any corporation, however, the ultimate measure of an FI's performance is the value of its common equity to its shareholders. This chapter discusses the financial statements of these institutions. Managers, stockholders, regulators, and other parties use financial statements to evaluate the performance of FIs. For example, Chase Manhattan made a balance sheet choice to hold emerging market bonds on its balance sheet, resulting in huge losses in 1997 (see Contemporary Perspectives Box 8–1). Given the extensive level of regulation and the accompanying requirements of public availability of financial information, the financial statements of commercial banks are ideal to use in examining the performance of these institutions.

Contemporary Perspectives 8–1

Chase Manhattan Pounded In Emerging Markets

Chase Manhattan Corp. sustained substantial losses in emerging-market securities from the tumult that roiled global markets over the past 10 days. Some people at the bank estimate that in the past week or so, Chase suffered pretax losses of $150 million to $200 million trading emerging-market debt. . . . These people say the bank was caught holding developing-country bonds on its books that it couldn't sell and trying to unwind complex, structured derivative securities.

"It's been a very difficult week for everybody," noted a Chase trader, who said that the bank had been hoping to limit its emerging-debt trading losses to $200 million, but added that Chase "had a big (bond) holding in Brazil" and was also significantly exposed to the Russian bond market. If those two and other emerging debt markets fall steeply again, Chase could have a hard time containing losses at that level. These markets have been caught up in the contagion sweeping global financial markets from the currency and stock market turmoil engulfing Southeast Asia. . . .

One Chase officer said, "From having a terrific year up to a week and a half ago, everybody is running scared, because it's bonus time. Everybody thought they were going to get enormous bonuses; now everybody is concerned about what they are going to get early next year," when bonuses reflecting 1997 performance are distributed.

SOURCE: Michael R. Sesit and Matt Murray, The *Wall Street Journal*, November 3, 1997, p. A4. Reprinted by permission of The *Wall Street Journal*, © 1997 Dow Jones & Company, Inc. All Rights Reserved Worldwide.

The chapter uses commercial banks to illustrate a return on equity (ROE) framework as a method of evaluating financial institutions' profitability. The ROE framework decomposes this frequently used measure of profitability into its various component parts to identify existing or potential financial management and risk exposure problems. The fact that bank size and/or niche (i.e., the financial market segment the bank specializes in servicing) may affect the evaluation of financial statements is highlighted.

The banking industry has experienced a series of mergers and acquisitions throughout the 1990s. The cause of many of these mergers and acquisitions has been the desire to achieve greater cost savings and revenue generation and to improve the bank's overall financial position and solvency. An acquiring bank may be concerned about the solvency and asset quality of a potential target bank and how an acquisition will affect its own balance sheet strength. It can analyze the financial statements of a target bank to identify its strengths and weaknesses. Indeed, acquiring banks use many of the ratios discussed in this chapter to identify appropriate target banks.

FINANCIAL STATEMENTS
OF COMMERCIAL BANKS

report of condition

Balance sheet of a
commercial bank
reporting information at a
single point in time.

report of income

Income statement of a
commercial bank
reporting revenues,
expenses, net profit or
loss, and cash dividends
over a period of time.

retail bank

A bank that focuses its
business activities on
consumer banking
relationships.

wholesale bank

A bank that focuses its
business activities on
commercial banking
relationships.

Financial information on commercial banks is reported in two basic documents. The **report of condition** (call report or balance sheet) presents financial information on a bank's assets, liabilities, and equity capital. The balance sheet reports a bank's condition at a single point in time. The **report of income** (or income statement) presents the major categories of revenues and expenses (or costs) and the net profit or loss for a bank over a period of time. Financial statements of commercial banks must be submitted to regulators and stockholders at the end of each calendar quarter: March, June, September, and December. The Federal Financial Institutions Examination Council (FFIEC) prescribes uniform principles, standards, and report forms of depository institutions.

Financial institutions are also engaging in an increased level of off-balance-sheet (OBS) activities. These activities produce income (and sometimes losses) for the FI that are reported on the income statement. This chapter summarizes off-balance-sheet activities (and the risks involved with such activities) which are discussed in more detail in Chapters 9 and 20.

To evaluate the performance of commercial banks, we use three bank holding companies of varying size and market niches: North Fork Bancorporation, Firstier Financial Inc., and Boatmen's Bancshares.

North Fork Bancorp (NFB) is a publicly traded commercial bank holding company headquartered in Melville, New York; it has $3.3 billion in assets. It is Long Island's largest independent commercial bank, operating 49 branch locations throughout Long Island, Queens, Westchester, and Rockland counties of New York. Emphasizing retail banking, NFB in recent years has been one of the most efficient and profitable banks in the country. **Retail banks** focus on individual consumer banking relationships; residential mortgages and consumer loans dominate their loan portfolios, and individual demand, NOW, savings, and time deposits dominate their liabilities. In contrast, **wholesale banks** focus their business activities on business banking relationships; they hold more business loans and fewer mortgages and consumer loans and use fewer consumer deposits and more purchased funds than retail banks do. In addition to providing a range of personal and commercial banking products, NFB also offers an array of financial services including trust, asset management, and brokerage services. NFB invests heavily in real estate loans and attempts to fund assets as much as possible with demand deposits. At the end of 1995, multifamily mortgage loans constituted more than half of the bank's loan portfolio.

In contrast to the strictly retail-oriented lines of business of North Fork Bancorp, Firstier Financial (FF) was known as a middle-market bank with a more balanced (both retail and wholesale) loan portfolio and a strong reputation. FF was a Nebraska-based multibank holding company with $3.8 billion in assets; it operated 45 full-service offices in 12 Nebraska and contiguous state communities. FF provided a full range of financial services to corporate, retail, and trust customers, the result of which was a balance of commercial and industrial, real estate, and consumer loans in its portfolio. FF's underperforming asset levels were exceptionally low and its noninterest income, net interest margin, and other key financial performance ratios (discussed later) were among the best of banks its size. Beginning in 1993, FF was the subject of takeover speculation, and in February 1996, it was purchased by First Bank Systems headquartered in Minneapolis, Minnesota. As we analyze the 1995 financial statements of these two comparably sized banks, we pay particular attention to how the choice of a niche strategy by North Fork Bancorp affected its financial ratios relative to Firstier Financial (which proved to be an attractive takeover target).

Boatmen's Bancshares (BB), headquartered in St. Louis, Missouri, was among the country's top 30 leading financial service providers in 1995, with assets totaling $33.7 billion at year-end. Boatmen's had offices in nine states and a nationally recognized trust and mortgage banking unit. Three major lines of business made up BB's organization: consumer and commercial banking, which included the delivery of commercial and consumer financial services by 54 banks; trust activities, providing fiduciary and advisory services to both individuals and institutions; and mortgage banking. The nine states in which BB operated plus the national reach of both the trust and mortgage banking units provided market and geographic diversity that cushioned potential downturns in any particular market segment. A large well-established institutional money manager, Boatmen's represented an attractive target for NationsBank, one of the nation's three largest banking organizations, which announced its takeover of Boatmen's in late summer of 1996. Chapter 26 presents the details of the acquisition and highlights the financial statement attributes that made Boatmen's an attractive target for NationsBank.

Balance Sheet Structure

Table 8–1 presents December 31, 1995, balance sheet information for the three commercial bank holding companies (hereafter called *banks*). As stated in Chapter 3, many banks are owned by parent bank holding companies. One-bank holding companies control only one subsidiary commercial bank; multiple bank holding companies control two or more subsidiary commercial banks. The financial statements reported in this chapter are for the consolidated bank holding company that includes the parent holding company plus bank subsidiaries. These data are taken from the Federal Deposit Insurance Corporation call reports and from annual reports. The assets listed are what the banks own, the liabilities are what they owe, and equity capital is the book value of the bank owner's capital investment stake. As with any company, assets (A) must equal liabilities (L) plus equity capital (E) or $A = L + E$. Pay particular attention to the fact that, unlike manufacturing corporations, the majority of a financial institution's assets are financial rather than physical or fixed. Additionally, a relatively large portion of an FI's liabilities are short-term deposits and borrowings; in general, banks have higher leverage than manufacturing corporations do.

Assets.   A bank's assets are grouped into four major subcategories: cash and balances due from depository institutions, investment securities, loans and leases, and other assets. Investment securities and loans and leases are the bank's earning assets. Cash and balances due from depository institutions (item 5 in Table 8–1) consist of vault cash, deposits at the Federal Reserve (the central bank), deposits at other financial institutions, and cash items in the process of collection. None of these items generates income for the bank, but each is held because they perform specific functions. Vault cash (item 1) is composed of the currency and coin needed to meet customer withdrawals. Deposits at the Federal Reserve (item 2) are used primarily to meet legal reserve requirements (see Chapter 14), to assist in check clearing, wire transfers, and in the purchase or sale of Treasury securities. Deposits at other financial institutions (item 3) are primarily used to purchase services from those institutions. These banks generally purchase from **correspondent banks** services such as check collection, check processing, fed funds trading, and investment advice. Cash items in the process of collection (item 4) are checks written against accounts at other institutions that have been deposited at the bank. Credit is given to the depositor of these checks only after they clear.

correspondent bank

A bank that provides services to another commercial bank.

Investment securities (item 14 in Table 8–1) consist of items such as interest-bearing deposits at other FIs, federal funds sold, repurchase agreements (RPs or repos), U.S. Treasury and agency securities, securities issued by states and political subdivisions (municipals), mortgage-backed securities, and other debt and equity securities. These securities generate some income for the bank and are used for liquidity risk management

Table **8–1**

BALANCE SHEET FOR THREE COMMERCIAL BANKS ON DECEMBER 31, 1995

(in millions of dollars)

	North Fork Bancorp*	Firstier Financial*	Boatmen's Bancshares†
Assets			
1. Vault cash	$20.19	$38.84	$396.44
2. Deposits at Federal Reserve	30.87	23.89	105.11
3. Deposits at other financial institutions	1.25	57.49	388.80
4. Cash items in process of collection	54.06	224.32	1,285.45
5. Cash and balances due from depository institutions	$106.37	$344.54	$2,175.80
6. Interest bearing deposits at other FIs	0.45	6.07	44.72
7. Federal funds sold	0.00	85.16	1,077.50
8. Repurchase agreements	0.00	40.00	22.20
9. U.S. Treasury securities	20.14	85.31	1,381.00
10. U.S. agency securities	88.52	195.51	987.00
11. Securities issued by state and political subdivisions	60.73	395.08	909.06
12. Mortgage-backed securities	961.40	253.46	4,842.90
13. Other debt and equity securities	16.17	29.94	916.04
14. Investment securities	$1,147.41	$1,090.53	$10,180.42
15. Commercial and industrial loans	181.69	702.64	9,623.20
16. Loans secured by real estate	1,683.02	730.16	4,669.20
17. Consumer loans	71.42	662.28	5,344.40
18. Other loans	8.84	161.84	20.90
19. Leases	40.06	5.86	169.20
20. Gross loans and leases	$1,985.03	$2,262.78	$19,826.90
21. Less: Unearned income	18.59	0.00	63.70
22. Reserve for loan and lease losses	50.21	50.60	383.00
23. Net loans and leases	1,916.23	2,212.18	19,380.20
24. Premises and fixed assets	43.31	47.63	637.50
25. Other real estate owned	4.93	1.28	26.78
26. Investments in unconsolidated subsidiaries	0.00	0.00	1.00
27. Intangible assets	19.21	9.25	345.50
28. Other	44.99	73.77	956.60
29. Other assets	$112.44	$131.93	$1,967.38
30. Total assets	$3,282.45	$3,779.18	$33,703.80

(continued)

Table 8-1

BALANCE SHEET FOR THREE COMMERCIAL BANKS ON DECEMBER 31, 1995 *(CONTINUED)*

(in millions of dollars)

	North Fork Bancorp*	Firstier Financial*	Boatmen's Bancshares†
Liabilities And Equity Capital			
31. Demand deposits	$452.28	$668.35	$5,824.56
32. NOW accounts	94.82	467.88	1,011.47
33. MMDAs	236.04	311.71	8,399.41
34. Other savings deposits	822.88	135.58	1,616.50
35. Retail CDs	753.81	1,154.94	7,570.32
36. Core deposits	$2,359.83	$2,738.46	$24,422.26
37. Wholesale CDs	176.11	244.37	1,471.90
38. Total deposits	$2,535.94	$2,982.83	$25,894.16
39. Federal funds purchased	0.00	97.81	1,608.82
40. Repurchase agreements	401.37	136.93	752.38
41. Other borrowed funds	10.00	170.49	1,398.90
42. Subordinated notes and debentures	0.00	0.00	615.13
43. Other liabilities	26.27	57.82	506.35
44. Total liabilities	$2,973.58	$3,445.88	$30,775.74
45. Preferred stock	0.00	0.00	0.96
46. Common stock	5.50	52.74	129.92
47. Surplus and paid-in capital	136.41	79.20	984.56
48. Retained earnings	166.96	201.36	1,812.62
49. Total equity capital	$308.87	$333.30	$2,928.06
50. Total liabilities and equity capital	$3,282.45	$3,779.18	$33,703.80

* Values are taken from the 1995 FDIC report of condition data tapes.

† Values are taken from the 1995 FDIC report of condition data tapes and annual report.

purposes (see Chapter 13). Investment securities are highly liquid,[1] have low default risk, and can usually be traded in a secondary market. Banks generally maintain significant amounts of these securities to ensure that they can easily meet liquidity needs.[2] However, because the revenue generated from investment securities is low, compared to that from loans and leases, many (particularly larger) banks attempt to minimize the amount of investment securities they hold.

Short-maturity investments such as interest-bearing deposits at other FIs (item 6), federal funds sold (item 7), repurchase agreements (item 8), and U.S. Treasury bills (item 9) have maturities ranging from overnight to one year. Returns on these investments vary

---

[1] Not all of a bank's investment securities can be sold immediately. Some securities, such as U.S. Treasury securities and municipals, can be pledged against certain types of borrowing by the bank and, therefore, must remain on the bank's books until the debt obligation is removed or another security is pledged as collateral.

[2] Most investment securities are debt rather than equity instruments because current regulations generally prohibit banks from owning equity securities as investments. Banks can hold equity securities only if they are acquired as collateral on a loan or if they are stocks issued by the Federal Reserve Bank.

directly with changes in market interest rates. Although banks with excess cash reserves invest some of this in interest-earning liquid assets such as T-bills and short-term securities, they have the option to lend excess reserves for short intervals to other banks seeking increased short-term funding. The interbank market for excess reserves is called the federal funds (fed funds) market. In the United States, federal funds are short-term uncollateralized loans made by one bank to another; more than 90 percent of such transactions have maturities of one day.

Repurchase agreements (RPs or repos) can be viewed as collateralized federal funds transactions. In a federal funds transaction, the bank with excess reserves sells fed funds for one day to the purchasing bank. The next day, the purchasing bank returns the fed funds plus one day's interest reflecting the fed funds rate. Since credit risk exposure exists for the selling bank because the purchasing bank may be unable to repay the fed funds the next day, the seller may seek collateral backing for the one-day loan of fed funds. In an RP transaction, the funds-selling bank receives government securities as collateral from the funds-purchasing bank. That is, the funds-purchasing bank temporarily exchanges securities for cash. The next day, this transaction is reversed; the funds-purchasing bank sends back the fed funds it borrowed plus interest (the RP rate); it receives in return (or repurchases) its securities used as collateral in the transaction.

Long-maturity investments such as U.S. Treasury bonds (item 9), U.S. agency securities (item 10), municipals (item 11), mortgaged-backed securities (item 12), and most other securities (item 13) are similarly liquid and offer somewhat higher expected returns than short-maturity investments. U.S. Treasury securities and one agency security (Government National Mortgage Association) are fully backed by the U.S. government and thus carry no default risk. Other U.S. government agency securities, such as those of the Federal National Mortgage Association and the Federal Home Loan Mortgage Corporation, are not directly backed by the full faith and credit of the U.S. government and therefore carry some default risk (see Chapter 12). Municipal securities held by commercial banks are generally high-rated, investment-grade (i.e., low-risk) securities issued as either general obligation or revenue bonds.[3] Interest paid on municipals is exempt from federal income tax obligations. Mortgage-backed securities include items such as collateralized mortgage obligations and mortgage-backed bonds (see Chapter 12). Other investment securities include investment-grade corporate bonds, foreign debt securities, and trading account securities, such as U.S. Treasury securities and municipals held for short-term trading purposes. The trading account securities earn interest for the bank and generate capital gains or losses from changes in the prices of these securities (see Chapter 19).[4]

Loans (items 15–18 in Table 8–1) are the major items on a bank's balance sheet and generate the largest flow of revenue income. However, loans are also the least liquid asset item and the major source of credit and liquidity risk for most banks. Leases (item 19) substitute for loans in which the bank, as owner of a physical asset, allows a customer to use the asset in return for periodic lease payments. The bank maintains ownership of the asset upon conclusion of the lease. Loans are categorized as commercial and industrial (C&I) loans (item 15), loans secured by real estate (item 16), individual or consumers loans (item

---

[3] Payments of principal and interest on general obligation bonds are backed by the full faith, credit, and taxing authority of the issuer. Payments of principal and interest on revenue bonds are backed only by the revenues generated from the facility or project that the proceeds of the bonds are financing.

[4] Investment securities included in the bank's trading portfolio and designated as *trading securities* or *available-for-sale securities* are listed on the balance sheet at their *market value*. All other items on the balance sheet are listed at their *book values*.

17), and other loans (item 18). The characteristics of each category of loan are discussed in more detail in Chapter 10. Foreign loans often carry an additional risk for the bank—called *country or sovereign risk*—beyond default risk (see Chapter 28). Each category can consist of domestic and foreign loans. C&I loans are used to finance a firm's capital needs, equipment purchases, and plant expansion. Real estate loans primarily include mortgage loans, as well as some revolving home equity loans. Consumer loans consist of auto loans, revolving loans (i.e., credit cards), and other (i.e., mobile home loans and personal loans). Other loans include a wide variety of borrowers and types such as loans to nonbank financial institutions, state and local governments, foreign banks, and sovereign governments. As discussed in Chapter 10, each category of loan entails a wide variety of characteristics that must be evaluated to determine the risk involved with the loan, whether the bank should grant the loan, and, if so, at what price.

Unearned income (item 21) and the allowance (reserve) for loan and lease losses (item 22) are deducted from the gross loans and leases on the balance sheet. Unearned income is the amount of income that the bank has received on a loan from a customer but has not yet recorded as income on the income statement because the customer has not had the use of these funds for a sufficient length of time. Over the life of the loan the bank earns (or accrues) interest income and accordingly transfers it out of unearned income into interest income. The allowance for loan and lease losses is an estimate by the bank's management of the percentage of the gross loans (and leases) that will not be repaid to the bank. Although the maximum amount of the reserve is influenced by tax laws, the bank's management actually sets the level based on loan growth and recent loan loss experience. The allowance for loan losses is an accumulated reserve that is adjusted each period as management recognizes the possibility of additional bad loans and makes appropriate provisions for such losses. Actual losses are then deducted from, and recoveries are added to, their accumulated loan and lease loss reserve balance.

Other assets on the bank's balance sheet (item 29) consist of items such as premises and fixed assets (item 24), other real estate owned (item 25), investments in unconsolidated subsidiaries (item 26), intangible assets (i.e., goodwill and mortgage servicing rights, item 27), and other (i.e., deferred taxes, prepaid expenses, and mortgage servicing fees receivable, item 28). These accounts are generally a small part of the bank's overall assets.

Liabilities. A bank's liabilities consist of various types of deposit accounts and other borrowings used to fund the investments and loans on the asset side of the balance sheet. Liabilities vary in terms of their maturity, interest payments, check-writing privileges, and deposit insurance coverage.

Demand deposits (item 31) are transaction accounts held by individuals, corporations, partnerships, and governments that pay no explicit interest. Corporations are prohibited from holding deposits other than demand deposits. This group therefore constitutes the major holders of demand deposits. Since 1980 all banks in the United States have been able to offer checkable deposits that pay interest and are withdrawalable on demand; they are called *negotiable order of withdrawal accounts* or **NOW accounts**[5] (item 32). The major distinction between these instruments and traditional demand deposits is these instruments require the depositor to maintain a minimum account balance to earn interest. If the minimum balance falls below some level, such as $500, the account formally converts to a status equivalent to a demand deposit and earns no interest. Also, there are restrictions on corporations holding NOW accounts.

NOW account

Negotiable order of withdrawal account; similar to a demand deposit account but has a minimum balance requirement and, when maintained, pays interest.

---

[5] Super-NOW accounts have very similar features to NOW accounts but require a larger minimum balance.

MMDAs

Money market deposit accounts; these accounts have features of retail savings accounts and limited checking account features.

Money market deposit accounts or **MMDAs** (item 33) are an additional liability instrument that banks can use. To make banks competitive with the money market mutual funds offered by groups such as Vanguard and Fidelity, the MMDAs they offer must be liquid but are not so liquid as demand deposits and NOW accounts. In the United States, MMDAs are checkable but subject to restrictions on the number of checks written on each account per month, the number of preauthorized automatic transfers per month, and the minimum denomination of the amount of each check. For example, one bank may allow a customer with an MMDA to make a maximum of six preauthorized automatic transfers, of which no more than three can be checks of not less than $500 each. In addition, MMDAs impose minimum balance requirements on depositors. The Federal Reserve does not require banks to hold reserves against MMDAs. Accordingly, banks generally pay higher rates on MMDAs than on NOW accounts. **Other savings deposits** (item 34) are all savings accounts other than MMDAs (i.e., regular passbook accounts) with no set maturity and no check-writing privileges. Like MMDAs, savings accounts currently carry zero reserve requirements.

other savings deposits

All savings accounts other than MMDAs.

The major categories of time deposits are retail certificates of deposit (CDs) and wholesale CDs. **Retail CDs** (item 35) are fixed-maturity instruments with face values under $100,000. Small time deposits carry early withdrawal penalties. Although the size, maturity, and rate on these CDs are negotiable, most banks issue standardized retail CDs. **Wholesale CDs** (item 37) were created by banks in the early 1960s as a contractual mechanism to allow depositors to liquidate their position in these CDs by selling them in the secondary market rather than settling up with the bank. Thus, a depositor can sell a relatively liquid instrument without causing adverse liquidity risk exposure for the bank. Thus, the unique feature of wholesale CDs is not so much their large minimum denomination size of $100,000 or more but the fact that they are **negotiable instruments**. That is, they can be resold by title assignment in a secondary market to other investors. This means, for example, that if IBM had bought a $1 million, three-month CD from Citibank but for unexpected liquidity reasons needed funds after only one month passed, it could sell this CD to another outside investor in the secondary market. This does not impose any obligation on Citibank in terms of an early funds withdrawal request. Wholesale funds obtained through a brokerage house that markets the bank's CDs are referred to as **brokered deposits**. CDs held in foreign offices and denominated in a currency other than that of the home country are referred to as *Eurodollar deposits.*

retail CDs

Time deposits with a face value below $100,000.

wholesale CDs

Time deposits with a face value above $100,000.

negotiable instrument

An instrument whose ownership can be transferred in the secondary market.

brokered deposits

Wholesale CDs obtained through a brokerage house.

Some banks separate foreign from domestic deposits on the balance sheet. Foreign deposits are not explicitly covered by government-provided deposit insurance guarantees (see Chapter 15). These deposits are generally large and held by corporations with a high level of international dealings.

The liabilities just described are all deposit liabilities, reflecting deposit contracts issued by banks in return for cash. However, banks not only fund their assets by issuing deposits but can also borrow in various markets for purchased funds. Since the funds generated from these purchases are borrowed funds, not deposits, they are subject to neither reserve requirements (as with demand deposits and NOW accounts) nor deposit insurance premium payments to the FDIC (as with all the domestic deposits described earlier).[6] The largest market available for purchased funds is the federal funds market (item 39). We

---

[6] Foreign deposits are not subject to deposit insurance premiums. However, in the exceptional event of a very large failure in which all deposits are protected, under the 1991 FDICIA, the FDIC is required to levy a charge on surviving large banks proportional to their total asset size. To the extent that assets are partially funded by foreign liabilities, this is an implied premium on foreign deposits.

discussed earlier that a bank with excess reserves can sell them in the fed funds market, recording them as an asset on the balance sheet. The bank that purchases fed funds shows them as a liability on its balance sheet. As with the fed funds market, the RP market (item 40) is a highly liquid and flexible source of funds for banks needing to increase their liabilities and to offset deposit withdrawals. Moreover, like fed funds, these transactions can be rolled over each day if the counterparty is willing. The major difference in flexibility of liability management for fed funds and RPs is that a fed funds transaction can be entered into at any time in the banking day as long as the Fedwire is open (see Chapter 24). In general, it is difficult to transact an RP borrowing late in the day since the bank sending the fed funds must be satisfied with the type and quality of the securities' collateral proposed by the borrowing bank. Although this collateral is normally T-bills, T-notes, T-bonds, and mortgage-backed securities, the maturities and other features, such as callability or coupons, may be unattractive to the fund seller.

Fed funds and RPs have been the major sources of borrowed funds, but banks have utilized other borrowing (item 41) sources to supplement their flexibility in liability management. Four of these sources include banker's acceptances (BAs), commercial paper, medium-term notes, and discount window loans. Banks often convert off-balance-sheet letters of credit into on-balance-sheet BAs by discounting the letter of credit when the holder presents it for acceptance. In addition, these BAs may then be resold to money market investors. Thus, BA sales to the secondary market are an additional funding source. Although a bank subsidiary itself cannot issue commercial paper, its parent holding company can; that is, Citicorp can issue commercial paper but Citibank cannot. This provides banks owned by holding companies—most of the largest banks in the United States—with an additional funding source.

A number of banks in search of stable sources of funds with low withdrawal risk have begun to issue subordinated notes and debentures (item 42), often in the five- to seven-year range. These notes are especially attractive because they are subject to neither reserve requirements nor deposit insurance premiums, and some can serve as capital for the bank to satisfy regulations regarding minimum capital requirements (see Chapter 16).

Finally, banks facing temporary liquidity crunches can borrow from the central bank's discount window at the discount rate. Since this rate is not market determined and usually lies below fed funds and government security rates, it offers a very attractive borrowing opportunity to a bank with deficient reserves as the reserve maintenance period comes to an end (see Chapter 14).[7]

core deposits

Deposits of the bank that are stable over short periods of time.

purchased funds

Rate-sensitive funding sources of the bank.

Some banks separate core deposits from purchased funds on the balance sheet. The stable deposits of the bank are referred to as **core deposits** (item 36). These deposits are not expected to be withdrawn over short periods of time and therefore are a more permanent source of funding for the bank. Core deposits generally are defined as demand deposits, NOW accounts, MMDAs, other saving accounts, and retail CDs. **Purchased funds** are a more volatile source of funds because they are highly rate sensitive. That is, these funds are likely to be immediately withdrawn or replaced as rates on competitive instruments change. Purchased funds are generally defined as brokered deposits, wholesale CDs, deposits at foreign offices, fed funds purchased, RPs, and subordinated notes and debentures.

---

[7] Although the low rate makes the discount window an attractive place to borrow, banks do not use it very often because such borrowings attract the Fed's attention (see Chapter 14).

Banks also list other liabilities (item 43) (that do not require interest to be paid). These items consist of accrued interest, deferred taxes, dividends payable, minority interest in consolidated subsidiaries, and other miscellaneous claims.

Equity Capital. The bank's equity capital (item 49) consists mainly of preferred (item 45) and common (item 46) stock (listed at par value), surplus or additional paid-in capital (item 47), and retained earnings (item 48). Regulations require banks to hold a minimum level of equity capital to act as a buffer against losses from its on- and off-balance-sheet assets (see Chapter 16).

Off-Balance-Sheet Assets and Liabilities

Off-balance-sheet items are *contingent* assets and liabilities that *may* affect the future status of a financial institution's balance sheet. OBS activities are less obvious and often invisible to financial statement readers because they usually appear "below the bottom line," frequently as footnotes to accounts. We discuss OBS activities in detail in Chapter 20. In this chapter, we introduce the items as they appear off the FI's balance sheet.

Although OBS activities are now an important source of fee income for many FIs, they have the potential to produce positive as well as negative *future* cash flows. Some OBS activities can involve risks that add to the institution's overall risk exposure; others can hedge or reduce their interest rate, credit, and foreign exchange risks. A financial institution's performance and solvency are also affected by the management of these items. The OBS activities for North Fork Bancorp, Firstier Financial Inc., and Boatmen's Bancshares are reported in Table 8–2.

Off-balance-sheet activities can be grouped into five major categories: loan commitments, letters of credit, when-issued securities, loans sold, and derivative securities. A **loan commitment** (item 1 in Table 8–2) is a contractual commitment to loan a certain maximum amount to a borrower at given interest rate terms over some contractual period in the future (e.g., one year). **Letters of credit** are essentially guarantees that FIs sell to underwrite the

loan commitment

Contractual commitment to loan to a firm a certain maximum amount at given interest rate terms.

letter of credit

Guarantee sold by an FI to underwrite the performance of the buyer of the guarantee.

Table **8–2**

OFF-BALANCE-SHEET ACTIVITIES FOR THREE COMMERCIAL BANKS ON DECEMBER 31, 1995

(in millions of dollars)

	North Fork Bancorp*	**Firstier Financial***	**Boatmen's Bancshares***
Commitments and contingencies			
1. Loan commitments	$189.53	$1,745.78	$12,191.10
2. Commercial letters of credit	0.72	4.23	92.00
3. Standby letters of credit	13.47	9.83	1,027.30
4. When-issued securities	0.00	0.83	0.00
5. Loans sold	5.25	0.00	86.60
Notional amounts for derivatives†			
6. Interest rate swaps	0.00	127.88	2,680.60
7. Total	$208.97	$1,888.55	$16,077.60

*Values are taken from 1995 FDIC report of condition data tapes and annual reports.

†Notional amounts reflect the face value of the contracts entered into.

Table 8–3

INCOME STATEMENT FOR THREE COMMERCIAL BANKS FOR 1995

(in millions of dollars)

	North Fork Bancorp*	Firstier Financial*	Boatmen's Bancshares†
Interest Income			
1. Income on C&I loans	$ 18.39	$ 64.67	$ 743.40
2. Income on real estate loans	145.63	64.25	582.67
3. Income on consumer loans	5.12	53.65	375.39
4. Income on other loans	0.86	10.83	1.53
5. Income on leases	2.14	0.42	8.56
6. Interest and fees on loans and leases	$172.14	$193.82	$1,711.55
7. Interest on deposits at other institutions	0.00	0.00	4.53
8. Interest on fed funds and RPs	0.80	8.13	33.67
9. Interest on U.S. Treasury and agency securities	42.76	33.85	249.99
10. Interest on municipals	2.49	24.16	56.11
11. Interest on other debt and equity securities	7.89	2.08	263.92
12. Interest income on investment securities	$53.94	$ 68.22	$ 608.22
13. Total interest income	$226.08	$262.04	$2,319.77
Interest Expense			
14. Interest on NOW accounts	1.28	9.79	64.78
15. Interest on MMDA accounts	5.75	9.80	207.58
16. Interest on other savings	20.76	2.94	44.53
17. Interest on retail CDs	8.33	14.35	86.21
18. Interest on wholesale CDs	40.18	68.99	394.16

when-issued securities

Commitments to buy or sell securities before they are issued.

loans sold

Loans originated by the FI and then sold to other investors that can be returned to the originating institution.

derivative securities

Future, forward, swap, and option positions taken by the FI for hedging or other purposes.

future performance of the buyers of the guarantees. Commercial letters of credit (item 2) are used mainly to assist a firm in domestic and international trade. The FI's role is to provide a formal guarantee that it will pay for the goods shipped or sold if the buyer of the goods defaults on its future payments. Standby letters of credit (item 3) cover contingencies that are potentially more severe, less predictable or frequent, and not necessarily trade related. **When-issued securities** (item 4) are forward or future commitments to buy or sell securities (e.g., Treasury bills) before they are issued. Because the FI locks in a price on the securities before their issuance, these off-balance-sheet commitments expose it to interest rate risk. **Loans sold** (item 5) are loans that the FI originated and then sold to other investors that can be returned to the originating institution in the future if the credit quality of the loans deteriorate (see Chapter 12). **Derivative securities** (item 6) are future, forward, swap, and option positions taken by the bank for hedging and other purposes (see Chapters 21 through 23).

Income Statement

See Table 8–3 for the report of income or income statement for North Fork Bancorp, Firstier Financial Inc., and Boatmen's Bancshares for the 1995 calendar year. The report of income identifies the interest income and expenses, net interest income, provision for loan

	North Fork Bancorp*	Firstier Financial*	Boatmen's Bancshares†
19. Interest on deposit accounts	$76.30	$105.87	$797.26
20. Interest on fed funds and RPs	6.32	12.77	257.23
21. Interest on other borrowed funds	1.10	10.64	3.87
22. Interest on subordinated notes and debentures	0.00	0.00	47.34
23. Total interest expense	$ 83.72	$129.28	$1,105.70
24. Net interest income	142.36	132.76	1,214.70
25. Provision for loan losses	9.00	1.21	46.70
Noninterest Income			
26. Income from fiduciary activities	1.79	16.72	196.18
27. Service charges on deposit accounts	10.84	17.22	190.80
28. Trading gains and fees from foreign exchange transactions	0.00	0.00	0.00
29. Other foreign transaction gains	0.00	0.27	0.00
30. Other gains from trading assets and liabilities	0.07	0.03	14.70
31. Other noninterest income	8.09	23.18	271.70
32. Total noninterest income	$ 20.79	$ 57.42	$ 673.38
Noninterest expense			
33. Salaries and employee benefits	33.89	49.25	597.21
34. Expenses of premises and fixed assets	11.36	13.11	175.83
35. Other noninterest expense	22.25	64.42	425.96
36. Total noninterest expense	$67.50	$126.78	$1,199.00
37. Income before taxes and extraordinary items	$86.65	$62.19	$641.75
38. Applicable income taxes	36.66	15.07	222.92
39. Extraordinary items	0.00	0.00	0.00
40. Net income	$49.99	$47.12	$418.83

*Values are taken from the 1995 FDIC report of income data tapes.

†Values are taken from the 1995 FDIC report of income data tapes and annual report.

losses, noninterest income and expenses, income before taxes and extraordinary items, and net income for the year for the banks. As we discuss the income statement, notice the direct relationship between it and the balance sheet (both on- and off-). The composition of an FI's assets and liabilities, combined with the interest rates earned or paid on them, directly determines the interest income and expense on the income statement. In addition, because the assets and liabilities of FIs are mainly financial, most of the income and expense reported on the income statement is interest rate related (rather than reflecting sales prices and cost of goods sold as seen with manufacturing corporations).

Interest Income.   The income statement for a commercial bank first shows interest and fee income on loans and leases (item 6 in Table 8–3), the largest interest income–producing category. Subcategories are often listed on the income statement (items 1–4) for each category of loan listed earlier. Most banks also list income from leases (item 5) as a separate item. Interest from investment securities held (item 12) is also included as interest income. These too may be listed by subcategories (items 7–11) described earlier. Interest income (item 13) is recorded on an accrued basis (see earlier discussion). Thus, loans on which interest payments are past due can still be recorded as generating income for a bank.[8] Interest income is taxable, except for that on municipal securities and tax-exempt income from direct lease financing. Tax-exempt interest can be converted to a taxable equivalent basis as follows

$$\text{Taxable equivalent interest income} = \frac{\text{Interest income}}{1 - \text{Bank's tax rate}}$$

Interest Expenses.   Interest expense (item 23) is the second item on a bank's income statement. Items listed here come directly from the liability section of the balance sheet: interest on deposits (item 19) (NOW accounts [item 14], MMDAs [item 15], other savings [item 16], retail CDs [item 17], and wholesale CDs [item 18]) and interest on purchased funds (fed funds [item 20], RPs [item 20], and other borrowed funds [item 21]). Interest on subordinated notes and debentures is generally reported as a separate item (item 22).

Net Interest Income.   Total interest income minus total interest expense is listed next on the income statement as net interest income (item 24). Net interest income is an important tool in assessing the bank's ability to generate profits and control interest rate risk (see Chapters 17 and 18).

Provision for Loan Losses.   The provision for loan losses (item 25) is a noncash, tax-deductible expense. The provision for loan losses is the current period's allocation to the allowance for loan losses listed on the balance sheet. This item represents the bank management's recognition of bad loans for the period. As mentioned earlier, the size of the provision is determined by management and in the United States is subject to a maximum allowable tax deductible amount set by the Internal Revenue Service.

Noninterest Income.   Noninterest income (item 32) includes all other income received by the bank as a result of its on- and off-balance sheet activities and is becoming increasingly important as the ability to attract core deposits and high-quality loan applicants becomes more difficult (see Chapter 24). Included in these categories are income from fiduciary activities (for example, earnings from operating a trust department; item 26), service charges on deposit accounts (generally the largest source of noninterest income; item 27), trading gains and losses and fees from foreign exchange transactions (gains and losses from trading account securities and OBS hedge transactions; item 28), other foreign transaction gains (item 29), other gains (losses) and fees from trading assets and liabilities (from cash instruments and OBS derivative instruments; item 30), and other noninterest income (fee income from OBS loan commitments and letters of credit, and revenue from one-time transactions such as sales of real estate owned, loans, premises, and fixed assets; item 31).

The sum of interest income and noninterest income is referred to as the bank's *total operating income or total revenue*. **Total operating income** for a bank is equivalent to total sales in a manufacturing firm and represents the bank's income received from all sources.

total operating income

The sum of the interest income and noninterest income.

Noninterest Expense.   Noninterest expense (item 36) items consist mainly of personnel expenses and are generally large relative to noninterest income. Items in this category include salaries and employee benefits (item 33), expenses of premises and fixed assets

---

[8] A bank can recognize income for at least 90 days after the due date of the interest payment.

(i.e., utilities, depreciation, and deposit insurance) (item 34), and other (expenses of one-time transactions such as losses on sale of real estate, loans, and premises) (item 35).

Income before Taxes and Extraordinary Items.   Net interest income minus provisions for loan losses plus noninterest income minus noninterest expense produces the operating profit or income before taxes and extraordinary items for the bank (item 37).

Income Taxes.   All federal, state, local, and foreign income taxes due from the bank are listed next on the income statement (item 38). Some of this amount may be recorded as a liability (deferred taxes) or may be paid to the Internal Revenue Service.

Extraordinary Items.   Extraordinary items and other adjustments (item 39) include such things as effects of changes in accounting rules, corrections of accounting errors made in previous years, and equity capital adjustments.

Net Income.   Income before taxes and extraordinary items minus income taxes plus (or minus) extraordinary items results in the net income for the bank (item 40). Net income is the *bottom line* on the income statement.

The Direct Relationship between the Income Statement and the Balance Sheet

As mentioned earlier, banks' financial statements are directly related (more so than nonfinancial companies). That is, the items on the income statement are determined by the balance sheet assets and liabilities along with the interest rates on each item. This direct relationship between the two financial statements can be seen by depicting the income statement as follows

$$NI = \sum_{n=1}^{N} r_n A_n - \sum_{m=1}^{M} r_m L_m - P + NII - NIE - T$$

where

NI = bank's net income
A_n = dollar value of the bank's nth asset
L_m = dollar value of the bank's mth liability
r_n = rate earned on the bank's nth asset
r_m = rate paid on the bank's mth liability
P = provision for loan losses
NII = noninterest income earned by the bank including income from off-balance-sheet activities
NIE = noninterest expenses incurred by the bank
T = bank's taxes and extraordinary items
N = number of assets the bank holds
M = number of liabilities the bank holds

Net income is the direct result of i) the amount and mix of assets and liabilities held by the bank taken from the balance sheet and ii) the interest rate on each of them. For example, increasing the dollar value of an asset, all else constant, results in a direct increase in the bank's net income equal to the size of the increase times the rate of interest on the asset. Likewise, decreasing the rate paid on a liability, all else constant, directly increases net income by the size of the rate decrease times the dollar value of the liability on the balance sheet. Finally, changing the mix of assets or liabilities on the balance sheet has a direct effect on net income equal to the size of the rate difference times the dollar value of the asset or liability being changed. For example, suppose that a bank replaces $100,000 of assets currently yielding 8 percent with assets yielding 10 percent. Net income increases by $2,000 [(10% − 8%) times $100,000].

Concept Questions

1. What is the difference between a wholesale bank and a retail bank?
2. What are the trade-offs in holding a large proportion of short-term securities, such as T-bills, versus long-term securities, such as loans?
3. What are the trade-offs in issuing short-term deposit accounts such as demand deposits and retail CDs versus long-term deposits and other funding sources, such as wholesale CDs and long-term debt?
4. What is the nature of the relationship between balance sheet and income statement items?
5. Suppose that a bank pays a lower rate for new deposits than it pays on other liabilities. How will this impact the bank's net income?

FINANCIAL STATEMENT ANALYSIS USING A RETURN ON EQUITY FRAMEWORK

In recent years, the commercial banking industry has experienced a period of record profits, quite a change from the late-1980s and early-1990s when banks were failing in record numbers. See Contemporary Perspectives Box 8–2 for a summary of the size and source of the record profits for the third quarter of 1997. Despite record profits, many FIs have weak and inefficient areas that still need to be addressed. One way to identify weaknesses and problem areas is by analyzing financial statements. In particular, an analysis of selected accounting ratios—so-called ratio analysis—allows a bank manager to evaluate the bank's current performance, the change in its performance over time (**time series analysis** of ratios over a period of time), and its performance relative to that of competitor banks (**cross-sectional analysis** of ratios across a group of banks).

time series analysis

Analysis of financial statements over a period of time.

cross-sectional analysis

Analysis of financial statements comparing one bank with others.

Figure 8–1 summarizes the return on equity (ROE) framework.[9] The ROE framework starts with a most frequently used measure of profitability, ROE, and then breaks it down to identify strengths and weaknesses in the bank's performance.[10] The resulting breakdown provides a convenient and systematic method to identify strengths and weaknesses of a bank's performance. Identification of strengths and weaknesses, and the reasons for them, provides an excellent tool for bank managers as they look for ways to improve per-

---

[9] The ROE framework is similar to the DuPont analysis that managers of nonfinancial institutions frequently use.

[10] Many large banks also use a risk-adjusted return on capital (RAROC) to evaluate the impact of credit risk on bank performance. ROE does not consider the bank's risk in lending as does RAROC. RAROC is described in Chapter 10.

Contemporary Perspectives 8–2

Banks' Profits Climbed To Record In Third Quarter

Commercial banks posted record profits in the third quarter, putting them on a trajectory toward their sixth straight year of record earnings following last year's $52.4 billion, the Federal Deposit Insurance Corp. said. Even as banks' core businesses produce stellar profits, regulators are continuing to open the door to new lines. In the latest move, the comptroller of the currency yesterday approved a bank's request to underwrite municipal bonds, applying for the first time rules that could eventually let banks into such areas as leasing and real-estate development.

The comptroller's decision to let banks into new businesses followed similar moves by the Federal Reserve earlier this year. The issue hasn't had much opposition in part because banks are currently in the best shape they've been in a generation. The industry's performance reflects strong economic growth. "The economy is a gift that keeps on giving," said FDIC Chairman Andrew Hove. Sharply rising consumer fees such as charges for using automatic teller machines and the boom in commercial lending helped boost profits to $14.8 billion in the latest third quarter, up from $13.2 billion in the third quarter of 1996. But bad credit-card debt climbed to a record as well, to $5.35 for every $100 in outstanding loans.

Still, earnings of the 74 credit-card banks rebounded sharply, with third-quarter net income more than double that of the prior quarter. Profits for the credit-card banks rose to $1.3 billion, from $623 million in the second quarter, when many of them were hit with one-time restructuring charges. The boost in profits at the credit-card banks helped save commercial banks' overall earnings, which would otherwise have slipped in the third quarter from the second quarter.

After the second quarter, the FDIC raised alarms about the sharp rise in bad credit-card debt, in part because it was accompanied by poor earnings at the credit-card banks. Because of the profit rebound in the latest quarter, however, FDIC officials think that problems may be largely under control. The third-quarter credit-card loss rate of 5.35 percent—amounting to $3 billion—compared with 5.22 percent in the second quarter and 4.41 percent in the third quarter of 1996. Credit-card losses were the largest portion of loan charge-offs of $4.8 billion in the latest quarter, the highest level since the fourth quarter of 1993, the FDIC said.

SOURCE: John R. Wilke, The *Wall Street Journal,* December 12, 1997, p. A2. Reprinted by permission of The *Wall Street Journal,* © 1997 Dow Jones & Company, Inc. All Rights Reserved Worldwide.

formance. Table 8–4 summarizes the role of ROE and the first two levels of the ROE framework (from Figure 8–1) in analyzing an FI's performance.

The remainder of this chapter applies the ROE framework to our three banks: North Fork Bancorp, Firstier Financial, and Boatmen's Bancshares. All of the ratios discussed as part of the ROE breakdown are reported in Table 8–5. We refer to these ratios by number (1 through 121). In addition, Figure 8–2 presents these ratios (by ratio number) as they fit into the ROE framework shown in Figure 8–1.

Return on Equity and Its Components

ROE is a frequently used measure of profitability for any firm. ROE (ratio 1 in Table 8–5) is defined as

$$ROE = \frac{\text{Net income}}{\text{Total equity capital}}$$

It measures the amount of net income after taxes earned for each dollar of equity capital contributed by the bank's stockholders. Taking these data from the financial statements for

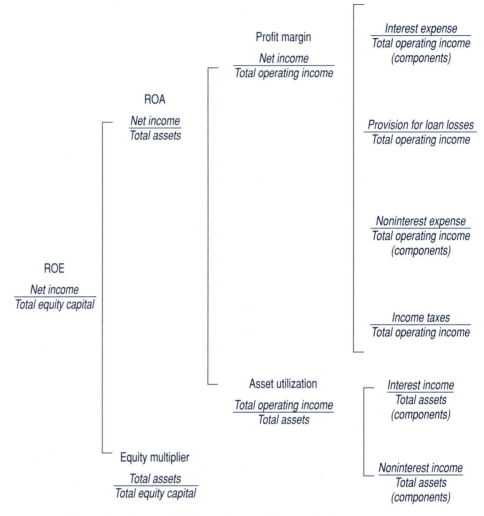

Figure **8-1**   *Breakdown of ROE into Various Financial Ratios*

Table **8-4**

ROLE OF ROE, ROA, EM, PM, AND AU IN ANALYZING FINANCIAL INSTITUTION PERFORMANCE

Return on Equity (ROE)	Measures overall profitability of the FI per dollar of equity.
Return on Assets (ROA)	Measures profit generated relative to the FI's assets.
Equity Multiplier (EM)	Measures the extent to which assets of the FI are funded with equity relative to debt.
Profit Margin (PM)	Measures the ability to pay expenses and generate net income from interest and noninterest income.
Asset Utilization (AU)	Measures the amount of interest and noninterest income generated per dollar of total assets.

Table **8-5**

FINANCIAL RATIOS FOR THREE COMMERCIAL BANKS FOR 1995

Ratio	North Fork Bancorp	Firstier Financial	Boatmen's Bancshares
1. ROE	16.18%	14.14%	14.30%
2. ROA	1.52%	1.25%	1.24%
3. Equity multiplier	10.63X	11.34X	11.51X
4. Profit margin	20.25%	14.75%	13.99%
5. Asset utilization	7.52%	8.45%	8.88%
6. Net interest margin	4.65%	4.02%	4.11%
7. Spread	4.02%	3.18%	3.32%
8. Overhead efficiency	30.80%	45.29%	56.16%
Profit margin components			
9. Interest expense ratio	33.91%	40.47%	36.94%
10. Provision for loan loss ratio	3.65	0.38	1.56
11. Noninterest expense ratio	27.34	39.69	40.06
12. Tax ratio	14.85	4.72	7.45
Interest expenses as a percentage of total operating income			
13. NOW accounts	0.52%	3.06%	2.16%
14. MMDAs	2.33	3.07	6.94
15. Other savings	8.41	0.92	1.48
16. Retail CDs	3.37	4.49	2.88
17. Wholesale CDs	16.28	21.60	13.17
18. Fed funds and RPs	2.56	4.00	8.59
19. Other borrowed funds	0.45	3.33	0.13
20. Subordinated notes and debentures	0.00	0.00	1.58
Noninterest expense as a percentage of total operating income			
21. Salaries and employee benefits	13.73%	15.42%	19.95%
22. Expenses of premises and fixed assets	4.60	4.10	5.87
23. Other noninterest expenses	9.01	20.17	14.23
Liability yields			
24. NOW accounts	1.34%	2.09%	6.40%
25. MMDAs	2.44	3.14	2.47
26. Other savings	2.52	2.17	2.75
27. Retail CDs	1.11	1.24	1.14
28. Wholesale CDs	22.82	28.23	26.78
29. Fed funds and RPs	1.57	5.44	10.89
30. Other borrowed funds	11.00	6.24	0.28
31. Subordinated notes and debentures	0.00	0.00	7.70
Liability accounts as a percentage of total assets			
32. Demand deposits	13.78%	17.69%	17.28%
33. NOW accounts	2.89	12.38	3.00
34. MMDAs	7.19	8.25	24.92
35. Other savings	25.07	3.59	4.80
36. Retail CDs	22.96	30.56	22.46
37. Core deposits	71.89	72.47	72.46
38. Wholesale CDs	5.37	6.47	4.37
39. Fed funds and RPs	12.23	6.21	4.77
40. Other borrowed funds	0.30	4.51	4.15

continued

Table **8-5**

FINANCIAL RATIOS FOR THREE COMMERCIAL BANKS FOR 1995 (CONTINUED)

Ratio	North Fork Bancorp	Firstier Financial	Boatmen's Bancshares
41. Subordinated notes and debentures	0.00	0.00	1.83
42. Purchased funds	17.90	17.19	15.12
43. Other liabilities	0.80	1.52	1.50
Liability items as a percentage of interest bearing liabilities			
44. NOW accounts	3.80%	17.20%	4.14%
45. MMDAs	9.46	11.46	34.36
46. Other savings	32.98	4.98	6.61
47. Retail CDs	30.21	42.47	30.97
48. Wholesale CDs	7.06	8.99	6.02
49. Fed funds and RPs	16.09	8.63	9.66
50. Other borrowed funds	0.40	6.27	5.72
51. Subordinated notes and debentures	0.00	0.00	2.52
Noninterest expense as a percentage of noninterest income			
52. Salaries and employee benefits	163.01%	85.77%	88.69%
53. Expenses of premises and fixed assets	54.64	22.83	26.11
54. Other noninterest income	107.02	112.19	63.26
Noninterest expense as a percentage of total assets			
55. Salaries and employee benefits	1.03%	1.30%	1.77%
56. Expenses of premises and fixed assets	0.35	0.35	0.52
57. Other noninterest income	0.68	1.70	1.26
Asset utilization breakdown			
58. Interest income ratio	6.89%	6.93%	6.88%
59. Noninterest income ratio	0.63	1.52	2.00
Interest income as a percentage of total assets			
60. C&I Loans	0.56%	1.71%	2.21%
61. Real estate loans	4.44	1.70	1.73
62. Consumer loans	0.16	1.42	1.11
63. Other loans	0.03	0.29	0.00
64. Leases	0.07	0.01	0.03
65. Deposits at other institutions	0.00	0.00	0.01
66. Fed funds and RPs	0.02	0.22	0.10
67. U.S. Treasury and agencies	1.30	0.90	0.74
68. Municipals	0.08	0.64	0.17
69. Other debt and equity securities	0.02	0.06	0.78
Asset yields			
70. C&I loans	10.12%	9.20%	7.73%
71. Real estate loans	8.65	8.80	12.48
72. Consumer loans	7.17	8.10	7.02
73. Other loans	9.73	6.69	7.32
74. Leases	5.34	4.82	5.06
75. Fed funds and RPs	0.00	6.50	10.13
76. U.S. Treasury and agencies	4.00	12.05	10.56
77. Municipals	4.10	6.12	6.17
78. Other debt and equity securities	0.81	0.73	4.58

Ratio	North Fork Bancorp	Firstier Financial	Boatmen's Bancshares
Asset items as a percentage of total assets			
79. Cash and balances due from institutions	3.24%	9.12%	6.46%
80. C&I loans	5.54	18.59	28.55
81. Real estate loans	51.27	19.32	13.85
82. Consumer loans	2.18	17.52	15.86
83. Other loans	0.27	4.28	0.06
84. Leases	1.22	0.16	0.50
85. Net loans and leases	58.38	58.54	57.50
86. Deposits at other institutions	0.01	0.16	0.13
87. Fed funds and RPs	0.00	3.31	3.26
88. U.S. Treasury and agencies	3.31	7.43	7.03
89. Municipals	1.85	10.45	2.70
90. Other debt and equity securities	29.78	7.50	17.09
91. Total investment securities	34.95	28.85	30.21
92. Other assets	3.43	3.49	5.84
Asset items as a percentage of earning assets			
93. C&I loans	5.93%	21.27%	32.55%
94. Real estate loans	54.94	22.11	15.80
95. Consumer loans	2.33	20.05	18.08
96. Other loans	0.29	4.90	0.07
97. Leases	1.31	0.18	0.57
98. Deposits at other institutions	0.01	0.18	0.15
99. Fed funds and RPs	0.00	3.79	3.72
100. U.S. Treasury and agencies	3.55	8.50	8.01
101. Municipals	1.98	11.96	3.08
102. Other debt and equity securities	31.91	8.58	19.48
Off-Balance-Sheet items as a percentage of total assets			
103. Loan commitments	5.77%	46.20%	36.17%
104. Standby letters of credit	0.41	0.26	3.05
105. Commercial letters of credit	0.02	0.11	0.27
106. When-issued securities	0.00	0.02	0.00
107. Loans sold	0.16	0.00	0.26
108. Interest rate swaps	0.00	3.38	7.95
109. Total off-balance-sheet items	6.36	49.97	47.70
Noninterest income as a percentage of total assets			
110. Fiduciary accounts	0.05%	0.44%	0.58%
111. Service charges	0.33	0.46	0.57
112. Trading gains	0.00	0.00	0.00
113. Other foreign transactions	0.00	0.01	0.00
114. Other gains from trading	0.00	0.00	0.00
115. Other noninterest income	0.25	0.61	0.81
Noninterest income as a percentage of total noninterest income			
116. Fiduciary accounts	8.61%	29.12%	29.13%
117. Service charges	52.14	29.99	28.34
118. Trading gains	0.00	0.00	0.00
119. Other foreign transaction	0.00	0.47	0.04
120. Other gains from trading	0.34	0.05	2.18
121. Other noninterest income	38.91	40.37	40.35

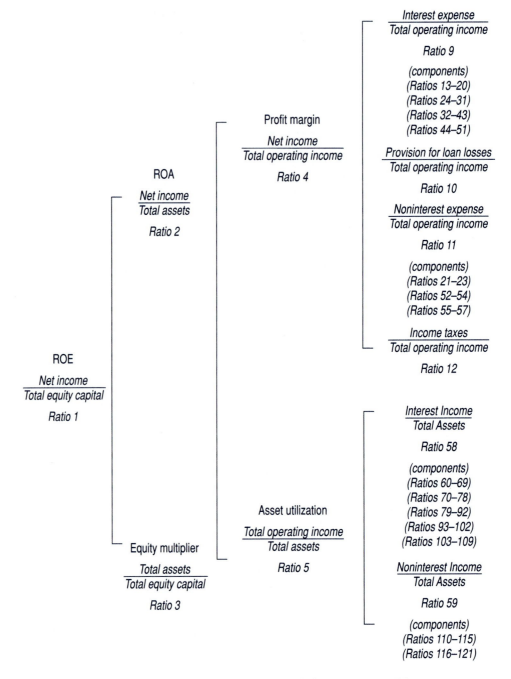

North Fork Bancorp, Firstier Financial, Inc., and Boatmen's Bancshares produces the following ROEs for 1995:[11]

	North Fork Bancorp	Firstier Financial	Boatmen's Bancshares
ROE	$\dfrac{49.99}{308.87} = 16.18\%$	$\dfrac{47.12}{333.30} = 14.14\%$	$\dfrac{418.83}{2,928.06} = 14.30\%$

Generally, bank stockholders prefer ROE to be high. It is possible, however, that an increase in ROE indicates increased bank risk. For example, ROE increases if total equity capital decreases relative to net income. A large drop in equity capital may result in a violation of minimum regulatory capital standards and an increased risk of insolvency for the bank (see Chapter 16). Thus, an increase in ROE may simply result from an increase in a bank's leverage (and consequently an increase in its solvency risk).

To identify potential problems, ROE (ratio 1) can be broken into component parts as follows

$$ROE = \frac{\text{Net income}}{\text{Total assets}} \times \frac{\text{Total assets}}{\text{Total equity capital}}$$

$$= ROA \times EM$$

where return on assets (ROA, ratio 2) is the return on assets and EM (ratio 3) is the equity multiplier. ROA determines the net income produced per dollar of assets; EM measures the dollar value of assets funded with each dollar of equity capital (the higher this ratio, the more leverage or debt the bank is using to fund its assets; thus, this ratio is a measure of the degree of leverage the bank is using). The values of these ratios for our three banks are as follows:

	North Fork Bancorp	Firstier Financial	Boatmen's Bancshares
ROA	$\dfrac{49.99}{3,282.45} = 1.52\%$	$\dfrac{47.12}{3,779.18} = 1.25\%$	$\dfrac{418.83}{33,703.80} = 1.24\%$
EM	$\dfrac{3,282.45}{308.87} = 10.63$ times	$\dfrac{3,779.18}{333.30} = 11.34$ times	$\dfrac{33,703.80}{2,928.06} = 11.51$ times

High values for these ratios produce high ROEs, but, as noted, managers should be concerned about the source of high ROE values. For example, an increase in ROE due to an increase in the EM means that the bank's leverage, and therefore its solvency risk, has increased.

---

[11]We are using year-end balance sheet data to calculate ratios. The use of these data may bias ratios in that they are data for one day in the year, but income statement data cover the full year. To avoid this bias, the use of average values for balance sheet data are often used to calculate ratios.

Return On Assets and Its Components

A further breakdown of a bank's profitability is that of ROA (ratio 2) into the profit margin (PM) and asset utilization (AU) ratios.

$$ROA = \frac{\text{Net income}}{\text{Total operating income}} \times \frac{\text{Total operating income}}{\text{Total assets}}$$

$$= PM \times AU$$

where PM (ratio 4) is the net income generated per dollar of total operating (interest and noninterest) income and AU (ratio 5) is the amount of interest and noninterest income generated per dollar of total assets. For our three banks, these are as follows:

	North Fork Bancorp	Firstier Financial	Boatmen's Bancshares
PM	$\dfrac{49.99}{226.08 + 20.79} = 20.25\%$	$\dfrac{47.12}{262.04 + 57.42} = 14.75\%$	$\dfrac{418.83}{2,319.77 + 673.38} = 13.99\%$
AU	$\dfrac{226.08 + 20.79}{3,282.45} = 7.52\%$	$\dfrac{262.04 + 57.42}{3,779.18} = 8.45\%$	$\dfrac{2,319.77 + 673.38}{33,703.80} = 8.88\%$

Again, high values for these ratios produce high ROAs and subsequently ROEs. PM measures the bank's ability to control expenses. The better the expense control, the more profitable is the bank. AU measures the bank's ability to generate income from its assets. The more income generated per dollar of assets, the more profitable is the bank. Again, bank managers should be aware that high values of these ratios may indicate underlying problems. For example, PM increases if the bank experiences a drop in salaries and benefits. However, if this expense decreases because the most highly skilled employees are leaving the bank, the increase in PM and in ROA is associated with a potential "labor quality" problem. Thus, it is often prudent to break down these ratios further.

Profit Margin.   As stated, PM measures a bank's ability to control expenses and thus its ability to produce net income from its operating income (or revenue). A breakdown of PM, therefore, can isolate the various expense items listed on the income statement as follows

$$\text{Interest expense ratio (ratio 9)} = \frac{\text{Interest expense}}{\text{Total operating income}}$$

$$\text{Provision for loan loss ratio (ratio 10)} = \frac{\text{Provision for loan losses}}{\text{Total operating income}}$$

$$\text{Noninterest expense ratio (ratio 11)} = \frac{\text{Noninterest expense}}{\text{Total operating income}}$$

$$\text{Tax ratio (ratio 12)} = \frac{\text{Income taxes}}{\text{Total operating income}}$$

These ratios measure the proportion of total operating income that goes to pay the particular expense item. The values of these ratios for North Fork Bancorp, Firstier Financial, and Boatmen's Bancshares are as follows:

	North Fork Bancorp	Firstier Financial	Boatmen's Bancshares
Interest expense ratio	$\dfrac{83.72}{226.08 + 20.79} = 33.91\%$	$\dfrac{129.28}{262.04 + 57.42} = 40.47\%$	$\dfrac{1,105.70}{2,319.77 + 673.38} = 36.94\%$
Provision for loan loss ratio	$\dfrac{9.00}{226.08 + 20.79} = 3.65\%$	$\dfrac{1.21}{262.04 + 57.42} = 0.38\%$	$\dfrac{46.70}{2,319.77 + 673.38} = 1.56\%$
Noninterest expense ratio	$\dfrac{67.50}{226.08 + 20.79} = 27.34\%$	$\dfrac{126.78}{262.04 + 57.42} = 39.69\%$	$\dfrac{1,199.00}{2,319.77 + 673.38} = 40.06\%$
Tax ratio	$\dfrac{36.66}{226.08 + 20.79} = 14.85\%$	$\dfrac{15.07}{262.04 + 57.42} = 4.72\%$	$\dfrac{222.92}{2,319.77 + 673.38} = 7.45\%$

The sum of the numerators of these four ratios subtracted from the denominator (total operating income) is the bank's net income.[12] Thus, the lower any of these ratios, the higher the bank's profitability (PM). As mentioned, however, although a low value for any of these ratios produces an increase in the bank's profit, it may be the result of a problem situation in the bank. Thus, an even more detailed breakdown of these ratios may be warranted. For example, the interest expense ratio can be broken down according to the various interest expense–generating liabilities (ratios 13–20; e.g., interest on NOW accounts/total operating income). Additionally, the noninterest expense ratio may be broken down according to its components (ratios 21–23; e.g., salaries and benefits/total operating income). These ratios allow for a more detailed examination of the generation of the bank's expenses.

A different method to evaluate the bank's expense management is to calculate such ratios as liability yields (ratios 24–31; e.g., interest expense on NOW accounts/dollar value of NOW accounts) or size of investment (e.g., dollar value of NOW accounts/total assets— ratios 32–43— or dollar value of NOW accounts/total interest bearing liabilities— ratios 44–51). The noninterest expense items can be evaluated using component percentages (ratios 52–54; e.g., salaries and benefits/noninterest income) or size of expense (ratios 55–57; e.g., salaries and benefits/total assets). Recent bank mergers that attempted to cut costs used these breakdowns as key variables in determining the desirability of the merger. For our banks, these ratios follow:

	North Fork Bancorp	Firstier Financial	Boatmen's Bancshares
$\dfrac{\text{Salaries and benefits}}{\text{Noninterest income}}$	$\dfrac{33.89}{20.79} = 163.01\%$	$\dfrac{49.25}{57.42} = 85.77\%$	$\dfrac{597.21}{673.38} = 88.69\%$
$\dfrac{\text{Expense of premises and fixed assets}}{\text{Noninterest income}}$	$\dfrac{11.36}{20.79} = 54.64\%$	$\dfrac{13.11}{57.42} = 22.83\%$	$\dfrac{175.83}{673.38} = 26.11\%$
$\dfrac{\text{Other noninterest expense}}{\text{Noninterest income}}$	$\dfrac{22.25}{20.79} = 107.02\%$	$\dfrac{64.42}{57.42} = 112.19\%$	$\dfrac{425.96}{673.38} = 63.26\%$

---

[12]For example, for Boatmen's Bancshares, the denominator of each of the four ratios ($2,319.77 + 673.38 = $2,993.15) less the sum of the numerators of the four ratios ($1,105.70 + 46.70 + 1,199.00 + 222.92 = $2,574.32) is $418.83, which is the net income reported for Boatmen's Bancshares in Table 8–3.

$\dfrac{\text{Salaries and benefits}}{\text{Total assets}}$	$\dfrac{33.89}{3{,}282.45} = 1.03\%$	$\dfrac{49.25}{3{,}779.18} = 1.30\%$ $\qquad$ $\dfrac{597.21}{33{,}703.80} = 1.77\%$
$\dfrac{\text{Expenses of premises and fixed assets}}{\text{Total assets}}$	$\dfrac{11.36}{3{,}282.45} = 0.35\%$	$\dfrac{13.11}{3{,}779.18} = 0.35\%$ $\qquad$ $\dfrac{175.83}{33{,}703.80} = 0.52\%$
$\dfrac{\text{Other noninterest expense}}{\text{Total assets}}$	$\dfrac{22.25}{3{,}282.45} = 0.68\%$	$\dfrac{64.42}{3{,}779.18} = 1.70\%$ $\qquad$ $\dfrac{425.96}{33{,}703.80} = 1.26\%$

Asset Utilization. The AU ratio measures the extent to which the bank's assets generate revenue. The breakdown of the AU ratio separates the total revenue generated into interest income and noninterest income as follows

$$\text{Asset utilization ratio} = \frac{\text{Total operating income}}{\text{Total assets}} = \frac{\text{Interest income}}{\text{ratio}} + \frac{\text{Noninterest income}}{\text{ratio}}$$

where

$$\text{Interest income ratio (ratio 58)} = \frac{\text{Interest income}}{\text{Total assets}}$$

$$\text{Noninterest income ratio (ratio 59)} = \frac{\text{Noninterest income}}{\text{Total assets}}$$

which measures the bank's ability to generate interest income and noninterest income, respectively. For the banks represented in Tables 8–1 and 8–3, the value of these ratios are as follows

	North Fork Bancorp	Firstier Financial	Boatmen's Bancshares
Interest income ratio	$\dfrac{226.08}{3{,}282.45} = 6.89\%$	$\dfrac{262.04}{3{,}779.18} = 6.93\%$	$\dfrac{2{,}319.77}{33{,}703.80} = 6.88\%$
Noninterest income ratio	$\dfrac{20.79}{3{,}282.45} = 0.63\%$	$\dfrac{57.42}{3{,}779.18} = 1.52\%$	$\dfrac{673.38}{33{,}703.80} = 2.00\%$

The interest income and noninterest income ratios are not necessarily independent. For example, the bank's ability to generate loans affects both interest income and, through fees and service charges, noninterest income. High values for these ratios signify the efficient use of bank resources to generate income and are thus generally positive for the bank. But some problematic situations that result in high ratio values could exist; for example, a bank that replaces low-risk, low-return loans with high-risk, high-return loans will experience an increase in its interest income ratio. However, high-risk loans have a higher default probability, which could result in the ultimate loss of both interest and principal payments. Further breakdowns of these ratios are therefore valuable tools in the financial performance evaluation process.

The interest income ratio can be broken down using the various components of interest income (ratios 60–69; e.g., income on C&I loans/total assets), or by using asset yield (ratios 70–78; e.g., income on C&I loans/dollar value of C&I loans), or by using size of investment (e.g., dollar value of C&I loans/total assets—ratios 79–92—or dollar value of C&I

loans/total earning assets—ratios 93–102). Off-balance-sheet activities can also be measured in terms of the size of the contingencies they create in relation to bank assets (ratios 103–109; e.g., loan commitments/total assets). The noninterest income ratio can also be subdivided into the various subcategories (e.g., income from fiduciary activities/total assets—ratios 110–115—or income from fiduciary activities/noninterest income—ratios 116–121).

Other Ratios

A number of other profit measures are commonly used to evaluate bank performance. Three of these are the net interest margin, the spread (ratio), and overhead efficiency.

net interest margin

Interest income minus interest expense divided by earning assets.

Net Interest Margin.   **Net interest margin** (ratio 6) measures the net return on the bank's earning assets (investment securities and loans and leases) and is defined as follows

$$\text{Net interest margin} = \frac{\text{Net interest income}}{\text{Earning assets}} = \frac{\text{Interest income} - \text{Interest expense}}{\text{Investment securities} + \text{Net loans and leases}}$$

Generally, the higher this ratio, the better. Suppose, however, that the preceding scenario (replacement of low-risk, low-return loans with high-risk, high-return loans) is the reason for the increase. This situation can increase risk for the bank; it highlights the fact that looking at returns without looking at risk can be misleading and potentially dangerous in terms of bank solvency and long-run survivability.

spread

The difference between lending and deposit rates.

The Spread.   The **spread** (ratio 7) measures the difference between the average yield of earning assets and average cost of interest-bearing liabilities and is thus another measure of return on the bank's assets. The spread is defined as

$$\text{Spread} = \frac{\text{Interest income}}{\text{Earning assets}} - \frac{\text{Interest expense}}{\text{Interest-bearing liabilities}}$$

The higher the spread, the more profitable is the bank but again, the source of a high spread and the potential risk implications should be considered.

overhead efficiency

A bank's ability to generate noninterest income to cover noninterest expense.

Overhead Efficiency.   **Overhead efficiency** (ratio 8) measures the bank's ability to generate noninterest income to cover noninterest expenses. It is represented as

$$\text{Overhead efficiency} = \frac{\text{Noninterest income}}{\text{Noninterest expense}}$$

The higher this ratio, the better, but, because of the high levels of noninterest expense relative to noninterest income, it is rarely higher than 1 (or in percentage terms, greater than 100 percent). The values of these ratios for the three banks are as follows:

	North Fork Bancorp	Firstier Financial	Boatmen's Bancshares
Net interest margin	$\dfrac{142.36}{3,063.64} = 4.65\%$	$\dfrac{132.76}{3,302.71} = 4.02\%$	$\dfrac{1,214.07}{29,560.62} = 4.11\%$
Spread	$\dfrac{226.08}{3,063.64} - \dfrac{83.72}{2,495.03} = 4.02\%$	$\dfrac{262.04}{3,302.71} - \dfrac{129.28}{2,719.71} = 3.18\%$	$\dfrac{2,319.77}{29,560.62} - \dfrac{1,105.70}{24,444.83} = 3.32\%$
Overhead efficiency	$\dfrac{20.79}{67.50} = 30.80\%$	$\dfrac{57.42}{126.78} = 45.29\%$	$\dfrac{673.38}{1,199.00} = 56.16\%$

Concept Questions

1. What are two scenarios in which a high value of ROE may signal a risk problem for a bank?
2. Into what ratios can ROA be broken down?
3. What does *spread* measure?

IMPACT OF MARKET NICHE ON FINANCIAL STATEMENTS: A COMPARATIVE ANALYSIS OF TWO BANKS OF SIMILAR SIZE

As mentioned earlier, in 1995 North Fork Bancorp was a profitable and efficient bank that specialized in real estate loans and low-cost funding methods. Firstier, on the other hand, operated more with a balanced portfolio of both assets and liabilities. Keeping the market niche of North Fork Bancorp in mind, let us make a comparative financial analysis using the ROE framework and the banks' 1995 financial statements.

ROE and Its Components. As stated, the ROE (ratio 1) of 16.18% for North Fork Bancorp (NFB) was significantly higher than the 14.14% ROE reported for Firstier Financial (FF). NFB's relatively high profitability compared to that of FF is also seen in the high NIM (ratio 6; 4.65 percent for NFB, 4.02 percent for FF) and spread (ratio 7; 4.02 percent for NFB, 3.18 percent for FF). NFB was earning an overall higher rate on its assets relative to FF (ratios 70–78). The breakdown of ROE indicates that NFB's higher profitability was due to its ROA of 1.52 percent compared with that of 1.25 percent for FF (ratio 2). NFB's equity multiplier or leverage (ratio 3) was, in fact, below that of FF. NFB's EM of 10.63X translated to an equity to asset ratio (=1/EM) of 9.41 percent, and the FF's EM of 11.34X translated to an equity to asset ratio of 8.82 percent. Thus, although both banks appeared to be well capitalized, NFB had less leverage. The nondiversified nature of NFB's loan portfolio (it held mainly real estate loans; see ratio 81) made it more susceptible to earnings swings. This may be one reason for its extra equity cushion.

ROA and Its Components. ROA can be broken down into profit margin (PM) and asset utilization (AU) ratios. NFB's PM (ratio 4) was also significantly higher than that of FF. NFB produced 20.25 cents of net profit per dollar of operating revenue while FF produced only 14.75 cents of net profit. By breaking the PM down into its components (ratios 9–12), we see that low levels of interest expense and noninterest expense were driving the high ROA ratio for NFB.

An examination of the liability expenses (ratios 13–20) indicates that NFB was using less of its operating income to cover each of its liability expenses except for Other Savings Deposits. Further, NFB was paying less than FF on each of its liabilities except Other Savings Deposits (2.52 percent for NFB, 2.17 percent for FF) and Other Borrowed Funds (11.00 percent for NFB, 6.24 percent for FF). Although at year-end 1995 NFB was using many more Other Savings relative to Total Assets than FF (item 35; 25.07 percent for NFB and 3.59 percent for FF), NFB was using few of the relatively expensive Other Borrowed Funds (item 40; 0.30 percent for NFB and 4.51 percent for FF). These year-end levels may explain the large difference in the rates on Other Borrowed Funds for the two banks.

Finally, the extra interest NFB paid on its Other Savings Deposits combined with its extensive use of these deposits was more than made up by the wide margins of savings NFB had over FF for the other liability accounts. NFB's use of more equity (i.e., less debt) also contributed to the low interest expense.

Looking at noninterest expense as a percentage of total operating income (ratios 21–23), NFB was using less of its operating income to cover salaries and employee benefits and other noninterest expenses than FF was and only slightly more for expenses of premises and fixed assets. The ratios of noninterest expenses to total assets (ratios 55–57) also highlight the differences in operating efficiency across the two banks. NFB's salaries and employee benefits (1.03 percent), expenses of premises and fixed assets (0.35 percent), and other noninterest expenses (0.68 percent) to total assets were in all cases less than or equal to those of FF (1.30 percent, 0.35 percent, and 1.70 percent, respectively). On the other hand, from ratios 52-54, salaries and employee benefits to noninterest income (163.01 percent) and expenses of premises and fixed assets to noninterest income (54.64 percent) for NFB were both significantly higher than those for FF (85.77 percent and 22.83 percent, respectively). As discussed later, this probably results from NFB's limited generation of noninterest income, not to a lack of expense control.

The asset utilization ratio (ratio 5) of 7.52 percent indicates that NFB was producing less income per dollar of assets than FF, which had an asset utilization ratio of 8.45 percent. Breaking the AU ratio into its components (interest income ratio and noninterest income ratio), we see that NFB was below FF on both sources of income. From ratios 58 and 59, NFB produced 6.89 cents of interest income and 0.63 cents of noninterest income per dollar of assets while FF produced 6.93 cents and 1.52 cents of income, respectively.

As for the generation of interest income, NFB had 51.27 percent of its assets in the form of real estate loans (ratio 81). The yield on these loans (ratio 71) was 8.65 percent, less than the 8.80 percent FF was earning. FF had a more balanced loan portfolio (see ratios 80–83) and was earning a higher yield than NFB on real estate and consumer loans (see ratios 70–73). In NFB's favor, it held fewer funds in cash and due from accounts compared to FF's holdings (3.24 percent of total assets for NFB and 9.12 percent for FF; see ratio 79). Instead, NFB appears to have put excess cash revenues into investment securities (mainly other debt and equity securities; see ratios 86–90). From ratios 75–78, however, we see that NFB was earning generally lower yields on investment securities.

Regarding the generation of noninterest income, NFB had little, if any, noninterest income to total assets relative to FF (see ratios 110–115). In addition, service charges represented the main source of noninterest income for NFB (52.14 percent) with trading accounts and foreign transactions sources of zero income (see ratios 116–120). FF generated noninterest income mainly from fiduciary activities and service charges. Again, NFB's niche strategy of customer service (i.e., retail banking) could explain such differences.

Summary Comments.   Although NFB was more profitable than FF, the sources of NFB's profits appear to have come from the cost side of the balance sheet rather than the revenue side, specifically because of its ability to fund assets cheaply (low interest expense) and to operate efficiently (low noninterest expense). NFB's income or revenue generation was, in fact, weaker than FF's. The niche NFB attempted to fill (concentration of real estate loans funded with cheap liabilities and provision of high-quality customer service) resulted in a more profitable bank compared to that of FF. However, the lack of diversification in NFB's loan portfolio and the relatively low rates on those loans left NFB susceptible to credit risk. Subsequent chapters evaluate credit risk as well as the other types of risks to which banks are exposed.

IMPACT OF SIZE ON FINANCIAL STATEMENT ANALYSIS

Bank size has traditionally affected the financial ratios of commercial banks, resulting in significant differences across size groups (see Chapter 3). Large banks' relatively easy access to purchased funds and capital markets compared to small bank's access is a reason for many of these differences. For example, large banks with easier access to capital markets operate with lower amounts of equity capital than do small banks. Also, large banks tend to use more purchased funds (such as fed funds and RPs) and fewer core deposits than do small banks. Large banks tend to put more into salaries, premises, and other expenses than small banks do, and they tend to diversify their operations and services more than small banks do. Large banks also generate more noninterest income (i.e., trading account, derivative security, and foreign trading income) than small banks do and when risky loans pay off, they earn more interest income. As a result, although large banks tend to hold less equity than small banks do, large banks do not necessarily return more on their assets. A recent study by the Federal Reserve Bank of St. Louis[13] reported that ROA consistently increased for banks grouped by size up to $15 billion in total assets but decreased for banks with more than $15 billion (see also Chapter 3).

Examining ratios for the relatively large Boatmen's Bancshares (BB) compared to the smaller FF and NFB banks, we see many of these size-related effects on accounting ratios. The EM (ratio 3) shows that BB (EM = 11.51X) uses slightly less equity to fund total assets than FF uses (EM = 11.34X) and much less than NFB uses (EM = 10.63X). Looking at ROA (ratio 2), BB is the least profitable of the three banks. Notice that BB is producing the lowest income per dollar of total operating income (ratio 4; PM for BB = 13.99 percent; for NFB = 20.25 percent; and for FF 14.75 percent) but is producing the most operating income per dollar of assets (AU for BB = 8.88 percent, for NFB = 7.52 percent, and for FF = 8.45 percent; see ratio 5). The generation of total operating income in the form of interest income (ratio 58) is about the same for all three banks (interest income ratio for BB = 6.88 percent, for NFB = 6.89 percent, and for FF = 6.93 percent). However, looking at ratio 59, BB generates more noninterest income (2.00 percent of total assets) than NFB (0.63 percent of total assets) or FF (1.52 percent of total assets). This is likely due to BB's relatively large amount of OBS activities (which is typical of large banks compared with small banks). In addition, BB's other assets (i.e., premises and equipment) are 5.84 percent of total assets compared to 3.43 percent for NFB and 3.49 percent for FF (ratio 92). The addition of ratios 21 and 22 indicates that salaries and employee benefits plus expenses of premises and fixed assets are much higher for BB (25.82 percent of total operating income) than for NFB (18.33 percent) or FF (19.52 percent).

Uncharacteristically, BB is using fewer purchased funds to total assets than NFB and FF (see ratio 42). Notice too that BB's net loans and leases (ratio 85) are 57.50 percent of total assets, compared with 58.38 percent and 58.54 percent for NFB and FF, respectively. Finally, despite the size-related differences across the three banks, BB's ROE (ratio 1) is only slightly higher than that of FF and is well below that of NFB.

---

[13]See D.C. Wheelock, "A Changing Relationship between Bank Size and Profitability," *Monetary Trends*, Federal Reserve Bank of St. Louis, September, 1996, p. 1.

Concept Questions

1. How did North Fork Bancorp's niche strategy affect its profitability relative to Firstier Financial?
2. How does the access of funds from the capital markets affect the financial ratios of large banks relative to small banks?

• •

SUMMARY

This chapter analyzed the financial statements of commercial banks. The financial statements of other FIs such as savings banks, credit unions, and insurance companies take a similar form as well. The assets, liabilities, and equity capital were described as they appear in the balance sheet (report of condition). The income and expenses were described as they appear in the income statement (report of income). From the items on the financial statements, the profitability of three banks was analyzed using a return on equity framework. Many problems and areas of managerial concern can be identified by performing a detailed breakdown of the financial ratios of FIs. What might appear as a favorable sign of profitability and performance can sometimes, in fact, indicate risk problems that management should address. Thus, both profitability and risk management are interlinked and should be of concern to managers. The chapter discussed how ideal ratios may vary for an FI depending on the niche it attempts to fill or its size. The various risks to which FIs are exposed are examined in more detail in the next several chapters.

PERTINENT WEB SITES

Federal Deposit Insurance Corp.   http://www.fdic.gov/.

Federal Financial Institutions Examination Council   http://www.ffiec.gov/

Federal Home Loan Mortgage Corp.   http://www.freddiemac.com/

Federal National Mortgage Association   http://www.fanniemae.com/

Government National Mortgage Assc.   http://www.ginniemae.gov/

Evaluating the Performance of Financial Intermediaries

1. How does a bank's report of condition differ from its report of income?
2. Match these three types of cash balances with the functions that they serve:

    a. Vault cash
    b. Deposits at the Federal Reserve
    c. Deposits at other FIs

    1. Meet legal reserve requirements
    2. Used to purchase services
    3. Meet customer withdrawals

3. Classify the following accounts (1–15) into one of the following categories (a–f):

    a. Assets
    b. Liabilities
    c. Equity
    d. Revenue
    e. Expense
    f. Off-Balance-Sheet activities

    1. Services charged on deposit accounts
    2. Retail CDs
    3. Surplus and paid-in capital
    4. Loan commitments
    5. Consumer loans
    6. Federal funds sold
    7. Swaps
    8. Interest on municipals
    9. Interest on NOW accounts
    10. NOW accounts

11. Commercial letters of credit
12. Leases
13. Retained earnings
14. Provision for loan losses
15. Interest on U.S. Treasury securities

4. If we examine a typical bank's asset portion of the balance sheet, how are the assets arranged in terms of expected return and liquidity?

5. Repurchase agreements are listed as both assets and liabilities in Table 8–1. How can an account be both an asset and a liability?

6. How does a NOW account differ from a demand deposit?

7. How does a retail CD differ from a wholesale CD?

8. How do core deposits differ from purchased funds?

9. What are the major categories of off-balance-sheet activities?

10. A bank is considering two securities: a 30-year Treasury bond yielding 7 percent and a 30-year municipal bond yielding 5 percent. If the bank's tax rate is 30 percent, which bond offers the higher tax-equivalent yield?

11. A bank is considering an investment in a municipal security that offers a yield of 6 percent. What is this security's tax equivalent yield if the bank's tax rate is 35 percent?

12. How does a bank's annual net income compare with its annual cash flow?

13. How might the use of an end-of-the-year balance sheet bias the calculation of certain ratios?

14. How does the asset utilization ratio for a bank compare to that of a retail company? How do the equity multipliers compare?

15. Smallville Bank has the following balance sheet, rates earned on its assets, and rates paid on its liabilities.

Balance Sheet (in thousands)

Assets		Rate Earned (%)
Cash and due from banks	$ 6,000	4
Investment securities	22,000	8
Repurchase agreements	12,000	6
Loans less allowance for losses	80,000	10
Fixed assets	10,000	0
Other assets	4,000	9
Total assets	$134,000	

Liabilities and Equity		Rate Paid (%)
Demand deposits	$9,000	0
NOW accounts	69,000	5
Retail CDs	18,000	7
Subordinated debentures	14,000	8
Total liabilities	$110,000	
Common stock	10,000	
Paid in capital surplus	13,000	
Retained earnings	11,000	
Total liabilities and equity	$134,000	

If the bank earns $120,000 in noninterest income, incurs $80,000 in noninterest expenses, and pays $2,500,000 in taxes, what is it's net income?

16. Megalopolis Bank has the following balance sheet and income statement.

Balance Sheet (in millions)

Assets

Cash and due from banks	$ 9,000
Investment securities	23,000
Repurchase agreements	42,000
Loans	90,000
Fixed assets	15,000
Other assets	4,000
Total assets	$183,000

Liabilities and Equity

Demand deposits	$19,000
NOW accounts	89,000
Retail CDs	28,000
Debentures	19,000
Total liabilities	$155,000
Common stock	12,000
Paid in capital	4,000
Retained earnings	12,000
Total liabilities and equity	$183,000

Income Statement

Interest on fees and loans	9,000
Interest on investment securities	4,000
Interest on repurchase agreements	6,000
Interest on deposits in banks	1,000
Total interest income	20,000
Interest on deposits	9,000
Interest on debentures	2,000
Total interest expense	11,000

Operating income	9,000
Provision for loan losses	2,000
Other income	2,000
Other expenses	1,000
Income before taxes	10,000
Taxes	3,000
Net income	7,000

For Megalopolis, calculate the following:

a. Return on equity
b. Return on assets
c. Asset utilization
d. Equity multiplier
e. Profit margin
f. Interest expense ratio
g. Provision for loan loss ratio
h. Noninterest expense ratio
i. Tax ratio

17. What is the likely relationship between the interest income ratio and the noninterest income ratio?

18. Anytown Bank has the following ratios:
a. Profit margin: 21%
b. Asset utilization: 11%
c. Equity multiplier: 12 times.
Calculate Anytown's ROE and ROA.

19. A security analyst calculates the following ratios for two banks. How should the analyst evaluate the financial health of the two banks?

	Bank A	Bank B
Return on equity	22%	24%
Return on assets	2%	1%
Equity multiplier	11 times	16 times
Profit margin	15%	14%
Asset utilization	13%	11%
Spread	3%	3%
Interest expense ratio	35%	40%
Provision for loan loss ratio	1%	4%

20. What problems or opportunities might ratio analysis fail to identify?

21. Go to the FDIC web site and find the total number of deposits for Fleet National Bank in Providence, Rhode Island.

Chapter Nine

Risks of Financial Intermediation

Chapter 8 looked at a method to evaluate the profitability, or return on equity (ROE), of a financial intermediary (FI). As has been mentioned, one objective of FI management is to increase the FI's returns. This often comes, however, at the cost of increased risk. The remainder of the textbook examines the measurement and management of the various returns and risks facing FIs beginning with those from traditional balance sheet activities (credit risk, liquidity risk, insolvency risk, interest rate risk, and market risk) followed by those off the balance sheet (off-balance-sheet risk), and ending with other types of risk (technology risk, operational risk, foreign exchange risk, and country or sovereign risk). Table 9–1 presents a brief definition of each of these risks. The effective management of these risks is central to an FI's performance. This chapter introduces the fundamental risks that modern FIs face. By the end of this chapter, you will have a basic understanding of the variety and complexity of the risks facing managers of modern FIs.

Table **9–1**

RISKS FACED BY FINANCIAL INTERMEDIARIES

Credit Risk   The risk that promised cash flows from loans and securities held by FIs may not be paid in full.

Liquidity Risk   The risk that a sudden surge in liability withdrawals may require an FI to liquidate assets in a very short period of time and at low prices.

Interest Rate Risk   The risk incurred by an FI when the maturities of its assets and liabilities are mismatched.

Market Risk   The risk incurred in trading assets and liabilities due to changes in interest rates, exchange rates, and other asset prices.

Off-Balance-Sheet Risk   The risk incurred by an FI as the result of activities related to contingent assets and liabilities.

Technology Risk   The risk incurred by an FI when its technological investments do not produce anticipated cost savings.

Operational Risk   The risk that existing technology or support systems may malfunction or break down.

Foreign Exchange Risk   The risk that exchange rate changes can affect the value of an FI's assets and liabilities located abroad.

Country or Sovereign Risk   The risk that repayments from foreign borrowers may be interrupted because of interference from foreign governments.

Insolvency Risk   The risk that an FI may not have enough capital to offset a sudden decline in the value of its assets.

CREDIT

RISK

credit risk

The risk that the promised cash flows from loans and securities held by FIs may not be paid in full.

Credit risk arises because of the possibility that promised cash flows on the financial claims held by FIs will not be paid in full. If the principal on all financial claims held by FIs was paid in full on maturity and interest payments were made on their promised dates, FIs would always receive the original principal lent plus an interest return. That is, they would face no credit risk. Should a borrower default, both the principal loaned and the interest payments expected to be received are at risk. As a result, many financial claims issued by individuals or corporations and held by FIs promise a limited or fixed upside return (principal and interest payments to the lender with a high probability) and a large downside risk (loss of loan principal and promised interest with a much smaller probability). Some examples of financial claims issued with these return-risk trade-offs are fixed coupon bonds issued by corporations and bank loans. In both cases, an FI holding these claims as assets earns the coupon on the bond or the interest promised on the loan if no borrower default occurs. In the event of default, the FI earns zero interest on the asset and may lose all or part of the principal lent, depending on its ability to access some of the borrower's assets through bankruptcy and insolvency proceedings. Accordingly, a key role of FIs involves screening and monitoring loan applicants to ensure that they fund only the most creditworthy loans (see Chapter 10).

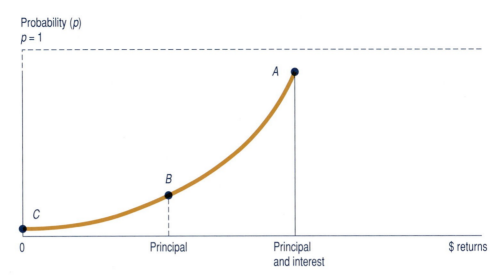

F i g u r e **9–1**   *The Probability Distribution of Dollar Returns on Risky Debt (Loans/Bonds)*

The effect of credit risk is evident in the high rate of delinquencies and charge-offs experienced by credit card companies (such as Advanta Corp. and Capital One Financial) in the late 1990s. Credit card delinquencies increased consistently from the early 1990s until February 1997, meaning that credit card holders were not paying off their debts (both interest and principal) as promised. Even though delinquencies began to decline after February 1997, charge-offs continued to increase, meaning that credit card companies simply gave up trying to collect the principal and interest owed to them by customers, thus writing these loans off as a loss.

Figure 9–1 presents the probability distribution of dollar returns from an FI investing in risky loans or bonds. The distribution indicates a high probability (but less than 1) of repayment of principal and promised interest in full (point *A*). Problems with a borrower's cash flows can result in varying degrees of default risk, including repayment of principal with a partial or complete default on interest payments (the range between point *A* and point *B*) and, if the problems are extreme, even partial or complete default on the principal lent, as well (the range between point *B* and point *C*). Notice too that the probability of a complete default of principal and interest (point *C*) is small (but greater than 0). Because this probability of partial or complete default on bond and loan interest and principal exists, FIs must estimate expected default risk on these assets and demand risk premiums on them equal to that risk exposure.

The return distribution for credit risk suggests that FIs need to monitor them and collect information about individuals and firms whose assets are in their portfolios. Thus, managerial efficiency and credit risk management strategy affect the shape of the loan return distribution. Moreover, the credit risk distribution in Figure 9–1 is for the investment in a single asset exposed to default risk. One of the advantages that FIs have over individual investors is the ability to diversify some credit risk by exploiting the law of large numbers in their asset investment portfolios (see Chapter 1). In the framework of Figure 9–1, diversification across assets exposed to credit risk reduces the overall credit risk in the asset portfolio and thus increases the probability of partial or full repayment of principal and/or interest.

In effect, diversification reduces individual **firm-specific credit risk,** such as the risk specific to holding the bonds or loans of General Motors or IBM, while still leaving the FI

firm-specific credit risk

The risk of default for the borrowing firm associated with the specific types of project risk taken by that firm.

systematic credit risk

The risk of default associated with general economywide or macroconditions affecting all borrowers.

exposed to **systematic credit risk,** such as factors that increase the default risk of all firms in the economy (e.g., an economic recession). Chapter 10 describes methods to measure the default risk of individual corporate claims such as bonds and loans. Chapter 11 investigates methods to measure the risk in portfolios of such claims. Chapter 12 discusses various methods—for example, loan sales and rescheduling—to manage and control credit risk exposures better.

Concept Questions

1. Why does credit risk exist for FIs?
2. How does diversification affect an FI's credit risk exposure?

LIQUIDITY RISK

liquidity risk

The risk that a sudden surge in liability withdrawals may require an FI to liquidate assets in a very short period of time and at low prices.

Liquidity risk arises when an FI's liability holders, such as depositors or insurance policyholders, demand immediate cash for their financial claims. When liability holders demand cash immediately—that is, "put" their financial claim back to the FI—the FI must either borrow additional funds or sell assets to meet the demand for the withdrawal of funds. The most liquid asset of all is cash, which FIs can use directly to meet liability holders' demands to withdraw funds. Although FIs minimize their cash assets because such holdings earn no interest, low holdings are generally not a problem. Day-to-day withdrawals by liability holders are, to a large extent, predictable, and large FIs can normally expect to borrow additional funds to meet any shortfalls of cash on the money and financial markets.

At times, however, FIs face a liquidity crisis. Due to either a lack of confidence in an FI or some unexpected need for cash, liability holders may demand larger withdrawals than normal. When all or many FIs face similar abnormally large cash demands, the cost of additional funds rises and the supply becomes restricted or unavailable. As a consequence, FIs may have to sell some of their less liquid assets to meet the withdrawal demands of liability holders. This results in a more serious liquidity risk; some assets with thin markets generate lower prices when the sale is immediate than when an FI has more time to negotiate the sale. As a result, the liquidation of some assets at low or "fire-sale" prices could threaten an FI's profitability and solvency. Good examples of such illiquid assets are bank loans to small firms. Such serious liquidity problems may eventually result in a run in which all liability claimholders seek to withdraw their funds simultaneously from an FI because they fear that it will be unable to meet their demands for cash in the future. This turns the FI's liquidity problem into a solvency problem and can cause it to fail.

The situation of several Ohio savings institutions in 1985 is an extreme case of liquidity risk. A group of 70 Ohio savings institutions were insured by a private fund, the Ohio Deposit Guarantee Fund (ODGF). One of these savings banks, Home State Savings Bank (HSSB), had invested heavily in a Florida-based government securities dealer, EMS Government Securities, Inc. Alleged fraudulent dealings of EMS resulted in a default on the investment made by HSSB (note the interaction between credit risk and liquidity risk) that in turn made it difficult for HSSB to meet withdrawals of deposits. HSSB's losses from the ESM default were, in fact, so large that the insurance fund could not cover them. Not only was HSSB unable to cover the deposit withdrawals, but also other Ohio savings institutions insured by ODGF were inundated with deposit withdrawals to the extent that they could not cover them. As a result, ODGF–insured institutions were temporarily closed and the state legislature had to step in to cover depositors' claims.

Chapter 13 examines the nature of normal, abnormal, and run-type liquidity risks and their impact on banks, thrifts, insurance companies, and other FIs in more detail. Chapter 14 then looks at liquidity and liability management. Finally, Chapter 15 presents information on deposit insurance and other liability guarantees that seek to deter deposit and other liability runs.

Concept Questions

1. Why might an FI face a sudden liquidity crisis?
2. What circumstances might lead an FI to liquidate assets at fire-sale prices?

INTEREST RATE RISK

interest rate risk

The risk incurred by an FI when the maturities of its assets and liabilities are mismatched.

Chapter 1 discussed asset transformation as a special key function of FIs. *Asset transformation* involves buying primary securities or assets and issuing secondary securities or liabilities. FIs that purchase primary securities often have different maturity characteristics from the secondary securities that the FIs sell. In mismatching the maturities of assets and liabilities as part of their asset transformation function, FIs potentially expose themselves to **interest rate risk.**

Consider, for example, an FI that issues liabilities of one-year maturity to finance the purchase of assets with a two-year maturity. We show this in the following time lines:

Suppose that the cost of funds (liabilities) for an FI is 9 percent per year and the interest return on an asset is 10 percent per year. Over the first year, the FI can lock in a profit spread of 1 percent (10 percent – 9 percent) by borrowing short term (for one year) and lending long term (for two years). Its profits for the second year, however, are uncertain. If the level of interest rates does not change, the FI can *refinance* its liabilities at 9 percent and lock in a 1 percent profit for the second year as well. The risk always exists, however, that interest rates will change between years 1 and 2. If interest rates rise and the FI can borrow only new one-year liabilities at 11 percent in the second year, its profit spread in the second year is actually negative; that is, 10 percent– 11 percent = –1 percent. The positive spread earned in the first year by the FI from holding assets with a longer maturity than its liabilities is offset by a negative spread in the second year. As a result, when an FI holds longer-term assets relative to liabilities, it potentially exposes itself to the interest rate risk that the cost of rolling over or refinancing funds can be more than the return earned on asset investments. The classic example of this mismatch in recent years was demonstrated by U.S. thrifts and savings banks in the 1980s (see Chapter 3).

An alternative balance sheet structure would have the FI borrowing for a longer term than the assets in which it invests. This is shown as follows:

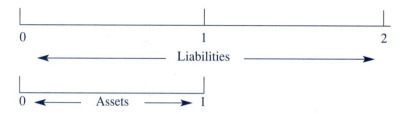

In this case, the FI is also exposed to an interest rate risk; by holding shorter-term assets relative to liabilities, it faces uncertainty about the interest rate at which it can *reinvest* funds borrowed for a longer period. In recent years, good examples of this exposure are banks operating in the Euromarkets that have borrowed fixed-rate deposits while investing in floating-rate loans; that is, loans whose interest rates are changed or adjusted frequently.

In addition to a potential refinancing or reinvestment affect that occurs when interest rates change, an FI faces *economic or present-value* uncertainty as well. Remember that the economic value or "fair" market price of an asset or liability is conceptually equal to the discounted future cash flows on that asset or liability. Therefore, rising interest rates increase the discount rate on those cash flows and reduce the market price or present value of that asset or liability. Conversely, falling interest rates increase the prices or present values of assets and liabilities. Moreover, mismatching maturities by holding longer-term

Contemporary Perspectives 9–1

Insurer Topics; Employee Recruiting and Training; Insurers Are Past the Point of No Return; Facing Volatility in Interest Rates and Squeezed Profit Margins, Companies Must Take a New Approach to Investment

Gone are the days when investment management for insurance companies appeared to work fairly well, and insurers counted on reasonably consistent and solid investment results. The circumstances in which insurers find themselves today have rendered traditional investment approaches inappropriate.

Since the 1970s significant changes have rocked the insurance environment and dramatically impacted the asset and liability sides of insurers' balance sheets. Interest rates became volatile, with rates climbing to unprecedented heights. Life insurers have introduced interest-sensitive products, such that their profits increasingly are driven by managing spreads between the rates they earn on their underlying portfolio and the rates they pay policyholders. . . .

These developments have led to the current predicament: Insurers have become more dependent on investment returns and spreads, in an environment where managing such returns and spreads has become more challenging. . . .

In an attempt to adapt to the changing environment, some managers have tried to address asset/liability management by simply matching the [maturity] of the asset portfolio to that of the liabilities. However, relying only on [maturity] matching can prove very dangerous in the event of significant interest rate changes.... It seems obvious that insurers' earnings targets and surplus needs should be incorporated in developing the investment strategy. . . .

Although a portfolio manager's work should be integrated within the insurer's overall operating framework and requirements, he or she usually is focused on understanding the investment markets. Added influences such as volatile interest rates, complex new securities and competitive pricing cause a widening gap between investment and insurance needs. In the U.S. market, there have been insolvencies because these pressures are not integrated and mastered.

SOURCE: Reprinted with permission from *Business Insurance*, September 16, 1996. © 1996, Crain Communications, Inc. All rights reserved.

assets than liabilities means that when interest rates rise, the economic or present value of the FI's assets fall by a larger amount than do its liabilities. This exposes the FI to the risk of economic loss and insolvency.

If holding assets and liabilities with mismatched maturities exposes FIs to interest rate risk, the FIs can approximately hedge or protect against interest rate risk by matching the maturity of their assets and liabilities. This has resulted in the general philosophy that matching maturities is somehow the best policy for FIs averse to risk. Note, however, that matching maturities is not necessarily consistent with an active asset transformation function for FIs. That is, FIs cannot be asset transformers and direct balance sheet matchers or hedgers at the same time. Although it does reduce exposure to interest rate risk, matching maturities may reduce the FI's profitability because any returns from acting as specialized risk-bearing asset transformers are eliminated. Contemporary Perspectives Box 9–1 highlights how increased interest rate risk has affected the management of insurance companies. We discuss these issues more fully in Chapters 17 and 18 and the methods and instruments to hedge interest rate risk in Chapters 21 through 23.

Concept Questions

1. What is refinancing risk? What type of FI best illustrated this concept in the 1980s?
2. Why does a rise in the level of interest rates adversely affect the market value of both assets and liabilities?
3. What does the concept of *maturity matching* mean?

MARKET RISK

market risk

The risk incurred in trading assets and liabilities due to changes in interest rates, exchange rates, and other asset prices.

Market risk arises when FIs actively trade assets and liabilities (and derivatives) rather than holding them for longer-term investment, funding, or hedging purposes. As discussed in Chapters 1 to 7, the traditional roles of commercial and investment banks have changed in recent years. For large commercial banks such as money center banks, the decline in income from traditional deposit taking and lending activities has been matched by an increase in reliance on income from trading. Similarly, the decline in underwriting and brokerage income for the large investment banks has also been met by more active and aggressive trading in securities and other assets.

To understand the type of risk involved in active trading, consider the case of Barings, the 200-year-old British merchant bank that failed in February 1995 as the result of trading losses. In this case, the bank (or, more specifically, one trader, Nick Leeson) bet that the Japanese Nikkei Stock Market Index would rise; he bought futures on that index (some $8 billion worth). For a number of reasons—including the Kobe earthquake—the index actually fell, however. As a result, over a period of one month, the bank lost more than $1.2 billion on its trading positions, rendering the bank insolvent.[1] That is, the losses on its futures positions exceeded the bank's own equity capital resources. Of course, if the Nikkei Index had actually risen, the bank would have made very large profits and might still be in business today.

---

[1] Barings was eventually acquired by ING, a Dutch bank.

Contemporary Perspectives 9–2

Risk-Management Models Kept Even Keel in Topsy-Turvy Week

Banks successfully used computerized risk-management models to limit their losses in this week's turbulent stock and bond markets, according to regulators and bankers. "There has been no material financial impact on any of the banks we regulate at this point," said Michael L. Brosnan, director of treasury and market risk at the Office of the Comptroller of the Currency. "That is an indicator that these models work." "People know what their exposure is," a Federal Reserve official said. "The models have been very useful. We expect this to be a wash for most banks."

This month's 12 percent drop in the Dow Jones Industrial Average, capped off by Monday's 554 point loss, was the first major test for market-risk models, which more than 50 banks are using to manage their exposure to fluctuations in securities prices.

Kevin Blakely, executive vice president for risk management at KeyCorp. said the company's losses and gains always remained within the range the model predicted. "So far, so good," Mr. Blakely said. "The model seems to be holding up and giving us the right kind of reads. There were no significant surprises." "Our model has worked during this turbulent week," said Louis A. Schmidt Jr., managing director at First Union Capital Markets. "The value-at-risk methodology told us what our risk was, and we have had no reason to question it."

Regulators said they plan an in-depth review of the performance of the models once the markets settle down. "This is not the right time to ask too many questions," the Fed official said. "Events are still occurring. But once things calm down, we will follow up." "If we see a hole where someone lost more than expected, then we are going to investigate," Mr. Brosnan said. Mr. Brosnan warned bankers not to become complacent. Computer models need to be updated and tested constantly to ensure they are working properly, he said. Also, bankers should limit their exposure to any single security. This is particularly important for securities in developing countries, where prices often fluctuate wildly. "If everyone does their job right, we will not see any material losses," he said.

SOURCE: Jaret Seiberg, *The American Banker,* October 31, 1997, p. 3. Reprinted with permission—American Banker.

As this example illustrates, trading or market risk is present when an FI takes an open or unhedged long (buy) or short (sell) position in bonds, equities, commodities, and derivatives and prices change in a direction opposite to that expected. As a result, the more volatile are asset prices, the greater are the market risks faced by FIs that adopt open trading positions. This requires FI management (and regulators) to establish controls to limit positions taken by traders as well as models to measure the market risk exposure of an FI on a day-to-day basis. As Contemporary Perspectives Box 9–2 points out, in their first major test, these controls did their job in protecting FIs against extreme market volatility experienced at the end of 1997 brought on by the collapse of most Southeast Asian currencies. These market risk measurement controls are discussed in Chapter 19.

Concept Questions

1. What is trading or market risk?
2. What modern conditions have led to an increase in this particular type of risk for FIs?
3. As the volatility of asset prices increases, does market risk increase, decrease, or remain constant? Why?

OFF-BALANCE-SHEET RISK

off-balance-sheet risk

The risk incurred by an FI as the result of activities related to contingent assets and liabilities.

letter of credit

A credit guarantee issued by an FI for a fee on which payment is contingent on some future event occurring, most notably default of the agent that purchases the letter of credit.

One of the most striking trends involving modern FIs has been the growth in their off-balance-sheet activities and thus, their **off-balance-sheet risk.** An off-balance-sheet activity, by definition, does not appear on the current balance sheet because it does not involve holding a *current primary claim* (asset) or the issuance of a *current secondary claim* (liability). Instead, off-balance-sheet activities affect the *future shape* of an FI's balance sheet because they involve the creation of contingent assets and liabilities. As such, accountants place them "below the bottom line" on an FI's balance sheet. A good example of off-balance-sheet activity is the issuance of standby **letter of credit** guarantees by insurance companies and banks to back the issuance of municipal bonds. Many state and local governments could not issue such securities without a bank or insurance company *letter of credit guarantees* promising principal and interest payments to investors should the municipality default on its obligations in the future. Thus, the letter of credit guarantees payment should a municipal government (e.g., New York state) face financial problems in paying either the promised interest and/or principal on the bonds it issues. If a municipal government's cash flow is sufficiently strong to pay off the principal and interest on the debt it issues, the letter of credit guarantee issued by an FI expires unused. Nothing appears on the FI's balance sheet today or in the future. The fee earned for issuing the letter of credit guaranty appears, however, on the FI's income statement (see Chapter 8).

As a result, the ability to earn fee income while not loading up or expanding the balance sheet has become an important motivation for FIs to pursue off-balance-sheet business. Unfortunately, this activity is not risk free. Suppose that a municipal government defaults on its bond interest and principal payments. Then the contingent liability or guarantee that the FI issued becomes an actual or real balance sheet liability. That is, the FI must use its own funds to compensate investors in municipal bonds.

A letter of credit is just one example of off-balance-sheet activities. Others include loan commitments by banks; mortgage servicing contracts by thrifts; and positions in forwards, futures, swaps, options, and other derivative securities by almost all large FIs. Some of these activities are structured to reduce an FI's exposure to credit, interest rate, or foreign exchange risks, but mismanagement or inappropriate use of these instruments can result in major losses for the FI. We detail the specific nature of the risks of off-balance-sheet activities more fully in Chapter 20.

Concept Questions

1. Why are letter of credit guarantees an off-balance-sheet item?
2. Why are FIs motivated to pursue off-balance-sheet business? What are the risks?

TECHNOLOGY AND OPERATIONAL RISKS

Central to FIs' decision-making process is the cost of inputs or factors used to produce bank services both on and off the balance sheet. Two important factors are labor (tellers, credit officers) and capital (building, machinery, furniture). Crucial to the efficient management and combination of these inputs (which result in financial outputs at the lowest cost) is technology. Technological innovation has been a major concern of FIs in recent years. In the 1980s and 1990s, banks, insurance companies, and investment companies have sought to improve operational efficiency with major investments in internal and external communications, computers, and an expanded technological infrastructure. Good examples are the automated teller machine (ATM) networks developed by banks at the retail level and the automated clearing houses (ACH) and wire transfer payment networks such as the Clearing House Interbank Payments Systems (CHIPS) developed at the wholesale level. Indeed, a global financial service firm such as Citicorp has operations in more than 80 countries connected in real time by a proprietary-owned satellite system.

The objectives of technological expansion are to lower operating costs, increase profits, and capture new markets for the FI. In current terminology, the object is to allow the FI to exploit better potential economies of scale and economies of scope in selling its products. **Economies of scale** imply an FI's ability to lower its average costs of operations by expanding its output of financial services. **Economies of scope** imply an FI's ability to generate cost synergies by producing more than one output with the same inputs. For example, an FI could use the same information on the quality of customers stored in its computers to expand the sale of both loan products and insurance products. That is, the same information (e.g., age, job, size of family, or income) can identify both potential loan and life insurance customers.

Technology risk occurs when technological investments do not produce the anticipated cost savings in economies of scale or scope. Diseconomies of scale, for example, arise because of excess capacity, redundant technology, and/or organizational and bureaucratic inefficiencies (red tape) that become worse problems as an FI grows. Diseconomies of scope arise when an FI fails to generate perceived synergies or cost savings through major new technology investments. Chapter 24 describes the measurement and evidence of economies of scale and scope in FIs. Technological risk can result in major losses in an FI's competitive efficiency and ultimately result in its long-term failure. Similarly, gains from technological investments can produce performance superior to an FI's rivals as well as allow it to develop new and innovative products enhancing its long-term survival chances.

Operational risk is partly related to technology risk and can arise when existing technology malfunctions or back-office support systems break down. For example, major banks use the federal funds market both to sell to and buy funds from other banks for periods as short as a day. Their payment messages travel along a wire transfer network called *Fedwire*. Suppose that the Bank of New York wished to lend federal funds to Bank of America. The Bank of New York transmits an electronic message instructing the Federal Reserve Bank of New York to deduct reserves from its account and sends a message by Fedwire to credit the Bank of America's account at its own Federal Reserve Bank. Thus, funds are credited to Bank of America's account at the Federal Reserve Bank of San Francisco. Normally, this system functions highly efficiently. Occasionally, however, risk exposures such as that actually faced by the Bank of New York in 1985 can arise. Specifically, the Bank of New York's computer system failed to register incoming payment (funds borrowed) messages on Fedwire but continued to process outbound (funds lent) messages. As a result, at the end of the day, the bank faced a huge net payment position on funds lent that it had to settle with other banks. The Bank of New York could do this only by arranging emergency loans from the Federal Reserve. Even though such computer glitches are rare, their occurrence can cause major problems for the FIs involved and potentially disrupt the financial system in general. Indeed, considerable concerns have been raised about FIs' computer systems and payment systems in the year 2000 as a result of the so-called millennium bug (i.e., the inability of computer codes to read the year 2000 correctly).

economies of scale

The degrees to which an FI's average unit costs to produce financial services fall as its output of services increases.

economies of scope

The degrees to which an FI can generate cost synergies by producing multiple financial service products.

technology risk

The risk incurred by an FI when its technological investments do not produce anticipated cost savings.

operational risk

The risk that existing technology or support systems may malfunction or break down.

Back-office support systems combine labor and technology to provide clearance, settlement, and other services to back FIs' underlying on- and off-balance-sheet transactions. Prior to 1975, most transactions among securities firms and their customers were paper based. As the market volume of trades rose, severe backlogs in settling and clearing transactions occurred because of the general inefficiency of decentralized paper-based systems. Such problems have stimulated the development of centralized depositories as well as computerized trading and settlement in the securities industry.

The failure of these systems as well as the downside of operational risk is evident in the Wells Fargo/First Interstate merger. Wells Fargo wanted to make the merger process easy for First Interstate customers by allowing them to use up their old checks and deposit forms, but customer account numbers had been changed as a result of the merger. Therefore, some deposits were not posted to the proper accounts, resulting in a deluge of unfairly bounced checks. Further, Wells Fargo's back-office operations were thinly staffed and unable to find where all the misplaced deposits had gone. Promising to reimburse all customers for the accounting mistakes, Wells Fargo eventually corrected the problem, incurring an operating loss of some $180 million.

Concept Questions

1. What is the difference between economies of scale and economies of scope?
2. How is operational risk related to technology risk?
3. How does technological expansion help an FI better exploit economies of scale and economies of scope? When might technology risk interfere with these goals?

FOREIGN EXCHANGE RISK

FIs have increasingly recognized that both direct foreign investment and foreign portfolio investments can extend the operational and financial benefits available from purely domestic investments. Thus, in the mid-1990s U.S. pension funds held approximately 5 percent of their assets in foreign securities; this is projected to rise to 10 percent by the year 2000. Japanese pension funds currently hold more than 30 percent of their assets in foreign securities plus an additional 10 percent in foreign currency deposits. To the extent that the returns on domestic and foreign investments are imperfectly correlated, FIs have risk-reduction opportunities.

The returns on domestic and foreign direct investments and portfolio investments are not perfectly correlated for two reasons. The first is that the underlying technologies of various economies differ as do the firms in those economies. For example, one economy may be agriculture based and another industry based. Given different economic infrastructures, one economy could be expanding while another is contracting. The second reason is that exchange rate changes are not perfectly correlated across countries. For example, the dollar-deutsche mark exchange rate may be appreciating while the dollar-yen exchange rate may be falling.

One potential benefit to an FI from becoming increasingly global in its outlook is the ability to expand abroad directly through branches or acquisition or by extending a financial asset portfolio to include foreign as well as domestic securities. Even so,

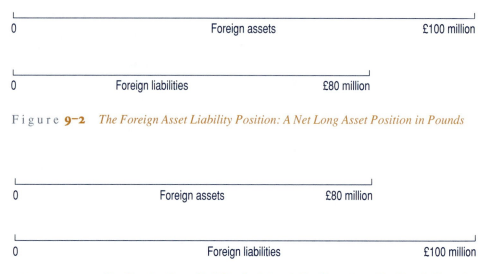

F i g u r e **9–2**   *The Foreign Asset Liability Position: A Net Long Asset Position in Pounds*

F i g u r e **9–3**   *The Foreign Asset Liability Position: A Net Short Asset Position in Pounds*

foreign exchange risk

The risk that exchange rate changes can affect the value of an FI's assets and liabilities located abroad.

undiversified foreign expansion—such as establishing operations in only one country or buying the securities of corporations in only one country—exposes an FI to **foreign exchange risk** in addition to interest rate risk and default risk.

To understand how foreign exchange risk arises, suppose that a U.S. FI makes a loan to a British company in pounds sterling (£). Should the British pound depreciate in value relative to the U.S. dollar, the principal and interest payments received by U.S. investors would be devalued in dollar terms. Indeed, were the British pound to fall far enough over the investment period, when cash flows were converted back into dollars, the overall return could be negative. That is, on the conversion of principal and interest payments from sterling into dollars, foreign exchange losses can offset the promised value of local currency interest payments at the original exchange rate at which the investment occurred.

An FI can hold assets denominated in a foreign currency and/or issue foreign liabilities. Consider an Fl that holds £100 million in British loans as assets and funds £80 million of them with British certificates of deposit. The difference between the £100 million in pound loans and £80 million in pound CDs is funded by dollar CDs (i.e., £20 million pounds worth of dollar CDs). See Figure 9–2. In this case, the U.S. FI is *net long* £20 million in British assets; that is, it holds more foreign assets than liabilities. The U.S. FI suffers losses if the exchange rate for pounds falls or depreciates against the dollar over this period. In dollar terms, the value of the British pound loan assets falls or decreases in value by more than the British pound CD liabilities do. That is, the FI is exposed to the risk that its net foreign assets may have to be liquidated at an exchange rate lower than the one that existed when the FI entered into the foreign asset-liability position.

Instead, the FI could have £20 million more foreign liabilities than assets; in this case, it holds a *net short* position in foreign assets, as shown in Figure 9–3. Under this circumstance, the FI is exposed to foreign exchange risk if the pound appreciates against the dollar over the investment period. This occurs because the value of its British pound liabilities in dollar terms rose faster than the return on its pound assets. Consequently, to be appropriately hedged, the FI must match its assets and liabilities in each foreign currency.

Note that the FI is fully hedged only if we assume that it holds foreign assets and liabilities of exactly the same maturity.[2] Consider what happens if the FI matches the size of its foreign currency book (British pound assets = British pound liabilities = £100 million in that currency) but mismatches the maturities, so that the pound sterling assets are of six-month maturity and the liabilities are of three-month maturity. The FI is then exposed to foreign interest rate risk—the risk that British interest rates will rise when it rolls over its £100 million British CD liabilities at the end of the third month. Consequently, the FI that matches both the size and maturities of its exposures in assets and liabilities of a given currency is hedged or immunized against both foreign currency and foreign interest rate risks. To the extent that FIs mismatch their portfolios and maturity exposures in different currency assets and liabilities, they face both foreign currency and foreign interest rate risks. As noted, if foreign exchange rate and interest rate changes are not perfectly correlated across countries, an FI can diversify part, if not all, of its foreign currency risk. Chapter 27 discusses the measurement and evaluation of an FI's foreign currency risk exposure in depth.

Concept Questions

1. Why are the returns on domestic and foreign portfolio investments not, in general, perfectly correlated?
2. A U.S. bank is net long in deutsche mark (DM) assets. If the DM appreciates against the dollar, will the bank gain or lose?
3. A U.S. bank is net short in DM assets. If the DM appreciates against the dollar, will the bank gain or lose?

• •

COUNTRY OR SOVEREIGN RISK

country or sovereign risk

The risk that repayments from foreign borrowers may be interrupted because of interference from foreign governments.

As noted in the preceding section, a globally oriented FI that mismatches the size and maturities of its foreign assets and liabilities is exposed to foreign currency and foreign interest rate risks. Even beyond these risks and even when investing in dollars, investing in assets in a foreign country can expose an FI to a third foreign investment risk, **country or sovereign risk.** Country or sovereign risk is a more serious credit risk than the risk faced by an FI that purchases domestic assets such as the bonds and loans of domestic corporations. For example, when a domestic corporation is unable or unwilling to repay a loan, an FI usually has recourse to the domestic bankruptcy court and eventually may recoup at least a portion of its original investment when the assets of the defaulted firm are liquidated or restructured.

By comparison, a foreign corporation may be unable to repay the principal or interest on its issued claims even if it would like to do so. For example, the government of the country may prohibit payment or limit payments due to foreign currency shortages and political events. For example, in 1982 the Mexican and Brazilian governments announced a debt

---

[2] Technically speaking, hedging requires matching the durations (average lives of assets and liabilities) rather than simple maturities.

moratorium (i.e., a delay in their debt repayments). The largest U.S. banks had made substantial loans to these countries and their government-owned corporations (such as Pemex, the Mexican state-run oil company). As a result, banks such as Citicorp had to make additional provisions to their loan loss reserves because expected losses on these loans were recognized as part of post–1982 attempts to restructure and reschedule these debts. In 1987 alone, Citicorp set aside more than $3 billion to cover expected losses (again note the interaction between credit risk and country risk). More recently, in 1997 and 1998, U.S., European, and Japanese banks had enhanced sovereign risk exposure to Southeast Asian countries such as Thailand, South Korea, Malaysia, and Indonesia. A bailout of these countries by the International Monetary Fund (IMF) and the U.S., Japanese, and European governments enabled the banks largely to avoid losses. Nevertheless, Indonesia had to declare a moratorium on some of its debt repayments.

In the event of restrictions or outright prohibitions on the payment of debt obligations by sovereign governments, the FI claimholder has little if any recourse to the local bankruptcy courts or to an international civil claims court. The major leverage available to an FI to ensure or increase repayment probabilities is its control of the future supply of loans or funds to the country concerned. Such leverage may be very weak, however, in the face of a country's collapsing currency. Chapter 28 discusses how country risk is measured and considers possible financial market solutions to the country risk exposure problems of a globally oriented FI.

Concept Questions

1. Can a bank be subject to sovereign risk if it lends only to the highest-quality foreign corporations?
2. What is one major way an FI can discipline a country that threatens not to repay its loans?

INSOLVENCY RISK

insolvency risk

The risk that an FI may not have enough capital to offset a sudden decline in the value of its assets relative to its liabilities.

Insolvency risk is a consequence or an outcome of one or more of the following risks: excessive interest rate, market, credit, off balance sheet, technological, foreign exchange, sovereign, and liquidity. Technically, insolvency occurs when the internal capital or equity resources of an FI's owners are at or near zero due to one or more risks described in the preceding sections. Consider the case of the 1984 near-failure of Continental Illinois National Bank and Trust. Continental's strategy in the late 1970s and early 1980s was to pursue growth through aggressive lending. Continental's loan portfolio grew an average of 19.8 percent per year from 1977 to 1981 compared to 14.7 percent for its peer banks. The downturn in the economy at the turn of the decade resulted in the default of many of these loans (credit risk). In addition, Continental had a very small core deposit base, relying instead on borrowed funds such as fed funds, RPs, and Eurodollar deposits. The increasing number of defaults in Continental's loan portfolio fueled concerns about the bank's ability to meet its liability payments, resulting in the eventual refusal by a number of money market lenders to renew or rollover their borrowed funds (liquidity risk). The substantial defaults on Continental's loans combined with its inability to obtain funds resulted in the rapid deterioration of Continental's market value of equity (insolvency risk). Continental was unable to survive, and the FDIC took control of it.

In general, the more equity capital to borrowed funds an FI has—that is, the lower its leverage—the better able it is to withstand losses, whether due to adverse liquidity changes, unexpected credit losses, or other reasons. Thus, both management and regulators focus on the management of an FI's capital and its capital adequacy as key measures of its ability to remain solvent and grow in the face of a multitude of risks. Chapter 16 discusses the issue of what is considered an adequate level of capital to manage an FI's risk exposure.

Concept Questions

1. When does insolvency risk occur?
2. How is insolvency risk related to credit risk and liquidity risk?

OTHER RISKS AND THE INTERACTION AMONG RISKS

This overview chapter concentrated on ten major risks continuously impacting FI managers' decision-making processes and risk management strategies. Even though the discussion described each independently, in reality these risks are often interdependent. For example, when interest rates rise, corporations find maintaining promised payments on their debt more difficult. Thus, over some range of interest rate movements, credit and interest rate risks are positively correlated. Furthermore, the FI may have been counting on the funds from these promised payments for liquidity purposes. Thus, liquidity risk also is correlated with interest rate and credit risk. The inability of the customer to make promised payments, of course, also affects the FI's income, and consequently, its equity or capital position. Thus, this situation ultimately affects solvency risk. The interaction of the various risks means that FI managers face making trade-offs among them. As they take actions in an attempt to affect one type of risk, FI managers must consider the possible impact on other risks.

Various other risks, often of a more discrete type, have an impact on an FI's profitability and risk exposure as well. Discrete risks include a sudden change in taxation such as the Tax Reform Act of 1986 which subjected banks to a minimum corporate tax rate of 20 percent (the alternative minimum tax) and limited their ability to expense the cost of funds used to purchase tax-free municipal bonds. Such changes can affect the attractiveness of some types of assets over others, as well as the liquidity of the balance sheet. For example, banks' demand for municipal bonds to hold as assets fell quite dramatically following the 1986 tax law change that affected their ability to deduct from their taxes the cost of reserves held against possible default on these securities. As a result, the municipal bond market became quite illiquid for a time.

Changes in regulatory policy contribute another type of discrete risk. These include lifting the regulatory barriers to lending or to entry or on products offered (see Chapters 3 and 26). The 1997 regulatory change removing lending "firewalls" between commercial banks and their investment banking subsidiaries is one example (see Chapter 24).

Other discrete risks—often called *event risks*—involve sudden and unexpected changes in financial market conditions due to war, revolution, or sudden collapse such as the 1929 and 1987 stock market crashes. These have a major impact on an FI's risk exposure. Other event risks include theft, malfeasance, and breach of fiduciary trust; all of these can ultimately cause an FI to fail or be severely harmed.

Finally, more general macroeconomic risks such as increased inflation, inflation volatility, and unemployment can directly and indirectly impact an FI's level of interest rate, credit, and liquidity risk exposure. For example, inflation was very volatile during the period 1979–1982 in the United States. Interest rates reflected this volatility. During periods in which an FI faces high and volatile inflation and interest rates, its interest rate risk exposure from mismatching its balance sheet maturities tends to rise. Its credit risk exposure also rises because borrowing firms with fixed price product contracts often find it difficult to keep up their loan interest payments when inflation and interest rates rise abruptly.

Concept Questions

1. What does the term *event risk* mean?
2. What are some examples of event and general macroeconomic risks that impact FIs?

SUMMARY

This chapter provided an overview of the ten major risks that modern FIs face. They face *credit risk* or default risk if their clients default on their loans and other obligations. They encounter *liquidity risk* as a result of excessive withdrawals or problems in refinancing liabilities. They face *interest rate risk* when the maturities of their assets and liabilities are mismatched. They incur *market risk* on their trading assets and liabilities if adverse movements in interest rates, exchange rates, or other asset prices occur. Modern-day FIs also engage in significant off-balance-sheet activities that expose them to *off-balance-sheet risks:* contingent asset and liability risks. The advent of sophisticated technology and automation exposes FIs to both *technological* and *operational risks.* If FIs conduct foreign business, they are subject to additional risks, namely *foreign exchange* and *sovereign risks.* FIs face *insolvency risk* when their capital is insufficient to withstand the losses they incur as a result of such risks. The effective management of these risks determines a modern FI's success or failure. The chapters that follow analyze each of these risks in greater detail, beginning with credit risk.

PERTINENT WEB SITES

Federal Deposit Insurance Corp. (FDIC)   http://www.fdic.gov/
Office of the Comptroller of the Currency   http://www.occ.treas.gov/

Risks of Financial Intermediation

1. What is the difference between refinancing risk and reinvestment risk? If an FI funds long-term assets with short-term liabilities, what will be the impact of an interest rate increase on earnings?

2. The sales literature of a mutual fund claims that the fund has no risk exposure since it invests exclusively in default risk-free federal government securities. Is this claim true? Why or why not?

3. Characterize the risk exposure(s) of the following FI transactions by choosing one or more of the following:

   a. Interest rate risk
   b. Credit risk
   c. Off-balance-sheet risk
   d. Technology risk
   e. Foreign exchange rate risk
   f. Country or sovereign risk

   (1) A bank finances a $10 million, six-year fixed rate commercial loan by selling one-year certificates of deposit.
   (2) An insurance company invests its policy premiums in a long-term municipal bond portfolio.
   (3) A French bank sells two-year fixed rate notes to finance a two-year fixed rate loan to a British entrepreneur.
   (4) A Japanese bank acquires an Austrian bank to facilitate clearing operations.
   (5) A mutual fund completely hedges its interest rate risk exposure using forward contingent contracts.
   (6) A bond dealer uses his own equity to buy Mexican debt on the lesser developed country (LDC) bond market.
   (7) A securities firm sells a package of mortgage loans as mortgage backed securities.

4. What is the difference between firm-specific credit risk and systematic credit risk? How can an FI alleviate firm-specific credit risk?

5. Consider two bonds; a 10-year premium bond with a coupon rate higher than its required rate of return and a zero coupon bond that pays only a lump-sum payment after 10 years with no interest over its life. Which do you think would have more interest rate risk, that is, which bond's price would change by a larger amount for a given change in interest rates? Explain your answer.

6. Off-balance-sheet risk encompasses several of the other nine sources of risk exposure (e.g., interest rate risk, credit risk, and foreign exchange rate risk). Discuss.

7. Corporate bonds usually pay interest semiannually. If a company decided to change from semiannual to annual interest payments, how would this affect the bond's interest rate risk?

8. What is the difference between technology risk and operational risk? How does internationalizing the payments system among banks increase operational risk?

9. If international capital markets are well integrated and operate efficiently, will banks be exposed to foreign exchange risk? What are the sources of foreign exchange risk for FIs?

10. A U.S. insurance company invests $1,000,000 in a private placement of German bonds. Each bond pays 300DM in interest per year for 20 years. If the current exchange rate is 1.7612DM/$, what is the nature of the insurance company's exchange rate risk? Specifically, what type of exchange rate movement concerns this insurance company?

11. What does the term *economic value risk* mean?

12. If you expect the French franc to depreciate in the near future, would a U.S.–based FI in Paris prefer to be net long or net short in its asset positions? Discuss.

13. In the 1980s, many S&Ls that failed had made loans to oil companies located in Louisiana, Texas, and Oklahoma. When oil prices fell, these companies, the regional economy, and the S&Ls all experienced financial problems. What types of risk were inherent in the loans that these S&Ls had made?

14. Discuss the interrelationships among the different sources of bank risk exposure.

15. A money market mutual fund bought $1,000,000 of two-year Treasury notes six months ago. During this time, the value of the securities has increased, but for tax reasons, the mutual fund wants to postpone any sale for two more months. What type of risk does the mutual fund face for the next two months?

16. If a bank invested $50 million in a two-year asset paying 10 percent interest per annum and simultaneously issued a $50 million, one-year liability paying 8 percent interest per annum, what would be the impact on the bank's net interest income if, at the end of the first year, all interest rates increased by one percentage point?

17. Consider these four types of risks: credit, foreign exchange, market, and sovereign. They can be separated into two pairs of risk types in which each pair consists of two related risk types, one being a subset of the other. How would you pair off the risk types and which risk types might be considered a subset of another?

18. Assume that a bank has assets located in Germany worth DM150 million earning an average of 8 percent on its assets. It also holds DM100 in liabilities and pays an average of 6 percent per year. The current spot rate is

DM1.50/$. If the exchange rate at the end of the year is DM2.00/$,

   a. What happened to the dollar? Did it appreciate or devalue against the mark?

   b. What is the effect of the exchange rate change on the net interest margin (interest received minus interest paid) in dollars from its foreign assets and liabilities?

   c. What is the effect of the exchange rate change on the value of the assets and liabilities in dollars?

19. Six months ago, Qualitybank, Ltd. issued a $100 million, one-year maturity CD, denominated in German deutsche mark (Euromark CD). On the same date, $60 million was invested in a DM-denominated loan and $40 million in a U.S. Treasury bill. The exchange rate on this date was 1.7382 DM/$. If you assume no repayment of principal and if today's exchange rate is 1.3905 DM/$,

   a. What is the current value of the Euromark CD principal (in dollars and DM)?

   b. What is the current value of the German loan principal (in dollars and DM)?

   c. What is the current value of the U.S. Treasury bill (in dollars and DM)?

   d. What is Qualitybank's profit/loss from this transaction (in dollars and DM)?

20. Suppose that you purchase a 10-year AAA-rated Swiss bond for par that is paying an annual coupon of 8 percent and has a face value of 1,000 Swiss francs (SF). The spot rate is SF1.50/$. At the end of the year, the bond is downgraded to AA and the yield increases to 10 percent. In addition, the SF depreciates to SF1.35/$.

   a. What is the loss or gain to a Swiss investor who holds this bond for a year?

   b. What is the loss or gain to a U.S. investor who holds this bond for a year?

Section
Two

Measuring and Managing Risk on the Balance Sheet

Chapter Ten

Credit Risk: Credit Analysis and Lending Risk

As discussed in Chapter 1, financial intermediaries (FIs) are special because of their ability to transform financial claims of household savers efficiently into claims issued to corporations, individuals, and governments. An FI's ability to evaluate information and control and monitor borrowers allows it to transform these claims at the lowest possible cost to all parties. One of the specific types of financial claim transformation discussed in Chapter 1 was credit allocation. That is, FIs transform claims of household savers (in the form of deposits) into loans issued to corporations, individuals, and governments. The FI accepts the credit risk on these loans in exchange for a fair return sufficient to cover the cost of funding (e.g., covering the cost of borrowing, or issuing deposits) to household savers and the credit risk involved in lending.

In this, the first of two chapters on credit risk, we discuss different approaches to analyze and measure the credit or default risk on individual (real estate, consumer, and commercial and industrial) loans. In the next chapter, we consider methods to analyze and measure the risk of loan portfolios or loan concentration risk. Methods for managing an FI's credit risk are left to Chapter 11. Measurement of the credit risk on individual loans is crucial if an FI manager is to (1) price a loan correctly and (2) set appropriate "limits" on the amount of credit extended to any one borrower or the loss exposure accepted from any particular counterparty. For example, in recent years, Japanese banks have suffered losses from an excessive number of loans to the Japanese real estate sector (see Contemporary Perspectives Box 10–1).

Contemporary Perspectives 10–1

Debt Dogs Japan's Banks Despite Write-Offs

The Japanese banks continue to make progress in writing off their huge burden of post bubble-economy bad debt but the pace is too slow for comfort, say banking officials.

With expected diminished profitability this year compared with last, the scope for maintaining, let alone accelerating, the rate of write-downs appears limited.

Japanese finance ministry figures show total nonperforming and restructured loans at all of the country's deposit-taking institutions (from leading commercial or "city" banks to credit cooperatives) declined by ¥5.57 trillion ($47 billion) or 16 percent to ¥29.23 trillion between the end of March and the end of September 1996.

Practically all of the write-downs during the half year were applicable to loans that banks had made to the notorious housing loan corporations, or Jusen, that have been rescued by the government with the help of taxpayers' money. Little headway was made on disposing of other bad debts.

Japan's 10 "city" or leading commercial banks hold the bulk of the total problem loans——¥10.95 trillion worth at 30 September—while the nation's seven trust banks hold a further ¥3.74 trillion and the three long-term credit banks ¥2.72 trillion. The remainder is held by regional and local banks and by credit co-operatives.

Usually, a senior Japanese finance ministry official used the presentation of the latest bad debt figures to publicly urge leading banks to accelerate the writing off of their nonperforming loans in general. His remarks came amid fresh turmoil in Tokyo financial markets and renewed concerns overseas over the health of the nation's financial system following the collapse of Hanwa Bank late last year.

After allowing for provisions that banks have already made against bad or doubtful debts, and for the fact that land and other collateral they hold has some residual market value (an assumed 35 percent of the original loan value), the finance ministry estimates that total problem loans still to be disposed of amounted to ¥7.86 trillion at 30 September. This was 12 percent down on the March figure of ¥8.41 trillion.

In theory, banks and other deposit-taking institutions could write off this remaining amount from one year's annual profits—which will amount to an estimated ¥7.86 trillion on an industry-wide basis during the year to 31 March. However, finance ministry officials acknowledge banking profits will almost certainly decline during 1997. This is because banks felt a huge benefit during 1996 from the lowering of the official discount rate to an historic low of 0.5 percent with short-term deposit rates moving down accordingly.

This year, however, with relatively high-interest loans being (paid) off and rates on new loans moving down in line with deposit rates some analysts calculate that lending margins will contract by as much as 20 percent. The outlook for disposing rapidly of bad debts is therefore becoming more clouded, especially as new loan growth continues to be extremely sluggish.

SOURCE: *The Banker*, February 1997, p. 4.

TYPES
OF LOANS

Although most FIs make loans, the types of loans they make and the characteristics of these loans differ considerably. This section analyzes the major types of loans made by U.S. commercial banks. Remember from Chapters 3 through 7, however, that other FIs, such as thrifts and insurance companies, also engage heavily in lending, especially in the real estate area. We also discuss important aspects of thrift and insurance company loan portfolios. See Table 10–1 for a recent list of the aggregate loan portfolio of U.S. commercial banks separated into four broad classes: real estate, individual, commercial and industrial (C&I), and all other. We briefly discuss each of these loan classes.

Real Estate Loans

Real estate loans are primarily mortgage loans and some revolving home equity loans (approximately 7.9 percent of banks' real estate loan portfolios).[1] See Table 10–2 for the distribution of mortgage debt for U.S. banks for the second quarter of 1997.

Table **10–1**

TYPES OF U.S. BANK LOANS, SEPTEMBER 1997
(in billions of dollars)

	Amount	Percent
Total Loans*	$2,725.1	100.0%
C&I	760.7	27.9
Real estate	1,112.3	40.8
Individual	517.3	19.0
Other	334.8	12.3

*Excluding interbank loans.

SOURCE: *Federal Reserve Bulletin,* December 1997, Table 1.26.

Table **10–2**

THE DISTRIBUTION OF U.S. COMMERCIAL BANK REAL ESTATE MORTGAGE DEBT, SECOND QUARTER 1997

	Percent
One- to four-family residences	61.3%
Multifamily residences	4.1
Commercial	32.4
Farm	2.2
	100.0%

SOURCE: *Federal Reserve Bulletin*, December 1997, Table 1.54.

---

[1] Under home equity loans, borrowers use the homes they fully own as collateral backing for new loans.

For banks (as well as thrifts), residential mortgages are still the largest component of the real estate loan portfolio; until recently, however, commercial real estate mortgages had been the fastest-growing component of real estate loans.[2] Moreover, commercial real estate loans make up more than 80 percent of life insurance companies' real estate portfolios. These loans caused banks, thrifts, and insurance companies significant default and credit risk problems in the early 1990s.

Residential mortgages are very long-term loans with an average maturity of approximately 25 years. To the extent that house prices can fall below the amount of the loan outstanding—that is, the loan-to-value (house) ratio rises—the residential mortgage portfolio can also be susceptible to default risk. For example, during the collapse in real estate prices in Houston, Texas, in the late 1980s, many house prices actually fell below their prices in the early 1980s. This led to a dramatic surge in the number of mortgage defaults and eventually to foreclosures by banks and thrifts.

As with C&I loans, the characteristics of residential mortgage loans differ widely. These include the size of loan, the loan-to-value ratio, and the maturity of the mortgage. Other important characteristics are the mortgage interest (or commitment) rate and fees and charges on the loan, such as commissions, discounts, and points paid by the borrower or the seller to obtain the loan.[3] In addition, the mortgage rate differs according to whether the mortgage has a fixed rate or a floating rate, also called an *adjustable rate*. The contractual rates of an **adjustable-rate mortgage (ARM)** are adjusted periodically to some underlying index such as the one-year T-bond rate. The proportion of fixed-rate to ARM mortgages in FI portfolios varies with the interest rate cycle. In low interest rate periods, borrowers prefer fixed-rate to ARM mortgages while FIs prefer ARM to fixed-rate mortgages. As a result, the proportion of ARMs to fixed-rate mortgages can vary considerably over the interest rate cycle. Note in Figure 10–1 the behavior of ARMs over one recent interest rate cycle—1992 to 1995—when interest rates fell dramatically. Notice that borrowers' preferences prevailed over this period as a consistently low percentage of total loans closed were ARMs. Table 10–3 includes a summary of the major contractual terms on the average conventional fixed-rate mortgage during September 1997.

adjustable-rate mortgage (ARM)

A mortgage whose interest rate adjusts with movements in an underlying market index interest rate.

Table **10–3**

CONTRACTUAL TERMS ON THE AVERAGE CONVENTIONAL NEW HOME MORTGAGE, SEPTEMBER 1997
(in thousands of dollars)

Purchase price	$190.6
Amount of loan	$147.0
Loan price ratio (percent)	79.3%
Maturity (years)	28.3
Fees and charges (percent of loan amount)	1.12%
Contract rate (percent)	7.43%

SOURCE: *Federal Reserve Bulletin*, December 1997, Table 1.53.

---

[2] Thrifts' proportion of one- to four-family loans in their real estate mortgage portfolio was 80 percent in the second quarter of 1997.

[3] *Points* are a certain percentage of the face value of the loan paid up front, as a fee, by the borrower to the lender.

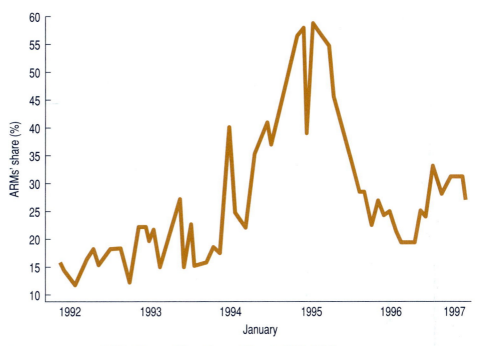

F i g u r e **10–1**   *ARMs' Share of Total Loans Closed, 1992–1997*
SOURCE: Federal Housing Finance Board.

T a b l e **10–4**

LARGEST CREDIT CARD ISSUERS AS OF JUNE 1997

Card Issuer	Total Outstanding Balances (in billions of dollars)	Change from Year Earlier (percentage)
Citicorp	$45.8	+7%
MBNA America	39.1	+35
Chase/Chemical	26.3	+12
First USA	24.6	+31
First Chicago NBD	17.1	−2

SOURCE: The Nilson Report.

Individual (Consumer) Loans

Another major type of loan is the individual or consumer loan such as personal and auto loans. Commercial banks, finance companies, retailers, savings banks, and gas companies also provide consumer loan financing through credit cards such as Visa, MasterCard, and proprietary credit cards issued by companies such as Sears and AT&T. A typical credit card transaction is illustrated in Figure 10–2. Data on the largest credit card issuers and their total outstanding balances are shown in Table 10–4.

See Table 10–5 for the three major classes of consumer loans at U.S. banks. The largest class of loans is revolving consumer loans, which include credit card debt. With a

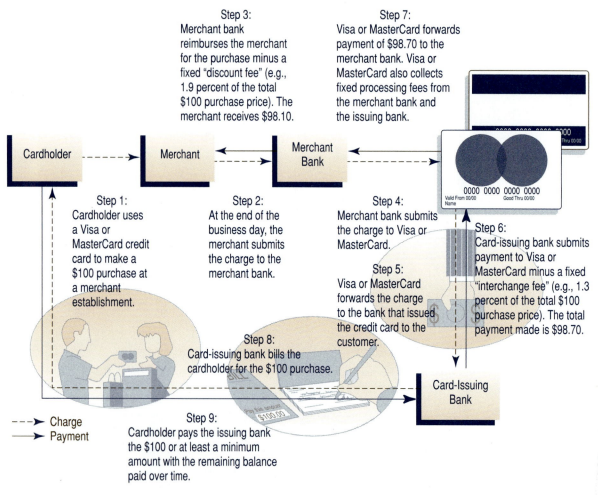

Step 3: Merchant bank reimburses the merchant for the purchase minus a fixed "discount fee" (e.g., 1.9 percent of the total $100 purchase price). The merchant receives $98.10.

Step 7: Visa or MasterCard forwards payment of $98.70 to the merchant bank. Visa or MasterCard also collects fixed processing fees from the merchant bank and the issuing bank.

Cardholder → Merchant ← Merchant Bank ← Card

Step 1: Cardholder uses a Visa or MasterCard credit card to make a $100 purchase at a merchant establishment.

Step 2: At the end of the business day, the merchant submits the charge to the merchant bank.

Step 4: Merchant bank submits the charge to Visa or MasterCard.

Step 5: Visa or MasterCard forwards the charge to the bank that issued the credit card to the customer.

Step 6: Card-issuing bank submits payment to Visa or MasterCard minus a fixed "interchange fee" (e.g., 1.3 percent of the total $100 purchase price). The total payment made is $98.70.

Step 8: Card-issuing bank bills the cardholder for the $100 purchase.

Card-Issuing Bank

- - -→ Charge
———→ Payment

Step 9: Cardholder pays the issuing bank the $100 or at least a minimum amount with the remaining balance paid over time.

F i g u r e **10–2**   *Payment Flows in a Typical Credit Card Transaction*

SOURCE:: GAO (GAO/GGD-94-23) (1994), p. 57.

T a b l e **10–5**

TYPES OF CONSUMER LOANS AT COMMERCIAL BANKS, AUGUST 1997

	Percentage
Automobile	32.6%
Revolving	42.6
Other	24.8
	100.0%

SOURCE: *Federal Reserve Bulletin,* December 1997, Table 1.55.

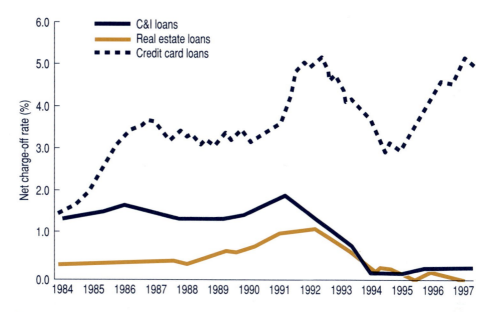

F i g u r e **10–3**   *Charge-Off Rates for Credit Card Lending and Commercial Bank Lending Activities, 1984–1997*

SOURCE: Federal Deposit Insurance Corporation.

T a b l e **10–6**

INTEREST RATE TERMS ON CONSUMER LOANS, AUGUST 1997

	Percentage
48-month car loan	8.99%
24-month personal	13.84
Credit card	15.78

SOURCE: *Federal Reserve Bulletin*, December 1997, Table 1.56.

revolving loan

A credit line on which a borrower can both draw and repay many times over the life of the loan contract.

revolving loan, the borrower has a credit line on which to draw as well as to repay up to some maximum during the life of the credit contract. In recent years, banks have normally faced charge-off[4] rates of between 2 and 5 percent on their credit card loans outstanding. These charge-off rates are significantly higher than those on commercial loans (see Figure 10–3). Such relatively high charge-off rates again point to the importance of evaluating risk prior to making the credit decision. The other major class of consumer loans is for new and used automobile purchases. Finally, other consumer loans include fixed-term consumer loans such as 24-month personal loans and loans to purchase mobile homes.

See Table 10–6 for interest rates on consumer loans as of August 1997. These rates differ widely, depending on features such as collateral backing, maturity, default rate experience, and noninterest rate fees. In addition, competitive conditions in each market as well

---

[4] A *charge-off* occurs when the FI recognizes the loan as bad (uncollectible) and writes it off the books.

usury ceilings

State-imposed ceilings on the maximum rate that FIs can charge on consumer and mortgage debt.

as regulations such as state-imposed **usury ceilings** affect the rate structure of consumer loans.

Commercial and Industrial Loans

The figures in Table 10–1 disguise a great deal of heterogeneity in the commercial and industrial loan portfolio. Indeed, commercial loans can be made in quite small amounts such as $100,000 to small businesses or in packages as large as $10 million or more to major corporations. Commercial loans can be made at either fixed rates or floating rates of interest. The interest rate on a fixed-rate loan is set at the beginning of the contract period. This rate remains in force over the loan contract period no matter what happens to market rates. Suppose, for example, that IBM borrowed $10 million at 10 percent for one year, but the bank's cost of funds rose over the course of the year. Because this is a fixed-rate loan, the bank bears all interest rate risk. This is the reason that many loans have floating-rate contractual terms. The loan rate can be adjusted periodically according to a formula so that the interest rate risk is transferred in large part from the bank to the borrower. As might be expected, longer-term loans are more likely to be made under floating-rate contracts than are relatively short-term loans.

In addition, commercial loans can be made for periods as short as a few weeks to as long as eight years or more. Traditionally, short-term commercial loans (those with an original maturity of one year or less) are used to finance firms' working capital needs and other short-term funding needs while long-term commercial loans are used to finance credit needs that extend beyond one year, such as the purchase of real assets (machinery), new venture start-up costs, and permanent increases in working capital.

secured loan

A loan that is backed by a first claim on certain assets (collateral) of the borrower if default occurs.

unsecured loan

A loan that has only a general claim to the assets of the borrower if default occurs.

spot loan

A loan that the borrower withdraws immediately.

loan commitment

A loan agreement with a maximum size and a maximum period of time over which the borrower can withdraw funds.

Commercial loans can be secured or unsecured. A **secured loan** (or asset-backed loan) is backed by specific assets of the borrower; if the borrower defaults, the lender has a first lien or claim on those assets. In the terminology of finance, secured debt is senior to an **unsecured loan** (or junior debt) that has only a general claim on the assets of the borrower should default occur. As we explain later in this chapter, a trade-off normally exists between the security or collateral backing of a loan and the loan interest rate or credit risk premium that the lender charges on a loan.[5]

Finally, loans can be made as either spot or commitment. A **spot loan** is made by the bank and the borrower uses—or takes down—the entire loan amount immediately. With a **loan commitment**, or a line of credit, in contrast, the lender makes an amount of credit such as $10 million available; the borrower has the option to take down any amount up to the $10 million at any time over the commitment period. In a fixed-rate loan commitment, the interest rate to be paid on any takedown is established when the loan commitment contract originates. In a floating-rate commitment, the borrower pays the loan rate in force when the loan is actually taken down. For example, suppose that the $10 million IBM loan was made under a one-year loan commitment. When the loan commitment was originated (say, January 1999), IBM borrowed nothing. Instead, it waited six months (say, June 1999) before taking down the entire $10 million. IBM pays the loan rate in force as of June 1999. We discuss the special features of loan commitments more fully in Chapter 20.

To determine the basic characteristics of C&I loans, the Federal Reserve surveys more than 300 banks each quarter. See Table 10–7 for a list of the major characteristics in a recent lending survey. Note that more short-term (under one year) loans than long-term

---

[5] A recent empirical study has confirmed such a trade-off; see A. Berger and G. Udell, "Relationship Lending and Lines of Credit in Small Firm Finance," *Journal of Business* 68 (1995), pp. 351–382.

Table **10–7**

CHARACTERISTICS OF COMMERCIAL LOAN PORTFOLIOS, AUGUST 1997

	Long-Term Loans	Short-Term Loans (31 to 365 days)
Amount outstanding	$2.69 billion	$23.62 billion
Average size of loan	$240,000	$795,000
Weighted-average maturity	52 months	387 days
Weighted-average effective loan rate	8.44%	6.70%
Percent of loans secured by collateral	65.5%	35.6%

SOURCE: *Federal Reserve Bulletin*, November 1997, Table 4.23.

loans were reported. Short-term loans are more likely to be fixed rate than are long-term loans and are less likely to be backed or secured by collateral.

Finally, as noted in Chapter 3, commercial loans are declining in importance in bank loan portfolios. The major reason for this has been the rise in nonbank loan substitutes, especially commercial paper. *Commercial paper* is a short-term debt instrument issued by corporations either directly or via an underwriter to purchasers in the financial markets, such as money market mutual funds. By using commercial paper, a corporation can sidestep banks and the loan market to raise funds often at rates below those banks charge. Moreover, since only the largest corporations can tap the commercial paper market, banks are often left with a pool of increasingly smaller and riskier borrowers in the C&I loan market. This makes credit risk evaluation more important today than ever before. As of September 1997, total commercial paper outstanding was $836.8 billion compared to C&I loans of $760.7 billion.

Other Loans

The other loans category includes a wide variety of borrowers and types. These borrowers include other banks, nonbank financial institutions (such as call loans to investment banks), state and local governments, foreign banks, and sovereign governments.[6] We discuss sovereign loans in Chapter 28.

Concept Questions

1. What are the four major types of loans that U.S. commercial banks make? What are the basic distinguishing characteristics of each type of loan?

---

[6] A *call loan* is a loan contract that allows the lender (e.g., the bank) to request repayment of a loan at any time in the contract period. A *noncallable loan* leaves the timing of the repayment in the hands of the borrower subject to the limit of the maturity of the loan. For example, most broker loans to investment banks are callable within the day and must be repaid immediately at the bank lender's request.

2. Will more ARMs be originated in high or low interest rate environments? Explain your answer.
3. Why are the credit card loan rates reported in Table 10–6 much higher than car loan rates?

- -

CREDIT QUALITY

PROBLEMS

junk bond

A bond rated as speculative or less than investment grade by bond-rating agencies such as Moody's.

Over the past two decades, the credit quality of many FIs' lending and investment decisions has attracted a great deal of attention. In the 1980s, tremendous problems occurred with bank and thrift loans for residential and farm mortgages. In the early 1990s, attention shifted to the problems of commercial real estate loans (to which banks, thrifts, and insurance companies are all exposed) and to **junk bonds** (rated as speculative or less than investment-grade securities by bond-rating agencies such as Moody's). As discussed in Chapter 1, concerns were expressed about the rapid increase in auto loans and credit cards as well as the declining quality in commercial lending standards.[7] For example, in October 1997, Sears, Roebuck & Co's stock fell nearly 11 percent when it announced that its future earnings would be deflated by rising delinquencies and charge-offs on its credit card business. More recently, attention has focused on the risk of lending to Southeast Asian countries and borrowers (such as, Thailand, Indonesia, South Korea, and Malaysia).

Nevertheless, the credit quality of most FIs has improved throughout the 1990's. For example, for FDIC-insured commercial banks, the ratio of nonperforming loans to assets has declined from 1990 to September 1997 except for loans to individuals (see Figure 10–4).[8] The decline in nonperforming C&I and real estate loans and the increase in banks' nonperforming loans to individuals are shown in Table 10–8.[9] Notice that the majority of the increase in nonperforming loans to individuals occurred in banks with more than $1 billion of consolidated assets, and the decrease in nonperforming C&I loans is attributable to the largest banks.

As Chapter 9 discussed, credit quality problems, in the worst case, can cause an FI to become insolvent or can result in such a significant drain on capital and net worth that they adversely affect its growth prospects and its ability to compete with other domestic and international FIs. For example, consider a FI with the following balance sheet:

Cash	$20 m.	Deposits	$90 m.
Gross loans	80 m.	Equity	10 m.
	$100 m.		$100 m.

---

[7] See, for example, "Bank Regulators Taking a Close Look at Lending Risks," *New York Times*, April 8, 1995, pp. 1 and 36. Specifically, the comptroller of the currency formed a special credit analysis committee to double-check whether the nation's largest banks were taking on excessive lending exposures.

[8] In addition, the increased securitization or sale of loans (see Chapter 12) has caused banks to hold loans for shorter periods of time, thus reducing the potential for credit quality problems.

[9] *Nonperforming loans* are defined as loans past due 90 days or more and loans that are not accruing interest due to problems of the borrower.

Table **10-8**

NONPERFORMING LOANS AS A PERCENTAGE OF TOTAL LOANS
Insured Commercial Banks by Consolidated Assets

Quarter	All Banks	$0–$100 million	$100 million–$1 billion	$1 billion–$10 billion	$10 billion+
Commercial and Industrial					
March 1995	1.27	1.52	1.35	0.97	1.22
June 1995	1.26	1.48	1.34	0.93	1.22
September 1995	1.22	1.46	1.43	0.92	1.16
December 1995	1.19	1.32	1.23	0.98	1.13
March 1996	1.20	1.60	1.36	1.03	1.08
June 1996	1.14	1.64	1.40	1.09	0.96
September 1996	1.11	1.59	1.46	1.07	0.92
December 1996	0.98	1.41	1.26	0.91	0.83
March 1997	0.97	1.60	1.34	0.96	0.77
June 1997	0.95	1.51	1.31	0.98	0.77
September 1997	0.93	1.41	1.33	0.92	0.75
Real Estate					
March 1995	1.77	1.05	1.19	1.44	2.56
June 1995	1.62	1.03	1.15	1.35	2.24
September 1995	1.53	1.01	1.12	1.35	2.01
December 1995	1.39	0.98	1.06	1.18	1.78
March 1996	1.41	1.04	1.06	1.20	1.81
June 1996	1.33	0.99	1.00	1.13	1.68
September 1996	1.29	0.95	0.99	1.13	1.59
December 1996	1.23	0.94	0.92	1.28	1.40
March 1997	1.18	0.95	0.90	1.10	1.41
June 1997	1.09	0.92	0.85	1.08	1.22
September 1997	1.05	0.91	0.82	1.06	1.19
Loans to Individuals					
March 1995	1.05	0.67	0.57	0.99	1.41
June 1995	1.07	0.66	0.57	1.03	1.38
September 1995	1.16	0.74	0.60	1.17	1.43
December 1995	1.22	0.72	0.64	1.14	1.56
March 1996	1.24	0.78	0.70	1.28	1.48
June 1996	1.22	0.79	0.68	1.24	1.41
September 1996	1.32	0.85	0.77	1.52	1.36
December 1996	1.36	0.84	0.79	1.42	1.50
March 1997	1.36	0.85	0.79	1.42	1.52
June 1997	1.34	0.85	0.76	1.44	1.47
September 1997	1.37	0.91	0.80	1.52	1.42

SOURCE: Federal Deposit Insurance Corporation.

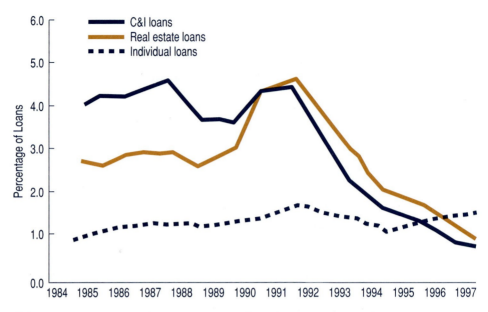

F i g u r e **10–4**   *Nonperforming Asset Ratio for U.S. Commercial Banks*

SOURCE: Federal Deposit Insurance Corporation.

Suppose that the managers of an FI recognize that $10 million of its $80 million in loans are unlikely to be repaid. Eventually, the managers must respond by charging (or writing) off the loans on the balance sheet. This means that loans fall from $80 million to $70 million, a loss that is charged off against the stockholder's equity capital (i.e., equity capital falls from $10 million to zero). Thus, both sides of the balance sheet shrink by the amount of the loss:

Cash		$20 m.	Deposits	$90 m.
Gross loans	80 m.		Equity after charge-off	0 m.
Less: Loan loss	−10 m.			
Loans after charge-off		70 m.		
		$90 m.		$90 m.

However, credit risk does not apply only to traditional areas of lending and bond investing. As banks and other FIs have expanded into credit guarantees and other off-balance-sheet activities (see Chapter 20), new types of credit risk exposure have occurred, causing concern among managers and regulators. Thus, credit analysis is now important for a variety of contractual agreements between FIs and counterparties.[10]

---

[10]This is one of the reasons for bank regulators' new approach to setting capital requirements against credit risk (see Chapter 16).

Concept Questions

1. What are some of the credit quality problems faced by FIs in the last two decades?
2. What are some of the consequences of credit quality problems?

CREDIT ANALYSIS

This section[11] discusses credit analysis for real estate lending, consumer and small business lending, mid-market commercial and industrial lending, and large commercial and industrial lending. This section provides insight into credit risk management from the perspective of the credit officer of an FI evaluating a loan application.

Real Estate Lending

Because of the importance of residential mortgages to banks, savings and loans, credit unions, and insurance companies, residential mortgage loan applications are among the most standardized of all credit applications. Two considerations dominate an FI's decision of whether to approve a mortgage loan application: (1) the applicant's ability and willingness to make timely interest and principal payments and (2) the value of the collateral underlying the loan.

Ability and willingness to service the mortgage debt are usually established by application of qualitative and quantitative models. The character of the applicant is also extremely important. Stability of residence, occupation, family status, previous history of savings, and bill payment history are used in assessing character. The loan officer must also establish that the applicant has sufficient income available to service the debt. The loan amortization (i.e., principal payments) should be reasonable when compared with the applicant's age. The loan officer should also consider the applicant's monthly expenditure budget. Family responsibilities and marital stability are also important. Monthly financial obligations from furniture, car, personal, and credit card loans should be ascertained, and an applicant's personal balance sheet should be constructed.

Two ratios are most useful in determining the customer's ability to make mortgage payments: the **gross debt service (GDS)** and the **total debt service (TDS) ratios**. They are defined as follows:

GDS ratio

Gross debt service ratio calculated as total accommodation expenses (mortgage, lease, condominium, management fees, real estate taxes, etc.) divided by gross income.

TDS ratio

Total debt service ratio calculated as total accommodation expenses plus all other debt service payments divided by gross income.

$$GDS = \frac{\text{Annual mortgage payments} + \text{Property taxes}}{\text{Annual gross income}}$$

$$TDS = \frac{\text{Annual total debt payments}}{\text{Annual gross income}}$$

---

[11]Except for minor changes, this section of the chapter was written by Hugh Thomas, School of Business, McMaster University, Hamilton, Ontario, Canada.

As a rule of thumb, for an FI to consider an applicant, the GDS and TDS ratios must both be less than an acceptable threshold. The threshold is commonly 25 to 30 percent for GDS and 35 and 40 percent for TDS.[12]

E X A M P L E   1 0 – 1

Calculation of GDS and TDS Ratios

Consider two customers who have applied for a mortgage from an FI with a GDS threshold of 25 percent and TDS threshold of 40 percent.

Customer	Gross Annual Income	Monthly Mortgage Payments	Annual Property Taxes	Monthly Other Debt Payments
1	$150,000	$3,000	$3,500	$2,000
2	60,000	500	1,500	200

The GDS and TDS ratios for the mortgage applicants are as follows:

Customer	GDS	TDS
1	$\dfrac{3,000(12) + 3,500}{150,000} = 26.33\%$	$\dfrac{3,000(12) + 3,500 + 2,000(12)}{150,000} = 42.33\%$
2	$\dfrac{500(12) + 1,500}{60,000} = 12.50\%$	$\dfrac{500(12) + 1,500 + 200(12)}{60,000} = 16.50\%$

Despite the higher level of gross income, Customer 1 does not meet the GDS or TDS thresholds because of relatively high mortgage, tax, and other debt payments. Customer 2, while earning less, has fewer required payments and meets both the FI's GDS and TDS thresholds.   •   •   •

credit scoring system

A mathematical model that uses observed loan applicant's characteristics to calculate a score that represents the applicant's probability of default.

FIs often combine the various factors assessing ability and willingness to make payments into a single **credit scoring system.** Credit scoring systems are quantitative models that use observed characteristics of the applicant to calculate a "score" that represents the applicant's probability of default. The scoring system may be on a paper scorecard or on the loan officer's computer terminal. Either way, the loan officer asks questions concerning the applicant's assets, income, monthly expenses, dependents, other credit obligations, and credit history and inputs the answers into the scoring model. The applicant's total score must be above a certain threshold to be considered for the loan. The theory behind credit scoring is that by selecting and combining different economic and financial applicant characteristics, an FI manager may be able to separate good from bad loan customers based on characteristics of past borrowers. Credit scoring assumes that factors that separated good from bad loan customers in the past will, with only a small margin of error, separate good from bad loan customers in the future.

---

[12]Other FIs may impose different thresholds. The numerator of the GDS is often increased to include home heating and property taxes. When the GDS ratio is used for consumer credit, rent is substituted for mortgage payments.

If the FI uses a scoring system, the loan officer can give an immediate answer—yes, maybe, or no (with yes being subject, of course, to a credit check to verify the applicant's responses, and to the determination that the property is acceptable as collateral)—and the reasons for that answer. A maybe occurs in borderline cases or when the loan officer is uncertain of the classification of certain input information. By reducing ambiguity and turnaround time and increasing the transparency of the credit approval process, the FI builds the applicant's respect even if the answer is no.

EXAMPLE 10–2

* * * * * * * *Credit Scoring of a Real Estate Loan*
An FI uses the following credit scoring model to evaluate real estate loan applications:

Characteristic	Characteristic Values and Weights				
Annual gross income	<$10,000	$10,000–$25,000	$25,000–$50,000	$50,000–$100,000	>$100,000 income
Score	0	15	35	50	75
TDS	>50%	35%–50%	15%–35%	5%–15%	<5%
Score	0	10	20	35	50
Relations with FI	None	Checking account	Savings account	Both	
Score	0	30	30	60	
Major credit cards	None	1 or more			
Score	0	20			
Age	<25	25–60	>60		
Score	5	30	25		
Residence	Rent	Own with mortgage	Own outright		
Score	5	20	50		
Length of residence	<1 year	1–5 years	>5 years		
Score	0	20	45		
Job stability	<1 year	1–5 years	>5 years		
Score	0	25	50		
Credit history	No record	Missed a payment in last 5 years	Met all payments		
Score	0	−15	50		

The loan is automatically rejected if the applicant's *total* score is less than 120; the loan is automatically approved if the total score is higher than 190. A score between 120 and 190 is reviewed by a loan committee for a final decision.

A loan customer listing the following information on the loan application receives the following points:

Characteristic	Value	Score
Annual gross income	$67,000	50
TDS	12%	35
Relations with FI	None	0
Major credit cards	4	20
Age	37	30
Residence	Own/Mortgage	20
Length of residence	2½ years	20
Job stability	2½ years	20
Credit history	Met all payments	50
	Total score =	245

The real estate loan is automatically approved.   •   •   •

Verification of the borrower's financial statements is essential. If the answer is yes to a loan application, the loan officer states that the FI is prepared to grant the loan subject to verification of creditworthiness and obtains the applicant's permission to make all necessary inquiries. The current employer should be contacted for a reference. Past pay stubs and tax filings may be used to establish the applicant's past income. A credit agency report should be obtained. Balances to current creditors should be confirmed directly (because credit reports can be out of date and are sometimes inaccurate). Following independent confirmation of employment, income, credit history (from a credit report), and outstanding **chattel mortgages** (on tangible or movable personal property, for example, a vehicle) and liens, the loan officer should reconcile any discrepancies with the applicant.

The collateral provided by the mortgage should be considered *only* after the loan officer has established that the applicant can and is committed to service the loan. No FI should become involved in a loan that is likely to go into default. In such case, the FI would at best seize the property in a **foreclosure** or **power of sale**. At worst, the FI would be defrauded.[13]

Before an FI accepts a mortgage, it must satisfy itself regarding the property involved in the loan by doing the following:

* Confirming the title and legal description of the property.
* Obtaining a surveyor's certificate confirming that a house is within the property boundaries.
* Checking with the tax office to confirm that no property taxes are unpaid.
* Requesting a land title search to determine that there are no other claims against the property.
* Obtaining an independent appraisal to confirm that the purchase price is in line with the market value.

chattel mortgage

A mortgage on movable property.

foreclosure

The process of taking possession of the mortgaged property in satisfaction of a defaulting borrower's indebtedness and forgoing claim to any deficiency.

power of sale

The process of taking the proceedings of the forced sale of a mortgaged property in satisfaction of the indebtedness and returning to the mortgagor the excess over the indebtedness or claiming any shortfall as an unsecured creditor.

---

[13]Good collateral coverage makes a loan relatively riskless only if the collateral is priced continuously in the market and can be disposed of without delay at the market price with minimal transaction costs. A margin account with a broker where the securities posted for collateral are traded in deep and liquid markets and where market crashes do not occur satisfies this condition. Real estate, on the other hand, is subject to large swings in value, illiquidity, and high transactions costs.

Contemporary Perspectives 10–2

Automated Loan Machines Migrate to the Net

Affinity Technology Group, a company that builds automated loan machines (ALMs), will come out with an Internet version of a loan machine by the end of the year. Affinity's technology allows consumers to take out loans through kiosks, similar to automated teller machines (ATMs), within 10 minutes and without human intervention. The Internet product should be available in December, said Jeff Norris, CEO of Affinity.

"Applied correctly to the Internet, Affinity's technology has great potential," said James Marks, v.p. of equity research at CS First Boston. Scott Nelson, research director at Stamford, Conn.–based Gartner Group, said several banks he con-

tacted were eager to implement the loan technology on their Web Sites. "[Banks] want to increase the value of their Web sites by changing from advertising venues to transaction sites," Nelson added.

The physical loan machines have proved increasingly popular with banks. NationsBank and Wells Fargo will start using ALM kiosks in their branches during the first quarter of 1997 and Mellon Bank, in November of this year, will have ALMs. ALMs cut loan origination costs by about one-third to one-half for banks, Norris said. He declined to name banks that have expressed an interest in the Internet version of the ALM.

The ALM allows consumers to take out loans ranging from a

minimum of $1,000 to a maximum of $10,000. Banks that use ALMs set their own criteria for loans and credit scoring, said Norris. The ALM has a touch screen that asks a series of questions, including Social Security number, date of birth and annual income. On approval, the consumer can elect to have a check issued by the ALM—which includes the consumer's signature and picture—have the money deposited in an existing account or open a new account to deposit the money. On the Internet, the consumer will be able to have the money deposited in an account or go to the nearest ALM to get a check, said Norris.

SOURCE: Mildred Wulff, *Financial NetNews*, October 7, 1996, p. 1. This copyrighted material is reprinted with permission of *Financial NetNews,* a publication of Institutional Investor, Inc. 488 Madison Avenue, New York, NY 10022.

Consumer (Personal) and Small Business Lending

The techniques used for mortgage loan analysis are very similar to those applied to personal and small business credits. Personal loans (discussed earlier) are scored like mortgages, often without the borrower ever meeting the loan officer. Unlike mortgage loans for which the focus is on the property, however, nonmortgage consumer loans focus on the individual (i.e., generally no specific asset backs the loan). Thus, credit scoring models (like that in Example 10–2) put more weight on personal characteristics such as annual gross income, TDS score, and so on. The advent of the automated lending machine (ALM) allows borrowers to apply for and receive loans of up to $10,000 within minutes from a machine (see Contemporary Perspectives Box 10–2).

Small business loans are more complex because the FI is frequently asked to assume the credit risk of an individual whose business's cash flows require considerable analysis often with incomplete accounting information. The payoff for this analysis is small by definition because loan principal amounts are small. A $50,000 loan with a 3 percent interest spread over the cost of funds provides only $1,500 of gross revenues before loan loss provisions and allocation of overheads. This level of gross revenue can pay for very little of the loan officer's analytical and monitoring time. This constraint has caused many FIs to build small business scoring models similar to, but more complex than, those used for mortgages and consumer credit. These models combine computer-based financial analysis of statements with behavioral analysis of the owner of the small business to tell the applicant immediately whether the credit is acceptable. Application of such models has reduced loan losses and shortened turnaround time.

It is not surprising that for small business credits, the focus remains on the creditworthiness of the individual (owner), even if a separate legal entity that is technically a business with limited liability exists. Frequently, because the business relies on an individual and separating personal from corporate accounts is difficult, the FI insists on a personal guarantee from an owner before granting a small business loan. Additional collateral for small business loans includes the assets of the small business (e.g., mortgages, **fixed charge** liens on specific assets—that is, a specific piece of equipment, specific items in inventory, and large receivables—and **floating charge** liens on a class of assets that may change in composition over time).

fixed charge

A lien that relates to specific identifiable assets.

floating charge

A lien over a class of assets in which the individual assets may change over time (such as receivables or inventories).

Mid-Market Commercial and Industrial Lending

Mid-market commercial and industrial lending offers some of the most profitable opportunities for the credit-granting FI. Although definitions of mid-market corporates vary, they typically have sales revenues from $5 million to $100 million per year, have a recognizable organization structure (unlike the more fluid small businesses), and do not have ready access to deep and liquid capital markets (unlike large corporations). Thus, mid-market credits are large enough to provide significant revenues to the FI but are too small to threaten the FI's position with disintermediation (e.g., borrowing in the commercial paper market).

Credit analysis of a mid-market corporate customer differs from that of a small business because, although it still assesses the character of the firm's management, its main focus is the business itself, not the owner. See Figure 10–5 for a flow chart of the credit process for a hypothetical mid-market credit in a large FI. The credit process begins with marketing efforts of the account officer, who gathers information by meeting existing customers, checking referrals, and making cold calls on new business prospects. Having gathered information about the credit applicant, the account officer must decide whether it is worthwhile to pursue the new business, given the applicant's needs, the FI's policies, the current economy, and the competitive environment. If it is, the account officer structures and prices the credit agreement with reference to FI policy and then negotiates with the applicant. At any time in this process, conditions could change or new information could be revealed to significantly change the situation, forcing the account officer to begin the process again. Booking a new mid-market loan is often an iterative process that proceeds until a mutually acceptable credit agreement is worked out or until one party stops negotiations.

Once the applicant and the account officer tentatively agree on the loan, the account officer must obtain internal approval from the FI's credit risk management team. Even for the smallest mid-market credit request, at least two officers must approve a new loan customer. Larger credit requests must be presented formally (either in hard copy or through a computer network) to a credit approval officer and/or committee before they can be signed. This means that, during the negotiations, the account officer must be very well acquainted with the FI's overall credit philosophy and current strategy.

To analyze the loan applicant's credit risk, the account officer must understand the customer's character, capacity, collateral, conditions, and capital (sometimes referred to as the five Cs of credit). Some important questions that provide information on the five Cs follow.

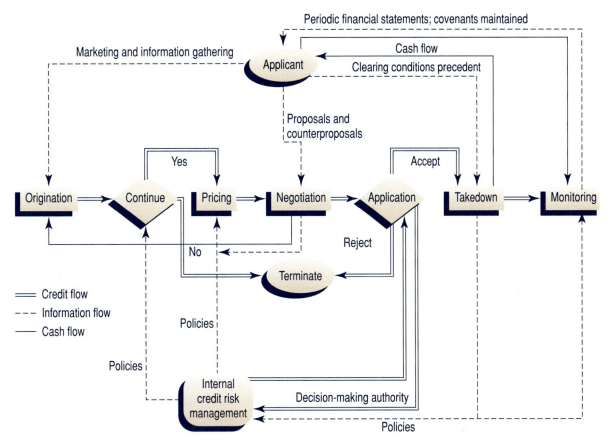

F i g u r e **10-5**   *Credit Process Flow Chart*

Production (measures of capacity and conditions)

- On what production inputs does the applicant depend? To what extent does this cause supply risk?
- How do input price risks affect the applicant?
- How do costs of production compare with those of the competition?
- How does the quality of goods and services produced compare with those of the competition?

Management (measures of character and conditions)

- Is management trustworthy?
- Is management skilled at production? Marketing? Finance? Building an effective organization?
- To what extent does the company depend on one or a few key players? Is there a successful plan?
- Are credible and sensible accounting, budgeting, and control systems in place?

Marketing (measures of conditions)

- How are the changing needs of the applicant's customers likely to affect the applicant?

- How creditworthy are the applicant's customers?
- At what stage of their life cycles are the applicant's products and services?
- What are the market share and share growth of the applicant's products and services?
- What is the applicant's marketing policy?
- Who are the applicant's competitors? What policies are they pursuing? Why are they able to remain in business?
- How is the applicant meeting changing market needs?

Capital (measures of capital and collateral)

- How much equity is currently funding the firm's assets?
- How much access does the firm have to equity and debt markets?
- Will the company back the loan with the firm's assets?

One frequently used source of much of this information is Robert Morris Associates (RMA). RMA has become a standard reference for thousands of commercial lenders by providing average balance sheet and income data for more than 400 industries, common ratios computed for each size group and industry, five-year trend data, and financial statement data for more than 100,000 commercial borrowers.

Cash Flow Analysis.   FIs require corporate loan applicants to provide cash flow information, which provides the FI with relevant information about the applicant's cash receipts and disbursements that are compared with the principal and interest payments on the loan. *Cash receipts* include any transaction that results in an increase in cash assets (i.e., receipt of income, decrease in a noncash asset, increase in a liability, and increase in an equity account). *Cash disbursements* include any transaction that results in a decrease in cash assets (i.e., cash expenses, increase in a noncash asset, decrease in a liability, and decrease in equity).[14] The cash flow statement (or cash-based income statement) reconciles changes in the cash account over some period according to three cash flow activities: operations, investing, and financing.

EXAMPLE 10-3

Computation of Cash Flow Statement

Consider the financial statements for the loan applicant presented in Table 10–9. The cash flow statement reconciles the change in the firm's cash account from 1998 to 1999 as equal to –$61 (see the first row of panel A). Construction of the cash flow statement begins with all cash flow items associated with the operations of the applicant. Panel A of Table 10–10 shows that the cash flows from operations total –$78. Next, cash flows from investment activities (i.e., fixed asset investments and other nonoperating investments of the firm) are calculated in Table 10–10, Panel B as –$168. Finally, cash flows from financing activities are shown in Panel C as $185. The sum of these cash flow activities, reported in Panel D, –$61, equals the change in the cash account from 1998 to 1999 (Table 10–9, Panel A, first row).

---

[14]For example, if a firm issues new bonds (increasing liabilities), it will have an (increased) cash flow from the purchasers of the newly issued bonds. Similarly, a sale of new equity (such as common stock) will create a positive cash inflow to the firm from purchasers of the equity.

Table **10-9**

FINANCIAL STATEMENTS USED TO CONSTRUCT A CASH FLOW STATEMENT

Panel A: Balance Sheets

Assets	1998	1999	Change from 1998 to 1999	Liabilities/Equity	1998	1999	Change from 1998 to 1999
Cash	$ 133	$ 72	($ 61)	Notes payable	$ 657	$ 967	$ 310
Accounts receivable	1,399	1,846	447	Accounts payable	908	1,282	374
Inventory	1,255	1,779	524	Accruals	320	427	107
Gross fixed assets	876	1,033	157	Long-term debt	375	300	(75)
Less: depreciation	(277)	(350)	(73)	Common stock	700	700	–0–
Net fixed assets	599	683	84	Retained earnings	465	754	289
Temporary investments	39	50	11	Total	$3,425	$4,430	$1,005
Total Assets	$3,425	$4,430	$ 1,005				

Panel B: Income Statement

	1999
Net sales	$12,430
Cost of goods sold	(8,255)
Gross profit	4,175
Cash operating expenses	(3,418)
Depreciation	(73)
Operating profit	684
Interest expense	(157)
Taxes	(188)
Net income	339
Dividends	(50)
Change in retained earnings	$ 289

Cash flows generated from operations—as in the preceding example—are the source of cash used to repay the loan to the FI and they thus play a key role in the credit decision process.

Ratio Analysis. In addition to cash flow information, an applicant requesting specific levels of credit substantiates the business needs by presenting historical audited financial statements and projections of future needs. Historical financial statement analysis can be very useful in determining whether cash flow and profit projections are plausible in quantifying many of the qualitative issues just discussed, and in highlighting the applicant's risks. Calculation of financial ratios is useful when performing financial statement analysis on a mid-market corporate applicant. Although stand-alone accounting ratios are essential for determining the size of the credit facility, the analyst may find relative ratios more informative when determining how the applicant's business is changing over time. Ratios are particularly informative when they differ either from an industry average (or FI-determined standard of what is appropriate) or from the applicant's own past history. An optimal value is seldom given for any ratio because no two companies are identical. A ratio that differs from an industry average or an FI-determined standard, however, should cause the account officer to investigate further. A ratio that shifts radically from accounting

Table **10-10**

CASH FLOW STATEMENT

Panel A: Cash Flow from Operations		Cash Flow Impact
Net sales	$12,430	↑
Change in accounts receivable	(447)	↓
Cash receipts from sales	11,983	
Cost of goods sold	(8,255)	↓
Change in inventory	(524)	↓
Change in accounts payable	374	↑
Cash margin	3,578	
Cash operating expenses	(3,418)	↓
Change in accruals	107	↑
Cash before interest and taxes	267	
Interest expense	(157)	↓
Taxes	(188)	↓
Cash flows from operations	(78)	
Panel B: Cash Flow from Investing Activities		
Change in gross fixed assets	(157)	↓
Change in temporary investments	(11)	↓
Cash flows from investing activities	(168)	
Panel C: Cash Flow from Financing Activities		
Retirement of long-term debt	(75)	↓
Change in notes payable	310	↑
Change in common stock	0	—
Dividends paid	(50)	↓
Cash flow from financing activities	185	
Panel D: Net Increase (Decrease) in Cash		
	(61)*	

*This is equal to the change in cash for 1998–1999 reported in Panel A of Table 10–9.

period to accounting period may reveal a company's weakness, change in policy, or normal business operations. The account officer must determine which is the case by obtaining additional information.

Hundreds of ratios could be calculated from any set of accounting statements. The following are a few that credit analysts find useful.

Liquidity Ratios.

$$\text{Current ratio} = \frac{\text{Current assets}}{\text{Current liabilities}}$$

$$\text{Quick ratio (acid-test ratio)} = \frac{\text{Cash} + \text{Cash equivalents} + \text{Receivables}}{\text{Current liabilities}}$$

Liquidity provides the defensive cash and near-cash resources to meet claims on the firm. Liquidity ratios express the variability of liquid resources relative to potential claims. As we discuss in Chapters 13 and 14 when considering the liquidity of FIs, high levels of liquidity effectively guard against liquidity crises, but at the cost of lower returns on investment. Note that a company with a very predictable cash flow can maintain low levels of liquidity without much liquidity risk. Account officers frequently request detailed cash flows from an applicant that specify exactly when cash inflows and outflows are anticipated.

Asset Management Ratios.

$$\text{Number of days' sales in receivables} = \frac{\text{Accounts receivable} \times 365}{\text{Credit sales}}$$

$$\text{Number of days in inventory} = \frac{\text{Inventory} \times 365}{\text{Cost of goods sold}}$$

$$\text{Sales to working capital} = \frac{\text{Sales}}{\text{Working capital}}$$

$$\text{Sales to fixed assets} = \frac{\text{Sales}}{\text{Fixed assets}}$$

$$\begin{matrix}\text{Sales to total assets} \\ \text{(asset turnover)}\end{matrix} = \frac{\text{Sales}}{\text{Total assets}}$$

The asset management ratios give the account officer clues to how well the applicant uses its assets relative to its past performance and the performance of the industry. For example, ratio analysis may reveal that the number of days that finished goods are in inventory is increasing. This suggests that finished goods inventories, relative to the sales they support, are not being used as well as in the past. If this increase is the result of a deliberate policy to increase inventories to offer customers a wider choice and if it results in higher sales volumes or increased margins that more than compensate for increased capital tied up in inventory, the increased relative size of finished goods inventories is good for the applicant and, thus, the FI. An FI should be concerned on the other hand, if increased finished goods inventories are the result of declining sales but steady purchases of supplies and production or worse, increasing stocks of stale inventory that should be written off. Inventory aging schedules give more information than single ratios and should be requested by the account officer concerned about deteriorating ratios.

The business the applicant describes in words often differs substantially from what the ratio analysis reveals. For example, a company that claims to be a high-volume producer but has low sales-to-assets ratios relative to the industry bears further investigation. In discussing the analysis with the applicant, the account officer not only gains a better appreciation of the applicant's industry, strategy, and needs, but also may help the applicant better understand the company relative to financial and industry norms.

Debt and Solvency Ratios.

$$\text{Debt-asset ratio} = \frac{\text{Short-term liabilities} + \text{Long-term liabilities}}{\text{Total assets}}$$

$$\text{Fixed-charge coverage ratio} = \frac{\text{Earnings available to meet fixed charges}}{\text{Fixed charges}}$$

EBIT

Earnings before interest and taxes.

$$\text{Cash-flow debt ratio} = \frac{\text{EBIT} + \text{Depreciation}}{\text{Debt}}$$

where **EBIT** represents earnings before interest and taxes.

Adequate levels of capital are as critical to the health of a credit applicant as they are to the health of FIs (see Chapter 16). The account officer analyzing a credit application or renewal wishes to know whether a sufficient equity cushion exists to absorb fluctuations in earnings and asset values and sufficient cash flow exists to make debt-service payments. Clearly, the larger the fluctuations or variability of cash flows, the larger is the need for equity cushions. Note that from a secured debtor's point of view, the unsecured creditors and subordinate lenders form part of the quasi-equity cushion in liquidation. The secured creditor must make sure, however, that it enjoys true seniority in cash payment so that the firm's assets are not liquidated in paying down the claims of the subordinate (junior) creditors and equity holders.

Whether a debt burden is too large can be analyzed with the help of a fixed-charge coverage ratio. This ratio can be tailored to the applicant's situation, depending on what really constitutes fixed charges that must be paid. One version of it follows

$$(\text{EBIT} + \text{Lease payments})/(\text{Interest} + \text{Lease payments} + \text{Sinking fund}/(1 - T))$$

where T is the marginal tax rate.[15] Here it is assumed that sinking fund payments must be made.[16] They are adjusted by the division of $(1 - T)$ into a before-tax cash outflow so they can be added to other before-tax cash outflows. The past variability of cash flows provides a clue as to how much higher than 1 the fixed-charge coverage ratio should be.

The cash-flow debt ratio is a variant of the fixed-charge coverage ratio. It measures the cash flow available for debt service in proportion to the debt being serviced. The more the ratio exceeds the interest rate, the larger is the debt-service cushion.

Profitability Ratios.

$$\text{Gross margin} = \frac{\text{Gross profit}}{\text{Sales}}$$

$$\text{Operating profit margin} = \frac{\text{Operating profit}}{\text{Sales}}$$

$$\text{Income to sales} = \frac{\text{EBIT}}{\text{Sales}}$$

$$\text{Return on assets} = \frac{\text{EAT} + \text{Interest charges} (1 - T)}{\text{Average total assets}}$$

$$\text{Return on equity} = \frac{\text{EAT}}{\text{Total equity}}$$

$$\text{Dividend payout} = \frac{\text{Dividends}}{\text{EAT}}$$

EAT

Earnings after taxes.

where **EAT** represents earnings after taxes.

---

[15] Another version adds to the denominator investments for replacing equipment that is needed for the applicant to remain in business.

[16] *Sinking funds* are required periodic payments into a fund that is used to retire the principal amounts on bonds outstanding.

A profitable firm that retains its earnings increases its level of equity capital as well as its creditworthiness. The analyst should be concerned about large swings in profitability as well as trends.

Market value ratios such as the share price growth rate, price-earnings ratio, and dividend yield are also valuable indicators if they are available. For a mid-market corporation, however, they are probably unavailable since the debt and equity claims of most mid-market corporations are not publicly traded. The account officer may find it informative to substitute a similarly listed firm (a so-called comparability test).

Common Size Analysis and Growth Rates.   An analyst can compute sets of ratios by dividing all income statement amounts by total sales revenue and all balance sheet amounts by total assets. These calculations yield common-size financial statements that can be used to identify changes in corporate performance. Year-to-year growth rates also give useful ratios for identifying trends. Common-size financial statements may provide quantitative clues as to the direction that the firm is moving and that the analysis should take.

Following Approval.   The credit process does not end when the applicant signs the loan agreement. As is the case for mortgage loans, before allowing takedown of a mid-market credit, the account officer must make sure that **conditions precedent** have been cleared. These include various searches, registration of collateral, confirmation of the officer's authority to borrow, and the like. Following takedown, the credit must be monitored throughout the loan's life to ensure that the borrower is living up to its commitments and to detect deterioration should it occur to protect the bank's interests.

conditions precedent

Those conditions specified in the credit agreement or terms sheet for a credit that must be fulfilled before drawings are permitted.

Typically, the borrower's credit needs change from time to time. A growing company has an expanding need for credit. A company moving into the international arena needs foreign exchange credit agreements. A contractor may have periodic guarantee requests. Even if the credit agreements being offered do not change, corporate credits are usually reviewed on an annual basis to ensure that they comply with the terms of the credit agreement. The FIs typically wish to maintain close contact with customers to meet their ongoing financial service requirements—both credit and noncredit—so that the relationship will develop into a permanent, mutually beneficial one.

Large Commercial and Industrial Lending

An FI's bargaining strength is severely diminished when it deals with creditworthy large corporate customers. Large corporations are able to disintermediate, issuing debt and equity directly in the capital markets and making private placements.[17] They typically maintain credit relationships with several FIs and have significant in-house financial expertise. They manage their cash position through the money markets by issuing their own commercial paper to meet fund shortfalls and using excess funds to buy Treasury bills, banker's acceptances, and other companies' commercial paper. Moreover, large corporate clients are not seriously restricted by international borders but have operations in may parts of the world. Typically, they also count nondomestic FIs among their advisers and creditors. They may wish to tap foreign markets and swap the proceeds into the currency of

---

[17]This additional source of funds for large corporations is a major reason for some of the mergers between large commercial banks and investment banks in the late 1990s (e.g., NaitonsBank/Montgomery Securities and U.S. Bancorp/Piper Jaffray). Such mergers offer commercial banks the opportunity to participate in new security issues of large corporations in addition to the traditional business of lending.

choice (either U.S. dollars or a third currency; see Chapter 23). Large corporate clients are very attractive to FIs because, although spreads and fees are small in percentage terms, the transactions are large enough to make them very profitable (and very often loan business can enable the FI to sell other products to the same client). Hence, competition for loans to large corporate clients tends to be intense.

Moreover, the FI's relationship with large corporate credits is fluid. The FI's role as broker, dealer, and adviser to the corporate client may rival or exceed the importance of its role as a lender. A large corporate client is likely to investigate several avenues for obtaining credit from several FIs at the same time and to compare, for example, the flexibility and cost of a bond, a private placement, and bank borrowings. The client may periodically poll FIs to determine opportune times to tap the financial market, even if that means inventorying funds. The account officer must often liaise with the FI's investment dealer to obtain information and indicative pricing on security offers. Clearly, the amount of time this involves means that a senior account officer for large corporations manages far fewer accounts than colleagues providing mid-market corporate credits.

In providing a credit service to large corporations, credit management remains an important issue. Large corporations frequently use loan commitments, performance guarantees, and term loans as do mid-market corporates. When underwriting securities for a client, an FI must have (or be able to obtain quickly) underwriting credit lines that provide temporary credit risk exposures well in excess of the FI's regular positions. If the FI is contracting in spot and forward foreign exchange or swaps or is engaging in other derivative activities with the corporate client as a counterparty, it must do so within the credit limits established by a regular credit review process.

An additional complicating factor is that large corporate accounts usually consist of several corporate entities with cross-holdings of ownership under a common management. A holding company may wholly own, control, or have substantial stakes in various operating subsidiaries. A subsidiary's credit risk may be better than, the same as, or worse than that of the holding company parent. An FI lending to a holding company with no assets but its equity in the subsidiaries puts itself in a subordinate lending position relative to the lenders to the operating subsidiaries, which have direct claims over the subsidiaries' operating assets. An FI lending to a risky subsidiary with no guarantee from its more stable parent is taking far more risk than if it lent directly to the well-capitalized parent. A parent can potentially walk away from the unguaranteed debts of its bankrupt subsidiary.

An account officer preparing a credit review for a large corporate customer often faces a complex task. The standard methods of analysis that we introduced when discussing mid-market corporates applies to large corporate clients, but with additional complications. The corporate business often crosses more than one business type and location. Hence, industry comparisons are difficult at best. Additional analytical aids are available to account officers; they can apply the market price of the client's publicly traded securities to market-based models of loan pricing. And the large corporates are tracked by rating agencies and market analysts, which can provide account officers a great deal of publicly available information to aid in their credit analysis. Also, because of these customers' additional complexities and large credit risk exposures, FIs also use sophisticated models in the credit review. The next section discusses two of these sophisticated models.

Credit Scoring Models.   Credit scoring models use data on observed borrower characteristics either to calculate the probability of default or to sort borrowers into different default risk classes. By selecting and combining different economic and financial borrower characteristics, an FI manager may be able to

1. Numerically establish which factors are important in explaining default risk.
2. Evaluate the relative degree or importance of these factors.
3. Improve the pricing of default risk.
4. Screen high-risk loan applicants.
5. Calculate any reserves needed to meet expected future loan losses.

To employ credit scoring models in this manner, the FI manager must identify objective economic and financial measures of risk for any particular class of borrower. For corporate debt, financial ratios such as the debt-equity ratio are usually key factors. After data are identified, a statistical technique quantifies or scores the default risk probability or default risk classification.

Altman's Z-Score.   E. I. Altman developed a Z-score model for analyzing publicly traded manufacturing firms in the United States. The indicator variable Z is an overall measure of the borrower's default risk classification. That, in turn, depends on the values of various financial ratios of the borrower (X_j) and the weighted importance of these ratios based on the observed experience of defaulting versus nondefaulting borrowers derived from a discriminant analysis model.[18]

Altman's credit scoring model takes the following form

$$Z = 1.2X_1 + 1.4X_2 + 3.3X_3 + 0.6X_4 + 1.0X_5$$

where

X_1 = working capital/total assets ratio
X_2 = retained earnings/total assets ratio
X_3 = earnings before interest and taxes/total assets ratio
X_4 = market value of equity/book value of long-term debt ratio
X_5 = sales/total assets ratio.

The higher the value of Z, the lower the borrower's default risk classification.[19] Thus, low or negative Z values may be evidence that the borrower is a member of a relatively high default risk class.

EXAMPLE   10 – 4

Calculation of Altman's Z-Score

Suppose that the financial ratios of a potential borrowing firm took the following values

$X_1 = .2$
$X_2 = 0$
$X_3 = -.20$
$X_4 = .10$
$X_5 = 2.0$

The ratio X_2 is zero and X_3 is negative, indicating that the firm has had negative earnings or losses in recent periods. Also, X_4 indicates that the borrower is highly leveraged. However,

---

[18]E. I. Altman, "Managing the Commercial Lending Process," in *Handbook of Banking Strategy*, ed. R C. Aspinwall and R. A. Eisenbeis (New York: John Wiley & Sons, 1985), pp. 473–510.
[19]Working capital is current assets minus current liabilities.

the working capital ratio (X_1) and the sales/assets ratio (X_5) indicate that the firm is reasonably liquid and is maintaining its sales volume. The Z-score provides an overall score or indicator of the borrower's credit risk since it combines and weights these five factors according to their past importance in explaining borrower default. For the borrower in question

$$Z = 1.2(.2) + 1.4(0) + 3.3(-.20) + 0.6(.10) + 1.0(2.0)$$
$$Z = 0.24 + 0 - .66 + 0.06 + 2.0$$
$$Z = 1.64$$ • • •

According to Altman's credit scoring model, any firm with a Z-score of less than 1.81 should be considered to be a high default risk.[20] Thus, the FI should not lend to this borrower until it improves its earnings performance.

Use of the Z-score model to make credit risk evaluations has a number of problems. The first problem is that this model usually discriminates only between two extreme cases of borrower behavior, no default and default. As discussed in Chapter 9, in the real world various gradations of default exist, from nonpayment or delay of interest payments (nonperforming assets) to outright default on all promised interest and principal payments. This problem suggests that a more accurate or finely calibrated sorting among borrowers may require defining more classes in the scoring model.

The second problem is that there is no obvious economic reason to expect that the weights in the Z-score model—or, more generally, the weights in any credit scoring model—will be constant over any but very short periods. The same concern also applies to the variables (X_j). Specifically, due to changing financial market conditions, other borrower-specific financial ratios may come to be increasingly relevant in explaining default risk probabilities.

The third problem is that these models ignore important, hard-to-quantify factors that may play a crucial role in the default or no-default decision. For example, the reputation of the borrower and the nature of the long-term borrower-lender relationship could be important borrower-specific characteristics, as could macro factors such as the phase of the business cycle. Credit scoring models often ignore these variables. Moreover, credit scoring models rarely use publicly available information, such as the prices in asset markets in which the outstanding debt and equity of the borrower are already traded.[21]

A fourth problem relates to default records kept by FIs. Currently, no centralized, publicly available database on defaulted loans for proprietary or other reasons exists. Some task forces run by consortiums of commercial banks and consulting firms are currently seeking to construct such databases, but it may well be many years before they are developed. This constrains the ability of many FIs to use credit scoring models for larger business loans.

KMV Model.   In recent years, following the pioneering work of Nobel prize winners in economics—Merton, Black, and Scholes—we now recognize that when a firm raises funds either by issuing bonds or increasing its bank loans, it holds a very valuable default or

---

[20]This "critical value" is calculated by taking the average or the mean Z-score for firms that defaulted in the FI's sample and the mean Z-score for firms that did not default. Thus, if defaulting firms had a mean Z-score of 1.61 and nondefaulting firms a mean Z-score of 2.01, the critical Z-score is 1.81 (i.e., half way between these two values).

[21]However, it might be noted that the X_4 variable in Altman's Z-score model includes a market value of equity measure.

repayment option.[22] That is, if a borrower's investment projects fail so that it cannot repay the bondholder or the FI, it has the option to default on its debt repayment and turn any remaining assets over to the debtholder (FI). Because of limited liability for equity holders, the borrower's loss is limited, on the downside, by the amount of equity invested in the firm.[23] On the other hand, if things go well, the borrower can keep most of the upside returns on asset investments after the promised principal and interest on the debt have been paid. The KMV Corporation has turned this relatively simple idea into a credit-monitoring model. Many of the largest U.S. banks are reputedly now using this model to determine the expected default risk frequency (EDF) of large corporations.[24]

The KMV model uses the option pricing model of a firm's equity price to extract an implied asset volatility (risk) of a given firm (σ). Using the implied value of risk for assets, the likely distribution of possible asset values of the firm relative to its current debt obligations can be calculated. The EDF reflects the probability that the market value of the firm's assets will fall below the promised repayments on debt liabilities in one year. If the value of a firm's assets falls below its debt liabilities, it can be viewed as being economically insolvent. Simulations by KMV have shown that this model outperforms both Z-score models and S&P rating changes as predictors of corporate failure and distress.[25] For example, Figure 10–6 illustrates the EDF for IBM in the period before it suffered two credit rating downgrades by Standard and Poor's in the fall of 1992 and the spring of 1993. IBM's EDF in this figure begins to rise more than two years before these downgrades.

Concept Questions

1. "As long as a mortgage loan is sufficiently overcollateralized, it is riskless." Do you agree? Why or why not?
2. What does a title search accomplish?
3. FIs have separate checks on account officers granting credit. Why do you think these are needed?
4. Why must the account officer be well versed in the FI's credit policy before talking to potential borrowers?
5. Why should a credit officer be concerned if a borrower's number of days' receivables increases beyond the industry norm?
6. Do you agree or disagree with the statement that disintermediation means that FIs have less business with large corporations? Why?
7. From a credit risk point of view, would you rather lend to a holding company or to its operating subsidiaries? Why?
8. What are the major problems with the Z-score model of credit risk?
9. How should a reduction in a borrower's leverage and the underlying volatility of its earnings affect the risk premium on its loan?

---

[22]R. C. Merton, "On the Pricing of Corporate Debt: The Risk Structure of Interest Rates," *Journal of Finance* 29 (1974), pp. 449–70; and F. Black and M. Scholes, "The Pricing of Options and Corporate Liabilities," *Journal of Political Economy* 81 (1973), pp. 737–759.

[23]Given limits to losses in personal bankruptcy, a similar analysis can be applied to retail and consumer loans.

[24]See KMV Corporation, *Credit Monitor* (San Francisco: KMV Corporation, 1994).

[25]KMV currently provides EDFs for more than 20,000 U.S. and foreign companies.

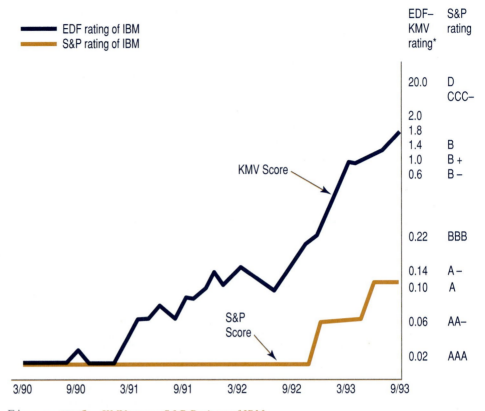

Figure 10-6   *KMV versus S&P Ratings of IBM*

*EDF's rating ranges from 0 percent to 20 percent.
SOURCE: KMV Corporation.

S U M M A R Y

This chapter discussed different approaches to measure credit or default risk on individual loans (bonds). The different types of loans that FIs make and some of their basic characteristics were first examined. The chapter then discussed the role of credit analysis and how it differs across different types of loans, espe-

cially mortgage loans, individual loans, mid-market corporate loans, and large corporate loans. Both qualitative and quantitative approaches to credit analysis were discussed. The next chapter discusses methods to evaluate the risk of loan portfolios or loan concentration risk.

P E R T I N E N T   W E B   S I T E S

Board of Governors of the Federal Reserve   http://www.bog.frb.
    fed.us/
Federal Deposit Insurance Corp. (FDIC)   http://www.fdic.gov/
Federal Housing Finance Board   http://www.fhfb.gov/
KMV Corp.   http://www.kmv.com/

Moody's Corp.   http://www.moodys.com/
Robert Morris Associates   http://www.rmahq.org/
Standard and Poor's Corp.   http://www.stockinfo.standardpoor.
    com/

Credit Risk: Credit Analysis and Lending Risk

1. Why is credit risk analysis an important component of bank risk management? What recent activities by FIs have made the task of credit risk assessment more difficult for both bank managers and regulators?

2. Differentiate between a *secured* and an *unsecured loan.* Who bears most of the risk in a fixed rate loan? Why would bankers prefer to charge floating rates, especially for longer maturity loans?

3. How does a spot loan differ from a loan commitment?

4. What are the advantages and disadvantages of borrowing through a loan commitment?

5. Why is commercial lending declining in importance in the United States? What effect does the decline have on overall commercial lending activities?

6. In what ways does the credit analysis of a mid-market borrower differ from that of a small business borrower?

7. Why could a lender's expected return be lower when the risk premium is increased on a loan?

8. Jane Doe earns $30,000 per year and has applied for an $80,000, 30-year mortgage at 8 percent interest. Property taxes on the house are expected to be $1,200 per year. If her bank requires a gross debt service ratio of no more than 30 percent, will Jane be able to obtain the mortgage?

9. How does ratio analysis help to answer questions about the production, management, and marketing capabilities of a prospective borrower?

10. How does a bank control its credit risks with respect to consumer and commercial loans?

11. What are some of the special risks and considerations when lending to small businesses rather than to large businesses?

12. What borrower-specific and market-specific factors need to be considered in evaluating a loan?

13. Consider the following company's balance sheet and income statement.

Balance Sheet

Assets		Liabilities and equity	
Cash	$4,000	Accounts payable	$30,000
Accounts receivable	52,000	Notes payable	12,000
Inventory	40,000		
Total current assets	96,000	Total current liabilities	42,000
Fixed assets	44,000	Long-term debt	36,000
		Equity	62,000
Total assets	$140,000	Total liabilities and equity	$140,000

Income Statement

Sales	$200,000
Cost of goods sold	130,000
Gross margin	70,000
Selling and administrative expenses	20,000
Depreciation	8,000
EBIT	42,000
Interest expense	4,800
Earning before tax	37,200
Taxes	11,160
Net income	$ 26,040

For this company, calculate the following:
  - (a) Current ratio
  - (b) Number of days' sales in receivables
  - (c) Sales to total assets
  - (d) Number of days in inventory
  - (e) Debt ratio
  - (f) Cash-flow debt ratio
  - (g) Return on assets
  - (h) Return on equity

14. In problem (13), how might we determine whether these ratios reflect a well-managed, creditworthy company?

15. Industrial Corporation has an income-to-sales ratio of .03, a sales-to-assets ratio of 1.5, and a debt-to-asset ratio of .66. What is Industrial's return on equity?

16. Consider the coefficients of Altman's Z-score. Can you tell by the size of the coefficients which ratio appears most important in assessing the creditworthiness of a loan applicant? Explain.

17. The following is ABC Inc's balance sheet (in thousands):

Assets		Liabilities	
Cash	$ 20	Accounts payable	$ 30
Accounts receivables	90	Notes payable	90
Inventory	90	Accruals	30
		Long-term debt	150
Plant and equipment	500	Equity	400
Total	$700		$700

Also, sales equal $500, cost of goods sold equals $360, taxes equal $56, interest payments equal $40, and net income equals $44.

  a. Calculate Altman's Z-score for ABC Inc. if ABC has a 50 percent dividend payout ratio and the market value of equity is equal to its book value. Recall the following:

   New working capital = Current assets − Current liabilities

Current assets = Cash + Accounts receivable + Inventory

Current liabilities = Accounts payable + Accruals + Notes payable

EBIT = Revenues – Cost of goods sold – Depreciation

Taxes = (EBIT – Interest)(Tax rate)

Net income = EBIT – Interest – Taxes

Retained earnings = Net income (1 – dividend payout ratio)

b. Should you approve ABC Inc.'s application to your bank for $500,000 for a capital expansion loan?

c. If ABC's sales were $300,000 and the market value of equity fell to half its book value (assume cost of goods sold and interest unchanged), how would that change ABC's income statement? ABC's tax liability can be used to offset tax liabilities incurred by the other divisions of the firm. Would your credit decision change?

d. What are some of the shortcomings of using a Z-score to evaluate credit risk?

The following questions are related to Appendix material.

18. Countrybank offers one-year loans with a stated rate of 10 percent but requires a compensating balance of 10 percent. What is the true cost of this loan to the borrower?

19. Metrobank offers one-year loans with a 9 percent stated rate, charges a .25 percent loan origination fee, imposes a 10 percent compensating balance requirement, and must pay a 6 percent reserve requirement to the Federal Reserve. What is the return to the bank on these loans?

20. A bank is planning to make a loan of $5,000,000 to a firm in the steel industry. It expects to charge an up-front fee of 1.5 percent and a service fee of 50 basis points. The loan has a maturity of eight years. The cost of funds (and the RAROC benchmark) for the bank is 10 percent. Assume that the bank has estimated the risk premium on the steel manufacturing sector to be appoximately 4.2 percent, based on two years of historical data. The current market interest rate for loans in this sector is 12 percent. Using the RAROC model, should the bank make the loan?

APPENDIX: CALCULATING
THE RETURN ON A LOAN

This Appendix demonstrates two ways to calculate the return on a loan: the traditional *return on assets approach* and a newer approach called (*risk-adjusted return on assets*) *RAROC* that considers loan returns in the context of the risk of the loan to the FI.

Return on Assets (ROA)

A number of factors impact the promised return that an FI achieves on any given dollar loan amount. These factors include the following:

1. The interest rate on the loan.
2. Any fees relating to the loan.
3. The credit risk premium on the loan.
4. The collateral backing the loan.
5. Other nonprice terms (especially compensating balances and reserve requirements).

First, let us consider an example of how to calculate the promised return on a C&I loan. Suppose that a bank makes a spot one-year, $1 million loan. The loan rate is set as follows

$$\text{Base lending rate} = 12\% = L$$
$$+$$
$$\underline{\text{Risk premium} = 2\% = m}$$
$$14\% = L + m$$

The base lending rate (L) could reflect the bank's weighted average cost of capital or its marginal cost of funds, such as the commercial paper rate, the federal funds rate, or **LIBOR**—the London interbank offered rate, which is the rate for interbank dollar loans in the foreign or Eurodollar market of a given maturity. Alternatively, it could reflect the **prime lending rate**. Traditionally, the prime rate has been the rate charged to the bank's lowest risk customers. Now it is more a base rate to which positive or negative risk premiums can be added. In other words, banks now charge their best and largest borrowers below prime rate to compete with the commercial paper market.[26]

Suppose that the bank does the following:

1. Charges a ⅛ percent (or 0.125 percent) loan origination fee (f) to the borrower.
2. Imposes a 10 percent compensating balance requirement (b) to be held as noninterest-bearing demand deposits. **Compensating balances** represent a percentage of a loan that a borrower cannot actively use for expenditures. Instead, these balances must be kept on deposit at the FI. For example, a borrower facing a 10 percent compensating balance requirement on a $100 loan would have to place $10 on deposit (traditionally on demand deposit) with the FI and could use only $90 of the $100 borrowed. This requirement raises the effective cost of loans for the borrower since the deposit rate earned on compensating balances is less than the borrowing rate. Thus,

LIBOR

The London interbank offered rate, the rate for interbank dollar loans in the foreign or Eurodollar market of a given maturity.

prime lending rate

The base lending rate periodically set by banks.

compensating balance

A proportion of a loan that a borrower is required to hold on deposit at the lending institution.

---

[26]For more information on the prime rate, see P. Nabar, S. Park, and A. Saunders, "Prime Rate Changes: Is There an Advantage in Being First?" *Journal of Business* 66 (1993), pp. 69–92; and L. Mester and A. Saunders, "When Does the Prime Rate Change?" *Journal of Banking and Finance* 19 (1995), pp. 743–764.

compensating balance requirements act as an additional source of return on lending for an FI.[27] Consequently, although credit risk may be the most important factor ultimately affecting the return on a loan, FI managers should not ignore these other factors in evaluating loan profitability and risk. Indeed, FIs can compensate for high credit risk in a number of ways other than charging a higher explicit interest rate or risk premium on a loan or restricting the amount of credit available. In particular, higher fees, high compensating balances, and increased collateral backing offer implicit and indirect methods to compensate an FI for lending risk.

3. Pays reserve requirements (R) of 10 percent imposed by the Federal Reserve on the bank's demand deposits, including any compensating balances (see Chapter 14).

Then the contractually promised gross return on the loan, k, per dollar lent—or ROA per dollar lent—equals[28]

$$1 + k = 1 + \frac{f + (L + m)}{1 - [b(1 - R)]}$$

This formula may need some explanation. The numerator is the promised gross cash inflow to the FI per dollar lent, reflecting fees (f) plus interest $(L + m)$. In the denominator, for every $1 in loans that the FI lends, it retains b as noninterest-bearing compensating balances. Thus, $1 - b$ represents the net proceeds of each $1 of loans received by the borrower from the FI, ignoring reserve requirements. However, since b (compensating balances) are held by the borrower at the FI as demand deposits, the Federal Reserve requires the FI to hold noninterest-bearing reserves at the rate R against these compensating balances. Thus, the FI's net benefit from requiring compensating balances must consider noninterest-bearing reserve requirements. The net outflow by the FI per $1 of loans is $1 - [b(1 - R)]$ or 1 minus the reserve adjusted compensating balance requirement.

Placing the numbers from our example into this formula, we have

$$1 + k = 1 + \frac{.00125 + (.12 + .02)}{1 - [(.10)(.9)]}$$

$$1 + k = 1 + \frac{.14125}{.91}$$

$$1 + k = 1.1552 \text{ or } k = 15.52\%$$

This is, of course, larger than the simple promised interest return on the loan, $L + m = 14$ percent.

In the special case in which fees (f) are zero and the compensating balance (b) is zero

$$f = 0$$
$$b = 0$$

the contractually promised return formula reduces to

$$1 + k = 1 + (L + m)$$

---

[27]They also create a more stable supply of deposits and, thus, mitigate liquidity problems.

[28]This formula ignores present value aspects that could easily be incorporated. For example, fees are earned in upfront undiscounted dollars while interest payments and risk premiums are normally paid on loan maturity and, thus, should be discounted by the bank's cost of funds.

That is, the credit risk premium is the fundamental factor driving the promised return on a loan once the base rate on the loan has been set.

Note that as credit markets have become more competitive, both origination fees (*f*) and compensating balances (*b*) have become less important. For example, when compensating balances are still required, banks may now allow them to be held as time deposits and earn interest. As a result, borrowers' opportunity losses from compensating balances have been reduced to the difference between the loan rate and the compensating balance time-deposit rate. In addition, in most foreign dollar loans, compensating balance requirements are very rare.

RAROC Models

An increasingly popular model used to evaluate the return on a loan to a large customer is the risk-adjusted return on capital (RAROC) model. RAROC, pioneered by Bankers Trust, has now been adopted by virtually all the large banks in the United States and Europe, although with some proprietary differences among them.

The essential idea behind RAROC is that rather than evaluating the actual or promised annual cash flow on a loan as a percentage of the amount (or the ROA) lent, as described in the earlier subsection, the lending officer balances expected loan income against the loan's risk (should the financial condition of the borrower deteriorate).[29] Thus, rather than dividing loan income by assets lent, it is divided by some measure of asset (loan) risk or FI capital at risk

$$\text{RAROC} = \frac{\text{One-year income on a loan}}{\text{Loan (asset) risk or capital at risk}}$$

A loan is approved only if RAROC is sufficiently high relative to a benchmark return on equity capital (ROE) for the FI. The idea here is that a loan should be made only if the risk-adjusted return on the loan adds to the FI's equity value as measured by the ROE required by the FI's stockholders. Thus, for example, if ROE is 15 percent, a loan should be made only if the estimated RAROC is higher than 15 percent. Alternatively, if the RAROC on an existing loan falls below an FI's RAROC benchmark, the lending officer should seek to adjust the loan's terms to make it "profitable" again.

One problem in estimating RAROC is the measurement of loan risk (the denominator in the RAROC equation). In calculating RAROC, most FIs divide one-year income—usually the spread between the loan rate and the cost of funds plus any fees directly earned from making the loan—by the product of an unexpected loss rate and the proportion of the loan that cannot be recaptured on default as a measure of risk per dollar loaned, thus

$$\text{RAROC} = \frac{\text{One-year income per dollar loaned}}{\text{Unexpected loss rate} \times \text{Proportion of loan lost on default}}$$

---

[29]Since loan defaults are charged to the FI's capital or equity account, the loan's risk is also a measure of "risk capital," or capital at risk.

EXAMPLE 10–1A

• • • • • •   *Calculation of RAROC*

Suppose that expected income per dollar lent is 0.3 cents, or .003. The 99th percentile (extreme case) loss rate for borrowers of this type is 4 percent, and the dollar proportion of loans of this type that cannot be recaptured on default is 80 percent.[30] Then

$$RAROC = \frac{.003}{(.04)(.8)} = \frac{.003}{(.032)} = 9.375\%$$

If the FI's ROE is less than 9.375 percent (e.g., it is 9 percent), the loan can be viewed as being profitable. If the ROE is higher than 9.375 percent (e.g., 15 percent), it should be rejected and/or the loan officer should seek higher spreads and fees on the loan.   • • •

---

[30]The extreme loss rate is usually calculated by taking the average annual loss rate and estimating the annual standard deviation of loan loss rates around that mean. If the standard deviation is multiplied by 2.33, as long as loan loss rates are normally distributed, this reflects the 99th percentile worst-loss case scenario (i.e., the FIs will experience a worse percentage loss on these loans only 1 year in every 100 years). In the example in the text, the standard deviation (σ) of the loss rate is 1.71 percent. Thus, $2.33 \times 1.71\% = 4\%$.

Chapter Eleven

Credit Risk: Loan Portfolio Risk

Chapter 10 described ways in which a financial intermediary (FI) manager can measure the returns and risks on individual debt instruments such as loans or bonds. This chapter concentrates on the ability of an FI manager to measure credit risk in a loan (asset) portfolio context and to benefit from loan (asset) portfolio diversification. The return-risk characteristics of each loan in the portfolio are a concern to an FI, but the return-risk status of the overall loan portfolio, with some of the risk of the individual loans diversified, affects the FI's overall credit risk exposure. Additionally, this chapter considers the potential use of loan portfolio models in setting maximum concentration (borrowing) limits for certain business or borrowing sectors; for example, sectors identified by their industry or sector Standard Industrial Classification (SIC) codes. The chapter also discusses regulatory models for measuring the default risk of a portfolio. In particular, the FDIC Improvement Act of 1991 required bank regulators to incorporate credit concentration risk into a bank's risk-based capital requirements. In 1996, the National Association of Insurance Commissioners (NAIC) developed limits for different types of assets and borrowers in insurers' portfolios, a so-called pigeonhole approach.

SIMPLE MODELS OF LOAN
CONCENTRATION RISK

migration analysis

A method to measure loan concentration risk by tracking credit ratings of firms in particular sectors for unusual declines.

concentration limits

External limits set on the maximum loan size that can be made to an individual borrower.

FIs widely employ two simple models to measure credit risk concentration in the loan portfolio beyond the purely subjective model of "we have already lent too much to this borrower."[1] The first model is **migration analysis**, by which lending officers track the S&P or Moody's credit ratings of certain sectors, for example, machine tools. If the credit ratings of a number of firms in a sector decline by a larger amount than usual, FIs curtail lending to that sector.[2] The problem with this approach is that it amounts to "locking the stable door after the horse has bolted."

The second credit risk model requires management to set some external limit on the maximum amount of loans that it will make to an individual borrower. The FI determines **concentration limits** on the proportion of the loan portfolio that can go to any single customer by assessing the borrower's current portfolio, its operating units' business plans, its economists' economic projections, and its strategic plans. Typically, FIs set concentration limits to reduce exposures to certain industries and increase exposures to others. When two industry groups' performances are highly correlated, an FI may set an aggregate limit of less than the sum of the two individual industry limits. FIs also typically set geographic limits. They may set aggregate portfolio limits or combinations of industry and geographic limits. For example, suppose that management is unwilling to permit losses exceeding 10 percent of an FI's capital to a particular sector. If management estimates that the amount lost per dollar of defaulted loans in this sector is 40 cents (i.e., the FI receives 60 cents on every dollar loaned out), the maximum loans to a single borrower as a percentage of capital, defined as the *concentration limit*, is as follows:

$$\text{Concentration limit} = \text{Maximum loss as a percent capital} \times \frac{1}{\text{Loss rate}}$$

$$= 10\% \times (1/.4)$$
$$= 25\%$$

Bank regulators in recent years have limited loan concentrations to *individual borrowers* to a maximum of 10 percent of a bank's capital.

Concept Questions

1. What is the concentration limit if the loss rate on bad loans is 25 cents on the dollar?
2. What is the concentration limit if the maximum loss (as a percentage of capital) is 15 percent instead of 10 percent?

· ·

---

[1] See Board of Governors of the Federal Reserve, "Revisions to Risk Based Capital Standards to Account for Concentration of Credit Risk and Risks of Non-Traditional Activities," Washington, D.C.: FDICIA, March 26, 1993, Section 305.

[2] Technically speaking, the rate of current downgrades exceeds the historical probability of downgrades for a particular industry or rating concentration.

Next we look at the use of more sophisticated portfolio theory–based models to set concentration limits. Although these models have a great deal of potential, data availability and other implementation problems have often prevented their reaching this potential.

LOAN PORTFOLIO DIVERSIFICATION
AND MODERN PORTFOLIO THEORY

To the extent that an FI manager holds widely traded loans and bonds as assets or can calculate or simulate loan or bond returns, the manager can use portfolio diversification models to measure and control the FI's aggregate credit risk exposure.[3] Suppose that the manager can estimate the expected returns of each loan or bond $(\bar{R}_i)$ in the FI's portfolio.

After calculating the individual security return series, the FI manager can compute the expected return (R_p) on a portfolio of assets as

$$R_P = \sum_{i=1}^{N} X_i \bar{R}_i$$

In addition, the variance of returns or risk of the portfolio (σ_P^2) can be calculated from:

$$\sigma_P^2 = \sum_{i=1}^{N} X_i^2 \sigma_i^2 + \sum_{i=1}^{N} \sum_{\substack{j=1 \\ i \neq j}}^{N} X_i X_j \sigma_{ij}$$

where

R_P = The expected or mean return on the asset portfolio
Σ = Summation sign
$\bar{R}_i$ = The mean return on the ith asset in the portfolio
X_i = The proportion of the asset portfolio invested in the ith asset
σ_i^2 = The variance of returns on the ith asset
σ_{ij} = The covariance of returns between the ith and jth assets

The fundamental lesson of modern portfolio theory (MPT) is that by taking advantage of its size, an FI can diversify considerable amounts of credit risk as long as the returns on different assets are imperfectly correlated.[4]

---

[3] J. P. Morgan's CreditMetrics model of the value at risk on loan portfolios (discussed later in this chapter) uses both direct calculation and simulation methods (so called Monte Carlo simulation). See J. P. Morgan, *Introduction to CreditMetrics* (New York: J.P. Morgan Securities, April 1997).

[4] One objection to using MPT for loans is that the returns on individual loans are not normally or symmetrically distributed. In particular, most loans have limited upside returns and long-tail downside risks (see the discussion in Chapter 9). Nevertheless, default correlations in general are likely to be low. For example, the joint probability of two major companies such as General Motors and Ford defaulting on their loans at exactly the same time is quite small, even though they are both in the same industry. For example, studies presented in J. P. Morgan's *Introduction to CreditMetrics*, Chapter 5, suggest that most default correlations lie in the .2 to .3 range. This suggests potentially large benefits from diversifying the loan portfolio.

Consider the equation for variance of returns, σ_p^2. If many loans have negative correlations or covariances of returns (σ_{ij} are negative)—that is, when one borrower's loans do badly, another's do well—the sum of the individual credit risks of loans viewed independently overestimates the risk of the whole portfolio. This is what we meant in Chapter 9 when we stated that by pooling funds, FIs can reduce risk by taking advantage of the law of large numbers in their investment decisions.

E X A M P L E   1 1 – 1

• • • • • • •

Calculation of Return and Risk on a Two-Asset Portfolio

Suppose that an FI holds two loans with the following characteristics:[5]

Loan i	X_i	$\bar{R}_i$	σ_i	σ_i^2	
1	.40	10%	9.80%	96.0%	$\sigma_{12} = -84\%$
2	.60	12	8.57	73.5	

The return on the loan portfolio is

$$R_P = .4\,(10\%) + .6\,(12\%) = 11.2\%$$

while the risk of the portfolio is

$$\sigma_p^2 = (.4)^2\,(96.0\%) + (.6)^2\,(73.5\%) + 2(.4)(.6)(-84\%) = 1.5\%$$

thus, $\sigma_p = \sqrt{1.5\%} = 1.22\%$.

Notice that the risk (or standard deviation of returns) of the portfolio, σ_p (1.22 percent), is less than the risk of either individual asset (9.8 percent and 8.57 percent, respectively). The negative covariance of the returns of the two loans (–84 percent) results in an overall reduction of risk when they are put together in an FI's portfolio.   • • •

Consider the advantages of diversification in Figure 11–1. Note that A is an undiversified portfolio with heavy investment concentration in just a few loans or bonds. By fully exploiting diversification potential with bonds or loans whose returns are negatively correlated or that have a low positive correlation with those in the existing portfolio, the FI manager can lower the credit risk on the portfolio from σ_{pA} to σ_{pB} while earning the same expected return. That is, portfolio B is the efficient (lowest risk) portfolio associated with portfolio return level R_p. By varying the required portfolio return level R_p up and down, the manager can identify an entire frontier of efficient portfolio mixes of loans and bonds. Each portfolio mix is efficient in the sense that it offers the lowest risk level to the FI manager at each possible level of portfolio returns. Figure 11–1 indicates, however, of all possible efficient portfolios that can be generated, portfolio B produces the lowest possible risk level for the FI manager. That is, it maximizes the gains from diversifying across all available loans and bonds so that the manager cannot reduce the risk of the portfolio below σ_{pB}. For this reason, σ_{pB} is usually considered the **minimum risk portfolio.**

Even though B is clearly the minimum *risk* portfolio, it does not generate the highest returns. Consequently, portfolio B may be chosen only by the most risk-averse FI managers, whose sole objective is to minimize portfolio risk regardless of the portfolio's return.

minimum risk portfolio

A portfolio for which a combination of assets reduces the variance of portfolio returns to the lowest feasible level.

---

[5]Note that variance (σ^2) is measured in percent squared; standard deviation (σ) is measured in percent.

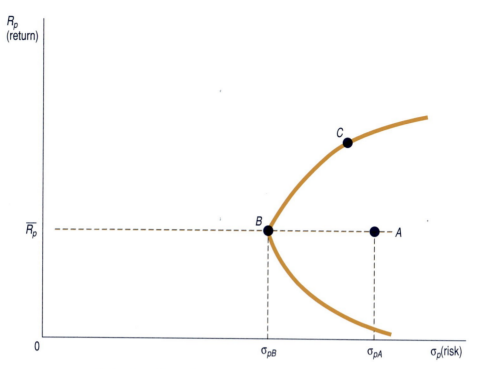

F i g u r e **11–1**   *FI Portfolio Diversification*

Most portfolio managers have some desired return–risk trade-off in mind; they are willing to accept more risk if they are compensated with higher expected returns.[6] One such possibility would be portfolio C in Figure 11–1. This is an efficient portfolio because the FI manager has mixed loans to produce a portfolio risk level that is a minimum for that higher expected return level. This portfolio dominates all other portfolios that can produce the same expected return level.[7]

CreditMetrics

CreditMetrics, released by J. P. Morgan and its co-sponsors (Bank of America, BZW, Deutsche Morgan Grenfell, Swiss Bank Corporation, Union Bank of Switzerland, and KMV Corporation) in 1997, is the first publicly available model that applies portfolio

---

[6] The point that is chosen depends on the manager's risk aversion and the degree of separation of ownership from control. If the FI is managed by agents who perform the task of maximizing the value of the firm, they act as risk-neutral agents. They would know that stockholders, who are well diversified, could, through homemade diversification, hold the shares of many firms to eliminate borrower-specific risk. Thus, managers would seek to maximize expected return subject to any regulatory constraints on risk-taking behavior (i.e., they would likely pick a point in the region C in Figure 11–1). However, if managers are risk averse because of their human capital invested in the FI and make lending decisions based on their own risk preferences rather than those of the stockholders, they are likely to choose a relatively low-risk portfolio, something closer to the minimum risk portfolio.

[7] For a detailed discussion of portfolio risk calculation, see R.A. Brealey, S.C. Myers, and A.J. Marcus, *Fundamentals of Corporate Finance* (New York, NY: McGraw-Hill, Inc., 1995), pp. 225–229.

theory and value-at-risk methodology to evaluate credit risk across a broad range of instruments and portfolios of these instruments, including traditional loans, commitments, and letters of credit; fixed income instruments; commercial contracts (such as trade credits and receivables); and derivative instruments (such as swaps, forwards, and futures).

CreditMetrics's approach to quantifying credit risk is different than traditional approaches. That is, traditional approaches usually consider only two states of the world: default and no default. These two-states-of-the-world approaches attempt to capture each loan's entire credit risk based only on the probability of default or full recovery at various intervals over the life of the loan. They do not allow for intermediate changes in the value of the loans in the portfolio as the credit "quality" of the borrower changes.

By contrast, CreditMetrics estimates portfolio *value at risk* due to credit events that include credit rating upgrades and downgrades, as well as defaults (thus, it adopts a mark-to-market framework). It also uses long-term estimates of credit quality changes rather than observations for some recent sample period. CreditMetrics is probabilistic in that it recalculates the market value of the loan in different rating downgrade/upgrade conditions, including default, weighting each new market value by the historical probability of occurrence and then calculates volatility or value-at-risk measures of the change in market value of the loan.

Specifically, CreditMetrics assesses both individual and portfolio value at risk due to credit in three steps:

1. It establishes the exposure profile of each item in a portfolio. It recognizes that many different types of instruments create credit risk and incorporates the exposures of conventional instruments such as floating rate loans; it also provides a framework in which to consider less straightforward exposure profiles such as unused loan commitments, letters of credit, and commercial credit arrangements (such as trade credits or receivables).
2. It computes each instrument's volatility in value caused by possible upgrades, downgrades, and defaults. Likelihoods are attributed to each possible credit event: upgrades, downgrades, and defaults. The probability that a change in rating will occur over time is estimated from a historically based "transition matrix" that reflects the historical patterns of upgrades/downgrades (e.g., a credit rating going from BB to B in one year might have a historical probability of 5 percent). Each rating change is converted into a market value effect from which each asset's expected market value and volatility of market value are computed.
3. It considers correlations between changes in the value of individual items in step (2) and combines the volatility of the individual instruments to give an aggregate portfolio volatility.[8]

EXAMPLE 11–2

• • • • • •   *Calculation of Value at Risk for a Loan Portfolio Using CreditMetrics*
An FI has a portfolio of loans with a current present value or market value of $4.3 million. It wants to estimate the value at risk of that loan portfolio from credit quality changes (such as credit rating upgrades and downgrades) and possible default. The relevant information

---

[8] For more information and details, see J.P. Morgan, *Introduction to CreditMetrics* (New York: J.P. Morgan Securities, April 1997).

Table **11–1**

POSSIBLE CREDIT QUALITY CHANGES ON AN FI'S LOAN PORTFOLIO

(1) Future Credit Rating	(2) Probability of Rating Changing (%) Based on Historical Data of Loan Rating Migrations	(3) Future Value of Loan (millions)
AAA	0.02%	$4.375
AA	0.33	4.368
A	5.95	4.346
BBB	86.93	4.300
BB	5.30	4.081
B	1.17	3.924
CCC	0.12	3.346
Default	0.18	2.125

should credit quality change is presented in Table 11–1.[9] Based on historical data, the data in Table 11–1 show that the probability of the loan portfolio maintaining its current BBB credit rating is 86.93 percent and the value of the loan portfolio at the end of the year if it stays BBB is $4.3 million. The historical probability of the loan portfolio falling to a B rating is 1.17 percent.

The loan portfolio's mean or expected value and value at risk (standard deviation) are calculated in Table 11–2. Data there indicate that if the distribution of loan returns is normal, there is a 68 percent probability that the loan portfolio value will fluctuate by one standard deviation (σ), that is, between ±$116,698 around its mean value of $4,281,911. If the distribution of loan returns is normal or bell-shaped, there is also a 1 percent chance, or probability, that the loan portfolio value will fall by 2.33σ or, in this case, by $2.33 \times$ $116,698 = $271,906 (the portfolio value falls to $4,010,005). In general, however, the returns on a portfolio of loans are not normally distributed. As discussed in Chapter 9 and shown in Figure 11–2, loans have a maximum upside return and a long-tailed downside risk. Specifically, the actual distribution of loan values relative to the mean in Table 11–1 indicates a 1.17 percent chance of losing $357,911 (the portfolio value falls to $3,924,000) if the bond is downgraded to B.

This loss is much larger than the 1 percent chance of a loss of $271,906 relative to the mean value of the loan portfolio implied by the normal distribution.[10] Such losses can

---

[9] Notice in Table 11–1, that if a loan borrower is downgraded, FIs (or investors) would require a high yield spread to hold the loan. Since, by assumption, the interest rate that the borrower paid on the loan is fixed, the higher required yield to hold the loan would be reflected in a higher discount rate on the remaining cash flows on the loan. This reduces the present value (or market value) of the loan. If the loan borrower is upgraded, the required yield on the loan falls and the present (or market) value of the loan rises. In the case of default, the $2.125 million represents the amount of the loan portfolio that can be recovered from the borrowers in bankruptcy.

[10] The 99 percent loss for the normal distribution is calculated as $2.33 \times \sigma$. Since σ is $116,698, $2.33 \times$116,698 = $271,906.

Table 11-2

CALCULATION OF VALUE AT RISK ON AN FI'S LOAN PORTFOLIO USING CREDITMETRICS

(a) Rating	(b) Probability Weighted Future Value*	(c) Difference in Value from Mean†	(d) Difference Squared (millions)	(e) Probability of Rating Change	(f) Probability Weighted Difference Squared (millions) (d) × (e)
AAA	$ 875	$ 93,089	$ 8,666	.0002	$ 1.733
AA	14,414	86,089	7,411	.0033	24.457
A	258,587	64,089	4,108	.0595	244.390
BBB	3,737,990	18,089	327	.8693	284.445
BB	216,293	(200,911)	40,365	.0530	2,139.375
B	45,911	(357,911)	128,100	.0117	1,498.773
CCC	4,015	(935,911)	875,928	.0012	1,051.115
Default	3,825	(2,156,911)	4,652,260	.0018	8,374.077

Mean = $4,281,911

Variance = $13,618.340

Standard Deviation (σ) = $\sqrt{\$13,618.340}$ = $116,698

*Equals Columns (2) × (3) from Table 11–1.

†Equals Column (3) from Table 11–1 minus the Mean

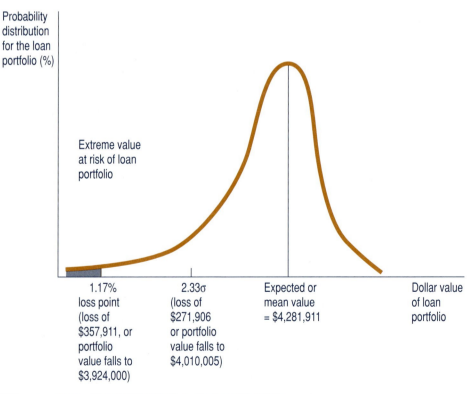

Figure 11-2   *Return Distribution of a Loan Portfolio*

threaten an FI's solvency. To avoid insolvency due to unexpected large losses on its credit portfolio that it has to charge off against its capital reserves, an FI would be better off holding capital reserves closer to $357,911 than $271,906.   • • •

Portfolio theory is a highly attractive tool, especially for mutual fund managers who invest in widely traded assets. Still, beyond the intuitive concept that diversification is generally positive, a question arises as to portfolio theory's applicability for small banks, insurance companies, and thrifts. These FIs often hold significant amounts of regionally specific nontraded or infrequently traded loans and bonds. At best, these FIs may be able to use only very simplified forms of portfolio diversification models. We look at modified forms of portfolio theory next.

Partial Applications of Portfolio Theory

Loan Volume–Based Models.   Direct application of modern portfolio theory is often difficult for depository institutions lacking information on market prices of assets since many of the assets—such as loans—are not bought and sold in established markets. Sufficient loan volume data may be available to allow managers to construct a modified or partial application of MPT to analyze an FI's overall concentration or credit risk exposure. Such loan volume data include the following:

1. *Commercial bank call reports.*   These reports to the Federal Reserve classify loans as real estate, agriculture, commercial and industrial (C&I), depository institution, individual, state and political subdivision, and international. Produced for individual banks, these data can be aggregated to estimate the notional allocation of loans among categories or types.
2. *Data on shared national credits.*   A national database on large syndicated commercial and industrial loans categorizes loan volume by two-digit SIC codes. For example, loans made to SIC code 49 are loans to public utilities. Because this database provides a national picture of the allocation of large loans across sectors, it is analogous to the market portfolio or basket of commercial and industrial loans.

These data, therefore, provide *market benchmarks* with which an individual bank can compare its own internal allocations of loans across major lending sectors such as real estate and C&I loans. For example, the Shared National Credit (SNC) database provides a market benchmark of all FIs allocations of large loans across various industries or borrowers.

By comparing its own allocation, or proportions (X_{ij}), of loans in any specific area with the national allocations across borrowers (X_i, where i designates different loan groups), the jth FI can measure the extent to which its loan portfolio allocation deviates from the national portfolio benchmark. This indicates the degree to which the FI has developed *loan concentrations* or relatively undiversified loan portfolios in various areas.

This partial use of modern portfolio theory provides an FI manager with a sense of the relative degree of loan concentration carried in the FI's asset portfolio. Finally, although the preceding discussion has referred to the loan portfolio of banks, any FI can use this portfolio theory for any asset group or, indeed, the whole asset portfolio, whether the asset is traded or not. The key data needed are the investment allocations of a peer group of regional or national financial institutions faced with similar investment decision choices.

systematic loan loss risk

A measure of the sensitivity of loan losses in a particular business sector relative to the losses in a bank's loan portfolio.

Loan Loss Ratio–Based Models.   A second partial application of MPT is a model based on historical loan loss ratios. This model involves estimating the **systematic loan loss risk** of a particular sector or industry relative to the loan loss risk of a bank's total loan portfolio. This systematic loan loss can be estimated by running a time-series regression of the quarterly loss rate in the ith sector on the quarterly loss rate of the bank's total loan portfolio:

$$\frac{\text{Sectoral losses in the } i\text{th sector}}{\text{Loans to the } i\text{th sector}} = \alpha + \beta_i \frac{\text{Total loan losses}}{\text{Total loans}}$$

where α measures the loan loss rate for a sector that has no sensitivity to losses on the aggregate loan portfolio (i.e., its $\beta = 0$) and β_i measures the systematic loss sensitivity of the ith sector loans to total loan losses. For example, regression results showing that the consumer sector has a β of 0.2 and the real estate sector has a β of 1.4 suggest that loan losses in the real estate sector are systematically higher relative to the total loan losses of the bank (by definition, the loss rate β for the whole loan portfolio is 1). Similarly, loan losses in the consumer sector are systematically lower relative to the total loan losses of the bank. Consequently, it may be prudent for the bank to maintain lower concentration limits for the real estate sector as opposed to the consumer sector. The implication of this model is that sectors with lower βs could have higher concentration limits than high β sectors—since low β loan sector risks (loan losses) are less systematic; that is, they are more diversifiable in a portfolio sense.

Regulatory Models

As the introduction to this chapter noted, bank and insurance regulators have been investigating ways to measure concentration risk. After examining the various quantitative approaches discussed here, the Federal Reserve in 1994 issued a final ruling on its proposed measure of credit concentration risk. The method adopted was largely subjective and based on examiner discretion. The reasons given for rejecting more technical models were that (1) at the time, the methods for identifying concentration risk were not sufficiently advanced to justify their use and (2) insufficient data were available to estimate more quantitative-type models. As noted in Chapter 10, currently no (publicly available) shared national database contains information about commercial loan defaults. The Federal Reserve is actively encouraging the development of such databases, however, as a necessary condition for the full implementation of MPT-type models and has issued a challenge to banks to adopt more sophisticated methods[11] (see Contemporary Perspectives Box 11–1). Indeed, J.P. Morgan's CreditMetrics can be viewed as one bank's response to this challenge.

Life and property-casualty insurance regulators have also been concerned with excessive industry sector and borrower concentrations. The Model Act supported by NAIC for state regulators (remember that insurance companies are regulated at the state level; see Chapter 4) proposes to set maximums on the investments an insurer can hold in securities or obligations of any single issuer.[12] These so-called **general diversification limits** are set at 3 percent for life-health insurers and 5 percent for property-casualty insurers, implying that the minimum number of different issues is 33 for life-health companies and for PC

general diversification limits

Maximums set on the amount of investments an insurer can hold in securities of any single issuer.

---

[11]Note that data on losses at the sector (rather than individual borrower) level are not really adequate since aggregating losses at the sector level basically assumes that the causes of default are similar across all firms in that sector. As we know, however, companies such as GM, Chrysler, and Ford have very different financial ratios (e.g., leverage) even though they are in the same sector. As discussed in Chapter 10, a highly levered firm is more likely to default than a low-levered firm.

[12]See Investments of Insurers Model Act (Washington, D.C.: NAIC draft, August 12, 1994).

Contemporary Perspectives 11–1

Greenspan's Challenge: A Reward for Improving Credit Risk

The chairman of the Federal Reserve Board is offering a challenge to bankers. Will they accept it? In his remarks before the Federal Reserve Bank of Chicago's 32nd Annual conference on Bank Structure and Competition in May, Fed Chairman Alan Greenspan suggests that the adoption by banks of more sophisticated methodologies to measure credit risk could lead to changes in the risk-based capital guidelines—changes that no doubt would benefit many banks. . . .

Risk-based capital guidelines do not differentiate among levels of credit risk, according the same risk weighting to all loans except residential real estate loans. They do not allow for consideration of actions management may have taken to limit credit risk, such as hedging or conservative underwriting standards. . . .

Historically, loan portfolio planning in many banks has involved setting some strategic goals, but not developing the tactical plans necessary to achieve these goals. Planning may be little more than establishing targets for the size of different types of portfolios (e.g., consumer, small business, or larger commercial loans) and perhaps setting some industry concentration limits in terms of capital at risk. How the portfolios are actually populated, that is, which loans are made, has been largely left to chance. Each time a potential customer requests a loan, lenders and credit administrators decide whether the borrower and the deal are a fit for the bank. As such, true portfolio planning—the ability of a bank to influence and shape the composition of its loan portfolio— has actually been ceded to the marketplace. Too often, as well, banks

have been slow to take into consideration changing market conditions.

Motivated by a number of considerations including revenue enhancement and cost cutting, improved customer service, and a desire to improve risk management, many larger banks have decided to influence and shape their loan portfolios more deliberately. They have done this by more proactively planning and prospecting for new business. In these instructions, portfolio planning involves identifying not only target markets, but also the acceptable risk criteria of borrowers within these markets.

Target market definitions establish the industries on which the bank or lending unit will focus, set limits for these industries, detail the types of financial products to be offered and the size range, structure, and pricing of facilities to be offered, establish the geographic lending territory, broadly define the characteristics of the targeted borrowers, and describe how the desired business will be developed. This is supplemented by the development of specific benchmarks—acceptable risk criteria—that are used to screen desirable borrowers from undesirable borrowers. New businesses are not entered until target market definitions and acceptable risk criteria have been established. Loans outside of the acceptable parameters can be made on an exception basis, but only after review and approval at higher levels of the organization. This type of approach brings both focus and efficiency to the lending process and, when appropriately linked to portfolio monitoring and review functions, provides the information and means to make timely changes to

portfolio standards in response to changing conditions. For such an approach to work successfully, a bank needs the right technology— systems that can transform data into information.

A number of banks, particularly larger institutions, are also attempting to make credit decisions more objective through the use of statistical rating models and rule-based systems that are predictors of default.

To date, much of this portfolio management technology has been based on the performance of large public companies and public bonds, but increasingly the technology is being improved to capture middle market and private companies as well. When coupled with a well-developed credit process, this technology can provide information that allows an institution to quantify its risks better and make more informed decisions about such issues as pricing and capital allocation.

So, what remains to be done before regulators can be convinced to replace the "one-size fits all" risk-based capital guidelines with customized models that allocate capital based on banks' own internal models?

In short, more banks need to demonstrate that they are taking an enlightened approach to lending, with a focus on process and technology that will allow them to manage more proactively and predict more accurately the risk involved.

If this can be accomplished on a wide scale, banks figure to reap many rewards—a more cost-effective credit process, improved customer response time and services, and more efficient use of capital.

SOURCE: Carol M. Beaumier, *Banking Policy Report,* August 5, 1996. Permission to reprint granted by Aspen Law & Business, a division of Aspen Publishers, Inc.

Contemporary Perspectives 11–2

Adopted But Unloved Model Investment Law May Not Stick

After five long years of painful labor, the NAIC finally gave birth last week to a model law governing company investments.

The model law could lead to restrictions on insurer investments. But there is an indication that even though it has been sanctioned by the NAIC, it might not get that much further. There was the lack of strong industry lobbying against its passage, one knowledgeable observer pointed out. Insurers maneuvered successfully to make it unlikely that the new model law will get serious consideration at the state level.

In addition, the NAIC decided not to include the investment model as an accreditation standard, which means there is little or no pressure for individual states to adopt the more restrictive approach. . . .

The model law has been called a "pigeonhole" law because it contains limits on how much insurers can invest in certain categories.

"The new model will give states that follow this approach a strong mechanism for promoting insurer solvency and financial strength," said NAIC President Brian Atchinson.

Before voting to adopt, the NAIC members added a preamble stating that the restrictive approach was not the only way to regulate insurer investments. The NAIC is also working on another model that takes a "prudent person" approach.

Michigan Commissioner D. Joseph Olson led the fight to keep the "pigeonhole" model from adoption. He couched his argument in terms of a state's right to determine its own regulatory destiny.

"This organization has been very successful in avoiding federal regulation, and I think it would be somewhat ironic if it turns out we have subjected ourselves to the type of regulation that we could expect from the federal government and imposed a one size fits all approach to regulation."

Olson argued that the model's restrictions set a dangerous precedent that could be imposed even in states that don't adopt it: the codification process may include model laws as part of the statutory accounting hierarchy, he noted. He also said individual examiners could use the model as a reference in reviewing the investment portfolio of an insurer.

SOURCE: *The Insurance Regulator*, October 7, 1996, p. 1. Courtesy of The *Insurance Regulator*, an *American Banker* newsletter.

companies is 20. The rationale for such a simple rule comes from MPT, which shows that *equal* investments across approximately 15 or more stocks can provide significant gains from diversification, that is, lowering asset portfolio risk or variance of returns. Regardless, insurers and even some NAIC members are working diligently to prevent these limits from becoming industry standards (see Contemporary Perspectives Box 11–2).

Concept Questions

1. Suppose that the returns on different loans are independent; would loan portfolio diversification provide any advantages?
2. How would you find the minimum risk loan portfolio in a modern portfolio theory framework?
3. Should FI managers select the minimum risk loan portfolio? Why or why not?
4. What is the reasoning behind the Federal Reserve's 1994 ruling to rely on a subjective rather than a quantitative approach to measure credit concentration risk?

SUMMARY

This chapter discussed the various approaches available to an FI manager to measure credit concentration risk. It demonstrated how portfolio diversification can reduce an FI's loan risk exposure. The chapter discussed two simple models to reduce loan concentration risk: migration analysis, which relies on S&P downgradings to provide information on loan concentrations, and a model that sets concentration limits based on an FI's capital exposure to different lending sectors. The chapter considered more sophisticated loan concentration limits built around the principles of modern portfolio theory. The chapter outlined one MPT–based model—J. P. Morgan's CreditMetrics. In addition, the chapter discussed two partial applications of portfolio theory: one based on loan volume and the other based on loan loss ratios in different sectors. Finally, the chapter described approaches by the Federal Reserve and the NAIC to measure loan concentrations.

PERTINENT WEB SITES

Board of Governors of the Federal Reserve
   http://www.bog.frb.fed.us/
Federal Deposit Insurance Corp.   http://www.fdic.gov/
National Association of Insurance Commissioners
   http://www.naic.org/

J.P. Morgan   http://www.jpmorgan.com/
J.P. Morgan (CreditMetrics)   http://www.jpmorgan.com/
   RiskManagement/CreditMetrics/CreditMetrics.htm

Credit Risk: Loan Portfolio Risk

1. How does loan portfolio risk differ from individual loan risk?
2. What is migration analysis? How do FIs use it to measure credit risk concentration? What are its shortcomings?
3. What does *loan concentration risk* mean?
4. A manager decides not to lend to any firm in sectors that generate losses in excess of 5 percent of equity.
    a. If the average historical losses in the automobile sector total 8 percent, what is the maximum loan a manager can lend to a firm in this sector, as a percentage of total capital?
    b. If the average historical losses in the mining sector total 15 percent, what is the maximum loan a manager can lend to a firm in this sector, as a percentage of total capital?
5. An FI has set a maximum loss of 12 percent of total capital as a basis for setting concentration limits on loans to individual firms. If it has set a concentration limit of 25 percent to a firm, what is the expected loss rate for that firm?
6. Explain how modern portfolio theory can be applied to lower the credit risk of an FI's portfolio.
7. Why is it difficult for small banks and thrifts to measure credit risk using modern portfolio theory?

8. The Bank of Tinytown has two $20,000 loans in its portfolio with the following characteristics:

Loan	Expected Return	Standard Deviation
A	10%	.1
B	12	.2

If the covariance between loans A and B is .015, calculate the expected return and standard deviation of this portfolio.

9. Repeat problem (8) with a covariance of –.015. How do your answers compare? What does this comparison tell you?
10. What databases that contain loan information at national and regional levels are available? How can they be applied to analyze credit concentration risk?
11. A bank vice president is evaluating the loan portfolios of three assistant vice presidents. How might the three portfolios be evaluated?

Portfolio	Expected Return	Standard Deviation
A	10%	.08
B	12	.09
C	11	.10

12. The following provides information concerning allocation of loan portfolios in different sectors in percentages:

Sectors	National	Bank A	Bank B
Commercial	30%	50%	10%
Consumer	40	30	40
Real estate	30	20	50

a. Bank A and Bank B would like to estimate how much their portfolios deviate from the national average. Which bank is farther from the national average?

b. Is a large standard deviation necessarily bad for a bank using this model?

13. Assume that the averages for national banks engaged primarily in mortgage lending have their assets diversified in the following proportions: 20 percent residential, 30 percent commercial, 20 percent international, and 30 percent mortgage-backed securities. A local bank has the following ratios: 30 percent residential, 40 percent commercial, and 30 percent international. How does the local bank differ from the national bank?

14. A bank has two loans of equal size, A and B, outstanding and has identified the returns each would earn in two different states of nature, 1 and 2, representing default and no default, respectively.

State	1	2
Security A	2%	14%
Security B	0	18

If the probability of state 1 is .2 and the probability of state 2 is .8, calculate

a. The expected return of each security.

b. The expected return on the portfolio in each state.

c. The expected return on the portfolio.

15. Using regression analysis on historical loan losses, a bank has estimated the following:

$$X_C = 0.002 + 0.8X_L \text{ and } X_h = 0.003 + 1.8X_L$$

where X_C = loss rate in the commercial sector, X_h = loss rate in the consumer (household) sector, and X_L = loss rate for its total loan portfolio.

a. If the bank's total loan loss rate is expected to be 10 percent, what are the expected loss rates in the commercial and consumer sectors?

b. In which sector should the bank limit its loans and why?

16. What reasons did the Federal Reserve Board offer for recommending the use of subjective evaluations of credit concentration risk instead of quantitative models?

17. What rules have been proposed by the National Association of Insurance Commissioners on credit concentrations? How are they related to modern portfolio theory?

18. How does the CreditMetrics approach to quantifying credit risk differ from the traditional approach?

19. An FI is limited to holding no more than 8 percent of securities of a single issuer. What is the minimum number of securities it should hold to meet this requirement? What if the requirements are 2 percent, 4 percent, and 7 percent?

20. The obvious benefit to holding a diversified portfolio of loans is to spread risk exposures so that a single event does not result in a great loss to the bank. Are there any benefits to not being diversified?

21. Go to the J.P. Morgan Web site. What data set information is provided for use with CreditMetrics?

Chapter Twelve

Loan Sales and Asset Securitization

asset securitization

The packaging and selling of loans and other assets backed by securities issued by an FI.

In Chapter 1, we distinguished between FIs that are asset transformers and those that are asset brokers. Loan sales and **asset securitization**—the packaging and selling of loans and other assets backed by loans or other securities issued by the FI—are mechanisms that FIs have used to hedge their interest rate exposure and credit risks. In addition, loan sales and securitization have allowed FI asset portfolios to become more liquid, provided an important source of fee income (with FIs acting as servicing agents for the assets sold) and helped to reduce the effects of regulatory "taxes" such as capital requirements, reserve requirements, and deposit insurance premiums. By increasingly relying on loan sales and securitization, depository institutions have begun moving away from being asset transformers that originate and hold assets to maturity to becoming more reliant on servicing and other fees. This makes depository institutions look increasingly similar to securities firms and investment banks in terms of enhanced importance of asset brokerage over asset transformation.

This chapter investigates the role of loan sales and other forms of asset securitization

Table **12–1**

BASIC DESCRIPTION OF LOAN SALES AND OTHER FORMS OF ASSET SECURITIZATION

Loan Sale   An FI originates a loan and subsequently sells it to an outside buyer.

Pass-Through Securities   Mortgages or other assets originated by an FI are pooled and investors are offered an interest in the pool in the form of pass-through certificates or securities. Examples of pass-through securities are Government National Mortgage Association (GNMA) or Federal National Mortgage Association (FNMA) securities.

Collateralized Mortgage Obligations (CMOs)   Similar to pass-throughs CMOs are securities backed by pools of mortgages or other assets originated by an FI. Pass-throughs give investors common rights in terms of risks and returns, but CMOs assign varying combinations of risk and return to different groups of investors in the CMO by repackaging the pool.

Mortgage-Backed Bonds (MBBs)   A bond issue backed by a group of mortgages on an FI's balance sheet. With MBBs, the mortgages remain on the FI's balance sheet, and funds used to pay the MBB holders' coupons and principal repayments may or may not come from the collateralized mortgages.

in improving the return-risk trade-off for FIs. It describes the process and details associated with loan sales and the major forms, or vehicles, of asset securitization and analyzes their unique characteristics. Table 12–1 presents a definition of the mechanisms that the chapter discusses.

LOAN

SALES

correspondent banking

A relationship between a small bank and a large bank in which the large bank provides a number of deposit, lending, and other services.

highly leveraged transaction (HLT) loan

A loan that finances a merger and acquisition; a leveraged buyout results in a high leverage ratio for the borrower.

Banks and other FIs have sold loans among themselves for more than 100 years. In fact, a large part of **correspondent banking** involves small banks making loans that are too big for them to hold on their balance sheets—either for lending concentration risk or capital adequacy reasons—and selling parts of these loans to large banks with which they have a long-term deposit-lending correspondent relationship. In turn, the large banks often sell parts of their loans called *participations* to smaller banks. Even though this market has existed for many years, it grew slowly until the early 1980s when it entered a period of spectacular growth, largely due to expansion in **highly leveraged transaction (HLT) loans** to finance leveraged buyouts (LBOs) and mergers and acquisitions (M&As). Specifically, the volume of loans sold by U.S. banks increased from less than $20 billion in 1980 to $285 billion in 1989. In the early 1990s, the volume of loan sales declined almost as dramatically, along with the decline in LBOs and M&As. In 1995, the volume of loan sales had fallen to approximately $32 billion. In the last few years, however, the volume of loan sales has started to increase again as M&As have increased.[1]

---

[1] Also, the composition of loan sales is changing with increasing amounts of commercial real estate loans being sold.

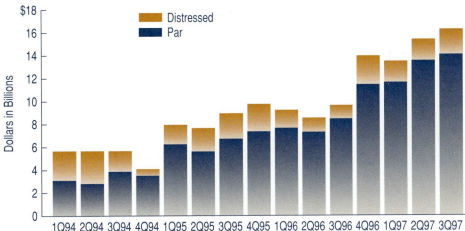

Figure **12–1**   *Recent Trends in the Loan Sales Market*

Secondary trading volume reached $16.26 billion for the third quarter, bringing year-to-date volume to $45.2 billion. Hungry investors continued to drive par volume, as that market totaled $14.12 billion for the third quarter. Distressed volume increased by 5.4% from the second quarter, to $2.14 billion. The abundance of leveraged paper already completed this year—along with a substantial amount in the pipeline—promises to push volume past $60 billion for 1997.
SOURCE: Loan Pricing Corporation, *Goldsheets,* November 10, 1997, p. 23.

Figure 12–1 shows recent trends in the loan sales market, in particular, the increasing number of loan sales during the period 1994–1997 and the increasing (relative) proportion of nondistressed (par loans) to distressed loans. The latter reflects the improving macroeconomic conditions that have moved many distressed firms out of Chapter 11 bankruptcy protection in recent years.

bank loan sale

Sale of loan originated by a bank with or without recourse to an outside buyer.

A **bank loan sale** occurs when a bank originates a loan and sells it with or without recourse to an outside buyer. As an extreme example, Westmark Group Holdings, Inc., of Delray Beach, Florida, one of the country's top 15 subprime lenders, issued in excess of $128 million in subprime mortgage loans in 1997. By year-end, Westmark had sold $125.4 million of these loans to secondary market investors and recorded revenues of $7.4 million in 1997 from its mortgage division, a 177 percent increase over 1996.

recourse

The ability of a loan buyer to sell the loan back to the originator should it go bad.

If the loan is sold without recourse, the bank not only removes it from its balance sheet but also has no explicit liability if the loan eventually goes bad. Thus, the buyer (not the FI that originated the loan) bears all the credit risk. If, however, the loan is sold with **recourse,** under certain conditions the buyer can put the loan back to the selling bank; therefore, the bank retains a contingent credit risk liability. In practice, most loan sales are without recourse because a loan sale is technically removed from the balance sheet only when the buyer has no future credit risk claim on the bank. Loan sales usually involve no creation of new types of securities such as those described later in the chapter, an important consideration. As such, loan sales are a primitive form of securitization because loan selling creates a secondary market for loans in which ownership of the loan is simply transferred to the loan buyer.

The Bank Loan Sale Market

LDC loans

Loans made to a less
developed country
(LDC).

The U.S. bank loan sale market has three segments; two involve sales and trading of domestic loans, and the third involves **less developed country (LDC) loans**, which are made to certain Asian, African, and Latin American countries. Because we fully describe the LDC loan sales market in Chapter 28, we concentrate on the domestic loan sales market here.

Traditional Short-Term Segment.   In the traditional short-term segment of the market, banks sell loans with short maturities, often one to three months. This market has characteristics similar to those of the market for commercial paper issued by corporations (see Chapter 2) in that loan sales have similar maturities and issue size. Loan sales, however, usually have yields that are 1 to 10 basis points above those of commercial paper of a similar rating. The key characteristics of the short-term loan sale market are these:

- Secured by assets of the borrowing firm.
- Made to investment-grade borrowers or better.
- Issued for a short term (90 days or less).
- Closely tied to the commercial paper rate.
- Sold in units of $1 million and up.

Traditional short-term loan sales predominated the market until 1984 and the emergence of the HLT and LDC loan markets. The growth of the commercial paper market (and its accessibility by more than 20,000 corporations) has also reduced the importance of this market segment.

HLT Loan Sales.   With the increase in M&As and LBOs financed via HTLs, especially from 1985 to 1989, a new segment in the loan sales market—HTL loan sales—appeared.[2] One measure of the increase in HLTs is that between January 1987 and September 1994 the Loan Pricing Corporation reported 4,122 M&A deals with a combined dollar amount in new-issue loans estimated at $593.5 billion and by 1997 alone, M&A activity topped the $200 billion mark. HLT loans mainly differ according to whether they are nondistressed (bid price exceeds 80 cents per $1 of loans) or distressed (bid price is less than 80 cents per $1 of loans or the borrower is in default).

Virtually all HLT loans have the following characteristics:

financial distress

The state when a
borrower is unable to
meet a payment
obligation to lenders and
other creditors.

- All term loans (TLs).
- Are secured by assets of the borrowing firm (usually given senior security status).
- Have long maturity (often three- to six-year maturities).
- Have floating rates tied to the London interbank offered rate (LIBOR), the prime rate, or a CD rate (HTL rates are normally 200–275 basis points above these rates).
- Have strong covenant protection.

Nevertheless, HLTs tend to be quite heterogeneous with respect to the size of the issue, the interest payment date, interest indexing, and prepayment features. After origination, some HLT borrowers such as Macy's and El Paso Electric suffered periods of **financial distress**.

---

[2] What constitutes an HLT loan has often caused dispute. In October 1989, however, the three U.S. federal bank regulators adopted a definition of HLT as a loan that involves (1) a buyout, acquisition, or recapitalization and (2) either doubles the company's liabilities and results in a leverage ratio higher than 50 percent, results in a leverage ratio higher than 75 percent, or is designated as an HLT by a syndication agent.

As a result, a distinction between the market for distressed and nondistressed HLTs is usually made.

Types of Loan Sales Contracts.   The two basic types of loan sale contracts or mechanisms by which loans can be transferred between seller and buyer are *participations* and *assignments*. Currently, assignments represent the bulk of loan sales trading.

Participations.   The unique features of **participations in loans** follow:

> **participation in a loan**
>
> The act of buying a share in a loan syndication with limited contractual control and rights over the borrower.

- The holder (buyer) is not a party to the underlying credit agreement so that the initial contract between loan seller and borrower remains in place after the sale.
- The loan buyer can exercise only partial control over changes in the loan contract's terms. The holder can vote on only material changes to the loan contract, such as the interest rate or collateral backing.

The economic implication of these features is that the buyer of the loan participation has a double-risk exposure—to the borrower as well as to the lender. Specifically, if the selling bank fails, the loan participation bought by an outside party may be characterized as an unsecured obligation of the bank rather than a true sale. Alternatively, the borrowers' claims against a failed selling bank may be netted against its loans, reducing the amount of loans outstanding and adversely impacting the buyer of a participation in those loans. As a result of these exposures, the buyer bears a double monitoring cost as well.

Assignments.   Because of the monitoring costs and risks involved in participations, loans are sold on an assignment basis in more than 90 percent of the cases on the U.S. domestic market. They key features of an **assignment** follow:

> **assignment**
>
> The purchase of a share in a loan syndication with some contractual control and rights over the borrower.

- Transfer of all rights on sale, meaning that the loan buyer holds a direct claim on the borrower.
- Transfer of U.S. domestic loans normally associated with a Uniform Commercial Code filing (as proof that a change of ownership has been completed).

Although ownership rights are generally much clearer in a loan sale by assignment, contractual terms frequently limit the seller's scope regarding to whom the loan can be sold. In particular, the loan contract may require either the bank agent or the borrower to agree to the sale. The loan contract may also restrict the sale to a certain class of institutions such as those that meet certain net worth/net asset size conditions. (A *bank agent* is a bank that distributes interest and principal payments to lenders in loan syndications with multiple lenders.) Currently, the trend appears to be toward originating loan contracts with very limited assignment restrictions. This is true in both the U.S. domestic and LDC loan sales markets. The most tradable loans are those that can be assigned without buyer restrictions. In evaluating ownership rights, the buyer of the loan also needs to verify the original loan contract and to establish the full implications of the purchase regarding the buyer's rights to collateral if the borrower defaults. Because of these contractual problems, trading frictions, and costs, some loan sales take as long as three months to complete; reportedly, up to 50 percent eventually fail to be completed at all.

The Buyers.   Of the wide array of potential buyers, some are interested in only a certain segment of the market for regulatory and strategic reasons. In particular, an increasingly specialized group of buyers of distressed HLT loans includes investment banks and **vulture funds**. For the nondistressed HLT market and the traditional U.S. domestic loan sales market, the five major buyers are other domestic banks, foreign banks, insurance companies and pension funds, closed-end bank loan mutual funds, and nonfinancial corporations.

> **vulture fund**
>
> A specialized fund that invests in distressed loans.

Investment Banks.   Investment banks are predominately buyers of HLT loans because (1) analysis of these loans[3] utilizes investment skills similar to those required for junk bond trading and (2) investment banks were often closely associated with the HLT distressed borrower in underwriting the original junk bond/HLT deals. As such, large investment banks—for example, First Boston, Merrill Lynch, and Goldman Sachs—are relatively more informed agents in this market, either by acting as market makers or in taking short-term positions on movements in the market prices of these loans.

Vulture Funds.   Vulture funds are specialized funds established to invest in distressed loans. These investments can be active, especially for those seeking to use the loans purchased for bargaining in a restructuring deal which generates restructuring returns that strongly favor the loan purchaser. Alternatively, such loans may be held as passive investments or high-yield securities in a well-diversified portfolio of distressed securities. Investment banks in fact manage many vulture funds. Most secondary market trading in U.S. loan sales occurs in this segment of the market.

Other Domestic Banks.   Interbank loan sales are at the core of the traditional market and historically have revolved around correspondent banking and *regional banking/branching restrictions* (such as the McFadden Act of 1927 and the Bank Holding Company Act of 1956 and its 1970 Amendments). Restrictions on nationwide banking have often led banks to originate regionally undiversified and borrower-undiversified loan portfolios. Small banks often sell loan participations to their large correspondents to improve regional/borrower diversification and to avoid regulatory imposed single-borrower loan concentration ceilings. (A loan to a single borrower should not exceed 10 percent of a bank's capital.) This arrangement can also work in the other direction, with the larger banks selling participations to smaller banks. The traditional interbank market, however, has been shrinking as the result of at least three factors. First, the traditional correspondent banking relationship is breaking down as markets become more competitive. Second, concerns about counterparty risk and moral hazard have increased. An extreme example of this is Penn Square, a small Texas bank which sold many risky (energy-based) loans to its larger correspondent bank, Continental Illinois, in the early 1980s. In 1984, Continental Illinois, then the eighth largest bank in the United States, failed. Third, the barriers to nationwide banking are being eroded. This erosion is likely to accelerate following the introduction of interstate banking in 1997 and the (continuing) contraction in the number of small banks (see Chapter 26).

Foreign Banks.   Foreign banks remain the dominant buyer of domestic U.S. loans. Because of the cost of branching, the loan sales market allows foreign banks to achieve a well-diversified domestic U.S. loan portfolio without developing a nationwide banking network. However, renewed interest in asset **downsizing,** especially among Japanese banks, has caused this source of demand to begin to contract.

downsizing

Shrinking an FI's asset size.

Insurance Companies and Pension Funds.   Subject to meeting liquidity and quality or investment-grade regulatory restrictions, insurance companies (such as Aetna) and pension funds are important buyers of long-term loans.

---

[3] Junk bonds are noninvestment-grade bonds (i.e., those issued with an investment credit rating of BB or below by Standard and Poor's).

Closed-End Bank Loan Mutual Funds.   First established in 1988, these leveraged mutual funds, such as Merrill Lynch Prime Fund, invest in domestic U.S. bank loans. Recent figures put their asset size at approximately $10 billion and their number at five publicly traded funds. Although they could purchase loans on the secondary market, such as loan resales, the largest funds have moved into primary loan syndications because of the attractive fee income available. That is, these mutual funds participate in funding loans originated by commercial banks. The mutual fund in turn receives a fee or part of the interest payment. Indeed, some money center banks, such as Citibank, have actively encouraged closed-end fund participation in primary loan syndications.

Nonfinancial Corporations.   Some corporations—primarily the financial services arms of the very largest U.S. and European companies (e.g., GE Capital and ITT Finance)—buy loans. This activity amounts to no more than 5 percent of total U.S. domestic loan sales.

The Sellers.   The sellers of domestic loans and HLT loans are major money center banks, small regional or community banks, foreign banks, and investment banks.

Major Money Center Banks.   The largest money center banks have dominated loan selling. In recent years, market concentration in loan-selling has been accentuated by the increase in HLTs (and the important role that major money center banks have played in originating loans in HLT deals) and in real estate problem loans as a result of the recession in the real estate market in the early 1990s.

Small Regional or Community Banks.   As mentioned, small banks sell loans and loan participations to larger FIs for diversification and regulatory purposes. Although they are not a major player in the loan sales market, small banks have found loan sales to be essential for diversifying credit risk and other risks created in their loan portfolios.

Foreign Banks.   To the extent that foreign banks are sellers rather than buyers of loans, these loans come from branch networks such as the Japanese-owned banks in California or through their market-making activities selling loans originated in their home country in U.S. loan sales markets. One of the major market makers in the U.S. loan sales market (especially the HLT market) is the Dutch FI, ING Barings.

Investment Banks.   Investment banks such as Salomon Brothers act as loan sellers either as part of their market-making function (selling loans they have originated) or as active traders. Again, these loan sales are generally confined to large HLT transactions.

Reasons That Banks and Other FIs Sell Loans

The introduction to this chapter stated that one reason that FIs sell loans is to manage their credit risk better. Loan sales remove assets (and credit risk) from the balance sheet and allow an FI to achieve better asset diversification. Other than credit risk management, however, FIs are encouraged to sell loans for a number of other economic and regulatory reasons. The benefits of loan sales are summarized in Table 12–2 and discussed in detail here.

Reserve Requirements.   Regulatory requirements, such as noninterest-bearing reserve requirements that a bank must hold at the central bank, represent a form of tax that adds to the cost of funding the loan portfolio. Regulatory taxes such as reserve requirements create

---

T a b l e **12–2**

BENEFITS OF LOAN SALES

Remove credit risk associated with loans from the balance sheet
Reduce regulatory requirements, such as noninterest-bearing reserve requirements
Generate fee income
Alleviate the burden of capital adequacy requirements
Reduce liquidity risk
Provide a substitute for securities underwriting

---

an incentive for banks to remove loans from the balance sheet by selling them without recourse to outside parties.[4] Such removal allows banks to shrink both their assets and deposits and, thus, the amount of reserves they have to hold against their deposits.

Fee Income.   A bank can often report any fee income earned from originating loans as current income, but interest earned on direct lending can be accrued (as income) only over time (see Chapter 8). As a result, originating and quickly selling loans can boost a bank's reported income under current accounting rules.

Capital Costs.   Like reserve requirements, the capital adequacy requirements imposed on banks are a burden as long as required capital exceeds the amount the bank believes to be privately beneficial. Debt is a cheaper source of funds than equity capital. Thus, banks struggling to meet a required capital-(K) to-assets (A) ratio can boost this ratio by reducing assets (A) rather than boosting capital (K) (see Chapter 16). One way to downsize or reduce A and boost the K/A ratio is through loan sales.

Liquidity Risk.   In addition to credit risk, holding loans on the balance sheet can increase the overall illiquidity of a bank's assets. This illiquidity is a problem because bank liabilities tend to be highly liquid. Asset illiquidity can expose the bank to harmful liquidity squeezes when depositors unexpectedly withdraw their deposits. To mitigate a liquidity problem, a bank's management can sell some of its loans to outside investors. (We discuss these issues in detail in Chapter 13.) Thus, the bank loan market has created a secondary market in loans that has significantly reduced the illiquidity of bank loans held as assets on the balance sheet.

Glass-Steagall and Securities Law Interpretations.   Loan sales can substitute for securities underwriting. Because the 1933 Glass-Steagall Act prohibited banks from underwriting corporate equity and bonds, questions have been raised about underwriting loans for sale in the secondary market.[5]

---

[4] Under current reserve requirement regulations (Regulation D, amended May 1986), bank loan sales with recourse are regarded as a liability and hence are subject to reserve requirements. The reservability of loan sales extends to a bank issuing a credit guarantee and a recourse provision. Loans sold without recourse (or credit guarantees by the selling bank) are free of reserve requirements. With the elimination of reserve requirements on nontransaction accounts and the lowering of reserve requirements on transaction accounts in 1991, the reserve tax effect is likely to become a less important feature driving bank loan sales (as well as the recourse/nonrecourse mix) in the future.

[5] Underwriting involves the origination, sale, and distribution of a security or loan.

Case law has been almost unanimous in deciding that a loan or a loan participation sold by one bank to another financial institution is not a security for the purposes of federal securities acts (or state securities laws).

Factors Deterring Future Loan Sales Growth

The loan sales market has experienced a number of up-and-down phases in recent years. Notwithstanding the value of loan sales as a credit risk management tool, however, two factors may deter the market's growth and development in the future. We discuss these next.

Access to the Commercial Paper Market.   Since 1987, large banks have enjoyed much greater powers to underwrite commercial paper directly without experiencing legal challenges by the securities industry's claim that underwriting by banks was contrary to the Glass-Steagall Act. These powers were expanded in 1996 when bank securities subsidiaries were allowed to generate up to 25 percent of their gross revenues from previously ineligible activities such as commercial paper underwriting. This means that the need to underwrite or sell short-term bank loans as an imperfect substitute for commercial paper underwriting has now become much less important. In addition, more and more smaller middle market firms (as many as 20,000) are gaining direct access to the commercial paper market. As a result, such firms have less need to rely on bank loans to finance their short-term expenditures.

fraudulent conveyance

A transaction such as a sale of securities or transference of assets to a particular party that is determined to be illegal.

Legal Concerns.   A number of legal concerns are currently hampering the loan sale market's growth, especially for distressed HLT loans. In particular, although banks are normally secured creditors, other creditors may attack this status if the borrowing firm enters bankruptcy. For example, **fraudulent conveyance** proceedings have been brought against the secured lenders to firms such as Revco, Circle K, Allied Stores, and RJR Nabisco. In these cases, the sale of securities to a particular party were found to be illegal. Such lawsuits represent one of the factors that have slowed the growth of the distressed loan market. Indeed, in many of the most recent HLT sales, loan buyers have demanded a put option feature that allows them to put the loan back to the seller at the purchase price if a transaction is proved to be fraudulent under the *Uniform Fraudulent Conveyance Act*. In addition, a second type of distressed-firm risk may result if, in the process of a loan workout, the bank lender acts more as an equity owner than an outside debtor. For example, the bank may become involved in the firm's day-to-day operations and make strategic investment and asset sales decisions. This could support claims that the bank's loans should be treated as equity rather than secured debt. That is, the bank's loans may be subordinated in the claims' priority ranking.

Factors Encouraging Future Loan Sales Growth

At least three factors in addition to the credit risk "hedging" value of loan sales point to an enhanced volume of loan sales in the future.

BIS Capital Requirements.   The rules of the Bank for International Settlements (BIS) require that an FI's capital include a 100 percent risk weighting on commercial loans (explained in detail in Chapter 16). This means that bankers will continue to have strong incentives to sell commercial loans to other FIs and investors to downsize their balance sheets and boost their bank capital ratios.

Market Value Accounting.   The Securities and Exchange Commission (SEC) and the Financial Accounting Standards Board (FASB) have advocated the replacement of book value accounting with market value accounting for financial services firms (see Chapter 18). In addition, proposed and current capital requirements for interest rate risk and market risk have moved banks toward a market value accounting framework (see Chapter 19). The effect of marking to market will be to make bank loans appear to be more like securities and, thus, make them easier to sell and/or trade.

Asset Brokerage and Loan Trading.   The increased emphasis of large money center banks (such as Bankers Trust and J. P. Morgan), as well as investment banks, on trading and trading income suggests that significant attention will still be paid to those segments of the loan sales market for which price volatility is high and thus potential trading profits can be made. Most HLT loans have floating rates so that their underlying values are in large part insulated from swings in the level of interest rates (unlike fixed-income securities such as Treasury bonds). Nevertheless, the low credit quality of many of these loans and their long maturities create an enhanced potential for credit risk volatility. As a result, a short-term, secured loan to an AAA–rated company is unlikely to show significant future credit risk volatility compared to eight-year HLT loans to a distressed company. This suggests that trading in distressed HLT loans will always be attractive to banks that use their specialized credit-monitoring skills as asset traders rather than as asset transformers in participating in the market.

Concept ? Questions

1. What are the reasons for the rapid growth and subsequent decline in loan sales over the last two decades?
2. Which loans should have the highest yields; loans sold with recourse or loans sold without recourse?
3. What are the two basic types of loan sale contracts by which loans can be transferred between seller and buyer? Describe each.
4. What institutions are the major buyers in the traditional U.S. domestic loan sales market? What institutions are the major sellers in this market?
5. What are some of the economic and regulatory reasons that FIs choose to sell loans?
6. What are some of the factors that are likely to deter the growth of the loan sales market in the future?
7. What are some of the factors that are likely to encourage loan sales growth in the future?

ASSET SECURITIZATION

Asset securitization is useful in improving the risk-return trade-off for FIs. This section discusses the three major forms of securitization—the pass-through security, the collateralized mortgage obligation (CMO), and the asset-backed security—and analyzes their unique characteristics. Although depository institutions mainly undertake asset securitization, the insurance industry has also entered into this area (see Contemporary Perspectives Box 12–1). In addition, although all three forms of securitization originated in the real estate

Contemporary Perspectives 12–1

Investors Warming to Developing CMBS Market

In the last three to four years, investors have gradually taken less of a "defensive approach" to commercial mortgage-backed securities and are now looking at them as more of an investment opportunity, two CMBS experts maintain. Insurers are participating in the market, largely as buyers but also in a number of cases as issuers of these securities, they added.

Estimates suggest that in the last four to five years, annual securitizations of commercial mortgages have grown to $20 billion with the potential for $40 billion to $50 billion in securitizations annually in five years. For 1996, the total could reach $25 billion.

The advantages of securitizing a commercial mortgage loan include "recognizing the real cost of holding loans in a portfolio," including the cost to administer and service those loans, said Stacey Berger, executive vice president at Midland Loan Services, Kansas City, Mo. Liquidity or the ability to quickly change the composition of a portfolio is another important consideration, he added.

In addition to more favorable risk-based capital treatment, commercial mortgage-backed securities offer benefits including a rating and more efficient pricing, according to Jonathan Adams, an analyst with Prudential Securities, New York. Another advantage, he explained, is

that insurers can leverage the risk in a commercial mortgage pool and "pick and choose a level of risk. If they retain the lower rated tranches, then they would receive higher yields." Knowing the assets in the lower tranches perform despite their lower rating makes this possible, he explained.

CMBSs also allow insurers that want to participate in the financing of a building—but are unable to because of the size of the mortgage—to share in that financing, he added. And although there is the risk of loan prepayments, Mr. Adams said, commercial mortgage-backed securities can offer approximately 90 basis points over a Treasury bond with a comparable average life and 40–50 basis points over a corporate bond with a comparable average life and a comparable rating, Mr. Adams added.

Spreads for commercial mortgage-backed securities have narrowed in the last year, however, he said. Consequently, although there is still "good value" in the market, "it is a less obvious choice for a fixed income portfolio manager" in terms of being compensated for prepayment risk, Mr. Adams explained.

For insurers issuing commercial mortgage-backed securities, the reverse is true, he added. In late August, Penn Mutual Life Ins. Co., Horsham, Pa., completed a $780 million CMBS issuance which Peter

Sherman, senior vice president and chief investment officer, said will free up sufficient capital to allow the insurer to focus efforts.

This is a more efficient way to invest in commercial mortgages, he added. There is "quite an improvement in net yield" as opposed to making investments in whole loans, Mr. Sherman explained. For, example, he said, a CMBS tranch with a "BBB" rating might offer 150 basis points over a Treasury bond minus 1–2 basis points in expenses while the commercial mortgage loan might offer 150 basis points minus 25 basis points in expenses.

Another benefit Mr. Sherman cited is the ability to "more easily pick and choose when to participate in the asset class." When loans are made, they have to be done on a fairly frequent basis in order for a company to maintain contacts, he explained.

Another point he raised is that with increased liquidity, arising from CMBSs, a company has a greater ability to invest in other less liquid investments such as private placement transactions. He also said that mid-sized insurers may not get the kind of look over all commercial mortgage real estate transactions available that would be available to larger entities.

SOURCE: Jim Connolly, *National Underwriter*, Life + Health/Financial Services Edition, September 16, 1996, p. 29.

lending market, these techniques are currently being applied to loans other than mortgages, for example, credit card loans and commercial and industrial (C&I) loans. Thus, a CMO might better be defined as collateralized loan obligations (CLOs) when C&I loans are involved in the securitization process or as certificates of amortizing revolving debt (CARDs) when credit card loans are involved.

The Pass-Through Security

FIs frequently pool the mortgages and other assets they originate and offer investors an interest in the pool in the form of *pass-through certificates or securities.* Although many different types of loans and assets on FIs' balance sheets are currently being securitized, the original use of securitization is a result of government-sponsored programs to enhance the liquidity of the residential mortgage market. These programs indirectly subsidize the growth of home ownership in the United States.

We begin by analyzing the government-sponsored securitization of residential mortgage loans. Three government agencies or government-sponsored enterprises are directly involved in the creation of mortgage-backed pass-through securities. Informally, they are known as *Ginnie Mae, Fannie Mae,* and *Freddie Mac.*

GNMA.   The Government National Mortgage Association (GNMA), or Ginnie Mae, began in 1968 when it split off from the Federal National Mortgage Association (FNMA). GNMA is a government-owned agency with two major functions: sponsoring mortgage-backed securities programs by FIs such as banks, thrifts, and mortgage bankers and acting as a guarantor to investors in mortgage-backed securities regarding the timely pass-through of principal and interest payments on their sponsored bonds. In other words, GNMA provides **timing insurance**. In acting as a sponsor and payment-timing guarantor, GNMA supports only those pools of mortgage loans whose default or credit risk is insured by one of three government agencies, the Federal Housing Administration (FHA), the Veterans Administration (VA), and the Farmers Home Administration (FMHA). Mortgage loans insured by these agencies target groups that might otherwise be disadvantaged in the housing market such as low-income families, young families, and veterans. As such, the maximum mortgage under the FHA/VA/FMHA–GNMA securitization program is capped.

timing insurance

A service provided by a sponsor of pass-through securities (such as GNMA) guaranteeing the bondholder interest and principal payments at the calendar date promised.

FNMA.   Originally created in 1938, FNMA, or Fannie Mae, is the oldest of the three mortgage-backed security-sponsoring agencies. It is now a private corporation owned by shareholders with stocks traded on major exchanges, but in the minds of many investors, it still has implicit government backing that makes it equivalent to a government-sponsored agency. Indeed, the fact that FNMA has a secured line of credit available from the U.S. Treasury should it need funds in an emergency supports this view. FNMA is a more active agency than GNMA in creating pass-through securities. GNMA merely sponsors such programs; FNMA actually helps create pass-throughs by buying and holding mortgages on its balance sheet; it also issues bonds directly to finance those purchases.

Specifically, FNMA creates mortgage-backed securities (MBSs) by purchasing packages of mortgage loans from banks and thrifts; it finances such purchases by selling MBSs to outside investors such as life insurers or pension funds. In addition, FNMA engages in swap transactions by which it swaps MBSs with an FI for original mortgages. Since FNMA guarantees securities as to the full and timely payment of interest and principal, the FI receiving the MBSs can then resell them on the capital market or can hold them in its portfolio. Unlike GNMA, FNMA securitizes conventional mortgage loans as well as FHA/VA insured loans, as long as the conventional loans have acceptable loan-to-value or collateral ratios not normally exceeding 80 percent. Conventional loans with high loan-to-value ratios usually require additional private sector credit insurance before they are accepted into FNMA securitization pools.

FHLMC.   The Federal Home Loan Mortgage Corporation (FHLMC), or Freddie Mac, performs a similar function to that of FNMA except that its major securitization role has historically involved thrifts. Like FNMA, FHLMC is a stockholder-owned corporation with a line of credit from the U.S. Treasury. Further, like FNMA, it buys mortgage loan pools from FIs and swaps MBS for loans. FHLMC also sponsors conventional loan pools as well as FHA/VA mortgage pools and guarantees timely payment of interest and ultimate payment of principal on the securities it issues.

The Incentives and Mechanics of Pass-Through Security Creation.   In beginning to analyze the securitization process, we trace the mechanics of a mortgage pool securitization to provide insights into the return-risk benefits of this process to the mortgage-originating FI, as well as the attractiveness of these securities to investors. Given that more than $2.13 trillion of mortgage-backed securities are outstanding—a large proportion sponsored by GNMA—we analyze an example of the creation of a GNMA pass-through security next.[6]

E X A M P L E   1 2 – 1

Creation of a GNMA Pass-Through Security
Suppose that a bank has just originated 1,000 new residential mortgages in its local area. The average size of each mortgage is $100,000. Thus, the total size of the new mortgage pool is

$$1,000 \times \$100,000 = \$100 \text{ million}$$

Each mortgage, because of its small size, receives credit risk insurance protection from the FHA. This insurance costs a small fee to the originating bank. In addition, each of these new mortgages has an initial stated maturity of 30 years and a mortgage rate—often called the *mortgage coupon*—of 12 percent per year. Suppose that the bank originating these loans relies mostly on liabilities such as demand deposits as well as its own capital or equity to finance its assets. Under current capital adequacy requirements, each $1 of new residential mortgage loans must be backed by some capital. Since residential mortgages fall into Category 3 (50 percent risk weight) in the risk-based capital standards (see Chapter 16) and the risk-based capital requirement is 8 percent, the bank capital needed to back the $100 million mortgage portfolio is

$$\text{Capital requirement} = \$100 \text{ million} \times .5 \times .08 = \$4 \text{ million}$$

We assume that the remaining $96 million needed to fund the mortgages comes from the issuance of demand deposits. Current regulations require that for every dollar of demand deposits held by the bank, however, $0.10 in cash reserves be held at the Federal Reserve Bank (see Chapter 14). Assuming that the bank funds the cash reserves on the asset side of the balance sheet with demand deposits, the bank must issue $106.67 ($96/[1 − .1]) in demand deposits (i.e., $96 to fund mortgages and $10.67 to fund the required cash reserves on these demand deposits). The reserve requirement on demand deposits is essentially an additional tax, over and above the capital requirement, on funding the bank's residential mortgage portfolio. Note that since a 0 percent reserve requirement currently exists on CDs and time deposits, the FI needs no extra funds to pay reserve requirements if it uses CDs to fund the mortgage portfolio.

---

[6]At the end of the second quarter 1997, outstanding mortgage pools were $2.13 trillion, with GNMA pools amounting to $521 billion; FNMA, $674 billion; and FHLMC, $567 billion.

Table 12–3

BANK BALANCE SHEET

(in millions of dollars)

Assets		Liabilities	
Cash reserves	$ 10.67	Demand deposits	$106.67
Long-term mortgages	100.00	Capital	4.00
	$110.67		$110.67

Given these considerations, the bank's initial postmortgage balance sheet may look like the one in Table 12–3. In addition to the capital and reserve requirement taxes, the bank also must pay an annual insurance premium to the FDIC based on the size of its deposits (see Chapter 15). Assuming a deposit insurance premium of 27 basis points,[7] the fee would be

$$\$106.67 \text{ million} \times .0027 = \$288,000$$

Although the bank is earning a 12 percent mortgage coupon on its mortgage portfolio, it is facing three levels of regulatory taxes:

1. Capital requirements
2. Reserve requirements
3. FDIC insurance premiums

Thus, one incentive to securitize is to reduce the regulatory "tax" burden on the FI to increase its after-tax return.[8] In addition to facing regulatory taxes on its residential mortgage portfolio earnings, the bank in Table 12–3 has two risk exposure problems:

1. *Interest Rate Risk Exposure.*   The FI funds the 30-year mortgage portfolio from (short-term) demand deposits; thus, it has a maturity mismatch (see Chapter 9). This is true even if the mortgage assets have been funded with short-term CDs, time deposits, or other purchased funds.
2. *Liquidity Risk Exposure.*   The bank is holding a very illiquid asset portfolio of long-term mortgages and no excess reserves; as a result, it is exposed to the type of potential liquidity shortages discussed in Chapter 13, including the risk of having to conduct mortgage asset fire-sales to meet large unexpected demand deposit withdrawals.

One possible solution to these interest rate and liquidity risk problems is to lengthen the bank's on-balance-sheet liabilities by issuing longer-term deposits or other liability claims such as medium-term notes. Another solution is to engage in interest rate swaps to transform the bank's liabilities into those of a long-term, fixed-rate nature (see Chapter 23). These techniques do not resolve the problem of regulatory taxes and the burden they impose on the FI's returns.

In contrast, creating GNMA pass-through securities can largely resolve the interest rate and liquidity risk problems on the one hand and reduce the burden of regulatory taxes on

---

[7] In 1998, this was the fee charged to the lowest-quality banks.

[8] Another reason for securitization is increased geographic diversification of the loan portfolio. Specifically, many FIs originate mortgages from the local community; the ability to securitize facilitates replacing them with MBSs based on mortgages from other cities and regions.

the other. This requires the bank to securitize the $100 million in residential mortgages by issuing GNMA pass-through securities. In our example, the bank can do this since each of the 1,000 underlying mortgages has FHA/VA mortgage insurance, the same stated mortgage maturity of 30 years, and coupons of 12 percent. Therefore, they are eligible for securitization under the GNMA program if the bank is an approved lender (which we assume it is).

The bank begins the securitization process by packaging the $100 million in mortgage loans. The packaged mortgage loans are removed from the balance sheet by placing them with a third-party trustee off the balance sheet. This third-party trustee may be another bank of high creditworthiness or a legal trustee. Next, the bank determines that (1) GNMA will guarantee, for a fee, the timing of interest and principal payments on the bonds issued to back the mortgage pool and (2) the bank itself will continue to service the pool of mortgages for a fee, even after they are placed in trust. Then GNMA issues pass-through securities backed by the underlying $100 million pool of mortgages. These GNMA securities or pass-through bonds are sold to outside investors in the capital market, and the proceeds (net of any underwriting fees) go to the originating bank. The steps followed in this securitization process are summarized in Figure 12–2.

fully amortized

The equal, periodic repayment on a loan that reflects part interest and part principal over the life of the loan.

Following the sale, each mortgagee makes a payment every month to the bank. The bank aggregates these payments and passes the funds through to GNMA bond investors via the trustee net of servicing fee and insurance fee deductions. To make things easy, most fixed-rate mortgages are **fully amortized** over the mortgage's life. This means that so long as the mortgagee does not seek to prepay the mortgage early within the 30-year period,

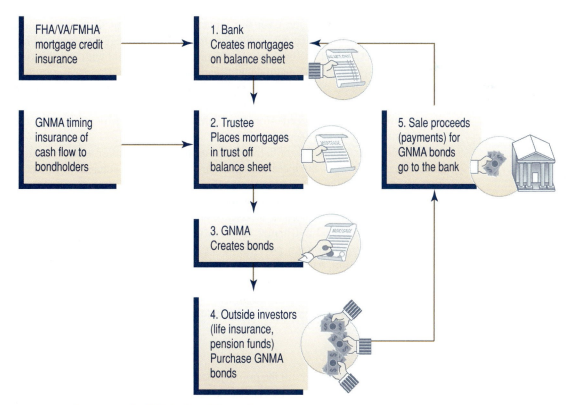

F i g u r e **12–2** *Summary of a GNMA Pass-Through*

Table **12–4**

THE BANK'S BALANCE SHEET POSTSECURITIZATION
(in millions of dollars)

Assets		Liabilities	
Cash reserves	$ 10.67	Demand deposits	$106.67
Cash proceeds from mortgage securitization	100.00	Capital	4.00
	$110.67		$110.67

prepay
To pay back a loan before its maturity to the FI that originated the loan.

either to buy a new house or to refinance the mortgage should interest rates fall, bondholders can expect to receive a constant stream of payments each month analogous to the stream of income on fixed-coupon, fixed-income bonds. In reality, however, mortgagees do not act in such a predictable fashion. For a variety of reasons, they relocate or refinance their mortgages (especially when current mortgage rates are below mortgage coupon rates). This propensity to **prepay** means that *realized* coupons/cash flows on pass-through securities can often deviate substantially from the stated or expected coupon flows in a no-prepayment world. This unique prepayment risk provides the attraction of pass-throughs to some investors but leads other more risk-averse investors to avoid these instruments. Collateralized mortgage obligations, discussed in the next section, provide a way to reduce this prepayment risk.

Assuming that a bank incurs no fees or underwriting costs in the securitization process, its balance sheet might be similar to the one in Table 12–4 immediately after the securitization has taken place. A dramatic change in the bank's balance sheet exposure has occurred. First, $100 million cash has replaced $100 million illiquid mortgage loans. Second, the maturity mismatch is reduced as long-term mortgages are replaced by cash (a short-term asset). Third, the bank has an enhanced ability to deal with and reduce its regulatory taxes. Specifically, it can reduce its capital since capital standards require none be held against cash on the balance sheet compared to residential mortgages that require 4 percent. The bank also reduces its reserve requirement and deposit insurance premiums if it uses part of the cash proceeds from the GNMA sale to pay off or retire demand deposits and downsize its balance sheet.

Of course, keeping an all- or highly liquid asset portfolio and/or downsizing is a way to reduce regulatory taxes, but these strategies are hardly likely to enhance an FI's profits. The real logic of securitization is that the bank can use cash proceeds from the mortgage/GNMA sale to create or originate new mortgages, which in turn can be securitized. In so doing, the bank is acting more as an asset (mortgage) broker than a traditional asset transformer, as we discussed in Chapter 1. The advantage of being an asset broker is that the bank profits from mortgage pool servicing fees plus up-front points and fees from mortgage origination. At the same time, the bank no longer must bear the illiquidity and maturity mismatch risks and regulatory taxes that arise when it acts as an asset transformer and holds mortgages to maturity on its balance sheet. Put more simply, the bank's profitability becomes more fee dependent than interest rate spread dependent. • • •

The Collateralized Mortgage Obligation

Although pass-throughs are still the primary mechanism for securitization, the collateralized mortgage obligation (CMO) is a second vehicle for securitizing bank assets that is used increasingly. Innovated in 1983 by FHLMC and First Boston, the CMO is a device for

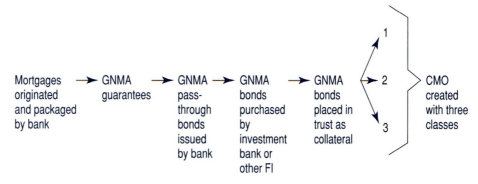

F i g u r e   **12-3**   *The Creation of a CMO*

making mortgage-backed securities more attractive to investors. The CMO does this by repackaging the cash flows from mortgages and pass-through securities in a different fashion to attract different types of investors. A pass-through security gives each investor a pro rata share of any promised and prepaid cash flows on a mortgage pool; the CMO is a multiclass pass-through with a number of different bondholder classes or tranches. Unlike a pass-through, each bondholder class has a different guaranteed coupon just as a regular T-bond has, but more important, the allocation of early cash flows due to mortgage prepayments is such that at any one time, all prepayments go to retire the principal outstanding of only one class of bondholders, leaving the other classes' prepayment protected for a period of time.

Creation of CMOs.   **CMOs** can be created either by packaging and securitizing whole mortgage loans or, more usually, placing existing pass-throughs in a trust off the balance sheet. The trust or third-party bank holds the GNMA pass-through as collateral and issues new CMO securities. The trust issues these CMOs in three or more different classes. For example, the first CMO that Freddie Mac issued in 1983, secured by 20,000 conventional home mortgages worth $1 billion, had three classes: A-1, $215 million; A-2, $350 million, and A-3, $435 million. We show a three-class or tranche CMO in Figure 12–3.

Clearly, issuing CMOs is often equivalent to offering double securitization. An FI packages mortgages and issues a GNMA pass-through. An investment bank such as Goldman Sachs or another CMO issuer such as FHLMC, a commercial bank, or a savings bank may buy this entire issue or a large part of it. Goldman Sachs, for example, then places these GNMA securities as collateral with a trust and issues three new classes of bonds backed by the GNMA securities as collateral.[9] As a result, the investors in each CMO class have a claim to the GNMA collateral should the issuer fail. The investment bank or other issuer creates the CMO to make a profit by repackaging the cash flows from the single-class GNMA pass-through into cash flows more attractive to different groups of investors. The sum of the prices at which the three CMO bond classes can be sold normally exceeds that of the original pass-through

$$\sum_{i=1}^{3} P_{iCMO} > P_{GNMA}$$

collateralized mortgage obligation (CMO)

A mortgage-backed bond issued in multiple classes or tranches.

---

[9]These trusts are sometimes called *real estate mortgage investment conduits (*REMICs).

Gains from repackaging come from the way CMOs restructure prepayment risk to make it more attractive to different classes of investors. Specifically, under a CMO, each class has a guaranteed or fixed coupon.[10] By restructuring the GNMA as a CMO, a bank can offer investors who buy bond class C a high degree of mortgage prepayment protection compared to a pass-through. Those who buy class B receive an average degree of prepayment protection; those who take class A have virtually no prepayment protection.

Each month mortgagees in the GNMA pool pay principal and interest on their mortgages (R) plus a prepayment of principal (some of the mortgage holders prepay principal either to refinance their mortgages or because they have sold their houses and are relocating). These cash flows are passed through to the owner of the GNMA bonds. The CMO issuer uses the cash flows to pay promised coupon interest to the three classes of CMO bondholders.

EXAMPLE 12–2

Calculation of Payments to Three Classes of CMO Bondholders
Suppose that an investment bank buys a $150 million issue of GNMAs and places them in trust as collateral. It then issues a CMO with these three classes as follows:

Class A: Annual fixed coupon 7 percent, class size $50 million.

Class B: Annual fixed coupon 8 percent, class size $50 million.

Class C: Annual fixed coupon 9 percent, class size $50 million.

Suppose that in month 1 the promised amortized cash flows (R) on the mortgages underlying the GNMA pass-through collateral are $1 million, but an additional $1.5 million cash flow results from early mortgage prepayments. Thus, in the first month the cash flows available to pay promised coupons to the three classes of bondholders is

$$R + \text{Prepayments} = \$1 \text{ million} + \$1.5 \text{ million} = \$2.5 \text{ million}$$

This cash flow is available to the trustee, who uses it in the following fashion:

1. *Coupon payments.* Each month (or more commonly, each quarter or half-year), the trustee pays the guaranteed coupons to the three classes of bondholders at annualized coupon rates of 7 percent, 8 percent, and 9 percent, respectively. Given the stated principal of $50 million for each class, the class A (7 percent annual coupon) bondholders receive approximately $291,667 in coupon payments in month 1; the class B (8 percent annual coupon) receives approximately $333,333 in month 1; and the class C (9 percent annual coupon) receives approximately $375,000 in month 1. Thus, the total promised coupon payments to the three classes amount to $1,000,000 (equal to R, the no-prepayment principal and interest cash flows in the GNMA pool).

2. *Principal payments.* The trustee has $2.5 million available to pay as a result of promised mortgage payments plus early prepayments, but the total payment of coupon interest amounts to $1 million. For legal and tax reasons, the remaining $1.5 million must be paid to the CMO bondholders. The unique feature of the CMO is that the trustee pays this remaining $1.5 million only to class A bondholders in order to retire some of these bondholders' principal amounts they have lent. At the end of month 1, only $48.5 million ($50 million – $1.5 million) of class A bonds remains

---

[10]Coupons may be paid monthly, quarterly, or semiannually.

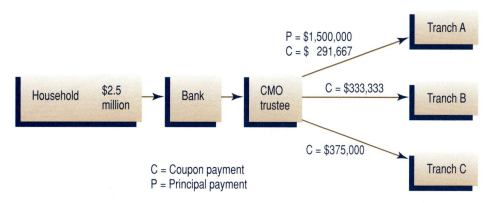

F i g u r e **12-4** *Allocation of Cash Flows to Owners of CMO Tranches*

outstanding, compared to $50 million of class B and $50 million of class C. These payments flows are shown graphically in Figure 12–4.

Let's suppose that the same thing happens in month 2. The cash flows from the mortgage/GNMA pool exceed the promised coupon payments to the three classes of bondholders. Again, the trustee uses any excess cash flows to pay off or retire the principal of class A bondholders. If the excess cash flows again amount to $1.5 million, at the end of month 2 only $47 million ($48.5 million – $1.5 million) of class A bonds is outstanding. This continues until the full amount of the principal of class A bonds is paid off. Once this happens, any subsequent prepayments go to retire the principal outstanding to class B bondholders and, after they are paid off, to class C bondholders. • • •

Figure 12–5 illustrates the typical pattern of outstanding principal balance for a three-tranche CMO over time. With no prepayment, the outstanding principal balance is represented in Figure 12–5 by the curved line *MN*. Given any positive flow of prepayments, within a few years, the class A bonds clearly would be fully retired, point *X* in Figure 12–5. In practice, this often occurs between 1.5 and 3 years after issue. After the trustee retires class A, only classes B and C remain. As the months pass, the trustee uses any excess cash flows over and above the promised coupon payments to class B and C bondholders to retire bond class B's principal. Eventually, all of the principal on class B bonds is retired (point *Y* in Figure 12–5), in practice, five to seven years after CMO issue. After class B bonds are retired, all remaining cash flows are dedicated to paying the promised coupon of class C bondholders and retiring the full amount of principal on class C bonds (point *Z* in Figure 12–5). In practice, class C bonds can have an average life of as long as 20 years.

Class A, B, and C Bond Buyers.   Class A bonds have the shortest average life with a minimum of prepayment protection. They are therefore of great interest to investors seeking short-duration mortgage-backed assets to reduce the duration of their mortgage-related asset portfolios. In recent years, savings banks and commercial banks have been large buyers of CMO class A securities.

Class B bonds have some prepayment protection and expected durations of five to seven years, depending on the level of interest rates. Pension funds and life insurance companies primarily purchase these bonds, although some depository institutions also buy them.

Because of their long expected duration, Class C bonds are highly attractive to insurance companies and pension funds seeking long-term assets to match their long-term liabilities.

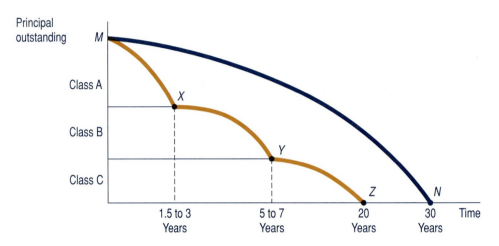

F i g u r e **12–5**   *Principal Balance Outstanding to Classes of Three-Tranch CMO*

Indeed, because of their failure to offer prepayment protection, regular GNMA pass-throughs may not have much attraction for these institutions. Class C CMOs, with their high but imperfect degree of prepayment protection, may be of more interest to the FI managers of these institutions.

In summary, by separating bondholders into different classes and by restructuring cash flows into forms more valued by different investor clienteles, the CMO issuer stands to make a profit.

The Mortgage-Backed Bond

mortgage- (asset-) backed bonds

Bonds collateralized by a pool of assets.

Mortgage- (asset-) backed bonds (MBBs) are the third asset-securitization vehicle. These bonds differ from pass-throughs and CMOs in two key dimensions. First, pass-throughs and CMOs help depository institutions remove mortgages from their balance sheets as forms of off-balance-sheet securitization, but MBBs normally remain on the balance sheet. Second, pass-throughs and CMOs have a direct link between the cash flows on the underlying mortgages and the cash flows on the bond vehicles, but the relationship for MBBs is one of collateralization; the cash flows on the mortgages backing the bond are not necessarily used to make interest and principal payments on the MBB.

Essentially, an FI issues an MBB to reduce risk to the MBB holders, who have a first claim to a segment of the FI's mortgage assets. Practically speaking, the FI segregates a group of mortgage assets on its balance sheet and pledges this group as collateral for the MBB issue. An example of an MBB issue is Society General Australia's 1997 A\$1 billion residential mortgage-backed commercial paper and A\$1 billion mortgage-backed term note programs. Society General calls these programs home owner mortgage enhanced securities (HOMES); Standard and Poors rates them A1-plus and AA-minus, respectively.

A trustee normally monitors the segregation of assets and ensures that the market value of the collateral exceeds the principal owed to MBB holders. That is, FIs back most MBB issues by excess collateral. This excess collateral backing of the bond, in addition to the priority rights of the bondholders, generally ensures the sale of these bonds with a high investment-grade credit rating (such as AA, as in the preceding Society General example).

Table **12–5**

BALANCE SHEET OF POTENTIAL MBB ISSUER
(in millions of dollars)

Assets		Liabilities	
Long-term mortgages	$20	Insured deposits	$10
		Uninsured deposits	10
	$20		$20

In contrast, the FI, when evaluated as a whole, could be rated as BB or even lower. A high credit rating results in lower coupon payments than would be required if significant default risk had lowered the credit rating. To explain the potential benefits and the sources of any gains to an FI from issuing MBBs we examine the following simple example.

EXAMPLE 12–3

Gains to an FI from Issuing MBBs

Consider a bank with $20 million in long-term mortgages as assets. It is financing these mortgages with $10 million in short-term uninsured deposits (e.g., wholesale deposits over $100,000) and $10 million in insured deposits (e.g., retail deposits under $100,000). In this example, we ignore the issues of capital and reserve requirements. Look at the balance sheet structure shown in Table 12–5.

This balance sheet poses problems for the FI manager. First, the bank has a significant interest rate risk exposure due to the mismatch of the maturities of its assets and liabilities. Second, because of this interest rate risk and the potential default risk on the bank's mortgage assets, uninsured depositors are likely to require a positive and potentially significant risk premium to be paid on their deposits. By contrast, the insured depositors may require approximately the risk-free rate on their deposits because they are fully insured by the FDIC (see Chapter 15).

To reduce its interest rate risk exposure and to lower its funding costs, the bank can segregate $12 million of the mortgages on the asset side of its balance sheet and pledge them as collateral backing a $10 million long-term MBB issue. Because the $10 million in MBBs is backed by mortgages worth $12 million, the mortgage-backed bond issued by the bank may cost less to issue, in terms of required yield, than uninsured deposits; that is, it may well be rated AA while uninsured deposits might be rated BB. The FI can then use the proceeds of the $10 million bond issue to replace the $10 million of uninsured deposits.

Consider the bank's balance sheet after the issue of the MBBs (Table 12–6). It might seem that the bank has miraculously engineered a restructuring of its balance sheet that has resulted in a better match of the maturities of its assets and liabilities and a decrease in funding costs. The bond issue has lengthened the average maturity of liabilities by replacing short-term deposits with long-term MBBs and has lowered funding costs because AA-rated bond coupon rates are below BB-rated uninsured deposit rates. This outcome occurs *only because the insured depositors do not worry about risk exposure since they are 100 percent insured by the FDIC*. The result of the MBB issue and the segregation of $12 million of assets as collateral backing the $10 million bond issue is that the insured deposits of $10 million are now backed only by $8 million in free or unpledged assets. If smaller depositors were not insured by the FDIC, they would surely demand very high risk

---

Table **12–6**

BANK'S BALANCE SHEET AFTER MBB ISSUE
(in millions of dollars)

Assets		Liabilities	
Collateral = (market value of segregated mortgages)	$12	MBB issue	$10
Other mortgages	8	Insured deposits	10
	$20		$20

---

premiums for holding these risky deposits. The implication of this is that the bank gains only because the FDIC is willing to bear enhanced credit risk through its insurance guarantees to depositors.[11] As a result, the bank is actually gaining at the expense of the FDIC. Consequently, it is not surprising that the FDIC is concerned about the growing use of this form of securitization by risky banks and thrifts. • • •

A bank might prefer to issue the pass-through/CMO forms of securitization rather than MBBs because of their regulatory discouragement and the risk of regulatory intervention, or for other return reasons. The first reason is that MBBs tie up mortgages on the bank's balance sheet for a long time. This decreases the asset portfolio's liquidity. Second, the illiquidity is enhanced by the need to overcollateralize to ensure a high-quality credit risk rating for the bond issue; in our example, the overcollateralization was $2 million. Third, by keeping the mortgages on the balance sheet, the bank continues to be liable for capital adequacy and reserve requirement taxes. Because of these problems, MBBs are the least used of the three basic vehicles of securitization.

Concept Questions

1. Describe the three forms of asset securitization. What are the major differences in the three forms?
2. How would a simple bank balance sheet change when a pass-through mortgage is securitized? Assume the mortgage is funded with demand deposits and capital and reserve regulations are in force.
3. Why would an investor in a securitized asset who is concerned about prepayment risk prefer a CMO over a pass-through security?
4. Would an AAA FI ever issue mortgage-backed bonds? Explain your answer.

---

[11]The FDIC does not make the risk-based deposit insurance premium to banks and thrifts sufficiently large to reflect this risk.

SECURITIZATION OF OTHER ASSETS

The major use of the three securitization vehicles—pass-throughs, CMOs, and mortgage-backed bonds—has been to package fixed-rate residential mortgage assets, but these techniques can and have been used for other assets including the following:

- Automobile loans.
- Credit card receivables (CARDs).
- Small business loans guaranteed by the Small Business Administration.
- Commercial and industrial loans.
- Junk bonds.
- Adjustable rate mortgages.[12]

Moreover, at one point in the mid-1990s, the U.S. Congress discussed creating another government-sponsored secondary market, the Venture Enhancement and Loan Development Administration for Small Undercapitalized Enterprises, VELDA SUE, for trading securitized small business loans. VELDA SUE never materialized, but the market is being organized in the private sector. Also, as the Contemporary Perspectives Box 12–2 indicates, the market for asset-backed securities now includes asset-backed securities from LDCs.

CAN ALL ASSETS BE SECURITIZED?

The extension of securitization technology to assets other than fixed-rate residential mortgages raises questions about the limits of securitization and whether all assets and loans can be securitized. Conceptually, the answer is that they can be so long as doing so is profitable or the benefits to the FI from securitization outweigh the costs of securitization. Table 12–7 summarizes the benefits versus the costs of securitization.

Table **12-7**

BENEFITS VERSUS COSTS OF SECURITIZATION

Benefits	Costs
New funding source (bonds versus deposits)	Public/private credit risk insurance and
Increased liquidity of bank loans	guarantees
Enhanced ability to manage the maturity gap and thus interest rate risk	Overcollateralization
A savings to the issuer, if off balance sheet, on reserve requirements, deposit insurance premiums, and capital adequacy requirements	Valuation and packaging (the cost of asset heterogeneity)

---

[12]As of November 1997, securitized automobile loans totaled $59.3 billion, credit card receivables totaled $216.4 billion, and commercial and industrial loans totaled $32.3 billion.

Contemporary Perspectives 12–2

Banks Joining Parade of Buyers of Asset-Backed Paper from Third World

Banks are joining insurance companies and pension funds as buyers in the fledgling market for asset-backed securities from emerging nations.

"Commercial banks are having a tremendous appetite for buying these instruments," said Fernando Guerrero, who puts together emerging market offerings at BT Securities Corp., the investment banking arm of Bankers Trust New York Corp. He declined to name banks, but said they have been investing in unrated deals with little collateral to support them.

About $8 billion of asset-backed securities have been originated in Latin America and other developing regions this year. Such issues are gaining in popularity because they carry yields of 200 basis points or more over the London interbank offering rate.

Unlike American securitizations, in which companies offer investors a stake in income-producing assets, many unrated Latin American deals are backed by "future flow"—from assets companies have not yet sold or manufactured. "In this sense, the deals are more like loans than securitizations," said Thomas McCormick, managing director at Financial Security Assurance, a company that insures the securities.

Investment banks have begun offering future flow deals more often in recent years as Latin American governments privatize industries and companies seek capital. Dealers say the risks in the future-flow deals are limited; the offerings are often small—$200 million or less—and short in duration. Timothy Hall, managing director at ING Barings Securities Inc., said investors are reluctant to buy anything that lasts longer than four years.

Deals are also structured to mitigate risks. They are in American dollars to protect against foreign currency rate changes. Investors said that despite instability in some countries, no asset-backed security from an emerging market has "defaulted" although payment on some deals has been delayed. But David Gold, investment manager at Transamerica Life Insurance Co., said his firm usually declines emerging market securities, because there are plenty of high-risk, high-yield deals originated in the U.S. The only exception, he said, was an investment in receivables from tequila-maker Jose Cuervo.

John Lapham, managing director at SunAmerica Corporate Finance, an annuity group, said he has invested cautiously—limiting his international security stakes to $28 million, or less than 2 percent of SunAmerica's assets.

Mr. Lapham said it remains to be seen how risky the deals are. Since securitization took off, the Latin American economy has been solid, so no one really knows what could happen to the deals in a downturn. "We're whistling past the graveyard if we think problems couldn't develop," he said.

SOURCE: Aaron Elstein, *The American Banker*, November 13, 1996, p. 32. Reprinted with permission—American Banker.

According to Table 12–7, given any set of benefits, the more costly and difficult it is to find asset packages of sufficient size and homogeneity, the more difficult and expensive it is to securitize. For example, C&I loans have maturities running from a few months to eight years; in addition, they have varying interest rate terms (fixed, LIBOR floating, federal funds–rate floating) and fees. In addition, C&I loans contain different contractual covenants (covering items such as dividend payments by firms and their M&A activity) and are made to firms in a wide variety of industries. Given this, it is difficult for investors, insurers, and bond rating agencies to value C&I loan pools.[13] The more difficult it is to

---

[13]Despite this, there has been some securitization of C&I loans. These are called collateralized loan obligations (CLOs). A CLO is modeled on the CMO. A bank collects a diversified pool of loans, places them in a trust, and usually issues three tranches of securities against the pool; usually, a senior tranche, a subordinated tranche, and a tranche that has features similar to the residual tranche of CMOs. Most issues so far have involved securitizing highly leveraged loans to finance mergers and acquisitions.

value such asset pools, the higher are the costs of securitization. Thus, the potential boundary to securitization may well be defined by the relative degree of homogeneity of an asset type or group. That is, the more homogeneous or similar are assets, the easier they are to securitize. Thus, it is not surprising that 30-year fixed-rate residential mortgages were the first assets to be securitized since they are the most homogeneous of all assets on bank balance sheets (i.e., have similar maturities and interest rates). Moreover, the existence of secondary markets for houses provides price information that allows for reasonably accurate market valuations of the underlying asset to be made in the event of mortgage defaults.

Concept Question

1. Can all assets and loans be securitized? Explain your answer.

SUMMARY

Loan sales provide a simple alternative to the full securitization of loans through bond packages. In particular, they provide a valuable tool to an FI that wishes to manage its credit risk exposure better. Recently, by increasingly relying on securitization, banks and thrifts have begun to move away from being asset transformers and have begun to become asset brokers. Thus, over time, we can expect the traditional financial technology differences between commercial banking and investment banking to diminish as more and more loans and assets are securitized. This chapter discussed the increasing role of loan sales in addition to the legal and regulatory factors that are likely to affect the future growth of this market. The chapter discussed three major forms of securitization—pass-through securities, collateralized mortgage obligations (CMOs), and mortgage-backed bonds—and described recent innovations in the securitization of other FIs' assets.

PERTINENT WEB SITES

Bank for International Settlements   http://www.bis.org/home.htm

Board of Governors of the Federal Reserve   http://www.bog.frb.fed.us/

Federal Deposit Insurance Corp.   http://www.fdic.gov/

Federal Home Loan Mortgage Corp. (FHLMC)   http://www.freddiemac.com/

Federal Housing Administration (FHA)   http://www.hud.gov/fha/fhahome.html

Federal National Mortgage Association (FNMA)   http://www.fanniemae.com/

Financial Accounting Standards Board (FASB)   http://www.rutgers.edu/accounting/raw/fasb/home.htm

Government National Mortgage Association (GNMA)   http://www.ginniemae.gov/

Loan Pricing Corporation   http://www.loanpricing.com

Securities and Exchange Commission (SEC)   http://www.sec.com/

Veterans Administration (VA)   http://www.va.gov/

Loan Sales and Asset Securitization

1. What is the difference between loans sold with recourse and without recourse from the perspective of both sellers and buyers?

2. What are some of the key features of short-term loan sales? How have banks used this sector of the loan market to circumvent Glass-Steagall limitations?

3. Why are yields higher on loan sales than on commercial paper issues for similar maturity and issue size?

4. What is the difference between loan participations and loan assignments?

5. Why have FIs been very active in loan securitization issuance of pass-through securities while they have reduced their volume of loan sales? Under what circumstances would you expect loan sales to dominate loan securitization?

6. Who are the buyers and sellers of U.S. loans? Why do they participate in this activity?

7. A bank has made a three-year, $10 million dollar loan that pays annual interest of 8 percent. The principal is due at the end of the third year.
   a. The bank is willing to sell this loan with recourse at an interest rate of 8.5 percent. What should it receive for this loan?
   b. The bank has the option to sell this loan without recourse at an interest rate of 8.75 percent. What should it receive for this loan?
   c. If the bank expects a .5 percent probability of default on this loan, is it better to sell this loan with or without recourse? The bank expects to receive no interest payments or principal if the loan is defaulted.

8. City Bank has made a 10-year, $2 million HLT loan that pays annual interest of 10 percent. The principal is expected at maturity.
   a. What should City Bank expect to receive from the sale of this loan if the current market rate on loans is 12 percent?
   b. The price of loans in this risk category is currently quoted in the secondary market at bid-offer prices 88–89 cents (on each dollar). Translate these quotes into actual prices for this loan.
   c. Do these prices reflect a distressed or nondistressed loan? Explain.

9. What role do reserve requirements play in the decision to sell a loan with or without recourse?

10. What three levels of regulatory taxes do FIs face when making loans? How does securitization reduce the levels of taxation?

11. How will a move toward market value accounting affect the market for loan sales?

12. An FI is planning to issue $100 million in commercial loans. It will finance the loans by issuing demand deposits.
   a. What is the minimum capital required if there are no reserve requirements?
   b. What is the minimum demand deposit it needs to attract to fund this loan if you assume a 10 percent average reserve requirement on demand deposits?
   c. Show a simple balance sheet with total assets and total liabilities and equity if this is the only project funded by the bank.

13. How do loan sales and securitization help a bank manage its interest rate and liquidity risk exposures?

14. Go to the Ginnie Mae web site and find the following for the most recent year available: number of new securities issued, cumulative issuances, and securities outstanding.

15. What are the differences between CMOs and MBBs?

16. Consider $200 million of 30-year mortgages with a coupon of 10 percent per annum paid quarterly.
   a. What is the quarterly mortgage payment?
   b. What are the interest repayments over the first year of life of the mortgages? What are the principal repayments?

   Construct a 30-year CMO using this mortgage pool as collateral. There are three tranches (A offers the least protection against prepayment and C offers the most): a $50 million Tranche A makes quarterly payments of 9 percent p.a.; a $100 million Tranche B makes quarterly payments of 10 percent; and a $50 million Tranche C makes quarterly payments of 11 percent.

   c. Assuming no amortization of principal and no prepayments, what are the total promised coupon payments to the three classes? What are the principal payments to each of the three classes for the first year?
   d. If, over the first year, the trustee receives quarterly prepayments of $10 million on the mortgage pool, how are the funds distributed?
   e. How can the CMO issuer earn a positive spread on the CMO?

17. Assume that an FI originates a pool of short-term real estate loans worth $20 million with maturities of five years paying annual interest rates of 9 percent. The average prepayment of loans is approximately 5 percent each year beginning at the end of year 3.

a. What average payment (both principal and interest) does the FI receive if no prepayment is expected over the life of the loans?

b. If the loans are converted into real estate certificates and the FI charges 50 basis points as a servicing fee (including insurance), what payments do the holders of the securities expect if no prepayment is expected?

c. If instead the payments are separated into interest-only (IO) and principal-only (PO) payments, what are the expected payments for each instrument, assuming prepayments of 5 percent at the end of years 3 and 4 and the repayment of the remaining principal in year 5? Assume discount rates of 9 percent.

18. How do FIs use securitization to manage their interest rate, credit, and liquidity risks?

19. Why do buyers of Class C tranches of CMOs demand a lower return than do purchasers of Class A tranches?

20. Go to the FHA web site and locate the most recent information on net prices and average yields for HUD-insured new home mortgages.

Chapter Thirteen

Liquidity Risk

T his chapter looks at the problems created by liquidity risk. Unlike the other risks that threaten the very solvency of an FI, liquidity risk is a normal aspect of the everyday management of an FI. In extreme cases, liquidity risk problems develop into solvency risk problems (see Contemporary Perspectives Box 13–1). Moreover, some FIs are more exposed to liquidity risk than others. At one extreme, depository institutions are highly exposed; in the middle life insurance companies are moderately exposed; at the other extreme, mutual and pension funds and property-casualty insurance companies have relatively low exposure. We examine the reasons for these differences in this chapter.

CAUSES OF LIQUIDITY RISK

Liquidity risk arises for two reasons, a liability side reason and an asset side reason. The liability side risk occurs when an FI's liability holders, such as depositors or insurance policyholders, seek to cash in their financial claims immediately. When liability holders demand cash by withdrawing deposits, the FI needs to borrow additional funds or sell assets to meet the withdrawals. The most liquid asset is cash; FIs use this asset to pay claimholders who seek to withdraw funds. As discussed in Chapter 8, however, FIs tend to minimize their holdings of cash reserves as assets because they pay no interest. To generate interest revenues, most FIs

Contemporary Perspectives 13–1

Public's Confidence In Bank System Tested

The weekend run on Bank of New England (BNE) and its subsequent seizure by the government underscore the public's fragile confidence in the banking system. While the large increase in troubled loans announced last Friday apparently prompted large withdrawals, the insolvency of Rhode Island's private deposit insurance fund earlier in the week and large losses reported in the national deposit fund played a role as well. "The psychological atmosphere in New England following the Rhode Island debacle is not good," said William Isaac, head of the Secura Group, a Washington consulting firm. Bert Ely, a financial consultant based in Alexandria, VA, chalked it up to "jitteriness, uncertainty and confusion." "I think we're asking too much of people to worry about how

sound their bank is," he said. Ely called the seizure a "terrible comment on the bank regulatory process."

To some extent, the run and seizure were unexpected, even though analysts noted that Bank of New England has been the nation's largest problem bank for the past year. The bank also had recently worked out a deal to swap some of its debt for equity. Yet, analysts said, failure may have been inevitable. "Failure was in the cards," said Gerard Cassidy, a banking analyst with Tucker Anthony based in Portland, Maine. "And the FDIC played them this weekend." "They were somewhat of an aberration in their lending and the way they ran the institution," said Ely . . . . "They were not representative of the New

England banks, and New England is not representative of the rest of the country." After years as the region's most aggressive real estate lender, BNE was particularly hard hit when that market headed south, analysts said. The large increase in troubled loans BNE reported Friday was mainly due to real estate and effectively wiped out its capital. . . .

All of BNE's depositors will be covered by deposit insurance, regardless of the amount. By contrast, the larger depositors at Freedom National Bank in Harlem, formerly the nation's largest minority-owned bank, got only 50 cents for each $1 above $100,000. But some of that money may be recovered after assets are sold, according to regulators.

SOURCE: Karen Padley, *Investor's Daily,* January 8, 1991, p. 1.

---

invest in less liquid and/or longer maturity assets. Although most assets can be turned into cash eventually, for some assets this can be done only at a high cost when the asset must be liquidated immediately. The price that the asset holder must accept for immediate sale may be far less than it would receive with a longer horizon over which to negotiate a sale. Thus, some assets may be liquidated only at low **fire-sale prices**, thus threatening the FI's solvency.

fire-sale price

The price received for an asset that has to be liquidated (sold) immediately.

To understand the connection between liquidity risk and solvency risk, consider the simple FI balance sheet in Table 13–1. Before the deposit withdrawals, the FI has $10 million in cash assets and $90 million in nonliquid assets. These assets are funded with $90 million in deposits and $10 million in equity. Suppose that depositors withdraw $20 million and the FI receives no new deposits to replace them. To meet the withdrawals, the FI first uses the $10 million in cash assets and then is forced to sell some nonliquid assets immediately. Let's assume that since it cannot wait to get better prices in the future because it needs the cash immediately to meet depositor withdrawals, the FI can sell the nonliquid assets at only 50 cents on the dollar. Thus, to cover the remaining $10 million in deposit withdrawals, the FI must sell $20 million in nonliquid assets, incurring a loss of $10 million from face value. The FI must write this loss off against its capital or equity funds. Since its equity fund was $10 million, the loss on the fire-sale of assets of $10 million leaves the FI insolvent (i.e., with zero equity capital).

The second cause of liquidity risk is asset side liquidity risk; a result of lending commitments. As we describe in Chapter 20, a loan commitment allows a borrower to take funds

Table **13–1**

ADJUSTING TO A DEPOSIT WITHDRAWAL USING ASSET SALES
(in millions)

Before the Drain				After the Drain			
Assets		**Liabilities/Equity**		**Assets**		**Liabilities/Equity**	
Cash assets	$ 10	Deposits	$ 90	Cash assets	$ 0	Deposits	$70
Nonliquid assets	90	Equity	10	Nonliquid assets	70	Equity	0
	$100		$100		$70		$70

from an FI (over a commitment period) on demand. When the borrower takes down the loan commitment, the FI must fund the loan on the balance sheet immediately; this creates a demand for liquidity. As it can for liability withdrawals, an FI can meet such liquidity needs by running down its cash assets, selling off other liquid assets, or borrowing additional funds.

To analyze the different degrees of importance of liquidity risk across FIs, we next consider liquidity risk problems that face depository institutions, insurance companies, and mutual and pension funds.

Concept Questions

1. What are the sources of liquidity risk?
2. What does the phrase liquidating assets at fire-sale prices mean?

LIQUIDITY RISK AND DEPOSITORY INSTITUTIONS

Liability Side Liquidity Risk

As discussed in Chapter 3, a depository institution's balance sheet typically has a large amount of short-term liabilities, such as demand deposits and other transaction accounts (discussed in Chapter 8), which fund relatively long-term assets. Demand deposit accounts and other transaction accounts are contracts that give the holders the right to put their claims back to the bank on any given day and demand immediate repayment of the face value of their deposit claims in cash.[1] Thus, an individual demand deposit account holder with $10,000 in an account can demand cash immediately as easily as a corporation with $100 million in its demand deposit account. In theory, at least, a bank that has 20 percent of

---

[1] Accounts with this type of put option include demand deposits, NOW accounts (checking accounts with minimum balance requirements), and money market accounts (checking accounts with minimum balance and restrictions as to the number of checks written). We describe these accounts in more detail in Chapter 8. Banks typically liquidate savings account contracts immediately upon request of the customer. Many savings account contracts, however, give a bank some powers to delay withdrawals by requiring notification of withdrawal a certain number of days before withdrawal or by imposing penalty fees such as loss of interest.

its liabilities in demand deposits and other transaction accounts must stand ready to pay out that amount by liquidating its assets on any banking day. Table 13–2 shows the aggregate balance sheet of the assets and liabilities of U.S. commercial banks; total deposits are 70.99 percent of total liabilities (with 16.68 percent demand deposits and transaction accounts). By comparison, cash assets are only 6.02 percent of total assets. Short-term borrowed funds are 17.59 percent of total liabilities.

In reality, a depository institution knows that in normal times only a small proportion of its depositors will withdraw funds from their accounts on any given day. Most demand deposits normally act as **core deposits** on a day-by-day basis, providing a relatively stable source of funds for an FI. Moreover, deposit withdrawals may in part be offset by the receipt of new deposits. The depository institution manager must monitor the resulting net deposit withdrawals or so-called **net deposit drains**. Specifically, over time a depository institution manager can predict the probability distribution of net deposit drains—the difference between deposit withdrawals and deposit additions—on any given normal banking day.

Consider the distribution in Figure 13–1. The distribution in Figure 13–1 is assumed to be strongly peaked at the 5 percent net deposit withdrawal level. That is, this FI expects approximately 5 percent of its net deposit funds to be withdrawn on any given day with the

core deposits

Deposits that provide a long-term funding source to a bank.

net deposit drains

The amount by which cash withdrawals exceed additions; a net cash outflow.

T a b l e **13–2**

ASSETS AND LIABILITIES OF U.S. BANKS, AUGUST 27, 1997
(in billions)

Assets			**Liabilities**		
Total securities	$1,027.7	21.97%	Total deposits	$3,029.0	70.99%
Total loans	3,083.4	65.91	Borrowings	750.4	17.59
Total cash assets	281.6	6.02	Other liabilities	487.4	11.42
Other assets	285.6	6.10	Total liabilities	$4,266.8	
Total assets	$4,678.3				

SOURCE: *Federal Reserve Bulletin*, November 1997, Table 1.26.

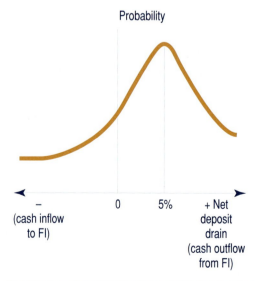

F i g u r e **13–1**   *Distribution of an FI's Net Deposit Drains (cash outflows)*

Table **13-3**

THE EFFECT OF NET DEPOSIT DRAINS ON THE BALANCE SHEET

(in millions)

Before the Drain				After the Drain			
Assets		**Liabilities**		**Assets**		**Liabilities**	
Assets	$100	Deposits	$ 70	Assets	$100	Deposits	$65
		Borrowed funds	10			Borrowed funds	10
		Other liabilities	20			Other liabilities	20
	$100		$100		$100		$95

highest probability. A net deposit drain means that a bank receives insufficient additional deposits (and other cash inflows) to offset deposit withdrawals. The bank represented in Figure 13–1 has a mean or expected net positive drain on deposits, so its new deposit funds and other cash flows are expected to be insufficient to offset deposit withdrawals. The liability side of its balance sheet is contracting. Table 13–3 illustrates an actual 5 percent net drain of deposit accounts (or, in terms of dollars, a drain of $5 million).

The bank can meet this $5 million drain on deposits in two major ways: purchased liquidity management and/or stored liquidity management. Traditionally, bankers have relied on *stored liquidity management* as the primary mechanism of adjustment. Today, many banks—especially the largest banks with access to the money market and other nondeposit markets for funds—rely on *purchased liquidity* to deal with the risk of cash shortfalls. A more extensive discussion of liquidity management techniques is left to Chapter 14. Here we briefly discuss the two methods of liquidity risk management.

Purchased Liquidity Management.   A manager who purchases liquidity turns to markets for purchased funds, such as the federal funds market and/or the repurchase (repo) agreement markets,[2] which are interbank markets for short-term loans to offset the deposit drain. Alternatively, the manager could have the bank issue additional fixed-maturity wholesale certificates of deposit or additional notes and bonds.[3] As long as the total amount of the funds raised equals $5 million, the bank in Table 13–3 could fully fund its net deposit drain. This can be expensive for the bank, however, since it is paying *market rates* for funds in the wholesale money market to offset net drains on low interest-bearing deposits.[4] Thus, the higher the cost of purchased funds relative to the rates earned on assets, the less attractive this approach to liquidity management becomes. Table 13–4 shows the bank's balance sheet if it responds to deposit drains by using purchased liquidity techniques and markets.

---

[2] Securities companies and institutional investors use the repo market extensively for liquidity management purposes.

[3] The *discount window* is also a source of funds but in emergency situations only. See the section Bank Runs, the Discount Window, and Deposit Insurance in this chapter and Chapter 15 for more discussion of the role of the discount window.

[4] Although checking accounts pay no explicit interest, other transaction accounts such as NOW and money market accounts do. The rates paid are normally slow to adjust to changes in market interest rates however, and lie below purchased fund rates; see Chapter 14.

Table **13–4**

ADJUSTING TO A DEPOSIT DRAIN BY PURCHASING FUNDS
(in millions)

Assets		Liabilities	
Assets	$100	Deposits	$ 65
		Borrowed funds	15
		Other liabilities	20
	$100		$100

Note that purchased liquidity has allowed the bank to maintain its overall balance sheet size of $100 million without disturbing the size and composition of the asset side of its balance sheet. That is, all the adjustments to the deposit drain occur on the liability side of the balance sheet. In other words, effective purchased liquidity can insulate the asset side of the balance sheet from normal drains in deposit accounts. This is one of the reasons for the enormous growth of bank-purchased liquidity techniques and associated purchased fund markets such as fed funds, repurchase agreements, and CDs in recent years. (We describe and discuss these instruments and markets in more detail in Chapters 2, 8, and 14.)

Stored Liquidity Management.   Instead of meeting the net deposit drain by borrowing in the wholesale money markets, the bank could liquidate some assets. Banks traditionally have held cash reserves in their vaults and at the Federal Reserve for this very purpose. The Federal Reserve sets minimum reserve requirements for the cash reserves that banks must hold. (Currently, the Fed requires a minimum 3 percent cash reserve on the first $47.8 million and 10 percent on the rest of a bank's demand deposit and transaction account holdings.[5]) Even so, banks still prudently tend to hold excess reserve assets or stored liquidity to meet liquidity drains. For example, the United Kingdom has no official central bank–designated cash reserve requirements although banks still hold 1 percent or more of their assets in stored liquidity.

Suppose in our example that on the asset side of the balance sheet the bank normally holds $9 million of its assets in cash (of which $3 million is for reserve requirements and $6 million is an excess cash reserve). We depict the situation before the net drain in liabilities in Table 13–5. As depositors withdraw $5 million in deposits, the bank meets this directly by using the excess cash held in its vaults or by withdrawing cash reserves (called *correspondent balances*) on deposit at other banks or at the Federal Reserve. If the reduction of $5 million in deposit liabilities is met by a $5 million reduction in cash assets held by the bank, its balance sheet is as shown in Table 13–6.

When the bank uses its cash reserve assets as the adjustment mechanism, both sides of its balance sheet contract; in this example, the bank's total assets shrink from $100 to $95 million. The cost to the bank of using stored liquidity, apart from shrinkage in bank asset size,[6] is that it must hold excess noninterest-bearing assets on its balance sheet.[7] Thus, the

---

[5] The $47.8 million figure is adjusted annually along with the increase in bank deposits. The first $4.7 million of the $47.8 million is not subject to reserve requirements. See Chapter 14.

[6] No empirical evidence indicates a significant correlation between a bank's asset size and its profits.

[7] Banks could hold highly liquid interest-bearing assets such as T-bills, but they are still less liquid than cash, and immediate liquidation may result in some small capital value losses.

Table **13-5**

COMPOSITION OF A BANK'S BALANCE SHEET
(in millions)

Assets		Liabilities	
Cash	$ 9	Deposits	$ 70
Other assets	91	Borrowed funds	10
		Other liabilities	20
	$100		$100

Table **13-6**

RESERVE ASSET ADJUSTMENT TO DEPOSIT DRAIN
(in millions)

Assets		Liabilities	
Cash	$ 4	Deposits	$65
Other assets	91	Borrowed funds	10
		Other liabilities	20
	$ 95		$95

cost is the forgone return (or opportunity cost) of being unable to invest these funds in loans and other higher income-earning assets.

Finally, note that although stored liquidity management and purchased liquidity management are alternative strategies for meeting deposit drains, a bank can combine the two methods by using some purchased liquidity management and some stored liquidity management to meet any given deposit drain.

Asset Side Liquidity Risk

Just as deposit drains can cause a bank liquidity problems, so can the exercise by borrowers of their loan commitments and other credit lines. Table 13–7 shows $5 million of an FI's loan commitment made to a customer exercised on a particular day. As a result, it must fund $5 million in additional loans on the balance sheet. Consider the Before columns in Table 13–7, the balance sheet before the commitment exercise, and the After columns, the balance sheet after it. In particular, the exercise of the loan commitment means that the bank needs to provide $5 million immediately to the borrower (other assets increase from $91 to $96 million). This can be done either by purchased liquidity management (borrowing an additional $5 million in the money market and lending these funds to the borrower) or by stored liquidity management (decreasing the bank's own cash assets from $9 million to $4 million). We present these two policies in Table 13–8.

Measuring a Bank's Liquidity Exposure

Sources and Uses of Liquidity.   As discussed, a bank's liquidity risk can arise either from a drain on deposits or from new loan demands, and the subsequent need to meet these

Table **13-7**

THE EFFECTS OF A LOAN COMMITMENT EXERCISE
(in millions)

Before				After			
Cash	$ 9	Deposits	$ 70	Cash	$ 9	Deposits	$ 70
Other assets	91	Borrowed funds	10	Other assets	96	Borrowed funds	10
		Other liabilities	20			Other liabilities	20
	$100		$100		$105		$100

Table **13-8**

ADJUSTING THE BALANCE SHEET TO A LOAN COMMITMENT EXERCISE
(in millions)

Liability Management				Cash Reserve Asset Adjustment			
Cash	$ 9	Deposits	$ 70	Cash	$ 4	Deposits	$ 70
Other assets	96	Borrowed funds	15	Other assets	96	Borrowed funds	10
		Other liabilities	20			Other liabilities	20
	$105		$105		$100		$100

demands by liquidating assets or borrowing funds. Therefore, an FI manager must be able to measure its liquidity position on a daily basis, if possible. A useful tool is *a net liquidity statement* that lists the sources and uses of liquidity and, thus, provides a measure of an FI's net liquidity position. Such a statement for a hypothetical U.S. money center bank is presented in Table 13–9.

The bank can obtain liquid funds in three ways. First, it can sell its cash-type assets such as T-bills immediately with little price risk and low transaction costs. Second, it can borrow funds in the money/purchased funds market up to a maximum amount (this is an *internal* guideline based on the manager's assessment of the credit limits that the purchased or borrowed funds market is likely to impose on the bank). Third, it can use any excess cash reserves over and above the amount held to meet regulatory imposed reserve requirements. The bank's *sources* of liquidity shown in Table 13–9 total $14,500 million. Compare this to the bank's *uses* of liquidity, in particular, the amount of borrowed or money market funds it has already utilized (e.g., fed funds, RPs borrowed) and the amount of cash it has already borrowed from the Federal Reserve through discount window loans. These total $7,000 million. As a result, the bank has a positive net liquidity position of $7,500 million. The position can be easily tracked on a day-by-day basis.

Peer Group Ratio Comparisons. Another way to measure a bank's liquidity exposure is to compare certain of its key ratios and balance sheet features—such as loans-to-deposits, borrowed funds-to-total assets, and commitments to lend-to-assets ratios—with those for banks of a similar size and geographic location (see Chapter 8). A high ratio of loans to deposits and borrowed funds to total assets means that the bank relies heavily on the short-term money market rather than on core deposits to fund loans. This could mean future liquidity problems if the bank is at or near its borrowing limits in the purchased funds market.

Table **13‒9**

NET LIQUIDITY POSITION
(in millions)

Sources of Liquidity

1.	Total cash-type assets	$ 2,000
2.	Maximum borrowed funds limit	12,000
3.	Excess cash reserves	500
	Total	$14,500

Uses of Liquidity

1.	Funds borrowed	$ 6,000
2.	Federal Reserve borrowing	1,000
	Total	7,000
	Total net liquidity	$ 7,500

Table **13‒10**

LIQUIDITY EXPOSURE RATIOS FOR THREE BANKS, 1995 VALUES

	North Fork Bancorp	Firstier Financial	Boatmen's Bancshares
Borrowed funds to total assets	17.90%	17.19%	13.29%
Core deposits to total assets	71.89	72.47	72.46
Loans to deposits	78.28	75.86	76.57
Commitments to lend to total assets	6.20	46.59	39.49

Similarly, a high ratio of loan commitments to assets indicates the need for a high degree of liquidity to fund any unexpected takedowns of these loans by customers. That is, high-commitment banks often face more liquidity risk exposure than do low-commitment banks.

Table 13–10 lists the 1995 values of these ratios for the banks we reviewed in Chapter 8: North Fork Bancorp (NFB), Firstier Financial (FF), and Boatmen's Bancshares (BB). None of the three banks relied heavily on borrowed funds (short-term money market instruments) to fund loans. The ratio of borrowed funds to total assets is 17.90 percent, 17.19 percent, and 13.29 percent, respectively. The ratio of core deposits (the stable deposits of the FI, such as demand deposits, NOW accounts, MMDAs, other savings accounts, and retail CDs) to total assets, on the other hand, is 71.89 percent, 72.47 percent, and 72.46 percent, respectively. Furthermore, NFB has a ratio of commitments to total assets of only 6.20 percent, FF and BB are exposed to substantially greater liquidity risk from unexpected takedowns of these commitments (i.e., the ratio of commitments to total assets is 46.59 percent for FF and 39.49 percent for BB).

Liquidity Index.   A third way to measure liquidity risk is to use a liquidity index. One such index was developed by Jim Pierce at the Federal Reserve. This index measures the potential losses an FI could suffer from a sudden or fire-sale disposal of assets compared to the amount it would receive at a fair market value established under normal market (sale) conditions, which might take a long period of time as a result of a careful search and bidding process. The larger the differences between immediate fire-sale asset prices (P_i) and fair market prices (P_i^*), the less liquid is the FI's portfolio of assets. That is, define an index I such that

$$I = \sum_{i=1}^{N} [(w_i)(P_i/P_i^*)]$$

where w_i is the percentage of each asset in the FI's portfolio and $\Sigma w_i = 1$.

E X A M P L E   1 3 – 1

• • • • • •   *Calculation of the Liquidity Index*

Suppose that an FI has two assets, 50 percent in one-month Treasury bills and 50 percent in real estate loans. If the FI must liquidate its T-bills today (P_1), it receives \$99 per \$100 of face value; if it can wait to liquidate them on maturity (in one month's time), it will receive \$100 per \$100 of face value (P_1^*). If the FI has to liquidate its real estate loans today, it receives \$85 per \$100 of face value (P_2); liquidation at the end of one month (closer to maturity) will produce \$92 per \$100 of face value (P_2^*). Thus, the one-month liquidity index value for this FI's asset portfolio is:

$$I = (\tfrac{1}{2})\,(.99/1.00) + (\tfrac{1}{2})\,(.85/.92)$$
$$= 0.495 + 0.462$$
$$= 0.957$$

Suppose alternatively that a slow or thin real estate market caused the FI to be only able to liquidate the real estate loans at \$65 per \$100 of face value (P_2). The one-month liquidity index for the FI's asset portfolio is:

$$I = (\tfrac{1}{2})\,(.99/1.00) + (\tfrac{1}{2})\,(.65/.92)$$
$$= 0.495 + 0.353$$
$$= 0.848$$

The value of the one-month liquidity index decreases from the first one due to the larger discount on the fire-sale price—from the fair (full value) market price of real estate—over the one-month period. The larger the discount from fair value, the smaller the liquidity index or higher the liquidity risk the FI faces.   • • •

The liquidity index is always between 0 and 1. The liquidity index for this FI could be compared with similar indexes calculated for a group of similar FIs.

Financing Gap and the Financing Requirement.   A fourth way to measure liquidity risk exposure is to determine the bank's financing gap. As we discussed earlier, even though demand depositors can withdraw their funds immediately, they do not do so in normal circumstances. On average, most demand deposits stay at banks for quite long periods, often two years or more.[8] Thus, a banker often thinks of the average deposit base, including demand deposits, as a core source of funds that over time can fund a bank's average amount of loans. We define a **financing gap** as

financing gap

The difference between a bank's average loans and average (core) deposits.

$$\text{Financing gap} = \text{Average loans} - \text{Average deposits}$$

---

[8] See Federal Reserve Board of Governors, "Risk-Based Capital and Interest Rate Risk," press release, July 30, 1992.

Table **13–11**

THE FINANCING REQUIREMENT OF A BANK
(in millions)

Assets		Liabilities	
Loans	$25	Core deposits	$20
		Financing gap	(5)
Liquid assets	5	Financing requirement	
		(borrowed funds)	10
Total	$30	Total	$30

If this financing gap is positive, the bank must fund it by using its cash and liquid assets and/or borrowing funds in the money market, thus

$$\text{Financing gap} = -\text{ Liquid assets} + \text{Borrowed funds}$$

We can write this relationship as

$$\text{Financing gap} + \text{Liquid assets} = \text{Financing requirement (borrowed funds)}$$

financing requirement

The financing gap plus a bank's liquid assets.

As expressed in this fashion, the liquidity and managerial implications of the **financing requirement** are that some level of core deposits and loans as well as some amount of liquid assets determines the bank's borrowing or purchased fund needs.[9] In particular, the larger a bank's financing gap and liquid asset holdings, the higher the amount of funds it needs to borrow on the money markets and the greater is its exposure to liquidity problems from such a reliance.

The balance sheet in Table 13–11 indicates the relationship between the financing gap, liquid assets, and the borrowed funds financing requirement. See also the following equation

$$\text{Financing gap} + \text{Liquid assets} = \text{Financing requirement}$$
$$(\$5 \text{ million}) \qquad (\$5 \text{ million}) \qquad (\$10 \text{ million})$$

A widening financing gap can warn of future liquidity problems for a bank since it may indicate increased deposit withdrawals (core deposits falling below $20 million in Table 13–11) and increasing loans due to more exercise of loan commitments (loans rising above $25 million). If the bank does not reduce its liquid assets—they stay at $5 million—the manager must resort to more money market borrowings. As these borrowings rise, sophisticated lenders in the money market may be concerned about the bank's creditworthiness. They may react by imposing higher risk premiums on borrowed funds or establishing stricter credit limits by not rolling over funds lent to the bank. If the bank's financing requirements dramatically exceed such limits, it may become insolvent. A good example of an excessive financing requirement resulting in bank insolvency is the failure of

---

[9] The bank holds cash and liquid assets to meet day-to-day variations in the actual level of deposits and loans. On any given day, however, cash and liquid asset balances may exceed those needed to meet daily variations in deposits and loans. These excess balances may be run down to fund the financing gap.

Continental Illinois in 1984.[10] This possibility of insolvency also highlights the need for FI managers to engage in active liquidity planning to avoid such crises.

Liquidity Planning. Liquidity planning is a key component in measuring (and being able to deal with) liquidity risk and its associated costs. Specifically, liquidity planning allows managers to make important borrowing decisions before relatively predictable events occur. Such forward planning can lower the cost of funds (by determining an optimal funding mix) and minimize the amount of excess reserves that a bank needs to hold.

A liquidity plan has a number of components. The first component is the delineation of managerial details and responsibilities. Responsibilities are assigned to key management personnel should a liquidity crisis occur; the plan identifies those managers responsible for interacting with various regulatory agencies such as the Federal Reserve, the FDIC, and Office of Thrift Supervision (OTS). It also specifies areas of managerial responsibility in disclosing information to the public, including depositors. The second component of a liquidity plan is a detailed list of fund providers most likely to withdraw as well as the pattern of fund withdrawals. For example, in a crisis, financial institutions such as mutual funds and pension funds are more likely than correspondent banks and small business corporations to withdraw funds quickly from banks and thrifts. In turn, correspondent banks and small corporations are more likely than individual depositors to withdraw funds quickly. This makes liquidity exposure sensitive to the effects of future funding composition changes. In addition, FIs such as depository institutions face particularly heavy seasonal withdrawals of deposits in the quarter before Christmas. The third component of liquidity planning is the identification of the size of potential deposit and fund withdrawals over various time horizons in the future (one week, one month, one quarter, etc.) as well as alternative private market funding sources to meet such runoffs (e.g., emergency loans from other FIs and the Federal Reserve). The fourth component of the plan sets internal limits on separate subsidiaries' and branches' borrowings as well as bounds for acceptable risk premiums to pay in each market (fed funds, RPs, CDs, etc.). In addition, the plan details a sequencing of assets for disposal in anticipation of various degrees or intensities of deposit/fund withdrawals. Such a plan may evolve from an FI's asset-liability management committee and may be relayed to various key departments of the FI, for example, the money desk and the treasury department, which play vital day-to-day roles in liability funding.

Consider, for example, Table 13–12. The data are for a bank that holds $250 million in deposits from mutual funds, pension funds, correspondent banks, small businesses, and individuals. The table includes the average and maximum expected withdrawals over the next one-week, one-month, and one-quarter periods. The liquidity plan for the bank outlines how to cover expected deposit withdrawals should they materialize. In this case, the bank will seek to cover expected deposit withdrawals over the next three months first with

---

[10]Continental Illinois, headquartered in Chicago, had a very small core deposit base due to restrictions on bank branching within the state. As a result, it had to rely extensively on borrowed funds such as fed funds, RPs, and Eurodollar deposits (wholesale CDs from Euromarkets). As these borrowings increased, concerns about the bank's ability to meet its payment commitments also increased—especially in view of its worsening loan portfolio. This resulted in the eventual refusal of a number of large money market lenders (such as Japanese banks) to renew or roll over their borrowed funds held by Continental Illinois on maturity. With the rapid withdrawal of such borrowed funds, Continental Illinois was unable to survive and was eventually taken over by the FDIC. For detailed descriptions of the Continental Illinois failure, see I. Swary, "Stock Market Reaction to Regulatory Action in the Continental Illinois Crisis," *Journal of Business* 59 (1986), pp. 451–473; and L. Wall and D. R. Peterson, "The Effect of Continental Illinois' Failure on the Performance of Other Banks," *Journal of Monetary Economics,* 1990, pp. 77–99.

Table **13–12**

DEPOSIT DISTRIBUTION AND POSSIBLE WITHDRAWALS
INVOLVED IN A BANK'S LIQUIDITY PLAN

(in millions)

Deposits	$250
From	
Mutual funds	60
Pension funds	50
Correspondent banks	15
Small businesses	70
Individuals	55

Expected withdrawals	Average	Maximum
One week	$40	$105
One month	55	140
Three months	75	200

Sequence of deposit withdrawal funding	One Week	One Month	Three Months
1. New deposits	$10	$35	$75
2. Investment portfolio asset liquidation	50	60	75
3. Borrowings from other FIs	30	35	45
4. Borrowings from Fed	15	10	5

new deposits, then with the liquidation of marketable securities in its investment portfolio, next with borrowings from other FIs, and finally, if necessary, with borrowings from the Federal Reserve.

Liquidity Risk, Unexpected Deposit Drains, and Bank Runs

Under normal conditions and with appropriate planning, net deposit withdrawals or the exercise of loan commitments poses few liquidity problems for banks because borrowed fund availability or excess cash reserves are adequate to meet anticipated needs. For example, even in December and the summer vacation season, when net deposit withdrawals are high, banks anticipate these *seasonal* effects by holding larger than normal excess cash reserves or borrowing more than normal on the wholesale money markets.

Major liquidity problems can arise, however, if deposit drains are abnormally *large* and *unexpected*. Such deposit withdrawal shocks may occur for a number of reasons, including these:

1. Concerns about a bank's solvency relative to that of other banks.
2. Failure of a related bank, leading to heightened depositor concerns about the solvency of other banks (a *contagion effect*).
3. Sudden changes in investor preferences regarding holding nonbank financial assets (such as T-bills or mutual fund shares) relative to deposits.

bank run

A sudden and unexpected increase in deposit withdrawals from a bank.

Any sudden unexpected surge in net deposit withdrawals risks triggering a **bank run** could eventually force a bank into insolvency.

Table **13-13**

BANK RUN INCENTIVES

Assets		Liabilities	
Assets	$90	Deposits	$100
			(100 × $1 each)

Deposit Drains and Bank Run Liquidity Risk.   At the core of bank run liquidity risk is the fundamental and unique nature of the *demand deposit contract*. Specifically, demand deposit contracts are first-come, first-served contracts in the sense that a depositor's place in line determines the amount he or she will be able to withdraw. In particular, a depositor receives either full payment or nothing. For example, suppose that a bank has 100 depositors, each of whom deposited $1. Suppose that each has a reason to believe—correctly or incorrectly—that the bank has assets valued at only $90 on its balance sheet (see Table 13–13).

As a result, each depositor has an incentive to go to the bank quickly to withdraw his or her $1 deposit because the bank pays depositors sequentially by liquidating its assets. If it has $90 in assets, it can pay in full only the first 90 depositors in the line. The 10 depositors at the end of the line get *nothing at all*. Thus, demand deposits are in essence either full-pay or no-pay contracts.

Because demand deposit contracts pay in full only a certain proportion of depositors when a bank's assets are valued at less than its deposits—and because depositors realize this—any line outside a bank encourages other depositors to join the line immediately even if they do not need cash today for normal consumption purposes.[11] Thus, even the bank's core depositors who really do not need to withdraw deposits for consumption needs rationally seek to withdraw their funds immediately when they observe a sudden increase in the lines at their bank.

As a bank run develops, the demand for net deposit withdrawals increases. The bank might initially meet this by decreasing its cash reserves, selling off liquid or readily marketable assets such as T-bills and T-bonds, and seeking to borrow in the money markets. As a bank run increases in intensity, more depositors join the withdrawal line, and a liquidity crisis develops. Specifically, the bank finds it difficult, if not impossible, to borrow on the money markets at virtually any price. Also, it has sold all its liquid assets, cash, and bonds as well as any salable loans (see Chapter 12). The bank is likely to have left only relatively illiquid loans on the asset side of the balance sheet to meet depositor claims for cash. However, these loans can be sold or liquidated only at very large discounts from face value.

A bank needing to liquidate long-term assets at fire-sale prices to meet continuing deposit drains faces the strong possibility that the proceeds from such asset sales are insufficient to meet depositors' cash demands. The bank's liquidity problem then turns into a solvency problem; that is, the bank must close its doors.

bank panic

A systemic or contagious run on the deposits of the banking industry as a whole.

The incentives for depositors to run first and ask questions later create a fundamental instability in the banking system so that an otherwise sound bank can be pushed into insolvency and failure by unexpectedly large depositor drains and liquidity demands. This is especially so in periods of contagious runs or **bank panics** (such as the panic involving the

---

[11]Here we assume no deposit insurance or discount window. The presence of deposit insurance and the discount window alters the incentives to engage in a bank run, as we describe later in this chapter and in Chapter 15.

Ohio savings banks in 1985 discussed in Chapter 9) when depositors lose faith in the banking system as a whole and engage in a run on all banks by not materially discriminating among them according to their asset qualities.[12]

Bank Runs, the Discount Window, and Deposit Insurance

Regulators have recognized the inherent instability of the banking system due to the all-or-nothing payoff features of the deposit contract. As a result, regulatory mechanisms are in place to ease banks' liquidity problems and to deter bank runs and panics. The two major liquidity risk insulation elements are *deposit insurance* and the *discount window*. Because of the serious social welfare effects that a contagious run on banks could have, government regulators of depository institutions have established guarantee programs offering deposit holders varying degrees of insurance protection to deter runs. Specifically, if a deposit holder believes a claim is totally secure, even if the bank is in trouble, the holder has no incentive to run. The deposit holder's place in line no longer affects his or her ability to obtain the funds. Deposit insurance deters runs as well as contagious runs and panics. In addition to deposit insurance, central banks, such as the Federal Reserve, have traditionally provided a discount window facility to meet banks' short-term nonpermanent liquidity needs. The central bank makes discount window loans, however, at its discretion, not necessarily to assist troubled banks. Consequently, the discount window is a partial, not a full, substitute for deposit insurance as a liquidity stabilizing mechanism. We discuss deposit insurance in detail in Chapter 15. As Chapter 15 discusses, deposit insurance has effectively deterred bank panics since 1933, although the provision of deposit insurance has not been without other costs and problems.

Concept Questions

1. What are two benefits and two costs of using (a) liability management and (b) reserve or cash assets to meet a deposit drain?
2. What are the three major sources of bank liquidity? What are the two major uses?
3. Which factors determine an FI's financing requirement?

LIQUIDITY RISK AND LIFE INSURANCE COMPANIES

Banks are not the only FIs exposed to liquidity risk or run problems. Like banks, life insurance companies hold some cash reserves to meet policy cancellations and other working capital needs. In the normal course of business, premium income and returns on the asset portfolio are sufficient to meet the cash outflows required when policyholders cash in or surrender their policies early (see Chapter 4). The distribution or pattern of

---

[12]See G. G. Kaufman, "Bank Contagion: A Review of Theory and Evidence," *Journal of Financial Services Research*, 1994, pp. 123–150, for an excellent review of the nature and causes of bank runs and panics. There is strong evidence that contagious bank runs or panics occurred in 1930–1932 in the United States (see A. Saunders and B. Wilson, "Contagious Bank Runs: Evidence From the 1929–1933 Period," *Journal of Financial Intermediation*, 1996, pp. 409–423). Such panics also cause a flight to safe assets such as T-bills.

surrender value

The amount that an insurance policyholder receives when cashing in a policy early.

premium income minus policyholder liquidations is normally predictable as it is with banks. When premium income is insufficient, a life insurer can sell some of its relatively liquid assets, such as government bonds. In this case, bonds act as a buffer or reserve asset fund for the insurer. Concerns about the solvency of the insurer or insurance companies in general can result in a run in which new premium income dries up and existing policyholders seek to cancel their policies by cashing them in for their **surrender values**. That is, life insurance policies with a savings component accumulate funds that are referred to as the policy's *surrender value*.[13] The policyholder may cancel the policy on demand and receive its surrender value. To meet exceptional demands for cash, a life insurer could be forced to liquidate the less liquid assets in its portfolio, such as commercial mortgage loans and other securities, at potentially fire-sale prices.[14] Forced asset liquidations can push an insurer, like banks, into insolvency. An insurance company run occurred in 1991 on First Capital, an $8.5 billion California-based insurer. With more than 300,000 life policies and 167,000 annuity policies, First Capital held more than 40 percent of its assets in junk bonds. Losses on its junk bond portfolio (estimated to be worth 75 cents on the dollar in May 1991) raised regulator and policyholder concerns about the quality of its balance sheet. New policyholder premiums dried up, and existing policyholders engaged in a run by seeking to cash in their policies for whatever surrender values they could obtain. Policy surrenders totaled $265 million in the first two weeks of May 1991 and rose to $100 million on May 10, 1991. To deter the run, the California state insurance regulator placed limits on the ability of existing policyholders to surrender their policies.[15]

Concept Questions

1. What is likely to be a life insurance company's first source of liquidity when premium income is insufficient?
2. Can a life insurance company be subjected to a run? If so, under what circumstances?

LIQUIDITY RISK AND PROPERTY-CASUALTY INSURERS

As discussed in Chapter 4, property-casualty (PC) insurers sell policies insuring against certain contingencies impacting either real property or individuals. Those contingencies (and policy coverages) are relatively short term, often one to three years, unlike those for

---

[13]A *surrender value* is usually some proportion or percentage less than 100 percent of the face value of the insurance contract. The surrender value continues to grow as funds invested in the policy earn interest. Earnings to the policyholder are taxed if and when the policy is actually surrendered or cashed in before the policy matures. Some insurance companies have faced run problems resulting from their sale of guaranteed investment contracts (GICs). A GIC, similar to a long-term, fixed-rate bank deposit, is a contract between an investor and an insurance company. As market interest rates rose, many investors withdrew their funds and reinvested elsewhere in higher return investments. This created both liquidity and refinancing problems for life insurers that supplied such contracts and eventually led to restrictions on withdrawals.

[14]Life insurers also provide a considerable amount of loan commitments, especially in the commercial property area. As a result, they face asset side loan commitment liquidity risk in a similar fashion to banks.

[15]State guaranty plans also deter policyholder runs. In general, the level of coverage and the value of the guarantees are less than deposit insurance. We discuss these guaranty plans in Chapter 15.

life insurers. As a result, PC insurers' assets tend to be shorter term and more liquid than those of life insurers. PC insurers' contracts and premium-setting intervals are usually relatively short term as well, so problems caused by policy surrenders are less severe. PC insurers' greatest liquidity exposure occurs when policyholders cancel or fail to renew policies because of insolvency risk, pricing, or competitive reasons. This may cause their premium cash inflow, when added to their investment returns, to be insufficient to meet policy claims. Or large unexpected claims may materialize and exceed the flow of premium income and income returns from assets. Disasters such as Hurricane Andrew in 1991 and the East Coast blizzard of the century in 1996 caused severe liquidity crises and failures among small PC insurers.[16]

Concept Questions

1. What is the greatest cause of liquidity exposure that property-casualty insurers face?
2. Is the liquidity risk of property-casualty insurers, in general, larger or smaller than that of life insurers?

MUTUAL FUNDS

closed-end fund

An investment fund that sells a fixed number of shares to outside investors.

open-end fund

An investment fund that sells an elastic or nonfixed number of shares to outside investors.

net asset value

The price at which mutual fund shares are sold (or can be redeemed), equals the total market value of the fund's assets less any accrued liabilities divided by the number of shares in the fund outstanding.

Mutual funds sell shares as liabilities to investors and then invest the proceeds in assets such as bonds and equities. Mutual funds are open end and closed end. **Closed-end funds** issue a fixed number of shares as liabilities; unless the issuing fund chooses to repurchase them, the number of outstanding shares does not change. As discussed in Chapter 7, by far the majority of U.S. mutual funds are **open-end funds;** that is, they can issue an unlimited supply of shares to investors. Open-end funds must stand ready to buy back previously issued shares from investors at the current market price for the fund's shares.

We show the supply function of open-end mutual fund shares in Figure 13–2. Thus, at a given market price—$0P$ in Figure 13–2—the supply of open-end fund shares is perfectly elastic. The price at which an open-end mutual fund stands ready to sell new shares or redeem existing shares is the **net asset value** (NAV) of the fund. NAV is the current or market value of the fund's assets less any accrued liabilities divided by the number of shares in the fund. A mutual fund's willingness to provide instant liquidity to shareholders while it invests funds in equities, bonds, and other long-term instruments could expose it to liquidity problems similar to those that banks, thrifts, and life insurance companies face when the number of withdrawals (or of mutual fund shares cashed in) rises to abnormally and unexpectedly high levels. Indeed, mutual funds can be subject to dramatic liquidity runs if investors become nervous about the NAV of the mutual funds' assets. The fundamental difference in the way that mutual fund contracts are valued compared to the valuation of bank deposit and insurance policy contracts, however, mitigates the incentives for mutual fund shareholders to engage in such runs. Specifically, if a mutual fund were to be liquidated, its

---

[16]Claims also may arise in so-called long-tail lines when a contingency takes place during the policy period but a claim is not lodged until many years later. As mentioned in Chapter 4, the claims regarding damage caused by asbestos contacts are in this category.

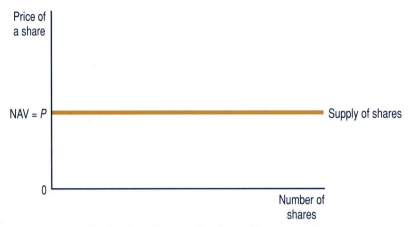

F i g u r e **13-2**   *The Supply of Shares of an Open-End Mutual Fund*

NAV = net asset value

P = market price

T a b l e **13-14**

**RUN INCENTIVES OF BANK DEPOSITORS VERSUS
MUTUAL FUND INVESTORS**

Bank			Open-End Mutual Fund		
Assets		**Liabilities**	**Assets**		**Liabilities**
Assets	$90	$100 Deposits (100 depositors with $1 deposits)	Assets	$90	$100 Shares (100 shareholders with $1 shares)

assets would be distributed to fund shareholders on a pro rata basis rather than the first-come, first-served basis employed under deposit and insurance policy contracts.

To illustrate this difference, we can compare the incentives for mutual fund investors to engage in a run directly with those of bank depositors. Table 13–14 shows a simple balance sheet of an open-end mutual fund and one of a bank. When they perceive that a bank's assets are valued below its liabilities, depositors have an incentive to engage in a run on the bank to be first in line to withdraw. In the example in Table 13–14, only the first 90 bank depositors would receive $1 back for each $1 deposited. The last 10 would receive nothing at all.

Now consider the mutual fund with 100 shareholders who invested $1 each for a total of $100 with assets worth $90. If these shareholders tried to cash in their shares, *none* would receive $1. Instead, a mutual fund values its balance sheet liabilities on a market value basis; the price of any share liquidated by an investor is

$$P = \frac{\text{Value of assets}}{\text{Shares outstanding}} = \text{NAV}$$

Thus, unlike deposit contracts that have fixed face values of $1, the value of a mutual fund's shares reflects the changing value of its assets divided by the number of shares outstanding. In Table 13–14, the value of each shareholder's claim is

Contemporary Perspectives 13-2

SEC Official Sees Small-Market Fund Liquidity Risk

A top U.S. mutual funds regulator said Tuesday he is concerned about potential liquidity problems confronting the growing number of mutual funds investing in emerging and other small markets.

"I have fears that we could see problems with some kinds of markets....It does concern me," said Barry Barbash, director of the division of investment management of the U.S. Securities & Exchange Commission.

Liquidity means the ability of a fund to buy and sell the securities it owns on short notice—an eventuality that can arise if mutual fund investors suddenly want their money back. Liquidity can be hard to come by,

though, in markets with limited numbers of active buyers and sellers. "The problem can arise in any sort of market that is smaller," Barbash said.

In search of superior returns, a growing number of mutual funds have poured money into small markets, such as emerging economies and small- and micro-cap stocks.

In the $3 trillion mutual fund business, with about 40,000 funds worldwide, potential liquidity problems at small-market funds likely do not pose a risk to the entire industry.

The risk faced by emerging country funds is that a political, military or other surprise—whether in

Russia, China or Latin America—could frighten investors, leading to a wave of share redemption requests.

In an illiquid market, that could cause big problems, Barbash said, adding that it may only be a matter of time before the mutual fund industry finds out just how big.

"At some point there will be a test and we'll see what happens."

Emerging country funds are not the only type of mutual funds that could be vulnerable to a liquidity crunch.

Micro-capitalization stock funds in the United States and other highly specialized funds run such risks, too.

SOURCE: *The Reuters Business Report*, November 12, 1996. Reprinted with permission of Reuters.

$$P = \frac{\$90}{100} = \$0.90$$

That is, each mutual fund shareholder participates in the fund's loss of asset value on a *pro rata,* or proportional, basis. Technically, whether first or last in line, each mutual fund shareholder who cashes in shares on any given day receives the same net asset value per share of the mutual fund. In this case, it is 90 cents, representing a loss of 10 cents per share. All mutual fund shareholders realize this and know that investors share asset losses on a pro rata basis; being first in line to withdraw has no overall advantage, as it has at banks.

This is not to say that mutual funds bear no liquidity risk (see, for example, Contemporary Perspectives Box 13–2) but that the incentives for mutual fund shareholders to engage in runs that produce the extreme form of liquidity problems faced by banks, thrifts, and life insurance companies are generally absent.[17] This situation has led some academics to argue for deposit contracts to be restructured in a form more similar to mutual fund or

---

[17]A sudden surge of mutual fund shareholder redemptions might require a mutual fund manager to sell some of its less marketable bonds and equities at fire-sale prices. For example, in 1996, Fidelity Investment's Magellan Fund had to sell significant blocks of securities when fundholder redemptions increased at the announcement of the resignation of the extremely successful fund manager.

equity contracts. This might also make the need for deposit insurance to deter bank runs unnecessary.[18]

Concept Questions

1. What would be the impact on a bank's liquidity needs if it offered deposit contracts of an open-end mutual fund type rather than the traditional all-or-nothing demand deposit contract?
2. How do the incentives of a mutual fund's investors to engage in runs compare with the incentives of bank depositors?

• •

---

[18]A common argument against this is that since deposits are money, and money is the unit of account in the economy, equity-type contracts could pose a problem if the value of a deposit were to fluctuate day to day. Note, however, that money market mutual funds offer depositlike contracts as well. As their NAV varies, they solve the fluctuating share value problem by setting the value of each share at $1 but allowing the number of shares an individual holds to fluctuate so that the value of the individual's overall holdings moves in line with asset values while the price of each money market mutual fund share remains at $1. A similar policy could be adopted for deposits at banks.

SUMMARY

Liquidity risk, as a result of heavier than anticipated liability withdrawals or loan commitment exercise, is a common problem that FI managers face. Well-developed policies for holding liquid assets or having access to markets for purchased funds are normally adequate to meet liability withdrawals. Very large withdrawals, however, can cause asset liquidity problems to be compounded by incentives for liability claimholders to engage in runs at the first sign of a liquidity problem. The incentives for depositors and life insurance policyholders to engage in runs can push normally sound FIs into insolvency. Mutual funds are able to avoid runs because their liabilities and assets are marked to market so that losses are shared equally among liability holders. Since FI insolvencies have costs to society as well as to private shareholders, regulators have developed mechanisms such as deposit insurance and the discount window to alleviate liquidity problems. We discuss these mechanisms in detail in Chapter 15.

PERTINENT WEB SITES

Board of Governors of the Federal Reserve http://www.bog.frb.fed.us/

Liquidity Risk

1. How does liquidity risk differ for different types of financial institutions?
2. How does the asset side reason for liquidity risk differ from the liability side reason?
3. The probability distribution of the net deposit drain on an FI has been estimated to have a mean of 2 percent and a standard deviation of 1 percent.

   a. Is this bank increasing or decreasing in size? Explain.
   b. If an FI has a net deposit drain, in what two ways can it offset this drain of funds? How do the two methods differ?
4. How is asset side liquidity risk likely to be related to liability side liquidity risk?
5. Why would an FI be forced to sell assets at fire-sale prices?

6. What are four measures of liquidity risk?
7. Acme Corporation has been acquired by Conglomerate Corporation. To help finance the takeover, Conglomerate will liquidate the overfunded portion of Acme's pension fund. The following assets will be liquidated. Their face values, liquidation values today, and anticipated liquidation values one year from now are given below.

Asset	Face Value	Liquidation 0	Liquidation 1
IBM stock	$10,000	$ 9,900	$10,500
GE bonds	5,000	4,000	4,500
Treasury securities	15,000	13,000	14,000

Calculate the one-year liquidity index for these securities.
8. AllStarBank has the following balance sheet:

Assets (in millions)		Liabilities	
Cash	30	Deposits	90
Other assets	140	Borrowed funds	40
	170	Other liabilities	40
			170

Its largest customer decides to exercise a $15 million loan commitment. Show how the new balance sheet changes if AllStar uses (a) asset management or (b) liability management.
9. Assume that an FI has assets of $10 million consisting of $1 million in cash and $9 million in loans. It has core deposits of $6 million. It also has $2 million in subordinated debt and $2 million in equity. Increases in interest rates are expected to result in a net drain of $2 million in core deposits over the year.
   a. The average cost of deposits is 6 percent and the average return on loans is 8 percent. The FI decides to reduce its loan portfolio to offset this expected decline in deposits. What is the cost? What will be the total asset size of the firm from this strategy after the drain?
   b. If the cost of issuing new short-term debt is 7.5 percent, what is the cost of offsetting the expected drain if it increases its liabilities? What will be the total asset size of the FI from this strategy after the drain?
10. What government safeguards are in place to lessen liquidity risk for banks?
11. Consider the Balance Sheet of an FI listed below:

Balance Sheet ($ millions)

Cash	$10	Deposits	$68
Loans	50	Equity	7
Securities	15		

The FI is expecting a $15 million net deposit drain. Show the FI's balance sheet under these two conditions:
   a. The bank purchases liabilities to offset this expected drain.
   b. The reserve asset adjustment method is used to meet the liquidity shortfall.
12. An FI has $10 million in T-bills, a $5 million line of credit to borrow in the repo market, and $5 million in cash reserves with the Fed in excess of its required reserve requirements. It has also borrowed $6 million in federal funds and $2 million from the federal discount window to meet seasonal demands.
   a. What is the bank's total available (sources of) liquidity?
   b. What are the bank's total uses of liquidity?
   c. What is the bank's net liquidity? What conclusions can you derive from the result?
13. An FI has the following assets in its portfolio: $20 million in cash reserves with the Fed, $20 million in T-bills, $50 million in mortgage loans, and $10 million in fixed assets. If it needs to dispose of its assets with short notice, it will receive only 99 percent of the fair market value of the T-bills and 90 percent of the fair market value of its mortgage loans. Estimate the liquidity index using this information.
14. What are the components of an FI's liquidity plan? How can the plan help an FI reduce liquidity shortages?
15. How is the liquidity problem faced by mutual funds different from that faced by banks and insurance companies?
16. Plainbank has $10 million in cash and equivalents, $30 million in loans, and $15 in core deposits. Calculate (a) the financing gap and (b) the financing requirement.
17. The following is a bank's balance sheet in millions:

Cash	$ 2	Demand deposits	$50
Loans	50		
Premises and equipment	3	Equity	5
Total	$55		$55

The asset-liability management committee has estimated that the loans, whose average coupon rate is 6 percent and average life is three years, will have to be discounted at 10 percent if they are to be sold in less than two days. If they can be sold in four days, they will have to be discounted at 8 percent. Loans are not amortized (i.e., principal is paid at maturity). If they can be sold later than a week, they will receive the full market value.
   a. What price does the bank receive for the loans if they have to be sold in (a) two days and (b) in four days?
   b. In a crisis, if the bank's depositors all demand payment on the first day, what amount will they receive? What

will they receive if they demand to be paid within the week?

18. How does the liquidity risk of an open-end mutual fund compare with that of a closed-end fund?

19. A mutual fund has the following assets in its portfolio: $40 million in fixed income securities and $40 million in stocks at current market values. In the event of a liquidity crisis, it can sell its assets at a 96 percent discount if they are disposed of in two days. It will receive 98 percent if disposed off in four days. Two shareholders, A and B, own 5 percent and 7 percent of equity (shares), respectively.
    a. Market uncertainty has caused shareholders to sell the shares back to the fund. What will the two shareholders receive if the mutual fund must sell all its assets in two days? In four days?
    b. How does this differ from a bank run? How have bank regulators mitigated the problem of bank runs?

20. A mutual fund has $1 million in cash and $9 million invested in securities. It currently has 1 million shares outstanding.

a. What is the NAV of this fund?
b. Assume that some of the shareholders decide to cash in their shares of the fund. How many shares at its current NAV can the fund take back without resorting to a sale of assets?
c. As a result of anticipated heavy withdrawals, it sells 10,000 shares of IBM stock currently valued at $40. Unfortunately, it receives only $35 per share. What is the NAV after the sale? What are the fund's cash assets after the sale?
d. Assume that after the sale of IBM shares, 100,000 shares are sold back to the fund. What is the current NAV? Is there a need to sell more stocks to meet this redemption?

21. Go to the Web site for the Board of Governors of the Federal Reserve and look up *money supply* and *debt levels* for the past six months. Does it appear that the economy has become more or less liquid?

Chapter Fourteen

Liability and Liquidity Management

D epository institutions and life insurance companies are especially exposed to liquidity risk (see Chapter 13). The essential feature of this risk is that a financial intermediary's assets are relatively illiquid when liability claims are suddenly withdrawn (or not renewed). The classic case is a bank run in which depositors demand cash as they withdraw their claims from a bank and the bank is unable to meet these demands because of the relatively illiquid nature of its assets. For example, the bank could have a large portfolio of nonmarketable small business or real estate loans.

To reduce the risk of a liquidity crisis, FIs can insulate their balance sheets from liquidity risk by efficiently managing their liquid asset positions or managing the liability structure of their portfolios. We address both management issues in this chapter. In reality, an FI manager can optimize both liquid asset and liability structures to insulate the FI against liquidity risk.

LIQUID ASSET MANAGEMENT

A liquid asset can be turned into cash quickly and at a low cost with little or no loss in principal value (see the discussion of the liquidity index in Chapter 13). Specifically, a liquid asset is traded in an active market so that even large transactions in that asset do not move the market price or move it very little. Good examples of liquid assets are newly issued T-bills, T-notes, and T-bonds. The ultimate liquid asset is cash, of course. Although it is obvious that an FI's liquidity risk can be reduced by holding large amounts of assets such as cash, T-bills, and T-bonds, FIs usually face a return or interest earnings penalty from doing this.[1] Because of their high liquidity and low default risks, such assets often bear low returns reflecting their essentially risk-free nature. By contrast, nonliquid assets often must promise additional returns or risk premiums to compensate an FI for the relative lack of marketability and often greater default risk of the instrument.

Holding relatively small amounts of liquid assets exposes an FI to enhanced illiquidity and risk of a *bank run*. Excessive illiquidity can result in an FI's inability to meet required payments on liability claims and, at the extreme, insolvency and can even lead to contagious effects that negatively impact other FIs (see Chapter 13). Consequently, regulators have often imposed minimum liquid asset reserve requirements on FIs. In general, these requirements differ in nature and scope for various FIs and even according to country. The requirements depend on the illiquidity risk exposure perceived for the FI's type and other regulatory objectives that relate to minimum liquid asset requirements.

Specifically, regulators often set minimum liquid asset requirements for at least two additional reasons than simply ensuring that FIs can meet expected and unexpected liability withdrawals. The other two reasons relate to monetary policy and taxation.

Monetary Policy Reasons

Many countries set minimum liquid asset reserve requirements to strengthen their monetary policy. Specifically, setting a minimum ratio of liquid reserve assets to deposits limits the ability of banks and bank-related institutions to expand lending and enhances the central bank's ability to control the money supply. Consider the following simple balance sheet:

Liquid reserve assets	$ 10 million	Deposits	$100 million
Loans	110 million	Equity	20 million
	$120 million		$120 million

If the minimum ratio of liquid asset reserves to deposits is set by regulators at 10 percent, this FI barely meets the minimum by holding $10 million in liquid reserve assets against

---

[1] Of course, at times Treasury bonds provide relatively high yields. When this occurs, FIs are motivated to purchase safe assets with relatively high returns instead of making loans and accepting potential default risks.

the $100 million in deposits. The FI cannot issue new deposits to fund new loans without also increasing the size of the liquid reserve assets it holds against the new deposits. An addition of $1 million in liquid assets would allow the bank to expand its deposit base by a maximum of $10 million (with an additional $9 million in loans). The new balance sheet after the full adjustment, including the addition of $1 million in liquid reserve assets, follows:

Liquid reserve assets	$ 11 million	Deposits	$110 million
Loans	119 million	Equity	20 million
	$130 million		$130 million

In this context, requiring depository institutions to hold minimum ratios of liquid assets to deposits allows the central bank to gain greater control over deposit growth and thus over the money supply (of which bank deposits are a highly significant portion; see Chapter 1) as part of its overall macrocontrol objectives.

Taxation Reasons

reserve requirement tax

The cost of holding reserves that pay no interest at the central bank. This cost is further increased if inflation erodes the purchasing power value of these reserve balances.

Another reason for requiring minimums on FI liquid asset holdings is to force FIs to invest in government financial claims rather than private sector financial claims. That is, a minimum required liquid asset **reserve requirement tax** is an indirect way for governments to raise additional "taxes" from FIs. Having banks hold cash in the vault or cash reserves at the central bank (when no interest rate compensation is paid) requires banks to transfer a resource to the central bank. In fact, the profitability of many central banks is contingent on the size of the reserve requirement that can be viewed as a tax levy on banks under their jurisdiction. This tax or cost effect is increased if inflation erodes the purchasing power value of those balances.

Concept Questions

1. Why do regulators set minimum liquid asset requirements for FIs?
2. Can we view reserve requirements as a tax when the consumer price index (CPI) is falling?

THE COMPOSITION OF THE
LIQUID ASSET PORTFOLIO

liquid assets ratio

A minimum ratio of liquid assets to total assets set by the central bank.

The composition of an FI's liquid asset portfolio, especially cash and government securities, is determined partly by earnings considerations and partly by the type of minimum liquid asset reserve requirements that the central bank imposes. In many countries, including the United Kingdom, reserve ratios have historically been imposed to encompass both cash and liquid government securities such as T-bills.[2] Thus, a 20 percent **liquid assets ratio** requires a commercial or savings bank in the United Kingdom to hold $1 of

---

[2] The United Kingdom no longer imposes minimum reserve requirements on banks.

cash plus government securities for every $5 of deposits. Many states in the United States impose liquid asset ratios on life insurance companies that require minimum cash and government securities holdings in their balance sheets.

By contrast, the minimum liquid asset requirements for banks in the United States have been cash based and have excluded government securities. As a result government securities are less useful because they are not counted as part of the reserves held by banks and at the same time yield lower promised returns than loans do. Nevertheless, many banks view government securities holdings as performing a useful secondary or **buffer reserve** function. In times of liquidity crisis, when significant drains on cash reserves occur, these securities can be turned into cash quickly and with very little loss of principal value because of the deep nature of the markets in which these assets are traded.

buffer reserve

Nonreserve asset that can be quickly turned into cash.

Concept Question

1. In general, would it be better to hold three-month T-bills or 10-year T-notes as buffer assets? Explain.

RETURN-RISK TRADE-OFF
FOR LIQUID ASSETS

In optimizing its holdings of liquid assets, an FI must trade the benefit of cash immediacy for lower returns. In addition, the FI manager's choice is one of *constrained optimization* in the sense that liquid asset reserve requirements imposed by regulators set a minimum bound on the level to which liquid reserve assets can fall in the balance sheet. Thus, an FI facing little risk of liquidity withdrawals and holding only a small amount of liquid assets for prudential reasons finds that it is forced to hold more than is privately optimal as a result of minimum reserve restrictions imposed by regulators.

The Liquid Asset Reserve Management Problem for U.S. Banks

This section examines the risk-return trade-off in running a liquid asset position and the regulatory constraints imposed on this position. The section presents a detailed example of U.S. bank liquidity management under the current minimum reserve requirements imposed by the Federal Reserve. Many of the issues and trade-offs are readily generalizable, however, to any FI facing liability withdrawal risk under conditions in which regulators impose minimum liquid asset reserve ratios.

The issues involved in the optimal management of a liquid asset portfolio are illustrated by the problems faced by the money desk manager in charge of a U.S. bank's reserve position. In the context of U.S. bank regulation, we concentrate on a bank's management of its **cash reserves,** defined as vault cash and cash deposits held by the bank at the Federal Reserve.[3] Currently in accordance with Regulation D of the Securities Act of 1933, banks

cash reserves

Vault cash and cash deposits held at the Federal Reserve.

---

[3] However, banks that are not members of the Federal Reserve System, mostly very small banks, may maintain reserve balances with a Federal Reserve Bank indirectly (on a pass-through basis) with certain approved institutions such as correspondent banks.

in the United States are required to hold the following "target" minimum cash reserves against net transaction accounts:[4]

< $4.7 million	0%
$4.7 million–$47.8 million	3
> $47.8 million	10

transaction accounts

Deposits that permit the account holders to make multiple withdrawals.

Transaction accounts include all deposits on which an account holder may make withdrawals by negotiable or transferrable instruments and may make more than three monthly telephone or preauthorized fund transfers for the purpose of making payments to third parties (for example, demand deposits, NOW accounts, and share draft accounts—offered by credit unions).[5] Transaction account balances are reduced by demand balances due from U.S. depository institutions and cash items in process of collection to obtain net transaction accounts.

To calculate the target amount of reserves and to determine whether it is holding too many or too few reserves, the bank reserve manager requires two additional pieces of information to manage the position. First, for which period's deposits does the manager compute the bank's reserve requirement? Second, for which period or periods must the bank maintain the target reserve requirement just computed?

The U.S. system is complicated by the fact that the period for which the bank manager computes the required reserve target differs from the period during which the reserve target is maintained or achieved. We describe the computation and maintenance periods for bank reserves next.

reserve computation period

Period over which required reserves are calculated.

Computation Period.   For the purposes of bank reserve management, a U.S. bank reserve manager must think of the year as being divided into two-week periods. The **reserve computation period** always begins on a Tuesday and ends on a Monday 14 days later.

E X A M P L E   1 4 – 1

Computation of Daily Average Required Reserves

Consider ABC Bank's reserve manager who wants to assess the bank's minimum cash reserve requirement target. Let's suppose that the manager knows the bank's net transaction accounts balance at the close of the banking day on each of the 14 days over the period Tuesday, July 23, to Monday, August 5. Of course, in reality, the manager knows these deposit positions with certainty only at the end of the two-week period. Consider the realized net transaction account positions of ABC bank in Table 14–l.

The minimum daily average reserves that a bank must maintain is computed as a percentage of the daily average net transaction accounts held by the bank over the two-week computation period, where Friday's balances are carried over for Saturday and Sunday. The

---

[4] The Garn-St. Germain Depository Institutions Act of 1982 (Public Law 97–320) requires that $2 million of reservable liabilities of each depository institution be subject to a zero percent reserve requirement. Each year, the Federal Reserve adjusts the amount of reservable liabilities subject to this zero percent reserve requirement for the succeeding calendar year by 80 percent of the percentage increase in the total reservable liabilities of all depository institutions, measured on an annual basis as of June 30. In 1998, this figure was $4.7 million.

As of 1998 these were the requirements. The reserve ratio was also reduced from 12 to 10 percent for transaction accounts in April 1992.

[5] Historically, U.S. banks also had to hold reserves against time deposits and personal savings deposits (including MMDAs). However, this was reduced from 3 to 0 percent at the beginning of 1991.

Table 14-1

NET TRANSACTION ACCOUNT BALANCES OF ABC BANK
(in millions of dollars)

Date	Transaction Accounts	Less Demand Balances due from U.S. Depository Institutions	Less Cash Items in Process of Collection	Net Transaction Accounts
Tuesday, July 23	$ 1,850	$ 240	$ 140	$ 1,470
Wednesday, July 24	1,820	235	135	1,450
Thursday, July 25	1,770	250	120	1,400
Friday, July 26	1,610	260	100	1,250
Saturday, July 27	1,610	260	100	1,250
Sunday, July 28	1,610	260	100	1,250
Monday, July 29	1,655	250	125	1,280
Tuesday, July 30	1,650	230	130	1,290
Wednesday, July 31	1,690	240	130	1,320
Thursday, August 1	1,770	275	135	1,360
Friday, August 2	1,820	280	140	1,400
Saturday, August 3	1,820	280	140	1,400
Sunday, August 4	1,820	280	140	1,400
Monday, August 5	1,785	260	135	1,390
Total	$24,280	$3,600	$1,770	$ 18,910
Daily average net transaction accounts				$1,350.7

minimum daily average for ABC Bank to hold against the daily average of $1,350.70 million in net transaction accounts is calculated as follows (amounts in millions):

Daily Average Net Transaction Accounts	× Reserve Percentage	=	Daily Average Reserves Required
$4.7	0%		$0.000
$47.8–$4.7	3		1.293
$1,350.7–$47.8	10		130.290
Minimum average reserves to be held			$131.583

Note that the daily average target in Example 14–1 is calculated by taking a 14-day average of net transaction accounts even though the bank is closed for 4 of the 14 days (two Saturdays and two Sundays). Effectively, Friday's deposit figures count three times compared to those of other days in the business week. This means that the bank manager who can engage in a strategy in which deposits are lower on Fridays can, on average, lower the bank's reserve requirements. This may be important if required liquid asset reserve holdings are above the optimal level from the bank's perspective to handle liquidity drains due to expected and unexpected deposit withdrawals.

One strategy employed in the past was for a bank to send deposits out of the country (e.g., transfer them to a foreign subsidiary) on a Friday when a reduction in deposits effectively counts for 3/14ths of the two-week period and to bring them back on the following Monday when an increase counts for only 1/14th of the two-week period. This action effectively reduces the average demand deposits in the balance sheet of the bank over the 14-day

Table **14–2**

ABC BANK'S DAILY VAULT CASH OVER THE JUNE 25–JULY 8 CASH COMPUTATION PERIOD

(in millions of dollars)

Date	
Tuesday, June 25	$ 30
Wednesday, June 26	28
Thursday, June 27	24
Friday, June 28	21
Saturday, June 29	21
Sunday, June 30	21
Monday, July 1	24
Tuesday, July 2	26
Wednesday, July 3	25
Thursday, July 4	25
Friday, July 5	27
Saturday, July 6	27
Sunday, July 7	27
Monday, July 8	29
Total	$355
Daily average vault cash	$25.357

weekend game

Name given to the policy of lowering deposit balances on Fridays since that day's figures count three times for reserve accounting purposes.

period by 2/14th times the amount sent out of the country and, thus, reduces the amount of reserves it needs to hold. Analysts term this the **weekend game.**[6]

Note that the $131.583 million figure is a *minimum* reserve target. The bank manager may hold excess cash reserves above this minimum level if the privately optimal or prudent level for the bank exceeds the regulatory specified minimum level because this bank is especially exposed to deposit withdrawal risk. In addition, the bank manager may hold some buffer reserves in the form of government securities that can quickly be turned into cash if deposit withdrawals are unusually high or to preempt the early stages of a bank run.

Maintenance Period.   We have computed a daily average minimum cash reserve requirement for ABC Bank but have yet to delineate the exact period over which the bank manager must maintain this $131.583 million daily average reserve target. Reserves may be held either as vault cash or as deposits held by the bank at the Federal Reserve. Under the current set of regulations, the vault cash portion of required reserves is determined using a two-week period starting 28 days prior to the start of the reserve computation period. For ABC Bank, this **cash computation period** is from June 25 through July 8. Thus, the bank's reserve manager knows the value of this part of its target reserves with perfect certainty throughout the reserve computation period. The daily balances in vault cash for ABC Bank for the 14-day cash computation period from June 25 through July 8 are shown in Table 14–2. The resulting average daily balance in vault cash for this period

cash computation period

Period over which vault cash is recorded against required reserve target.

---

[6] In fact, the weekend game is a special case of bank window dressing, in which transactions are undertaken to reduce reported deposits below their true or actual figures. For a discussion of window dressing in banking and the incentives for bankers to window dress, see L. Allen and A. Saunders, "Bank Window Dressing: Theory and Evidence," *Journal of Banking and Finance*, 1992, pp. 585–624.

is $25.357 million. The bank must therefore hold an average daily balance of $106.226 million (i.e., $131.583 million – $25.357 million) at the Federal Reserve during the **reserve maintenance period.**

Currently, regulators have set the two-week reserve maintenance period for meeting the reserve target beginning two days after the start of the reserve computation period and ending two days after the end of that period. Regulators set this almost **contemporaneous reserve accounting system** to give the bank reserve manager a two-day leeway or grace period in which to meet target reserves.

EXAMPLE 14-2

• • • • • • •

reserve maintenance period

Period over which deposits at the Federal Reserve Bank must meet or exceed the required reserve target.

contemporaneous reserve accounting system

An accounting system in which the reserve computation and reserve maintenance periods overlap.

Computation of Required Reserves to Be Held Over the Last Two Days of the Reserve Maintenance Period

In our example, the reserve computation period runs from Tuesday, July 23, to Monday, August 5, but the reserve maintenance period runs from Thursday, July 25, to Wednesday, August 7. As a result, for the last two days of the reserve maintenance period, August 6 and 7, the bank manager knows with absolute certainty the minimum reserves to hold at the Federal Reserve (here, it is $106.226 million per day). For the first 12 days of the reserve period, however, the manager is uncertain as to the final daily average target. We show these almost contemporaneous reserve requirements in Figure 14–1. Basically, the reserve manager has two days, August 6 and August 7, to correct any major amount under or over the required reserve target during the preceding 12 days when there was target uncertainty.

Table 14–3 presents ABC Bank's reserve position as of the close of the day on August 5, when the federal reserve target can be calculated with certainty and two days are left in the reserve maintenance period in which to make adjustments to reserves held to meet the required target. On the close of the Monday, August 5, banking day, the average daily cash reserve position of ABC Bank held at the Federal Reserve (over the first 12 days of the

Table **14-3**

ABC BANK'S DAILY RESERVE POSITIONS OVER THE JULY 23–AUGUST 5 RESERVE MAINTENANCE PERIOD
(in millions of dollars)

Date		
Thursday, July 25	$ 98	
Friday, July 26	100	
Saturday, July 27	100	
Sunday, July 28	100	
Monday, July 29	98	
Tuesday, July 30	91	
Wednesday, July 31	102	
Thursday, August 1	101	
Friday, August 2	99	
Saturday, August 3	99	
Sunday, August 4	99	
Monday, August 5	107	(Last day of the reserve computation period)
12-day total	$1,194	
Tuesday, August 6	?	
Wednesday, August 7	?	(Last day of the reserve maintenance period)

JUNE

SUN	MON	TUES	WED	THUR	FRI	SAT
						1
2	3	4	5	6	7	8
9	10	11	12	13	14	15
16	17	18	19	20	21	22
23	24	25	26	27	28	29
30						

JULY

SUN	MON	TUES	WED	THUR	FRI	SAT
	1	2	3	4	5	6
7	8	9	10	11	12	13
14	15	16	17	18	19	20
21	22	23	24	25	26	27
28	29	30	31			

AUGUST

SUN	MON	TUES	WED	THUR	FRI	SAT
				1	2	3
4	5	6	7	8	9	10
11	12	13	14	15	16	17
18	19	20	21	22	23	24
25	26	27	28	29	30	31

Cash Computation Period
Reserve Computation Period
Reserve Maintenance Period

F i g u r e **14–1**   *Almost Contemporaneous Reserve Requirements*

reserve maintenance period) was $99.5 million ($1,194 million/12). Based on deposits held over the full reserve computation period, however, the manager must hold an average reserve level of $106.226 million per day at the Federal Reserve over the full 14-day reserve maintenance period. Thus, as of that Monday evening, the manager can easily calculate that during the preceding 12 days, the minimum reserve target was short by $6.726 million per day ($106.226 million − $99.5 million), or cumulatively $80.712 million (12 × $6.726 million).

This information presents the manager with a clear target for the two remaining days of the reserve maintenance period, Tuesday, August 6, and Wednesday, August 7. The manager must hold an average of $106.226 million on each of those days and must make up the cumulative shortfall of $80.712 million over the previous 12 days. The bank manager must hold a minimum of $293.164 million ($106.226m. + $106.226m. + $80.712 m.) over the last two days of the reserve maintenance period (or an average of $146.582 million for the two days) at the Federal Reserve. The manager could hold different amounts of reserves on each of these two days, such as $144.108 million on Tuesday and $149.056 million on Wednesday, but the total for the two days must be at least $293.164 million so that the manager can meet the regulatory imposed minimum reserve ratio target for the full 14-day period. • • •

Undershooting/Overshooting the Reserve Target

Undershooting.   What happens if, at the end of the reserve maintenance period on August 7, the bank *undershoots* the regulatory required daily minimum reserve ratio—that is, holds less that the required amount ($131.583 million daily average in our example)? The Federal Reserve allows the bank to make up as much as a 4 percent daily average error without penalty.[7] Thus, if the bank is 4 percent in the red on its reserve target by $5.263 million per day (4 percent × $131.583 million),[8] it must make this up in the next two-week reserve maintenance period that runs from August 8 to August 21.[9] When a bank holds a deficit in its required reserves in a given two-week period, it must hold a surplus amount of reserves in the subsequent two-week period.

If the reserve shortfall exceeds 4 percent, the bank is liable to explicit and implicit penalty charges from the Federal Reserve. The explicit charges include the imposition of a penalty interest rate charge equal to the central bank's discount rate plus a 2 percent markup; the implicit charges can include more frequent monitoring, examinations, and surveillance if bank regulators view the inadequate reserve amount as a reflection of an unsafe

---

[7] The carryover was changed from 2 percent to 4 percent on September 3, 1992. See Federal Reserve Board of Governors (1992), CSC no. 92–35, Attachment Docket no. R-0750, p. 5.

[8] This means the allowable deficiency over the full 14 days could be $73.686 million ($131.583 million × .04 × 14).

[9] Suppose, on the other hand, that ABC Bank carried forward a deficit of $1.5 million in reserves from the previous reserve maintenance period (July 11 through July 24). As a result, the $106.226 million in reserve deposits to be held for the period July 25 through August 7 must increase to $107.726 million to make up the previous deficit. Given the daily reserves reported in Table 14–3 from July 25 through August 5, the manager now can calculate that for the first 12 days of the reserve maintenance period, the minimum target was short by $8.226 million per day ($107.726 million − $99.5 million) or $98.712 million cumulatively (12 × $8.226 million). The bank manager must now hold a minimum of $314.164 million ($107.726 million + $107.726 million + $98.712 million) in deposits at the Federal Reserve on Tuesday, August 6, and Wednesday, August 7 (the last two days of the reserve maintenance period), or an average daily balance for these two days of $157.082 million.

and unsound practice by the bank's manager. Such a view is likely to be taken only if the bank consistently undershoots its reserve targets.

A bank that undershoots the reserve target has two principal ways to build up reserves to meet the target as the reserve maintenance period comes to an end: it can (1) liquidate assets (e.g., by selling some buffer assets such as Treasury bills) or (2) borrow in the interbank market for reserves, especially in the federal funds and repurchase agreement markets described later. The bank manager is likely to choose the least costly method to meet any reserve deficiency such as borrowing fed funds if this rate is less than the cost of selling off liquid assets.

Overshooting.   The cost of *overshooting*, or holding cash reserves in excess of the minimum required level, depends on whether the bank perceives its prudent level of reserves to meet expected and unexpected deposit withdrawals to be higher or lower than the regulatory-imposed minimum reserve amount.

If its required minimum reserves are higher than the amount managers perceive to be optimal, the first 4 percent of excess reserves can be carried forward to the next reserve period. The Federal Reserve allows this amount to count toward meeting the reserve requirement in the next two-week maintenance period. After that, any reserves held above the required minimum plus 4 percent constitute a drag on bank earnings since every dollar that is held as excess reserves—either in cash or on deposit at the central bank—earns no interest and could have been lent out at the bank lending rate. For example, if the bank's lending rate to its best customers is 12 percent, the bank and its shareholders have suffered an opportunity cost of 12 percent for every dollar of excess cash reserves held by the bank.

In contrast, if the bank manager perceives that the regulatory required minimum level of reserves is lower than it needs for expected and unexpected deposit withdrawal exposure, the FI overshoots the required minimum reserve target. This policy maintains the bank's liquidity position at a prudently adequate level. In choosing to overshoot the target, the manager must consider the least cost instrument in which to hold such reserves.

Thus, although some excess reserves might be held in some highly liquid (noninterest-bearing) cash form, at least part of any excess reserve position might be held in buffer assets such as short-term securities or Treasury bills that earn interest but are not quite as liquid as cash. The proportion between cash and Treasury bills held depends in large part on yield spreads.

For example, suppose that the loan rate is 12 percent, the T-bill rate is 7 percent, and the interest earned on excess cash holdings is 0 percent. The opportunity cost of a forgone return to the bank from holding excess reserves in cash form or T-bill form is

$$\text{Opportunity cost of cash } = 12\% - 0\% = 12\%$$
$$\text{Opportunity cost of T-bills } = 12\% - 7\% = 5\%$$

Thus, T-bills have a significantly lower opportunity cost than cash has, and the manager must weigh the 7 percent net opportunity cost savings of holding excess reserves in T-bill form against the ease with which such instruments can be sold and turned into cash to meet liability withdrawals or liquidity crunches. Table 14–4 data indicate excess cash reserves of U.S. banks between December 1991 and December 1997. Because of their opportunity cost, excess reserves are invariably kept at very low levels; this was 3.7 percent of required reserves in 1997.

Liquidity Management as a Knife-Edge Management Problem.   The management of an FI's liquidity position is something of a knife-edge situation because holding too many liquid assets penalizes a bank's earnings and, thus, its stockholders. An FI manager who

Table **14–4**

RESERVES AND EXCESS RESERVES OF U.S. BANKS
(in millions)

	December						
	1991	**1992**	**1993**	**1994**	**1995**	**1996**	**1997**
Total reserves	$59,120	$55,532	$62,858	$61,319	$57,900	$51,243	$47,197
Required reserves	57,456	54,553	61,795	60,171	56,622	49,819	45,513
Excess reserves	1,664	979	1,063	1,147	1,278	1,424	1,684

SOURCE: *Federal Reserve Bulletin,* various issues.

holds excessive amounts of liquid assets is unlikely to survive long. Similarly, a manager who undershoots the reserve target faces enhanced risks of liquidity crises and regulatory intervention. Again, such a manager's tenure at the FI may be relatively short.

Avoiding the costs of excessive overshooting or undershooting is made even more difficult for U.S. banks because the exact minimum required reserve target is not known until two days before the end of the reserve maintenance period. This makes the optimal management of the reserve position of a bank similar to a complex dynamic control problem with a moving target. A number of quite sophisticated attempts have been made to solve the management control problem. The Contemporary Perspectives Box 14–1 looks at one such attempt related to the sweeping of retail transaction deposits. This method of avoiding

Contemporary Perspectives 14–1

Sweeps of Retail Transaction Deposits

In January 1994, depository institutions began implementing sweep programs for retail customers. In such programs, balances in household transaction accounts (typically NOW accounts, but also some demand deposits, both of which are included in M1) are swept into savings deposits. Such sweeps shift deposits from reservable (transaction) accounts to nonreservable (savings) accounts without impairing depositors' ability to access the funds for transactions purposes. Depositories have an incentive to establish these programs because reserves held at the Federal Reserve earn no interest.

Retail sweep programs have been established either as daily sweeps or as weekend sweeps. Under a daily sweep, a depositor's transaction balances above a target level are shifted each night into a special savings account created for the purpose. If debits threaten to reduce the remaining transaction account balances below zero, enough funds are transferred back from the savings account to reestablish the target level of transaction balances. Because only six transfers are allowed out of a savings account within a statement month, on the sixth transfer, the entire savings balance is returned to the transaction account. Alternatively, in a weekend sweep program, all affected transaction account balances are swept into the special purpose savings account over the weekend and then returned on Monday. Some "weekend sweep"

programs undertake sweeps on certain holidays as well.

No information is available on the current amounts of transaction balances that are being swept into savings accounts. The Federal Reserve has obtained data from depositories only on the initial amounts swept on the date each program was established. The [data] shows that the initial amounts swept under programs implemented through May 1996 have cumulated to $98 billion. With a marginal reserve requirement of 10 percent on most of these balances, the cumulative reduction of required reserves attributable to the initial amounts swept has been nearly $10 billion.

SOURCE: *Federal Reserve Bulletin,* August 1996, p. 715.

Contemporary Perspectives 14–2

Reliance on Sweep Accounts May Prompt Fed to Revise Reserve Requirement Rules

The banking industry's increasing reliance on sweep accounts may prompt the Federal Reserve Board to revise reserve requirements. Tucked inside a Dec. 26 final rule updating Regulation D, which governs reserve requirements, the Fed signaled substantial changes may be on the way. "Many depository institutions have implemented so-called 'retail sweep' programs in order to reduce their reserve requirements," the rule states. "These programs have already resulted in a substantial decline in transaction accounts and required reserves. . . . These developments could eventually suggest changes in the structure of reserve requirements."

"We are putting people on notice that this is a situation we are watching closely," a senior central bank official said this week. . . . Two alternatives are under consideration: banks could be required to hold reserves against money market accounts or, less likely, the Fed could ask Congress for authority to pay interest on reserves. The Fed is concerned because sweep programs, which transfer funds regularly from checking accounts into higher-yielding investment accounts, circumvent reserve requirements.

Sweep-account balances stood at $98 billion in May (1996), up from $10 billion in January 1995. The proliferation of sweep programs caused funds on deposit with the Fed to drop by 33 percent over that period . . . the Fed is concerned that the decrease in reserves affects its ability to influence interest rates. . . . If reserves dry up, banks no longer will look to this market for overnight credit. That would make the interest rate the Fed sets irrelevant.

SOURCE: Jaret Seiberg, *The American Banker,* January 2, 1997, p. 1. Reprinted with permission—American Banker.

holding noninterest-bearing reserve deposits has become so popular that the Federal Reserve is considering changing the calculation of required reserves (see Contemporary Perspectives Box 14–2).

Concept Questions

1. In addition to the target reserve ratio, what other pieces of information does the bank reserve manager require to manage the bank's reserve requirement position?
2. What ways are available to a reserve manager whose bank undershot its reserve target to build up reserves to meet the target?
3. Prior to 1984, U.S. banks operated under a lagged reserve accounting system in which the reserve computation period ended one week before the start of the reserve maintenance period. Did the reserve manager face any uncertainty at all in managing a bank's reserve position in this system? Explain your answer.

LIABILITY MANAGEMENT

Liquidity and liability management are closely related. One aspect of liquidity risk control is the buildup of a prudential level of liquid assets. Another aspect is the management of the FI's liability structure to reduce the need for large amounts of liquid assets to meet liability withdrawals. Excessive use of purchased funds in the liability structure can result, however, in a liquidity crisis if investors lose confidence in the bank and refuse to roll over such funds.

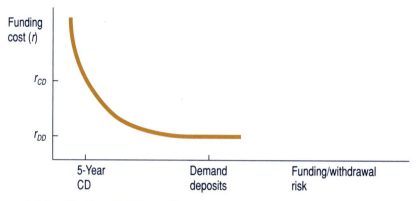

Figure 14-2   *Funding Risk Versus Cost*

Funding Risk and Cost

Unfortunately, constructing a low-cost, low-withdrawal-risk liability portfolio is more difficult than it sounds. This is true because those liabilities, or sources of FI funds, that are the most subject to withdrawal risk are often the least costly to the FI. That is, an FI must trade off the benefits of attracting liabilities at a low funding cost with a high chance of withdrawal against liabilities with a high funding cost and low liquidity. For example, demand deposits are relatively low funding cost vehicles for banks but can be withdrawn without notice.[10] By contrast, a five-year, fixed-term certificate of deposit may have a relatively high funding cost but can be withdrawn before the five-year maturity is up only if the deposit holder pays a substantial interest rate penalty. Thus, in structuring the liability, or funding, side of the balance sheet, the FI manager faces a trade-off (see Figure 14–2 for a graphic representation).

Although we have discussed commercial banks' funding risk, thrifts and other FIs face a similar trade-off.[11] For example, investment banks can finance through overnight funds (repurchase agreements and brokered deposits) or longer-term sources such as notes and bonds. Finance companies have a choice between commercial paper and longer-term notes and bonds.

The next section looks at the spectrum of liabilities available to a bank manager in seeking to actively impact liquidity risk exposure through the choice of liability structure.

Concept ? Questions

1. How are liquidity and liability management related?
2. What is the trade-off that the FI manager faces in structuring the liability side of the balance sheet?

• •

---

[10]Depositors do not always exercise this option; therefore, some demand deposits behave as longer-term core deposits.

[11]The trade-off faced by thrifts is essentially the same as that faced by banks with the exception of thrifts' access to borrowings from Federal Home Loan banks, but banks tend to have more direct access to the federal funds and repurchase agreement markets.

CHOICE OF LIABILITY STRUCTURE
IN DEPOSITORY INSTITUTIONS

This section considers in more detail the withdrawal risk and funding cost characteristics of the major liabilities (introduced in Chapter 8) available to a modern depository institution manager. These characteristics are summarized in Table 14–5.

Demand Deposits

Withdrawal Risk.   Demand deposits issued by banks have a high degree of withdrawal risk. Withdrawals can be instantaneous and largely expected by the bank manager, such as preweekend cash withdrawals, or unexpected, such as those made during economic crisis situations (so-called bank runs; see Chapter 13).

Costs.   In the United States, demand deposits have paid zero explicit interest since the 1930s by law. This does not mean that they are a costless source of funds for banks or that banks have no price or interest mechanisms available to control partially the withdrawal risk associated with these contracts.

T a b l e 14–5

WITHDRAWAL RISKS AND FUNDING COSTS ASSOCIATED WITH MAJOR LIABILITY SOURCES OF DEPOSITORY INSTITUTIONS

Funding Source	Withdrawal Risk	Cost
Demand deposit	High withdrawal risk Withdrawals instantaneous and sometimes predictable	Zero explicit interest paid High implicit interest costs
Interest-bearing checking (NOW) accounts	Less prone to withdrawal risk due to interest payments and minimum balance requirements	Low rate of explicit interest paid Implicit interest paid
Passbook savings	Low withdrawal risk relative to demand deposits	Explicit interest paid at rates slightly higher than NOW accounts
Money market deposit accounts (MMDA)	Low withdrawal risk Withdrawals subject to restrictions	Explicit interest paid at rates generally competitive with those of competing instruments, such as MMMF rates
Retail time deposits and CDs	Low withdrawal risk Penalties imposed for early withdrawal	Explicit interest paid at close to Treasury bill rates
Wholesale CDs	Low withdrawal risk due to existence of secondary market	Explicit interest paid at close to Treasury bill rates
Federal funds	No withdrawal risk, but rollover risk is present	Explicit interest paid at fed funds rate
Repurchase agreements	No withdrawal risk, but rollover risk is present	Explicit interest paid at less than fed funds rate

---

Despite the zero explicit interest paid on demand deposit accounts, competition among banks and other FIs (e.g., money market mutual funds) has resulted in the payment of implicit interest, or payments of interest in kind, on these accounts. Specifically, in providing demand deposits through checkable accounts, a bank must provide a whole set of associated services from providing checkbooks to clearing checks to sending out statements with cleared checks or check images. Because such services absorb real resources of labor and capital, they are costly for banks to provide. Banks can recapture these costs by charging fees, such as 10 cents a check cleared. To the extent that these fees do not fully cover the bank's cost of providing such services, the depositor receives a subsidy or an implicit interest payment.

E X A M P L E   1 4 – 3

Calculation of Average Implicit Interest Rate

If a bank pays 15 cents to clear a check but charges a fee of only 10 cents per check cleared, the customer receives a 5 cent subsidy. We can calculate implicit yields for each service, or an average implicit interest rate, for each demand deposit account. For example, an average implicit interest rate for a bank's demand deposits might be calculated as

$$\text{Average implicit interest rate (IRR)} = \frac{\text{Bank's average management costs per account per annum} - \text{Average fees earned per account per annum}}{\text{Average annual size of account}}$$

Suppose the following

$$\text{Bank's average management costs per account per annum} = \$\ 150$$
$$\text{Average fees earned per account per annum} = \$\ 100$$
$$\text{Average annual size of account} = \$1,200$$

Then

$$\text{IRR} = \frac{\$150 - \$100}{\$1,200} = 4.167\%$$

The payment of implicit interest means that the bank manager is not absolutely powerless to stop deposit withdrawals, especially if rates on competing instruments are rising. In particular, the FI could lower check-clearing fees, which in turn raises implicit interest payments to deposits. Such payments are *payments in kind* or *subsidies* that are not paid in actual dollars and cents because interest is earned on competing instruments. Nevertheless, implicit payments of interest are tax free to the depositor, but explicit interest payments are taxable. Finally, demand deposits have an additional cost in the form of noninterest-bearing reserve requirements that the bank must hold at the Federal Reserve.

Interest-Bearing Checking (NOW) Accounts

Withdrawal Risk.   The payment of explicit interest and the existence of the minimum balance requirement makes NOW accounts potentially less prone to withdrawal risk than demand deposits. Nevertheless, NOW accounts are still highly liquid instruments from the depositor's perspective.

Costs.   Like demand deposits, the FI can influence the potential withdrawability of these accounts by paying implicit interest or fee subsidies such as not charging the full cost to clear checks. However, the manager has two other ways to impact the yield paid to the depositor. The first is by varying the minimum balance requirement. By lowering the minimum balance requirement—say from $500 to $250—a larger portion of a NOW account becomes subject to interest payments and thus the explicit return and attractiveness of these accounts increases.[12] The second way is to vary the explicit interest rate payment itself, such as increasing it from 5 to 5¼ percent. Thus, the FI manager has three pricing mechanisms to increase or decrease the attractiveness and therefore impact the withdrawal rate of NOW accounts: implicit interest payments, minimum balance requirements, and explicit interest payments.[13]

E X A M P L E   1 4 – 4

Gross Interest Return

Consider a depositor who holds on average $250 per month for the first three months of the year, $500 per month for the next three months, and $1,000 per month for the final six months of the year in a NOW account. The NOW account pays 5 percent interest per annum if the minimum balance is $500 or more, and it pays no interest if the account falls below $500. The depositor writes an average of 50 checks per month and pays a service fee of 10 cents for each check although it costs the bank 15 cents to process each check. The account holder's gross interest return, consisting of implicit plus explicit interest, is

$$\text{Gross interest return} = \text{Explicit interest} + \text{Implicit interest}$$

$$= \$500(.05)(.25) + \$1000(.05)(.5) + (\$.15 - \$.10)(50)(12)$$
$$= \$6.25 + \$25 + \$30 = \$61.25$$

Suppose that the minimum balance was lowered to $250 and check service fees were lowered from 10 cents to 5 cents per check

$$\text{Gross interest return} = \$250(.05)(.25) + \$500(.05)(.25) + \$1000(.05)(.5) +$$
$$(\$.15 - \$.05)(50)(12)$$
$$= \$3.125 + \$6.25 + \$25 + \$60$$
$$= \$94.375$$

Passbook Savings

Withdrawal Risk.   Passbook savings are generally less liquid than demand deposits and NOW accounts for two reasons. First, they are noncheckable and usually involve physical presence at the institution for withdrawal. Second, the FI has the legal power to delay payment or withdrawal requests for as long as one month. This is rarely done and FIs

---

[12]This is subject to any regulatory requirement on the minimum balance.

[13]As transaction accounts, these deposits are also subject to reserve requirements at the same rate as demand deposits as well as deposit insurance premiums. Using a 5 percent NOW account rate, a 10 percent reserve ratio, and a 27-basis-point insurance premium and ignoring implicit interest, the effective cost of the marginal dollar of NOW accounts to the issuing bank is

$$\text{Effective cost} = [r_{NOW}/1 - R] + \text{Premium} = [.05/.90] + .0027 = .0583, \text{ or } 5.83\%$$

normally meet withdrawal requests with immediate cash payment, but they have the legal right to delay, which provides an important withdrawal risk control to FI managers.

Costs.   Since these accounts are noncheckable, any implicit interest rate payments are likely to be small; thus, the principal costs to the FI are the explicit interest payments on these accounts. In recent years, FIs have normally paid slightly higher explicit rates on passbook savings than on NOW accounts.

Money Market Deposit Accounts

Withdrawal Risk.   Depository institutions can use money market deposit accounts (MMDAs) as an additional liability instrument to control their overall withdrawal risk, in particular, the risk of funds disintermediating from depository institutions and flowing to money market mutual funds (MMMFs). Although MMDAs are checkable, they are subject to restrictions on the number of checks written on each account per month, the number of preauthorized automatic transfers per month, and the minimum denomination of the amount of each check. For example, a customer with an MMDA may make a maximum of six preauthorized transfers, of which no more than three can be checks for less than $500 each. In addition, MMDAs impose minimum balance requirements on depositors.

Costs.   The explicit interest paid to depositors is the major cost of MMDAs; it is also the pricing mechanism FIs use to control withdrawal risk. Since MMDAs are in direct competition with MMMFs, an FI manager can influence their net withdrawal rate by varying the rate the FI pays on such accounts. In particular, although the rate that MMMFs pay on their shares directly reflects the rates earned on the underlying money market assets in which the portfolio manager invests, such as commercial paper, banker's acceptances, repurchase agreements, and T-bills, the rates that FI managers pay on MMDAs are not directly based on any underlying portfolio of money market assets. In general, FI managers have considerable discretion to alter the rates paid on MMDAs and, thus, the spread on MMMF–MMDA accounts. This can directly impact the rate of withdrawals and withdrawal risk on such accounts. Allowing MMDA rates to have a large negative spread with MMMFs increases the net withdrawal rate on such accounts.

Retail Time Deposits and Certificates of Deposit

Withdrawal Risk.   By contractual design, time deposits and retail certificates of deposit (CDs) reduce the withdrawal risk to issuers. In a world of no early withdrawal requests, the FI manager knows the exact schedule of interest and principal payments to depositors holding such deposit claims, since these payments are contractually specified. Therefore, the FI manager can directly control fund inflows and outflows by varying the maturities of the time deposits and CDs it offers to the public. In general, depository institutions offer time deposits and CDs with maturities varying from two weeks to eight years.

When depositors wish to withdraw before the maturity of their time deposit or CD contract, regulation empowers FIs to impose penalties on the withdrawing depositor such as the loss of a certain number of months' interest depending on the maturity of the deposit. Although this does impose a friction or transaction cost on withdrawals, it is unlikely to stop withdrawals when the depositor has exceptional liquidity needs. In addition, withdrawals may increase if depositors perceive the FI to be insolvent, despite interest penalties and deposit insurance coverage up to $100,000. Nevertheless, under normal conditions, these instruments have relatively low withdrawal risk compared to transaction accounts such as demand deposits and NOW accounts and can be used as an important liability management tool to control withdrawal/liquidity risk.

Costs.   Similar to the costs for passbook savings, the major costs of time deposits and CDs are explicit interest payments. Short-term CDs are often competitive with T-bills; their rates are set with the T-bill rate in mind. Note that depositors who buy CDs are subject to state and local taxes on their interest payments, whereas T-bill investors do not pay state and local taxes on T-bill interest income.[14] Short-term CDs, however, can be issued in relatively small denominations compared to T-bills (i.e., $1,000 for CDs versus $10,000 for T-bills). Finally, time deposits and CDs do not, at present, require the FI to hold noninterest-bearing reserves at the central bank.

Wholesale CDs

Withdrawal Risk.   The distinctive feature of wholesale CDs is not their large minimum denomination size of $100,000 but their negotiability. That is, they can be resold by title assignment in a secondary market to other investors. This does not impose any obligation on the CD holder in terms of an early funds withdrawal request. Thus, a depositor can sell a relatively liquid instrument without causing adverse withdrawal risk exposure for the FI. Essentially, the only withdrawal risk (which can be substantial) is that these wholesale CDs are not rolled over and reinvested by the holder of the deposit claim on maturity.[15]

Costs.   The rates that banks pay on these instruments are competitive with other wholesale money market rates, especially those on commercial paper and T-bills. This competitive rate aspect is enhanced by the highly sophisticated nature of investors in CDs, such as money market mutual fund managers, and the fact that these deposits are not covered by explicit deposit insurance guarantees, only the first $100,000 invested in these CDs (per investor, per institution) are covered by insurance. To the extent that these CDs are offered by large depository institutions perceived as being too big to fail, the required credit risk premium on CDs is less than that required for similar quality instruments issued by the nonbank private sector (e.g., commercial paper). In addition, required interest yields on CDs reflect investors' perceptions of the depth of the secondary market for CDs. In recent

---

[14]Thus, the marginal investor is indifferent between Treasury bills and insured bank CDs when

$$r_{TB} = r_{CD} (1 - T_L)$$

where r_{TB} is the rate on T-bills, r_{CD} is the CD rate, and T_L is the local income tax rate. T. Cook has estimated the average local tax rate at 8 percent. Thus, if the T-bill rate is 3 percent, insured CDs must pay

$$r_{CD} = r_{TB} /(1 - T_L) = 3.00\%/(1 - .08) = 3.26\%$$

See T. Cook, "Treasury Bills," in *Instruments of the Money Market* (Richmond, VA: Federal Reserve Bank of Richmond, 1986), pp, 81–93.

[15]Wholesale CDs are also offered in countries other than the U.S., in which case they are called *Eurodollar CDs*. Eurodollar CDs may sell at slightly different rates than domestic CDs because of differences in demand and supply for CDs between the domestic and Euromarket and differences in credit risk perceptions of depositors buying a CD from a foreign branch (e.g., Citibank in London) rather than a domestic branch (Citibank in New York). To the extent that it is believed that banks are too big to fail, a guaranty that extends only to domestic branches, a higher risk premium may be required of foreign CDs. Indeed, FDICIA has severely restricted the ability of the FDIC to rescue foreign depositors of a failed U.S. bank.

years, the liquidity of the secondary market in CDs appears to have diminished as dealers have withdrawn. This has increased FIs' relative cost of issuing such instruments.[16]

Federal Funds

Withdrawal Risk.   Liability-funding depository institutions have no risk that the fed funds they have borrowed can be withdrawn within the day, although there is settlement risk at the end of each day (see Chapter 24). Some risk that fed funds will not be rolled over by the lending FI the next day if roll over is desired by the borrowing FI exists, however. In reality, this has occurred only in periods of extreme crisis such as the failure of Continental Illinois Bank in 1984. Nevertheless, since fed funds are uncollateralized loans, institutions selling fed funds normally impose maximum bilateral limits or credit caps on borrowing institutions. This may constrain the ability of an FI to expand its federal funds–borrowing position very rapidly if this is part of its overall liability management strategy.

Costs.   The cost of fed funds for the purchasing institution is the federal funds rate. The federal funds rate is set by FIs (mostly banks) that trade in the fed funds market and can vary considerably both within the day and across days. In particular, the federal funds rate shows considerable variability around the last days of each two-week reserve maintenance period; that is, around the second Tuesday and Wednesday of each successive period. For example, on some Wednesdays, the fed funds rate can rise as high as 30 percent and fall close to zero. This happens because FIs use federal funds as a major liability management tool in offsetting deposit withdrawals that deplete their cash reserve positions. For example, suppose that ABC Bank had experienced a large unexpected withdrawal of demand deposits on the afternoon of the second Wednesday of the reserve maintenance period. As deposits are withdrawn, ABC's cash-liquid asset reserve position is depleted in meeting these deposit withdrawals. To offset the possible undershooting of its required minimum and prudential reserve targets, the FI can purchase immediately available funds on the interbank federal funds market. Since the FI has few alternative market sources on the second Wednesday afternoon and it fears the regulatory penalties from reserve target undershooting, the institution is often willing to pay a high one-day rate to borrow such funds. The rate it pays depends on how many FIs wish to generate a one-day return by selling excess reserves on the federal funds market that day. Similarly, if an FI has excess reserves on the last afternoon of the reserve maintenance period, it prefers to lend them for one day—even at rates as low as 0.5 percent—since this is better than earning 0 percent on excess cash reserves held at the Federal Reserve.[17]

---

[16]In addition, for all the liability instruments considered so far (with the exception of Euro CDs), the FI must pay an FDIC insurance premium depending on its perceived riskiness (see Chapter 15). For example, consider an AAA bank issuing CDs at 3.26 percent, at which rate a depositor might just be indifferent to holding T-bills at 3.00 percent, given a local tax rate of 8 percent. However, the cost of the CD issue to the FI is not 3.26 percent but

$$\text{Effective CD cost} = 3.26\% + \text{Insurance premium} = 3.26\% + 0.27\% = 3.53\%$$

where 27 basis points is the assumed size of the deposit insurance premium. Thus, deposit insurance premiums add to the cost of deposits as a source of funds. However, in 1996, the FDIC reduced the insurance premium to zero for most banks, with only the riskiest banks having to pay 27 basis points.

[17]The minimum required rate would have to exceed the fees the Federal Reserve charges for transacting wire transfers over Fedwire (the wire transfer system that underlies the fed funds market).

Repurchase Agreements

Withdrawal Risk.   As with the fed funds market, the repurchase agreement (RP) market is a highly liquid and flexible source of funds for FIs needing to increase their liabilities and to offset deposit withdrawals. Moreover, these transactions, like federal funds, can be rolled over each day. The major liability management flexibility difference between fed funds and RPs is that a fed funds transaction can be entered into at any time in the business day so long as the Fedwire is open (see Chapter 24).[18] In general, it is difficult to transact an RP borrowing late in the day since the FI sending the fed funds must be satisfied with the type and quality of the securities collateral proposed by the borrowing institution. This collateral is normally in the form of T-bills, T-notes, T-bonds, and mortgage-backed securities, but their maturities and other features such as callability or coupons may be unattractive to the funds seller. Negotiations over the collateral package can delay RP transactions and make them more difficult to arrange than simple uncollateralized fed fund loans.

Costs.   Because of their collateralized nature, RP rates normally lie below federal funds rates. In addition, RP rates generally show less interday fluctuation than do fed funds over the reserve maintenance period, especially the last two days of the reserve maintenance period. This is in part due to less intraday flexibility of RPs relative to fed fund transactions.

Other Borrowings

Although fed funds and RPs have been the major sources of borrowed funds, depository institutions have utilized a host of other borrowing sources (such as banker's acceptances, commercial paper, medium-term notes, and discount window loans) to supplement their liability management flexibility.

Liquidity and Liability Structures for U.S. Banks

We summarize the preceding discussion by considering some balance sheet data for U.S. banks. Table 14–6 shows the liquid asset–nonliquid asset composition of insured U.S. banks in 1997 and in 1960. We use 1960 as a benchmark year since the next year (1961) is widely viewed as the date when banks first began to actively manage their liabilities—with Citibank's innovation of wholesale CDs that can be sold in secondary markets. Until the 1960s, banks had to take funding (basically deposits) as a given. With the advent of wholesale CDs, banks had more control over the amount of funding they had. They could therefore determine the size of the investments (mainly loans) they wanted to make and the purchased funds (such as new wholesale CDs) they needed to make the loans.

Clearly, the ratio of traditional liquid to total assets has declined since 1960, with cash plus securities in 1997 totaling 28.0 percent of the asset balance sheet of insured banks versus 52 percent in 1960. However, it may be argued that such a comparison misrepresents and overstates the fall in bank asset liquidity since bank loans themselves became significantly more liquid during this 30-year period. As we discuss in Chapter 12, bank loans are increasingly being securitized and/or sold in secondary markets. This has fundamentally altered the illiquidity of bank loan portfolios and has made them more similar to securities than in the past. The more liquid the loan portfolio, the less need for large amounts

---

[18]Normally, Fedwire closes at 6:30 PM EST.

Table **14–6**

LIQUID ASSETS VERSUS NONLIQUID ASSETS FOR INSURED COMMERCIAL BANKS, 1960 AND 1997

Assets	1960	1997
Cash	20.0%	6.0%
Government and agency securities	24.0	15.4
Other securities*	8.0	6.6
Loans†	46.0	65.9
Other assets	2.0	6.1
	100.0%	100.0%

*Other securities include state and local and mortgage-backed securities.

†Loans include C&I, mortgage, consumer, and other loans.

SOURCE: *Federal Reserve Bulletin,* various issues.

Table **14–7**

LIABILITY STRUCTURE OF INSURED COMMERCIAL BANKS, 1960 AND 1997

Liabilities	1960	1997
Transaction accounts	61.0%	15.2%
Retail CDs and time deposits	29.0	36.5
Wholesale CDs and time deposits	0.0	13.0
Borrowings and other liabilities	2.0	26.5
Bank capital	8.0	8.8
	100.0%	100.0%

SOURCE: *Federal Reserve Bulletin,* various issues.

of traditional liquid assets, such as cash and securities, to act as buffer reserves against unexpected liability withdrawals.

Table 14–7 presents the liability structure of commercial banks in 1960 and 1997. The most striking feature of Table 14–7 is the banks' shift from funds sources with relatively high withdrawal risk—transaction accounts (demand deposits and NOW accounts) and retail savings and time deposit accounts—to accounts or instruments over which the banks have greater potential control of the supply. Specifically, the sum of retail savings and time deposit accounts fell from 90 percent in 1960 to 51.7 percent in 1997. In contrast, wholesale CDs and time deposits plus borrowed funds (fed funds, RPs, other borrowed funds) have increased from 2 percent in 1960 to 39.5 percent in 1997. As discussed in Chapters 1–7 of this textbook, the increased competition between banks and nonbank intermediaries for funds over this period certainly attributed to the change in the composition of liabilities presented in Table 14–7. Banks have intentionally managed liabilities, however, to reduce withdrawal risk. Having a liability management strategy that reduces liability withdrawal risk does not come without a cost. As the data in Figure 14–2 imply, there is often a trade-off between withdrawal risk and funding cost. Banks' attempts to reduce their withdrawal risk by relying more on borrowed and wholesale funds have added to their interest expenses.

Finally, relying too heavily on borrowed funds can be a risky strategy in itself. Even though withdrawal risk may be reduced if lenders in the market for borrowed funds have confidence in the borrowing bank, perceptions that the bank is risky can lead to nonrenewals of fed fund and RP loans and the nonrollover of wholesale CDs and other purchased funds as they mature. The best example of a bank's failure as the result of excessive reliance on large CDs and purchased funds is the Continental Illinois Bank case of 1984 with more than 80 percent of its funds borrowed from wholesale lenders. Consequently, excessive reliance on borrowed funds may be as bad an overall liability management strategy as excessive reliance on transaction accounts and passbook savings. Thus, a well-diversified portfolio of liabilities may be the best strategy to balance withdrawal risk and funding cost considerations.

Concept Questions

1. Describe the withdrawal risk and funding cost characteristics of some of the major liabilities available to a modern bank manager.
2. Transaction accounts are subject to both reserve requirements and deposit insurance premiums, but fed funds are not. Why shouldn't a bank fund all of its assets through fed funds? Explain your answer.
3. Consider the information in Table 14–6. How has the ratio of traditional liquid to total assets changed since 1960?
4. Consider the information in Table 14–7. How did the liability composition of banks change from 1960 to 1997?

LIQUIDITY RISK MANAGEMENT IN INSURANCE COMPANIES

Insurance companies use a variety of sources to meet liquidity needs. As discussed in Chapters 4 and 13, liquidity is required to meet the claims on the insurance policies that these FIs have written, as well as unexpected surrenders of such policies. These contracts therefore represent a potential future liability to the insurance company. Ideally, liquidity management in insurance companies is conducted so that funds needed to meet claims on insurance contracts written can be met with premiums received on new and existing contracts. However, a high frequency of claims at a single point in time (e.g., an unexpectedly severe hurricane season) could force insurers to liquidate assets for something less than their fair market value.

Insurance companies can reduce their exposure to liquidity risk by diversifying the distribution of risk in the contracts they write. For example, property-casualty insurers can diversify across the types of disasters they cover (e.g., in 1996 the top two property-casualty insurance companies—in terms of premiums sold—held policies for 18 different business lines from commercial auto liability, for which they wrote 10.9 percent of all industry premiums, to homeowners multiple peril, for which they wrote 35.1 percent of all industry premiums).[19]

---

[19]See "Industry Underwriting by Lines," *Best's Review*, August, 1997, p. 33.

Alternatively, insurance companies can meet liquidity needs by holding relatively marketable assets to cover claim payments. Assets such as government and corporate bonds and corporate stock usually can be liquidated quickly at close to their fair market value in financial markets to pay claims on insurance policies when premium income is insufficient. For example, at the end of 1997, life insurance companies held 81.2 percent of their assets in the form of government securities and corporate securities (see Chapter 4). Because of the less predictable timing of claims against property-casualty insurers (i.e., fires, earthquakes, and floods), these FIs typically hold more bonds and common stock than do life insurance companies. In 1997 property-casualty companies held 89.5 percent of their assets in the form of these assets.

Concept Questions

1. What are two strategies that insurance companies can use to reduce liquidity risk?
2. Why would property-casualty insurers hold more short-term liquid assets to manage liquidity risk than life insurers would hold?

LIQUIDITY RISK MANAGEMENT IN OTHER FIs

Other FIs (such as securities firms, investment banks, and finance companies) may experience liquidity risk if they rely on short-term financing (such as commercial paper or bank loans), and investors may become reluctant to roll these funds over. Remember the discussion in Chapter 5; the main source of funding for securities firms are repurchase agreements, bank call loans,[20] and short positions in securities. Liquidity management for these FIs requires the ability to have sufficient cash and other liquid resources at hand to underwrite (purchase) new securities from quality issuers before reselling these securities to other investors. Liquidity management also requires a securities firm to be able to act as a market maker, which requires the firm to finance an inventory of securities in its portfolio. Similarly, Chapter 6 discusses finance companies that fund assets mainly with commercial paper and long-term debt. Liquidity management for these FIs requires the ability to fund loan requests and loan commitments of sufficient quality without delay.

The experience of Drexel Burnham Lambert in 1989 is a good example of a securities firm being subjected to a liquidity challenge. Throughout the 1980s, Drexel Burnham Lambert captured the bulk of the junk bond market by promising investors to act as a dealer for the junk bonds in the secondary market. Investors were, therefore, more willing to purchase these junk securities because Drexel provided an implied guarantee that it would buy them back or find another buyer at market prices should an investor need to sell. The junk bond market experienced difficulties in 1989, however, as their prices fell, reflecting the economy's move into recession. Serious concerns about the creditworthiness of Drexel's junk bond–ladened asset portfolio led creditors to deny Drexel extensions of its vital short-term commercial paper financings. As a result, Drexel declared bankruptcy. Drexel's

---

[20]A *bank call loan* is a loan that a lending bank can call in from an investment bank with very little notice.

sudden collapse makes frighteningly clear that access to short-term purchased funds is crucial to the health of securities firms.[21]

Concept  Question

1. How did poor liquidity risk management cause the demise of Drexel Burnham Lambert?

• •

---

[21]For additional discussion of the failure of Drexel Burnham Lambert, see W. S. Haraf, "The Collapse of Drexel Burnham Lambert: Lessons for Bank Regulators," *Regulation,* Winter 1991, pp. 22–25.

SUMMARY

Liquidity and liability management issues are intimately linked for the modern FI. Many factors, both cost and regulatory, impact an FI manager's choice of the amount of liquid assets to hold and the types of liabilities to issue. An FI's choice of liquidity is something of a knife-edge situation, trading off the costs and benefits of undershooting or overshooting regulatory specified (and prudentially specified) reserve asset targets.

An FI can manage its liabilities in a fashion that affects the overall withdrawal risk of its funding portfolio and, therefore, the need for liquid assets to meet such withdrawals. However, reducing withdrawal risk often comes at a cost, because liability sources that are easier to control from a withdrawal risk perspective are often more costly for the bank to utilize.

PERTINENT WEB SITES

Board of Governors of the Federal Reserve   http://www.bog.frb.fed.us/

Liquidity and Liability Management

1. What are the benefits and costs to an FI of holding large amounts of liquid assets?
2. Consider the balance sheets (in millions) of two banks, A and B. How would you assess their respective liquidity positions?

Bank A

Assets	
Cash	10
Treasury securities	40
Commercial loans	90
	140

Liabilities and Equity	
Deposits	120
Equity	20
	140

Bank B

Assets	
Cash	20
Consumer loans	30
Commercial loans	90
	140

Liabilities and Equity	
Deposits	120
Equity	20
	140

3. What concerns motivate regulators to require FIs to hold minimum amounts of liquid assets?
4. Compare the liquidity of these four securities:
   a. Cash
   b. Corporate bonds
   c. NYSE-traded stocks
   d. T-bills

5. City Bank has estimated that its average daily demand deposits over the recent 14-day computation period was $225 million. Its average daily balance with the Fed over the 14-day maintenance period was $11 million. Its average daily vault cash over the two-week period prior to the computation period was $7 million.
   a. Under the rules effective in 1998, what is the amount of average daily reserves required to be held during the reserve maintenance period for these demand deposit balances?
   b. Has the bank met its reserve requirements for this period? If not, is the amount higher or lower than its requirements?
   c. If the bank had managed to transfer $20 million of its deposits every Friday over the two-week computation period to one of its foreign facilities, what would be its average daily reserve requirement?

6. If the reserve computation period extends from May 18 through May 31, what is the corresponding reserve maintenance period? What accounts for the difference?

7. A bank's average demand deposits during the most recent reserve computation period is estimated at $225 million over a 14-day period (Tuesday to Monday). The amount of average daily reserves at the Fed during the 14-day reserve maintenance period was $16 million; the corresponding daily vault cash during this period was $4 million. Note that the vault cash estimation is calculated four weeks prior to the reserve computation period.
   a. What are the average daily required reserves to be held by the bank during the maintenance period?
   b. Is the bank in compliance with the requirements?
   c. What is the amount higher than or lower than required that can be carried over to the following computation period?
   d. What is the loss of the excess carryover if the opportunity cost is 6 percent?

8. The following demand deposits and cash reserves at the Fed have been documented by a bank for the computation of its reserve requirements (in millions).

	Mon. 10	Tue. 11	Wed. 12	Thur. 13	Fri. 14
Demand deposits	$200	$300	$250	$280	$260
Reserves at Fed	$20	$22	$21	$18	$27

	Mon. 17	Tue. 18	Wed. 19	Thur. 20	Fri. 21
Demand deposits	$280	$300	$270	$260	$250
Reserves at Fed	$20	$35	$21	$18	$28

	Mon. 24	Tue. 25	Wed. 26	Thur. 27	Fri. 28
Demand deposits	$240	$230	$250	$260	$270
Reserves at Fed	$19	$19	$21	$19	$24

The average vault cash for the computation period has been estimated to be $2 million per day.
   a. What is the amount of the average daily required reserves to be held by the bank during the maintenance period?
   b. Is the bank in compliance with the requirements?
   c. What is the amount higher than or lower than required that can be carried over to the following computation period?
   d. If the average cost of funds to the bank is 6 percent per year, what is the loss or gain to the bank over the 14-day period if it has kept excess or deficient reserves?

9. How is an FI's liability and liquidity risk management problem related to the maturity of its assets relative to its liabilities?

10. Prior to February 1984, reserve requirements in the United States were computed on a lagged reserve accounting system. Under lagged reserve accounting, the reserve computation period preceded the reserve maintenance period by two weeks.
   a. Contrast the contemporaneous reserve accounting (CRA) system with the lagged reserve accounting (LRA) system.
   b. Under which accounting system, CRA or LRA, were bank reserves higher? Why?
   c. Under which accounting system, CRA or LRA, was bank uncertainty higher? Why?
   d. Why do you think that the Fed moved from LRA to CRA?

11. What is the "weekend game"? Contrast a bank's ability and incentive to play the weekend game under LRA as opposed to CRA.

12. Under CRA, when is the uncertainty about the reserve requirement resolved? Discuss the feasibility of making large reserve adjustments during this period of complete information.

13. An investor is considering two possible fixed income investments: a six-month insured CD that yields 8 percent before taxes and a six-month T-bill that yields 6.5 percent before taxes. For this investor, the federal tax rate is 30 percent; state and local taxes are 15 percent. Which security should the investor choose?

14. An FI has estimated the following costs for its demand deposits per year: management cost per account = $140,

average account size = $1,500, average number of checks processed per account per month = 75, cost of clearing a check = $0.10, fees charged to customer per check = $0.05, and average fee charged per customer per month = $8.

a. What is the FI's implicit interest cost of demand deposits?

b. If the FI must keep an average of 8 percent as required reserves on demand deposits with the Fed, what is the FI's implicit interest cost of demand deposits?

c. By how much should the FI raise its check-clearing fees to reduce the imputed interest costs to 3 percent? Ignore the reserve requirements.

15. A NOW account requires a minimum balance of $750 for interest to be earned at a rate of 4 percent per year. An account holder has maintained an average balance of $500 for the first six months and $1,000 for the remaining six months. She writes an average of 60 checks a month and pays $0.02 per check, although it costs the bank $0.05 to clear a check.

a. What average return does the account holder earn on the account?

b. What is the average return if the bank lowers the minimum balance to $400?

c. What is the average return if the bank pays interest on only the amount in excess of $400? Assume that the minimum required balance is $400.

d. How much should the bank increase its check-clearing fee to ensure that the average interest it pays on this account is 5 percent? Assume that the minimum required balance is $750.

16. What does a low federal fund rate indicate about the level of bank reserves?

17. Contrast the following liabilities with respect to funding risk and funding cost:

a. Demand deposits

b. Certificates of deposit

c. Federal funds

d. Repurchase agreements

18. How does the withdrawal risk differ for federal funds and repurchase agreements?

19. How does an FI's cash balance determine the size of the repurchase agreements into which it would enter?

20. What trends have been observed between 1960 and 1997 as to liquidity and liability structures of commercial banks?

Chapter Fifteen

Deposit Insurance and Other Liability Guarantees

Chapter 13 discussed the liquidity risks that FIs face and Chapter 14 described ways in which FIs can better manage that risk. If they have concerns about an FI's asset quality or solvency, liability holders such as depositors and life insurance policyholders (and to a lesser extent mutual fund shareholders) have incentives to engage in runs; that is, to withdraw all their funds. As Chapter 13 discusses, the incentive to run is accentuated in banks, thrifts, and insurance companies by the place in line rule used to meet liability withdrawals. As a result, deposit and liability holders who are first in line to withdraw funds get preference over those last in line.

Although a run on an unhealthy FI is not necessarily a bad thing—it can discipline the performance of managers and owners—there is a risk that runs on bad FIs can become contagious and spread to well-run FIs in the same industry and even across FI sectors. In contagious runs or panic conditions, liability holders do not bother to distinguish between poorly and well-run FIs but seek to turn their liabilities into cash or safe securities as quickly as possible. Contemporary Perspectives Box 15–1 highlights such a run on a Rhode Island private insurance fund. Contagious runs such as that one can have a major contractionary effect on the supply of credit as well as the money supply.

Moreover, a contagious run on FIs can have serious social welfare effects (e.g., inability to transfer wealth, inability to implement monetary policy, inability to allocate credit to various sectors of the economy in special need of financing (see Chapter 1)). For example, a major run on banks can adversely affect the level of savings deposited in all types of FIs and, therefore, can inhibit individuals' abilities to transfer wealth through time to protect themselves against major risks such as future ill-health or falling income as they age.

Because of the effects on wealth, money supply, and credit supply, government regulators of financial service firms have introduced guaranty programs to deter runs by offering liability holders varying degrees of failure protection. Specifically, a liability holder who believes that a claim is totally secure even if the FI is in trouble has no incentive to run. The liability holder's place in line no longer affects getting his or her funds back. Regulatory guaranty or insurance programs for liability holders deter runs and, thus, deter contagious runs and panics.[1]

Federally backed insurance programs include the Federal Deposit Insurance Corporation (FDIC) created in 1933 for banks and thrifts, the National Credit Union Share Insurance Fund (NCUSIF) created in 1970 for credit unions, the Securities Investors Protection Corporation (SIPC) created in 1970 for securities firms, and the Pension Benefit Guaranty Corporation (PBGC) created in 1974 for private pension funds.[2] In addi-

---

[1] Alternatives to these insurance programs have been proposed, but federally backed insurance programs remain the guaranty system of choice in the United States. The principal two alternatives proposed have been the *narrow-bank* (in which risk averse depositors have their deposits backed by T-bills as assets while more risk-loving depositors hold funds in a bank subsidiary that can invest in any type of risky asset, including loans). This basically renders deposits held in the narrow-bank default free and interest rate risk-free. The concern here is whether sufficient fire walls can be put in place to keep the narrow bank insulated from the risk-taking activities of the risk-taking bank subsidiary. The other alternative is to replace publicly (government) run deposit insurance funds with *privately operated funds* (i.e., by the banks and insurance companies). The concern here is whether such a contract could ever be credible during a major panic. For example, the total assets of all U.S. property-casualty insurance companies are less than the amount outstanding of U.S. deposits.

[2] Until its insolvency in 1989, the Federal Savings and Loan Insurance Corporation (FSLIC) insured the deposits of most thrifts. Since 1989, both banks and thrifts have been insured under the umbrella of the FDIC, as we discuss later in this chapter.

Contemporary Perspectives 15–1

Rhode Island Governor Orders Closure of Half the State Banks

Some 300,000 account holders in Rhode Island, USA, yesterday were unable to withdraw funds after the new governor closed more than half the state's banks. The move was ordered by Governor Bruce Sundlun, a 71-year-old millionaire Democrat businessman just three hours after taking office on Tuesday. The governor said he had taken the action "to protect depositors and taxpayers" following the collapse of the private insurance fund which guarantees deposits at 45 banks not insured by the federal government. . . .

State officials were last night working feverishly to patch together federal deposit insurance for the 45 local banks that were shut down and which are not guaranteed by the Federal Deposit Insurance Corporation. . . . The governor's decision means that some 300,000 account holders at 45 of the state's 83 banks are unable to withdraw funds. The 45 institutions, which include 33 credit unions, or state-chartered locally owned co-operative banks, have $1.7 billion of deposits. . . . . While some of the 45 banks will be allowed to reopen within days, others, including many of the credit unions, may need to be liquidated and depositors may not recover all of their money.

The cause for the action was the failure on Monday of the Rhode Island Share and Deposit Indemnity Corporation (RISDIC), the private insurer. RISDIC's resources were drained by the costs associated with the seizure last November of Heritage Loan and Investment, a two-branch bank in Providence, Rhode Island. Mr. Joseph Molincone, the bank's president, has been charged with embezzlement in state and federal arrest warrants and has been missing since November 8.

SOURCE: Alan Friedman, *Financial Times,* January 3, 1991, p. 1. Reprinted with permission of Financial Times.

tion, because of their state rather than federal regulation, state-organized guaranty funds back up most life and property-casualty insurance companies.

This chapter analyzes the deposit insurance funds for banks and thrifts and then considers the special features of the guaranty funds for other FIs. The chapter specifies which deposits or liabilities are insured and paid off by a guaranty fund when an FI fails.

THE HISTORY OF BANK AND THRIFT GUARANTY FUNDS

The FDIC

The FDIC was created in 1933 in the wake of the banking panics of 1930–1933, when approximately 10,000 commercial banks failed. Between 1945 and 1980, commercial bank deposit insurance clearly worked; no runs or panics occurred, the number of individual bank failures was very small (see Figure 15–1), and the FDIC was consistently overfunded. Beginning in 1980, however, the number of bank failures increased, with more than 1,039 in the decade ending in 1990, peaking at 221 in 1988. This number of failures was actually higher than that in the entire 1930–1979 period. Moreover, the costs of each of these failures to the FDIC were often larger than the total costs for the mainly small bank failures in 1933–1979. As the number and costs of these closures mounted in the 1980s, the FDIC

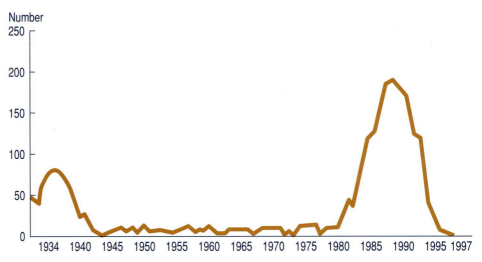

F i g u r e **15-1**   *Number of Failed Banks by Year, 1934–1997*

SOURCE: "BIF Closings and Assistance Transactions," various years, FDIC.

fund was rapidly drained. Indeed, the FDIC's resources were virtually depleted by early 1991 when it received permission to borrow $30 billion from the Treasury. Even then, it ended 1991 with a deficit of $7 billion. In response to this crisis, Congress passed the FDIC Improvement Act (FDICIA) in December 1991 to restructure the bank insurance fund and prevent its potential insolvency.

Since 1991, the fund's finances have dramatically turned around, and bank failures have decreased significantly—partly in response to banks' record profit levels as a result of a very strong U.S. economy. Specifically, by the end of 1997, the FDIC's Bank Insurance Fund (BIF) had reserves of $28.0 billion, and the number of bank failures for 15 months prior to the fourth quarter of 1997 was zero. The fund's reserves now stand at a record high and exceed 1.35 percent of insured deposits.

The Federal Savings and Loan Insurance Corporation (FSLIC) and Its Demise

The Federal Savings and Loan Insurance Corporation (FSLIC) covered deposits of savings and loan associations (S&Ls).[3] Like the FDIC, this insurance fund was in relatively good shape until the end of the 1970s. Beginning in 1980, its resources were rapidly depleted as more and more thrifts failed and were closed or merged. Between 1980 and 1988, 514 thrifts failed, at an estimated cost of $42.3 billion. Moreover, between 1989 and 1992, an additional 734 thrifts failed, at a cost of $78 billion. As a result of these failures,

---

[3] As discussed in Chapter 3, credit union depositors enjoy a degree of coverage similar to bank, S&L, and savings bank depositors via coverage through NCUIF (established in 1971). See Edward J. Kane and Robert Hendershott, "The Federal Deposit Insurance Fund That Didn't Put a Bite on U.S. Taxpayers," *Journal of Banking and Finance* 20 no. 5 (1996), pp. 1305–1327. In their working paper "Deposit Insurance and Risk-Taking Behavior in the Credit Union Industry," Christine A. McClatchey and Gordon V. Karels look at whether credit unions increased their risk-taking behavior after share deposits became federally insured. They find that asset quality and liquidity improved over the period following the institution of deposit insurance. Other thrifts, such as mutual savings banks, often choose to be insured under the FDIC–BIF fund rather than FDIC–SAIF (or the now deceased FSLIC) fund (see discussion later in this chapter).

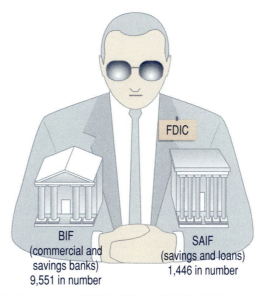

F i g u r e **15–2** *The Structure of FDIC, BIF, and SAIF in 1998*

by 1989 the FSLIC fund had a negative net worth; the present value of its liabilities exceeded that of its assets. Lacking the resources to close or resolve failing thrifts, the FSLIC followed a policy of *forbearance* (leniency) toward the closure of failed and failing thrifts. This meant that it allowed many bad thrifts to stay open and continue to accumulate losses.

In August 1989, Congress passed the Financial Institutions Reform, Recovery, and Enforcement Act (FIRREA), largely in response to the deepening crisis in the thrift industry and the growing insolvency of the FSLIC. This act completely restructured the savings bank fund and transferred its management to the FDIC.[4] At the same time, the restructured savings bank insurance fund became the Savings Association Insurance Fund (SAIF). Currently, the FDIC manages the SAIF separately from the commercial bank fund, which is now called the Bank Insurance Fund (BIF). At the end of 1997, SAIF had 9.3 billion in reserves, representing 1.32 percent of insured deposits. See Figure 15–2 for the organizational structure of FDIC and the number of depository institutions insured by these funds.

Based on performance of banks and thrifts in the 1990s, the FDICIA and FIRREA appear to have been successful in helping strengthen the financial condition of FIs in these industries. Whether these regulations will continue to work (particularly in the event of a major economic downturn in the U.S. economy) remains to be seen. One argument is that the continued success of these regulations depends on the political will of bank regulators to carry out the intent of the legislation, even at the cost of reducing their own discretionary power.[5]

---

[4] At that time, the FSLIC ceased to exist.

[5] This argument includes a call for fully implementing market-value accounting and increasing the thresholds for all capital adequacy categories (see Chapter 16) to levels more consistent with those the market imposes on uninsured competitors of banks and thrifts. See G.J. Benston and G.G. Kaufman, "FDICIA after Five Years," *Journal of Economic Perspectives,* Summer 1997, pp. 139–158.

Concept  Q u e s t i o n s

1. What events led Congress to pass the FDICIA?
2. What events brought about the demise of the FSLIC?

• •

THE CAUSES OF THE DEPOSITORY FUND INSOLVENCIES

There are at least two not necessarily independent views on the reason that depository institution insurance funds became insolvent in the 1980s. In addition, some factors offer better explanations of the FSLIC insolvency than the FDIC insolvency, especially because the FSLIC insolvency was far worse than the FDIC insolvency.

The Financial Environment

One view of the cause of insolvency is that a number of external events or shocks adversely impacted U.S. banks and thrifts in the 1980s. The first of these was the dramatic rise in interest rates during the 1979–1982 period. This rise in rates had a major negative effect on those thrifts funding long-term, fixed-rate mortgages with short-term deposits. The second event was the collapse in oil, real estate, and other commodity prices, which particularly harmed oil, gas, and agricultural loans in the southwestern United States. The third event was the increased financial service firm competition at home and abroad, which eroded the value of bank and thrift charters during the 1980s (see Chapters 25 and 26).

Moral Hazard

moral hazard

The loss exposure an insurer faces when providing insurance encourages the insured to take more risks.

implicit premiums

Deposit insurance premiums or costs imposed on a bank through activity constraints rather than direct monetary charges.

The other view is that these financial environment effects were catalysts for, rather than the causes of, the crisis. At the heart of the crisis was deposit insurance itself, especially some of its contractual features. Although deposit insurance had deterred depositors and other liability holders from engaging in runs prior to 1980, in so doing it had also removed or reduced depositor discipline. Deposit insurance allowed banks to borrow at rates close to the risk-free rate and, if they chose, to undertake high-risk asset investments. Bank owners and managers knew that insured depositors had little incentive to restrict such risky behavior, either by withdrawing funds or by requiring risk premia on deposit rates since they were fully insured by the FDIC if the bank failed. Given this scenario, losses on oil, gas, and real estate loans in the 1980s are viewed as the outcome of bankers exploiting underpriced or mispriced risk under the deposit insurance contract. The provision of insurance that encourages rather than discourages risk taking is called **moral hazard** because it increases the scope of the risk exposure faced by insurers.[6]

In the absence of depositor discipline, regulators could have controlled bankers' risk taking by charging either explicit deposit insurance premiums linked to bank risk or **implicit premiums** through increased monitoring and restrictions on the risky activities of

---

[6] The precise definition of *moral hazard* is the loss exposure of an insurer (the FDIC) that results from the character or circumstances of the insured (here, the bank).

banks. This potentially could have substituted for depositor discipline (i.e., those banks that took more risk would have paid directly or indirectly for this risk-taking behavior). However, from 1933 until January 1, 1993, regulators based deposit insurance premiums on the amount of (domestic) deposits that a bank held rather than its risk. The decade of the 1980s was also a period of deregulation and leniency in capital adequacy rather than stringent activity regulation and tough capital requirements. Moreover, for the FSLIC, the number of savings and loan examinations and examiners actually fell between 1981 and 1984.[7] Finally, prompt corrective action for undercapitalized banks did not begin until the end of 1992 (see Chapter 16).

Concept Questions

1. What two basic views are offered to explain the insolvency of depository institution insurance funds during the 1980s?
2. Why was interest rate risk less a problem for banks than for thrifts in the early 1980s?

PANIC PREVENTION
VERSUS MORAL HAZARD

A great deal of attention has focused on the moral hazard reason for the collapse of the bank and thrift insurance funds in the 1980s. The less bank owners have to lose from taking risks, the greater are their incentives to take excessively risky asset positions. When asset investment risks or gambles pay off, bank owners make windfall gains in profits. Should they fail, however, the FDIC, as the insurer, bears most of the costs, given that owners of banks—like owners of regular corporations—have limited liability. It's a heads I win, tails I don't lose (much) situation.

Note that even without deposit insurance, the limited liability of bank owners or stockholders always creates incentives to take risk at the expense of fixed claimants such as depositors or debt holders.[8] Ideally, actuarially fairly priced insurance is insurance pricing based on the perceived risk of the insured institution. The difference between banks and other firms, however, is that mispriced deposit insurance, that is, when risk taking does not result in **actuarially fairly priced insurance,** adds to bank stockholders' incentives to take additional risk with little penalty if the risk does not pay off.

Nevertheless, even though mispriced deposit insurance potentially accentuates bank risk taking, deposit insurance effectively deterred bank panics and runs of the type experienced in 1930–1933 during the postwar period (see Figure 15–1). That is, insurance has ensured a good deal of stability in the credit and monetary system.

This suggests that regulators ideally should design the deposit insurance contract with the trade-off between moral hazard risk and bank panic or run risk in mind. For example, by providing 100 percent coverage of all depositors and reducing the probability of runs to

actuarially fairly priced insurance

Insurance pricing based on the perceived risk of the insured.

---

[7] L. J. White points to a general weakness of thrift supervision and examination in the 1980s. The number of examinations fell from 3,210 in 1980 to 2,347 in 1984 and examinations per billion dollars of assets from 5.41 in 1980 to 2.4 in 1984. See L. J. White, *The S and L Debacle* (New York: Oxford University Press, 1991), p. 89.

[8] See K. John, T. John, and L. W. Senbet, "Risk Shifting Incentives of Depository Institutions: A Perspective on Federal Deposit Insurance Reform," *Journal of Banking and Finance* 36 (1991), pp. 335–367.

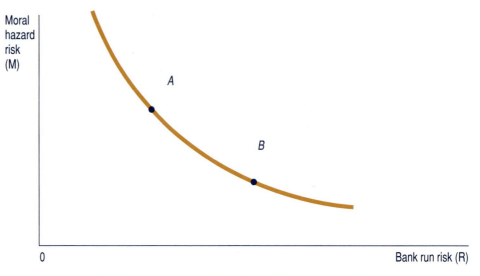

Figure **15–3**   *Bank Run Risk versus Moral Hazard Risk Trade-Off*

zero, the insurer may be encouraging certain banks to take a significant degree of moral hazard risk-taking behavior. On the other hand, a very limited degree of deposit insurance coverage might encourage runs and panics, although moral hazard behavior would be less evident. Figure 15–3 depicts the potential trade-off between bank run risk and moral hazard risk.

In the 1980s, extensive insurance coverage for deposit holders and the resulting lack of incentive for deposit holders to monitor and restrict bank owners' and managers' risk taking resulted in small levels of bank run risk but high levels of moral hazard risk (point *A* in Figure 15–3). By restructuring the deposit insurance contract, it may be possible to reduce moral hazard risk quite a bit without a very large increase in bank run risk. Such a point might be *B* in Figure 15–3. To some extent, these were the objectives behind the passage of the FDICIA of 1991 and the depositor preference legislation contained in the Omnibus Budget Reconciliation Act of 1991. Of course, Figure 15–3 is only illustrative. The actual shape of the moral hazard bank run risk trade-off as the deposit insurance contract changes is not known, but the relationship is expected to be inverse. That is, more explicit pricing of bank run risk should discourage moral hazard behavior.

Concept Questions

1. Historically, what effect has deposit insurance had on bank panics and runs?
2. How would levying actuarially fairly priced deposit insurance premiums on banks change the trade-off shown in Figure 15–3?
3. Suppose that the FDIC provides deposit insurance free of charge to banks and covered all depositors. Roughly where would we be on the trade-off curve in Figure 15–3?

CONTROLLING BANK
RISK TAKING

The three ways in which deposit insurance could be structured to reduce moral hazard behavior are as follows:

1. Increase stockholder discipline.
2. Increase depositor discipline.
3. Increase regulator discipline.

Specifically, redesigning the features of the insurance contract can either directly impact bank stockholders' risk-taking incentives or indirectly affect their risk-taking incentives by altering the behavior of depositors and regulators. In the wake of the FDIC's insolvency in 1991, FDICIA was passed with the objective to increase discipline in all three areas.

Stockholder Discipline

As discussed, the provision of mispriced (or not actuarially fairly priced) deposit insurance encourages risk-taking activities on the part of depository institution owners since they know that the insurance fund, and not stockholders, will largely cover the downside risk of asset investments. Restructuring the insurance contract to increase the risk exposure of stockholders should create greater discipline of their risk-taking incentives (i.e., risk taking becomes more expensive for stockholders).

Insurance Premiums.   One approach to make stockholders' risk taking more expensive is to link FDIC insurance premiums to a bank's risk profile. We now consider ways to do this, including the risk-based premium plan adopted by the FDIC since 1993.

Theory.   A major feature of the pre–1993 FDIC deposit insurance contract was the flat deposit insurance premium levied on banks and thrifts. Specifically, each year a bank paid a given sum or premium to the FDIC based on a fixed proportion of its domestic deposits.[9] Until 1989, the premium was 8.33 cents per $100 in domestic deposits.[10] As the FDIC fund became increasingly depleted, the level of the premium was raised several times but its risk-insensitive nature was left unaltered. By 1993, the premiums that banks paid had risen to 23 cents per $100 of their domestic deposits, almost tripling their premiums since 1988.[11]

To see why a flat or size-based premium schedule does not discipline a bank's risk taking, consider two banks of the same domestic deposit size, as shown in Table 15–1. Banks A and B have domestic deposits of $100 million and pay the same premium to the FDIC (.0023 × $100 million = $230,000 per year). However, their risk-taking behavior is completely different. Bank A is excessively risky, investing all its assets in real estate loans. Bank B is almost risk free, investing all of its assets in government T-bills. Figure 15–4 shows the insurance premium rates by the two banks compared to their asset risks.

---

[9] In actual practice, premiums were levied and paid semiannually.

[10] In the pre–1980 period, the FDIC was able to rebate some of these premiums because it was believed that it had adequate reserves at the time. See S.A. Buser, A.H. Chen, and E.J. Kane, "Federal Deposit Insurance, Regulatory Policy, and Optimal Bank Capital," *Journal of Finance* 36 (1981), pp. 51–60.

[11] This was also the rate for thrifts insured under SAIF.

Table **15–1**

FLAT DEPOSIT INSURANCE PREMIUMS AND RISK TAKING

Bank A (values in millions)				Bank B (values in millions)			
Assets		**Liabilities**		**Assets**		**Liabilities**	
Real estate loans	100	Domestic deposits	100	T-bills	100	Domestic deposits	100

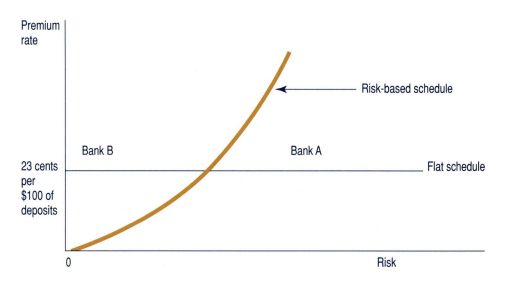

Figure **15–4**   *Premium Schedules Relative to Risk*

Note in Figure 15–4 that under the pre–1993 flat premium schedule, both banks A and B would have been charged the same deposit insurance premium based on the size of their domestic deposits. Critics of flat premiums argue that the FDIC should act more as a private property-casualty (PC) insurer. That is, PC insurance premiums are normally set to have those with higher risks pay higher premiums. Under the pre–1993 FDIC flat premium pricing plan, low-risk banks (such as Bank B) paid more than their fair share for insurance while high-risk banks (such as Bank A) paid less than their fair share. The result is that low-risk banks partially subsidized the insurance premiums of high-risk banks. Knowing that they will pay less than their actuarially fair price for it, banks consider that this insurance mispricing gives them an incentive to take additional risk. If premiums had increased as bank risk increased, banks would have considered this an incentive to reduce their risk taking. Therefore, the ultimate goal is to price risk in an actuarially fair fashion, similar to the way a private PC insurer prices it, so that premiums reflect the expected private costs or losses to the insurer from the provision of deposit insurance.[12]

---

[12]Note that there are arguments against imposing an actuarially fair risk-based premium schedule. If the deposit insurer's mandate is not to act as if it were a private cost-minimizing insurer such as a PC insurance company because of social welfare considerations, some type of subsidy to banks and thrifts can be justified. Remember that the FDIC is a quasi-government agency, and broader banking market stability concerns and savers' welfare

Calculating the Actuarially Fair Premium.   Economists have suggested a number of approaches for calculating the fair deposit insurance premium that a cost-minimizing FDIC should charge. One approach is to set the premium equal to the expected loss times the frequency of losses due to bank failure plus some load or markup factor. This would exactly mimic the approach toward premium setting in the property-casualty industry. The most commonly suggested approach, the **option pricing model (OPM),** has been, however, to view the FDIC's provision of deposit insurance as virtually identical to the FDIC's writing a put option on the assets of the bank that buys the deposit insurance. Figure 15–5 illustrates the cash flows for the FDIC (Panel A) and the bank and its deposit holders (Panel B) resulting from this deposit insurance scheme. Notice that if the bank maintains its ability to pay off all deposits (all points to the right of and including point X), it incurs the cost of deposit insurance premiums (the FDIC retains these funds) and receives nothing in return. If the bank defaults on the repayment to deposit holders (points to the left of point X), the FDIC covers these payments to deposit holders. The smaller the percentage of deposits the bank is able to pay off, the greater the cash flows paid out by the FDIC to the bank's deposit holders. The pay-off relationship is formally equivalent to the FDIC's writing a put option on the assets of the bank, with the bank's deposits acting as the exercise price. The actuarially fair insurance (or option) premium charged by the FDIC in this framework is positively related to bank asset risk and its leverage.

Although the option pricing model is a conceptually and theoretically elegant tool, it is difficult to apply in practice, and the FDIC has not adopted it. The next section discusses the risk-based deposit premium plan introduced by the FDIC in January 1993. Although not a direct application of the put option approach, the schedule adopts important aspects or features of this approach by directly linking insurance premiums to both bank asset quality and leverage.

Implementing Risk-Based Premiums.   The FDICIA required the FDIC to establish risk-based premiums by January 1, 1994. The FDIC must now base premiums on the following:[13]

1. Different categories and concentrations of assets.
2. Different categories and concentrations of liabilities—insured, uninsured, contingent, and noncontingent.
3. Other factors that affect the probability of loss.
4. The deposit insurer's revenue needs.[14]

The FDIC first introduced a **risk-based deposit insurance program** on January 1, 1993. Under this program, which applies equally to all depository-insured institutions, a bank or thrift's risk is ranked along a capital adequacy dimension and a supervisory

option pricing model

A model for calculating deposit insurance as a put option on the bank's assets.

risk-based deposit insurance program

A program that assesses insurance premiums on the basis of capital adequacy and supervisory judgments on bank quality.

---

concerns might arguably override private cost minimizing concerns and require subsidies. Other authors have argued that if an actuarially fair premium is imposed on a banking system that is fully competitive, banking itself cannot be profitable. That is, some subsidy is needed for banks to exist profitably. Indeed, the 1995 level of deposit insurance was estimated to absorb around 6 to 10 percent of bank earnings. Large banks such as Bank of America and NationsBank, which have significant domestic deposit bases, paid $284 million and $210 million, respectively, in premiums to the FDIC in 1994 alone. However, although U.S. banking is competitive, it probably deviates somewhat from the perfectly competitive model.

[13]The FDIC is also allowed to reinsure up to 10 percent of an insured institution's risk and to use reinsurance prices to set the insured's premiums.

[14]In particular, the FDIC cannot cut premiums until the fund's reserves exceed 1.25 percent of insured deposits. This target level was exceeded by 1995 for BIF and by 1996 for SAIF.

Panel A: Cash Flows for FDIC

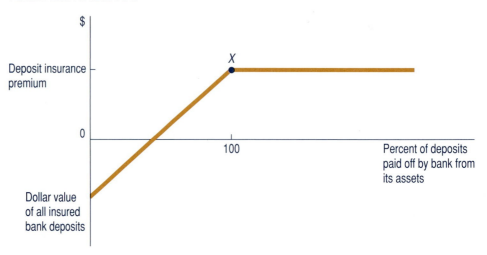

Panel B: Cash Flows for Bank and Its Deposit Holders

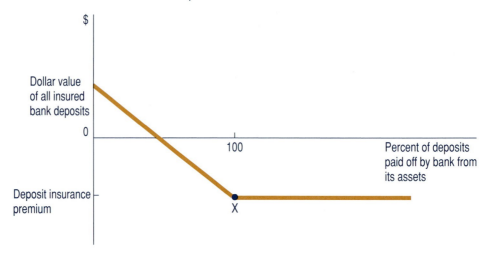

F i g u r e 15–5   *Option Pricing Model Approach to Deposit Insurance*

dimension. That is, rankings are based partly on regulators' judgments regarding asset quality, loan underwriting standards, and other operating risks. Since each dimension has three categories, a bank or thrift is placed in any one of nine cells. See Table 15–2 for the original structure of premiums.

The best banks, those that were well capitalized and healthy, paid an annual insurance premium of 23 cents per $100 of deposits; the worst banks paid 31 cents. Although the 8 cent differential in insurance premiums between the safest and riskiest banks was a first step in risk-based pricing, it was widely considered to be so small that it did not effectively price insurance according to risk. At the time of the risk-based premiums' introduction, the

Table 15-2

SHIFTING THE DEPOSIT INSURANCE BURDEN

The fee structure for deposit insurance, effective January 1, 1993

	Supervisory Groups		
Capital Category	**Healthy***	**Supervisory Concern**	**Substantial Supervisory Concern†**
Well capitalized‡	23 cents per $100	26 cents per $100	29 cents per $100
Adequately capitalized§	26 cents per $100	29 cents per $100	30 cents per $100
Undercapitalized#	29 cents per $100	30 cents per $100	31 cents per $100

*Financially sound and only a few weaknesses.

†Substantial probability of loss to the fund unless effective corrective action is taken.

‡Total risk-based capital ≥ 10 percent, Tier I risk-based capital ≥ 6 percent, Tier I leverage ≥ 5 percent.

§Total risk-based capital ≥ 8 percent, Tier I risk-based capital ≥ 4 percent, Tier I leverage ≥ 4 percent.

#Does not meet the capital criteria for well or adequately capitalized depository institution.

SOURCE: From the *New York Times,* September 16, 1992, p. D2. Copyright © 1992 by The New York Times Company. Reprinted by permission.

FDIC estimated that about 75 percent of the more than 12,000 insured commercial banks and savings banks (with 51 percent of the bank deposit base) and 60 percent of the 2,300 insured thrifts (with approximately 43 percent of the thrift deposit base) were in the group paying the lowest premium of 23 cents. Only about 220 banks (2 percent of all insured commercial and savings banks) and 160 thrifts (7 percent of all insured thrifts) were in the group paying the highest insurance premium of 31 cents. However, the improving solvency position of the FDIC (and of the institutions it insures) has resulted in a considerable reduction in insurance premiums for banks since 1996 (see Contemporary Perspectives Box 15–2) and for thrifts since 1997. Indeed, since 1996, the large majority of banks and thrifts have had to pay only a small fee and no explicit insurance premiums at all.

Increased Capital Requirements and Stricter Closure Rules.   A second way to reduce stockholders' incentives to take excessive risks is to (1) require higher capital-lower leverage ratios (so that stockholders have more at stake in taking risky investments) and (2) impose stricter bank closure rules. Bank owners' moral hazard risk-taking incentives increase as their capital or net worth approaches zero and their leverage increases. The risk taking incentives of the owners of those thrifts allowed to operate in the 1980s with virtually no book equity capital and with negative net worth were enormous.

capital forbearance

Regulatory policy that allows an FI to continue operating even when its capital is fully depleted.

By failing to close such thrifts, regulators exhibited excessive **capital forbearance.** In the short run, capital forbearance may save the insurance fund some liquidation costs. In the long run, however, owners of bad banks or thrifts have continuing incentives to grow and take additional risks in the hope that it would have a large payoff that could turn the institution around. This strategy potentially adds to the future liabilities of the insurance fund and to the costs of bank liquidation. We now know that huge additional costs were the actual outcome of the regulators' capital forbearance policy in the thrift industry.

Contemporary Perspectives 15–2

FDIC Cuts Commercial Bank Premiums

The Federal Deposit Insurance Corporation decided today to virtually eliminate deposit insurance premiums for most commercial banks after concluding that its insurance fund had enough money to cover bank failures in the coming months.

Bankers welcomed the unanimous decision by the agency's board, which will take effect on January 1 and save them $946 million a year in premiums. Industry lobbyists waged a vigorous campaign to eliminate the premiums, arguing that they were unnecessary after the Bank Insurance Fund late last spring reached its congressionally mandated target of $1.25 in reserves for every $100 of insured deposits.

Rick Helfer, the chairman of the FDIC, said premiums needed to be reduced because of the banking industry's current health, the economy's strength and the expectation of FDIC examiners that few banks would fail soon. Premiums will still be collected for some banks with risky business practices and less solid finances. Still, the income from premiums as a share of insured deposits will fall to the lowest level in the 62 years of federal deposit insurance.

Consumer activists and even some of the board's members criticized the decision. "Under a better system, we would be allowed to build up a surplus in better times that we would run off in bad times," said Jonathan L. Fiechter, the acting director of the Office of Thrift Supervision and one of the four sitting members of the FDIC's board.

But Mr. Fiechter voted for the premium reduction anyway, saying that current law left the board with little choice once the fund had clearly met the target for reserves.

Ralph Nader, the consumer activist, contended that the $25.08 billion now in the Bank Insurance Fund could be exhausted easily by the collapse of one or two of the giant banks now forming from the industry's many mergers, leaving taxpayers with the burden of paying for any further failures. Today's decision "is a prescription for another round of corporate bank welfare," he said.

SOURCE: Keith Bradsher, The *New York Times,* November 15, 1995, p. D2. Copyright © 1995 by The New York Times Co. Reprinted with Permission.

As discussed in Chapter 16, a system of risk-based capital requirements mandates that those banks and thrifts taking greater on- and off-balance-sheet credit and interest rate risks must hold more capital. Thus, risk-based capital supports risk-based deposit insurance premiums by increasing the cost of risk taking for bank stockholders.[15] In addition, the 1991 FDICIA sought to increase significantly the degree of regulatory discipline over bank stockholders by introducing a prompt corrective action program. This imposed five capital zones for banks and thrifts, with progressively harsher mandatory actions being taken by regulators as capital ratios fall. Under this carrot-and-stick approach, a bank or thrift is placed into receivership when its capital falls below some positive book value level (currently 2 percent of assets for banks).

The extent to which the book value of capital approximates true net worth, or market value, of capital, enhances stockholder discipline by imposing additional costs on bank owners for risk taking. It also increases the degree of coinsurance, in regard to risks taken, between bank owners and regulators, such as the FDIC.

---

[15]This is under the assumption that new equity is more costly for banks to raise than deposits.

Concept Question

1. Do we need both risk-based capital requirements and risk-based premiums to discipline shareholders?

• •

Depositor Discipline

An alternative, more indirect method to discipline riskier banks is to create conditions for a greater degree of depositor discipline. Depositors could either require higher interest rates and risk premiums on deposits or ration the amount of deposits they are willing to hold in riskier banks.

Critics argue that under the current deposit insurance regulations, neither insured depositors nor uninsured depositors have sufficient incentives to discipline riskier banks. To understand these arguments, we consider the risk exposure of both insured and uninsured depositors under the current deposit insurance contract.

Insured Depositors.   When the deposit insurance contract was introduced in 1933, the level of coverage per depositor was $2,500. This coverage cap gradually rose over the years to $100,000 in 1980. The $100,000 cap concerns a depositor's beneficial interest and ownership of deposited funds. In actuality, by structuring deposit funds in a bank or thrift in a particular fashion, a depositor can achieve many times the $100,000 coverage cap on deposits. To see this, consider the different categories of deposit fund ownership available to an individual shown in Table 15–3. Each of these categories represents a distinct accumulation of funds toward the $100,000 insurance cap; the coverage ceiling is *per bank*. We give an example of how depositors can raise the coverage level by adopting certain strategies.

Table 15–3

DEPOSIT OWNERSHIP CATEGORIES

Individual ownership, such as a simple checking account

Joint ownership, such as the savings account of a husband and wife

Revocable trusts, in which the beneficiary is a qualified relative of the settlor, and the settlor has the ability to alter or eliminate the trust

Irrevocable trusts, whose beneficial interest is not subject to being altered or eliminated

Employee benefit plans, whose interests are vested and thus not subject to being altered or eliminated

Public units, that is, accounts of federal, state, and municipal governments

Corporations and partnerships

Unincorporated businesses and associates

Individual retirement accounts (IRAs)

Keogh accounts

Executor or administrator accounts

Accounts held by banks in an agency or fiduciary capacity

SOURCE: U.S. Department of the Treasury, "Modernizing the Financial System: Recommendations for Safer More Competitive Banks," (Washington, DC: Department of Treasury, February 1991).

EXAMPLE 15–1

Calculation of Insured Deposits

IRA and Keogh accounts

Private pension plans self-funded by individuals, with banks or other FIs acting as trustees.

For example, a married couple with one child that has **Individual Retirement Accounts (IRA)** and **Keogh** private pension plans for both the husband and the wife at the bank could accrue a total coverage cap of $800,000 as a family: his individual deposit account, her individual deposit account, their joint deposit account, their child's deposit account held in trust, his IRA account, his Keogh account, her IRA account, and her Keogh account. By expanding the range of ownership in this fashion, the coverage cap for a family per bank can rapidly approach $1 million or more. • • •

The 1991 FDICIA left the insured depositor coverage cap unchanged at $100,000. Lowering the coverage cap would increase the incentives of depositors to monitor and run from more risky banks, but it would also increase the number of bank failures and the probability of panics. Thus, the gains to the FDIC from covering a smaller dollar amount of deposits per head would have to be weighed against the possibility of more failures and their attendant liquidation costs. This suggests that setting the optimal level of the insurance cap per depositor per bank is far from an easy problem.

too big to fail

A term describing banks that regulators view as being too big to be closed and liquidated without imposing a systemic risk to the banking and financial system.

least-cost resolution

Policy requiring that the lowest cost method of closure be used for failing banks.

insured depositor transfer

A method to resolve failures by requiring uninsured depositors to take a loss or haircut on failure equal to the difference between their deposit claims and the estimated value of the failed bank's assets minus insured deposits.

Uninsured Depositors.   The primary intention of deposit insurance is to deter bank runs and panics. A secondary and related objective has been to protect the smaller, less-informed saver against the reduction in wealth that would occur if that person were last in line when a bank fails. Under the current deposit insurance contract, the small, less-informed depositor is defined by the $100,000 ceiling. Theoretically, at least, larger, more informed depositors with more than $100,000 on deposit are at risk should a bank fail. As a result, these large uninsured depositors should be sensitive to bank risk and seek to discipline riskier banks by demanding either higher interest rates on their deposits or withdrawing their deposits completely. Until recently, the manner in which bank failures have been resolved meant that both large and small depositors were often fully protected against losses. This was especially true when large banks got into trouble and were viewed as being **too big to fail** (TBTF). That is, they were too big to be liquidated by regulators either because of the draining effects on the resources of the insurance fund or for fear of contagious or systemic runs spreading to other major banks. Thus, although uninsured depositors tended to lose in small bank failures, the failure resolution methods employed by regulators in large bank failures usually resulted in implicit 100 percent deposit insurance. As a result, for large banks in particular, neither small nor large depositors had sufficient incentives to impose market discipline on riskier banks. Table 15–4 summarizes the resolution procedures that the FDIC used prior to the implementation of the FDICIA of 1991. Table 15–5 compares the relative sizes of liquidation methods during the period 1986–1997.[16]

We next look at the FDICIA's creation of exposure for uninsured depositors and creditors and the way it reduced the FDIC's bank failure resolution costs. Since the passage of FDICIA, the FDIC is now required to use a **least-cost resolution** policy by which it selects the lowest cost method of all closure methods available. Table 15–6 summarizes the least-cost resolution requirements imposed under FDICIA. To this end, the FDIC has been increasingly using an **insured depositor transfer** (IDT) or "haircut" method to resolve a number of post–1991 failures. Under the IDT method of resolution, the insured deposits of

---

[16]There were five payoffs in 1993, and zero for 1994 through 1997 out of, respectively, 42, 13, 6, 5, and 1 failure resolutions in those years. The remaining resolutions were all purchase and assumptions (P&As).

Table **15-4**

BANK FAILURE RESOLUTION PROCEDURES USED PRIOR TO THE FDIC IMPROVEMENT ACT OF 1991

Payoffs and Transfers: Regulators liquidate the bank's assets and pay off the insured deposits in full (insured deposit payoff) or transfer these deposits in full to another local bank (insured deposit transfer).

Purchase and Assumption (P&A): Regulators merge a failed bank with a healthy bank. Under an *insured deposit P&A*, only the insured deposits of the failed bank are assumed by the healthy bank. In a "*clean*" *P&A*, the healthy bank purchases and assumes both the insured and uninsured deposits of the failed bank as well as its remaining good assets (mostly securities). The healthy bank also receives a cash infusion from the FDIC equal to the difference in the value of the liabilities minus the good assets assumed. In a *total P&A*, the healthy bank assumes all assets and liabilities of the failed bank and receives a cash infusion from the FDIC for the difference in value of the total deposits and the market value of the total assets (good and bad) of the failed bank.

Open Assistance: The FDIC assists the failing bank by issuing promissory notes, net worth certificates, cash, infusions of equity, and so on to keep the bank afloat.

Table **15-5**

SUMMARY STATISTICS FOR BANKS RESOLVED BY THE FEDERAL DEPOSIT INSURANCE CORPORATION BY TYPE OF RESOLUTION, 1986–1997

Type of Resolution	Bank Resolved, 1986–1997		Estimated Losses to the Bank Insurance Fund		Assets Recorded at Time of Resolution		Losses as a Percentage of Assets*	Average Asset Size of Resolved Banks (millions of dollars)*
	Number of Banks	(percentage of total)	(millions of dollars)	(percentage of total)	(millions of dollars)	(percentage of total)		
Payoffs and transfers								
Deposit payoff	75	6	$ 1,337	4	$ 3,969	2	34	$ 52.9
Deposit transfer	153	12	2,865	10	9,725	4	29	63.6
Subtotal	228	18	4,202	14	13,694	6	31	60.1
Purchases and assumption								
Total bank	291	23	9,802	32	72,120	32	14	247.8
Insured deposits only	90	7	2,470	8	23,176	10	11	257.5
Clean and other	596	48	12,103	40	102,670	45	12	172.5
Subtotal	972	78	24,375	80	197,966	87	12	202.6
Assistance transactions	54	4	1,860	6	16,914	7	11	313.2
Total	1,259	100	$30,437	100	$228,574	100	13	$181.6

NOTES: Sample includes commercial and savings banks insured by the Bank Insurance Fund that were resolved between 1986 and 1997. Assets are those recorded at time of resolution.

*Figures represent averages for each type of resolution.

SOURCE: Congressional Budget Office analysis based on Federal Deposit Insurance Corporation, Division of Finance, Financial Reporting Branch, Washington, DC: *Failed Bank Cost Analysis,* 1985–1995, and FDIC Historical Statistics, "BIF Closings and Assistance Transactions," 1997.

Table 15–6

LEAST-COST RESOLUTIONS (LCR) REQUIREMENTS UNDER FDICIA

The FDIC must

- Consider and evaluate all possible resolution alternatives by computing and comparing their costs on a present value basis using realistic discount rates
- Select the least costly alternative based on the evaluation
- Document the evaluation and the assumptions on which it is based, including any assumptions with regard to interest rates, asset recovery rates, asset holding costs, and contingent liabilities
- Retain documentation for at least five years

SOURCE: GAO, *1992 Bank Resolutions,* GAO/GGD-94-147 (Washington, D.C.: GAO, 19), p. 14.

a closed bank are usually transferred in full to another local bank in the community to conduct a direct payoff of the depositors for the FDIC. By contrast, uninsured depositors and general creditors of the failed bank (such as fed fund lenders) must file a claim against the receiver of the failed bank and share with the FDIC in any receivership distributions from the liquidation of the closed bank's assets. This usually results in a loss for uninsured depositors (a so-called haircut). For example, in 115 out of 182 failures between 1992 and 1997, the FDIC imposed initial losses or haircuts on uninsured depositors ranging from 13 to 100 percent. The size of haircut depends mostly on the FDIC–estimated value of the failed bank's assets.[17]

There is a very important and controversial exception to using the least-cost resolution in all cases. Specifically, a *systemic risk* exemption applies when a large bank failure could threaten the entire financial system. Then methods that could involve the full protection of uninsured depositors as well as insured depositors could be used. This appears to allow the too big to fail guarantee to large bank uninsured depositors prevalent in the pre–1991 system (see Table 15–4) to carry over after the passage of the FDICIA. However, the act has restricted the circumstances when this systemic risk exemption can be used. Such an exemption is allowed only if a two-thirds majority of the boards of the Federal Reserve and the FDIC recommend it to the secretary of the Treasury, and if the secretary of the Treasury, in consultation with the president of the United States, agrees. Further, any cost of such bailout of a big bank must be shared among all other banks by charging them an additional deposit insurance premium based on their size as measured by their domestic and foreign deposits as well as their borrowed funds, excluding subordinated debt. Because large banks have more foreign deposits and borrowed funds, they will have to make larger contributions (per dollar of assets) to any future bailout of a large bank than will smaller banks.

depositor preference

Priority given to depositors (insured and uninsured) over all other unsecured creditors in the event of the insolvency of a bank or a thrift.

Legislation that also seems to be contrary to the spirit of the least-cost resolution requirement is the depositor preference legislation included in the 1993 budget bill. **Depositor preference** gives depositors, including uninsured domestic depositors, priority over all other unsecured creditors in the event of the insolvency of a bank or thrift. It

---

[17]In some cases, the FDIC transfers a proportion of the failed bank's uninsured deposits to the local bank (e.g., 50 cents of every $1 of uninsured deposits). This haircut (50 cents) is based on the FDIC's expectations as to how much it will receive by liquidating the failed bank's assets.

requires junior creditors of failed institutions (foreign depositors, fed fund lenders, banker's acceptance holders, counterparties in swaps and options, etc.) to be completely wiped out before the FDIC and uninsured domestic depositors suffer any losses. Therefore, contrary to FDICIA, depositor preference lessens the importance of depositor discipline because this group of potential monitors now faces little or no risk of loss. This is offset to at least some extent, however, in that uninsured claimants, such as large interbank borrowers of fed funds, have an increased incentive to discipline poor bank management. More than 30 states had depositor preference statutes prior to the 1993 legislation, but several large states (i.e., California and New York) did not.

Concept Questions

1. What is the difference between the payoff method and the purchase and assumption method to resolve a bank failure?
2. What are four factors that might influence an acquirer to offer a large premium when bidding for a failed bank?
3. Under what conditions will uninsured depositors be protected in the event of a bank or thrift insolvency?

Regulatory Discipline

In the event that stockholder and deposit holder discipline does not reduce moral hazard by banks and thrifts, regulations can require regulators to act more promptly and in a more consistent and predictable fashion to restrain risk taking. To bolster increased regulatory discipline, FDICIA perceived two areas of regulatory weakness: (1) the frequency and thoroughness of examinations and (2) the forbearance shown to weakly capitalized banks in the pre–1991 period. FDICIA included provisions to address these weaknesses.

Examinations. First, FDICIA required improved accounting standards for banks, including the market evaluaton of an increasing number of balance sheet assets and liabilities. This would improve examiners' abilities to monitor banks' net worth positions off-site and would be consistent with monitoring the true net worth of the bank (see Chapters 17 and 18). Second, beginning in December 1992, the FDICIA required an annual on-site examination of every bank.[18] Third, the requirement of independent audits has given private accountants a larger role in monitoring a bank's performance.[19]

Capital Forbearance. The introduction of prompt corrective action capital zones (see Chapter 16) and the mandatory actions required by regulators in each of those zones

---

[18]Although the timing of examinations is secret, M. Flannery and J. Houston, in "Market Responses to Federal Examinations of U.S. Bank Holding Companies," Graduate School of Business Administration, University of Florida, October 1993, mimeograph, find that examinations have a positive effect on bank equity values since an examination is seen as certifying (or reducing uncertainty surrounding) the reported accounting values of banks—for example, the size of nonperforming loans.

[19]This is similar to the practice in the United Kingdom, where the 1987 Bank Act recommended an enhanced role for private auditors as a backup for regulatory examiners.

(including closure), is symptomatic of a movement toward a regulatory policy based on rules rather than discretion. Such rules clearly direct the behavior of regulators to act in a certain manner even if they are reluctant to do so out of self-interest or for other reasons. The weakness of such rules is that if a policy is bad, regulators can not quickly change it.[20]

Concept Questions

1. Why is stockholder, depositor, and regulator discipline important?
2. What additional measures did FDICIA mandate to bolster stockholder and depositor discipline?

NON–U.S. DEPOSIT INSURANCE SYSTEMS

Most European countries have historically operated without explicit deposit insurance programs. Despite this, European countries have not seen the 1930s type of bank run and panic experienced in the United States. In respect to our earlier discussion of the moral hazard problem, the question of how this can happen arises. The answer is that European governments have often given implicit deposit guarantees at no cost to the largest banks in their countries. This has been possible as the result of the higher degree of concentration of deposits among the largest banks in European countries. However, deposit insurance systems are being increasingly adopted worldwide. One view of this trend toward implementation of explicit deposit programs is that governments are now simply collecting premiums as a fee to offset an obligation (implicit deposit insurance) that they previously offered for free.

Many of these systems offer quite different degrees of protection to depositors compared to the U.S. system. For example, in response to the single banking and capital market in Europe, the European Community (EC) has proposed establishing a single deposit insurance system covering all EC–located banks by the end of 1999. This would insure deposit accounts up to 20,000 ECUs (approximately $25,000). However, depositors would be subject to a 10 percent deductible to create incentives for them to monitor banks. Currently, the United Kingdom insures up to £20,000 with a 25 percent deductible, and Germany provides virtually 100 percent insurance to depositors (each nonbank depositor is insured up to 30 percent of a bank's capital). In contrast, neither Greece nor Portugal offers explicit insurance plans. The idea underlying the EC plan is to create a level playing field for banks across all European Community countries. The appendix to this chapter summarizes deposit insurance plans for commercial banks in the European Union (EU) and G–10 major industrial countries.

---

[20]Similar arguments have been made in the area of monetary policy, whose proponents (such as monetarist Milton Friedman) have argued for a rules-based policy on a constant growth rate of the money supply. However, most central bankers prefer discretion in deciding the timing and size of monetary policy actions such as those affecting their open market operations.

THE DISCOUNT
WINDOW

Deposit Insurance versus the Discount Window

The previous sections have discussed how a well-designed deposit insurance system might impose stockholder, depositor, and regulator discipline. Such system has the potential to stop bank runs and extreme liquidity problems arising in the banking system without introducing significant amounts of moral hazard risk-taking behavior among insured institutions.

Only time will tell whether the FDICIA has priced risk accurately enough to stop all but the most egregious cases of moral hazard. It has certainly increased the incentives of bank owners, uninsured depositors, and regulators to monitor and control bank risk. As such, the changes made under the FDICIA are considerable improvements over the old deposit insurance contract.

However, deposit insurance is not the only mechanism by which regulators help offset bank liquidity risk problems. A second mechanism has been the central bank's provision of a lender of last resort facility through the discount window.

The Discount Window

discount window

A central bank lender of last resort used to meet banks' short-term, nonpermanent liquidity needs.

Traditionally, central banks such as the Federal Reserve have provided a **discount window** facility to meet the short-term, nonpermanent, liquidity needs of banks.[21] For example, suppose that a bank has an unexpected deposit drain near the end of a reserve requirement period but cannot meet its reserve target (see Chapter 14). It can seek to borrow from the central bank's discount window facility. Alternatively, discount window loans can also meet short-term seasonal liquidity needs due to crop-planting cycles. Normally, banks make such loans by discounting short-term high-quality securities such as Treasury bills and bankers' acceptances with the central bank. The interest rate at which such securities are discounted is called the *discount rate* and is set by the central bank. In the United States, the central bank has traditionally set the discount rate below market rates, such as the overnight bank-determined federal funds rates, shown in Table 15–7.[22]

Table **15–7**

THE SPREAD BETWEEN THE DISCOUNT RATE AND THE FED FUNDS RATE

	1990	1991	1992	1993	1994	1995	1996	1997
Federal funds	8.10	5.69	3.52	3.02	4.21	5.83	5.30	5.50
Discount window	6.98	5.45	3.25	3.00	3.60	5.21	5.02	5.00

SOURCE: *Federal Reserve Bulletin,* Table A26, various issues.

---

[21]In times of extreme crisis, the discount window can meet the liquidity needs of securities firms as well.

[22]As the level of market rates drops, however, fed fund rates can lie below the discount rate. This occurred in October 1992, when the fed funds rate was 2.96 percent and the discount rate was 3 percent.

The Discount Window Does Not Substitute for Deposit Insurance

Bank access to the discount window is unlikely to deter bank runs and panics the way deposit insurance does for a number of reasons. The first reason is that to borrow from the discount window, a bank is required to pledge high-quality liquid assets as collateral. Failing, highly illiquid banks are, by definition, unlikely to have such assets available to discount. The second reason is that unlike deposit insurance coverage, discount window borrowing is not automatic. Specifically, banks gain access to the window only on a "need-to-borrow" basis. If the central bank considers that a borrowing request is the result of a profit motive because the discount rate is set below bank-determined fed fund rates, the bank would refuse the borrowing request. That is, the central bank makes discount window loans at its discretion. Third, discount window loans are meant to provide temporary liquidity for inherently solvent banks, not permanent long-term support for otherwise insolvent banks.[23]

This narrow role of the discount window was confirmed in the 1991 FDICIA, which limited the discretion of the Federal Reserve to make extended loans to troubled banks. Specifically, discount window loans to troubled, undercapitalized banks are limited to no more than 60 days in any 120-day period, unless both the FDIC and the institution's primary regulator certify that the bank is viable. Additional extensions of up to 60 days are allowed subject to regulator certification. Finally, any discount window advances to undercapitalized banks that eventually fail would cause the Federal Reserve to compensate the FDIC for incremental losses caused by the delay in keeping the troubled bank open longer than necessary.[24] Consequently, the discount window is a partial, but not a full, substitute for deposit insurance as a liquidity stabilizing mechanism.

Concept Question

1. Is a bank's access to the discount window as effective as deposit insurance in deterring bank runs and panics? Why or why not?

. . . .

OTHER GUARANTY PROGRAMS

As Chapter 13 discusses, other FIs (such as insurance companies) are also subject to liquidity crises and liability holder runs. To deter such runs and protect small claim holders, guaranty programs have appeared in other sectors of the financial services industry. We next describe these programs and their similarities to and differences from deposit insurance of banks and thrifts.

---

[23]Note that all three of these reasons are the result of regulations set by U.S. regulators. If regulators and politicians want to use the discount window as a substitute for deposit insurance, it is within their jurisdiction to alleviate these barriers.

[24]In practice, the Fed would be penalized by a loss in the interest income on discount window loans made to banks that eventually fail.

National Credit Union Administration

The National Credit Union Administration (NCUA) is an independent federal agency that charters, supervises, examines, and insures the nation's 11,300 federal credit unions (see Chapter 3). Through its insurance fund, the National Credit Union Insurance Fund (NCUIF), NCUA provides deposit insurance guarantees of up to $100,000 for insured credit unions. The fund's reserves come entirely from premiums paid by member credit unions.

Because credit unions hold almost 30 percent of their assets in government securities and hold relatively small amounts of residential mortgages, they have been less affected by the crises experienced by other thrifts, such as S&Ls. In addition, more than 40 percent of their assets are in small consumer loans, often for amounts less than $10,000. Thus, credit unions have a significant degree of credit risk diversification, which also lowers their risk of insolvency.

Property-Casualty and Life Insurance Companies

Both life insurance and property-casualty (PC) insurance companies are regulated at the state level; see Chapter 4. Unlike banks and thrifts, neither life nor PC insurers have a federal guaranty fund. Beginning in the 1960s, most states began to sponsor state guaranty funds for firms selling insurance in that state.[25] These state guaranty funds differ in a number of important ways from deposit insurance. First, although these programs are sponsored by state insurance regulators, they are actually run and administered by the private insurance companies themselves.

Second, unlike SAIF or BIF, in which the FDIC established a permanent reserve fund by requiring banks to pay annual premiums in excess of payouts to resolve failures, no such permanent guaranty fund exists for the insurance industry, with the sole exception of the PC and life guaranty funds in the state of New York. This means that contributions are paid into the guaranty fund by surviving firms only after an insurance company has failed.

Third, the size of the required contributions that surviving insurers make to protect policyholders in failed insurance companies differs widely from state to state. In those states that have guaranty funds, each surviving insurer is normally levied a pro rata amount, according to the size of its statewide premium income. This amount either helps pay off small policyholders after the assets of the failed insurer have been liquidated or acts as a cash injection to make the acquisition of a failed insurer attractive. The definition of small policyholders generally varies among states from $100,000 to $500,000.[26]

Finally, because no permanent fund exists and the annual pro rata contributions are often legally capped, a delay usually occurs before small policyholders receive the cash surrender values of their policies or other payment obligations from the guaranty fund. This contrasts with deposit insurance, which normally provides insured depositors immediate coverage of their claims. For example, the failure of Executive Life Insurance in 1991 left approximately $117.3 million in outstanding claims in Hawaii. But the Hawaii life insurance guaranty fund can raise only $13.1 million a year due to legal caps on surviving

---

[25]However, Louisiana, New Jersey, and Washington, D.C. have no fund for life insurance industry failures; Colorado has only recently established one. Moreover, New York has a permanent fund into which insurers pay premiums regardless of the failure rate.

[26]Since insurance industry guaranty fund premiums are size based, they are similar to the pre-1993 flat insurance premiums under deposit insurance.

firms' contributions. This means that it will take up to nine years for surviving firms to meet the claims of Executive Life policyholders in Hawaii. In the failure of Baldwin United in 1983, the insurers themselves raised additional funds, over and above the guaranty fund, to satisfy policyholders' claims.

Thus, the private nature of insurance industry guaranty funds, their lack of permanent reserves, and low caps on annual contributions mean that they provide less credible protection to claimants than do bank and thrift insurance funds. As a result, the incentives for insurance policyholders to engage in a run, should they perceive that an insurer has asset quality problems or insurance underwriting problems, is quite strong even in the presence of such guaranty funds.

The Securities Investor Protection Corporation

Since the passage of the Securities Investor Protection Act in 1970 and the creation of the Securities Investor Protection Corporation (SIPC), customers of securities firms have been given specific, but limited, protection against insolvencies. Basically, customers receive pro rata shares of a liquidated securities firm's assets and SIPC satisfies the remaining claims up to a maximum of $500,000 per individual. Since its inception, SIPC has had to intervene in approximately 1 percent of the 20,000 security dealers-brokers that have failed or ceased operations. Most of these firms had less than 1,000 customers, with the biggest loss involving 6,500 customers (and a payout of $31.7 million) following the failure of Bell and Beckwith. Thus, compared to either the banking or insurance funds, SIPC losses have been very small. In 1997, the fund's reserves stood at $1.082 billion; its premium rate was a flat assessment of $150 per member. However, some concerns have been raised regarding the adequacy of this fund in the wake of increased stock and bond market volatility and the increase in highly complex derivative instruments.[27]

The Pension Benefit Guaranty Corporation

In 1974, the Employee Retirement Income Security Act (ERISA) established the Pension Benefit Guaranty Corporation (PBGC). Currently, PBGC protects the retirement benefits of more than 41 million workers and has 58,000 insured private pension plan sponsors. Prior to 1974, an employee's pension benefits with a private corporation had very limited backing from that firm's assets. The establishment of PBGC resulted in the insurance of corporations' underfunded plans.[28]

When PBGC was created in 1974, the single-employer premium was a flat-rate $1 per plan participant. Congress raised the premium to $2.60 in 1979 and to $8.50 in 1986. In 1987, the basic premium was raised to $16 and an additional variable-rate premium was imposed on underfunded plans up to a maximum of $50. In 1991, Congress set the maximum at $72 per participant for underfunded plans and $19 per participant for fully funded plans.

Despite these premiums, however, PBGC has operated at a deficit since its inception. This reflects the fact that unlike the FDIC, the PBGC has little regulatory power over the

---

[27]See U.S. General Accounting Office, *Securities Investor Protection*, GAO/GGD-92-109 (Washington, D.C.: GAO, September 1992).

[28]Regulators created the PBGC to insure underfunded pension plans by corporations. No such insurance fund exists for public pension plans, such as the U.S. Social Security fund, which is currently severely underfunded.

pension plans it insures. Thus, it cannot use portfolio restrictions or implicit insurance premiums to restrict the risk taking of plan managers.[29]

Partly in response to the growing PBGC deficit, the 1994 Retirement Protection Act was passed. Under the act, the $72 premium cap was phased out in 1997. As a result, underfunded programs are now subjected to even higher premiums (80 percent of underfunded plans were at the cap in 1997). As a result of these changes, the PGBC's deficit has decreased and it is estimated that these changes will eliminate the PGBC's deficit within 10 years. Thus, like the FDIC in 1993, the PBGC has changed to an overtly risk-based premium plan.

Concept Questions

1. How do state-sponsored guaranty funds for insurance companies differ from deposit insurance?
2. What specific protection against insolvencies does the SIPC provide to customers of securities firms?

---

[29]To the extent that regulation restricts the asset and liability activities of a firm or FI, the restriction is similar to imposing an implicit premium or tax on the activities of the firm.

SUMMARY

A contagious run on FIs can have serious social welfare effects. Because of adverse wealth, money supply, and credit supply effects, government regulators of FIs have introduced guaranty programs to deter runs by offering liability holders varying degrees of failure protection. Mispriced insurance, however, can lead to moral hazard behavior by FI owners/managers. That is, since insurance guarantees result in little risk to FI owners/managers in the event of losses, they have an incentive to take excessively risky asset positions.

In recent years, bank and other financial industry guaranty programs have weakened and in some cases been rendered insolvent. This chapter looked at the causes of the deposit insurance fund insolvencies in the late 1980s, including external economic events and moral hazard behavior induced by the insurance plan itself. These deposit insurance fund insolvencies led to a major restructuring of the FDIC and deposit guarantees in general. We discussed the post–1991 restructuring of deposit insurance, including the introduction of risk-related premiums, risk-based capital, and increased market and regulatory discipline on FI owners and deposit holders. As a result, the provision and cost of deposit insurance is currently much more sensitive to a bank's risk exposure. This chapter also examined liability guaranty programs for other FIs, including the NCUIF, SIPC, PGBC, and the state-organized life and PC guaranty insurance funds.

P E R T I N E N T   W E B   S I T E S

Board of Governors of the Federal Reserve   http://www.bog.frb.fed.us/

Federal Deposit Insurance Corp. (FDIC)   http://www.fdic.gov/

National Credit Union Administration (NCUA)   http://www.ncua.org/

Pension Benefit Guaranty Corp. (PBGC)   http://www.pbgc.gov/

Securities Investor Protection Corp. (SIPC)   http://www.sipc.org/

Deposit Insurance and Other Liability Guarantees

1. Compared to banks, to what extent are other FIs subject to contagious runs?

2. What major changes did the Financial Institutions Reform, Recovery, and Enforcement Act of 1989 make to the FDIC and the FSLIC?

3. How did the fixed-rate deposit insurance program of the FDIC contribute to the savings and loan crisis?

4. How does a risk-based insurance program solve the moral hazard problem of excess risk taking by FIs? Is an actuarially fair premium for deposit insurance always consistent with a competitive banking system?

5. How does federal deposit insurance help mitigate the problem of bank runs? What are some other elements of the safety net available to banks in the United States?

6. Contrast the two views of the reasons that depository institution insurance funds became insolvent in the 1980s.

7. What are some of the ways to impose stockholder discipline to prevent FIs from engaging in excessive risk taking?

8. What type of tradeoff is inherent in the capital forbearance of regulators?

9. Why did the fixed-rate deposit insurance system fail to induce insured and uninsured depositors to impose discipline on risky banks in the United States in the 1980s?

10. Match the following policies with their intended consequences:

    _____ a.   Lower FDIC insurance levels
    _____ b.   Stricter reporting standards
    _____ c.   Risk-based deposit insurance

    (1) Increased stockholder discipline
    (2) Increased depositor discipline
    (3) Increased regulator discipline

11. When can the systemic risk exemption be used as an exception to the least-cost resolution policy of bank closure methods?

12. Why is access to the discount window of the Fed less effective as a deterrent than deposit insurance for bank runs?

13. What are some of the essential features of the FDICIA of 1991 with regard to the resolution of failing banks?

14. How should mandatory automobile insurance affect driving behavior? How can a state try to promote safe driving and insured drivers?

15. The following is a balance sheet of a commercial bank (amounts in millions of dollars).

Cash	$5	Insured deposits	$30
Loans	40	Uninsured deposits	10
		Equity	5

    The bank experiences a run on its deposits after it declares that it will write off $10 million of its loans as the result of nonpayment. The bank has the option to meet withdrawals by first drawing on its cash and then selling off its loans. Fire-sale of loans in one day can be accomplished at a 90 percent discount. They can be sold at a 95 percent discount if sold in two days. The full market value will be obtained if sold after two days.

    a. What is the amount of loss to the insured depositors if a run on the bank occurs on the first day? on the second day?

    b. What amount do the uninsured depositors lose if the FDIC uses the insured depositor transfer method to close the bank immediately? It plans to sell the assets after the two-day period.

16. What type of insurance, life or property-casualty, is more likely to result in a moral hazard problem? Explain.

17. How is the 1994 Retirement Protection Act expected to reduce the deficits currently experienced by the PBGC?

18. What types of activities will the risk-based insurance premium of the PBCG prevent?

19. Go to the FDIC Web site and look up the amount of total deposits and assets of failed banks during the most recent year available.

20. Go to the Web site of the Board of Governors of the Federal Reserve and update Table 15–7.

APPENDIX: DEPOSIT-INSURANCE PLANS FOR COMMERCIAL BANKS IN THE EU AND G-10 COUNTRIES: 1995

Panel A: Administration of and Membership in the System

Country	Name of Guarantee/ Insurance System	Year First Established	Date Current System Took Effect	Administration of System: Government or Industry	Agency Responsible for Administering System	Membership: Voluntary or Compulsory
Austria	Deposit Guarantee System	1979	July 1, 1995	Industry	Sectoral Associations	Compulsory
Belgium	Guarantee Scheme for Deposits with Credit Institutions	1974	January 1, 1995	Government/Industry—joint	Herdiscontering-en Waarborginstituut- Institute of Resolution and Guarantee	Compulsory
Canada	Canada Deposit Insurance System	1967	1967	Government (Crown Corporation)	Canada Deposit Insurance Corporation	Compulsory
Denmark	Deposit Insurance Fund	1987	July 17, 1995	Government	Deposit Insurance Fund	Compulsory
Finland*	Quarantee Fund of Commercial Banks and Postipankki Ltd.	1966	July 1, 1995	Industry	Quarantee Fund of Commercial Banks and Postipankki Ltd.	Compulsory
France	Deposit Guarantee Fund	1980	No information	Industry	French Bankers' Association	Compulsory
Germany	Deposit Protection Fund of the Federal Association of German Banks	1966	1976	Industry	Federal Association of German Banks	Voluntary
Greece	Deposit Guarantee Fund	1995†	July 1, 1995	Government/Industry—joint	Deposit Guarantee Fund	Compulsory
Ireland	Deposit Protection Account (Central Bank)	1989	July 1, 1995	Government	Central Bank of Ireland	Compulsory
Italy	Bank Fund for the Guarantee of Deposits	1987	1987	Industry	Independently Administered	Voluntary
Japan	Deposit Insurance Corporation	1971	No information	Government/Industry—joint	Deposit Insurance Corporation	Compulsory
Luxembourg	Association for the Guarantee of Deposits, Luxembourg (AGDL)	1989	October 1995	Industry	AGDL	Compulsory
Netherlands	Collective Guarantee System	1979	July 1, 1995	Government/Industry—joint	DeNetherlandsche Bank N.V.	Compulsory
Portugal	Deposit Guarantee Fund	1992	1994	Government	Deposit Guarantee Fund	Compulsory
Spain	Deposit Guarantee Fund	1977	End of 1995	Government/Industry—joint	Deposit Guarantee Fund	Compulsory
Sweden	Swedish Deposit-Guarantee Scheme	1974	January 1, 1996	Government	The Bank Support Authority	Compulsory
Switzerland	Deposit Guarantee Scheme	1982	July 1, 1993	Industry	Swiss Banker's Association	Voluntary
United Kingdom	Deposit Protection Fund	1982	July 1, 1995	Government	Deposit Protection Board	Compulsory
United States	Bank Insurance Fund	1933	January 1, 1996	Government	Federal Deposit Insurance Corporation	Compulsory
European Union (EC Directive on Deposit-Guarantee Schemes)	Determined within each member state	Adopted on May 30, 1994	July 1, 1995	Only directs that each member state shall ensure within its territory one or more deposit guarantee schemes that are introduced and officially recognized	Determined with each member state	Compulsory

Panel B: Coverage or Protection

Country	Extent Amount of Coverage	Interbank Deposits Covered	Deposits of Foreign Branches of Domestic Banks Covered		Deposits of Domestic Branches of Foreign Banks Covered		Foreign-Currency Denominated Deposits Covered	Nonresident Depositors Covered
			Branches located in EU Country	Branches located in Non-EU Country	Branches of EU Banks	Branches of Non-EU Banks		
Austria	ATS 260,000 (per physical person-depositor)	No	Yes	Yes	Yes, amount depends on home country	Yes	Yes	Yes
Belgium	15,000 ECU until Dec. 1999 20,000 ECU thereafter	No	Yes	No	Yes‡	Yes	Yes, but only deposits expressed in ECU or another EU currency	Yes
Canada	Can $60,000 (per depositor)	Yes	No	No	Yes§	Yes§	No	Yes
Denmark	300,000 DKK or 42,000 ECU (per depositor)	No	Yes	Yes	Yes‡	Yes	Yes	Yes
Finland	100 percent (per depositor)	No	Yes	Yes	Yes‡	Yes	Yes	Yes
France	FF 400,000 (per depositor)	No	Yes	No, except for EEA Countries	Yes	Yes	Yes, but only deposits expressed in ECU or another EU currency	No information
Germany	100% up to a limit of 30% of the bank's liable capital (per depositor)	No	Yes	Yes	Yes	Yes	Yes	Yes
Greece	20,000 ECU (per depositor)	No	Yes#	Yes#	Yes**	Yes‡	Yes	Yes
Ireland	90% of deposit—Max. Compensation is 15,000 ECU	No	Yes	Yes	No	Yes	Yes	Yes
Italy	100% of first 200 million Lira and 75% of next 800 million Lira (per deposit)	No	Yes	Yes††	Yes	Yes	Yes	Yes
Japan	10 million Yen (per depositor)	No	No	No	No	No	No	Yes
Luxembourg	Lux F 500,000 (per depositor), only natural persons	No	No	No	Yes	Yes	Yes	Yes
Netherlands	20,000 ECU (per depositor) compensation paid in Guilders	No	Yes	No	Yes‡	Yes‡‡	Yes	Yes
Portugal	100% up to 15,000 ECU 75%—15,000–40,000 ECU 50%—30,000–45,000 ECU (per depositor)	No	Yes	No	Yes‡	Yes	Yes	Yes
Spain	Ptas 1.5 million (per depositor): to be increased to 20,000 ECU	No	Yes	Yes	Yes	Yes	Yes	Yes
Sweden	SEK 250,000 (per depositor)	No	Yes§§	No##	Yes***	Yes	Yes	Yes
Switzerland	SF 30,000 (per depositor)	No	No	No	Yes	Yes	Yes	Yes

United Kingdom	90% of projected deposits, with the maximum amount of deposits protected for each depositor being L20,000 (unless the sterling equivalent of ECU 22,222 is greater). Thus, the most an individual can collect in a bank failure is L18,000 (per depositor) or ECU 20,000 if greater	No	Yes, throughout EEA.	No	Yes†††	Yes‡‡‡	Yes, but only deposits in other EEA currencies and the ECU, as well as sterling	Yes
United States	100,000 USD (per depositor)	No	No	No	No, unless engaged in retail deposit-taking activities	No, unless engaged in retail deposit-taking activities	Yes	Yes
European Union	The aggregate deposits of each depositor must be covered up to ECU 20,000. Until December 31, 1999, member states in which deposits are not covered up to ECU 20,000 may retain the maximum amount laid down on their guarantee schemes, provided that this amount is not less than ECU 15,000 (per depositor)	No	If located within the EU, but until December 13, 1999, not to exceed the maximum amount laid down in their guarantee scheme within the territory of the host member state. If the host member state has greater coverage a branch may voluntarily supplement its coverage	This issue is determined by each member state	Yes, either by having coverage equivalent to the Directive or by joining the host-country deposit-guarantee scheme if it is more favorable for the extra coverage	NA	Yes, if denominated in ECU or currencies of member states of EU	Yes, determine within each member state

Part C: Funding

Country	Ex ante or Ex post Funding	Fund Minimum Reserve Level	Base for Premium	Premium Rate	Risk-Based Premiums
Austria	Ex post, system organized as an incident-related guarantee facility	NA	The deposit guarantee system shall obligate its member institutions, in case of paying-out of guaranteed deposits, to pay without delay pro rata amounts which shall be computed according to the share of the remaining member institution at the preceding balance sheet date as compared to the sum of such guaranteed deposits of the deposit guarantee system	See adjacent column to left	NA
Belgium	Ex ante, but in case of insufficient reserves, banks may be asked to pay, each year if necessary, an exceptional additional contribution up to 0.04 percent	No	Total amount of customers' deposits which qualify for reimbursement and which are expressed either in BEF, ECU, or another EU currency	0.02 percent	No
Canada	Ex ante	No	Insured deposits	One-sixth of one percent	No
Denmark	Ex ante	Yes, 3 billion DKK	Deposits	Max 0.2 percent	No
Finland	Ex ante	No	Total assets	Between 0.01 and 0.05 percent	No
France	Ex post	NA	The contribution consists of two parts: 1. A fixed part, irrespective of the size of the bank, equal to 0.1% of any claim settled and with a FFR 200,000 ceiling; 2. A proportional part, varying according to a regressive scale relative to the size of the bank contributing, based on deposits and one-third credits	See adjacent column to left	NA
Germany	Ex ante; however, additional assessments may be made if necessary to discharge the fund's responsibilities. These contributions are limited to twice the annual contribution	No	Balance sheet item "Liabilities to Customers"	0.03 percent	No
Greece	Ex ante	No	Total deposits	0–200 billion GRD 2% 200–500 billion GRD 1% 500–1,000 billion GRD 0.4% Above 1,000 billion GRD 0.1%	No
Ireland	Ex ante	No, but see information under Premium Rate column	Total deposits excluding interbank deposits and deposits represented by negotiable certificates of deposit	0.2 percent, with a minimum of L 20,000	No
Italy	Ex post; banks commit ex ante, however contributions are ex post	NA	Max. limit for funding the whole system: 4,000 Billion Lire. Contributions are distributed among participants on the basis of (Deposits + Loans - Own funds) with a correction mechanism linked to deposit growth	See adjacent column to left	NA
Japan	Ex ante	No	Insured deposits	0.012 percent	No
Luxembourg	Ex post	NA	Banks' premiums based on percentage of loss to be met	See adjacent column to left	NA

356

Country	Funding	Fund required	Assessment base	Premium/Contribution	Coverage
Netherlands	Ex post	NA	Amount repaid in compensation to insured is apportioned among participating institutions. However, the contribution in any one year shall not exceed 5% per an institution's own funds and per all institutions' own funds	See adjacent column to left	NA
Portugal	Ex ante. However, the payment of the annual contributions may be partly replaced, with a legal maximum of 75% by the commitment to deliver the amount due to the Fund, at any moment it proves necessary	No	Guaranteed deposits	0.08 to 0.12 percent	Yes
Spain	Ex ante	No	Deposits	Max. 2 per thousand. Premiums will be interrupted when the fund reaches 2%	No
Sweden	Ex ante	No	Covered deposits	0.25% percent***	Yes
Switzerland	Ex post	NA	Two components: Fixed fee in relation to gross profit; variable fee depending on share of total protected deposits of an individual bank	See adjacent column to left	NA
United Kingdom	Ex ante; banks make initial contributions of £10,000 when a bank is first authorized, further contributions if the fund falls below £3 million, not exceeding £300,000 per bank based on the insured deposit base of the banks involved, and special contributions, again based on the insured deposit base on the banks involved, but with no contribution limit	Yes, the fund is required by law to maintain a level of £5 million to £6 million, but the DPB can decide to borrow to meet its needs	All deposits in EEA currencies less deposits by credit institutions; financial institutions, insurance undertakings, directors, controllers and managers, secured deposits, CDs, deposits by other group companies and deposits which are part of the bank's own funds	Initial contributions are 0.01 percent. The rate of other contributions depends on the sum required to be raised	No
United States	Ex ante	Yes, 1.25 percent of insured deposits	Domestic deposits	0 to 0.27 percent, subject to a flat minimum of $2,000 for the highest rated banks	Yes
European Union	Determined within each member state	Determined within each member state	Determined within each member state	Determined within each member state	Determined within each member state

SOURCE: J.R. Barth, D.E. Nolle, and T.N. Rice, "Commercial Banking Structure, Regulation, and Performance: An International Comparison," Working Paper, Office of the Comptroller of Currency, March, 1997.

NOTE: The EU and the 7-member European Free Trade Association (EFTA)—except Switzerland—form the European Economic Area (EEA), a single market of 18 countries. In addition to the EU countries, it includes Iceland, Liechtenstein, and Norway. EFTA includes Austria, Finland, Iceland, Norway, Sweden, Switzerland, and Liechtenstein. The EEA was initially established in May of 1992 and came fully into effect in January of 1994.

*A government guarantee fund was also established in 1992.
†There was no deposit guarantee scheme prior to 1995.
§Foreign banks must incorporate subsidiaries to operate in Canada. Deposits of foreign bank subsidiaries are covered by CDIC insurance.
‡Yes, if they join for supplementary coverage.
#Unless covered by an equivalent host country scheme.
**Unless covered by an equivalent home country scheme.
††Only if bank does not participate in local system.
‡‡If the coverage by their home state is equivalent.
§§Covers EEA countries.
##Unless application for non-EEA country is approved.
***Premium rate varies by institution based upon several factors.
†††For depositors of UK branches of EEA banks whose coverage is less generous, they have the option to pay for equivalent coverage.
‡‡‡Unless the Deposit Protection Board is satisfied that the home country scheme provides equivalent coverage to UK depositors.

Chapter Sixteen

Capital Adequacy

Throughout the book we examine the major areas of risk exposure facing a modern FI manager. These risks can emanate from both on- and off-balance-sheet (OBS) activities and can be either domestic or international in source. To ensure survival, an FI manager needs to protect the institution against the risk of insolvency—that is, to shield it from risks sufficiently large to cause the institution to fail. The primary means of protection against the risk of insolvency and failure is an FI's capital. This leads to the first function of capital:

1. To absorb unanticipated losses with enough margin to inspire confidence and enable the FI to continue as a going concern.

In addition, capital protects nonequity liability holders—especially those uninsured by an external guarantor such as the FDIC—against losses. This leads to the second function of capital:

2. To protect uninsured depositors in the event of insolvency and liquidation.

When FIs fail, regulators such as the FDIC must intervene to protect insured claimants (see Chapter 15). An FI's capital offers protection to insurance funds and ultimately the taxpayers who bear the cost of insurance fund insolvency. This leads to the third function of capital:

3. To protect FI insurance funds and the taxpayers.

At this time, each of the government deposit insurance funds is completely funded with monies obtained from industry participants. By holding capital and reducing the risk of insolvency, an FI protects its industry from larger insurance premiums. Thus, a fourth function of capital is as follows:

4.   To protect the industry against increases in insurance premiums.

Finally, as it is for any firm, equity or capital is an important source of financing for an FI. In particular FIs have a choice, subject to regulatory constraints, between debt and equity to finance new projects and business expansion. Thus, the traditional factors that affect a business firm's choice of capital structure—for instance, the tax deductibility of the interest on debt or the private costs of failure or insolvency—also affect the FI's capital decision.[1] This leads to a fifth function of capital:

5.   To fund new assets and business expansion.[2]

The following sections focus mostly on the first four functions concerning the role of capital in reducing insolvency risk and the related costs of insolvency for depositors, regulators, and industry participants.

CAPITAL AND INSOLVENCY RISK

Capital

net worth

A measure of an FI's capital that is equal to the difference between the market value of its assets and the market value of its liabilities.

book value

Value of assets and liabilities based on their historical costs.

To understand how capital protects an FI against insolvency risk, we must define *capital* more precisely. The problem is that capital has many definitions; an economist's definition of capital may differ from an accountant's definition, which, in turn, may differ from regulators' definition. Specifically, the economist's definition of an FI's capital or owners' equity stake in an FI is the difference between the market values of its assets and its liabilities. This is also called an FI's **net worth** (see Chapter 8). This is the *economic* meaning of capital, but regulators have found it necessary to adopt definitions that depart by a greater or lesser degree from economic net worth. The concept of an FI's economic net worth is really a *market value accounting concept*. With the exception of the investment banking industry, regulatory-defined capital and required leverage ratios are based in whole or in part on historical or **book value** accounting concepts.

We begin by looking at the role of economic capital or net worth as a device to protect against two major types of risk: credit risk and interest rate risk. We then compare this market value concept with the book value concept of capital. Because it can actually distort an FI's true solvency position, the book value of capital concept can be misleading to managers, owners, liability holders, and regulators. We also examine some possible reasons that FI regulators continue to rely on book value concepts when such economic value transparency problems exist. Finally, we consider in detail the actual minimum capital requirements imposed by regulators in commercial banking, thrift or savings banking, PC and life insurance, and investment banking.

---

[1] See S. Ross, R. Westerfield, and J. Jaffe, *Corporate Finance,* 4th edition (Burr Ridge, IL: Irwin, 1996).

[2] A sixth function might be added; it would focus on the role of capital regulation restraining the rate of asset growth.

The Market Value of Capital

market value or mark-to-market

Balance sheet values that reflect current rather than historical prices.

To understand how economic net worth or equity insulates an FI against risk, consider the following example. Table 16–1 presents a simple balance sheet on which all of an FI's assets and liabilities are valued in **market value** terms at current prices on a **mark-to-market basis** (see Chapter 17). On a market value or mark-to-market basis, the economic value of the FI's equity is $10 million, which is the difference between the market value of its assets and liabilities. On a market value basis, the FI is economically solvent and imposes no failure costs on depositors or regulators if it were to be liquidated today. Let's consider the impact of two classic types of FI risk—credit and interest rate—on this FI's net worth.

Market Value of Capital and Credit Risk.   The balance sheet in Table 16–1 indicates that the FI has $20 million in long-term loans. Suppose that as the result of a recession, a number of its borrowers have cash flow problems and are unable to keep up their promised loan repayment schedules. A decline in the current and expected future cash flows on loans lowers the market value of the FI's loan portfolio below $20 million. Suppose that loans are really worth only $12 million (the price the FI would receive if it could sell these loans in a secondary market). This means the market value of the loan portfolio has fallen from $20 million to $12 million. The revised market value balance sheet is presented in Table 16–2.

The loss of $8 million in the market value of loans appears on the liability side of the balance sheet as a loss of $8 million of the FI's net worth. That is, the loss of asset value is directly charged against the equity owners' capital or net worth. As you can see, the liability holders (depositors) are fully protected because the total market value of their claims is still $90 million. This is due to the fact that debt holders legally are senior claimants and equity holders are junior claimants to the FI's assets. Consequently, equity holders bear losses on the asset portfolio first. In fact, in this example, liability holders are hurt only when losses

Table 16–1

AN FI'S MARKET VALUE BALANCE SHEET
(in millions of dollars)

Assets		Liabilities	
Long-term securities	$ 80	Liabilities (short-term, floating-rate deposits)	$ 90
Long-term loans	20	Net worth	10
	$100		$100

Table 16–2

AN FI'S MARKET VALUE BALANCE SHEET AFTER A DECLINE IN THE VALUE OF LOANS
(in millions of dollars)

Assets		Liabilities	
Long-term securities	$80	Liabilities	$90
Long-term loans	12	Net worth	2
	$92		$92

Table **16–3**

**AN FI'S BALANCE SHEET AFTER A MAJOR DECLINE
IN THE VALUE OF THE LOAN PORTFOLIO**
(in millions of dollars)

Assets		Liabilities	
Long-term securities	$80	Liabilities	$90
Long-term loans	8	Net worth	–2
	$88		$88

on the loan portfolio exceed $10 million (which was the FI's original net worth). Let's consider a larger credit risk shock in which the market value of the loan portfolio plummets from $20 million to $8 million, a loss of $12 million (see Table 16–3).

This larger loss renders the FI insolvent; the market value of its assets ($88 million) is now less than the value of its liabilities ($90 million). The owners' net worth stake has been completely wiped out—reduced from $10 million to –$2 million, resulting in a negative net worth. Therefore, this hurts liability holders, but only a bit. Specifically, the equity holders bear the first $10 million of the $12 million loss in value of the loan portfolio. Only after the equity holders are completely wiped out do the liability holders begin to lose. In this example, the economic value of their claims on the FI has fallen from $90 million to $88 million, or a loss of $2 million (a percentage loss of 2.22 percent). After insolvency, the remaining $88 million in assets is liquidated and distributed to deposit holders. Note here that we are ignoring deposit insurance.[3]

This example clearly demonstrates the concept of net worth or capital as an insurance fund protecting liability holders, such as depositors, against insolvency risk. The larger the FI's net worth relative to the size of its assets, the more insolvency protection, or insurance its liability holders and liability guarantors such as the FDIC have. This is the reason that regulators focus on capital requirements such as the ratio of net worth to assets in assessing an FI's insolvency risk exposure and in setting deposit insurance premiums (see Chapter 15).

Market Value of Capital and Interest Rate Risk. Consider the market value balance sheet in Table 16–1 after interest rates rise. As we discuss in Chapter 17, rising interest rates reduce the market value of the FI's long-term fixed income securities and loans while floating-rate instruments find their market values largely unaffected if interest rates are instantaneously reset. Suppose that a rise in interest rates reduces the market value of the FI's long-term securities investments to $75 million from $80 million and the market value of its long-term loans from $20 million to $17 million. Because all deposit liabilities are assumed to be short-term floating-rate deposits, their market values are unchanged at $90 million.

After the shock to interest rates, the market value balance sheet is represented in Table 16–4. The loss of $8 million in the market value of the FI's assets is once again reflected on the liability side of the balance sheet by an $8 million decrease in net worth to $2 million. Thus, as for increased credit risk, the equity holders first bear losses in asset values due to

---

[3] In the presence of deposit insurance, the insurer, such as the FDIC, bears some of the depositors' losses; for details, see Chapter 15.

Table **16–4**

**AN FI'S MARKET VALUE BALANCE SHEET AFTER
A RISE IN INTEREST RATES**
(in millions of dollars)

Assets		Liabilities	
Long-term securities	$75	Liabilities	$90
Long-term loans	17	Net worth	2
	$92		$92

Table **16–5**

AN FI'S BOOK VALUE BALANCE SHEET
(in millions of dollars)

Assets		Liabilities	
Long-term securities	$ 80	Short-term liabilities	$ 90
Long-term loans	20	Net worth	10
	$100		$100

adverse interest rate changes. Only if the fall in the market value of assets exceeds $10 million are the liability holders, as senior claimants to the FI's assets, adversely affected.

These examples show that market valuation of the balance sheet produces an economically accurate picture of the net worth and, thus, an FI's solvency position. The equity holders directly bear credit risk and interest rate risk shocks that result in losses in the market value of assets in the sense that such losses are charges against the value of their ownership claims in the FI. So long as the owners' capital or equity stake is adequate, or sufficiently large, liability holders (and implicitly regulators that back the claims of liability holders) are protected against insolvency risk. That is, if regulators were to close an FI before its economic net worth became zero, neither liability holders nor those regulators guaranteeing the claims of liability holders would stand to lose. Thus, many academics and analysts advocate the use of market value accounting and market value of capital closure rules for all FIs, especially because of the book value of capital rules associated with the savings and loan disaster in the 1980s (discussed in Chapter 15).

The Book Value of Capital

We contrast market value or economic net worth with book value of capital or net worth. As we discuss in later sections, FI regulators most commonly use book value capital and capital rules based on book values. Table 16–5 uses the same initial balance sheet as in Table 16–1, but you should assume that assets and liabilities are now valued at their historical book values.

In Table 16–5, the $80 million in long-term securities and $20 million in long-term loans reflect the historic or original book values of those assets. That is, they reflect the values at the time the loans were made and bonds were purchased, which may have been many years ago. Similarly, on the liability side, the $90 million in liabilities reflects their historical cost, and net worth or equity is now the book value of the stockholders' claims rather than the market value of those claims. For example, the book value of capital—the difference between the book value of assets and the book value of liabilities—usually comprises the following four components in banking:

1. *Par value of shares.* The face value of the common stock shares issued by the FI (the par value is usually $1 per share) times the number of shares outstanding.
2. *Surplus value of shares.* The difference between the price the public paid for common stock or shares when originally offered (e.g., $5 per share) and their par values (e.g., $1) times the number of shares outstanding.
3. *Retained earnings.* The accumulated value of past profits not yet paid in dividends to shareholders. Since these earnings could be paid in dividends, they are part of the equity owners' stake in the FI.
4. *Loan loss reserve.* A special reserve from retained earnings set aside to meet expected and actual losses on the portfolio. As discussed in Chapter 8, loan loss reserves reflect an estimate by the FI's management of the losses in the loan portfolio. Tax laws influence the reserve's size, but the FI's managers actually set the level.

Consequently, book value of capital equals par value plus surplus plus retained earnings plus loan loss reserves. As the example in Table 16–5 is constructed, the book value of capital equals $10 million. However, invariably the *book value of equity does not equal the market value of equity* (the difference between the market value of assets and liabilities).

This inequality in book and market value of equity can be understood by examining the effects of the same credit and interest rate shocks on the FI's capital position, but assuming book value accounting methods.

The Book Value of Capital and Credit Risk. Suppose that some of the $20 million in loans is in difficulty regarding repayment schedules. We assumed in Table 16–2 that the revaluation of cash flows leads to an immediate downward adjustment of the loan portfolio's market value from $20 million to $12 million, a market value loss of $8 million. By contrast, under historic book value accounting methods such as generally accepted accounting principles (GAAP), FIs have more discretion in reflecting or timing problem loan loss recognition on their balance sheets and thus in the impact of such losses on capital. Indeed, FIs may well resist writing down the values of bad assets as long as possible to try to present a more favorable picture to depositors and regulators. Such resistance might be expected if managers believe that the recognition of such losses could threaten their jobs. Only pressure from auditors and regulators such as bank, thrift, or insurance examiners may force loss recognition and write-downs in the values of problem assets. For example, in recent years on-site examinations of property insurance companies have occurred as infrequently as once every three years; regulators analyze off-site balance sheet information as infrequently as once every 18 months. Although bank call report data and on-site examinations are more frequent,[4] the tendency is still to delay writing down the book values of loans. In the United States, recent low interest rates and a strong economy have significantly reduced this type of delaying activity, but the financial crisis of the late 1990s in Japan resulted in the Finance Ministry's call for banks to discontinue the delay in the writing off of their non-performing loans (see Contemporary Perspectives Box 16–1).

---

[4] The FDIC Improvement Act of 1991 requires bank examinations at least annually. Banks produce *call reports* (balance sheet data) quarterly.

Contemporary Perspectives 16–1

Japanese Banks Urged to Step Up Loan Write-Offs

A senior Japanese finance ministry official last night called on the country's leading banks to accelerate the writing off of their non-performing loans caused by the collapse of the bubble economy. His remarks came amid signs of fresh turmoil in Japanese financial markets and renewed concern overseas over the health of the nation's financial system.

Figures released yesterday by the Ministry of Finance showed that the amount of non-performing and restructured loans among all Japanese deposit taking institutions

fell by 5.57 trillion yen or 16 per cent to 29.23 trillion yen ($356 billion) between end-March and end-September. . . .

"Banks need to make more efforts to write off other non-performing loans . . . in order to demonstrate the health of the Japanese financial system to international markets," the official said after the release of the figures. . . .

After allowing for special provisions that Japanese banks have made against bad or doubtful debts, and for the fact that land and other collateral held by banks has some market

value, the finance ministry estimates that total problem loans at mid-March were 7.86 trillion yen. This is 12 percent down on the September figure of 8.41 trillion.

In theory, banks and other deposit-taking institutions as a whole could completely write off this remaining amount from annual profits—which amounted to 7.86 trillion yen on an annualized, industry-wide basis for fiscal 1996. But finance ministry officials admitted last night that Japanese bank profits will probably decline in 1997.

SOURCE: *Business Times,* December 27,1996, p. 7, courtesy of Anthony Rowley.

Book Value of Capital and Interest Rate Risk.   Although book value accounting systems recognize credit risk problems, albeit only partially and usually with a long and discretionary time lag, their failure to recognize the impact of interest rate risk is more extreme.

In the market value accounting example in Table 16–4 a rise in interest rates lowered the market values of long-term securities and loans by $8 million and led to a fall in the market value of net worth from $10 million to $2 million. In a book value accounting world, when all assets and liabilities reflect their original cost of purchase, the rise in interest rates has no effect on the value of assets, liabilities, or the book value of equity. That is, the balance sheet remains unchanged; Table 16–5 reflects the position both before and after the interest rate rise. Consider those thrifts that continued to report long-term fixed rate mortgages at historical book values even though interest rates rose dramatically in the early 1980s, and, therefore, a positive book capital position. On a market value net worth basis, however, their mortgages were worth far less than the book values shown on their balance sheets.[5] Indeed, more than half of the firms in the industry were economically insolvent; many massively so.[6]

The Discrepancy between the Market and Book Values of Equity

The degree to which the book value of an FI's capital deviates from its true economic market value depends on a number of factors, especially

---

[5] Note that although book values were not directly affected by changes in interest rates, the increase in interest rates resulted in shrinking spreads and accounting earnings. As a result, the rise in interest rates did not leave the book value accounting results entirely unaffected.

[6] See L. J. White, *The S and L Debacle* (New York: Oxford University Press, 1991), p. 89.

1. *Interest rate volatility.*   The higher the interest rate volatility, the greater the discrepancy.
2. *Examination and enforcement.*   The more frequent on-site and off-site examinations and the stiffer the examiner/regulator standards regarding charging off problem loans, the smaller the discrepancy.

In actual practice, we can get an idea of the discrepancy between book values (BV) and market values (MV) of equity for large publicly traded FIs even when the FI does not mark its balance sheet to market.

Specifically, in an efficient capital market, the FI's stock price reflects the market value of the FI's outstanding equity shares. This valuation is based on the FI's current and expected future net earnings or dividend flows. The market value (MV) of equity per share is therefore

$$\text{MV} = \frac{\text{Market value of equity ownership in shares outstanding}}{\text{Number of shares}}$$

By contrast, the historical or book value of the FI's equity per share (BV) is equal to

$$\text{BV} = \frac{\text{Par value of equity} + \text{Surplus value} + \text{Retained earning} + \text{Loan loss reserves}}{\text{Number of shares}}$$

market-to-book ratio

A ratio that shows the discrepancy between the stock market value of an FI's equity and the book value of its equity.

The ratio MV/BV is often called the **market-to-book ratio** and shows the degree of discrepancy between the market value of an FI's equity capital as perceived by investors in the stock market and the book value of capital on its balance sheet.

The higher the market-to-book ratio, the more the book value of capital *understates* an FI's true equity or economic net worth position as perceived by investors in the capital market. Figure 16–1 graphically indicates the size of some of these differences; it shows

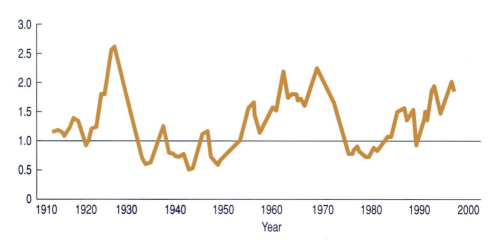

F i g u r e **16–1**   *Average Market Value (MV) to Book Value (BV) of Banks, 1914–1996*

SOURCE: A. Saunders and B. Wilson, "Bank Capital Structure: An Analysis of the Charter Value Hypothesis," Working Paper (New York: Salomon Center–New York University, December 1996); and New York: Salomon Brothers, Commercial Bank U.S. Equity Research, June 1996. Copyright 1997 Salomon Brothers, Inc. This table and table statistics contain data from Salomon Brothers, Inc. Although the information in this table was obtained from sources that Salomon Brothers, Inc., believes to be reliable, Salomon does not guarantee its accuracy, and such information may be incomplete or condensed. All figures included in this table constitute Salomon's judgement as of the original publication date.

the average MV/BV ratio for all available banks whose stocks were traded during the period 1914–1996. Given such discrepancies, why do regulators and FIs continue to oppose the implementation of market value accounting?

Concerns with Market Value Accounting

The first concern about market value (MV) accounting is that it is difficult to implement. This may be especially true for small commercial banks and thrifts with large amounts of nontraded assets such as small loans in their balance sheets. When it is impossible to determine accurate market prices or values for assets, marking to market may be done only with error. A counterargument to this is that the error resulting from the use of market valuation of nontraded assets is still likely to be less than the one resulting from the use of original book or historical valuation since the market value approach does not require all assets and liabilities to be traded. So long as current and expected cash flows on an asset or liability and an appropriate discount rate can be specified, approximate market values can always be imputed (see Chapter 17). Further, with the increase of loan sales and asset securitization (see Chapter 12), indicative market prices are available on an increasing variety of loans.[7]

A second concern with market value accounting is that it introduces an unnecessary degree of variability into an FI's earnings—and thus net worth—because paper capital gains and losses on assets are passed through the income statement. Critics argue that reporting unrealized capital gains and losses is distortionary if the FI actually plans to hold these assets to maturity. Insurers and bankers argue that in many cases, they do hold loans and other assets to maturity and, therefore, never actually realize capital gains or losses. Regulators also argue that they may be forced to close banks too early under the prompt corrective action requirements imposed by the FDIC Improvement Act (FDICIA) of 1991 (discussed later in this chapter), especially if an interest rate spike is only temporary (as much empirical evidence shows) and capital losses on securities can be quickly turned into capital gains as rates fall again. The counterargument is that FIs are increasingly trading, selling, and securitizing assets rather than holding them to maturity. In addition, the failure to reflect capital gains and losses from interest rate changes means that the FI's equity position fails to reflect its true interest rate risk exposure.

A third concern with market value accounting is that FIs are less willing to accept longer-term asset exposures, such as commercial mortgage loans and C&I loans, if these assets must be continually marked to market to reflect changing credit quality and interest rates. For example, as discussed in Chapter 17, long-term assets are more interest rate sensitive than are short-term assets. The concern is that market value accounting may interfere with FIs' special functions (see Chapter 1) as lenders and monitors and may even result in (or accentuate) a major credit crunch. Of the three arguments against market value accounting, this one is probably the most persuasive to regulators concerned about small business finance and economic growth.[8]

---

[7] Congress recently proposed a number of initiatives to securitize small business loans using a public agency similar to the Government National Mortgage Association (GNMA), the public agency that facilitates residential mortgage securitization. Additionally, Angbazo, Mei, and Saunders (1996) analyze the pricing of loans in the secondary market, by looking at highly leveraged transactions loans. See "Credit Spreads in the Market for Highly Leveraged Transactions Loans," Working Paper, New York University.

[8] This was a particularly sensitive issue in the early 1990s when a credit crunch was already perceived to exist and the proportion of C&I loans in bank portfolios was falling (also see Chapter 3).

Concept Questions

1. Why is an FI economically insolvent when its net worth is negative?
2. What are the four major components of a bank's book value of equity?
3. Is book value accounting for loan losses backward or forward looking?
4. What does a market-to-book ratio that is less than 1 imply about an FI's performance?

CAPITAL ADEQUACY IN THE COMMERCIAL BANKING AND THRIFT INDUSTRY

Actual Capital Rules

As noted in the discussion of the advantages and disadvantages of book- and market-based measures of an FI's capital, most FI regulators have chosen some form of book value accounting standard to measure an FI's capital adequacy.[9] This section examines the capital adequacy rules imposed in key FI sectors: (1) commercial banking and thrifts, (2) PC insurance, (3) securities firms, and (4) life insurance. Although capital adequacy rules currently differ across these sectors, a clear movement is toward similar risk-based capital rules in banking, the thrift industry, and insurance (both PC and life). The FDICIA of 1991 requires banks and thrifts to adopt essentially the same capital requirements. Some minor differences exist, but for capital requirements the two industries have converged on a level playing field. Given this, we concentrate on the recent evolution of capital requirements in commercial banking.

Since 1987, U.S. commercial banks have faced two different capital requirements: a capital-assets (leverage) ratio and a risk-based capital ratio that is subdivided into a Tier I capital risk-based ratio and a total capital (Tier I plus Tier II capital) risk-based ratio.

The Capital-Assets (or Leverage) Ratio

leverage ratio

Ratio of an FI's core capital to its assets.

The capital-assets or **leverage ratio** measures the ratio of a bank's book value of primary or core capital to the book value of its assets. The lower this ratio, the more highly leveraged the bank is. Primary or core capital is a bank's common equity (book value) plus qualifying cumulative perpetual preferred stock plus minority interests in equity accounts of consolidated subsidiaries.

With the passage of the FDICIA of 1991, a bank's capital adequacy is assessed according to where its leverage ratio (L) places it in one of five target zones listed in the Leverage Ratio column of Table 16–6. The leverage ratio is

$$L = \frac{\text{Core capital}}{\text{Assets}}$$

If a bank's leverage ratio is higher than 5 percent, it is well capitalized. At 4 percent or more, it is adequately capitalized; at less than 4 percent, it is undercapitalized; at less than

---

[9] The major exception is the Securities and Exchange Commission. Along with the NYSE and major stock exchanges, the SEC imposes on securities firms, retail brokers, and specialists a capital or net worth rule that is in effect a market value accounting rule.

Table **16–6**

SPECIFICATIONS OF CAPITAL CATEGORIES FOR PROMPT CORRECTIVE ACTION

Zone	(1) Leverage Ratio		(2) Total Risk- Based Ratio		(3) Tier I Risk- Based Ratio		Capital Directive/Other
1. Well-capitalized	5% or above	*and*	10% or above	*and*	6% or above	*and*	Not subject to a capital directive to meet a specific level for any capital measure
2. Adequately capitalized	4% or above*	*and*	8% or above	*and*	4% or above	*and*	Does not meet the definition of well capitalized
3. Undercapitalized	Under 4%†	*or*	Under 8%	*or*	Under 4%		
4. Significantly undercapitalized	Under 3%	*or*	Under 6%	*or*	Under 4%		
5. Critically undercapitalized	Under 2%	*or*	Under 2%	*or*	Under 2%		

*3 percent or higher for banks and savings associations that are not experiencing or anticipating significant growth.

†Under 3 percent for composite one-rated banks and savings associations that are not experiencing or anticipating significant growth.

SOURCE: Federal Reserve Board of Governors, Press Release, September 10, 1993.

3 percent, it is significantly undercapitalized; and at 2 percent or less, it is critically undercapitalized. Since 1995, less than 0.5 percent of the banking industry assets have been classified as undercapitalized. This compares to 31.3 percent undercapitalized in the fourth quarter of 1990 (i.e., during the 1989–1991 recession). Associated with each zone is a mandatory set of actions as well as a set of discretionary actions for regulators to take. The idea here is to enforce minimum capital requirements and to limit regulators' ability to show forbearance to the worst capitalized banks.

Since December 18, 1992, under the FDICIA legislation, regulators must take specific actions—**prompt corrective action** (PCA)—when a bank falls outside zone 1, or the well-capitalized category. Most importantly, a receiver must be appointed when a bank's book value of capital-to-assets (leverage) ratio falls to 2 percent or lower.[10] That is, receivership is mandatory even before the book value ratio falls to 0 percent.

Unfortunately, the leverage ratio as a measure of capital adequacy has three problems:

prompt corrective action

Mandatory action that regulators must take as a bank's capital ratio falls.

1. *Market value.* Even if a bank is closed when its leverage ratio falls below 2 percent, a 2 percent book capital-asset ratio could be consistent with a massive *negative* market value net worth. That is, there is no assurance that depositors and regulators (including taxpayers) are adequately protected against losses.[11]
2. *Asset risk.* By taking the denominator of the leverage ratio as total assets, the leverage ratio fails to consider, even partially, the different credit and interest rate risks of the assets that comprise total assets.

---

[10]Admittedly, managers and stockholders might exploit a number of loopholes and delaying tactics, especially through the courts.

[11]Many thrifts that were closed with low book capital values in the 1980s had negative net worths on a market value basis exceeding 30 percent.

3. *Off-balance-sheet activities.* Despite the massive growth in banks' off-balance-sheet activities, banks are not required to hold capital to meet the potential insolvency risks involved with such contingent assets and liabilities.

Risk-Based Capital Ratios

Considering the weaknesses of the simple capital-assets ratio just described, U.S. bank regulators formally agreed with other member countries of the Bank for International Settlements (BIS) to implement two new risk-based capital ratios for all commercial banks under their jurisdiction. The BIS phased in and fully implemented these risk-based capital ratios on January 1, 1993, under what has become known as the **Basel (or Basle) Accord.**

Basel (or Basle) Accord

An agreement that requires the imposition of risk-based capital ratios on banks in major industrialized countries.

Regulators currently enforce the Basel Accord's risk-based capital ratios as well as the traditional leverage ratio. Unlike the simple capital-asset (leverage) ratio, the calculation of these risk-based capital adequacy measures is quite complex. Their major innovation is to distinguish among the different credit risks of assets on the balance sheet and to identify the credit risk inherent in instruments off the balance sheet by using a risk-adjusted assets denominator in these capital adequacy ratios. In a very rough fashion, these capital ratios mark to market a bank's on- and off-balance-sheet positions to reflect its credit risk.

Capital. A bank's capital is divided into Tier I and Tier II. Tier I capital is primary or core capital; Tier II capital is supplementary capital. The total capital that the bank holds is defined as the sum of Tier I and Tier II capital. The definitions of Tier I core capital and Tier II supplementary capital are listed in Table 16–7.

Tier I Capital. Tier I capital is closely linked to a bank's book value of equity reflecting the concept of the core capital contribution of a bank's owners.[12] Basically, it includes the book value of common equity plus an amount of perpetual (nonmaturing) preferred stock plus minority equity interests held by the bank in subsidiaries minus goodwill. Goodwill is an accounting item that reflects the amount a bank pays above market value when it purchases or acquires other banks or subsidiaries.

Tier II Capital. Tier II capital is a broad array of secondary capital resources. It includes a bank's loan loss reserves up to a maximum of 1.25 percent of risk-adjusted assets plus various convertible and subordinated debt instruments with maximum caps.

Risk-Adjusted Assets. Risk-adjusted assets represent the denominator of the risk-based capital ratio. Two components comprise **risk-adjusted assets**: (1) risk-adjusted on balance sheet assets, and (2) risk-adjusted off balance sheet assets.

risk-adjusted assets

On- and off-balance-sheet assets whose value is adjusted for approximate credit risk.

To be adequately capitalized, a bank must hold a minimum total capital (Tier I core capital plus Tier II supplementary capital) to risk-adjusted assets ratio of 8 percent; that is, its **total risk-based capital ratio** is calculated as

total risk-based capital ratio

The ratio of an FI's total capital to its risk-adjusted assets.

$$\text{Total risk-based capital ratio} = \frac{\text{Total capital (Tier I plus Tier II)}}{\text{Risk-adjusted assets}} \geq 8\%$$

---

[12]However, loan loss reserves are assigned to Tier II capital because they often reflect losses that have already occurred rather than losses or insolvency risks that may occur in the future.

Table **16-7**

SUMMARY DEFINITION OF QUALIFYING CAPITAL FOR BANK HOLDING
COMPANIES USING YEAR-END 1992 STANDARDS

Components	Minimum Requirements after Transition Period
Core capital (Tier I)	Must equal or exceed 4 percent of weighted-risk assets
Common stockholders' equity	No limit
Qualifying cumulative and noncumulative perpetual preferred stock	Limited to 25 percent of the sum of common stock, minority interests, and qualifying perpetual preferred stock
Minority interest in equity accounts of consolidated subsidiaries	Organizations should avoid using minority interests to introduce elements not otherwise qualifying for Tier I capital
Less: Goodwill*	
Supplementary capital (Tier II)	Total of Tier II is limited to 100 percent of Tier I†
Allowance for loan and lease losses	Limited to 1.25 percent of weighted-risk assets
Perpetual preferred stock	No limit within Tier II
Hybrid capital instruments, perpetual debt and mandatory convertible securities	No limit within Tier II
Subordinated debt and intermediate-term preferred stock (original weighted-average maturity of 5 years or more)	Subordinated debt and intermediate-term preferred stock are limited to 50 percent of Tier I; amortized for capital purposes as they approach maturity†
Revaluation reserves (equity and buildings)	Not included; organizations encouraged to disclose; may be evaluated on a case-by-case basis for international comparisons; considered in making an overall assessment of capital
Deductions (from sum of Tier I and Tier II)	
Investments in unconsolidated subsidiaries	
Reciprocal holdings of banking organizations' capital securities	As a general rule, one-half of the aggregate investments would be deducted from Tier I capital and one-half from Tier II capital‡
Other deductions (such as other subsidiaries or joint ventures) as determined by supervisory authority	On a case-by-case basis or as a matter of policy after formal rule making
Total capital (Tier I + Tier II − deductions)	Must equal or exceed 8 percent of weighted-risk assets

*Goodwill on the books of bank holding companies before March 12, 1988, would be grandfathered for the transition period.

†Amounts in excess of limitations are permitted but do not qualify as capital.

‡A proportionately larger amount may be deducted from Tier I capital if the risks associated with the subsidiary so warrant.

SOURCE: Federal Reserve Board of Governors, Press Release, January 1989, Attachment II.

In addition, the Tier I core capital component of total capital has its own minimum guideline. The **Tier I (core) capital ratio** is calculated as follows:

tier I (core) capital ratio

The ratio of an FI's core capital to its risk-adjusted assets.

$$\text{Tier I (core) capital ratio} = \frac{\text{Core capital (Tier 1)}}{\text{Risk-adjusted assets}} \geq 4\%$$

That is, of the 8 percent total risk-based capital ratio, a bank must hold a minimum of 4 percent in core or primary capital. Thrifts also must operate according to these ratios. Capital ratios for credit unions vary by state, but they must maintain minimums. Contemporary Perspectives Box 16–2 highlights the growth of capital in the credit union industry; the growth is so large that some argue that the capital levels of credit unions are now excessive.

Contemporary Perspectives 16–2

Industry's Reserves Top 10%, Sparking Calls to Cut Back

When it comes to capital-to-asset ratios, credit unions have been hell-bent on raising reserves since the early 1980s and could have billions more than they need. The industry's ratio in June was 10.61%, or $31.8 billion. Ten years earlier credit unions had a 6.84% ratio, or $7.3 billion.

William N. Cox, a columnist for the industry newspaper Credit Union News, maintains that 8% capital is sufficient for typical credit unions—those that stick to consumer lending and have a stable membership base. If that's the case, credit unions have roughly $2.1 billion in capital that could be used more constructively or simply returned to members.

Other industry analysts are reluctant to set a hard-and-fast number for an adequate capital ratio, but most agree that if the industry keeps padding its cushion it could jeopardize future competitiveness.

"It think it's too much," said Tun Wai, chief economist for the National Association of Federal Credit Unions. "At some point you have to ask if you're taking away any services you could provide or are you taking away dividends you could give to members."

"It's a double-edged sword," said James Barth, a finance professor at Auburn (Ala.) University. "It means it's less likely that there will be failures, but it also means they're not leveraging that capital to make as many loans."

In the trenches, credit union executives are split between those who believe in maintaining capital commensurate with their risk and those who like an extra layer of protection, sometimes to help keep examiners off their backs. James C. Blaine, chief executive of State Employee Credit Union, Raleigh, N.C., said in an interview that building up capital is merely a matter of prudence. The $3.9 billion-asset institution now has a 7.75% capital ratio and is trying to build it to 8%. "Six is the statutory minimum" for the state, Mr. Blaine said. "Eight is reasonable. Above 10, you're taking away money from today's members."

Excess capital is a relatively new concern for the industry, said William F. Hampel, chief economist for the Credit Union National Association. Credit unions traditionally kept a minimum of capital and routinely returned much of their net income to members in the form of bonus dividends and loan interest refunds. The industry, and CUNA, began stressing the need for reserves during the economic upheaval of the early 1980s, Mr. Hampel said. The industry's average then was about 6.5%. But progress was slow until the early 1990s, when declining interest rates helped credit union earnings sky-rocket and deposits tumble, he said.

Although it took 11 years for credit union capital to increase 150 basis points in 1991, since then it has jumped 250 basis points, Mr. Hampel said. "That growth wasn't planned," he said. But some credit unions very consciously increased capital because of the regulators, Mr. Hampel and other observers said. During the 1980s the NCUA clamped down on institutions it considered undercapitalized, and other credit unions followed suit. "The regulators have done a good job of pressuring credit unions into building capital," Mr. Cox said.

Also, the NCUA adopted a new rating system—the Camel code, which grades institutions according to their capital, assets, management, earnings, and liquidity—that rewarded credit unions for keeping high capital levels. But now the NCUA has backed off from its capital demands, and Mr. Hampel and other observers expect credit unions to maintain capital and offer better prices and invest in new services, including technology. "I doubt credit unions are going to want to wholesale reduce capital, but I think more credit unions are going to be content to let it stay around current levels," Mr. Hampel said.

SOURCE: James B. Arndorfer, *The American Banker*, January 22, 1996. Reprinted with permission—American Banker.

In addition to their use to define adequately capitalized banks, risk-based capital ratios—along with the traditional leverage ratio—also define well-capitalized, undercapitalized, significantly undercapitalized, and critically undercapitalized banks as part of the prompt corrective action program under FDICIA. As with the simple leverage ratio for both the total risk-based capital ratio and the Tier I risk-based capital ratio, these five zones—specified in columns (2) and (3) of Table 16–6—assess capital adequacy and the actions regulators are mandated to take. Table 16–8 summarizes these regulatory actions.

Table **16–8**

SUMMARY OF PROMPT CORRECTIVE ACTION PROVISIONS OF THE FEDERAL DEPOSIT INSURANCE CORPORATION IMPROVEMENT ACT OF 1991

Zone	Mandatory Provisions	Discretionary Provisions
1. Well capitalized		
2. Adequately capitalized	1. Prohibit brokered deposits, except with FDIC approval	
3. Undercapitalized	1. Suspend dividends and management fees	1. Order recapitalization
	2. Require capital restoration plan	2. Restrict interaffiliate transactions
	3. Restrict asset growth	3. Restrict deposit interest rates
	4. Require approval for acquisitions	4. Restrict certain other activities
	5. Prohibit brokered deposits	5. Allow any other action that would better carry out prompt corrective action
4. Significantly undercapitalized	1. Same as for Zone 3	1. Enforce any Zone 3 discretionary actions
	2. Order recapitalization*	2. Appoint conservatorship or receivership if fails to submit or implement plan or recapitalize pursuant to order
	3. Restrict interaffiliate transactions*	
	4. Restrict deposit interest rates*	
	5. Restrict pay of officers	3. Enforce any other Zone 5 provision, if such action is necessary to carry out prompt corrective action
5. Critically undercapitalized	1. Same as for Zone 4	
	2. Appoint receiver/conservator within 90 days*	
	3. Appoint receiver if still in Zone 5 four quarters after becoming critically undercapitalized	
	4. Suspend payments on subordinated debt*	
	5. Restrict certain other activities	

*Not required if primary supervisor determines action would not serve purpose of prompt corrective action or if certain other conditions are met.

SOURCE: Federal Reserve Board of Governors, Press Release, September 10, 1993.

Next we discuss how to calculate a bank's or a thrift's risk-based capital ratio.

Calculating Risk-Based Capital Ratios

Risk-Adjusted On-Balance-Sheet Assets.   Under the risk-based capital plan, each bank assigns its assets to one of four categories of credit risk exposure: 0 percent, 20 percent, 50 percent, or 100 percent. Table 16–9 lists the key categories and assets in these categories. The risk-adjusted value of the bank's on-balance-sheet assets are

$$\sum_{i=1}^{n} w_i\, a_i$$

where

w_i = risk weight of the ith asset

a_i = dollar (book) value of the ith asset on the balance sheet

---

Table **16-9**

SUMMARY OF THE RISK-BASED CAPITAL STANDARDS FOR ON-BALANCE-SHEET ITEMS

Risk Categories

Category 1 (0% weight)

Cash, Federal Reserve Bank balances, U.S. Treasury securities, OECD* governments, and some U.S. agencies (e.g., GNMAs)

Category 2 (20% weight)

Cash items in the process of collection, U.S. and OECD interbank deposits and guaranteed claims

Some non–OECD bank and government deposits and securities, general obligation municipal bonds

Some mortgage-backed securities, claims collateralized by the U.S. Treasury and some other government securities

Category 3 (50% weight)

Loans fully secured by first liens on one- to four-family residential properties, other (revenue) municipal bonds, credit-equivalent amounts of interest rate and foreign exchange–related contracts except those assigned to a lower risk category

Category 4 (100% weight)

All other on-balance-sheet assets not listed above, including loans to private entities and individuals, some claims on non–OECD governments and banks, real assets, and investments in subsidiaries, contingent or guarantee contracts (e.g., loan commitments, letters of credit) except those assigned to a lower risk category

---

*Organization for Economic Cooperation and Development

SOURCE: Federal Reserve Board of Governors, Press Release, January 1989, Attachment III.

Risk-Adjusted Off-Balance-Sheet Activities. The calculation of the risk-adjusted values of the off-balance-sheet (OBS) activities involves some initial segregation of these activities. In particular, the calculation of the credit risk exposure or the risk-adjusted asset amount of contingent or guaranty contracts such as letters of credit or loan commitments differs from the calculation of the risk-adjusted asset amounts for foreign exchange and interest rate forward, option, and swap contracts. We next consider the risk-adjusted asset value of off-balance-sheet guaranty-type contracts and contingent contracts and then derivative or market contracts.

The Risk-Adjusted Asset Value of Off-Balance-Sheet Contingent Guaranty Contracts. The beginning step in calculating the risk-adjusted asset values of these off-balance-sheet items is to convert them into credit equivalent amounts—amounts equivalent to an on-balance-sheet item. The conversion factors are listed in Table 16–10.

> **credit equivalent amount**
>
> The amount of credit risk exposure of an off-balance-sheet item calculated by multiplying the face value of an off-balance-sheet instrument by a conversion factor.

To find the risk-adjusted asset value for off-balance-sheet items, we follow a two-step process. In the first step, we multiply the dollar amount outstanding of these items by the conversion factors listed in Table 16–10 to derive the **credit equivalent amounts.** These conversion factors convert an off-balance-sheet item into an equivalent credit or on-balance-sheet item. In the second step, we multiply these credit equivalent amounts by their

---

T a b l e **16–10**

CONVERSION FACTORS FOR OFF-BALANCE-SHEET CONTINGENT
OR GUARANTY CONTRACTS

Direct credit substitute standby letters of credit (100%)
Performance-related standby letters of credit (50%)
Unused portion of loan commitments with original maturity of more than one year (50%)
Commercial letters of credit (20%)
Bankers acceptances conveyed (20%)
Other loan commitments (0%)

SOURCE: Federal Reserve Board of Governors, Press Release, January 1989, Attachment IV.

appropriate risk weights as listed in Table 16–9. The appropriate risk weight in each case depends on the underlying counterparty, such as a municipality, a government, or a corporation, to the off-balance-sheet activity. For example, if the underlying party being guaranteed were a municipality issuing general obligation (GO) bonds and a bank issued an off-balance-sheet standby letter of credit backing the credit risk of the municipal GO issue, the risk weight is 0.2. If, on the other hand, the counterparty being guaranteed is a *private entity*, the appropriate risk weight is 1. Note that if the counterparty had been the central government, the risk weight is zero.

The Risk-Adjusted Asset Value of Off-Balance-Sheet Market Contracts or Derivative Instruments.   Modern FIs engage heavily in buying and selling OBS futures, options, forwards, swaps, caps, and other derivative securities contracts for interest rate and foreign exchange (FX) management and hedging reasons and to buy and sell such products on behalf of their customers (see Chapter 20). Each of these positions potentially exposes banks to **counterparty credit risk**, that is, the risk that the counterparty (or other side of a contract) will default if it suffers large actual or potential losses on its position. Such defaults mean that a bank must go back to the market to replace such contracts at (potentially) less favorable terms.

counterparty credit risk

The risk that the other party to a contract will default on payment obligations.

The calculation of the risk-adjusted asset values of OBS market contracts also requires a two-step approach. First, we calculate a conversion factor to create credit equivalent amounts. Second, we multiply the credit equivalent amounts by the appropriate risk weights.

Specifically, we convert the notional or face values of all nonexchange-traded swap, forward, and other derivative contracts into credit equivalent amounts. The credit equivalent amount itself is divided into a *potential exposure* element and a *current exposure* element. That is

$$\text{Credit equivalent amount of OBS derivative security items (\$)} = \text{Potential exposure (\$)} + \text{Current exposure (\$)}$$

potential exposure

The risk that a counterparty to a derivative securities contract will default in the future.

The **potential exposure** component reflects the credit risk if the counterparty to the contract defaults in the *future*. The probability of such an occurrence depends on future volatility of either interest rates for an interest rate contract or exchange rates for an exchange rate contract. The Bank of England and the Federal Reserve performed an enormous number of simulations and found that FX rates are far more volatile than interest rates. Thus, the potential exposure conversion factors in Table 16–11 are larger for foreign

Table **16–11**

CREDIT CONVERSION FACTORS FOR INTEREST RATE AND FOREIGN EXCHANGE CONTRACTS IN CALCULATING POTENTIAL EXPOSURE

Remaining Maturity	(1) Interest Rate Contracts	(2) Exchange Rate Contracts
1. 1 year or less	0.0%	1.0%
2. 1–5 years	0.5	5.0
3. More than 5 years	1.5	7.5

SOURCE: Federal Reserve Board of Governors, Press Release, August 1995, Section II.

exchange contracts than for interest rate contracts. Also note the larger potential credit risk exposure for longer-term contracts of both types.

In addition to calculating the potential exposure of an OBS market instrument, a bank also must calculate its **current exposure** with the instrument. This reflects the cost of replacing a contract should a counterparty default *today*. The bank calculates this *replacement cost* or *current exposure* by replacing the rate or price initially in the contract with the current rate or price for a similar contract and recalculates all the current and future cash flows that the current rate or price terms generate.[13] The bank discounts any future cash flows to give a current present value measure of the contract's replacement cost. If the contract's replacement cost is negative (i.e., the bank is out of the money—potentially losing on the contract—and profits if the counterparty defaults), regulations require the replacement cost (current exposure) to be set to zero. If the replacement cost is positive (i.e., the contract is profitable to the bank but it is harmed if the counterparty defaults), this value is used as the measure of current exposure. Since each swap or forward is in some sense unique, calculating current exposure involves a considerable task for the FI's management information systems. Indeed, specialized service firms are likely to perform this task for small banks.[14]

Once we total the current and potential exposure amounts to produce the credit equivalent amount for each contract, we multiply this dollar number by a risk weight to produce the final risk-adjusted asset amount for OBS market contracts. In general, the appropriate risk weight is .5, or 50 percent, that is

$$\text{Risk-adjusted asset value of OBS market contracts} = \text{Total credit equivalent amount} \times \text{Risk weight}$$

current exposure

The cost of replacing a derivative securities contract at today's prices.

---

[13]For example, suppose that a two-year forward foreign exchange contract was entered into in January 1997 at $1.55/£. In January 1998, the bank must evaluate the credit risk of the contract, which now has one year remaining. To do this, the bank replaces the agreed forward rate $1.55/£ with the forward rate on a current one-year forward contract, $1.65/£. It then recalculates its net gain or loss on the contract if it had to be replaced at this price. This is the contract's *replacement cost*.

[14]One large New York money center bank calculates, on average, the replacement cost of more than 6,000 different forward contracts alone.

Table **16-12**

BANK'S BALANCE SHEET
(in millions of dollars)

Weight	Assets		Liabilities/Equity		Capital Class
0%	Cash	$ 8	Demand deposits	$ 150	
	Balances due from Fed	13	Time deposits	500	
	Treasury bills	60	CDs	400	
	Long-term Treasury securities	50	Fed funds purchased	80	
	Long-term government agencies (GNMAs)	42	Convertible bonds	15	Tier II
20	Items in process of collection	10	Subordinated bonds	15	Tier II
	Long-term government agencies (FNMAs)	10			
	Munis (general obligation)	20	Perpetual preferred stock	5	Tier II
50	University dorm bonds (revenue)	34	Retained earnings	28	Tier I
	Residential 1–4 family mortgages	308	Common stock	12	Tier I
100	Commercial loans	530	Surplus	10	Tier I
	Third World loans	118		$1,215	
	Premises, equipment	22			
N/A	Reserve for loan losses	(10)			Tier II
	Total Assets	$1,215			

Off-balance-sheet items

100%	$80m in 2-year loan commitments to a large U.S. corp.
	$10m in standby letters of credit backing an issue of commercial paper
	$50m in commercial letters of credit
50%	One fixed-floating interest rate swap for 4 years with notational dollar value of $100m and replacement cost of $3m
	One two-year Euro$ contract for $40m with a replacement cost of –$1m

EXAMPLE 16 – 1

• • • • • •   *Calculation of Risk-Adjusted Value of Assets*

This example highlights six steps in calculating the risk-adjusted value of assets for a hypothetical bank balance sheet shown in Table 16–12.

Step 1:   The risk-adjusted value of the bank's on-balance-sheet assets are calculated as the book value of each asset times the percentage risk weight assigned to it.

Risk-adjusted on-balance-sheet assets = 0(8m + 13m + 60m + 50m + 42m) + .2 (10m + 10m + 20m) +.5(34m + 308m) + 1(530m + 118m + 22m) = $849 million

Although the simple book value of on-balance-sheet assets is $1,215 million, the risk-adjusted value is $849 million.

Step 2:   To find the risk-adjusted asset value for off-balance-sheet contingent or guaranty contracts, we first multiply the dollar amount outstanding of these items by the conversion factors listed in Table 16–10 to derive the credit equivalent amounts.

OBS Item	Face Value (in millions)		Conversion Factor		Credit Equivalent Amount (in millions)
Two-year loan commitment	$80	×	.5	=	$40
Standby letter of credit	10	×	1.0	=	10
Commercial letter of credit	50	×	.2	=	10

Step 3: Next we multiply the credit equivalent amounts calculated in step 2 by their appropriate risk weight. Since the counterparty for each of these contracts is a private agent, the appropriate weight is 1 (see Table 16–9).

OBS Item	Credit Equivalent Amount (in millions)		Risk Weight (w_i)		Risk-Adjusted Asset Amount (in millions)
Two-year loan commitment	$40	×	1.0	=	$40
Standby letter of credit	10	×	1.0	=	10
Commercial letter of credit	10	×	1.0	=	10
					$60

The bank's risk-adjusted asset value of its OBS contingencies and guarantees is $60 million.

Step 4: To determine the risk-based asset value for off-balance-sheet interest rate and foreign exchange contracts, we first calculate the credit equivalent amount for each item or contract using the conversion factors listed in Table 16–11 to find the potential exposure and add the current exposure or replacement cost should the counterparty default.

		Potential Exposure + Current Exposure					
Type of Contract (remaining maturity)	Notational Principal	×	Potential Exposure Conversion Factor =	Potential Exposure ($)	Replacement Cost	Current Exposure =	Credit Equivalent Amount
4-year fixed-floating interest rate swap	$100m	×	.005 =	$.5m	3m	3m	3.5m
2-year forward foreign exchange contract	$ 40m	×	.05 =	2m	−1m	0m	2m

Note that the replacement cost for the two-year forward contract is *minus* $1 million. That is, in this example, our bank actually stands to *gain* if the counterparty were to default. Exactly why the counterparty would do this when it is "in the money" is unclear. Regulators cannot permit a bank to gain from a default by a counterparty, however, because this might produce all types of perverse risk-taking incentives. Consequently, the current exposure must be set equal to zero (as shown). Thus, the sum of potential exposure ($2 million) and current exposure ($0) produces a total credit equivalent amount of $2 million for this contract.

Step 5:   Since the bank has only two OBS derivative contracts, summing the two credit equivalent amounts produces a total credit equivalent amount of $5.5 million ($3.5m + $2m) for the bank's OBS market contracts. Next we multiply this credit equivalent amount by the appropriate risk weight. Specifically, to calculate the risk-adjusted asset value for the bank's OBS derivative or market contracts, we multiply the credit equivalent amount by the appropriate risk weight, which for virtually all over-the-counter derivative security products is .5, or 50 percent.

$$\begin{array}{c} \text{Risk-adjusted asset} \\ \text{value of OBS derivatives} \end{array} = \begin{array}{c} \$5.5 \text{ million} \\ \text{(credit equivalent} \\ \text{amount)} \end{array} \times \begin{array}{c} 0.5 \\ \text{(risk weight)} \end{array} = \$2.75 \text{ million}$$

Step 6:   According to these calculations, the total risk-adjusted assets for the bank are the sum of the risk-adjusted assets on the balance sheet ($849 million), the risk-adjusted value of the OBS contingencies and guarantees ($60 million), and the risk-adjusted value of OBS derivatives ($2.75 million), or $911.75 million.   • • •

From Table 16–12, the bank's Tier I capital (retained earnings, common stock, and surplus) totals $50 million; Tier II capital (convertible bonds, subordinate bonds, perpetual preferred stock, and reserve for loan losses) totals $45 million. The resulting total capital is therefore $95 million.

We can now calculate our bank's overall capital adequacy in light of the risk-based capital requirements

$$\text{Tier I (core) capital} = \frac{\$50m}{\$911.75m} = 5.48\%$$

and

$$\text{Total risk-based capital ratio} = \frac{\$95m}{\$911.75m} = 10.42\%$$

Since the minimum Tier I capital ratio required is 4 percent and the minimum risk-based capital ratio required is 8 percent, this bank has more than adequate capital, exceeding the required minimums by 1.48 percent and 2.42 percent, respectively. (In fact it is in capital zone 2 under the prompt corrective action (PCA) plan; see Table 16–6.)

The book value of assets, risk-weighted assets, Tier I capital ratio, total capital ratio, and leverage ratio for the 25 largest banks studied in 1997 by Salomon Brothers are shown in Table 16–13. As the table data indicates, all exceeded the 4 and 8 percent minimum requirements by significant margins. All but one (SunTrust Banks) meet the well-capitalized (zone 1) criteria specified under the PCA regulations (see Table 16–6). If anything, these major U.S. banks were significantly overcapitalized.

Interest Rate Risk, Market Risk, and Risk-Based Capital.   From a regulatory perspective, existing risk-based capital ratios are adequate only so long as a bank is not exposed to undue interest rate or market risk. The reason is that the existing 8 percent risk-based capital ratio considers only the adequacy of a bank's capital to meet both its on- and off-balance-sheet credit risks. Not explicitly accounted for is the insolvency risk emanating from interest rate risk (maturity mismatches) and market (trading) risk.

Table 16–13

RISK-BASED CAPITAL RATIOS FOR LARGE U.S. BANKS

Ticker	Name	Total Assets (in millions)	Risk-Weighted Assets (in millions)	Tier I Capital Ratio	Total Capital-Asset	Leverage Ratio
CMB	Chase Manhattan Corp.	$303,989	$230,887	8.22%	12.27%	6.68%
CCI	Citicorp	256,853	224,915	8.40	12.30	7.45
BAC	BankAmerica Corp.	232,446	205,433	7.30	11.40	6.92
NB	NationsBank	187,298	149,053	7.24	11.58	6.27
JPM	J.P. Morgan & Co.	184,879	103,122	8.80	13.00	6.10
CHL	Chemical Bank	182,926	130,909	8.45	12.10	6.43
FTU	First Union Corp.	131,880	98,966	6.51	10.36	5.49
FCN	First Chicago NBD Corp.	122,002	99,454	7.80	11.90	6.90
BT	Bankers Trust NY	104,002	53,021	8.50	13.90	5.06
ONE	Banc One Corp.	90,454	78,180	9.97	13.94	8.87
FLT	Fleet Financial Group	84,432	69,384	7.62	11.24	6.41
PNC	PNC Bank Corp.	73,404	59,539	8.00	11.56	6.37
NOB	Norwest Corp.	72,134	49,255	8.16	10.23	5.69
KEY	KeyCorp.	66,339	53,933	7.53	10.85	6.20
I	First Interstate	58,071	45,085	7.61	10.52	6.28
BK	Bank of New York Co	53,685	53,492	8.39	13.04	8.46
WFC	Wells Fargo & Co.	50,316	41,200	8.80	12.45	7.45
BKB	Bank of Boston Corp.	42,397	42,636	7.95	12.78	7.38
STI	SunTrust Banks, Inc.	46,471	36,742	7.78	9.71	6.71
WB	Wachovia Corp.	44,981	38,470	9.43	13.64	8.36
RNB	Republic NY Corp.	43,882	23,367	14.72	24.96	6.24
BBI	Barnett Banks Inc.	41,554	30,188	8.25	11.51	6.16
MEL	Mellon Bank Corp.	40,646	38,295	8.30	11.37	7.80
NCC	National City Corp.	36,199	29,806	8.54	13.13	7.37
CMA	Comerica Inc.	35,470	30,969	7.63	11.21	6.87

SOURCE: Salomon Brothers, *Commercial Banks, U.S. Equity Research* (New York: 1996). Copyright 1997 Salomon Brothers, Inc. This table and table statistics contain data from Salomon Brothers, Inc. Although the information in this table was obtained from sources that Salomon Brothers, Inc., believes to be reliable, Salomon does not guarantee its accuracy, and such information may be incomplete or condensed. All figures included in this table constitute Salomon's judgment as of the original publication date.

To meet these deficiencies, the Federal Reserve (along with the BIS) has developed additional capital requirement proposals and capital requirements for interest rate risk (see Chapter 17) and market risk (see Chapter 18). Although the Fed relies primarily on examiners' judgments as to what is excessive interest rate exposure, it still focuses on the change in the FI's market value of equity when rates change. The Fed implemented capital requirements for market risk in 1998 at which time two alternative models (explained in Chapter 19) may be used to measure market risk by most large banks. The market risk capital requirement must be held in addition to the 8 percent risk-based capital ratio for credit risk discussed earlier (i.e., it can be viewed as an "add on").

Criticisms of the Risk-Based Capital Ratio.   The risk-based capital requirement seeks to improve on the simple leverage ratio by (1) more systematically accounting for credit risk differences among assets, (2) incorporating off-balance-sheet risk exposures, and (3) applying a similar capital requirement across all the major banks (and banking centers) in the world. Unfortunately, the risk-based capital requirement has a number of conceptual and applicability weaknesses in achieving these objectives.

1. *Risk weights.* It is unclear how closely the four risk weight categories reflect true credit risk. For example, residential mortgage loans have a 50 percent risk weight; commercial loans have a 100 percent risk weight. Taken literally, these relative weights imply that commercial loans are exactly twice as risky as mortgage loans.[15]

2. *Balance sheet incentive problems.* The fact that different assets have different risk weights may induce bankers to engage in balance sheet asset allocation games. For example, given any amount of total capital, a bank can always increase its reported risk-based capital ratio by reducing its risk-adjusted assets, the denominator of the ratio. An FI manager has a number of interesting opportunities to do this under the new plan. For example, residential mortgages have a 50 percent risk weight, and GNMA mortgage-backed securities have 0 percent risk weight. Suppose that a bank pools all its mortgages and then sells them to outside investors (see Chapter 12). If it then replaced the mortgages it sold with GNMA securities backing similar pools of mortgages to those securitized, it could significantly reduce its risk-adjusted asset amount.

3. *Portfolio aspects.* The new plan also ignores credit risk portfolio diversification opportunities. As we discuss in Chapter 11, when returns on assets have negative or less than perfectly positive correlations, an FI may lower its portfolio risk through diversification. As constructed, the new capital adequacy plan is essentially a linear risk measure that ignores correlations or covariances among assets and asset group credit risks, such as between residential mortgages and commercial loans.[16] That is, the banker weights each asset separately by the appropriate risk weight and then sums those numbers to get an overall measure of credit risk.

4. *Bank specialness.* Giving private sector commercial loans the highest credit risk weighting may reduce the incentive for banks to make such loans relative to holding other assets. This may reduce the amount of bank loans to business as well as the degree of bank monitoring and may have associated negative externality effects on the economy. That is, one aspect of banks' special functions—bank lending—may be muted.[17]

5. *Equal weight of all commercial loans.* Loans made to an AAA-rated company have a credit risk weight of 1, as do loans made to a CCC-rated company. That is, within a broad risk-weight class such as commercial loans, credit risk quality differences are

---

[15]However, R. B. Avery and A. Berger show evidence that these risk weights do a good job in distinguishing between failing and nonfailing banks. See "Risk-Based Capital and Deposit Insurance Reform," *Journal of Banking and Finance* (1991), pp. 847–74. By contrast, David S. Jones and Kathleen Kuester King, "The Implementation of Prompt Corrective Action: An Assessment," *Journal of Banking and Finance* (1995) find that risk-based capital would have done a poor job in identifying failing banks in the 1984–1989 period had it been used for prompt corrective action purposes.

[16]In a portfolio context, the new capital adequacy plan assumes that asset and OBS risks are independent of each other.

[17]This effect has been of great concern and controversy in recent years. Indeed, the high-risk weight given to commercial loans relative to securities has been blamed in part for inducing a credit crunch and a reorientation of bank portfolios from commercial loans toward securities.

not recognized. This may create perverse incentives for banks to pursue lower-quality customers, thereby increasing the risk of the bank.[18]

6. *Other risks.*   Although market risk exposure has now been integrated into the risk-based capital requirements, the plan does not yet account for other risks such as foreign exchange rate risk, asset concentration risk, and operating risk. A more complete risk-based capital requirement would include these risks.[19]

7. *Competition.*   As a result of tax and accounting differences across banking systems and in safety net coverages, the 8 percent risk-based capital requirement has not created a level competitive playing field across banks as intended by many proponents of the plan. In particular, Japan and the United States have very different accounting, tax, and safety net rules that significantly affect the comparability of U.S. and Japanese bank risk-based capital ratios. The provisions of the Basle Accord also allow differences in bank capital rules to persist among countries. Different capital elements are allowed for both Tier I and Tier II capital across countries. Also, many countries use a 10 percent risk category that is not used in the United States.[20]

Concept Questions

1. What are the major strengths of the risk-based capital ratios?
2. You are an FI manager with a total risk-based capital ratio of 6 percent. What are four strategies to meet the required 8 percent ratio in a short period of time without raising new capital? Discuss each.
3. Why isn't a capital ratio levied on exchange-traded derivative contracts?
4. What are three problems with the simple leverage ratio measure of capital adequacy?
5. What is the difference between Tier I and Tier II capital?
6. What is one asset in each of the four risk-weight categories?

CAPITAL REQUIREMENTS FOR OTHER FINANCIAL INTERMEDIARIES

Securities Firms

Unlike the book value capital rules employed by bank and thrift regulators, the capital requirements for broker-dealers set by the SEC's Rule 15C 3–1 in 1975 are close to a market value accounting rule. Essentially, broker-dealers must calculate a market value for their net worth on a day-to-day basis and ensure that their net worth–assets ratio exceeds 2 percent:

---

[18]One possible argument in support of the same risk weight for all commercial loans is that if the bank holds a well-diversified commercial loan portfolio, the unsystematic risk of each individual loan is diversified away, leaving only systematic credit risk. However, the betas or systematic risk sensitivity of loans may still differ across loans.

[19]Interestingly, the risk-based capital plans for property-casualty and life insurers (discussed later in this chapter) have more complete coverage of risks than does the bank plan.

[20]See J. Wagster, "Impact of the Basle Accord on International Banks," *Journal of Finance*, September 1996, pp. 1321–1346 and J. Wagster, J. Kolari, and K. Cooper, "Market Reaction to National Discretion in Implementing the Basle Accord," *Journal of Financial Research,* Fall 1996, pp. 339–357.

$$\frac{\text{Net worth}}{\text{Assets}} \geq 2\%$$

The essential idea is that if a broker-dealer must liquidate all assets at near market values, a capital cushion of 2 percent should be sufficient to satisfy all customer liabilities such as brokerage accounts held with the firm.[21]

Specifically, to compute net capital, the broker-dealer calculates book capital or net worth—the difference between the book values of its assets and liabilities—and then makes a number of adjustments: subtracts (1) all assets such as fixed assets not readily convertible into cash and (2) securities that cannot be publicly offered or sold. Moreover, the dealer must make other deductions, or "haircuts," reflecting potential market value fluctuations in assets. For example, the net capital rule requires haircuts on illiquid equities of up to 40 percent and on debt securities generally between 0 and 9 percent. Finally, other adjustments must reflect unrealized profits and losses, subordinated liabilities, contractual commitments, deferred taxes, options, commodities and commodity futures, and certain collateralized liabilities.

Thus, broker-dealers must make significant adjustments to the book value of net worth to reach an approximate market value net worth figure. This figure must exceed 2 percent of assets.

Life Insurance

In 1993, the life insurance industry adopted a model risk-based capital plan. Although similar in nature to that adopted by banks and thrifts, it is more extensive in that it also covers other types of risk (discussed later in this chapter). The capital requirements which are imposed at the state level are heavily influenced by recommendations from the National Association of Insurance Commissioners (NAIC). We describe the NAIC approach next.

The model begins by identifying four risks faced by the life insurer: C1, asset risk; C2, insurance risk; C3, interest rate risk; and C4, business risk.

C1: Asset Risk.   Asset risk reflects the riskiness of the life insurer's asset portfolio. It is similar in spirit to the risk-adjusted asset calculations for banks and thrifts in that a credit risk weight is multiplied by the dollar or face value of the assets on the balance sheet. Table 16–14 shows the relative asset risk weights for life and PC insurers. Thus, an insurer with $100 million in common stocks would have a risk-based capital requirement of $30 million, while one with $100 million in BBB corporate bonds would have a requirement of only $1 million.

mortality risk

The risk of death.

morbidity risk

The risk of ill-health.

C2: Insurance Risk.   Insurance risk captures the risk of adverse changes in **mortality risk** and **morbidity risk.** As we discuss in Chapter 4, mortality tables give life insurers an extremely accurate idea of the probability that an insured will die in any given year. Epidemics such as AIDS, however, can upset these predictions quite drastically. As a result, insurers must adjust insurance by an *insurance risk factor*. They perform similar calculations for accident and health insurance, which cover morbidity risk.

---

[21]If a broker fails with negative net worth, the SIPC provides guarantees of up to $500,000 per customer (see Chapter 15).

Table **16–14**

RISK-BASED CAPITAL (RBC) FACTORS FOR SELECTED ASSETS OF LIFE AND PROPERTY-CASUALTY INSURERS

	Insurer	
	---	---
Assets	**Life**	**Property-Casualty**
Bonds		
U.S. government	0.0%	0.0%
NAIC 1: AAA-A*	0.3	0.3
NAIC 2: BBB	1.0	1.0
NAIC 3: BB	4.0	2.0
NAIC 4: B	9.0	4.5
NAIC 5: CCC	20.0	10.0
NAIC 6: In or near default	30.0	30.0
Mortgages		
Residential mortgages (whole loans)	0.5†	5.0
Commercial mortgages	3.0†	5.0
Stocks		
Common stock	30.0	15.0
Preferred stock—bond factor for same NAIC category plus	2.0	2.0

*Includes agencies and most collateralized mortgage obligations.

†Mortgage factors are for loans in good standing. These factors will be adjusted for a company's default experience relative to the industry.

SOURCE: Salomon Brothers, *Insurance Strategies* (New York: 1993). Copyright 1997 Salomon Brothers, Inc. This table and table statistics contain data from Salomon Brothers, Inc. Although the information in this table was obtained from sources that Salomon Brothers, Inc., believes to be reliable, Salomon does not guarantee its accuracy, and such information may be incomplete or condensed. All figures included in this table constitute Salomon's judgment as of the original publication date.

C3: Interest Rate Risk.   Interest rate risk in part reflects the fixed-rate, long-term nature of liabilities and the probability of withdrawal as interest rates change. For example, insurance company-issued guaranteed investment contracts (GICs) have similar characteristics to long-term, fixed-rate bank deposits, and withdrawals and values are highly sensitive to interest rate movements. As we discuss also in Chapter 13, liquidity problems have led to a number of insurer insolvencies in recent years. With respect to interest rate risk, insurers must divide liabilities into three risk classes: low risk (0.5 percent risk-based capital requirement), medium risk (1 percent capital requirement), and high risk (2 percent capital requirement).

C4: Business Risk.   As we discuss in Chapter 15, states have organized guaranty funds that pay partially for insurer insolvencies by levying a charge on surviving firms. Thus, the capital requirement for business risk is set to equal the maximum potential assessment by state guaranty funds (2 percent for life and annuity premiums and 0.5 percent for health premiums for each surviving insurer). Also, company-specific fraud and litigation risks might require an additional capital charge.

After calculating the dollar values ($C1$, $C2$, $C3$, and $C4$), the life insurance manager computes a risk-based capital measure (RBC) based on the following equation

Table **16–15**

CALCULATION OF TOTAL RISK-BASED CAPITAL (RBC) FOR PROPERTY-CASUALTY INSURERS

Risk	Type	Description
R0	Asset	RBC for investments (common and preferred) in property-casualty affiliates
R1	Asset	RBC for fixed income
R2	Asset	RBC for equity; includes common and preferred stocks (other than in property-casualty affiliates) and real estate
R3	Credit	RBC for reinsurance recoverables and other receivables
R4	Underwriting	RBC for loss and loss adjustment expense (LAE) reserves plus growth surcharges
R5	Underwriting	RBC for written premiums plus growth surcharges

$$RBC = R0 + \sqrt{R1^2 + R2^2 + R3^2 + R4^2 + R5^2}$$

$$RBC = \sqrt{(C1 + C3)^2 + C2^2} + C4$$

Because the four risks are unlikely to move in the same direction at the same time, the formula sums the risks together and adjusts, when appropriate, for correlations among the risks. As calculated, the RBC is the minimum required capital for the life insurer. The insurer compares this risk-based capital measure to the actual capital and surplus (total capital) held

$$\frac{\text{Total surplus and capital}}{\text{RBC}}$$

If this ratio is higher than 1, the life insurance manager is meeting or exceeds the minimum capital requirements. If the ratio falls below 1, the manager is subject to regulatory scrutiny.[22]

Property-Casualty Insurance

Capital requirements for property-casualty insurers are quite similar to those for life insurance companies. For this industry, the risk-based capital requirements—introduced by the NAIC in 1994—are quite similar to the life insurance industry's RBC except that they have six (instead of four) risk categories, including three separate asset risk categories. The risk weights for these different types of assets are shown in Table 16–14. The risk weights in some areas—especially common stock—are lower than those for life insurers because of the relatively smaller exposures of PC companies to this type of asset risk. The six different types of risk and the calculation of RBC (to be compared with a PC insurer's total capital and surplus) are shown in Table 16–15.

---

[22]NAIC testing found that 87 percent of the industry had a total surplus and capital-RBC ratio above 1 at the time of the RBC ratio's introduction. This description of the life insurance risk-based capital ratio is based on L. S. Goodman, P. Fischer, and C. Anderson, "The Impact of Risk-Based Capital Requirements on Asset Allocation for Life Insurance Companies," *Insurance Executive Review,* Fall 1992, pp. 14–21; and P. J. Bouyoucos, M. H. Siegel, and E. B. Raisel, *Risk-Based Capital for Insurers: A Strategic Opportunity to Enhance Franchise Value*, (New York: Goldman Sachs, Industry Resource Group, 1992).

Table **16–16**

RISK-BASED CAPITAL (RBC) CHARGES FOR TYPICAL INSURANCE COMPANY

Risk	Description	RBC Charge (millions)
R0	Affiliated property-casualty	$ 10
R1	Fixed income	5
R2	Common stock	10
R3	Credit	10
R4	Reserve	40
R5	Premium	25
Total charges before covariance		$100

$$RBC = 10 + \sqrt{5^2 + 10^2 + 10^2 + 40^2 + 25^2} = \$59.50$$

SOURCE: Salomon Brothers, *Insurance Strategies* (New York: 1993). Copyright 1997 Salomon Brothers, Inc. This table and table statistics contain data from Salomon Brothers, Inc. Although the information in this table was obtained from sources that Salomon Brothers, Inc., believes to be reliable, Salomon does not guarantee its accuracy, and such information may be incomplete or condensed. All figures included in this table constitute Salomon's judgment as of the original publication date.

The calculation of RBC assumes that risks R1 to R5 are independent of each other—that is, they have a zero correlation coefficient so that a change in one risk component has no effect on any other component, whereas investments in PC affiliates, R0, are assumed to be perfectly correlated with the net risk of the R1 to R5 components so that a $1 change in R0 results in a $1 change in RBC.[23] If total capital and surplus of a PC insurer exceed the calculated RBC, the insurer is viewed as being adequately capitalized. For example, suppose that a PC insurer has total capital and surplus of $60 million and its RBC charge is calculated as $59.5 million (as shown in Table 16–16); it has a capital-RBC ratio exceeding 1 (i.e., 60/59.5 = 1.008) and is adequately capitalized.[24]

Concept Questions

1. How do the capital requirements for securities firms differ from the book value capital rules for banks and thrifts?
2. What types of risks does the NAIC include in estimating life insurance firms' RBC?
3. How do the NAIC's model risk-based capital requirements for PC insurers differ from the life insurance industry's RBC?

● ●

[23]See Alfred Weinberger, *Insurance Strategies* (New York: Salomon Brothers, 1993).

[24]For a critical evaluation of the NAIC's RBC plan, see J. Cummins, S. E. Harrington, and R. Klein, "Insolvency Exercise, Risk-Based Capital and Prompt Corrective Action in Property-Liability Insurance," *Journal of Banking and Finance*, 1995, pp. 511–527.

S U M M A R Y

This chapter reviewed the role of an FI's capital in insulating it against credit, interest rate, and other risks. According to economic theory, shareholder capital or net worth should be measured on a market value basis as the difference between the market value of assets and liabilities. In actuality, regulators use book value accounting rules. A book value capital adequacy ratio accounts for credit risk exposure in a rough fashion, but it overlooks the effects of interest rate changes and interest rate exposure on net worth. We analyzed the specific capital rules adopted by banks and thrifts, insurance companies, and securities firms and discussed their problems and weaknesses. In particular, we looked at ways that bank, thrift, PC, and life insurance regulators are now adjusting book value–based capital rules to account for different types of risk as part of their imposition of risk-based capital adequacy ratios. As a result, actual capital requirements in banks, life insurance companies, PC insurance companies, and thrifts are moving closer to market value-based capital requirements.

P E R T I N E N T   W E B   S I T E S

Bank for International Settlements   http://www.bis.org/home.htm

Board of Governors of the Federal Reserve   http://www.bog.frb.fed.us/

Federal Deposit Insurance Corp.   http://www.fdic.gov/

Government National Mortgage Association   http://www.ginniemae.gov/

National Association of Securities Dealers   http://www.nasd.com/

National Association of Insurance Commissioners   http://www.naic.org/

Salomon Brothers   http://www.sbil.com.uk/

Securities and Exchange Commission http://www.sec.com

Security Investors Protection Corp.   http://www.sipc.org/

Capital Adequacy

1. What five functions does an FI's capital play?
2. What is one of the new and major features in the estimation of credit risk under the 1988 Basle capital requirements?
3. What is the difference between Tier I and Tier II capital?
4. What are some of the arguments for and against the use of market value versus book value of capital?
5. Why is the market value of equity a better measure of a bank's ability to absorb losses than book value of equity?
6. Simplebank has the following balance sheet (in millions):

Assets		Liabilities and Equity	
Cash	$ 20	Deposits	$ 950
T-bills	40	Subordinated	50
Residential		debentures	
mortgages	600	Common stock	60
Other loans	430	Retained Earnings	30
	1,090		1,090

If Simplebank has no off-balance sheet activities, what is its

a. Total risk-based capital ratio?
b. Tier I capital ratio?

7. What is the contribution to the asset base of the following items under the Basle requirements? Under the U.S. capital-assets rule?
a. $10 million cash reserves.
b. $50 million 91-day U.S. Treasury bills.
c. $25 million cash items in the process of collection.
d. $5 million U.K. government bonds.
e. $5 million Australian short-term government bonds.
f. $1 million general obligation municipal bonds.
g. $40 million repurchase agreements (against U.S. Treasuries).
h. $500 million 1–4 family home mortgages.
i. $500 million commercial and industrial loans.
j. $100,000 performance-related standby letters of credit to a blue chip corporation.
k. $100,000 performance-related standby letters of credit to a municipality issuing general obligation bonds.

l. $7 million commercial letter of credit to a foreign corporation.

m. $3 million 5-year loan commitment to an OECD government.

n. $8 million bankers' acceptance conveyed to a U.S. corporation.

o. $17 million 3-year loan commitment to a private agent.

p. $17 million 3-month loan commitment to a private agent.

q. $30 million standby letter of credit to back a corporate issue of commercial paper.

r. $4 million 5-year interest rate swap with no current exposure (the counter party is a private agent).

s. $4 million 5-year interest rate swap with no current exposure (the counter party is a municipality).

t. $6 million 2-year currency swap with $500,000 current exposure (the counter party is a private agent).

8. Onshore Bank has $20 million in assets. It recently calculated the risk-adjusted value of its assets at $10 million. It has $500,000 of Tier I capital and $400,000 of Tier II capital. How do the following transactions affect the value of its Tier I and total capital ratios? What will the new values be?

a. The bank repurchases $100,000 worth of stock.

b. The bank issues $2,000,000 of CDs and uses the proceeds for loans to homeowners.

c. The bank receives $500,000 in deposits and invests them in T-bills.

d. The bank issues $800,000 in common stock and lends it to help finance a new shopping mall.

e. The bank issues $1,000,000 in nonqualifying perpetual preferred stock and purchases general obligation municipal bonds.

f. Homeowners pay back $4,000,000 of mortgages; the proceeds are used to build new ATMs.

The following information is for questions 9–12. Consider a bank's balance sheet as follows:

On-Balance-Sheet Items	Category	Face Value
Cash	1	$ 121,600
Short-term government securities (< 92 days)	1	5,400
Long-term government securities (> 92 days)	1	414,400
Federal Reserve stock	1	9,800
Repos secured by Federal agencies	2	159,000
Claims on U.S. depository institutions	2	937,900
Short-term (< 1 yr.) claims on foreign banks	2	1,640,000
General obligation municipals	2	170,000
Claims on or guaranteed by Federal agencies	2	26,500
Municipal revenue bonds	3	112,900
Loans	4	6,645,700
Claims on foreign banks (> 11 yr.)	4	5,800

Off-Balance-Sheet Items

Guaranteed by U.S. Government (risk weight category 1)

	Conversion Factor	Face Value
Loan commitments		
< 1 year	0%	$ 300
1–5 year	50	1,140
Standby letters of credit		
Performance related	5	200
Other	100	100

Backed by Domestic Depository Institution (risk weight category 2)

	Conversion	Face Value
Loan commitments		
< 1 year	0	1,000
> 1 year	50	3,000

	Conversion Factor	Face Value
Standby letters of credit		
Performance related	50	200
Other	100	56,400
Commercial letters of credit	20	400

Backed by State or Local Government Revenues (risk weight category 3)

	Conversion	Face Value
Loan Commitments		
> 1 year	50	100
Standby letters of credit		
Non-performance related	50	135,400

	Conversion Factor	Face Value
Extended to Corporate Customers (risk weight category 4)		
Loan Commitments		
< 1 year	0	2,980,000
>1 year	50	3,046,278
Standby letters of credit		
Performance related	50	101,543
Other	100	485,000
Commercial letters of credit	20	78,978
Note issuance facilities	50	20,154
Forward agreements	100	5,900
Category II Interest Rate Market Contracts (Current Exposure assumed to be zero)		
< 1 year (notional amount)	0	2,000
> 1-5 year (notional amount)	.5	5,000

9. What is the bank's risk-adjusted asset base?
10. What are the bank's Tier I and total risk-based capital requirements?
11. Using the leverage ratio requirement, what is the bank's minimum regulatory capital required to keep it in the well capitalized zone?
12. What is the bank's capital level if the par value of its equity is $150,000; surplus value of equity is $200,000; qualifying perpetual preferred stock is $50,000? Does the bank meet Basle (Tier I) capital standards? Does the bank comply with the well capitalized leverage ratio requirement?
13. How does the leverage ratio test impact the stringency of regulatory monitoring of bank capital positions?
14. What are some arguments against the risk-based capital ratios?
15. Third Bank has the following balance sheet in millions of dollars with the risk weights in parentheses. All assets are held by corporate customers.

Assets			Liabilities and Equity	
Cash	(0%)	$20	Deposits	$175
OECD interbank deposits	(20)	25	Subordinated debt (2.5 yrs.)	3
Mortgage loans	(50)	70	Cumulative preferred stock	5
Consumer loans	(100)	70	Equity	2
Total		$185		$185

In addition, the bank has $30 million in performance-related standby letters of credit (LCs), $40 million in 2-year forward FX contracts that are in the money by $1 million, and $300 million in 6-year interest rate swaps that are out of the money by $2 million. Credit conversion factors follow:

Performance-related standby LCs	50%
1–5 year foreign exchange contracts	5
11–5 year interest rate swaps	0.5
5–10 year interest rate swaps	1.5

a. What are the risk-adjusted *on-balance-sheet* assets of the bank as defined under the Basle Accord?
b. What is the total capital required for both *off- and on-balance-sheet* assets?
c. Does the bank have enough capital to meet the Basle requirements? If not, what minimum Tier I or total capital does it need to meet the requirement?

16. Second Bank has the following balance sheet in millions of dollars with the risk weights in parentheses. Assume that all clients are corporate clients.

Assets			Liabilities and Equity	
Cash	(0%)	$20	Deposits	$130
Mortgage loans	(50)	50	Subordinated debt (over 5 yrs.)	5
Commercial loans	(100)	70	Equity	5
		$140		$140

In addition, the bank has $20 million (100 percent) in commercial standby letters of credit and $40 million in 10-year forward contracts that are in the money by $1 million.

a. What is the risk-adjusted on-balance-sheet assets of the bank as defined under the Basle Accord?
b. What is the total capital required for both off- and on-balance-sheet assets?
c. Does the bank have enough capital to meet the Basle requirements?

17. A securities firm has the following balance sheet (in millions):

Assets		Liabilities and Equity	
Cash	40	5-day commercial paper	20
Debt securities	300	Bonds	550
Equity securities	500	Debentures	300
Other assets	60	Equity	30
	900		900

The debt securities are $1,000 face value bonds with a coupon rate of 6 percent issued at par five years ago with 20 years remaining until maturity. These bonds now have a required return of 8 percent. The equity securities were recently purchased; their book value is approximately equal to their market values. The other assets, primarily its own building and equipment, were recently assessed at $80 million. The company has 1 million shares outstanding and

its stock price is $35 per share. Is this company in compliance with SEC Rule 15C 3–1?

18. A life insurance company has estimated the following capital requirements for each of the risk classes: asset risk (C1) = $5 million, insurance risk (C2) = $4 million, interest rate risk (C3) = $1 million, and business risk (C4) = $3 million.

    a. What is the required risk-based capital for the life insurance company?

    b. If surplus and capital held by the company total $9 million, does it meet the minimum requirements?

    c. How much capital does it need to raise to meet the minimum requirements?

19. A property-casualty firm has estimated the following required charges for its various risk classes (in millions)

Risk	Description	RBC Charge
R0	Affiliated P/C	$ 2
R1	Fixed income	3
R2	Common stock	4
R3	Reinsurance	3
R4	Loss adjustment expense	2
R5	Written premiums	3
Total		$17

    a. What is the RBC charge as per the model recommended by the NAIC?

    b. If the firm currently has $7 million in capital, what should its surplus be to meet the minimum requirement?

20. Go to the FDIC web site and look up the assets, deposits, liabilities, and equity capital of all insured banks for the five most recent years available. How has the ratio of equity to assets changed over this period?

Chapter
Seventeen

Management of Interest Rate Risk I

C hapter 9 established the fact that while performing their asset-transformation functions, financial intermediaries (FIs) often mismatch the maturities of their assets and liabilities. In so doing, they expose themselves to interest rate risk. For example, in the 1980s, a large number of thrifts suffered economic insolvency (i.e., the **net worth** or equity of their owners was eradicated) due to major increases in interest rates. This chapter discusses the Federal Reserve's monetary policy which is a key determinant of interest rate risk. This chapter also analyzes two of the simpler methods to measure an FI's interest rate risk: the *repricing model* and the *maturity model*. The repricing model, sometimes called the *funding gap model*, concentrates on the impact of interest rate changes on an FI's net interest income (NII) which is the difference between an FI's interest income and interest expense (see Chapter 8). The discussion compares and contrasts this model to the market value–based, maturity model that includes the impact of interest

net worth

The value of the FI to its owners; equal to the difference between the market value of assets and liabilities.

Chapter Outline

rate changes on the overall market value of an FI's assets and liabilities and ultimately its net worth. Until recently, U.S. bank regulators had been content to base their evaluations of bank interest rate risk exposures on the repricing model. As explained later in this chapter, however, the repricing model has some serious weaknesses. In 1995, the Federal Reserve developed a new measure of exposure grounded in market value accounting (analyzed in Chapter 18) that it now applies in addition to supervisory examinations to help evaluate the interest rate risk exposures of banks.[1]

THE CENTRAL BANK AND INTEREST RATE RISK

Underlying the movement of interest rates is the central bank's monetary policy strategy. The central bank in the United States is the Federal Reserve Bank (the Fed). Through its daily open-market operations such as buying and selling Treasury bonds and Treasury bills, the Fed seeks to influence the money supply and the level of interest rates (particularly short-term interest rates). In turn, interest rates impact financial variables that influence economic decisions, such as whether to spend or save. When the Fed finds it necessary to slow down the economy, it tightens monetary policy by raising interest rates. The normal result is a decrease in business and household spending (especially that financed by credit or borrowing). Conversely, if business and household spending declines to the extent that the Fed finds it necessary to stimulate the economy, it allows interest rates to fall (an expansionary monetary policy). The drop in rates promotes borrowing and spending.

Furthermore, if the Fed smooths or targets the level of interest rates, unexpected interest rate shocks and interest rate volatility tend to be small. Accordingly, in a low interest rate volatility environment, the risk exposure to an FI from mismatching the maturities of its assets and liabilities tends to be small. On the other hand, to the extent that the Fed is willing to let interest rates find their own levels, the volatility of interest rates can be very high. See Figure 17–1 for the yields of U.S. 91-day T-bills for the period 1950–1997.

In addition to the Fed's impact on rates via its monetary policy strategy is the increasing level of financial market integration throughout the world. Financial market integration increases the speed of interest rate transmission among countries, making interest rates more volatile and their control by the Federal Reserve more difficult and less certain. The increased globalization of financial market flows in recent years has put the measurement and management of interest rate risk at the head of the problems facing modern FI managers. For example, investors across the world carefully evaluate the biannual statements by Alan Greenspan (chairman of the Federal Reserve Board of Governors) before Congress. Even hints of increased U.S. interest rates may have a major effect on world interest rates (as well as foreign exchange rates and stock prices).

This chapter and Chapter 18 analyze the different ways an FI might measure the risk exposure it faces when it mismatches the maturity between its assets and liabilities when

---

[1] See *Risk-Based Capital Standards: Interest Rate Risk,* Final Ruling, Federal Reserve Document R-0802, August 2, 1995.

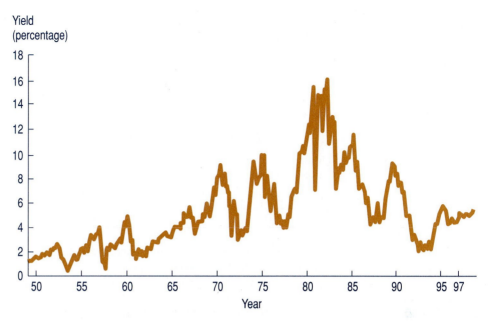

F i g u r e **17–1**   *Yields of 91-Day U.S. Treasury Bills*

SOURCE: *Federal Reserve Bulletin,* Table A26, various issues.

interest rates are volatile. In particular, this chapter concentrates on two ways, or models, to measure what FI managers call their asset-liability "gap" (or interest rate risk) exposure:

The repricing (or funding gap) model; and

The maturity model.

Chapter 18 discusses the duration model.

Concept Questions

1. When the Federal Reserve finds it necessary to slow down or to stimulate the economy, what type of actions would it take and what are the consequences?
2. What events occurred in the 1990s that affected the need for FIs to carefully manage interest rate risk?

repricing or funding gap

The difference between those assets whose interest rates will be repriced or changed over some future period (RSAs) and liabilities whose interest rates will be repriced or changed over some future period (RSLs).

THE REPRICING

MODEL

The **repricing or funding gap** model is essentially a book value accounting cash flow analysis of the interest revenue earned on an FI's assets and the interest expense paid on its liabilities (or net interest income) over some particular period. This contrasts with the market value–based maturity and duration models discussed later in this chapter and in Chapter 18.

Table 17–1

REPRICING GAPS FOR AN FI
(in millions of dollars)

	Assets	Liabilities	Gaps
1. 1 day	$ 20	$ 30	$–10
2. More than 1 day–3 months	30	40	–10
3. More than 3 months–6 months	70	85	–15
4. More than 6 months–12 months	90	70	+20
5. More than 1 year–5 years	40	30	+10
6. More than 5 years	10	5	+ 5
	$260	$260	–0–

In recent years, the Fed has required commercial banks to report quarterly repricing gaps for assets and liabilities with these maturities:

1. One day.
2. More than 1 day to 3 months.
3. More than 3 months to 6 months.
4. More than 6 months to 12 months.
5. More than 1 year to 5 years.
6. More than 5 years.

rate sensitivity

The time to repricing an asset or liability.

Under this plan, a bank reports the gaps in each maturity bucket (or bin) by calculating the **rate sensitivity** of each asset (RSA) and each liability (RSL) on its balance sheet. *Rate sensitivity* means that the asset or liability is repriced at or near current market interest rates within a maturity bucket. More simply, it indicates how long the FI manager must wait to change the posted interest rates on any asset or liability.

Refer to Table 17–1 to see how the assets and liabilities of a bank are categorized into each of the six previously defined buckets according to their time to repricing (or interest rate changes). Although the cumulative gap over the whole balance sheet must be zero by definition, the advantage of the repricing model lies in its information value and its simplicity in pointing to an FI's *net interest income exposure* (or profit exposure) to interest rate changes in different maturity buckets.[2]

For example, suppose that an FI's report indicates a negative $10 million difference between assets and liabilities being repriced in one day. Assets and liabilities that are repriced each day are likely to be interbank borrowings on the federal funds or repurchase agreement markets (see Chapter 2). Thus, this gap indicates that a rise in the federal funds rate would lower the bank's *net interest income* because the bank has more rate-sensitive liabilities than assets in this bucket. In other words, assuming equal changes in interest rates on RSAs and RSLs, interest expense will increase by more than interest revenue. Specifically, let

ΔNII_i = change in net interest income in the *i*th maturity bucket

GAP_i = the dollar size of the gap between the book value of rate sensitive assets and liabilities in maturity bucket *i*

---

[2] This is so if we include equity capital as a long-term (over five years) liability.

$\Delta R_i =$ the change in the level of interest rates impacting assets and liabilities in the *i*th maturity bucket.

Then

$$\Delta NII_i = (GAP_i) \, \Delta R_i = (RSA_i - RSL_i) \, \Delta R_i$$

In this first bucket, if the gap is negative $10 million and the fed fund rate rises by 1 percent, the annualized change in the bank's future net interest income is

$$\Delta NII = (-\$10 \text{ million}) \times .01 = -\$100,000$$

This approach is very simple and intuitive. We will see later in this chapter and in Chapter 18, however, that market or present-value losses (and gains) also occur on assets and liabilities when interest rates change. These effects are not accounted for in the funding gap model because asset and liability values are reported at their *historic* values or costs (i.e., on a book value basis rather than a market value basis). Thus, in this model, interest rate changes affect only current interest income earned and interest costs paid—that is, the net interest income on the FI's income statement rather than the market values of assets and liabilities on the balance sheet.[3]

The FI manager can also estimate cumulative gaps (CGAP) over various repricing categories or buckets. A common cumulative gap of interest is the one-year repricing gap estimated from Table 17–1 as

$$CGAP = (-\$10m) + (-\$10m) + (-\$15m) + \$20m = -\$15 \text{ million}$$

If ΔR_i is the average rate change affecting assets and liabilities that can be repriced within a year, the cumulative effect on the bank's net interest income is

$$\Delta NII = (CGAP) \, \Delta R_i$$
$$= (-\$15 \text{ million})(.01) = -\$150,000$$

We can now look at how an FI manager calculates the cumulative one-year gap from a balance sheet. Remember that the manager considers whether this asset or liability will or can have its interest rate changed within the next year. If it will or can, it is a rate-sensitive asset or liability; if not, it is not rate sensitive.

Consider the simplified balance sheet in Table 17–2. Rather than the original maturities, the maturities are those remaining on different assets and liabilities at the time the repricing gap is estimated.

Rate-Sensitive Assets

Looking down the asset side of the balance sheet, in Table 17–2 we see the following one-year rate-sensitive assets (RSA):

1. *Short-term consumer loans: $50 million*, which are repriced at the end of the year and just make the one-year cutoff.
2. *Three-month T-bills: $30 million*, which are repriced on maturity (rollover) every three months.

---

[3]For example, a 30-year bond purchased 10 years ago when rates were 13 percent would be reported as having the same book (accounting) value as when rates are 7 percent. Using market values, capital gains and losses would be reflected on the balance sheet as rates change.

Table **17-2**

SIMPLE BANK BALANCE SHEET

(in millions of dollars)

Assets		Liabilities	
1. Cash and due from	$ 5	1. Equity capital (fixed)	$ 20
2. Short-term consumer loans (one-year maturity)	50	2. Demand deposits	40
3. Long-term consumer loans (two-year maturity)	25	3. Passbook savings	30
4. Three-month T-bills	30	4. Three-month CDs	40
5. Six-month T-notes	35	5. Three-month banker's acceptances	20
6. Three-year T-bonds	60	6. Six-month commercial paper	60
7. 10-year, fixed-rate mortgages	20	7. One-year time deposits	20
8. 30-year, floating-rate mortgages	40	8. Two-year time deposits	40
9. Premises	5		
	$270		$270

3. *Six-month T-notes: $35 million*, which are repriced on maturity (rollover) every six months.

4. *30-year floating-rate mortgages: $40 million*, which are repriced (i.e., the mortgage rate is reset) every nine months. Thus, these long-term assets are RSA in the context of the repricing model with a one-year repricing horizon.

Summing these four items produces one-year RSA of $155 million. The remaining $115 million is not rate sensitive over the one-year repricing horizon. A change in the level of interest rates will not affect the interest revenue generated by these assets over the next year. The $5 million in the cash and due from category and the $5 million in premises are nonearning assets. Although the $105 million in long-term consumer loans, three-year Treasury bonds, and 10-year, fixed-rate mortgages generate interest revenue, the level of revenue generated will not change over the next year since the interest rates on these assets are not expected to change (i.e., they are fixed over the next year).

Rate-Sensitive Liabilities

Looking down the liability side of the balance sheet in Table 17–2, we see that the following liability items clearly fit the one-year rate or repricing sensitivity test:

1. *Three-month CDs: $40 million*, which mature in three months and are repriced on rollover.

2. *Three-month bankers acceptances: $20 million*, which mature in three months and are repriced on rollover.

3. *Six-month commercial paper: $60 million*, which mature and are repriced every six months.

4. *One-year time deposits: $20 million*, which are repriced at the end of the one-year gap horizon.

Summing these four items produces one-year rate-sensitive liabilities (RSL) of $140 million. The remaining $130 million is not rate sensitive over the one-year period. The $20 million in equity capital and $40 million in demand deposits (see the following discussion) do not pay interest and are therefore classified as nonpaying. The $30 million in passbook savings (see the following discussion) and $40 million in two-year time deposits generate interest expense over the next year, but the level of the interest generated will not change if the general level of interest rates change. Thus, we classify these items as *fixed-rate liabilities*.

core deposits

Those deposits that act as an FI's long-term sources of funds.

Note that demand deposits (or transaction accounts in general) were not included as RSLs here, but we can make strong arguments for and against their inclusion as RSLs.

Against Inclusion.   The explicit interest rate on demand deposits is zero by regulation. Further, although explicit interest is paid on transaction accounts such as NOW accounts, the rates paid by banks are very sticky. Moreover, many demand deposits act as **core deposits** for banks, meaning that they are a long-term source of funds.

For Inclusion.   Even though they pay no explicit interest, demand deposits pay implicit interest because FIs do not charge fees that fully cover their cost for checking services. Further, if interest rates rise, individuals draw down (or run off) their demand deposits, forcing the bank to replace them with higher-yielding, interest-bearing, rate-sensitive funds. This is most likely to occur when the interest rates on alternative instruments are high. In such an environment, the opportunity cost to holding funds in demand deposit accounts is likely to be larger than in a low-interest-rate environment.

Similar arguments both for and against inclusion of retail passbook savings accounts can be made. Although Federal Reserve Regulation Q ceilings regarding the maximum rates to be charged for these accounts were abolished in March 1986, banks still adjust these rates only infrequently. However, savers tend to withdraw funds from these accounts when rates rise, forcing banks into more expensive fund substitutions.[4]

The four repriced liabilities ($40 + $20 + $60 + $20) sum to $140 million, and the four repriced assets of $50 + $30 + $35 + $40 sum to $155 million. Given this, the cumulative one-year repricing gap (CGAP) for the bank is

$$\begin{aligned} \text{CGAP} &= (\text{One-year RSA}) - (\text{One-year RSL}) \\ &= \text{RSA} - \text{RSL} \\ &= \$155 \text{ million} - \$140 \text{ million} = \$15 \text{ million} \end{aligned}$$

Interest rate sensitivity can also be expressed as a percentage of assets (*A*) (typically called the *gap ratio*)

$$\frac{\text{CGAP}}{A} = \frac{\$15 \text{ million}}{\$270 \text{ million}} = .056 = 5.6\%$$

Expressing the repricing gap in this way is useful since it tells us (1) the direction of the interest rate exposure (positive or negative CGAP) and (2) the scale of that exposure as indicated by dividing the gap by the asset size of the institution. In our example, the bank has 5.6 percent more RSA than RSL in the one-year and less bucket.

---

[4] The Fed's repricing report has traditionally viewed transaction accounts and passbook savings accounts as rate-*in*sensitive liabilities, as we have done in this example.

Table **17–3**

IMPACT OF CGAP ON THE RELATION BETWEEN CHANGES IN INTEREST RATES AND CHANGES IN NET INTEREST INCOME, ASSUMING RATE CHANGES FOR RSAs EQUAL RATE CHANGES FOR RSLs

	CGAP	Change in Interest Rates	Change in Interest Revenue		Change in Interest Expense	Change in *NII*
1	> 0	⇑	⇑	>	⇑	⇑
2	> 0	⇓	⇓	>	⇓	⇓
3	< 0	⇑	⇑	<	⇑	⇓
4	< 0	⇓	⇓	<	⇓	⇑

Equal Changes in Rates on RSAs and RSLs

The CGAP provides a measure of a bank's interest rate sensitivity. Table 17–3 highlights the relation between CGAP and changes in *NII* when interest rate changes for RSAs are equal to interest rate changes for RSLs. For example, when CGAP (or the gap ratio) is positive (or the bank has more RSAs than RSLs), *NII* will rise when interest rates rise (line 1, Table 17–3) since interest revenue increases more than interest expense does.

EXAMPLE 17–1

Impact of Rate Changes on Net Interest Income When CGAP Is Positive

Suppose that interest rates rise by 1 percent on both RSAs and RSLs. The CGAP would project the expected annual change in net interest income (ΔNII) of the bank as approximately

$$\Delta NII = \text{CGAP} \times \Delta R$$
$$= (\$15 \text{ million}) \times .01$$
$$= \$150,000$$

Similarly, if interest rates fall equally for RSAs and RSLs (line 2, Table 17–3), *NII* will fall when CGAP is positive. As rates fall, interest revenue falls by more than interest expense. Thus, *NII* falls. Suppose that for our bank, rates fall by 1 percent. The CGAP predicts that *NII* will fall by approximately

$$\Delta NII = \text{CGAP} \times \Delta R$$
$$= (\$15 \text{ million}) \times (-.01)$$
$$= -\$150,000$$

It is evident from this equation that the larger the CGAP, the larger the expected swing in *NII* (i.e., the larger the increase or decrease in the FI's interest revenue relative to interest expense). In general, when CGAP is positive, the change in *NII* is positively related to the change in interest rates.

Conversely, when CGAP (or the gap ratio) is negative, if interest rates rise by equal amounts for RSAs and RSLs (line 3, Table 17–3), *NII* will fall. Since the bank has more

RSLs than RSAs, interest expense increases by more than interest revenue, and *NII* decreases.

E X A M P L E   1 7 – 2

* * * * * * *

Impact of Rate Changes on Net Interest Income When CGAP Is Negative
Suppose for our bank that RSAs equal \$140 million and RSLs equal \$155 million. Now CGAP equals – \$15 million (\$140 million – \$155 million). If rates rise by 1 percent the annual change in *NII* is

$$\Delta NII = (-\$15 \text{ million}) \times (.01)$$
$$= -\$150{,}000$$

* * *

CGAP effect

The relation between changes in interest rates and changes in net interest income.

Similarly, if interest rates fall equally for RSAs and RSLs (line 4, Table 17–3), *NII* will increase when CGAP is negative. As rates fall, interest expense decreases by more than interest revenue. Thus, *NII* increases. In general then, when CGAP is negative, the change in *NII* is negatively related to the change in interest rates. We refer to these relationships as **CGAP effects**.

Unequal Changes in Rates on RSAs and RSLs

The previous section considered changes in net interest income as interest rates changed, assuming that the change in rates on RSAs was exactly equal to the change in rates on RSLs (in other words, assuming the interest rate spread between rates on RSAs and RSLs remained unchanged). This is often not the case, however; rather, rate changes on RSAs generally differ from those on RSLs (i.e., the spread between interest rates on assets and liabilities changes along with the levels of these rates). See Figure 17–2, which plots quarterly CD rates (liabilities) and prime lending rates (assets) for the period 1990–1997. Notice that although the rates generally move in the same direction, they are not perfectly correlated.[5] In this case, as we consider the impact of rate changes on *NII*, we have a *spread effect* in addition to the CGAP effect.

E X A M P L E   1 7 – 3

* * * * * *

Impact of Spread Effect on Net Interest Income
To understand spread effect, assume for a moment that RSAs equal RSLs equal \$155 million. Suppose that rates rise by 1.2 percent on RSAs and by 1 percent on RSLs (i.e., the spread between the rate on RSAs and RSLs increases by 1.2 percent–1 percent = 0.2 percent). The resulting change in *NII* is calculated as

$$\Delta NII = [RSA \times \Delta R_{RSA}] - [RSL \times \Delta R_{RSL}]$$
$$= \Delta \text{interest revenue} - \Delta \text{interest expense}$$
$$= [\$155 \text{ million} \times 1.2\%] - [\$155 \text{ million} \times 1.0\%]$$
$$= \$155 \text{ million} (1.2\% - 1.0\%)$$
$$= \$310{,}000$$

* * *

---

[5] The spread effect therefore presents a type of so-called basis risk for the FI. That is, the FI's net interest income varies as the difference (basis) between interest rates on RSAs and interest rates on RSLs varies. We discuss basis risk in detail in Chapter 21.

F i g u r e 17–2 *Three-Month CD Rates versus Prime Rate for 1990–1997*

RSA stands for rate-sensitive assets.
RSL stands for rate-sensitive liabilities.
SOURCE: *Federal Reserve Bulletin,* various issues.

spread effect

The affect that a change in the spread between rates on RSAs and RSLs has on *NII* as interest rates change.

If the spread between the rate on RSAs and RSLs increases, when interest rates rise (fall), interest revenue increases (decreases) by more (less) than interest expense. The result is an increase in *NII*. Conversely, if the spread between the rates on RSAs and RSLs decreases, when interest rates rise (fall), interest revenue increases (decreases) less (more) than interest expense, and *NII* decreases. In general, the **spread effect** is such that, regardless of the direction of the change in interest rates, a positive relation occurs between changes in the spread (between rates on RSAs and RSLs) and changes in *NII*.

See Table 17–4 for various combinations of CGAP and spread changes and their effects on *NII*. The first four lines in Table 17–4 consider a bank with a positive CGAP; the last four consider a bank with a negative CGAP. Notice in Table 17–4 that the CGAP and spread effects can both have the same effect on *NII*. In these cases, bank managers can accurately predict the direction of the change in *NII* as interest rates change. When the two work in opposite directions, however, the change in *NII* cannot be estimated without knowing the size of the CGAP and expected change in the spreads.

Consider the one-year percentage gaps ((RSA – RSL)/Assets) of various large regional and money center banks over a period of interest rate volatility (1993–1996) in Table 17–5. Notice that some banks accept quite large interest rate exposures relative to their asset sizes. For example, the average one-year repricing gap of National City Corporation was –26.0 percent at the end of 1993 (i.e., it had considerably more RSLs than RSAs). If interest rates had fallen after the period, its net interest income would have risen. If rates had risen, however, National City Corp. would have been exposed to significant net interest income losses due to the cost of refinancing its large amount of RSLs relative to RSAs. As

Table **17-4**

IMPACT OF CGAP ON THE RELATION BETWEEN CHANGES IN INTEREST RATES AND CHANGES IN NET INTEREST INCOME ALLOWING FOR DIFFERENT CHANGES ON RSAs AND RSLs

	CGAP	Change in Interest Rates	Change in Spread	Change in *NII*
1	> 0	⇑	⇑	⇑
2	> 0	⇑	⇓	⇑⇓
3	> 0	⇓	⇑	⇑⇓
4	> 0	⇓	⇓	⇓
5	< 0	⇑	⇑	⇑⇓
6	< 0	⇑	⇓	⇓
7	< 0	⇓	⇑	⇑
8	< 0	⇓	⇓	⇑⇓

Table **17-5**

RATE-SENSITIVITY GAP AS A PERCENTAGE OF TOTAL ASSETS

	1993	1994	1995	1996
Bank of America	0.0%	0.8%	−1.0%	0.8%
Bankers Trust Company	2.3	−1.5	−0.4	−3.5
Barnett Banks	9.7	4.9	7.7	3.9
Boatmen's Bancshares	3.6	−5.9	3.3	n.a.
Chemical Bank	−5.0	−5.0	4.0	n.a.
CoreStates Financial	0.5	−0.8	0.4	0.1
Comerica	1.0	−5.0	−1.0	−3.7
First Bank System	7.2	3.2	1.1	0.4
First Interstate Bank, CA	10.0	7.4	3.1	n.a.
Fleet Financial	−4.4	−3.2	2.1	2.4
J.P. Morgan & Company	−15.8	−0.5	−1.3	−2.3
Mellon Bank	0.3	3.8	8.4	3.4
NationsBank	−9.9	−11.6	−16.8	−21.4
National City	−26.0	−3.4	4.0	7.1
Norwest	4.2	−4.4	−4.2	−4.2
PNC Bank	−8.6	−1.5	7.0	4.4
State Street Boston	8.0	−14.0	−3.0	−8.4
U.S. Bancorp	3.8	−10.2	−6.8	0.8
Wachovia	−1.5	−1.0	−4.2	−10.6
Wells Fargo Bank	2.7	1.0	−0.8	−1.3
Average	−0.9	−1.4	0.1	−2.0

NOTES: Rate-sensitive assets are all assets repricing or maturing within one year and include loans and leases, debt security, and other interest-bearing assets. Rate-sensitive liabilities are all liabilities scheduled to reprice or mature within one year and include domestic time certificates of deposits of $100,000 or more, all other domestic time deposits, total deposits in foreign offices, money market deposit accounts, Super NOWs, and demand notes issued to the U.S. Treasury.

SOURCE: Annual reports.

Contemporary Perspectives 17–1

Rate Risks Spur Banks to Cut Exposure

Banks learned some hard lessons from being burned by interest rate risks to their investment securities, and they've worked to reduce their exposure, analysts said. Banc One Corp., PNC Bank Corp., and a number of others suffered lower-than-expected earnings in 1994 because they had bet that interest rates would remain low.

Indeed, some analysts estimated that interest rate bets caused more than half of the bank group to underperform. "Banks got very complacent with interest rate risk in 1994," said Dennis Shea, a bank analyst at Morgan Stanley & Co. "We had steady declines in interest rates for quite a period of time. The easiest thing to do was position yourself for a continued decline." Nonetheless, as a group, banks have reduced that kind of risk because they got "punched in the nose" and they still remember it well, Mr. Shea said.

Moshe A. Orenbuch, a bank analyst at Sanford C. Bernstein & Co., in New York, said banks have cut their average interest rate sensitivity about in half. They have reduced the gap between assets and liabilities that reprice in 12 months to 0.6 percent from 1.0 percent of earning assets, according to research by Bernstein. Additionally, the standard deviation in interest rate sensitivity has fallen to 4.9 percent from 5.8 percent. That means the riskiest banks "got their acts together," Mr. Orenbuch said.

To be sure, interest rate risk remains a fundamental issue that can affect a bank's balance sheet, causing periodic drops in earnings. "I don't think as a result of a few banks having problems that the issue is either larger or smaller," said Diane Glossman, a bank analyst at Salomon Brothers Inc. "It's still an issue and has been so ever since there have been banks." Nonetheless, Ms. Glossman said, banks' balance sheets have become less tied to fixed rates.

SOURCE: Reprinted with permission—American Banker, Daniel Dunaief, The *American Banker,* June 4, 1996, p. 3A.

it turned out, National City Corp. was not so lucky—or its interest rate forecasts were incorrect—because rates actually rose for most of 1994 (see Figure 17–1). Commercial banks have recently paid much closer attention to interest rate risk exposure (see Contemporary Perspectives Box 17–1), significantly reducing the gaps between RSAs and RSLs. Commercial banks are not the only FIs to actively manage interest rate risk (see Contemporary Perspectives Box 17–2). All FIs with both the asset and liability sides of their balance sheets loaded with financial assets must actively manage the interest rate risk on their assets and liabilities.

The preceding discussion indicates that the rate-sensitivity gap can be a useful tool for managers and regulators in identifying interest rate risk opportunities or exposure. Nevertheless, the repricing gap model has a number of serious weaknesses that are discussed in the next section.

Concept Questions

1. How can banks change the size and the direction of their repricing gap?
2. What is the difference between CGAP affect and spread affect on the relation between interest rate changes and *NII* changes?
3. For a bank with a negative CGAP, if rates rise and spread increases, what happens to *NII*? Why?

Contemporary Perspectives 17–2

CRIIMI MAE Refinances $142 Million of Floating-Rate Debt Replacing It with Longer-Term, Fixed-Rate Financing

CRIIMI MAE Inc., a full service commercial mortgage company structured as a REIT, refinanced $142 million of existing floating-rate financing in exchange for longer-term, fixed rate debt in a transaction that is believed to be the largest repackaging of subordinated commercial mortgage-backed securities (CMBS) to date.

The innovative transaction replaces a significant portion of the company's existing repurchase agreement financing with fixed-rate funding and creates liabilities with maturities that closely match the maturities of the underlying mortgage assets. In addition, the transaction provides approximately $22 million to support CRIIMI MAE's 1997 business plan.

"This refinancing helps to match the maturities of our assets and liabilities and further reduces CRIIMI MAE's exposure to interest rate volatility," said chairman William B. Dockser. "This transaction completes a key part of our 1996 business plan and follows three major refinancings we completed in 1995." In those transactions last year, CRIIMI MAE replaced floating-rate debt with long-term, fixed-rate financing secured by $650 million of government-insured mortgages.

Mr. Dockser explained CRIIMI MAE's overall financing strategy as follows: "Our business plan focuses on the acquisition of mortgage investments, including subordinated CMBS, using a combination of equity and short-term financing. As we continue to grow, our strategy involves fixing the rates and matching the maturities of our debt with our acquired assets through major refinancings. The current refinancing accomplishes these goals, allowing us to lock-in spreads, match maturities and reduce our short-term interest rate exposure."

SOURCE: *PR Newswire,* December 20, 1996.

WEAKNESSES OF THE REPRICING MODEL

The repricing model has four major shortcomings: (1) it ignores market value effects, (2) it is overaggregative, (3) it fails to deal with the problem of asset and liability cash flow runoffs, and (4) it ignores cash flows from off-balance-sheet activities. This section discusses each of these weaknesses.

Market Value Effects

As discussed in the next section, interest rate changes have a market (or present-) value effect in addition to an income effect on asset and liability values. That is, the present value of the cash flows on assets and liabilities changes in addition to the interest received or paid on them as interest rates change. In fact, the present values of both rate-sensitive and fixed-rate assets and liabilities change as interest rates change. As such, the repricing gap is only a *partial* measure of an FI's true or overall interest rate risk exposure.

Overaggregation

The problem of defining buckets over a range of maturities ignores information regarding the distribution of assets and liabilities within that bucket. For example, the dollar value of RSAs and RSLs within any maturity bucket range may be equal; however, on average,

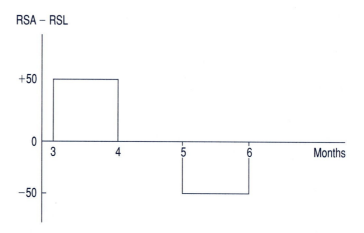

F i g u r e **17–3**   *The Overaggregation Problem: The Three-Month to Six-Month Bucket*

RSA stands for rate-sensitive assets.
RSL stands for rate-sensitive liabilities.

liabilities may be repriced toward the end of the bucket's range, and assets may be repriced toward the beginning.

Consider the simple example for the three-month to six-month bucket in Figure 17–3. Note that $50 million more RSAs than RSLs are repriced between months 3 and 4 while $50 million more liabilities than assets are repriced between months 5 and 6. In its gap analysis, the bank would show a zero repricing gap for the three-month to six-month bucket (+50 + (−50) = 0). But the bank's assets and liabilities are *mismatched* within the bucket. Clearly, the shorter the range over which bucket gaps are calculated, the smaller is this problem. If an FI manager calculated one-day bucket gaps out into the future, this would give a very good idea of the net interest income exposure to rate changes. Many large banks reportedly have internal systems that indicate their repricing gaps on any given day in the future (252 days' time, 1,329 days' time, etc.). This suggests that although regulators require the reporting of repricing gaps over only relatively wide maturity bucket ranges, FI managers could set in place internal information systems to report the daily future patterns of such gaps.

The Problem of Runoffs

runoffs

Periodic cash flow of interest and principal amortization payments on long-term assets such as conventional mortgages that can be reinvested at market rates.

The simple repricing model in the first section assumed that all consumer loans matured in one year or that all conventional mortgages matured in 30 years. In reality, a bank continually originates and retires consumer and mortgage loans as it creates and retires deposits. For example, today, some 30-year original maturity mortgages may have only one year left before they mature; that is, they are in their 29th year. In addition, virtually all long-term mortgages pay at least some principal back to the bank each month. As a result, the bank receives a **runoff** cash flow from its conventional mortgage portfolio that it can reinvest at current market rates; that is, this runoff of cash flow component is rate sensitive. The bank manager can easily deal with this in the repricing model by identifying for each asset and liability item the proportion that will run off, reprice, or mature within the next year. For example, consider Table 17–6.

Table **17–6**

RUNOFFS OF DIFFERENT ASSETS AND LIABILITIES
(in millions of dollars)

	Assets			Liabilities	
Item	**Amount Runoff in Less than One Year**	**Amount Runoff in More than One Year**	**Item**	**Amount Runoff in Less than One Year**	**Amount Runoff in More than One Year**
1. Short-term consumer loans	$ 50	—	1. Equity	$ —	$20
2. Long-term consumer loans	5	$20	2. Demand deposits	30	10
3. Three-month T-bills	30	—	3. Passbook savings	15	15
4. Six-month T-bills	35	—	4. Three-month CDs	40	—
5. Three-year notes	10	60	5. Three-month banker's acceptances	20	—
6. 10-year mortgages	2	18	6. Six-month commercial paper	60	—
7. 30-year floating-rate mortgages	40	—	7. One-year time deposits	20	—
			8. Two-year time deposits	20	20
	$172	$98		$205	$65

Notice in this table that although the original maturity of an asset or liability may be long term, these assets and liabilities still generate some cash flows that can be reinvested at market rates this year. Table 17–6 presents a more sophisticated measure of the one-year repricing gap that considers all the cash flows received on each asset and liability item during that year. Adjusted for runoffs, the repricing gap (in millions of dollars) is

$$GAP = \$172 - \$205 = -\$33$$

Note that the runoffs themselves are not independent of interest rate changes. Specifically, when interest rates rise, many people may delay repaying their mortgages (and the principal on those mortgages), causing the runoff amount of $2 million on 10-year mortgages in Table 17–6 to be overly optimistic. Similarly, when interest rates fall, people may prepay their fixed-rate mortgages to refinance at a lower interest rate. Then runoffs could balloon to a number much larger than $2 million. This sensitivity of runoffs to interest rate changes is another weakness of the repricing model.

Cash Flows from Off-Balance-Sheet Activities

The RSAs and RSLs used in the repricing model included only assets and liabilities listed on the balance sheet. Obviously, changes in interest rates affect values of off-balance-sheet activities as well and, therefore, the value of the FI. For example, an FI might have hedged its repricing gap with interest rate futures contracts (see Chapter 21). As interest rates change, these futures contracts produce a daily cash flow (either positive or negative) for the FI that may offset any on-balance-sheet repricing gap exposure. These offsetting cash flows from futures contracts are ignored by the simple repricing model and should (and could) be included in the model.

Concept  Questions

1. What are four major weaknesses of the repricing model?
2. What does runoff mean?

• •

THE MATURITY MODEL

book value accounting

Recording an FI's assets and liabilities at historic values.

market value accounting

Revaluing an FI's assets and liabilities according to the current level of interest rates.

marking to market

Valuing securities at their current market price.

As mentioned in the previous section, a weakness of the repricing model is its reliance on book values rather than market values of assets and liabilities. Indeed, in most countries, FIs report their balance sheets using **book value accounting**. This method records the historic values of securities purchased, loans made, and liabilities sold. For example, for U.S. banks, investment assets (i.e., those expected to be held for more than a year) are recorded at book values while those assets expected to be used for trading (held for less than one year) are reported according to market values.[6] Recording market values means that assets or liabilities are revalued to reflect current market conditions. Thus, if a fixed-coupon bond had been purchased at $100 per $100 of face value in a low interest rate environment, a rise in current market rates reduces the present value of the cash flows from the bond to the investor. Such a rise also reduces the price—say, to $97—at which the bond could be sold in the secondary market today. That is, the **market value accounting** method reflects economic reality or the true values of assets and liabilities if the FI's portfolio were to be liquidated at today's securities prices rather than at the prices when the assets and liabilities were originally purchased or sold. This practice of valuing securities at their market value is referred to as **marking to market**.

Fixed-Income Securities and the Maturity Model

EXAMPLE 17–4

Impact of Interest Rate Changes on Bond Value

Consider the value of a bond held by an FI that has one year to maturity, a face value of $100 ($F$) to be paid on maturity, a single coupon payment at a rate of 10 percent of the face value—or $10 (C)—and a current yield to maturity (R) (reflecting current interest rates) of 10 percent. The fair market price of the one-year bond, P_1^B, is equal to the present value of the cash flows on the bond

$$P_1^B = \frac{F+C}{(1+R)} = \frac{\$100 + \$10}{1.1} = \$\,100m$$

---

[6] More accurately, they are reported at the lower of cost or current market value (LOCOM). However, both the SEC and the Financial Accounting Standards Board (FASB) have strongly advocated that FIs switch to full market value accounting in the near future. Currently, *FASB 115* requires FIs to value certain bonds but not loans at market prices.

Suppose that the Fed tightens monetary policy so that the required yield on the bond rises instantaneously to 11 percent. The market value of the bond (or what is the same thing, the present value of the cash flows from the bond) falls to

$$P_1^B = \frac{\$100 + \$10}{1.11} = \$99.10$$

Thus, the market value of the bond is now worth only $99.10 per $100 of face value if it were sold to other investors, but its original book value was $100. The FI has suffered a capital loss (ΔP_1) of $0.90 per $100 of face value in holding this bond

$$\Delta P_1 = \$99.10 - \$100 = -\$0.90$$

Also the percent change in the price is

$$\%\Delta P_1 = \frac{\$99.10 - \$100}{\$100} = -0.90\%$$ • • •

This example simply demonstrates the fact that fixed income security price changes are negatively related to interest rate changes or that a rise in the required yield to maturity reduces the price of fixed income securities held in FI portfolios. Note that if the FI issued bond under consideration was a liability (e.g., a fixed interest deposit such as a CD) rather than an asset, the effect is the same—the market value of the FI's deposits would fall. However, the economic interpretation is different. Although rising interest rates that reduce the market value of assets is bad news for an FI's management, the reduction in the market value of liabilities is good news. The economic intuition is straightforward. Suppose that the bank issued a one-year deposit with a promised interest rate of 10 percent and principal or face value of $100.[7] When the current level of interest rates is 10 percent, the market value of the liability is $100. Should interest rates on new one-year deposits rise instantly to 11 percent, the bank has gained by locking in a promised interest payment to depositors of only 10 percent. The market value of the bank's liability to its depositors would fall to $99.10.[8] That is, the bank gained from paying only 10 percent on its deposits rather than 11 percent if they were newly issued after the rise in interest rates.[9]

As a result, in a market value accounting framework, rising interest rates generally lower the market values of both assets and liabilities on an FI's balance sheet. Clearly, falling interest rates have the reverse effect; they increase the market values of both assets and liabilities.

In the preceding example, both the bond and deposit were of one-year maturity. We can easily show that if the bond or deposit had a two-year maturity with the same annual coupon rate, the same increase in market interest rates from 10 to 11 percent would have had a more *negative* effect on the market value of the bond's price (value).

---

[7] In this example, we assume for simplicity that the promised interest rate on the deposit is 10 percent. In reality, for returns to intermediation to prevail, the promised rate on deposits would be less than the promised rate (coupon) on assets.

[8] $P_1^D = \dfrac{\$100 + \$10}{1.1} = \$99.10$

[9] Alternatively, this would be the price the bank would need to pay the depositor if it repurchased the deposit in the secondary market.

Impact of Maturity on Change in Bond Value

Before the rise in required yield, the present value of a two-year, 10 percent bond is

$$P^B_2 = \frac{\$10}{(1.1)} + \frac{\$10 + \$100}{(1.1)^2} = \$100$$

After a rise in market interest rates from 10 to 11 percent

$$P^B_2 = \frac{\$10}{(1.11)} + \frac{\$10 + \$100}{(1.11)^2} = \$98.29$$

and

$$\Delta P_2 = \$\,98.29 - \$100 = -\$1.71$$

The resulting percentage change in the bond's value is

$$\%\,\Delta P_2 = \frac{\$98.29 - \$100}{\$100} = -1.71\%$$

Let's extend the analysis one more year. The market value of a bond with three years to maturity, a face value of $100, and a coupon rate of 10 percent is

$$P^B_3 = \frac{\$10}{(1.1)} + \frac{\$10}{(1.1)^2} + \frac{\$10 + \$100}{(1.1)^3} = \$100$$

After the rise in market rates from 10 to 11 percent, the market value of the bond is

$$P^B_3 = \frac{\$10}{(1.11)} + \frac{\$10}{(1.11)^2} + \frac{\$10 + \$100}{(1.11)^3} = \$97.56$$

This is a change in the market value of

$$\Delta P_3 = \$\,97.56 - \$100 = -\$2.44$$

or

$$\%\,\Delta P_3 = \frac{\$97.56 - \$100}{\$100} = -2.44\%$$

This example demonstrates another general rule of portfolio management for FIs: the *longer* the maturity of a fixed income asset or liability, the larger is its fall in price and market value for any given increase in the level of market interest rates. For a given change in market interest rates, the change in the market value of a bond with 2 years left to maturity is larger than that of a bond with 1 year left to maturity (also the change in the value of a three-year bond is larger than a bond with 2 years to maturity, etc.). Note that although the two-year bond's fall in price is larger than the fall of the one-year bond, the difference between the two price falls, $\%\Delta P_2 - \%\,\Delta P_1$, is $-1.71\% - (-0.9\%) = -0.81\%$. The fall in a three-year, 10 percent coupon bond's price when the yield increases to 11 percent is -2.44 percent. Thus, $\%\Delta P_3 - \%\Delta P_2 = -2.44\% - (-1.71\%) = -0.73\%$. This establishes a third important result: while P_3 falls more than P_2 and P_2 falls more than P_1, the size of the capital loss increases at a diminishing rate as we move into the higher maturity ranges. This effect is graphed in Figure 17–4.

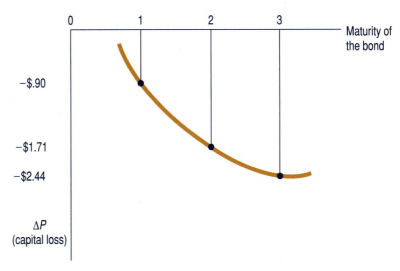

F i g u r e **17-4**   *The Relationship between ΔR, Maturity, and ΔP (Capital Loss)*

So far, we have shown that for an FI's fixed income assets and liabilities:

1. A rise (fall) in interest rates generally leads to a fall (rise) in the market value of an asset or liability.
2. The longer the maturity of a fixed income asset or liability, the larger the fall (rise) in market value for any given interest rate increase (decrease).
3. The fall in the value of longer-term securities increases at a diminishing rate for any given increase in interest rates.

The Maturity Model With a Portfolio of Assets and Liabilities

The preceding general rules can be extended beyond an FI holding an individual asset or liability to holding a portfolio of assets and liabilities. Let M_A be the weighted-average maturity of an FI's assets and M_L be the weighted-average maturity of an FI's liabilities.[10] In a portfolio context, the same three relationships prevail as for an individual security:

---

[10] M_A and M_L can be calculated as

$$M_i = W_{i1}M_{i1} + W_{i2}M_{i2} + ... + W_{in}M_{in}$$

where

M_i = the weighted-average maturity of an FI's assets (liabilities), $I = A \ or \ L$
W_{ij} = the importance of each asset (liability) in the asset (liability) portfolio as measured by the market value of that asset (liability) position relative to the market value of all the assets (liabilities)
M_{ij} = the maturity of the jth asset (or liability), $j = 1 \ldots n$

This equation shows that the maturity of a portfolio of assets or liabilities is a weighted average of the maturities of assets or liabilities that compose that portfolio.

Table **17-7**

THE MARKET VALUE BALANCE SHEET OF A BANK

Assets	Liabilities
Long-term assets (*A*)	Short-term liabilities (*L*)
	Net worth (*E*)

1. A rise in interest rates generally reduces the market values of an FI's asset and liability portfolios.
2. The longer the maturity of the asset or liability portfolio, the larger the fall in value for any given interest rate increase.
3. The fall in value of the asset or liability portfolio increases with its maturity at a diminishing rate.

Given the preceding information, the net effect of rising or falling interest rates on an FI's balance sheet depends on the extent and direction in which the FI mismatches the maturities of its asset and liability portfolios. That is, the effect depends on whether its **maturity gap**, $M_A - M_L$, is more than, equal to, or less than zero.

Consider the case in which $M_A - M_L > 0$; that is, the maturity of assets is longer than the maturity of liabilities. This is the case for most commercial banks and thrifts. These FIs tend to hold large amounts of relatively longer-term fixed income assets such as conventional mortgages, consumer loans, commercial loans, and bonds, while issuing shorter-term liabilities, such as certificates of deposit with fixed interest payments promised to the depositors.[11]

Consider the simplified portfolio of a representative bank in Table 17–7 and notice that all assets and liabilities are marked to market; that is, it uses a market value accounting framework.[12] In Table 17–7, the difference between the market value of the bank's assets (*A*) and the market value of its liabilities such as deposits (*L*) is the net worth or true equity value (*E*) of the bank. This is the economic value of the bank owners' stake in the FI. In other words, this is the money the owners would receive if they could liquidate the bank's assets and liabilities at today's prices in the financial markets by selling off loans, bonds, and repurchasing deposits at the best prices they can get. This is also clear from the balance sheet identity

$$E = A - L$$

As was demonstrated earlier, when interest rates rise, the market values of both assets and liabilities fall. However, in this example, because the maturity on the asset portfolio is longer than the maturity on the liability portfolio, for any given increase in interest rates, the market value of the asset portfolio (*A*) falls by more than the market value of the liability portfolio (*L*). For the balance sheet identity to hold, the difference between the

maturity gap

Difference between the weighted-average maturity of the FI's assets and liabilities.

---

[11]These assets generate periodic interest payments such as coupons that are fixed over the assets' lives. Chapter 18 discusses interest payments fluctuating with market interest rates, such as on an adjustable-rate mortgage.

[12]Note that in the real world, reported balance sheets differ from that in Table 17–7 because historic or book value accounting rules are used.

Table **17–8**

INITIAL VALUES OF A BANK'S ASSETS AND LIABILITIES

(millions of dollars)

Assets	Liabilities
$A = \$100 \ (M_A = 3 \text{ years})$	$L = \$\ 90 \ (M_L = 1 \text{ year})$
	$E = \underline{\quad 10 \quad}$
$\underline{\$100}$	$\$100$

changes in the market value of the bank's assets and liabilities must be made up by decreasing the bank's equity or net worth (E). That is,

$$\underset{\substack{\text{change in bank} \\ \text{net worth}}}{\Delta E} = \underset{\substack{\text{change in market value} \\ \text{of assets}}}{\Delta A} - \underset{\substack{\text{change in market value} \\ \text{of liabilities}}}{\Delta L}$$

To see the effect on bank net worth of having longer-term assets than liabilities, suppose that initially the bank's balance sheet looks like the one in Table 17–8. The $100 million of assets is invested in three-year, 10 percent coupon bonds, and the liabilities consist of $90 million of one-year deposits paying a promised interest rate of 10 percent. The resulting maturity gap ($M_A - M_L$) is two years. We showed earlier that if market interest rates rise by 1 percent from 10 to 11 percent, the value of three-year bonds falls by 2.44 percent while the value of one-year deposits falls by 0.90 percent.[13] Table 17–9 depicts this fall in asset and liability market values and the associated effects on bank net worth.

Because the bank's assets have a three-year maturity compared to its one-year maturity liabilities, the value of its assets have fallen by more than the value of its liabilities. The bank's net worth declines from $10 million to $8.37 million, a loss of $1.63 million, or 16.3 percent! A 1 percentage point rise in interest rates can cause the bank's owners or stockholders' net worth to take a big loss. Indeed, if a 1 percent rise in interest rates leads to a fall of 16.3 percent in the bank's net worth, it is not unreasonable to ask how large an interest rate change would need to occur to render the bank economically insolvent by reducing its owners' equity stake or net worth to zero. That is, what increase in interest rates would make E fall by $10 million so that all the owners' net worth is eliminated? For the answer to this question, consider Table 17–10. If interest rates were to rise a full 7 percent from 10

---

[13]Specifically, the market value of the deposits (in millions of dollars) is initially

$$P^D_1 = \frac{\$9 + \$90}{1.1} = \$90$$

When rates increase to 11 percent, the market value decreases to

$$P^D_1 = \frac{\$9 + \$90}{1.11} = \$89.19$$

The resulting change is

$$\Delta P^D_1 = \$89.19 - \$90 = -\$0.81 \quad \text{and} \quad \%\Delta P^D_1 = \frac{\$89.19 - \$90}{\$90} = -0.90\%$$

Table **17–9**

A BANK'S MARKET VALUE BALANCE SHEET AFTER A RISE IN INTEREST RATES OF 1 PERCENT WITH LONGER-TERM ASSETS
(millions of dollars)

Assets	Liabilities	
$A = \$97.56$	$L = \$89.19$	
	$E = \underline{8.37}$	
$\underline{}$		
$\$97.56$	$\$97.56$	

or

$$\Delta E = \Delta A - \Delta L$$
$$-1.63 = (-2.44) - (-0.81)$$

Table **17–10**

BANK BECOMES INSOLVENT AFTER A 7 PERCENT RATE INCREASE
(millions of dollars)

Assets	Liabilities	
$A = \$84.53$	$L = \$84.62$	
	$E = \underline{-0.09}$	
$\underline{}$		
$\$84.53$	$\$84.53$	

or

$$\Delta E = \Delta A - \Delta L$$
$$-10.09 = -15.47 - (-5.38)$$

to 17 percent, the market value balance sheet would look similar to that in Table 17–10.[14] As you can see, the bank's equity (E) falls by just over $10 million, rendering the FI economically insolvent.[15]

---

[14]Specifically (in millions of dollars),

$$P^B_3 = \frac{\$10}{1.17} + \frac{\$10}{(1.17)^2} + \frac{\$10 + \$100}{(1.17)^3} = \$84.53$$

and

$$P^D_1 = \frac{\$9 + \$90}{1.17} = \$84.62$$

[15]Here we are talking about *economic insolvency*. The legal and regulatory definition may vary, depending on what type of accounting rules are used. In particular, under the Federal Deposit Insurance Corporation Improvement Act or FDICIA (November 1991), a bank is required to be placed in conservatorship when the book value of its net worth falls below 2 percent. However, the true or market value of net worth may well be less than this figure at that time.

Table **17–11**

A BANK WITH AN EXTREME MATURITY MISMATCH
(millions of dollars)

Assets	Liabilities
$A = \$100\ (M_A = 30\ \text{years})$	$L = \$\ 90\ (M_L = 1\ \text{year})$
	$E = \underline{\ \ 10}$
$\underline{\hspace{3em}}$	
$\$100$	$\$100$

Table **17–12**

THE EFFECT OF A 1.5 PERCENT RISE IN INTEREST RATES ON THE NET WORTH OF A BANK WITH AN EXTREME ASSET AND LIABILITY MISMATCH

(millions of dollars)

Assets	Liabilities
$A = \$87.45$	$L = \$88.79$
	$E = \underline{-1.34}$
$\underline{\hspace{3em}}$	
$\$87.45$	$\$87.45$

or

$$\Delta E = \Delta A - \Delta L$$
$$-11.34 = (-12.55) - (-1.21)$$

EXAMPLE 17 – 6

Extreme Maturity Mismatch

Suppose that the bank had adopted an even more extreme maturity gap by investing all its assets in 30-year fixed-rate mortgages paying 10 percent coupons while continuing to raise funds by issuing 1-year deposits with promised interest payments of 10 percent, as shown in Table 17–11. Assuming annual compounding and a current level of interest rates of 10 percent, the market price of the mortgages (in millions of dollars) is initially

$$P^B_{30} = \frac{\$10}{(1.1)} + \frac{\$10}{(1.1)^2} + \cdots + \frac{\$10}{(1.1)^{29}} + \frac{\$10 + \$100}{(1.1)^{30}} = \$100$$

If interest rates were to rise by 1.5 percent, the fall in the price (in millions of dollars) of the 30-year mortgage would be

$$P^B_{30} = \frac{\$10}{(1.115)} + \frac{\$10}{(1.115)^2} + \cdots + \frac{\$10}{(1.115)^{29}} + \frac{\$10 + 100}{(1.115)^{30}} = \$87.45$$

a drop of \$12.55, or as a percentage change, $\%\Delta P^B_{30} = (\$87.45 - \$100)/\$100 = -12.55\%$. The market value of the bank's one-year deposits would fall to

$$P^D_1 = \frac{\$9 + \$90}{1.115} = \$88.79$$

a drop of \$1.21 or $(\$88.97 - \$90)/\$90 = -1.34\%$. • • •

immunize

To protect an FI's equity from interest rate changes.

See Table 17–12 for the effect on the market value balance sheet and the bank's net worth after a rise of 1.5 percent in interest rates. It is clear from Table 17–12 that a mere 1.5 percent increase in interest rates eliminates the bank's $10 million dollars in net worth and renders it insolvent (net worth has decreased by –$11.34 million to –$1.34 million after the rise in rates). Given this example, it is not surprising that savings and loans with 30-year fixed-rate mortgages as assets and 1-year or less CDs as liabilities suffered badly during the period 1979–1982 when interest rates rose dramatically.

From the preceding examples, you might infer that the best way for an FI to **immunize** or protect itself from interest rate risk is for its managers to match the maturities of its assets and liabilities; that is, to construct its balance sheet so that its maturity gap, the difference between the weighted-average maturity of its assets and liabilities, is zero ($M_A - M_L = 0$). As we discuss next, however, maturity matching does not always completely protect an FI against interest rate risk.

Concept Questions

1. How does book value accounting differ from market value accounting?
2. In a market value accounting framework, what impact do rising interest rates have on the market values of an FI's assets and liabilities?
3. Refer to Example 17–6. What would be the effect on this FI's net worth if it held one-year discount bonds (with a yield of 10 percent) as assets? Explain your findings.

MATURITY MATCHING AND INTEREST RATE RISK EXPOSURE

Although a strategy of matching asset and liability maturities moves the bank in the direction of hedging itself against interest rate risk, it is easy to show that this strategy does not always eliminate all interest rate risk for an FI. Indeed, we show in Chapter 18 that immunization against interest rate risk requires the bank to consider the following

duration

The average life of an asset or liability, or more technically, the weighted-average time to maturity using the relative present values of the asset or liability cash flows as weights.

1. The degree of leverage in the bank's balance sheet; that is, the proportion of assets funded by liabilities (such as deposits) rather than equity.
2. The **duration** or average life of asset or liability cash flows rather than the maturity of assets and liabilities.

To show the effect of leverage on the ability to immunize the FI, assume that the bank is initially set up as shown in Table 17–13. The $100 million in assets is invested in one-year,

Table **17–13**

INITIAL MARKET VALUES OF A BANK'S ASSETS AND LIABILITIES WITH A MATURITY GAP OF ZERO
(millions of dollars)

Assets	Liabilities
$A = \$100$ ($M_A = 1$ year)	$L = \$\ 90$ ($M_L = 1$ year)
	$E = \underline{\ \ 10}$
$\underline{\$100}$	$\$100$

Table **17–14**

BANK'S MARKET VALUE BALANCE SHEET AFTER A 1 PERCENT RISE IN INTEREST RATES
(millions of dollars)

Assets	Liabilities
$A = \$99.09$	$L = \$89.19$
	$E = \underline{\quad 9.90}$
$\overline{\quad\quad}$	
$\$99.09$	$\$99.09$

or

$$\Delta E = \Delta A - \Delta L$$
$$-0.10 = -0.91 - (-0.81)$$

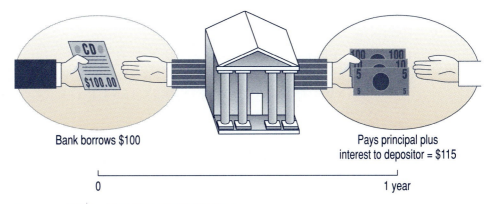

Bank borrows $100   Pays principal plus
                                            interest to depositor = $115

0   1 year

F i g u r e **17–5**   *One-Year CD Cash Flows*

10 percent coupon bonds, and the $90 million in liabilities are in one-year deposits paying 10 percent. The maturity gap $(M_A - M_L)$ is now zero. A 1 percent increase in interest rates results in the balance sheet in Table 17–14. In Table 17–14, even though the maturity gap is zero, the bank's equity value falls by $0.10 million.

The drop in equity value is due to the fact that not all of the assets (bonds) were financed with deposits; rather equity was used to finance a portion of the bank's assets. As interest rates increased, only $90 million in deposits was directly affected while $100 million in assets was directly affected.

Using a simple example, we show next that even when an FI chooses to directly match the maturities and initial dollar market values of assets and deposits (so that leverage is zero, i.e., $M_A = M_L$ and $\$A = \$L$) it does not necessarily achieve perfect immunization or protection for its equity holders against interest rate risk. Consider the example of a bank that issues a one-year CD to a depositor. This CD has a face value of $100 and an interest rate of 15 percent promised to the depositors. Thus, on maturity at the end of the year, the bank must repay the depositor $100 plus $15 interest, or $115, as shown in Figure 17–5.

Suppose that the bank lends the $100 for one year to a corporate borrower at a 15 percent annual interest rate (thus, $\$A = \$L$). However, the bank contractually requires half of the loan ($50) to be repaid after six months and the last half to be repaid at the end of the year. Note that although the maturity of the loan equals the maturity of the deposit equals

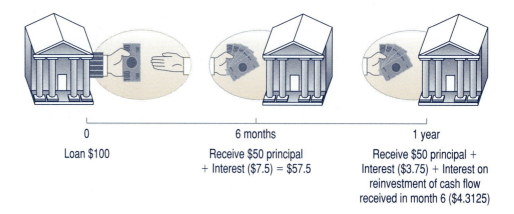

0   6 months   1 year
Loan $100   Receive $50 principal   Receive $50 principal +
                    + Interest ($7.5) = $57.5   Interest ($3.75) + Interest on
                                                       reinvestment of cash flow
                                                       received in month 6 ($4.3125)

F i g u r e 17-6   *One-Year Loan Cash Flow*

T a b l e 17-15

CASH FLOW ON A LOAN WITH A 15 PERCENT INTEREST RATE AND A 15 PERCENT REINVESTMENT RATE

Cash flow at ½ year
Principal	$ 50.00	
Interest	7.50	(= $100 × ½ year × 15 percent)
Cash flow at 1 year		
Principal	$ 50.00	
Interest	3.75	(= $50 × ½ year × 15 percent)
Reinvestment income	4.3125	(= $57.50 × ½ year × 15 percent)
	$115.5625	

---

one year and the loan is fully funded by deposit liabilities, the cash flow earned on the loan may be more or less than the $115 required to pay off depositors, depending on what happens to interest rates over the one-year period. You can see this in Figure 17-6.

At the end of the first six months, the bank receives a $50 repayment in loan principal plus $7.50 in interest ($100 × ½ year × 15 percent) for a total midyear cash flow of $57.50. Rather than allow the $57.50 to sit unproductively, the bank managers will reinvest it at the current interest rate. At the end of the year, the bank receives $50 as the final repayment of loan principal plus $3.75 interest ($50 × ½ year × 15 percent), plus the reinvestment income earned from relending the $57.50 received six months earlier. If interest rates do not change over the period, the bank's extra return from its ability to reinvest part of the cash flow for the last six months would be ($57.50 × ½ × 15 percent) = $4.3125. We summarize the total cash flow on the bank's one-year loan in Table 17–15.

By the end of the year, the cash paid in on the loan exceeded the cash paid out on the deposit by $0.5625 (= $4.3125 – $3.7500). The reason for this is the bank's ability to reinvest part of the principal and interest over the second half of the year at 15 percent.

Suppose that instead of interest rates remaining unchanged at 15 percent throughout the whole one-year period, they had fallen to 12 percent over the last six months in the year.

Table **17–16**

CASH FLOW ON THE LOAN WITH A 15 PERCENT INTEREST RATE AND 12 PERCENT REINVESTMENT RATE

Cash flow at ½ year		
Principal	$ 50.00	
Interest	7.50	(= $100 × ½ year × 15 percent)
Cash flow at 1 year		
Principal	$ 50.00	
Interest	3.75	(=$100 × ½ year × 15 percent)
Reinvestment income	3.45	(=$57.5 × ½ year × 12 percent)
	$114.70	

This fall in rate would affect neither the promised deposit rate of 15 percent nor the promised loan rate of 15 percent because they are set at time 0 when the deposit and loan were originated and do not change throughout the year. What is affected is the bank's *reinvestment income* on the $57.50 cash flow received on the loan at the end of six months. It can be relent only for the final six months of the year at the new lower interest rate of 12 percent (see Table 17–16).

The only change to the asset cash flows for the bank is from the reinvestment of the $57.50 received at the end of six months at the lower interest rate of 12 percent. This produces the smaller reinvestment income of $3.45 ($57.50 × ½ × 12 percent) rather than $4.3125 when rates stayed at 15 percent throughout the year. Rather than making a profit of $0.5625 from intermediation, the bank loses $0.30 (= $3.45 – $3.75). Note that this loss occurs as the result of interest rate change, even when the FI had matched the maturity of its assets and liabilities ($M_A - M_L = 0$) as well as the dollar amount of loans (assets) and deposits (liabilities) (i.e., $A = L).

Despite matching the maturities and dollar amounts, the FI is still exposed to interest rate risk because the *timing* of the *cash flows* on the deposit and loan are not perfectly matched. In a sense, the cash flows on the loan are received, on average, earlier than cash flows are paid out on the deposit when all cash flows occur at the end of the year. The next chapter shows that only by matching the average lives of assets and liabilities—that is, by considering the precise timing of arrival and payment of cash flows—can an FI fully immunize itself against interest rate risk. Table 17–17 summarizes the weaknesses of the repricing and maturity models discussed in this chapter.

Concept Questions

1. Can an FI achieve perfect immunization against interest rate risk by matching the maturities of its assets and liabilities? Explain your answer.
2. Suppose that the average maturity of an FI's assets equals its liabilities. If interest rates fall, why could an FI's net worth still decline? Explain your answer.

Table **17–17**

WEAKNESSES OF THE REPRICING AND MATURITY MODELS

Repricing Model
1. Ignores the effect of market value changes of assets and liabilities when interest rates change.
2. Ignores information regarding the maturity distribution of assets and liabilities within a time bucket by defining time buckets over a range of maturities. Thus, this model overaggregates the maturity of assets and liabilities.
3. Ignores the fact that FIs continuously originate and retire RSAs and RSLs, receiving a runoff cash flow that can be reinvested at current market rates.
4. Ignores cash flows from off-balance-sheet activities.

Maturity Model
1. Ignores the degree of leverage in the bank's balance sheet and thus the impact of leverage on equity value due to a change in interest rates.
2. Ignores the timing of cash flows on assets and liabilities and thus fails to achieve perfect immunization of equity value against interest rate changes.

S U M M A R Y

This chapter introduced two methods to measure an FI's interest rate gap and thus its risk exposure, the repricing model and the maturity model. The repricing model concentrates only on the net interest income effects of rate changes and ignores balance sheet or market value effects. As such it gives a partial, but potentially misleading, picture of an FI's interest rate risk exposure. The maturity model uses the difference between the average maturity of an FI's assets and liabilities to measure interest rate risk.

Specifically, the chapter showed that by mismatching the maturities of assets and liabilities, an FI exposes its equity holders to a risk of insolvency. Because the maturity model ignores the timing of the arrival of cash flows on assets and liabilities, however, it is an incomplete measure of an FI's interest rate exposure. More complete and accurate measures of interest rate risk are duration and the duration gap, which are explained in the next chapter.

P E R T I N E N T   W E B   S I T E S

Board of Governors of the Federal Reserve   http://www.bog.frb.fed.us/

Federal Deposit Insurance Corp.   http://www.fdic.gov/

Financial Accounting Standards Board (FASB)   http://www.rutgers.edu/Accounting/raw/fasb/home.html

Securities and Exchange Commission   http://www.sec.gov/

Management of Interest Rate Risk I

1. Why is the length of time selected for repricing assets and liabilities important when using the repricing model?
2. Calculate the repricing gap and impact on net interest income of a 1 percent increase in interest rates for the following positions:
   a. Rate-sensitive assets = $100 million. Rate-sensitive liabilities = $50 million.
   b. Rate-sensitive assets = $50 million. Rate-sensitive liabilities =$150 million.
   c. Rate-sensitive assets = $75 million. Rate-sensitive liabilities = $70 million.
   d. What conclusions can you draw about the repricing model from these results?

3. Consider the repricing model.
   a. What are some of its weaknesses?
   b. How have large banks solved the problem of choosing the optimal time period for repricing?
4. Which of the following assets or liabilities fit the one-year rate or repricing sensitivity test?
   a. 91-day U.S. T-bills.
   b. 1-year U.S. T-notes.
   c. 20-year U.S. T-bonds.
   d. 20-year floating-rate corporate bonds with annual repricing.
   e. 30-year floating-rate mortgages with repricing every two years.
   f. 30-year floating-rate mortgages with repricing every six months.
   g. Overnight fed funds.
   h. 9-month fixed-rate CDs.
   i. 1-year fixed-rate CDs.
   j. 5-year floating-rate CDs with annual repricing.
   h. Common stock.
5. Consider the following income statement for WatchoverU Savings Inc. (in millions):

Assets		Liabilities	
Floating-rate mortgages (currently 10% annually)	$ 50	Demand deposits (currently 6% annually)	$ 70
30-year fixed-rate loans (currently 7% annually)	$ 50	Time deposits (currently 6% annually)	$ 20
		Equity	$ 10
Total	$100		$100

   a. What is WatchoverU's expected net interest income at year-end?
   b. What will be the net interest income at year-end if interest rates rise by 2 percent?
   c. Using the cumulative repricing gap model, what is the expected net interest income for a 2 percent increase in interest rates?
6. Use the following information about a hypothetical government security dealer named J.P. Groman. (Market yields are in parentheses; amounts are in millions.)

J. P. Groman

Cash	$ 10	Overnight repos	$170
1 month T-bills (7.05%)	75	Subordinated debt	
3 month T-bills (7.25%)	75	7-year fixed (8.55%)	150
2-year T-notes (7.50%)	50		
8-year T-notes (8.96%)	100		

5-year munis (floating rate) (8.20% reset every six months)	25	Equity	15
Total	$335		$335

   a. What is the repricing or funding gap if the planning period is 30 days? 91 days? 2 years? (Recall that cash is a noninterest-earning asset.)
   b. What is the impact over the next 30 days on net interest income if all interest rates rise by 50 basis points?
   c. The following one-year runoffs are expected: $10 million for two-year T-notes, $20 million for the eight-year T-notes. What is the one-year repricing gap?
   d. If runoffs are considered, what is the effect on net interest income at year-end if interest rates rise by 50 basis points?
7. What is the difference between book value accounting and market value accounting? How do interest rate changes affect the value of bank assets and liabilities under the two methods?
8. What is maturity gap? How can one use it to immunize an FI's portfolio?
9. Local Bank has the following balance sheet (in millions):

Assets		Liabilities and equity	
Cash	$60	Demand deposits	$140
5-year T-notes	60	2-year CDs	160
30-year mortgages	200	Net worth	20
	$320		$320

   What is Local Bank's maturity gap?
10. What is one major disadvantage to using the maturity gap model to immunize an FI's portfolio?
11. Consider a 10-year, 10 percent annual coupon bond with a required return of 8 percent.
    a. What is the price of the bond?
    b. If interest rates rise to 9 percent, what is the price of the bond?
    c. Repeat parts (a) and (b) for a 15-year bond.
    d. What do the respective changes in bond prices tell us?
12. Consider a five-year, 15 percent annual coupon bond with a face value of $1,000.
    a. If the current market yield is 8 percent, what is the bond's price?
    b. If the current market yield increases by 1 percent, what is the bond's new price?

c. Using your answers to parts (a) and (b), what is the percentage change in the bond's price as a result of the 1 percent increase in interest rates?

13. Towne Bank has the following market value balance sheet (in millions):

Assets

Cash	$ 20
15-year commercial loan @ 10% annual interest (balloon payment)	160
30-year mortgages @ 8% annual interest, payable monthly (amortizing)	300
	$480

Liabilities and Equity

Demand deposits	$100
5-year CDs @ 6% annual interest (balloon payment)	210
20-year debentures @ 7% annual interest rate	120
Net worth	50
	$480

a. What is Towne Bank's maturity gap?
b. What will the maturity gap be if the interest rates on all assets and liabilities rise by 1 percent?

14. A company issues a three-year bond and a five-year bond simultaneously paying an annual coupon of 8 percent. The face value is $1,000.
   a. If the yield to maturity is 8 percent, what should the bonds sell for?
   b. If the yield to maturity increases to 9 percent, what should the bonds sell for?
   c. If the yield increases to 10 percent, what should the bonds sell for?
   d. What three principles of bond pricing can you derive from the results?

15. If a bank manager was quite certain that interest rates were going to rise within the next six months, how should the bank manager adjust the bank's maturity gap to take advantage of this anticipated rise? What if the manager believed rates would fall?

16. Assume that an FI holds a portfolio of two bonds, seven-year Acme International bonds and two-year Beta Corporation bonds. Acme's bonds are yielding 12 percent and Beta's are yielding 14 percent under current market conditions.
   a. What is the weighted-average maturity of the FI's portfolio if it holds 40 percent of Acme and 60 percent of Beta bonds?
   b. What amount of Acme and Beta bonds should the FI hold to have a weighted-average yield of 13.5 percent?
   c. What is the weighted-average maturity of the portfolio if the proportions held are those as estimated in (b)?

17. An insurance company has invested in three fixed-income securities: $10,000,000 of 5-year T-notes paying 5 percent interest and selling at par value, $5,800,000 of 10-year bonds paying 7 percent interest with a par value of $6,000,000, and $6,200,000 of 20-year subordinated debentures paying 9 percent interest with a par value of $6,000,000. What is the weighted-average maturity of this portfolio of assets? If interest rates change so that the yields on all of the securities decrease by 1 percent, how does the weighted-average maturity of the portfolio change? What if the yields increase by 1 percent? Explain the changes in the maturity values.

18. The following is a simplified balance sheet of an FI. All items are reported in *book values:*

Assets		Liabilities and Net Worth	
Loans	$1,000	Deposits	$850
		Equity	$150
		Total liabilities and	
Total assets	$1,000	net worth	$1,000

The average maturity of loans is four years; that of deposits is two years.
   a. What is the effect on net worth if interest rates on loans and deposits increase to 9 percent? Treat both loans and deposits as zero-coupon instruments (i.e., interest is paid only once, at maturity).
   b. How much should interest rates on deposits increase for net worth to become negative?
   c. What should the average maturity of deposits be for net worth to be zero when interest rates for both loans and deposits increase to 9 percent?

19. Consider the following balance sheet of Mesa Insurance Inc. Amounts are reported in thousands.

Assets		Liabilities	
2-year T-note	$175	1-year commercial paper	$135
15-year munis	165	5-year note	160
		Net worth	45

NOTE: All securities are selling at par equal to book value. The 2-year notes are yielding 5 percent. The 15-year munis are yielding 9 percent; the 1-year commercial paper pays 4.5 percent; and the 5-year notes pay 8 percent. Assume that all instruments pay coupons annually.

a. What is the weighted-average maturity of the FI's assets?

b. What is the weighted-average maturity of the FI's liabilities?

c. What is the FI's maturity gap?

d. What does your answer to part (c) imply about the interest rate exposure of Mesa Insurance Inc.?

e. Calculate the values of all four securities of Mesa Insurance's balance sheet if all interest rates increase by 2 percent.

f. What is the impact on the equity (net worth) of Mesa Insurance Inc. if interest rates increase by 2 percent? Calculate the percentage change in the value of the equity.

g. What would be the impact on Mesa Insurance's net worth if its liabilities paid interest semiannually instead of annually?

20. Scandia Bank has issued a one-year, $1 million CD paying 5.75 percent to fund a one-year loan paying an interest rate of 6 percent. The principal of the loan will be paid in two installments, $500,000 in six months and the balance at the end of the year.

a. What is the maturity gap of this FI? What does the maturity model state about the interest rate exposure with this maturity gap?

b. What is the expected net interest income at the end of the year?

c. What is the effect of an interest rate increase of 2 percent on net interest income as soon as the loan was made? What is the effect on net interest income at the end of the year, if interest rates decrease by 2 percent as soon as the loan was made?

d. What does this say about the maturity model's ability to immunize portfolios against interest rate exposure?

21. EDF bank has a very simple balance sheet. It has a two-year $1 million loan outstanding paying an interest rate of LIBOR + 4 percent annually. It has funded this loan by issuing a two-year deposit paying LIBOR + 3.5 percent interest (annually). The LIBOR is currently at 4 percent.

a. What is the maturity gap of this portfolio?

b. What is the expected net interest income in year 1 and year 2?

c. At the beginning of year 2, LIBOR rates increase to 6 percent. What is the expected net interest income in year 2? What is the effect on net interest income if LIBOR had instead declined to 2 percent?

d. How would your results be affected if the interest on the loan were paid semiannually?

e. What implications do the results have on the effectiveness of the maturity model as an immunization strategy?

Chapter Eighteen

Management of Interest Rate Risk II

This second chapter on measuring interest rate risk looks at a second market-based model of managing interest rate risk: the duration model. We explain the concept of *duration* and see that duration and the duration gap are more accurate measures of an FI's interest rate risk exposure than is the simple maturity model. We begin by presenting the basic arithmetic needed to calculate the duration of an asset or liability. Then we analyze the economic meaning of the number we calculate for duration. This number, which measures the average life of the asset or liability, also has *economic* meaning as the interest sensitivity (or interest elasticity) of that asset's or liability's value. Next we show the way to use the duration measure to protect an FI (or immunize its portfolio) against interest rate risk. Finally, we examine some problems in applying the duration measure to real-world FIs.

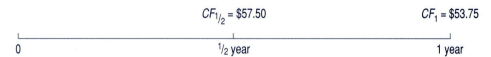

Figure **18–1**   *Promised Cash Flows on the One-Year Loan*

Figure **18–2**   *Present Value of the Cash Flows from the Loan*

DURATION

Duration is a more complete measure of an asset's or liability's interest rate sensitivity than maturity because duration considers the time of arrival of all cash flows as well as the asset's or liability's maturity. Consider the example of the one-year loan examined in Chapter 17. This loan had a 15 percent interest rate and required repayment of half of the $100 in principal at the end of six months and the other half at the end of the year. The bank receives the promised cash flows (*CF*) from the borrower and at the end of one-half year and at the end of one year (see Figure 18–1).

$CF_{1/2}$ is the $50 promised repayment of principal plus the $7.5 promised interest payment ($100 \times 1/2 \times 15\%$) received after six months. CF_1 is the promised cash flow at the end of year; it is equal to the second $50 promised principal repayment plus $3.75 promised interest ($50 \times 1/2 \times 15\%$). To compare the relative size of these two cash flows, we should put them in the same dimensions because $1 of principal or interest received at the end of one year is worth less to the bank in terms of the time value of money than is $1 of principal or interest received at the end of six months. Assuming that current required interest rates are 15 percent per year, we calculate the present values (*PV*) of the two cash flows (CF) as

$$
\begin{array}{ll}
CF_{1/2} = \$57.5 & PV_{1/2} = \$57.5/(1.075) = \$53.49 \\
CF_1 = \$53.75 & PV_1 = \$53.75/(1.075)^2 = \$46.51 \\
CF_{1/2} + CF_1 = \$111.25 & PV_{1/2} + PV_1 = \$100.00
\end{array}
$$

Note that since $CF_{1/2}$, the cash flows received at the end of one-half year, are received earlier, they are discounted at $(1 + R/2)$ where R is the current yield to maturity; this is smaller than the discount rate on the cash flow received at the end of the year $(1 + R/2)^2$. Figure 18–2 summarizes the *PVs* of the cash flows from the loan.[1]

---

[1] Here we use the Treasury formula for calculating the present values of cash flows on a security that pays cash flows semiannually.

duration

The weighted-average time to maturity on an investment.

Technically speaking, **duration** is the *weighted-average* time to maturity using the relative present values of the cash flows as weights. On a time value of money basis, duration also measures the period of time required to recover the initial investment. Any cash flows received after the period of duration and before maturity are the profits or returns paid to the investor. The FI receives some cash flows at one-half year and some at one year (Figure 18–2). Duration analysis weights the time at which cash flows are received by the relative importance in present value terms of the cash flows arriving at each point in time. In present value terms, the relative importance of the cash flows arriving at time $t = ½$ year and time $t = 1$ year are as follows:

Time (t)	Weight (x)
1/2 year	$X_{1/2} = \dfrac{PV_{1/2}}{PV_{1/2} + PV_1} = \dfrac{53.49}{100.00} = .5349 = 53.49\%$
1 year	$X_1 = \dfrac{PV_1}{PV_{1/2} + PV_1} = \dfrac{46.51}{100.00} = .4651 = 46.51\%$
	$\overline{1.0} \quad \overline{100\%}$

That is, in present value terms, the FI receives 53.49 percent of cash flows on the loan with the first payment at the end of six months $(t_{1/2})$ and 46.51 percent with the second payment at the end of the year (t_1). By definition, the sum of the (present value) cash flow weights must equal 1

$$X_{1/2} + X_1 = 1$$
$$.5349 + .4651 = 1$$

We can now calculate the duration (D) or the weighted-average life of the loan, using the present value of its cash flows as weights

$$D_L = X_{1/2}(t_{1/2}) + X_1(t_1)$$
$$= .5349(1/2) + .4651(1) = .7326 \text{ years}$$

Thus, although the maturity of the loan is one year, its duration or average life in a cash flow sense is only .7326 years. On a time value of money basis, the initial investment in the loan is recovered in .7326 years. After that time, the FI earns a profit or return on the loan. The duration is less than maturity because in present value terms 53.49 percent of the cash flows is received at the end of one-half year.

To learn why the bank was still exposed to interest rate risk while it was matching maturities under the maturity model in the example at the end of Chapter 17, we next calculate the duration of the one-year, $100, 15 percent interest certificate of deposit. The bank promises to make only one cash payment to depositors at the end of the year; that is, $CF_1 = \$115$, which is the sum of the promised principal ($100) and interest repayment ($15) to the depositor. Since weights are calculated in present value terms[2]

$$CF_1 = \$115, PV_1 = \$115/1.15 = \$100$$

---

[2]Since the CD is like an annual coupon bond, the annual discount rate is $1/1 + R = 1/1.15$.

$$0 \qquad\qquad\qquad\qquad\qquad\qquad 1 \text{ year}$$
$$PV_1 = \$100 \qquad\qquad\qquad\qquad\qquad CF_1 = \$115$$

F i g u r e **18–3** *Present Value of the Cash Flows of the Deposit*

We show this in Figure 18–3. Because all cash flows are received in one payment at the end of the year, $X_1 = PV_1/PV_1 = 1$, the duration of the deposit is

$$D_D = X_1 \times (1)$$
$$D_D = 1 \text{ x } (1) = 1 \text{ year}$$

Thus, only when all cash flows on a security are limited to one payment at the end of the period with no intervening cash flows does duration equal maturity. This example also illustrates that although the maturity gap between the loan and the deposit is zero, the duration gap is negative

$$M_L - M_D = 1 - 1 = 0$$
$$D_L - D_D = .7326 - 1 = -.2674 \text{ years}$$

As will become clearer, the bank needs to manage its duration gap rather than its maturity gap to measure and to hedge interest rate risk.

Concept Questions

1. Why is duration considered a more complete measure of an asset's or liability's interest rate sensitivity than maturity?
2. When does the duration of an asset equal its maturity?

A GENERAL FORMULA FOR DURATION

You can calculate the duration for any fixed income security that pays interest annually using the following formula:

$$D = \frac{\sum\limits_{t=1}^{N} \dfrac{CF_t * t}{(1+R)^t}}{\sum\limits_{t=1}^{N} \dfrac{CF_t}{(1+R)^t}} = \frac{\sum\limits_{t=1}^{N} PV_t * t}{\sum\limits_{t=1}^{N} PV_t}$$

where

D = duration measured in years

CF_t = cash flow received on the security at end of period t

R = annual yield or current required market interest rate on the investment

N = number of years to maturity

$\sum\limits_{t=1}^{n}$ = summation sign for addition of all terms from $t=1$ to $t=N$

PV_t = present value of the cash flow at the end of the period t

For bonds that compound (pay) interest semiannually, the duration equation becomes[3]

$$D = \frac{\sum\limits_{t=\frac{1}{2}}^{N} \dfrac{CF_t * t}{(1+R/2)^{2t}}}{\sum\limits_{t=\frac{1}{2}}^{N} \dfrac{CF_t}{(1+R/2)^{2t}}}$$

Notice that the denominator of the duration equation is nothing but the present value of the cash flows on the security. The numerator is the present value of each cash flow received on the security multiplied or weighted by the length of time to receive the cash flow. To help you fully understand this formula, we next look at some examples.

The Duration of Bonds Paying Periodic Interest

EXAMPLE 18–1

The Duration of a Four-Year Bond

Suppose that you have a bond that offers a coupon rate of 10 percent paid semiannually. The face value of the bond is $1,000, it matures in four years, and the current yield to maturity (R) is 8 percent. See Table 18–1 for the calculation of its duration. As the calculation indicates, the duration or weighted-average time to maturity on this bond is 3.42 years. In other words, on a time value of money basis, the initial investment of $1,067.34 is recovered after 3.42 years. Between 3.42 years and maturity (4 years), the bond produces a profit or return to the investor. Table 18–2 shows that if the annual coupon rate is lowered

---

[3] In general, the duration equation is written as

$$D = \frac{\sum\limits_{t=1/m}^{N} \dfrac{CF_t * t/m}{(1+R/m)^{mt}}}{\sum\limits_{t=1/m}^{N} \dfrac{CF_t}{(1+R/m)^{mt}}}$$

where

m = the number of times per year interest is paid

Table **18-1**

DURATION OF A FOUR-YEAR BOND WITH 10 PERCENT COUPON PAID SEMIANNUALLY AND 8 PERCENT YIELD

t	CF_t	$\dfrac{1}{(1+4\%)^{2t}}$	$\dfrac{CF_t}{(1+4\%)^{2t}}$	$\dfrac{CF_t * t}{(1+4\%)^{2t}}$
½	50	0.9615	48.08	24.04
1	50	0.9246	46.23	46.23
1½	50	0.8890	44.45	66.67
2	50	0.8548	42.74	85.48
2½	50	0.8219	41.10	102.75
3	50	0.7903	39.52	118.56
3½	50	0.7599	38.00	133.00
4	1,050	0.7307	767.22	3,068.88
			1,067.34	3,645.61

$$D = \frac{3,645.61}{1,067.34} = 3.42 \text{ years}$$

Table **18-2**

DURATION OF A FOUR-YEAR BOND WITH 6 PERCENT COUPON PAID SEMIANNUALLY AND 8 PERCENT YIELD

t	CF_t	$\dfrac{1}{(1+4\%)^{2t}}$	$\dfrac{CF_t}{(1+4\%)^{2t}}$	$\dfrac{CF_t * t}{(1+4\%)^{2t}}$
½	30	0.9615	28.84	14.42
1	30	0.9246	27.74	27.74
1½	30	0.8890	26.67	40.00
2	30	0.8548	25.64	51.28
2½	30	0.8219	24.66	61.65
3	30	0.7903	23.71	71.13
3½	30	0.7599	22.80	79.80
4	1,030	0.7307	752.62	3,010.48
			932.68	3,356.50

$$D = \frac{3,356.50}{932.68} = 3.60 \text{ years}$$

to 6 percent, duration rises to 3.60 years.[4] Since 6 percent coupon payments are lower than 10 percent, it takes longer to recover the initial investment in the bond. In Table 18–3 duration is calculated for the original 10 percent bond assuming that the yield to maturity

---

[4] We could also allow for a variable rate bond by adjusting the semiannual coupon payment by the expected change in interest rates.

Table **18-3**

DURATION OF A FOUR-YEAR BOND WITH 10 PERCENT COUPON PAID SEMIANNUALLY AND 10 PERCENT YIELD

t	CF_t	$\dfrac{1}{(1+5\%)^{2t}}$	$\dfrac{CF_t}{(1+5\%)^{2t}}$	$\dfrac{CF_t * t}{(1+5\%)^{2t}}$
½	50	0.9524	47.62	23.81
1	50	0.9070	45.35	45.35
1½	50	0.8638	43.19	64.78
2	50	0.8227	41.14	82.28
2½	50	0.7835	39.18	97.95
3	50	0.7462	37.31	111.93
3½	50	0.7107	35.53	124.36
4	1,050	0.6768	710.68	2,842.72
			1,000.00	3,393.18

$$D = \frac{3,393.18}{1,000.00} = 3.39 \text{ years}$$

Table **18-4**

DURATION OF A THREE-YEAR BOND WITH 10 PERCENT COUPON PAID SEMIANNUALLY AND 8 PERCENT YIELD

t	CF_t	$\dfrac{1}{(1+4\%)^{2t}}$	$\dfrac{CF_t}{(1+4\%)^{2t}}$	$\dfrac{CF_t * t}{(1+4\%)^{2t}}$
½	50	0.9615	48.08	24.04
1	50	0.9246	46.23	46.23
1½	50	0.8890	44.45	66.67
2	50	0.8548	42.74	85.48
2½	50	0.8219	41.10	102.75
3	1,050	0.7903	829.82	2,489.46
			1,052.42	2,814.63

$$D = \frac{2,814.63}{1,052.42} = 2.67 \text{ years}$$

increases to 10 percent. Now duration falls from 3.42 years (in Table 18–1) to 3.39 years. The higher the yield to maturity on the bond, the more the investor earns on reinvested coupons and the shorter the time needed to recover the initial investment. Finally, the maturity on the original bond decreases to 3 years in Table 18–4 and duration falls to 2.67 years (i.e., the shorter the maturity on the bond, the more quickly the initial investment is recovered). • • •

The Duration of a Zero-Coupon Bond

The U.S. Treasury has created zero-coupon bonds that allow securities firms and other investors to strip individual coupons and the principal from regular Treasury bonds and sell them to investors as separate securities. Elsewhere, such as in the Eurobond markets, corporations have issued discount or zero-coupon bonds directly. U.S. T-bills and commercial paper are usually issued on a discount basis and are additional examples of discount bonds. These bonds sell at a discount from face value on issue and pay the face value (e.g., $1,000) on maturity. These bonds have no intervening cash flows, such as coupon payments, between issue and maturity. The current price that an investor is willing to pay for such a bond, assuming annual compounding of interest, is equal to its present value

$$P = \frac{1,000}{(1 + R)^N}$$

where R is the required annually compounded yield to maturity, N is the number of years to maturity, and P is the price. Because the only cash flow received on these securities is the final payment at time N, the following must be true

$$D_{ZC} = N_{ZC}$$

That is, the duration of a zero-coupon instrument equals its maturity.

EXAMPLE 18–2

• • • • • • • *The Duration of a Zero-Coupon Bond*
Suppose that you have a zero-coupon bond with a face value of $1,000, a maturity of four years, and a current yield to maturity of 8 percent. Since the bond pays no interest, the duration equation consists of only one term; that for cash flows at the end of year 4:

t	CF_4	$\dfrac{1}{(1 + 8\%)^4}$	$\dfrac{CF_4}{(1 + 8\%)^4}$	$\dfrac{CF_4 * 4}{(1 + 8\%)^4}$
4	$1,000	0.7350	735	2,940

$$D = \frac{2,940}{735} = 4 \text{ years}$$

or duration equals the maturity of the zero-coupon bond. • • •

The Duration of a Consol Bond (Perpetuities)

consol bond

A bond that pays a fixed coupon each year forever.

Although *consol bonds* have yet to be issued in the United States, they are of theoretical interest in exploring the differences between maturity and duration. A **consol bond** pays a fixed coupon each year; its novel feature is that it *never* matures; that is, it is a perpetuity

$$M_c = \infty$$

In fact, consol bonds issued by the British government in the 1890s to finance the Boer Wars in South Africa are still outstanding. However, although its maturity is theoretically infinity, the formula for the duration of a consol bond is[5]

$$D_C = 1 + \frac{1}{R}$$

---

[5] For reasons of space, we do not provide formal proof here. Interested readers might refer to Hawawini, "Controlling the Interest Rate Risk of Bonds: An Introduction to Duration Analysis and Immunization Strategies," *Finance Market and Portfolio Management* 1 (1986–1987), pp. 8–18.

where R is the required yield to maturity. Suppose that the yield curve implies $R = 5$ percent annually; the duration of the consol bond is

$$D_C = 1 + \frac{1}{.05} = 21 \text{ years}$$

Thus, maturity is infinite but duration is finite. Specifically, on the basis of the time value of money recovery of the initial investment on this perpetual bond takes 21 years. After 21 years, the bond produces profit for the bondholder. Moreover, as interest rates rise, the duration of the consol bond falls. For example, consider the 1979–1982 period when some yields rose to around 20 percent on long-term government bonds

$$D_C = 1 + \frac{1}{.2} = 6 \text{ years}$$

Concept Questions

1. What does the denominator of the duration equation measure?
2. What does the numerator of the duration equation measure?
3. What is the duration of a one-year, 8 percent coupon, 10 percent yield bond that pays coupons quarterly?
4. What is the duration of a zero-coupon bond?
5. What feature is unique about a consol bond compared to other bonds?

FEATURES OF DURATION

From the preceding examples, we derive several important features of duration relating to the maturity, yield, and coupon interest of the security being analyzed. These features are summarized in Table 18–5.

Duration and Coupon Interest

A comparison of Tables 18–1 and 18–2 indicates that the higher the coupon or promised interest payment on the security, the lower is its duration. This is due to the fact that the larger the coupons or promised interest payments, the more quickly investors receive cash flows and the higher are the present value weights of those cash flows in the duration calculation. On a time value of money basis, the investor recoups the initial investments faster when coupon payments are higher.

Table **18-5**

FEATURES OF DURATION

1. The higher the coupon or promised interest payment on a security, the lower is its duration.
2. The higher the yield on a security, the lower is its duration.
3. Duration increases with maturity at a decreasing rate.

Table **18–6**

DURATION OF A TWO-YEAR BOND WITH 10 PERCENT COUPON PAID SEMIANNUALLY AND 8 PERCENT YIELD

t	CF_t	$\dfrac{1}{(1+4\%)^{2t}}$	$\dfrac{CF_t}{(1+4\%)^{2t}}$	$\dfrac{CF_t * t}{(1+4\%)^{2t}}$
½	50	0.9615	48.08	24.04
1	50	0.9246	46.23	46.23
1½	50	0.8890	44.45	66.67
2	1,050	0.8548	897.54	1,795.08
			1,036.30	1,932.02

$$D = \frac{1,932.02}{1,036.30} = 1.86 \text{ years}$$

In the extreme case when no coupon payments are made (zero-coupon bond), the duration is equal to the maturity of the security. Both the initial investments and any return are received when the security matures. So long as cash flows of some kind are received prior to maturity, a security's duration is less than its maturity.

Duration and Yield

A comparison of Tables 18–1 and 18–3 also indicates that duration decreases as yield increases. This makes sense intuitively because the higher the yield the lower is the cost of waiting to receive a return on the investment. Higher yields discount later cash flows more heavily and the relative importance, or weights, of those later cash flows decline when compared to earlier cash flows on an asset or liability.

Duration and Maturity

A comparison of Tables 18–1, 18–4, and 18–6 indicates that duration *increases* with the maturity of a fixed income asset or liability but at a *decreasing* rate. As maturity of a 10 percent coupon bond decreases from four years to three years (Tables 18–1 and 18–4), duration decreases by 0.75 years, from 3.42 years to 2.67 years. Decreasing maturity for an additional year, from three years to two years (Tables 18–4 and 18–6), decreases duration by 0.81 years from 2.67 years to 1.86 years.

Concept Questions

1. Which has the longest duration, a 30-year, 8 percent, zero-coupon or discount bond, or an 8 percent infinite maturity consol bond?
2. What is the relationship between duration and yield to maturity on a financial security?
3. Do high-coupon bonds have high or low durations?

THE ECONOMIC MEANING
OF DURATION

So far, we have calculated duration for a number of different fixed income assets and liabilities. Now we are ready to make the direct link between duration and the interest rate sensitivity of an asset or liability or of an FI's entire portfolio (i.e., its duration gap).

In addition to being a measure of the average life of an asset or liability, duration is also a direct measure of the interest rate sensitivity or elasticity of an asset or liability. In other words, the larger the numerical value of D calculated for an asset or liability, the more sensitive is the price of that asset or liability to changes or shocks in interest rates. The specific relationship between these factors is represented as

$$\frac{\frac{dP}{P}}{\frac{dR}{(1+R)}} = -D$$

for securities with annual compounding of interest and is represented as

$$\frac{\frac{dP}{P}}{\frac{dR/2}{(1+R/2)}} = -D$$

for securities with semiannual compounding of interest.

interest elasticity

The percentage change in the price of a bond for any given change in interest rates.

The economic interpretation of this equation is that the number D is the **interest elasticity,** or sensitivity, of the security's price to small interest rate changes. That is, D describes the percentage price fall or capital loss of the bond (dP/P) for any given (present value) increase in required interest rates or yields ($dR/1+R$).

The definition of duration can be rearranged in another useful way for interpretation regarding interest sensitivity

$$\frac{dP}{P} = -D\left[\frac{dR}{1+R}\right]$$

or

$$\frac{dP}{P} = -D\left[\frac{dR/2}{(1+R/2)}\right]$$

for annual and semiannual compounding of interest, respectively. This equation shows that for small changes in interest rates, bond prices move *in an inversely proportional* manner according to the size of D. The duration equation can be rearranged, combining D and $(1+R)$ into a single variable $D/(1+R)$ to produce what practitioners call **modified duration** (MD). For annual compounding of interest

modified duration

Duration divided by 1 plus the interest rate.

$$\frac{dP}{P} = -MD \times dR$$

where

$$MD = \frac{D}{1+R}$$

For semiannual compounding of interest

$$\frac{dP}{P} = -MD \times dR/2$$

where

$$MD = \frac{D}{1 + R/2}$$

This form is more intuitive because we multiply $-MD$ by the simple change in interest rates rather than the discounted change in interest rates. Next, we use duration to measure the interest sensitivity of an asset or liability.

The Interest-Paying Bond

EXAMPLE 18–3

Four-Year Bond

Consider the four-year bond with a 10 percent coupon paid semiannually and an 8 percent yield. According to calculations in Table 18–1, the bond's duration is $D = 3.42$ years. Suppose that yields were to rise by one basis point (1/100th of 1 percent) from 8 to 8.01 percent (or one-half a basis point, .00005, for each semiannual period), then using the semi-annual compounding version of the duration model, the percentage change in the bond's price is

$$\frac{dP}{P} = -(3.42)\left[\frac{.00005}{1.04}\right]$$
$$= -.000164$$

or

$$-0.0164\%$$

The bond price had been $1,067.34, which was the present value of a four-year bond with 10 percent coupons and 8 percent yield. However, the duration model predicts that the price of the bond would fall by 0.0164 percent or $0.175, to $1,067.165 after the increase in annual yield by one basis point.[6]

With a lower coupon rate of 6 percent, as in Table 18–2, the bond's duration, D, is 3.6 and the bond price changes by

$$\frac{dP}{P} = -(3.60)\left[\frac{.00005}{1.04}\right] = -.000173$$
$$= -0.0173\%$$

The bond price drops by 0.0173 percent, or $0.161, from $932.68 (reported in Table 18–2) to $932.519. Notice again that, all else constant, the higher the coupon rate on the bond, the shorter is the duration and the smaller is the percentage change in price for a given change in interest rates.

When the yield increased from 8 percent to 10 percent in Table 18–3 with a coupon of 10 percent, duration decreased to 3.39 years. With a one basis point increase in this yield

---

[6] That is, a price fall of 0.0164 percent in this case translates into a dollar fall of $0.175. To calculate the dollar change in value, we can rewrite the equation as $dP = (P)(-D)(dR/1 + R) = (\$1,067.34)(-3.42)(.00005/1.04) = \$0.175$.

$$\frac{dP}{P} = -(3.39)\left[\frac{.00005}{1.05}\right] = -.000161$$
$$= -0.0161\%$$

The bond price drops by 0.016 percent, or $0.161, from $1,000 (reported in Table 18–3) to $999.839. Compared to the original bond with 10 percent coupon and 8 percent yield (see Table 18–1), this bond experiences a smaller percentage price drop. In other words, all else constant, the higher the yield on a bond, the shorter is the duration, and the smaller is the percentage change in price for a given change in interest rates.

Finally, the maturity of the 10 percent coupon bond decreased to three years (Table 18–4), and its duration decreased to 2.67 years. Now for a one basis point increase in yield

$$\frac{dP}{P} = -(2.67)\left[\frac{.00005}{1.04}\right] = -.000128$$
$$= -0.0128\%$$

The bond price drops by 0.0128 percent, or $0.135, from $1,052.42 (Table 18–4) to $1,052.285. All else constant, the shorter the maturity of a bond, the shorter is the duration and the smaller is the percentage change in price. • • •

The Consol Bond

Consider a consol bond with an 8 percent coupon paid annually, an 8 percent yield, and a calculated duration of 13.5 years ($D_C = 1 + 1/.08 = 13.5$). Thus, for a one basis point change in the yield from 8 percent to 8.01 percent

$$\frac{dP}{P} = -(13.5)\left[\frac{.0001}{1.08}\right]$$
$$= -.00125$$

or a 0.125 percent price fall.

Clearly, for any given change in yield, long-duration securities suffer a larger capital loss or receive a higher capital gain than do short-duration securities.

Concept Question

1. What is the relationship between the duration of a bond and its interest elasticity?

• •

DURATION AND IMMUNIZATION

So far, you have learned how to calculate duration and have come to understand that the duration measure has economic meaning because it indicates the interest sensitivity or elasticity of an asset's or liability's value. For FIs, the major relevance of duration is as a measure for managing interest rate risk exposure. Also important is duration's role in allowing an FI to hedge or immunize its balance sheet or some subset on that balance sheet against interest rate risk. The following sections consider two examples of an FI's use of the duration measure for immunization purposes. The first is its use by insurance company and pension fund managers to help meet promised cash flow payments to policyholders or beneficiaries at a particular time in the future. The second is its use in immunizing or insulating an FI's balance sheet against interest rate risk.

Duration and Immunizing Future Payments

Frequently, pension fund and life insurance company managers face the problem of structuring their asset investments so they can pay a given cash amount to policyholders in some future period. The classic example of this is an insurance policy that pays the holder some lump sum when the holder reaches retirement age. The risk to the life insurance company manager is that interest rates on the funds generated from investing the holder's premiums could fall. Thus, the accumulated returns on the premiums invested could not meet the target or promised amount. In effect, the insurance company would be forced to draw down its reserves and net worth to meet its payout commitments. (See Chapter 4 for a discussion of this risk.)

Suppose that it is 1998 and the insurer must make a guaranteed payment to an investor in five years, 2003. For simplicity, we assume that this target guaranteed payment is $1,469, a lump-sum policy payout on retirement, equivalent to investing $1,000 at an annually compounded rate of 8 percent over five years. Of course, realistically, this payment would be much larger, but the underlying principles of the example do not change by scaling up or down the payout amount.

To immunize or protect itself against interest rate risk, the insurer needs to determine which investments would produce a cash flow of exactly $1,469 in five years, regardless of what happens to interest rates in the immediate future. By investing either in a five-year maturity and duration zero-coupon bond or a coupon bond with a five-year duration, the FI would produce a $1,469 cash flow in five years, no matter what happens to interest rates in the immediate future.

Next we consider the two strategies: buying five-year deep-discount bonds and buying five-year duration coupon bonds.

Buy Five-Year Deep-Discount Bonds.   Given a $1,000 face value and an 8 percent yield and assuming annual compounding, the current price per five-year discount bond is $680.58 per bond

$$P = 680.58 = \frac{1,000}{(1.08)^5}$$

If the insurer buys 1.469 of these bonds at a total cost of $1,000 in 1998, these investments would produce $1,469 on maturity in five years. The reason is that the duration of this bond portfolio exactly matches the target horizon for the insurer's future liability to its policyholders. Intuitively, since the issuer of the zero-coupon discount bonds pays no intervening cash flows or coupons, future changes in interest rates have no reinvestment income effect. Thus, the return would be unaffected by intervening interest rate changes.

Buy a Five-Year Duration Coupon Bond.   Suppose that no five-year discount bonds exist. In this case, the portfolio manager may seek to invest in appropriate duration coupon bonds to hedge interest rate risk. In this example, the appropriate investment is in five-year duration coupon-bearing bonds. Consider a six-year maturity bond with an 8 percent coupon paid annually, an 8 percent yield, and $1,000 face value. The duration of this six-year maturity bond is computed as 4.993 years or approximately 5 years (Table 18–7). By buying this six-year maturity, five-year duration bond in 1998 and holding it for five years

Table **18-7**

DURATION OF A SIX-YEAR BOND WITH 8 PERCENT COUPON PAID ANNUALLY AND AN 8 PERCENT YIELD

t	CF_t	$\dfrac{1}{(1+8\%)^t}$	$\dfrac{CF_t}{(1+8\%)^t}$	$\dfrac{CF_t * t}{(1+8\%)^t}$
1	80	0.9259	74.07	74.07
2	80	0.8573	68.59	137.18
3	80	0.7938	63.51	190.53
4	80	0.7350	58.80	235.20
5	80	0.6806	54.45	272.25
6	1,080	0.6302	680.58	4,083.48
			1,000.00	4,992.71

$$D = \frac{4{,}992.71}{1{,}000.00} = 4.993 \text{ years}$$

until 2003, the term exactly matches the insurer's target horizon. We show in the next set of examples that cash flows generated at the end of five years is $1,469 whether interest rates stay at 8 percent or instantaneously (immediately) rise to 9 percent or fall to 7 percent. Thus, buying a coupon bond whose duration exactly matches the investment time horizon of the insurer also immunizes the insurer against interest rate changes.

EXAMPLE 18 – 4

Interest Rates Remain at 8 Percent

The cash flows received by the insurer on the bond if interest rates stay at 8 percent throughout the five years are as follows:

1.	Coupons, 5 × $80	$ 400
2.	Reinvestment income	69
3.	Proceeds from sale of bond at end of the fifth year	1,000
		$1,469

We calculate each of the three components of the insurer's income from the bond investment as follows

1. *Coupons.* The $400 from coupons is simply the annual coupon of $80 received in each of the five years.
2. *Reinvestment income.* Because the coupons are received annually, they can be reinvested at 8 percent as they are received, generating an additional cash flow of $69. To understand this, consider the coupon payments as an annuity stream of $80 invested at 8 percent at the end of each year for five years. The future value of the annuity stream[7] is calculated using a future value of an annuity factor (FVAF) as $80 (FVAF$_{5 \text{ years}, 8\%}$) = 80 (5.867) = $469. Subtracting the $400 of invested coupon payments leaves $69 of reinvestment income.

---

[7] Tables for future value of an annuity factor (FVAF) are at the end of this book.

3. *Bond sale proceeds.*   The proceeds from the sale are calculated by recognizing that the six-year bond has just one year left to maturity when the insurance company sells it at the end of the fifth year (i.e., year 2003). That is:

```
↓ Sell                              $1,080
|_____|
Year 5                          Year 6
(2003)                          (2004)
```

What fair market price can the insurer expect to receive upon selling the bond at the end of the fifth year with one year left to maturity? A buyer would be willing to pay the present value of the $1,080—final coupon plus face value—to be received at the end of the one remaining year, or

$$P_5 = \frac{1,080}{1.08} = \$1,000$$

Thus, the insurer would be able to sell the one remaining cash flow of $1,080, to be received in the bond's final year, for $1,000   • • •

Next we show that since this bond has a duration of five years, matching the insurer's target period, even if interest rates were to instantaneously fall to 7 percent or rise to 9 percent, the expected cash flows from the bond still would sum exactly to $1,469. That is, the coupons plus reinvestment income plus principal received at the end of the fifth year would be immunized. In other words, the cash flows on the bond are protected against interest rate changes.

E X A M P L E   1 8 – 5

Interest Rates Fall to 7 Percent
In this example with falling interest rates, the cash flows over the five years are as follows

1.	Coupons, 5 × $80	$ 400
2.	Reinvestment income	60
3.	Bond sale proceeds	1,009
		$1,469

Thus, the amount of the total proceeds over the five years is unchanged from proceeds generated when interest rates were 8 percent. To see why this occurs, consider what happens to the three parts of the cash flow when rates fall to 7 percent:

1. *Coupons.*   These are unchanged since the insurer still receives five annual coupons of $80 ($400).
2. *Reinvestment income.*   The coupons can now be reinvested only at the lower rate of 7 percent. Thus, at the end of five years $80(FVAF$_{5 \text{ years},7\%}$) = 80(5.751) = $460. Subtracting the $400 in original coupon payments leaves $60. Because interest rates have fallen, the investor has $9 less in reinvestment income at the end of the five-year planning horizon.
3. *Bond sale proceeds.*   When the six-year maturity bond is sold at the end of the fifth year with one cash flow of $1,080 remaining, investors would be willing to pay more

$$P_5 = \frac{1,080}{1.07} = \$1,009$$

That is, the bond can be sold for $9 more than when rates were 8 percent. The reason is that investors can get only 7 percent on newly issued bonds, but this older bond was issued with a higher coupon of 8 percent.

A comparison of reinvestment income with bond sale proceeds, indicates that the decrease in rates has produced a *gain* of $9 on the bond sale proceeds. This offsets the loss of reinvestment income of $9 as a result of reinvesting at a lower interest rate. Thus, total cash flows remain unchanged at $1,469.   •   •   •

•   •   •   •   •   •   •

Interest Rates Rise to 9 Percent

In this example with rising interest rates, the proceeds from the bond investment are as follows:

1. Coupons, 5 × $80 $ 400
2. Reinvestment income [(FVAF$_{5 \text{ years, } 9\%}$) 80 – 400]   78   [FVAF$_{5 \text{ years, } 9\%}$ = 5.985]
3. Bond sale proceeds (1,080/1.09)   991
                                                         $1,469

Notice that the rise in interest rates from 8 to 9 percent leaves the final terminal cash flow unaffected at $1,469. The rise in rates has generated $9 extra reinvestment income ($78 – $69), but the price at which the bond can be sold at the end of the fifth year has declined from $1,000 to $991, equal to a capital loss of $9. Thus, the gain in reinvestment income is exactly offset by the capital loss on the sale of the bond.   •   •   •

The preceding examples demonstrate that matching the duration of a coupon bond—or any fixed interest rate instrument such as a loan or mortgage—to the FI's target or investment horizon *immunizes* it against instantaneous shocks to interest rates. The gains or losses on reinvestment income that result from an interest rate change are exactly offset by losses or gains from the bond proceeds on sale.

Immunizing an FI's Entire Balance Sheet

So far we have looked at the durations of individual instruments and ways to select individual fixed income securities to protect FIs, such as life insurance companies and pension funds, with certain precommitted liabilities, such as future pension plan payouts. The duration model can also evaluate an FI's overall interest rate exposure, that is, measure the **duration gap** on its balance sheet.

duration gap

A measure of overall interest rate risk exposure for an FI.

The Duration Gap for a Financial Institution. To estimate the overall duration gap, we first determine the duration of an FI's asset portfolio (A) and the duration of its liability portfolio (L). These can be calculated as

$$D_A = X_{1A}D_1^A + X_{2A}D_2^A + ... + X_{nA}D_n^A$$

and

$$D_L = X_{1L}D_1^L + X_{2L}D_2^L + ... + X_{nL}D_n^L$$

where

$$X_{1j} + X_{2j} + ... + X_{nj} = 1 \text{ and } j = A,L$$

The *X*s in the equation represent the market value proportions of each asset or liability held in the respective asset and liability portfolios. Thus, if new 30-year Treasury bonds were 1 percent of a life insurer's portfolio and D_1^A the duration of those bonds, was equal to 9.25 years, then $X_{1A}D_1^A = .01 (9.25) = 0.0925$. More simply, the duration of a portfolio of assets or liabilities is a market value weighted average of the individual durations of the assets or liabilities on the FI's balance sheet.[8]

Consider an FI's simplified market value balance sheet:

Assets ($)	Liabilities ($)
A = 100	L = 90
	E = 10
100	100

From the balance sheet

$$A = L + E$$

and

$$\Delta A = \Delta L + \Delta E$$

or

$$\Delta E = \Delta A - \Delta L$$

That is, when interest rates change, the change in the FI's net worth equals the difference between the change in the market values of assets and liabilities on each side of the balance sheet. This was part of the discussion of the maturity model in Chapter 17. The difference here is that the goal is to relate the sensitivity of an FI's net worth (ΔE) to its duration mismatch rather than its maturity mismatch. As we have already shown, duration is a more accurate measure of the interest rate sensitivity of an asset or liability than is maturity since duration accounts for the timing of receiving and paying cash flows on assets and liabilities.

Since $\Delta E = \Delta A - \Delta L$, we need to determine how ΔA and ΔL—the changes in the market values of assets and liabilities on the balance sheet—are related to duration.[9] From the duration model (assuming annual compounding of interest)

$$\frac{\Delta A}{A} = (-D_A) \frac{\Delta R}{(1 + R)}$$

$$\frac{\Delta L}{L} = (-D_L) \frac{\Delta R}{(1 + R)}$$

Here we have simply substituted $\Delta A/A$ or $\Delta L/L$, the percentage change in the market values of assets or liabilities, for $\Delta P/P$, the percentage change in any single bond's price,

---

[8] This derivation of an FI's duration gap closely follows G. G. Kaufman, "Measuring and Managing Interest Rate Risk: A Primer," *Economic Perspectives*, (Chicago: Federal Reserve Bank of Chicago, 1984), pp. 16–29.

[9] In what follows, we use the Δ (change) notation instead of *d* (derivative notation) to recognize that interest rate changes tend to be discrete rather than infinitesimally small. For example, in real-world financial markets, the smallest observed rate change is usually one basis point or 1/100th of 1 percent.

and D_A or D_L, the duration of the FI's asset or liability portfolio, for D, the duration on any given bond, deposit, or loan. The term $\Delta R/(1 + R)$ reflects the shock to interest rates as before.[10] To show dollar changes, these equations can be rewritten as:

$$\Delta A = A \times (-D_A) \times \frac{\Delta R}{(1 + R)}$$

and

$$\Delta L = L \times (-D_L) \times \frac{\Delta R}{(1 + R)}$$

Since $\Delta E = \Delta A - \Delta L$, we can substitute these two expressions into this equation. Rearranging and combining these equations[11] results in a measure of the change in the market value of equity

$$\Delta E = -[D_A - kD_L] \times A \times \frac{\Delta R}{(1 + R)}$$

where $k = L/A$ is a measure of the FI's leverage, that is, the amount of borrowed funds or liabilities rather than owners' equity used to fund its asset portfolio. The effect of interest rate changes on the market value of an FI's equity or net worth (ΔE) breaks down into three effects:

1. *The leverage-adjusted duration gap* $= [D_A - kD_L]$. This gap is measured in years and reflects the degree of duration mismatch in an FI's balance sheet. Specifically, the larger this gap *in absolute terms,* the more exposed the FI is to interest rate risk.
2. *The size of the FI.* The term A measures the size of the FI's assets. The larger the scale of the FI, the larger is the dollar size of the potential net worth exposure from any given interest rate shock.

---

[10]For simplicity, we assume that the interest rate changes are the same for both assets and liabilities. This assumption is standard in "Macauley" duration analysis.

[11]

$$\Delta E = \left[A \times (-D_A) \times \frac{\Delta R}{(1 + R)}\right] - \left[L \times (-D_L) \times \frac{\Delta R}{(1 + R)}\right]$$

Assuming that the level of interest rates and expected shock to interest rates are the same for both assets and liabilities

$$\Delta E = [(-D_A)A + (D_L)L] \frac{\Delta R}{(1 + R)}$$

or

$$\Delta E = -[D_A A - D_L L] \frac{\Delta R}{(1 + R)}$$

To rearrange the equation in a slightly more intuitive fashion, we multiply and divide both the terms $D_A A$ and $D_L L$ by A (assets):

$$\Delta E = -[(A/A)D_A - (L/A)D_L] \times A \times (\Delta R/(1 + R))$$

Therefore

$$\Delta E = -[D_A - (L/A)D_L] \times A \times (\Delta R/(1 + R))$$

and thus

$$\Delta E = -[D_A - kD_L] \times A \times (\Delta R/(1 + R))$$

where $k = L/A$.

3. *The size of the interest rate shock* = ΔR/(1 + R).   The larger the shock, the greater is the FI's exposure.[12]

Given this, we express the exposure of the net worth of the FI as

$$\Delta E = -[\text{Adjusted duration gap}] \times \text{Asset size} \times \text{Interest rate shock}$$

Interest rate shocks are largely external to the bank and often result from changes in the Federal Reserve's monetary policy or from international capital movements (as discussed in the first section of Chapter 17). The size of the duration gap and the size of the FI, however, are largely under the control of management.

The next section uses an example to explain how a manager can utilize information on an FI's duration gap to restructure the balance sheet to immunize stockholders' net worth against interest rate risk.

E X A M P L E   1 8 – 7

Duration Gap Measurement and Exposure
Suppose that the FI manager calculates that

$$D_A = 5 \text{ years}$$
$$D_L = 3 \text{ years}$$

Then the manager learns from an economic forecasting unit that rates are expected to rise from 10 to 11 percent in the immediate future, that is,

$$\Delta R = 1\% = .01$$
$$1 + R = 1.10$$

The FI's initial balance sheet is assumed to be

Assets ($ millions)	Liabilities ($ millions)	
A = 100	L =	90
	E =	10
100		100

The FI manager calculates the potential loss to equity holders' net worth (E) if the forecast of rising rates proves true

$$\Delta E = -(D_A - kD_L) \times A \times \frac{\Delta R}{(1 + R)}$$

$$= -(5 - (.9)(3)) \times \$100 \text{ million} \times \frac{.01}{1.1} = -\$2.09 \text{ million}$$

---

[12]We assume that the level of rates and the expected shock to interest rates are the same for both assets and liabilities. This assumption is standard in "Macauley" duration analysis. Although restrictive, this assumption can be relaxed. Specifically, if ΔR_A is the shock to assets and ΔR_L is the shock to liabilities, we can express the duration gap model as

$$\Delta E = -[[D_A \times A \times \frac{\Delta R_A}{1 + R_A}] - [D_L \times L \times \frac{\Delta R_L}{1 + R_L}]]$$

That is, the bank could lose $2.09 million in net worth if rates rise by 1 percent. The FI started with $10 million in equity, so the loss of $2.09 million is almost 21 percent of its initial net worth. The market value balance sheet after the rise in rates by 1 percent then appears as follows:[13]

Assets ($ millions)	Liabilities ($ millions)	
A = 95.45	L =	87.54
	E =	7.91
95.45		95.45

Even though the rise in interest rates would not push the FI into economic insolvency, it reduces the FI's net worth-to-assets ratio from 10 (10/100) to 8.29 percent (7.91/95.45). To counter this effect, the manager might reduce the FI's adjusted duration gap. In an extreme case, the gap might be reduced to 0

$$\Delta E = -[0] \times A \times \Delta R/(1 + R) = 0$$

To do this, the FI should not directly set $D_A = D_L$, which ignores the facts that the bank's assets (A) do not equal its borrowed liabilities (L) and that k (which reflects the ratio L/A) is not equal to 1. To see the importance of factoring in leverage (or L/A), suppose that the manager increases the duration of the FI's liabilities to five years, the same as D_A then

$$\Delta E = -[5 - (.9)(5)] \times \$100 \text{ million} \times (.01/1.1) = -\$0.45 \text{ million}$$

The FI is still exposed to a loss of $0.45 million if rates rise by 1 percent.

An appropriate strategy involves changing D_L until

$$D_A = kD_L = 5 \text{ years}$$

For example,

$$\Delta E = -[5 - (.9)5.55] \times \$100 \text{ million} \times (.01/1.1) = 0$$

In this case, the FI manager sets $D_L = 5.55$ years, or slightly longer than $D_A = 5$ years, to compensate for the fact that only 90 percent of assets are funded by borrowed liabilities, with the other 10 percent funded by equity. Note that the FI manager has at least three other ways to reduce the adjusted duration gap to zero:

1. *Reduce D_A.* Reduce D_A from 5 years to 2.7 years (equal to kD_L or (.9)(3)) so that

$$[D_A - kD_L] = [2.7 - (.9)(3)] = 0$$

---

[13]These values are calculated as follows:

$$\frac{\Delta A}{A} = -5\left(\frac{.01}{1.1}\right) = -.04545 = -4.545\%$$

$$100 + (-.04545)100 = 95.45$$

and

$$\frac{\Delta L}{L} = -3\left(\frac{.01}{1.1}\right) = -.02727 = -2.727\%$$

$$90 + (-.02727)90 = 87.54$$

Contemporary Perspectives 18–1

Pitcairn Cuts Govies

Pitcairn Trust recently purchased $1–2 million each of Lehman Brothers 7 1/2% senior subordinated notes of 2003, Ford Motor Credit 6 3/8% notes of 2008 and Weyerhaeuser 7 1/2% debentures of 2013 to pick up spread in the anticipated choppy interest rate environment, according to Patrick Kennedy, port-folio manager. The move, financed by selling Treasuries of similar duration, left Government/Corporate Bond Index benchmark.

Kennedy says recent interest-rate volatility makes it difficult to predict the direction of near-term rates so he is maintaining a duration-neutral approach while buying short-term spread products. The $37 million Jenkintown, Pa.-based fund allocates 41% to investment-grade corporates, 25% to Treasuries, 12% to mort-gages, 14% to asset-backed secu-rities, 3% to international credits and 5% to cash.

SOURCE: *Bondweek,* May 26,1997, p. 8. This copyrighted material is reprinted with the permission of Bondweek, a publication of Institu-tional Investor, Inc., 488 Madison Avenue, New York, NY 10022.

Contemporary Perspectives 18–2

Federated Cuts Duration Ahead of FOMC

Federated Investors recently shortened duration in its $10 million Limited Term Fund by selling $4 million in credit card-backed bonds, the fund's longest duration instruments, for money-market paper and floating-rate notes. The move is designed to preempt a likely Federal Reserve monetary policy tightening at tomorrow's Federal Open Market Committee meeting, says Randall Bauer, portfolio manager.

Bauer expects a Fed tightening to cause the yield curve to flatten overall, but has built a defensive position in the short-term fund because he expects short maturity bonds will trade off on a rate hike. Bauer's move trimmed duration to a short 1.7 years from a neutral 1.87 years. The fund tracks the Merrill Lynch One- to Three-Year Corporate Bond Index.

SOURCE: Elizabeth Roy, *The Bond Buyer,* November, 13, 1996, p. 6. Reprinted with permission—*American Banker.*

2. *Reduce* D_A *and increase* D_L. Shorten the duration of assets and lengthen the duration of liabilities at the same time. One possibility is to *reduce* D_A to 4 years and to *increase* D_L to 4.44 years so that

$$[D_A - kD_L] = [4 - (.9)(4.44)] = 0$$

3. *Change* k *and* D_L. Increase k (leverage) from .9 to .95 and increase D_L from 3 years to 5.26 years so that

$$[D_A - kD_L] = [5 - (.95)(5.26)] = 0 \qquad \bullet \quad \bullet \quad \bullet$$

Contemporary Perspectives Boxes 18–1 and 18–2 show how two FIs used duration to immunize interest rate volatility.

Concept Questions

1. Refer to Example 18–4. Suppose that rates fall to 6 percent. Is the FI's portfolio still immunized? What if rates rise to 10 percent?
2. How is an FI's overall duration gap calculated?
3. How can a manager use information about an FI's duration gap to restructure, and thereby immunize, the balance sheet against interest rate risk?
4. Suppose that D_A = 3 years, D_L = 6 years, k = .8, and A = \$100 million; what is the effect on owners' net worth if $\Delta R/(1 + R)$ rises by 1 percent?

DIFFICULTIES IN APPLYING THE DURATION MODEL TO REAL-WORLD FI BALANCE SHEETS

Critics of the duration model have often claimed that it is difficult to apply in real-world situations. However, duration measures and immunization strategies are useful in most real-world situations. In fact, the model recently proposed by the Federal Reserve and the Bank for International Settlements to monitor bank interest rate risk taking, which we discuss later in this chapter, is heavily based on the duration model. We next consider the various criticisms of the duration model and discuss ways in which a modern FI manager would deal with these criticisms in practice.

Duration Matching Can Be Costly

Critics charge that although in principle an FI manager can change D_A and D_L to immunize the FI against interest rate risk, restructuring the balance sheet of a large and complex FI can be both time consuming and costly. This argument may have been true historically, but the growth of purchased funds, asset securitization, and loan sales markets has considerably eased the speed and lowered the transaction costs of major balance sheet restructurings. (See Chapter 12 for a discussion of these strategies.) Moreover, an FI manager could still manage risk exposure using the duration model by employing techniques other than direct portfolio rebalancing to immunize against interest rate risk. Managers can obtain many of the same results of direct duration matching by taking hedging positions in the markets for derivative securities, such as futures and forwards (Chapter 21); options, caps, floors, and collars (Chapter 22); and swaps (Chapter 23).

Immunization Is a Dynamic Problem

Immunization is an aspect of the duration model that is not well understood. Let's go back to the earlier immunization example in which an insurer sought to buy bonds to provide an accumulated cash flow of \$1,469 in five years no matter what happened to interest rates. We showed that buying a six-year maturity, 8 percent coupon bond with a five-year duration immunizes the insurer against an instantaneous change in interest rates. The word *instantaneous* is very important here; it means a change in interest rates immediately after purchasing the bond. However, interest rates can change at any time over the holding period. In addition, the duration of a bond changes as time passes, that is, as it approaches maturity or the target horizon date. In addition, duration changes at a different rate than does real or calendar time.

To understand this time effect, consider the initially hedged position of the insurer that bought the five-year duration (six-year maturity), 8 percent coupon bond in 1998 to match its cash flow target of $1,469 in 2003. Suppose that the FI manager puts the bond in the bottom drawer of a desk and does not think about it for a year, believing that the insurance company's position is fully hedged. After one year (in 1999), the manager opens the drawer of the desk and finds the bond. Knowing that the target date is now only four years away, the manager recalculates the duration of the bond. Imagine the manager's shock on finding that the same 8 percent coupon bond with an 8 percent yield and only five years left to maturity has a duration of 4.31 years. This means the insurance company is no longer hedged; the 4.31 year duration of this bond portfolio *exceeds* the investment horizon of four years. As a result, the manager must restructure the bond portfolio to remain immunized. One way to do this is to sell some of the 5-year bonds (4.31 year duration) and buy some bonds of shorter duration so that the overall duration of the investment portfolio is four years.

For example, suppose that the insurer sold 50 percent of the 5-year bonds with a 4.31-year duration and invested the proceeds in zero-coupon bonds with a remaining maturity and duration of 3.69 years. Because duration and maturity are the same for discount bonds, the duration of the asset portfolio is

$$D_A = [4.31 \times .5] + [3.69 \times .5] = 4 \text{ years}$$

This simple example demonstrates that immunization based on duration is a dynamic strategy. In theory, the strategy requires the portfolio manager to rebalance the portfolio continuously to ensure that the duration of the investment portfolio exactly matches the investment horizon (i.e., the duration of liabilities). Because continuous rebalancing may not be easy to do and involves costly transaction fees, most portfolio managers seek to be only approximately dynamically immunized against interest rate changes by rebalancing at discrete intervals such as quarterly. That is, there is a trade-off between being perfectly immunized and the transaction costs of maintaining an immunized balance sheet over time.

Large Interest Rate Changes and Convexity

Duration accurately measures the price sensitivity of fixed-income securities for small changes in interest rates of the order of one basis point. But suppose that interest rate shocks are much larger, of the order of 2 percent or 200 basis points. Then duration becomes a less accurate predictor of how much the prices of securities will change and, therefore, a less accurate measure of interest rate sensitivity. Figure 18–4 is a graphic representation of the reason for this. Note first the change in a bond's price due to yield changes according to the duration model and then the true relationship, as calculated directly, using the exact present value calculation for bond valuation.

The duration model predicts that the relationship between interest rate shocks and bond price changes will be proportional to *D* (duration). By precisely calculating the true change in bond prices, however, we would find that for large interest rate increases, duration overpredicts the *fall* in bond prices and for large interest rate decreases, it underpredicts the *increase* in bond prices. That is, the duration model predicts symmetric effects for rate increases and decreases on bond prices. As Figure 18–4 shows, in actuality, the *capital loss effect* of rate increases tends to be smaller than the *capital gain effect* of rate decreases. This is the result of the bond price–yield relationship exhibiting a property called **convexity** rather than *linearity,* as assumed by the basic duration model.

convexity

The degree of curvature of the price-yield curve around some interest rate level.

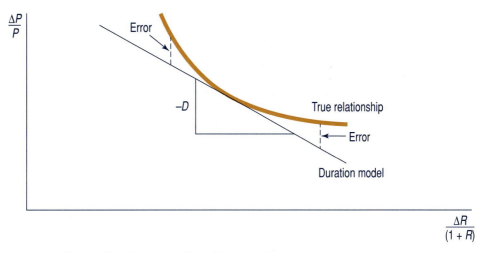

F i g u r e **18–4**   *Duration versus True Relationship*

Concept Questions

1. Why do critics argue that the duration model is difficult to apply in real-world situations? How can these arguments be countered?
2. What is convexity? Is it a desirable feature for assets?

• •

NEW REGULATORY APPROACHES TO
INTEREST RATE RISK MEASUREMENT

Congress passed the Federal Deposit Insurance Corporation Improvement Act (FDICIA) at the end of 1991 in the wake of record numbers of bank and thrift failures. This act requires federal regulators to review capital adequacy standards for banks and thrifts and to revise the way they measure interest rate risk exposure.

In 1993, the Bank for International Settlements (BIS), an organization encompassing the largest central banks in the world (such as the Federal Reserve), made a specific proposal for measuring the interest rate gap exposure of banks and other credit-generating FIs based on the duration gap model. The proposal was to use a common model (and capital requirement) to measure the duration gap exposures of banks in all BIS member countries. This supplements the 8 percent capital requirement for credit risk currently imposed on the world's major banks (see Chapter 16).[14]

However, the 1993 BIS proposal came under attack for a number of reasons. These attacks—especially from the banking industry—focused on a number of areas. Most specifically, the proposal (1) imposes an additional reporting burden on small, low-risk

---

[14]For more details, see Federal Reserve Board of Governors, Press Release, July 30, 1992.

banks, (2) requires an approach that is too crude and that ignores the complexity of many large FI portfolios, and (3) results in an inaccurate duration as a measure of interest rate risk for large interest rate changes (the so-called convexity problem).

In 1995, the Federal Reserve revised the BIS proposal as part of its new approach to evaluating a bank's interest rate risk exposure. The Fed proposes to rely primarily on examiners' judgment as to what is excessive interest rate exposure, but it includes a quantitative (market value–based) model that examiners could use to make their overall evaluations of bank interest rate risk exposures. Specifically, quantitative models evaluate the effect on a bank's net worth (ΔE) of hypothetical 2 percent increases and decreases in the level of interest rates on the present-value cash flows from a bank's assets and liabilities and off-balance-sheet positions.[15]

Concept Question

1.   What are the criticisms of the 1993 BIS model?

• •

_____

[15]Conceptually, these quantitative models can be viewed as a duration model approach with an adjustment for convexity.

S U M M A R Y

This chapter analyzed the duration model approach to measuring interest rate risk. The duration model is superior to the simple maturity and repricing models because it incorporates the timing of cash flows as well as maturity effects into a simple measure of interest rate risk. FIs can use the duration measure to immunize a particular liability as well as their entire balance sheet. However, the duration model itself is not completely accurate. Specifically, it can under- or overestimate the effects of interest rate changes on asset and liability values when interest rate changes or shocks are large.

P E R T I N E N T   W E B   S I T E S

Bank for International Settlements   http://www.bis.org/home.htm

Board of Governors of the Federal Reserve   http://www.bog.frb.fed.us/

Management of Interest Rate Risk II

1.   Consider the following.
   a.   What is the duration of a two-year bond that pays an annual coupon of 10 percent and has a current yield to maturity of 12 percent? Use $1,000 as the face value.
   b.   What is the duration of a two-year zero-coupon bond that is yielding 11.5 %? Use $1,000 as the face value.
   c.   Given these answers, how does duration differ from maturity?
2.   Consider the following two banks:
   Bank 1 has assets composed solely of a 10-year, 12 percent, $1 million loan. It is financed by a 10-year, 10 percent, $1 million CD.

Bank 2 has assets composed solely of a 7-year, 12 percent zero-coupon bond with a current value of $894,006.2 and a maturity value of $1,976,362.88. It is financed by a 10-year, 8.275 percent coupon, $1,000,000 face value CD with a yield to maturity (ytm) of 10 percent. All securities except the zero-coupon bond pay interest annually.

    a. If interest rates rise by 1 percent (100 basis points), how do the values of the assets and liabilities of each bank change?

    b. What accounts for the differences between the two banks' accounts?

3. Consider the following.

    a. What is the duration of a five-year Treasury bond with a 10 percent semiannual coupon selling at par?

    b. What is the duration of this bond if the ytm increases to 14 percent? What if the ytm increases to 16 percent?

    c. What can you conclude about the relationship between duration and yield to maturity?

4. A six-year, $10,000 CD pays 6 percent interest annually.

    a. What is the CD's duration?

    b. Recalculate the duration if interest is paid semiannually.

5. Consider the following.

    a. What is the duration of a four-year Treasury bond with a 10 percent semiannual coupon selling at par?

    b. What is the duration of a three-year Treasury bond with a 10 percent semiannual coupon selling at par?

    c. What is the duration of a two-year Treasury bond with a 10 percent semiannual coupon selling at par?

    d. What conclusions can you draw from these results between duration and maturity?

6. Consider the following.

    a. What is the duration of a consol bond that has a discount rate of 8 percent? What is the duration if it increases to 10 percent? If it increases to 12 percent?

    b. What are some examples of consol bonds?

7. Suppose that you purchase a five-year, 13.76 percent bond that is priced to yield 10 percent.

    a. Show that the duration is equal to four years.

    b. Show that if interest rates rise to 11 percent next year and your investment horizon is four years from today, you will still earn a 10 percent yield on your investment.

8. An insurance company is analyzing the following three bonds and is using duration as its measure of interest rate risk:

  A. $10,000 par value, coupon rate = 8%, ytm = 10%

  B. $10,000 par value, coupon rate = 10%, ytm = 10%

  C. $10,000 par value, coupon rate = 12%, ytm = 10%

What is the duration of each of the three bonds?

9. How is duration related to the interest elasticity of a fixed income security? What is the relationship between duration and the price of a fixed income security?

10. You have discovered that when the required return of a bond you own fell by 0.5 percent from 9.75 percent to 9.25 percent, the price rose from $975 to $995. What is the duration of this bond?

11. You can obtain a loan for $100,000 at a rate of 10 percent for two years. You have a choice of either paying the principal at the end of the second year or amortizing the loan (i.e., pay principal and interest per year). The loan is priced at par (i.e., you can discount it at 10 percent).

    a. What is the duration of the loan under both methods of payments?

    b. Explain the difference in the two results.

12. The duration of an 11-year Treasury bond paying a 10 percent semiannual coupon and selling at par has been estimated at 6.9 years. Assume a face value of $1,000.

    a. What is the modified duration of the bond?

    b. What is the effect on the price of the bond if interest rates increase by 0.10 percent?

13. If you use duration only to immunize your portfolio, what three factors affect changes in an FI's net worth when interest rates change?

14. What are the three criticisms of using the duration model to immunize an FI's portfolio?

15. Consider the following.

    a. What is the duration of a two-year bond that pays an annual coupon of 10 percent and whose current yield to maturity is 14 percent? Use $1,000 as the face value.

    b. What is the expected change in the price of the bond if interest rates are expected to decline by 0.5 percent?

16. Consider the following.

    a. Calculate the leverage-adjusted duration gap of an FI that has assets of $1 million invested in 30-year, 10 percent semiannual coupon Treasury bonds selling at par and whose duration has been estimated at 9.94 years. It has liabilities of $900,000 financed through a two-year, 7.25 percent semiannual coupon note selling at par.

    b. What is the impact on equity values if all interest rates fall 20 basis points, that is, $(\Delta R/2)/(1 + R/2) = -0.0020$?

17. If interest rates rise and an investor holds a bond for a time longer than the duration, will the return earned exceed or fall short of the original required rate of return?

18. Use the data provided for Gotbucks Bank, Inc. to answer the questions.

Gotbucks Bank, Inc. ($ millions)

Assets		Liabilities	
Cash	30	Core deposits	20
Federal funds	20	Federal funds	50
Loans (floating)	105	Euro CDs	130
Loans (fixed)	65	Equity	20
Total assets	220	Total liab. & equity	220

NOTES TO THE BALANCE SHEET: Currently the Fed funds rate is 8.5%. Variable rate loans are priced at 4% over LIBOR (currently at 11%). Fixed rate loans have five-year maturities with 12% interest paid annually. Core deposits are all fixed rate for two years at 8% paid annually. Euros currently yield 9%.

a. What is the duration of Gotbucks Bank's (GBI) fixed-rate loan portfolio if the loans are priced at par?
b. If the average duration of GBI's floating rate loans (including Fed fund assets) is .36 years, what is the duration of the bank's assets? (Note that the duration of cash is zero.)
c. What is the duration of GBI's core deposits if they are priced at par?
d. If the duration of GBI's Euro CD and Fed fund liabilities is .401 years, what is the duration of the bank's liabilities?
e. What is GBI's duration gap? What is its interest rate risk exposure? If *all* yields increase by 1 percent, what is the impact on the market value of GBI's equity? (That is, $\Delta R/1 + R = .01$ for all assets and liabilities).

19. An insurance company issued a $90 million, one-year, zero-coupon note at 8 percent add-on annual interest (paying one coupon at the end of the year) and used the proceeds to fund a $100 million, face-value, two-year commercial loan at 10 percent annual interest. Immediately after these transactions were (simultaneously) undertaken, all interest rates went up 1.5 percent.

a. What is the market value of the insurance company's loan investment after the changes in interest rates?
b. What is the duration of the loan investment when it was first issued?
c. Using duration, what is the expected change in the value of the loan if interest rates are predicted to increase to 11.5 percent from the initial 10 percent?
d. What is the market value of the insurance company's $90 million liability when interest rates rose by 1.5 percent?
e. What is the duration of the insurance company's liability when it is first issued?

20. Use the following balance sheet information to answer the questions.

Balance Sheet ($ thousands) and Duration (in years)

	Duration	Amount
T-bills	0.5	90
T-notes	0.9	55
T-bonds	x	176
Loans	7	2,274
Deposits	1	2,092
Federal funds	.01	238
Equity		715

NOTES: Treasury bonds are five-year maturities paying 6% semiannually and selling at par.

a. What is the duration of the *T*-bond portfolio? (Calculate the value of x in the balance sheet.)
b. What is the average duration of all the assets?
c. What is the average duration of all the liabilities?
d. What is the FI's leverage-adjusted duration gap? What is the FI's interest rate risk exposure?
e. If the entire yield curve shifted upward 0.5 percent (i.e., $\Delta R/1 + R = .0050$), what is the impact on the FI's market value of equity?
f. If the entire yield curve shifted downward 0.25 percent (i.e., $\Delta R/1 + R = -.0025$), what is the impact on the FI's market value of equity?

Chapter Nineteen

Market Risk

In recent years, the trading activities of financial intermediaries (FIs) have raised considerable concern among investors, regulators, and FI analysts. The profit of major FIs such as Merrill Lynch, Salomon Brothers, and J. P. Morgan have taken big hits from losses in trading.[1] Moreover, in February 1995, Barings, the U.K. merchant bank, was forced into insolvency as a result of losses on its trading in Japanese stock index futures. In September 1995, a similar incident took place at the New York branch of a leading Japanese bank, Daiwa Bank. The largest trading loss in recent history involving an alleged "rogue trader occurred" in June 1996 (see Contemporary Perspectives Box 19–1). As traditional commercial and investment banking franchises shrink and markets become more liquid and complex (e.g., emerging country equity and bond markets and new sophisticated derivative contracts), concerns regarding the threats to an FI's solvency from its trading activities are likely only to increase.

Conceptually, an FI's trading portfolio can be differentiated from its investment portfolio on the basis of time horizon and liquidity. The trading portfolio contains assets and derivative contracts that can be

---

[1] For example, one trader cost Merrill Lynch more than $370 million in 1987 by taking a position in mortgage-backed security strips.

Contemporary Perspectives 19–1

Sumitomo Puts Its Copper Losses at $2.6 Billion, Will Sue Ex-Trader

Sumitomo Corp., disclosing that its copper-trading losses have mounted to $2.6 billion, said it intends to sue its former chief copper trader, Yasuo Hamanaka, and any other participants in what the firm is calling his elaborate scheme to defraud it.

The announcement confirmed months of speculation that the Sumitomo scandal's cost would climb well past Sumitomo's original forecast of $1.8 billion made in June when it fired the trader. The new figure makes the Sumitomo scandal by far the largest in history involving an alleged "rogue trader." Mr. Hamanaka hasn't been formally charged with wrongdoing either in Japan or the U.S.

Kenji Miyahara, Sumitomo's president and chief executive officer, said the firm will sue Mr. Hamanaka on the grounds of breach of trust, claiming he falsified documents, forged signatures and destroyed business records to hide losses that began to mount a decade ago. Such a suit by Sumitomo is widely con-

sidered to be the first step toward any move by Tokyo prosecutors to pursue criminal charges against Mr. Hamanaka, as Japanese prosecutors in corporate fraud cases prefer that a company act first to sue offending individuals.

Sumitomo executives said the company may also sue Saburo "Steve" Shimizu, a former boss of Mr. Hamanaka's who the company believes may have been involved in any fraudulent activities. Mr. Shimizu left the company in 1987, but retained close ties with Mr. Hamanaka. Neither Mr. Hamanaka nor Mr. Shimizu returned calls seeking comment.

Copper market participants fear brokers and merchants closely associated with Mr. Hamanaka could also face legal action by Sumitomo as the Japanese firm strives to rid itself of the reputation of a company with lax risk-management controls. Those fears were fueled by comments from Sumitomo officials that Mr. Hamanaka borrowed heavily from foreign banks and brokers to disguise

his losses. Those loans ultimately magnified the damage from the trading strategy when it went awry.

In particular, **Winchester Commodities Group,** a British brokerage firm that helped Mr. Hamanaka execute trades on the London Metal Exchange, and **Global Minerals & Metals Corp.,** a New York metals merchant that helped implement Sumitomo's strategy in the physical copper market, could face intensified scrutiny from regulators and criminal prosecutors. The U.S. attorney's office in Manhattan launched a probe into Global following the disclosure of the Sumitomo losses, while Britain's Serious Fraud Office last month raided the homes of Winchester's two founders, Charles Vincent and Ashley Levett. People close to the continuing regulatory investigation, which includes the Commodity Futures Trading Commission as well as Britain's Securities and Investment Board and the Securities and Futures Authority, confirm that the two firms are an integral part of their inquiries.

SOURCE: Norihiko Shirouzu, Stephen Frank, and Suzanne McGee, The *Wall Street Journal*, September 20, 1996, p. C1. Reprinted by permission of The Wall Street Journal, © 1996 Dow Jones & Company, Inc. All Rights Reserved Worldwide.

quickly bought or sold over the counter or on organized financial markets. With the increasing securitization of bank loans (e.g., mortgages), more and more assets have become liquid and tradable. Of course, with time, every asset and liability can be sold. Bank regulators have normally viewed tradable assets as those being held for horizons of less than one year, but private FIs take an even shorter-term view. In particular, FIs are concerned about the fluctuation in value of their trading account assets and liabilities for periods as short as one day—so-called daily earnings at risk (DEAR)—especially if such fluctuations pose a threat to their solvency.

market risk

Risk related to the uncertainty of an FI's earnings on its trading portfolio caused by changes in market conditions.

Market risk can be defined as the risk related to the uncertainty of an FI's earnings on its trading portfolio caused by changes in market conditions such as the price of assets, interest rates, market volatility, and market liquidity.[2] This earnings uncertainty can be measured over periods as short as one day or as long as one year. Moreover, market risk can be defined in absolute terms as a *dollar* exposure amount or as a *relative* amount against some benchmark. The sections that follow concentrate on absolute dollar measures of market risk.

MARKET RISK MEASUREMENT

Market risk measurement (MRM) is important for at least five reasons:

1. *Management information.*   MRM provides senior management with information on the risk exposure taken by the FI's traders. Management can then compare this risk exposure with the FI's capital resources. Such an information system appears to have been lacking in the Barings' failure.
2. *Establishment of limits.*   MRM considers the market risk of traders' portfolios, which will lead to the establishment of economically logical position limits per trader in each area of trading.
3. *Resource allocation.*   MRM involves the comparison of returns with market risks in different areas of trading, which may allow the identification of areas with the greatest potential return per unit of risk into which more capital and resources can be directed.
4. *Performance evaluation.*   MRM considers the return-risk ratio of traders, which may allow a more rational bonus (compensation) system to be put in place. That is, those traders with the highest returns may simply be the ones who have taken the largest risks. It is not clear that they should receive higher compensation than traders with lower returns and lower risk exposures.
5. *Regulation.*   With the Bank for International Settlements (BIS) and Federal Reserve now regulating market risk through capital requirements (discussed later in this chapter), private sector benchmarks are important since it is possible that regulators will overprice some risks. MRM conducted by the FI can be used to point to potential misallocations of resources as a result of prudential regulation.[3]

---

[2] J.P. Morgan, *Introduction to RiskMetrics* (New York: J. P. Morgan Securities, October 1994), p. 2.

[3] Since regulators are concerned with the social costs of a failure or insolvency, including contagion effects and other externalities, regulatory models normally tend to be more conservative than private sector models that are concerned with only the private costs of failure.

Table **19–1**

JPM'S TRADING BUSINESS

	Fixed Income	Foreign Exchange STIRT*	Commodities	Derivatives	Equities	Emerging Markets	Proprietary	Total
Number of active locations	14	12	5	11	8	7	11	14
Number of independent risk-taking units	30	21	8	16	14	11	19	120
Thousands of dollars of transactions per day	>5	>5	<1	<1	>5	<1	<1	>20
Billions of dollars in daily trading volume	>10	>30	1	1	<1	1	8	>50

*Note: STIRT denotes Short-term interest rate instruments.

SOURCE: J.P. Morgan, *Introduction to RiskMetrics* (New York: J. P. Morgan Securities, October 1994).

J.P. MORGAN'S
RISKMETRICS MODEL

The following quote indicates the ultimate objective of market risk measurement models: "Every afternoon at 4:15, Dennis Weatherstone, chairman of J.P. Morgan, is handed a sheet of paper. Written on it are estimates of how much money the bank would lose should prices in the markets in which it has open positions move by a certain amount."[4] In a nutshell, the chairman of JPM wants a single *dollar* number, at 4:15 PM New York time, that tells him JPM's expected market or trading risk exposure over the next 24 hours (or day).

This is nontrivial, given the extent of JPM's trading business (see Table 19–1). JPM has 14 active trading locations with 120 independent units trading fixed income securities, foreign exchange, commodities, derivatives, emerging market securities, and proprietary assets, with a total daily volume exceeding $50 billion. This scale and variety of activities are typical of the major money center banks, large overseas banks (e.g., CS Holdings, UBS, Deutsche Bank, and Barclays), and major insurance companies and investment banks.

Essentially, the FI is concerned with how much it can potentially lose should market conditions move adversely; that is

Market risk = Estimated potential loss under adverse circumstances

daily earnings at risk (DEAR)

Market risk exposure over the next 24 hours.

More specifically, the market risk in terms of the FI's **daily earnings at risk** has three measurable components:

Daily earnings at risk = Dollar market value of the position × Price sensitivity of position × Potential adverse move in yield

---

[4] "Safety in Numbers," *The Economist*, October 15, 1994, p. 102.

Since price sensitivity multiplied by adverse move in yield measures the degree of price volatility of an asset, we can also write the preceding equation as the following equation

Daily earnings at risk = Dollar market value of the position × Price volatility

How price sensitivity and an "adverse move" will be measured depends on the FI and its choice of a price-sensitivity model as well as its view of what exactly is a potentially adverse price (yield) move.

We concentrate here on measuring the market risk exposure of a major FI on a daily basis using JPM's RiskMetrics model.[5] As discussed later, measuring the risk exposure for periods longer than a day (e.g., five days) is, under certain assumptions, a simple transformation of the daily risk exposure number. In recent years, JPM has made its RiskMetrics model publicly available and provides data through Reuters to estimate this market risk model on a daily basis. Thus, in principle, any FI can use JPM's model as a benchmark for its own proprietary models. Because of its public availability, we concentrate on how JPM's RiskMetrics model calculates daily earnings at risk (DEAR) in three trading areas— foreign exchange (FX), fixed income, and equities[6]—and then how it estimates the aggregate risk of the entire trading portfolio to meet Dennis Weatherstone's objective of a single aggregate dollar exposure measure across the whole bank at 4:15 PM each day.

The Market Risk of Foreign Exchange Positions

Like most large FIs, JPM actively trades in FX. Remember that

DEAR = Dollar market value position × Price volatility

EXAMPLE 19–1

Daily Earnings at Risk of Foreign Exchange Contracts

Suppose that a bank has a 1.6 million long trading position in spot German deutsche marks (DM) at the close of business on a particular day. The bank wants to calculate the daily earnings at risk from this (i.e., the risk exposure on this position should tomorrow be a "bad" day in the FX markets with respect to the value of the deutsche mark against the dollar).

The first step is to calculate the dollar-equivalent amount of the position

$$\begin{aligned} \text{Dollar equivalent value of DM position} &= \text{FX position} \times \$/\text{DM spot exchange rate} \\ &= \text{DM 1.6 million} \times \$ \text{ per unit of foreign} \\ &\quad \text{currency} \end{aligned}$$

If the exchange rate is DM1.60/\$1, or \$0.625/DM, at the daily close

$$\begin{aligned} \text{Dollar value of DM position} &= \text{DM 1.6 million} \times \$0.625/\text{DM} \\ &= \$1 \text{ million} \end{aligned}$$

---

[5] Other banks have adopted different approaches to measure market risk exposure. The two most popular alternatives to RiskMetrics are based on simulations using either actual past rates or prices on assets (historical or back simulation) or generating theoretical rates or prices (Monte Carlo simulation).

[6] JPM's RiskMetrics model also includes three approaches to calculating value at risk for options. The BIS standardized model currently considers option risk as well.

Suppose that, looking back at the daily changes in the exchange rate of deutsche marks to dollars for the past year, we find that the volatility or standard deviation (σ) of the spot exchange rate was 56.5 basis points (bp). However, suppose that the bank is interested in adverse moves—that is, (bad) moves that will not occur more than 5 percent of the time, or 1 day in every 20. Statistically speaking, if changes in exchange rates are historically "normally" distributed, the exchange rate must change in the adverse direction by 1.65σ (1.65×56.5 bp) for this change to be viewed as likely to occur only 1 day in every 20 days.[7]

$$\text{FX volatility} = 1.65 \times 56.5 \text{ bp} = 93.2 \text{ bp, or } 0.932\%$$

In other words, during the last year, the deutsche mark declined in value against the dollar by 93.2 bp 5 percent of the time. As a result,

$$\begin{aligned} \text{DEAR} &= \text{Dollar value of DM position} \times \text{FX volatility} \\ &= \$1 \text{ million} \times .00932 \\ &= \$9,320 \end{aligned}$$

This is the potential daily earnings exposure to adverse deutsche mark to dollar exchange rate changes for the bank from the DM 1.6 million spot currency holding in German currency.   •   •   •

Fixed Income Securities

Suppose that an FI has a $1 million market value position in zero-coupon bonds of seven years to maturity with a face value of $1,631,483.[8] Today's yield on these bonds is 7.243 percent per annum. These bonds are held as part of the trading portfolio.

$$\text{Dollar market value of position} = \$1 \text{ million}$$

The FI manager wants to know the potential exposure the FI faces should interest rates move against the FI due to an adverse or reasonably bad market. How much the FI will lose depends on the bond's price volatility. From the duration model (presented in Chapter 18), and when MD represents modified duration, we know that

$$\begin{aligned} \text{Daily price volatility} &= \text{Price sensitivity to a small change in yield} \\ &\quad \times \text{Adverse daily yield move} \\ &= (-MD) \times \text{Adverse daily yield move} = \frac{-D}{1+R} \times \Delta R \end{aligned}$$

The *MD* of this bond is[9]

$$MD = \frac{D}{1+R} = \frac{7}{(1.07243)} = 6.527$$

given that the yield on the bond is $R = 7.243$ percent. To estimate price volatility, multiply the bond's *MD* by the expected adverse daily yield move.

---

[7] Technically, 90 percent of the area under a normal distribution lies between $\pm 1.65\sigma$ from the mean. This means that 5 percent of the time, daily exchange rate changes will increase by more than 1.65σ and 5 percent of the time, will decrease by 1.65σ. This case concerns only adverse moves in the exchange rate of deutsche marks to dollars (i.e., a depreciation of 1.65σ).

[8] The face value of the bonds is $1,631,483; that is, $1,631,483/(1.07243)^7 = \$1,000,000$ market value.

[9] We assume annual compounding for simplicity.

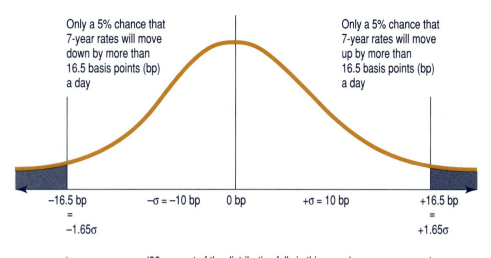

Figure **19–1**   *Adverse Rate Move, Seven-Year Rates*

E X A M P L E   1 9 – 2

Daily Earnings at Risk on Fixed Income Securities

Suppose that we want to obtain maximum yield changes so that there is only a 5 percent chance the yield changes will be higher than this maximum in either direction or, since we are concerned only with bad outcomes, that there is 1 chance in 20 that the next day's yield change (or shock) will exceed this given adverse move. If we assume that yield changes are normally distributed,[10] we can fit a normal distribution to the histogram of recent past changes in seven-year interest rates to determine an estimate of the size of this adverse rate move. From statistics, we know that 90 percent of the area under the normal distribution is to be found within ± 1.65 standard deviations from the mean, that is, 1.65σ. Suppose that during the last year the mean change in daily yields on seven-year zero-coupon bonds was 0 percent while the standard deviation, σ, was 10 bp (or 0.001). Thus, 1.65σ is 16.5 bp.[11] In other words, over the last year, daily yields on seven-year, zero-coupon bonds have fluctuated (either positively or negatively) by more than 16.5 bp only 10 percent of the time.[12] Adverse moves in yield are those that decrease the value of the security (i.e., the yield increases). These occurred 5 percent of the time, or 1 in 20 days. This is shown in Figure 19–1.

We can now calculate the potential daily price volatility on seven-year discount bonds as

$$\text{Price volatility} = (-MD) \times \text{Potential adverse move in yield}$$
$$= -6.527 \times .00165$$
$$= -.01077, \text{ or } -1.077\%$$

---

[10]In reality, many distributions of asset returns—such as exchange rates and interest rates—have "fat tails." Thus, the normal distribution tends to underestimate extreme outcomes.

[11]When JPM calculates σ for RiskMetrics, it weights recent observations more heavily that past observations (called *exponential weighting*). This allows more recent news to be more heavily reflected in the calculation of σ. Regular σ calculations put an equal weight on all past observations.

[12]If the mean were nonzero (e.g., –1 basis point), this could be added to the 16.5 bp to project the yield shock.

Given this price volatility and the initial market value of the seven-year bond portfolio[13]

$$\text{Daily earnings at risk} = \text{Dollar market value of position} \times \text{Price volatility}$$
$$= \$1,000,000 \times .01077$$
$$= \$10,770$$

That is, the potential daily loss on the position is $10,770 if the one bad day in 20 occurs tomorrow.[14] • • •

We can extend this analysis to calculate the potential loss over 2,3, . . . , N days. If we assume that yield shocks are independent, the N-day market value at risk (VAR) is related to daily earnings at risk (DEAR) by

$$\text{VAR} = \text{DEAR } \sqrt{N}$$

That is, the value of the FI that is at risk should interest rate yields move against the FI over several days is a function of the value or earnings at risk for one day (DEAR) and the (square root of the) number of days being considered. If N is five days,[15] then

$$\text{VAR} = \$10,770 \times \sqrt{5} = \$24,082$$

If N is 10 days,[16] then

$$\text{VAR} = \$10,770 \times \sqrt{10} = \$34,057$$

Equities

Many large FIs also take positions in equities. According to the Capital Asset Pricing Model (CAPM),[17] an equity position in an individual stock involves two types of risk.[18]

$$\text{Total risk} = \text{Systematic risk} + \text{Unsystematic risk}$$
$$\sigma_{it}^2 = \beta_i^2 \sigma_{mt}^2 + \sigma_{eit}^2$$

---

[13]Since we are calculating loss here, we drop the minus sign.

[14]These calculations estimated price sensitivity using modified duration. However, the JPM model generally prefers using the present value of cash flow changes as the price-sensitivity weights instead of modified durations. Essentially, each cash flow is discounted by the appropriate zero-coupon rate to generate the daily earnings at risk measure. If we used the direct cash flow calculation in this case, the loss would be $10,771.2. The initial market value of the seven-year zero-coupon was $1,000,000, or $1,631,483/(1.07243)^7$. The (loss) effect of a rise in rates by 1 bp on each $1 (market value) invested in the bond is .0006528. However, the adverse rate move is 16.5 bp. Thus

$$\text{DEAR} = \$1 \text{ million} \times .0006528 \times 16.5 = \$10,771.2$$

The estimate in this case is very close to that using modified duration.

[15]To understand why we take the square root of N, consider a five-day holding period. The σ_5^2, or five-day variance, equals the current one-day variance, σ_1^2 times five, or

$$\sigma_5^2 = \sigma_1^2 \times 5$$

The standard deviation of this equation is

$$\sigma_5 = \sigma_1 \times \sqrt{5}$$

[16]In the April 1995 BIS proposal (a revision of the 1993 BIS proposal), a 10-day holding period ($N = 10$) is assumed to measure exposure.

[17]The CAPM theorizes that the fair rate of return on a security should be equal to the risk-free rate plus a risk premium to compensate for the risk on the security relative to the risk in the overall market.

[18]This assumes that systematic risks are independent of each other.

Beta

Systematic (undiversifiable) risk reflecting the comovement of the returns of a specific stock and the returns on the market portfolio.

Systematic risk reflects the co-movement of that stock with the market portfolio—reflected by the stock's **beta** (β_i) and the volatility of the market portfolio (σ_{mt})—while unsystematic risk is specific to the firm itself (σ_{eit}).

In a very well-diversified portfolio, unsystematic risk (σ_{eit}^2) can be largely diversified away (i.e., will equal zero), leaving behind systematic (undiversifiable) market risk ($\beta_i \sigma_m^2$). If the returns on the FI's trading portfolio follow (replicate) the returns on the stock market index, the β of that portfolio will be 1 since the movement of returns on the FI's portfolio will be one to one with the market, and the standard deviation of the portfolio, σ_{it}, will be equal to the standard deviation of the stock market index, σ_{mt}.[19]

E X A M P L E   1 9 – 3

Daily Earnings at Risk on Equities

Suppose that the FI holds a $1 million trading position in stocks that reflect the U.S. stock market index (e.g., the S&P 500). Then β equals 1, and the DEAR for equities is

$$\text{DEAR} = \text{Dollar market value of position} \times \text{Stock market return volatility}$$
$$= \$1,000,000 \times 1.65\sigma_m$$

If, over the last year, the σ_m of the daily returns on the stock market index was 2 percent, then $1.65\sigma_m = 3.3$ percent (i.e., the adverse change or declines in the daily return on the stock market exceeded 3.3 percent only 5 percent of the time). In this case

$$\text{DEAR} = \$1,000,000 \times 0.033$$
$$= \$33,000$$

That is, the FI stands to lose at least $33,000 in earnings if adverse stock market returns materialize tomorrow.   •   •   •

Portfolio Aggregation

The preceding sections analyzed the daily earnings at risk of individual trading positions. The examples considered a position in spot deutsche marks ($1 million market value), a seven-year, zero-coupon, fixed income security ($1 million market value), and a position in the U.S. stock market index ($1 million market value). The individual DEARs were as follows:

1. DM spot = $9,320.
2. Seven-year, zero-coupon bonds = $10,770.
3. U.S. equities = $33,000.

However, senior management, such as Dennis Weatherstone at JPM, wants to know the aggregate risk of the entire trading position. To calculate this, we *cannot* simply sum the three DEARs—$10,770 + $9,320 + $33,000 = $53,090—because this ignores any degree of offsetting covariance or correlation among the fixed income, FX, and equity trading positions. In particular, some of these asset shocks (adverse moves) may be negatively correlated. According to modern portfolio theory, negative correlations across asset shocks will reduce the degree of portfolio risk (see Chapter 11).

---

[19]In less well-diversified portfolios or portfolios of individual stocks, the effect of unsystematic risk σ_{eit} on the value of the trading position would need to be added. Moreover, if the CAPM does not offer a good explanation of asset pricing compared to, say, multi-index arbitrage pricing theory (APT), a degree of error will be built into the DEAR calculation.

Table **19–2**

CORRELATIONS (ρ_{ij}) AMONG ASSETS

	Seven-year zero-coupon	DM/$	U.S. stock index
Seven-year zero-coupon	—	−.2	.4
DM/$	—	—	.1
U.S. stock index	—	—	—

Table 19–2 shows a hypothetical correlation matrix between daily seven-year, zero-coupon bond yield changes, deutsche mark–dollar spot exchange rate changes, and changes in daily returns on a U.S. stock market index (S&P 500). The correlation shown in Table 19–2, between the seven-year, zero-coupon bond and deutsche mark–dollar exchange rate, $\rho_{z,DM}$, is negative (–.2), while the seven-year, zero-coupon yield changes with, respectively, U.S. stock returns, $\rho_{z,U.S.}$, (.4), and DM/$ shocks, $\rho_{U.S.,DM}$, (.1) are positively correlated.

Using this correlation matrix along with the individual asset DEARs, we can calculate the risk (or standard deviation) of the whole (three-asset) trading portfolio as

$$
\begin{aligned}
\text{DEAR portfolio} = [&(\text{DEAR}_Z)^2 + (\text{DEAR}_{DM})^2 + (\text{DEAR}_{U.S.})^2 \\
&+ (2 \times \rho_{z,DM} \times \text{DEAR}_Z \times \text{DEAR}_{DM}) \\
&+ (2 \times \rho_{z,U.S.} \times \text{DEAR}_Z \times \text{DEAR}_{U.S.}) \\
&+ (2 \times \rho_{U.S.,DM} \times \text{DEAR}_{U.S.} \times \text{DEAR}_{DM})]^{1/2}
\end{aligned}
$$

This is a direct application of modern portfolio theory (MPT) since DEARs are directly similar to standard deviations. Substituting the calculated individual DEARs (in thousands of dollars) in the preceding equation, we get

$$
\begin{aligned}
\text{DEAR portfolio} = [&(10.77)^2 + (9.32)^2 + (33)^2 \\
&+ 2(-.2)(10.77)(9.32) \\
&+ 2(.4)(10.77)(33) \\
&+ 2(.1)(9.32)(33)]^{1/2} \\
= \ &\$39{,}969
\end{aligned}
$$

The equation indicates that considering the risk of each trading position as well as the correlation structure among those positions' returns results in a lower measure of portfolio trading risk ($39,969) than when the risks of the individual trading positions (the sum of which was $53,090) are added. A quick check will reveal that had we assumed that all three assets were perfectly positively correlated (i.e., $\rho_{ij} = 1$), DEAR for the portfolio would have been $53,090. Clearly, even in abnormal market conditions, assuming that asset returns are perfectly correlated will exaggerate the degree of trading risk exposure.

Table 19–3 shows the type of spreadsheet used by banks such as J.P. Morgan to calculate its DEAR. Positions can be taken in at least 15 different country (currency) bonds in eight different maturity buckets.[20] There is also a column for FX risk (and, if necessary,

---

[20]Bonds held with different maturity dates (e.g., six years) are split into two and allocated to the nearest two of the eight maturity buckets (here, five years and seven years) using three criteria:

  a. The sum of the current market *value* of the two resulting cash flows must be identical to the market value of the original cash flow.

Table **19–3**

PORTFOLIO DEAR SPREADSHEET

	Interest Rate Risk Notional Amounts (U.S. $ millions equivalents)									FX Risk		Total	
	1 Month	1 Year	2 Years	3 Years	4 Years	5 Years	7 Years	10 Years	Interest DEAR	Spot FX	FX DEAR	Portfolio Effect	Total DEAR
Australia											AUD		
Belgium											BEF		
Canada											CAD		
Denmark											DKK		
France	19		−30					11	48		FFR		48
Germany	−19		30					−11	27		DEM		27
Italy											LIR		
Japan											YEN		
Netherlands											NLG		
Spain											ESB		
Sweden											SEK		
Switzerland											CHF		
United Kingdom											BP		
ECU											ECU		
United States						10		10	76		USD		76
Total						10		10	151				151
							Portfolio effect		(62)				(62)
RISK DATA PRINT CLOSE							Total DEAR ($000s)		89				89

SOURCE: J.P. Morgan, *Introduction to RiskMetrics* (New York: J. P. Morgan Securities, 1994).

equity risk) in these different country markets, although in this example the bank has no FX risk exposure (all of the cells are empty).

In the example in Table 19–3, the bank is holding offsetting long and short positions in both German and French bonds, but it is still exposed to trading risk of $48,000 and $27,000, respectively (see the column Interest DEAR). This happens because the French yield curve is more volatile than the German one and shocks at different maturity buckets are not equal. The DEAR figure for a U.S. bond position of long $20 million is $76,000. Adding these three positions yields a DEAR of $151,000. However, this ignores the fact that German, French, and U.S. yield shocks are not perfectly correlated. Allowing for diversification effects results in a total DEAR of only $89,000. This would be the number reported to JPM's senior management.[21]

---

b. The market *risk* of the portfolio of the two cash flows must be identical to the overall market risk of the original cash flow.

c. The two cash flows must have the same *sign* as the original cash flow.

See J.P. Morgan, RiskMetrics—Technical Document (New York: J. P. Morgan Securities, November, 1994), pp. 35–36.

[21]This calculation of DEAR ignores the potential exposure of the positions in foreign bonds (German, French) to foreign exchange stocks. For completeness, the foreign exchange DEARs also should be calculated for the foreign exchange positions backing these bonds, as well as the correlations among the foreign exchange and bond exposures.

In actuality, the number of markets covered by JPM's traders and the number of correlations among those markets require the daily production and updating of more than 450 volatility estimates (σ) and 250,000 correlations (ρ). In association with JPM, Reuters provides these data for a fee.

Concept Questions

1. Why is market risk measurement important to FIs?
2. What is the ultimate objective of market risk measurement model?
3. Referring to Example 19–2, what is the DEAR for this bond if (σ) had been 15 bp?
4. Referring to Table 19–2, what is the DEAR of the portfolio if the returns on the three assets are independent of each other?

• •

REGULATORY MODELS: THE BIS STANDARDIZED FRAMEWORK

The development of internal trading risk models by FIs such as JPM and Chase were partly in response to proposals by the Bank for International Standards (BIS) in 1993 to measure and regulate the market risk exposures of banks by imposing capital requirements on their trading portfolios.[22] The BIS is an organization encompassing the largest central banks in the world. We look briefly at the BIS regulatory 1993 proposal, since it provides a useful benchmark—or standardized measurement framework—for comparison with private sector FI models. We then review the BIS April 1995 revised proposal, which made some minor adjustments to the standardized measurement framework introduced in 1993. In addition, we discuss the implications of the 1995 BIS proposal, which became effective in 1998, and allows the largest banks in the world (approximately 100) to use their own internal models to calculate exposure for capital adequacy (regulatory) purposes, leaving the standardized framework as the relevant model for smaller banks.

The next sections describe the standardized methodology for smaller banks to use to calculate their market risk exposures. We divide the measurement of the trading portfolio's risk into its three components: fixed income, FX, and equities.

Fixed Income

We can examine the 1993 BIS standardized framework for measuring the market risk on the fixed income (or debt security) trading portfolio by using the example for a typical bank provided by the BIS; see Table 19–4. Panel A in Table 19–4 lists the security holdings of a bank in its trading account. The bank holds long and short positions—column (3)—in various quality debt issues—column (2)—with maturities ranging from one month to more than 20 years—column (1). Long positions have positive values; short positions have negative values. To measure the risk of this trading portfolio, the BIS uses two capital charges:

---

[22]Basle Committee on Banking Supervision, "The Supervisory Treatment of Market Risks" (Basle, Switzerland: BIS, April 1993); and "Proposal to Issue a Supplement to the Basle Accord to Cover Market Risks" (Basle, Switzerland: BIS, April 1995).

(1) a specific risk charge—columns (4) and (5)—and (2) a general market risk charge—columns (6) and (7).

specific risk charge

A charge reflecting the risk of a decline in the liquidity or credit risk quality of the trading portfolio.

general market risk charge

A charge reflecting the modified durations and interest rate shocks for each maturity.

Specific Risk Charge.   The **specific risk charge** is meant to measure the risk of a decline in the liquidity or credit risk quality of the trading portfolio over the bank's holding period. As column (4) of Panel A indicates, Treasuries have a zero risk weight; junk bonds (e.g., 10–15 year nonqualifying "NonQual" corporate debt) have a risk weight of 8 percent. According to Table 19–4, multiplying the absolute dollar values of all of the long and short positions in these instruments—column (3)—by the specific risk weights—column (4)—produces a specific risk capital or requirement charge for each position—column (5).[23] Summing the individual charges for specific risk gives the total specific risk charge of $229.

General Market Risk Charge.   The **general market risk** charges or weights—column (6)—reflect the modified durations and interest rate shocks for each maturity. The weights

Table **19-4**

BIS MARKET RISK CALCULATION: DEBT SECURITIES, SAMPLE MARKET RISK CALCULATIONS

Panel A: Bank Holdings and Risk Charges

(1)	(2)	(3)	(4)	(5)	(6)	(7)
			Specific Risk		**General Market Risk**	
Time Band	**Issuer**	**Position ($)**	**Weight (%)**	**Charge ($)**	**Weight(%)**	**Charge($)**
0–1 month	Treasury	5,000	0.00%	0.00	0.00%	0.00
1–3 months	Treasury	5,000	0.00	0.00	0.20	10.00
3–6 months	Qual Corp*	4,000	0.25	0.00	0.40	16.00
6–12 months	Qual Corp	(7,500)	1.00	75.00	0.70	(52.50)
1–2 years	Treasury	(2,500)	0.00	0.00	1.25	(31.25)
2–3 years	Treasury	2,500	0.00	0.00	1.75	43.75
3–4 years	Treasury	2,500	0.00	0.00	2.25	56.25
3–4 years	Qual Corp	(2,000)	1.60	32.00	2.25	(45.00)
4–5 years	Treasury	1,500	0.00	0.00	2.75	41.25
5–7 years	Qual Corp	(1,000)	1.60	16.00	3.25	(32.50)
7–10 years	Treasury	(1,500)	0.00	0.00	3.75	(56.25)
10–15 years	Treasury	(1,500)	0.00	0.00	4.50	(67.50)
10–15 years	NonQual†	1,000	8.00	80.00	4.50	45.00
15–20 years	Treasury	1,500	0.00	0.00	5.25	78.75
> 20 years	Qual Corp	1,000	1.60	16.00	6.00	60.00
Specific risk				$229.00		
Residual general market risk						$66.00

continued

---

[23]Note that the risk weights for both specific and general market risk are based on no theory, empirical research, or past experience. Rather, the weights are based on regulators' perceptions of what was appropriate when the model was established.

Table **19-4**

BIS MARKET RISK CALCULATION: DEBT SECURITIES, SAMPLE MARKET RISK CALCULATIONS (*CONTINUED*)

Panel B: Calculation of Total Capital Charge

(1)	(2)	(3)	(4)	(5)	(6)	(7)
1. Specific risk						Charge ($)
						229.00
General Market Risk						66.00
Time band	Longs	Shorts	Residual‡	Offset	Disallowance	Charge
2. Vertical offsets within same time bands						
3–4 years	56.25	(45.00)	11.25	45.00	10.00%	4.50
10–15 years	45.00	(67.50)	(22.50)	45.00	10.00	4.50
						$9.00
3. Horizontal offsets within same time zones						
Zone 1						
0–1 month	0.00					
1–3 months	10.00					
3–6 months	16.00					
6–12 months		(52.50)				
Total zone 1	26.00	(52.50)	(26.50)	26.00	40.00%	10.40
Zone 2						
1–2 years		(31.25)				
2–3 years	43.75					
3-4 years	11.25					
Total zone 2	55.00	(31.25)	23.75	31.25	30.00%	9.38
Zone 3						
4–5 years	41.25					
5–7 years		(32.50)				
7–10 years		(56.25)				
10–15 years		(22.50)				
15–20 years	78.75					
>20 years	60.00					
Total zone 3	180.00	(111.25)	68.75	111.25	30.00%	33.38
						53.16
4. Horizontal offsets between time zones						
Zones 1 and 2	23.75	(26.50)	(2.75)	23.75	40.00%	9.50
Zones 1 and 3	68.75	(2.75)	66.00	2.75	150.00%	4.12
						13.62
5. Total capital charge						
Specific risk						229.00
Vertical disallowances						9.00
Horizontal disallowances						
Offsets within same time zones						53.16
Offsets between time zones						13.62
Residual general market risk after all offsets						66.00
Total						370.78

*Qual Corp is an investment grade debt issue (e.g., rated BBB and above).

†NonQual is a debt issue below investment grade (e.g., rated BB and below), that is, a "junk bond."

‡Residual amount carried forward for additional offsetting as appropriate.

in Table 19–4 range from zero for the 0–1 month Treasuries to 6 percent for the long-term (longer than 20 years to maturity) quality corporate debt securities. The positive or negative dollar values of the positions in each instrument—column (3)—are multiplied by the general market risk weights—column (6)—to determine the general market risk charges for the individual holdings—column (7). Summing these gives the total general market risk charge of $66.

Vertical Offsets.   The BIS model assumes that long and short positions in the same maturity bucket, but in different instruments, cannot perfectly offset each other. Thus, the $66 general market risk charge tends to underestimate interest rate or price risk exposure. For example, the bank is short $1,500 in 10–15 year U.S. Treasuries (producing market risk charge of $67.50) and is long $1,000 in 10–15 year junk bonds (with a risk charge of $45). Because rates on Treasuries and junk bonds do not fluctuate together exactly, we cannot assume that a $45 charge for a short position in junk bonds is hedging an equivalent ($45) value of U.S. Treasuries of the same maturity. Similarly, the bank is long $2,500 in three- to four-year Treasuries (with a general market risk charge of $56.25) and short $2,000 in three- to four-year quality corporate bonds (with a risk charge of $45). To account for this, the BIS requires additional capital charges called **vertical offsets** or disallowance factors. We show these calculations in part 2 of panel B in Table 19–4.

vertical offset

The assignment of additional capital charges because long and short positions in the same maturity bucket, but in different instruments, cannot perfectly offset each other.

   In panel B, column 1 lists the time bands for which the bank has both a long and short position. Columns (2) and (3) list the general market risk charges—from column (7) of panel A—resulting from the positions, and column (4) lists the difference (or "residual") between the charges. Column (5) reports the smallest value of the risk charges for each time band (or "offset"). As listed in column (6), the BIS disallows 10 percent[24] of the $45 position in corporate bonds in hedging $45 of the Treasury bond position. This results in an additional capital charge of $4.50 ($45 × 10 percent). The total charge for all vertical offsets is $9.

Horizontal Offsets Within Time Zones.   In addition, the debt trading portfolio is divided into three maturity zones: 1 (1 month to 12 months), 2 (more than 1 year to 4 years), and 3 (more than 4 years to 20 years plus). Again because of basis risk (i.e., the imperfect correlation of interest rates on securities of different maturites), short and long positions of different maturities in these zones will not perfectly hedge each other. This results in additional (horizontal) disallowance factors of 40 percent (zone 1), 30 percent (zone 2), and 30 percent (zone 3).[25] Part 3 of panel B shows these calculations. The **horizontal offsets** are calculated using the sum of the general market risk charges from the long and short positions in each time zone—columns (2) and (3) of panel B. As with the vertical offsets, the smallest of these totals is the "offset" value against which the disallowance is applied. For example, the total zone 1 charges for long positions is $26.00 and for short positions is ($52.00). A disallowance of 40 percent of the offset value (the smaller of these two values), $26.00, is charged, that is, $10.40 ($26 × 40 percent). Repeating this process for each of the three zones produces additional (horizontal offset) charges totaling $53.16.

horizontal offset

The assignment of additional charges because short and long positions of different maturities do not perfectly hedge each other.

Horizontal Offsets Between Time Zones.   Finally, because interest rates on short maturity debt and long maturity debt do not fluctuate exactly together, a residual long or short

---

[24]Note again that the disallowance factors were set subjectively by regulators.
[25]The zones were also set subjectively by regulators.

Table **19–5**

EXAMPLE OF THE SHORTHAND MEASURE OF FOREIGN EXCHANGE RISK
(in millions of dollars)

Once an FI has calculated its net position in each foreign currency, it converts each position into its reporting currency and calculates the shorthand measure as in the following example, in which the position in the reporting currency has been excluded:

Yen*	Deutsche Mark	British Pounds	French Franc	Swiss Franc
+50	+100	+150	–20	–180

+ 300   – 200

The capital charge would be 8 percent of the higher of the longs and shorts (i.e., 300)

* All currencies in dollar equivalent*s*.

SOURCE: Basle Committee on Banking Supervision, "The Supervisory Treatment of Market Risks," Basle, Switzerland: April 1993.

position in each zone can only partly hedge an offsetting position in another zone. This leads to a final set of offsets or disallowance factors between time zones, part 4 of panel B of Table 19–4. Here the BIS model compares the residual charges from time zones 1 ($26.50) and 2 ($23.75). The difference, $2.75, is then compared to the residual from zone 3 ($68.75). The smaller of each zone comparison is again used as the "offset" value against which a disallowance of 40 percent for adjacent zones and 150 percent for nonadjacent zones, respectively, is applied.[26] The additional charges here total $13.62.

Summing the specific risk charges ($229), the general market risk charge ($66), and the basis risk or disallowance charges ($9.00 + $53.16 + $13.62) produces a total capital charge of $370.78 for this fixed income trading portfolio.

Foreign Exchange

The BIS originally proposed alternative methods to calculate FX trading exposure, a shorthand and a back-simulation method. The Federal Reserve uses only the shorthand method, so we demonstrate only it in this section.[27] The shorthand method requires the FI to calculate its net exposure in each foreign currency—yen, deutsche mark, and so on — and then convert this amount into dollars at the current spot exchange rate. As Table 19–5 shows, the FI is net long (million dollar equivalent) $50 yen, $100 DM, and $150 British

[26]For example, zone 1 and zone 2 are adjacent to each other in terms of maturity. By comparison, zone 1 and zone 3 are not adjacent to each other.
[27]The final plan, adopted in 1998 in the United States, dropped the longhand method, although European central banks such as the Bank of England continue to use it since this methodology is consistent with the European Community's Capital Adequacy Directive Act, which came into force in January 1996.

Table **19-6**

BIS CAPITAL REQUIREMENT FOR EQUITIES: ILLUSTRATION OF *X* PLUS *Y* METHODOLOGY

(in millions of dollars)

Under the two-part calculation, there are separate requirements for the position in each individual equity (i.e., the gross position) and for the net position in the market as a whole. Here we show how the system works for a range of hypothetical portfolios, assuming a capital charge of 4 percent for the gross positions and 8 percent for the net positions.

Stock	Sum of Long Positions	Sum of Short Positions	*x* Factor — Gross Position (sum of columns 1 and 2)	*x* Factor — 4 Percent of Gross	*y* Factor — Net Position (difference between columns 1 and 2)	*y* Factor — 8 Percent of Net	Capital Required (gross + net)
1	100	0	100	4	100	8	12
2	100	25	125	5	75	6	11
3	100	50	150	6	50	4	10
4	100	75	175	7	25	2	9
5	100	100	200	8	0	0	8
6	75	100	175	7	25	2	9
7	50	100	150	6	50	4	10
8	25	100	125	5	75	6	11
9	0	100	100	4	100	8	12

SOURCE: Basle Committee on Banking Supervision, "The Supervisory Treatment of Market Risks," Basle, Switzerland, April 1993.

pounds while being short $20 French francs and $180 Swiss francs. Its total currency long position is $300 and short position is $200. The BIS proposes a capital requirement equal to 8 percent times the maximum absolute value of either the aggregate long or short positions. In this example, 8 percent times $300 million equals $24 million. This shorthand method of calculating FX exposure assumes some partial but not complete offsetting of currency risk by holding opposing long or short positions in different currencies.

Equities

As discussed in the context of JPM's RiskMetrics market value model, the two sources of risk in holding equities are (1) a firm-specific, or unsystematic, risk element and (2) a market, or systematic, risk element. The BIS charges for unsystematic risk by adding the long and short positions in any given stock and applying a 4 percent capital charge against the gross position in the stock (called the *x* factor). Suppose that stock 2 in Table 19–6 is IBM. The FI has a long $100 million and a short $25 million position in that stock. Its gross position that is exposed to unsystematic (firm-specific) risk is $125 million, which is multiplied by 4 percent, to give a capital charge of $5 million.

Market or systematic risk is reflected in the net long or short position (the so-called *y* factor). In the case of IBM stock, this risk is $75 million ($100 long minus $25 short). The capital charge would be 8 percent against the $75 million, or $6 million. The total capital charge (*x* factor + *y* factor) is $11 million for this stock.

This approach is very crude and basically assumes the same systematic risk factor (or beta) for every stock. It also does not fully consider the benefits from portfolio diversification (i.e., that unsystematic risk is not diversified away).

Concept Questions

1. What is the difference between the BIS–specific risk and general market risk in measuring trading portfolio risk?
2. What two methods did the BIS model originally propose in 1993 for calculating FX trading exposure? How does each method work?
3. How are unsystematic and systematic risks in equity holdings by FIs reflected in charges assessed under the 1993 BIS model?

BIS CAPITAL REQUIREMENT VERSUS INTERNAL BANK MODELS

Large banks have heavily criticized the BIS (standardized) framework for measuring market risk on a number of grounds. First, the framework does not employ the most accurate risk measurement techniques. Second, the standardized framework is incompatible with large bank internal systems (such as the JPM's RiskMetrics).

As a result, the BIS's final capital regulations, in the 1995 revised proposal allow, effective in 1998, large banks (subject to regulator permission) to use their own internal models—instead of the standardized model—to calculate market risk and thus their capital requirement to protect themselves against such risk. However, this calculation must be relatively conservative and is subject to a number of regulatory constraints. A comparison of the BIS requirements for large banks using their internal model with JPM's RiskMetrics indicates the following in particular:

1. A bank must define an adverse change in rates as being in the 99th percentile rather than in the 95th percentile (multiply σ by 2.33 rather than by 1.65 as under RiskMetrics).
2. A bank must assume the minimum holding period to be 10 days (this means that RiskMetrics' daily DEAR would have to be multiplied by $\sqrt{10}$).
3. A bank must consider its proposed capital charge as the *higher* of
   a. The previous day's VAR (value at risk or DEAR $\times \sqrt{10}$).
   b. The average daily VAR over the previous 60 days times a multiplication factor with a minimum value of 3 (i.e., capital charge = DEAR $\times \sqrt{10} \times 3$).

In general, the multiplication factor makes required capital significantly higher than the VAR produced from private models.[28]

However, to reduce the burden of capital needs, FIs can raise an additional type of capital—so-called Tier 3 capital—to meet the capital change (or requirement). For example, suppose the portfolio DEAR were $10 million.[29] The minimum capital charge or market risk capital requirement for the bank is[30]

---

[28]In April 1996, the BIS proposal allowed the multiplication factor of 3 to be increased to as high as 4 if the bank's model fails to perform adequately in back-testing examination by regulators. The idea behind the increase is to make private sector models incentive compatible (i.e., to avoid cheating and make them more conservative).

[29]Using 2.33 σ rather than 1.65 σ.

[30]The idea of a minimum multiplication factor of 3 is to create a plan that is "incentive compatible." Specifically, if FIs using internal models constantly underestimate the amount of capital they need to meet their market risk exposures, regulators can punish those FIs by raising the multiplication factor (theoretically, to any level they like). Such a response may effectively put the FI out of the trading business.

Contemporary Perspectives 19–2

Going Metric

Within the past few years, risk control techniques in major financial institutions have been revolutionized, as state-of-the-art statistical risk models have displaced traditional risk assessment methods.

First we had the development of individual proprietary risk models covering securities trading books; subsequently J.P. Morgan made available its RiskMetrics framework for those who wanted to acquire an off-the-shelf risk modelling capacity. More recently, banks have been applying sophisticated credit scoring techniques to their loan portfolios; and now we have the CreditMetrics framework, also from J.P. Morgan, for evaluating credit risks on a portfolio basis.

Advances in financial technology have therefore had two opposite effects on risk management at the institutional level. On the one hand such technology has given individual players the capacity to change their risk profile, in whichever direction, at unprecedented speed and on the hitherto unimaginable scale. On the other hand, that same technology provides firms with the means to control those risks on a real-time portfolio basis. The real difficulty has arisen in the back office, where verification and reconciliation procedures have not kept up with the hectic pace of change on the trading side.

At the national supervisory level the same influences are at work. Early last year the Basle Committee on Banking Supervision introduced a new framework for regulating banks' market risks, which for the first time gave formal recognition to banks' internal risk models. It is now surely only a matter of time before the 1988 Basle Accord on capital adequacy is amended to allow credit risk models to be used as a basis for calculating capital requirements on loan portfolios (and other credit-risk exposures). However, just as management is finding it difficult to develop robust back-office controls to support the new risk management techniques, so national supervisory authorities are having to focus increasing attention on institutions' internal controls and back-office procedures. A balance has to be struck between increasing on-site inspections, greater reliance on external auditors and strengthened accountability of top management.

Meanwhile the globalization of financial markets is forcing regulatory authorities to address more explicitly the "top tier" of supervision—that is, the monitoring of national supervisory arrangements. In order to establish truly global supervisory standards three things are necessary: first, an agreed set of principles; secondly, a means of

assessing national adherence to these principles; and, finally, the application of sanctions to regimes that fall short of agreed standards.

The Basle Committee has now published a consultative paper on "Core Principles for Effective Banking Supervision" which is intended to meet the first of these requirements. The Committee also proposes to monitor compliance with these principles and for this purpose is enlisting the support of the IMG—a major step towards supernational regularly oversight of financial markets.

The third requirement, namely sanctions, already exists in so far as national authorities are obligated under the Basle framework to prevent their own financial institutions from operating in weakly supervised jurisdictions, and to exclude from their territory banks headquartered in such jurisdictions.

What all this amounts to is that the two major forces reshaping financial markets—financial innovation and globalization—are also reshaping approaches to risk management at the individual firm level, the national regulatory level, and at the level of international supervisory oversight.

SOURCE: *Financial Regulation Report*, May 1997.

$$\text{Capital charge} = \$10 \text{ million} \times \sqrt{10} \times 3 = \$94.868 \text{ million}$$

As explained in more detail in Chapters 9 and 16, capital provides an internal insurance fund to protect an FI, its depositors, and the FDIC fund against losses. The BIS permits three types of capital to be held to meet this capital requirement: Tier 1, Tier 2, and Tier 3. Tier 1 capital is essentially retained earnings and common stock, Tier 2 is essentially long-term subordinated debt (more than five years), and Tier 3, a new type of capital created to meet market risk capital requirements, is short-term subordinated debt with an original maturity of at least two years.[31] Chapter 16 discusses the different types of capital and capital requirements in more detail.

This discussion should make clear that the process of measuring market risk is ongoing. So long as financial innovation and globalization of financial markets continue to evolve (see Contemporary Perspectives Box 19–2), both internal models and standardized (regulatory) models will continue to be revised.

Concept Questions

1. On what basis did large banks criticize the April 1993 BIS framework for measuring market risk?
2. What concessions did the April 1995 BIS proposals make for large banks?

---

[31]Thus, the $94.86 million in this example can be raised by any of the three capital types subject to the two following limitations: (1) Tier 3 capital is limited to 250 percent of Tier 1 capital and (2) Tier 2 capital can be substituted for Tier 3 capital up to the same 250 percent limit. For example, suppose that Tier 1 capital was $27.10 million and the bank issued short-term Tier 3 debt of $67.76 million. Then the 250 percent limit means that no more Tier 3 (or Tier 2) debt could be issued to meet a target higher than $94.86 ($27.1 $\times$ 2.5 = $67.76). The capital charge for market risk is added to the capital charge for credit risk to determine the bank's total capital requirement.

SUMMARY

This chapter highlighted the importance of measuring an FI's market risk exposure. This risk is likely to continue to increase in importance as more and more loans and previously illiquid assets become marketable and as the traditional franchises of commercial and investment banks decrease. Given the risks involved, both private FI management and regulators are investing resources in models to measure and track market risk exposures. The chapter provided a detailed analysis of two approaches to this problem: J.P. Morgan's RiskMetrics model and the standardized market risk capital requirement model used by BIS and the Federal Reserve.

PERTINENT WEB SITES

Bank for International Settlements http://www.bis.org/home.htm

J.P. Morgan http://www.jpmorgan.com/

RiskMetrics   http://www.jpmorgan.com/RiskManagement/RiskMetrics/RiskMetrics.htm

Market Risk

1. What does the term *market risk* mean?
2. Why is the measurement of market risk important to an FI manager?
3. Consider daily earnings at risk (DEAR) and value at risk (VAR).
   a. Define DEAR and VAR.
   b. What is the statistical relationship between them?
4. If a bank's DEAR is $8,500, what is its VAR
   a. If a 10-day period is used?
   b. If a 20-day period is used?
5. The mean change in the daily yields of a 15-year, zero-coupon bond has been five basis points (bp) over the past year with a standard deviation of 15 bp. Using these data and assuming that the yield changes are normally distributed
   a. What is the highest yield change expected if adverse moves will not occur more than 1 day in every 20?
   b. What is the highest yield change expected if adverse moves will not occur more than 1 day in every 100 (i.e., use 2.33σ)?
6. In what sense is duration a measure of market risk?
7. Bank Alpha has an inventory of AAA–rated, 15-year, zero-coupon bonds with a face value of $400 million. They are currently yielding 9.5 percent in the over-the-counter market.
   a. What is the modified duration of these bonds?
   b. What is the price volatility if the potential adverse move in yields is 25 basis points?
   c. What is the DEAR?
8. Bank One has in its portfolio bonds outstanding with a market value of $200 million. The price volatility of these bonds has been estimated at 0.0095. What are the DEAR and the 10-day VAR?
9. Bank of Southern Vermont has estimated that its inventory of 20 million German deutsche marks (DM) and 25 million British pounds (BP) is subject to market risk. The spot exchange rates are $0.40/DM and $1.28/BP, respectively. The σs of the spot exchange rates of the DM and BP, based on the daily changes of spot rates over the past six months, are 65 bp and 45 bp, respectively. Determine the bank's 10-day VAR for both currencies. Use adverse rate changes as being in the 95th percentile.
10. Bank of Alaska's stock portfolio has a market value of $10,000,000. The beta of the portfolio approximates the market portfolio whose standard deviation, σ_m, has been estimated at 1.5 percent. What is the five-day VAR of this portfolio, using adverse rate changes being in the 99th percentile?

11. Jeff Resnick, vice-president of operations, Choice Bank, is estimating the aggregate DEAR of the bank's portfolio of assets consisting of loans, foreign currencies, and common stock. The individual DEARs are $300,700, $274,000 and $126,700, respectively. If the correlation coefficients ρ_{ij} between loans (L) and foreign currencies (FX), loans and common stock (EQ), and FX and common stock are 0.3, 0.7 and 0.0, respectively, what is the DEAR of the aggregate portfolio?
12. Calculate the DEAR for the following portfolio with and without the correlation coefficients.

Asset	Estimated Dear	$\rho_{S,FX}$	$\rho_{S,B}$	$\rho_{FX,B}$
Stocks (S)	$300,000	–0.10	0.75	0.20
Foreign exchange (FX)	200,000	—	—	—
Bonds (B)	250,000	—	—	—

13. Chase Choice Bank has the following positions outstanding overnight in foreign currencies (FX) (in millions of U.S. dollars): $80 million long in DM, $40 million short in BP, and $20 million long in FF. Using the BIS shorthand method, determine the capital charge required against market risk.
14. Bank Metals, Inc., has positions in the following precious metals: $30 million long in silver, $25 million long in gold, and $45 million short in platinum. What is the required capital charge using the BIS shorthand method?
15. An FI has the following stocks in its portfolio:

Company	Long	Short
Texaco	$45 million	$25 million
Microsoft	55 million	12 million
Robeco	20 million	—
Cifra	—	15 million

Using the 1993 BIS standardized framework, determine the total capital charge required for this portfolio of stocks.
16. What were the major criticisms of the BIS standardized framework for measuring risk?
17. Bank Dark Star has estimated its average VAR for the previous 60 days to be $35.5 million. Its DEAR for the previous day was $30.2 million. Under the revised April 1995 BIS standards
   a. Determine the amount of capital to be held for market risk.
   b. The Bank has $15 million of Tier 1 capital, $37.5 million of Tier 2 capital, and $55 million of Tier 3 capital. Is this capital sufficient? If not, what minimum amount of new Tier 1 capital should it raise?

18. An FI has the following bonds in its portfolio: long 1-year U.S. Treasury bills, short 3-year Treasury bonds, long 3-year AAA–rated corporate bonds, and long 12-year B-rated (nonqualifying) bonds worth $40, $10, $25, and $10 million, respectively (market values). Using Table 19–4, determine the following:

a. Charges for specific risk.

b. Charges for general market risk.

c. Charges for basis risk: *vertical offsets within same time bands* only (i.e., ignore the horizontal offsets).

d. What is the total capital charge using the information from parts a–c?

19. What are some of the important changes in the 1995 BIS proposals to measure market risk?

20. Go to the Risk Management Advisory section of the J. P. Morgan web site and find the 1.65 standard deviation confidence band for the firm's daily trading revenues.

Section
Three

Managing Risk off the Balance Sheet

Chapter Twenty

Off-Balance-Sheet Activities

O ff-balance-sheet activities can involve risks that add to the overall risk exposure of a financial intermediary (FI). Indeed, the failure of the U.K. investment bank Barings (see Contemporary Perspectives Box 20–1), the legal problems of Bankers Trust (relating to swap deals involving Procter & Gamble and Gibson Greeting Cards), and the bankruptcy of Orange County in California have been linked to FIs' off-balance-sheet activities in derivatives. However, some off-balance-sheet activities can hedge or reduce FIs' interest rate, credit, and foreign exchange risks. That is, off-balance-sheet activities have both risk-increasing and risk-reducing attributes. In addition, off-balance-sheet activities are now an important source of fee income for many FIs.[1]

---

[1] This fee income can be both direct (e.g., a fee from the sale of a letter of credit) and indirect (e.g., from improved customer relations) effects that have a positive income impact in other product areas. In cases in which customers have a grievance with respect to derivatives purchased from a dealer FI (e.g., Gibson Greeting Cards and Proctor & Gamble), off-balance-sheet activities can have important negative reputational effects that have an adverse impact on the future flow of fees and other income (see "Bankers Trust Clients Complaining," *New York Times,* January 20, 1995, p. DI).

C o n t e m p o r a r y   Perspectives 20–1

Barings Pays the Price of Ignoring Warning Signs

As a Bank of England inquiry got under way into the collapse of Barings, the City dismissed the official line that Nick Leeson's trading losses of up to 1 billion pounds were simply the work of a "rogue trader" which could not have been foreseen. "They're bound to say this," said one banking analyst. "It gets Barings off the hook."

But the City remains unconvinced. Derivatives market insiders claim that responsibility for the bank's collapse lies squarely with Barings' management, which ignored a series of warning signs. This has been compounded by unsubstantiated reports that Mr. Leeson's 24-year-old wife, Lisa, worked in the back office of the bank's Singapore operation which monitored the trading activities of her husband.

While the financial markets had been agog with rumors of Mr. Leeson's colossal 27 billion dollars (17 billion pounds) market position days before the crisis came to a head, Barings either knew nothing of it or failed to react to the danger signs. "Any professional follower of the derivatives market and many of the integrated securities houses were more than aware some time ago of the large positions Barings was building up," said Martin Burton, managing director of derivatives trader Monument Derivatives.

To discover this position, management need have looked no further than the data published by the Oska Securities Exchange, one of the two exchanges where Mr. Leeson traded heavily. Between early January and mid-February, Barings' "buy" futures commitments on the Nikkei 225 spiraled from a sizable 3,000 contracts to an amazing 20,000. The Singapore International Monetary Exchange (SIMEX) must also have known.

But Barings failed to act. Fellow traders speculate that this was because the bank believed the position to be hedged—largely balanced by offsetting positions—or that it was being built for a client. But as one dealer points out: "This is still a huge position to build for a client." And Barings should have checked it out.

That it didn't illustrates the breakdown of control systems throughout the bank, and particularly in the Singapore office. Mr. Leeson was invested with trust way beyond his youth. As one Barings trader put it: "He'd taken big positions before, some long, some short. And management just assumed they were covered."

But there was also a more fundamental problem. In the Singapore office, according to persistent market rumors, Mr. Leeson was also allowed to settle his own transactions—banks normally keep trading and settlement rigidly apart. "This is so basic, it's unbelievable," commented the head of market risk at one London bank.

Blaming Barings' collapse on the failure of its internal control systems in Singapore, Derek Ross, a leading consultant on capital markets operations at Touche Ross, says: "As in the past, where there have been huge losses in the derivatives market, they have not been due to the complexity of the derivatives contracts or the failure of computer systems. They have been due to a lack of control at a very fundamental level."

SOURCE: *Investors Chronicle* (London: The Financial Times Limited, March 3,1995).

OFF-BALANCE-SHEET ACTIVITIES
AND FINANCIAL INTERMEDIARY SOLVENCY

contingent asset and liability

Asset and liability off the balance sheet that potentially can produce positive or negative future cash flows for an FI.

One of the most important choices facing an FI manager is the relative scale of the FI's on- and off-balance-sheet activities. Most of us are aware of on-balance-sheet activities because they appear on FI's published asset and liability balance sheets. For example, a bank's deposits and holdings of bonds and loans are on-balance-sheet activities. In contrast, off-balance-sheet activities are less obvious and are often invisible to all but the very well-informed investor or regulator. In accounting terms, *off-balance-sheet items* usually appear "below the bottom line," frequently only in the footnotes to the financial statements. In economic terms, however, off-balance-sheet items are **contingent assets and liabilities** that affect the future, rather than the current, shape of an FI's balance sheet. As such, they have a direct impact on the FI's future profitability and solvency performance. Consequently, efficient management of these off-balance-sheet items is central to a modern FI's control of overall risk exposure.

From a valuation perspective, off-balance-sheet assets and liabilities have the potential to produce positive or negative *future* cash flows. As a result, the true value of an FI's capital or net worth should not simply present the difference between the market value of assets and liabilities on its balance sheet today but should also reflect the difference between the current market value of its off-balance-sheet or contingent assets and liabilities as well.

This section discusses the effect of off-balance-sheet activities on an FI's risk exposure and return performance. The following section describes different types of off-balance-sheet activity and the risks associated with each.

An item or activity is an **off-balance-sheet (OBS) asset** if, when a contingent event occurs, the item or activity moves onto the asset side of the balance sheet. Conversely, an item or activity is an **off-balance-sheet (OBS) liability** if, when a contingent event occurs, the item or activity moves onto the liability side of the balance sheet. For example, as we discuss in more detail later, FIs sell various performance guarantees, especially guarantees that its customers will not default on their financial and other obligations. Examples of such guarantees include letters of credit and standby letters of credit. Should a customer default occur, the bank's contingent liability (its guarantee) becomes an actual liability and it moves onto the liability side of the balance sheet.

Since off-balance-sheet items are contingent assets and liabilities and move onto the balance sheet with a probability lower than 1, their valuation is difficult and often highly complex. However, determining their value is less difficult as the result of (1) the fact that they are often traded over the counter or in organized financial markets and (2) the availability of high-powered mathematical models and techniques (e.g., RiskMetrics—see Chapter 19). Consider Table 20–1. In Panel A, the value of the FI's net worth (*E*) is calculated in the traditional way as the difference between the market values of its on-balance-sheet assets (*A*) and liabilities (*L*).

off-balance-sheet (OBS) asset

An item that moves onto the asset side of the balance sheet when a contingent event occurs.

off-balance-sheet liability

An item that moves onto the liability side of the balance sheet when a contingent event occurs.

Table 20–1

VALUATION OF AN FI'S NET WORTH WITH AND WITHOUT CONSIDERATION OF OFF-BALANCE-SHEET ACTIVITIES

Panel A: Traditional Valuation of an FI's Net Worth

Assets		Liabilities	
Market value of assets (A)	100	Market value of liabilities (L)	90
		Net worth (E)	10
	100		100

Panel B: Valuation of an FI's Net Worth with On- and Off-Balance-Sheet Activities Valued

Assets		Liabilities	
Market value of assets (A)	100	Market value of liabilities (L)	90
		Net worth (E)	5
Market value of contingent assets (CA)	50	Market value of contingent liabilities (CL)	55
	150		150

$$E = A - L$$
$$10 = 100 - 90$$

Under this calculation, the market value of the stockholders' equity stake in the FI is 10 and the ratio of the FI's capital to assets (or capital assets ratio) is 10 percent. Regulators and FIs often use the latter ratio as a simple measure of solvency (see Chapter 16 for more details).

A more accurate picture of the FI's economic solvency should consider the market values of both its on-balance-sheet and OBS activities (Panel B of Table 20–1). Specifically, the FI manager should value contingent or future asset and liability claims as well as current assets and liabilities. In our example, the current market value of the FI's contingent assets (CA) is 50; the current market value of its contingent liabilities (CL) is 55.[2] Since CL exceed CA by 5, this difference is an additional obligation, or claim, on the FI's net worth. That is, stockholders' true net worth (E) is really

$$E = (A - L) + (CA - CL)$$
$$= (100 - 90) + (50 - 55)$$
$$= 5$$

rather than 10 when we ignored off-balance-sheet activities. Thus, economically speaking, contingent assets and liabilities are contractual claims that directly impact the economic value of the equity holders' stake in an FI. Indeed, from both the stockholders' and regulators' perspectives, large increases in the value of OBS liabilities can render the FI economically insolvent just as effectively as losses due to mismatched interest rate gaps and default or credit losses from on-balance-sheet activities. For example, in the fourth quarter of 1994, after a number of highly publicized legal cases, Bankers Trust forgave $72 million owed by its clients as part of its sales transactions of derivatives. Moreover, it reclassified $351 million of its derivative deals as "nonperforming loans," thereby emphasizing the credit risk potential of OBS activities. In addition, in January 1995, Chase Manhattan deducted $20 million from trading profits because some clients could not pay the bank what they owed on derivative transactions.

Concept Questions

1. What do the terms *contingent asset* and *contingent liability* mean?
2. Suppose that an FI had a market value of assets of 95 and a market value of liabilities of 88. In addition, it had contingent assets valued at 10 and contingent liabilities valued at 7. What is the FI's true net worth position?

RETURNS AND RISKS OF OFF-BALANCE-SHEET ACTIVITIES

In the 1980s, increasing losses on loans to less-developed and Eastern European countries, increased interest rate volatility, and squeezed interest margins for on-balance-sheet lending as the result of nonbank competition led many large commercial banks to seek

---

[2] As noted earlier, such valuation can be achieved either by observing the market prices of such investments (e.g., on options or future exchanges) or by using high-powered mathematical techniques.

profitable OBS activities. By moving activities off the balance sheet, banks hoped to earn more fee income to offset declining margins or spreads on their traditional lending business. At the same time, they could avoid regulatory costs or taxes since reserve requirements, deposit insurance premiums, and capital adequacy requirements were not levied on off-balance-sheet activities. Thus, banks had both earnings and regulatory tax-avoidance incentives to move activities off their balance sheets.[3]

The dramatic increase in OBS activities caused the Federal Reserve to introduce a tracking plan in 1983. As part of the quarterly call reports they file, banks began submitting schedule L on which they listed the notional dollar size and variety of their OBS activities. We show these OBS activities and their distribution and growth for 1991 to 1997 in Table 20–2.

Notice the relative growth of OBS activities in Table 20–2. By the third quarter of 1997, the notional or face value of OBS bank activities was $28,409.3 billion compared to the $4,869.4 billion value of on-balance-sheet activities (see Tables 20–3 and 20–4). The use of derivative contracts accelerated during the period 1991–1997. Although the notional dollar value of OBS items overestimates their current market or contingent claims values, the increase in these activities is still nothing short of phenomenal.[4] Indeed, this phenomenal increase has pushed regulators to impose capital requirements on such activities and to explicitly recognize FIs' solvency risk exposure from pursuing such activities. These capital requirements[5] came into effect on January 1, 1993; we describe them in detail in Chapter 16.

As noted in Tables 20–2, 20–3, and 20–4, major types of OBS activities for U.S. banks include the following:

- Loan commitments.
- Standby letters of credit and letters of credit.
- Derivative contracts: futures, forward contracts, swaps, and options.
- When-issued securities.
- Loans sold.

The notational/dollar amounts of derivative contracts reported by seven major U.S. bank OTC derivatives dealers from year-end 1990 through September 1997 are reported in Table 20–5. Securities firms, insurance companies, and pension funds engage in most of these OBS activities as well.[6] The use of derivatives to hedge risk by some sectors of the financial services industry has recently decreased, however; see Contemporary Perspectives Box 20–2.

The next section analyzes these OBS activities in more detail, and pays particular attention to the types of risk exposure an FI faces when it engages in such activities. A summary of these risks is presented in Table 20–6. As we discussed earlier, precise market valuation of these contingent assets and liabilities can be extremely difficult because of their complex features. At a very minimum, FI managers should understand not only the general features of the risk associated with each major OBS asset and liability but also how each can impact an FI's return and profitability.

---

[3] Chapter 12 presents more detail on incentives relating to loan sales.

[4] This occurs because the value of contingent claims is usually less than the face value of most contingent assets and liabilities.

[5] In actual practice, the capital requirements on OBS activities were phased in over the 1988–1992 period.

[6] See, for example, M. K. Hassan and W. H. Sackley, "Determinants of Thrift Institution Off-Balance-Sheet Activities: An Empirical Investigation," Working Paper 70148, Department of Finance, University of New Orleans.

Table **20-2**

AGGREGATE VOLUME OF OFF-BALANCE-SHEET COMMITMENTS AND CONTINGENCIES BY U.S. COMMERCIAL BANKS, ANNUAL DATA AS OF DECEMBER*

(in billions of dollars)

	1991	1992	1993	1994	1995	1996	1997	Distribution 1997
Commitments to lend	$1,183.4	$1,272.0	$1,455.3	$1,768.3	$2,157.4	$2,528.7	$2,966.9	10.4%
Future and forward contracts (exclude FX†)								
On commodities and equities	24.9	26.3	43.9	54.3	115.0	101.6	101.2	0.4
On interest rates	1,226.5	1,738.1	2,496.7	3,434.3	3,063.1	3,201.2	4,170.9	14.7
Notional amount of credit derivatives								
Bank is guarantor	3.4	4.1	10.4	7.6	4.1	14.1	14.7	0.0
Bank is beneficiary	3.0	4.5	8.0	8.4	7.9	14.5	24.1	0.1
Standby contracts and other option contracts								
Written option contracts on interest rates	427.6	504.7	950.2	1,024.4	1,261.7	1,588.6	2,148.0	7.6
Purchased option contracts on interest rates	426.5	508.0	818.8	1,015.0	1,223.8	1,567.6	2,046.7	7.2
Written option contracts on foreign exchange	236.3	245.7	263.3	341.4	406.6	529.9	764.9	2.7
Purchased option contracts on foreign exchange	226.7	249.1	254.5	312.0	409.9	502.6	711.5	2.5
Written option contracts on commodities	40.1	30.9	50.3	77.5	111.6	106.8	159.6	0.6
Purchased option contracts on commodities	36.0	29.4	46.3	71.1	102.6	97.1	129.8	0.5
Commitments to buy FX (includes $U.S.), spot, and forward	2,624.1	3,015.5	3,689.4	4,620.4	4,525.4	5,000.8	5,844.2	20.6
Standby LCs‡ and foreign office guarantees								
To U.S. addresses	37.0	34.5	32.2	35.7	39.6	44.5	45.5	0.2
To non-U.S. addresses								
(Amount of these items sold to others via participations)								
Commercial LCs	29.7	28.1	28.0	32.5	31.9	30.9	31.7	0.1
Participations in acceptances sold to others	0.8	0.8	0.9	0.8	1.1	1.2	1.3	0.0
Participations in acceptances bought from others	0.3	0.2	0.2	0.2	0.3	0.2	0.2	0.0
Securities borrowed	9.1	10.8	21.4	14.6	17.9	25.5	24.6	0.1
Securities lent	66.4	96.4	127.0	140.4	149.8	208.0	288.3	1.0
Other significant commitments and contingencies	13.7	8.7	7.8	3.5	3.6	14.0	10.3	0.0
Memoranda								
Notional value of all outstanding interest rate swaps	1,755.9	2,122.0	2,946.3	4,451.1	5,546.8	7,069.4	8,904.5	31.3
Mortgages sold, with recourse								
Outstanding principal balance of mortgages sold or swapped	18.5	10.7	8.8	7.5	9.4	11.4	12.1	0.0
Amount of recourse exposure on these mortgages	9.2	6.3	4.9	4.2	5.6	8.2	8.3	0.0
Total, including memoranda items	$8,510.8	$10,072.3	$13,365.5	$17,409.1	$19,195.1	$22,666.8	$28,409.3	100.00%
Total assets (on-balance-sheet items)	$3,402.2	$3,476.4	$3,673.7	$3,972.9	$4,312.7	$4,578.3	$4,869.4	—

*1997 figures are as of September.

†Foreign exchange

‡Letter of credit

SOURCES: FDIC, *Statistics on Banking,* various issues.

Table **20–3**

DERIVATIVE CONTRACTS BY PRODUCT, ALL COMMERCIAL BANKS*

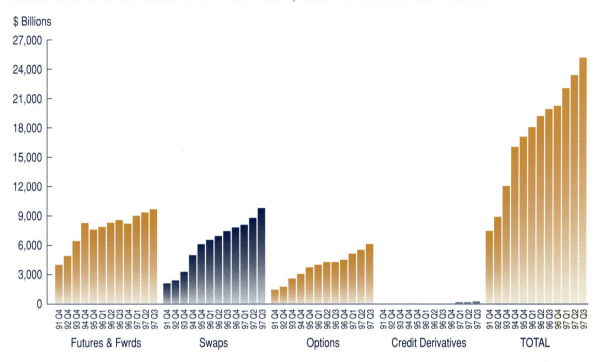

Derivative by Contract Product ($ billions)†

	91 Q4	92 Q4	93 Q4	94 Q4	95 Q4	96 Q1	96 Q2	96 Q3	96 Q4	97 Q1	97 Q2	97 Q3
Futures & forwards	3,876	4,780	6,229	8,109	7,399	7,653	8,138	8,304	8,041	8,866	9,165	9,465
Swaps	2,071	2,417	3,260	4,823	5,945	6,336	6,727	7,288	7,601	7,950	8,723	9,563
Options	1,393	1,568	2,384	2,841	3,516	3,858	4,171	4,227	4,393	5,052	5,411	5,961
Credit derivatives	—	—	—	—	—	—	—	—	—	19	26	39
TOTAL	7,339	8,764	11,873	15,774	16,861	17,847	19,036	19,818	20,035	21,887	23,325	25,028

*Data are preliminary.

†In billions of dollars; notional value of futures, total exchange traded options, total over the counter options, total forwards, and total swaps. Note that data after 1994 do not include spot fx in the total notional amount of derivatives.

Credit derivatives were reported for the first time in the first quarter of 1997. Currently, the Call Report does not differentiate credit derivatives by product, which have therefore been added as a separate category. As of 1997, credit derivatives have been included in the sum of total derivatives in this chart.

NOTE: Numbers may not add due to rounding.

SOURCE: Call reports and Office of the Comptroller of the Currency.

loan commitment agreement

A contractual commitment to make a loan up to a stated amount at a given interest rate in the future.

Loan Commitments

These days, most commercial and industrial loans are made by firms that take down (or borrow against) prenegotiated lines of credit or loan commitments rather than borrow spot loans (see discussion on C&I loans in Chapter 10). A **loan commitment agreement** is a contractual commitment by a bank or another FI (such as an insurance company) to loan a

Table **20–4**

DERIVATIVE CONTRACTS BY TYPE, ALL COMMERCIAL BANKS*

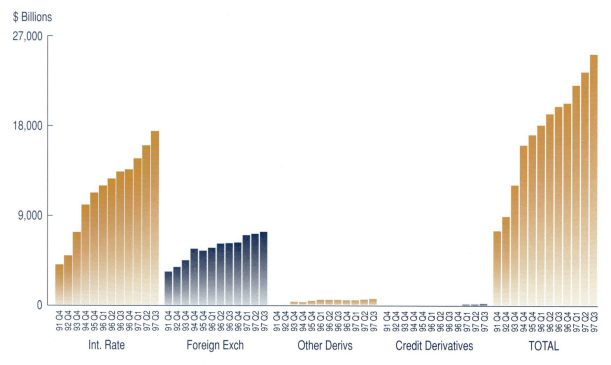

Derivative Contracts by Type ($ billions)†

	91 Q4	92 Q4	93 Q4	94 Q4	95 Q4	96 Q1	96 Q2	96 Q3	96 Q4	97 Q1	97 Q2	97 Q3
Interest rate	3,837	4,872	7,210	9,926	11,096	11,820	12,517	13,257	13,427	14,562	15,802	17,270
Foreign exchange	3,394	3,789	4,484	5,605	5,387	5,650	6,125	6,210	6,241	6,919	7,084	7,268
Other derivatives	109	102	179	243	378	378	394	351	367	387	413	452
Credit derivatives	—	—	—	—	—	—	—	—	—	19	26	39
TOTAL	7,339	8,764	11,873	15,774	16,861	17,847	19,036	19,818	20,035	21,887	23,325	25,028

*Data are preliminary.

†In billions of dollars; notional value of futures, total exchange traded options, total over the counter options, total forwards, and total swaps. Note that data after 1994 do not include spot fx in the total notional amount of derivatives.

Credit derivatives were reported for the first time in the first quarter of 1997. Currently, the Call Report does not differentiate credit derivatives by contract type, which have therefore been added as a separate category. As of the first quarter of 1997, credit derivatives have been included in the sum of total derivatives.

NOTE: Numbers may not add due to rounding.

SOURCE: Call reports and Office of the Comptroller of the Currency.

up-front fee

The fee charged for making funds available through a loan commitment.

firm a certain maximum amount (say, $10 million) at given interest rate terms (say, 12 percent). The loan commitment agreement also defines the length of time over which the borrower has the option to take down this loan. In return for making this loan commitment, the bank may charge an **up-front fee** (or facility fee) of, say, 1/8 percent of the commitment size, or $12,500 in this example. In addition, the bank must stand ready to supply the full

Table **20–5**

NOTIONAL/CONTRACT AMOUNTS OF DERIVATIVES REPORTED BY THE SEVEN MAJOR U.S. BANK OTC DERIVATIVES DEALERS*

(in billions of dollars)

	1990	1991	1992	1993	1994	1995	1996	1997*
Banks	$5,350	$5,811	$7,574	$10,353	$13,724	$15,809	$14,552	$20,645

*Amounts reported year-end 1990 through September 1997.

Note 1: These amounts have not been adjusted for double counting.

Note 2: The seven major U.S. bank OTC derivatives dealers are The Chase Manhattan Corporation; Citicorp; J.P. Morgan & Co., Inc.; Bankers Trust New York Corporation; BankAmerica Corporation; NationsBank Corporation; First Chicago.

SOURCE: Annual reports of the seven dealers; GAO *Report on Financial Derivatives,* November, 1996; OCC figures.

Contemporary Perspectives 20–2

Institutions Cut Derivative Use

Fixed-income derivatives trading volume plummeted among pension funds, investment managers and mutual funds, a Greenwich Associates report shows. In addition, the share of trading in exchange-traded futures and derivatives among investment managers and mutual fund managers fell, although pension funds' share held steady. . . .

In a survey of many types of institutional derivatives users, pension fund use of interest rate and cross-currency swaps fell to $100 million on average from $6.2 billion; investment manager use fell to $100 million on average from $1 billion; and mutual fund use fell to $100 million on average from $6.1 billion.

Pension fund use of interest rate options, caps, collars, floors or swaptions among survey respondents rose to $500 million on average from $100 million, while investment manager use fell to $800 million on average from $2.2 billion, and mutual fund use fell to $300 million on average from $600 million.

Frank Feenstra, principal with Greenwich, said the big derivatives-linked losses taken in the past few years woke up a lot of senior people at institutional investment firms to the realization that they didn't know how derivatives were being used. Because the firms didn't want to get burned, they curtailed the use of all derivatives, he said. The number of users also declined, with smaller investors possibly getting out for good, Mr. Feenstra said. The cost of managing positions and understanding what they're doing might be too great for smaller investors, he said. . . .

Robert Arnott, chief investment officer and chief executive of First Quadrant Corp., . . . said he isn't surprised by the drop in volume among pension funds and money managers in using over-the-counter derivatives. He said the decline "is probably, in fact almost certainly, happening in the OTC swap market, where some of the exotic custom-designed fixed-income swaps and other over-the-counter derivatives have turned out

to be so costly—indeed, devastatingly costly to some institutional investors who did not have the sophistication to fully understand what they were buying. But we have seen no evidence at all of a decline in interest in using exchange-traded bond futures (plain-vanilla derivatives—where the daily settlement of gains and losses makes it much more difficult to get into serious trouble unexpectedly building up losses over months)."

William Miller, chairman of the End Users of Derivatives Association . . . noted other factors—like a less volatile interest rate environment—might have contributed to decreased use of derivatives. If interest rates don't move as much, there's less of a need to use derivatives to try to limit volatility, Mr. Miller said. He also said if derivatives use by pension funds and investment managers has fallen as overall use increases, maybe those investors should question whether they are managing risk properly.

SOURCE: Paul G. Barr, *Pensions & Investments,* July 22, 1996, p. 3. Reprinted with permission, Pension & Investments, July 22, 1996. Copyright, Crain Communications, Inc.

T a b l e **20–6**

MAJOR TYPES OF RISKS ASSOCIATED WITH VARIOUS OFF-BALANCE-SHEET ACTIVITIES

Loan Commitments

Interest rate risk—Risk resulting from the fact that the bank precommits to make loans available over the commitment period at either some fixed interest rate or some variable rate.

Take-down risk—Future liquidity risk or uncertainty due to the fact that the FI can never be absolutely sure when the borrower will arrive to take down the loan commitment and what amount will actually be taken down.

Credit risk—Risk that the creditworthiness of the borrower will change between the time the interest rate on the loan commitment is set and the time the borrower takes down the loan commitment.

Aggregate funding risk—Risk of a rise in the cost of funds to FIs and increased level of take downs due to macroeconomic events such as restrictive monetary policy actions of the Federal Reserve.

Letters of credit

Commercial letter of credit (CLC) and standby letter of credit (SLC) risk—Risk that the holder of the CLC or SLC will default on a promised payment, forcing the FI to make good on its guarantee that it will cover any default.

Derivative contracts

Credit risk—Risk that the counterparty to a derivative contract may default on its payment obligations.

When-issued securities

Interest rate risk—Risk introduced when FIs make commitments to buy or sell at a stated price before issue.

Loans sold

Credit risk—Risk created when an FI sells a loan with recourse, meaning that if loan payments are defaulted on, the holder of the loan can give (or put) the loan back to the FI at face value.

---

back-end fee

The fee charged on the unused component of a loan commitment.

$10 million at any time over the commitment period, for example, one year. Meanwhile, the borrower has a valuable option to take down any amount between $0 and $10 million. The bank may also charge the borrower a **back-end fee** (or commitment fee) on any unused balances in the commitment line at the end of the period. In this example, if the borrower takes down only $8 million in funds over the year and the fee on *unused* commitments is 1/4 percent, the bank generates additional revenue of 1/4 percent times $2 million, or $5,000.

Note that only when the borrower actually draws on the commitment do the loans made under the commitment appear on the balance sheet. Thus, only when the $8 million loan is taken down exactly halfway through the one-year commitment period (i.e., *six months later*) does the balance sheet show the creation of a new $8 million loan. When the $10 million commitment is made at time 0, nothing shows on the balance sheet. Nevertheless, the bank must stand ready to supply the full $10 million in loans on any day within the one-year commitment period; that is, at time 0 a new contingent claim on the resources of the bank was created.

This raises a question. What contingent risks does the loan commitment provision create? At least four types of risk are associated with the extension of loan commitments: interest rate risk, take-down risk, credit risk, and aggregate funding risk.

Interest Rate Risk.   *Interest rate risk* is a contingent risk emanating from the fact that the bank precommits to make loans available to a borrower over the commitment period at either (1) some fixed interest rate as a fixed-rate loan commitment or (2) some variable rate as a variable-rate loan commitment. Suppose that the bank precommits to lend a maximum of $10 million at a fixed rate of 12 percent over the year and then its cost of funds rises. The cost of funds may well rise to such a level to make the spread between the 12 percent commitment rate and the bank's cost of funds negative or very small. Moreover, 12 percent may be much less than the rate the customer would have to pay if it were forced to borrow on the spot loan market under current interest rate conditions. When rates do rise during the commitment period, the FI stands to lose on its portfolio of fixed-rate loan commitments as borrowers exercise to the full amount their very valuable options to borrow at below market rates.

One way the FI can control this risk is by making commitment rates float with spot loan rates, for example, by indexing loan commitments to the prime rate. If the prime rate rises during the commitment period, so does the cost of commitment loans to the borrower; the borrower pays the market rate in effect when the commitment is drawn on. Nevertheless, this fixed formula rate solution does not totally eradicate interest rate risk on loan commitments. For example, suppose that the prime rate rises by 1 percent but the cost of funds rises by 1.25 percent; the spread between the indexed commitment loan and the cost of funds narrows by .25 percent. This spread risk is often called **basis risk.**[7]

basis risk

The variable spread between a lending rate and a borrowing rate, or between any two interest rates or prices.

Take-Down Risk.   Another contingent risk is take-down risk. Specifically, in making the loan commitment, the FI must always stand ready to provide the maximum of the commitment line—$10 million in our example. The borrower has the flexible option to borrow anything between $0 and the $10 million ceiling on any business day in the commitment period. This exposes the FI to a degree of future liquidity risk or uncertainty (see Chapter 13). The FI can never be absolutely sure when during the commitment period the borrower will demand the full $10 million or some proportion thereof in cash.[8] To some extent, at least, the back-end fee on unused amounts is designed to create incentives for the borrower to take down lines in full to avoid paying this fee. In actuality, however, many lines are only partially drawn on.[9]

Credit Risk.   FIs also face a degree of contingent credit risk in setting the interest or formula rate on a loan commitment. Specifically, an FI often adds a risk premium based on its current assessment of the borrower's creditworthiness. For example, the borrower may

---

[7] Basis risk occurs because loan rates and deposit rates do not move in unison; that is, they are not perfectly correlated in their movements over time (see Chapter 21).

[8] Indeed, the borrower could borrow different amounts over the period ($1 million in month 1, $2 million in month 2, etc.). The only constraint is the $10 million ceiling. We discuss this liquidity risk aspect of loan commitments more in Chapter 13.

[9] A recent study by E. Asarnow and J. Marker, "Historical Performance of the U.S. Corporate Loan Market 1988–1993," *The Journal of Commercial Lending,* Spring 1995, pp. 13–22, indicates that the average take-down rates varied widely according to the borrower's credit rating, from a take-down rate of only 0.1 percent by a AAA borrower to 20 percent for BBB, and 75 percent for CCC.

be judged as a AA credit risk paying 1 percent above prime rate. Suppose, however, that over the one-year commitment period the borrowing firm gets into difficulty; its earnings decline so that its creditworthiness is downgraded to BBB. The FI's problem is that the credit risk premium on the commitment had been preset to the AA level for the one-year commitment period. To avoid being exposed to dramatic declines in borrower creditworthiness over the commitment period, most FIs include an *adverse material change in conditions clause* by which the FI can cancel or reprice a loan commitment. Exercising such a clause, however, is really a last resort tactic for the FI because it may put the borrower out of business and result in costly legal claims related to breach of contract.[10]

Aggregate Funding Risk.   Many large borrowing firms, such as GM, Ford, or IBM, take out multiple commitment or credit lines with many banks as insurance against future credit crunches.[11] A credit crunch restricts the supply of spot loans to borrowers possibly as the result of restrictive monetary policy actions by the Federal Reserve. Another cause is an FI's aversion to lending. In such credit crunches, borrowers with long-standing loan commitments are unlikely to be as credit constrained as those without loan commitments. This also implies, however, that borrowers' aggregate demand to take down loan commitments is likely to be greatest when the FI's borrowing and funding conditions are most costly and difficult. In difficult credit conditions, this aggregate commitment take-down effect can increase the cost of funds above normal levels while many FIs scramble for funds to meet their commitments to customers. This is similar to the *externality effect* common in many markets when all participants simultaneously act together and adversely affect the costs of each individual participant.

The four contingent risk effects just identified—interest rate, take-down, credit, and aggregate funding risk—appear to imply that loan commitment activities increase the insolvency exposure of FIs that engage in such activities. However, an opposing view holds that loan commitment contracts may make an FI less risky than had it not engaged in them. This view maintains that to be able to charge fees and sell loan commitments or equivalent credit-rationing insurance, the FI must convince borrowers that it will still be around to provide the credit needed in the *future*.[12] To convince borrowers that an FI will be around to meet its future commitments, managers may have to adopt *lower* risk portfolios *today* than otherwise. By adopting lower risk portfolios, managers increase the probability that the FI will be able to meet all its long-term on- and off-balance-sheet obligations. Interestingly, recent empirical studies have confirmed that banks making more loan commitments have lower on-balance-sheet portfolio risk characteristics than those with relatively low levels of commitments; that is, safer banks have a higher tendency to make loan commitments.

---

[10]Potential damage claims could be enormous if the borrower goes out of business and attributes the failure to the cancellation of loans under the commitment contract. Important reputational costs also must be considered when deciding whether to cancel a commitment to lend.

[11]Recent research by D.P. Morgan, "The Credit Effects of Monetary Policy: Evidence Using Loan Commitments," *Journal of Money, Credit, and Banking*, February 1998, pp. 102–118, has found evidence of this type of insurance effect. Specifically in credit crunches, spot loans may decline but loans made under commitment do not.

[12]See A.W.A. Boot and A.V. Thakor, "Off-Balance-Sheet Liabilities, Deposit Insurance, and Capital Regulation," *Journal of Banking and Finance* 15 (1991), pp. 825–46.

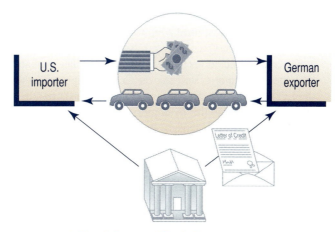

F i g u r e **20-1**   *A Simple Letter of Credit Transaction*

Commercial Letters of Credit and Standby Letters of Credit

letters of credit

Contingent guarantees sold by an FI to underwrite the trade or commercial performance of the buyer of the guaranty.

standby letters of credit

Guarantees issued to cover contingencies that are potentially more severe and less predictable than contingencies covered under trade-related or commercial letters of credit.

In selling commercial **letters of credit** (LCs) and **standby letters of credit** (SLCs) for fees, FIs add to their contingent future liabilities. Both LCs and SLCs are essentially *guarantees* that an FI sells to underwrite the *performance* of the buyer of the guarantee (such as a corporation). In economic terms, the FI that sells LCs and SLCs is selling insurance against the frequency or severity of some particular future occurrence. Further, similar to the different lines of insurance sold by property-casualty insurers, LC and SLC contracts differ as to the severity and frequency of their risk exposures. We look next at an FI's risk exposure from engaging in LC and SLC OBS activities.

Commercial Letters of Credit.   Commercial letters of credit are widely used in both domestic and international trade. For example, they ease the shipment of grain between a farmer in Iowa and a purchaser in New Orleans or the shipment of goods between a U.S. importer and a foreign exporter. The FI's role is to provide a formal guarantee that payment for goods shipped or sold will be forthcoming regardless of whether the buyer of the goods defaults on payment. We show a very simple LC example in Figure 20–1 for an international transaction between a U.S. importer and a German exporter.

Suppose that a U.S. importer sent an order for $10 million worth of machinery to a German exporter, as shown in Figure 20–l. However, the German exporter may be reluctant to send the goods without some assurance or guarantee of being paid once the goods are shipped. The U.S. importer may promise to pay for the goods in 90 days but the German exporter may feel insecure either because it knows little about the creditworthiness of the U.S. importer or because the U.S. importer has a low credit rating (i.e., B or BB). To persuade the German exporter to ship the goods, the U.S. importer may have to turn to a large U.S. bank with which it has developed a long-term customer relationship. In its role as a lender and monitor, the U.S. bank can better appraise the U.S. importer's creditworthiness. The U.S. bank can issue a contingent payment guarantee—that is, an LC to the German exporter on the importer's behalf—in return for an LC fee paid by the U.S. importer. In our example, the bank would send the German exporter an LC guaranteeing payment for the goods in 90 days regardless of whether the importer defaults on its obligation to the German exporter. Implicitly, the bank is replacing the U.S. importer's credit risk with its own credit risk guarantee. For this substitution to work effectively, the bank, in guaranteeing payment, must have a higher credit standing or better credit quality reputation than the U.S. importer. Once the bank issues the LC and sends it to the German exporter, the exporter ships the goods to the U.S. importer. The probability is very high that in 90 days' time the U.S. importer will pay the German exporter for the goods sent and the bank keeps the LC fee as profit. The fee is perhaps 10 basis points of the face value of the letter of credit, or $10,000 in this example.

A small probability exists, however, that the U.S. importer will be unable to pay the $10 million in 90 days and will default. Then the bank is obliged to make good on its guarantee. The cost of such a default could mean that the bank must pay $10 million, although it would have a creditor's claim against the importer's assets to offset this loss. Clearly, the fee should exceed the expected default risk on the LC, which equals the probability of default times the expected payout on the LC after adjusting for the bank's ability to reclaim assets from the defaulting importer and any monitoring costs.

Standby Letters of Credit.   Standby letters of credit perform an insurance function similar to commercial and trade letters of credit. The structure and type of risk covered differ, however. FIs may issue SLCs to cover contingencies that are potentially more *severe,* less *predictable* or frequent, and not necessarily trade related. These contingencies include performance bond guarantees by which an FI may guarantee that a real estate development will be completed in some interval of time. Alternatively, the FI may offer default guarantees to back an issue of commercial paper (CP) or municipal revenue bonds to allow issuers to achieve a higher credit rating and a lower funding cost than otherwise.

Without credit enhancements, for example, many firms would be unable to borrow in the CP market or would have to borrow at a higher funding cost. P1 borrowers, who offer the highest-quality commercial paper, normally pay 40 basis points less than P2 borrowers, the next quality grade. By paying a fee of perhaps 25 basis points to a bank, an FI guarantees to pay CP purchasers' principal and interest on maturity should the issuing firm itself be unable to pay. The SLC backing of commercial paper issues normally results in the paper's placement in the lowest default risk class (P1) and the issuer's savings of up to 15 basis points on issuing costs—40 basis points (the P2 –P1 spread) minus the 25-basis-point SLC fee equals 15 basis points.

Note that in selling the SLCs, banks are competing directly with another of their OBS products, loan commitments. Rather than buying an SLC from a bank to back a CP issue, the issuing firm might pay a fee to a bank to supply a loan commitment. This loan commitment would match the size and maturity of the commercial paper issue, for example, a $100 million ceiling and 45 day maturity. If, on maturity, the commercial paper issuer had insufficient funds to repay the commercial paper holders, the issuer has the right to take down the $100 million loan commitment and to use these funds to meet CP repayments. Often, the up-front fees on such loan commitments are less than those on SLCs; therefore, many CP-issuing firms prefer to use loan commitments.

Finally, remember that U.S. banks are not the only issuers of SLCs. Not surprising, property-casualty insurers have an increasingly important business line of performance bonds and financial guarantees. The growth in these lines for property-casualty insurers has come at the expense of U.S. banks. Moreover, foreign banks increasingly are taking a share of the U.S. market in SLCs. The reason for the loss in this business line by U.S. banks is that to sell guarantees such as SLCs credibly, the seller must have a better credit rating than the customer. In recent years, few U.S. banks or their parent holding companies have had AAA ratings. Other domestic FIs and foreign banks, on the other hand, have more often had AAA ratings. High credit ratings not only make the guarantor more attractive from the buyer's perspective but also make the guarantor more competitive because its cost of funds is lower than that of less creditworthy FIs.

Derivative Contracts: Futures, Forwards, Swaps, and Options

FIs can be either users of derivative contracts for hedging (see Chapter 21 through 23) and other purposes or dealers that act as counterparties in trades with customers for a fee. It has been estimated that only 600 U.S. banks use derivatives and that only five large dealer banks—Bankers Trust, Bank of America, Chase, Citicorp, and Morgan—accounting for some 70 percent of the derivatives that user banks hold.[13]

forward contract

A nonstandard contract inferred laterally between two parties.

Contingent credit risk is likely to be present when FIs expand their positions in forward, futures, swaps, and option contracts. This risk relates to the fact that the counterparty to one of these contracts may default on payment obligations, leaving the FI unhedged and having to replace the contract at today's interest rates, prices, or exchange rates, which may be relatively unfavorable. In addition, such defaults are most likely to occur when the counterparty is losing heavily on the contract and the FI is in the money on the contract. As noted earlier, both Chase and Bankers Trust suffered significant losses on their derivative positions in 1994 due to counterparty defaults. This type of default risk is much more serious for **forward contracts** than for futures contracts. This is so because forward contracts are nonstandard contracts entered into bilaterally by negotiating parties such as two banks and all cash flows are required to be paid at one time (on contract maturity). Thus, they are essentially over-the-counter arrangements with no external guarantees should one or the other party default on the contract. For example, the contract seller might default on a forward foreign exchange contract that promises to deliver £10 million in three months' time at the exchange rate $1.70 to £1 if the cost to purchase £1 for delivery is $1.90 when the forward contract matures. By contrast, **futures contracts** are standardized contracts guaranteed by organized exchanges such as the New York Futures Exchange (NYFE). Futures contracts, like forward contracts, make commitments to deliver foreign exchange (or some other asset) at some future date. If a counterparty were to default on a futures contract, however, the exchange assumes the defaulting party's position and payment obligations. Consider the case of Barings, the 200-year-old British merchant bank that failed as the result of trading losses in February 1995. In this case, Barings (specifically, one trader, Nick Leeson) bought $8 billion worth of futures on the Japanese Nikkei Stock Market Index, betting that the Nikkei Index would rise. For a number of reasons, the index actually fell, and the bank lost more than $1.2 billion on its trading position over a period of one month. When Barings was unable to meet its margin calls on Nikkei Index futures traded on the Singapore futures exchange (SIMEX) in 1995, the exchange stood ready to assume Barings' futures contracts and ensure that no counterparty lost money (leaving Barings liable to SIMEX rather than the futures contracts counterparty). Thus, unless a systematic financial market collapse threatens the exchange itself, futures are essentially default risk free.[14] In addition, the daily marking to market of future contracts reduces default risk. This

futures contract

A standardized contract guaranteed by organized exchanges.

---

[13]See *GAO Report on Financial Derivatives*, Washington, DC: U.S. Government Printing Office, November 1996.

[14]More specifically, the default risk of a futures contract is less than that of a forward contract for at least four reasons: (1) daily marking to market of futures, (2) margin requirements on futures that act as a security bond, (3) price limits that spread extreme price fluctuations over time, and (4) default guarantees by the futures exchange itself.

prevents the accumulation of losses and gains that occur with forward contracts. These differences are discussed in more detail in Chapter 21.

Option contracts can also be traded over the counter (OTC) or bought/sold on organized exchanges. If the options are standardized options traded on exchanges, such as bond options, they are virtually default risk free.[15] If they are specialized options purchased OTC such as interest rate caps (see Chapter 22), some element of default risk exists.[16] Similarly, swaps are OTC instruments normally susceptible to counterparty risk (see Chapter 23).[17] In general, default risk on OTC contracts increases with the time to maturity of the contract and the fluctuation of underlying prices, interest rates, or exchange rates.[18]

Forward Purchases and Sales of When-Issued Securities

when-issued (WI) trading

Trading in securities prior to their actual issue.

Very often, banks and other FIs—especially investment banks—enter into commitments to buy and sell securities before issue. This is called **when-issued (WI) trading**. These OBS commitments can expose an FI to future or contingent interest rate risk.

Good examples of WI commitments are those taken on with new T-bills in the week prior to the announcement of the T-bill auction results. Every Tuesday, the Federal Reserve, on behalf of the Treasury, announces the auction size of new three- and six-month bills to be allotted the following Monday. Between the announcement of the total auction size on Tuesday and the announcement of the winning bill allotments on the following Monday, primary dealers sell WI contracts. Large investment banks and commercial banks (currently approximately 40 in number) normally are primary dealers. They sell the yet-to-be-issued T-bills for forward delivery to customers in the secondary market at a small margin above the price they expect to pay at the primary auction. This can be profitable if the primary dealer obtains all the bills needed at the auction at the appropriate price or interest rate to fulfill these forward WI contracts. A primary dealer that makes a mistake regarding the tenor of the auction (i.e., level of interest rates) faces the risk that the commitments entered into to deliver T-bills in the WI market can be met only at a loss. For example, an overcommitted dealer (resulting from a miscalculation of interest rate changes) may have to buy T-bills from other dealers at a loss right after the auction results are announced to meet the WI T-bill delivery commitments that the dealer made to its customers. This type of problem occurred for many commercial and investment bank primary dealers when Salomon Brothers cornered (or squeezed) the market for new two-year Treasury bonds in

---

[15]Note that the options still can be subject to interest rate risk; see the discussion in Chapter 22.

[16]Under an interest rate cap, the seller, in return for a fee, promises to compensate the buyer should interest rates rise above a certain level. If rates rise much more than expected, the cap seller may have an incentive to default to truncate the losses. Thus, selling a cap is similar to a bank's selling interest rate risk insurance (see Chapter 22 for more details).

[17]In a swap, two parties contract to exchange interest rate payments or foreign exchange payments. If interest rates (or foreign exchange rates) move a good deal, one party can face considerable future loss exposure, creating incentives to default.

[18]Reputational considerations and the need for future access to markets for hedging deter the incentive to default (see Chapter 22 as well). However, most empirical evidence suggests that derivative contracts have reduced FI risk. See for example, G. Gorton and R. Rosen, "Banks and Derivatives," Working Paper, University of Pennsylvania Wharton School, February 1995. Gorton and Rosen find that swap contracts have generally reduced the systematic risk of the U.S. banking system.

1990. As a result, the Treasury instituted a wholesale reform program to change the way bills and bonds are auctioned.[19]

Loans Sold

We discuss the types of loans that FIs sell, their incentives to sell, and the way in which they can sell them in more detail in Chapter 12. Banks and other FIs increasingly originate loans on their balance sheets, but rather than holding the loans to maturity, they quickly sell them to outside investors. These outside investors include other banks, insurance companies, mutual funds, or even corporations. In acting as loan originators and loan sellers, FIs are operating more as loan brokers than as traditional asset transformers (see Chapter 1).

recourse

The ability to put an asset or loan back to the seller should the credit quality of that asset deteriorate.

When an outside party buys a loan with absolutely no **recourse** to the seller of the loan should the loan eventually go bad, loan sales have no OBS contingent liability implications for FIs. Specifically, *no recourse* means that if the loan the FI sells should go bad, the buyer of the loan must bear the full risk of loss. In particular, the buyer cannot put the bad loan back to the seller or originating bank. Suppose that the loan is sold with recourse. Then, loan sales present a long-term contingent credit risk to the seller. Essentially, the buyer of the loan holds a long-term option to put the loan back to the seller, which the buyer can exercise should the credit quality of the purchased loan deteriorate. In reality, the recourse or nonrecourse nature of loan sales is often ambiguous. For example, some have argued that banks generally are willing to repurchase bad no recourse loans to preserve their reputations with their customers. Obviously, reputation concerns may extend the size of a selling bank's contingent liabilities for OBS activities.

Concept Questions

1. What four risks are related to loan commitments?
2. What is the major difference between a commercial letter of credit and a standby letter of credit?
3. What does counterparty risk in a forward contract mean?
4. Which is riskier for a bank, loan sales with recourse or loan sales without recourse?

SCHEDULE L AND NONSCHEDULE L OFF-BALANCE-SHEET RISKS

So far we have discussed five different off-balance-sheet activities that banks must report to the Federal Reserve each quarter as part of their Schedule L section of the call report. Remember that many other FIs engage in these activities as well. Thus, thrifts, insurance companies, and investment banks engage in futures, forwards, swaps, and option transactions in varying forms. Life insurers engage heavily in making loan commitments in commercial mortgages, property-casualty companies underwrite large amounts of financial

---

[19]Under the auction rules, no bidder could bid for or attain more than 35 percent of an issue. By bidding using customers' names (without their knowledge) in addition to bidding under its own name, however, Salomon Brothers vastly exceeded the 35 percent limit and thus created a shortage in the availability of newly issued securities for other dealers.

guarantees, and investment banks trade when-issued securities. Moreover, the five activities just discussed are not the only off-balance-sheet activities that can create contingent liabilities or risks for an FI. Next, we briefly introduce two other activities that can create them and discuss these activities in more depth in later chapters.

Settlement Risk

FIs send the bulk of their wholesale dollar payments along wire transfer systems such as Fedwire and the Clearing House InterBank Payments System (CHIPS). The Federal Reserve owns Fedwire, a domestic wire transfer network. CHIPS is an international and private network owned by 140 or so participating or member banks. Currently, these two networks transfer more than $1.7 trillion a day.

Unlike the domestic Fedwire system, funds or payment messages sent on the CHIPS network *within* the day are provisional messages that become final and are settled only at the *end* of the day. For example, bank X sends a fund transfer payment message to bank Z at 11 AM EST. The actual cash settlement and physical transfer of funds between X and Z takes place at the end of the day, normally by transferring cash held in reserve accounts at the Federal Reserve banks. Because the transfer of funds is not finalized until the end of the day, bank Z—the message-receiving bank—faces an *intraday* or within-day **settlement risk.** Specifically, bank Z assumes that the funds message it received at 11 AM from bank X will result in the actual delivery of the funds at the end of the day and may then lend them to bank Y at 11:15 AM. However, if bank X does not deliver (settle) the promised funds at the end of the day, bank Z may be pushed into a serious net funds deficit position and may therefore be unable to meet its payment commitment to bank Y. Conceivably, bank Z's net debtor position may be large enough to exceed its capital and reserves, rendering it technically insolvent. Such a disruption can occur only if a major fraud were discovered in bank X's books during the day and bank regulators closed it the same day. That situation would make payment to bank Z impossible to complete at the end of the day. Alternatively, bank X might transmit funds it does not have in the hope that it can keep its "name in the market" to be able to raise funds later in the day. Other banks may revise their credit limits for this bank during the day, however, making bank X unable to deliver all the funds it promised to bank Z.

The essential feature of settlement risk is that bank Z is exposed to a within-day or intraday credit risk that does not appear on its balance sheet. The balance sheet, at best, summarizes only the bank's closing position or book at the end of the day. Thus, intraday settlement risk is an additional form of OBS risk that FIs participating on private wholesale wire transfer system networks face. (See Chapter 24 for a more detailed analysis of this risk and recent policy changes designed to reduce this risk.)

settlement risk

Intraday credit risk associated with CHIPS wire transfer activities.

Affiliate Risk

Many FIs operate as holding companies. A *holding company* is a corporation that owns the shares (normally more than 25 percent) of other corporations. For example, Citicorp is a one-bank holding company (OBHC) that owns all the shares of Citibank. Citicorp engages in certain permitted nonbank activities such as data processing through separately capitalized affiliates or companies that it owns. Similarly, a number of other holding companies are multibank holding companies (MBHC) that own shares in a number of different banks. First InterState is an MBHC that holds shares in banks in more than 10 states. The organization structures for these two holding companies is presented in Figure 20–2.

Legally, in the context of OBHCs, the bank and the nonbank affiliate are separate companies, as are bank 1 and bank 2 in the context of MBHCs. Thus, the failure of the nonbank

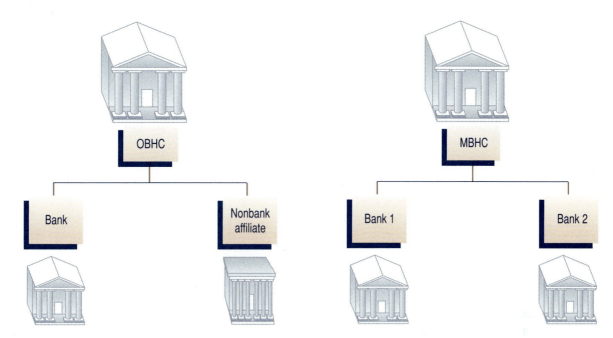

F i g u r e **20-2** *The Organization Structures of a One-Bank Holding Company and a Multibank Holding Company*

affiliate and bank 2 should have no effect on the financial resources of the bank in the OBHC or on bank 1 in the MBHC. This is the essence of the principle of corporate separateness underlying a legal corporation's limited liability in the United States. In reality, the failure of an affiliated firm or bank imposes **affiliate risk** on another bank in a holding company structure in a number of ways. We next discuss two ways this happens.

First, *creditors* of the failed affiliate may lay claim to the surviving bank's resources on the grounds that operationally, in name or in activity, the bank is not really a separate company from its failed affiliate. This *estoppel argument* made under the law is based on the idea that the customers of the failed institution are relatively unsophisticated in their financial affairs. They probably can't distinguish between the failing corporation and its surviving affiliate because of name similarity or some other reason.[20] Second, *regulators* have tried to enforce a *source of strength doctrine* in recent years for large MBHC failures. Under this doctrine, which directly challenges the principle of corporate separateness, the resources of sound banks may be used to support failing banks. The Federal Reserve has tried to implement this principal, as in the failure of MCorp in Texas, but the courts have generally prevented this.[21]

affiliate risk

Risk imposed on one holding company affiliate due to the potential failure of the other holding company affiliates.

---

[20]For example, suppose that the failing nonbank affiliate is Town Data Processing and the affiliated bank is Town Bank.

[21]Nevertheless, the attempts by regulators to impose the source of strength doctrine appears to have had an adverse effect on the equity values of holding companies operating with a large number of subsidiaries. The number of subsidiaries of holding companies has fallen each year since 1987—the first year in which the Fed tried to impose the source of strength doctrine. See J. Houston, "Corporate Separateness and the Organizational Structure of Bank Holding Companies," Working Paper, Department of Finance, University of Florida–Gainesville, April 1993.

If either of these breaches of corporate separateness is legally supported, the risks related to the activities of a nonbank affiliate or an affiliated bank impose an additional contingent liability on a healthy bank. This is true for banks and potentially true for many other FIs such as insurance companies and investment banks that adopt holding company organization structures in which corporate separateness is in doubt.[22]

Concept Questions

1. What is the source of settlement risk on the CHIPS payments system?
2. What are two major sources of affiliate risk?

NONRISK-INCREASING OFF-BALANCE-SHEET ACTIVITIES

This chapter has emphasized that OBS activities may add to the riskiness of an FI's activities. Indeed, most contingent assets and liabilities have various characteristics that may accentuate an FI's default and/or interest rate risk exposures. Even so, FIs use some OBS instruments—especially forwards, futures, options, and swaps—to reduce or manage their interest rate risk, foreign exchange risk, and credit risk exposures in a manner superior to what would exist in their absence.[23] When used to hedge on-balance-sheet interest rate, foreign exchange, and credit risks, these instruments can actually work to reduce FIs' overall insolvency risk. Although we do not fully describe the role of these instruments as hedging vehicles in reducing an FI's insolvency exposure until Chapters 21 through 23, you can now recognize the inherent danger in the overregulation of OBS activities and instruments. For example, the risk that a counterparty might default on a forward foreign exchange contract is very small. It is probably much lower than the insolvency risk an FI faces if it does not use forward contracts to hedge its foreign exchange assets against undesirable fluctuations in exchange rates. (See Chapters 21 and 27 for some examples of this.) As the regulatory costs of hedging rise—for example by imposing special capital requirements or restrictions on the use of such instruments (see Chapter 16)—FIs may have a tendency to underhedge, resulting in an increase, rather than a decrease, in their insolvency risk.

Finally, fees from OBS activities provide a key source of noninterest income for many FIs, especially the largest and most creditworthy ones. The importance of noninterest income for large banks is shown in Table 24–1. Thus, increased OBS earnings can potentially compensate for increased OBS risk exposure and actually reduce the probability of insolvency for some FIs.[24]

---

[22]A good example is the failure of Drexel Burnham Lambert in February 1991. For a good discussion of affiliate risk in this case, see W.S. Haraf, "The Collapse of Drexel Burnham Lambert: Lessons for Bank Regulators," *Regulation,* Winter 1991, pp. 22–25.

[23]As we discuss in Chapter 21, the use of derivatives for purposes other than direct hedging has strong tax disincentives.

[24]In addition, by allowing risk-averse managers to hedge risk, derivatives may lead managers to follow more value-maximizing investment strategies. That is, derivatives may reduce manager-stockholder agency conflicts over the level of risk taking.

Concept  Questions

1. How do OBS activities work to reduce an FI's overall insolvency risk even though they can add to an FI's risk?
2. Other than hedging and speculation, what reasons do FIs have for engaging in OBS activities?

• •

S U M M A R Y

This chapter showed that an FI's net worth or economic value as a going concern is linked not only to the value of its traditional on-balance-sheet activities but also to the values of its off-balance-sheet activities. The chapter discussed in detail the risks and returns of several OBS items: loan commitments; commercial and standby letters of credit; derivative contracts such as futures, options, and swaps; forward purchases; sales of when-issued securities; and loans sold. In all cases, these instruments clearly have a major impact on an FI's future profitability and risk. The chapter also discussed two other risks associated with OBS activities, settlement risk and affiliate risk. The chapter concluded by noting that although OBS activities can increase risk, they can also be used to hedge on-balance-sheet exposures, resulting in lower risks as well.

P E R T I N E N T   W E B   S I T E S

Federal Deposit Insurance Corp.   http://www.fdic.gov/

General Accounting Office (GAO)   http://www.gao.gov/

Office of the Comptroller of Currency   http://www.occ.treas.gov/

Off-Balance-Sheet Activities

1. Classify the following items as either (i) on-balance sheet assets, (ii) on-balance-sheet liabilities, (iii) off-balance-sheet assets, (iv) off-balance-sheet liabilities, or (v) capital account.
   a. Loan commitments
   b. Loan loss reserves
   c. Letter of credit
   d. Banker's acceptance
   e. Rediscounted banker's acceptance
   f. Loan sales without recourse
   g. Loan sales with recourse
   h. Forward contracts to purchase
   i. Forward contracts to sell
   j. Swaps
   k. Loan participations
   l. Securities borrowed
   m. Securities lent
   n. Loss adjustment expense account (PC insurers)
   o. Net policy reserves

2. How does one distinguish between an off-balance-sheet asset and an off-balance-sheet liability?

3. Contingent Bank has the following balance sheet in market value terms ($ millions):

Assets		Liabilities and Equity	
Cash	20	Deposits	220
Mortgages	220	Equity	20
	240		240

   In addition, the bank has contingent assets with $100 million market value and contingent liabilities with $80 million market value. What is the stockholders' true net worth?

4. What factors explain the growth of off-balance-sheet activities in the 1980s and 1990s for U.S. FIs?

5. What role does Schedule L play in reporting off-balance-sheet activities?

6. What total fees does a bank earn when it makes each of the following loan commitments?

a. A loan commitment of $2,500,000 with an up-front fee of 50 basis points and 25 basis points back-end fee on the unused portion of the loan. The take down on the loan is 50 percent.

b. A loan commitment of $1,000,000 with an up-front fee of 1 percent and a back-end fee of 50 basis points. The take down on the loan is 85 percent.

c. What are the total fees earned at the end of the year by both (a) and (b)? Assume that the cost of capital of the firm is 6 percent.

7. Long Bank has assets that consist mostly of 30-year mortgages. Its liabilities are principally short-term time and demand deposits. Will an interest rate futures contract the bank sells add to or subtract from the bank's risk?

8. How is a bank exposed to interest rate risk and credit risk when it makes loan commitments? How are these two contingent risks related?

9. How is a bank exposed to take-down risk and aggregate funding risk? How are these two contingent risks related?

10. A German bank issues a three-month letter of credit on behalf of its customer in Germany that is planning to import $100,000 worth of goods from the U.S. It charges an up-front fee of 100 basis points.

a. What up-front fee does the bank earn?

b. If the U.S. exporter decides to discount this letter of credit after it has been accepted by the German bank, how much will the exporter receive, assuming that the interest rates are currently 5 percent and 90 days are left to maturity?

c. What risks does the German bank incur by issuing this letter of credit?

11. A corporation is planning to issue $1,000,000 of 270-day commercial paper for an effective yield of 5 percent. It plans to either use an SLC or a loan commitment to back its issue. It expects to save 30 basis points in interest rates if it uses either one of these instruments as collateral.

a. What are the net savings to the corporation if a bank agrees to provide a 270-day SLC for an up-front fee of 20 basis points to back the commercial paper issue?

b. What are the net savings to the corporation if a bank agrees to provide a 270-day loan commitment to back the issue and charges 10 basis points for an up-front fee and 10 basis points for a back-end fee for any unused portion of the loan (assume no use of the loan)?

12. Explain the similarities between a letter of credit and an insurance contract.

13. Explain how forward purchases of when-issued government T-Bills can expose FIs to contingent interest rate changes.

14. Distinguish between loan sales with and without recourse. Why would banks want to sell loans with recourse? Explain how loan sales can leave banks exposed to contingent interest rate risks.

15. The manager of Shakey Bank sends a $2 million funds transfer payment message via CHIPS to the Trust Bank at 10 AM. Trust Bank then sends a $2 million funds transfer message via CHIPS to Hope Bank later that same day. What type of risk is inherent in this transaction?

16. Explain how settlement risk is incurred in the interbank payment mechanism and how it is another form of off-balance-sheet risk.

17. What is the difference between a one-bank holding company and a multibank holding company? How does the principle of corporate separateness ensure that a bank is safe from the failure of its affiliates?

18. Discuss how the failure of an affiliate can affect the holding company or its affiliates even if the affiliates are structured separately.

19. Defend the statement that although off-balance-sheet activities expose FIs to several forms of risks, they could also alleviate the banks' risks.

20. Go to the FDIC web site and find the total amount of unused commitments and letters of credit and the notional value of interest rate swaps of FDIC–insured commercial banks for the most recent year available.

Chapter Twenty-one

Futures and Forwards

C hapter 20 described the increase of FIs' off-balance-sheet activities. A major component of this growth has been the increase in derivative contracts such as futures and forwards. Although large banks and other FIs are responsible for a significant amount of derivatives trading activity, many financial intermediaries (FIs) of all sizes have used these instruments to hedge their asset-liability risk exposures. Contemporary Perspectives Box 21–1 demonstrates the success of one small bank in using futures contracts to hedge interest rate risk. Indeed, as this chapter will discuss, derivative contracts—such as futures and forwards—have the potential to allow an FI to manage (or hedge) its interest rate, foreign exchange (FX), and credit risk exposures.

Table 21–1 lists the derivative contract holdings of all commercial banks and specifically for 25 large U.S. banks as of September 1997. The table shows notional (dollar) contract volumes for these 25 banks exceeding $24 trillion; the other 450 bank and trust companies with derivatives activity

Contemporary Perspectives 21–1

Afraid of Derivatives? Not These Three Little Banks

Greene County Bank is an unlikely pioneer in currency futures trading. But the $23 million-asset bank in Strafford, Mo.—population 1,166—is one of a handful of tiny banks that have latched onto futures trading as a tool for important balance sheet management. It is using Eurodollar futures to hedge the interest rate risk of its certificates of deposit. Only three banks with under $100 million in assets are making extensive use of futures, data from the Office of Comptroller of the Currency (OCC) show.

Greene County Bank posted net income of $40,000 for 1995, and most of its liabilities are six-month certificates of deposit. But Greene County's financial report to regulators stands out from those filed by its peers because it hedges those liabilities with an eye-popping $160 million of derivatives contracts. . . .

But experts say Greene County is using the derivatives safely, albeit creatively. Unable to afford swap contracts used by larger banks to hedge against interest rate changes, Greene County gets the benefits of swaps by buying inexpensive, publicly traded Eurodollar futures contracts. . . .

Because the Eurodollar futures market is highly liquid and the contracts are affordable, it is an ideal venue for small banks seeking to hedge their portfolios for a short time. . . .

Greene County Bank began buying three-month Eurodollar contracts four years ago, to minimize the rate exposure of its growing portfolio. The bank buys futures partly because its balance sheet has changed in recent years. Last year, for example, deposits increased 20 percent and loans 26 percent.

Mr. Bernard Rullman [president of Greene County Bank] says Greene County Bank divides its contracts $80 million short and $80 million long. Thus its credit exposure to the contracts nets out to zero.

The notional value of the derivatives is much higher than the bank's liabilities because the bank buys new contracts every quarter for several years in advance at $1 million in notional value each. . . .

Banks can do this by selling Eurodollar contracts every time they issue a new CD. Selling enough Eurodollar contracts to cover the duration of the CD provides a (fixed) rate of interest. This protects the bank against quarterly fluctuations in interest rates that may affect how much money the bank can make from the CD.

According to OCC records, 507 banks reported using derivatives in the second quarter. But only 2 percent of banks with under $100 million in assets use derivatives at all, according to the American Bankers Association.

SOURCE: Aaron Elstein, *The American Banker,* October 22, 1996. Reprinted with permission—American Banker.

---

report notional contract volume of $356 billion. Table 21–1 categorizes those positions into futures/forwards, swaps, options, and credit derivatives. Swaps ($9.56 trillion) represent the largest group of derivatives, followed by futures/forwards ($9.47 trillion), and options ($5.96 trillion). The replacement cost of these derivative contracts for the top 25 derivative users is reported at $156 billion; credit exposure is $312 billion (or 96.8% of the capital of the banks).[1]

This chapter considers the role that futures and forward contracts play in managing an FI's interest rate risk. (The appendix to this chapter discusses the role in hedging credit risk of these contracts. Appendix A to Chapter 27 on FX risk discusses their role in hedging FX risk.) Chapters 22 and 23 discuss option-type derivatives and swaps, respectively.

---

[1]See Chapter 16 for a discussion of the calculation of credit exposure of derivatives for regulatory reporting.

Table 21–1
DERIVATIVE CONTRACTS
Notional Amount and Credit Equivalent Exposure of the 25 Commercial Banks and Trust Companies with the Most Derivative Contracts, September 1997 (in millions of dollars)

| Rank Bank Name | Total Assets | Derivative Contracts | | | | | Replacement Cost of All Contracts | RBC* Add-On | Credit Exposure from All Contracts | Credit Exposure to Capital Ratio |
		Futures & Forwards	Total Swaps	Total Options	Credit Derivatives	Total Derivatives				
1. Chase Manhattan Bank	$291,529	$3,176,381	$3,455,313	$ 999,928	$ 4,886	$7,636,508	$35,376	$39,618	$ 74,994	308.2
2. Morgan Guaranty Tr Co	201,145	1,465,381	2,873,646	1,741,057	23,592	6,103,678	56,798	46,558	103,356	736.9
3. Citibank NA	253,929	1,572,070	609,964	676,148	4,343	2,862,525	24,052	21,238	45,290	184.2
4. Bankers Trust Co	106,152	837,325	867,474	391,282	2,439	2,098,520	15,923	16,175	32,098	400.1
5. Nationsbank of NC NA	186,021	245,931	403,826	1,092,708	353	1,742,817	3,379	6,103	9,482	61.8
6. Bank of America NT & SA	235,952	943,508	518,075	168,956	204	1,630,743	7,892	10,828	18,720	83.4
7. First NB of Chicago	56,109	599,537	309,368	341,063	0	1,249,968	3,804	7,600	11,404	19.2
8. Republic NB of New York	51,350	158,848	42,843	105,438	251	307,380	3,458	2,374	5,833	159.5
9. Bank of New York	57,537	56,219	15,301	140,228	0	211,748	1,192	1,041	2,232	40.4
10. Bankboston NA	60,188	83,438	20,333	51,231	700	155,702	528	619	1,147	21.4
11. First Union NB of NC	109,113	35,414	60,335	19,510	6	115,265	542	500	1,042	11.0
12. State Street Bank & TC	35,892	105,544	3,645	755	0	109,944	976	989	1,965	100.1
13. Fleet National Bank	50,059	5,113	19,641	34,890	0	59,644	164	271	435	7.9
14. Wells Fargo Bank NA	89,529	7,172	18,998	30,286	0	56,455	285	223	508	6.5
15. Mellon Bank NA	37,806	31,994	12,974	6,333	0	51,300	405	373	778	18.0
16. Citibank South Dakota	14,757	12,278	13,378	11,928	0	37,584	103	55	158	7.6
17. Keybank NA	68,989	9,275	18,680	8,710	0	36,664	180	152	333	4.9
18. Nationsbank of Texas NA	54,012	2,487	13,401	18,461	0	34,348	170	177	347	8.2
19. Citibank Nevada NA	9,673	3,257	11,264	16,395	0	30,916	93	83	175	11.8
20. National City Bank	11,500	3,086	20,210	5,430	0	28,726	123	160	283	27.3
21. PNC Bank NA	57,649	6,071	9,981	11,523	0	27,573	153	77	230	4.0
22. Marine Midland Bank	31,196	3,222	10,544	9,396	0	23,162	61	36	97	3.8
23. Corestates Bank NA	44,430	4,518	11,869	5,844	0	22,231	182	116	298	6.6
24. Bank One NA	24,941	0	19,941	953	10	20,903	110	127	237	7.6
25. Chase Manhattan USA	27,176	8,967	8,675	765	0	18,407	108	58	166	5.1
Total 25 commercial banks	**$2,166,632**	**$9,377,033**	**$9,369,679**	**$5,889,216**	**$36,783**	**$24,672,712**	**$156,057**	**$155,552**	**$311,610**	**96.8†**
Other 450 commercial banks	**$1,565,410**	**$88,261**	**$193,864**	**$71,383**	**$2,096**	**$355,605**	**$2,234**	**$1,761**	**$3,995**	**N/A**
Total for all banks	**$3,732,042**	**$9,465,294**	**$9,563,543**	**$5,960,600**	**$38,880**	**$25,028,316**	**$158,292**	**$157,313**	**$315,604**	**6.4**

*Risk-based capital

†Average

SOURCE: Office of the Comptroller of the Currency.

Table **21–2**

SPOT, FORWARD, AND FUTURES CONTRACTS

Spot Contract   Agreement made between a buyer and a seller at time 0 for the seller to deliver the asset immediately and the buyer to pay for the asset immediately.

Forward Contract   Agreement between a buyer and a seller at time 0 to exchange a nonstandardized asset for cash at some future date. The details of the asset and the price to be paid at the forward contract maturity date are set at time 0. The price of the forward contract is fixed over the life of the contract.

Futures Contract   Agreement between a buyer and a seller at time 0 to exchange a standardized asset for cash at some future date. Each contract has a standardized maturity, and transactions occur in a centralized market. The price of the futures contract changes daily as the market value of the asset underlying the futures fluctuates.

FORWARD AND
FUTURES CONTRACTS

To present the essential nature and characteristics of forward and futures contracts, we compare them with spot contracts. We show appropriate time lines for each of the three contracts in Figure 21–1 and define each in Table 21–2.

Spot Contract

spot contract

An agreement to transact involving the immediate exchange of assets and funds.

A **spot contract** is an agreement between a buyer and a seller at time 0, when the seller of the asset agrees to deliver it immediately and the buyer agrees to pay for that asset immediately.[2] Thus, the unique feature of a spot market is the immediate and simultaneous exchange of cash for securities, or what is often called *delivery versus payment*. A spot bond quote of $97 for a 20-year maturity bond is the price the buyer must pay the seller, per $100 of face value, for immediate delivery of the 20-year bond.

Forward Contract

forward contract

An agreement to transact involving the future exchange of a set amount of assets at a set price.

A **forward contract** is a contractual agreement between a buyer and a seller at time 0, to exchange a prespecified asset for cash at some later date. For example, in a three-month forward contract to deliver 20-year bonds, the buyer and seller agree on a price and amount today (time 0) but the delivery (or exchange) of the 20-year bond for cash does not occur until three months hence. If the forward price agreed to at time 0 was $97 per $100 of face value, in three months' time the seller delivers $100 of 20-year bonds and receives $97 from the buyer. This is the price the buyer must pay and the seller must accept no matter what happens to the spot price of 20-year bonds during the three months between the time the contract was entered into and the time the bonds are delivered for payment.

Forward contracts often involve underlying assets that are nonstandardized (e.g., six-month pure discount bonds). As a result, the buyer and seller involved in a forward contract

---

[2] Technically, physical settlement and delivery may take place one or two days after the contractual spot agreement in bond markets. In equity markets, delivery and cash settlement normally occur three business days after the spot contract agreement.

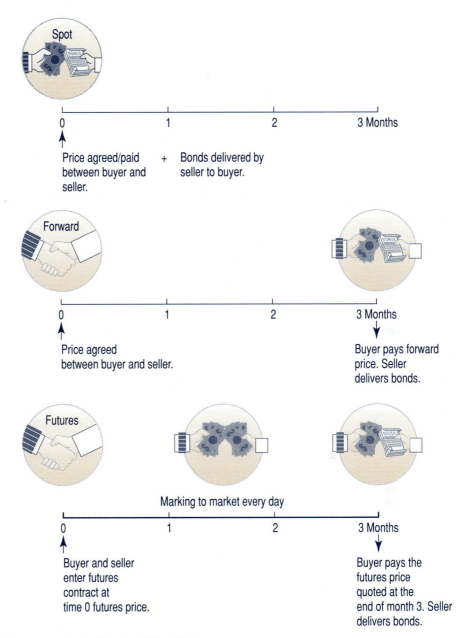

F i g u r e **21–1**   *Contract Time Lines*

must locate and deal directly with each other to set the terms of the contract rather than transacting the sale in a centralized market. Accordingly, once a party has agreed to a forward position, canceling the deal prior to expiration is generally difficult.

futures contract

An agreement to transact involving the future exchange of a set amount of assets for a price that is settled daily.

Futures Contract

A **futures contract** is normally arranged by an organized exchange. It is an agreement between a buyer and a seller at time 0 to exchange a standardized, prespecified asset for cash at some later date. As such, a futures contract is very similar to a forward contract. The

marked to market

Describes the prices on outstanding futures contracts that are adjusted each day to reflect current futures market conditions.

difference relates to the price, which in a forward contract is fixed over the life of the contract ($97 per $100 of face value for three months), but a futures contract is **marked to market** daily. This means that the contract's price is adjusted each day as the futures price for the contract changes. Therefore, actual daily cash settlements occur between the buyer and seller in response to this marking-to-market process. This can be compared to a forward contract for which cash payment from buyer to seller occurs at the end of the contract period.[3]

Concept Questions

1. What is the difference between a futures contract and a forward contract?
2. What are the major differences between a spot contract and a forward contract?

FORWARD CONTRACTS AND HEDGING INTEREST RATE RISK

naive hedge

A hedge of a cash asset on a direct dollar-for-dollar basis with a forward or futures contract.

To understand the usefulness of forward contracts in hedging an FI's interest rate risk, consider a simple example of a **naive hedge**. Suppose that an FI portfolio manager holds a 20-year, $1 million face value government bond on the balance sheet. At time 0, the market values these bonds at $97 per $100 of face value, or $970,000 in total. Assume that the manager receives a forecast that interest rates are expected to rise by 2 percent from their current level of 8 percent to 10 percent over the next three months. Knowing that rising interest rates mean that bond prices will fall, the manager stands to make a capital loss on the bond portfolio. Having read Chapters 17 and 18, the manager is an expert in duration and has calculated the weighted-average life of the 20-year maturity bonds to be exactly nine years. Thus, the manager can predict a capital loss or change in bond values (ΔP) from the duration equation of Chapter 18.[4]

$$\frac{\Delta P}{P} = -D \times \frac{\Delta R}{1 + R}$$

where

$\Delta P =$ capital loss on bonds = ?
$P =$ initial value of bond position = $970,000
$D =$ duration of the bonds = 9 years
$\Delta R =$ change in forecast yield = .02
$1 + R =$ 1 plus the current yield on 20-year bonds = 1.08

$$\frac{\Delta P}{\$970,000} = -9 \times \left[\frac{.02}{1.08} \right]$$

$$\Delta P = -9 \times \$970,000 \times \left[\frac{.02}{1.08} \right] = -\$161,667$$

---

[3] Another difference between forwards and futures is that forward contracts are bilateral contracts subject to counterparty default risk, but the default risk on futures is significantly reduced by the futures exchange guaranteeing to indemnify counterparties against credit or default risk.

[4] For simplicity, we ignore issues relating to convexity here.

As a result, the FI portfolio manager expects to incur a capital loss on the bond of $161,667—as a percentage loss $(\Delta P/P) = 16.67\%$—or a drop in price from $97 per $100 face value to $80.833 per $100 face value. To offset this loss—in fact, to reduce the risk of capital loss to zero—the manager may hedge this position by taking an off-balance-sheet hedge, such as selling $1 million face value of 20-year bonds for forward delivery in three months' time.[5] Suppose that at time 0, the portfolio manager can find a buyer willing to pay $97 for every $100 of 20-year bonds delivered in three months' time.

Now consider what happens to the FI portfolio manager if the gloomy forecast of a 2 percent rise in interest rates is accurate. The portfolio manager's bond position has fallen in value by 16.67 percent, equal to a capital loss of $161,667. After the rise in interest rates, the manager can buy $1 million face value of 20-year bonds in the spot market at $80.833 per $100 of face value, a total cost of $808,333, and deliver these bonds to the forward contract buyer. Remember that the forward contract buyer agreed to pay $97 per $100 of face value for the $1 million of face value bonds delivered, or $970,000. As a result, the portfolio manager makes a profit on the forward transaction of

$$\begin{array}{ccccc} \$970,000 & - & \$808,333 & = & \$161,667 \\ \text{(price paid by} & & \text{(cost of purchasing} & & \\ \text{forward buyer to} & & \text{bonds in the spot market} & & \\ \text{forward seller)} & & \text{at } t = \text{month 3 for delivery} & & \\ & & \text{to the forward buyer)} & & \end{array}$$

immunized

Describes an FI that is fully hedged or protected against adverse movements in interest rates (or other asset prices).

As you can see, the on-balance-sheet loss of $161,667 is exactly offset by the off-balance-sheet gain of $161,667 from selling the forward contract. Thus, the FI's net interest rate exposure is zero, or, in the parlance of finance, it has **immunized** its assets against interest rate risk.

Concept Questions

1. How does a naive hedge work?
2. An FI has immunized its portfolio against a particular risk. What does this mean?

HEDGING INTEREST RATE RISK WITH FUTURES CONTRACTS

Even though some hedging of interest rate risk does take place using forward contracts—such as forward rate agreements commonly used by insurance companies and banks prior to mortgage loan originations—most FIs hedge interest rate risk either at the micro level (called *microhedging*) or at the macro level (called *macrohedging*) using futures contracts. Before looking at futures contracts, we explain the difference between microhedging and macrohedging and between routine hedging and selective hedging.

---

[5] Since a forward contract involves the delivery of bonds at a future time period, it does not appear on the balance sheet, which records only current and past transactions. Thus, forwards are one example of off-balance-sheet items (see Chapter 20).

Microhedging

microhedging

Using a futures (forward) contract to hedge a specific asset or liability.

An FI is **microhedging** when it employs a futures or a forward contract to hedge a particular asset or liability risk. For example, we earlier considered a simple example of microhedging asset-side portfolio risk, in which an FI manager wanted to insulate the value of the institution's bond portfolio fully against a rise in interest rates. An example of microhedging on the liability side of the balance sheet occurs when an FI attempting to lock in a cost of funds to protect itself against a possible rise in short-term interest rates takes a short (sell) position in futures contracts on CDs or T-bills. In microhedging, the FI manager often tries to pick a futures or forward contract whose underlying deliverable asset closely matches the asset (or liability) position being hedged. The earlier example of exactly matching the asset in the portfolio with the deliverable security underlying the forward contract (20-year bonds) was unrealistic. Because such exact matching cannot be achieved often, this situation produces a residual unhedgable risk termed **basis risk**. We discuss basis risk in detail later in this chapter; this risk occurs mainly because the prices of the assets or liabilities that an FI wishes to hedge are imperfectly correlated over time with the prices on the futures or forward contract used to hedge risk.

basis risk

A residual risk that occurs because the movement in a spot (cash) asset's price is not perfectly correlated with the movement in the price of the asset delivered under a futures or forward contract.

Macrohedging

macrohedging

Hedging the entire duration gap of an FI.

Macrohedging occurs when an FI manager wishes to use futures or other derivative securities to hedge the entire balance sheet duration gap. This contrasts with microhedging, in which an FI manager identifies specific assets and liabilities and seeks individual futures and other derivative contracts to hedge those individual risks. Note that macrohedging and microhedging can lead to quite different hedging strategies and results. In particular, a macrohedge takes a whole portfolio view and allows for individual asset and liability interest sensitivities or durations to net out each other. This can result in a very different aggregate futures position than when an FI manager disregards this netting or portfolio effect and hedges only individual asset and liability positions on a one-to-one basis.[6]

Routine Hedging versus Selective Hedging

routine hedging

Hedging all interest rate risk exposure.

Routine hedging occurs when an FI reduces its interest rate or other risk exposure to the lowest possible level by selling sufficient futures to offset the interest rate risk exposure of its whole balance sheet or cash positions in each asset and liability. For example, this reduction might be achieved by macrohedging the duration gap, as described later. However, since reducing risk also reduces expected return, not all FI managers seek to do this. Figure 21–2 illustrates the trade-off between expected return and risk and the minimum risk fully hedged portfolio.[7]

Rather than taking a fully hedged position, many FIs choose to bear some interest rate risk as well as credit and FX risks because of their comparative advantage as FIs (see

---

[6] P. H. Munter, D. K. Clancy, and C.T. Moores found that macrohedges provided better hedge performance than microhedges in a number of different interest rate environments. See "Accounting for Financial Futures: A Question of Risk Reduction," *Advances in Accounting* (1986), pp. 51–70. See also R. Stoebe, "Macrohedging Bank Investment Portfolios," *Bankers Magazine,* November–December 1994, pp. 45–48.

[7] The minimum risk portfolio is not shown here as zero because of basis risk that prevents perfect hedging. In the absence of basis risk, a zero risk position becomes possible.

F i g u r e **21–2**   *The Effects of Hedging on Risk and Expected Return*

hedging selectively

Only partially hedging the gap or individual assets and liabilities.

Chapter 1). One possibility is that an FI may choose to **hedge selectively** its portfolio. For example, an FI manager may generate expectations regarding future interest rates before deciding on a futures position. As a result, the manager may selectively hedge only a percentage of its balance sheet position. Alternatively, the FI manager may decide to remain unhedged or even to overhedge by selling more futures than the cash position requires, although regulators may view this as speculative. Thus, the fully hedged position—and the minimum risk portfolio—becomes one of several choices depending, in part, on managerial interest rate expectations, managerial objectives, and the nature of the return-risk trade-off from hedging. Finally, an FI may selectively hedge in an attempt to arbitrage profits between a spot asset's price movements and movements in a futures price.

Microhedging with Futures

The number of futures contracts that an FI should buy or sell in a microhedge depends on the interest rate risk exposure created by a particular asset or liability on the balance sheet. The key is to take a position in the futures market to offset a loss on the balance sheet due to a move in interest rates with a gain in the futures market. Figure 21–3 lists interest rate futures contracts that are currently available. In this list, a March 1998 Treasury bill futures contract can be bought (long) or sold (short) on October 24, 1997, for 95.10 percent of the face value of the T-bill, or the yield on the T-bill deliverable in March 1998 will be 4.90 percent (100% − 95.10%). The minimum contract size on one of these futures is $1,000,000, so a position in one contract can be taken at a price of $951,000.

The subsequent profit or loss from a position in March 1998 T-bills taken on October 24, 1997 is graphically described in Figure 21–4. A short position in the futures will produce a profit when interest rates rise (meaning that the value of the underlying T-bill decreases). Therefore, a short position in the futures market is the appropriate hedge when the FI stands to lose on the balance sheet if interest rates are expected to rise (e.g., the FI

INTEREST RATE

TREASURY BONDS (CBT)-$100,000; pts. 32nds of 100%

	Open	High	Low	Settle	Change	Lifetime High	Lifetime Low	Open Interest
→ Dec	116-11	117-02	115-27	116-25	+ 15	118-16	100-08	663,835
→ Mr98	116-08	116-23	115-20	116-15	+ 15	118-07	104-21	69,513
June	115-31	116-09	115-23	116-02	+ 13	117-15	104-03	9,338
Sept	....	....	....	115-26	+ 15	115-21	103-22	2,006
Dec	....	....	....	115-17	+ 15	116-10	103-13	4,704

Est vol 600,000; vol Thu 736,678; open int 749,452, +24,677.

TREASURY BONDS (MCE)-$50,000; pts. 32nds of 100%

	Open	High	Low	Settle	Change	Lifetime High	Lifetime Low	Open Interest
Dec	115-29	117-01	115-28	116-30	+ 18	118-17	105-20	17,086

Est vol 5,050; vol Thu 7,394; open int 17,114, −34.

TREASURY NOTES (CBT)-$100,000; pts. 32nds of 100%

	Open	High	Low	Settle	Change	Lifetime High	Lifetime Low	Open Interest
Dec	110-16	110-27	110-07	110-22	+ 5	111-29	104-10	370,503
Mr98	109-31	110-16	109-31	110-12	+ 5	111-18	105-24	18,858

Est vol 110,001; vol Thu 169,180; open int 389,363, −5,096.

5 YR TREAS NOTES (CBT)-$100,000; pts. 32nds of 100%

	Open	High	Low	Settle	Change	Lifetime High	Lifetime Low	Open Interest
Dec	107-18	07-255	107-12	07-225	+ 3.5	108-19	04-005	230,795
Mr98	107-18	107-22	107-12	107-20	+ 3.5	108-10	106-07	4,311

Est vol 64,500; vol Thu 82,438; open int 235,106, −2,435.

2 YR TREAS NOTES (CBT)-$200,000; pts. 32nds of 100%

	Open	High	Low	Settle	Change	Lifetime High	Lifetime Low	Open Interest
Dec	103-20	103-23	103-17	103-21	+ .703	03-305	02-265	37,829

Est vol 3,000; vol Thu 4,436; open int 37,849, −852.

30-DAY FEDERAL FUNDS (CBT)-$5 million; pts. of 100%

	Open	High	Low	Settle	Change	Lifetime High	Lifetime Low	Open Interest
Oct	94.495	94.500	94.495	94.500	....	94.510	93.900	7,781
Nov	94.43	94.44	94.43	94.44	....	94.46	93.88	7,318
Dec	94.36	94.39	94.36	94.39	+ .01	94.43	93.78	4,367
Ja98	94.32	94.36	94.32	94.36	+ .01	94.43	93.97	2,384
Feb	94.32	94.35	94.32	94.35	+ .01	94.44	93.84	1,657

Est vol 2,222; vol Thu 6,406; open int 23,872, +1,430.

MUNI BOND INDEX (CBT)-$1,000; times Bond Buyer MBI

	Open	High	Low	Settle	Change	Lifetime High	Lifetime Low	Open Interest
Dec	119-22	120-21	119-21	120-13	+ 14	122-19	109-22	21,222
Mr98	118-13	119-06	118-13	119-03	+ 14	119-19	116-29	134

Est vol 8,000; vol Thu 6,593; open int 21,356, +464.
The Index: Close 120-20; Yield 5.69.

TREASURY BILLS (CME)-$1mil.; pts. of 100%

	Open	High	Low	Settle	Chg	Discount Settle	Discount Chg	Open Interest
Dec	95.03	95.08	95.02	95.05	+ .01	4.95	− .01	4,455
→ Mr98	95.04	95.10	95.04	95.10	+ .03	4.90	− .03	4,453
June	....	....	....	95.02	+ .04	4.98	− .04	384

Est vol 1,112; vol Thu 1,463; open int 9,304, +271.

LIBOR-1 MO. (CME)-$3,000,000; points of 100%

	Open	High	Low	Settle	Chg	Yield Settle	Yield Chg	Open Interest
Nov	94.30	94.32	94.27	94.32	+ .02	5.68	− .02	40,920
Dec	94.16	94.16	94.11	94.15	+ .01	5.86	− .01	13,527
Mr98	94.20	94.20	94.16	94.22	+ .04	5.79	− .04	753

Est vol 6,616; vol Thu 13,432; open int 61,090, −1,792.

EURODOLLAR (CME)-$1 million; pts. of 100%

	Open	High	Low	Settle	Chg	Yield Settle	Yield Chg	Open Interest
Nov	94.15	94.19	94.15	94.18	+ .02	5.82	− .02	24,505
Dec	94.15	94.18	94.11	94.17	+ .03	5.83	− .03	552,891
Mr98	94.10	94.14	94.05	94.13	+ .04	5.87	− .04	423,088
June	94.03	94.07	93.97	94.06	+ .04	5.94	− .04	347,330
Sept	93.96	94.01	93.90	93.97	+ .03	6.03	− .03	255,889
Dec	93.86	93.90	93.79	93.86	+ .02	6.14	− .02	227,954
Mr99	93.85	93.88	93.78	93.85	+ .02	6.15	− .02	162,382
June	93.76	93.85	93.76	93.82	+ .02	6.18	− .02	143,533
Sept	93.77	93.82	93.73	93.78	+ .01	6.22	− .01	109,540
Dec	93.65	93.75	93.65	93.72	+ .02	6.28	− .02	89,014
Mr00	93.70	93.76	93.65	93.73	+ .03	6.27	− .03	72,091
June	93.67	93.73	93.62	93.70	+ .03	6.30	− .03	59,129
Sept	93.64	93.70	93.59	93.67	+ .03	6.33	− .03	50,880
Dec	93.54	93.64	93.54	93.61	+ .03	6.39	− .03	41,290
Mr01	93.54	93.64	93.54	93.61	+ .03	6.39	− .03	37,775
June	93.51	93.61	93.45	93.58	+ .03	6.42	− .03	34,930
Sept	93.48	93.58	93.42	93.55	+ .03	6.45	− .03	34,496
Dec	93.41	93.51	93.36	93.48	+ .03	6.52	− .03	18,297
Mr02	93.41	93.51	93.36	93.48	+ .03	6.52	− .03	18,874
June	93.38	93.48	93.33	93.45	+ .03	6.55	− .03	14,500
Sept	93.35	93.45	93.30	93.42	+ .03	6.58	− .03	12,826
Dec	93.34	93.38	93.32	93.36	+ .03	6.64	− .03	7,826
Mr03	93.34	93.38	93.32	93.36	+ .03	6.64	− .03	6,565
June	93.31	93.35	93.29	93.33	+ .03	6.67	− .03	5,654
Sept	93.28	93.32	93.26	93.30	+ .03	6.70	− .03	5,608
Dec	93.25	93.25	93.19	93.23	+ .03	6.77	− .03	5,091
Mr04	....	....	....	93.23	+ .03	6.77	− .03	4,486
June	....	....	....	93.20	+ .03	6.80	− .03	6,283
Sept	....	....	....	93.17	+ .03	6.83	− .03	4,395
Dec	....	....	....	93.10	+ .03	6.90	− .03	4,523
Mr05	....	....	....	93.10	+ .03	6.90	− .03	2,262
June	....	....	....	93.06	+ .03	6.94	− .03	2,510
Sept	....	....	....	93.03	+ .03	6.97	− .03	2,361
Dec	....	....	....	92.97	+ .03	7.03	− .03	1,712
Mr06	....	....	....	92.97	+ .03	7.03	− .03	2,731
June	....	....	....	92.93	+ .03	7.07	− .03	1,882
Sept	....	....	....	92.90	+ .03	7.10	− .03	1,781
Dec	....	....	....	92.84	+ .03	7.16	− .03	1,514
Mr07	....	....	....	92.84	+ .03	7.16	− .03	1,503

Est vol 586,535; vol Thu 895,549; open int 2,804,348, −11,233.

F i g u r e **21–3** *Futures Contracts on Interest Rates, October 24, 1997*

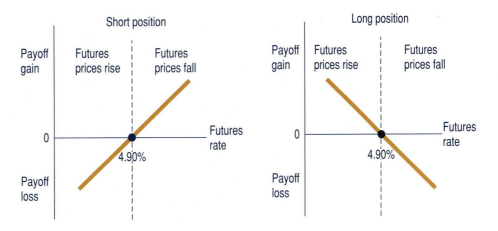

F i g u r e **21–4** *Profit or Loss on a Futures Position in Treasury Bills Taken on October 24, 1997*

T a b l e **21–3**

SUMMARY OF GAINS AND LOSSES ON MICROHEDGES USING FUTURES CONTRACTS

Type of Hedge	Change in Interest Rates	Cash Market	Futures Market
Long hedge (buy)	Decrease	Loss	Gain
Short hedge (sell)	Increase	Loss	Gain

---

holds bonds in its asset portfolio[8]). A long position in the futures market produces a profit when interest rates fall (meaning that the value of the underlying T-bill increases).[9] Therefore, a long position is the appropriate hedge when the FI stands to lose on the balance sheet if interest rates are expected to fall.[10] Table 21–3 summarizes the long and short position.

The Risk-Minimizing Futures Position. The objective is to hedge interest rate risk exposure by constructing a futures position that, should interest rates rise, would make a gain on the futures position that just offsets the loss on the balance sheet.

When interest rates rise, the price of a futures contract falls since its price reflects the value of the underlying bond that is deliverable against the contract. The amount by which a bond price falls when interest rates rise depends on its duration. Thus, we expect the price

---

[8] We assume that the balance sheet has no liability of equal size and maturity (or duration) as the bond. If the bank has such a liability, any loss in value from the bond could be offset with an equivalent decrease in value from the liability. In this case there is no interest rate risk exposure and thus there is no need to hedge.

[9] Notice that if rates move in an opposite direction from that expected, losses are incurred on the futures position. That is, if rates rise and futures prices drop, the long hedger loses. Similarly, if rates fall and futures prices rise, the short hedger loses.

[10] This might be the case when the FI is financing itself with long-term, fixed rate certificates of deposit.

of the 20-year T-bond futures contract to be more sensitive to interest rate changes than the price of the three-month T-bill futures contract since the former futures price reflects the price of the 20-year T-bond deliverable when the contract matures. Thus, the sensitivity of the price of a futures contract depends on the duration of the deliverable bond underlying the contract, or

$$\frac{\Delta F}{F} = -D_F \frac{\Delta R_F}{1 + R_F}$$

where

ΔF = change in dollar value of futures contracts
F = dollar value of the initial futures contracts
D_F = duration of the bond to be delivered against the futures contracts such as a 20-year, 8 percent coupon T-bond[11]
ΔR_F = expected change in interest rates on T-bond to be delivered against the futures contract
$1 + R_F$ = 1 plus the T-bond interest rate

This can be rewritten as:

$$\Delta F = -D_F \times F \times \frac{\Delta R_F}{1 + R_F}$$

The left side of this expression (ΔF) shows the dollar gain or loss on a futures contract when interest rates change.

To see this dollar gain or loss more clearly, we can decompose the initial dollar value position in futures contracts, F, into its two component parts:

$$F = N_F \times P_F$$

The dollar value of the outstanding futures position depends on the number of contracts bought or sold (N_F) and the price of each contract (P_F).

Futures contracts are homogeneous in size. Thus, futures exchanges sell T-bond futures in minimum units of $100,000 of face value; that is, one T-bond futures (N_F = 1) equals $100,000. T-bill futures are sold in larger minimum units: one T-bill future (N_F = 1) equals $1,000,000. The price of each contract quoted in the newspaper is the price per $100 of face value for delivering the underlying bond. A price quote of $116^{25}\!/_{32}$ on October 24, 1997, for the Chicago Board of Trade T-bond futures contract maturing in December 1997 means that the buyer is required to pay $116,781.25 for one contract (see Figure 21–3).[12]

Recall from Chapter 18 that the change in value of an asset or liability on the FI's balance sheet from a change in interest rates equals

$$\Delta P = -D \times P \times \frac{\Delta R}{1 + R}$$

---

[11]Note the difference between D and D_F. D is the duration on a bond currently held; D_F is the duration on a pre-specified bond that will be delivered in the future (when the futures contract matures).

[12]In practice, the futures price changes daily, and gains or losses accumulate to the seller/buyer over the period from the time the contract is entered into until it matures or is sold. See the later discussion of this unique marking-to-market feature.

We can now solve for the number of futures contracts to buy or sell to microhedge an FI's assets or liabilities. We have shown the following:

1. *Loss on balance sheet* from a change in interest rates is:

$$\Delta P = -D \times P \times \frac{\Delta R}{1 + R}$$

2. *Gain off the balance sheet* from a position in the futures contract is

$$\Delta F = -D_F \times (N_F \times P_F) \times \frac{\Delta R_F}{1 + R_F}$$

Hedging can be defined as buying or selling a sufficient number of futures contracts (N_F) so that the loss on the balance sheet (ΔP) due to rate changes is just offset by a gain off the balance sheet on the position in futures contracts (ΔF), or

$$\Delta F = \Delta P$$

Substituting the appropriate expressions for each

$$-D_F \times (N_F \times P_F) \times \frac{R_F}{1 + R_F} = -D \times P \times \frac{\Delta R}{1 + R}$$

Canceling $\Delta R/1 + R$ and $\Delta R_F/1 + R_F$, we get[13]

$$-D_F \times (N_F \times P_F) = -D \times P$$

Solving for N_F (the number of futures contracts to buy or sell):

$$N_F = \frac{D \times P}{D_F \times P_F}$$

The following example shows how the microhedge protects the FI against interest rate risk exposure.

Short Hedge.   An FI takes a short position in a futures contract when rates are expected to rise; that is, the FI loses value on the asset side of its balance sheet if rates rise, so it seeks to hedge the value of its assets by selling an appropriate number of futures contracts.

EXAMPLE   21 – 1

• • • • • •   *Hedge of Interest Rate Risk Using a Short Hedge*
Consider the FI described in the section Forward Contracts and Hedging Interest Rate Risk. It has a 20-year, $1 million face value bond in its asset portfolio. The duration on the bond is nine years. Assume that on October 24, 1997, the bond is valued at $97 per $100 of face value, or $970,000, and the FI manager expects interest rates to rise by 2 percent from the

---

[13]This amounts to assuming that the interest changes of the cash asset position match those of the futures position; that is, there is no basis risk. This assumption is discussed and relaxed later.

Table 21–4

ON- AND OFF-BALANCE-SHEET EFFECTS OF A SHORT HEDGE

	On Balance Sheet	Off Balance Sheet
Begin hedge October 24, 1997	$970,000 bond held in asset portfolio. Current interest rate = 8%. Duration = 9 years.	Short 7.89008 March 1998 T-bond futures contracts at a price of $116,468.75. Duration = 9.5 years.
End hedge January 24, 1998	Interest rate increases to 10%.	Long 7.89008 March 1998 T-bond futures contracts.
	Capital value loss on-balance-sheet: $\Delta P = -9 \text{ years} \times \$970,000 \times \dfrac{.02}{1.08}$ $= -\$161,667$	Gain off-balance-sheet: $-\Delta F = -\left(-9.5 \text{ years} \times 7.89008 \times \$116,468.75 \times \dfrac{.02}{1.08}\right)*$ $= \$161,667$

*Assuming no basis risk (i.e., $\Delta R/1 + R = \Delta R_F/1 + R_F$)

current level of 8 percent over the next three months. We saw earlier that the expected rate increase results in a loss in capital value of $161,667 on the balance sheet

$$\Delta P = -9 \times \$970,000 \times \frac{.02}{1.08} = -\$161,667$$

To hedge this expected loss in value, the FI can take a short position in T-bond futures for the three-month period. Given that the hedge period covers the next three months (October 24, 1997, through January 24, 1998), the FI needs to hedge with a futures contract that trades for the entire period of the hedge. Since the December 1997 T-bond futures contract matures before January 24, 1998, the bank needs to take a short position in the March 1998 T-bond futures contract on October 24, 1997. The initial price of this contract is $116\tfrac{15}{32}$ per $100 of face value (see Figure 21–3). The minimum contract size on these futures is $100,000, so P_F equals $116,468.75. Suppose that the duration of the deliverable T-bond is 9.5 years. The appropriate number of T-bond futures to short (sell) is

$$N_F = \frac{9 \text{ years} \times \$970,000}{9.5 \text{ years} \times \$116,468.75} = 7.89008 \text{ contracts to short (sell)}$$

Since the FI cannot sell a fraction of the futures contract, the number of contracts should be rounded down to the nearest whole number, or seven.[14]   •   •   •

Table 21–4 shows the resulting on- and off-balance sheet effects from the increase in interest rates. To see the effect of the perfect hedge, we also assume that the FI can short exactly 7.89008 T-bond futures contracts. The 2 percent interest rate increase produces a

---

[14]The reason for rounding down rather than rounding up is technical. The target number of contracts to sell is the number that minimizes interest rate risk exposure. By slightly underhedging rather than overhedging, the FI can generate the same risk exposure level, but the underhedging policy produces a slightly higher return (see Figure 21–2).

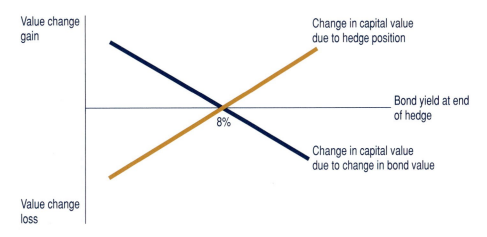

F i g u r e 21–5 *FI Value Change On- and Off-Balance-Sheet from a Perfect Short Hedge*

loss on the bond of $161,667 (see Table 21–4). If the bank could short hedge 7.89008 T-bond contracts, it exactly offsets the on-balance-sheet loss with a gain of $161,667 on the futures hedge. That is, assuming no basis risk ($\Delta R/1 + R = \Delta R_F/1 + R_F$) and ignoring the problem that the FI can only sell (short) T-bond contracts in increments of $100,000, then

$$-\Delta F = -(-9.5 \text{ years} \times 7.89008 \times \$116,468.75 \times \frac{.02}{1.08}) = \$161,667$$

The FI fully hedged the interest rate risk exposure.[15]

In fact, the FI is hedged against interest rate risk regardless of the change in the interest rate over the period of the hedge. Because the FI is perfectly hedged, any loss in value from the bond should interest rates rise in the next three months is exactly offset by a gain on the short position in the T-bond futures contract (see Figure 21–5). If, on the other hand, the bond's interest rate or yield falls below 8 percent over the next three months, the resulting gain in the bond's value to the FI is exactly offset by a loss in the T-bond futures contract.

Long Hedge.   An FI will take a long position in a futures contract when an expected drop in interest rates would result in a loss in capital value on the balance sheet (e.g., if the FI held short positions in bonds on its balance sheet). Taking the appropriate long position in the futures market produces a gain over the period of the hedge should rates fall so that any loss on the balance sheet is offset by a gain from the futures position.

Macrohedging with Futures

Macrohedging is similar to microhedging except that rather than hedging a single asset or liability, the bank hedges the total value of assets or liabilities. Chapter 18 showed that an

---

[15]Since the FI in reality can short only seven contracts, its actual gain is $143,429. The result, in this case, is a net exposure or loss of $18,238 (that is, $161,667 − $143,429).

FI's net worth exposure to interest rate shocks is directly related to its leverage-adjusted duration gap as well as its asset size. Again, this is

$$\Delta E = -[D_A - kD_L] \times A \times \frac{\Delta R}{1 + R}$$

where

ΔE = change in an FI's net worth
D_A = duration of its asset portfolio
D_L = duration of its liability portfolio
k = ratio of an FI's liabilities to assets (L/A)
A = size of an FI's asset portfolio
$\dfrac{\Delta R}{1 + R}$ = Shock to interest rates

E X A M P L E   2 1 – 2

Calculation of Change in FI Net Worth as Interest Rates Rise
To see how futures might fully hedge a positive or negative portfolio duration gap, consider an FI for which

$$D_A = 5 \text{ years}$$
$$D_L = 3 \text{ years}$$

Suppose that the FI manager receives information from an economic forecasting unit that interest rates are expected to rise from 10 to 11 percent over the next six months. The FI's initial balance sheet is as follows:

Assets (in millions)		Liabilities (in millions)	
A	$100	L	$90
		E	10
	$100		$100

so that k equals L/A equals 90/100 equals 0.9.

The FI manager wants to calculate the potential loss to the FI's net worth (E) if the forecast of rising rates proves to be true. As Chapter 18 showed

$$\Delta E = - (D_A - kD_L) \times A \times \frac{\Delta R}{1 + R}$$

so that

$$\Delta E = - (5 - (.9)(3)) \times \$100 \times \frac{.01}{1.1} = -\$2.09 \text{ million}$$

The bank could expect to lose $2.09 million in shareholders' net worth should the interest rate forecast be accurate. Since the FI started with a net worth of $10 million, the loss of $2.09 million is almost 21 percent of its initial net worth position. Clearly, as this example illustrates, the impact of the rise in interest rates could be quite threatening to the FI and its insolvency risk exposure. • • •

We now solve the problem of how many futures contracts to sell (to hedge against an interest rate increase) to fully macrohedge an FI's on-balance-sheet interest rate risk exposure. Fully hedging can be defined as selling a sufficient number of futures contracts (N_F) so that the loss of net worth on the balance sheet (ΔE) when rates rise is just offset by the gain from off-balance-sheet selling of futures (ΔF) when rates rise, or

$$\Delta F = \Delta E$$

Substituting in the appropriate expressions for each:

$$-D_F(N_F \times P_F)\frac{\Delta R_F}{1 + R_F} = -(D_A - kD_L)A\frac{\Delta R}{1 + R}$$

If we continue to assume that basis risk is zero (i.e., $\Delta R/1 + R = \Delta R_F/1 + R_F$), then

$$-D_F(N_F \times P_F) = -(D_A - kD_L)A$$

and solving for N_F (the number of futures to sell)

$$N_F = \frac{(D_A - kD_L) \times A}{D_F \times P_F}$$

EXAMPLE 21 – 3

Calculation of the Number of Futures Contracts Needed for Macrohedge
From the equation for N_F, we can now solve for the correct number of futures positions to sell (N_F) in the context of Example 21–2 in which the bank was exposed to a balance sheet loss of net worth (ΔE) amounting to \$2.09 million when interest rates rose

$$D_A = 5 \text{ years}$$
$$D_L = 3 \text{ years}$$
$$k = .9$$
$$A = \$100 \text{ million}$$

Suppose that the current futures price quote is \$97 per \$100 of face value for the benchmark 20-year, 8 percent coupon bond underlying the T-bond futures contract that is nearest to maturity; the minimum contract size is \$100,000, so P_F equals \$97,000, and the duration of the deliverable bond is 9.5 years. Inserting these numbers into the expression for N_F, we can now solve for the number of futures to sell

$$N_F = \frac{(5 - (.9)3) \times \$100 \text{ million}}{9.5 \times \$97,000}$$

$$= 249.59 \text{ contracts to be sold}$$

or rounded down to the nearest whole number, 249 contracts.   • • •

Next, we verify that selling T-bond futures contracts will indeed hedge the FI against a sudden increase in interest rates from 10 to 11 percent, or a 1 percent interest rate shock. Table 21–5 summarizes the on- and off-balance-sheet changes resulting from the shock to interest rates. As indicated, the bank loses \$2.09 million on the balance sheet while the short position in the futures market produces an offsetting gain from the futures hedge. That is, as the seller of futures contracts, the FI makes a gain of \$2.09 million.

Table 21-5

ON- AND OFF-BALANCE-SHEET EFFECTS OF A MACROHEDGE HEDGE

	On Balance Sheet	Off Balance Sheet
Begin hedge $t = 0$	Equity value of $10m exposed to impact of rise in interest rates in next 6 months.	Sell 249.59 T-bond futures contracts at $97,000. Underlying T-bond coupon rate is 8%.
End hedge $t = 6$ months	Interest rates rise on assets and liabilities by 1%.	Buy 249.59 T-bond futures.
	Opportunity loss on-balance-sheet: $$\Delta E = -(5 - .9(3)) \times \$100m \times \frac{.01}{1.1}$$ $$= -\$2.09 \text{ million}$$	Real gain on futures hedge: $$-\Delta F = -\left(-9.5 \times (249.59 \times \$97,000) \times \frac{.01}{1.1}\right)^*$$ $$= \$2.09 \text{ million}$$

*Assuming no basis risk (i.e., $\Delta R/1 + R = \Delta R_F/1 + R_F$)

Suppose that instead of using the 20-year T-bond futures to hedge, the bank had used the three-month T-bill futures.[16] For example, assume that the P_F equals $97 per $100 of face value, or $970,000, per contract (the minimum contract size is $1,000,000), and D_F equals .25 (the duration of a three-month T-bill that is the discount instrument deliverable under the contract).[17] Then

$$N_F = \frac{(5 - (.9)3) \times \$100 \text{ million}}{.25 \times \$970,000}$$

$$= 948.45 \text{ contracts to be sold.}$$

Rounding down to the nearest whole contract, N_F equals 948.

As this example illustrates, we can hedge an FI's on-balance-sheet interest rate risk when its D_A is greater than kD_L by selling either T-bond or T-bill futures. In general, fewer T-bond than T-bill contracts need to be sold, in our case, 948 T-bill versus 249 T-bond contracts. This suggests that on a simple transaction cost basis, the FI normally prefers to use T-bond futures. Other considerations can be important, however, especially if the FI holds the futures contracts until the delivery date. The FI needs to consider the availability of the deliverable set of securities and any possible supply shortages or squeezes. Such liquidity concerns may favor T-bills.[18]

---

[16]As Figure 21–3 shows, three-month T-bill futures are an alternative interest rate futures contract to the long-term T-bond futures contract.

[17]We assume the same futures price ($97) here for purposes of comparison. Of course, the actual prices of the two futures contracts are very different (see Figure 21–3).

[18]When rates change, however, the loss of net worth on the balance sheet and the gain on selling the futures are instantaneous; therefore, delivery need not be a concern. Indeed, because of the daily marking-to-market process, an FI manager can close out a futures position by taking an exactly offsetting position. That is, a manager who had originally sold 100 futures contracts could close out a position on any day by buying 100 contracts. Because of the unique marking-to-market feature, the marked-to-market price of the contracts sold equals the price of any new contracts bought on that day.

The Problem of Basis Risk

It is important to recognize that in the previous examples the bank perfectly hedged interest rate risk exposure because interest rate changes in both the cash and futures markets moved by the same relative amounts (i.e., we assumed $\Delta R/1 + R = \Delta R_F/1 + R_F$). This is rarely the case. The shift in yields, $\Delta R/1 + R$, affecting the values of the on-balance-sheet cash portfolio often differs from the shift in yields, $\Delta R_F/1 + R_F$, affecting the value of the underlying bond in the futures contract; that is, changes in spot and futures prices or values are not perfectly correlated. As defined earlier, this lack of perfect correlation is called *basis risk*.

Basis risk occurs for two reasons. First, the asset or liability being hedged is not the same as the underlying security on the futures contract. For instance, in Example 21–1 we hedged rate changes on the FI's 9-year duration bonds with T-bond futures contracts written on 20-year maturity bonds with a duration of 9.5 years. Generally, the interest rates on bonds of different maturities and durations do not move in a perfectly correlated manner. The second source of basis risk comes from the difference in movements in spot rates versus futures rates. Because spot securities (e.g., government bonds) and futures contracts (e.g., on the same bonds) are traded in different markets, the shift in spot rates may differ from the shift in futures rates (i.e., they are not perfectly correlated).

Let b reflect the relative sensitivity of rates underlying the bond in the futures market relative to interest rates on bonds in the spot market.[19] Then the number of futures to sell (N_F) equals

$$N_F = \frac{(D_A - kD_L) \times A}{D_F \times P_F \times b}$$

The only difference between these and the previous formulas is an adjustment for basis risk (b) in the preceding equation, which measures the degree to which the futures price yields move more or less than spot bond price yields.

In macrohedge Example 21–3, let b equal 1.1. This means that for every 1 percent change in discounted spot rates ($\Delta R/1 + R$), the implied rate on the deliverable T-bond in the futures market moves by 1.1 percent. That is, futures prices are more sensitive to interest rate shocks than are spot market prices. Solving for N_F, the number of futures contracts that needs to be sold to hedge the $2.09 million loss in net worth on the balance sheet should rates increase by 1 percent for the FI's assets and liabilities, we have:

$$N_F = \frac{(5 - (.9)(3)) \times \$100 \text{ million}}{9.5 \times \$97,000 \times 1.1}$$

$$= 226.9 \text{ contracts to be sold}$$

or 226 contracts rounded down. This compares to 249 when we assumed equal rate shocks in both the spot and futures markets ($\Delta R/1 + R = \Delta R_F/1 + R_F$). We need fewer futures contracts than was the case when we ignored basis risk because futures rates and prices are more volatile so that selling fewer futures would be sufficient to provide the same change in ΔF (the value of the futures position) than before when we implicitly assumed no basis risk (i.e., $b = 1$).

[19]That is, $b = (\Delta R_F/(1 + R_F)) / (\Delta R / (1 + R))$.

Concept  Questions

1. What is the difference between microhedging and macrohedging and between routine hedging and selective hedging?
2. Regarding Example 21-1, how many futures should have been sold if the duration of the 20-year, $1 million, face value bond was 15 years?
3. Regarding Example 21-3, suppose the FI had the reverse duration gap, that is, the duration of its assets was shorter ($D_A = 3$) than the duration of its liabilities ($D_A = 5$). (This might be the case of a bank that borrows with long-term notes or time deposits to finance floating-rate loans.) How should it hedge using futures?

ACCOUNTING GUIDELINES, REGULATIONS, AND MACROHEDGING VERSUS MICROHEDGING

A number of accounting rules and regulations determine whether an FI should use futures to macrohedge or microhedge and affect its choice of hedging instrument.

Accounting Rules and Futures Contracts

The Financial Accounting Standards Board (FASB) has made a number of rulings regarding the accounting and tax treatment of futures transactions.[20] In hedge accounting, a futures position is a hedge transaction if it can be linked to a particular asset or liability. An example is using a T-bond futures contract to hedge a bank's holdings of long-term bonds as investments.

Prior to 1997, if this hedging condition were met, when the bank's on-balance-sheet position is carried at book value, it could defer gains or losses on its futures contract until the position is closed out. Any gains or losses are then amortized over the remaining life of the asset or liability; that is, they are reflected in bank income slowly. Requiring that hedges be linked to an identifiable asset or liability mitigates pursuing macrohedging or aggregate duration gap hedging. Since this type of hedge cannot be directly associated with any particular underlying asset or liability, it can be viewed as speculative and requires immediate recognition of losses and gains in the profit and loss statement. Unfortunately, although the FASB accounting rules required a close correlation between the instrument being hedged and the futures contract, it failed to actually define quantitatively what close correlation means or to state the precise statistical technique that could establish such a close correlation.

This situation resulted in some disputes among FI managers and regulators. Perhaps the most publicized involved the closure of Franklin Savings Bank in February 1990.[21] Franklin Savings Bank operated in a nontraditional fashion for a thrift. It relied heavily on brokered deposits for its growth, increasing its asset size from $0.5 billion in 1982 to more than $9 billion by the end of 1989. More important, it invested heavily in junk bonds and mortgage-backed securities and took very active positions in futures, swaps, and options.

---

[20]*FASB Statement No. 80,* "Accounting for Futures Contracts" (1984), is probably the most important.

[21]The following discussion is based on S. Holifield, M. Madaris, and W. H. Sackley, "Regulatory Risk and Hedging Accounting Standards in Financial Institutions," Working Paper, University of Southern Mississippi, April 1994.

At the end of 1989, it had a notional value of $1.7 billion in long-term futures (short positions) with $119 million in futures contract losses it wished to defer.

The dispute revolved around whether these losses could be deferred. Franklin pursued a general policy of macrohedging (hedging the duration gap) rather than directly hedging specific assets or liabilities. Because its hedging practices were not closely correlated with specific or identifiable assets or liabilities, the Office of Thrift Supervision denied Franklin's request for loss deferral and placed it under the conservatorship in 1990.[22]

Possibly as a result of opportunities to defer losses on futures positions so that an insolvent FI appears solvent, the FASB in 1997 reversed its position and required that all gains and losses on derivatives used to hedge assets and liabilities on the balance sheet be recognized immediately as earnings, in the period of change, together with the offsetting gain or loss on the hedged item. Gains or losses on derivatives used to hedge forecasted changes in the values of balance sheet items should also be recognized in a new section on the balance sheet called Other Comprehensive Income outside of earnings. When the forecasted change actually occurs, the gain or loss is taken out of other comprehensive income and placed in earnings. Thus, the 1997 ruling effectively requires derivatives to be marked to market. Additionally, U.S. companies that hold or issue derivatives must report their trading objectives and strategies for reaching these objectives on all disclosures.[23]

Futures and Forward Policies of Regulators

The main bank regulators—the Federal Reserve, the FDIC, and the Comptroller of the Currency—have issued uniform guidelines for banks taking positions in futures and forwards. These guidelines require a bank to (1) establish internal guidelines regarding its hedging activity, (2) establish trading limits, and (3) disclose large contract positions that materially affect bank risk to shareholders and outside investors. Overall, regulators' policy is to encourage the use of futures for hedging and to discourage their use for speculation, although—as noted—on a practical basis, it is often difficult to distinguish between the two.

Finally, as Chapter 16 discusses, futures contracts are not subject to risk-based capital requirements with respect to credit risk; by contrast, over-the-counter forward contracts are potentially subject to capital requirements. Other things being equal, the risk-based capital requirements favor the use of futures over forwards. To the dismay of some regulators, the use of derivative securities in some nondepository FIs remains virtually unregulated (see Contemporary Perspectives Box 21–2).

Concept Questions

1. According to FASB rules, when is a futures position a hedge transaction?
2. Discuss how the FASB's position on accounting and tax treatment of futures transactions led to a dispute between regulators and FI managers in the Franklin Savings Bank case.

---

[22]Another interesting case is that of Metallgesellschaft, the German conglomerate with strong ownership and control links to Deutsche Bank. Under German accounting rules, losses on futures, even for hedging purposes, cannot be deferred and must be recognized immediately. In the United States, on the other hand, losses (and gains) for hedging purposes can be realized when the underlying asset to be hedged matures or is sold. This forced realization of its losses on all futures nearly forced Metallgesellschaft into insolvency in 1993. (See F. R. Edwards, "Derivatives Can Be Hazardous to Your Health," London School of Economics, Working Paper, December 1994.)

[23]See "Called to Account," *Risk Magazine,* August 1996, pp. 15–17.

Contemporary Perspectives 21–2

GAO Calls Insurance "Regulatory Gap"

The volume of derivative activities of insurance companies increased at a greater rate than banks or securities firms during four of the five years in a recent study, according to the Government Accounting Office's new report, *Financial Derivatives Actions Taken or Proposed Since May 1994.*

However, the watchdog arm of Congress said that "state insurance regulators do not directly oversee the financial condition of affiliates of insurance companies that are OTC derivatives dealers."

Reiterating its stance in its 1994 report, GAO said that derivatives dealer affiliates of insurance companies are subject to minimal reporting requirements, continue to have no capital requirements and are not examined. . . .

GAO added, "A regulatory gap remains for the three insurance companies that are OTC derivatives dealers. While the National Association of Insurance Commissioners has recommended improvements in derivatives disclosures and examinations for insurance companies, these recommendations do not apply to the activities of the OTC derivatives dealer affiliates of insurance companies."

In sum, the report pointed out that "Insurance companies' OTC derivatives dealer affiliates remain virtually unregulated." . . .

While the NAIC has been reworking its policies and procedures to enhance derivatives disclosures and examinations, the report noted that NAIC's proposals have no power over the affiliates. "Thus, even if the states adopt the NAIC proposals, the resulting requirements would apply only to the insurance companies, not to their derivatives dealer affiliates." . . .

GAO focused on five areas of improvement between 1994 and the present for its follow-up report, with one of them being "to provide federal oversight of major derivatives dealers that are unregulated affiliates of securities firms and insurance companies."

SOURCE: Michele Clayton, *The Insurance Accountant,* November 18, 1996, p. 1. Courtesy of *The Insurance Accountant,* an *American Banker* newsletter.

SUMMARY

This chapter analyzed the risk-management role of futures and forwards. We saw that although they are close substitutes, they are not perfect substitutes. A number of characteristics such as maturity, liquidity, flexibility, marking to market, and capital requirements differentiate these products and make one or the other more attractive to any given FI manager. Although the chapter concentrated on their role in hedging interest rate risk, these products might be used to partially or fully hedge other types of risk commonly faced by an FI, such as foreign exchange risk (see Chapter 27, Appendix A) and credit risk (see the appendix to this chapter). An FI can engage in microhedging or macrohedging as well as selective or routine hedging. In all cases, perfect hedging was shown to be difficult because of basis risk. Finally, accounting rules are shown to affect FIs' strategies in taking positions in futures contracts, with regulators mainly concerned about preventing speculation.

PERTINENT WEB SITES

Board of Governors of the Federal Reserve   http://www.bog. frb.fed.us/

Chicago Board of Trade   http://www.cbot.com/

Chicago Mercantile Exchange   http://www.cme.com/

Federal Deposit Insurance Corporation   http://www.fdic.gov/

Financial Accounting Standards Board   http://www.rutgers.edu/accounting/raw/fasb/home.html

Office of the Comptroller of Currency   http://www.occ.treas.gov/

Office of Thrift Supervision   http://www.ustreas.gov/treasury/bureaus/ots/ots.html

Futures and Forwards

1. What are some of the major differences between futures and forward contracts?

2. In each of the following cases, indicate whether it would be appropriate for an FI to buy or sell a forward contract to hedge the appropriate risk.
   a. A commercial bank plans to issue CDs in three months.
   b. An insurance company plans to buy bonds in two months.
   c. A thrift is going to sell Treasury securities next month.
   d. A U.S. bank lends to a French company; the loan is payable in francs.
   e. A mutual fund plans to sell its holding of stock in a German company.
   f. A finance company has assets with a duration of six years and liabilities with a duration of 13 years.

3. Suppose that you purchase a Treasury bond futures contract at 95.
   a. What is your obligation when you purchase this futures contract?
   b. If an FI purchases this contract, in what kind of hedge is it engaged?
   c. Assume that the Treasury bond futures price falls to 94. What is your loss or gain?
   d. Assume that the Treasury bond futures price rises to 97. Mark your position to market.

4. Answer the following.
   a. What is the duration of a 20-year, 8 percent coupon (paid semiannually) Treasury bond (deliverable against the Treasury bond futures contract) selling at par?
   b. What is the impact on the Treasury bond price if interest rates increase 50 basis points?
   c. What is the meaning of the following Treasury bond futures price quote: 101-13?

5. An FI holds a 15-year, par value, $10,000,000 bond that is priced at 104 and yields 7 percent. The FI plans to sell the bond but for tax purposes must wait two months. The bond has a duration of eight years. The FI's market analyst is predicting that the Federal Reserve will raise interest rates within the next two months and doing so will raise the yield on the bond to 8 percent. Most other analysts are predicting no change in interest rates, so presently plenty of two-month forward contracts for 15-year bonds are available at 104. The FI would like to hedge against this interest rate forecast with an appropriate position in a forward contract. What will this position be? Show that if rates raise by 1 percent as forecasted, the hedge will protect the FI from loss.

6. Why is it generally more efficient for FIs to employ a macrohedge than a series of microhedges?

7. A mutual fund plans to purchase $500,000 of 30-year Treasury bonds in four months. These bonds have a duration of 12 years and are priced at 96–08. The mutual fund is concerned about interest rates changing over the next four months and is considering a hedge with six-month T-bond futures that are currently selling for 98-24 and have a duration of 8.5 years. Assume that interest rate changes in the spot market exactly match those in the futures market. What type of futures position should the mutual fund enter into? How many contracts should be used?

8. What are the sources of basis risk?

9. Consider the following FI's balance sheet:

Assets ($000)		Liabilities ($000)	
Duration = 10 years	$950	Duration = 2 years	$860
		Equity	90

   a. What is the FI's duration gap?
   b. What is the FI's interest rate risk exposure?
   c. How can the FI use futures and forward contracts to macrohedge?
   d. What is the impact on the FI's equity value if all interest rates increase by 1 percent? That is,
   $$\frac{\Delta R}{1 + R} = 0.01$$
   e. Suppose that the FI in part (c) macrohedges using Treasury bond futures that are currently priced at 96. What is the impact on the FI's futures position if all interest rates increase by 1 percent? That is,
   $$\frac{\Delta R}{1 + R} = 0.01 \text{ Assume that the deliverable Treasury}$$
   bond has a duration of nine years.
   f. If the FI wanted a perfect macrohedge, how many Treasury bond futures contracts does it need?

10. Hedge Row Bank has the following balance sheet:

Assets (in millions)		Liabilities (in millions)	
A	$150	L	$135
		E	15
	$150		$150

    The duration of the assets is six years, and the duration of the liabilities is four years. The bank is expecting interest rates to fall from 10 percent to 9 percent over the next year. What is Hedge Row's change in net worth if the forecast is accurate?

11. Assume that you are planning to hedge your $100 million bond instruments with a cross-hedge using Euromark futures. How would you estimate the

$$b = \frac{\Delta R_F / 1 + R_F}{\Delta R / (1 + R)}$$ to determine the exact number of

Euromark futures contracts to hedge?

12. Village Bank has $240 million of assets with a duration of 14 years and liabilities worth $210 million with a duration of 4 years. It is concerned about preserving the value of its equity in the event of an increase in interest rates. It is contemplating a macrohedge with interest rate futures contracts now selling at 102-21. Assuming that the spot and futures interest rates move together, how many futures contracts must Village Bank sell to hedge effectively?

13. Assume that an FI has assets of $250 million and liabilities of $200 million. The duration of the assets is six years and the duration of the liabilities is three years. The price of the futures contract is $115,000, and its duration is 5.5 years. What is the number of contracts needed to construct a macrohedge?

14. Suppose that you purchase a $1 million, 91-day Eurodollar futures contract trading at 98.50.

   a. If you reverse the position two days later by purchasing the contract at 98.60, what is your net profit?

   b. What is the loss or gain if the price at reversal is 98.40?

15. An FI has decided to hedge its asset portfolio with S&P 500 Index futures because it expects the market to decline in the near future. It sells 20, six-month S&P Index futures contracts currently trading at 505.

   a. What is the profit for the FI if a month later the Index is trading at $498?

   b. If instead the predictions are not accurate and the economy recovers, what is the FI's loss or gain if the Index settles at 511?

16. Why is it important that an FI separate its derivative contracts used for hedging against those used for proprietary (speculative) trading?

17. What guidelines have regulators given banks for taking futures and forward positions?

18. Go to the Office of the Comptroller of the Currency web site and update Table 21–1.

   The following questions are related to Appendix material.

19. What is a credit forward?

20. What is the gain on the purchase of a $20,000,000 credit forward contract with a modified duration of seven years if the credit spread between a benchmark Treasury bond and a borrowing firm's debt decreases by 50 basis points?

APPENDIX: HEDGING CREDIT RISK WITH FORWARDS

Chapter 11 demonstrated that by diversifying their loan portfolios across different borrowers, sectors, and regions, FIs could diversify away much of the borrower-specific or unsystematic risk of the loan portfolio. Of course, the ability of an FI manager to diversify sufficiently depends in part on the size of the loan portfolio under management. Thus, the potential ability to diversify away borrowers' specific risk increases with the FI's size. An FI can also seek to hedge individual credit risk exposure with credit forward contracts on a loan-by-loan basis or even seeking to hedge the systematic risk component of the loan portfolio.[24]

Forward Contracts and Credit Risk Hedging

credit forward

Forward agreement that hedges against an increase in default risk on a loan after the loan terms have been determined and the loan issued.

A **credit forward** is a forward agreement that hedges against an increase in default risk on a loan (decline in credit quality of a borrower) after the loan rate is determined and the loan issued. The credit forward agreement specifies a credit spread (a risk premium above the risk-free rate to compensate for default risk) on a benchmark bond issued by the borrower from the bank. For example, suppose that the benchmark bond of the borrower was rated BBB at the time the loan was originated and that it had an interest spread over a U.S. Treasury bond of the same maturity of 2 percent. Then S_F equals 2 percent defines the credit spread on which the credit forward contract is written. Figure 21–A1 illustrates the payment pattern on a credit forward. In Figure 21–A1, S_T is the actual credit spread on the bond when the credit forward matures, for example, one year after the loan was originated and the credit forward contract was entered into. MD is the modified duration on the benchmark BBB bond, and A is the principal amount of the forward agreement.

From the payment pattern established in the credit forward agreement, Figure 21–A1 shows that the credit forward buyer bears the price risk of an increase in default risk on the benchmark bond of the borrowing firm while the credit forward seller (the bank lender) hedges itself against an increase in the borrower's default risk. That is, if the borrower's

Credit Spread at End of Forward Agreement	Credit Spread Seller	Credit Spread Buyer
$S_T > S_F$	Receives $(S_T - S_F) \times MD \times A$	Pays $(S_T - S_F) \times MD \times A$
$S_F > S_T$	Pays $(S_F - S_T) \times MD \times A$	Receives $(S_F - S_T) \times MD \times A$

Figure **21–A1**   *Payment Pattern on a Credit Forward*

---

[24]The use of credit derivatives is also becoming more common in hedging certain credit risks. The notional amount of credit derivatives for commercial banks at the end of 1997 was $38.9 billion (see Table 21–1).

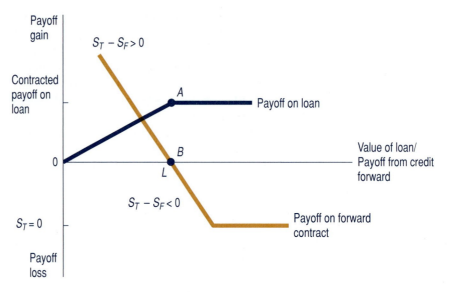

F i g u r e **21–A2**   *Payoff to an FI from Hedging Default Risk on a Loan with a Credit Forward*

default risk increases so that when the forward agreement matures, the market requires a higher credit spread on the borrower's benchmark bond, S_T, than that originally agreed to in the forward contract, S_F, (i.e., $S_T > S_F$), the credit forward buyer pays the credit forward seller—the bank—$(S_T - S_F) \times MD \times A$. For example, suppose that the credit spread between BBB bonds and U.S. Treasury bonds widened to 3 percent from 2 percent over the year, the modified duration (MD) of the benchmark BBB bond was five years, and the size of the forward contract, A, was \$10,000,000. Then the gain on the credit forward contract to the seller is \$500,000 [(3% – 2%) × 5 × \$10,000,000]. This amount could be used to offset the loss in the loan's market value as the result of the rise in default risk on loans. However, should the borrower's default risk and credit spread decrease, the credit forward seller pays the credit forward buyer $(S_F - S_T) \times MD \times A$.[25]

Thus, an FI concerned about an increase in the default risk on a loan can sell (short) a credit forward to hedge against this possibility. Figure 21–A2 illustrates the impact on the FI from the hedged loan. If the default risk on the loan increases, the value of the loan falls below L (to the left of point A in Figure 21–A2), its value at the beginning of the hedge period. However, the FI hedged the change in default risk by selling a credit forward contract. Assuming that the credit spread on the borrower's benchmark bond also increases, the FI receives $(S_T - S_F) \times MD \times A$ (to the left of point B in Figure 21–A2). If the characteristics of the benchmark bond (i.e., change in credit spread, modified duration, and principal value) are the same as those of the FI's loan to the borrower, the loss on the balance sheet is offset completely by the gain from the credit forward (i.e., in our example, a \$500,000 market value loss in the loan is offset by a \$500,000 gain from selling the credit forward contract).

---

[25]For additional discussion, see J. D. Finnerty, "Credit Derivatives, Infrastructure Finance, and Emerging Market Risk, *The Financier, ACMT,* February 1996, pp. 64–75.

If the default risk does not increase or even decreases, the FI selling the forward contract will pay $(S_F - S_T) \times MD \times A$ to the credit forward buyer. However, importantly, this payout by the FI is limited to a maximum amount at which S_T equals 0 (i.e., the default spread on BBB bonds falls to zero or the original BBB bonds of the borrower are viewed as having the same default risk as government bonds, in other words, the credit spread or rate on the benchmark bond cannot fall below the risk free rate). In this case, the maximum fixed loss on the credit forward mirrors (offsets) the maximum fixed rate gain on the loan.

Chapter Twenty-two

Options

F Is have a wide variety of forward and futures contracts to use in hedging and an even wider array of option products, including exchange-traded options, over-the-counter (OTC) options, options embedded in securities, and caps, collars, and floors. Not only has the type of option products increased in recent years, but the use of options has increased as well (see Contemporary Perspectives Box 22–1). However, option positions and a crisis in another part of the world can also lead to huge losses for FIs (see Contemporary Perspectives Box 22–2).

This chapter discusses the role of options in hedging interest rate risk. The use of options to hedge credit risk is discussed in Appendix C to this chapter. The use of options to hedge foreign exchange (FX) risk is discussed in Appendix B to Chapter 27 on FX risk. This chapter begins by reviewing the four basic option strategies: buying a call, writing (selling) a call, buying a put, and writing (selling) a put.[1]

---

[1] The two basic option contracts are *puts* and *calls*. However, an FI could potentially be a buyer or seller (writer) of each.

Contemporary Perspectives 22–1

News and Trends: Derivatives Showed Gains in All Sectors, ISDA Survey Says

Worldwide derivatives volume in interest rate swaps, currency swaps, and interest rate options rose by 56.7 percent in 1995 from 1994, according to a survey released last week by the International Swaps and Derivatives Association. The survey of 71 derivatives dealers indicated strong gains in all sectors of the business, the association said.

"The growing market clearly reflects recognition that privately negotiated derivatives have become a major risk-management tool to hedge financial uncertainty in business and investment portfolios," said Gay Evans, chairwoman of ISDA and a managing director at Bankers Trust International.

The notional principal amount of transactions in interest rate swaps, currency swaps, and interest rate options stood at $17.713 trillion at the end of 1995, up from $11.303 trillion in 1994, according to the survey compiled for ISDA by accounting firm Arthur Andersen.

Notional principal, the measure ISDA uses to track market behavior, is the base amount for calculating cash flows in swaps and interest rate options. The financial risk involved in these transactions amounts to a small fraction of the notional principal. . . .

Interest rate options—caps, collars, floors, and swaptions—that were outstanding at year-end 1995

stood at $3.704 trillion compared with $1.573 trillion a year earlier, reflecting a gain of 136 percent for the full year and 79.3 percent for the second half.

New transactions in interest rate options grew 33.2 percent to $2.015 trillion from $1.513 trillion. Activity in the second half amounted to $1.34 trillion, almost double to the $675.8 billion in activity in the first half.

"The robust activity in these options can largely be attributed to increased mortgage hedging, increased market volatility, and the general pickup in business," said Tom Montag, vice chairman of ISDA and a partner at Goldman, Sachs & Co.

SOURCE: Joanne Morrison, *The Bond Buyer,* July 16, 1996, p. 30. Reprinted with permission.

BASIC FEATURES OF OPTIONS

In describing the features of the four basic option strategies that FIs might employ to hedge interest rate risk, we discuss their return payoffs in terms of interest rate movements. These are summarized in Table 22–1. Specifically, we consider bond options whose payoff values

Table **22-1**

SUMMARY OF GAINS AND LOSSES ON OPTION CONTRACTS

Position	Change in Interest Rates	Gain/Loss
Buy call option	Increase	Loss limited to option premium
	Decrease	Gain unlimited
Write call option	Increase	Gain limited to option premium
	Decrease	Loss unlimited
Buy put option	Increase	Gain unlimited
	Decrease	Loss limited to option premium
Write put option	Increase	Loss unlimited
	Decrease	Gain limited to option premium

Contemporary Perspectives 22–2

Blind Faith

Full details about the derivatives losses at Union Bank of Switzerland (UBS) are still not known. But according to sources at UBS and at SBC Warburg Dillon Read, the investment-banking arm of Swiss Bank Corporation (SBC), two familiar factors may be at fault. One is that UBS traders may have fed incorrect data into the computer models that the bank used to price derivatives, particularly options. The other is that the bank had too much faith in its models.

Many of UBS's losses appear to have involved huge amounts of convertible preference shares, arcane securities issued last year in copious amounts by Japanese banks. . . . Normally, a bank with such large positions protects itself against a drop in the value of its options. The best way, buying offsetting options in particular shares, is difficult and expensive, particularly in Japan. A second way for UBS to have hedged its risk was to sell the banks' shares. UBS apparently did relatively little of this at the start: it thought that bank shares would not fall below the lowest price at which the preferred

shares could be converted, so that its downside risks were limited.

Not so. Shares in Japanese banks fell precipitously when Yamaichi Securities, then Japan's fourth-largest securities firm, went bust in November. Share prices also became much more volatile, making it even more expensive for UBS to hedge its risk. UBS seems to have had a particularly large exposure to Fuji Bank, whose shares stopped trading altogether for three days.

UBS desperately tried to cut its losses by selling some of the Japanese banks' shares, to the point that in November and December it became the biggest seller of bank stocks. The result was to drive share prices down even more, magnifying the losses on its options. It also tried to sell futures contracts on the Nikkei 225 stockmarket average. But there were days when the Nikkei rose and bank shares fell. As a result, losses mounted alarmingly. UBS refuses to say whether it has incurred any losses on derivatives trading in Japan.

And why did UBS's global equity derivatives department sell so many options on Japanese banks' shares?

The answer is that it seems to have systematically overestimated the value of these contracts. That value depends in part on the expected dividend yield on the underlying shares. Sources suggest that people in the global equity derivatives department may have fed inflated estimates of future dividends into the computers. To the bank's bosses, this would have made the positions in Japanese preference shares seem far more profitable than they were.

On top of that, the department seemingly had blind faith in the accuracy of the assumptions used to build price-setting models. This may be the best-known danger in derivatives dealing: everyone in the markets knows that if shares stop trading or the share prices become much more volatile than expected, an option's market value will differ from the model's valuation. UBS seems to have ignored this risk. And when some of its chief assumptions proved less than robust, it was caught on the hop.

SOURCE: *The Economist*, January 31, 1998, p. 76. © 1998 The Economist Newspaper Group, Inc. Reprinted with permission. Further reproduction prohibited.

are inversely linked to interest rate movements in a manner similar to bond prices and interest rates in general (see Chapter 17).

Buying a Call Option on a Bond

call option

An option that gives a purchaser the right, but not the obligation, to buy the underlying security from the writer of the option at a prespecified exercise price on a prespecified date.

The first strategy of buying (or taking a long position in) a call option on a bond is shown in Figure 22–1. A **call option** gives the purchaser the right (but not the obligation) to buy an underlying security—a bond—at a prespecified price called the *exercise* or *strike price* (X). In return, the buyer of the call option must pay the writer or seller an up-front fee known as a *call premium* (C). This premium is an immediate negative cash flow for the buyer of the call that potentially stands to make a profit should the underlying bond's price rise above the exercise price by an amount exceeding the premium. If the price of the bond

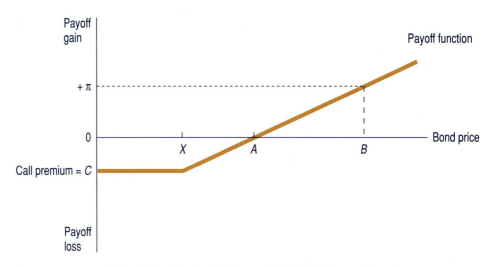

F i g u r e   **22–1**   *Payoff Function for the Buyer of a Call Option on a Bond*

never rises above X, the buyer of the call never exercises the option (i.e., buying the bond at X when its market value is less than X). In this case, the option matures unexercised. The call buyer incurs a cost C for the option, and no other cash flows result.

As Figure 22–1 shows, if the price of the bond underlying the option rises to price B, the buyer makes a profit of π, which is the difference between the bond price (B) and the exercise price of the option (X) minus the call premium ($C = XA$). If the bond price rises to A, the buyer of the call has broken even because the profit from exercising the call ($A - X$) just equals the premium payment for the call (C).

Notice two important things about bond call options in Figure 22–1:

1. As interest rates fall, bond prices rise and the call option buyer has unlimited profit potential; the more that rates fall, the higher bond prices rise and the larger the profit on the exercise of the option.
2. As interest rates rise, bond prices fall and the potential for a negative payoff (loss) for the buyer of the call option increases. If rates rise so that bond prices fall below the exercise price X, the call buyer is not obligated to exercise the option. Thus, the buyer's losses are truncated by the amount of the up-front premium payment (C) made to purchase the call option.

Thus, buying a call option is a strategy to take when interest rates are expected to fall. Notice that unlike interest rate futures, whose prices and payoffs move symmetrically with changes in the level of rates, the payoffs on bond call options move asymmetrically with interest rates (see Chapter 21).

Writing a Call Option on a Bond

The second strategy is writing (or taking a short position in) a call option on a bond. In writing a call option on a bond, the writer or seller receives an up-front fee or premium (C) and must stand ready to sell the underlying bond to the purchaser of the option at the exercise price, X. Note the payoff from writing a call option on a bond in Figure 22–2. Notice two important things about this payoff function:

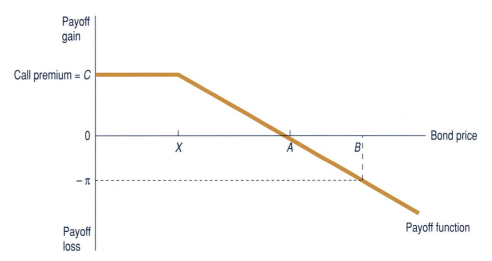

F i g u r e **22–2** *Payoff Function for the Writer of a Call Option on a Bond*

1. When interest rates *rise* and bond prices *fall,* the potential for the writer of the call to receive a positive payoff or profit increases. The call buyer is less likely to exercise the option, which would force the option writer to sell the underlying bond at the exercise price. However, this profit has a maximum equal to the call premium (*C*) charged up front to the buyer of the option.

2. When interest rates fall and bond prices rise, the probability that the writer will take a loss increases. The call buyer will exercise the options, forcing the option writer to sell the underlying bonds. Since bond prices are theoretically unbounded in the upward direction, although they must return to par at maturity, these losses could be very large.

Thus, writing a call option is a strategy to take when interest rates are expected to rise. Caution is warranted, however, because profits are limited but losses are unlimited. A fall in interest rates and a rise in bond prices to *B* results in the writer of the option losing π (in Figure 22–2).

Buying a Put Option on a Bond

put option

An option that gives a purchaser the right, but not the obligation, to sell the underlying security to the writer of the option at a prespecified exercise price on a prespecified date.

The third strategy is buying (or taking a long position in) a put option on a bond. The buyer of a **put option** on a bond has the right (but not the obligation) to sell the underlying bond to the writer of the option at the agreed exercise price (*X*). In return for this option, the buyer of the put option pays a premium (*P*) to the writer. We show the potential payoffs to the buyer of the put option in Figure 22–3. Note the following:

1. When interest rates rise and bond prices fall, the probability that the buyer of the put will make a profit from exercising the option increases. Thus, if bond prices fall to *D*, the buyer of the put option can purchase bonds in the bond market at that price and put them (sell them) back to the writer of the put at the higher exercise price *X*. As a result, after deducting the cost of the put premium, the buyer makes a profit of πp in Figure 22–3. The put option buyer has unlimited profit potential; the higher the rates rise, the more the bond prices fall and the larger the profit on the exercise of the option.

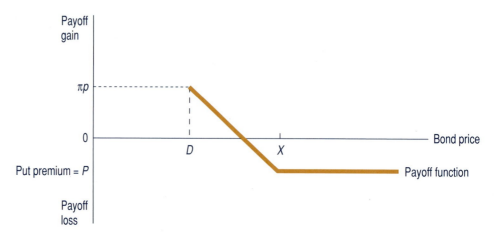

F i g u r e **22–3**   *Payoff Function for the Buyer of a Put Option on a Bond*

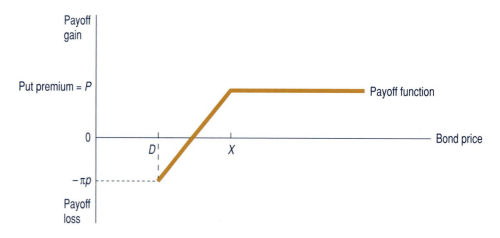

F i g u r e **22–4**   *Payoff Function for the Writer of a Put Option on a Bond*

2. When interest rates fall and bond prices rise, the probability that the buyer of a put will lose increases. If rates fall so that bond prices rise above the exercise price X, the put buyer does not have to exercise the option. Thus, the maximum loss is limited to the size of the up-front put premium (P).

Thus, buying a put option is a strategy to take when interest rates are expected to rise.

Writing a Put Option on a Bond

The fourth strategy is writing (or taking a short position in) a put option on a bond. To do this, the writer or seller receives a fee or premium (P) in return for standing ready to buy bonds at the exercise price (X) should the buyer of the put choose to exercise the option to sell. See the payoff function for writing a put option on a bond in Figure 22–4. Note the following:

1. When interest rates fall and bond prices rise, the writer has an enhanced probability of making a profit. The put buyer is less likely to exercise the option, which would force the option writer to buy the underlying bond. However, the writer's maximum profit is constrained to equal the put premium (P).
2. When interest rates rise and bond prices fall, the writer of the put is exposed to potentially large losses (e.g., $-\pi p$ if bond prices fall to D in Figure 22–4). The put buyer will exercise the option, forcing the option writer to buy the underlying bond at the exercise price. Since bond prices are theoretically unbounded in the downward direction, these losses can be unlimited.

Thus, writing a put option is a strategy to take when interest rates are expected to fall. However, profits are limited and losses are potentially unlimited.

Concept Questions

1. How do interest rate increases affect the payoff from buying a call option on a bond? How do they affect the payoff from writing a call option on a bond?
2. How do interest rate increases affect the payoff from buying a put option on a bond? How do they affect the payoff from writing a put option on a bond?

WRITING VERSUS BUYING OPTIONS

Many small FIs are restricted to buying rather than writing options. Of the two reasons for this, one is economic and the other is regulatory. As we note later, however, large FIs such as money center banks often both write and buy options including caps, floors, and collars, which are complex forms of interest rate options.

Economic Reasons for Not Writing Options

In writing an option, the upside profit potential is truncated, but the downside losses are not. Although such risks may be offset by writing a large number of options at different exercise prices and/or hedging an underlying portfolio of bonds, the writer's downside risk exposure may still be significant. Figure 22–5 indicates this; an FI is long in a bond in its portfolio and seeks to hedge the interest rate risk on that bond by writing a bond call option.

Note that writing the call may hedge the FI when rates fall and bond prices rise; that is, the increase in the value of the bond is offset by losses on the written call. When the reverse occurs and interest rates rise, the FI's profits from writing the call may be insufficient to offset the loss on its bonds. This occurs because the upside profit (per call written) is truncated and equals the premium income (C). If the decrease in the bond value is larger than the premium income (to the left of point A in Figure 22–5), the FI is unable to offset the associated capital value loss on the bond with profits from writing options.

By contrast, hedging the FI's risk by buying a put option on a bond offers the manager a much more attractive alternative. Figure 22–6 shows the gross payoff of a bond and the payoff from buying a put option on it. In this case, any losses on the bond (as rates rise and bond values decrease) are offset with profits from the put option that was bought (points to

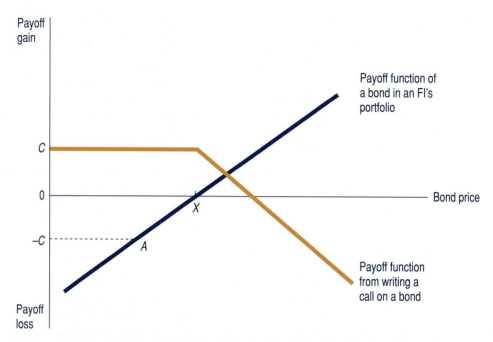

Figure **22–5**   *Writing a Call Option to Hedge the Interest Rate Risk on a Bond*

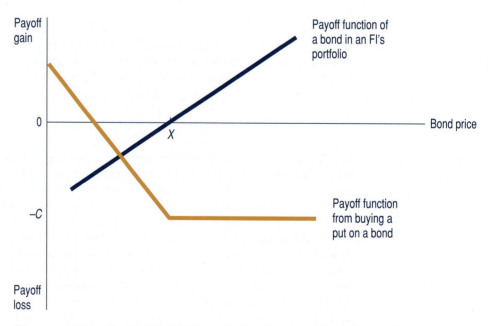

Figure **22–6**   *Buying a Put Option to Hedge the Interest Rate Risk on a Bond*

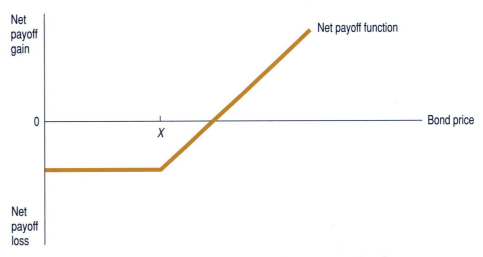

F i g u r e **22–7**   *Net Payoff of Buying a Bond Put and Investing in a Bond*

the left of point X in Figure 22–6). If rates fall, the bond value increases, yet the accompanying losses on the purchased put option positions are limited to the option premiums paid (points to the right of point X). Figure 22–7 shows the net overall payoff from the bond investment combined with the put option hedge. Note in Figure 22–7 that buying a put option truncates the downside losses on the bond following interest rate rises to some maximum amount and scales down the upside profits by the cost of bond price risk insurance—the put premium—leaving some positive upside profit potential. Notice too that the combination of being long in the bond and buying a put option on a bond mimics the payoff function of buying a call option (compare Figures 22–1 and 22–7).

Regulatory Reasons

naked options

Option positions that do not identifiably hedge an underlying asset or liability.

FIs also buy options rather than write options for regulatory reasons. Regulators consider writing options, especially **naked options** that do not identifiably hedge an underlying asset or liability position, to be risky because of the unlimited loss potential. Indeed, bank regulators prohibit banks from writing puts or calls in certain areas of risk management.

Futures versus Options Hedging

To understand the differences between using futures versus options contracts to hedge interest rate risk, compare the payoff gains illustrated in Figure 22–8 (for futures contracts) with those in Figure 22–6 (for option contracts). A hedge with futures contracts reduces volatility in payoff gains on both the upside and downside of interest rate movements. That is, if the FI in Figure 22–8 loses value on the bond resulting from an interest rate increase (to the left of point X), a gain on the futures contract offsets the loss. If the FI gains value on the bond due to an interest rate decrease (to the right of point X), however, a loss on the futures contract offsets the gain.

In comparison, the hedge with the option contract completely offsets losses but only partly offsets gains. That is, in Figure 22–6, if the FI loses value on the bond due to an interest rate increase (to the left of point X), a gain on the options contract offsets the loss.

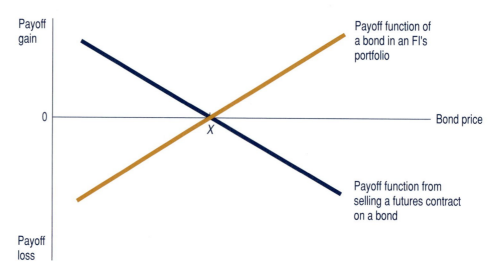

F i g u r e **22–8**   *Buying a Futures Contract to Hedge the Interest Rate Risk on a Bond*

However, if the FI gains value on the bond due to an interest rate decrease (to the right of point *X*), the gain is offset only to the extent that the FI loses the option premium (because it never exercises the option). Thus, the option hedge protects the FI against value losses when interest rates move against the on-balance-sheet securities but, unlike futures hedging, does not reduce value when interest rates move in favor of on-balance-sheet securities.

Concept Q u e s t i o n s

1.   What are the economic reasons that FIs do not write options?
2.   What are the regulatory reasons that an FI might choose to buy options rather than write them?

A C T U A L
B O N D   O P T I O N S

open interest

The outstanding stock of put or call contracts.

futures option

An option contract that, when exercised, results in the delivery of a futures contract as the underlying asset.

FIs have a wide variety of OTC and exchange-traded options available. Figure 22–9 is from the *Wall Street Journal's* business section reporting exchange-traded interest rate options traded on the Chicago Board of Options Exchange (CBOE) on October 24, 1997. These contracts are rarely traded, however. In actual practice, most pure bond options trade OTC. This happens not because interest rate or bond options are not used, although the **open interest** is relatively small, but because the preferred method of hedging is an option on an interest rate futures contract. See these **futures options** on bonds in Figure 22–10. Bond or interest rate futures options are generally preferred to options on the underlying bond because they combine the favorable liquidity, credit risk, homogeneity, and marking-to-market features of futures with the same asymmetric payoff functions as regular puts and calls.

CBOE INTEREST OPTIONS

Friday, October 24, 1997

OPTIONS ON SHORT-TERM INTEREST RATES (IRX)

Strike	Calls-Last			Puts-Last		
Price	Nov	Dec	Jan	Nov	Dec	Jan
52 ½	....	3/16	....	....	....	.....

Total call volume 80   Total call open int. 1

Total put volume 0   Total put open int. 391

IRX levels: high 50.40; Low 49.80; Close 50.10, +0.40

30 YEAR TREASURY YIELD OPTION (TYX)

Strike	Calls-Last			Puts-Last		
Price	Nov	Dec	Jan	Nov	Dec	Jan
60	3 1/4	....	....	....	....	13/16
62½	1 7/8	2 1/8	2 ½	7/8	....	....
65	7/16	7/8	1 ½	2 9/16	....	....
70	.....	.....	.....	7 1/8	....	....

Total call volume 150   Total call open int. 2,846

Total put volume 145   Total put open int. 1,866

TYX levels: high 63.55; Low 62.65; Close 62.92, -0.28

F i g u r e **22–9**   *Interest Rate Options, October 24, 1997*

Specifically, when the FI hedges by buying put options on bond futures, if interest rates rise and bond prices fall, the exercise of the put causes the FI to deliver a bond futures contract to the writer. The futures price itself reflects the price of the underlying deliverable bond such as a 20-year, 8 percent coupon T-bond; see Figure 22–10. As a result, a profit on futures options may be made to offset the loss on the market value of bonds held directly in the FI's portfolio. If interest rates fall and bond and futures prices rise, the buyer of the futures option will not exercise the put, and the losses on the bond futures put option are limited to the put premium. Thus, if on October 24, 1997, the FI had bought one $100,000 November 1997 T-bond futures put option at a strike price of $117 but did not exercise the option, the FI's loss equals the put premium of 34/64 per $100, or $531.25 per $100,000 contract. Offsetting these losses, however, would be an increase in the market value of the FI's underlying bond portfolio. Unlike futures positions in Chapter 21, a net upside profit potential remains when interest rates fall and FIs use put options on futures to hedge interest rate risk.

Concept Questions

1. Why are bond or interest rate futures options generally preferred to options on the underlying bond?
2. What is the outcome if an FI hedges by buying put options on futures and interest rates rise (i.e., bond prices fall)?

INTEREST RATE

T-BONDS (CBT)
$100,000; points and 64ths of 100%

Strike Price	Calls-Settle Nov	Dec	Mar	Puts-Settle Nov	Dec	Mar
115	1-49	2-18	....	cl	0-33	....
116	0-50	1-37	2-49	0-02	0-53	2-19
117	0-08	1-03	....	0-34	1-17	....
118	0-01	0-41	1-54	1-19	1-56	3-22
119	cl	0-24	....	2-17	2-38	....
120	cl	0-15	1-11	3-17	3-29	4-42

Est. vol. 170,000;
Th vol. 140,797 calls; 111,659 puts
Op. Int. Thur 613,857 calls; 525,772 puts

T-NOTES (CBT)
$100,000; points and 64ths of 100%

Strike Price	Calls-Settle Nov	Dec	Mar	Puts-Settle Nov	Dec	Mar
108	2-26	2-47	2-57	0-01	0-04	0-35
109	1-26	1-53	2-12	0-01	0-09	0-53
110	0-24	1-03	1-37	0-01	0-23	1-13
111	0-05	0-32	1-07	0-24	0-52	1-47
112	0-01	0-13	0-49	1-22	1-32	2-23
113	0-01	0-04	0-32	....	2-23	....

Est vol 35,000 Th 23,575 calls 15,647 puts
Op int Thur 227,566 calls 233,255 puts

5 YR TREAS NOTES (CBT)
$100,000; points and 64ths of 100%

Strike Price	Calls-Settle Nov	Dec	Mar	Puts-Settle Nov	Dec	Mar
10650	....	1-19	....	0-01	0-06	0-32
10700	0-44	0-56	1-19	0-01	0-12	0-43
10750	0-13	0-35	1-00	0-02	0-22	0-56
10800	0-03	0-19	0-49	0-22	0-38	1-09
10850	0-01	0-10	0-38	0-52	0-61	....
10900	0-01	0-05	0-26	1-20	1-23	....

Est vol 12,000 Th 3,375 calls 8,948 puts
Op int Thur 51,702 calls 62,802 puts

MUNI BOND INDEX (CBT)
$1,000; times Bond Buyer MBI

Strike Price	Calls-Settle Oct	Dec	Mar	Puts-Settle Oct	Dec	Mar
118	....	....	....	....	0-42	....
119	1-26	2-18	....	0-01	0-56	....
120	0-01	1-58	2-50	....	1-22	....
121	0-01	0-52	....	....	....	....
122	0-01	0-33	....	....	....	....
123	....	0-27	....	....	....	....

Est vol 700 Th 0 calls 1,500 puts
Op int Thur 4,937 calls 13,181 puts

EURODOLLAR (CME)
$ million; pts. of 100%

Strike Price	Calls-Settle Nov	Dec	Jan	Puts-Settle Nov	Dec	Jan
9375	....	0.42	....	0.00	0.01	0.02
9400	0.18	0.19	0.20	0.01	0.02	0.07
9425	0.02	0.03	0.07	0.10	0.11	0.19
9450	0.00	0.01	0.02	0.33	0.34	....
9475	....	0.00	....	....	0.58	....
9500	....	0.00	....	....	0.83	....

Est. vol. 141,659;
Th vol. 124,856 calls; 91,478 puts
Op. int. Thur 1,288,073 calls; 1,288,371 puts

1 YR. MID-CURVE EURODLR (CME)
$1,000,000 contract units; pts. of 100%

Strike Price	Calls-Settle Nov	Dec	Jan	Puts-Settle Nov	Dec	Jan
9325	....	0.63	....	0.00	0.02	....
9350	0.38	0.41	....	0.02	0.05	0.07
9375	0.18	0.22	0.25	0.07	0.11	0.15
9400	0.05	0.10	0.13	0.19	0.24	....
9425	0.01	0.04	0.05	0.40	0.43	....
9450	....	0.01	....	....	....	....

Est vol 21,445 Th 16,650 calls 10,835 puts
Op Int Thur 151,639 calls 165,131 puts

2 YR. MID-CURVE EURODLR (CME)
$1,000,000 contract units; pts. of 100%

Strike Price	Calls-Settle Dec	Mar	....	Puts-Settle Dec	Mar
9325	....	....	....	0.02	0.08
9350	0.29	0.38	....	0.07	0.15
9375	0.14	0.23	....	0.17	0.25
9400	0.05	0.12	....	....	....
9425	0.01	0.06	....	....	....
9450	....	....	....	....	....

Est vol 450 Th 0 calls 0 puts
Op Int Thur 22,515 calls 22,855 puts

EUROMARK (LIFFE)
$1 million; pts. of 100%

Strike Price	Calls-Settle Nov	Dec	Jan	Puts-Settle Nov	Dec	Jan
9575	0.43	0.44	0.19	....	0.01	0.06
9600	0.19	0.21	0.06	0.01	0.03	0.18
9625	0.03	0.05	0.02	0.10	0.12	0.39
9650	0.01	0.01	....	0.33	0.33	0.62
9675	....	....	....	0.57	0.57	0.87
9700	....	....	....	0.82	0.82	1.12

Vol Fr 9,749 calls 4,179 puts
Op Int Thur 361,763 calls 305,900 puts

LONG GILT (LIFFE)
£50,000; 64ths of 100%

Strike Price	Calls-Settle Nov	Dec	Jan	Puts-Settle Nov	Dec	Jan
117	1-50	2-08	2-24	....	0-22	0-40
118	0-50	1-26	1-47	....	0-40	0-63
119	....	0-54	1-13	0-14	1-04	1-29
120	....	0-29	0-51	1-14	1-43	2-03
121	....	0-15	0-32	2-14	2-29	2-48
122	....	0-08	0-19	3-14	3-22	3-35

Vol Fr 2,500 calls 816 puts
Op Int Thur 66,360 calls 37,310 puts

GERMAN GOVT BOND (LIFFE)
$250,000 marks; pts. of 100%

Strike Price	Calls-Settle Nov	Dec	Jan	Puts-Settle Nov	Dec	Jan
1.13	1.13	1.35	1.06	....	0.22	0.66
10150	0.63	0.97	0.79	....	0.34	0.89
10200	0.13	0.66	0.56	....	0.53	1.16
10250	....	0.41	0.39	0.37	0.78	1.49
10300	....	0.24	0.26	0.87	1.11	1.86
10350	....	0.13	0.16	1.37	1.50	2.26

Vol Fr 28,239 calls 22,791 puts
Op Int Thur 274,045 calls 317,538 puts

F i g u r e **22–10**   *Futures Options on Interest Rates, October 24, 1997*

CAPS, FLOORS, AND COLLARS

cap

A call option on interest rates, often with multiple exercise dates.

Buying a **cap** means buying a call option or a succession of call options on interest rates.[2] Specifically, if interest rates rise above the cap rate, the seller of the cap—usually a bank—

---

[2] Note that a *cap* can be viewed as a *call option on interest rates* (as discussed here) or as a *bond option on bond prices* since rising interest rates mean falling bond prices. Similarly, *a floor* (discussed in the next paragraph) can be viewed as a put option on interest rates or a call option on bond prices. We follow market convention and discuss caps and floors as options on interest rates rather than on bond prices.

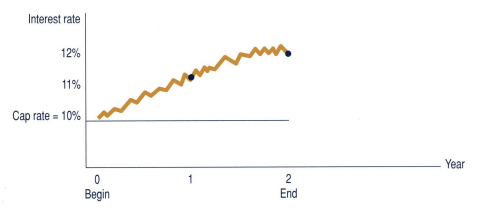

F i g u r e **22–11**   *Hypothetical Path of Interest Rates during a Cap Agreement*

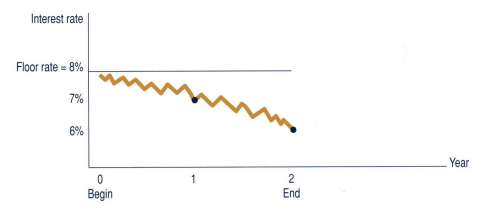

F i g u r e **22–12**   *Hypothetical Path of Interest Rates during a Floor Agreement*

compensates the buyer—for example, another FI—in return for an up-front premium. Suppose that two FIs enter a two-year cap agreement with a notional value of $1 million. The cap rate is 10 percent and payments are settled once a year based on year-end interest rates. For interest rate movements shown in Figure 22–11, the cap writer owes the cap buyer (11 percent minus 10 percent) times $1 million, or $100,000 at the end of year 1 and (12 percent minus 10 percent) times $1 million, or $200,000 at the end of year 2. As a result, buying an interest rate cap is like buying insurance against an (excessive) increase in interest rates. A cap agreement can have one or many exercise dates.

floor

A put option on interest rates, often with multiple exercise dates.

Buying a **floor** is similar to buying a put option on interest rates. If interest rates fall below the floor rate, the seller of the floor compensates the buyer in return for an up-front premium. For example, suppose that two FIs enter a two-year floor agreement with a notional value of $1 million. The floor rate is 8 percent and payments are settled once a year based on year-end rates. For interest rate movements shown in Figure 22–12, the floor writer owes the floor buyer (8 percent minus 7 percent) times $1 million, or $100,000 at the end of year 1 and (8 percent minus 6 percent) times $1 million, or $200,000 at the end of year 2. As with caps, floor agreements can have one or many exercise dates.

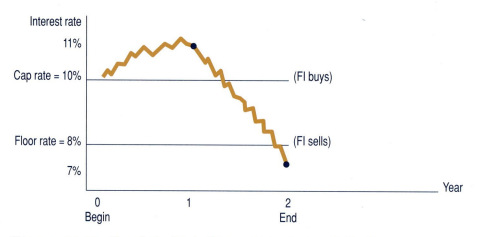

F i g u r e **22–13**   *Hypothetical Path of Interest Rates during a Collar Agreement*

collar

A position taken simultaneously in a cap and a floor.

A **collar** occurs when an FI takes a simultaneous position in a cap and a floor, usually *buying* a cap and *selling* a floor. The idea here is that the FI wants to hedge itself against rising rates but wants to finance the cost of the cap. One way to do this is to sell a floor and use the premiums on the floor to pay the premium on the purchased cap. For example, suppose that a FI enters into a two-year collar agreement with a notional value of $1 million. The floor rate is 8 percent and the cap rate is 10 percent. Payments are settled once a year based on year-end rates. For interest rate movements shown in Figure 22–13, the collar buyer, the FI, gains (11 percent minus 10 percent) times $1 million, or $100,000 at the end of year 1. However, since the FI has written or sold a floor to another FI to finance the cap purchase, it pays (8 percent minus 7 percent) times $1 million, or $100,000 at the end of year 2.

In general, FIs purchase interest rate caps if they are exposed to losses when interest rates rise. Usually, this happens if FIs are funding assets with floating-rate liabilities such as notes indexed to the London interbank offering rate (or some other cost of funds) and they have fixed rate assets or they are net long in bonds, or—in a macrohedging context—their duration gap, or D_A minus kD_L, is greater than 0. By contrast, FIs purchase floors when they have fixed costs of debt and have variable rates (returns) on assets or they are net short in bonds, or D_A minus kD_L is less than 0. Finally, FIs purchase collars when they are concerned about excessive volatility of interest rates or more commonly to finance cap or floor positions.

Concept   Q u e s t i o n s

1.   What is the difference between a *cap* and a *collar*?
2.   Under what conditions would an FI buy a floor?

S U M M A R Y

This chapter discussed the use of option-type contracts available to FI managers to hedge interest rate risk. In particular, it noted that the unique nature of the asymmetric payoff function of option-type contracts often makes them more attractive to FIs than other hedging instruments such as forwards and futures. The appendixes to this chapter discuss some technical issues related to the determination of how many options should be used to hedge a particular asset position and a particular duration gap position and the role of credit options in hedging loans and loan portfolio risk.

P E R T I N E N T   W E B   S I T E S

Chicago Board of Options Exchange (CBOE)   http://www.cboe.com/

Chicago Board of Trade (CBT)   http://www.cbot.com/

Chicago Mercantile Exchange (CME)   http://www.cme.com/

London International Financial Futures Exchange (LIFFE)   http://www.liffe.com/

Options

1. How does hedging with options differ from hedging with forward or futures contracts?
2. Consider the following.
   a. What are the two ways to use call and put options on T-bonds to generate positive cash flows when interest rates decline?
   b. When and how can an FI use options on T-bonds to hedge its assets and liabilities against interest rate declines?
   c. Is it more appropriate for FIs to hedge against a decline in interest rates with long calls or short puts?
3. In each of the following cases, indicate whether it is appropriate for an FI to buy a put or a call option to hedge the appropriate risk.
   a. A commercial bank plans to issue CDs in three months.
   b. An insurance company plans to buy bonds in two months.
   c. A thrift plans to sell Treasury securities next month.
   d. A U.S. bank lends to a French company; the loan is payable in francs.
   e. A mutual fund plans to sell its holding of stock in a German company.
   f. A finance company has assets with a duration of 6 years and liabilities with a duration of 13 years.
4. Consider Figure 22–10. What are the prices paid for the following futures options:
   a. March T-bond calls at 116.
   b. March 5 Year T-note puts at 10750.
   c. January Eurodollar calls at 9450.
5. Consider Figure 22–10 again.
   a. What happens to the price of a call when
      1. The exercise price increases?
      2. The time until expiration increases?
   b. What happens to the price of the put when these two variables increase?
6. Suppose that an FI manager writes a call option on a T-bond futures contract with an exercise price of 114 at a quoted price of 0-55. What type of opportunities or obligations does the manager have?
7. Suppose that a pension fund manager anticipates the purchase of a 20-year, 8 percent coupon T-bond at the end of two years. Interest rates are assumed to change only once every year at year-end. At that time, it is equally probable that interest rates will increase or decrease 1 percent. When purchased in two years, the T-bond will pay interest semiannually. Currently, it is selling at par.
   a. What is the pension fund manager's interest rate risk exposure?
   b. How can the pension fund manager use options to hedge that interest rate risk exposure?
8. In what sense do options on interest rate futures contracts offer more favorable liquidity than options on bond contracts?
9. Contrast the use of financial futures options with the use of options on cash instruments to construct interest rate hedges.
10. When would an FI prefer to use caps and floors as hedging devices? When would an FI use collars as hedging devices?

11. An FI has purchased a $200 million cap (i.e., call options on interest rates) of 9 percent at a premium of 0.65 percent of face value. A $200 million floor (i.e., put options on interest rates) of 4 percent is also available at a premium of 0.69 percent of face value.

    a. If interest rates rise to 10 percent, what amount does the FI receive? What is its net savings after deducting the premium?

    b. If the FI *also* purchases a floor, what is its net savings if interest rates rise to 11 percent? What is its net savings if interest rates fall to 3 percent?

    c. If instead the FI sells (writes) the floor, what is its net savings if interest rates rise to 11 percent? What if rates fall to 3 percent?

    d. What amount of floors should the FI sell to compensate for its purchases of caps given the stated premiums?

12. Go to the CBOT web site and look up the contract specifications for its Long-Term Inflation-Indexed U.S. Treasury Note Futures and Options.

The following questions are related to the Appendix material.

13. When an FI buys a default option, is it buying a put option or a call option?

14. A mutual fund plans to purchase $10,000,000 of 20-year T-bonds in two months. These bonds have a duration of 11 years. The mutual fund is concerned about interest rates changing over the next four months and is considering a hedge with a two-month option on a T-bond futures. Two-month calls with a strike price of 105 are priced at 1-25, and puts of the same maturity and exercise price are priced at 2-09. The δ of the call is .5 and the δ of the put is –.7. The current price of a deliverable T-bond is 103-08 per $100 of face value, and its modified duration is nine years.

    a. What type of option should the mutual fund purchase?

    b. How many options should it purchase?

    c. What is the cost of these options?

15. Corporate Bank has $840 million of assets with a duration of 12 years and liabilities worth $720 million with a duration of 7 years. It is concerned about preserving the value of its equity in the event of an increase in interest rates and is contemplating a macrohedge with interest rate options. The call and put options have a δ of .4 and -.4, respectively, the price of an underlying T-bond is 104-34, and its modified duration is 7.6 years.

    a. What type of option should Corporate Bank use to hedge?

    b. How many options should it purchase?

16. An FI has a $200 million asset portfolio with an average duration of 6.5 years. The average duration of its $160 million liabilities is 4.5 years. It uses put options on T-bonds to hedge against unexpected rises in interest rates. The average δ of the put options has been estimated at –0.3, and the average duration of T-bonds is –7 years. The current market value of the T-bonds is $96,000.

    a. What is the modified duration of the T-bonds if the current level of interest rates is 10 percent?

    b. How many put option contracts should it purchase to hedge its exposure against rises in interest rates? The face value of the T-bonds is $100,000.

    c. If put options on T-bonds are selling at a premium of $1.25 per face value of $100, what is the total cost of hedging using options on T-bonds?

17. What is a credit spread call option?

APPENDIX A:
MICROHEDGING WITH OPTIONS

Figures 22–6 and 22–7 graphically describe the way that buying a put option on a bond can potentially hedge the interest rate risk exposure of an FI that holds bonds as part of its asset investment portfolio. This section uses a simple example to demonstrate how buying a put option works mechanically as a device to hedge a bond held as an asset. Given the economic and regulatory reasons for not writing options, the examination is limited to buying or taking a long position in put options.

Microhedging with Options

Recall from Chapter 18 that for an asset or liability on the FI's balance sheet

$$\Delta P = -D \times P \times \frac{\Delta R}{1 + R} \tag{1A}$$

Let ΔO be the total change in the value of a put position in T-bonds. This can be decomposed into

$$\Delta O = (N_o \times \Delta o) \tag{2A}$$

where N_o is the number of \$100,000 options on T-bond contracts to be purchased (the number for which we are solving), and Δo is the change in the dollar value for each \$100,000 face value T-bond put option contract.

The change in the dollar value of each contract (Δo) can be further decomposed into

$$\Delta o = \frac{do}{dB} \times \frac{dB}{dR_b} \times \frac{\Delta R_b}{1 + R_b} \tag{3A}$$

This decomposition needs some explanation. The first term (do/dB) shows the change in the value of an option for each \$1 dollar change in the underlying bond. This is called the *delta of an option* (δ) and lies between 0 and 1. For call options, the delta has a positive sign since the value of the call rises when bond prices rise. For put options, the delta has a negative sign since the value of the put option falls when bond prices rise. The second term (dB/dR_b) shows how the market value of a bond changes if interest rates rise by 1 basis point. This value of 1 basis point term can be linked to duration. Specifically, we know from Chapter 18 that

$$\frac{dB}{B} = -MD \times dR_b \tag{4A}$$

That is, the percentage change in the bond's price for a small change in rates is proportional to the bond's modified duration (MD). Equation (4A) can be rearranged by cross multiplying as

$$\frac{dB}{dR_b} = -MD \times B \tag{5A}$$

Thus, the term dB / dR_b is equal to minus the modified duration on the bond (MD) times the current market value of the T-bond (B) underlying the option contract. As a result, we can rewrite Equation (3A) as

$$\Delta o = [(\delta) \times (-MD) \times B \times \frac{\Delta R_b}{1 + R_b}] \tag{6A}$$

for a call option contract and

$$\Delta o = [(-\delta) \times (-MD) \times B \times \frac{\Delta R_b}{1 + R_b}] \tag{7A}$$

for a put option contract, where $\Delta R_b / 1 + R_b$ is the discounted shock to interest rates (i.e., the number of basis points by which rates change).

Decomposing Δo, the change in the total value of an option position (ΔO) is

$$\Delta O = N_o \times [\delta \times (-MD) \times B \times \frac{\Delta R_b}{1 + R_b}] \tag{8A}$$

for a call option, and

$$\Delta O = N_o \times [-\delta \times (-MD) \times B \times \frac{\Delta R_b}{1 + R_b}] \tag{9A}$$

for a put option,[3] where B is the value of the bond underlying the option contract, δ is the value change of an option for a \$1 change in the value of the underlying bond, and MD is the underlying bond's modified duration.

To hedge net worth exposure, we require the profit on the OBS put options to just offset the loss of on-balance-sheet assets (bonds) when rates rise (or bond prices fall). That is

$$\Delta O = \Delta P \tag{10A}$$

or

$$N_o \times [|\delta| \times (-MD) \times B \times \frac{\Delta R_b}{1 + R_b}] = -D \times P \times \frac{\Delta R}{1 + R} \tag{11A}$$

If we assume there is no basis risk (i.e., $\Delta R / 1 + R = \Delta R_b / 1 + R_b$) we can solve for N_o, the number of put options to buy

$$N_o = \frac{D \times P}{|\delta| \times MD \times B} \tag{12A}$$

Buying a Put Option.   An FI buys a put option when interest rates are expected to rise in such a way that the FI will lose value on its balance sheet assets such as T-bonds.

E X A M P L E   2 2 – 1 A

Hedge of Interest Rate Risk Using a Put Option

Consider the FI in Example 21–1 that on October 24, 1997, has a 20-year, \$1 million face value bond in its asset portfolio. The bond's duration is nine years and the bond is valued at

---

[3] Rather than make this distinction for the remaining derivation, we shall simply use the absolute value of δ for the rest of the discussion. The sign appended to δ changes from positive for a call option to negative for a put option because the call option gives the option holder the right to buy the underlying security at the exercise price, and the put option gives the option holder the right to sell the underlying security. Thus, the call option increases in value but the put option decreases in value as the underlying security's value increases (i.e., the call option holder makes more on the exercise while the put option holder makes less on exercise).

$97 per $100 of face value, or $970,000. The FI manager expects interest rates to rise by 2 percent from the current level of 8 percent over the next three months, which would result in a loss in capital value of $161,667 on the balance sheet.

$$\Delta P = -9 \times \$970,000 \times \frac{.02}{1.08} = -\$161,667$$

To hedge this loss, the FI could buy a put option on T-bond futures for the three-month period (October 24, 1997, through January 24, 1998). According to the data in Figure 22–10, the bank can purchase March 1998 put options on T-bond futures contracts with an exercise price of $116 per $100 of face value for a put premium of $2 19/64 per $100 of face value or at a premium cost of $2,296.875 per $100,000 put option contract. The δ on the put option is $-.7$ (i.e., the value of the put option increases by 70 cents as the value—price—of the underlying T-bond decreases by $1—due to an interest rate increase). Suppose that the current price on the deliverable T-bond is 105 9/32 per $100 of face value (or for the minimum $100,000 face value of one option contract, $B = \$105,281.25$) and the modified duration on the T-bond underlying the option on T-bond futures contract is 7.5 years.

Solving for N_o, the number of put options to buy, we get

$$N_o = \frac{9 \text{ years} \times \$970,000}{.7 \times 7.5 \text{ years} \times \$105,281.25}$$

$$= 15.7944 \text{ put option contracts}$$

Like futures contracts, options cannot be bought in fractions of a contract. Thus, the bank buys 15 put options. The total premium cost to the FI of buying these puts is the price (premium) of each put times the number of puts

$$\text{Cost} = N_o \times \text{Put premium per contract} \qquad (13A)$$
$$= 15 \times 2,296.875$$
$$= \$34,453.125$$

Remember that the value of the asset being hedged is $970,000.   • • •

Table 22–1A shows the on- and off-balance-sheet effects of the increase in interest rates on the bond and the hedge in the put option market. To see the effect of a perfect hedge, we assume that the FI can buy exactly 15.7944 put option contracts. Notice that the gain from the bank's position in the put option market, $161,667, exactly offsets the loss on the balance sheet from the bond held in the asset portfolio (see Table 22–1A). The long hedge in the put option market allows the bank to fully hedge against interest rate risk (see Figure 22–6). The cost of doing this is the cost of the put premiums paid to the writer of the option.

In fact, the FI is hedged against any increase in interest rates. Because the FI is fully hedged, a gain in the value of the put option on T-bond futures contracts offsets a loss in value from the bond should rates rise in the next three months (see Figure 22–1A). Notice, however, that if bond rates fall, the change in the FI's capital or net worth strictly increases. As the put option moves out of the money due to the interest rate drop, the opportunity for exercise is eliminated and the FI loses the put premium. This loss is offset, however, by the gains on the bond position (balance sheet assets) that occur as interest rates drop. The larger the drop in interest rates, the more likely are the gains on the bond portfolio to offset the loss of the put premium on the option.

Table **22–1A**

ON- AND OFF-BALANCE-SHEET EFFECTS FROM BUYING A PUT OPTION TO HEDGE

	On-Balance-Sheet	**Off-Balance-Sheet**
Begin hedge October 24, 1997	$1million bond held in asset portfolio. Current interest rate = 8%, duration = 9 years	Buy 15.7944 put options on March 98 T-bond futures
End hedge January 24, 1998	Interest rate increases to 10%	Sell 15.7944 put options on March 98 T-bond futures

Capital value loss on balance sheet:

$$\Delta P = -9 \times \$970,000 \times \frac{.02}{1.08}$$

$$= -\$161,667$$

Real gain on option hedge:

$$\Delta O = 15.7944 \times (-.7) \times (-7.5) \times \$105,281.25 \times \frac{.02^*}{1.08}$$

$$= \$161,667$$

Cost of options = $34,453.125

*Assuming no basis risk (i.e., $\Delta R / 1 + R = \Delta R_b / 1 + R_b$).

F i g u r e **22–1A**   *FI Value Changes On- and Off-Balance-Sheet from Perfect Hedge with a Put Option*

Basis Risk.   It is again important to recognize that in the previous examples, the bank hedged interest rate risk exposure perfectly because basis risk was assumed to be zero (i.e., $\Delta R / 1 + R = \Delta R_b / 1 + R_b$). As discussed in Chapter 21, the introduction of basis risk means that the FI must adjust the number of option contracts it holds to account for the degree to which the rate on the option's underlying security (i.e., T-bond) moves relative to the spot rate on the asset or liability the FI is hedging.

Allowing basis risk to exist, the equation used to determine the number of options to buy to hedge interest rate risk becomes

$$N_o = \frac{D \times P}{|\delta| \times MD \times B \times b} \tag{14A}$$

where b is a measure of the volatility of interest rates (R_b) on the bond underlying the options contract relative to the interest rate that impacts the bond on the bank's balance sheet (R). That is

$$b = \frac{\dfrac{\Delta R_b}{1 + R_b}}{\dfrac{\Delta R}{1 + R}} \tag{15A}$$

EXAMPLE 22–2A

Put Option Hedge with Basis Risk

Refer to Example 22–1A. Suppose that basis risk, b, is 0.92 (i.e., the rate on the option's underlying bond changes by 92 percent of the spot rate change on the asset—bond—being hedged). In Example 22–1A, with no basis risk, the number of options needed to hedge interest rate risk on the bond position is 15.7944 put option contracts. Introducing basis risk, $b = 0.92$

$$N_o = \frac{9 \text{ years} \times \$970,000}{.7 \times 7.5 \text{ years} \times \$105,281.25 \times 0.92} = 17.17 \text{ put option contracts}$$

Additional put option contracts are needed to hedge the risk on the asset because interest rates on the bond underlying the option contract do not move as much as interest rates on the bond held as an asset on the balance sheet.   • • •

APPENDIX B:
MACROHEDGING WITH OPTIONS

Our previous examples show that an option can hedge the interest rate risk on an underlying position in the asset or liability portfolio. Next we determine the put option position that can hedge the interest rate risk of the overall balance sheet; that is, we analyze macrohedging rather than microhedging. As with futures, the use of hedge accounting by regulators and hedging selectivity—the need and desire to bear some interest rate risk for return on equity reasons—favors microhedging over macrohedging.

Chapter 18 discussed the fact that an FI's net worth exposure to an interest rate shock could be represented as

$$\Delta E = -(D_A - kD_L) \times A \times \frac{\Delta R}{1 + R} \tag{1B}$$

where

$$\Delta E = \text{change in the FI's net worth}$$
$$(D_A - kD_L) = \text{FI's duration gap}$$
$$A = \text{size of the FI's assets}$$
$$\frac{\Delta R}{1 + R} = \text{size of the interest rate shock}$$
$$k = \text{FI's leverage ratio } (L/A)$$

Let's say that we wish to determine the optimal number of put options on bonds to buy to insulate the FI against changes in interest rates, given that the FI has a positive duration gap. That is, we want to adopt a bond put option position to generate profits that just offset the loss in on-balance-sheet net worth resulting from a rate shock (where E_0 is the bank's initial equity position).

Fully hedging can be defined as buying a sufficient number of put options (N_o) so that the loss of net worth on the balance sheet (ΔE) when rates rise is just offset by the gain from the hedge, or

$$\Delta O = \Delta E \tag{2B}$$

Substituting in the appropriate expressions for each, we get

$$N_o \times [\delta \times (-MD) \times B \times \frac{\Delta R_b}{1 + R_b}] = -[D_A - kD_L] \times A \times \frac{\Delta R}{1 + R} \tag{3B}$$

Assuming that no basis risk (i.e., $\Delta R/1 + R = \Delta R_b/1 + R_b$) exists, we can solve for N_o (the optimal number of put options to buy)

$$N_o = \frac{(D_A - kD_L) \times A}{\delta \times MD \times B} \tag{4B}$$

E X A M P L E   2 2 – 1 B

Calculation of the Number of Option Contracts Needed for a Macrohedge

Suppose, as in Chapter 21, that D_A equals 5, D_L equals 3, k equals .9, and A equals $100 million. Rates are expected to rise from 10 to 11 percent over the next six months, which would result in a $2.09 million loss in value to the bank. Suppose also that δ of the put option is .5, MD equals 8.82 for the bond underlying the option contract, and that the current market value of $100,000 face value long-term Treasury bonds underlying the option contract, B, equals $97,000. Solving for N_o, the number of put option contracts to buy

$$N_o = \frac{(5 - .9(3)) \times \$100 \text{ million}}{.5 \times 8.82 \times \$97,000} = 537.672 \text{ contracts}$$

If we slightly underhedge, this can be rounded down to 537 contracts.

Suppose that T-bond put option premiums are quoted at $2½ per $100 of face value for the contract nearest to maturity, or $2,500 per $100,000 put contract. Then the cost of macrohedging the gap with put options is

$$\text{Cost} = 537 \times \$2,500 = \$1,342,500$$

Remember that the total assets of the bank were assumed to be $100 million.

Figure 22–1B summarizes the change in the FI's overall value from a movement in interest rates and the offsetting change in value from the hedge in the put option market. If rates increase as predicted, the bank's gap exposure results in a decrease in net worth. This decrease is offset with a gain on the put options position held by the FI. Should rates decrease, however, the resulting increase in net worth is not offset by a decrease in an out-of-the-money put option.

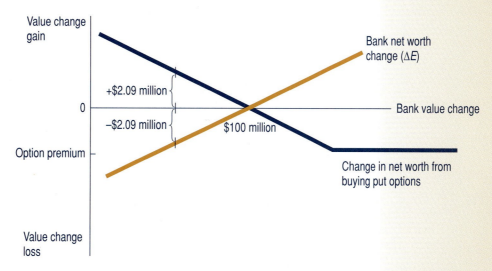

F i g u r e **22–1B**   *Buying Put Options to Hedge an FI's Interest Rate GAP Risk Exposure*

APPENDIX C:

HEDGING CREDIT RISK WITH OPTIONS

Options also have a potential use in hedging an FI's credit risk. Although FIs are always likely to be willing to bear some credit risk as part of the intermediation process (i.e., exploiting their comparative advantage to bear such risk), options may allow them to modify that level of exposure selectively. In Chapter 21, we stated that an FI could seek an appropriate credit risk hedge by selling credit forward contracts. Rather than using credit forwards to hedge, an FI has at least two alternative credit option derivatives with which it can hedge its on-balance-sheet credit risk, a credit spread call option and a default option.

credit spread call option

A call option whose payoff increases as a yield spread decreases below a stated spread.

A **credit spread call option** is a call option whose payoff increases as the (default) yield spread on the borrower's specified benchmark bond increases above some exercise spread, S*. An FI concerned that the risk on a loan will increase can purchase a credit spread call option to hedge the increased credit risk.

Figure 22–1C illustrates the change in the FI's capital value and its payoff from the credit risk call option as a function of the credit spread. As the credit spread increases on the FI's loan to a borrower, the value of the loan and, consequently, of the FI's net worth decreases. If the characteristics of the benchmark bond (i.e., change in credit spread) are the same as that on the FI's loan, however, the loss of net worth on the balance sheet is offset with a gain from the credit spread call option. Should the required credit spread on the FI's loan decrease (perhaps because the credit quality of the borrower improves over the loan period), the value of the FI's net worth increases but the credit spread call option will expire out of the money. As a result, the FI will suffer a maximum loss equal to the required (call) premium on the credit option, which will be offset against the market value gain of the loan in the portfolio (which is reflected in a positive increase in the FI's net worth).[4]

---

[4] For additional discussion, see J. D. Finnerty, "Credit Derivatives, Infrastructure Finance, and Emerging Market Risk, *The Financier, ACMT,* February 1996, pp. 64–75.

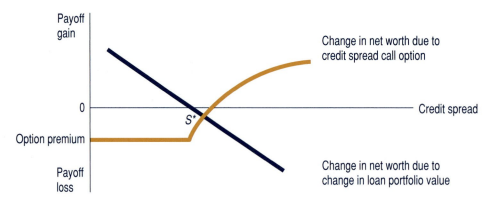

Figure 22–1C   *Buying Credit Spread Call Options to Hedge Credit Risk*

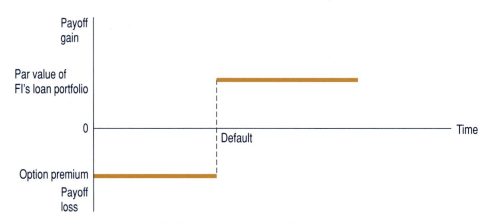

Figure 22–2C   *Buying a Default Option to Hedge Credit Risk*

default option

An option that pays the par value of a loan in the event of a loan default.

A **default option** is an option that pays a stated amount in the event of a loan default (the extreme case of increased credit risk). As shown in Figure 22–2C, the FI can purchase a default option covering the par value of a loan (or loans) in its portfolio. In the event of a loan default, the option writer pays the FI the par value of the defaulted loans. If the loans are paid off in accordance with the loan agreement, however, the default option expires unexercised. As a result, the FI will suffer a maximum loss on the option equal to the premium (cost) of buying the default option from the writer (seller).

Chapter Twenty-three

Swaps

The market for swaps has grown enormously in recent years; the notional value of swap contracts outstanding by U.S. commercial banks was $9.56 trillion in 1997 (see Chapter 20). Currently such a glut of swaps exists in the marketplace that trading revenue generated is deteriorating (see Contemporary Perspectives Box 23–1). Commercial banks and investment banks are major participants in the market as dealers, traders, and users for proprietary hedging purposes. Insurance companies have only recently adopted hedging strategies using swaps, but their interest in this market is growing quickly (see Contemporary Perspectives Box 23–2). A dealer can act as an intermediary or third party by putting a swap together and/or creating an over-the-counter (OTC) secondary market for swaps. This massive growth of the swap market, especially in the 1980s, raised regulatory concerns regarding the credit risk exposures of banks engaging in this market. This growth was one of the motivations behind the introduction of the Bank for International Settlements (BIS)-sponsored risk-based capital adequacy reforms described in Chapter 16. In addition, in recent years there has been a growth in exotic swap products such as "inverse floater" swaps that have raised considerable controversy, especially since the bankruptcy of Orange County.

The five generic types of swaps, in order of their quantitative importance, are *interest*

Contemporary Perspectives 23–1

Risk Management: Oversupply of Interest Swaps Slows Growth in Trade

A glut of "plain vanilla" derivatives in the marketplace apparently is slowing trading revenue growth for banks that deal in the financial contracts.

The Office of the Comptroller of the Currency reported a 6 percent increase in total notional value of derivatives in the second quarter, but a 3 percent drop in trading revenues, mainly due to a drop in interest rate contract revenues.

Traders say the oversupply in 5- and 10-year fixed rate contracts is depressing trading revenues, and may prompt dealers to return to marketing more exotic, high-yielding instruments.

Volume in the interest rate swap market has grown in recent months because banks and other corporations have been issuing a lot of debt, said

Simon Lack, head of derivatives and proprietary trading at Chase Manhattan Bank. These businesses generally want to hedge interest-rate risk, so they arrange swaps of fixed-rate for floating from a derivatives dealers.

"It's been a case of everything trying to go the same way at the same time," Mr. Lack said.

Because more seek fixed-rate deals than usual, the swap spread above U.S. Treasury notes has tightened as derivatives dealers are becoming less willing to buy fixed-rate instruments.

Spreads on 5- and 10-year interest rate swaps fell to 22.5 basis points and 30 basis points, respectively, over underlying securities, according to a recent report by Salomon Brothers.

The decline, which picked up steam in April, means the derivatives are less attractive to users, because the difference between the hedge and the cost of comparable Treasury securities has dwindled.

"It is difficult to quantify the effects" of these developments, said Charbel E. Abouchared, managing director and head of U.S. trading at CIBC Woody Gundy. "There are lower spreads, but also higher volume. But overall I'd say the higher volume has not made up for the lower spreads."

Mr. Abourchared said his shop is pursuing more structured deals, arbitrages, and other kinds of trades that mean more complexity as well as more profits.

SOURCE: Aaron Elstein, The *American Banker,* November 7, 1996, p. 20. Reprinted with permission–American Banker.

rate swaps, currency swaps, commodity swaps, equity swaps, and *credit risk swaps*.[1] The instrument underlying the swap may change, but the basic principle of a swap agreement is the same in that it involves the transacting parties' restructuring of asset or liability cash flows in a preferred direction. We consider next the role of the two major generic types of swaps—interest rate and currency—in hedging FI risk. We then examine the credit risk characteristics of these instruments and their possible use in hedging and arbitraging credit risk.

---

[1] There are also *swaptions*, which are options to enter into a swap agreement at some preagreed contract terms (e.g., a fixed rate of 10 percent) at some time in the future in return for the payment of an up-front premium.

Contemporary Perspectives 23–2

Insurance Investors Sharpen Skills

The insurance industry is moving toward the investment practices of mutual fund managers and institutional managers, says a study by Coopers & Lybrand Consulting, the management consulting division of the professional services firm.

The study was sponsored by 24 major insurance companies with combined assets of more than $700 billion. The survey covered approximately 55 percent of the life insurance industry's general account

assets and 12 percent of the property and casualty sector's assets.

Here are some of the key findings, which were released on Oct.22: 71 percent of respondents have altered investment management oversight or risk management practices in the last two years, by establishing tighter controls and upgrading risk management controls. 92 percent of respondents use simulation of interest rate shifts to stress test their portfolios. 88 percent use derivatives,

and of these users 90 percent use plain vanilla interest rate swaps, 62 percent use basic currency swaps and 57 percent use structured nonvanilla swaps. 79 percent of participants use duration matching targets. The three factors that have the greatest impact on actively managed bond portfolios are relative value considerations, duration cash/flow matching and asset/liability management.

SOURCE: Michelle Clayton, The *Insurance Accountant,* October 28, 1996, p. 1. Courtesy of The *Insurance Accountant,* an *American Banker* newsletter.

INTEREST RATE SWAPS

interest rate swap

An exchange of fixed-interest payments for floating-interest payments by two counterparties.

swap buyer

By convention, a party that makes the fixed-rate payments in an interest rate swap transaction.

swap seller

By convention, a party that makes the floating-rate payments in an interest rate swap transaction.

By far the largest segment of the U.S. commercial bank swap market comprises **interest rate swaps.** Conceptually, an interest rate swap is a succession of forward contracts on interest rates arranged by two parties.[2] As such, it allows a financial intermediary (FI) to put in place a long-term hedge (sometimes for as long as 15 years). This hedge reduces the need to roll over contracts if futures or forward contracts had been relied on to achieve such long-term hedges.

In a swap, the **swap buyer** agrees to make a number of fixed interest rate payments on periodic settlement dates to the **swap seller.** The swap seller, in turn, agrees to make floating-rate payments to the swap buyer on the same periodic settlement dates. In undertaking this transaction, the FI that is the fixed-rate payer is seeking to transform the variable-rate nature of its liabilities into fixed-rate liabilities to better match the fixed returns earned on its assets. Meanwhile, the FI that is the variable-rate payer seeks to turn its fixed-rate liabilities into variable-rate liabilities to better match the variable returns on its assets.

To explain the role of a swap transaction in hedging FI interest rate risk, we use a simple example. Consider two FIs; the first is a money center bank that has raised $100 million of its funds by issuing four-year, medium-term notes with 10 percent annual fixed coupons rather than relying on short-term deposits to raise funds (see Table 23–1). On the asset side

---

[2] For example, a four-year swap with annual swap dates involves four net cash flows between the parties to a swap. This is essentially similar to arranging four forward rate agreement (FRA) contracts: a one-year, a two-year, a three-year, and a four-year contract.

Table 23–1

MONEY CENTER BANK BALANCE SHEET

Assets		Liabilities	
C&I loans (rate indexed to LIBOR)	$100 million	Medium-term notes (coupons fixed at 10% annually)	$100 million

Table 23–2

SAVINGS BANK BALANCE SHEET

Assets		Liabilities	
Fixed-rate mortgages	$100 million	Short-term CDs (one year)	$100 million

London interbank offered rate (LIBOR)

A base rate for prime interbank dollar loans in the Eurodollar market of a given maturity. FIs use LIBOR as an index for annual changes on variable rate loans.

of its portfolio, the bank makes commercial and industrial (C&I) loans whose rates are indexed to annual changes in the **London interbank offered rate (LIBOR)**. As we discuss in Chapter 10, banks currently index most large commercial and industrial loans to either LIBOR or the federal funds rate in the money market.

As a result of having floating-rate loans and fixed-rate liabilities in its asset-liability structure, the money center bank has a negative duration gap; the duration of its assets is shorter than that of its liabilities.

$$D_A - kD_L < 0$$

One way for the bank to hedge this exposure is to shorten the duration or interest rate sensitivity of its liabilities by transforming them into short-term floating-rate liabilities that better match the duration characteristics of its asset portfolio. The bank can make changes either on or off the balance sheet. On the balance sheet, the bank could attract an additional $100 million in short-term deposits that are indexed to the LIBOR rate (at say LIBOR plus 2.5 percent) in a manner similar to its loans. The proceeds of these deposits can be used to pay off the medium-term notes. This reduces the duration gap between the bank's assets and liabilities. Alternatively, the bank could go off the balance sheet and sell an interest rate swap, that is, enter into a swap agreement to make the floating-rate payment side of a swap agreement.

The second party of the swap is a thrift institution (savings bank) that has invested $100 million in fixed-rate residential mortgages of long duration. To finance this residential mortgage portfolio, the savings bank had to rely on short-term certificates of deposit with an average duration of one year (see Table 23–2). On maturity, these CDs must be rolled over at the current market rate.

Consequently, the savings bank's asset-liability balance sheet structure is the reverse of the money center bank's, that is

$$D_A - kD_L > 0$$

The savings bank could hedge its interest rate risk exposure by transforming the short-term floating-rate nature of its liabilities into fixed-rate liabilities that better match the long-term maturity/duration structure of its assets. On the balance sheet, the thrift could issue long-term notes with a maturity equal or close to that on the mortgages (at, say, 12 percent).

The proceeds of the sale of the notes can be used to pay off the CDs and reduce the duration gap. Alternatively, the thrift can buy a swap; that is, take the fixed-payment side of a swap agreement.

The opposing balance sheet and interest rate risk exposures of the money center bank and the savings bank provide the necessary conditions for an interest rate swap agreement between the two parties. This swap agreement can be arranged directly between the parties. However, it is likely that an FI—another bank or an investment bank—would act either as a broker or an agent, receiving a fee for bringing the two parties together or to intermediate fully by accepting the credit risk exposure and guaranteeing the cash flows underlying the swap contract. By acting as a principal as well as an agent, the FI can add a credit risk premium to the fee. However, the credit risk exposure of a swap to an FI is somewhat less than that on a loan (this is discussed later in this chapter). Conceptually, when a third-party FI fully intermediates the swap, that FI is really entering into two separate swap agreements, one with the money center bank and one with the savings bank.

plain vanilla

A standard agreement without any special features.

For simplicity, we consider a **plain vanilla** fixed-floating rate swap in which a third-party intermediary acts as a simple broker or agent by bringing together two banks with opposing interest rate risk exposures to enter into a swap agreement or contract.

E X A M P L E   2 3 – 1

Expected Cash Flows on an Interest Rate Swap

In this example, the notional value of the swap is $100 million—equal to the assumed size of the money center bank's medium-term note issue—and the four-year maturity is equal to the maturity of the bank's note liabilities. The annual coupon cost of these note liabilities is 10 percent and the money center bank's problem is that the variable return on its assets may be insufficient to cover the cost of meeting these coupon payments if market interest rates *rise* and therefore asset returns *fall*. By comparison, the fixed returns on the thrift's mortgage asset portfolio may be insufficient to cover the interest cost of its CDs should market rates *rise*. As a result, the swap agreement might dictate that the thrift send fixed payments of 10 percent per annum of the notional $100 million value of the swap to the money center bank to allow the money center bank to cover fully the coupon interest payments on its note issue. In return, the money center bank sends annual payments indexed to the one-year LIBOR to help the thrift cover the cost of refinancing its one-year renewable CDs. Suppose that the money center bank agrees to send the thrift annual payments at the end of each year equal to one-year LIBOR plus 2 percent.[3] We depict this fixed-floating rate swap transaction in Figure 23–1; the expected net financing costs for the FIs are listed in Table 23–3.

As a result of the swap, the money center bank has transformed its fixed-rate interest payments into variable-rate payments matching the variability of returns on its assets. Further, through the interest rate swap, the money center bank effectively pays LIBOR plus 2 percent for its financing. Had it gone to the debt market, the money center bank would pay LIBOR plus 2.5 percent (a savings of .5 percent with the swap). The thrift also has transformed its variable-rate interest payments into fixed-rate payments similar to those received on its assets. • • •

---

[3] These rates implicitly assume that this is the cheapest way each party can hedge its interest rate exposure. For example, LIBOR plus 2 percent is the lowest-cost way that the money center bank can transform its fixed-rate liabilities into floating-rate liabilities.

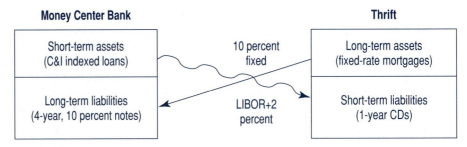

F i g u r e **23-1**   *Fixed-Floating Rate Swap*

T a b l e **23-3**

FINANCING COST RESULTING FROM INTEREST RATE SWAP
(in millions of dollars)

	Money Center Bank	Thrift
Cash outflows from balance sheet financing	− 10% × $100	− (CD) × $100
Cash inflows from swap	10% × $100	(LIBOR +2%) × $100
Cash outflows from swap	− (LIBOR +2%) × $100	− 10% × $100
Net cash flows	− (LIBOR +2%) × $100	− (8%+CD Rate − LIBOR) × $100
Rate available on		
Variable-rate debt	LIBOR + 2½%	
Fixed-rate debt		12%

Note in Example 23–1 that in the absence of default/credit risk, only the money center bank is really fully hedged. This happens because the annual 10 percent payments it receives from the savings bank at the end of each year allows it to meet the promised 10 percent coupon rate payments to its note holders regardless of the return it receives on its variable-rate assets. By contrast, the savings bank receives variable-rate payments based on LIBOR plus 2 percent. It is quite possible that the CD rate that the savings bank must pay on its deposit liabilities does not exactly track the LIBOR–indexed payments sent by the money center bank. That is, the savings bank is subject to basis risk exposure on the swap contract. This basis risk can come from two sources. First, CD rates do not exactly match the movements of LIBOR rates over time since the former are determined in the domestic money market and the latter in the Eurodollar market. Second, the credit/default risk premium on the savings bank's CDs may increase over time; thus, the plus 2 percent add-on to LIBOR may be insufficient to hedge the savings bank's cost of funds. The savings bank might be better hedged by requiring the money center bank to send it floating payments based on U.S. domestic CD rates rather than on LIBOR. To do this, the money center bank would probably require additional compensation since it would then bear basis risk. Its asset returns would be sensitive to LIBOR movements while its swap payments were indexed to U.S. CD rates.

In analyzing this swap, one must distinguish between how the swap should be priced at time 0 (now); that is, how the exchange rate of fixed (10 percent) for floating (LIBOR plus

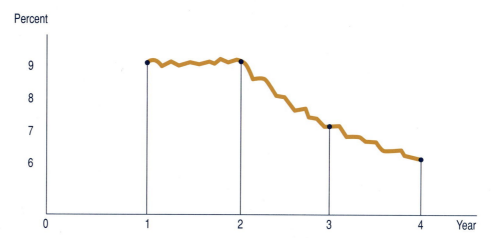

F i g u r e **23–2** *Actual Path of One-Year LIBOR over the Four Years of the*
Swap Agreement

2 percent) is set when the swap agreement is initiated and the actual realized cash flows on
the swap. *Fair pricing* on initiation of the swap depends on the market's expectations of
future short-term rates while realized cash flows on the swap depend on the actual market
rates (here, LIBOR) that materialize over the life of the swap contract.

Realized Cash Flows on an Interest Rate Swap

E X A M P L E   2 3 – 2

Calculation of Realized Cash Flows
We assume that the realized or actual path of interest rates (LIBOR) over the four-year life
of the contract would look similar to Figure 23–2. Given this actual path of LIBOR, we can
see that at the end of each year's settlement date for the four-year swap, the rates would be
as follows:

End of Year	LIBOR
1	9%
2	9
3	7
4	6

The money center bank's variable payments to the thrift were indexed to these rates by the
formula

$$(\text{LIBOR} + 2\%) \times \$100 \text{ million}$$

By contrast, the fixed annual payments the thrift made to the money center bank were
the same each year: 10 percent times $100 million. We summarize the actual or realized
cash flows among the two parties over the four years in Table 23–4. The savings bank's net
gains from the swap in years 1 and 2 are $1 million per year. The enhanced cash flow
offsets the increased cost of refinancing its CDs in a higher interest rate environment; that

Table **23–4**

REALIZED CASH FLOWS ON SWAP AGREEMENT
(in millions of dollars)

End of Year	One-Year LIBOR	One-Year LIBOR +2 Percent	Cash Payment by Money Center Bank	Cash Payment by Savings Bank	Net Payment Made by Money Center Bank
1	9%	11%	$11	$10	$1
2	9	11	11	10	1
3	7	9	9	10	− 1
4	6	8	8	10	− 2
Total			$39	$40	$– 1

is, the savings bank is hedged against rising rates. By contrast, the money center bank makes net gains on the swap in years 3 and 4 when rates fall; thus, it is hedged against falling rates. The positive cash flow from the swap offsets the decline in the variable returns on the money center bank's asset portfolio. Overall, the money center bank made a net dollar gain of $1 million in nominal dollars; its true realized gain is the present value of this amount. • • •

In effect, the money center bank has transformed its four-year, fixed-rate liability notes into a variable-rate liability (a floating-rate swap payment to the savings bank). Meanwhile, the thrift has transformed its variable-rate liability of one-year CDs into a fixed-rate liability (a 10 percent fixed-rate swap payment to the money center bank).

Swaps can be molded or tailored to the needs of the transacting parties as long as one party is willing to compensate the other party for accepting nonstandard terms or **off-market swap** arrangements—usually in the form of an up-front fee or payment. Relaxing a standardized swap agreement can include special interest rate terms and indexes and can allow for varying notional values underlying the swap.

For example, in the example we just considered, the notional value of the swap was fixed at $100 million for each of the four annual swap dates. However, swap notional values can be allowed to decrease or increase over a swap contract's life. This flexibility is useful when one of the parties (in our example, the savings bank) has heavy investments in **fully amortized** mortgages, meaning that the annual and monthly cash flows on the mortgage portfolio reflect repayments of both principal and interest so that the periodic payment is kept constant (see Chapter 12). Fixed-rate mortgages normally have larger payments of interest than principal in the early years with the interest component falling as mortgages approach maturity. One possibility is for the savings bank to enter into a mortgage swap to hedge the amortizing nature of the mortgage portfolio or to allow the notional value of the swap to decline at a rate similar to the decline in the principal component of the mortgage portfolio.

off-market swaps

Swaps that have nonstandard terms that require one party to compensate another.

fully amortized mortgages

Mortgage portfolio cash flows that have constant payment.

Macrohedging with Interest Rate Swaps

The duration model can be used to estimate the optimal number of swap contracts to enter into. In particular, the optimal notional value of swap contracts should be set so that the gain on swap contracts entered into off the balance sheet just offsets the loss in net worth on the balance sheet when rates rise.[4]

Assume that an FI (such as a thrift) has a positive duration gap so that its net worth will fall if interest rates rise

$$\Delta E = -(D_A - kD_L)A \; \frac{\Delta R}{1 + R} < 0$$

As discussed earlier, the thrift can seek to hedge by paying fixed and receiving floating payments through an interest rate swap. However, many different maturity swaps are available. The size of the notional value of the interest rate swap entered into depends on the maturity of the swap contract. Specifically, as long as $D_{Fixed} > D_{Float}$, when interest rates rise, the market (present) value of fixed-rate payments will fall by more than the market (present) value of floating-rate payments; in market (or present) value terms, the fixed-rate payers gain when rates rise and lose when rates fall, and the longer the maturity of the contract, the more the present value of fixed payments falls relative to the present value of the floating rate payments.

That is, if the FI engages in a long rather than a short maturity swap, the notional value of swap contracts would fall the most for the long-term swap. This happens because the longer the maturity of the swap, the larger the change in the market value of the fixed swap payments as interest rates change and the greater the ability to offset a loss in net worth on the balance sheet.

Concept Questions

1. In Example 23–2, which of the two FIs has its liability costs fully hedged? Which is only partially hedged? Explain your answer.
2. What are some nonstandard terms that might be encountered in an off-market swap?
3. How is the optimal notional value of a swap contract set for a macrohedge?

---

[4] That is, let N_S be the optimal notional value of swap contracts, then

$$N_S = \frac{(D_A - kD_L) \times A}{D_{Fixed} - D_{Floating}}$$

For example, if $D_A = 5$, $D_L = 3$, $k = .9$, and $A = \$100$ million, while $D_{Fixed} = 7$ and $D_{Floating} = 1$ (where D_{Fixed} and $D_{Floating}$ reflect, respectively, the duration or interest sensitivity of the fixed payer's cash flows and the duration of the floating payer's cash flows over the life of the swap contract)

$$N_S = \frac{(5 - (.9)\, 3) \times \$100 \text{ m.}}{7 - 1}$$

$$= \frac{\$230,000,000}{6}$$

$$= \$38.3 \text{ million}$$

If each swap contract is $100,000 in size, the FI should enter into 383 contracts.

CURRENCY
SWAPS

Interest rate swaps are long-term contracts that can be used to hedge an FI's interest rate risk exposure and its currency risk exposures. The following section considers a plain vanilla example of how **currency swaps** can immunize FIs against exchange rate risk when they mismatch the currencies of their assets and liabilities.

Fixed-Fixed Currency Swaps

currency swap

A swap used to hedge against exchange-rate risk from mismatched currencies on assets and liabilities.

Consider a U.S. FI with all of its fixed-rate assets denominated in dollars. It is financing part of its asset portfolio with a £50 million issue of four-year, medium-term British pound sterling notes that have a fixed annual coupon of 10 percent. By comparison, an FI in the United Kingdom has all its assets denominated in sterling; it is partly funding those assets with a $100 million issue of four-year, medium-term dollar notes with a fixed annual coupon of 10 percent.

These two FIs are exposed to opposing currency risks. The U.S. FI is exposed to the risk that the dollar will depreciate against the pound over the next four years, which would make it more costly to cover the annual coupon interest payments and the principal repayment on its pound-denominated notes. On the other hand, the U.K. FI is exposed to the risk that the dollar will appreciate against the pound, making it more difficult to cover the dollar coupon and principal payments on its four-year, $100 million note issue from the sterling cash flows on its assets.

The FIs can hedge the exposures either on or off the balance sheet. Assume that the dollar/pound exchange rate is fixed at $2/£1. On the balance sheet, the U.S. FI can issue $100 million in four-year, medium-term dollar notes (at, say, 10.5 percent). The proceeds of the sale can be used to pay off the £50 million of four-year, medium-term sterling notes. Similarly, the U.K. FI can issue £50 million in four-year, medium-term sterling notes (at, say, 10.5 percent), using the proceeds to pay off the $100 million of four-year, medium-term dollar notes. Both FIs have taken actions on the balance sheet so that they are no longer exposed to movements in the exchange rate between the two currencies.

EXAMPLE 23–3

* * * * * * * *

Expected Cash Flows on Fixed-Fixed Currency Swap

The U.K. and U.S. FIs can enter into a currency swap by which the U.K. FI sends annual payments in pounds to cover the coupon and principal repayments of the U.S. FI's pound sterling note issue, and the U.S. FI sends annual dollar payments to the U.K. FI to cover the interest and principal payments on its dollar note issue.[5] We summarize this currency swap in Figure 23–3, Table 23–5, and Table 23–6. As a result of the swap, the U.K. FI transforms fixed-rate dollar liabilities into fixed-rate sterling liabilities that better match the sterling fixed-rate cash flows from its asset portfolio. Similarly, the U.S. FI transforms fixed-rate sterling liabilities into fixed-rate dollar liabilities that better match the fixed-rate dollar cash

---

[5] In a currency swap, it is usual to include both principal and interest payments as part of the swap agreement. For interest rate swaps, it is usual to include only interest rate payments. The reason for this is that both principal and interest are exposed to foreign exchange risk.

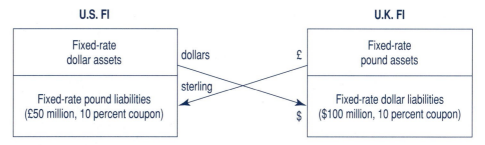

F i g u r e **23–3** *Fixed-Fixed Pound/Dollar Currency Swap*

T a b l e **23–5**

FINANCING COSTS RESULTING FROM THE FIXED-FIXED CURRENCY SWAP AGREEMENT
(in millions)

	U.S. FI	U.K. FI
Cash outflows from balance sheet financing	− 10% × £50	− 10% × $100
Cash inflows from swap	10% × £50	10% × $100
Cash outflows from swap	− 10% × $100	− 10% × £50
Net cash flows	− 10% × $100	− 10% × £50
Rate available on		
Dollar-denominated notes	10.5%	
Pound-denominated notes		10.5%

T a b l e **23–6**

CASH FLOWS UNDER THE FIXED-FIXED CURRENCY SWAP AGREEMENT
(in millions)

	Cash Flow Payments		**Payments by U.K. FI in**	
End of Year	**U.S. FI ($s)**	**U.K. FI (£s)**	**$s (at $2/£1 exchange rate)**	**Net Cash Flow ($s)**
1	$ 10	£ 5	$ 10	0
2	10	5	10	0
3	10	5	10	0
4	110	55	110	0

flows from its asset portfolio. Further, both FIs transform the pattern of their payments at a lower rate than had they made changes on the balance sheet. Both FIs effectively obtain financing at 10 percent while hedging against exchange rate risk. Had they gone to the market, they would have paid 10.5 percent to do this. In undertaking this exchange of cash flows, the two parties normally agree on a fixed exchange rate for the cash flows at the beginning of the period.[6] In this example, the fixed exchange rate is $2/£1.　• • •

In Example 23–3, both liabilities bear a fixed 10 percent interest rate, but this is not a necessary requirement for the fixed-fixed currency swap agreement. For example, suppose that U.S. note coupons were 5 percent per annum while U.K. note coupons were 10 percent. The swap dollar payments of the U.S. FI in Table 23–6 would remain unchanged, but the U.K. FI's sterling payments would be reduced by £2.5 million (or $5 million) in each of the four years. This difference could be met either by some up-front payment by the U.K. FI to the U.S. FI, reflecting the difference in the present value of the two fixed cash flows, or by annual payments that result in zero net present value differences among the fixed-fixed currency swap participants' payments. Also note that should the exchange rate change from the rate agreed in the swap ($2/£1), either of the sides would lose in the sense that they might enter into a new swap at a more favorable exchange rate to one party. Specifically, if the dollar were to appreciate (rise in value) against the pound over the life of the swap, the agreement would become more costly for the U.S. FI. If, however, the dollar were to depreciate (fall in value) against the pound, the U.K. FI would find the agreement increasingly costly over the swap's life.

By combining an interest rate swap of the fixed-floating type described earlier with a currency swap, we can also produce a fixed-floating currency swap that is a hybrid of the two plain vanilla swaps we have considered so far.

Fixed-Floating Currency Swaps

E X A M P L E 2 3 – 4

• • • • • • •   *Financing Costs Associated with a Fixed-Floating Currency Swap*
Consider a U.S. FI that primarily holds floating-rate, short-term, U.S. dollar-denominated assets. It has partly financed this asset portfolio with a £50 million, four-year note issue with fixed 10 percent annual coupons denominated in sterling. By comparison, a U.K. FI that holds primarily long-term, fixed-rate assets denominated in sterling has partly financed this portfolio with $100 million, short-term, dollar-denominated Euro CDs whose rates reflect changes in one-year LIBOR plus a 2 percent premium. As a result, the U.S. FI is faced with both an interest rate risk and a foreign exchange risk. Specifically, if dollar short-term rates fall and the dollar depreciates against the pound, the FI may face a problem in covering its promised fixed-coupon and principal payments on the pound-denominated note. Consequently, it may wish to transform its fixed-rate, pound-denominated liabilities into variable-rate, dollar-denominated liabilities. The U.K. FI also faces interest rate and foreign exchange rate risk exposure. If U.S. interest rates rise and the dollar appreciates against the pound, the U.K. FI would find it more difficult to cover its promised coupon and principal payments on its dollar-denominated CDs out of the cash flows from its fixed-rate pound asset portfolio. Consequently, it may wish to transform its floating-rate, short-term dollar-denominated liabilities into fixed-rate pound liabilities.

Both FIs can make changes on the balance sheet to hedge the interest rate and foreign exchange rate risk exposure. The U.S. FI can issue $100 million U.S. dollar-dominated,

---

[6] As with interest rate swaps, this exchange rate reflects the contracting parties' expectations as to future exchange rate movements.

Table **23–7**

FINANCING COSTS RESULTING FROM THE FIXED-FLOATING CURRENCY SWAP

(in millions)

	U.S. FI	U.K. FI
Cash outflows from balance sheet financing	$-10\% \times £50$	$-(\text{LIBOR} + 2\%) \times \$100$
Cash inflows from swap	$10\% \times £50$	$(\text{LIBOR} + 2\%) \times \$100$
Cash outflows from swap	$-(\text{LIBOR} + 2\%) \times \$100$	$-10\% \times £50$
Net cash flows	$-(\text{LIBOR} + 2\%) \times \$100$	$-10\% \times £50$
Rate available on		
Dollar-denominated variable-rate debt	$\text{LIBOR} + 2\frac{1}{2}\%$	
Pound-denominated fixed-rate debt		11%

floating-rate, short-term debt (at, say, LIBOR plus 2.5 percent), the proceeds of which can be used to pay off the existing £50 million four-year note. The U.K. FI can issue £50 million in four-year notes (at, say, 11 percent) and use the proceeds to pay off the $100 million in short-term Euro CDs. Both FIs, by changing the financing used on the balance sheet, hedge both the interest rate and foreign exchange rate risk. We again assume that the dollar/pound exchange rate is $2/£1.

Alternatively, each FI can achieve its objective of liability transformation by engaging in a fixed-floating currency swap. Each year, the two FIs swap payments at some pre-arranged dollar/pound exchange rate, assumed to be $2/£1. The U.K. FI sends fixed payments in pounds to cover the cost of the U.S. FI's pound-denominated note issue, and the U.S. FI sends floating payments in dollars to cover the U.K. FI's floating-rate dollar CD costs. The resulting expected financing costs are calculated in Table 23–7. As a result of the fixed-floating currency swap, both FIs have hedged interest rate and foreign exchange rate risk and have done so at a rate below what they could have achieved by making on-balance-sheet changes. The U.S. FI's net financing cost is LIBOR plus 2 percent with the swap compared to LIBOR plus 2.5 percent in the debt market. The U.K. FI's net financing cost is 10 percent with the swap compared to 11 percent had it refinanced on the balance sheet.

Given the realized LIBOR rates in column 2, we show the relevant payments among the contracting parties in Table 23–8. The realized cash flows from the swap result in a net nominal payment of $2 million by the U.S. FI to the U.K. FI over the life of the swap. • • •

Concept Questions

1. Referring to the fixed-fixed currency swap in Table 23–6, if the net cash flows are zero, why does either bank enter into the swap agreement?

2. Referring to Table 23–8, suppose that the U.S. FI had agreed to make floating payments of LIBOR plus 1 percent instead of LIBOR plus 2 percent. What would its net payment have been to the U.K. FI over the four-year swap agreement?

Table 23–8
REALIZED CASH FLOWS ON FIXED-FLOATING CURRENCY SWAP
(in millions)

Year	LIBOR	LIBOR +2 Percent	Floating Rate Payment by U.S. FI ($s)	Fixed Rate Payment by U.K. FI (£)	Fixed Rate Payment by U.K. FI ($ at $2/£1)	Net Payment by U.S. FI ($s)
1	9%	11%	$11	£5	$10	$1
2	7	9	9	5	10	− 1
3	8	10	10	5	10	0
4	10	12	112	55	110	2
Total net payment						$2

CREDIT RISK AND SWAPS

Hedging interest rate risk and foreign exchange rate risk have been important reasons for the increase in swaps, and FIs have originated a significant number of swaps to *arbitrage* (or *exploit for a profit*) the differences in credit risk pricing in the markets for short-term, floating-rate and long-term, fixed-rate debt. This type of swap—in which an FI might be on either side—is generally called a **quality swap.** FIs have more recently used swaps to try to hedge directly the credit risk of their on-balance-sheet assets, so-called total return swaps. We look at quality swaps next (*total return swaps*—another type of credit risk related swap—are described in the Appendix to this chapter).

quality swap

A fixed-floating rate swap between two parties of different credit ratings.

Quality Swap

Consider a U.S. money center bank with predominantly interest-sensitive, floating-rate dollar-denominated assets. Because of its good profit and capital adequacy performance, the rating agencies rate it AAA (the highest possible). Consider a life insurance company with predominantly fixed-rate, long-term dollar assets such as government bonds and mortgages in its portfolio. Because of general concerns about its performance and its property portfolio, the life insurer's debt rating is currently BBB (the bottom of the investment-grade rating).

Because the bank has a short duration of assets and the life insurer has a long duration of assets, direct hedging dictates that the bank borrow short term in the floating-rate market and the insurance company borrow long term in the fixed-rate market. The motivation behind the quality swap is that these parties can achieve the same hedging outcome at a lower price by borrowing in the "wrong" market and then entering into a swap. Under a quality swap, the bank borrows long-term fixed and the life insurer borrows short-term floating, and then they enter into a swap agreement in which the life insurer sends fixed payments to cover the bank's fixed cost of debt and the bank sends floating-rate payments to cover the life insurer's floating cost of debt. The net result of this swap transaction is that the bank has transformed a fixed-rate liability into a floating-rate liability that matches the

Table **23–9**

QUALITY SPREADS IN THE FIXED- AND FLOATING-RATE MARKETS

	Floating-Rate Market	Fixed-Rate Market
Insurer (BBB)	LIBOR + 1%	12%
Bank (AAA)	LIBOR + .5%	10%
Quality spread	.5%	2%
Net quality spread = 2% –.5% = 1.5%		

duration structure of its assets. Similarly, the life insurer has transformed a floating-rate liability into a fixed-rate liability that better matches the relatively long-term duration of its assets.

The question arises as to how and why borrowing in the "wrong" market and then swapping payments lowers the costs of funding for both parties over the costs of direct hedging. To understand the rationale for a quality swap, consider the representative cost of funds facing the AAA bank and the BBB insurer in the floating-rate and fixed-rate markets for debt (see Table 23–9).

According to Table 23–9, the high credit–quality AAA bank's rate advantage (over the BBB insurer) in borrowing in the short-term floating-rate market is only .5 percent compared to its 2 percent advantage in the long-term debt market. The bank has a borrowing cost advantage over the insurer in both markets, but it has the larger *comparative* advantage in the long-term debt market. To exploit this comparative advantage and to generate gains, the bank can borrow in the debt market where its *comparative advantage* is largest (fixed, long term) and the life insurer can borrow in the debt market where its *comparative disadvantage* is lowest (floating, short term); then the two can engage in a swap. The net quality spread—the difference between the credit spreads in the fixed and floating markets—can then be saved and shared between the bank and the life insurer. That is, the **net quality spread** reflects the potential aggregate gains to the bank and life insurer from entering into a quality swap. In the example in Table 23–9, the net quality spread is

$$\text{Net quality spread} = \text{Spread in fixed-rate market} - \text{Spread in floating-rate market} = 2\% - .5\% = 1.5\%$$

net quality spread

The net interest rate spread between rates paid by high-quality borrowers relative to low-quality borrowers in the long-term (fixed) and short-term (floating) rate markets.

That is, the combined debt costs of the participants can theoretically be reduced by 1.5 percent by entering into a quality swap. To see how these gains occur and are shared, let's follow each part of the swap transaction in detail.

The Bank.   The bank borrows long-term, fixed rate at 10 percent. It then wishes to convert this fixed-rate liability into a floating-rate liability by selling a swap (i.e., being the floating-payment party). It contracts to send floating payments to the insurer equal to LIBOR plus 1 percent, which exactly matches the insurer's cost of debt when borrowing short term. In return, it receives from the insurer fixed payments equal to 11 percent per annum. These fixed payments exactly match the bank's 10 percent cost of debt plus an additional 1 percent markup payment. As a result, the bank's net cost of funds (shown by a negative sign) is as follows:

1.   Direct fixed-rate borrowing cost, – 10 percent.
2.   Fixed-rate payment received from insurer,+ 11 percent.

Table **23–10**

FINANCING COSTS RESULTING FROM THE QUALITY SPREAD

	Bank	Insurer
Rate on existing balancing sheet financing	– 10%	– (LIBOR +1%)
Rate on inflow from quality swap	11%	LIBOR + 1%
Rate on outflow from quality swap	– (LIBOR +1%)	– 11%
Net financing rate from swap	– LIBOR	– 11%
Rate available on		
Variable-rate debt	LIBOR + .5%	
Fixed-rate debt		12%
Savings from swap over debt market	.5%	1%

3. Floating payment to insurer, – (LIBOR + 1 percent).
4. Net payments, – 10 percent + 11 percent – (LIBOR + 1 percent) = – LIBOR.

Therefore, the postswap cost of funds to the bank is LIBOR. If the bank had engaged in direct hedging by borrowing in the short-term floating rate market directly, its cost of funds would have been higher, at LIBOR plus .5 percent. That is, the quality swap has saved the bank .5 percent in financing costs. These costs are summarized in column 2 of Table 23–10.

The Insurer.   The life insurer borrows short-term floating rate at LIBOR plus 1 percent. It then participates in the quality swap with the bank as the buyer (the fixed-rate payer) to convert its floating-rate liabilities into fixed-rate liabilities. The life insurer agrees to send fixed-rate payments to the bank equal to 11 percent and to receive floating-rate payments from the bank equal to LIBOR plus 1 percent. As a result, the life insurer has transformed its floating-rate debt liabilities into fixed-rate liabilities. The insurer's net cost of funds is as follows:

1. Direct floating-rate borrowing cost, – (LIBOR + 1 percent).
2. Floating-rate payment received from the bank, (LIBOR + 1 percent).
3. Fixed-rate payment made to bank, – 11 percent.
4. Net payment, – (LIBOR + 1 percent) + (LIBOR + 1 percent) – 11 percent = – 11 percent.

As a result, the after swap cost of funds to the life insurer is 11 percent. This compares to the cost to the life insurer of direct hedging in the fixed-rate market of 12 percent. That is, the quality swap has saved the life insurer 1 percent in debt costs. These costs are summarized in column 3 of Table 23–10.

The 1.5 percent net quality spread is shared between the bank and the life insurer, with .5 percent going to the bank and 1 percent to the life insurer

$$1.5\% \qquad = \qquad .5\% \qquad + \qquad 1\%$$
(net quality spread)   (debt cost savings, bank)   (debt cost savings, insurer)

Note that the two parties could share the 1.5 percent very differently. In fact, the degree to which the 1.5 percent is shared reflects the relative bargaining power of the two parties. The only limitation is that each needs to make some positive gains from entering into the quality swap. As a result, each party's share must be positive to result in a win-win situation.

Nevertheless, many observers are skeptical about whether the net quality spread reflects a true arbitrage opportunity. Indeed, if this were the case, the market forces of demand and supply would probably eliminate these spread differentials over time. Only gross inefficiencies or barriers to the entry of good credit-rated parties into credit markets and quality swap deals would prevent such an equalizing of fixed-floating spreads.[7] Few believe that credit markets are so inefficient that quality spreads of 1.5 percent or more could persist for any length of time nor that credit risk in each market is so grossly mispriced. One view is that the supposed gains from a quality swap are really illusory and come from ignoring the value of important option features on loans. That is, borrowing fixed directly or borrowing floating and converting these liabilities into fixed via the swap are not the same from an option perspective. This is true because a direct fixed-rate borrower (the life insurer in our case) always has the option to pay back a fixed-rate loan early; that is, it can prepay or put the fixed-rate loan back to the lender should fixed market rates fall. However, the synthetic fixed-rate borrowing created via the quality swap does not provide such an opportunity. This synthetic loan cannot be prepaid. Thus, the 1 percent savings to the life insurer may reflect, in part, the sale or sacrifice of a valuable prepayment (or refinancing) option that exists when fixed-rate borrowing occurs directly.

Credit Risk Concerns with Swaps

The growth of the over-the-counter (OTC) swap market was one of the major factors underlying the imposition of the BIS risk-based capital requirements in January 1993 (see Chapter 16). The fear was that in a long-term OTC swap-type contract, the out-of-the-money counterparty would have incentives to default on such contracts to deter current and future losses. Consequently, BIS imposed a required capital ratio for banks against their holdings of both interest rate and currency swaps. Many analysts have argued that these capital requirements work against the growth of the swap market since they can be viewed as a cost or tax on market participants.

Both regulators and market participants have a heightened awareness of credit risk. Merrill Lynch and Salomon Brothers are heavy participants as intermediaries in the swap market; for example, they act as counterparty guarantors to both the fixed and floating sides in swaps. To act as counterparty guarantors successfully and to maintain market share, a high—if not the highest—credit rating is beginning to be required. For example, Merrill Lynch and Salomon Brothers were rated only single A in 1993. To achieve a AAA rating, each established a separately capitalized subsidiary in which to conduct the swap business. Merrill Lynch had to invest $350 million in its swap subsidiary, and Salomon invested $175 million in its subsidiary.

This raises some questions. What, exactly, is the default risk on swaps? Is it high or low? Is it the same as or different from the credit risk on loans? In fact, the credit risk on swaps and the credit risk on loans differ in three major ways. As a result, the credit risk on a swap is generally much less than that on a loan of equivalent dollar size.[8] We discuss these differences next.

---

[7] This assumes that enough good-credit parties are available. If not, then the good-credit parties with AAA ratings have implicit monopoly power.

[8] As with loans, swap participants deal with the credit risk of counterparties by setting bilateral limits on the notional amount of swaps entered into (similar to credit rationing on loans) and adjusting the fixed and/or floating rates by including credit risk premiums. For example, a low credit–quality, fixed-rate payer may have to pay an additional spread to a high credit–quality, floating-rate payer.

Netting and Swaps.   One factor that mitigates the credit risk on swaps is the netting of swap payments. On each swap payment date, one party makes a fixed payment and the other makes a floating payment. In general, however, each party calculates the net difference between the two payments, and one party makes a single payment for the net difference to the other. This netting of payments implies that the default exposure of the in-the-money party is limited to the net payment rather than either the total fixed or floating payment itself. In addition, when two parties have large numbers of contracts outstanding against each other, they tend to net across contracts. This process called *netting by novation*—often formalized through a master netting agreement in the United States— further reduces the potential risk of loss if some contracts are in the money and others out of the money to the same counterparty.[9] However, note that netting by novation has not been fully tested in all international courts of law. For example, in 1990, a number of municipal officials in the United Kingdom engaged in swaps with U.S. and U.K. banks and investment banks. After taking major losses on some swap contracts, these municipal officials defaulted on further payments. The U.K. High Court supported their right to default by stating that they did not have the authority to enter into such swaps in the first place. This still has not prevented these municipal officials from seeking to collect on in-the-money swaps (to them).

Payment Flows Are Interest, not Principal.   Currency swaps involve swaps of interest and principal, but interest rate swaps involve swaps of interest payments only measured against some notional principal value. This suggests that the default risk on such interest rate swaps is less than on a regular loan in which both interest and principal are exposed to credit risk.

Standby Letters of Credit.   When swaps are made between parties of different credit standings, so that one party perceives a significant risk of default by the other party, the poor-quality credit risk party may be required to buy a standby letter of credit (or another form of performance guaranty) from a third-party high-quality (AAA) FI so that should default occur, the standby letter of credit would provide the swap payments in lieu of the defaulting party. In addition, low-quality counterparties are increasingly required to post collateral in lieu of default. This collateral is an incentive mechanism to deter swap defaults.[10]

Concept Questions

1. For AAA borrowers, short-term rates are 10 percent and long-term rates are 10.5 percent. For BBB borrowers, short-term rates are 11 percent and long-term rates are 13 percent. What is the net quality spread?

---

[9] In January 1995, the Financial Accounting Standards Board's *Interpretation No. 39* established the *right to setoff* under a master netting agreement. Also, in 1995 the BIS allowed for the bilateral netting of swap contracts in calculating risk-based capital requirements. This has been estimated to have reduced banks' capital requirements against swaps by up to 40 percent.

[10] One solution being considered by market participants (such as the International Association of Swap Dealers) is to use collateral to mark to market a swap contract in a way similar to marking futures to market to prevent credit risk building up over time. Remember that a swap contract is like a succession of forward contracts. A 1994 survey by Arthur Andersen showed that approximately $6.9 billion was posted as collateral against a net replacement value of $77.9 billion of swaps. (See "A Question of Collateral," *Euromoney*, November 1995, pp. 46–49.)

2. In a swap, how is the net quality spread shared between the AAA and the BBB firms?
3. What are the major differences between the credit risk on swaps and the credit risk on loans?

SUMMARY

This chapter evaluated the role of swaps as risk-management vehicles for FIs. It analyzed the major types of swaps: interest rate and currency swaps as well as the credit quality swap. Swaps have special features of long maturity, flexibility, and liquidity that make them attractive alternatives relative to shorter-term hedging vehicles such as futures, forwards, and options discussed in Chapters 21 and 22. However, even though the credit risk of swaps is generally less than that of loans, because of their OTC nature and long maturities, their credit risk is still generally larger than that for other OTC derivative instruments such as caps and floors. Also, the credit risk on swaps compares unfavorably with that on exchange-traded futures and options, whose credit risk is approximately zero.

PERTINENT WEB SITES

Bank for International Settlements   http://www.bis.org/home.htm

Swaps

1. Explain the similarity between a *swap* and a *forward contract*.
2. FIs used forward, futures, and options contracts to hedge risk for many years before swaps were invented. If FIs already had these hedging instruments, why do they need swaps?
3. Distinguish between a *swap seller* and a *swap buyer*.
4. An insurance company owns $50 million of floating-rate bonds yielding LIBOR plus 1 percent. These loans are financed by $50 million of fixed rate guaranteed investment contracts (GICs) costing 10 percent. A finance company has $50 million of auto loans with a fixed rate of 14 percent. They are financed by $50 million of CDs with a variable rate of LIBOR plus 4 percent. If the thrift is going to be the swap buyer and the insurance company the swap seller, what is an example of a feasible swap?
5. Two multinational corporations enter their respective debt markets to issue $100 million of two-year notes. Firm A can borrow at a fixed annual rate of 11 percent or a floating rate of LIBOR plus 50 basis points, repriced at the end of the year. Firm B can borrow at a fixed annual rate of 10 percent or a floating rate of LIBOR, repriced at the end of the year.

a. If Firm A is a positive duration gap insurance company and Firm B is a money market mutual fund, in what market(s) should both firms borrow to reduce their interest rate risk exposures?
b. In which debt market does Firm A have a comparative advantage over Firm B?
c. Although Firm A is riskier than Firm B and therefore must pay a higher rate in both the fixed- and floating-rate markets, there are possible gains to trade. Set up a swap to exploit Firm A's comparative advantage over Firm B. What are the total gains from the swap trade? (Assume a swap intermediary fee of 10 basis points.)
d. The gains from the swap trade can be apportioned between Firm A and B through negotiation. What terms of trade would give all the gains to Firm A? What terms of trade would give all the gains to Firm B?
e. Assume swap pricing that allocates all of the gains from the swap to Firm A. If Firm A buys the swap from Firm B and pays the swap intermediary's fee, what are the end-of-year net cash flows if LIBOR equals 8.25 percent?
f. If Firm A buys the swap in part (e) from Firm B and pays the swap intermediary's fee, what are the end-of-year net cash flows if LIBOR equals 11 percent? (Be

sure to net swap payments against cash market payments for both firms.)

g. If all barriers to entry and pricing inefficiencies between the debt markets of Firm A and Firm B are eliminated, how would that affect the swap transaction?

6. A commercial bank has $200 million of floating-rate loans yielding the T-bill rate plus 2 percent. These loans are financed by $200 million of fixed-rate deposits costing 9 percent. An S&L has $200 million of mortgages with a fixed rate of 13 percent. They are financed by $200 million of CDs with a variable rate of T-bill plus 3 percent.

a. Discuss the type of interest rate risk each FI faces.

b. Propose a swap that would result in each FI having the same type of assets and liabilities (i.e., one has fixed assets and fixed liabilities, and the other has assets and liabilities all tied to some floating rate).

c. Show that this swap would be acceptable to both parties.

d. What are some practical difficulties in arranging this swap?

7. A German bank issues a $100 million, three-year Eurodollar CD at a fixed annual rate of 7 percent. The proceeds of the CD are lent to a German company for three years at a fixed rate of 9 percent. The spot exchange rate is deutsche mark (DM) 1.50/US$.

a. Is this expected to be a profitable transaction? What are the cash flows if exchange rates are unchanged over the next three years? What is the risk exposure of the bank's underlying cash position? How can the German bank reduce that risk exposure?

b. If the U.S. dollar is expected to appreciate against the DM to DM1.65/$, DM1.815/$, and DM2.00/$ over the next three years, what will be the cash flows on this transaction?

c. If the German bank swaps U.S. dollar payments for DM payments at the current spot exchange rate, what are the cash flows on the swap? What are the cash flows on the entire hedged position? Assume that the U.S. dollar appreciates at the same rates as in part (b).

d. What are the cash flows on the swap and the hedged position if actual spot exchange rates are as follows:
End of year 1: DM1.55/US$.
End of year 2: DM1.47/US$.
End of year 3: DM1.48/US$.

8. Bank 1 can issue five-year CDs at an annual rate of 11 percent fixed or at a variable rate of LIBOR plus 2 percent. Bank 2 can issue five-year CDs at an annual rate of 13 percent fixed or at a variable rate of LIBOR plus 3 percent.

a. Is a mutually beneficial swap possible between the two banks?

b. What is the comparative advantage of the two banks?

c. What is an example of a feasible swap?

d. What is the net quality spread?

9. Consider the German bank's cash position in problem (7).

a. What would be the bank's risk exposure if the fixed-rate German loan were financed with a floating-rate U.S. $100 million, three-year Eurodollar CD? What type(s) of hedge is (are) appropriate if the German bank wants to reduce its risk exposure?

b. The annual Eurodollar CD rate is set at LIBOR so that LIBOR at the end of years 1, 2, 3 is expected to be 7 percent, 8 percent, and 9 percent, respectively. What are the cash flows on the bank's unhedged cash position? (Assume no change in exchange rates.)

c. What are the cash flows on the bank's unhedged cash position if exchange rates are as follows:
End of year 1: DM1.55/US$.
End of year 2: DM1.47/US$.
End of year 3: DM1.48/US$

d. What are both the swap and total hedged position cash flows if the bank swaps out its floating-rate U.S. dollar-denominated CD payments in exchange for 7.75 percent fixed-rate DM payments at current spot exchange rates (DM1.50/U.S.$)?

10. First Bank can issue one-year, floating CDs at prime plus 1 percent or fixed-rate CDs at 12.5 percent. Second Bank can issue one-year, floating-rate CDs at prime plus .5 percent or fixed-rate at 11 percent. Give an example of a feasible swap between the two banks.

11. A money center bank swaps its fixed-rate payments on its liabilities for floating-rate payments because its assets are short term paying floating rates. What are the two sources of basis risk it faces that prevent constructing a perfect hedge?

12. Why is it *not* necessary to consider the principal in the pricing of interest rate swap instruments (except to ensure that they are the same) but it *is* necessary in the case of currency swaps?

13. An FI has $500 million of assets with a duration of nine years. It has $450 of liabilities with a duration of three years. It wants to hedge its duration gap with a swap that has fixed-rate payments with a duration of six years and floating-rate payments with a duration of two years. What is the optimal amount of the swap to effectively macrohedge against the adverse effect of a change in interest rates on the value of equity?

14. Explain why the credit risk on an interest rate swap is lower than that of a regular loan.

15. Use the balance sheet information to construct a swap hedge against interest rate risk exposure.

Balance Sheet ($millions)

Rate-sensitive assets	$ 50	Rate-sensitive liabilities	$ 75
Fixed-rate assets	150	Fixed-rate liabilities	100
		Net worth	25

Rate-sensitive assets are repriced quarterly at the 91-day Treasury bill rate plus 150 basis points. Fixed-rate assets have five years until maturity and pay 9 percent annually. Rate-sensitive liabilities are repriced quarterly at the 91-day Treasury bill rate plus 100 basis points. Fixed-rate liabilities have two years until maturity and pay 7 percent annually. Currently, the 91-day Treasury bill rate is 6.25 percent.

a. What is the bank's current net interest income? If T-bill rates increase 150 basis points, what will be the change in the bank's net interest income?

b. What is the bank's repricing or funding gap? Use the repricing model to calculate the change in the bank's net interest income if interest rates increase 150 basis points.

c. How can swaps be used as an interest rate hedge in the preceding example?

Use the following additional information for parts d through g. The bank is a price taker in both the fixed-rate (at 9 percent) and rate-sensitive asset (at T-bill plus 1.5 percent) markets. A securities dealer is a price taker in another fixed-rate market (paying 8.5 percent) and another floating-rate asset market (paying the 91-day T-bill rate plus 1.25 percent). All interest is paid annually.

d. If the securities dealer has a positive funding gap, what is its interest rate risk exposure? How can the bank and the securities dealer use a swap to hedge their respective interest rate risk exposures? What are the total potential gains to the swap trade?

e. Consider the following two-year swap of asset cash flows: an annual fixed-rate asset cash inflow of 8.6 percent in exchange for a floating-rate asset cash inflow of T-bill plus 125 basis points. The total swap intermediary fee is 5 basis points. How are the swap gains apportioned between the bank and the securities dealer if each hedges its interest rate risk exposures using this swap?

f. What are the swap net cash flows if T-bill rates at the end of the first year are 7.75 percent and at the end of the second year are 5.5 percent?

g. What are the sources of the swap gains? What are the implications for the efficiency of cash markets?

16. What is the credit risk in a swap, and how does netting reduce the credit risk on swaps?

17. A U.S. thrift has most of its assets in the form of French franc-denominated, floating-rate loans. Its liabilities consist mostly of fixed-rate, dollar-denominated CDs. What type of currency risk and interest rate risk does this FI face? How might it use a swap to eliminate some of these risks?

18. Consider the following currency swap of coupon interest on the following assets:

5 percent (annual coupon) fixed-rate US $1 million bond.

5 percent (annual coupon) fixed-rate bond denominated in deutsche marks (DM).

Spot exchange rates: DM1.5/$

a. What is the face value of the DM bond if the investments are equivalent at spot rates?

b. What are the end-of-year cash flows, assuming no change in spot exchange rates? What are the net cash flows on the swap?

c. What are the cash flows if spot exchange rates fall to DM 0.50/$? What are the net cash flows on the swap?

d. What are the cash flows if spot exchange rates rise to DM 2.25/$? What are the net cash flows on the swap?

e. Describe the underlying cash position that would prompt the FI to hedge by swapping dollars in exchange for deutsche marks.

19. Consider the following fixed-floating rate currency swap of assets: 5 percent (annual coupon) fixed-rate US$1 million bond. Floating-rate bond denominated in deutsche marks (DM) set at LIBOR annually. Currently LIBOR is 4 percent. Face value is DM 1.5 million. Spot exchange rates: DM 1.5/$.

a. What are the end-of-year cash flows, assuming no change in spot exchange rates? What are the net cash flows on the swap at spot exchange rates?

b. If the one-year forward rate is DM 1.538 per US$, what are the end-of-year net cash flows on the swap? (Assume LIBOR remains unchanged.)

c. If LIBOR increases to 6 percent, what are the end-of-year net cash flows on the swap? (Evaluate at the forward rate.)

20. An FI arranges an interest rate swap between two counterparties, Intel and Digital. Assume the following:

Intel
Bond Rating: AA

a. Can borrow at fixed rate of 8 percent
or

b. Can borrow at floating rate of LIBOR plus 2 percent

Digital
Bond Rating: A

Can borrow at fixed rate of 10 percent
or

Can borrow at floating rate of LIBOR plus 3 percent

Assume that LIBOR is currently at 5 percent. The face value of borrowing is $10 million. Show how an FI can arrange a fixed-floating rate swap that will generate a 50-basis-point spread. Intel and Digital will share equally any other savings.

APPENDIX: TOTAL
RETURN SWAP

total return swap

A swap involving an obligation to pay interest at a specified fixed or floating rate for payments representing the total return on a specified amount.

Although FIs spend significant resources attempting to evaluate and price expected changes in a borrower's credit risk over the life of a loan, a borrower's credit situation (credit quality) sometimes deteriorates unexpectedly after the loan terms are determined and the loan issued. A lender can use a total return swap to hedge this possible change in credit risk exposure. A **total return swap** involves swapping an obligation to pay interest at a specified fixed or floating rate for payments representing the total return on a loan or a bond (interest and principal value changes) of a specified amount.

For example, suppose that an FI lends $100 million to a Brazilian manufacturing firm at a fixed rate of 10 percent. Should the firm's credit risk increase unexpectedly over the life of the loan, the market value of the loan and consequently the FI's net worth will fall. The FI can hedge an unexpected increase in the borrower's credit risk by entering into a total return swap in which it agrees to pay a total return based on an annual fixed rate plus changes in the market value of Brazilian government debt (changes in the value of these bonds reflect the political and economic events in the firm's home country and will thus be correlated with the credit risk of the Brazilian borrowing firm). In return, the FI receives a variable market rate payment of interest annually (e.g., one-year LIBOR rate). Figure 23–1A illustrates the cash flows associated with the typical total return swap for the FI.

Using the total return swap, the FI agrees to pay a fixed rate of interest annually and the capital gain or loss on the market value of the Brazilian bond (e.g., a Brazilian Brady bond; see Chapter 28) over the period of the hedge. In Figure 23–1A, P_0 denotes the market value of the bond at the beginning of the swap period, and P_T represents the market value of the bond at the end of the swap period. If the Brazilian bond decreases in value over the period of the hedge ($P_0 > P_T$), the FI pays a relatively small (possibly negative) amount to the counterparty equal to the fixed payment on the swap minus the capital loss[11] on the reference bond. For example, suppose the Brazilian bond was priced at par ($P_0 = 100$) at the beginning of the swap period. At the end of the swap period or the payment date, the Brazilian bond had a market value of 90 ($P_T = 90$) due to an increase in Brazilian sovereign country risk. Suppose that the fixed rate payment as part of the total return swap was 12 percent, then the FI would send to the swap counterparty the fixed rate of 12 percent minus 10 percent (the capital loss on the Brazilian reference bond), or a total of 2 percent and would receive in return the floating payment (e.g., LIBOR = 11 percent). Thus, the net profit on the swap is 9 percent (11 percent minus 2 percent) times the notional amount of the swap contract. This gain can be used to offset the loss of market value of the loan. This example is illustrated in Figure 23–1A.

If the Brazilian bond increases in value ($P_T > P_0$), the FI pays this capital gain to the swap counterparty plus any fixed rate payment. Thus, the FI benefits from the total return swap if the Brazilian bond value deteriorates as a result of a political or economic shock. Assuming that the Brazilian firm's credit risk deteriorates along with the local economy, the FI will offset some of this loss of the Brazilian loan on its balance sheet with a gain from the total return swap.[12]

---

[11]Total return swaps are typically structured so that the capital gain or loss is paid at the end of the swap. However, an alternate structure does exist in which capital gain or loss is paid at the end of each interest period during the swap.

[12]For additional discussion, see J.D. Finnerty, "Credit Derivatives, Infrastructure Finance, and Emerging Market Risk," *The Financier, ACMT*, February 1996, pp. 64–75.

	Annual Cash Flow for Years 1 through Final Year	Additional Final Payment by FI	Total Return
Cash inflow on swap to FI	1-year LIBOR (11%)	–	1-year LIBOR (11%)
Cash outflow on swap to FI	Fixed rate $(\overline{F})$ (12%)	$P_T - P_0$ (90 – 100)	$[\overline{F} + \dfrac{P_T - P_0}{P_0}]$,
			$(12\% + \dfrac{90 - 100}{100} = 12\% - 10\% = 2\%)$
		Net profit	9%

F i g u r e 23–1A   *Total Return Swap*

In March 1997, Bears Stearns used a total return swap to hedge credit risk exposure on the 1998 refinancing of Revlon Worldwide's $1.15 billion, zero-coupon, high-yield bonds. In this swap, Bears Stearns paid the total return of the Revlon zero-coupon bonds and received LIBOR plus a spread. Bears Stearns was betting that Revlon would be unable to issue new debt to refinance the zero-coupon bonds and that it would profit from the deterioration in Revlon bonds' values. Revlon successfully refinanced the issue, however, and Bears Sterns paid the counterparty in the swap the full return on Revlon's zero-coupon bonds.

Section
Four

Measurement and Management of Other Types of Risk

Chapter Twenty-four

Operating Cost and Technology Risk

The preceding chapters concentrated on the financial risks that occur as financial intermediaries (FIs) perform their asset transformation and/or brokerage functions both on and off the balance sheet. However, financial risk is only one part of a modern FI's risk profile. As with regular corporations, FIs have a real or production side to their operations that results in additional costs and revenues. This chapter focuses on (1) the risk-return considerations and factors that impact the operational costs of FIs and (2) the importance of optimal management and control of labor, capital, and other input sources and their costs. In particular, well-managed FIs can use cost savings to increase the FI's value to its stockholders and thus reduce the probability of insolvency.

For example, J.P. Morgan's recent $900 million acquisition of American Century Companies (a Kansas City–based mutual fund company) was billed as an example of large synergies and few overlaps. American Century gave J.P. Morgan a more extensive product line as well as technology and an infrastructure to handle many more mutual fund clients. J.P. Morgan offered American Century access to its corporate and institutional relationships in the United States and foreign countries. One expected result is a reduction in overall operational cost per dollar of assets for the combined firm.

TECHNOLOGICAL INNOVATION AND PROFITABILITY

technology

The application of computers, visual and audio communication systems, and other information systems to an FI's production of services.

Central to FIs' real or operating decisions are the costs of the inputs and the factors used in producing services both on and off the balance sheet. The two most important factors are labor (tellers, credit officers) and capital (buildings, machinery, furniture). Crucial to the efficient management and combination of these inputs resulting in financial outputs at the lowest possible cost is *technology*. Broadly defined, **technology** includes computers, visual and audio communication systems, and other information systems. See Figure 24–1 for a depiction of U.S. banks' spending on information technology. Notice that technology spending in 1996 was more than 150 percent higher than that in 1987.

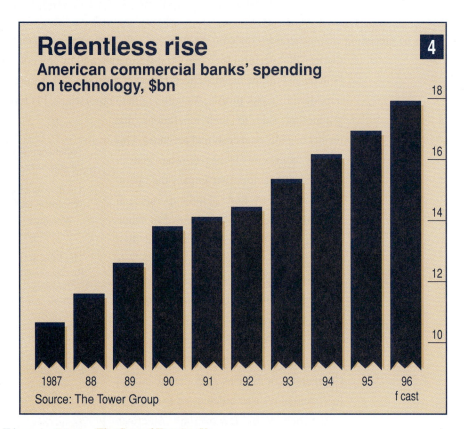

Figure **24–1**   *The Cost of Keeping Up*

Spending on IT systems by American commercial banks (in billions of dollars)
SOURCE: *The Economist,* October 26, 1996, p. 7. © 1992 The Economist Newspaper Group, Inc. Reprinted with permission. Further reproduction prohibited.

An efficient technological base for an FI can result in the following:

1. Lower costs by combining labor and capital in a more efficient mix.
2. Increased revenues by allowing a wider array of financial services to be produced or innovated and sold to customers.

The importance of an FI's operating costs and the efficient use of technology impacting these costs is clearly demonstrated by this simplified gross profit function:

$$\text{Gross profit} = (\text{Interest income} - \text{Interest expense}) +$$
$$(\text{Other income} - \text{Noninterest expense})$$
$$- \text{Provision for loan losses}$$

See Table 24–1 for a breakdown of the earnings data for U.S. banks for the period 1987–1997 into the different components impacting profits. In 1997 (through the third quarter), interest income of $250,915 million and interest expense of $121,110 million produced net interest income of $129,805 million. However, U.S. banks also had total other income of $77,326 million and noninterest expenses of $125,556 million. Thus, banks' other net income was –$48,230 million. After considering provisions for loan losses of $14,269 million and other (unreported) adjustments, the gross profit of U.S. banks was $68,280 million; net profit after tax was $43,927. Underscoring the importance of operating costs is the fact that since 1992, noninterest expenses were actually higher than interest expenses.

Technology is important because well-chosen technological investments have the potential to increase both the FI's net interest margin—the difference between interest income and interest expense—and other net income. Therefore, technology can directly improve profitability, as the following examples indicate:

1. *Interest income* can increase if the FI sells a wider array of financial services resulting from technological developments. These may include cross-selling financial products by having the computer identify customers and then telemarket financial service products such as life insurance and bank products to them.
2. *Interest expense* can be reduced if access to markets for liabilities is directly linked to the FI's technological capability. For example, Fedwire and CHIPS (two wire transfer systems discussed later in the chapter) connect the domestic and international interbank lending markets; they are based on interlocking computer network systems. Moreover, an FI's ability to originate and sell commercial paper is becoming increasingly computer driven. Thus, failure to invest in the appropriate technology may lock an FI out of a lower-cost funding market.[1]
3. *Other income* increases when fees for FI services, especially those from off-balance-sheet activities, are linked to the quality of the FI's technology. For example, customers can now electronically originate letters of credit; swaps, caps, options, and other complex derivatives (such as mortgage-backed securities and collateralized mortgage obligations) are usually traded, tracked, and valued using high-powered computers and algorithms. FIs could not offer innovative derivative products to customers without investments in suitable IT.

---

[1] Corporations alone are not responsible for selling commercial paper. In recent years, financial firms such as bank holding companies, investment banks, and finance companies have sold approximately 75 percent of all commercial paper. Thus, commercial paper is now an important source of funds for many FIs.

Table **24–1**

EARNINGS AND OTHER DATA FOR ALL INSURED BANKS
(in millions of dollars)

Financial Data	R1987	R1988	R1989	R1990	R1991	R1992	R1993	R1994	R1995	R1996	1997*
Interest income	$244,784	$272,351	$316,362	$319,987	$289,440	$256,524	$244,595	$257,829	$302,663	$312,783	$250,915
Interest expense	144,975	165,001	204,581	204,703	167,693	122,494	105,531	111,278	148,441	150,007	121,110
Net interest income	$ 99,809	$107,350	$111,781	$115,284	$121,747	$134,030	$139,064	$146,551	$154,222	$162,776	$129,805
Provision for loan losses	37,711	17,486	31,034	32,206	34,351	26,775	16,597	10,963	12,550	16,278	14,269
Miscellaneous	33,132	36,084	41,347	44,184	48,062	53,097	61,062	60,939	66,395	76,730	——
Service charges	8,735	9,455	10,235	11,423	12,818	14,117	14,869	15,337	16,045	16,937	——
Total other income	$ 41,867	$ 45,539	$ 51,582	$ 55,607	$ 60,880	$ 67,214	$ 75,931	$ 76,276	$ 82,440	$ 93,667	$ 77,326
Personnel expenses	45,333	46,878	49,293	52,030	53,536	55,487	58,460	60,600	63,440	67,054	——
Other operating expenses	52,333	55,127	59,265	64,350	72,425	77,351	81,834	83,634	86,231	93,659	——
Noninterest expenses	$ 97,666	$102,005	$108,558	$116,380	$125,961	$132,838	$140,294	$144,234	$149,671	$160,713	$125,556
Net securities gains or losses	$ 1,441	$ 275	$ 794	$ 476	$ 2,897	$ 3,957	$ 3,042	$ 1,571	$ 545	$ 1,114	$ 947
Income before taxes	5,741	33,672	24,569	22,780	25,214	45,589	61,146	67,059	74,986	80,566	68,280
Taxes	5,407	10,016	9,550	7,720	8,274	14,500	19,925	22,420	26,176	28,209	24,353
Net earnings	$ 2,536	$ 24,468	$ 15,307	$ 15,705	$ 17,927	$ 31,502	$ 43,295	$ 44,624	$ 48,810	$ 52,357	$ 43,927
Average total assets ($ billion)	2,922	3,048	3,188	3,339	3,380	3,441	3,565	3,880	4,313	4,578	4,869
Return on assets	0.09	0.80	0.48	0.47	0.53	0.92	1.21	1.15	1.13	1.19	1.24

R = Revised.

* Through the third quarter.

SOURCE: Federal Reserve Board and FDIC.

4. *Noninterest expenses* can be reduced if collecting and storing of customer information as well as processing and settling numerous financial products are computer based rather than paper based. This is particularly true of security-related back-office activities. Indeed, overall technological developments present an opportunity to continue to change the basic principles of financial intermediation such as the asset and liability management of interest gaps and liquidity gaps and the management of credit risk.

Concept Questions

1. What are some of the advantages of an efficient technological base for an FI? How can it be used to directly improve profitability?
2. Review Table 24–1. During the period 1987–1997, did noninterest expenses increase or decrease as a percentage of total bank costs?

THE IMPACT OF TECHNOLOGY ON WHOLESALE AND RETAIL BANKING

The previous discussion established that modern technology has the potential to directly affect all of a modern FI's profit-producing areas. The following discussion focuses on some specific technology-based products found in modern retail and wholesale banking. Note that this list is far from complete.

Wholesale Banking Services

Probably the most important area on which technology has impacted wholesale or corporate customer services is a bank's ability to provide cash management or working capital services. Cash management service needs have largely resulted from (1) corporate recognition that excess cash balances result in a significant opportunity cost due to lost or forgone interest and (2) corporate need to know cash or working capital positions on a real-time basis. Among the services that modern banks provide to improve the efficiency with which corporate clients manage their financial positions are these:

1. *Controlled disbursement accounts.*   An account feature that establishes for the customer in the morning almost all payments to be made in a given day. The bank informs the corporate client of the total funds it needs to meet disbursements, and the client wire transfers the amount needed. These checking accounts are debited early each day so that corporations can obtain an early insight into their net cash positions.
2. *Account reconciliation.*   A checking feature that records which of the firm's checks have been paid by the bank.
3. *Lockbox services.*   A centralized collection service for corporate payments to reduce the delay in check clearing, or the **float**. In a typical lockbox arrangement, a local bank sets up a lockbox at the post office for a corporate client located outside the area. Local customers mail payments to the lockbox rather than to the out-of-town corporate headquarters. The bank collects these checks several times per day and deposits them directly into the customer's account. Details of the transaction are wired to the corporate client.

float

The time between depositing a check and the availability of the funds for depositor use; that is, the time it takes a check to clear at a bank.

4. *Funds concentration.*   Redirects funds from accounts in a large number of different banks or branches to a few centralized accounts at one bank.

5. *Electronic funds transfer.*   Includes overnight payments via CHIPS or Fedwire, automated payment of payrolls or dividends via automated clearinghouses (ACHs), and automated transmission of payment messages by SWIFT, an international electronic message service owned and operated by U.S. and European banks that instructs banks to make specific payments.

6. *Check deposit services.*   Encoding, endorsing, microfilming, and handling customers' checks.

7. *Electronic initiation of letters of credit.*   Allows customers in a network to access bank computers to initiate letters of credit.

8. *Treasury management software.*   Allows efficient management of multiple currency and security portfolios for trading and investment purposes.[2]

9. *Electronic data interchange.*   A specialized application of electronic mail, allowing businesses to transfer and transact invoices, purchase orders, and shipping notices automatically, using banks as clearinghouses.

Retail Banking Services

Retail customers have demanded efficiency and flexibility in their financial transactions. The limitation of using only checks or holding cash is often more expensive and time-consuming than using retail-oriented electronic payments technology.[3] See Figure 24–2 for a comparison of paying bills by mail with paying by an electronic bill payment system. Some of the most important retail payment product innovations include the following:

1. *Automated teller machines (ATMs).*   Allow customers 24-hour access to their checking accounts. They can pay bills as well as withdraw cash from these machines. In addition, if the bank's ATMs are part of a bank network (such as CIRRUS, PLUS, or HONOR), retail depositors can gain direct nationwide—and in many cases international—access to their deposit accounts by using the ATMs of other banks in the network to draw on their accounts.

2. *Point-of-sale debit (POS) cards.*   Allows customers who choose not to use cash, checks, or credit cards for purchases to buy merchandise and have the funds immediately deducted from their checking accounts and immediately transferred to the merchants' accounts.[4]

3. *Home banking.*   Usually connects customers to their deposit and brokerage accounts and provides a bill-paying service via personal computers.

4. *Preauthorized debits/credits.*   Includes direct deposit of payroll checks into bank accounts and direct payment of mortgages and utility bills.

5. *Paying bills via telephone.*   Allows direct transfer of funds from the customer's bank account to outside parties either by voice command or by touch-tone telephone.

---

[2] Computerized pension fund management and advisory services could be added to this list.

[3] The downside of electronic bill payment systems, for FI customers, however, is they lose the advantages of the float (the time between writing a check and debiting the check writer's bank account) that are inherent in a check (paper-based) system.

[4] In the case of bank-supplied credit cards, the merchant normally is compensated very quickly but not instantaneously (usually one or two days) by the credit card issuer. The bank then holds an account receivable against the card user. However, even a short delay can represent an opportunity cost for the merchant.

Perfecting the Paperless Path

Paying the bills electronically is not new, but the few electronic payments sent today lack the account information usually found on a billing stub. As a result, even computer banking services often send payments using paper checks. Now several companies say they are close to solving this problem. They have developed systems that can both send bills and receive payments electronically, in the process eliminating the use of paper. Here is how the paper trail created by the current process of paying bills compares with an electronic bill payment system.

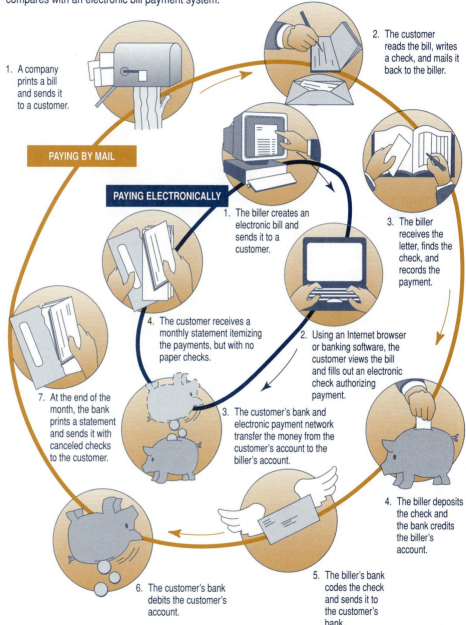

1. A company prints a bill and sends it to a customer.

2. The customer reads the bill, writes a check, and mails it back to the biller.

PAYING BY MAIL

PAYING ELECTRONICALLY

1. The biller creates an electronic bill and sends it to a customer.

3. The biller receives the letter, finds the check, and records the payment.

4. The customer receives a monthly statement itemizing the payments, but with no paper checks.

2. Using an Internet browser or banking software, the customer views the bill and fills out an electronic check authorizing payment.

7. At the end of the month, the bank prints a statement and sends it with canceled checks to the customer.

3. The customer's bank and electronic payment network transfer the money from the customer's account to the biller's account.

4. The biller deposits the check and the bank credits the biller's account.

6. The customer's bank debits the customer's account.

5. The biller's bank codes the check and sends it to the customer's bank.

F i g u r e **24–2**   *Comparison of Bill Payment System by Mail Compared with an Electronic Payment System*

SOURCE: The *New York Times,* July 5, 1996, p. D1. Copyright © 1996 by the New York Times Co. Reprinted with permission.

6.   *Retail sweep accounts.*   Allow customers to sweep balances in household transaction accounts into savings deposits overnight or over the weekend.

Contemporary Perspectives Box 24–1 discusses the role the Internet is playing in providing retail banking services. More and more FIs are applying technology to enable customers to transact from their homes. It will only be a matter of time before all FI services are available on the Internet.

Contemporary Perspectives 24–1

Home Banking Crossroads: The Web, The PC, or Both?

The latest stir in the unfolding world of home banking has been instigated, not surprisingly, by the Internet. More banks are adopting home-banking transaction capabilities via the World Wide Web.

The Internet certainly has momentum. The ubiquitous Internet makes it possible for consumers to access banking services directly through a bank's Web site: they need not buy PC-based home banking software and load it onto their computers. . . .

Booz, Allen & Hamilton (Booz, Allen), a consulting firm in New York, predicts that more than 16 million households will bank through the Internet by the year 2000, up from about 1 million in 1997. These 16 million will be a profitable sort. Even though they will comprise about 16 percent of U.S. households, they will account for almost 30 percent of total retail banking profits, says Booz, Allen.

To get a piece of this action, more than 1,500 banks will build Internet sites by the year 2000, predicts Booz, Allen, and 500 of these will offer full-fledged home banking services. And though PC banking is a cheap delivery method compared to the branch, Internet banking is even cheaper. Compared to PC banking's estimated $.015 cost per transaction, Internet banking is estimated by

Booz, Allen to cost $.010 per transaction. . . .

Christian Frederick, managing director of financial services at the consulting firm, Dove Associates in Boston, notes that consumers are not yet using the Web fluently due to security concerns. Banks should plan on implementing Web-based home banking services when it's more secure, he says. "If I were a banker, I wouldn't be putting significant transactions on the Internet now. It's a mistake to get ahead of the curve. All we need is to have some bank on the Internet and a little old lady losing $10,000 from a hacker—then banking on the Internet is over." . . .

"We will be seeing financial institutions heading for the Web in all directions," says Karen Epper, an analyst of money and technology strategies at Forrester Research, Cambridge, MA. "Some institutions are beginning to offer transactions via the Web, and we already see institutions going straight to the Web (bypassing the PC altogether). It's just the tip of the iceberg."

Certainly, Internet-based banking has come a long way. San Francisco–based Wells Fargo is credited as the first major bank to open its Web site to banking transactions. It was followed shortly by Security First Network Bank, an Internet-based bank headquartered in

Pineville, KY, as well as larger institutions, including Bank of America and Huntington National Bank, Columbus, OH.

Since May 1995, Wells Fargo customers have been able to view account balances and historical information by connecting to the bank's Web site. As of May of this year, customers have been able to transfer funds between accounts. Bill payment capabilities were added in July. Wells Fargo boasts that its site allows consumers to pay bills and send payments anywhere in the U.S. (Other bank sites allow payments to be sent only to a predesignated list of payees.) The bank currently processes all the payments in-house.

"Making payments is just the latest development in an ongoing process of our offering Internet banking services," says Gailyn Johnson, senior vice president of Wells Fargo's Online Financial Services. Customers can sign up for the Internet bill payment service through Wells' home page, says Johnson. The service costs a flat fee of $5 per month. Customers also have the option of downloading transactions to their personal financial software through an integrated export function. Wells also offers home banking services through Prodigy.

SOURCE: Joanna Kolor, *Bank Technology*, September 1996, p. 1.

Concept Q u e s t i o n s

1. What are some of the wholesale banking services provided to corporate customers that have been improved by technology?
2. What are some of the automated retail payment products available today? What advantages do these products offer the retail customer?

THE EFFECTS OF TECHNOLOGY
ON REVENUES AND COSTS

The previous section presented a list of some current products or services being offered by FIs that are built around a strong technological base. Technological advances allow an FI to offer such products to its customers and potentially to earn higher profits. The investment of resources in many of these products is risky, however, because product innovations may fail to attract sufficient business relative to the initial cash outlay and the future costs related to these investments once in place. In the terminology of finance, a number of technologically based product innovations may turn out to be *negative* net present value projects due to uncertainties about revenues and costs and how quickly rivals will mimic or copy any innovation. Another factor is agency conflicts, in which managers undertake growth-oriented investments to increase an FI's size; such investments may be inconsistent with stockholders' value-maximizing objectives.[5] As a result, losses on technological innovations and new technology could weaken an FI because scarce capital resources are invested in value-decreasing products.

This leads one to consider whether direct or indirect evidence is available as to whether technology investments to update the operational structure of FIs have either increased revenues or decreased costs. Most of the direct or indirect evidence has concerned the effects of size on financial firms' operating costs; indeed, the largest FIs appear to be investing most in IT and other technological innovations.

We first discuss the evidence on the product revenue side and then discuss it on the operating cost side. Before looking at these revenue and cost aspects, however, we should stress that the success of a technologically related innovation cannot be evaluated independently from regulation and regulatory changes. To a large extent, the growth and success of the retail and wholesale cash management products just described depend on continuing frictions and restrictions on full interstate banking (see Chapter 26). Historically, restrictions on U.S. banks' ability to branch across state lines have created problems for large corporations with national and international franchises; these firms needed to consolidate and centralize their deposit funds for working capital purposes. Thus, innovations such as wholesale lockboxes and funds concentration have eased these problems. It is more than a coincidence that cash management services have not attracted customers in Europe to the degree that they have in the United States. One reason for this is that in European

---

[5] A good example of the cost of failed technological innovation was the problem Fleet Financial experienced in its 1995 takeover of Shawmut National Bank. Fleet ran into problems assimilating Shawmut's check-clearing operations in Connecticut. The result was a computer nightmare that produced late checks to customers, $10 million in added costs, and a delay in the conversion of all of Shawmut's systems. (See Chapter 26 for additional details.)

countries nationwide branching and banking have been more prevalent and interregional banking restrictions notably absent. As a result, the 1997 introduction of full interstate banking for banks in the United States may well reduce the future demand for such services.

Technology and Revenues

One potential benefit of technology is that it allows an FI to cross-market both new and existing products to customers. For example, a commercial bank may link up with an insurance company to jointly market the other's loan and insurance products. Such joint selling does not require the FI to produce all the services sold within the same branch or financial services outlet. This arrangement has proven popular in Germany, where the second and third largest banks (Dresdner and Commerzbank) have developed sophisticated cross-marketing arrangements with large insurance companies. In the United States, Citicorp is using computerized information on its customers to cross-sell bank-sponsored mutual funds, brokerage accounts, and insurance products. Unfortunately, concrete data for the revenue synergy benefits from such ventures are unavailable.

Technology also increases the rate of innovation of new financial products. In recent years, many notable failures as well as successes have occurred. For example, despite large investments by banks, new product innovations such as POS/debit cards have not found a sufficiently large market. On the other hand, paying bills via telephone and using preauthorized debits and credits, including direct payroll systems, are proving to be high growth areas in modern banking.

Finally, we cannot ignore the issue of *service quality*. For example, ATMs may potentially lower bank operating costs when compared to employing full-service tellers, but the machine's inability to address customers' concerns and questions flexibly may drive retail customers away. That is, revenue losses may counteract any cost-savings effects. The survival of many small banks may well be due to customers' belief that overall service quality is higher from tellers who provide a human touch rather than from ATMs.

Technology and Costs

Traditionally, FIs have considered the major benefits of technological advances to be on the cost side rather than the revenue side. After a theoretical look at how technology favorably or unfavorably affects an FI's costs, we look at the direct and indirect evidence of technology-based cost savings for FIs. In general, technology may favorably affect an FI's cost structure by allowing it to exploit either economies of scale or economies of scope.

Economies of Scale.   As financial firms become larger, the potential scale and array of the technology in which they can invest generally expands. As noted, the largest FIs make the largest expenditures on technology-related innovations. If enhanced or improved technology lowers an FI's average costs of financial service production, larger FIs may have an **economy of scale** advantage over smaller financial firms. Economies of scale imply that the unit or average cost of producing FI services in aggregate (or some specific service such as deposits or loans) falls as the size of the FI expands.

economy of scale

 The degree to which an FI's average unit costs to produce financial services fall as its output of services increases.

Figure 24–3 depicts economies of scale for three FIs of different-sizes. The average cost of producing an FI's output of financial services is measured as

$$AC_i = \frac{TC_i}{S_i}$$

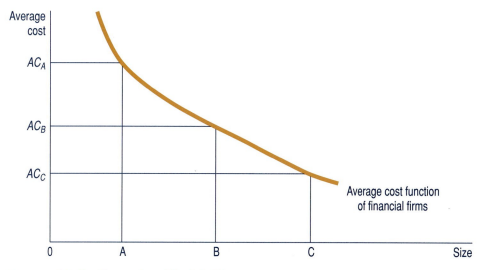

F i g u r e **24-3**   *Economies of Scale in FIs*

where

$$AC_i = \text{average costs of the } i\text{th bank}$$
$$TC_i = \text{total costs of the } i\text{th bank}$$
$$S_i = \text{size of the bank measured by assets, deposits, or loans.}[6]$$

The average cost to the largest FI in Figure 24–3 (size C) to produce financial services is lower than the cost to smaller firms B and A. This means that at any given price for financial service firm products, firm C can make a higher profit than either B or A. Alternatively, firm C can undercut B and A in price and potentially gain a larger market share.

For example, First Union Corporation's $3.2 billion acquisition of Signet Banking Corporation was billed as a cost-savings acquisition. Because of overlapping operations with Signet, First Union said it expected annual cost savings of approximately $240 million. In the framework of Figure 24–3, Signet, firm A, might be operating at AC_A and First Union might be represented as firm B at AC_B. First Union and Signet had significant back-office operations in Virginia that could be combined and consolidated. The consolidation of such overlapping activities would lower the average costs for the combined (larger) bank to point C in Figure 24–3, operating at AC_C.

The long-term implication of economies of scale on the FI sector is that the larger and most cost-efficient FIs will drive out smaller FIs, leading to increased large-firm dominance and concentration in financial services production. Such an implication is reinforced if time-related operating or technological improvements increasingly benefit large FIs more than small FIs. For example, satellite technology and supercomputers, in which enormous operating or technological advances are being made, may be available to only the largest FIs. The effect of improving operations or technology over time, which is biased toward larger projects, is to shift the AC curve downward over time but with a larger downward shift for large FIs; see Figure 24–4.

---

[6] It is arguable that the size of the modern FI should be measured by including off-balance-sheet assets (contingent value) as well.

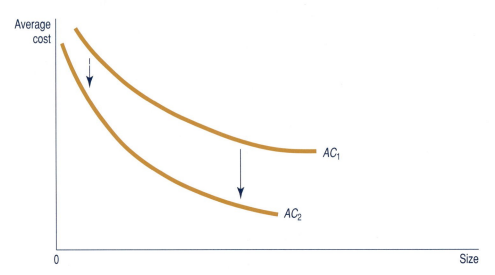

F i g u r e **24–4**   *The Effects of Technological Improvement*

In Figure 24–4, AC_1 is the hypothetical *AC* curve prior to cost-reducing innovations. AC_2 reflects the cost-lowering effects of technology and consolidation on FIs of all sizes but with the greatest benefit accruing to those of the largest size.

As noted earlier, technological investments are risky; if their future revenues do not cover their costs of development, they reduce the value of the FI and its net worth. On the cost side, large-scale investments may result in excess capacity problems and integration problems as well as cost overruns and cost control problems. Then small FIs with simple and easily managed computer systems and/or those leasing time on large FIs' computers without bearing the fixed costs of installation and maintenance may have an average cost advantage. In this case, the technological investments of large-size FIs result in higher than average costs of financial service production, causing the industry to operate under conditions of **diseconomies of scale**. See this in Figure 24–5. Diseconomies of scale imply that small FIs are more cost efficient than large FIs and that in a freely competitive environment for financial services, small FIs prosper.

Wells Fargo & Co.'s purchase of First Interstate Bancorp (in April 1996) is an example of potential diseconomies of scale. More than a year after the purchase, Wells Fargo was still having organization and systems problems integrating First Interstate. Specifically, 1997 profits were deflated as a result of expenses produced from the resolution of various operational and back-office issues related to the First Interstate acquisition, including clearing checking accounts with other banks. Wells Fargo had trouble keeping up with the integrated check-clearing system, resulting in such costs as write-offs for bounced checks that were not reconciled properly. As a result of managerial inefficiencies, Wells Fargo also had problems converting First Interstate's branches to its method of doing business.

At least two other possible shapes for the *AC* function exist (see Figure 24–6). In Figure 24–6(a), the financial services industry reflects economies of scale at first and then diseconomies of scale as firms grow larger. This suggests that a best or most efficient size for an FI exists at point S* and that too much technology investment could be as bad as too little. Figure 24–6(b) represents constant returns to scale. Any potential cost-reducing effects of technology are spread evenly over FIs of all sizes. That is, technology investments are neutral rather than favoring one size of FI over another.

diseconomy of scale

The degree to which an FI's average costs to produce financial services increase as its output of services increases.

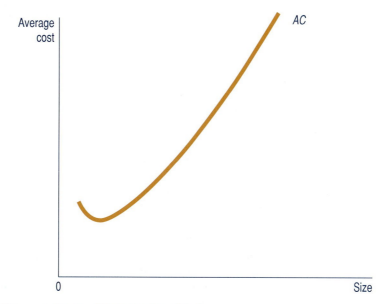

Figure **24-5**   *Diseconomies of Scale*

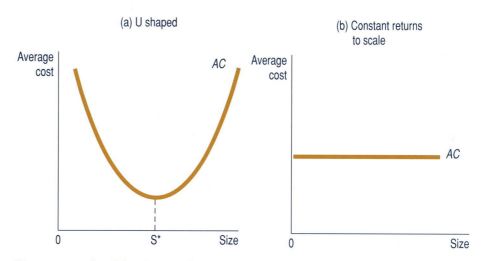

Figure **24-6**   *Other Average Cost Functions*

Economies of Scope.   Although technological investments may have positive or negative effects on FIs in general and these effects may well differ across FIs of different size, technology tends to be used more in some product areas than others. That is, FIs are multiproduct firms producing services involving different technological needs. Moreover, technological improvements or investments in one financial service area (such as lending) may have incidental and synergistic benefits in lowering the costs to produce financial services in other areas (such as securities underwriting or brokerage). Specifically, computerization allows the storage of important information on customers and their needs that can be used by more than one service area. The simple *economy of scale* concept ignores

economy of scope

The degree to which an
FI can generate cost
synergies by producing
multiple financial service
products.

these interrelationships among products and the "jointness" in the costs to produce financial products. In particular, FIs' abilities to generate synergistic cost savings through joint use of inputs in producing multiple products is called **economies of scope** as opposed to economies of scale.

The mergers and acquisitions in the FI industry in recent years (a result of the loosening of federal regulations) provide numerous examples of attempts to take advantage of economies of scope. For example, in 1997 Travelers Group acquired Salomon Brothers for $9 billion. Then in 1998 Travelers and Citicorp announced an $83 billion merger. Travelers' chairman, Sanford I. Weill, decided to build the largest financial services company in the United States. Travelers had long been involved in the insurance and mutual fund business before the acquisition of Salomon (it already owned Smith Barney), but it had lacked foreign influence and recognition as well as respect on Wall Street. The Salomon Brothers acquisition and the Citicorp merger were attempts to alleviate these deficiencies. Another example of a merger/acquisition for economies of scope is NationsBank's $1.2 billion purchase of Montgomery Securities (a San Francisco–based investment bank). NationsBank viewed this acquisition as a way to expand its operations to California (economies of scale) and to give it entry into the investment banking business of underwriting securities (economies of scope). A final example is Lincoln National Corp. (an Indiana-based insurance company), which is attempting to become one of the nation's premier sellers of life insurance, annuities, mutual funds, and 401(k) retirement plans through a series of acquisitions of firms such as Delaware Management Holdings (for $510 million) and Voyageur Fund Management (for $70 million), both mutual fund companies. Technology played a particularly large role in Lincoln National's plans as it committed major resources to technology purchases needed to support late night calls from mutual fund, 401(k), and variable annuity customers who expect to be able to make investment selections 24-hours a day.

Technology may allow two FIs to jointly use their input resources such as capital and labor to produce a set of financial services at a lower cost than if the financial service products were produced independently of one another. Specifically, let X_1 and X_2 be two financial products; each is produced by one firm as a specialized producer. That is, firm A produces only X_1 but no X_2, and firm B produces only X_2 but no X_1. The average cost functions (AC) of these firms are

$$AC_A[X_1, 0] \text{ and } AC_B[0, X_2]$$

Economies of scope exist if these firms merge and jointly produce X_1 and X_2, resulting in

$$AC_{A+B}[X_1, X_2] < AC_A[X_1, 0] + AC_B[0, X_2]$$

That is, the cost of joint production via cost synergies is less than the separate and independent production of these services.

EXAMPLE 24–1

• • • • • •   *Calculation of Average Costs*

Let TC_B be a specialized bank's total cost to produce lending services to a corporate client. Suppose that the total operating costs of producing these services is $50,000 for a loan volume (L_B) of $10 million. Such costs include collecting and monitoring information as well as maintaining and processing accounts. Thus, the average cost (AC_B) of loan production for the bank is

$$AC_B = \frac{TC_B}{L_B} = \frac{\$50,000}{\$10,000,000} = .005 = .5\%$$

At the same time, a specialized securities firm is selling commercial paper for the same corporate customer. The securities firm's total cost (TC_S) to run the commercial paper operation is $10,000 for a $1 million issue ($P_S$). These costs include underwriting the issue as well as placing it with outside buyers.

$$AC_S = \frac{TC_S}{P_S} = \frac{\$10,000}{\$1,000,000} = .01 = 1\%$$

Consequently, the total average cost (*TAC*) for the bank to produce the loan services and the securities firm to issue commercial paper is

$$TAC = \frac{\$60,000}{\$11,000,000} = 0.54\%$$

Suppose, instead, that a single FI acting as a provider of multiproduct finance services (FS) produced both $10 million of lending services and $1 million commercial paper issuance services for the same customer (i.e., P_{FS} = $11,000,000). Loans and commercial paper are sources of funds substitutes for corporate customers. For an FI to originate a loan and commercial paper requires very similar expertise in funding that issue and in credit risk assessment and monitoring. To the extent that most loans are quickly sold after origination, loan origination is very similar to the original underwriter's sale of commercial paper to outside buyers. Common technologies in the loan and commercial paper production functions suggest that a single FI, simultaneously (or jointly) producing both loan and commercial paper services for the same client at a total cost TC_{FS}, should be able to do this at a lower average cost than could the specialized FIs that separately produce these services. That is, the single FI should be able to produce the $11,000,000 ($P_{FS}$) of financial services at a lower cost (say TC_{FS} = $51,000) than should two specialized FIs. Accordingly

$$AC_{FS} = \frac{TC_{FS}}{P_{FS}} = \frac{\$51,000}{\$11,000,000} = 0.46\% < 0.54\% \qquad \bullet \quad \bullet \quad \bullet$$

Formally, if AC_{FS} is the total average cost of a nonspecialized financial services firm, economies of scope would imply that

$$AC_{FS} < TAC$$

That is, the average cost to jointly produce many financial services may be less than the average cost to produce these products separately.

diseconomy of scope

The degree to which the costs of joint production of FI services are higher than if they were produced independently.

Nevertheless, **diseconomies of scope** may occur instead. This happens when FIs find costs actually higher from joint production of services than had they been produced independently. For example, suppose that an FI purchases some very specialized information-based technology to ease its loan production and processing functions. The FI could use any excess capacity this system has in other service areas. This process could be a relatively inefficient technology for other service areas, however, and could add to the overall costs of production when compared to using a specialized technology for each service or product area.

Of course, not all technological innovation is appropriate and profitable for the FI. Consider the $8.9 billion merger of Aetna Inc. (a Hartford, Connecticut, based insurance company) with U.S. Healthcare Inc. In September 1997, Aetna's stock price plunged 10 percent as a result of glitches in its integration of U.S. Healthcare. Aetna attempted to meld its operations with those of U.S. Healthcare and tried to consolidate customer service centers too quickly, creating a backlog of claims. The resolution of the backlog produced higher than expected costs. The inability to accurately predict the costs early on meant that Aetna signed many contracts with employers based on out-of-date pricing assumptions. Since Aetna did not have the backing of claims in its system, it did not know what costs were doing and, as a result, did not set its insurance premiums high enough.

Concept Questions

1. What are two risk factors involved in an FI's investment of resources in innovative, technological products?
2. What is the link between interstate banking restrictions and the wholesale demand for electronic payment services?
3. Does the existence of economies of scale for FIs mean that in the long run small FIs cannot survive?
4. If diseconomies of scope exist, do specialized FIs have a relative cost advantage or disadvantage over product-diversified FIs?
5. What are the potential economies of scope or cost synergies if a commercial bank merges with an investment bank?

EMPIRICAL FINDINGS ON ECONOMIES OF SCALE AND SCOPE AND IMPLICATIONS FOR TECHNOLOGY EXPENDITURES

A large number of studies have examined economies of scale and scope in different financial service industry sectors.[7] With respect to banks, most of the early studies failed to find economies of scale for any but the smallest banks. More recently, better data sets and improved methodologies have suggested that economies of scale may exist for banks in the $100 million to $5 billion range. Many large regional and superregional banks are in this size range. With respect to economies of scope, either among deposits, loans, and other traditional banking product areas or between on-balance-sheet products and off-balance-sheet products such as loan sales, the evidence that cost synergies exist is at best very weak. Similarly, the smaller number of studies involving nonbank financial service firms such as

---

[7] Good reviews are found in J.A. Clark, "Economies of Scale and Scope in Depository, Financial Institutions: A Review of the Literature," *Economic Review*, Federal Reserve Bank of Kansas City, September–October 1988, pp. 16–33; L. Mester, "Efficient Production of Financial Services; Scale and Scope Economies," *Economic Review*, Federal Reserve Bank of Philadelphia, January–February 1987, pp. 15–25; and A. Berger, W. C. Hunter, and S. G. Timme, "The Efficiency of Financial Institutions: A Review and Preview of Research Past, Present and Future" *Journal of Banking and Finance* 17 (1993), pp. 221–249.

thrifts, insurance companies, and securities firms almost always report that neither economies of scale nor economies of scope exist.

Economies of Scale and Scope and X-Inefficiencies

Finally, a number of very recent studies have investigated the *dispersion* of costs in any given FI size class rather than the shape of the average cost functions. These efficiency studies find quite dramatic cost differences among banks, thrifts, and insurance companies in any given size class (e.g., $100 million asset size class, $200 million asset size class). Moreover, these studies find that sometimes as little as 5 percent of the cost differences among FIs in any size class can be attributed to economies of scale or scope.[8] This suggests that cost inefficiencies related to managerial performance and other hard-to-quantify factors (so-called *X-inefficiencies*) may better explain cost differences and operating cost efficiencies among financial firms than do technology-related investments per se.[9]

No strong direct evidence exists that larger multiproduct financial service firms enjoy cost advantages over smaller, more specialized financial firms. Nor do economies of scope and scale explain many of the cost differences among FIs of the same size. These empirical findings raise questions as to the benefits of technology investments and technological innovation. Although a majority of the existing studies tested for economies of scope and scale rather than the benefits of technology, these results are consistent with the relatively low payoff from technological innovation. To the extent that large FIs obtain benefits, they may well be on the revenue generation/new product innovation side rather than on the cost side.[10] This is not to say that small FIs do not innovate but that large FIs that have sufficient funds to invest are able to innovate before small FIs do.

Moreover, the real benefits of technological innovation may also be long term and dynamic, related to the evolution of the U.S. payments system away from cash and checks (first introduced in the 1700s and 1800s) and toward electronic means of payment (see Contemporary Perspectives Box 24–2 for a brief review of this evolution). Indeed, many commercial banks have created Web pages (a list of which can be found on the Internet at www.mybanks.com) and are very close to introducing home banking via the Internet. Additionally, NatWest Bank and MasterCard's Mondex is a card that can handle five different currencies at any one time, allowing a user to pay (or receive) the local currency appropriate to wherever he or she is doing business. Mondex's security resides in the chip on the card, allowing money to be moved safely over any network, including the Internet. Although the technology of such a paperless system may be implementable, convincing consumers to use the technology may take some time. Such benefits are difficult to obtain in traditional economy of scale and scope studies, which are largely static and ignore the more dynamic aspects of efficiency gains. This dynamic technological evolution not only has affected the fundamental role of FIs in the financial system but also has generated some new and subtle risks for FIs and their regulators. The next section discusses the effects of technology on the payments system.

---

[8] See A. Berger and D. B. Humphrey, "The Dominance of Inefficiencies over Scale and Product Mix in Banking," *Journal of Monetary Economics* 28 (1991) and *Journal of Banking and Finance* 17, Special Issue on Efficiency (1993). The task for future research is to identify more precisely the source of these relative cost inefficiencies.

[9] Research to date suggests that cost inefficiencies may explain 20 percent or more of costs in banking. See Berger, Hunter, and Timme, "The Efficiency of Financial Institutions."

[10] See A. Berger, D. Hancock, and D. B. Humphrey, "Bank Efficiency Derived from the Profit Function," *Journal of Banking and Finance* 17 (1993), pp. 317–347.

Contemporary Perspectives 24–2

Brief History of Money in the United States—Goodbye Dollar Bills: Digital Cash Is Coming

Colonial era–A variety of currencies from countries such as Great Britain, Portugal, Spain, France, and Germany was used. In addition to local currency issued by the colonies, they used wampum, livestock, and local crops, such as tobacco to conduct business and other daily transactions of commerce. This variety caused confusion and slowed trade and economic growth. Thomas Jefferson proposed the decimal coinage system that we use today; his efforts culminated in the enactment of the Mint Act of 1792, authored by Treasury secretary Alexander Hamilton, which also authorized construction of the first mint in Philadelphia.

1832–1863 Banks issued their own dollars backed by the collateral of their choosing. Bank notes were supposed to be convertible, on demand, to gold or silver, but many bank note holders found themselves stuck with worthless paper. It was sometimes difficult or impossible to detect which notes were sound and which were not because of the staggering number of different ones. By 1860, nearly 10,000 different bank notes circulated throughout the country. Demand grew for a uniform national currency acceptable anywhere without risk.

1863–1864 National Currency Act and National Bank Act, Congress authorized the U.S. Treasury to issue paper currency, the first standardized national bank dollar bill. The paper currency was to be 90 percent backed by U.S. Treasury securities, purchased by the issuing bank.

1913 The Federal Reserve Act created the 12 Federal Reserve banks and a national currency. Federal Reserve notes were first issued. Additional historical information is available from the Office of the Comptroller of Currency's Web-based history exhibit: (http://www.occ.treas.gov/exhibits/histor1.htm).

E-Money Forms: The End of the Fed's Currency Monopoly?

Stored value cards are prepaid instruments for which a record of funds owned by or available to the consumer is stored on an electronic device in the consumer's possession and the amount of stored "value" increases or decreases when the consumer uses the device to make a purchase or other transaction.

An alternative is a "digital token" plan that utilizes computer networks. Token products typically involve a standard personal computer with appropriate software to allow a consumer to purchase units of digital currency, store it on his or her computer's hard drive, and spend it over computer networks such as the Internet.

Backing During the early mercantile period in Europe, gold and silver were deposited (often with goldsmiths) in exchange for paper receipts. The metal was the collateral that "backed" the paper receipt, which was an early form of paper money and functioned as currency. Soon banks that ensured the value of currency notes emerged, diminishing the need to exchange a note that had been received for the original deposit backing the note.

Notice that any form of cash is a *claim* on the issuing party, most commonly in the form of a currency note. Consumers purchase the claim with traditional money and exchange the claims for goods and services with merchants who are willing to accept the claim as payment. E-cash is such a claim stored in digital form (e.g., computer code on a card about the size of a credit card, or on the hard drive of a computer). The confidence in any currency or store of value depends on the issuer's resources and its ability to make good on the claim. Placing collateral in a depository is a way for an issuer to win confidence. Depending on the (nonbank) issuer of e-cash, customers risk buying a card or transferring value to one that may become worthless if the issuer becomes insolvent. Because of this risk, consumers may prefer "electronic money" that banks or other regulated financial institutions issue.

SOURCE: "A Note on the Impact of Financial Technology: Money and Electronic Money," by Bruce Weber, Information Systems Department, Stern School of Business, New York University, September 1997.

Concept Questions

1. What does the empirical evidence reveal about economies of scale and scope?
2. What conclusion is suggested by recent studies that have focused on the dispersion of costs across banks of a given asset size?

TECHNOLOGY AND THE EVOLUTION
OF THE PAYMENTS SYSTEM

To better understand the changing nature of the U.S. payments system, consider Table 24–2. Nonelectronic methods accounted for 96.3 percent of noncash transactions, but this represented only 7.2 percent of the dollar *value* of noncash transactions. By comparison, electronic methods of payment accounted for only 3.7 percent in volume but 92.8 percent in value. Wire transfer systems alone accounted for 91.2 percent of all dollar transactions measured in value.

The two wire transfer systems that dominate the U.S. payments system are Fedwire and the Clearing House Interbank Payments System (CHIPS). Fedwire is a network linking more than 10,000 domestic banks with the Federal Reserve System. Banks use this network to make deposit and loan payments, to transfer book entry securities among themselves, and to act as payment agents on behalf of large corporate customers, including other financial service firms. CHIPS operates as a private network. At the core of the CHIPS system are approximately 115 large U.S. and foreign banks acting as correspondent banks for a larger number of domestic and international banks in clearing mostly international payments (foreign exchange, Eurodollar loans, certificates of deposit).

Together, the value of payments sent over these two wire transfer networks has been growing at around 25 percent per year. Indeed, since 1986, the combined value of payments sent over these two networks has often exceeded $2 trillion a day.[11] Another way to indicate the tremendous growth in these wire transfer payment networks is to compare their dollar payment values to bank reserves, as we do in Table 24–3. Thus, the value of wire transfers has increased approximately fortyfold relative to bank reserves, over the period 1970–1995.[12] According to data in Table 24–4, the United States is not the only country in

---

Table **24–2**

VOLUME AND VALUE COMPOSITION OF NONCASH U.S. PAYMENTS

	Volume Composition	**Value Composition**	**Average Value per Transaction**
Nonelectronic			
Checks	96.3%	7.2%	$ 660
Electronic			
Fedwire	0.1	38.5	2,937,500
CHIPS	0.1	52.7	6,478,070
ACH	3.5	1.6	3,971
	100%	100%	

SOURCE: Office of Technology Assessment Statistics, September 1995.

---

[11]See Office of Technology Assessment, *U.S. Banks and International Telecommunications*. Washington, D.C., September 1995. In the mid-1990s, the daily value of transactions on CHIPS alone exceeded $1.2 trillion.

[12]Interestingly, the slow growth in the ratio after 1990 is despite a fall in bank reserves over the period (due to a decline in required cash reserve ratios for banks). For example, bank reserves fell from $62 billion in 1987 to $48 billion in 1997.

Table **24–3**

RATIO OF FEDWIRE AND CHIPS DOLLAR PAYMENTS TO BANK RESERVES

	Average Daily Fedwire and CHIPS Payments ($) to Bank Reserves
1970	2%
1980	17
1990	80
1995	76

SOURCE: D. B. Humphrey, "Future Directions in Payment Risk Reduction," *Journal of Cash Management*, 1988; and Federal Reserve figures.

Table **24–4**

WHOLESALE WIRE TRANSFER SYSTEMS IN DIFFERENT COUNTRIES

	Number of Transactions (thousands)	Value of Transactions (billions of US $)	Ratio of Transactions Value to GDP (at annual rate)
Japan			
FEYCS	8,839	$ 81,624	16.0
BOJ-NET	3,849	434,677	85.0
Netherlands			
BGC-CH	1,410.9	1,363	3.4
8007-SWIFT	2.1	6,438	16.3
FA	0.4	5,261	13.3
Sweden			
RIX	119	7,509	32.8
Data-Clearing	249,153	318	1.4
Switzerland			
SIC	95,990	27,235	88.9
DTA/LSV	80,368	238	0.8
United Kingdom			
CHAPS	12,569	42,171	38.1
BACS	2,268,000	1,664	1.5
Cheque/credit	2,377,000	2,010	1.9
United States			
Fedwire	75,900	222,954	30.7
CHIPS	51,000	310,021	42.7

SOURCE: The Bank for International Settlements, *Statistics on Payment Systems in the Group of 10 Countries* (Basle, Switzerland: BIS, 1996), Table 10b, p. 126.

Table **24-5**

RISKS OF A WIRE TRANSFER PAYMENT SYSTEM

Daylight Overdraft Risk   Risk that a bank's overdraft on its reserve account at the Federal Reserve Bank run during the business day cannot be alleviated by the close of the business day.

International Technology Transfer Risk   Risk from the inability to transfer profitable domestic technological innovations to international markets.

Crime and Fraud Risk   Risk of internal or external interference with security codes and practices that protect wire transfers.

Regulatory Risk   Risk that FI telecommunications improvements render regulations toothless.

Tax Avoidance   Risk that FIs may use technology and wire transfer networks to minimize their tax burden.

Competition Risk   Risk resulting from increased competition with nontraditional financial service suppliers as financial services become more technology based.

---

which wholesale wire transfer systems have come to dominate the payments systems; the United Kingdom, Switzerland, and Japan also have very large wire transfer systems measured as a percentage of local gross domestic product (GDP).

Risks in the Wire Transfer Payment System

At least six important risks are possible with the use of the wire transfer systems. We mentioned some while discussing off-balance-sheet activities in Chapter 20; we present these in more detail here. The risks are summarized in Table 24–5.

Daylight Overdraft Risk.   Some analysts and regulators view *settlement* or *daylight overdraft risk* as one of the largest potential sources of instability in the financial markets today. To understand daylight overdrafts better, review Figure 24–7. It shows a typical daily pattern of net wire payment transfers—payment messages sent (debits) minus payment messages received (credits)—for a large money center bank using Fedwire.

Under the Federal Reserve Act, banks must maintain cash reserves on deposit at the Fed; Fedwire settlement normally occurs at the end of the banking day at 6:30 PM EST. At that time, the Fed adjusts each member bank's reserve account to reflect its net debit (credit) position with other banks.[13] Under current regulations, a member bank's end-of-day reserve position cannot be negative. What is true at the end of the day is not true, however, during the day; that is, the Fed allows banks to run real-time **daylight overdrafts** (or negative intraday balances) on their reserve accounts. These negative reserve balances occur under the current payments system because large banks and their customers often send messages repaying overnight loans and making interest payments at the beginning of the banking day and borrow funds (i.e., receive payment messages) toward the end of the banking day. For periods during the day, banks frequently run daylight overdrafts on their reserve accounts at the Fed by having their payment outflow messages exceed their payment inflow messages (see Figure 24–7).

daylight overdraft

A bank's intraday negative balance on its reserve account with the Federal Reserve.

---

[13]Technically, CHIPS transactions settle on Fedwire by 5:30 PM before Fedwire closes.

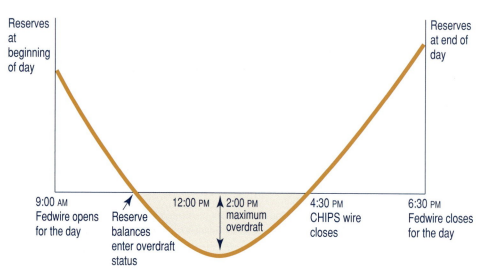

Figure **24–7**   *Daylight Overdrafts on Fedwire*

In effect, the Fed is implicitly lending banks within-day reserves. This process involves two other important institutional factors. First, until recently, the Fed did not charge banks an explicit interest rate or fee for these daylight overdrafts. As a result, neither banks nor their large corporate customers had any incentive to economize on these transactions. Daylight Fedwire overdrafts were effectively free and therefore oversupplied.[14] Second, under Regulation J, the Fed guarantees payment finality for every wire transfer message. Therefore, if the representative bank in Figure 24–7 were to fail at 12 PM, the Federal Reserve would be liable for all of the bank's Fedwire transactions until 12 PM. This eliminates any risk that a payment message–receiving bank or its customers would be left short of funds at the end of the day. Thus, the Fed bears the Fedwire credit risk of bank failures by granting overdrafts.

A technological failure or malfunction that exposed the Federal Reserve and the financial system to massive settlement risk exposure occurred at the Bank of New York (BONY). It is a major dealer in government securities and uses Fedwire to pay for secu-

book entry securities

Securities held in computerized account form rather than in paper form.

rities. Since the vast majority of U.S. Treasury securities are **book entry securities** (i.e., computerized accounts rather than paper claims), they are usually transferred by securities Fedwire at the same time that payments are made on cash Fedwire.[15] The problem occurred in November 1985. On November 20, BONY had a very large number of securities transactions that were too extensive for its clearing and settlement software to handle efficiently. Indeed, because of a software breakdown, it was still processing November 20 transactions on November 21. As a result, BONY could not make any new securities deliveries on November 21 or receive federal funds as payments. Its daylight overdraft on its reserve account built up throughout the day. Even though the Fed extended the Fedwire hours, the software problem was still not solved late into the evening of the 21st. When settlement

---

[14]Beginning in 1993, a small annual interest charge was levied on a bank's maximum daily overdraft amount. The maximum size of this charge is 0.25 percent and was phased in over a three-year period. This is clearly well below a bank's opportunity cost of funds.

[15]Technically, there are two Fedwires, one for securities and one for cash and reserve transfers.

finally occurred early in the morning of the 22nd, the Fed had to extend a one-day loan to BONY equal to nearly two-thirds of BONY's total domestic and worldwide assets and more than 24 times the size of its primary equity capital. Clearly, failure to extend the loan would have resulted in a large number of settlement failures by BONY and other banks. The fact that the loan size was so enormous, relative to BONY's capital, is symptomatic of the risk exposure that can potentially occur on the wire transfer networks and the sensitivity of banks to operational and technological breakdowns.[16] In particular, this technological breakdown brings into focus the question of whether BONY could have survived without a Federal Reserve bailout.

Similarly, concerns about technology malfunctions related to the impending "millennium bug" have been expressed. Many FI settlement computer systems currently date transactions by the last two digits of the year (e.g., 98 for 1998). In the year 2000, computer systems may read 00 (the last two digits) as 1900 rather than 2000. U.S. banks have addressed this problem more quickly than European banks have. Unless the problem is resolved, the number of settlement failures will increase, the use of wire transfer systems will decrease, and the cost of financial transactions will increase. Indeed, some banks may fail if the payment system becomes seriously gridlocked.

On CHIPS, net payment flows often have a daily pattern similar to that in Figure 24–7 except that, as a privately owned pure net settlement system, the beginning-of-day position must be zero for all banks. As with Fedwire, big banks often run a daylight overdraft, but this is generally larger and more pronounced early in the morning than on Fedwire. Again, large banks then seek to borrow funds in the afternoon to cover net debit positions created earlier in the day. CHIPS does not charge banks explicit fees for running daylight overdrafts, but it treats a bank's failure to settle at the end of the day very differently than Fedwire does. On Fedwire, all payments are in good funds—the Fed guarantees the finality of any wire transfer at the time it is made. By contrast, since CHIPS is a private network, all within-day transfers are provisional and become final only on settlement among CHIPS members at the end of the day. In this case, if a bank (Bank Z) with a daylight overdraft were to fail, CHIPS might have to resolve this by unwinding all of the failing bank's transactions over that day with the other (N–1) remaining banks. Bank Z's individual failure could result in a systemic crisis in the banking and financial system among the remaining (N–1) banks in the system.

In particular, suppose that Bank Y had been in a net creditor position at the end of the banking day had the failing bank settled. Bank Y might have found that after Bank Z's failure and any CHIPS unwinding of message transactions, it, too, could not settle its transactions with the other remaining banks. As a result, all of Bank Y's transactions with those banks had to be unwound. Such a process would have to continue until all banks could settle their transactions with each other. Although no settlement failure has occurred recently on CHIPS,[17] any such failure could be potentially disastrous, with financial ramifications far exceeding the October 1987 stock market crash.

To lower this settlement risk problem and to introduce an element of payment finality, CHIPS members have contributed more than $4 billion to a special escrow fund that became operational in October 1990. They can use this fund to replace the message commitments of any failed bank, therefore preventing the potentially disastrous unwinding

---

[16]This description of the BONY crisis is based on R. J. Herring, "Innovations to Enhance Liquidity: The Implications for Systemic Risk," University of Pennsylvania, Wharton School, October 1992.

[17] There was a failure in the early 1970s by the Herstatt Bank of Germany.

effects just described. However, $4 billion is probably an insufficient amount to cover the failure of a major bank such as a U.S. money center bank. At the end of the day, the Federal Reserve and other central banks would have to mount a rescue to prevent an international failure contagion from spreading throughout the domestic and international financial system. Of course, this implies yet another subsidy from U.S. regulators and taxpayers to the private domestic and international banking system.

Because of these concerns, the FDICIA, passed in 1991, required the Federal Reserve to implement Regulation F, under which banks, thrifts, and foreign banks must develop internal procedures or benchmarks to limit their settlement and other credit exposures to depository institutions with which they do business (so-called correspondent banks). Accordingly, since December 1992, banks have been required to limit their exposure to an individual correspondent to no more than 25 percent of the correspondent bank's capital. For adequately capitalized banks, however, this can be raised to 50 percent, although no set benchmark is required for well-capitalized banks. Thus, it is now easier for the most solvent banks to transact on the wire transfer networks and run daylight overdrafts than for less well-capitalized banks.[18] In addition, as long as the benchmarks are adhered to, regulators' exposure to settlement risk is reduced.

International Technology Transfer Risk.   In 1974, 5 of the top 20 banks in the world measured by assets were from the United States. In 1997, not one U.S. bank made the top 20. Over this period, however, the United States has been at the forefront in making technology investments and financial service innovations in the payments system. One possible reason for the relative decline of U.S. banks is that domestic payment system innovations may not be transferable to other countries' financial systems as a result of different cultures, financial practices, and stages of technological development. For example, the United States has been a major pioneer of ATMs (with more than 90,000 currently in place), yet, the use of such facilities has occurred slowly in countries such as Germany, Italy, and Belgium, often because of prohibitive charges imposed on the use and leasing of domestic telephone lines (see Table 24–6).

This differential technological development suggests that U.S. financial service firms have often been unable to transfer profitably their domestic technological innovations to international markets to gain competitive advantage, at least in the short term.[19] In contrast, foreign financial service firms entering the U.S. market gain direct access to, and knowledge of, U.S. technology-based products at a very low cost. For example, since the passage of the International Banking Act in 1978, foreign banks have had direct access to U.S. Fedwire.

Crime and Fraud Risk.   The increasing replacement of checks and cash by wire transfer as payment method or exchange has resulted in new problems regarding theft, data snooping, and white-collar crime. Because huge sums are transferred across the wire networks each day and some bank employees have knowledge of personal identification numbers (PINs) and other entry codes, the incentive for white-collar crime appears to have increased. For example, a manager at the Sri Lankan branch of the now defunct BCCI reportedly stole a computer chip from a telex machine in the bank's Oman branch and used

---

[18] See Federal Reserve Board of Governors press release, July 14, 1992, for more details.

[19] Longer-term benefits may yet be realized as the result of telecommunications deregulation globally and better customer recruitment and marketing of products in foreign environments.

Table 24-6

CASH DISPENSERS AND ATMS

	1991	1992	1993	1994	1995
Number of machines per 1,000,000 inhabitants					
Belgium	105	109	119	313	360
Canada	467	510	554	578	595
France	284	305	325	356	395
Germany	171	235	308	361	436*
Italy	204	245	266	326	378
Japan	795	870	935	978	1,013
Netherlands	222	260	291	324	355
Sweden	258	254	255	259	267
Switzerland	347	387	439	481	532
United Kingdom	309	316	321	334	358
United States	331	342	367	418	467
Number of transactions per inhabitant					
Belgium	8.1	8.8	9.1	11.9	14.2
Canada	33.6	36.0	37.5	41.0	45.9
France	11.0	12.0	13.3	14.2	15.7
Germany	—	—	—	11.5	13.4*
Italy†	2.9	3.6	4.1	4.6	5.3
Japan	2.4	3.0	3.3	3.6	3.8
Netherlands	13.7	17.2	20.4	23.8	27.5
Sweden	24.1	25.1	28.3	30.7	31.8
Switzerland	6.6	7.4	8.3	9.1	10.3
United Kingdom	18.5	19.8	20.6	22.1	25.2
United States	25.3	28.2	29.0	31.8	36.9
Average value of transactions (US $)‡					
Belgium	117.4	113.2	110.3	125.2	137.5
Canada§	56.7	55.5	53.5	51.2	51.3
France	82.7	86.1	77.0	76.4	81.3
Germany	—	—	—	157.6	196.6*
Italy	239.2	245.4	196.8	195.3	194.4
Japan	356.5	355.4	392.9	419.3	450.6
Netherlands	92.2	98.5	96.4	97.9	108.4
Sweden	120.6	128.6	101.2	104.7	112.6
Switzerland	224.6	225.1	207.8	217.8	242.1
United Kingdom	81.0	83.0	72.7	71.2	77.3
United States	67.0	66.9	70.0	67.2	67.7

†Estimated figures referring to the entire system.

*Increase partly due to new data source.

‡Converted at yearly average exchange rates.

§Average value of a cash withdrawal only.

SOURCE: The Bank for International Settlements, *Statistics on Payment Systems in the Group of 10 Countries* (Basle, Switzerland: BIS, 1996), Table 5, p. 117.

it to transfer $10 million from three banks in the United States and Japan to his own account in Switzerland.[20]

Considerable security problems exist in trying to develop the Internet as a form of electronic payment or electronic cash. Internet transactions can be intercepted by third parties. Financial institutions are accordingly concerned about open credit or debit card details on the Internet. Such transmissions are potential invitations to fraud. Any version of electronic cash on the Internet must meet the requirements of universal recognition and acceptability associated with physical cash but must provide the high level of security that is demanded of cash but the Internet itself cannot provide. In the future, more bank and regulatory resources will be spent on surveillance and employee monitoring as well as on developing fail-safe and unbreakable entry codes to wire transfer accounts.

Regulatory Risk.   The improvement in FIs' telecommunications networks also enhances the power of FIs vis-à-vis regulators, effectively aiding regulatory avoidance. Thus, as implied earlier, regulation not only can affect the profitability of technological innovations but also can spur or hinder the rate and types of innovation. For example, many states in the U.S. impose usury ceilings on banks. **Usury ceilings** place caps and controls on the fees and interest rates that bankers can charge on credit cards, consumer loans, and residential mortgages in-state. Because credit card operations are heavily communications based and do not need to be located directly in the bank's market, the two states that now dominate the credit card market are South Dakota and Delaware. These two states are among the most liberal regarding credit card fee and interest rate usury regulations.[21] As a result of regulation in the United States, banking in the relatively unregulated Cayman Islands has experienced considerable growth. The 500 or more banks located there do most of their banking business via public and private telecommunications networks.[22] The use of telecommunications networks and technological improvements has changed, perhaps irreversibly, the balance of power between large multinational FIs and governments—both local and national—in favor of the former. Such a shift may create incentives for countries to lower their regulations to attract entrants; that is, this shift may increase the incentives for competitive deregulation. This trend may be potentially destabilizing to the market in financial services, with the weakest regulators attracting the most entrants.[23]

Tax Avoidance.   The development of international wire networks as well as international financial service firm networks has enabled FIs to shift funds and profits by using internal pricing mechanisms, thereby minimizing their overall U.S. tax burden and maximizing their foreign tax credits. For example, prior to 1986, many large U.S. banks paid almost no corporate income taxes, despite large reported profits, by rapidly moving profits and funds across different tax regimes. This raised considerable public policy concerns and was a

usury ceiling

A cap or ceiling on consumer and mortgage interest rates imposed by state governments.

---

[20]Office of Technology Assessment, *U.S. Banks and International Telecommunications*, chapter 5, pp. 27–35, Washington, D.C. September 1995.

[21]For example, Citibank, the U.S. bank with the largest credit card franchise, has located its credit card operations in South Dakota.

[22] A major reason for the growth in Cayman Islands banking is the desire of large U.S. banks to avoid or reduce the cost of the Federal Reserve's noninterest-bearing reserve requirements. Many attribute its current popularity to drug or crime-related secret money transactions.

[23]A closely associated risk for regulators is that increased use of international wire transfer systems weakens the power of central banks to control the domestic money supply and foreign exchange markets and exchange rates. A good example of this was the rapid depreciation of currencies in Southeast Asia (e.g., Malaysia, Singapore, Thailand, Indonesia) in the summer, fall, and winter of 1997–1998 due to the rapid transfer of currencies across countries by hedge and other mutual funds.

major reason underlying the 1986 tax reforms in the United States. These reforms imposed a minimum corporate income tax rate of 20 percent on U.S. banks and limited their ability to use foreign tax credits to offset their domestic income tax burdens.

Competition Risk. As financial services become more technologically based, they are increasingly competing with nontraditional financial service suppliers. For example, in addition to offering its own enhanced credit card in competition with bank-supplied credit cards, AT&T now owns a finance company.[24] Once established, nonfinancial firms can easily purchase financial services technology. General Motors has also established a credit card operation linked to the purchase of its vehicles at a discount. Currently, banks issue less than half of all new credit cards; much of the new business is going to nontraditional firms such as AT&T and General Motors. As a result, technology exposes existing FIs to the increased risk of erosion of their franchises as costs of entry fall and the competitive landscape changes.

Concept Questions

1. What six risks do FIs face with the growth of wire transfer payment systems?
2. Why do daylight overdrafts create a larger risk problem for banks on CHIPS than on Fedwire?
3. What steps have the members of CHIPS taken to lower settlement or daylight overdraft risk?

---

[24] AT&T's universal card began operation in March 1990. It is both a credit card and a calling card. Its finance company subsidiary—AT&T Capital Corp—does leasing, project financing, and small business lending.

SUMMARY

This chapter analyzed the operating cost of FIs' activities, including the effects of the growth of technology-based innovations. The impact of technology was first examined separately for wholesale and retail services before analyzing its impact on cost and revenues. Technology-based investments can potentially result in new product innovations and lower costs, but the evidence of such cost savings is mixed. Moreover, modern technology appears to have created new and different risks. These include settlement or daylight overdraft risk, international technology transfer risk, crime or fraud risk, regulatory avoidance risk, taxation avoidance risk, and competition risk. Nevertheless, although the chapter focuses on the costs and benefits of technology to an FI, a more fundamental issue may not be technology's costs and benefits but the need to invest in technology to survive as a modern full-service FI.

PERTINENT WEB SITES

Board of Governors of the Federal Reserve   http://www.bog.frb.fed.us/

Bank for International Settlements   http://www.bis.org/home.htm

Bank Web Addresses   http://www.mybanks.com/

Fedwire   http://www.fedwire.com/

Office of the Comptroller of Currency   http://www.occ.treas.gov/

Office of Technology Assessment   http://www.ota.nap.edu/

Operating Cost and Technology Risk

1. Explain how technological improvements can increase FIs' interest and noninterest income and reduce interest and noninterest expenses. Use specific examples.

2. How do the effects of technology on banks' wholesale operations compare with the effects of technology on their retail operations?

3. What are some of the risks inherent in being the first to introduce a financial innovation?

4. How has technology impacted interest income, fee income, and expenses of FIs' provision of services of wholesale lockboxes and electronic initiation of letters of credit?

5. Sometimes, as in the case of ATMs, a technological innovation may be perceived to lower the quality of service. How can technological innovations also increase an FI's service quality?

6. The operations department of a major FI is planning to reorganize several of its back-office functions. Its current operating expense is $1,500,000, of which $1,000,000 is for staff expenses. The FI uses a 12 percent cost of capital to evaluate cost-saving projects.

   a. One way to reorganize is to send part of its data entry functions out of the country. This will require an initial cost of approximately $500,000 after taxes. The FI expects to save $100,000 in annual operating expenses. Should it undertake this project, assuming that this change will lead to permanent savings?

   b. Another option is to automate the entire process by installing new state-of-the-art computers and software. The FI expects to reduce after-tax personnel cost by more than $500,000, but the initial investment is approximately $3,000,000. In addition, the life of this project is limited to seven years (when new computers and software will have to be installed). Using this seven-year planning horizon, should it invest in this project?

7. What is the link between technology risk and regulation?

8. City Bank upgrades its computer equipment every five years to keep up with changes in technology. Its next update is two years from today and is budgeted to cost $1,000,000. Management is considering moving the date up by two years to install some new computers with a breakthrough software that could generate significant savings. The cost for this new set of equipment is the same (i.e., $1,000,000). What should the savings per year be to justify moving up the planned update by two years? Assume a cost of capital of 15 percent.

9. Distinguish between *economies of scale* and *economies of scope*.

10. What information on the operating costs of FIs does the measurement of economies of scale provide? If economies of scale exist, what implications do they have for regulators?

11. What information on the operating costs of FIs does the measurement of economies of scope provide? If economies of scope exist, what implications do they have for regulators?

12. Bank 1, with $130 million in assets and $20 million in costs, acquires Bank 2, which has $50 million in assets and $10 million in costs. After the acquisition, the bank has $180 million in assets and $35 million in costs. Did this acquisition produce economies of scale or economies of scope?

13. Bank 3, with assets of $2 billion and costs of $200 million, acquires as a subsidiary an investment banking firm with assets of $40 million and costs of $15 million. After the acquisition, the commercial bank's costs are $180 million and the investment bank's costs are $20 million. Does this represent economies of scale or economies of scope?

14. Table 24–1 shows data on earnings, expenses, and assets for all insured banks. If the growth rates in earnings and expenses from 1987 to 1997 are compared to that of assets, and if part of the growth rates in assets and expenses can be attributed to technological change, in what areas of the firms' operations does technological change appear to have the greatest impact?

15. You obtain the following average costs from a survey of a local market: Bank A, specializing in mortgage loans, has assets of $3 million. Its average cost, measured as a proportion of assets, is 20 percent. Insurance company B, specializing in life insurance, has assets of $4 million and an average cost, measured as a proportion of assets, of 30

percent. Pension fund C, specializing in corporate pension fund management, has assets of $4 million and an average cost of 25 percent. Bank A is planning to acquire firms B and C and expects to reduce overall average costs by eliminating duplication of services.

    a. What should the average cost be after acquisition, measured as a proportion of total assets, for the bank to justify this merger?

    b. If Bank A plans to reduce operating costs by $500,000 after the merger, what is the new firm's average cost?

16. What are some of the conclusions of empirical studies on economies of scale and scope? How important is the impact of cost reductions on total average costs?

17. What are the differences between the Fedwire and CHIPS payment systems?

18. How do FIs' overdraft risks incurred during the day differ for each of the two competing electronic payment systems, Fedwire and CHIPS?

19. How is Regulation F of the 1991 FDICIA expected to reduce the problem of daylight overdraft risk?

20. How have crime and fraud risk and the avoidance of regulation been made easier by the rapid technological improvements in the electronic payment systems?

Chapter Twenty-five

Product Diversification

T he U.S. financial system has traditionally been structured along separatist or segmented product lines. Regulatory barriers and restrictions have often inhibited an FI's ability to operate in one area of the financial services industry and expand its product set into other areas. FIs operating in the United States can be compared with those operating in Germany, Switzerland, and the United Kingdom, where a more **universal FI** structure allows any single financial services organization to offer a far broader range of banking, insurance, securities, and other financial services products.[1]

This chapter first analyzes the problems and risks that can arise, and have arisen, for U.S. FIs constrained to limited financial service sectors or franchises as well as the potential benefits from product expansion. Second, the chapter analyzes the laws and regulations that have restricted product

universal FI

An FI that can engage in a broad range of financial service activities.

---

[1] For a thorough analysis of universal banking systems overseas, see A. Saunders and I. Walter, *Universal Banking in the U.S.?* (New York: Oxford University Press, 1994); and A. Saunders and I. Walter, eds., *Financial System Design: Universal Banking Considered* (Burr Ridge, IL: Irwin/McGraw-Hill Professional Publishing, 1996).

expansions for banks, insurance companies, and securities firms in the United States and elsewhere, and the current modification of many of these laws and regulations. In addition, the chapter discusses barriers to product expansion between the financial sector and the real or commercial sector of the economy. Third, it evaluates the advantages and disadvantages of allowing U.S. FIs to adopt more universal franchises similar to those found in many European countries.

RISKS OF PRODUCT SEGMENTATION

In recent years, many financial service firms have faced return and risk problems due to constraints on product diversification. Arguably, product expansion restrictions have affected commercial banks the most. For example, to the extent that regulations have limited the franchise of banks to traditional areas such as deposit taking and commercial lending, banks have been increasingly susceptible to nonbank competition on both the liability and asset sides of their balance sheets. Specifically, the increased use of **money market mutual funds** (MMMFs) that offer checking accountlike deposit services with high liquidity, stability of value, and an attractive return has proven very strong competition for bank deposit and transaction account products.[2] From virtually no assets in 1972, MMMFs had acquired more than $1,005.1 billion by September 1997; this compares to time deposits and money market accounts of approximately $1,708.4 billion in commercial banks.

money market mutual funds (MMMFs)

Mutual funds that offer high liquidity, check-writing ability, and a money market return to small individual investors.

In addition, banks have been threatened by the increase in types of annuities offered by the life insurance industry. An annuity is a savings product that has many of the same features as bank CDs. By 1997, fixed and variable annuities were selling at the rate of more than $110 billion a year.[3]

On the asset side of the balance sheet, banks' commercial and industrial (C&I) loans have faced increased competition from the dynamic commercial paper market as an alternative source of short-term finance for large- and middle-sized corporations. For example, in January 1988, C&I loans outstanding totaled $565 billion versus $380 billion of commercial paper; in September 1997, C&I loans totaled $830.4 billion versus $836.8 billion of commercial paper outstanding. In addition, relatively unregulated finance companies compete for the business credit market. In September 1997, the ratio of finance company business loans to bank C&I loans was approximately 41 percent.

These trends mean that the economic value of narrowly defined bank franchises has declined. In particular, product line restrictions inhibit an FI's ability to optimize the set of

---

[2] As Chapter 7 discusses, MMMFs collect small savers' funds and invest in a diversified portfolio of short-term money market instruments. This allows the small saver indirect access to the wholesale money market and to the relatively more attractive rates in those markets.

[3] An annuity is a contract in which the purchaser makes one or more payments up front to receive a fixed or variable flow of payments over time. These instruments are normally tax sheltered (see Chapter 4).

financial services it can offer, potentially forcing it to adopt a riskier set of activities than it would have adopted if it could fully diversify.[4]

Product restrictions also limit an FI manager's ability to adjust flexibly to shifts in the demand for financial products by consumers and to shifts in costs due to technology and related innovations. We analyze the advantages and disadvantages of increased product line diversification in more detail after more closely considering the major laws and regulations segmenting the U.S. financial services industry and ways in which U.S. FIs have tried to overcome the effects of such regulations.

Concept Questions

1. What supports the claim that product expansion restrictions have affected commercial banks more than any other type of financial services firm?
2. What sources of competition have had an impact on the asset side of banks' balance sheets?

SEGMENTATION IN THE U.S. FINANCIAL SERVICES INDUSTRY

Commercial and Investment Banking Activities

commercial banking

Banking activity of deposit taking and lending.

investment banking

Banking activity of underwriting, issuing, and distributing securities.

Since 1863, the United States has experienced several phases of regulating the links between the commercial and investment banking industries. Simply defined, **commercial banking** is the activity of deposit taking and commercial lending; **investment banking** is the activity of underwriting, issuing, and distributing (via public or private placement) securities. Early legislation, such as the 1863 National Bank Act, prohibited nationally chartered commercial banks from engaging in corporate securities activities such as underwriting and distributing corporate bonds and equities. As the United States industrialized and the demand for corporate finance increased, however, the largest banks such as National City Bank (today's Citibank) found ways around this restriction by establishing state-chartered affiliates to do the underwriting. By 1927, these bank affiliates were underwriting approximately 30 percent of the corporate securities being issued. In that year, the Comptroller of the Currency, the regulator of national banks, relaxed the controls on national banks underwriting securities, thereby allowing them to pursue an even larger market share of securities underwritings.

After the 1929 stock market crash, the United States entered a major recession and approximately 10,000 banks failed between 1930 and 1933. A commission of inquiry (the Pecora Commission) established in 1931 began investigating the causes of the crash. Its findings resulted in new legislation, the 1933 Banking Act, or the Glass-Steagall Act (summarized in Table 25–1). The Glass-Steagall Act sought to impose a rigid separation

---

[4] Although it is true that banks earned very high profits in 1993 through 1997, this was in large part due to relatively low interest rates for deposits and the stickiness of lending rates that dramatically increased bank margins, especially in the consumer lending areas. The increased profitability of banks in the mid-1990s may well be more cyclical than secular (or long term).

Table 25–1

PROVISIONS OF GLASS-STEAGALL ACT (1933 BANKING ACT)

The 1933 Glass-Steagall Act imposed rigid separation between commercial banking and investment banking with three exemptions:

1. The underwriting of new issues of Treasury securities.
2. The underwriting of municipal general obligation bonds.
3. The private placements of corporate debt and equity securities.

---

between commercial banking—taking deposits and making commercial loans—and investment banking—underwriting, issuing, and distributing stocks, bonds, and other securities. The act defined three major securities underwriting exemptions. First, banks were to continue to underwrite new issues of Treasury bills, notes, and bonds. Thus, the largest banks today such as Citibank and Morgan Guaranty actively compete with Salomon Brothers and Goldman Sachs in government bond auctions. Second, banks were allowed to continue underwriting municipal general obligation (GO) bonds.[5] Third, banks were allowed to continue engaging in private placements of all types of bonds and equities, corporate and noncorporate. In a **private placement,** a bank seeks to find a large institutional buyer or investor, such as another FI, for a new securities issue. As such, the bank acts as an agent for a fee. By comparison, in a public offering of securities, a bank normally acts as a direct principal and has an underwriting stake in the issue. This principal position, such as in **firm commitment underwriting,** involves buying securities from the issuer at one price and seeking to resell them to public investors (large and small) at a slightly higher price. Failure to sell these securities can result in a major loss to the underwriter of publicly issued securities. Thus, the act distinguished between the private placement of securities, which was allowed, and public placement, which was not.

For most of the period 1933–1963, commercial banks and investment banks generally appeared to be willing to abide by the letter and spirit of the Glass-Steagall Act. Between 1963 and 1987, however, banks challenged restrictions on municipal revenue bond underwriting, commercial paper underwriting, discount brokerage, managing and advising open- and closed-end mutual funds, underwriting mortgage-backed securities, and selling annuities.[6] In most cases, the courts eventually permitted these activities for commercial banks.[7]

private placement

The placement of a whole issue of securities with a single (or a few) large investors by a bank acting as a placing agent.

firm commitment underwriting

The process by which an underwriter buys securities from an issuer and reoffers them to the public at a slightly higher price.

---

[5] A municipal general obligation bond is a bond issued by a state, city, or local government whose interest and principal payments are backed by the full faith and credit of that local government, that is, its full tax and revenue base (see Chapter 2).

[6] Municipal revenue bonds are riskier than municipal GO bonds since their interest and principal are guaranteed only by the revenue from the project they finance. One example is the revenue from road tolls of a bond funding the constuction of a new section of highway.

[7] Of the type of issues involved, *discount brokerage* was held to be legal since it was not viewed as being the same as *full-service brokerage* supplied by securities firms. In particular, a full-service brokerage combines both the agency function of securities purchase along with investment advice (e.g., hot tips). By contrast, discount brokers only carry out the agency function of buying and selling securities for clients; they do not give investment advice. For further discussion of these issues, see M. Clark and A. Saunders, "Judicial Interpretation of Glass-Steagall: The Need for Legislative Action," *The Banking Law Journal* 97 (1980), pp. 721–740; and "Glass-Steagall Revisited: The Impact on Banks, Capital Markets, and the Small Investor," *The Banking Law Journal* 97 (1980), pp. 811–840.

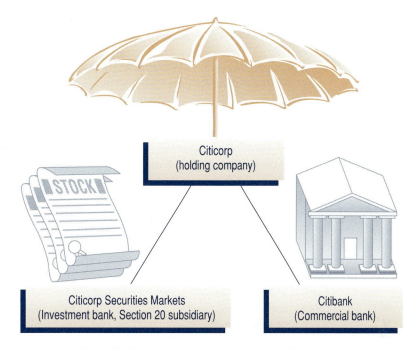

Figure **25-1**   *Bank Holding Company and Its Bank and Section 20 Subsidiary*

Section 20 affiliate

A securities subsidiary of a bank holding company through which a banking organization can engage in investment banking activities.

firewalls

Legal barriers separating the activities of a bank from those of the other subsidiaries.

With this onslaught and the de facto erosion of the act by legal interpretation, the Federal Reserve Board in April 1987 allowed commercial bank holding companies—such as Citicorp, the parent of Citibank—to establish separate **Section 20 securities affiliates**. Currently, approximately 40 Section 20 subsidiaries have been established, most representing the largest U.S. and international banks in the world. Through these Section 20 affiliates, bank holding companies can conduct all their "ineligible" or gray area securities activities, such as commercial paper underwriting, mortgage-backed securities underwriting, and municipal revenue bond underwriting. Banks such as Citibank and J.P. Morgan were quick to capitalize on the new opportunities and established Section 20 subsidiaries in April 1987. Note the organization structure of a bank holding company, its bank, and the Section 20 subsidiary or investment bank in Figure 25–1 for Citicorp. These Section 20 subsidiaries do not violate Section 20 of the Glass-Steagall Act, which restricts affiliation of banks and securities firms as long as the revenue generated from the subsidiaries' ineligible securities activities amounted to no more than 5 percent (increased to 25 percent in 1996) of the total revenues they generate.[8] For example, in the mid-1990s, revenues from Citicorp's Section 20 subsidiary generated approximately 5 percent of Citicorp's total revenue.

Moreover, in 1987 the Fed placed very stringent **firewalls,** or barriers, between the bank and its Section 20 securities subsidiary to protect the bank from the risks of the subsidiary's

---

[8] This means that 75 percent of the revenues of the Section 20 subsidiary must be generated from eligible securities activities such as government bond underwritings, which the Glass-Steagall Act permitted. Also note that the 25 percent revenue restriction has created incentives for banks to make the eligible business they put into these subsidiaries as large as possible on the basis that 25 percent of a very large number is itself a large number.

securities activities. These firewalls were both legal and economic in nature (we later discuss the elimination of some of these firewalls in 1997).[9] Therefore, Citibank in this example could neither make loans to nor buy assets from its Section 20 securities subsidiary, Citicorp Securities Markets (CSMI).

In 1989, the Federal Reserve expanded the set of permitted activities of selected Section 20 subsidiaries to include corporate bond underwriting and, in 1990, corporate equity underwriting. The Section 20 firewalls introduced in the 1987 and 1989 orders are listed in Table 25–2, which also lists the actions the Fed took in 1997 to remove many of the firewalls (these actions are discussed in more detail later in the chapter).

The erosion of the product barriers between commercial and investment banking was also helped by the fact that many states allow state-chartered banks to engage in securities activities beyond those permitted by Glass-Steagall for national banks. Because state-chartered banks are smaller than nationally chartered banks, however, few state-chartered banks have actually taken advantage of such powers.[10]

The erosion of the product barriers between the commercial and investment banking industries has not been all one way. Large investment banks such as Merrill Lynch have increasingly sought to offer banking products. For example, in the late 1970s, Merrill Lynch created the cash management account (CMA), which allowed investors to own a money market mutual fund with check-writing privileges into which bond and stock sale proceeds could be swept on a daily basis. This account allows the investor to earn interest on cash held in a brokerage account. In addition, many investment banks act as deposit brokers. As we discuss in Chapter 15, deposit brokers charge a fee to break large deposits into $100,000 deposit units and place them in banks across the country. Finally, investment banks have been major participants as traders and investors in the secondary market for loans to less-developed countries and other loans (see Chapters 12 and 28).

In summary, although the Glass-Steagall Act remains the defining piece of legislation concerning the mix of commercial and investment banking, the "homemade" deregulation by banks and securities firms is gradually eroding its provisions.[11]

Banking and Insurance

Traditionally, very strong barriers have restricted the entry of banks into insurance and vice versa. Insurance activities can be either of the property-casualty type (e.g., homeowners insurance, auto insurance) or the life/health type (e.g., term life insurance). Moreover, we

---

[9] For banks and the Section 20 securities affiliates, some 28 firewalls were established (see General Accounting Office, "Bank Powers: Issues Relating to Banks Selling Insurance," GAO/GGO 90-113, [Washington, DC: Government Printing Office, 1990]). The idea of a firewall is to insulate or protect the bank (and thus the deposit insurance fund) from the risks of nonbank activities.

[10] Moreover, 17 foreign banks can engage in securities activities because they were legally engaged in such activities prior to the passage of the International Banking Act of 1978. This act imposed the Glass-Steagall Act restrictions on the securities activities of all new foreign bank entrants to the United States. However, all foreign banks established prior to 1978 had their securities activities in the United States grandfathered (i.e., an affiliate established prior to the passage of restrictive laws regarding new entrants into an activity area is not subject to that law). Prior to 1978, foreign banks entering into the United States were largely regulated by state laws. Since these state laws often allowed more extensive securities activities than did federal law, a number of major foreign banks engaged in securities activities through affiliates. This has meant that foreign banks have been allowed to pursue securities activities even though they have a competitive advantage over domestic banks.

[11] Although the 1991 Treasury Report to Congress recommended eliminating most of the restrictive provisions of the Glass-Steagall Act, the final piece of legislation—the FDIC Improvement Act of 1991—did not materially change the Glass-Steagall Act's provisions.

Table **25–2**

SECTION 20 FIREWALLS ENACTED IN 1987 AND 1989 AND THE FEDERAL RESERVE BOARD ACTION TAKEN FOR EACH IN 1997

Firewall	1997 Action Taken
A. Capital Adequacy Conditions	
1. Deduction of investment in subsidiary from bank holding company capital. Deduction of extensions of credit from holding company capital.	1. Eliminated the investment deduction from bank holding company capital but required holding company to maintain adequate capital as a condition for operating a Section 20 subsidiary.
2. Prior approval requirement for investments in subsidiaries.	2. Repealed restriction.
3. Requirement of capital plan before commencing new activities.	3. Eliminated restriction as superfluous since Board analysis is normal part of Board authority.
4. Capital adequacy requirement for underwriting subsidiary.	4. Board sought comment on necessity, since no such restriction is imposed on other subsidiary and capital requirements are still required at holding company level.
B. Credit Extensions to Customers of Underwriting Subsidiary	
5. Restriction on credit enhancement by underwriting subsidiary.	5. Eliminated restriction.
6. Restriction on funding purchases of securities by nonunderwriting subsidiary to underwriting subsidiary customers.	6. Retained restriction but sought comments on need.
7. Restrictions on extensions of credit for repayment of underwritten securities.	7. Eliminated restriction.
8. Procedures for extensions of credit for repayment of underwritten securities.	8. Eliminated firewall.
9. Restriction on thrift subsidiaries to follow same restrictions as bank subsidiaries in dealings with underwriting subsidiary.	9. Made restriction superfluous with passage of Home Owners' Loan Act.
10. Restrictions on industrial revenue bonds consistent with firewalls 5 through 9.	10. Changed restrictions as in firewalls 5 through 9.
11. Loan documentation and exposure limits adopted for all bank and thrift subsidiaries.	11. Retained restriction.
12. Procedures for limiting exposure to one customer.	12. Retained restriction but sought comment.
C. Limitations to Maintain Separateness of an Underwriting Affiliate's Activity	
13. Restriction on directors, officers, or employees of a bank or thrift subsidiary with underwriting subsidiary interlocked.	13. Retained but amended to majority restriction. Eliminated separate subsidiary office requirement.
D. Disclosure by the Underwriting Subsidiary	
14. Customer disclosure on distinctness of bank/thrift and underwriting subsidiaries.	14. Retained restriction.
E. Marketing Activities on Behalf of an Underwriting Subsidiary	
15. Restriction on advertising bank connections with underwriting subsidiary.	15. Eliminated restriction.
16. Cross-marketing and agency activities by banks.	16. Eliminated restriction.
F. Investment Advice by Bank/Thrift Affiliates	
17. Restriction on comment by bank/thrift affiliates on value of underwriting subsidiary services.	17. Retained restriction.
18. Restriction on fiduciary purchases during underwriting period or from market maker.	18. Eliminated restriction.

continued

Table **25–2**

SECTION 20 FIREWALLS ENACTED IN 1987 AND 1989 AND THE FEDERAL RESERVE BOARD ACTION TAKEN FOR EACH IN 1997 (CONTINUED)

Firewall	1997 Action Taken
G. Extensions of Credit and Purchases and Sales of Agents	
19. Restrictions on purchases as principal during underwriting period or from market maker.	19. Eliminated restriction.
20. Restriction on underwriting and dealing in affiliates securities.	20. Eliminated restriction.
21. Prohibition on extensions of credit to Section 20 subsidiary.	21. Eliminated restriction except for intra-day extensions of credit.
22. Financial asset restrictions on bank or thrift to purchase or sell such assets of or to an underwriting subsidiary for its own account.	22. Eliminated restriction.
H. Limitations on Transfers of Information	
23. Disclosure of nonpublic information restricted across subsidiaries.	23. Retained restriction.
I. Reports	
24. Federal Reserve reports required quarterly from underwriting subsidiaries.	24. Retained restriction.
J. Transfer of Activities and Formation by Subsidiaries of an Underwriting Subsidiary to Engage in Underwriting and Dealing	
25. Scope of order complete.	25. Eliminated restriction.
K. Limitations on Reciprocal Arrangements and Discriminatory Treatment	
26. Prohibition on reciprocity arrangements.	26. Eliminated restriction.
27. Prohibition on discriminatory treatment based on customer's use of affiliate services.	27. Retained restriction but requested comment.
L. Requirement for Supervisory Review Before Commencement of Activities	
28. Infrastructure review required.	28. Retained restriction.

SOURCE: *Federal Reserve Bulletin,* January 1997.

must distinguish between a bank selling insurance as an agent by selling others' policies for a fee and a bank acting as an insurance underwriter and bearing the direct risk of underwriting losses. In general, the risks of insurance agency activities are quite low in loss potential when compared to insurance underwriting. Certain types of insurance, e.g., credit life insurance, mortgage insurance, and auto insurance, tend to have natural synergistic links to bank lending products.[12]

Nevertheless, banks are under stringent restrictions when selling and underwriting almost every type of insurance. For example, national banks have been restricted to offering credit-related life, accident, health, or unemployment insurance. Moreover, national banks can act as insurance agents only in towns of less than 5,000 people (although they

---

[12]See Saunders and Walter, *Universal Banking in the U.S.,* for an elaboration of these arguments.

Table **25-3**

PERMISSIBLE BANK HOLDING COMPANIES INSURANCE ACTIVITIES*

A. Banks may act as agent, broker, or principal (i.e., underwriter) for credit-related life, accident, health, or unemployment insurance.

B. Bank holding company finance subsidiaries may act as agent or broker for credit-related property insurance in connection with loans not exceeding $10,000[†] made by finance company subsidiaries of bank holding companies.

C. Banks may act as agent for any insurance activity in a place with a population not exceeding 5,000, or with insurance agency facilities that the bank holding company demonstrates to be inadequate. Sales may take place from these offices.

D. A bank holding company or its subsidiaries may engage in any insurance agency activity performed on or approved as of May 1, 1982.[‡]

E. Banks may act, on behalf of insurance underwriters, for insurance on bank holding company assets or group insurance for the employees of a bank holding company or its subsidiaries.

F. A bank holding company (or subsidiary) having total assets of $50 million or less may engage in any insurance agency activity.[§]

G. Any insurance agency activity that was performed by a registered bank holding company prior to January 1, 1971 may be continued.

---

*These are the seven statutory exemptions to the Bank Holding Company Act's prohibition on insurance activities under Title VI of the Garn-St. Germain Depository Institutions Act of 1982, Public Law 97-320 (October 15, 1982).

[†]$25,000 in the case of a mobile home loan.

[‡]Including (a) insurance sales at new locations of the same bank holding company or subsidiaries in the state of the bank holding company's principal place of business or adjacent states, or any states in which insurance activities were conducted by the bank holding company or any of its subsidiaries on May 1, 1982, or (b) insurance coverages functionally equivalent to those engaged in or approved by the Board as of May 1, 1982.

[§]Except that life insurance and annuities sold under this provision must be authorized by (A), (B), or (C).

SOURCE: S. D. Felgren, "Banks as Insurance Agencies: Local Constraints and Competitive Advances," Federal Reserve Bank of Boston, *New England Economic Review,* September–October 1985, pp. 34–39.

---

can sell insurance from these offices anywhere in the United States). In addition, the Bank Holding Company Act of 1956 (and its 1970 amendments) severely restricts bank holding companies from establishing separately capitalized insurance affiliates. The Garn-St. Germain Depository Institutions Act of 1982 sets out these restrictions explicitly (see Table 25–3). Most states also have taken quite restrictive actions regarding the insurance activities of state-chartered banks. A few states, most notably Delaware, have passed liberal laws allowing state-chartered banks to underwrite and broker various types of property-casualty and life insurance. This has encouraged large bank holding companies such as Citicorp and Chase to enter Delaware and establish state-chartered banking subsidiaries with their own insurance affiliates.

One area in which banks have successfully survived legal challenges—in this case from the insurance industry—is the annuity. In 1986, NationsBank began selling annuities, and was aggressively challenged in court. In the meantime, a large number of other banks also began offering annuities. By the end of 1995, the Supreme Court upheld the legality of banks to sell annuities; its decision argued that annuities should be viewed more as investment products than insurance products. Such sales are estimated to add nearly $1 billion a year to bank profits.

nonbank bank

A bank divested of its commercial loans and/or its demand deposits.

Unlike banks, insurance companies are regulated solely at the state level.[13] Although few states explicitly restrict insurance companies from acquiring banks and, therefore, pursuing banking activities, banking laws have essentially restricted such expansions. In particular, the Bank Holding Company Act of 1956 has severely restricted insurance companies' ability to own, or to be affiliated with, full-service banks. Nevertheless, beginning in the early 1980s, several insurance companies and commercial firms found indirect ways to engage in banking activities. They did so by the organizational mechanism of establishing **nonbank bank** subsidiaries (see Chapter 3). The 1956 Bank Holding Company Act legally defined a bank as an organization that both accepts demand deposits and makes commercial and industrial loans. An insurance company could circumvent this restrictive provision by buying a full-service bank and then divesting its demand deposits or its commercial loans. This converts a bank into a nonbank bank. In 1987, Congress passed the Competitive Equality Banking Act (CEBA), blocking the nonbank bank loophole. Although CEBA grandfathered nonbank banks established prior to 1987, it capped their growth rates.[14]

A new avenue that will allow expanded access for banks into the insurance market may soon exist. Legislation pending in Congress proposes merging the banking and thrift industries. Among other details, Congress must still decide which activities will be permissible for the new companies. Thrifts currently have broader charters than banks in that they are allowed to engage in insurance underwriting and other activities. An FDIC study on the merger of the industries submitted to Congress in December 1996 suggested that the common charter could include broad insurance powers because such insurance powers do not present safety and soundness issues. This proposed legislation presents the first real opportunity for banks to enter the insurance market.

Commercial Banking and Commerce

Although the direct holdings of other firms' equity by national banks has been constrained since 1863, the restrictions on the commercial activities of bank holding companies are more recent phenomena. In particular, the 1970 amendments to the 1956 Bank Holding Company Act required bank holding companies to divest themselves of nonbank-related subsidiaries over a 10-year period following the amendment. When Congress passed the amendments, bank holding companies owned approximately 3,500 commercial sector subsidiaries ranging from public utilities to transportation and manufacturing firms. Nevertheless, bank holding companies today can still hold up to 4.9 percent of the voting shares in any commercial firm without regulatory approval.[15]

The 1956 Bank Holding Company Act has also effectively restricted acquisitions of banks by commercial firms (as was true for insurance companies). The major vehicle for a

---

[13]This state level of regulation was reaffirmed by the McCarran-Ferguson Act of 1945. For an excellent discussion of the background to this act, see K. J. Meier, *The Political Economy of Regulation: The Case of Insurance* (Albany, NY: State University of New York Press, 1988).

[14]Specifically, nonbank banks established before March 5, 1987, were allowed to continue in business but were limited to a maximum growth in assets of 7 percent during any 12-month period beginning one year after the act's enactment. It also permitted those nonbank banks allowed to remain in business to engage only in those activities in which they were engaged as of March 1987 and limited the cross-marketing of products and services by nonbank banks and affiliated companies.

[15]The Bank Holding Company Act defines *control* as a holding company's equity stake in a subsidiary bank or affiliate that exceeds 25 percent.

commercial firm's entry into commercial banking has been through nonbank banks or nonbank financial service firms that offer banking-type services.

Nonbank Financial Service Firms and Commerce

In comparison with the barriers separating banking and either securities, insurance, or commercial sector activities, the barriers among nonbank financial service firms and commercial firms are generally less stringent. For example, in recent years, nonbank financial service firms and commercial firms have faced few barriers to entering into and exiting from various areas of nonbank finance service activity. For example, in 1997 Travelers Group undertook a $9 billion acquisition of Salomon Brothers one year after acquiring Smith Barney. Travelers had long been involved in insurance and mutual funds, and with these acquisitions became a powerhouse on Wall Street as well. The combination of Travelers, Salomon, and Smith Barney created an investment bank that ranks third in equity underwriting in the United States, first in municipal underwriting, fourth in global equity underwriting, and second in underwriting of all U.S. and international debt offerings. The new firm has five million customer accounts and 10,400 financial consultants operating in 438 offices in the United States and 26 foreign countries.

Various major nonbank financial service acquisitions and divestitures have occurred since 1990, many involving commercial firms such as Sears Roebuck, Xerox, and Gulf and Western (see Table 25–4). Sears Roebuck sought to expand its financial services network through acquisitions in the 1980s but subsequently sought to divest most of them in the 1990s (see Contemporary Perspectives Box 25–1).

Concept Questions

1. What was the rationale for the passage of the Glass-Steagall Act in 1933? What permissible underwriting activities did it identify for commercial banks?
2. Why do you think that a 25 percent rather than a 50 percent maximum ceiling has been imposed on the revenues earned from the ineligible underwriting activities of a Section 20 subsidiary?
3. Does a bank that currently specializes in making consumer loans but makes no commercial loans qualify as a nonbank bank?
4. How do the provisions of the National Bank Act of 1863 affect the participation of today's national banks in establishing nonbank subsidiaries?

ACTIVITY RESTRICTIONS

IN THE UNITED STATES

The preceding section described the essentially separatist or segmented nature of the U.S. financial services industry. Although many of the barriers are gradually being eroded and are relatively minor in some areas, the restrictions have a particularly significant effect on this nation's commercial banks. The Appendix to this chapter shows this; it compares the range of activities that U.S. commercial banks are allowed to perform with the range of product activities banks in other major industrialized countries and financial centers can engage in. With the possible exception of Japan, the range of nonbank product activities

Table **25-4**

SELECTED NONBANK FINANCIAL SERVICE INDUSTRY DIVESTITURES AND ACQUISITIONS SINCE 1990

Insurance Services

National Organization of Life, Health Guaranty Associations acquires Executive Life
Primerica acquires 27 percent of Travelers
Sears divests itself of Allstate
American Express divests itself of American Express Life
Prudential divests itself of Prudential Reinsurance
Transamerica divests itself (through an IPO) of Transamerica Insurance Group
Aetna divests itself of Aetna Life & Casualty
AXA acquires Equitable Insurance
Unum acquires Colonial
Penn Central acquires National
Met Life acquires United Mutual
Reliance Life acquires GECC

Consumer Finance Services

Gulf & Western Finance acquires Capitol Finance
Associates acquires First Family
Associates acquires Allied
Beneficial Mortgage closed
Sears divests itself of Coldwell Banker
Paine Webber divests itself of Paine Webber Mortgage
Primerica acquires Landmark
Primerica sells Margaretten

Investment Services

Gregg Mason acquires Fairchild
Franklin merges with Templeton
Kemper sells its Securities Division
Primerica acquires Shearson
Sears divests itself of Dean Witter
Weyerhauser sells its Annuities Division
Dun & Bradstreet acquires Gratner Group
Mellon Bank acquires Dreyfus
American Express spins off Lehman Brothers
Dean Witter merges with Morgan Stanley
BankAmerica acquires Robertson Stephens
NationsBank acquires Montgomery Securities
Bankers Trust NY acquires Alex Brown
U.S. Bancorp acquires Piper Jaffray
Travelers Group acquires Smith Barney
Travelers Group acquires Salomon Brothers
Citicorp merges with Travelers Group

Contemporary Perspectives 25–1

THE SEARS FINANCIAL SUPERMARKET: A TIMELINE

Sears Roebuck & Co. bought and spent ambitiously in the 1980s in a drive to offer consumers one-stop shopping for financial services. In the mid-1990's it divested itself of the empire just as ambitiously, returning Sears almost entirely to its retailing origins.

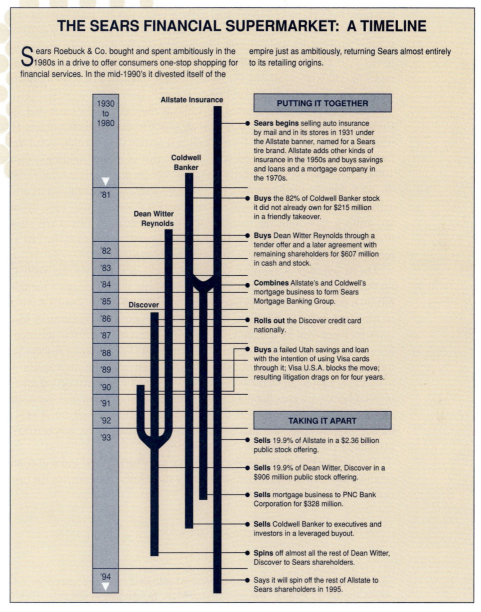

1930 to 1980	**PUTTING IT TOGETHER**
Allstate Insurance	**Sears begins** selling auto insurance by mail and in its stores in 1931 under the Allstate banner, named for a Sears tire brand. Allstate adds other kinds of insurance in the 1950s and buys savings and loans and a mortgage company in the 1970s.
Coldwell Banker	
'81	**Buys** the 82% of Coldwell Banker stock it did not already own for $215 million in a friendly takeover.
Dean Witter Reynolds	**Buys** Dean Witter Reynolds through a tender offer and a later agreement with remaining shareholders for $607 million in cash and stock.
'82	
'83	
'84	**Combines** Allstate's and Coldwell's mortgage business to form Sears Mortgage Banking Group.
'85 Discover	
'86	**Rolls out** the Discover credit card nationally.
'87	
'88	**Buys** a failed Utah savings and loan with the intention of using Visa cards through it; Visa U.S.A. blocks the move; resulting litigation drags on for four years.
'89	
'90	
'91	
'92	**TAKING IT APART**
'93	**Sells** 19.9% of Allstate in a $2.36 billion public stock offering.
	Sells 19.9% of Dean Witter, Discover in a $906 million public stock offering.
	Sells mortgage business to PNC Bank Corporation for $328 million.
	Sells Coldwell Banker to executives and investors in a leveraged buyout.
	Spins off almost all the rest of Dean Witter, Discover to Sears shareholders.
'94	Says it will spin off the rest of Allstate to Sears shareholders in 1995.

SOURCES: Company reports; *Hoover's Handbook;* Bloomberg Financial Market. Copyright © 1995 by The New York Times Company. Reprinted by permission.

that U.S. banks are permitted to engage in is the most constrained of banks in all of the major industrialized countries.[16] For example, no restrictions comparable to Glass-Steagall have been imposed on non-U.S. banks.

This situation has created considerable pressure on Congress to bring U.S. banks' activities in line with their global competitors and counterparts. Especially surprising is the fact that prior to 1998, no U.S. bank was in the world's top 20 (measured by assets). In contrast, in 1975 the United States had the top 2 banks (as well as 5 of the top 20)(see Table 25–5). While Congress did actively consider these issues in the debate leading up to the passage of the 1991 FDIC Improvement Act, it left the restrictions on nonbank activities defined under the Glass-Steagall Act, the Bank Holding Company Act and its amendments, and the Competitive Equality Bank Act largely intact.[17]

Significant changes occurred in 1997 as the Federal Reserve and the Office of the Comptroller of the Currency (OCC) took action to expand bank holding companies' activities. As shown in Table 25–1 and discussed earlier, the Fed eliminated the majority of the firewalls imposed on the Section 20 subsidiaries of a bank holding company in 1987 and 1989. Moreover, the OCC, which is responsible for regulating the 2,800 national banks that do not fall under the Fed's direct regulation, also expanded the set of allowable nonbank activities. Specifically, the OCC allowed national banks, on a "case-by-case" basis, to set up "arm's-length" subsidiaries that could underwrite securities or sell insurance. The OCC proposal was seen as a much easier route to diversification than the Fed's mechanism that requires the establishment of a bank holding company.

The result was a number of mergers and acquisitions between commercial and investment banks in 1997 and 1998. Some of the largest mergers include Citicorp's $83 billion merger with Travelers Group in April 1998, Bankers Trust's April 1997 acquisition of Alex Brown for $1.7 billion, NationsBank's June 1997 purchase of Montgomery Securities for more than $1 billion, U.S. Bancorp's December 1997 acquisition of Piper Jaffray for $730 million, and Bank of America's June 1997 purchase of Robert Stephens for $540 million. In each case, the bank stated that one motivation for the acquisition was the desire to establish a presence in the securities business since laws separating investment and commercial banking were changing. Also noted as a motivation in these acquisitions was the opportunity to expand business lines, taking advantage of economies of scale and scope to reduce overall costs and merge the customer bases of the respective commercial and investment banks involved in the acquisitions.

The next section discusses the issues that have been raised and will continue to be raised when the question of expanded product (or more universal) powers for banks and other FIs is debated.

---

[16]Many of Japan's postwar regulations were modeled on those of the United States. Thus, Article 65 in Japan separates commercial banking from investment banking in a fashion similar to the Glass-Steagall Act. Japan recently passed a major deregulation, however, that will considerably weaken the historic barriers between commercial and investment banking in that country. Specifically, under the 1992 Comprehensive Financial Reform Law, Japanese banks are permitted to establish subsidiaries to engage in a full range of securities activities. To protect small brokers, however, the law withholds permission to engage in retail equities brokerage. Interestingly, U.S. banking organizations currently are permitted to engage in this activity.

[17]See the U.S. Treasury Report, "Modernizing the Financial System" (United States Treasury Press Office, Department of Treasury, Washington, DC, 1991), for a description of these proposals. The prompt corrective action procedures implemented by the act did link the scope of permitted activities to the capitalization of the bank (see Chapter 16).

Table **25–5**

THE 20 LARGEST BANKS IN THE WORLD
(in millions of dollars)

	1975			1985			1995	
Bank	Total Assets	Capital and Reserves	Bank	Total Assets	Capital and Reserves	Bank	Total Assets	Capital and Reserves
1. BankAmerica Corp.	$65,789	$2,020	1. Citicorp	$167,201	$7,758	1. Deutsche Bank	$503,429	$18,929
2. Citicorp	52,775	2,717	2. Dai-Ichi Kangyo Bank	157,659	3,752	2. Sanwa Bank	501,043	17,687
3. Cassisse Nationale de Credit Agricole	49,060	2,382	3. Fuji Bank	142,128	4,008	3. Sumitomo Bank	499,933	18,598
4. Chase Manhattan	40,733	1,621	4. Sumitomo Bank	135,388	3,859	4. Dai-Ichi Kangyo Bank	498,625	19,197
5. Banque Nationale de Paris	38,333	305	5. Mitsubishi Bank	132,939	3,829	5. Fuji Bank	487,341	15,449
6. Deutsche Bank	34,639	1,218	6. Banque Nationale de Paris	123,081	2,486	6. Sakura Bank	478,050	15,967
7. Crédit Lyonnais	34,308	297	7. Sanwa Bank	123,008	3,321	7. Mitsubishi Bank	475,010	16,673
8. Société Générale	33,078	218	8. Crédit Agricole	122,891	5,321	8. Norinchukin Bank	429,517	3,221
9. Barclays Bank	33,044	1,809	9. BankAmerica Corp.	114,751	4,544	9. Crédit Agricole	386,388	20,405
10. Dai-Ichi Kangyo Bank	31,561	1,425	10. Crédit Lyonnais	111,458	1,371	10. Bank of China	373,614	10,050
11. National Westminster Bank	29,676	2,010	11. Norinchukin Bank	106,754	50	11. Industrial Bank of Japan	361,372	12,503
12. Banco do Brasil	29,125	2,450	12. National Westminster	104,677	4,281	12. CS Holding	358,734	13,740
13. Fuji Bank	28,059	1,323	13. Industrial Bank of Japan	102,770	2,919	13. HSBC Holdings	351,601	21,448
14. Dresdner Bank	28,003	747	14. Société Générale	97,627	2,216	14. ABN-Amro Bank	340,642	13,387
15. Sumitomo Bank	27,432	1,333	15. Deutsche Bank	95,751	3,820	15. Crédit Lyonnais	339,394	7,840
16. Manufacturers Hanover	27,394	998	16. Barclays Group	94,169	4,774	16. Union Bank of Switzerland	336,188	19,902
17. Mitsubishi Bank	26,458	1,273	17. Tokai Bank	90,423	2,396	17. Dresdner Bank	332,909	9,188
18. Sanwa Bank	25,554	722	18. Mitsui Bank	88,501	2,089	18. Société Générale	326,507	10,481
19. J.P. Morgan & Co.	24,983	1,221	19. Chase Manhattan Corp.	84,865	4,455	19. Banque Nationale de Paris	325,250	11,448
20. Banca Nazionale del Lavoro	24,452	856	20. Midland Bank	83,886	2,668	20. Tokai Bank	298,311	9,009

SOURCE: *The Banker*, June 1976, p. 653–655; July 1986, p. 113; and July 1996, p. 143.

Concept Questions

1. How does the range of product activities permitted U.S. commercial banks compare to that of banks in other major industrialized countries?
2. How are the product activities of U.S. commercial banks likely to change in the future?

• •

ISSUES INVOLVED IN THE DIVERSIFICATION OF PRODUCT OFFERINGS

Whether the debate concerns bank expansion into securities activities, insurance, or commerce, or vice versa, similar issues arise. These include the following:

1. Safety and soundness issues.
2. Economy of scale and scope issues.
3. Conflict of interest issues.
4. Deposit insurance issues.
5. Regulatory oversight issues.
6. Competition issues.

This section evaluates these issues in the context of banks entering into securities activities. The issues are summarized in Table 25–6.

Consider the three alternative organization structures for linking banking and securities activities in Figure 25–2. The bank holding company structure in parts (c) of the figure is the organization form within which we will evaluate the six issues just identified. The Fed has already adopted this form to accommodate bank organization expansions into nonbank activities, for example, the creation of Section 20 subsidiaries to engage in limited amounts of ineligible securities activities.

Figure 25–2 (a) shows the fully integrated universal bank, in which banking and securities activities are conducted in different departments. This is typical of the way in which large banks in Germany engage in securities activities. Figure 25–2 (b) is the universal subsidiary model in which a bank engages in securities activities through a separately owned securities affiliate. This is typical of the way in which commercial banks in the United Kingdom and Canada conduct their securities activities (and that the OCC recently approved as a model for U.S. nationally chartered banks).

Note that the degree of bank-nonbank integration is much less with the holding company model—part (c)—than with either the full or subsidiary universal banking model. For example, in the subsidiary universal banking model, the bank holds a direct ownership stake in the securities subsidiary.[18] By comparison, in the holding company model, the bank and securities subsidiary are separate companies with their own equity capital; the

---

[18]The comptroller of the currency recently advocated the establishment of direct subsidiaries along the lines of those shown in part (b). See "U.S. Proposes Letting Banks Enter New Fields," *New York Times,* November 29, 1994, p. D1.

Table **25-6**

ISSUES INVOLVED IN THE DIVERSIFICATION OF PRODUCT OFFERINGS

Safety and Soundness Issues: How risky is securities underwriting? If losses occur in a securities subsidiary, can this cause the affiliated bank to fail?

Economies of Scope and Scale Issues: As firewalls are reduced, are there economy of scale and scope opportunities available to banks that might undertake new activities?

Conflict of Interest Issues: What type of incentive structures can be implemented to prevent conflicts of interest? These conflicts include (1) salesperson stake in pushing the bank's own products to the customer's disadvantage, (2) stuffing fiduciary accounts with unplaceable securities underwritten by the securities subsidiary, (3) transference of bankruptcy risk of a loan customer by underwriting and selling bonds of the risky customer to unsuspecting bond buyers, (4) third-party loans used to guarantee purchase of underwritten securities, (5) tie-ins or coercion of loan customers to other products sold by the bank's securities affiliate, and (6) information transfer of private information from a bank subsidiary to the securities offering subsidiary, or vice versa.

Deposit Insurance Issues: Will banks, whose deposits are FDIC insured, pass along any funding subsidy by giving low-cost loans to affiliates?

Regulatory Oversight Issues: Is the multilayered regulatory structure overseeing the bank holding company and its subsidiaries efficient from a public policy perspective?

Competition Issues: What are the effects of bank affiliation with securities subsidiaries on competition in investment banking product lines? Procompetitive effects include (1) increased capital market access for small firms, (2) lower commission fees, and (3) reduced degree of underpricing of new issues. Anticompetitive effects include aggressive bank competition for new business driving traditional, single-line investment banking product firms out of business.

link is that their equity is held by the same parent company, the bank holding company (such as Citicorp).[19]

Safety and Soundness Concerns

Chapter 5 discussed and illustrated the risks of securities underwriting. With respect to the securities activities of commercial banks and the possible effects on their safety and soundness, one key question is whether securities activities can cause the affiliated bank to fail given the risk associated with securities underwriting.

Proponents of allowing banking organizations to expand their securities activities argue that the answer to this question is no, so long as the bank subsidiary is sufficiently insulated from the risk problems of the securities affiliate. As noted earlier, in a bank holding company structure, the bank is legally a separate corporation from the securities affiliate. As shown in Figure 25–3, its only link to its securities affiliate is indirect, through the holding company that owns a controlling equity stake in both the bank and the securities affiliate. However, even this indirect link raises the concern that the effects of losses by the

---

[19]In general, the advantages of the full universal banking are greater resource flexibility and integration of commercial bank and investment bank product lines. Its perceived disadvantages include greater monopoly power and large number of potential conflicts of interest.

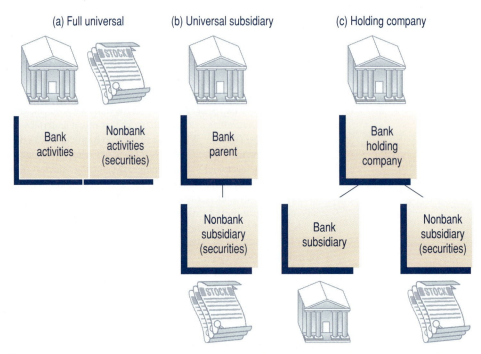

F i g u r e **25–2**   *Alternative Organization Forms for Nonbank Product Expansions of Banking Organizations*

securities affiliate could threaten the safety of the bank unless additional firewalls or regulatory barriers are introduced to insulate the bank against such losses.

A bank could be harmed by losses of a securities affiliate in a holding company structure in at least three ways. First, a bank holding company might be tempted to drain capital and funds from the bank by requiring excessive dividends and fees from the bank (this is called *upstreaming*). The holding company could then *downstream* these funds to prevent its failing securities affiliate from becoming insolvent. As a result, the bank would be weakened at the expense (or because) of the securities affiliate. Currently, the Federal Reserve closely monitors bank dividend payments to holding company owners and must restrict dividend payments of the bank if it is undercapitalized under the prompt corrective action plan (see Chapter 16). Also, Section 23B of the 1982 Federal Reserve Act limits the size of management and other fees that banks can pay for services provided by the holding company to the fee that the market for such services has established.[20]

A second way in which a bank could be harmed is through interaffiliate loans. For example, the holding company may induce the bank to extend loans to the securities subsidiary to keep it afloat, even though such loans are excessively risky. To prevent this, Section 23A of the Federal Reserve Act limits bank loans to any single nonbank subsidiary

---

[20]Nevertheless, in 1994 alone, at least seven cases of bank holding companies infusing funds into their mutual funds occurred, including $50.5 million by BankAmerica Corp. into its Pacific Horizon Prime MMF, to prevent fund holders from taking losses. So far, the Fed has not taken any punitive action against these banks. See E. J. Kane, "What Is the Value-Added Large U.S. Banks Find in Offering Mutual Funds?" Working Paper, Boston College, November 1994.

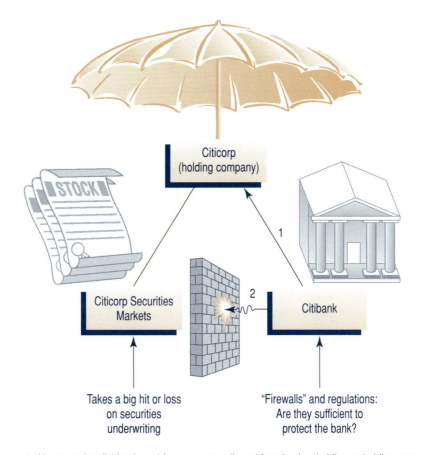

Takes a big hit or loss
on securities
underwriting

"Firewalls" and regulations:
Are they sufficient to
protect the bank?

1. No excessive dividends and fee payments allowed from bank subsidiary to holding company.
2. Bank loans to any single affiliate limited to 10 percent of bank's capital.

Figure **25–3**   *The Role of Firewalls in Protecting Banks*

to 10 percent of a bank's capital. If bank capital is approximately 5 percent of bank assets, this limits loans to a subsidiary to $.05 \times 10$ percent of bank assets, or 0.5 percent of bank assets. Prior to 1997, firewalls prohibited a bank from lending anything at all to its Section 20 securities subsidiary.[21]

The third way that may affect a bank is through a contagious confidence problem. Specifically, difficulty of an affiliated securities firm may result in a negative information signal to financial service consumers and investors regarding the quality of the management of the holding company and its bank affiliate. Such negative information can create incentives for large depositors and investors to withdraw their money from the bank in the manner described in Chapter 15. This bank run possibility seems more likely to occur if the bank and its securities subsidiary share similar names and logos; for example, if Citibank and Citicorp Securities Markets had joint management and office space and extensively cross-marketed each other's products. Until 1997, firewall regulations required Section 20 securities subsidiaries of banks to have separate offices and separate managements. Also, cross-marketing

---

[21]Prior to 1997, this also held for the sale of assets by the affiliate to the bank.

each other's products was absolutely prohibited. In general, however, nonbank subsidiaries have retained names similar to their bank subsidiaries, so a contagious confidence problem exists. With the reduction of these firewalls (see Table 25–2) the probability of a contagious confidence problem has increased.

Obviously, big losses taken by the securities subsidiary can potentially threaten the safety and solvency of the affiliated bank, especially through the confidence effect. At least two countervailing risk-reducing effects, however, may enhance the safety and soundness of a bank indirectly linked to a securities subsidiary in a holding company framework. The first effect is a **product diversification benefit**. A well-diversified financial services firm (bank holding company) potentially enjoys a far more stable earnings and profit stream over time than does a product-specialized bank. As demand and cost shifts reduce earnings in one activity area such as banking, offsetting demand and cost shifts may take place in other activity areas, such as securities or insurance, increasing bank holding company earnings. Advocates argue that a more stable and diversified earnings stream for the holding company enables it to act as a source of strength in keeping the affiliated bank well capitalized.

A number of empirical studies in the academic literature have evaluated the gains from bank activity diversification by observing the correlations of accounting earnings for segmented financial firms or industries and analyzing correlations between firms' stock market returns. Essentially, the lower these correlations, the higher the potential gains from activity diversification and the lower the variability of a banking organization's earnings flows. Other studies have sought to evaluate the potential effects of activity diversification on the risk of failure of banks and to simulate the effects of bank-nonbank mergers on bank risk. The majority of the studies find that bank holding company risk could be reduced by expansion into nonbank product lines. However, the optimal proportion of investment in individual nonbank product lines often falls in the 5 to 25 percent range. This suggests that excessive product expansion in some nonbank lines could actually increase banking organization's total risk exposure.

In addition to the potential risk-reducing gains of product diversification, by diversifying its earnings stream geographically, a bank holding company can generate additional risk reduction gains when regional imperfections exist in the costs of raising debt and equity (see Chapter 27).

product diversification benefit

Stabilization of earnings and profit resulting from a well-diversified bank holding company.

Economies of Scale and Scope

A second issue concerning the expansion of banks into securities and other nonbank activities is the potential for additional economies of scale and scope. As we discuss in Chapter 24, limited economy of scale opportunities appear to exist for financial firms in the $100 million to $5 billion range. Moreover, most studies find that cost-based economies of scope are negligible, although revenue-based economies of scope may occur for the largest FIs. Arguably, the pre-1997 restrictive firewalls between banks and their Section 20 investment banking affiliates covering finance, management, and cross-marketing severely limited economies of scope and related revenue and cost synergies. Such economies might be generated only in a more integrated universal banking structure of the German or British type with fewer cross-marketing and finance firewalls between the bank and its non-bank product activities.[22] Post-1997 U.S. bank holding companies may realize greater

---

[22]Nevertheless, Saunders and Walter, *Universal Banking in the United States,* could find no evidence of cost economies of scope for the world's 100 largest banks, many of which are universal banks.

economies of scope as the firewalls are reduced and they become more like German and British universal banks.

Conflicts of Interest

A third issue, the potential for conflicts of interest, lies at the very heart of opposition to the expansion of banking powers into other financial service areas. Indeed, concerns regarding conflicts of interest provided the main foundation for the passage of the Glass-Steagall Act in 1933.[23] The two principal concerns are (1) the potential conflicts of interest arising from the expansion of banks' securities activities and (2) the type of incentive structures that change potential conflicts into actual conflicts.

Six Potential Conflicts of Interest.   We discuss the six most common potential conflicts of interest identified by regulators and academics in this section.

Salesperson's Stake.   Critics argue that when banks have the power to sell nonbank products, bank staff no longer dispense dispassionate advice to their customers as to which products to buy. Instead, they have a salesperson's stake in pushing the bank's own products, often to the disadvantage of the customer.

Stuffing Fiduciary Accounts.   Suppose that a bank is acting as a securities underwriter and is unable to place these securities in a public offering. To avoid being exposed to potential losses, the bank may "stuff" these unwanted securities in accounts managed by its own trust department and over which it has discretionary investment powers.

Bankruptcy Risk Transference.   Assume that a bank has a loan outstanding to a firm and has private knowledge that the firm's credit or bankruptcy risk has increased. With this private knowledge, the bank may have an incentive to induce the firm to issue bonds underwritten by the bank's securities affiliate to an unsuspecting public. The proceeds of this bond issue could then be used to pay down the bank loan. As a result, the bank would have transferred the borrowing firm's credit risk from itself to less-informed outside investors while the securities affiliate also earned an underwriting fee.

Third-Party Loans.   To ensure that an underwriting goes well, a bank may make cheap loans to third-party investors on the implicit condition that this loan is used to purchase securities underwritten by its securities affiliate.

Tie-Ins.   A bank may use its lending powers to coerce or tie in a customer to the products that its securities affiliate sells. For example, the bank may threaten to ration credit unless the customer agrees to let the bank's securities affiliate do its securities underwritings.

Information Transfer.   In acting as a lender, the bank may become privy to certain inside information about its customers or its rivals that it can use to set the prices or help the distribution of securities offerings by its affiliate. This information could also flow from the securities affiliate to the bank. The details of one such case involving conflicts of interest and information transfer are presented in Comptemporary Perspectives Box 25–2.

---

[23]See G. J. Benston, *The Separation of Commercial and Investment Banking: The Glass-Steagall Act Revisited and Reconsidered* (New York: St. Martin's Press, 1989).

Contemporary Perspectives 25–2

ADT versus Chase: Testing Limits of Bank's Role in Takeovers

ADT Inc., continuing to resist a hostile $3.5 billion bid by Western Resources, will drag the takeover battle into the courtroom on Monday, saying that Chase Manhattan Bank violated fiduciary and contractual obligations by allying itself with Western.

Whatever the merits of the case, the wrangling between ADT and Chase in State Supreme Court in Manhattan may well portend the pitfalls that await those commercial banks that are aggressively pushing into Wall Street's domain, providing investment banking services, merger advice and underwriting, as well as loans.

The commercial banks are much larger and have many more clients than investment banks and law firms and are therefore exposed to far more potential conflicts of interest. ADT contends in the lawsuit that it filed on Feb. 10 that Chase Manhattan, which was ADT's lender and financial adviser, used confidential information in providing financing and advice for Western's attempted takeover.

ADT . . . contends that Chase's alliance with Western Resources con-

tradicted oral statements by Chase executives in 1993 that the bank would never back a hostile bid for ADT . . . Chase's response states that no such oral promises were made and that under New York law the bank "owes no fiduciary duties" to ADT. . . . Finally, Chase says that its actions on behalf of Western do not harm ADT shareholders and that ADT managers, fearing for their jobs, are merely trying to obstruct Western's effort to acquire ADT. . . .

"This is an indication of how life has gotten complex for everyone in the financial world," said Harvey Goldschmid, a professor of corporate law at Columbia University Law School. "It means they're going to have to be very careful. The banks have to build impregnable walls between the mergers and acquisitions work and the traditional banking relationships, otherwise they run the risk of being accused of using confidential information. . . ."

Stephen J. Ruzika, president of ADT, contends in an affidavit that Chase's involvement with the Western bid contradicted statements made to him by Chase executives in

1993, when he was negotiating a $500 million loan agreement. Mr. Ruzika's affidavit states that Chase, which aggressively sought to be ADT's financial adviser as well as a lender, assured him that the bank would not "fund or otherwise assist a hostile takeover effort." ADT provided the bank with sensitive documents and discussed corporate strategy. In similar cases, courts have ruled that banks, unlike lawyers and investment banks, do not owe a fiduciary duty to a borrower. But ADT contends that there was a relationship of trust and confidence that went well beyond that of a simple borrower-lender connection.

The Chase Manhattan executives named by Mr. Ruzika, however, have denied that the conversations took place and have stated that impregnable walls existed between its investment bankers who worked with Western Resources and its lending officers who dealt with ADT and acquired confidential information about the company.

Chinese wall

An internally imposed barrier within an organization that limits the flow of confidential client information among departments or areas.

Potential Conflicts of Interest and Their Actual Exploitation.   On their own these conflicts are unquestionably extremely troublesome. Remember, however, that specific and general checks and balances limit their exploitation. Many of these conflicts are likely to remain potential rather than become actual conflicts of interest. Specifically, many of these conflicts, such as tie-ins and third-party loans, breach existing bank regulations and laws.[24] Also, internal barriers or **Chinese walls** in most banks prohibit internal information

---

[24]Involuntary tie-ins are illegal under various sections of the Clayton Act, the Sherman Antitrust Act, and the Bank Holding Company Act.

transfers when they potentially conflict with the customer's best interests. In addition, sales of debt issues to a less-informed public to pay down bank loans may result in future lawsuits against the underwriter once investors discover their losses.[25]

More generally, conflicts of interest can be exploited only under three conditions. First, markets for bank services are uncompetitive, so that banks have monopoly power over their customers, for example, in making loans. Second, information flows between the customer and the bank are imperfect, so that the bank possesses an information advantage over its customers. Third, the bank places a relatively low value on its reputation. The discovery of having exploited a conflict can result in considerable market and regulatory penalties. Despite such penalties in recent years, some banks such as NationsBank have been subject to a number of lawsuits alleging overzealous selling tactics and incomplete information disclosure that amount to conflicts of interest.[26]

Deposit Insurance

A possible argument against expanded powers is that the explicit and implicit protection given to banks by deposit insurance coverage gives banks a competitive advantage over other financial service firms (see Chapter 15). For example, because explicit deposit insurance covers bank deposits up to $100,000, banks are able to raise funds at subsidized, lower-cost rates than are traditional securities firms. This may allow banks to pass on these lower costs in cheaper loans to their affiliates. An indirect deposit insurance–related advantage to banking organizations undertaking securities activities when compared to traditional securities firms may exist. This advantage may result if bank regulators regard certain large banking organizations as being too big to fail (TBTF), thereby encouraging these institutions to take excessive risks such as placing aggressive underwriting bids for new issues. This situation would limit the underwriting shares of traditional investment banks, especially because TBTF guarantees do not appear to exist for them—as shown in the failure of Drexel Burnham Lambert in February 1990. Consequently, TBTF guarantees tend to give banks some unfair competitive advantages.[27]

Regulatory Oversight

Currently, most bank holding companies with extensive nonbank subsidiaries face a diffused and multilayered regulatory structure that would potentially hinder the monitoring and control of conflicts of interest abuses and excessive risk taking should banks be allowed to expand their securities activities. Specifically, the Federal Reserve is the primary regulator for a bank holding company such as Citicorp. For its bank subsidiary such as Citibank, the Office of the Comptroller of the Currency, which charters national banks, shares regulatory oversight with the Federal Reserve and the FDIC. The primary regulator of a bank's Section 20 securities subsidiary is the SEC, although the Federal Reserve also has some oversight powers. It is far from clear that such a complex and overlapping regulatory structure is efficient from a public policy perspective[28] because the

---

[25]In particular, the underwriter may be accused of lack of due diligence in not disclosing information in the new issue's prospectus.

[26]See "NationsBank: An Excess of Zeal," *Business Week,* November 28, 1994, pp. 104-106.

[27]This point has also been made with respect to bank sales of mutual funds.

[28]In the context of allowing banks to expand into insurance activities, the problem of aligning the differences between (largely) federal bank regulation and state-based insurance regulation would have to be faced as well.

structure is prone to waste monitoring and surveillance resources and to cause unnecessary disputes over bureaucratic turf. Furthermore, coordination problems can weaken monitoring and surveillance efficiency. Thus, a case can be made for placing all regulatory power in a single regulatory body should the securities powers of banks be extended further.[29]

Competition

The final issue concerns the effects of bank product diversification on competition in investment banking product lines. In securities underwriting, three primary factors are cited as reasons that bank expansions would enhance competition. One factor is cited as a reason that it would do the reverse; that is, bank expansions would increase both market concentration and the monopoly power of commercial banks over customers.

Procompetitive Effects.   The three factors that explain the enhancement of competition should banks engage in securities underwriting are discussed in the following sections.

Increased Capital Market Access for Small Firms.   Most large investment banks are headquartered in New York and the Northeast. As a result, small U.S. firms based in the Midwest and Southwest often have had a more difficult time accessing national capital markets than have firms of a similar size located in the Northeast. Consequently, the entry of regional and superregional banks into securities underwriting through securities affiliates could potentially expand smaller firms' access to the national capital market.[30]

Lower Commissions and Fees.   Increased competition for securities underwritings should reduce the underwriter's spread. That is, it should reduce the spread between the new issue bid price paid to the issuing firm and the offer price at which these shares are resold to the market. This potentially raises the amount of new issue proceeds for the issuing firm by raising the underwriter's bid price. (Such an effect was claimed when banks expanded their municipal bond underwritings, although this has been disputed.[31]) In recent years, the spreads on debt underwritings have fallen by half, or from approximately 50 basis points in the mid-1980s to around 25 basis points today. The extent to which this decline has been due to increased competition from Section 20 subsidiaries remains to be tested.[32]

Reduced Degree of Underpricing of New Issues.   The greatest risk to the underwriter is to price a new issue too high relative to the market's valuation of that security. That is, under-

---

[29]Despite numerous attempts in recent years to reform and rationalize the regulatory structure through Congress, none has been successful.

[30]Some support for this case can be found in A. Gande, M. Puri, A. Saunders, and I. Walter, "Bank Underwriting of Debt Securities: Modern Evidence," *Review of Financial Studies,* 1997. They find that the size of debt issues underwritten by Section 20 subsidiaries was significantly smaller than those underwritten by investment banks in the period 1993–1994.

[31]For a review of this debate and the evidence, see W. L. Silber, "Municipal Revenue Bond Costs and Bank Underwriting: A Survey of the Evidence," Monograph Series in Finance and Economics, Salomon Center for the Study of Financial Institutions, New York University, 1979.

[32]The spreads on equity underwritings also have fallen from 6.8 percent in 1990 (when banks first achieved equity underwriting powers) to 6.1 percent in 1997; see "Banks Push Into Securities Squeezes Fees," The *Wall Street Journal,* December 16, 1997, p. C1.

writers stand to lose when they overprice new issues. Given this, underwriters have an incentive to underprice new issues by setting the public offer price below the price established for the security in the secondary market once trading begins. The investment banker stands to gain by underpricing as it increases the probability of selling out the issue without affecting the fixed underwriting spread. That is, a spread of $.50 at a bid-offer price spread of $93 and $93.50 produces the same gross revenue (spread) of $.50 per share to the underwriter as a bid-offer price spread of $97 and $97.50. The major difference is that a lower offer price (i.e., $93 rather than $97) increases investors' demand for the shares and the probability that the entire issue will sell to the public very quickly. Both the underwriter and the outside investor may benefit from underpricing; the loser is the firm issuing the securities because it obtains lower proceeds than had the offer price been set at a higher price reflecting a more accurate market valuation. In this example, the issuer receives only $93 per share rather than $97. Consequently, underpricing new issues is an additional cost of the issuance of securities that issuing firms bear. Most empirical research on the underpricing of U.S. new issues, or **initial public offerings** (IPOs), has found that they are underpriced in the range of 8 to 48 percent, depending on the sample and time period chosen.[33] In contrast, **secondary issues** tend to be underpriced by less than 3 percent.[34]

If a major cause of IPO underpricing is a lack of competition among existing investment banks, bank entry and competition should lower the degree of underpricing and increase the new issue proceeds for firms. Nevertheless, many economists argue that monopoly power is not the primary reason for underpricing new issues but that underpricing reflects a risk premium that must be paid to investors and investment bankers for information imperfections. That is, underpricing is a risk premium for the information advantage possessed by issuers who better know the true quality of their firm's securities and its assets.[35] If this is so, bank entry into securities activities may reduce only the degree of underpricing to the extent that it reduces the degree of information imperfection among issuers and investors. This might reasonably be expected given the specialized role of banks as delegated monitors (see Chapter 1).

Anticompetitive Effects.   Although bank entry may be procompetitive in the short term, considerable concern about potential anticompetitive behavior in the long term still exists. The large money center banks, measured by either capital or assets, are many times larger than the largest securities firms—or insurance firms, for that matter. Indeed, this is one

---

IPO (initial public offering)

A corporate equity or debt security offered to the public through an underwriter for the first time.

secondary issue

A new issue of equity or debt by firms whose securities are already traded in the market.

---

[33] See the review of approximately 20 studies of underpricing by A. Saunders, "Why Are So Many Stock Issues Underpriced?" Federal Reserve Bank of Philadelphia, *Business Review,* March–April 1990, pp. 3–12.

[34] See C. F. Loderer, D. P. Sheehan, and G. B. Kadler, "The Pricing of Equity Offerings," *Journal of Financial Economics,* 1991, pp. 35–57. Interestingly, S. Dalta, M. Iskandar-Dalton, and A. Patel, "The Pricing of Initial Public Offers of Corporate Straight Debt," *Journal of Finance,* March 1997, pp. 379–396, find no evidence of underpricing of IPOs of investment grade bonds (i.e., rated BBB and higher). However, they do find underpricing for straight debt IPOs rated below investment grade (i.e., BB or below). That is, junk bond new issues appear to be underpriced in a fashion similar to equity IPOs.

[35] See R. Beatty and J. Ritter, "Investment Banking, Reputation, and the Underpricing of Initial Public Offerings," *Journal of Financial Economics* 15 (1986), pp. 213–232; and K. Rock, "Why New Issues Are Underpriced," *Journal of Financial Economics* 15 (1986), pp. 187–212; and C. Muscarella and M. R. Vetsuypens, "A Simple Test of Baron's Model of IPO Underpricing," *Journal of Financial Economics* 24 (1989), pp. 125–136. They found that when investment banks themselves (such as Morgan Stanley) went public, their stocks were underpriced. This tends to support an information role in underpricing, although the average underpricing of investment banks was less than that found, on average, for other firms.

reason for large nonbank financial services firms to merge (e.g., Travelers and Smith Barney in 1996, and Travelers and Salomon Brothers in 1997). The largest banks may aggressively compete for business in the short term, trying to force traditional investment banks out of business. If successful, they would assume quasi-oligopoly positions, market concentration may rise, and in the long run, prices for investment banking services would rise rather than fall. Such a long-term outcome would outweigh any short-term procompetitive benefits.[36]

Nevertheless, in recent years, regulators and Congress have shown a greater appreciation of the potential benefits of financial service activity expansions, resulting in 1997 in major legislative changes for banks to allow them to integrate their banking and non-banking services more fully. Given that, prior to 1998, no United States bank was among the world's top 20 banks—measured by assets—and that the countries of the European Community have now adopted a *single capital market* in which universal banking is viewed as the norm, the larger and more powerful financial service conglomerates may pose an increasing competitive threat to financial firms headquartered in segmented financial systems such as the United States. If this occurs, pressure on Congress and regulators is likely to increase to allow U.S. financial firms to expand further their activities beyond the traditional boundaries defined by laws such as Glass-Steagall, the National Banking Act, and the Bank Holding Company Act.

Concept Questions

1. What are some of the issues concerning bank expansion into securities, insurance, and commercial activities?
2. How is firm commitment underwriting of securities similar to writing put options on assets?
3. What are three ways in which the losses of a securities affiliate in a holding company structure can be transmitted to a bank?
4. In addition to the six potential conflicts of interest discussed in this section, can you think of any other possible conflicts that might occur if commercial banks were allowed to expand their investment banking activities?
5. What three factors are cited in support of banks' expansion into securities activities? What reason is given to support the opposite claim (i.e., that bank expansion would *not* enhance competition)?

---

[36]One possible reason for the slow development of the German corporate bond market is that German universal banks wish to preserve their monopoly power over corporate debt. This may be best done by encouraging corporate loans rather than bond issues.

S U M M A R Y

The U.S. financial system is structured on segmented product lines. Unlike the situation in other countries, several legislative acts, including the Glass-Steagall Act of 1933 and the Bank Holding Company Act of 1956, have separated commercial banking, investment banking, and insurance activities. The restrictions that these acts place on product or activity expansion may inhibit several benefits from financial services conglomeration both at the private and the social welfare levels. Most important are the potential risk-reducing gains from both regional and product diversification as well as gains from the potential generation of cost and revenue synergies. However, a set of important public policy or social welfare concerns relates to conflicts of interest, safety and soundness, competition, and regulation. These latter concerns have restricted the expansion of the financial product sets of traditional FIs such as commercial banks.

P E R T I N E N T   W E B   S I T E S

Board of Governors of the Federal Reserve   ttp://www.bog.frb.fed.us/

Office of the Comptroller of the Currency   http://www.occ.treas.gov/

Product Diversification

1. How does product segmentation reduce FIs' risks? How does it increase FIs' risks?
2. In what ways have other FIs taken advantage of the restrictions on product diversification imposed on commercial banks?
3. How does product segmentation reduce FI's profitability? How does product segmentation increase FI's profitability?
4. What insurance activities are permitted for U.S. commercial bank holding companies?
5. What restrictions are placed on Section 20 subsidiaries of U.S. commercial banks that make investment banking activites other than those permitted by the Glass-Steagall Act less attractive? How does this differ from banking activities in other countries?
6. A Section 20 subsidiary of a major United States bank is planning to underwrite coprorate securities and expects to generate $5 million in revenues. It currently underwrites U.S. Treasury securities and general obligation municipal bonds, earning annual fees of $40 million.
   a. Is the bank in compliance with the laws regulating the revenue generation of Section 20 subsidiaries?
   b. The bank plans to increase its private placement activities and expects to generate $11 million in revenue. Is it in compliance with the revenue generation requirements?
   c. If it plans to increase underwriting of corporate securities and generate $11 million in revenues, is it in compliance? If not, what should it do to ensure that it is in compliance?
7. Why have small state-chartered banks not taken advantage of their ability to engage in securities activities such as underwriting?
8. The Garn-St. Germain Act of 1982 and several subsequent banking laws have clearly established the separation of banking and insurance firms. What are the likely reasons for maintaining this separation?
9. What is the consensus from academic studies evaluating the gains from bank activity diversification?
10. What types of insurance products are commercial banks permitted to offer?
11. How have nonbanks managed to exploit the loophole in the Bank Holding Company Act of 1956 and engage in banking activities? What law closed this loophole?
12. How might the Congressional proposal to merge the commercial bank and thrift industries offer commercial banks an entry into the insurance underwriting business?
13. How will the absence of any U.S. commercial banks from the top 20 world banks likely affect bank industry reform in Congress?
14. How is underwriting on a firm commitment basis similar to writing a put option?
15. What do empirical studies reveal about the effect of activity diversification on the risk of failure of banks?

16. What role does bank activity diversification play in the ability of a bank to exploit economies of scale and scope?

17. A bank could be affected negatively in three ways if its securities affiliate, under a holding company organizational form, fails. How has the Fed attempted to prevent a breakdown of the firewalls between banks and its affiliates?

18. Big Bank has assets of $2 billion and capital equal to 6 percent of assets. What is the maximum amount that Big Bank could lend to its thrift affiliate?

19. What are some of the legal, institutional, and market conditions that lessen the likelihood that an FI can exploit any conflict of interest from the expansion of commercial banks into other financial service areas?

20. Go to the web site of the Federal Reserve Board and find the most recent information about the supervision and regulation of nonbank activities of commercial banks.

PERMISSIBLE ACTIVITIES FOR BANKING ORGANIZATIONS IN VARIOUS FINANCIAL CENTERS[1]

	Securities[2]	Insurance[3]	Real Estate[4]	Bank Investment in Industrial Firms[5]	Industrial Firm Investments in Banks
Argentina	Permitted; certain activities must be conducted through subsidiaries	Permitted through subsidiaries	Limited; based on bank capital and investment objective	Limited	Permitted but subject to prior approval of authorities
Australia	Permitted	Permitted through subsidiaries subject to controls of insurance legislation	Limited	Limited by prudential guidelines	Acquisition of more than 10% of a bank's voting stock requires regulatory approval
Austria	Permitted	Permitted through subsidiaries	Permitted	Permitted, but subject to limits based on the bank's capital	Permitted, but subject to notification and prohibition under certain circumstances
Bahrain	Permitted, but limited by terms of license and supervisory guidelines	Not permitted	Generally limited to holding bank premises	Not permitted	No legal restriction, but subject to approval of banking authorities
Belgium	Permitted; some activities must be conducted through subsidiaries	Permitted through subsidiaries	Generally limited to holding bank premises	Single shareholding may not exceed 10% of bank's own funds, and such share-holdings on an aggregate basis may not exceed 35% of own funds	Permitted, but subject to prior approval of authorities
Bolivia	Permitted through subsidiaries	Permitted through subsidiaries	Not permitted	Not permitted	No legal restriction, but subject to approval of banking authorities
Brazil	Permitted through subsidiaries	Permitted through subsidiaries	Generally limited to holding bank premises	Limited to suppliers to the bank	Permitted
Canada	Permitted through subsidiaries	Permitted through subsidiaries	Permitted through subsidiaries	Permitted to hold up to 10% interest, with aggregate shareholdings not to exceed 70% of bank capital	Permitted to hold up to 10% interest
Cayman Islands	Permitted	Permitted on issuance of a license	Permitted	Not restricted by law	Permitted, but subject to consultations with authorities

continued

	Securities[2]	Insurance[3]	Real Estate[4]	Bank Investment in Industrial Firms[5]	Industrial Firm Investments in Banks
Chile	Permitted to some extent; certain activities through subsidiaries	Not permitted	Not permitted	Not permitted	Permitted
China	Permitted through subsidiaries	Permitted through subsidiaries	Permitted through subsidiaries	Not permitted	Not permitted
Denmark	Permitted	Permitted through subsidiaries	Limited to 20% of capital	Permitted with restrictions; permanent controlling holdings in industrial companies are prohibited	Not prohibited, but such investments are generally not made
European Union[6]	Not applicable; permissibility is subject to home country authorization and limited host country regulation	Not applicable; permissibility is subject to home country host country regulation	Not applicable; permissibility is subject to home country host country regulation	Each 10% or more shareholding may not exceed 15% of the bank's own funds, and such shareholdings on an aggregate basis may not exceed 60% of own funds	No general restrictions; does not allow investments of 10% or more if home country supervisor is not satisfied with the suitability of the shareholder
Finland	Permitted	Permitted, but only selling of insurance policies as an agent	Permitted to hold real estate and shares in real estate companies up to 13% of total assets	Permitted to hold directly up to 10% of shares of nonfinancial companies, and up to 20% on an aggregate basis through subsidiaries	Permitted
France	Permitted	Permitted, usually through subsidiaries	Permitted	Permitted with regulatory approval of interests in excess of 10%	Not prohibited
Germany	Permitted	Permitted, but only through insurance subsidiaries	Permitted, but subject to limits based on bank's capital; unlimited through subsidiaries	Limited to 15% of bank's capital; in the aggregate, limited to 60% of the bank's capital	Permitted (subject to regulatory consent based on the suitability of the shareholder)
Greece	Underwriting permitted by certain credit institutions; brokerage and dealing permitted through subsidiaries	Permitted to hold shares in insurance companies subject to limits based on bank's capital and the insurance company's capital	Generally permitted	Permitted, but subject to the EU directive on qualified holdings	Permitted, but subject to the EU directive on qualified holdings
Hong Kong	Permitted (except for limitation on shareholding in certain listed companies and subject to limits based on the capital of the bank)	Permitted (subject to limits based on the capital of the bank)	Permitted (subject to limits based on the capital of the bank)	Permitted (subject to regulatory consent based on the capital of the bank)	Permitted (subject to regulatory consent based on the suitability of the shareholder)

India	Permitted; some activities through subsidiaries	Not permitted	Generally limited to holding bank premises	Limited to 30% of the share capital and reserves of the company or the bank, whichever is less	Permitted, but subject to acknowledgement of Reserve Bank of India to transfer 1% or more of the capital of the bank
Ireland	Permitted; usually through a subsidiary	Permitted agency and certain life assurance activities through a subsidiary, which must be separate and independent	Permitted	Acquisition of more than 10% of voting rights of a firm requires Central Bank approval	Permitted, but subject to Central Bank prior approval for acquisition more than 10% of total bank shares
Italy	Permitted, but not to operate directly on the stock exchange	Limited to 10% of own funds for each insurance company and 20% aggregate investment in insurance company	Generally limited to holding bank premises	Not permitted	Permitted up to 15% of shares of the bank, subject to approval of the Bank of Italy
Japan	Permitted through subsidiaries, except for equity brokerage for the time being	Not permitted	Generally limited to holding bank premises	Limited to holding 5% interests	Permitted, provided total investment does not exceed investing firm's capital or net assets
Korea	Permitted through affiliates	Not permitted	Limited to banking activities and to 40% of bank capital	Subject to prior approval for investments in excess of 10%	Permitted up to 8% of the bank's shares
Mexico	Permitted through affiliates	Permitted through affiliates	Not permitted	Not permitted	Not permitted
The Netherlands	Permitted	Permitted through subsidiaries	Permitted	Subject to regulatory approval for voting shares in excess of 10%	Subject to regulatory approval for voting shares in excess of 5%
New Zealand	Permitted, but in practice through a subsidiary	Permitted through subsidiaries	Permitted through subsidiaries	Permitted	Permitted, but subject to approval of authorities
Norway	Generally permitted through subsidiaries; stock brokerage activities need no longer be conducted in separate subsidiaries	Permitted through subsidiaries	Permitted subject to restrictions based on the total assets of the bank	Investments of up to 49% in single companies permitted; only 4% of total bank assets permitted to be invested in shares	Generally, a maximum ownership limit of 10% for any single owner of a financial institution; some exceptions, the most important relating to subsidiaries of foreign institutions
Pakistan	Permitted, except for some specifically disallowed securities	Not permitted	Generally limited to holding bank premises	Permitted as a form of financing, subject to the central bank's prudential guidelines	Permitted

continued

635

	Securities[2]	Insurance[3]	Real Estate[4]	Bank Investment in Industrial Firms[5]	Industrial Firm Investments in Banks
Panama	Permitted	Not permitted	Generally limited to holding bank premises	Permitted up to 25% of the bank's capital	Not prohibited, but such investments would require approval by the National Banking Commission
Peru	Permitted through subsidiaries; banks have recently been authorized to issue mortgage-backed securities	Not permitted	Generally limited to holding bank premises	Generally not permitted	Permitted subject to approval of superintendent of banks if investments exceed 15% of bank's capital
Poland	Permitted	Permitted	Permitted	Permitted up to 25% of the bank's capital	Permitted
Portugal	Generally permitted; mutual funds only through subsidiaries	Permitted through subsidiaries	Generally limited to holding bank premises	Permitted up to 15% of bank's own funds (but not to exceed 25% of the voting rights of the company), and such investments may not in the aggregate exceed 60% of the bank's own funds	Subject to regulatory approval for acquisitions of voting shares in excess of 20, 33, and 50%
Singapore	Banks may hold equity participants in stock brokering firms with the Monetary Authority of Singapore's approval	Locally incorporated banks may own insurance companies with MAS's approval	Limited in the aggregate to 40% of bank's capital	Limited in the aggregate to 40% of bank's capital	Acquisition of 5% or more requires regulatory approval
Spain	Permitted; banks are permitted to own up to 100% of stock exchange members	Permitted through subsidiaries	Permitted	Permitted, subject to capital-based limits	Acquisition of 5% or more require the approval of the Bank of Spain
Sweden	Permitted	Permitted	Generally limited to holding bank premises	Limited	Not prohibited, but such investments are generally not made
Switzerland	Permitted	Permitted through subsidiaries	Permitted	Permitted	Not prohibited, but such investments are generally not made

636

	Securities[2]	Insurance[3]	Real estate[4]		
Thailand	Permitted through subsidiaries; banks recently given authority to underwrite debt securities	Permitted through subsidiaries	Generally limited to holding bank premises	Permitted to hold up to 10% interest	Maximum equity interest limited to 5%
United Kingdom	Permitted; usually through subsidiaries	Permitted through subsidiaries	Permitted	Permitted subject to consultations with the Bank of England	No prohibitions contained in The Banking Act of 1987[7]
United States	Permitted for government securities; stock brokerage activities also generally permitted; however, corporate securities underwriting and dealing activities must be conducted through specially authorized affiliates, which must limit such activities to 25% of gross revenues	Generally not permitted	Generally limited to holding bank premises	Permitted to hold up to 5% of the voting shares through a holding company	Permitted to make noncontrolling investments of up to 25% of the voting shares
Uruguay	Underwriting authority permitted; dealing limited to public debt; brokerage and mutual funds not permitted	Not permitted; however in some cases, banks permitted to sell insurance policies to their customers	Generally limited to holding bank premises	Not permitted	Not permitted

[1] With respect to the activities described, the chart indicates which *types* of financial activities are permitted. The chart is not intended to summarize the complete range of prudential restrictions that may apply to any such activities.

[2] Securities activities include underwriting, dealing, and brokering all types of securities and all aspects of the mutual fund business.

[3] Insurance activities include underwriting and selling insurance as principal and as agent.

[4] Real estate activities include real estate investment, development, and management.

[5] Including investments through holding company structures.

[6] The Second Banking Directive contains a broad list of securities and commercial banking activities that European Union (EU) "credit institutions" (i.e., entities engaged in deposit taking and lending) may conduct directly or through branches throughout the EU so long as their home countries authorize the activities. Subsidiaries of credit institutions governed by the law of the same member state may also conduct activities on the list throughout the EU, subject to conditions that include 90% ownership and a guaranty of commitments by the parent credit institutions. Insurance and real estate activities are not on the list and are therefore determined by home country and host country regulations.

[7] No statutory prohibitions, but the Bank of England has indicated it would not favor controlling investments by industrial firms in major banks.

SOURCE: Institute of International Bankers, *1994 Global Survey of Regulatory and Market Developments in Banking, Securities and Insurance.* New York, NY.

Chapter Twenty-six

Geographic Expansion: Domestic and International

Both product expansion (see Chapter 25) and geographic expansion may enable an FI to reduce risk and increase returns. Geographic expansions can have a number of dimensions. In particular, they can be either domestic within a state or region or international by participating in a foreign market. Expansions also can be affected by opening a new office or branch or by acquiring another FI. This chapter traces the potential benefits and costs to an FI from expanding domestically—especially through acquisition—and considers international or cross-border expansions. In addition, it presents some empirical evidence on the gains from geographic expansions.

639

DOMESTIC
EXPANSIONS

de novo office

A newly established
office.

In the United States, the ability of FIs to expand domestically is constrained by regulation. By comparison, no special regulations inhibit the ability of commercial firms such as General Motors, IBM, or Sears from establishing new or **de novo offices**, factories, or branches anywhere in the country. Nor are such companies generally prohibited from acquiring other firms—as long as they are not banks. Although securities firms and insurance companies face relatively few restrictions in expanding their business domestically, other FIs, especially banks, face a complex and changing network of rules and regulations. Such regulations may inhibit expansions, but they also may create potential opportunities to increase an FI's returns. In particular, regulations may create locally uncompetitive markets with monpolistically economic rents that new entrants can potentially exploit. Thus, for the most innovative FIs, regulation can provide profit opportunities as well as costs. As a result, regulation acts both as an inhibitor and an incentive to engage in geographic expansions.[1]

In addition, the economic factors that impact commercial firm expansion and acquisition decisions are likely to impact FIs' decisions as well. Two major groups of factors are cost and revenue synergies and firm- and market-specific attractions, such as the specialized skills of an acquired firm's employees or the markets of the firm to be acquired. Thus, the attractiveness of a geographic expansion, whether through acquisition, branching, or opening a new office, depends on a broad set of factors:

1. Regulation and the regulatory framework.
2. Cost and revenue synergies.
3. Firm- or market-specific factors.

These are summarized in Table 26–1.

The following sections consider how the first factor, regulation, impacts a U.S.–based FI's geographic expansion decision. Specifically, the chapter briefly discusses the restrictions applying to insurance companies and thrifts and then discusses in more detail the regulations affecting commercial banks.

Concept Questions

1. Why does regulation act as an inhibitor and as an incentive to an FI to engage in geographic expansion?
2. What three basic factors influence the attractiveness of geographic expansion to an FI?

---

[1] E. Kane has called this interaction between regulation and incentives the regulatory dialectic. See "Accelerating Inflation, Technological Innovation, and the Decreasing Effectiveness of Banking Regulation," *Journal of Finance* 36 (1981), pp. 335–367. Expansions that are geographic market extensions involving firms in the same product areas are part of a broader set of horizontal mergers.

Table **26-1**

FACTORS IMPACTING GEOGRAPHIC EXPANSION

Regulatory Factors

Insurance companies   No national (federal) regulations exist to prohibit insurance companies' entry into states throughout the country since insurance companies are state regulated.

Thrifts   The crisis in the thrift industry in the 1980s resulted in the allowance of interstate geographic expansion for these FIs.

Banks' intrastate regulations   Most states allow intrastate expansion.

Banks' interstate regulations   Prior to passage of Riegle-Neal Interstate Banking Act, nationwide branching was not generally allowed.

Cost and Revenue Synergy Factors

Cost synergies   Synergies may result from economies of scale, economies of scope, or managerial efficiency sources.

Revenues synergies   Revenues may be enhanced by acquiring an FI in a growing market, revenues may be stabilized as various risks are diversified, or revenues may be enhanced by expanding into markets that are less than fully competitive.

Market- and Firm-Specific Factors

Solvency and asset quality of potential target   The acquisition decision may be influenced by the target's leverage or capital ratio, its loss reserves, and the size of its nonperforming loans and other assets.

REGULATORY FACTORS IMPACTING GEOGRAPHIC EXPANSION

Insurance Companies

As Chapter 4 discussed, insurance companies are state-regulated firms. By establishing a subsidiary in one state, an insurance company normally has the opportunity to sell insurance anywhere in that state and often to market the product nationally by telemarketing and direct sales. To deliver a financial service effectively, however, establishing a physical presence in a local market is often necessary. To do this, insurance companies establish subsidiaries and offices in other states. This is usually easy since the initial capital requirement for establishing a new subsidiary is set at relatively low levels by state regulators. Thus, most large insurance companies such as Aetna, Allstate, and Prudential have a physical presence in virtually every state in the union.

Thrifts

A thrift's ability to branch or expand geographically—whether intrastate (within a state) or interstate (between states)—was under the power of the Federal Home Loan Bank Board until 1989. Since 1989, the Office of Thrift Supervision has regulated the ability to branch as part of the 1989 Financial Institutions Reform, Recovery, and Enforcement Act (FIRREA) legislation. Generally, the policy historically had prohibited a federally chartered thrift from branching across state lines. In the 1980s, a considerable loosening of these restrictions occurred. Both the Garn-St. Germain Act of 1982 and FIRREA allowed sound banks and thrifts to acquire failing thrifts across state lines and to run them either as

Table **26–2**

SUMMARY OF VALUATION MEASURES FOR SELECTED
THRIFT ACQUISITIONS BY ALL COMPANIES, 1986
THROUGH APRIL 20, 1996

Year Transaction Announced	Number of Transactions	Median Price Paid as Multiple of Earnings*	Median Premium† as Percentage of Deposits	Median Price Paid as Percentage of Tangible Book Value‡
1986	14	14.3×	7.3%	197%
1987	25	13.8	4.6	156
1988	10	16.5	4.5	138
1989	12	12.9	3.1	139
1990	8	12.5	1.9	125
1991	10	11.8	1.4	118
1992	35	11.0	3.7	135
1993	47	15.7	6.3	171
1994	56	14.2	6.2	169
1995	44	17.6	7.1	152
1996	14	18.5	7.2	151
Total all thrifts	261	14.2×	4.6%	146%

*Calculated using trailing 12-month fully diluted earnings net of extraordinary items.

†Premium defined as excess of purchase price over book value.

‡Calculated using fully diluted book value based on the latest relevant period-end financial statements.

SOURCE: Salomon Brothers, *Bank Annual: 1996 Edition.* Salomon Brothers Inc. New York, NY. Copyright 1997 Salomon Brothers Inc. This table and table statistics contains data from Salomon Brothers Inc. Although the information in this table and table statistics were obtained from sources that Salomon Brothers Inc. believes to be reliable, Salomon does not guarantee its accuracy and such information may be incomplete or condensed. All figures included in this table and table statistics constitute Salomon's judgement as of the original publication date.

separate subsidiaries or convert them into branches. For example, the Resolution Trust Corporation (RTC), which was established under FIRREA to resolve failing thrift institutions (but was closed in 1995), had wide-ranging powers to enable out-of-state acquisitions of failing thrifts to lower the costs of failure resolution. Thus, the RTC allowed banks to acquire thrifts and convert them into branches, overriding state laws in Colorado, New Mexico, and Arkansas. The RTC also allowed banks to acquire a thrift in another industry, eroding barriers to geographic expansion for this class of FIs. Table 26–2 lists the thrift acquisitions that Salomon Brothers tracked between 1986 and April 20, 1996. Note the increase in the number of acquisitions over the period, and the price paid for them.

Commercial Banks

unit bank

A bank with a single office.

Restrictions on Intrastate Banking. At the beginning of the century, most U.S. banks were **unit banks** with a single office. Improving communications and customer needs resulted in a rush to branching in the first two decades of the 20th century. This movement ran into increasing opposition from the smallest unit banks and the largest money center banks. The smallest unit banks perceived a competitive threat to their retail business from the larger branching banks; money center banks feared a loss of valuable correspondent business such as check-clearing and other payment services. As a result, several states restricted the banks' ability to branch within the state. Indeed, some states prohibited intrastate branching per se, effectively constraining a bank to unit bank status. Over the years and in a very piecemeal fashion, states have liberalized their restrictions on within-state branching. As of 1997, only six states had laws that limited intrastate banking, which usually means that banks are limited to setting up branches in counties bordering the county in which the bank's head office is established.

Restrictions on Interstate Banking. The defining piece of legislation affecting interstate branching was the McFadden Act, passed in 1927 and amended in 1933. The McFadden Act and its amendments restricted nationally chartered banks' branching abilities to the same extent allowed to state-chartered banks. Given the McFadden prohibition on interstate branching, bank organizations expanding across state lines between 1927 and 1956 relied on establishing subsidiaries rather than branches. Some of the largest banking organizations established **multibank holding companies** for this purpose. A multibank holding company (MBHC) is a parent company that acquires more than one bank as a direct subsidiary.

In 1956, Congress recognized the potential loophole to interstate banking posed by the MBHC movement and passed the Douglas Amendment to the Bank Holding Company Act. This act permitted MBHCs to acquire bank subsidiaries only to the extent allowed by the laws of the state in which the proposed bank target resided. Any MBHCs with out-of-state subsidiaries established prior to 1956 were **grandfathered**; that is, MBHCs were allowed to keep them. (One such example was First Interstate.) The passage of the 1956 Douglas Amendment did not close all potential interstate banking loopholes. Because the amendment pertained to MBHC acquisitions, it still left open the potential for **one-bank holding company** (OBHC) geographic extensions. An OBHC is a parent bank holding company that has a single bank subsidiary and a number of other nonbank subsidiaries. By creating an OBHC and establishing across state lines various nonbank subsidiaries that sell financial services such as consumer finance, leasing, and data processing, a bank could almost replicate an out-of-state banking presence.

In 1970, Congress again acted, recognizing that bankers had creatively innovated yet another loophole to interstate banking restrictions. The 1970 Bank Holding Company Act Amendments effectively restricted the nonbank activities that an OBHC could engage in to those "closely related to banking," as defined by the Federal Reserve under Section 4(c)(8) of the act. Thus, the year 1970 and the passage of the Bank Holding Company Act Amendments are probably the low point of interstate banking in the United States.

Riegle-Neal Interstate Banking and Branching Efficiency Act of 1994. It has long been recognized that the expansion of nationwide banking through multibank holding companies is potentially far more expensive than through branching. Separate corporations and boards of directors must be established for each bank in an MBHC, and it is hard to achieve the same level of economic and financial integration as with branches. Moreover, most of the major banking competitor countries such as Japan, Germany, France, and the United Kingdom have nationwide branching.

In the fall of 1994, the U.S. Congress passed an interstate banking law that allows U.S. and nondomestic banks to branch interstate by consolidating out-of-state bank subsidiaries into a branch network and/or acquiring banks or individual branches of banks by merger

multibank holding company (MBHC)

A parent banking organization that owns a number of individual bank subsidiaries.

grandfathered subsidiaries

Subsidiaries established prior to the passage of a restrictive law and not subject to that law.

one-bank holding company

A parent banking organization that owns one bank subsidiary and nonbank subsidiaries.

and acquisition. (The effective beginning date for these new branching powers was June 1, 1997.) Although the act is silent on the ability of banks to establish de novo branches in other states—essentially leaving it to individual states to pass laws allowing de novo branching—it is possible under the new law for a New York bank such as Citibank to purchase, for example, a single branch of Bank of America in San Francisco. To date, the most common approach to interstate branching among the states has been to allow branching through acquisition and merger. Most states have barred de novo interstate branching by out-of-state banks.[2] States that bar de novo branching also have tended to prohibit the acquisition of individual in-state branches, preferring to require the out-of-state institutions to acquire an entire bank (and hence branch network). States were given the opportunity to "opt out" of interstate banking. As of April 1997, only Texas (until 1999) and Montana (until 2001) have decided to opt out. Many states opted to adopt interstate banking even before the June 1997 date. The passage of the Riegle-Neal Act is a major reason for the renewed merger wave (and increased consolidation) in U.S. banking since 1993. The result of the Riegle-Neal Act is that full interstate banking is becoming a reality in the United States.

Concept Questions

1. What is the difference between the interstate banking restrictions imposed under the 1956 Bank Holding Company Act and those passed under the 1970 Amendments to the Bank Holding Company Act?
2. How has the Riegle-Neal Act affected geographic expansion opportunities of banks?

COST AND REVENUE SYNERGIES IMPACTING GEOGRAPHIC EXPANSION

megamerger

The merger of two large banks.

One reason that an FI decides to expand (or not to expand) geographically by acquisition relates to the regulations defining its merger opportunities. Another reason relates to the exploitation of potential cost and revenue synergies from merging. Indeed, in recent years, a merger wave among banks has occurred, including some **megamergers** among large banks, driven by the desire to achieve greater cost and revenue synergies. Table 26–3 shows some of the largest bank merger activity in recent years.

X efficiencies

Cost savings due to the greater managerial efficiency of the acquiring bank.

Cost Synergies

A reason frequently given for bank mergers is the potential cost synergies that may result from economies of scale, economies of scope, or managerial efficiency sources (often called **X efficiencies**[3] because they are difficult to specify in a quantitative fashion). For

---

[2] The reason for the restriction on de novo branching is to protect small community banks' franchise values. If branching can be accomplished only by acquisition, the franchise values of small banks will be higher than when larger banks have the option to branch de novo.

[3] X efficiencies are those cost savings not directly due to economies of scope or economies of scale. As such, they are usually attributed to superior management skills and other difficult-to-measure managerial factors. To date, the explicit identification of what composes these efficiencies remains to be established in the empirical banking literature.

Table **26-3**

LARGE U.S. BANK MERGERS, 1990–1998

Year	Banks	Value (billions)
1990	Citizens & Southern/Sovran Financial	2.05
1991	Chemical/Manufacturers Hanover	2.04
1991	NCNB/C&S Sovran	4.26
1991	BankAmerica/Security Pacific	4.21
1993	KeyCorp/Society	3.88
1994	BankAmerica/Continental Bank	1.90
1995	Fleet Financial/Shawmut	4.50
1996	Chase Manhattan/Chemical Bank	11.36
1996	Wells Fargo/First Interstate	11.20
1997	NationsBank/Boatmen's Bancshares	8.70
1997	NationsBank/Barnett Banks	15.50
1997	First Union/CoreStates Financial	17.10
1997	First Bank System/US Bancorp	19.20
1998	Bank America/NationsBank	60.00
1998	BancOne/First Chicago	30.00

SOURCE: Securities Data Corp. and The *Wall Street Journal,* various issues.

example, in 1996, Chase Manhattan and Chemical Bank merged, creating the (then) largest banking organization in the United States with assets of $300 billion. Annual cost savings from the merger were estimated at $1.5 billion, to be achieved by consolidating certain operations and eliminating redundant costs; including the elimination of some 12,000 positions from a combined staff of 75,000 located in 39 states and 51 countries. Similarly, the $30 billion merger of BancOne and First Chicago in 1998 was estimated to produce $930 million in cost savings and $275 million in additional revenue resulting from synergies in their credit card and retail and commercial banking businesses.

Wells Fargo's $11.2 billion merger with First Interstate, also in 1996, was expected to reap cost savings of up to $1 billion per year through the elimination of branches and layoffs. The cutbacks would eliminate 365 of the 430 First Interstate branches in California and result in the layoff of 5,100 of its approximately 6,000 employees. Moreover, the merger gave Wells Fargo entrance into new markets to implement its strategy of providing bank services through supermarket outlets rather than through the traditional bank branches.

Another example of the search for cost savings and synergies through acquisition is Fleet Financial's 1995 acquisitions of Shawmut National and National Westminster Bank PLC's U.S. operations. Fleet's acquisitions doubled its customers to 6 million, fortified its New England stronghold, gave it a major presence in New York and New Jersey, and made Fleet the 11th largest U.S. bank. Fleet has reduced costs from the merged banks by $600 million and is trying to transition itself into a more consumer-oriented bank, maximizing the distribution power of its 1,200 branches to sell new products such as insurance. However, Fleet has had problems as a result of the mergers and, as a result, its earnings and stock price are suffering. Fleet had difficulty assimilating Shawmut's check-clearing operations in Connecticut, resulting in computer problems that produced late checks to customers, $10 million in added costs, and a delay in the conversion of all Shawmut's systems. Additionally, Fleet's mortgage subsidiary, the third largest mortgage originator in the United States, saw earnings fall to between $10 million and $15 million in 1996, mainly due to the unit's inability to originate sufficient loan volume and the loss of six senior executives.

Although Chase/Chemical Bank, BancOne/First Chicago, Wells Fargo/First Interstate, and Fleet/Shawmut are interesting examples of megamergers, they are still essentially mergers in the same or closely related geographic banking markets. Whether similar cost synergies are available for more geographically dispersed acquisitions is important. For example, the retail-oriented, California-based Bank of America acquired the wholesale-oriented, Chicago-based Continental Bank for $1.9 billion in 1994. Bank of America's objective was to sell fee-based services—especially those with a strong technology base—to Continental's corporate customers.[4] Research has shown that corporate customers stay very loyal to a bank even postacquisition. Another example (discussed in detail later in the chapter) is North Carolina–based NationsBank's acquisition of Boatmen's Bancshares of St. Louis, Missouri. The acquisition gave NationsBank entry into markets in Missouri, Arkansas, Kansas, Oklahoma, and New Mexico. The shift to statewide banking groups and the use of technology as a result of the acquisition were expected to produce cost savings of $335 million. These two banks (Bank America and NationsBank) became the first truly nationwide bank when they merged in 1998, a transaction valued at $60 billion. The banks estimated the merger would cut their combined expenses by $1.3 billion and would eliminate between 5,000 to 8,000 jobs (3 to 4 percent of their workforce).

In a comprehensive study, Berger and Humphrey used data from 1981 to 1989 to analyze the cost savings from megamergers, which they defined as assets of the acquirer and the target bank exceeding $1 billion. They could find very little evidence of potential gains from economies of scale and scope. Indeed, any cost savings they could find were related to improved managerial efficiency (so called X efficiencies). Their study had three major findings. First, the managerial efficiency of the acquirer tends to be superior to that of the acquired bank. Second, the 57 megamergers analyzed produced small but significant X efficiency gains. Third (and perhaps surprisingly), the degree of cost savings in market overlap mergers (e.g., as in the Chase/Chemical or Wells Fargo/First Interstate cases) was apparently no greater than for geographic extension mergers (as in the Bank of America/Continental or NationsBank/Boatmen's cases). Overall, they could not find the sizable cost synergies of 30 percent or so that are often given as the motivational forces behind such mergers. More recently, J. Houston and M. Ryngaert found that the greater the degree of market overlap, the more favorably shareholders see the merger.[5]

Revenue Synergies

The revenue synergies argument has three dimensions. First, acquiring an FI in a growing market may enhance revenues. Thus, acquisitions of banks in Florida and the Southwest by Nationsbank are apparently a key of its strategy to expand its retail banking network.

Second, the acquiring bank's revenue stream may become more stable if the asset and liability portfolio of the target institution exhibits different credit, interest rate, and liquidity risk characteristics from the acquirer. For example, real estate loan portfolios have shown

---

[4] These services include derivatives, FX trading, and cash management.

[5] A. Berger and D.B. Humphrey, "Megamergers in Banking and the Use of Cost Efficiency as an Antitrust Defense," *The AntiTrust Bulletin* 37 (1992), pp. 541–600; and J. Houston and M. Ryngaert, "The Overall Gains from Large Bank Mergers," *Journal of Banking and Finance* 18 (1994), pp. 1155–1176.

very strong regional cycles. Specifically, in the 1980s, U.S. real estate declined in value in the Southeast, then in the Northeast, and then in California with a long and variable lag. Thus, a geographically diversified real estate portfolio may be far less risky than one in which both acquirer and target specialize in a single region.[6] Recent studies confirm risk diversification gains from geographic expansions.[7]

Third, expanding into markets that are less than fully competitive offers opportunity for revenue enhancement. That is, banks may be able to identify and expand geographically into those markets in which *economic rents* potentially exist, but in which regulators will not view such entry as potentially anticompetitive. Indeed, to the extent that geographic expansions are viewed as enhancing an FI's monopoly power by generating excessive rents, regulators may act to prevent a merger unless it produces potential efficiency gains that cannot be reasonably achieved by other means.[8] In recent years, the ultimate enforcement of antimonopoly laws and guidelines has fallen to the U.S. Department of Justice. In particular, the Department of Justice has established guidelines regarding the acceptability or unacceptability of acquisitions based on the potential increase in concentration in the market in which an acquisition takes place with the cost-efficiency exception just noted.[9]

Interestingly, a comparison of asset concentrations by bank size indicates that the recent merger wave in banking appears to have reduced the national asset share of the very smallest banks (under $100 million) from 16.1 percent in 1984 to 5.7 percent in 1997 while increasing the relative size of the very largest banks (over $10 billion) from 34.5 percent in 1984 to 60.2 percent in 1997. The relative market shares of intermediate-sized banks appear to have remained relatively stable (see Table 26–4).

Concept Questions

1. What recent bank mergers have been motivated by cost synergies?
2. What are the three dimensions to revenue synergy gains?

---

[6] As a result, the potential revenue diversification gains for more geographically concentrated mergers such as Bank of America and Security Pacific are likely to be relatively low because both are heavily exposed to California real estate loans.

[7] M. Levonian, "Interstate Banking and Risk," Federal Reserve Bank of San Francisco, *Weekly Letter* 94–26 (1994); and W. Lee, "The Value of Risk Reduction to Investors," Research Paper 9312, Federal Reserve Bank of New York, 1993.

[8] U.S. Department of Justice, "Horizontal Merger Guidelines," April 2, 1992.

[9] The Federal Reserve also has the power to approve or disapprove mergers among state member banks and bank holding companies. The comptroller of the currency has similar powers over nationally chartered banks. The Federal Reserve's criteria are similar to those of the Department of Justice in that it considers a market concentration index called the *Herfindahl-Hirschman Index* (HHI). However, it also evaluates the risk effects of the merger. The Department of Justice has authority to review the decisions made by the bank regulatory agencies. For example, in 1990 and 1991, the Department of Justice successfully challenged two mergers approved by the Federal Reserve Board. These two mergers eventually were accomplished only after the acquiring bank had divested some branches and offices. The two mergers were First Hawaiian's acquisition of First Interstate of Hawaii and the Society–Ameritrust merger. See D. Palia, "Recent Evidence of Bank Mergers," *Financial Markets, Instruments, and Institutions* 3, no. 5 (1994), pp. 36–59, for further details.

Table **26-4**

U.S. BANK ASSET CONCENTRATION, 1984 VERSUS 1997

	1997				1984			
	Number	Percentage of Total	Assets	Percentage of Total	Number	Percentage of Total	Assets	Percentage of Total
All FDIC-insured commercial banks	**9,308**		**$4,771,200**		**14,483**		**$2,508,871**	
Under $100 million	6,047	65.0%	273,400	5.7%	12,044	83.2%	404,223	16.1%
$100 million–$1 billion	2,888	31.0	711,000	14.9	2,161	14.9	513,912	20.5
$1–$10 billion	306	3.3	916,000	19.2	254	1.7	725,947	28.9
$10 billion or more	67	0.7	2,870,800	60.2	24	0.2	864,789	34.5

SOURCE: General Accounting Office, *Interstate Banking,* GAO/GGD, 95-35, December 1994, p. 101, and *FDIC Quarterly Banking Profile,* September 1997.

OTHER MARKET- AND FIRM-SPECIFIC FACTORS IMPACTING GEOGRAPHIC EXPANSION DECISIONS

In addition to regulation and cost and revenue synergies, other factors may affect an acquisition decision. For example, an acquiring FI may be concerned about the solvency and asset quality of a potential target FI in another region. Thus, important factors influencing the acquisition decision may include the target FI's leverage or capital ratio, its loss reserves, and the amount of nonperforming loans in its portfolio. In addition, a potential acquirer may be concerned about the dilution effect of an acquisition on the FI's EPS. (The mechanics of a merger on EPS are discussed in the Appendix to this chapter.) The next section discusses these concerns as they affected the 1997 acquisition of Boatmen's Bancshares by NationsBank.

Analysis of a Geographic Expansion Acquisition

On August 30, 1996, NationsBank Corp, headquartered in Charlotte, North Carolina, announced an acquisition bid for Boatmen's Bancshares Inc., of St. Louis, Missouri. This was an unusual acquisition for NationsBank whose previous acquisition transactions had involved targets saddled with problems. With this acquisition, NationsBank obtained a leading market share in the banking markets in Missouri, Arkansas, Kansas, Oklahoma, and New Mexico. Its trust and investment management business was enhanced, soaring from $67 billion to $111 billion in managed assets. Yet many analysts and the stock market viewed the acquisition as a bad deal for NationsBank. Its stock price dropped 8 percent when it announced Boatmen's acquisition. Many analysts concluded that the price offered was too high. NationsBank offered $61 per share of Boatmen's stock, 2.7 times Boatmen's book value (when two times book value is considered normal). The following section discusses several financial and other considerations involved in this acquisition.

Cost Synergies.   Panel (a) of Table 26–5 lists cost synergies that NationsBank expected from 1997 through 1999 resulting from the acquisition of Boatmen's. The largest savings

Table **26-5**

PRO FORMA FINANCIAL DATA FOR NATIONSBANK'S ACQUISITION OF BOATMEN'S BANCSHARES

	1997	1998	1999
Panel (a) NationsBank—Expected Cost Savings*, 1997–1999			
Pretax dollars in millions*			
Corporate activities	$ 63	$111	$125
Services company consolidation	26	60	80
Delivery system optimization	29	64	70
Business line consolidation	11	35	35
Vendor leverage	11	25	25
Annual savings	**$140**	**$ 295**	**$335**
Panel (b) NationsBank—Expected Revenue Enhancements†, 1997–1999			
Pretax dollars in millions†			
Improved product delivery process, including model bank	$14	$30	$40
Higher fee revenues, including ATM surcharges	15	20	20
Increased credit card and asset management penetration	6	15	20
Total enhancements	**$35**	**$ 65**	**$80**
Panel (c) NationsBank—Pro Forma Earnings, 1997–1999 (dollars in millions)			
Combined net income adjusted (after tax)	$3,272	$3,522	$3,790
Merger savings	$ 98	$ 200	$ 217
Funding advantages	26	62	62
Revenue enhancements	22	40	49
Opportunity cost for shares repurchased	(36)	(54)	(74)
Goodwill amortization	(245)	(245)	(245)
Interest cost on debt (at 5% after tax)	(203)	(203)	(203)
Pro forma earnings	**$2,934**	**$3,322**	**$3,596**
Pro forma cash earnings	**$3,329**	**$3,717**	**$3,991**

Panel (d) NationsBank—Pro Forma Ratios (Year End), 1995–1998

	1995	1996	1997	1998
Return on tangible assets	1.11%	1.27%	1.42%	1.53%
Return on assets	1.03	1.20	1.21	1.32
Return on tangible equity	20.81	21.64	28.13	29.35
Return on equity	17.01	17.75	14.66	16.25
Equity to assets			8.85	8.90
Tangible equity to tangible assets			5.71	6.03
Tier 1 capital ratio			6.67	7.05
Total capital ratio			11.18	11.39

*$335 million by 1999, or 22% reduction

†$80 million by 1999, or 8% improvement

NOTE: Reflects IBES estimates for both companies, *not* management forecasts.

SOURCE: Statistics printed in U.S. Equity Research: NationsBank Acquires Boatmen's, September 4, 1996. Salomon Brothers Inc., New York, NY. Copyright 1997 Salomon Brothers Inc. This table and table statistics contain data from Salomon Brothers Inc. Although the information in this table and table statistics were obtained from sources that Salomon Brothers Inc. believes to be reliable, Salomon does not guarantee its accuracy, and such information may be incomplete or condensed. All figures included in this table and table statistics constitute Salomon's judgement as of the original publication date.

were expected to come from corporate activities (a shift to statewide banking groups rather than multiple separately operated banks.) NationsBank's ability to use its technology and systems in Boatmen's operations (Boatmen's had not invested in equivalent technology) was also expected to produce savings from consolidation of its services company and optimization of its delivery system. The cost savings expected by the end of 1999 is $335 million.

Revenue Synergies.   Panel (b) of Table 26–5 reports NationsBank's expected revenue synergies from 1997 through 1999 from the acquisition. The majority of the increased revenue was expected to come from improved product delivery processes of NationsBank applied to Boatmen's banks. This was followed by increased fee revenues and increased credit card and asset management penetration. The expected increase in revenues was $80 million by 1999.

Financial Statement Measures.   The financial statements for Boatmen's Bancshares as of December 31, 1995, were presented and discussed in Chapter 8. Certainly, NationsBank's management examined these in detail prior to its acquisition bid and several items were mentioned as reasons for the acquisition bid. These items also produce the revenue gain and cost reduction estimates mentioned earlier. First, Boatmen's had a very low loan-to-deposit ratio. This, combined with NationsBank's large size, is expected to significantly reduce the cost of funding. Second, Boatmen's had a very well-established institutional money manager, Boatmen's Trust Co., which managed $44 billion in assets. NationsBank's plans were not only to leave this area untouched but to add some of its trust assets to it. NationsBank also cited Boatmen's relatively high loan growth rates, excess balance sheet liquidity, low loan loss or charge-off ratio, and high noninterest revenue growth as other strengths making Boatmen's an attractive target. Panel (c) of Table 26–5 lists the expected earnings, and Panel (d) lists selected pro forma financial ratios for NationsBank as a result of the acquisition. The combined bank's earnings are expected to increase to almost $3.6 billion by 1999 as a result of the acquisition. Further, return on assets is expected to decrease during this period from 17.01 percent in 1995 to 16.25 percent in 1998; however, return on equity is expected to increase significantly from 20.81 percent in 1995 to 29.35 percent in 1998.

Earnings per Share Dilution. NationsBank expected that the acquisition would dilute earnings per share (EPS) by 5.5 percent in 1997 but would actually increase EPS by 2 percent in 1999. Some analysts argued, however, that despite the favorable expectations and projections regarding the acquisition, NationsBank shareholders were getting too little for the risk involved in this megamerger. Others speculated that NationsBank obtained a large, well-established bank with much to offer for a fair price. The final results are yet to be seen, and, as a result of the merger with Bank America, may never be specifically identified.

Concept Questions

1. Suppose that you are a manager of a bank that is considering another bank as a target for acquistion. What three characteristics of the target bank would most attract you?
2. Given the same scenario as in question (1), what three characteristics would most discourage you?

THE SUCCESS OF
GEOGRAPHIC EXPANSIONS

A variety of regulatory and economic factors affects the attractiveness of geographic expansions to an FI manager. This section evaluates some of the empirical evidence on the success of market extension mergers. Such an evaluation can be done on at least two levels: first, how did investors react when an interstate bank merger was announced? Second, once interstate bank mergers have taken place, do they produce, in aggregate, the expected gains in efficiency and profitability?[10]

Investor Reaction

abnormal returns

Risk-adjusted stock returns above expected levels.

Researchers have conducted a number of studies on both nonbank and bank mergers investigating the announcement effects of mergers on the share values of both the bidding firm and the target firm. The studies have measured the announcement effect by the reaction of investors in the stock market to the news of a merger event. In particular, economists have been interested in whether a merger announcement generates positive **abnormal returns—** risk-adjusted stock returns above normal levels—for the bidding and/or target firms. Unlike the situation with commercial firms, for which the typical study finds that only target firms' shareholders gain from merger announcements through significantly positive abnormal returns, studies in banking find that occasionally both the acquiring bank and the target bank gain.[11] For example, Cornett and De studied interstate merger proposals during the period 1982–1986. They found that on the day of the merger announcement, bidding bank stockholders enjoyed positive abnormal returns of 0.65 percent while target bank shareholders enjoyed 6.08 percent abnormal returns. They also found that bidding bank returns were higher for those banks seeking to acquire targets in states with more restrictive banking pact laws that prohibited nationwide entry and where target banks were not failed banks. Houston and Ryngaert studied a subsequent period, 1985 through 1992, and found that although target bank shareholders continue to receive positive abnormal returns of 17.7 percent around merger proposals, bidding bank shareholders do not, on average, gain. The abnormal return for this group was found to be −2.3 percent.[12]

Postmerger Performance

Even though the expectation, on announcement, might be favorable for enhanced profitability and performance as a result of an interstate geographic expansion, do such mergers actually prove successful in the postmerger period? Cornett and Tehranian studied the postacquisition performance of large bank mergers between 1982 and 1987. Using operating cash flow (defined as earnings before depreciation, goodwill, interest on long-term debt, and taxes) divided by assets as a performance measure, they found that merged banks

---

[10]We have already noted that the Berger and Humphrey "Megamergers in Banking" study casts doubts on the actual size of the cost savings from megamergers.

[11]See, for example, N. Travlos, "Corporate Takeover Bids, Methods of Payment, and Bidding Firm Stock Returns," *Journal of Finance* 42 (1987), pp. 943–963.

[12]M. M. Cornett and S. De, "Common Stock Returns in Corporate Takeover Bids: Evidence of Interstate Bank Mergers," *Journal of Banking and Finance* 15 (1991), pp. 273–295; and J. Houston and M. Ryngaert, "Equity Issuance and Adverse Selection: A Direct Test Using Conditional Stock Offers," *Journal of Finance* 52 (1997), pp. 197–219.

tended to outperform the banking industry.[13] They found that superior performance resulted from improvements in these banks' abilities to (1) attract loans and deposits, (2) increase employee productivity, and (3) enhance asset growth. Spong and Shoenhair studied the postmerger performance of banks that merged interstate in 1985, 1986, and 1987; they found that acquired banks either maintained or increased earnings and demonstrated some success in controlling and reducing overhead and personnel costs. The acquired banks also tended to become more active lenders.[14] Boyd and Graham studied small bank mergers (with combined total deposits less than $400 million) from 1989 through 1991. Comparing industry-adjusted return on assets (ROA) before and after a merger, they found that 1989 mergers resulted in large ROA increases, 1991 mergers resulted in decreases, and 1990 mergers had results somewhere in the middle. For all years, however, the merged banks outperformed the banking industry. Further, the merged banks all experienced decreases in interest expense to total assets and all outperformed the industry on this measure.[15] Finally, Akhavein, Berger, and Humphrey found that bank megamergers in the 1980s produced large increases in profit efficiency relative to other banks. The improvements are found to come mainly from increasing revenues including a shift from securities to loans. Improvements were greatest for banks with lowest efficiencies prior to merging (i.e., those with the greatest room for improvement).[16]

Thrift expansion has also been found to produce superior performance. Cebernoyan, Cooperman, Register, and Bauer found evidence suggesting that interstate thrifts have superior performance when compared to a national benchmark of all thrifts.[17] The superior performance was particularly significant during recessionary periods (e.g., 1989–1991), when net interest margins were significantly above the national benchmark and noninterest expense and provision for loan losses relative to assets were significantly below the national benchmark. Interstate thrifts also experienced lower volatility in earnings than did benchmark thrifts.

Thus, both the announcement effect studies and the postmerger performance studies generally support the existence of gains from domestic geographic expansions by U.S. commercial banks and thrifts.

Concept Questions

1. If the abnormal returns on target banks are usually positive, does this mean that managers of acquiring banks tend to overpay the shareholders of the target bank?
2. In general, what do studies of the announcement effect and postmerger performance conclude?

- -

[13]M. M. Cornett and H. Tehranian, "Changes in Corporate Performance Associated with Bank Acquisitions," *Journal of Financial Economics* 31 (1992), pp. 211–234.

[14]K. Spong and J. D. Shoenhair, "Performance of Banks Acquired on an Interstate Basis," Federal Reserve Bank of Kansas City, *Financial Industry Perspectives*, December 1992, pp. 15–23.

[15]J. D. Boyd and S. L. Graham, "Consolidation in U.S. Banking: Implications for Efficiency and Competition Risk," Conference on Mergers of Financial Institutions, New York University, October 1996.

[16]J. Akhavein, A. N. Berger, and D. B. Humphrey, "The Effects of Megamergers on Efficiency and Prices: Evidence from a Bank Profit Function," Conference on Mergers of Financial Institutions, New York University, October 1996.

[17]A. S. Cebenoyan, E. S. Cooperman, C. A. Register, and D. L. Bauer, "Interstate Savings and Loans in the 1990s: A Performance and Risk Appraisal," Working Paper, University of Colorado at Denver, 1997.

GLOBAL OR INTERNATIONAL
EXPANSIONS

Many FIs can potentially diversify domestically, but only the very largest can aspire to diversify beyond national frontiers. An FI can establish a global or international presence in at least three ways: (1) selling financial services from its domestic offices to foreign customers, such as a loan originated in the New York office of Citibank made to a Brazilian manufacturer; (2) selling financial services through a branch, agency, or representative office established in the foreign customer's country, such as making a loan to the Brazilian customer through Citibank's branch in Brazil; and (3) selling financial services to a foreign customer through subsidiary companies in the foreign customer's country, such as Citibank buying a Brazilian bank and using that wholly owned bank to make loans to the Brazilian customer. Note that these three methods of global activity expansion are not mutually exclusive; an FI could use all three simultaneously to expand the scale and scope of its international operations.

U.S. banks, insurance companies, and securities firms have expanded into foreign countries in recent years, often through branches and subsidiaries; this has been reciprocated by the increased entrance of foreign FIs in U.S. financial service markets. The world's most active 15 banks based on the percent of their assets outside their home countries are listed in Table 26–6. These include the big three Swiss banks—Union Bank of Switzerland, Swiss Bank Corporation, and Credit Suisse[18]—as well as U.S. banks such as Bankers

Table 26–6

TOP GLOBAL BANKS

	Banks	Home Country	Percentage of Overseas Business*
1.	Standard Chartered	United Kingdom	74.3%
2.	Credit Suisse	Switzerland	74.2
3.	Union Bank of Switzerland	Switzerland	71.0
4.	Credit Agricole Indosuez	France	71.0
5.	Swiss Bank Corporation	Switzerland	64.6
6.	HSBC Holdings	United Kingdom	62.8
7.	Citicorp	USA	59.6
8.	Comp Financièrede Paribas	France	55.6
9.	Crédit Lyonnais	France	52.5
10.	Creditanstalt-Bankverein	Austria	52.3
11.	Erste Bank	Austria	51.0
12.	J.P. Morgan & Co.	USA	50.9
13.	Bankers Trust	USA	49.5
14.	ABN-Amro Bank	Netherlands	49.4
15.	Allied Irish Bank	Ireland	48.8

Overseas business refers to the percent of assets banks hold outside their home country.

SOURCE: "Top 50 Global Banks," *The Banker,* February 1998, pp. 41–42.

---

[18]Union Bank of Switzerland and Swiss Bank Corporation announced a merger in 1998.

Trust, J. P. Morgan, and Citicorp. Interestingly, although prior to 1998, Japanese banks occupied 8 of the top 15 banks in the world in terms of asset size (see Table 25–5), they are absent from the list of banks with the most active international operations. Contemporary Perspectives Box 26–1 explains some reasons for their absence.

The next section concentrates on the growth of global banking. It begins with U.S. bank expansions into foreign countries and the factors motivating these expansions and then discusses foreign bank expansions into the United States.

U.S. Banks in Foreign Countries

Although some U.S. banks such as Citibank and J. P. Morgan have had foreign offices since the beginning of the century, the major phase of expansion began in the early 1960s following passage of the Overseas Direct Investment Control Act of 1964. This law restricted U.S. banks' ability to lend to U.S. corporations that wanted to make foreign investments. This law was eventually repealed, but it created incentives for U.S. banks to establish foreign offices to service the funding and other business needs of their U.S. clients in other countries. This offshore funding and lending in dollars created the beginning of a market we now call the *Eurodollar market*. The term *Eurodollar transaction* denotes any transaction involving dollars that takes place outside the United States. For example, any deposit (loan) in dollars taken (made) externally to the United States normally qualifies as a Euro transaction. "Euro" markets in other currencies include the yen, deutsche mark, and pound sterling.

Factors Encouraging U.S. Bank Expansions into Foreign Countries. Regulation of foreign lending was the original impetus for the early growth of the Eurodollar market and the associated establishment of U.S. branches and subsidiaries outside the United States. Other regulatory and economic factors that have encouraged the increase of U.S. banking in foreign countries are discussed next.

The Dollar as an International Medium of Exchange. The growth of international trade after World War II and the use of the dollar as an international medium of exchange encouraged foreign corporations and investors to demand dollars. A convenient way to do this was to use U.S. banks' foreign offices to intermediate such fund flows between the United States and foreign investors. Today, trade-related transactions underlie much of the activity in the Eurodollar market.[19]

Political Risk Concerns. Political risk concerns among countries from the old Eastern or Communist bloc countries and Latin America have led to enormous flows of dollars out of the United States, often to U.S. branches and subsidiaries in the Cayman Islands and the Bahamas, where very stringent bank secrecy rules exist.

Domestic Activity Restrictions. As Chapter 25 discusses, the securities, insurance, and commercial activities of U.S. banks have faced considerable activity restrictions at home. With certain exceptions, however, Federal Reserve Regulation K has allowed U.S. banking offices in other countries to engage in the foreign country's permitted banking activities,

---

[19]The decline in the dollar relative to the yen and mark in recent years has weakened the role of the dollar as the international medium of exchange.

Contemporary Perspectives 26–1

Japan: There's Even Further to Fall

The Japanese banks' fall from grace and top positions was ascribed to post-bubble traumas and to a weakening of the yen, when *The Banker* published its annual rankings of the world's Top 1,000 banks in July. But that is not the end of the story: in the next few years there will be a continued contraction of banks' assets at home and overseas.

This asset downsizing will need to be accompanied by a parallel process of upgrading as Japanese banks seek to shed archaic methods of credit assessment and to modernize their management practices.

Thus, even though the newly created Bank of Tokyo-Mitsubishi will move back to the top of the 1,000 list next year by virtue of its size, that will not signal a true recovery in Japanese banks' international prowess. . . .

Fuji Bank chairman Toru Hashimoto suggested recently that mergers might be a "good option" for banks to improve their global competitiveness. But while further mergers are likely—involving perhaps Fuji and other leaders such as Sumitomo and Daiwa—greater size is no panacea for banks' ills. . . .

The reluctance of bank management to relinquish this insistence upon collateral, even after the post-bubble collapse of asset prices, makes it hard to mesh domestic credit practices with those overseas. . . .

Another problem is the reluctance of Japanese banks to assimilate foreign managers and other specialists into their operations overseas. . . .The

prospect of foreign nationals sitting on the boards of Japanese banks appears remote. Some analysts argue that unless banks absorb foreign expertise, it will be hard for them to pursue global strategies.

No Japanese bank can expect to rank among the truly globalized banking institutions of the future without first undergoing a fundamental change in management culture. Some Japanese bankers acknowledge that even BoT-Mitsubishi probably cannot expect to be a global player on the scale of Citibank, J.P. Morgan, Deutsche Bank or Credit Suisse First Boston.

Meanwhile at least some Japanese banks are expected to withdraw altogether from international business in line with growing capital constraints. One senior finance ministry official says boldly that Japan has "too many banks operating overseas at present" and indicates that some contraction of their presence would have official blessing.

Officials worry about the vulnerability of Japanese banks to a funding crisis in their overseas operations. The banks, notes one, suffer from "basic funding constraint." This arises from the fact that the overseas assets and liabilities of Japanese banks are mainly denominated in US dollars and yet with few exceptions (such as BoT-Mitsubishi which owns two banks in California) the banks have no natural dollar deposit base. . . .

Another problem Japanese banks face in maintaining their international presence is that of capital adequacy.

All the city banks have ratios of capital to risk assets in excess of the 8 percent minimum mandated by the BIS to support international lending. But the need to provision at a high level against domestic bad debts is preventing Japanese banks from emulating their competitors in North America and Europe in applying retained profits to capital building. . . .

Japanese banks have already significantly reduced the size of their international operations since 1990 when the high level of profits enabled them to undertake overseas business at low margins. According to the BIS, total international assets of Japanese banks peaked at $2.12 trillion in 1990 (when it represented one third of international assets held by all the world's bank). By 1993, this figure had declined to under $1.7 trillion or less than 27 percent of international assets held globally by all banks.

By 1994, Japanese banks had raised international asset levels to $1.82 trillion, according to the BIS. This reflected an increase in lending within the Asia region. This in turn was associated with strong outflows of foreign direct investment by Japanese manufacturers into the Asia region.

But overseas activity continues to diminish as a proportion of banks' total activity. According to the Bank of Japan, overseas assets as a proportion of total assets has fallen from 20 percent in 1990 to 15 percent now. . . .

SOURCE: *The Banker,* September 1996, p. 47.

even if the United States did not permit such activities. For example, U.S. banks setting up foreign subsidiaries can lease real property, act as general insurance agents, and underwrite and deal in foreign corporate securities (up to a maximum commitment of $2 million).

Technology and Communication Improvements.   The improvements in telecommunications and other communication technologies such as the Clearing House Interbank Payment System (CHIPS) and the development of communication networks by large FIs have allowed U.S. parent FIs to extend and maintain real-time control over their foreign operations at a decreasing cost. The decreasing operating costs of such expansions have made it feasible to locate offices in an even wider variety of international locations.

NAFTA

North American Free
Trade Agreement.

Factors Deterring U.S. Expansions in Foreign Countries.   A number of potential factors deter international expansion, as discussed next.

Emerging Market Problems.   The financial collapse of Mexico in 1994 and the problems of emerging market countries such as Korea, Thailand, Malaysia, and Indonesia in 1997 and 1998 have made many U.S. banks more cautious in expanding outside traditional foreign markets. This is despite the existence of an increasingly favorable regulatory environment. For example, the 1994 **NAFTA** agreement enabled U.S. (and Canadian) banks to expand into Mexico (see Table 26–7 for details on the NAFTA agreement[20]), and the December 1997 agreement by 100 countries, reached under the auspices of the World Trade Organization, heralds an important step toward dismantling barriers inhibiting the entry of foreign banks, insurance companies, and securities firms into emerging market countries.[21]

Competition.   In the 1990s, the United States faced extensive and increasing competition from Japanese and European banks for foreign business. Aiding the Japanese banks was their access to a large domestic savings base at a relatively low funding cost, given the relatively slow pace of deregulation in the Japanese domestic financial markets and their size.

For example, for most of the 1990s, Japan has had 9 of the 10 largest banks measured by asset size in the world. Although large size does not necessarily mean high profits,[22] it does allow a bank greater ability to diversify across borders (and products) and to attract business by aggressively cutting fees and spreads in selected areas.

Aiding the competitive position of European banks has been the passage of the European Community (EC) Second Banking Directive, which created a single banking market in Europe. This Directive allowed European banks to branch and acquire banks throughout the European Community—that is, they had a single European Community passport.[23] Although the Second Banking Directive did not come into effect fully until the

---

[20]For an excellent discussion of the potential effects of NAFTA on U.S. banks, securities firms, and insurance companies, see R. S. Sczudio, "NAFTA: Opportunities Abound for U.S. and Canadian Financial Institutions," *Bankers Magazine*, July–August 1993, pp. 28–32.

[21]See *The New York Times*, "Accord Is Reached to Lower Barriers in Global Finance," *The New York Times*, December 12, 1997, pp. A1.

[22]In fact, Crédit Lyonnais, the French bank, is a good example of large size not necessarily correlating with high profitability. In spring 1995, the French government had to bail out the bank by shifting its bad loans into a newly created entity. In addition, most of the Japanese banks have had severe problems with bad loans in recent years, which has meant a reduced tendency to expand further abroad.

[23]Direct branching by non-European Community banks into member states is not governed by the Second Banking Directive but by the laws of each member state. Currently, all European Community countries allow foreign banks to branch.

Table **26-7**

THE NAFTA AGREEMENT AND U.S. BANKS

Any bank chartered in Canada or the United States, including Canadian or U.S. banks owned by nondomestic banks, may establish a bank subsidiary in Mexico that may expand in Mexico without geographic restriction. Canadian and U.S. banks, however, may not branch directly into Mexico.

Banks from Mexico and Canada may establish direct branches and subsidiaries in the United States subject to the same geographic restrictions imposed on direct branches of other nondomestic banks and on other U.S. chartered banks, respectively.

Banks from the United States and Mexico that are not controlled by investors from other countries may establish Schedule II bank subsidiaries in Canada, which subsidiaries enjoy nationwide branching powers. Mexican and U.S. banks may not branch directly into Canada.

NOTES:

1. Nondomestic banks cannot open branches but are allowed to establish Schedule II subsidiary banks in Canada. Schedule II subsidiary banks owned by banks from the United States or Mexico have the same nationwide branching privileges as domestic Canadian banks. Schedule II banks owned by banks from other countries must seek government approval to open additional branches. This geographic restriction on Schedule II subsidiaries will be eliminated when the latest round of General Agreement on Tariff and Trade comes into effect.

2. Mexico does not permit nondomestic banks to establish domestic branches. However, nondomestic banks can establish representative offices and offshore branches and take minority interests in local banking institutions. In addition, under NAFTA, banks from the United States and Canada, including U.S. and Canadian banks owned by banks from other countries, are allowed to establish bank subsidiaries with the same nationwide branching privileges as Mexican banks.

SOURCE: Institute of International Bankers, *1994 Global Survey of Regulatory and Market Developments in Banking, Securities and Insurance,* September 1994, p. 17.

---

end of 1992, it had been announced as early as 1988. As a result, a merger wave among European banks has paralleled the U.S. domestic merger and acquisition wave during the period 1991–1998; not all, however, have been successful (see Contemporary Perspectives Box 26–2). This greater consolidation in European banking has created more intense competition for U.S. and other foreign banks in European wholesale markets and has made their penetration into European retail markets more difficult.

Nevertheless, despite these capital, emerging market, and competitive concerns and pressures, U.S. banks have been accelerating their foreign business in recent years. U.S. bank claims held outside the country rose from $320.1 billion in 1990 to $680.5 billion in June 1997 (see Table 26–8). Interestingly, the fastest-growing segment has been "offshore banking." Possible reasons for this—including foreign regulatory laxity—will be discussed later in this chapter. The U.S. bank claims held in the United Kingdom reflect its importance as the center of the Eurodollar market.

Foreign Banks in the United States

Just as U.S. banks can profitably expand into foreign markets, foreign banks have historically viewed the United States as an attractive market for entry. The following sections discuss foreign banks in the United States.

Organization Form.   Foreign banks use five primary forms of entry into the U.S. market.

Contemporary Perspectives 26–2

The End of a European Banking Dream: Crédit Lyonnais Is Preparing to Sell Much of Its Network Outside France

Potential buyers are starting to scrutinize the European operations of Crédit Lyonnais, the French state-owned bank, as it prepares—through gritted teeth—to sell some of them.

In the coming months, as part of a restructuring plan to prepare it for privatization, Crédit Lyonnais is likely to unwind much of its remaining retail banking network in western Europe outside France.

The move represents the abrupt end of the attempt by the discredited former chairman, Mr. Jean-Yves Haberer, to create a pan-European retail banking network, which started in the early 1990s. . . .

Crédit Lyonnais has little choice. The European Commission in Brussels approved a first restructuring plan, which included support from the French taxpayer of up to 45 billion French francs, in 1995. . . . Crédit Lyonnais has already sold its branch banking operation in London, and its stake in Banca Olombarda in Italy. It has modest specialist business in Sweden, Luxembourg, Ireland and Switzerland, and significant operations in Belgium. . . .

But these are not considered prime candidates for sale. That leaves activities in four principal countries, which could be open to tenders before the end of the year. They are:

• In Germany, BfG Bank, a medium-sized bank based in Frankfurt previously controlled by labor unions, which still hold a significant stake.

Crédit Lyonnais took a controlling 50.01 percent share in the bank in 1993. BfG employs 5,200 staff and operates 230 branches around the country. After wide-ranging restructuring, it is profitable. But the high price that Crédit Lyonnais paid means the sale is likely to trigger a capital loss of about 2.5 billion French francs. The cost to the bank will be twice as high, because when it took control, Credit Lyonnais agreed to compensate the other shareholders for any capital loss if it sold its stake.

• In Italy, it has 56.8 percent of Credito Bergamasco, with some 2,000 staff in 170 branches, mainly in the north. It acquired the stake in 1989 and has since merged the bank with Banco San Marco, based in Venice.

In the highly-fragmented Italian banking sector, its market share—less than 1 percent—makes Bergamasco a tempting candidate for disposal. Its current market value comfortably exceeds the 1,144 billion lire ($737m) that Credit Lyonnais paid. . . .

• In Spain, it paid high multiples in 1990 to acquire from Banco Santander two subsidiary networks, Banca Jover in Barcelona and what is now Crédit Lyonnais Espana, with 8,000 staff and 94 branches, in which it owns 99.6 percent and 98.6 percent, respectively.

The subsequent recession in Spain and a squeeze on margins in the battle for high-interest bearing accounts helped contribute to large recent losses in both operations.

• Crédit Lyonnais Portugal, a long-standing investment which was one of only three banks to escape nationalization in 1974, and in which it owns 93.7 percent.

The unit has suffered heavily from non-performing loans, triggering a large restructuring in 1994. Its 20 branches have become a likely acquisition target in the face of recent takeovers by domestic banks and their Spanish rivals.

SOURCE: Andrew Jack, *Financial Times,* January 16, 1997, p. 34. Reprinted with permission of *Financial Times.*

Subsidiary.   A foreign bank subsidiary has its own capital and charter; it operates like any U.S. domestic bank, with access to both retail and wholesale markets.

Branch.   A branch bank is a direct expansion of the parent bank into a foreign or U.S. banking market. As such, it relies on its parent bank, such as Sumitomo Bank in Japan, for capital support; normally, it has access to both wholesale and retail deposit and funding markets in the United States.

Table **26-8**

U.S. BANK CLAIMS HELD OUTSIDE THE UNITED STATES*

	1990	1991	1992	1993	1994	1995	1996	June 1997
Total	320.1	343.6	346.5	403.7	496.6	551.7	645.0	680.5
United Kingdom	60.9	68.5	60.8	84.5	90.1	82.4	104.6	109.7
Offshore banking centers†	44.7	54.2	58.5	72.5	71.4	99.0	134.9	129.5

*Billions of dollars held by U.S. offices and foreign branches of U.S. banks (including U.S. banks that are subsidiaries of foreign banks).

†Includes Bahamas, Bermuda, and Cayman Islands.

SOURCE: *Federal Reserve Bulletin,* January 1998, Table 3.21, and earlier issues.

Agency.   An agency is a restricted form of entry; this organization form restricts fund access to those funds borrowed on the wholesale and money markets (i.e., an agency cannot accept deposits). A special agency case is New York Agreement Company, which has both agency functions and limited investment banking functions.

Edge Act Corporation.   An Edge Act corporation is a specialized organization form open to U.S. domestic banks since 1919 and to foreign banks since 1978. These banks specialize in international trade–related banking transactions or investments.

Representative Office.   Even though a representative office neither books loans nor deposits in the United States, it acts as a loan production office, generating loan business for its parent bank at home. This is the most limited organization form for a foreign bank entering the United States.[24]

Trends and Growth.   Table 26–9 shows the rapid expansion of foreign banks in the United States between 1980 and 1997. In 1980, foreign banks had $166.7 billion in assets (10.8 percent of the size of total U.S. bank assets). This activity reached a peak in 1992, when foreign banks had $514.3 billion in assets (16.4 percent of the size of U.S. assets). Since 1997, a modest retrenchment in the asset share of foreign banks in the United States has occurred. In 1997, their U.S. assets totaled $601.8 billion (14.7 percent of the size of U.S. assets). This recent retrenchment reflects a number of factors, including the highly competitive market for wholesale banking in the United States, a decline in U.S. loan quality, capital constraints on Japanese banks at home and their poor lending performance at home, and the introduction of the Foreign Bank Supervision and Enforcement Act (FBSEA) of 1991, which tightened regulations on foreign banks in the United States (discussed next). Whether this retrenchment is temporary or permanent remains to be seen and may well depend on the competitive effects of recent regulatory actions in the United States and the

[24]Also note the existence of international banking facilities (IBF) in the United States since 1981. These are specialized vehicles allowed to take deposits from and make loans to foreign (non-U.S.) customers only. As such, they are essentially foreign banking units that operate in the United States; most are located in New York, Illinois, and California and are generally free of U.S. bank regulation and taxes.

Table **26–9**

U.S. AND FOREIGN BANK ASSETS 1980–1997

| | Bank Assets Held in United States (billions of dollars) | |
	U.S.–owned	Foreign–owned
1980	$1,537.0	$166.7
1985	2,284.8	175.5
1990	3,010.3	389.6
1991	3,068.7	467.3
1992	3,138.4	514.3
1993	3,204.6	427.9
1994	3,409.9	471.1
1995	3,660.6	530.1
1996	3,812.6	601.8
1997	4,083.6	642.3

SOURCE: *Federal Reserve Bulletin*, various issues, Tables 1.25 and 1.26.

restructuring of the Japanese financial system (especially in regard to Japan's problem loans domestically and to other Asian countries[25]).

Regulation of Foreign Banks in the United States.   Prior to 1978, foreign branches and agencies entering the United States were primarily licensed at the state level. As such, their entry, regulation, and oversight were almost totally confined to the state level. Beginning in 1978 with the passage of the International Banking Act (IBA) and the more recent passage of FBSEA, and Title II of the FDICIA of December 1991, federal regulators have exerted increasing control over foreign banks operating in the United States.

The International Banking Act of 1978

Pre-IBA.   Before the passage in 1978 of the IBA, foreign agencies and branches entering the United States with state licenses had some competitive advantages and disadvantages relative to most domestic banks. On the one hand, as state-licensed organizations, they were not subject to the Federal Reserve's reserve requirements, audits, and exams; interstate branching restrictions (the McFadden Act); and restrictions on corporate securities underwriting activities (the Glass-Steagall Act). However, they had no access to the Federal Reserve's discount window (i.e., lender of last resort); no direct access to Fedwire, and, thus, the fed funds market; and no access to FDIC deposit insurance.

Their inability to gain access to deposit insurance effectively precluded them from the U.S. retail banking market and its deposit base. As a result, prior to 1978, foreign banks in the United States largely concentrated on wholesale banking.

Post-IBA. The unequal treatment of domestic and foreign banks regarding federal regulation and the lobbying by domestic banks regarding the unfairness of this situation provided the impetus for Congress to pass the IBA in 1978. The fundamental regulatory

---

[25]See for example, "Japan Banks That Ventured Abroad Come Back Home," *International Herald Tribune*, December 10, 1997, p. 20.

philosophy underlying the IBA was one of **national treatment**, a philosophy that attempted to create a level playing field for domestic and foreign banks in U.S. banking markets. As a result of this act, foreign banks were required to hold Federal Reserve–specified reserve requirements if their worldwide assets exceeded $1 billion and became subject to Federal Reserve examinations and to both the McFadden and Glass-Steagall Acts. With respect to the latter, an important grandfather provision in the act allowed foreign banks established in the United States prior to 1978 to keep their "illegal" interstate branches and securities-activity operations. That is, interstate and security activity restrictions were applied only to foreign banks entering the United States after 1978.[26]

national treatment

Regulation of foreign banks in the same fashion as domestic banks or the creation of a level playing field.

If anything, the passage of the IBA accelerated the expansion of foreign bank activities in the United States. A major reason for this was that for the first time, the IBA gave foreign banks access to the Federal Reserve's discount window, Fedwire, and FDIC insurance. In particular, access to FDIC insurance allowed access to retail banking. For example, in 1979 alone, foreign banks acquired four large U.S. banks (Crocker, National Bank of North America, Union Planters, and Marine Midland). In addition, in the early 1980s, the Bank of Tokyo, Mitsubishi Bank, and Sanwa Bank invested $1.3 billion in California bank acquisitions.[27] Overall, Japanese banks owned more than 25 percent of California bank assets at the end of the 1980s.

The Foreign Bank Supervision Enhancement Act (FBSEA) of 1991

Along with the growth of foreign bank assets in the United States came concerns about foreign banks' rapidly increasing share of U.S. banking markets and about the weakness of regulatory oversight of many of these institutions. Three events focused attention on the weaknesses of foreign bank regulation. The first event was the collapse of the Bank of Credit and Commerce International (BCCI), which had a highly complex international organization structure based in the Middle East, the Cayman Islands, and Luxembourg and had undisclosed ownership stakes in two large U.S. banks. BCCI was not subject to any consolidated supervision by a home country regulator; this quickly became apparent after its collapse, when massive fraud, insider lending abuses, and money-laundering operations were discovered. The second event was the issuance of more than $1 billion in unauthorized letters of credit to Saddam Hussein's Iraq by the Atlanta agency of the Italian bank, Banca Nazionale del Lavoro. The third event was the unauthorized taking of deposit funds by the U.S. representative office of the Greek National Mortgage Bank of New York.

These events and related concerns led to the passage of the FBSEA in 1991. The objective of this act was to extend federal regulatory authority over foreign banking organizations in the United States, especially when these organizations had entered using state licenses. The act's five main features have significantly enhanced the powers of federal bank regulators over foreign banks in the United States:

1. *Entry.* Under FBSEA, a foreign banking organization must now have the Fed's approval to establish a subsidiary, branch, agency, or representative office in the United States. The approval applies to both a new entry and an entry by acquisition. To secure Fed approval, the organization must meet a number of standards, two of

---

[26]For example, in 1978, approximately 60 foreign banks had branches in at least three states. As noted earlier, the McFadden Act prevented domestic banks from interstate branching.

[27]Thus, the newly formed bank—as a result of the 1996 Bank of Tokyo–Mitsubishi Bank merger—controls 70 percent of the Union Bank of San Francisco (a $17 billion bank with 200 branches) and 100 percent of the Bank of California (a $7 billion bank with 50 branches).

which are mandatory. First, the foreign bank must be subject to comprehensive supervision on a consolidated basis by a home country regulator. Second, that regulator must furnish all the information that the Federal Reserve requires to evaluate the application. Both standards attempt to avoid the lack of disclosure and lack of centralized supervision associated with BCCI's failure.

2. *Closure.* FBSEA also gives the Federal Reserve authority to close a foreign bank if its home country supervision is inadequate, if it violates U.S. laws, or if it engages in unsound and unsafe banking practices.

3. *Examination.* The Federal Reserve has the power to examine each office of a foreign bank, including its representative offices. Further, each branch or agency must be examined at least once a year.

4. *Deposit taking.* Only foreign subsidiaries with access to FDIC insurance can take retail deposits under $100,000. This effectively rolls back the provision of the IBA that gave foreign branches and agencies access to FDIC insurance.

5. *Activity powers.* Beginning December 19, 1992, state-licensed branches and agencies of foreign banks were not allowed to engage in any activity that was not permitted to a federal branch.

Overall, then, the FBSEA considerably increased the Federal Reserve's authority over foreign banks and added to the regulatory burden or costs of entry into the United States for foreign banks. This has made the post–FBSEA U.S. banking market much less attractive to foreign banks than it had been over the period in 1980–1992. Indeed, perhaps the strongest punitive action taken so far against a foreign bank was the Federal Reserve's closure of all operations of Daiwa Bank in the United States for six weeks in 1995 for not reporting a bond trader's losses of nearly $1 billion and the resulting four-year prison sentence and $2.57 million fine imposed on the offending trader by a New York court. This closure may signal a willingness of the authorities to be much tougher on foreign banks in the United States in the future.

Concept Questions

1. What regulatory and economic factors have encouraged the growth of U.S. offshore banking? What factors have deterred U.S. offshore banking?
2. What are the primary forms of entry by foreign banks into the U.S. market?
3. What impact did the passage of the International Banking Act of 1978 have on foreign bank activities in the United States?

ADVANTAGES AND DISADVANTAGES OF INTERNATIONAL EXPANSION

The historical and recent trends affecting the expansion of FIs both into and outside the United States have been discussed. The chapter next discusses the economic and regulatory advantages and disadvantages of international expansion to an individual FI seeking to generate additional returns or to better diversify its risk (see Table 26–10).

Table **26-10**

ADVANTAGES AND DISADVANTAGES OF INTERNATIONAL
EXPANSION

Advantages

Risk diversification   International activities enhance the opportunity to diversify the risk of
domestic earnings flows.
Economies of scale   Expansion beyond domestic boundaries can potentially lower average
operating costs.
Innovations   New product innovations offered internationally can generate extra returns.
Funds source   International expansion allows the FI to search for the cheapest and most
available sources of funds.
Customer relationships   International expansion allows the FI to maintain contact with
domestic multinational corporations with which the FI does business.
Regulatory avoidance   Domestic regulations do not apply to all international activities.

Disadvantages

Information/Monitoring costs   International expansion increases the FI's exposure to default
risk and thus the need for additional information and monitoring.
Nationalization/Expropriation   A change in a foreign government may lead to the
nationalization of fixed assets, such as branches owned in the foreign country.
Fixed costs   The fixed costs of establishing overseas organizations may be extremely high.

Advantages

International expansion has six major advantages:

Risk Diversification.   As with domestic geographic expansions, an FI's international
activities potentially enhance its opportunity to diversify the risk of its earning flows. Often
domestic earnings flows from financial services are strongly linked to the state of that
economy. Therefore, the less integrated the economies of the world are, the greater is the
potential for earnings diversification through international expansions.[28]

Economies of Scale.   To the extent that economies of scale exist, an FI can potentially
lower its average operating costs by expanding its activities beyond domestic boundaries.

Innovations.   An FI can generate extra returns from new product innovations if it can sell
such services internationally rather than just domestically. For example, consider complex
financial innovations, such as securitization, caps, floors, and options, that FIs have innovated in the United States and sold to new foreign markets with few domestic competitors
until recently.[29]

---

[28]This, of course, assumes that stockholders are sufficiently undiversified to value FIs diversifying on their behalf.
[29]One reason that Sumitomo Bank took a limited partnership stake in Goldman Sachs in 1986 was to acquire
knowledge and expertise about the management and valuation of complex financial instruments.

Funds Source.   International expansion allows an FI to search for the cheapest and most available sources of funds. This is extremely important with the very thin profit margins in domestic and international wholesale banking. It also reduces the risk of fund shortages (credit rationing) in any one market.

Customer Relationships.   International expansions also allow an FI to maintain contact with and service the needs of domestic multinational corporations. Indeed, one of the fundamental factors determining the growth of FIs in foreign countries has been the parallel growth of foreign direct investment and foreign trade by globally oriented multinational corporations from the FI's home country.[30]

Regulatory Avoidance.   To the extent that domestic regulations such as activity restrictions and reserve requirements impose constraints or taxes on the operations of an FI, seeking low regulatory tax countries can allow an FI to lower its net regulatory burden and to increase its potential net profitability.

Disadvantages

International expansion has three major disadvantages:

Information/Monitoring Costs.   Although global expansions allow an FI the potential to better diversify its geographic risk, the absolute level of exposure in certain areas such as lending can be high, especially if the FI fails to diversify in an optimal fashion. For example, the FI may fail to choose a loan portfolio combination on the efficient portfolio frontier (see Chapter 11). Foreign activities may also be riskier for the simple reason that monitoring and information collection costs are often higher in foreign markets. For example, Japanese and German accounting standards differ significantly from the generally accepted accounting principles that U.S. firms use. In addition, language, legal, and cultural issues can impose additional transaction costs on international activities. Finally, because the regulatory environment is controlled locally and regulation imposes a different array of net costs in each market, a truly global FI must master the various rules and regulations in each market.

Nationalization/Expropriation.   To the extent that an FI expands by establishing a local presence through investing in fixed assets such as branches or subsidiaries, it faces the political risk that a change in government may lead to the nationalization of those fixed assets.[31] If foreign FI depositors take losses following a nationalization, they may seek legal recourse from the FI in U.S. courts rather than from the nationalizing government. For example, the resolution of the outstanding claims of depositors in Citicorp's branches in Vietnam following the Communist takeover and expropriation of those branches took many years.

Fixed Costs.   The fixed costs of establishing foreign organizations may be extremely high. For example, a U.S. FI seeking an organizational presence in the Tokyo banking market

---

[30]Foreign direct investment increased worldwide from $48 billion in 1985 to $318 billion in 1995. In the United States, foreign direct investment increased from $19 billion to $60 billion.

[31]Such nationalizations have occurred with some frequency in African countries.

faces real estate prices some five to six times higher than in New York. Such relative costs can be even higher if an FI chooses to enter by buying an existing Japanese bank rather than establishing a new operation because of the considerable cost of acquiring Japanese FI equities measured by price-earnings ratios. These high acquisition costs exist despite the significant bank loan problems of Japanese banks in recent years and the secular decline in Japanese share prices. These relative cost considerations become even more important if the expected volume of business to be generated and, thus, the revenue flows from foreign entry are uncertain. The failure of U.S. acquisitions to realize expected profits following the 1986 deregulation in the United Kingdom is a good example of unrealized revenue expectations vis-à-vis the high fixed costs of entry and the costs of maintaining a competitive position.[32]

Concept Questions

1. What are the major advantages of international expansion to an FI?
2. What are the major disadvantages of international expansion to an FI?
3. Compare the advantages and disadvantages of an FI's international expansion. Why do you think so few U.S. banks have established branches in Russia?

---

[32]However, U.S. banks and securities firms have fared better since the Canadian deregulation of securities business in 1987 (see "Canada's Borrowing with Its Fat Fees Lures Wall Street," The *New York Times*, April 15, 1995, p. D1).

S U M M A R Y

This chapter examined the potential return-risk advantages and disadvantages to FIs from both domestic and international geographic expansions. Although regulatory considerations and costs are fundamental to such decisions, several other economic factors play an important role in the net return or benefit-cost calculus for any given FI. For example, earnings diversification and economies of scale and scope add to the potential benefits from geographic expansions. However, costs or risks of geographic expansions include monitoring costs, expropriation of assets, and the costs of market entry. Managers need to weigh carefully each of these factors before making a geographic expansion decision, whether domestic or international.

P E R T I N E N T   W E B   S I T E S

Board of Governors of the Federal Reserve   http://www.bog.frb.fed.us/

Federal Deposit Insurance Corp.   http://www.fdic.gov/

Federal Home Loan Bank Board   http://www.fhlbanks.com/

NationsBank   http://www.nationsbank.com/

Salomon Brothers   http://www.salomon.com/

Geographic Expansion: Domestic and International

1. How do limitations on geographic diversification affect FI profitability?
2. How are insurance companies able to offer services in states beyond their state of incorporation?
3. How did the Resolution Trust Corporation make it easier for banks to expand across state lines?
4. Why were unit banks and money center banks opposed to bank branching in the early 1990s?
5. What are the new provisions on interstate banking in the Riegle-Neal Interstate Banking and Branching Efficiency Act of 1994?
6. What is the difference between an MBHC and an OBHC? What are the implications of this difference for bank expansion?
7. Bank mergers are likely to produce hard-to-quantify benefits and costs. The former are called *X efficiencies,* and we may call the latter *X inefficiencies.* What is an example of each?
8. What does the Berger and Humphrey study reveal about the cost savings from bank mergers?
9. What are the three revenue synergies that an FI may obtain from expanding geographically?
10. What are some plausible reasons for the percentage of small bank decreases and the percentage of large bank increases while the percentage of intermediate size banks has stayed constant since 1984?
11. What are the results of studies that examined the mergers of banks including postmerger performances? How do they differ from the studies examining mergers of nonbanks?
12. What are some of the important firm-specific financial factors that influence the acquisition decision of an FI?
13. How has the performance of merged banks compared to bank industry averages?
14. How can an FI establish a global or international presence?
15. How has the International Banking Act of 1978 and FDICIA of 1991 been detrimental to foreign banks in the United States?
16. What are some of the benefits for banks engaging in geographic expansion?
17. What are some of the main features of the Foreign Bank Supervision Enhancement Act of 1991?
18. What are the disadvantages of international expansion?

The following questions are related to Appendix material.

19. If a bank with a low PE ratio acquires a bank with a high PE ratio in a stock-financed deal, what will be the likely effect on the acquiring firm's earnings per share?
20. A Bank is planning to acquire B Bank and is concerned about a possible dilution of EPS. A Bank expects earnings to increase by 5 percent per year while the B Bank expects annual earnings to increase by 10 percent. The merged bank expects earnings to increase by 8 percent. From the information presented here, calculate the current and pro forma EPS dilution.

	A Bank	B Bank	Merged Bank
Net income	$200 million	$100 million	$300 million
Shares outstanding	40 million	25 million	75 million
EPS	$5.00	$4.00	

APPENDIX:
EPS DILUTION

A measure of the attractiveness of a merger or acquisition is earnings per share (EPS) dilution. Regardless of how much additional value a merger or acquisition creates, the mathematics of combining common equity shares and net income of the two firms can create increases or decreases in EPS that are not attributable to cost savings or revenue generation. From the bidder's viewpoint, reductions in EPS of this kind are bothersome. The bidder wants to make sure that the acquisition does not produce significant EPS dilution and that any EPS dilution will not be long-lived. EPS dilution is measured as

$$\frac{\text{Current or pro forma EPS of acquiring bank} - \text{Pro Forma EPS of combined banks}}{\text{Current or pro forma EPS of acquiring bank}}$$

EXAMPLE 26–1A

Calculation of EPS Dilution

Bank 1 is considering the purchase of Bank 2. Bank 2 shareholders would receive two shares in Bank 1 for every one share owned in Bank 2. Bank 1, whose revenues and expenses increase at 10 percent a year, is interested in Bank 2 because its revenues are increasing at 11 percent a year while its expenses are increasing only at 10 percent a year. The current financial data for the two banks individually and on a consolidated basis follow:

	Bank 1	**Bank 2**	**Consolidated Banks**
Revenues	$800 million	$250 million	—
Expenses	$720 million	$220 million	—
Net income	$ 80 million	$ 30 million	$110 million
Shares outstanding	20 million	5 million	30 million
EPS	$ 4.00	$6.00	—
Total assets	$ 5 billion	$ 1 billion	$ 6 billion

The consolidated bank is expected to experience 11 percent growth per year. Bank 1 will not undertake the acquisition if EPS dilution is larger than 4 percent in the first year or if any EPS dilution is evident four years after the merger.

Based on growth expectations, the bank's financial data one year after the acquisition are as follows:

	Bank 1	**Bank 2**	**Consolidated Banks**
Net income[33]	$88 million	$35.5 million	$122.1 million
Shares outstanding	20 million	5 million	30 million
EPS	$ 4.40	$ 7.10	$ 4.07

---

[33]Net income for Bank 1 = $80 million $(1.1)^1$ = $88 million, for Bank 2 = $250 million $(1.11)^1$ − $220 million $(1.1)^1$ = $35.5 million, and for Consolidated Banks = $110 million $(1.11)^1$ = $122.1 million.

and

$$\text{Current EPS dilution} = \frac{4.00 - 4.07}{4.00} = -1.75\%$$

$$\text{Pro forma EPS dilution} = \frac{4.40 - 4.07}{4.40} = 7.50\%$$

There would be no EPS dilution one year after the acquisition based on Bank 1's current EPS ($4). In fact, the consolidated bank would experience a 1.75 percent increase in EPS after the first year. On a pro forma basis, EPS dilution after the first year would be 7.50 percent (i.e., had Bank 1 remained independent, its EPS would be 7.5 percent higher than it would experience with the acquisition).

After four years the financial data are as follows:

	Bank 1	Bank 2	Consolidated Banks
Net income[34]	$117.13 million	$57.42 million	$166.99 million
Shares outstanding	20 million	5 million	30 million
EPS	$ 5.86	$11.48	$ 5.57

and

$$\text{Pro forma EPS dilution} = \frac{5.86 - 5.57}{5.86} = 4.95\%$$

Even four years after the acquisition the consolidated bank's EPS would not have recovered so that it is higher than that of independent Bank 1. This does not meet Bank 1's requirements for EPS dilution.   •   •   •

The problem with the acquisition in the above example is that the consolidated bank's growth in net income was not sufficient to raise its pro forma EPS to levels that Bank 1 could achieve if it remained independent after four years. The level of growth in EPS needed to do this can be calculated as follows

$$\begin{array}{c} \text{Growth rate needed for} \\ \text{consolidated bank to} \\ \text{alleviate EPS dilution} \\ \text{after } n \text{ years} \end{array} = \left[\frac{\text{EPS}_{b,n} \times \text{Outstanding shares}_{con}}{\text{Initial consolidated bank net income}} \right]^{\frac{1}{n}} - 1$$

where

$$\text{EPS}_{b,n} = \text{EPS of the bidder bank } n \text{ years after the acquisition}$$

and

$$\text{Outstanding shares}_{con} = \text{Number of shares outstanding in the consolidated bank}$$

For the preceding example

---

[34]Net income for Bank 1 = $80 million $(1.1)^4$ = $117.13 million, for Bank 2 = $250 million $(1.11)^4$ − $220 million $(1.1)^4$ = $57.42 million, and for Consolidated Bank = $110 million $(1.11)^4$ = $166.99 million.

$$\left[\frac{5.86 \times 30 \text{ million}}{110 \text{ million}} \right]^{1/4} - 1 = 12.44\%$$

With this growth in the consolidated bank's net income, no EPS dilution would occur after four years, that is,

	Bank 1	Bank 2	Consolidated Banks
Net income	$117.13 million	$57.42 million	$175.82 million
Shares outstanding	20 million	5 million	30 million
EPS	$ 5.86	$11.48	$ 5.86

and pro forma EPS dilution would be zero.

Chapter Twenty-seven

Foreign Exchange Risk

The globalization of the U.S. financial services industry has meant that managers of financial intermediaries (FIs) are increasingly exposed to foreign exchange (FX) risk. Chapter 2 introduced the basics of FX markets and risks by discussing how events in other countries affect an FI's return-risk opportunities. Foreign exchange risks can occur either directly as the result of trading in foreign currencies, making foreign currency loans (a loan in sterling to a corporation), buying foreign-issued securities (U.K. sterling-denominated bonds or German deutsche mark government bonds), or issuing foreign currency–denominated debt (sterling certificates of deposit) as a source of funds.

Extreme foreign exchange risk was evident in 1997 when a currency crisis occurred in Asia. The crisis began July 2 when the Thai baht fell nearly 50 percent in value relative to the U.S. dollar. This drop led to contagious drops in the value of other Asian currencies and eventually affected currencies other than those in Asia (e.g., the Brazilian real and Russian ruble). For example, on November 20, 1997, almost five months after the drop in the value of the baht, the South Korean currency, the won,

Figure 27–1   *1997 Currency Devaluation in Southeast Asian Countries*

SOURCE: The *New York Times,* December 10, 1997, p. D1. Copyright © 1997 by The New York Times Co. Reprinted by Permission.

dropped by 10 percent relative to the dollar. See Figure 27–1 for the drop in the value of several currencies experienced in the fall of 1997 and Contemporary Perspectives Box 27–1, which describes the sequence of events that pushed many currencies beyond the brink. As a result of these currency shocks, the earnings of some U.S. FIs were adversely impacted. For example, in November 1997, Chase Manhattan Corp. announced a $160 million loss for October from foreign currency trading and holdings of foreign currency bonds. Similarly, in 1998, J.P. Morgan was forced to discharge about 700 employees (nearly 5 percent of its workforce) as a result of losses, including those experienced when Asian currency values dropped in value in 1997 and 1998 (see Contemporary Perspectives Box 27–2). In addition, the stability of the Japanese banking system has been questioned, given its foreign currency exposure to troubled Asian countries including Indonesia, South Korea, and Thailand.

This chapter evaluates the risks that FIs face when their assets and liabilities are denominated in foreign (as well as domestic) currencies and when they take major positions as traders in the spot and forward foreign currency markets. The Appendices to this chapter discuss FI management and hedging of foreign exchange risk with futures and options contracts.

SOURCES OF FOREIGN EXCHANGE RISK EXPOSURE

The nation's largest commercial banks are major players in foreign currency trading and dealing, with large money center banks such as Citicorp and J. P. Morgan also taking significant positions in foreign currency assets and liabilities (refer to Chapter 19 on trading

Contemporary Perspectives 27–1

Many Players, Many Losers: How and Why Asian Currencies Tumbled So Quickly

There is no way to re-create the exact train of selling that pushed the currencies beyond the brink. But in interviews with bankers, economists, currency traders, portfolio managers, hedge fund executives and corporate treasurers in Asia and elsewhere, a picture has emerged of the sequence of events and the players who were central to the drama.

First, the talk of a Japanese interest rate increase raised fears among commercial bankers, investment bankers and others about the safety of big investment positions that were predicated on currency stability.

As these investors scurried to liquidate holdings in local currencies, the anxiety spread. Big foreign companies operating in the region became frightened, too, and scrambled to convert local revenues into dollars. And finally, local companies rushed to get yen and dollars. With everyone running for the exits, the Thai baht, the Indonesian rupiah and other regional currencies were trampled.

"Big movements in asset markets don't tend to happen unless all the actors move from one side of the ship to the other," said Peter Fisher, head of market intervention at the Federal Reserve Bank of New York.

The underlying cause of the rout . . . was the mistaken faith of millions of investors in the stability of the smaller Asian currencies. . . . So certain were many investors of that stability that they refused to pay the cost of insurance, through hedging, against a currency fall. . . . A currency trader based in Singapore for a major American investment bank, who spoke on condition of anonymity, said: "Nobody is going to admit that they did not hedge well. We have people who are still lying about their exposure. . . . The difference between hedging and speculation becomes blurred when most market participants become convinced—rightly or wrongly—that a nontrivial change in exchange rates is coming, and that the change is likely to be in one direction, . . . In that circumstance, everyone gets into the act."

SOURCE: Jonathan Fuerbringer, The *New York Times*, December 10, 1997, p. D1. Copyright © 1997 The New York Times Co. Reprinted by Permission.

Contemporary Perspectives 27–2

J.P. Morgan Plans to Fire 700 Staffers Amid Surging Costs, Crimpled Earnings

J.P. Morgan & Co., plagued by surging costs and recent losses in Asia and elsewhere that have crimped profits, plans to fire about 700 employees, or nearly 5 percent of its work force worldwide. . . .

The latest cuts aren't concentrated in any one area, though people familiar with the firm said there may be relatively more job eliminations in Asian operations than elsewhere. In addition, the layoffs are expected to affect workers at all levels, from clerical staff to managing directors.

The cuts are likely to be accompanied by a one-time serverance-related charge in the first quarter, though Morgan officials haven't yet determined how big that charge will be, people familiar with the situation said.

The cutbacks cap what has in many respects been a disappointing month for J.P. Morgan. In January, the bank said its fourth-quarter earnings plummeted 35 percent, hurt by losses in swaps contracts with Asian counterparties, as well as lower income from stock derivatives and bond trading in developed markets. Since then, all three major credit-rating agencies have placed Morgan on review for possible ratings downgrades. In addition, the bank—which last month designated nearly $600 million in swaps contracts with Asian counterparties as nonperforming—has been involved in a messy series of lawsuits over those swaps with several companies in South Korea.

SOURCE: Stephen E. Frank, The *Wall Street Journal*, February 24, 1998, p. A3. Reprinted by permission of The Wall Street Journal, © 1998 Dow Jones & Company, Inc. All rights reserved worldwide.

spot market for FX

The market in which
foreign currency is traded
for immediate delivery.

forward market for FX

The market in which
foreign currency is traded
for future delivery.

or market risk). See Table 27–1 for the outstanding (dollar value) of U.S. banks' foreign
assets and liabilities for the period 1993 to June 1997. The June 1997 figure for foreign
assets was $84.7 billion, with foreign liabilities of $109.4 billion. See Table 27–2 for the
categories of foreign currency positions of all U.S. banks in five major currencies.

Columns 1 and 2 of Table 27–2 refer to the assets and liabilities denominated in foreign
currencies that U.S. banks' financial portfolios include. Columns 3 and 4 refer to foreign
currency trading activities (the **spot** and **forward foreign exchange** contracts bought and
sold in each major currency). Foreign currency trading dominates direct portfolio investments. Even though the aggregate trading positions appear very large—for example, U.S.
banks bought 180,804 billion yen—their overall or net exposure positions can be relatively
small.

An FI's overall FX exposure in any given currency can be measured by the net book or
position exposure, which is measured in column 5 of Table 27–2 as

$$\text{Net exposure}_i = (\text{FX assets}_i - \text{FX liabilities}_i) + (\text{FX bought}_i - \text{FX sold}_i)$$
$$= \text{Net foreign assets}_i + \text{Net FX bought}_i$$

where

$$i = i\text{th country's currency}$$

Clearly, an FI could match its foreign currency assets to its liabilities in a given currency
and match buys and sells in its trading book in that foreign currency to avoid FX risk. It
could also offset an imbalance in its foreign asset-liability portfolio by an opposing
imbalance in its trading book so that its **net exposure** position in that currency would
be zero.

Notice in Table 27–2 that U.S. banks' net FX exposures in September 1997 varied
across currencies: they carried a positive net exposure position in Canadian dollars,
German marks, and British pounds and a negative net exposure position in Japanese yen

---

T a b l e **27–1**

**LIABILITIES TO AND CLAIMS ON FOREIGNERS REPORTED BY BANKS IN THE
UNITED STATES, PAYABLE IN FOREIGN CURRENCIES**
(millions of dollars, end of period)

				1996		1997	
Item	**1993**	**1994**	**1995**	**June**	**December**	**March**	**June**
Banks' liabilities	$78,259	$89,284	$109,713	$111,651	$103,383	$109,238	$109,433
Banks' claims	62,017	60,689	74,016	65,825	66,018	72,589	84,665
Deposits	20,993	19,661	22,696	20,890	22,467	24,542	26,503
Other claims	41,024	41,028	51,320	44,935	43,551	48,047	58,162
Claims of banks' domestic customers*	12,854	10,878	6,145	7,554	10,978	9,357	11,292

NOTE: Data on claims exclude foreign currencies held by U.S. monetary authorities.

*Assets owned by customers of the reporting bank located in the United States that represent claims on foreigners held by reporting banks for
the accounts of the domestic customers.

SOURCE: *Federal Reserve Bulletin*, Table 3.16, various issues.

Table **27-2**

WEEKLY U.S. BANK POSITIONS IN FOREIGN CURRENCIES AND FOREIGN ASSETS AND LIABILITIES, SEPTEMBER 1997

(in currency of denomination)

	(1) **Assets**	(2) **Liabilities**	(3) **FX Bought***	(4) **FX Sold***	(5) **Net Position****
Canadian dollars (millions)	82,156	71,754	272,658	271,655	11,405
German marks (millions)	275,079	274,374	2,188,964	2,177,715	11,954
Japanese yen (billions)	24,979	24,295	180,804	184,456	−2,968
Swiss francs (millions)	33,194	45,512	637,016	652,715	−28,017
British pounds (millions)	73,248	76,550	395,007	386,919	4,786

*Includes spot, future, and forward contracts.

**Net position = Assets − Liabilities + FX bought − FX sold

SOURCE: *Treasury Bulletin*, December 1997, pp. 98–102.

net exposure

The degree to which a bank is net long (positive) or net short (negative) in a given currency.

net long (short) in a currency

A position of holding more (less) assets than liabilities in a given currency.

and Swiss francs. A *positive* net exposure position implies that a U.S. FI is overall **net long in a currency** and faces the risk that the foreign currency will fall in value against the U.S. dollar, the domestic currency. A *negative* net exposure position implies that a U.S. FI is **net short** in a foreign currency and faces the *risk* that the foreign currency could rise in value against the dollar. Thus, failure to maintain a fully balanced position in any given currency exposes a U.S. FI to fluctuations in the FX rate of that currency against the dollar.

We have given the FX exposures for U.S. banks only, but most large nonbank FIs also have some FX exposure either through asset-liability holdings or currency trading. The absolute sizes of these exposures are smaller than for major U.S. money center banks. The reasons for this are threefold: smaller asset sizes, prudent person concerns,[1] and regulations.[2] See Figure 27–2 for foreign investments by pension fund companies from 1990 to 2000 (projected). During the actual period reported, U.S. pension funds invested from 7 to 15 percent of their asset portfolios in foreign securities. Interestingly, U.S. FIs' holdings of foreign assets on a percentage basis are slightly less than those of Japanese FIs and much below those of British FIs. U.S. life insurance companies generally hold less than 10 percent of their assets in foreign securities.

The levels of claims in foreign currencies and positions in foreign currencies held by FIs have increased in recent years, but the level of foreign currency trading has decreased. Some estimates are that half of all foreign exchange traders employed in 1995 will be gone by the year 2000. Reduced volatility in European country FX rates in the 1990s and the movement toward a single currency in Europe as part of the 1999 European Monetary

---

[1] *Prudent person concerns,* which require financial institutions to adhere to investment and lending policies, standards, and procedures that a reasonable and prudent person would apply with respect to a portfolio of investments and loans to avoid undue risk of loss and obtain a reasonable return, are especially important for pension funds.

[2] For example, New York State restricts foreign asset holdings of New York–based life insurance companies to less than 10 percent of their assets.

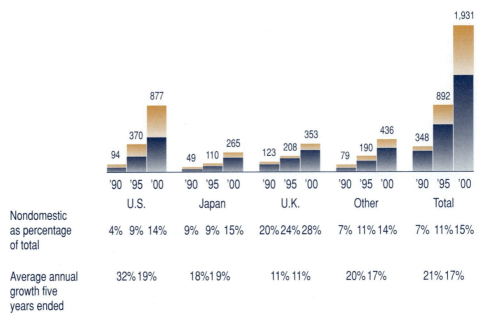

	'90	'95	'00	'90	'95	'00	'90	'95	'00	'90	'95	'00	'90	'95	'00
		U.S.			Japan			U.K.			Other			Total	
Nondomestic as percentage of total	4%	9%	14%	9%	9%	15%	20%	24%	28%	7%	11%	14%	7%	11%	15%
Average annual growth five years ended		32%	19%		18%	19%		11%	11%		20%	17%		21%	17%

F i g u r e   27–2   *Pension Fund Foreign Investments, Current and Projected, 1990, 1995, and 2000*

SOURCE: InterSec Research Corp., 1996.

Union (EMU) have reduced the need for foreign exchange trading with these countries and thus, traders. For example, when EMU goes into effect, cash flows from subsidiaries based in one European country can be put directly into the accounts of the parent country without complicated foreign exchange adjustments. As a result, after EMU is effective (i.e., after 2000) large multinational companies will likely reduce the number of their banking relationships and FX transactions.

Foreign Exchange Rate Volatility and Exposure

As Chapter 19 on market risk discussed, we can measure the potential size of an FI's FX exposure by analyzing the asset, liability, and currency trading mismatches on its balance sheet and the underlying volatility of exchange rate movements. Specifically, we can use this equation

Dollar loss/gain in currency i = (Net exposure in foreign currency i measured in U.S. dollars) $\times$ Shock (volatility) to the \$/Foreign currency i exchange rate

The larger the FI's net exposure in a foreign currency and the larger the foreign currency's exchange rate volatility, the larger is the potential dollar loss or gain to an FI's earnings (i.e., the greater its daily earnings at risk, DEAR). See Chapter 19 for more details on measuring the DEAR of FX exposure.

We next consider the underlying determinants and risks of the two components of an FI's net exposure in a foreign currency; its foreign currency trading book and its foreign financial asset and liability book.

Concept Questions

1. How is the net foreign currency exposure of an FI measured?
2. If a bank is long in deutsche marks (DM), does it gain or lose if the dollar appreciates in value against the DM?
3. A bank has £10 million in assets and £7 million in liabilities. It also bought £52 million in foreign currency trading. What is its net exposure in pounds?

FOREIGN CURRENCY TRADING

The FX markets of the world have become the largest of all financial markets with turnover often exceeding $3 trillion a day in 1997. London continues to be the largest center for trading in foreign exchange; it handles almost twice as much as New York, the second largest market. Third-ranked Tokyo handles approximately one-third the amount of London. Moreover, the FX market is essentially a 24-hour market, moving from Tokyo, London, and New York throughout the day. Therefore, FX trading risk exposure continues into the night even when some FI operations are closed. This clearly adds to the risk from holding mismatched FX positions.

Foreign Exchange Trading Activities

An FI's position in the FX markets generally reflects four trading activities:

1. The purchase and sale of foreign currencies to allow customers to partake in and complete international commercial trade transactions.
2. The purchase and sale of foreign currencies to allow customers (or the FI itself) to take positions in foreign real and financial investments.
3. The purchase and sale of foreign currencies for hedging purposes to offset customer (or FI) exposure in any given currency.
4. The purchase and sale of foreign currencies for speculative purposes through forecasting or anticipating future movements in FX rates.

In the first two activities, the FI normally acts for a fee as an *agent* of its customers but does not assume the FX risk itself. Citicorp is the dominant supplier of FX to retail customers in the United States. As of December 31, 1996, the aggregate value of Citicorp's notional principal amounts of foreign exchange products totaled $1,397 billion. In the third activity, the FI acts defensively as a hedger to reduce FX exposure. Thus, risk exposure essentially relates to those **open positions** taken as a principal for speculative purposes, the fourth activity. An FI usually creates open positions by taking an unhedged position in a foreign currency in its FX trading with other FIs. The Federal Reserve estimates that 200 FIs are active market makers in foreign currencies in the U.S. FX market, with about 30 commercial and investment banks making a market in five major currencies. FIs can make speculative trades directly with other FIs or arrange them through specialist FX brokers. The Federal Reserve Bank of New York estimates that approximately 44 percent of speculative or position trades are accomplished through specialized brokers who receive a fee for arranging trades between FIs. Speculative trades can be instituted through a variety of FX instruments. Spot currency trades are the most common, with FIs seeking to make a profit

open position

An unhedged position in a particular currency.

on the difference between buy and sell prices (i.e., movements in the bid–ask prices over time). However, FIs can also take speculative positions in foreign exchange forward contracts, futures, and options.

The Profitability of Foreign Currency Trading

Profits or losses on foreign trading can come from taking an open position or speculating in currencies. Revenues from market making—the bid-ask spread—or from acting as agents for retail or wholesale customers generally provide only a secondary or supplementary revenue source.

Note the trading income from FX trading for some large U.S. banks in Table 27–3. For large U.S. banks such as Bankers Trust, Citibank, and J. P. Morgan, FX trading has become an extremely important source of income. FX trading income is a highly volatile income source, however, for example, FX income at Bankers Trust varied from a low of –$54 million in 1994 to a high of $425.0 million in 1990.[3]

Table **27-3**

FOREIGN EXCHANGE TRADING INCOME OF MAJOR U.S. BANKS

	1988	1989	1990	1991	1992	1993	1994	1995	1996	1997[*]
1. Bank of America[†]	$135.0	$143.2	$207.0	$246.0	$300.0	$325.0	$237.0	303.0	316.0	312.0
2. Bankers Trust	153.9	296.5	425.0	272.0	331.0	191.0	(54.0)	36.0	178.0	205.0
3. Chase Manhattan Bank	249.7	227.0	217.2	215.0	327.0	354.4	280.0	241.0	444.0	572.0
4. Chemical Bank	143.2	153.9	207.2	289.0	363.0	302.0	152.9	291.0	—	—
5. Manufacturers Hanover	103.0	95.0	106.0	—	—	—	—	—	—	—
6. Citibank[§]	616.0	471.9	657.0	709.0	1,005.0	995.0	573.0	1,053.0	864.0	924.0
7. Continental Bank Corp.[#]	20.9	(1.0)	187.0	18.0	13.0	17.0	—	—	—	—
8. First Chicago NBD[**]	148.6	75.9	102.8	95.1	109.5	105.0	42.0	106.0	63.0	NR[‡‡]
9. Bank of New York[††]	30.9	29.0	47.6	71.0	66.0	54.2	27.0	42.0	57.0	87.0
10. Marine Midland	5.0	3.3	3.4	3.1	3.5	7.3	3.6	3.8	3.8	NR[‡‡]
11. J. P. Morgan & Co.	186.8	191.0	309.0	218.3	359.6	304.4	131.0	253.0	320.0	270.0
12. Republic New York Corp.	35.4	55.0	77.3	81.4	102.6	111.6	91.0	113.1	98.0	86.3
Total	**$1,828.4**	**$1,740.7**	**$2,546.5**	**$2,217.9**	**$2,980.2**	**$2,766.9**	**$1,483.5**	**$2,441.9**	**$2,343.8**	**$2,456.3**

[†]Millions of dollars, exclusive of translation income.

[§]Includes translation gains and losses.

[#]1988 and 1989 only; other years for Continental Illinois.

[**]1994 and prior years for First Chicago.

[††]1988 for Irving Trust.

[‡‡]NR=not reported.

[*] Through third quarter.

SOURCE: Annual reports, 10-Qs, call report data.

---

[3] In 1996, almost 30 percent of Bankers Trust's net profits came from FX and securities trading. The four largest New York banks plus Bank of America made more than $1,802 million from trading in that year, representing almost 20 percent of their combined total profits. These data are taken from companies' annual reports.

Concept  Questions

1. What are the four major FX trading activities?
2. In which trades do FIs normally act as agents and in which as principals?
3. What is the source of most profits or losses on foreign exchange trading? What foreign currency activities provide a secondary source of revenue?

· ·

FOREIGN ASSET AND LIABILITY POSITIONS

A second dimension of an FI's FX exposure results from any mismatches between its foreign financial asset and foreign financial liability portfolios. Foreign financial assets might include Swiss franc–denominated bonds, British pound–denominated securities, or even peso-denominated Mexican bonds. Foreign financial liabilities might include issuing British pound CDs or a yen-denominated bond in the Euromarkets to raise yen finance. The globalization of financial markets has created an enormous range of possibilities for raising funds in currencies other than the home currency. This is important for FIs that wish not only to diversify their sources and uses of funds but also to exploit imperfections in foreign banking markets that create opportunities for higher returns on assets or lower funding costs.

The Return and Risk of Foreign Investments

This section discusses the extra dimensions of return and risk from adding foreign currency assets and liabilities to an FI's portfolio. Like domestic assets and liabilities, returns result from the contractual income from or costs paid on a security. With foreign assets and liabilities, however, returns are also affected by changes in foreign exchange rates.

EXAMPLE 27–1

Calculating the Return of Foreign Investments

Suppose that a bank has the following assets and liabilities:

Assets	Liabilities
$100 million U.S. loans (one year) in dollars	$200 million U.S. CDs (one year) in dollars
$100 million equivalent U.K. loans (one year) (loans made in sterling)	

The U.S. FI is raising all of its $200 million liabilities in dollars (one-year CDs) but is investing 50 percent in U.S. dollar assets (one-year maturity loans) and 50 percent in U.K. pound sterling assets (one-year maturity loans).[4] In this example, the FI has matched the

---

[4] For simplicity, we ignore the leverage or net worth aspects of the FI's portfolio.

duration of its assets and liabilities ($D_A = D_L = 1$ year) but has mismatched the currency composition of its asset and liability portfolios. Suppose that the promised one-year U.S. CD rate is 8 percent to be paid in dollars at the end of the year and that one-year, credit risk–free loans in the United States are yielding only 9 percent. The FI would have a positive spread of 1 percent from investing domestically. Suppose, however, that credit risk–free one-year loans are yielding 15 percent in the United Kingdom.

To invest $100 million (of the $200 million in CDs issued) in one-year loans in the United Kingdom, the U.S. FI engages in the following transactions:

1. At the beginning of the year, sell $100 million for pounds on the spot currency markets. If the exchange rate is $1.60 to £1, this translates into $100 million/1.6 = £62.5 million.
2. Take the £62.5 million and make one-year U.K. loans at a 15 percent interest rate.
3. At the end of the year, sterling revenue from these loans will be £62.5(1.15) = £71.875 million.[5]
4. Repatriate these funds back to the United States at the end of the year. That is, the U.S. bank sells the £71.875 million in the foreign exchange market at the spot exchange rate that exists at that time, the end of the year spot rate.

Suppose that the spot foreign exchange rate has not changed over the year; it remains fixed at $1.60/£1. Then the dollar proceeds from the U.K. investment is:

$$£71.875 \text{ million} \times \$1.60/£1 = \$115 \text{ million or as a return}$$

$$\frac{\$115 \text{ million} - \$100 \text{ million}}{\$100 \text{ million}} = 15\%$$

Given this, the weighted return on the bank's portfolio of investments would be

$$(.5)(.09) + (.5)(.15) = .12, \text{ or } 12\%$$

This exceeds the cost of the bank's CDs by 4 percent ($12\% - 8\%$).

Suppose, however, that the exchange rate had fallen from $1.60/£1 at the beginning of the year to $1.45/£1 at the end of the year when the bank needed to repatriate the principal and interest on the loan. At an exchange rate of $1.45/£1, the pound loan revenues at the end of the year translate into

$$£71.875 \text{ million} \times \$1.45/£1 = \$104.22 \text{ million}$$

or as a return on the original dollar investment of:

$$\frac{\$104.22 - \$100}{\$100} = .0422 = 4.22\%$$

The weighted return on the bank's asset portfolio would be

$$(.5)(.09) + (.5)(.0422) = .0661 = 6.61\%$$

In this case, the bank actually has a loss or has a negative interest margin ($6.61\% - 8\% = -1.39\%$) on its balance sheet investments.   •   •   •

---

[5] No default risk is assumed.

The reason for the loss is that the depreciation of the pound from $1.60 to $1.45 has offset the attractive high yield on British pound sterling loans relative to domestic U.S. loans. If the pound had instead appreciated (risen in value) against the dollar over the year— say, to $1.70/£1—the U.S. bank would have generated a dollar return from its U.K. loans of

$$£71.875 \times \$1.70 = \$122.188 \text{ million}$$

or a percentage return of 22.188 percent.

The U.S. bank would receive a double benefit from investing in the United Kingdom, a high yield on the domestic British loans and an appreciation in sterling over the one-year investment period.

Risk and Hedging

Since a manager cannot know in advance what the pound/dollar spot exchange rate will be at the end of the year, a portfolio imbalance or investment strategy in which the bank is *net long* $100 million in pounds (or £62.5 million) is risky. As we discussed, the British loans would generate a return of 22.188 percent if the pound appreciated from $1.60 to $1.70 but would produce a return of only 4.22 percent if the pound were to depreciate in value against the dollar to $1.45.

In principle, an FI manager can better control the scale of its FX exposure in two major ways: on-balance-sheet hedging and off-balance-sheet hedging. On-balance-sheet hedging involves making changes in the on-balance-sheet assets and liabilities to protect FI profits from FX risk. Off-balance-sheet hedging involves no on-balance-sheet changes but a position in forward or other derivative securities to hedge FX risk.

On-Balance-Sheet Hedging.   The following example illustrates how an FI manager can control FX exposure by making changes on the balance sheet.

E X A M P L E   2 7 – 2

Hedging on the Balance Sheet

Suppose that instead of funding the $100 million investment in 15 percent British loans with U.S. CDs, the FI manager funds the British loans with $100 million equivalent one-year pound sterling CDs at a rate of 11 percent. Now the balance sheet of the bank would be as follows:

Assets	Liabilities
$100 million U.S. loans (9%)	$100 million U.S. CDs (8%)
$100 million U.K. loans (15%) (loans made in sterling)	$100 million U.K. CDs (11%) (deposits raised in sterling)

In this situation, the bank has both a matched maturity and currency foreign asset–liability book. We might now consider the bank's profitability or spreads between the return on assets and cost of funds under two scenarios: first, when the pound depreciates in value against the dollar over the year from $1.60/£1 to $1.45/£1 and, second, when the pound appreciates in value during the year from $1.60/£1 to $1.70/£1.

The Depreciating Pound.   When the pound falls in value to $1.45/£1, the return on the British loan portfolio is 4.22 percent. Consider what happens to the cost of $100 million in pound liabilities in dollar terms:

1. At the beginning of the year, the bank borrows $100 million equivalent in sterling CDs for one year at a promised interest rate of 11 percent. At an exchange rate of $1.60/£1, this is a sterling equivalent amount of borrowing of $100 million/1.6 = £62.5 million.
2. At the end of the year, the bank must pay the sterling CD holders their principal and interest, £62.5 million (1.11) = £69.375 million.
3. If the pound had depreciated to $1.45/£1 over the year, the repayment in dollar terms would be $100.59 million (£69.375 million $\times$ $1.45/£1) or a dollar cost of funds of 0.59 percent.

Thus, at the end of the year, the following occurs:

Average return on assets

$$(0.5)(0.9) + (0.5)(.0422) = .0661 = 6.61\%$$
U.S. asset return + U.K. asset return = Overall return

Average cost of funds

$$(0.5)(.08) + (0.5)(.0059) = .04295 = 4.295\%$$
U.S. cost of funds + U.K. cost of funds = Overall cost

Net return

Average return on assets – Average cost of funds
$$6.61\% - 4.295\% = 2.315\%$$

The Appreciating Pound.   When the pound appreciates over the year from $1.60/£1 to $1.70/£1, the return on British loans equals 22.188 percent. Now consider the dollar cost of British one-year CDs at the end of the year when the U.S. FI must pay the principal and interest to the CD holder:

$$£69.375 \text{ million} \times \$1.70/£1 = \$117.9375 \text{ million}$$

or a dollar cost of funds of 17.9375 percent. Thus, at the end of the year

Average return on assets

$$(0.5)(.09) + (0.5)(.22188) = .15594 \text{ or } 15.594\%$$

Average cost of funds

$$(0.5)(.08) + (0.5)(.179375) = .12969 \text{ or } 12.969\%$$

Net return

$$15.594\% - 12.969\% = 2.625\%$$ • • •

Thus, by directly matching its foreign asset and liability book, an FI can lock in a positive return or profit spread whichever direction exchange rates change over the investment period. For example, even if domestic U.S. banking is a relatively low profit activity (i.e., there is a low spread between the return on assets and the cost of funds), the bank could be very profitable overall. Specifically, it could lock in a large positive spread—if it exists—between deposit rates and loan rates in foreign markets. In our example, a 4 percent positive spread occurred between British one-year loan rates and deposit rates compared to only a 1 percent spread domestically.

Note that for such imbalances in domestic spreads and foreign spreads to continue over long periods of time, financial service firms would have to face significant barriers to entry in foreign markets. Specifically, if real and financial capital is free to move, banks would increasingly withdraw from the U.S. market and reorient their operations toward the United Kingdom. Reduced competition would widen loan deposit interest spreads in the United States, and increased competition would contract U.K. spreads until the profit opportunities from overseas activities disappeared. Chapter 26 discusses banks' abilities and limits on them to engage in cross-border financial and real investments.

Hedging with Forwards. Instead of matching its $100 million foreign asset position with $100 million of foreign liabilities, the FI may have chosen to remain unhedged on the balance sheet. Instead, as a lower cost alternative, it could hedge by taking a position in the forward or other derivative markets for foreign currencies, for example, the one-year forward market for selling sterling for dollars. (We consider the role of futures contracts and options in hedging FX risk in Appendices A and B to this chapter.) Any forward position taken would not appear on the balance sheet; it would appear as a contingent off-balance-sheet claim, which we described as an item below the bottom line in Chapter 20. The role of the forward FX contract is to offset the uncertainty regarding the future spot rate on sterling at the end of the one-year investment horizon. Instead of waiting until the end of the year to transfer sterling back into dollars at an unknown spot rate, the FI can enter into a contract to sell forward its *expected* principal and interest earnings on the loan at today's known **forward exchange rate** for dollars/pounds, with delivery of sterling funds to the buyer of the forward contract taking place at the end of the year. Essentially, by selling the expected proceeds on the sterling loan forward, at a known (forward FX) exchange rate today, the FI removes the future spot exchange rate uncertainty and thus the uncertainty relating to investment returns on the British loan.

forward exchange rate

The exchange rate agreed on today for future (forward) delivery of a currency.

E X A M P L E 2 7 – 3

Hedging with Forwards

Consider the following transactional steps when the FI hedges its FX risk by immediately selling its expected one-year sterling loan proceeds in the forward FX market:

1. The U.S. bank sells $100 million for pounds at the *spot* exchange rate *today* and receives $100 million/1.6 = £62.5 million.
2. The bank then immediately lends the £62.5 million to a British customer at 15 percent for one year.
3. The bank also sells the expected principal and interest proceeds from the sterling loan forward for dollars at *today's* forward rate for one-year delivery. Let the current forward one-year exchange rate between dollars and pounds stand at $1.55/£ or at a 5 cent discount to the spot pound; as a percentage discount

$$(\$1.55 - \$1.60)/\$1.6 = -3.125\%$$

This means that the forward buyer of sterling promises to pay

£62.5 million (1.15) × $1.55/£ = £71.875 × $1.55/£ = $111.406 million

to the FI seller in one year when the bank delivers the £71.875 million proceeds of the loan to the FI seller.

4. In one year, the British borrower repays the loan to the bank plus interest in sterling (£71.875 million).
5. The bank delivers the £71.875 million to the buyer of the one-year forward contract and receives the promised $111.406 million.

Barring the sterling borrower's default on the loan or the pound forward buyer's reneging on the forward contract, the bank knows from the very beginning of the investment period that it has locked in a guaranteed return on the British loan of

$$\frac{\$111.406 - \$100}{\$100} = .11406 = 11.406\%$$

Specifically, this return is fully hedged against any dollar/pound exchange rate changes over the one-year holding period of the loan investment. Given this return on British loans, *the overall expected return* on the bank's asset portfolio is

$$(.5)(.09) + (.5)(.11406) = .10203, \text{ or } 10.203\%$$

Since the cost of funds for the bank's $200 million U.S. CDs is an assumed 8 percent, it has been able to lock in a return spread over the year of 2.203 percent regardless of spot exchange rate fluctuations between the initial overseas (loan) investment and repatriation of the foreign loan proceeds one year later.   •   •   •

In the preceding example, it is profitable for the FI to drop domestic U.S. loans and to hedge foreign U.K. loans since the hedged dollar return on foreign loans of 11.406 percent is so much higher than the 9 percent domestic loans. As the FI seeks to invest more in British loans, it needs to buy more spot sterling. This drives up the spot price of sterling in dollar terms to more than $1.60/£1. In addition, the bank could sell more sterling forward (the proceeds of these sterling loans) for dollars, driving the forward rate to below $1.55/£1. The outcome would widen the dollar forward spot exchange rate difference on sterling, making forward hedged sterling investments less attractive than before. This process would continue until the U.S. cost of bank funds just equals the forward hedged return on British loans. That is, the FI could make no further profits by borrowing in U.S. dollars and making forward contract–hedged investments in U.K. loans (see also Chapter 2 on the interest rate parity theorem).

Concept Questions

1. The cost of one-year U.S. dollar CDs is 8 percent, one-year U.S. dollar bank loans yield 10 percent, and U.K. sterling loans yield 15 percent. The dollar/pound spot exchange is $1.50/£1, and the one-year forward exchange rate is $1.48/£1. Are one-year U.S. dollar loans more or less attractive than U.K. sterling loans?
2. What are the two ways in which an FI manager can control FX exposure?

S U M M A R Y

This chapter analyzed the sources of FX risk that modern FI managers face. Such risks result from mismatching foreign currency trading and/or foreign asset–liability positions in individual currencies. Although such mismatches can be profitable if FX forecasts prove to be correct, unexpected outcomes and volatility can impose significant losses on an FI. They threaten its profitability and, ultimately, its solvency in a fashion similar to interest rate, off-balance-sheet, and technology risks. This chapter discussed possible ways to reduce such risks, including direct hedging through matched foreign asset–liability books and hedging through forward contracts. The Appendices to the chapter discuss ways in which FIs may also use foreign currency futures and option contracts to hedge their FX risk.

P E R T I N E N T   W E B   S I T E S

Foreign Exchange Risk

1. What are the four FX trading activities undertaken by FIs? How do they earn from these activities?

2. X-M bank has 14 million DM in assets and 23 million DM in liabilities and sold 8 DM in foreign currency trading. What is X-M's net exposure? For what type of exchange rate movement does the exposure put the bank at risk?

3. City Bank issued $200 million of one-year CDs in the United States at a rate of 6.50 percent. It invested part of this money, $100 million, in a one-year bond issued by a U.S. firm at a annual rate of 7.00 percent. The remaining $100 million was invested in a one-year Brazilian government bond paying an annual interest rate of 8 percent. The current exchange rate is real 1/$.
   a. What is the net return on this $200 million investment in bonds if the exchange rate between Brazilian real and the U.S. dollar remains the same?
   b. What is the net return on this $200 million investment in bonds if the exchange rate changes to real 1.20/$?
   c. What is the net return on this $200 million investment in bonds if the exchange rate changes to real 0.80/$?

4. Sun Bank USA purchased a 16 million one-year deutsche mark loan that pays 12 percent interest annually. The spot rate for deutsche marks is DM 1.60/$. The bank has funded this loan by accepting a British pound (BP)–denominated deposit for the equivalent amount and maturity at an annual rate of 10 percent. The current spot rate of the British pound to US $ is $1.60/£.
   a. What is the net interest income earned in dollars on this one-year transaction if the spot rates at the end of the year are DM1.70/$ and $1.85/£?
   b. What should the BP to US $ spot rate be for the bank to earn a net interest margin of 4 percent?

5. North Bank has been borrowing in the U.S. markets and lending abroad, thereby incurring foreign exchange risk. In a recent transaction, it issued a one-year, $2 million CD at 6 percent and is planning to fund a loan in German marks at 8 percent for a 2 percent spread. The spot rate for the German mark is DM1.45/$. However, new information now indicates that the German mark will depreciate to DM1.47/$ by year-end.
   a. What should the bank charge on the loan to maintain the 2 percent spread?
   b. The bank has an opportunity to sell one-year forward marks at DM1.46. What is the spread on the loan if the bank hedges its forward foreign exchange exposure?
   c. How should the loan rates be increased to maintain the 2 percent spread if the bank intends to hedge its exposure using the forward rates?

6. One way for an FI to hedge its foreign exchange exposure is to match its foreign currency assets and liabilities by currency. Explain why it may still not be a perfect hedge.

7. The following are the foreign currency positions of an FI, expressed in dollars:

Currency	Assets	Liabilities	FX Bought	FX Sold
Deutsche mark (DM)	$125,000	$50,000	$10,000	$15,000
British pound (BP)	50,000	22,000	15,000	20,000
Japanese yen (JY)	75,000	30,000	12,000	88,000

a. What is the FI's net exposure in deutsche marks?
b. What is the FI's net exposure in British pounds?
c. What is the FI's net exposure in Japanese yen?
d. What is the expected loss or gain if the DM exchange rates appreciate by 1 percent?
e. What is the expected loss or gain if the BP exchange rates depreciate by 1 percent.
f. What is the expected loss or gain if the JY exchange rates appreciate by 2 percent?

8. A money market mutual fund manager is looking for some profitable investment opportunities and observes the following one-year interest rates on government securities and exchange rates: r_{us} = 12%, r_{uk} = 9%, S = $1.50/£, f = $1.6/£, where S is the spot exchange rate and f is the forward exchange rate. Which of the two types of government securities would constitute a better investment?

9. If an FI wants to hedge its FX risk exposure, what are the advantages and disadvantages of off-balance-sheet hedging in comparison to on-balance-sheet hedging?

10. What motivates FIs to hedge foreign currency exposures? What are the limitations to hedging foreign currency exposures?

11. A bank purchases a six-month, $1 million Eurodollar deposit at an interest rate of 6.5 percent per year. It invests the funds in a six-month Swedish krone bond paying 7.5 percent per year. The current spot rate is $0.18/SK.
a. The six-month forward rate on the Swedish krone is being quoted at $0.1810/SK. What is the net spread earned on this investment if the bank covers its foreign exchange exposure using the forward market?
b. At what forward rate will the spread be only 1 percent per year?

12. If financial markets are not perfectly correlated, do they help or hinder FIs holding multicurrency foreign assets and liabilities?

13. What does the fact that returns of financial assets in different countries are not perfectly correlated imply about the extent of integration of the markets? Does it provide more or fewer opportunities for FIs?

14. Bank USA recently made a $10 million loan that pays 10 percent interest annually. It has funded this loan by accepting a deutsche mark-denominated deposit for the equivalent amount and maturity at an annual rate of 8 percent. The current spot rate of the US$ to DM is DM1.60/$.
a. What is the net interest income earned in dollars on this one-year transaction if the spot rate at the end of the year is DM1.58/$?
b. What is the rate beyond which any appreciation of the DM will lead to a loss?
The following four questions refer to material found in Appendix A.

15. Suppose that an FI has assets denominated in British pound sterling of $125 million and sterling liabilities of $100 million.
a. What is the FI's net exposure?
b. Is the FI exposed to a dollar appreciation or depreciation?
c. How can the FI use futures or forward contracts to hedge its FX rate risk?
d. What are the number of futures contracts to be utilized to fully hedge the FI's currency risk exposure?
e. If the exchange rate of British pound to US$ falls from $1.60/£ to $1.50/£, what would be the impact on the FI's cash position? Assume that the FI has not hedged.
f. If the British pound to US$ futures price falls from $1.55/£ to $1.45/£, what would be the impact on the FI's futures position?

16. Refer to Problem 15(f).
a. If the British pound to US$ futures price fell from $1.55/£ to $1.43/£, how would this impact the FI's futures position?
b. Does your answer to part (a) differ from your answer to problem 15(f)? Why or why not?
c. How would you fully hedge the FX rate risk exposure in problem 15 using the futures price change of 16(a)?

17. An FI is planning to hedge its one-year, $100 million deutsche mark (DM)–denominated loan against exchange rate risk. The current spot rate is $0.60/DM. A one-year DM futures contract is currently trading at $0.58/DM. DM futures are sold in standardized units of DM62,500.
a. Should the FI be worried about the DM appreciating or depreciating?
b. Should it buy or sell futures to hedge against exchange rate exposure?

18. Suppose that a U.S. FI has assets denominated in deutsche marks (DM) of 75 million and DM liabilities of 125 million. The spot rate is $0.6667/DM. One-year DM futures are available for $0.6579/DM.
    a. What is the FI's net exposure?
    b. Is the FI exposed to a dollar appreciation or depreciation?
    c. What are the number of futures contracts to be utilized to fully hedge the FI's currency risk exposure if the contract size is DM62,500 per contract?
    d. If the DM spot rate falls from $0.6667/DM to $0.6897/DM, how would this impact the FI's currency exposure? Assume no hedging.
    e. If the British pound futures price falls from $0.6579/DM to $0.6349/DM, what would be the impact on the FI's futures position?

The following questions refer to material covered in Appendix B.

19. An FI is expecting to make a single payment of 500,000 Swiss francs in six months when a CD it had issued earlier expires. The current spot rate is $0.80/SF. Your in-house analyst expects the spot price of the franc to remain fairly stable (i.e., at $0.80/SF), but cautions you that it could rise as high as $0.85/SF or fall to as low as $0.75/SF. In lieu of this uncertainty, you recommend that the FI hedge this expected payment using either options or futures. Six-month call and put options on the Swiss franc with an exercise price of $0.80/SF are trading at 4 cents and 2 cents, respectively. A six-month futures contract on the Swiss franc is trading at $0.80/SF.
    a. Should you be worried about the dollar depreciating or appreciating?
    b. If you decide to hedge using options, should you be buying put or call options to hedge this payment. Why?
    c. If you decide to hedge using futures, should you be buying or selling Swiss franc futures to hedge this payment? Why?

20. Use the information in question 19 to answer the following questions.
    a. What will your net payments be if you use the selected call or put options in question 19(b) to hedge your payment? Assume that that the spot price in six months will be either $0.75, $0.80, or $0.85/SF. Also assume that the options will be exercised instead of being sold.
    b. What will your net payments be if you had instead used futures to hedge the payment? Use the same three amounts as in part (a).
    c. Which method of hedging is preferable?

21. Suppose that a U.S. insurance company issued $10 million of one-year, zero-coupon guaranteed investment contracts denominated in deutsche marks at a rate of 5 percent. The insurance company holds no DM-denominated assets and has neither bought nor sold DM in the foreign exchange market.
    a. What is the insurance company's net exposure in DM?
    b. What is the insurance company's risk exposure to foreign exchange rate fluctuations?
    c. How can the insurance company use futures to hedge the risk exposure in part (b)? How can it use options to hedge?
    d. If the strike price on a DM call and put option is $0.6667/DM and the spot price is $0.6452/DM, what is the intrinsic value (upon expiration) of the call option on DM? What is the intrinsic value (upon expiration) of the DM put option? (Note: DM futures options traded on the Chicago Mercantile Exchange are set at 125,000 DM per contract.)
    e. If the June delivery call option premium is 0.32 cents per DM and the June delivery put option is 10.7 cents per DM, what is the dollar premium cost per contract? (Assume that today's date is April 15.)
    f. Why is the call option premium lower than the put option premium?

22. An FI has made a loan commitment of DM10 million that is likely to be withdrawn in six months. The current spot rate is $0.60/DM.
    a. Is the FI exposed to the dollar's depreciating or appreciating? Why?
    b. If it decides to hedge using DM futures, should it buy or sell DM futures?
    c. If the spot rate six months from today is $0.64/DM, what amount in dollars is needed in six months if the loan is drawn down and if it had remained unhedged?
    d. A six-month DM futures contract is available for $0.61/DM. What net amount is needed at the end of six months if the FI had hedged using the DM10 million of futures contract? Assume that futures prices are equal to spot prices at the time of payment (i.e., at maturity).
    e. If it decides to use options to hedge, should it purchase call or put options?
    f. Call and put options with an exercise price of $0.61/DM are selling for $0.02 and $0.03, respectively. What net amount does the FI need at the end of six months if it had used options instead of futures to hedge this exposure?

23. An FI is planning to hedge its three-month, $250 million deutsche mark (DM)–denominated discount loan against exchange rate risk. The current spot rate is $0.50/DM. Three-month calls with an exercise price of $.50/DM can be bought for $.015/DM; three-month puts with the same exercise price can be bought for $.0321/DM. DM options are sold in standardized units DM125,000.

    a. Should the FI be worried about the DM's appreciating or depreciating?

    b. Should it buy calls or puts to hedge against exchange rate exposure?

    c. How many option contracts should it hedge if the FI wants to hedge its entire position?

    d. Show exactly how the FI is hedged if it repatriates its principal of DM 100 million at year-end and if the spot price of DM at year-end is $0.55/DM.

    e. Given the relative prices of the options, what is the market expecting to happen to the mark against the dollar?

APPENDIX A: HEDGING FOREIGN EXCHANGE RISK WITH FUTURES

open interest

The number of futures contracts outstanding at the start of the trading day.

Just as futures can hedge an FI against losses due to interest rate changes (as demonstrated in Chapter 21), they can also hedge against foreign exchange rate risk. The major foreign currency futures contracts available are shown in Figure 27–1A. As indicated by the trading data on October 24, 1997, measured by **open interest,** or the number of contracts outstanding at the end of the day, the Japanese yen, German deutsche mark, Canadian dollar, Swiss franc, and British pound were the most popular currencies for futures positions.

Consider a U.S.–based FI wishing to hedge a one-year British pound loan of £100 million principal plus £15 million interest (or £115 million) against the risk of the pound falling in value against the dollar over the following year. As shown for October 24, 1997, there were two British pound futures contracts: the December 1997 contract and the March 1998 contract. Thus, the futures market did not allow the FI to institute a long-term, one-year hedge that day. The longest maturity contract available matured in just over four months, in March 1998. Measured by open interest, however, this contract is quite illiquid compared to the December 1997 contract. Thus, the FI could use futures only by rolling over its hedging activity into a new futures contract on maturity. How many futures should it sell? It should sell the amount that produces a sufficient profit on the pound futures contract just to offset any exchange rate losses on the pound loan portfolio should the pound fall in value relative to the dollar. For simplicity, we assume that the dollar/pound "price"

CURRENCY

	Open	High	Low	Settle	Change	Lifetime High	Low	Open Interest
JAPAN YEN (CME)-12.5 million yen; $ per yen (.00)								
Dec	.8267	.8334	.8230	.8265	....	.9320	.8135	94,008
Mr98	.8384	.8435	.8355	.8377	....	.9375	.8269	992
June	....	....	....	.8491	....	.9090	.8510	230
Est vol 19,132; vol Th 35,270; open int 95,231, +9,209.								
DEUTSCHEMARK (CME)-125,000 marks; $ per mark								
Dec	.5674	.5680	.5616	.5640	− .0033	.6610	.5343	61,091
Mr98	.5648	.5680	.5648	.5668	− .0033	.6160	.5383	2,560
June	....	....	....	.5693	− .0033	.5995	.5490	2,618
Sept	....	....	....	.5715	− .0033	.5825	.5687	105
Est vol 23,202; vol Th 38,704; open int 66,377, −1,379.								
CANADIAN DOLLAR (CME)-100,000 dlrs.; $ per Can $								
Dec	.7210	.7216	.7197	.7199	− .0011	.7685	.7197	54,656
Mr98	.7240	.7245	.7230	.7232	− .0011	.7670	.7230	2,610
June	.7265	.7266	.7265	.7256	− .0011	.7470	.7260	529
Sept	.7285	.7290	.7280	.7276	− .0011	.7463	.7280	229
Est vol 6,400; vol Th 10,887; open int 58,114, +1,089.								
BRITISH POUND (CME)-62,500 pds.; $ per pound								
Dec	1.6294	1.6336	1.6252	1.6304	+ .0010	1.6970	1.5630	36,463
Mr98	....	....	....	1.6250	+ .0010	1.6840	1.5680	258
Est vol 4,452; vol Th 5,751; open int 36,792, +327.								
SWISS FRANC (CME)-125,000 francs; $ per franc								
Dec	.6866	.6874	.6796	.6857	− .0008	.7740	.6602	42,013
Mr98	.6857	.6932	.6857	.6919	− .0007	.7450	.6754	2,150
June	....	....	....	.6980	− .0007	.7135	.6750	265
Sept	....	....	....	.7039	− .0007	.7150	.6965	109
Est vol 18,165; vol Th 23,264; open int 44,537, −1,357.								
AUSTRALIAN DOLLAR (CME)-100,000 dlrs.; $ per A.$								
Dec	.7045	.7090	.6928	.6933	− .0103	.7860	.6928	20,242
Est vol 1,430; vol Th 4,901; open int 20,268, +985.								
MEXICAN PESO (CME)-500,000 new Mex. peso, $ per MP								
Dec	.12580	.12680	.12370	.12412	− .0160	.12720	.0985	27,952
Mr98	.12280	.12280	.11950	.12010	− .0162	.12340	.1040	10,225
June	.11920	.11920	.11600	.11660	− .0175	.11985	.10050	2,833
Sept	.11620	.11620	.11300	.11350	− .0190	.11680	.10575	2,762
Dec	.11350	.11350	.11050	.11150	− .0150	.11440	.10960	1,344
Est vol 18,356; vol Th 17,338; open int 45,116, +1,838.								

F i g u r e **27–1A**   *Foreign Currency Futures Contracts, October 24, 1997*

(or exchange rate) in the futures market is expected to change in exactly the same fashion as the spot dollar/pound price over the course of the year. That is, futures and spot price changes are perfectly correlated (i.e., there is no "basis" risk).

EXAMPLE 27-1A

* * * * * * *

A Hedge of Foreign Exchange Risk Using Futures Contracts
On October 24, 1997, the *Wall Street Journal* reported the following

S_t = spot exchange rate (\$/£): \$1.634 per £1
f_t = futures price (\$/£) for the nearby contract (December 1997): \$1.6304 per £1

Suppose that the FI made a £100 million loan at 15 percent interest and wished to hedge fully the risk that the dollar value of the proceeds would be eroded by a declining British pound sterling over the year. Also suppose that the FI manager receives a forecast that in one year's time the spot and futures will be

$$S_{t+1} = \$1.5840 \text{ per } £1$$
$$f_{t+1} = \$1.5804 \text{ per } £1$$

So that over the year

$$\Delta S_t = 5 \text{ cents}$$
$$\Delta f_t = 5 \text{ cents}$$

For a manager who believes this forecast of a depreciating pound against the dollar, the correct full-hedge strategy is to cover the £115 million principal and expected interest earnings on the British loan by selling, or shorting, £115 million of British pound futures contracts on October 24, 1997. As the exchange rate falls, so does the value of the futures contract. Thus, the short hedger (the contract seller) will profit from the drop in price on the futures position. We assume here that the FI manager continually rolls over the futures position into new futures contracts and will get out of futures on October 24, 1998.

The size of each British pound futures contract is £62,500 (see Figure 27–1A). Therefore the number (N_F) of futures to be sold is

$$N_F = \frac{£115,000,000}{£62,500} = \frac{\text{Size of a long position}}{\text{Size of a pound futures contract}}$$

$$= 1,840 \text{ contracts}$$

Next, consider whether losses on the long asset position (the British loan) would just offset gains on the futures should the FI sell 1,840 British pound futures contracts and should spot and futures prices change in the direction and amount expected.

Loss on British Pound Loan.   The loss on the British pound loan in dollars would be

$$[£ \text{ Principal} + \text{Interest}] \times \Delta S_t$$
$$[£115 \text{ million}] \times [\$1.634/£ - \$1.584/£] = \$5.75 \text{ million}$$

That is, the dollar value of the British pound loan proceeds would be \$5.75 million less should the pound depreciate against the dollar from \$1.634/£ to \$1.584/£ in the spot market over the year.

Gain on Futures Contracts.   The gain on futures contracts would be

$$[N_F \times £62,500] \times \Delta f_t$$
$$[1,840 \times £62,500] \times [\$1.6304/£ - \$1.5804/£] = \$5.75 \text{ million}$$

By selling 1,840 futures contracts at £62,500 each, the seller makes $5.75 million in the futures market. This cash flow of $5.75 million results from marking to market the futures contract. As the futures price falls, resulting from daily marking to market, the pound futures contract buyer has the contract repriced to a lower level in dollars to be paid per pound. But the seller must be compensated from the buyer's margin account for the difference between the original contract price and the new lower marked-to-market contract price. Thus, over the one year, the buyer compensates the seller by a net of 5 cents per £1 of futures purchased: that is, $1.6304/£1 minus $1.5804/£1 as the futures price falls, or a total of 5 cents times the number of contracts (1,840) times the pound size of each contract (62,500). Note that on October 24, 1997, when the borrower pays the principal and interest on the pound loan, the FI seller of the pound futures terminates its position in 1,840 short contracts by taking an opposing position of 1,840 long in the same contract. This effectively ends any net cash flow implications from futures positions beyond this date.[6] •   •   •

APPENDIX B: HEDGING FOREIGN EXCHANGE RISK WITH OPTIONS

An FI can also hedge foreign exchange risk using currency options. To see this, suppose that a U.S. FI bought, or is long in, a sterling asset in October 1997. This sterling asset is a one-month T-bill worth £100 million in November 1997. Since the FI's liabilities are in dollars, it may wish to hedge the FX risk that the pound sterling will depreciate over the forthcoming month. Suppose that if the pound were to fall from the current exchange rate of $1.634/£1, the FI would incur a loss on its British T-bill investment when measured in dollar terms. For example, if the pound depreciated from $1.634/£1 in October to $1.4939/£1 in November, the £100 million asset would be worth only $149.39 million on maturity instead of the expected $163.4 million when it was purchased in October. If the foreign exchange rate depreciation is sufficiently severe, the FI might be unable to meet its dollar liability commitments used to fund the T-bill purchase. To offset this exposure, the FI may buy one-month put options on sterling at an exercise price of $1.60/£1. Thus, if the exchange rate does fall to $1.4939/£1 in November, the FI manager can put the £100 million proceeds from the T-bill on maturity to the writer of the option. Then the bank receives $160 million instead of the $149.39 million if the pounds were sold at the open market spot exchange rate at the end of the month. If the pound actually appreciates in value or does not depreciate below $1.60/£1, the option expires unexercised and the FI manager realizes the proceeds of the £100 million asset by a sale of pounds for dollars in

---

[6] This example ignores the interest income effects of marking to market. In reality, the FI seller would receive the $5.75 million from the futures position over the course of the year. As a result, this cash flow can be reinvested at the current short-term dollar interest rate and generate a cash flow of more than $5.75 million. Given this, an FI hedger can sell slightly fewer contracts in anticipation of this interest income. The number of futures that could be sold, below the 1,840 suggested, depends on the level and pattern of short-term rates over the hedging horizon as well as the precise expected pattern of cash flows from marking to market. In general, the higher the level of short-term interest rates, the more an FI manager could tail the hedge (i.e., reduce the number of futures contracts that are needed to hedge a cash position because of the interest income that is generated from reinvesting the marking to market cash flows generated by the futures contract).

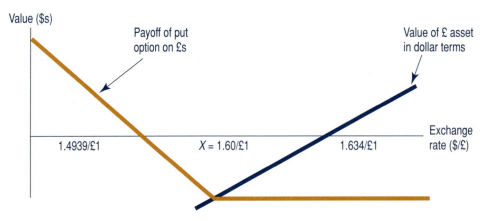

F i g u r e **27–1B**   *Hedging FX Risk by Buying a Put Option on British Pounds*

the spot foreign exchange market one month into the future (with the proceeds not being less than $160 million). See Figure 27–1B.

The cost of this one-month hedge and the number of put options required to hedge depends on the put premium and the options available, as well as the exchange on which the FX option is traded. Figure 27–2B shows the cost to buy a one-month European option on the British pound on the Philadelphia Options Exchange. As you can see, the premium cost of a November 1997 put option with a strike price of 158 (or $1.58 per £1) as of October 24, 1997, was 0.20 cents per pound or ($.002 per £). Since each contract has a value of £31,250, the dollar premium cost per put contract would be $62.50. If the bank wished to microhedge its whole £100 million position in the sterling T-bill assets, it would need to buy[7]

$$\frac{£100,000,000}{£31,250} = 3,200 \text{ contracts (puts)}$$

Thus, the total premium cost of this put position would be $200,000 ($62.50 × 3,200 contracts). This is the cost to buy foreign currency risk insurance in the options market against a major fall in the value of the pound.

Instead of taking a direct position in an option on the underlying pound asset, the bank could have bought put options on foreign currency futures contracts. The futures option contracts for foreign currencies traded on the Chicago Mercantile Exchange (CME) are shown in Figure 27–3B. A put position in one foreign currency futures contract with expiration in November 1997 and exercise price of $1.61/£ would have cost the bank a premium of $.0032 per pound on October 24, 1997.[8] Since each futures option contract is £62,500 in size, the cost would have been $200 per contract. If we ignore the question of basis risk—that is, the imperfect correlation between the dollar/pound exchange rate in the spot and options on futures markets—the optimal number of futures options purchased would be

---

[7] That is, on the Philadelphia exchange, no put option on the pound was available at $1.60/£1. The result was the put option with the lower strike price of $1.58/£1.

[8] No put option on futures was available with a strike price of $1.60. Thus, the put contract with the strike price of $1.61 was the nearest available.

PHILADELPHIA OPTIONS
Friday, October 24, 1997

	Calls Vol. Last	Puts Vol. Last			Calls Vol. Last	Puts Vol. Last
ADollr		69.40	**6,250,000 J. Yen -100ths of a cent per unit.**			
50,000 Australian Dollar EOM-cents per un			80½	Dec	....	400 0.58
73½ Oct	40 0.06	....	81½	Nov	....	10 0.52
Australian Dollar		69.40	81½	Dec	....	194 1.05
50,000 Australian Dollars-cents per unit.			82	Dec	....	350 1.18
70 Mar	....	10 1.20	82	Mar	....	37 1.80
British Pound		163.39	83	Dec	2 1.42	....
31,250 British Pounds-cents per unit.			84	Nov	2 0.42	....
158 Nov	....	10 0.20	84	Dec	3 0.88	....
Canadian Dollar		71.81	94	Dec	6 0.05	....
50,000 Canadian Dollars-cents per unit.			**6,250,000 J. Yen-European Style.**			
73½ Dec	....	6 1.60	82	Nov	....	20 0.60
German Mark		56.20	**Swiss Franc**			68.07
62,500 German Mark EOM-European style.			62,500 Swiss Francs EOM-cents per unit.			
56 Oct	....	300 0.20	68	Oct	....	100 0.23
62,500 German Marks EOM-European style.			62,500 Swiss Francs-European Style.			
56½ Oct	300 0.25	....	66	Dec	10 2.23	....
62,500 German Marks-European Style.			67	Nov	66 1.16	....
56 Dec	....	16 0.60	68	Nov	20 0.90	....
62,500 German Marks-cents per unit.			68	Dec	10 1.00	....
54 Mar	5 2.90	....	68½	Dec	....	20 1.12
55 Dec	....	10 0.37	69	Nov	32 0.22	....
55 Mar	....	1 0.83	70	Nov	....	34 1.70
55½ Dec	....	10 0.45	71	Nov	....	48 2.89
56 Nov	....	229 0.43	71	Dec	....	5 3.12
56 Dec	....	30 0.73	72	Dec	....	5 4.00
56 Mar	....	20 1.19	62,500 Swiss Francs-cents per unit.			
57 Dec	2 0.51	5 1.16	66	Mar	....	5 0.66
58 Dec	20 0.23	....	67	Mar	....	5 1.04
Japanese Yen		82.01	68	Mar	....	2 1.55
6,250,000 J. Yen EOM-European style.			68½	Nov	....	25 1.08
82 Oct	....	20 0.28	69	Nov	....	34 1.05
6,250,000 J. Yen EOM-European style.			69	Mar	....	1 1.92
82½ Oct	80 0.50	80 0.65	Call vol 4,716		Open Int 132,287	
6,250,000 J. Yen EOM 100ths of a cent per unit.			Put vol 8,636		Open Int ... 131,826	
80½ Oct	....	400 0.12				
6,250,000 J. Yen EOM 100ths of a cent per unit.						
82 Oct	....	200 0.46				

F i g u r e **27–2B**   *Currency Put Options, October 24, 1997*

$$\frac{£100,000,000}{£62,500} = 1,600 \text{ contracts}$$

with a total premium cost of $320,000.

CURRENCY

JAPANESE YEN (CME)
12,500,000 yen; cents per 100 yen

Strike Price	Calls-Settle Nov	Dec	Jan	Puts-Settle Nov	Dec	Jan
8150	....	....	....	0.36	0.86	....
8200	1.16	1.70	....	0.51	1.05	1.12
8250	0.86	1.42	....	0.71	1.27	....
8300	0.62	1.17	....	0.97	1.52	1.48
8350	0.44	0.96	....	1.29	1.80	....
8400	0.31	0.78	....	1.66	2.12	1.96

Est vol 6,166 Th 6,373 calls 2,578 puts
Op int Thur 61,249 calls 46,962 puts

DEUTSCHEMARK (CME)
125,000 marks; cents per mark

Strike Price	Calls-Settle Nov	Dec	Jan	Puts-Settle Nov	Dec	Jan
5550	1.05	1.29	....	0.15	0.40	0.56
5600	0.69	0.96	....	0.29	0.56	0.73
5650	0.41	0.70	....	0.51	0.80	....
5700	0.23	0.49	0.89	0.83	1.09	....
5750	0.12	0.34	0.70	1.22	1.43	1.51
5800	0.07	0.23	....	....	1.82	....

Est vol 2,580 Th 5,524 calls 2,797 puts
Op int Thur 39,055 calls 50,636 puts

CANADIAN DOLLAR (CME)
100,000 Can.$, cents per Can.$

Strike Price	Calls-Settle Nov	Dec	Jan	Puts-Settle Nov	Dec	Jan
7100	....	1.06	....	0.03	0.08	....
7150	....	0.66	....	0.08	0.17	....
7200	....	0.37	....	0.24	0.38	....
7250	0.08	0.19	....	0.59	0.70	....
7300	0.03	0.09	....	1.04	1.09	....
7350	0.02	0.04	....	1.53	1.54	....

Est vol 716 Th 1,504 calls 297 puts
Op int Thur 13,695 calls 7,027 puts

BRITISH POUND (CME)
62,500 pounds; cents per pound

Strike Price	Calls-Settle Nov	Dec	Jan	Puts-Settle Nov	Dec	Jan
16100	2.36	3.00	....	0.32	0.96	1.82
16200	1.64	2.36	2.76	0.60	1.32	....
16300	1.06	1.82	2.28	1.02	1.78	....
16400	0.64	1.38	1.86	1.60	....	....
16500	0.38	1.00	1.50	2.34	....	....
16600	0.20	0.72	1.20	....	3.66	....

Est vol 1,048 Th 367 calls 306 puts
Op int Thur 26,946 calls 24,903 puts

SWISS FRANC (CME)
125,000 francs; cents per franc

Strike Price	Calls-Settle Nov	Dec	Jan	Puts-Settle Nov	Dec	Jan
6750	1.26	1.56	2.28	0.19	0.50	0.61
6800	0.88	1.24	....	0.31	0.67	....
6850	0.57	0.96	....	0.50	0.89	....
6900	0.36	0.74	....	0.79	1.17	....
6950	0.21	0.56	....	1.14	1.48	....
7000	0.13	0.41	....	1.56	1.83	....

Est vol 958 Th 1,807 calls 395 puts
Op int Thur 19,854 calls 15,547 puts

BRAZILIAN REAL (CME)
100,000 Braz. reals; $ per reals

Strike Price	Calls-Settle Nov	Dec	Jan	Puts-Settle Nov	Dec	Jan
895	....	....	....	....	....	....
900	....	....	....	0.01	....	....
905	....	....	....	....	....	....
910	....	....	....	....	....	....
915	....	....	....	....	....	....
920	....	....	....	....	....	....

Est vol 6,645 Th 0 calls 2,900 puts
Op int Thur 0 calls 26,330 puts

MEXICAN PESO (CME)
500,000 new Mex. pesos; $ per MP

Strike Price	Calls-Settle Nov	Dec	Jan	Puts-Settle Nov	Dec	Jan
1212	....	....	....	....	0.35	....
1225	....	2.27	....	0.15	0.65	....
1238	....	....	....	....	1.02	....
1250	....	0.70	....	....	1.60	5.00
1262	....	0.35	....	....	2.45	....
1275	....	0.17	....	....	3.52	....

Est vol 1,656 Th 669 calls 1,779 puts
Op int Thur 18,568 calls 16,445 puts

F i g u r e   **27–3B**   *Futures Options on Currencies, October 24, 1997*

Chapter Twenty-eight

Sovereign Risk

I n the 1970s, commercial banks in the United States and other countries rapidly expanded their loans to Eastern bloc, Latin American, and other less-developed countries (LDCs). This was largely to meet their demand for funds beyond those provided by the World Bank and the International Monetary Fund (IMF) to aid their development and to allow commercial banks to recycle petrodollar funds from huge dollar holders such as Saudi Arabia. In many cases, loans appear to have been made with little judgment regarding the credit quality of the sovereign country in which the borrower resided or whether that body was a government-sponsored organization (such as Pemex) or a private corporation.

The debt repayment problems of Poland and other Eastern bloc countries at the beginning of the 1980s and the **debt moratoria** announced by the Mexican and Brazilian governments in the fall of 1982 had a major and long-lasting impact on commercial banks' balance sheets and profits. Indeed, at the time of the 1982 moratoria, the 10 largest U.S. money center banks had overall sovereign risk exposure of $56 billion, 80 percent of which was to Latin America. As a result, large banks such as Citicorp had to make provisions to their **loan loss reserves** because they had to write down the value of these loans in their

debt moratoria

Delay in repaying interest and/or principal on debt.

loan loss reserves

Special reserves created on the balance sheet against which to write off bad loans.

Chapter Outline

LATIN AMERICA	
Mexico	−22.2%
Peru	−19.2
Brazil	−10.2
Chile	−6.9
Argentina	−5.8
Venezuela	−4.8

EUROPE	
Hungary	−21.1
Poland	−13.0
Turkey	−12.9
Czech Republic	−7.0

ASIA	
Pakistan	−13.4%
Philippines	−13.2
China	−12.5
India	−12.2
South Korea	−11.4
Taiwan	−11.3
Hong Kong	−10.3
Thailand	−10.3
Malaysia	−9.2
Indonesia	−8.3
Singapore	−6.5
Sri Lanka	−2.3

Figure 28–1   *Ripple Effects of the Peso*

A drop in investor confidence brought on by the sudden fall of the value of the Mexican peso has hurt the stock markets of many emerging countries. This is the change in leading market indexes of some of those countries in January 1995.

SOURCE: *New York Times*, February 1, 1995, p. C1. Copyright © 1995 by The New York Times Company. Reprinted by permission.

portfolios. For example, in 1987, more than 20 U.S. banks announced major additions to their loan loss reserves, with Citicorp alone setting aside $3 billion.

Notwithstanding their experience with LDC lending a decade earlier, U.S. FIs and others began again to invest considerable amounts in these emerging market countries in the late 1980s to early 1990s. Rather than making loans, however, these investments were concentrated in debt and equity claims.

With rising trade deficits and declining foreign exchange reserves as the result of an overvalued peso, Mexico devalued the peso on December 20, 1994.[1] The Mexican devaluation—as with the Mexican loan moratorium 12 years earlier—had devastating short-term repercussions on the Mexican capital market as well as on other emerging markets. Figure 28–1

---

[1] Mexico's foreign exchange reserves fell from $25 billion at the end of 1993 to $6 billion at the end of 1994.

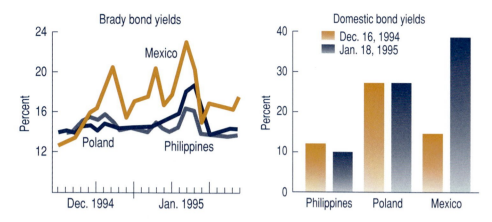

Figure **28–2** *Taking Fright; Yields on Brady versus Domestic Bonds*

SOURCES: J. P. Morgan; Citibank; Barings Securities; and "Taking Fright," *The Economist,* January 21, 1995, p. 78. © 1995 The Economist Newspaper Group, Inc. Reprinted with permission. Further reproduction prohibited.

illustrates the decline in Mexican and other emerging market country share prices in January 1995, and Figure 28–2 illustrates the rise in relevant bond yields as investors and FIs sought to withdraw funds from these countries after the Mexican devaluation.[2] This "run" on emerging market debt and equity markets was ameliorated only when the Clinton administration put together an international aid package for Mexico amounting to some $50 billion. Specifically, the United States provided loan guarantees, over three to five years, that would amount to as much as $20 billion to help restructure Mexican debt. The IMF and the Bank for International Settlements also provided loans of $17.8 billion and $10 billion, respectively. Mexican oil revenues were promised as collateral for the U.S. financial guarantees.[3]

Emerging markets in Asia faltered in 1997 when an economic and financial crisis in Thailand, a relatively small country (in terms of financial markets), produced worldwide reactions. In early July, the devaluation of the Thai baht resulted in contagious devaluations of currencies throughout Southeast Asia, including those of Indonesia, Singapore, Malaysia, and eventually South Korea (see Chapter 27, Figure 1). Hong Kong's pegging of currency to the U.S. dollar forced its monetary authority to take precautionary action by increasing interest rates

---

[2] Foreign investors held approximately 70 percent of Mexico's outstanding peso-denominated bonds (cetes) and 80 percent of its dollar-denominated bonds (tesobonos). Interestingly, domestic (Mexican) investors appear to have been the first to "run."

[3] See The *New York Times*, February 1, 1995, p. 1.

and to use China's foreign currency reserves to stabilize the Hong Kong dollar. In these countries, stock market indexes fell dramatically as well.

As Asian currencies collapsed, financial institutions in countries such as Japan and Hong Kong failed or were forced to merge or restructure. Investment bank powerhouses such as Yamaichi Securities, Japan's fourth largest securities firm, and Peregrine Investment Holding, Ltd., one of Hong Kong's largest investment banks, failed as currency values fell. Commercial banks in Japan and Hong Kong that had lent heavily to other Southeast Asian countries failed in record numbers as well. Estimates of problem loans held by Japanese banks totaled $577.5 billion in September 1997, compared with $210 billion in early August 1997.[4]

The large number of bank failures led to runs on the rumored failing banks. For example, rumors that the International Bank of Asia (IBA) was in trouble led crowds to descend on the bank to withdraw their deposit balances. Depositor withdrawals from IBA were, in fact, all paid and the bank remained in business. The run mentality, however, spilled over to the non-financial services sectors. For example, hints that Saint Honore Cake Shops, owned by a bankrupt Japanese company, was about to close sent crowds stampeding to cash in the gift certificates that the cake shops had sold. "Cakes leaped from shelves (and shelves collapsed), bakers worked overtime . . . and Saint Honore carried on."[5] The wealth effect of this financial and economic collapse is that net capital inflows from overseas to the most severely affected countries (Indonesia, Malaysia, Philippines, South Korea, and Thailand) have fallen dramatically, from $93 billion in 1996 to a $12 billion outflow in 1997 and a similar outflow forecasted for 1998.[6]

Possibly as a reaction to events (losses) experienced with the Latin American countries in the 1980s or to improved sovereign risk assessment techniques (see later discussion), U.S. FIs held their exposure in Asia (in the mid- and late 1990s) to approximately one-third of the investment made by Japanese and European banks (see Figure 28–3). Concerns regarding possible effects of the Asian crisis on the U.S. economy and FIs are still serious, however; see Contemporary Perspectives Box 28–1. Although most U.S. FIs limited their involvement to originating loans on debt securities to add fees and then sold them off, protecting themselves from the possibility of sudden economic swings,

---

[4] See "Japan Plans Crackdown on Bad Loans," The *Wall Street Journal*, December 26, 1997, p. A5.
[5] See "In Hong Kong, Runs on Banks and Cakes," The *New York Times*, December 19, 1997, p. D3.
[6] See "Economic Indicators," *The Economist*, February 7, 1998, p. 110.

Source: Bank for International Settlements

F i g u r e **28–3**   *Foreign Loans Outstanding in Asia in 1997*

Contemporary Perspectives 28–1

Asia Turmoil

Asian Turmoil

Financial crisis has spread from Thailand throughout south-east Asia and then from south-east to north-east Asia and Latin America. It has moved to Japan and even threatens the US and Europe. As the tropical storm has turned into a hurricane, it is agitating policymakers in Washington. The questions confronting them are how worried to be and what to do.

In yesterday's testimony to the banking and financial services committee of the US house of representatives, Alan Greenspan, chairman of the Federal Reserve, was his usual balanced self. "The financial disturbances that have afflicted a number [of] currencies in Asia do not at this point . . . threaten prosperity in this country, but we need to work closely with their leaders and the international finance community to assure their situations stabilize."

As Mr. Greenspan notes, only 4 percent of US exports go to Thailand,

the Philippines, Indonesia, and Malaysia. But Hong Kong has been tested and Korea is under severe pressure. A big worry is the risk to the fragile Japanese economy. Japan, Hong Kong, Korea, Singapore, and Taiwan take almost a quarter of US exports.

Turmoil is not restricted to Asia but has spread to Latin America, notably Brazil, and affected the stock markets of Europe and the US. In a time of financial panic, any economic weakness becomes a reason to sell. The attempt to flee then aggravates the fragility the frightened are trying to escape. What is, for the moment, no great danger to the world economy, however painful to affected countries, could become far worse. What needs to be done to stop that from happening?

Robert Rubin, a worried US Treasury secretary, has written a letter to his Japanese counterpart urging action on the banking crisis.

Larry Summers, his deputy, remarked earlier this month, in the same context: "International experience in dealing with the consequences of financial institutions' mistakes . . . has taught the benefits of acting . . . as quickly and openly as possible."

Mr. Greenspan provides a broader view: "Companies should be allowed to default, private investors should take their losses and government policies should be directed towards laying the macroeconomic and structural foundations for renewed expansion." This approach must be right. But the panic must also be halted. That means offering those governments able to undertake serious policy reform the funds needed to tide them over. In most places that ought to work. But nobody, except for the Japanese, can save Japan.

SOURCE: *The Financial Times Limited,* November 14, 1997, p. 15. Reprinted with permission of Financial Times.

Contemporary Perspectives 28–2

JP Morgan Warns of Global Blow to Earnings

J.P. Morgan, the U.S. bank, yesterday warned that its fourth quarter earnings would be lower than expected, adding fuel to growing fears about the impact of weak Asian markets on the profits of internationally active banks and industrial companies. The news—following indications from Oracle, the U.S. software company, and Corning, the U.S. manufacturer, that their profits were being affected by the weak Asian economies—contributed to a 100-point slide in the Dow Jones Industrial Average in morning trading.

J.P. Morgan said its earnings in October and November were "adversely affected by unsettled market conditions globally, resulting in lower levels of client activity and lower trading revenues." An official declined to comment on which areas of trading had been affected. A month ago, J.P. Morgan said it had "nothing material to report" on October trading results. J.P. Morgan's trading revenues typically account for around a quarter of total revenues.

Ron Mandle, bank analyst at Sanford C. Bernstein, said that following the sharp falls in Asian bond and equity markets in October, banks had been further hurt by weak trading volume in emerging markets. "Client interest in emerging market stocks and bonds has really tailed off" in the fourth quarter, he said.

Last month, Chase Manhattan announced a trading loss of about $160 million in October as a result of the sharp correction in Asian and other markets. Mr. Mandle said he expected fourth quarter earnings from trading at Citicorp and Bankers Trust to be more than 40 percent lower than in the third quarter.

SOURCE: Tracy Corrigan, The *Financial Times,* December 11, 1997, p. 23. Reprinted with permission of Financial Times.

not all U.S. FIs had limited exposure. For example, in November 1997, Chase Manhattan Corp. announced that losses from emerging market securities holdings would be in the $150 million to $200 million range. This was followed by a similar announcement of poor earnings by J.P. Morgan (see Contemporary Perspectives Box 28–2).

These experiences confirmed the importance of assessing the country or sovereign risk of a borrowing country before making lending or other investment decisions such as buying foreign bonds or equities. This chapter first defines *sovereign* or *country risk*. It then discusses measures of country risk FI managers can use as screening devices before making loans or other investment decisions. Finally, the chapter discusses the ways that banks have reacted to sovereign debt problems.

CREDIT RISK VERSUS SOVEREIGN RISK

rescheduling

Changing the contractual terms of the loan such as its maturity and interest payments.

To understand the difference between the sovereign risk and the credit risk on a loan or a bond, consider what happens to a domestic firm that refuses to repay, or is unable to repay, its loans. The lender would probably seek to work out the loan with the borrower by **rescheduling** its promised interest and principal payments on the loan into the future. Ultimately, continued inability or unwillingness to pay would likely result in bankruptcy proceedings and eventual liquidation of the firm's assets. Consider next a dollar loan made by a U.S. bank to a private Mexican corporation. Suppose that this first-class corporation has always maintained its debt repayments in the past; however, the Mexican economy and Mexican government's dollar reserve position are in bad shape. As a result, the Mexican government refuses to allow any further debt repayment to be made in dollars to outside creditors. This puts the Mexican borrower automatically into default even though, when viewed on its own, the company is a good credit risk. The Mexican government's decision is a *sovereign* or *country risk event* in large part independent of the credit standing of the individual loan to the borrower. In addition, unlike the situation in the United States, where the lender might seek a legal remedy in the local bankruptcy courts, there is no international bankruptcy court to which the lender can take the Mexican government. That is, the lenders' legal remedies to offset a sovereign country's default or moratoria decisions are very limited. For example, lenders can and have sought legal remedies in U.S. courts, but such decisions pertain only to Mexican government or Mexican corporate assets held in the United States itself.

This situation suggests that making a lending decision to a party residing in a foreign country is a *two-step* decision. First, a lender must assess the borrower's underlying *credit quality*, as it would do for a normal domestic loan, including setting an appropriate credit risk premium or credit limit (see Chapter 10). Second, the lender must assess the *sovereign risk quality* of the country in which the borrower resides. Should the credit risk or quality of the borrower be assessed as good but the sovereign risk be assessed as bad, the lender should not make the loan. When making international lending or foreign bond investment decisions, an FI manager should consider sovereign risk above private credit risk.

A good deal of misunderstanding exists regarding the nature of a sovereign risk event. In general, a sovereign country's (negative) decisions on its debt obligations or the obligations of its public and private organizations may take two forms, repudiation and rescheduling.

Debt Repudiation

repudiation

Outright cancellation of all current and future debt obligations by a borrower.

Repudiation is an outright cancellation of all current and future foreign debt and equity obligations. Since World War II, only China (1949), Cuba (1961), and North Korea (1964) have followed this course.[7] Repudiations on debt obligations were far more common before World War II.

Debt Rescheduling

Rescheduling has been the most common form of sovereign risk event. Specifically, a country declares a moratorium or delay on its current and future debt obligations and then seeks to ease credit terms by rescheduling the contractual terms such as debt maturity or interest rates. Such delays may relate to the principal and/or the interest on the debt.

Concept Questions

1. What is the difference between credit risk and sovereign risk?
2. In deciding to lend to a party residing in a foreign country, what two considerations must an FI weigh?
3. What is the difference between debt repudiation and debt rescheduling?

---

[7] With respect to equity, repudiation can include *direct nationalization* of private sector assets.

COUNTRY RISK
EVALUATION

In evaluating sovereign risk, an FI can use methods varying from the highly quantitative to the very qualitative. Moreover, as in domestic credit analysis, an FI may rely on outside evaluation services or develop its own internal evaluation models. Of course, to make a final assessment, many models and sources may be used together because different measures of country risk are not mutually exclusive.

The discussion begins with the country risk assessment services available to outside investors and FIs: the *Euromoney Index* and the *Institutional Investor Index*. It then discusses ways in which an FI manager might make internal risk assessments regarding sovereign risk.

Outside Evaluation Models

Euromoney Index.   When originally published in 1979, the *Euromoney Index* was based on the spread in the Euromarket of the required interest rate on that country's debt over the London interbank offered rate (**LIBOR**), adjusted for the volume and maturity of the issue. More recently, this has been replaced by an index based on a large number of economic and political factors weighted subjectively according to their perceived relative importance in determining country risk problems.

LIBOR

The London interbank offered rate, the rate charged on prime interbank loans in the Eurodollar market.

The Economist Intelligence Unit.   A sister company to *The Economist*, The Economist Intelligence Unit (EIU) rates country risk by combined economic and political risk on a 100 (maximum)-point scale. The higher the number, the worse the sovereign risk rating of the country. The EIU country risk ratings reported in 1997 are presented in Table 28–1.

The Institutional Investor Index.   Normally published twice a year, this index is based on surveys of the loan officers of major multinational banks. These officers give subjective scores regarding the credit quality of given countries. Originally, the score was based on 10, but since 1980, it has been based on 100, with a score of 0 indicating certainty of default and 100 no possibility of default. The *Institutional Investor* then weights the scores received from the officers surveyed by the exposure of each bank to the country in question. For the *Institutional Investor's* country credit ratings as of March 1998, see Table 28–2.

Internal Evaluation Models

Statistical Models.   By far, the most common approach to evaluating sovereign country risk has been to develop risk-scoring models based on key economic ratios for each country similar to the domestic credit risk-scoring models discussed in Chapter 10.

An FI analyst begins by selecting a set of macro- and microeconomic variables and ratios that might be important in explaining a country's probability of rescheduling. Then the analyst uses past data on rescheduling and nonrescheduling countries to see which variables best discriminate between those countries that rescheduled their debt and those that did not. This helps the analyst identify a set of key variables that best explain rescheduling and a group of weights that indicate the relative importance of these variables. Domestic credit risk analysis can employ discriminant analysis to calculate a Z-score rating of the probability of corporate bankruptcy. Similarly, in sovereign risk analysis, we can develop a Z-score to measure the probability that a country will reschedule (see Chapter 10 for discussion of the Z-score model).

Table **28-1**

THE ECONOMIST INTELLIGENCE UNIT COUNTRY RISK RATINGS

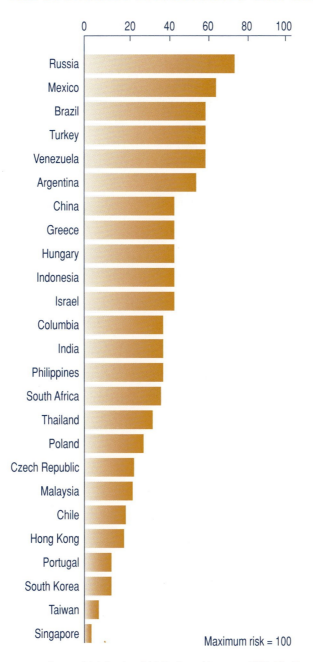

Maximum risk = 100

Table 28-2

INSTITUTIONAL INVESTOR'S 1998 COUNTRY CREDIT RATINGS

March 1998	September 1997	Country	Institutional Investor Credit Rating	Six-Month Change	One-Year Change
1*	1	Switzerland	92.6	0.4	0.1
2*	2	United States	92.6	0.5	1.4
3	4	Germany	92.3	1.0	0.8
4	3	Japan	90.8	−0.7	−0.5
5	5	Netherlands	90.5	−0.1	0.8
6*	6	France	89.3	0.9	1.1
7*	7	United Kingdom	89.3	0.9	0.9
8	8	Luxembourg	88.3	0.4	1.0
9	9	Austria	87.4	0.9	2.8
10	10	Norway	87.3	1.5	2.6
11	12	Denmark	83.4	0.8	1.8
12	13	Canada	83.1	1.0	2.3
13	11	Singapore	82.9	−1.3	−1.0
14	14	Belgium	82.0	0.7	1.3
15	15	Ireland	78.0	1.3	2.3
16	17	Finland	77.9	1.3	3.0
17	19	Spain	77.3	1.8	2.6
18	18	Sweden	77.1	0.9	2.8
19	20	Italy	76.6	1.2	2.3
20	16	Taiwan	75.5	−1.2	−1.6
21	21	Australia	73.7	0.4	1.5
22	22	New Zealand	73.4	0.3	1.7
23	23	Portugal	72.7	1.5	3.1
24	25	Malaysia	64.5	−2.2	−3.0
25	24	South Korea	64.4	−5.3	−7.0
26	30	Iceland	63.9	2.4	3.8
27	27	Chile	63.2	−0.3	1.2
28	26	Hong Kong	62.9	−1.0	−2.0
29	29	Malta	62.1	−0.6	−1.3
30	31	United Arab Emirates	61.4	1.3	0.6
31	28	Czech Republic	60.7	−2.4	−2.1
32	33	China	57.6	−0.2	−0.4
33	34	Cyprus	57.2	0.0	0.4
34	35	Kuwait	55.8	0.8	1.6
35	37	Slovenia	55.5	1.5	3.4
36	36	Saudi Arabia	55.4	0.6	1.7
37	38	Greece	53.7	0.7	2.4
38	39	Oman	53.2	0.2	0.4
39	41	Qatar	53.1	0.9	0.7
40	40	Israel	52.5	−0.4	0.3
41	32	Thailand	52.3	−7.6	−8.8
42	46	Hungary	52.2	2.5	4.6
43*	44	Botswana	51.9	0.7	2.4
44*	45	Poland	51.9	1.7	4.0
45	42	Mauritius	51.8	−0.1	0.9
46	43	Indonesia	49.9	−1.9	−1.7

47	47	Bahrain	49.8	0.1	0.1
48	48	Tunisia	48.0	0.1	1.7
49	49	Colombia	46.9	−0.3	−0.8
50*	51	South Africa	46.5	0.1	0.5
51*	50	India	46.5	−0.4	0.2
52	54	Mexico	45.2	1.7	2.6
53	55	Uruguay	44.6	1.2	2.9
54	56	Trinidad & Tobago	43.5	0.6	3.8
55	53	Philippines	43.3	−1.0	1.0
56	52	Slovakia	43.1	−1.7	−0.8
57	57	Barbados	42.3	−0.6	0.4
58	58	Argentina	41.6	0.3	1.7
59	59	Morocco	41.5	0.6	1.8
60	60	Egypt	41.3	1.6	4.6
61	63	Estonia	38.9	2.0	5.3
62	61	Brazil	38.7	−0.8	−0.1
63	62	Turkey	37.8	−0.8	−3.0
64	—	Namibia	36.4	—	—
65	65	Venezuela	36.1	0.7	3.0
66	71	Croatia	36.0	2.4	6.7
67	64	Costa Rica	35.8	−0.2	1.3
68	66	Jordan	35.5	0.6	1.7
69	70	Panama	34.9	1.3	4.7
70	67	Romania	34.5	0.4	1.8
71	74	Latvia	34.0	1.4	4.9
72*	78	Sri Lanka	33.6	1.5	0.4
73*	68	Zimbabwe	33.6	−0.2	1.3
74	69	Peru	33.5	−0.2	1.5
75	77	Papua New Guinea	33.2	0.9	0.7
76	73	Swaziland	33.1	−0.2	1.3
77	80	Lithuania	32.9	1.8	5.5
78	72	Paraguay	32.8	−0.7	0.8
79	75	Vietnam	32.7	0.2	0.2
80	76	Lebanon	32.5	0.1	1.0
81	79	Ghana	31.4	−0.1	0.8
82	88	Russia	31.2	3.7	7.7
83	81	Jamaica	30.1	0.4	2.6
84	86	El Salvador	29.0	1.5	5.1
85	85	Libya	28.3	0.5	−0.4
86	82	Seychelles	28.2	−1.3	0.9
87	86	Iran	28.1	0.6	2.0
88	89	Pakistan	27.5	0.3	−0.2
89	84	Bangladesh	27.2	−1.3	−0.2
90	90	Guatemala	27.0	0.2	2.9
91*	83	Kenya	26.7	−1.9	−1.2
92*	91	Ecuador	26.7	0.4	0.1
93	92	Bolivia	26.5	0.3	1.6
94	98	Kazakhstan	26.4	2.4	5.5
95	94	Dominican Republic	25.8	1.0	3.3
96	93	Nepal	25.5	−0.4	0.3
97	96	Algeria	25.1	0.6	1.9
98†	95	Gabon	24.7	0.2	0.6
	97	Syria	24.7	0.4	−0.3

continued

Table **28-2**

INSTITUTIONAL INVESTOR'S 1998 COUNTRY CREDIT RATINGS (CONTINUED)

March 1998	September 1997	Country	Institutional Investor Credit Rating	Six-Month Change	One-Year Change
100	99	Bulgaria	22.9	0.7	0.4
101	102	Myanmar	21.7	0.7	0.4
102	100	Senegal	21.6	0.4	1.8
103	104	Cote d'Ivoire	21.4	1.3	2.5
104	103	Uganda	21.1	1.1	3.5
105	105	Ukraine	20.5	0.7	2.9
106*	106	Burkina Faso	20.1	0.4	2.4
107*	101	Malawi	20.1	−0.9	0.3
108	108	Honduras	19.8	0.9	1.5
109	107	Uzbekistan	19.6	0.1	2.5
110	110	Tanzania	19.3	0.6	1.2
111	109	Cameroon	18.5	−0.3	0.4
112*	113	Ethiopia	17.5	0.4	1.5
113*	115	Zambia	17.5	1.5	1.4
114	114	Togo	17.4	0.5	0.7
115*	111	Benin	17.3	−0.1	1.3
116*	117	Grenada	17.3	2.3	4.4
117	111	Mali	16.7	−0.7	0.0
118	118	Guinea	16.4	1.5	2.6
119	119	Mozambique	16.1	1.5	1.2
120	116	Nigeria	15.2	−0.1	0.4
121	124	Nicaragua	13.5	0.0	1.6
122	121	Belarus	12.9	−1.3	−1.6
123	122	Haiti	12.7	−1.3	1.3
124	123	Angola	12.5	−1.1	0.0
125	126	Cuba	12.2	0.9	1.4
126	125	Albania	11.1	−0.5	−3.2
127	120	Congo Republic	10.7	−3.5	−3.3
128	128	Georgia	10.6	1.1	1.1
129	127	Yugoslavia	10.2	0.0	0.3
130	129	Sudan	7.6	−1.5	−2.8
131	130	Iraq	7.4	−0.5	−0.9
132	131	Liberia	7.0	−0.4	0.1
133	132	Congo (formerly Zaire)	6.8	−0.4	−1.3
134	134	Afghanistan	6.1	−0.2	−0.2
135	133	Sierra Leone	5.7	−0.8	−0.9
136	135	North Korea	5.1	0.4	−0.7
		Global average rating	**41.2**	**0.2**	**1.1**

*Order determined by actual results before rounding.

†Actual tie.

SOURCE: *Institutional Investor,* March 1998, p. 164. This copyrighted material is reprinted with the permission of Institutional Investor, a publication of Institutional Investor, Inc., 488 Madison Avenue, New York, NY 10022.

Table **28–3**

ACTUAL DEBT SERVICE RATIOS, 1990 AND 1995

Interest and principal paid as percentage of exports of goods and services

SOURCES: World Bank; and *The Economist,* April 6, 1995, p. 110. © 1995 The Economist Newspaper Group, Inc. Reprinted with permission. Further reproduction prohibited.

The first stage of this country risk analysis (CRA) is to pick a set of variables that may be important in explaining rescheduling probabilities. In many cases, analysts select more than 40 variables. Here we identify the variables most commonly included in sovereign risk assessment models.

The Debt Service Ratio (DSR)

$$\text{DSR} = \frac{\text{Interest plus amortization on debt}}{\text{Exports}}$$

An LDC's exports are its primary way to generate dollars and other hard currencies. The larger the debt repayments in hard currencies are in relation to export revenues, the greater the probability that the country will have to reschedule its debt. Thus, there should be a *positive* relationship between the size of the **debt service ratio** and the probability of rescheduling. Table 28–3 shows the scheduled debt service ratios of various geographic regions versus the actual amount that they paid as a percentage of export income (i.e., *actual* debt service ratios). For example, Latin American countries' debt was 30 percent of gross domestic product in 1995, and debt service costs exceeded exports (the DSR) by 254 percent.

debt service ratio

The ratio of a country's interest and amortization obligations to the value of its exports.

The Import Ratio (IR)

$$IR = \frac{\text{Total imports}}{\text{Total foreign exchange reserves}}$$

Many LDCs must import manufactured goods since their inadequate infrastructures prohibit producing them. In times of famine, even food becomes a vital import. To pay for imports, the LDC must run down its stock of hard currencies, its foreign exchange reserves. The greater its need for imports—especially vital imports—the more quickly a country can be expected to deplete its foreign exchange reserves. Since the first use of reserves is to buy vital imports, the larger the ratio of imports to foreign exchange reserves, the higher the probability that the LDC will have to reschedule its debt repayments. This is so because these countries generally view repaying foreign debtholders as being less important than supplying vital goods to the domestic population. Thus, the **import ratio** and the probability of rescheduling should be *positively* related.

import ratio

The ratio of a country's imports to its total foreign currency reserves.

Investment Ratio (INVR)

$$INVR = \frac{\text{Real investment}}{\text{GNP}}$$

investment ratio

The ratio of a country's real investment to its GNP.

The **investment ratio** measures the degree to which a country is allocating resources to real investment in factories, machines, and so on, rather than to consumption. The higher this ratio is, the more productive the economy should be in the future and the lower the probability that the country would need to reschedule its debt; this implies a *negative* relationship between INVR and the probability of rescheduling. An opposing view is that a higher investment ratio allows an LDC to build up its investment infrastructure. The higher ratio puts it in a stronger bargaining position with external creditors since the LDC would rely less on funds in the future and would be less scared about future threats of credit rationing by FIs should it request a rescheduling. This view argues for a *positive* relationship between the investment ratio and the probability of rescheduling, especially if the LDC invests heavily in import-competing industries.

Variance of Export Revenue (VAREX)

$$VAREX = \sigma^2_{ER}$$

An LDC's export revenues may be highly variable due to two risk factors. *Quantity risk* means that the production of the raw commodities that the LDC sells abroad—for example, coffee or sugar—is subject to periodic gluts and shortages. *Price risk* means that the international dollar prices at which the LDC can sell its exportable commodities are subject to high volatility as world demand and supply for a commodity such as copper vary. The more volatile an LDC's export earnings, the less certain creditors can be that at any time in the future it will be able to meet its repayment commitments. That is, there should be a *positive* relationship between σ^2_{ER} and the probability of rescheduling.

Domestic Money Supply Growth (MG)

$$MG = \frac{\Delta M}{M}$$

The faster the domestic growth rate of an LDC's money supply ($\Delta M/M$), the higher the domestic inflation rate and the weaker that country's currency becomes in domestic and international markets.[8] When a country's currency loses credibility as a medium of exchange, real output is often adversely impacted, and the country must rely increasingly on hard currencies for both domestic and international payments. These inflation, output, and payment effects suggest a *positive* relationship between domestic money supply growth and the probability of rescheduling.

We can summarize the expected relationships among these five key economic variables and the probability of rescheduling (P) for any country as

$$P = f(\text{DSR, IR, INVR, VAREX, MG} \ldots)$$
$$+ \quad + \quad + \text{ or } - \quad + \quad \quad +$$

After selecting the key variables, the FI manager normally places countries into two groups or populations:

$$P_1 = \text{bad (reschedulers)}$$
$$P_2 = \text{good (nonreschedulers)}$$

Then the manager uses a statistical methodology such as discriminant analysis (see Chapter 10) to identify which of these variables best discriminates between the population of rescheduling borrowers and that of nonrescheduling borrowers. Once the key variables and their relative importance or weights have been identified, the discriminant function can classify as good or bad current sovereign loans or sovereign loan applicants using currently observed values for the DSR, IR, and so on. Again, the methodology is very similar to the credit-scoring models discussed in Chapter 10.

EXAMPLE 28-1

Calculation of Probability of Rescheduling

Suppose that for a particular country (j) the values of the key variables described and the weight the FI manager assigns to each are as follows:

	Country j Value	**Weight (must sum to 1)**
DSR	1.75	.10
IR	1.50	.20
INVR	1.10	.20
VAREX (σ)	.24	.30
MG	.08	.20

That is, the manager had estimated a country risk credit scoring system of the form

$$Z = .1(\text{DSR}) + .2(\text{IR}) + .2(\text{INVR}) + .3(\text{VAREX}) + .2(\text{MG})$$

Plugging in values for the variables for country j results in a Z-score of 0.783.

The FI categorizes nonreschedulers as those countries with a total Z-score of .500 or less and reschedulers as those with a total Z-score of .700 or higher. Scores between .500 and .700 are not predictable in their probability of rescheduling. With a total score of .783, country j is classified as a probable rescheduler and is likely to have its loan application refused or the amount lent significantly reduced.   • • •

---

[8] The purchasing power parity theorem (PPP) argues that high relative inflation rates lead to a country's currency depreciating in value against other currencies (see Chapter 2).

Using Market Data to Measure Risk: The Secondary Market for LDC Debt

Since the mid-1980s, a secondary market for trading LDC debt has developed among large commercial and investment banks in New York and London. Indeed, trading in LDC loans often takes place in the high-yield (or junk bond) departments of the participating banks. These markets provide quoted prices for LDC loans and other debt instruments that an FI manager can use for CRA. Before we discuss how this is done, we describe the structure and development of the markets for LDC loans and related debt instruments, including the determinants of market demand and supply.

The Structure of the Market.   The secondary market in LDC debt has considerably enhanced the liquidity of LDC loans on bank and other FI balance sheets.[9] The following are the market players that sell and buy LDC loans.

Sellers
- Large FIs willing to accept write-downs of loans on their balance sheets.
- Small FIs wishing to disengage themselves from the LDC loan market.
- FIs willing to swap one country's LDC debt for another's to rearrange their portfolios of country risk exposures.

Buyers
- Wealthy investors, FIs, and corporations seeking to engage in debt-for-equity swaps or speculative investments.
- FIs seeking to rearrange their LDC balance sheets by reorienting their LDC debt concentrations.

Consider the quote sheets from Salomon Brothers in Tables 28–4 and 28–5 for May 2, 1988—a relatively early stage of LDC loan market development—and November 14, 1996, respectively. As indicated in Table 28–4, FIs such as investment banks and major commercial banks act as market makers, quoting two-way bid-ask prices for LDC debt.[10] Thus, an FI or an investor could have bought $100 of Peruvian loans from Salomon for $9 in May 1988, or a 91 percent discount from face value. In selling the same loans to Salomon, however, the investor would have received only $7 per $100, or a 93 percent discount. The bid-ask spreads for certain countries were very large in this period; for example, Sudan's $2 bid and $10 ask exemplified a serious lack of market demand for the sovereign loans of many countries.

The quote sheet of a later date in Table 28–5 suggests a large number of changes in the structure of the market. These reflect programs under which the U.S. and other banks have exchanged their dollar loans for dollar bonds issued by the relevant countries. These bonds have a much longer maturity than that promised on the original loans and a lower promised original coupon (yield) than the interest rate on the original loan. These loans for bond restructuring programs, also called *debt-for-debt swaps*, have developed under the auspices

---

[9] LDC loans exchange hands when one creditor assigns the rights to all future interest payments and principal payments to a buyer. In most early market transactions, the buyer was required to obtain the permission of the sovereign debtor country before the loan could be assigned to a new party. The reason for this was that the country might have concerns as to whether the buyer was as committed to any new money deals as part of restructuring agreements as the original lender. Most recent restructuring agreements, however, have removed the right of assignment from the borrower (the sovereign country). This has increased liquidity in the LDC loan market.

[10] Major market makers include the Dutch ING bank, Lehman, Salomon Bros., Citibank, J.P. Morgan, Bankers Trust, and Merrill Lynch.

Table **28-4**

INDICATIVE PRICES FOR LESS-DEVELOPED COUNTRY BANK LOANS

Country	Indicative Cash Prices		Swap Index		Trading Commentary
	Bid	**Offer**	**Sell**	**Buy**	
Algeria	$91.00	$93.00	5.22	6.71	Longer-dated paper resurfacing as cash substitute in swaps.
Argentina	29.00	30.00	0.66	0.67	Less volume this period; consolidation exercise slows note trades.
Bolivia	10.00	13.00	0.52	0.54	Minimal current activity.
Brazil	53.00	54.00	1.00	1.02	Rally topping out as supply catches up with auction interest.
Chile	60.50	61.50	1.19	1.22	Market firm and rising as deal calendar fills.
Colombia	67.00	68.00	1.42	1.47	Resurgence of interest as high-quality exit.
Costa Rica	13.00	16.00	0.54	0.56	Market building reserves of patience to deal with this name again.
Dominican Republic	17.00	20.00	0.57	0.59	Trading picks up at lower levels.
Ecuador	31.00	33.00	0.66	0.70	Occasional swaps surfacing.
Honduras	25.00	28.00	0.63	0.65	Viewed as expensive on a relative value basis.
Ivory Coast	30.00	33.00	0.67	0.70	Newly sighted by fee swappers.
Jamaica	33.00	36.00	0.70	0.73	Slow, but serious, inquiry continues.
Mexico	52.50	53.50	0.99	1.01	Prices continue upward drift on lower, lumpy flow.
Morocco	50.00	51.00	0.94	0.96	Fee swappers oblige sellers by jumping into the wider breach versus Latins.
Nicaragua	3.00	4.00	0.48	0.49	Avoided by the surviving court tasters.
Nigeria	28.50	30.50	0.66	0.68	Retail stonewalls dealer interest.
Panama	20.00	23.00	0.59	0.61	Recent bidding stirs the mud.
Peru	7.00	9.00	0.51	0.52	Debt-for-debt workouts and debt-for-goods deals continue.
Philippines	52.00	53.00	0.98	1.00	Prices drift higher with good interest in non-CB names.
Poland	43.25	44.50	0.83	0.85	Somewhat slower trading this period.
Romania	82.00	84.00	2.61	2.94	Bidding improves on expectations of '88 principal payments.
Senegal	40.00	45.00	0.78	0.85	Trading talk more serious.
Sudan	2.00	10.00	0.48	0.52	Still on the mat.
Turkey	97.50	99.00	18.80	47.00	CTLDs remain well bid.
Uruguay	59.50	61.50	1.16	1.22	Remains a patience-trying market.
Venezuela	55.00	55.75	1.04	1.06	Trading stronger as uptick in Chile brings swaps back into range.
Yugoslavia	45.50	47.00	0.86	0.89	More frequent trading.
Zaire	19.00	23.00	0.58	0.61	New interest develops.

SOURCE: Salomon Brothers Inc., May 2, 1988. Copyright 1997 Salomon Brothers Inc. This table and table statistics contain data from Salomon Brothers Inc. Although the information in this table was obtained from sources that Salomon Brothers believes to be reliable, Salomon does not guarantee the accuracy, and such information may be incomplete or condensed. All figures included in this table constitute Salomon's judgement as of the original publication date.

of the U.S. Treasury's Brady Plan and other international organizations such as the IMF. Once banks and other FIs have swapped loans for bonds, they can sell them on the secondary market. For example, 30-year Venezuelan discount bonds with a remaining life of 23.4 years had a bid price of $78.12 per $100 of face value.

Approximately $132 billion of LDC loans has been converted into bonds under the Brady Plan, with the top issuers being Brazil (33.3 percent), Mexico (16.8 percent), Argentina (16.5 percent), and Venezuela (12.1 percent). These bond-for-loan swap programs seek to restore LDCs' creditworthiness and thus the value of bank holdings of such debt by creating longer-term, lower fixed-interest but more liquid securities in place of shorter-term, floating-rate loans; see Table 28–6. The creation of these bonds was the result

Table 28-5
THE SECONDARY MARKET FOR LDC LOANS AND BONDS

Security & Country Sectors	Amount ($MM)	Pct. of Index	Market Value ($MM)	Pct. of Index	Bid Price*	Cash Flow		Current		Collateral Pct. of Price	Avg. life (yrs)	Final Maturity
						Yield	Spread	Yield	Coupon			
Brady Bond Index	**$135,935**	**—**	**$99,434**	**—**	**73.15**	**10.65%**	**418bp**	**8.43%**	**6.083%**	**18.9%**	**17.9**	**—**
Argentina discount	4,104	3.02	3,083	3.10	75.12	10.88	424	8.89	6.438	32.7	26.4	3/31/23
Argentina FRB	8,073	5.94	6,696	6.73	82.94	11.74	561	8.04	6.625	0.0	5.5	3/31/05
Argentina par	12,206	8.98	7,530	7.57	61.69	10.43	376	8.82	5.250	36.7	26.4	3/31/23
Argentina	**24,383**	**17.94**	**17,308**	**17.41**	**70.98**	**11.02**	**456**	**8.53**	**5.905**	**21.8**	**19.5**	
Brazil C-bond	8,040	5.91	5,592	5.62	69.55	12.67	620	10.00	8.000	0.0	12.5	4/15/14
Brazil DCB	8,500	6.25	6,112	6.15	71.91	12.27	583	9.16	6.562	0.0	11.5	4/15/12
Brazil discount Ser. Z	7,123	5.24	5,273	5.30	74.03	10.66	402	8.81	6.500	31.7	27.5	4/15/06
Brazil El bond	5,600	4.12	4,776	4.80	85.29	10.60	440	7.65	6.500	0.0	6.5	4/15/06
Brazil FLIRB	1,700	1.25	1,172	1.18	68.94	11.97	560	6.55	4.500	6.6	9.5	4/15/09
Brazil IDU	6,461	4.75	6,349	6.39	98.27	8.78	291	6.97	6.688	0.0	2.5	1/1/01
Brazil new money	2,100	1.54	1,665	1.67	79.29	11.45	514	8.31	6.562	0.0	8.5	10/14/99
Brazil par series Y	10,226	7.52	6,170	6.20	60.34	10.15	349	8.32	5.000	34.5	27.5	4/15/24
Brazil	**49,750**	**36.60**	**37,110**	**37.32**	**74.59**	**10.89**	**452**	**8.64**	**6.403**	**10.5**	**15.3**	
Bulgaria discount	1,686	1.24	877	0.88	52.02	15.33	880	13.31	6.688	43.0	27.7	7/28/24
Bulgaria FLIRB	1,488	1.10	481	0.48	32.33	20.43	1404	7.09	2.250	8.9	10.7	7/28/12
Bulgaria IAB	1,610	1.18	733	0.74	45.53	20.25	1388	15.29	6.688	0.0	11.8	7/28/11
Bulgaria	**4,784**	**3.52**	**2,091**	**2.10**	**43.71**	**18.23**	**1179**	**12.57**	**5.307**	**20.1**	**17.1**	
Ecuador discount	1,443	1.06	969	0.97	67.15	11.85	525	9.85	6.500	32.5	28.3	—
Ecuador PAR	1,913	1.41	863	0.87	45.11	10.81	415	7.43	3.250	41.9	28.3	—
Ecuador PDI	2,573	1.89	1,460	1.47	56.74	14.15	760	8.87	6.500	0.0	14.4	—
Ecuador	**5,929**	**4.36**	**3,292**	**3.31**	**55.52**	**12.60**	**600**	**10.01**	**5.451**	**20.5**	**22.3**	
Mexico discount	5,989	4.41	5,030	5.06	83.99	9.64	295	7.79	6.403	41.2	23.2	12/31/19
Mexico par	13,468	9.91	9,931	9.59	70.77	9.43	273	8.90	6.250	41.6	23.2	12/31/19
Mexico	**19,457**	**14.31**	**14,561**	**14.64**	**74.84**	**9.50**	**281**	**8.51**	**6.297**	**41.5**	**23.2**	
Nigeria par	**2,020**	**1.49**	**1,321**	**1.33**	**65.40**	**10.58**	**390**	**10.00**	**6.250**	**39.0**	**24.0**	**11/15/20**
Panama IRB	1,569	1.15	1,049	1.05	66.86	10.70	423	5.31	3.500	2.6	11.2	12/31/10
Panama PDI	1,346	0.99	1,019	1.02	75.71	10.58	395	5.37	4.000	0.0	16.2	12/31/14
Panama	**2,915**	**2.14**	**2,068**	**2.08**	**70.94**	**10.64**	**409**	**5.34**	**3.731**	**2.3**	**13.5**	
Philippine DCB	692	0.51	682	0.69	98.55	8.17	188	6.71	6.438	0.0	17.1	12/1/09
Philippine FLIRB	577	0.42	551	0.55	95.49	8.28	201	5.38	5.000	6.2	7.3	1/5/10
Philippine PCIRB	1,636	1.20	1,430	1.44	87.41	8.09	137	7.37	6.250	34.5	21.1	12/1/17
Philippine new money	715	0.53	713	0.72	99.72	7.83	173	6.73	6.562	0.0	4.7	1/5/09

Philippines	**3,620**	**2.66**	**3,375**	**3.39**	**93.23**	**8.08**	**165**	**6.78**	**6.148**	**15.6**	**13.0**	—
Poland discount	3,000	2.21	2,876	2.88	95.57	8.18	149	6.81	6.500	16.0	28.0	10/27/24
Poland par	930	0.68	505	0.51	54.30	7.93	120	5.07	2.750	28.3	28.0	10/27/24
Poland PDI	2,650	1.95	2,187	2.20	82.53	8.07	151	4.55	3.750	0.0	13.3	10/27/14
Poland RSTA	894	0.66	530	0.53	59.28	8.13	142	4.64	2.750	25.9	28.0	10/27/24
Poland	**7,474**	**5.50**	**6,089**	**6.12**	**81.47**	**8.12**	**147**	**5.66**	**4.610**	**12.2**	**22.8**	—
Venezuela DCB	5,154	3.79	4,361	4.39	84.61	11.74	555	8.07	6.625	0.0	6.1	12/18/07
Venezuela discount	1,179	0.87	921	0.93	78.12	10.26	359	8.25	6.386	39.6	23.4	3/31/20
Venezuela FLIRB	2,600	1.91	2,178	2.19	83.77	11.91	576	7.96	6.625	0.0	5.4	3/31/07
Venezuela par	6,670	4.91	4,760	4.79	71.36	9.95	327	9.49	6.750	38.8	23.4	3/31/20
Venezuela	**15,603**	**11.48**	**12,220**	**12.29**	**78.32**	**10.96**	**455**	**8.62**	**6.660**	**18.1**	**14.7**	—
Fixed Rate	**65,987**	**48.54**	**43,672**	**43.92**	**66.18**	**10.30**	**367**	**8.63**	**5.639**	**28.7**	**22.0**	—
Floating Rate	**69,948**	**51.46**	**55,763**	**56.08**	**79.72**	**10.93**	**458**	**8.27**	**6.502**	**11.2**	**14.1**	—
Latin	**118,037**	**86.83**	**86,559**	**87.75**	**73.33**	**10.75**	**429**	**8.57**	**6.203**	**19.2**	**17.7**	—
Non-Latin	**17,898**	**13.17**	**12,876**	**12.95**	**71.94**	**10.00**	**344**	**7.52**	**5.292**	**17.1**	**19.4**	—
Collateralized	**74,487**	**54.80**	**51,659**	**51.95**	**69.35**	**10.02**	**335**	**8.60**	**5.870**	**36.0**	**25.5**	—
Uncollateralized	**61,448**	**45.20**	**47,776**	**48.05**	**77.75**	**11.34**	**508**	**8.25**	**6.342**	**0.4**	**8.7**	—

*Offer Prices are from 1/4 to 1/2 percent above bid prices.

SOURCES: Salomon Brothers, Inc., *Emerging Market Research*, November 14, 1996. Copyright 1997 Salomon Brothers Inc. This table and table statistics contain data from Salomon Brothers Inc. Although the information in this table was obtained from sources that Salomon Brothers Inc. believes to be reliable, Salomon does not guarantee its accuracy, and such information may be incomplete or condensed. All figures included in this table constitute Salomon's judgment as of the original publication date.

Table **28-6**

SPECIAL CHARACTERISTICS OF BRADY BONDS

Par Bonds   So named because they are exchanged dollar for dollar for existing debt, par bonds also are known as *interest reduction bonds*. Because the face amount of debt remains the same, debt relief is provided by a below market rate coupon. These bonds typically have principal and interest guarantees, a fixed coupon or coupon schedule, and bullet maturities of 25–30 years.

Discount Bonds   These bonds are named for the manner in which they are exchanged for loans. The debt holder receives a face amount of these bonds, which is reduced by the discount negotiated in the Brady agreement. Because of the discount, these bonds are also known as *principal reduction bonds*. Like the par bonds, discount bonds typically have principal and interest guaranteed and bullet maturities of 25–30 years. Since the principal was reduced, these bonds pay a "market" rate, usually LIBOR + 13/16.

Front-Loaded Interest Reduction Bonds (FLIRBs)   These bonds usually have fixed coupons that step up from low levels for the first few years, after which they pay a floating rate. FLIRBs carry no principal collateral, and their interest collateral is released after the step-up period. These bonds have amortization schedules that give them a shorter average life (about 10 years) than par or discount bonds to compensate investors for the lack of principal collateral.

New Money Bonds and Debt Conversion Bonds (DCBs)   These bonds are generally issued together through the new money option of an exchange menu, which is designed to give debt holders an incentive to invest additional capital or "new money." For every dollar of new money bond that is purchased with cash, the investor may exchange existing debt for DCBs in a ratio negotiated in the Brady agreement (usually $4 to $6 of DCBs for every dollar of new money). This provides an incentive to invest new money because the DCBs are usually made more attractive than the bonds available in other options. New money bonds and DCBs typically pay LIBOR + 7/8 and amortization schedules that give them a 10- to 15-year average life. The name "new money bond" also has been used for bonds issued both outside a Brady Plan (Brazil) and as a prelude to a Brady Plan (Philippines).

Principal Collateralization   In a number of Brady Plans, the U.S. Treasury has issued 30-year, zero-coupon bonds to collateralize the principal of the bonds. The market value of the principal guarantee, which tends to increase as the bond ages, depends on the yield of 30-year U.S. Treasury strips. The collateral has been paid for by a combination of International Monetary Fund (IMF) and World Bank loans with the country's own reserves.

Rolling Interest Guarantees   In addition, in most Brady Plans, two or three semiannual interest payments are guaranteed by securities of at least double-A credit quality. All collateral is held by the New York Federal Reserve Bank in an escrow account to protect the investor against a temporary suspension of interest payments or default. If an interest payment is missed, the bond holder will receive the missed payment from the escrow account. Interest collateral is often referred to as *rolling interest guarantees*—if the interest collateral is not utilized, it will roll forward over the life of the bonds. The bonds are excluded by their terms from further new money requests.

Value Recovery Rights   Investors in the Mexican and Venezuelan bonds also may benefit from additional interest income from 1996 to maturity through value-recovery warrants, if both oil export volume and world oil prices increase. Attached to each bond is a series of value recovery rights entitling the holder to extra interest payments if the price of oil during a range of payment periods exceeds a certain price per barrel, adjusted for inflation. The holder may separate the right from the bond four years before the right's first payment.

of three factors. First is LDC central bank's assumption of the various loans made to individual borrowers in that country. Thus, for example, U.S. FIs' loans to Mexico, Brazil, and Argentina have been increasingly consolidated at the local central bank. As a result, a foreign FI such as Citibank becomes the owner or creditor of a consolidated account denominated in dollars at the LDC central bank.[11]

Second, the frequent restructurings of the stock of LDC loans, along with their consolidation at the local central bank, has made loan terms increasingly homogeneous. For example, the August 1987 restructuring of Argentinean debt to a maturity of 19 years and an interest rate of LIBOR + 13/16 percent involved the whole stock of Argentinean loans outstanding as of January 1986, or $30.5 billion.

Third, banks have received increasing demands to make their LDC loan portfolios more liquid. In particular, by converting loans into **Brady bonds** (a bond that is swapped for an outstanding loan to an LDC), LDC's assets become more liquid[12] because these bonds are often partially collateralized. Thus, the Venezuelan discount bonds in Table 28–5 have their principal repayments collateralized by a U.S. Treasury bond maturing in March 2020 that is held in escrow. This means that foreign bondholders, such as U.S. FIs, are exposed to Venezuelan default only on interest payments (in this case coupons of 6.386 percent) on these bonds.[13] To date, no defaults or reschedulings have occurred for Brady bonds.

Brady bond

A bond that is swapped for an outstanding loan to an LDC.

LDC Market Prices and Country Risk Analysis.   By combining LDC asset prices with key variables, FI managers have the ability to predict future repayment problems. For example, in the markets for which LDC debt is quite heavily traded, such as in Mexico and Brazil (both of which have more than $80 billion in debts outstanding), these prices reflect the market consensus regarding the current and expected future cash flows on these loans and, implicitly, the probability of rescheduling or repudiation of these loans. Because market prices on LDC loans have been available monthly since 1985, the FI manager might construct a statistical CRA model to analyze which key economic and political variables or factors have driven changes in secondary market prices. Basically, this involves relating periodic changes in the prices of LDC debt in the secondary market to changes in key variables such as those described earlier in this chapter.

Concept Questions

1. Are the credit ratings of countries in the *Institutional Investor* rating scheme forward or backward looking?
2. What variables are most commonly included in sovereign risk prediction models? What does each one measure?
3. What are the major problems involved with using traditional CRA models and techniques?

---

[11]Usually, a local company or state organization swaps its dollar loans owed to a U.S. bank for a peso loan at the central bank. That is, the debt to the U.S. bank is transferred to the central bank of that country.

[12]The Brady bond is usually created on an interest rate rollover date. On that date, the floating rate loans are usually converted into fixed-rate coupon bonds on the books of an agent bank. The agent bank is the bank that kept the records of loan ownership and distributed interest payments made by the LDC to individual bank creditors. Once converted, the bonds can start trading.

[13]In fact, this instrument has hybrid sovereign risk, part U.S. and part Venezuelan.

4. Which sovereign risk indicators are the most important for a large FI, those with a high or a low systematic element?
5. What three factors led to the creation of the Brady bonds?

• •

MECHANISMS FOR DEALING
WITH SOVEREIGN RISK EXPOSURE

Earlier we identified methods and models that FI managers can use to measure sovereign risk exposure before making credit decisions. In this section, we consider the benefits and costs of using four alternative mechanisms to deal with problem sovereign credits once they have arisen. The four mechanisms (summarized in Table 28–7) are the following:

1. Debt-for-equity swaps.
2. Multiyear restructuring agreements (MYRAs).
3. Sale of LDC loans on the secondary market.
4. Debt-for-debt swaps (Brady bonds).

Although restructuring keeps the loans in the portfolio, the other three mechanisms change the fundamental nature of the FI's claim or remove it from the balance sheet.

The following section presents the mechanics of loan restructuring and debt-for-equity swaps. Because we have already described LDC loan sales and debt-for-debt swaps (e.g., Brady bonds), we only summarize their benefits and costs here. Understanding each of these mechanisms, especially its benefits and costs, is important because an FI can choose among the four in dealing with a problem sovereign loan or credit.

Debt-for-Equity Swaps

The market for LDC loan sales has a close link to debt-for-equity swap programs arranged by certain LDCs, such as Chile and Mexico, with outside investors that wish to make equity investments in debtor countries. Indeed, although banks are the major sellers of LDC loans, important buyers are parties that wish to engage in long-term equity or real investments in those debtor countries. For example, the 1985 Mexican debt-for-equity swap program allowed Mexican dollar loans to be swapped for Mexican equity in certain priority investment areas. These were the motor, tourism, and chemical industries. For example, American Express Bank was an FI that exploited the opportunities of the Mexican debt-for-equity swap program by building seven hotels in Mexico. The estimated annual amount of debt-for-equity swaps is currently around $10 billion.[14]

To demonstrate the costs and benefits of a debt-for-equity swap for the FI and other parties participating in the transaction, we present a hypothetical example. Suppose that in November 1998, Citibank had $100 million loans outstanding to Chile and could have sold those loans on the secondary market for a bid price of $91 million, or $91 per $100. The advantages to Citibank from selling loans are the removal of these loans from its books and the freeing up of funds for other investments. However, Citibank must accept a loss of $9 million on the loan. Given that the rest of the bank is profitable, the bank can offset this loss against other profits. In addition, if the corporate tax rate is 34 percent, Citibank's after-tax loss is $9 (1 − .34) million, or $5.94 million.

---

[14]Countries with debt-for-equity swap programs include Argentina, Brazil, Chile, Costa Rica, Ecuador, Jamaica, Mexico, Uruguay, and Venezuela.

Table **28–7**

MECHANISMS FOR DEALING WITH SOVEREIGN RISK EXPOSURE

Debt for Equity Swaps   Programs arranged by certain LDCs with outside investors that wish to make equity investments to debtor countries. Loans are swapped with equity in certain priority investment areas.

Multiyear Restructuring Agreements (MYRAs)   An agreement rescheduling the contractual payments on a loan over several years when a country is unable to maintain its interest and principal payments on the loan.

Loan Sales   Sale of a loan in the secondary market specializing in the trading of LDC loans.

Debt-for-Debt Swap (Brady Bonds)   Transformation of an LDC loan into a more marketable and liquid debt instrument with a longer maturity and a lower promised interest rate.

If Citibank sold this loan to Salomon Brothers for $91 million, Salomon as a market maker[15] could reoffer the loan to an outside buyer at a slightly higher price, perhaps $93 million (or $93 per $100 of face value). Suppose that IBM wants to build a computer factory in Chile and buys the $100 million face value loan from Salomon for $93 million to finance its investments in Chile. Thus, Salomon earns a $2 million profit ($93 million – $91 million), and IBM knows that Chile has a debt-for-equity swap program. This means that at a given exchange rate, the Chilean government will allow IBM to convert the $100 million loan it has purchased into local currency or pesos. However, the Chilean government will be willing to do this only if it receives something. Thus, it may be willing to convert the dollars into pesos at only a 5 percent discount from the true free market dollar/peso exchange rate. If the free market exchange rate were 380 Chilean pesos to the U.S. dollar, the Chilean government will convert the dollars at only 361 pesos to the U.S. dollar. Thus, IBM must bear a 5 percent discount on the face value of the purchased loan; that is, when converting the $100 million loan at the Chilean Central Bank, IBM receives $95 million equivalent in pesos.[16] Remember that IBM had originally bought the loan for only $93 million on the secondary market. Thus, its net saving from this debt-for-equity conversion program is $2 million.[17] However, note that the $95 million is in pesos that must be invested in Chilean equity, such as real estate or factories. In general, debt-for-equity swap investors face long periods before they can repatriate dividends (12 years in the Mexican case) and often large withholding taxes (55 percent in the Mexican case). Moreover, they face the risk of future expropriation or nationalization of those assets as well as peso currency risk. Thus, the $2 million spread reflects IBM's expectations about such risks.

Finally, what does the Chilean government receive from this debt-for-equity swap program? On the one hand, it has retired relatively expensive hard-currency dollar debt with local currency pesos at a discount. Implicitly, it has retired a $100 million face-value debt at a cost of $95 million in pesos; the difference reflects the debt-for-equity swap official exchange rate (361 pesos/$1) and the true exchange rate (380 pesos/$1). The cost to Chile is printing $95 million more pesos. This may lead to a higher domestic inflation

---

[15]As the market maker, Salomon offers the best available price to Citibank for the loan. Citibank could have gone directly to IBM with the loan, but the loss (adjustment) on the loan would likely have been larger than $9 million after considering search and other transaction costs involved in trying to find a direct corporate buyer of the loan.

[16]In practice, debt-for-equity swaps convert into pesos at an official rate, which is often less attractive than the rate quoted in official or unofficial parallel markets for private transactions.

[17]That is, in general, the swap is cheaper than direct local borrowing, if this is an available alternative.

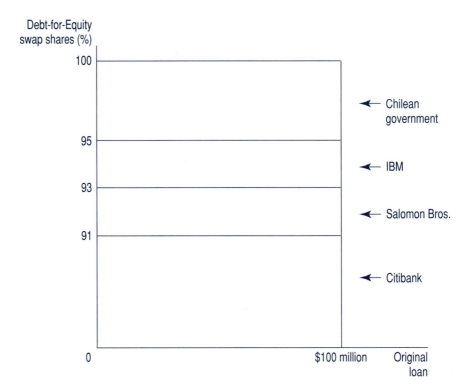

F i g u r e   **28–4**   *Debt-for-Equity Swaps and Loan Sales, Chilean Example*

rate, as well as increased foreign ownership and control of Chilean real assets as a result of IBM's equity purchases.

We illustrate the division of the original $100 million face value loan among the four parties as a result of the loan sale and debt-for-equity swap in Figure 28–4. Citibank gets 91 percent of the original face value of the loan; Salomon Brothers, 2 percent; IBM, 2 percent; and Chile, 5 percent. That is, three parties share the 9 percent discount from face value accepted by Citibank: the investment bank, the corporation involved in the debt-for-equity swap, and the sponsoring country's government.

One puzzle from the preceding example is why Citibank does not sidestep both the investment bank and IBM and engage in a local currency debt-for-equity swap itself. That is, why doesn't Citibank directly swap its $100 million loan to Chile into the $95 million equivalent of local equity? The problem is that in the United States, Federal Reserve Regulation K restricts U.S. banks' ability to buy real equity or engage in commerce in overseas countries.[18] If a U.S. bank can buy and hold Chilean real assets, this might lower its potential losses from restructuring its LDC loan portfolio. Nevertheless, note that although a loan sale directly removes a problem loan from the balance sheet, a debt-for-equity swap replaces that problem loan with a risky long-term peso-denominated equity position on its

---

[18]Specialized U.S. bank subsidiaries called Edge Act corporations are allowed limited amounts of equity purchases. Such corporations have been established since 1919 under the Edge Act to allow banks to finance international transactions. In 1987, the Federal Reserve approved bank acquisitions of 100 percent stakes in nonfinancial companies in 33 extremely poor LDCs as part of debt-for-equity swaps. Unfortunately, most of these countries do not operate debt-for-equity programs or have very little attractive equity. However, the building of seven hotels in Mexico by American Express Bank was a direct debt-for-equity swap engaged in by a bank.

balance sheet. Thus, the improvement of the liquidity of the balance sheet through such a transaction is far from certain.

Multiyear Restructuring Agreements

MYRA

A multiyear restructuring agreement that is the official terminology for a sovereign loan rescheduling.

If a country is unable to keep its payments on a loan current and an FI chooses to maintain the loan on its balance sheet rather than selling it or swapping it for equity or debt, the loan and its contractual terms would be rescheduled under a **multiyear restructuring agreement (MYRA)**. The agreement reached between Argentina and its major creditors to restructure $30.5 billion of its loans in August 1987 is an example of a MYRA.

As with the loan sale, the debt-for-equity swap, and the debt-for-debt swap, the crucial aspect for an FI is the amount it is willing to concede or give up to the borrower in the sovereign loan rescheduling process. The benefits and costs of this policy depend on a number of factors that are usually built into any MYRA, including the following:

1. The *fee* charged by the bank to the borrower for the costs of restructuring the loan. This fee may be as high as 1 percent of the face value of the loan if a large lending syndicate is involved in the negotiations.
2. The *interest rate* charged on the new loan. This is generally lower than that on the original loan to ease the repayment cash flow problem of the borrower. (In the 1987 Argentinean case, the restructured loan rate was set equal to LIBOR + 13/16 percent.)
3. A *grace period* may be involved before interest and/or principal payments begin on the new loan to give the borrower time to accumulate hard-currency reserves to meet its future debt interest and principal obligations. In the Argentinean case, the grace period was seven years.
4. The *maturity* of the loan is lengthened, normally to extend the interest and principal payments over a longer period. In the Argentinean case, the restructured loan's maturity was 19 years.
5. *Option features* are often built into the MYRA to allow the lender (and sometimes the borrower) to choose the currency for repayment of interest and/or principal.[19]

concessionality

The amount a bank gives up in present value terms as a result of a MYRA.

The magnitude and interaction of these factors determine the degree of a MYRA's **concessionality** (the net cost) to an FI. In general, the net cost or degree of concessionality can be defined as

$$\text{Concessionality} = \frac{\text{(Present value of}}{\text{original loan)}} - \frac{\text{(Present value of}}{\text{restructured loan)}}$$

$$= PV_O - PV_R$$

The lower the present value of the restructured loan relative to the original loan, the higher are the *concessions* that the bank has made to the borrower, that is, the higher the cost of loan restructuring.

Loan Sales

The third mechanism for dealing with problem sovereign loans, LDC loan sales, was discussed in some detail earlier in this chapter. This section summarizes the main benefits and

---

[19]For example, the lender may choose to be repaid in dollars or another currency. Such option features add value to the cash flow stream for either the borrower or lender, depending on who can exercise the currency option.

costs of these sales to the FI. The first major benefit is the removal of these loans from the balance sheet, and as such, the freeing of resources for other investments. Second, being able to sell these loans at a discount or loss signifies that the rest of the bank's balance sheet is sufficiently strong to bear the cost. In fact, a number of studies have found that announcements of banks taking reserve additions against LDC loans—prior to their charge-off and sale—have a positive effect on bank stock prices. Third, the bank shares part of the loan sale loss with the government because such losses provide a tax write-off for the lender.

The major cost is one of the loss itself, the tax-adjusted difference between the face value of the loan and its market value at the time of the sale. In addition, many banks engaged in LDC loan sales in 1987 and 1988 after taking big loan-loss reserve additions in May and June 1987. Since 1988, and in particular in the period 1991–1993, the secondary market loan prices of many LDC countries have risen in value. This suggests an additional cost related to loan sales—the optimal market timing of such sales. That is, at what point can FIs minimize the spread between the loan sale price and face value at the time of sale.

Debt-for-Debt Swaps (Brady Bonds)

The primary benefit of debt-for-debt swaps is that they transform an LDC loan into a highly marketable and liquid instrument, a bond. For example, FIs trade and clear Brady bonds (the most common debt-for-debt swap) in a fashion similar to the trade and clear of most Eurobonds with relatively low transaction costs, small bid-ask spreads, and an efficient clearing and settlement system. In addition, because of full or partial collateral backing, these bonds are normally senior in status to any remaining LDC loans of the country. The major cost occurs when the bond is swapped for the loan because it usually has a longer stated maturity and a fixed coupon set below the promised floating rate on the loan. Also, the swap of loan face value for debt face value is often less than dollar for dollar.

Choice between the Four Mechanisms

As described earlier in this section, FIs use four major mechanisms to deal with a problem sovereign LDC credit: a debt-for-equity swap, a MYRA, a loan sale, and a debt-for-debt (or loan-for-bond) swap. The extent to which each is used, however, varies. Specifically, debt-for-debt swaps and loan sales currently dominate MYRAs and debt-for-equity swaps as sovereign loan risk exposure control mechanisms. Indeed, the combined annual trading volume for emerging-market debt (Brady bonds) and LDC loan sales exceeded $5 trillion in 1996. This can be compared to $10 billion per annum in debt-for-equity swaps and an infrequent use of MYRAs among major creditor FIs in the 1990s.

Concept Questions

1. What are the four alternative mechanisms for dealing with problem sovereign loans?
2. What are the major benefits and costs of each of the mechanisms in question (1)?
3. Which alternative is most popular among FI managers today?

S U M M A R Y

This chapter discussed the problems that FIs face from sovereign or country risk exposures. Sovereign risk is the risk that a foreign government will limit or prevent domestic borrowers in its jurisdiction from repaying the principal and interest on debt owed to external lenders. In recent years, this risk has caused enormous problems for U.S. banks lending to LDCs and Latin American, Asian, and east European countries. The chapter presented various models for country risk analysis (CRA), including those produced by external monitoring agencies such as *Euromoney* and the *Institutional Investor* and those that an FI manager could construct for internal evaluation purposes. Such statistical CRA models have problems. The chapter also presented an alternative approach using secondary market prices on LDC loans and bonds. Finally, the chapter discussed the advantages and disadvantages of using four alternative mechanisms for dealing with problem sovereign credits from the perspective of the lender; namely, debt-for-equity swaps, MYRAs, loan sales, and debt-for-debt (or loan-for-bond) swaps.

P E R T I N E N T   W E B   S I T E S

The Economist   http://www.economist.com/
International Monetary Fund (IMF)   http://www.imf.org/

Salomon Brothers   http://www.salomon.com/
World Bank   http://www.worldbank.org/

Sovereign Risk

1. What additional risks do FIs incur when making loans to borrowers based in foreign countries? Explain.
2. What is the difference between debt repudiation and debt rescheduling?
3. Assume that countries A and B have exports of $2 and $6 billion, respectively. The total interest and amortization on foreign loans for both countries are $1 and $2 billion, respectively.
   a. What is the debt service ratio (DSR) of each country?
   b. Based only on the preceding information, which country should lenders charge a higher risk premium?
   c. What are the shortcomings of using the ratios in (a) to determine your answer in (b)?
4. How did the collapse of the Asian currencies in 1997 affect the Asian financial institutions?
5. Compare the effect of the 1997 Asian currency crisis on Asian banks with the effect on U.S. banks.
6. How do price risk and quantity risk affect the variability of a country's export revenue?
7. Explain the following relation

$$p = f \text{ (IR, INVR)}$$
$$+, \quad + \text{ or } -$$

   p = Probability of rescheduling
   IR = Total imports/Total foreign exchange reserves
   INVR = Real investment/GNP

8. What are the benefits and costs of debt rescheduling
   a. To a borrower?
   b. To a lender?
9. An FI manager has calculated the following values and weights to assess the credit risk and likelihood of having to reschedule the loan. From the *Z*-score calculated from these weights and values, is the manager likely to approve the loan?

Variable	Country Value	Weight
DSR	1.25	.05
IR	1.6	.10
INVR	0.6	.35
VAREX	0.15	.35
MG	0.02	.15

10. Who are the primary sellers of LDC debt?
11. Why are FIs both buyers and sellers of LDC debt in the secondary markets?
12. What are the risks to an investing company participating in a debt-to-equity swap?
13. A bank is in the process of renegotiating a loan. The principal outstanding is $50 million and is to be paid back in two installments of $25 million each, plus interest of 8 percent. The new terms will extend the loan to five years with no principal payments except for interest payments of 6 percent for the first three years. The cost of funds for the

bank is 6 percent for both the old loan and the renegotiated loan. An up-front fee of 1 percent is to be included for the renegotiated loan.

a. What is the present value of the existing loan for the bank?

b. What is the present value of the rescheduled loan for the bank?

c. Is the concessionality positive or negative for the bank?

14. How has the restructuring of sovereign bonds affected their interest rate risk?

15. A $20 million loan outstanding to the Nigerian government is currently in arrears with City Bank. After extensive negotiations, City Bank agrees to reduce the interest rates from 10 percent to 6 percent and to lengthen the maturity of the loan to 10 years from the present 5 years remaining to maturity. The principal of the loan is to be paid at maturity. There will be no grace period, and the first interest payment is expected at the end of the year.

a. If the cost of funds is 5 percent for the bank, what is the present value of the loan prior to the rescheduling?

b. What is the present value of the rescheduled loan to the bank?

c. What is the concessionality of the rescheduled loan if the cost of funds remain at 5 percent and an up-front fee of 5 percent is charged?

d. What up-front fee should the bank charge to make the concessionality equal zero?

16. What are major benefits and costs of loan sales to an FI?

17. What are an FI's major costs and benefits of converting debt to Brady bonds?

18. A bank is in the process of renegotiating a three-year, nonamortizing loan. The principal outstanding is $20 million and the interest rate is 8 percent. The new terms will extend the loan to 10 years at a new interest rate of 6 percent. The cost of funds for the bank is 7 percent for both the old and the renegotiated loan. An up-front fee of 50 basis points is to be included for the renegotiated loan.

a. What is the present value of the existing loan for the bank?

b. What is the present value of the rescheduled loan for the bank?

c. What is the concessionality for the bank?

d. What should the up-front fee be to make the concessionality zero?

19. Which of the four mechanisms used to deal with problem LDC debt have FIs used most widely?

20. Go to the World Bank web site and find the overview of the East Asia economic region.

Glossary

Abnormal returns Risk-adjusted stock returns above expected levels.

Actuarially fairly priced insurance Insurance pricing based on the perceived risk of the insured.

Adjustable-rate mortgage (ARM) A mortgage whose interest rate adjusts with movements in an underlying market index interest rate.

Affiliate risk Risk imposed on one holding company affiliate due to the potential failure of the other holding company affiliate(s).

Agency costs The risk that owners and managers of firms receiving savers' funds will take actions with those funds contrary to the best interests of the savers.

Asset securitization The packaging and selling of loans and other assets backed by securities issued by an FI.

Asset transformer Financial claims issued by an FI that are more attractive to household savers than are the claims directly issued by corporations.

Assignment The purchase of a share in a loan syndication with some contractual control and rights over the borrower.

Back-end fee The fee charged on the unused component of a loan commitment.

Bank loan sale Sale of loan originated by a bank with or without recourse to an outside buyer.

Bank panic A systemic or contagious run on the deposits of the banking industry as a whole.

Bank run A sudden and unexpected increase in deposit withdrawals from a bank.

Basel (or Basle) accord An agreement that requires imposition of risk-based capital ratios on banks in major industrialized countries.

Basis risk The variable spread between a lending rate and a borrowing rate, or between any two interest rates or prices. The lack of perfect correlation results in a residual risk.

Best efforts underwriting An underwriting in which the investment banker acts as an agent rather than as a principal that bears risk.

Beta Systematic (undiversifiable) risk reflecting the movement of the returns of a specific stock and the returns on the market portfolio.

Bond and income funds Funds consisting of fixed-income capital market debt securities.

Book entry securities Securities held in computerized account form rather than in paper form.

Book value Values of assets and liabilities based on their historical costs.

Book value accounting Recording an FI's assets and liabilities at historic values.

Brady bond A bond that is swapped for an outstanding loan to an LDC.

Broker-dealers Firms that assist in the trading of existing securities.

Brokered deposits Wholesale CDs obtained through a brokerage house.

Buffer reserve Nonreserve asset that can be quickly turned into cash.

Business credit institutions Finance companies specializing in business loans.

Call option An option that gives a purchaser the right, but not the obligation, to buy the underlying security from the writer of the option at a prespecified exercise price on a prespecified date.

Cap A call option on interest rates, often with multiple exercise dates.

Capital forbearance Regulatory policy that allows an FI to continue operating even when its capital is fully depleted.

Capital markets Markets that trade debt and equity instruments with maturities of more than one year.

Captive finance company A finance company wholly owned by a parent corporation.

Cash computation period Period over which vault cash is recorded against required reserve target.

Cash management account Money market mutual fund sold by investment banks that offer check-writing privileges.

Cash reserves Vault cash and cash deposits held at the Federal Reserve.

CGAP Effect The relation between changes in interest rates and changes in net interest income.

Chattel mortgage A mortgage on movable property.

Chinese wall An internally imposed barrier within an organization that limits the flow of confidential client information among departments or areas.

Closed-end fund An investment fund that sells a fixed number of shares to outside investors.

Closed-end investment companies Specialized investment companies that have a fixed supply of outstanding shares but invest in the securities and assets of other firms.

Collar A position taken simultaneously in a cap and a floor.

Collateralized mortgage obligation (CMO) A mortgage-backed bond issued in multiple classes or tranches.

Combined ratio A measure of the overall underwriting profitability of a line; equals the loss ratio plus the ratios of loss adjustment expenses to premiums earned, and commission and other acquisition costs to premiums written minus any dividends paid to policyholders as a proportion of premiums earned.

Commercial banking Banking activity of deposit taking and lending.

Community bank A bank that specializes in retail or consumer banking.

Compensating balances A proportion of a loan that a borrower is required to hold on deposit at the lending institution.

Concentration limits External limits set on the maximum loan size that can be made to an individual borrower.

Concessionality The amount a bank gives up in present value terms as a result of a MYRA.

Conditions precedent Those conditions specified in the credit agreement or terms sheet for a credit that must be fulfilled before drawings are permitted.

Consol bond A bond that pays a fixed coupon each year forever.

Contemporaneous reserve accounting system An accounting system in which the reserve computation and reserve maintenance periods overlap.

Contingent asset and liability Asset and liability off the balance sheet that potentially can produce positive or negative future cash flows for an FI.

Convexity The degree of curvature of the price-yield curve around some interest rate level.

Core deposits Deposits of the bank that are stable over short periods of time and act as long-term sources of funds.

Correspondent bank A bank that provides services to another commercial bank.

Correspondent banking A relationship between a small bank and a large bank in which the large bank provides a number of deposit, lending, and other services.

Counterparty credit risk The risk that the other party to a contract will default on payment obligations.

Country or sovereign risk The risk that repayments from foreign borrowers may be interrupted because of interference from foreign governments.

Covenant Legal clauses in a bond contract that require the issuer of bonds to take or avoid certain actions.

Credit equivalent amount The amount of credit risk exposure of an off-balance-sheet item calculated by multiplying the face value of an off-balance-sheet instrument by a conversion factor.

Credit forward Forward agreement that hedges against an increase in default risk on a loan after the loan terms have been determined and the loan issued.

Credit risk The risk that the promised cash flows from loans and securities held by FIs may not be paid in full.

Credit scoring system A mathematical model that uses observed loan applicants' characteristics to calculate a score that represents the applicant's probability of default.

Credit spread call option A call option whose payoff increases as a yield spread decreases below a stated spread.

Cross-sectional analysis Analysis of financial statements comparing one bank with others.

Currency swap A swap used to hedge against exchange rate risk from mismatched currencies on assets and liabilities.

Current exposure The cost of replacing a derivative securities contract at today's prices.

Daily earnings at risk (DEAR) Market risk exposure over the next 24 hours.

Daylight overdraft A bank's intraday negative balance on its reserve account with the Federal Reserve.

Debt moratoria Delay in repaying interest and/or principal on debt.

Debt service ratio The ratio of a country's interest and amortization obligations to the value of its exports.

Default option An option that pays the par value of a loan in the event of a loan default.

Default risk The risk that a security's issuer will default on that security by missing an interest or principal payment.

Delegated monitor An economic agent appointed to act on behalf of smaller agents in collecting information and/or investing funds on their behalf.

De novo office A newly established office.

Depositor preference Priority given to depositors (insured and uninsured) over all other unsecured creditors in the event of insolvency of a bank or a thrift.

Deposits Those deposits that act as long-term sources of funds for an FI.

Derivative securities Futures, forward, swap, and option positions taken by the financial intermediary for hedging or other purposes.

Discount broker A stockbroker that conducts trades for customers but does not offer investment advice.

Discount window A central bank lender facility of last resort used to meet banks' short-term, nonpermanent liquidity needs.

Diseconomy of scale The degree to which an FI's average costs to produce financial services increase as its output of financial services increases.

Diseconomy of scope The degree to which costs of joint production of FI services are higher than if they were produced independently.

Disintermediation Withdrawal of deposits from S&Ls and other depository institutions to be reinvested elsewhere.

Diversify The ability of an economic agent to reduce risk by holding a number of securities in a portfolio.

Downsizing Shrinking an FI's asset size.

Dual banking system The coexistence of both nationally and state-chartered banks as in the United States.

Duration The average life of an asset or liability, or more technically, the weighted-average time to maturity using the relative present values of the asset or liability cash flows as weights; the weighted-average time to maturity on an investment.

Duration gap A measure of overall interest rate risk exposure for an FI.

EAT Earnings after taxes.

EBIT Earnings before interest and taxes.

Economies of scale   The degrees to which an FI's average unit costs to produce financial services fall as its output of services increases; for example, the cost reduction in trading and other transaction services resulting from increased efficiency when FIs perform these services.

Economies of scope   The degrees to which an FI can generate cost synergies by producing multiple financial service products.

Equity funds   Funds consisting of common and preferred stock securities.

Factoring   The process of purchasing accounts receivable from corporations (often at a discount), usually with no recourse to the seller should the receivables go bad.

Federal funds market   An interbank market for short-term borrowing and lending of bank reserves.

Financial distress   The state in which a borrower is unable to meet a payment obligation to lenders and other creditors.

Financing gap   The difference between a bank's average loans and average (core) deposits.

Financing requirement   The financing gap plus a bank's liquid assets.

Fire-sale price   The price received for an asset that has to be liquidated (sold) immediately.

Firewalls   Legal barriers separating the activities of a bank subsidiary from those of the other subsidiaries.

Firm commitment offering   Securities being offered from the issuing firm purchased by an underwriter.

Firm commitment underwriting   The process by which an underwriter buys securities from an issuer and reoffers them to the public at a slightly higher price.

Firm-specific credit risk   The risk of default for the borrowing firm associated with the specific types of project risk taken by that firm.

Fixed charge   A lien that relates to specific identifiable assets.

Float   The time between depositing a check and the availability of the funds for depositor use; the time it takes a check to clear at a bank.

Floating charge   A lien over a class of assets in which the individual assets may change over time (such as receivables or inventories).

Floor   A put option on interest rates, often with multiple exercise dates.

Foreclosure   The process of taking possession of the mortgaged property in satisfaction of a defaulting borrower's indebtedness and forgoing claim to any deficiency.

Foreign exchange risk   The risk that exchange rate changes can affect the value of an FI's assets and liabilities located abroad.

Forward contract   A nonstandard contract inferred bilaterally between two parties; an agreement to transact involving the future exchange of a set amount of assets at a set price.

Forward exchange rate   The exchange rate agreed on today for future (forward) delivery of a currency.

Forward foreign exchange transactions   A transaction that involves the exchange of currencies at a specified time in the future and at a specified rate (or forward exchange rate).

Forward market for FX   The market in which foreign currency is traded for future delivery.

Fraudulent conveyance   A transaction such as a sale of securities or transference of assets to a particular party that is determined to be illegal.

Frequency of loss   The probability that a loss will occur.

Fully amortized   The equal, periodic repayment on a loan that reflects part interest and part principal over the life of the loan.

Fully amortized mortgages   Mortgage portfolio cash flows that have a constant payment.

Futures contract   A standardized contract guaranteed by organized exchanges; an agreement to transact involving the future exchange of a set amount of assets for a price that is settled daily.

Futures option   An option contract that, when exercised, results in the delivery of a futures contract as the underlying asset.

GDS ratio   Gross debt service ratio calculated as total accommodation expenses (mortgage, lease, condominium, management fees, real estate taxes, etc.) divided by gross income.

General diversification limits   Maximums set on the amount of investments an insurer can hold in securities of any single issuer.

General market risk charges   A charge reflecting the modified durations and interest rate shocks for each maturity.

General obligation bonds   Municipal bonds backed by the full faith and credit of the municipality that issued the debt.

Grandfathered subsidiaries   Subsidiaries established prior to the passage of a restrictive law and not subject to that law.

Hedge ratio   The dollar value of futures contracts that should be sold per dollar of cash position exposure.

Hedging selectively   Only partially hedging the gap or individual assets and liabilities.

Highly leveraged transaction (HLT) loan   A loan that finances a merger and acquisition; a leveraged buyout results in a high leverage ratio for the borrower.

Holding company   A parent company that owns a controlling interest in a subsidiary bank or other FI.

Horizontal offset   The assignment of additional charges because short and long positions of different maturities do not perfectly hedge each other.

Immunized   To protect an FI's equity from adverse interest rate (or other asset price) changes.

Implicit premiums   Deposit insurance premiums or costs imposed on a bank through activity constraints rather than direct monetary charges.

Import ratio   The ratio of a country's imports to its total foreign currency reserves.

Inflation   The continual increase in the price level of a basket of goods and services.

Initial public offering (IPO)   The first public issue of (equity or debt) securities by a firm through an underwriter.

Inside money   That part of the money supply produced by the private banking system.

Insolvency risk   The risk that an FI may not have enough capital to offset a sudden decline in the value of its assets relative to its liabilities.

Insurance guaranty fund   A fund of required contributions from within-state insurance companies to compensate insurance company policyholders in the event of a failure.

Insured depositor transfer A method to resolve failures by requiring uninsured depositors to take a loss or haircut on failure equal to the difference between their deposit claims and the estimated value of the failed bank's assets minus insured deposits.

Interest elasticity The percentage change in the price of a bond for any given change in interest rates.

Interest rate parity theorem (IRPT) The theory that the domestic interest rate should equal the foreign interest rate minus the expected appreciation of the domestic currency.

Interest rate risk The risk incurred by an FI when the maturities of its assets and liabilities are mismatched.

Interest rate swap An exchange of fixed-interest payments for floating-interest payments by two counterparties.

Investment banking Banking activity of underwriting, issuing, and distributing securities.

Investment-grade bond Bond rated BBB or better by bond-rating agencies such as Moody's.

Investment ratio The ratio of a country's real investment to its GNP.

IRA and Keogh accounts Private pension plans self-funded by individuals, with banks or other FIs acting as trustees.

Junk bond A bond rated as speculative or less than investment grade by bond-rating agencies such as Moody's.

LDC loans Loans made to a less-developed country (LDC).

Least-cost resolution Policy requiring that the lowest cost method of closure be used for failing banks.

Letter of credit Guarantee sold by a financial institution to underwrite the performance of the buyer of the guarantee; issued by an FI for a fee on which payment is contingent on some future event occurring, most notably default of the agent that purchases the letter of credit.

Leverage ratio Ratio of an FI's core capital to its assets.

LIBOR The London Interbank Offered Rate; the base rate for prime interbank dollar loans in the foreign or Eurodollar market of

a given maturity; used as an index for annual changes on variable rate loans.

Liquid assets ratio A minimum ratio of liquid assets to total assets set by the central bank.

Liquidity The ease with which an asset can be converted into cash.

Liquidity risk The risk that a sudden surge in liability withdrawals may require an FI to liquidate assets in a very short period of time and at low prices. Also, the risk that a security can be sold at a predictable price with low transaction costs on short notice.

Load fund A mutual fund with an up-front sales or commission charge that the investor must pay.

Loan commitment A contractual commitment to loan to a firm a certain maximum amount over a maximum period of time at given interest rate terms.

Loan commitment agreement Contractual commitment to make a loan up to a stated amount at a given interest rate in the future.

Loan loss reserves Special reserves created on the balance sheet against which to write off bad loans.

Loan sharks Subprime lenders that charge unfairly exhorbitant rates to desperate, subprime borrowers.

Loans sold Loans originated by the financial institution and then sold to other investors that can be returned to the originating institution.

Long-tail loss A loss for which a claim is made some time after a policy was written.

Loss ratio A measure of pure losses incurred to premiums earned.

Macrohedging Hedging the entire duration gap of an FI.

Market risk The risk incurred in trading assets and liabilities due to changes in interest rates, exchange rates, market conditions and other asset prices; risk related to the uncertainty of an FI's earnings on its trading portfolio caused by changes in market conditions.

Market to book ratio A ratio that shows the discrepancy between the stock market value of an FI's equity and the book value of its equity.

Market value accounting Recording an FI's assets and liabilities according to the current level of interest rates.

Marking to market Valuing securities at their current market price; the process by which the prices on outstanding futures contracts are adjusted each day to reflect current futures market conditions, or by which balance sheet values reflect current rather than historical prices.

Maturity gap Difference between the weighted-average maturity of the FI's assets and liabilities.

McCarran-Ferguson Act of 1945 Regulation confirming the primacy of state over federal regulation of insurance companies.

Megamerger The merger of two large banks.

Microhedging Using a futures (forward) contract to hedge a specific asset or liability.

Migration analysis A method to measure loan concentration risk by tracking credit ratings of firms in particular sectors for unusual declines.

Minimum risk portfolio A portfolio for which a combination of assets reduces the variance of portfolio returns to the lowest feasible level.

MMDAs Money market deposit accounts; retail savings accounts with some limited checking account features.

Modified duration Duration divided by 1 plus the interest rate.

Money center bank A bank that relies heavily on nondeposit or borrowed sources of funds.

Money market mutual funds (MMMFs) A specialized mutual fund that offers high liquidity, check-writing ability, and a money market return to small individual investors; consists of various mixtures of money market securities.

Money markets Markets that trade debt instruments with maturities of less than one year.

Moral hazard The loss exposure an insurer faces when providing insurance encourages the insured to take more risks.

Morbidity risk The risk of ill-health.

Mortality risk The risk of death.

Mortgage (asset)-backed bonds Bonds collateralized by a pool of assets.

Multibank holding company (MBHC) A parent banking organization that owns a number of individual bank subsidiaries.

Mutual organization Savings bank in which the depositors also own the bank.

MYRA A multiyear restructuring agreement that is the official terminology for a sovereign loan rescheduling.

NAFTA North American Free Trade Agreement.

Naive hedge A hedge of a cash asset on a direct dollar-for-dollar basis with a forward or futures contract.

Naked options Option positions that do not identifiably hedge an underlying asset or liability.

National treatment Regulation of foreign banks in the same fashion as domestic banks or the creation of a level playing field.

NAV See **Net asset value.**

Negative externality An action by an economic agent that imposes costs on other economic agents.

Negotiable CDs Fixed-maturity interest-bearing deposits with face values over $100,000 that can be resold in the secondary market.

Negotiable instrument An instrument whose ownership can be transferred in the secondary market.

Net asset value (NAV) The price at which mutual funds shares are sold (or can be redeemed); equals the total market value of the fund's assets less any accrued liabilities divided by the number of shares in the fund outstanding.

Net deposit drains The amount by which cash withdrawals exceed additions; a net cash outflow.

Net exposure The degree to which a bank is net long (positive) or net short (negative) in a given currency.

Net interest margin Interest income minus interest expense divided by earning assets.

Net long (short) in a currency A position of holding more (less) assets than liabilities in a given currency.

Net premiums written The entire amount of premiums on insurance contracts written.

Net quality spread The net interest rate spread between rates paid by high-quality borrowers relative to low-quality borrowers in the long-term (fixed) and short-term (floating) rate markets.

Net regulatory burden The difference between the private costs of regulations and the private benefits for the producers of financial services.

Net worth A measure of an FI's capital that is equal to the difference between the market value of its assets and the market value of its liabilities; the value of an FI to its owners.

No-load fund A mutual fund that does not charge up-front sales or commission charges on the sale of mutual fund shares to investors.

Nonbank bank A financial intermediary that undertakes many of the activities of a commercial bank without meeting the legal definition of a bank; a bank divested of its commercial loans and/or its demand deposits.

NOW account Negotiable order of withdrawal account, or interest-bearing checking account; similar to a demand deposit account but has a minimum balance requirement and, when maintained, pays interest.

Off-balance-sheet (OBS) asset An item that moves onto the asset side of the balance sheet when a contingent event occurs.

Off-balance-sheet (OBS) liability An item that moves onto the liability side of the balance sheet when a contingent event occurs.

Off-balance-sheet (OBS) risk The risk incurred by an FI as the result of activities related to contingent assets and liabilities.

Off-market swaps Swaps that have non-standard terms that require one party to compensate another.

One-bank holding company A parent banking organization that owns one bank subsidiary and nonbank subsidiaries.

Open-end fund An investment fund that sells an elastic or nonfixed number of shares to outside investors.

Open-end mutual fund A mutual fund for which the supply of shares is not fixed but can increase or decrease daily with purchases and redemptions of shares.

Open interest The outstanding stock of put or call contracts.

Open position An unhedged position in a particular currency.

Operating ratio A measure of the overall profitability of a PC insurer; equals the combined ratio minus the investment yield.

Operational risk The risk that existing technology or support systems may malfunction or break down.

Option pricing model A model for calculating deposit insurance as a put option on the bank's assets.

Other savings deposits All savings accounts other than MMDAs.

Outside money That part of the money supply directly produced by the government or central bank, such as notes and coin.

Overhead efficiency A bank's ability to generate noninterest income to cover noninterest expense.

Participation in a loan The act of buying a share in a loan syndication with limited, contractual control, and rights over the borrower.

Personal credit institutions Finance companies specializing in installment and other loans to consumers.

Plain vanilla Standard agreement without any special features.

Policy loans Loans made by an insurance company to its policyholders using their policies as collateral.

Policy reserves A liability item for insurers that reflects their expected payment commitments on existing policy contracts.

Potential exposure The risk that a counterparty to a derivative securities contract will default in the future.

Power of sale The process of taking the proceedings of the forced sale of a mortgaged property in satisfaction of the indebtedness and returning to the mortgagor the excess over the indebtedness or claiming any shortfall as an unsecured credit.

Premiums earned Premiums received and earned on insurance contracts because time has passed with no claim filed.

Prepay To pay back a loan before its maturity to the FI that originated the loan.

Price risk The risk that an asset's sale price will be lower than its purchase price.

Primary markets Markets in which corporations raise funds through new issues of securities.

Primary securities Financial obligations (e.g., equities, bonds) issued by corporations and backed by the real assets of those corporations. The corporation directly issues these securities in exchange for funds.

Prime lending rate The base lending rate periodically set by banks.

Private placement The placement by a bank acting as a placing agent of an entire issue of securities with a single (or a few) large institutional investors.

Product diversification benefit Stabilization of earnings and profit resulting from a well-diversified bank holding company.

Profit margin Net income divided by total operating income.

Prompt corrective action Mandatory action that regulators must take as a bank's capital ratio falls.

Purchased funds Rate-sensitive funding sources of the bank.

Purchasing power parity The theory explaining the change in foreign currency exchange rates as inflation rates in the countries change.

Put option An option that gives a purchaser the right, but not the obligation, to sell the underlying security to the writer of the option at a prespecified exercise price on a prespecified date.

QTL test Qualified thrift lender test that sets a floor on the mortgage-related assets that thrifts can hold (currently, 65 percent).

Quality swap A fixed-floating rate swap between two parties of different credit ratings.

Rate sensitivity The time to repricing an asset or liability.

Real interest rate The interest rate that would exist on a default-free security if no inflation were expected, calculated as the difference between a nominal interest rate and the expected rate of inflation.

Recourse The ability of a loan buyer to sell the loan back to the originator should it go bad.

Redlining The procedure by which a banker refuses to make loans to residents living inside given geographic boundaries.

Regional or superregional bank A bank that engages in a complete array of wholesale commercial banking activities.

Regulation Q ceiling An interest ceiling imposed on small savings and time deposits at banks and thrifts until 1986.

Regulator forbearance A policy not to close economically insolvent FIs but to allow them to continue in operation.

REIT A real estate investment trust; a closed-end investment company that specializes in investing in mortgages, property, or real estate company shares.

Report of condition Balance sheet of a commercial bank reporting information at a single point in time.

Report of income Income statement of a commercial bank reporting revenues, expenses, net profit or loss, and cash dividends over a period of time.

Repricing or funding gap The difference between those assets whose interest rates will be repriced or changed over some future period (rate-sensitive assets) and liabilities whose interest rates will be repriced or changed over some future period (rate-sensitive liabilities).

Repudiation Outright cancellation of all current and future debt obligations by a borrower.

Rescheduling Changing the contractual terms of the loan such as its maturity and interest payments.

Reserve computation period Period over which required reserves are calculated.

Reserve maintenance period Period over which deposits at the Federal Reserve Bank must meet or exceed the required reserve target.

Reserve requirement tax The cost of holding reserves that pay no interest at the central bank; increases if inflation erodes the purchasing power value of these reserve balances.

Retail bank A bank that focuses its business activities on consumer banking relationships.

Retail CDs Time deposits with a face value below $100,000.

Revenue bonds Municipal bonds backed by cash flows from the specific assets being financed.

Revolving loan A credit line on which a borrower can both draw and repay many times over the life of the loan contract.

Risk-adjusted assets On- and off-balance-sheet assets whose values are adjusted for approximate credit risk.

Risk-based deposit insurance program A program that assesses insurance premiums on the basis of capital adequacy and supervisory judgments on bank quality.

Routine hedging Hedging all interest rate risk exposure.

Runoff Periodic cash flow of interest and principal amortization payments on long-term assets such as conventional mortgages that can be reinvested at market rates.

Sales finance institution Finance companies specializing in loans to customers of a particular retailer or manufacturer.

Secondary issues A new issue of equity or debt by firms whose securities are already traded in the market.

Secondary market A market that trades existing securities.

Secondary securities Financial obligations (e.g., deposits, commercial paper) issued by FIs and backed by primary securities of corporations; serve as indirect investments in the issuing corporation.

Section 20 affiliate A securities subsidiary of a bank holding company through which a banking organization can engage in investment banking activities.

Secured loan A loan that is backed by a first claim on certain assets (collateral) of the borrower if default occurs.

Securitized mortgage assets Mortgages packaged and used as assets backing secondary market securities.

Separate account Annuity program sponsored by life insurance companies in which payoff on the policy is linked to the assets in which policy premiums are invested.

Settlement risk Intraday credit risk associated with CHIPS wire transfer activities.

Severity of loss The size of a loss.

Specific risk charge A charge reflecting the risk of a decline in the liquidity or credit risk quality of the trading portfolio.

Spot contract An agreement to transact involving the immediate exchange of assets and funds.

Spot foreign exchange transaction A transaction that involves the immediate exchange of currencies at the current (or spot) exchange rate.

Spot loan A loan that the borrower withdraws immediately.

Spot market for FX The market in which foreign currency is traded for immediate delivery.

Spread The difference between lending and deposit rates.

Spread effect The effect that a change in the spread between rates on rate-sensitive assets and rate-sensitive liabilities has on *NII* as interest rates change.

Standby letters of credit Guarantees issued to cover contingencies that are potentially more severe and less predictable than contingencies covered under trade-related or commercial letters of credit.

Subprime lender A finance company that lends to high-risk customers.

Surrender value of a policy   The cash value of a policy received by an insurance policyholder from the insurer if the policy-holder surrenders the policy prior to maturity; normally only a portion of the contract's face value.

Swap buyer   By convention, a party that makes the fixed-rate payments in an interest rate swap transaction.

Swap seller   By convention, a party that makes the floating-rate payments in an interest rate swap.

Systematic credit risk   The risk of default associated with general economywide or macroconditions affecting all borrowers.

Systematic loan loss risk   A measure of the sensitivity of loan losses in a particular business sector relative to the losses in a bank's loan portfolio.

TDS ratio   Total debt ratio calculated as total accommodation expenses plus all other debt service payments divided by gross income.

Technology   Computers, visual and audio communication systems, and other information systems central to an FI's production of services.

Technology risk   The risk incurred by an FI when its technological investments do not produce anticipated cost savings.

Term structure of interest rates   A comparison of market yields on securities, assuming all characteristics except maturity are same.

Tier I core capital ratio   The ratio of an FI's core capital to its risk-adjusted assets.

Time series analysis   Analysis of financial statements over a period of time.

Timing insurance   A service provided by a sponsor of pass-through securities (such as GNMA) guaranteeing the bondholder interest and principal payments at the calendar date promised.

Tombstone   A public announcement of a new issue of securities in the financial press.

Too big to fail   A term describing banks that regulators view as being too big to be closed and liquidated without imposing a systemic risk to the banking and financial system.

Total operating income   The sum of the interest income and noninterest income.

Total return swap   A swap involving an obligation to pay interest at a specified fixed or floating rate for payments representing the total return on a specified amount.

Total risk-based capital ratio   The ratio of an FI's total capital to its risk-adjusted assets.

Transaction accounts   Deposits that permit the account holders to make multiple withdrawals; the sum of noninterest-bearing demand deposits and interest-bearing checking accounts.

12b-1 fees   Fees relating to the distribution costs of mutual fund shares.

Underwriting   Assisting in the issue of new securities.

Underwriting cycle   A pattern that the profits in the PC industry tend to follow.

Unearned premiums   Reserves set aside that contain the portion of a premium that has been paid before insurance coverage has been provided.

Unit bank   A bank with a single office.

Universal FI   An FI that can engage in a broad range of financial service activities.

Unsecured loan   A loan that has only a general claim to the assets of the borrower if default occurs.

Up-front fee   The fee charged for making funds available through a loan commitment.

Usury ceilings   State-imposed ceilings on the maximum rate that FIs can charge on consumer and mortgage debt.

Vertical offset   The assignment of additional capital charges because long and short positions in the same maturity bucket, but in different instruments, cannot perfectly offset each other.

Vulture fund   A specialized fund that invests in distressed loans.

Weekend game   Name given to the policy of lowering deposit balances on Fridays since that day's figures count three times for reserve accounting purposes.

When-issued securities   Commitments to buy or sell securities before they are issued.

When-issued (WI) trading   Trading in securities prior to their actual issue.

Wholesale bank   A bank that focuses its business activities on commercial banking relationships.

Wholesale CDs   Time deposits with a face value above $100,000.

X efficiency   Cost savings due to the greater managerial efficiency of the acquiring bank.

Appendix

Table A-1

FUTURE VALUE OF $1 AT THE END OF t PERIODS $= (1 + r)^t$

Period	Interest Rate								
	1%	2%	3%	4%	5%	6%	7%	8%	9%
1	1.0100	1.0200	1.0300	1.0400	1.0500	1.0600	1.0700	1.0800	1.0900
2	1.0201	1.0404	1.0609	1.0816	1.1025	1.1236	1.1449	1.1664	1.1881
3	1.0303	1.0612	1.0927	1.1249	1.1576	1.1910	1.2250	1.2597	1.2950
4	1.0406	1.0824	1.1255	1.1699	1.2155	1.2625	1.3108	1.3605	1.4116
5	1.0510	1.1041	1.1593	1.2167	1.2763	1.3382	1.4026	1.4693	1.5386
6	1.0615	1.1262	1.1941	1.2653	1.3401	1.4185	1.5007	1.5869	1.6771
7	1.0721	1.1487	1.2299	1.3159	1.4071	1.5036	1.6058	1.7138	1.8280
8	1.0829	1.1717	1.2668	1.3686	1.4775	1.5938	1.7182	1.8509	1.9926
9	1.0937	1.1951	1.3048	1.4233	1.5513	1.6895	1.8385	1.9990	2.1719
10	1.1046	1.2190	1.3439	1.4802	1.6289	1.7908	1.9672	2.1589	2.3674
11	1.1157	1.2434	1.3842	1.5395	1.7103	1.8983	2.1049	2.3316	2.5804
12	1.1268	1.2682	1.4258	1.6010	1.7959	2.0122	2.2522	2.5182	2.8127
13	1.1381	1.2936	1.4685	1.6651	1.8856	2.1329	2.4098	2.7196	3.0658
14	1.1495	1.3195	1.5126	1.7317	1.9799	2.2609	2.5785	2.9372	3.3417
15	1.1610	1.3459	1.5580	1.8009	2.0789	2.3966	2.7590	3.1722	3.6425
16	1.1726	1.3728	1.6047	1.8730	2.1829	2.5404	2.9522	3.4259	3.9703
17	1.1843	1.4002	1.6528	1.9479	2.2920	2.6928	3.1588	3.7000	4.3276
18	1.1961	1.4282	1.7024	2.0258	2.4066	2.8543	3.3799	3.9960	4.7171
19	1.2081	1.4568	1.7535	2.1068	2.5270	3.0256	3.6165	4.3157	5.1417
20	1.2202	1.4859	1.8061	2.1911	2.6533	3.2071	3.8697	4.6610	5.6044
21	1.2324	1.5157	1.8603	2.2788	2.7860	3.3996	4.1406	5.0338	6.1088
22	1.2447	1.5460	1.9161	2.3699	2.9253	3.6035	4.4304	5.4365	6.6586
23	1.2572	1.5769	1.9736	2.4647	3.0715	3.8197	4.7405	5.8715	7.2579
24	1.2697	1.6084	2.0328	2.5633	3.2251	4.0489	5.0724	6.3412	7.9111
25	1.2824	1.6406	2.0938	2.6658	3.3864	4.2919	5.4274	6.8485	8.6231
30	1.3478	1.8114	2.4273	3.2434	4.3219	5.7435	7.6123	10.063	13.268
40	1.4889	2.2080	3.2620	4.8010	7.0400	10.286	14.974	21.725	31.409
50	1.6446	2.6916	4.3839	7.1067	11.467	18.420	29.457	46.902	74.358
60	1.8167	3.2810	5.8916	10.520	18.679	32.988	57.946	101.26	176.03

Table A-1
(CONCLUDED)

					Interest Rate					
10%	12%	14%	15%	16%	18%	20%	24%	28%	32%	36%
1.1000	1.1200	1.1400	1.1500	1.1600	1.1800	1.2000	1.2400	1.2800	1.3200	1.3600
1.2100	1.2544	1.2996	1.3225	1.3456	1.3924	1.4400	1.5376	1.6384	1.7424	1.8496
1.3310	1.4049	1.4815	1.5209	1.5609	1.6430	1.7280	1.9066	2.0972	2.3000	2.5155
1.4641	1.5735	1.6890	1.7490	1.8106	1.9388	2.0736	2.3642	2.6844	3.0360	3.4210
1.6105	1.7623	1.9254	2.0114	2.1003	2.2878	2.4883	2.9316	3.4360	4.0075	4.6526
1.7716	1.9738	2.1950	2.3131	2.4364	2.6996	2.9860	3.6352	4.3980	5.2899	6.3275
1.9487	2.2107	2.5023	2.6600	2.8262	3.1855	3.5832	4.5077	5.6295	6.9826	8.6054
2.1436	2.4760	2.8526	3.0590	3.2784	3.7589	4.2998	5.5895	7.2058	9.2170	11.703
2.3579	2.7731	3.2519	3.5179	3.8030	4.4355	5.1598	6.9310	9.2234	12.166	15.917
2.5937	3.1058	3.7072	4.0456	4.4114	5.2338	6.1917	8.5944	11.806	16.060	21.647
2.8531	3.4785	4.2262	4.6524	5.1173	6.1759	7.4301	10.657	15.112	21.199	29.439
3.1384	3.8960	4.8179	5.3503	5.9360	7.2876	8.9161	13.215	19.343	27.983	40.037
3.4523	4.3635	5.4924	6.1528	6.8858	8.5994	10.699	16.386	24.759	36.937	54.451
3.7975	4.8871	6.2613	7.0757	7.9875	10.147	12.839	20.319	31.691	48.757	74.053
4.1772	5.4736	7.1379	8.1371	9.2655	11.974	15.407	25.196	40.565	64.359	100.71
4.5950	6.1304	8.1372	9.3576	10.748	14.129	18.488	31.243	51.923	84.954	136.97
5.0545	6.8660	9.2765	10.761	12.468	16.672	22.186	38.741	66.461	112.14	186.28
5.5599	7.6900	10.575	12.375	14.463	19.673	26.623	48.039	85.071	148.02	253.34
6.1159	8.6128	12.056	14.232	16.777	23.214	31.948	59.568	108.89	195.39	344.54
6.7275	9.6463	13.743	16.367	19.461	27.393	38.338	73.864	139.38	257.92	468.57
7.4002	10.804	15.668	18.822	22.574	32.324	46.005	91.592	178.41	340.45	637.26
8.1403	12.100	17.861	21.645	26.186	38.142	55.206	113.57	228.36	449.39	866.67
8.9543	13.552	20.362	24.891	30.376	45.008	66.247	140.83	292.30	593.20	1178.7
9.8497	15.179	23.212	28.625	35.236	53.109	79.497	174.63	374.14	783.02	1603.0
10.835	17.000	26.462	32.919	40.874	62.669	95.396	216.54	478.90	1033.6	2180.1
17.449	29.960	50.950	66.212	85.850	143.37	237.38	634.82	1645.5	4142.1	10143.
45.259	93.051	188.88	267.86	378.72	750.38	1469.8	5455.9	19427.	66521.	*
117.39	289.00	700.23	1083.7	1670.7	3927.4	9100.4	46890.	*	*	*
304.48	897.60	2595.9	4384.0	7370.2	20555.	56348.	*	*	*	*

*The factor is greater than 99,999.

Table **A-2**

PRESENT VALUE OF $1 TO BE RECEIVED AFTER t PERIODS $= 1/(1 + r)^t$

					Interest Rate				
Period	**1%**	**2%**	**3%**	**4%**	**5%**	**6%**	**7%**	**8%**	**9%**
1	0.9901	0.9804	0.9709	0.9615	0.9524	0.9434	0.9346	0.9259	0.9174
2	0.9803	0.9612	0.9426	0.9246	0.9070	0.8900	0.8734	0.8573	0.8417
3	0.9706	0.9423	0.9151	0.8890	0.8638	0.8396	0.8163	0.7938	0.7722
4	0.9610	0.9238	0.8885	0.8548	0.8227	0.7921	0.7629	0.7350	0.7084
5	0.9515	0.9057	0.8626	0.8219	0.7835	0.7473	0.7130	0.6806	0.6499
6	0.9420	0.8880	0.8375	0.7903	0.7462	0.7050	0.6663	0.6302	0.5963
7	0.9327	0.8706	0.8131	0.7599	0.7107	0.6651	0.6227	0.5835	0.5470
8	0.9235	0.8535	0.7894	0.7307	0.6768	0.6274	0.5820	0.5403	0.5019
9	0.9143	0.8368	0.7664	0.7026	0.6446	0.5919	0.5439	0.5002	0.4604
10	0.9053	0.8203	0.7441	0.6756	0.6139	0.5584	0.5083	0.4632	0.4224
11	0.8963	0.8043	0.7224	0.6496	0.5847	0.5268	0.4751	0.4289	0.3875
12	0.8874	0.7885	0.7014	0.6246	0.5568	0.4970	0.4440	0.3971	0.3555
13	0.8787	0.7730	0.6810	0.6006	0.5303	0.4688	0.4150	0.3677	0.3262
14	0.8700	0.7579	0.6611	0.5775	0.5051	0.4423	0.3878	0.3405	0.2992
15	0.8613	0.7430	0.6419	0.5553	0.4810	0.4173	0.3624	0.3152	0.2745
16	0.8528	0.7284	0.6232	0.5339	0.4581	0.3936	0.3387	0.2919	0.2519
17	0.8444	0.7142	0.6050	0.5134	0.4363	0.3714	0.3166	0.2703	0.2311
18	0.8360	0.7002	0.5874	0.4936	0.4155	0.3503	0.2959	0.2502	0.2120
19	0.8277	0.6864	0.5703	0.4746	0.3957	0.3305	0.2765	0.2317	0.1945
20	0.8195	0.6730	0.5537	0.4564	0.3769	0.3118	0.2584	0.2145	0.1784
21	0.8114	0.6598	0.5375	0.4388	0.3589	0.2942	0.2415	0.1987	0.1637
22	0.8034	0.6468	0.5219	0.4220	0.3418	0.2775	0.2257	0.1839	0.1502
23	0.7954	0.6342	0.5067	0.4057	0.3256	0.2618	0.2109	0.1703	0.1378
24	0.7876	0.6217	0.4919	0.3901	0.3101	0.2470	0.1971	0.1577	0.1264
25	0.7798	0.6095	0.4776	0.3751	0.2953	0.2330	0.1842	0.1460	0.1160
30	0.7419	0.5521	0.4120	0.3083	0.2314	0.1741	0.1314	0.0994	0.0754
40	0.6717	0.4529	0.3066	0.2083	0.1420	0.0972	0.0668	0.0460	0.0318
50	0.6080	0.3715	0.2281	0.1407	0.0872	0.0543	0.0339	0.0213	0.0134

Table A-2
(CONCLUDED)

					Interest Rate					
10%	**12%**	**14%**	**15%**	**16%**	**18%**	**20%**	**24%**	**28%**	**32%**	**36%**
0.9091	0.8929	0.8772	0.8696	0.8621	0.8475	0.8333	0.8065	0.7813	0.7576	0.7353
0.8264	0.7972	0.7695	0.7561	0.7432	0.7182	0.6944	0.6504	0.6104	0.5739	0.5407
0.7513	0.7118	0.6750	0.6575	0.6407	0.6086	0.5787	0.5245	0.4768	0.4348	0.3975
0.6830	0.6355	0.5921	0.5718	0.5523	0.5158	0.4823	0.4230	0.3725	0.3294	0.2923
0.6209	0.5674	0.5194	0.4972	0.4761	0.4371	0.4019	0.3411	0.2910	0.2495	0.2149
0.5645	0.5066	0.4556	0.4323	0.4104	0.3704	0.3349	0.2751	0.2274	0.1890	0.1580
0.5132	0.4523	0.3996	0.3759	0.3538	0.3139	0.2791	0.2218	0.1776	0.1432	0.1162
0.4665	0.4039	0.3506	0.3269	0.3050	0.2660	0.2326	0.1789	0.1388	0.1085	0.0854
0.4241	0.3606	0.3075	0.2843	0.2630	0.2255	0.1938	0.1443	0.1084	0.0822	0.0628
0.3855	0.3220	0.2697	0.2472	0.2267	0.1911	0.1615	0.1164	0.0847	0.0623	0.0462
0.3505	0.2875	0.2366	0.2149	0.1954	0.1619	0.1346	0.0938	0.0662	0.0472	0.0340
0.3186	0.2567	0.2076	0.1869	0.1685	0.1372	0.1122	0.0757	0.0517	0.0357	0.0250
0.2897	0.2292	0.1821	0.1625	0.1452	0.1163	0.0935	0.0610	0.0404	0.0271	0.0184
0.2633	0.2046	0.1597	0.1413	0.1252	0.0985	0.0779	0.0492	0.0316	0.0205	0.0135
0.2394	0.1827	0.1401	0.1229	0.1079	0.0835	0.0649	0.0397	0.0247	0.0155	0.0099
0.2176	0.1631	0.1229	0.1069	0.0930	0.0708	0.0541	0.0320	0.0193	0.0118	0.0073
0.1978	0.1456	0.1078	0.0929	0.0802	0.0600	0.0451	0.0258	0.0150	0.0089	0.0054
0.1799	0.1300	0.0946	0.0808	0.0691	0.0508	0.0376	0.0208	0.0118	0.0068	0.0039
0.1635	0.1161	0.0829	0.0703	0.0596	0.0431	0.0313	0.0168	0.0092	0.0051	0.0029
0.1486	0.1037	0.0728	0.0611	0.0514	0.0365	0.0261	0.0135	0.0072	0.0039	0.0021
0.1351	0.0926	0.0638	0.0531	0.0443	0.0309	0.0217	0.0109	0.0056	0.0029	0.0016
0.1228	0.0826	0.0560	0.0462	0.0382	0.0262	0.0181	0.0088	0.0044	0.0022	0.0012
0.1117	0.0738	0.0491	0.0402	0.0329	0.0222	0.0151	0.0071	0.0034	0.0017	0.0008
0.1015	0.0659	0.0431	0.0349	0.0284	0.0188	0.0126	0.0057	0.0027	0.0013	0.0006
0.0923	0.0588	0.0378	0.0304	0.0245	0.0160	0.0105	0.0046	0.0021	0.0010	0.0005
0.0573	0.0334	0.0196	0.0151	0.0116	0.0070	0.0042	0.0016	0.0006	0.0002	0.0001
0.0221	0.0107	0.0053	0.0037	0.0026	0.0013	0.0007	0.0002	0.0001	*	*
0.0085	0.0035	0.0014	0.0009	0.0006	0.0003	0.0001	*	*	*	*

*The factor is zero to four decimal places.

Table A-3

PRESENT VALUE OF AN ANNUITY OF $1 PER PERIOD FOR *t* PERIODS
$= [1 - 1/(1 + r)^t]/r$

Period	1%	2%	3%	4%	5%	6%	7%	8%	9%
1	0.9901	0.9804	0.9709	0.9615	0.9524	0.9434	0.9346	0.9259	0.9174
2	1.9704	1.9416	1.9135	1.8861	1.8594	1.8334	1.8080	1.7833	1.7591
3	2.9410	2.8839	2.8286	2.7751	2.7232	2.6730	2.6243	2.5771	2.5313
4	3.9020	3.8077	3.7171	3.6299	3.5460	3.4651	3.3872	3.3121	3.2397
5	4.8534	4.7135	4.5797	4.4518	4.3295	4.2124	4.1002	3.9927	3.8897
6	5.7955	5.6014	5.4172	5.2421	5.0757	4.9173	4.7665	4.6229	4.4859
7	6.7282	6.4720	6.2303	6.0021	5.7864	5.5824	5.3893	5.2064	5.0330
8	7.6517	7.3255	7.0197	6.7327	6.4632	6.2098	5.9713	5.7466	5.5348
9	8.5660	8.1622	7.7861	7.4353	7.1078	6.8017	6.5152	6.2469	5.9952
10	9.4713	8.9826	8.5302	8.1109	7.7217	7.3601	7.0236	6.7101	6.4177
11	10.3676	9.7868	9.2526	8.7605	8.3064	7.8869	7.4987	7.1390	6.8052
12	11.2551	10.5753	9.9540	9.3851	8.8633	8.3838	7.9427	7.5361	7.1607
13	12.1337	11.3484	10.6350	9.9856	9.3936	8.8527	8.3577	7.9038	7.4869
14	13.0037	12.1062	11.2961	10.5631	9.8986	9.2950	8.7455	8.2442	7.7862
15	13.8651	12.8493	11.9379	11.1184	10.3797	9.7122	9.1079	8.5595	8.0607
16	14.7179	13.5777	12.5611	11.6523	10.8378	10.1059	9.4466	8.8514	8.3126
17	15.5623	14.2919	13.1661	12.1657	11.2741	10.4773	9.7632	9.1216	8.5436
18	16.3983	14.9920	13.7535	12.6593	11.6896	10.8276	10.0591	9.3719	8.7556
19	17.2260	15.6785	14.3238	13.1339	12.0853	11.1581	10.3356	9.6036	8.9501
20	18.0456	16.3514	14.8775	13.5903	12.4622	11.4699	10.5940	9.8181	9.1285
21	18.8570	17.0112	15.4150	14.0292	12.8212	11.7641	10.8355	10.0168	9.2922
22	19.6604	17.6580	15.9369	14.4511	13.1630	12.0416	11.0612	10.2007	9.4424
23	20.4558	18.2922	16.4436	14.8568	13.4886	12.3034	11.2722	10.3741	9.5802
24	21.2434	18.9139	16.9355	15.2470	13.7986	12.5504	11.4593	10.5288	9.7066
25	22.0232	19.5235	17.4131	15.6221	14.0939	12.7834	11.6536	10.6748	9.8226
30	25.8077	22.3965	19.6004	17.2920	15.3725	13.7648	12.4090	11.2578	10.2737
40	32.8347	27.3555	23.1148	19.7928	17.1591	15.0463	13.3317	11.9246	10.7574
50	39.1961	31.4236	25.7298	21.4822	18.2559	15.7619	13.8007	12.2335	10.9617

Table A-3
(CONCLUDED)

				Interest Rate					
10%	**12%**	**14%**	**15%**	**16%**	**18%**	**20%**	**24%**	**28%**	**32%**
0.9091	0.8929	0.8772	0.8696	0.8621	0.8475	0.8333	0.8065	0.7813	0.7576
1.7355	1.6901	1.6467	1.6257	1.6052	1.5656	1.5278	1.4568	1.3916	1.3315
2.4869	2.4018	2.3216	2.2832	2.2459	2.1743	2.1065	1.9813	1.8684	1.7663
3.1699	3.0373	2.9137	2.8550	2.7982	2.6901	2.5887	2.4043	2.2410	2.0957
3.7908	3.6048	3.4331	3.3522	3.2743	3.1272	2.9906	2.7454	2.5320	2.3452
4.3553	4.1114	3.8887	3.7845	3.6847	3.4976	3.3255	3.0205	2.7594	2.5342
4.8684	4.5638	4.2883	4.1604	4.0386	3.8115	3.6046	3.2423	2.9370	2.6775
5.3349	4.9676	4.6389	4.4873	4.3436	4.0776	3.8372	3.4212	3.0758	2.7860
5.7590	5.3282	4.9464	4.7716	4.6065	4.3030	4.0310	3.5655	3.1842	2.8681
6.1446	5.6502	5.2161	5.0188	4.8332	4.4941	4.1925	3.6819	3.2689	2.9304
6.4951	5.9377	5.4527	5.2337	5.0286	4.6560	4.3271	3.7757	3.3351	2.9776
6.8137	6.1944	5.6603	5.4206	5.1971	4.7932	4.4392	3.8514	3.3868	3.0133
7.1034	6.4235	5.8424	5.5831	5.3423	4.9095	4.5327	3.9124	3.4272	3.0404
7.3667	6.6282	6.0021	5.7245	5.4675	5.0081	4.6106	3.9616	3.4587	3.0609
7.6061	6.8109	6.1422	5.8474	5.5755	5.0916	4.6755	4.0013	3.4834	3.0764
7.8237	6.9740	6.2651	5.9542	5.6685	5.1624	4.7296	4.0333	3.5026	3.0882
8.0216	7.1196	6.3729	6.0472	5.7487	5.2223	4.7746	4.0591	3.5177	3.0971
8.2014	7.2497	6.4674	6.1280	5.8178	5.2732	4.8122	4.0799	3.5294	3.1039
8.3649	7.3658	6.5504	6.1982	5.8775	5.3162	4.8435	4.0967	3.5386	3.1090
8.5136	7.4694	6.6231	6.2593	5.9288	5.3527	4.8696	4.1103	3.5458	3.1129
8.6487	7.5620	6.6870	6.3125	5.9731	5.3837	4.8913	4.1212	3.5514	3.1158
8.7715	7.6446	6.7429	6.3587	6.0113	5.4099	4.9094	4.1300	3.5558	3.1180
8.8832	7.7184	6.7921	6.3988	6.0442	5.4321	4.9245	4.1371	3.5592	3.1197
8.9847	7.7843	6.8351	6.4338	6.0726	5.4509	4.9371	4.1428	3.5619	3.1210
9.0770	7.8431	6.8729	6.4641	6.0971	5.4669	4.9476	4.1474	3.5640	3.1220
9.4269	8.0552	7.0027	6.5660	6.1772	5.5168	4.9789	4.1601	3.5693	3.1242
9.7791	8.2438	7.1050	6.6418	6.2335	5.5482	4.9966	4.1659	3.5712	3.1250
9.9148	8.3045	7.1327	6.6605	6.2463	5.5541	4.9995	4.1666	3.5714	3.1250

Table **A-4**

FUTURE VALUE OF AN ANNUITY OF $1 PER PERIOD FOR *t* PERIODS
$= [(1 + r)^t - 1]/r$

| | | | | | Interest Rate | | | | |
Period	1%	2%	3%	4%	5%	6%	7%	8%	9%
1	1.0000	1.0000	1.0000	1.0000	1.0000	1.0000	1.0000	1.0000	1.0000
2	2.0100	2.0200	2.0300	2.0400	2.0500	2.0600	2.0700	2.0800	2.0900
3	3.0301	3.0604	3.0909	3.1216	3.1525	3.1836	3.2149	3.2464	3.2781
4	4.0604	4.1216	4.1836	4.2465	4.3101	4.3746	4.4399	4.5061	4.5731
5	5.1010	5.2040	5.3091	5.4163	5.5256	5.6371	5.7507	5.8666	5.9847
6	6.1520	6.3081	6.4684	6.6330	6.8019	6.9753	7.1533	7.3359	7.5233
7	7.2135	7.4343	7.6625	7.8983	8.1420	8.3938	8.6540	8.9228	9.2004
8	8.2857	8.5830	8.8932	9.2142	9.5491	9.8975	10.260	10.637	11.028
9	9.3685	9.7546	10.159	10.583	11.027	11.491	11.978	12.488	13.021
10	10.462	10.950	11.464	12.006	12.578	13.181	13.816	14.487	15.193
11	11.567	12.169	12.808	13.486	14.207	14.972	15.784	16.645	17.560
12	12.683	13.412	14.192	15.026	15.917	16.870	17.888	18.977	20.141
13	13.809	14.680	15.618	16.627	17.713	18.882	20.141	21.495	22.953
14	14.947	15.974	17.086	18.292	19.599	21.015	22.550	24.215	26.019
15	16.097	17.293	18.599	20.024	21.579	23.276	25.129	27.152	29.361
16	17.258	18.639	20.157	21.825	23.657	25.673	27.888	30.324	33.003
17	18.430	20.012	21.762	23.698	25.840	28.213	30.840	33.750	36.974
18	19.615	21.412	23.414	25.645	28.132	30.906	33.999	37.450	41.301
19	20.811	22.841	25.117	27.671	30.539	33.760	37.379	41.446	46.018
20	22.019	24.297	26.870	29.778	33.066	36.786	40.995	45.762	51.160
21	23.239	25.783	28.676	31.969	35.719	39.993	44.865	50.423	56.765
22	24.472	27.299	30.537	34.248	38.505	43.392	49.006	55.457	62.873
23	25.716	28.845	32.453	36.618	41.430	46.996	53.436	60.893	69.532
24	26.973	30.422	34.426	39.083	44.502	50.816	58.177	66.765	76.790
25	28.243	32.030	36.459	41.646	47.727	54.865	63.249	73.106	84.701
30	34.785	40.568	47.575	56.085	66.439	79.058	94.461	113.28	136.31
40	48.886	60.402	75.401	95.026	120.80	154.76	199.64	259.06	337.88
50	64.463	84.579	112.80	152.67	209.35	290.34	406.53	573.77	815.08
60	81.670	114.05	163.05	237.99	353.58	533.13	813.52	1253.2	1944.8

Table A–4
(CONCLUDED)

					Interest Rate					
10%	12%	14%	15%	16%	18%	20%	24%	28%	32%	36%
1.0000	1.0000	1.0000	1.0000	1.0000	1.0000	1.0000	1.0000	1.0000	1.0000	1.0000
2.1000	2.1200	2.1400	2.1500	2.1600	2.1800	2.2000	2.2400	2.2800	2.3200	2.3600
3.3100	3.3744	3.4396	3.4725	3.5056	3.5724	3.6400	3.7776	3.9184	4.0624	4.2096
4.6410	4.7793	4.9211	4.9934	5.0665	5.2154	5.3680	5.6842	6.0156	6.3624	6.7251
6.1051	6.3528	6.6101	6.7424	6.8771	7.1542	7.4416	8.0484	8.6999	9.3983	10.146
7.7156	8.1152	8.5355	8.7537	8.9775	9.4420	9.9299	10.980	12.136	13.406	14.799
9.4872	10.089	10.730	11.067	11.414	12.142	12.916	14.615	16.534	18.696	21.126
11.436	12.300	13.233	13.727	14.240	15.327	16.499	19.123	22.163	25.678	29.732
13.579	14.776	16.085	16.786	17.519	19.086	20.799	24.712	29.369	34.895	41.435
15.937	17.549	19.337	20.304	21.321	23.521	25.959	31.643	38.593	47.062	57.352
18.531	20.655	23.045	24.349	25.733	28.755	32.150	40.238	50.398	63.122	78.998
21.384	24.133	27.271	29.002	30.850	34.931	39.581	50.895	65.510	84.320	108.44
24.523	28.029	32.089	34.352	36.786	42.219	48.497	64.110	84.853	112.30	148.47
27.975	32.393	37.581	40.505	43.672	50.818	59.196	80.496	109.61	149.24	202.93
31.772	37.280	43.842	47.580	51.660	60.965	72.035	100.82	141.30	198.00	276.98
35.950	42.753	50.980	55.717	60.925	72.939	87.442	126.01	181.87	262.36	377.69
40.545	48.884	59.118	65.075	71.673	87.068	105.93	157.25	233.79	347.31	514.66
45.599	55.750	68.394	75.836	84.141	103.74	128.12	195.99	300.25	459.45	700.94
51.159	63.440	78.969	88.212	98.603	123.41	154.74	244.03	385.32	607.47	954.28
57.275	72.052	91.025	102.44	115.38	146.63	186.69	303.60	494.21	802.86	1298.8
64.002	81.699	104.77	118.81	134.84	174.02	225.03	377.46	633.59	1060.8	1767.4
71.403	92.503	120.44	137.63	157.41	206.34	271.03	469.06	812.00	1401.2	2404.7
79.543	104.60	138.30	159.28	183.60	244.49	326.24	582.63	1040.4	1850.6	3271.3
88.497	118.16	158.66	184.17	213.98	289.49	392.48	723.46	1332.7	2443.8	4450.0
98.347	133.33	181.87	212.79	249.21	342.60	471.98	898.09	1706.8	3226.8	6053.0
164.49	241.33	356.79	434.75	530.31	790.95	1181.9	2640.9	5873.2	12941.	28172.3
442.59	767.09	1342.0	1779.1	2360.8	4163.2	7343.9	22729.	69377.	*	*
1163.9	2400.0	4994.5	7217.7	10436.	21813.	45497.	*	*	*	*
3034.8	7471.6	18535.	29220.	46058.	*	*	*	*	*	*

*The factor is greater than 99,999.

References

"Adopted But Unloved Model Investment Law May Not Stick." *The Insurance Regulator*, October 7, 1996, p. 1.

"Aggregate Condition and Income Data, FDIC-Insured Commercial Banks." *FDIC Quarterly Banking Profile*. Washington, DC: FDIC, September 1997.

Akhavein, J., A. N. Berger, and D. B. Humphrey. "The Effects of Megamergers on Efficiency and Prices: Evidence from a Bank Profit Function." Conference on Mergers of Financial Institutions, New York University, October 1996.

Allen, L., and A. Saunders. "Bank Window Dressing: Theory and Evidence." *Journal of Banking and Finance* 16 (1992), pp. 585–624.

Altman, E. I. "Managing the Commercial Lending Process." In *Handbook of Banking Strategy*, ed. R. C. Aspinwall and R. A. Eisenbeis. New York: John Wiley, 1985, pp. 473–510.

American Council of Life Insurance. *Life Insurance Fact Book*, 1994.

Andersen, Arthur. "A Question of Collateral." *Euromoney*, November 1995, pp. 46–49.

Angbazo, L., J. Mei, and A. Saunders. "Credit Spreads in the Market for Highly Leveraged Transactions Loans." New York University, September 1996.

Asarnow, E., and J. Marker. "Historical Performance of the U.S. Corporate Loan Market 1988–1993." *The Journal of Commercial Lending*, Spring 1995, pp. 13–22.

"Asian Turmoil." *The Financial Times Limited*, November 14, 1997, p. 15.

Avery, R. B., and A. Berger. "Risk-Based Capital and Deposit Insurance Reform." *Journal of Banking and Finance* 15 (1991), pp. 847–874.

Bagli, C. V. "ADT versus Chase: Testing Limits of Bank's Role in Takeovers." The *New York Times*, February 22, 1997, Section 1, p. 35.

Bagli, C. V. "Insurer Grows, Equating Size and Survival." The *New York Times*, February 14, 1997, p. D1.

The Banker, June 1976, July 1986, February 1996, and July 1996.

"Bankers Trust Clients Complaining." The *New York Times*, January 20, 1995, p. D1.

Bank for International Settlements. "Proposal to Issue a Supplement to the Basle Accord to Cover Market Risks." Basle, Switzerland: Bank for International Settlements, April 1995.

———. *Statistics on Payment Systems in the Group of 10 Countries*. Basle, Switzerland: Bank for International Settlements, Table 5, p. 117; Table 10b, p. 126.

———. "The Supervisory Treatment of Market Risks." Basle, Switzerland: Bank for International Settlements, April 1993.

"Bank Regulators Taking a Close Look at Lending Risks." The *New York Times*, April 8, 1995.

"Banks Push into Securities Squeezes Fees." The *Wall Street Journal*, December 16, 1997, p. C1.

"Barings Pays the Price of Ignoring Warning Signs." *Investors Chronicle*, March 3, 1995.

Barr, P. G. "Institutions Cut Derivative Use." *Pensions & Investments*, July 22, 1996, p. 3.

Beatty, R., and J. Ritter. "Investment Banking, Reputation, and the Underpricing of Initial Public Offerings." *Journal of Financial Economics* 15 (1986), pp. 213–232.

Beaumier, C. M. "Greenspan's Challenge: A Reward for Improving Credit Risk." *Banking Policy Report*, August 5, 1996.

Benston, G. J. *The Separation of Commercial and Investment Banking: The Glass-Steagall Act Revisited and Reconsidered*. New York: St. Martin's Press, 1989.

———. "Universal Banking." *Journal of Economic Perspectives* 8 (1994), pp. 121–143.

Benston, G. J., and G. G. Kaufman. "FDICIA after Five Years." *Journal of Economic Perspectives*, Winter 1997, pp. 139–158.

Berger, A., D. Hancock, and D. B. Humphrey. "Bank Efficiency Derived from the Profit Function." *Journal of Banking and Finance* 17 (1993), pp. 317–347.

Berger, A., and D. B. Humphrey. "Megamergers in Banking and the Use of Cost Efficiency as an Antitrust Defense." *The Antitrust Bulletin* 37 (1992), pp. 541–600.

———. "The Dominance of Inefficiencies over Scale and Product Mix in Banking." *Journal of Monetary Economics* 28 (1991), and the *Journal of Banking and Finance* 17 (1993), Special Issue on Efficiency.

Berger, A., W. C. Hunter, and S. G. Timme. "The Efficiency of Financial Institutions: A Review and Preview of Research Past, Present and Future." *Journal of Banking and Finance* 17 (1993), pp. 221–249.

Berger, A., and G. Udell. "Relationship Lending and Lines of Credit in Small Firm Finance." *Journal of Business* 68 (1995), pp. 351–382.

Best's Aggregates & Averages, Life-Health, 1997, p. 3.

Best's Aggregates & Averages, Property-Casualty, 1994, pp. 2, 158, 183; 1997, p. 2.

Best's Review, August 1987; October 1996; May 1997; August 1997, p. 32.

Black, F., and M. Scholes. "The Pricing of Options and Corporate Liabilities." *Journal of Political Economy* 81 (1973), pp. 737–759.

"Blind Faith." *The Economist*, January 31, 1998, p. 76.

Bloch, E. *Inside Investment Banking*, 2nd ed.Chicago: Irwin, 1989.

Boot, A. W. A., and A. V. Thakor. "Off-Balance-Sheet Liabilities, Deposit Insurance, and Capital Regulation." *Journal of Banking and Finance* 15 (1991), pp. 825–846.

Bouyoucos, P. J., M. H. Siegel, and E. B. Raisel. "Risk-Based Capital for Insurers: A Strategic Opportunity to Enhance Franchise Value." Goldman Sachs, Industry Resource Group, New York, September 1992.

Boyd, J. D., and S. L. Graham. "Consolidation in U.S. Banking: Implications for Efficiency and Competition Risk." Conference on Mergers of Financial Institutions, New York University, October 1996.

Boyd, J. H., and M. Gertler. "Are Banks Dead? Or, Are the Reports Greatly Exaggerated?" Working Paper, Federal Reserve Bank of Minneapolis, May 1994.

Brealey, R. A., S. C. Myers, and A. J. Marcus. *Fundamental of Corporate Finance*. New York: McGraw-Hill, 1995, pp. 225–229.

Brewer, E. "Bank Gap Management and the Use of Financial Futures." *Economic Perspectives*, Federal Reserve Bank of Chicago, March–April 1985.

Buser, S. A., A. H. Chen, and E. J. Kane. "Federal Deposit Insurance, Regulatory Policy, and Optimal Bank Capital." *Journal of Finance* 36 (1981), pp. 51–60.

"Canada's Borrowing with Its Fat Fees Lures Wall Street." The *New York Times*, April 15, 1995, p. D1.

Cebenoyan, A. S., E. S. Cooperman, C. A. Register, and D. L. Bauer. "Interstate Savings and Loans in the 1990s: A Performance and Risk Appraisal." Working Paper, University of Colorado at Denver, 1997.

"Chase, Chemical Form America's Largest Bank." *Mergers & Acquisitions in Canada*, September 1, 1995.

Clark, J. A. "Economics of Scale and Scope at Depository Financial Institutions: A Review of the Literature." *Economic Review*, Federal Reserve Bank of Kansas City, September–October (1988), pp. 16–33.

Clark, M., and A. Saunders. "Judicial Interpretation of Glass-Steagall: The Need for Legislative Action." *The Banking Law Journal* 97 (1980), pp. 721–740.

———. "Glass-Steagall Revisited: The Impact on Banks, Capital Markets, and the Small Investor." *The Banking Law Journal* 97 (1980), pp. 811–840.

Clary, I. "US Debt Going into 'Uncharted Territory'—Experts." The *Reuters Financial Service*, January 24, 1996.

Clayton, M. "Insurance Investors Sharpen Skills." *The Insurance Accountant*, October 28, 1996, p. 1.

———. "GAO Calls Insurance 'Regulatory Gap.'" *The Insurance Accountant*, November 18, 1996, p. 1.

Connolly, J. "Investors Warming to Developing CMBS Market." National Life Underwriters, September 16, 1996, p. 29.

Cook, T. "Treasury Bills." *Instruments of the Money Market*. Richmond, VA: Federal Reserve Bank of Richmond, 1986, pp. 81–93.

Cornett, M. M., and S. De. "Common Stock Returns in Corporate Takeover Bids: Evidence of Interstate Bank Mergers." *Journal of Banking and Finance* 15 (1991), pp. 273–295.

Cornett, M. M., and H. Tehranian. "Changes in Corporate Performance Associated with Bank Acquisitions." *Journal of Financial Economics* 31 (1992), pp. 211–234.

Corrigan, T. "JP Morgan Warns of Global Blow to Earnings." *The Financial Times*, December 11, 1997, p. 23.

"CRIMI MAE Refinances $142 Million of Floating-Rate Debt Replacing It with Longer-Term, Fixed-Rate Financing." *PR Newswire*, December 20, 1996.

Cummins, J., S. E. Harrington, and R. Klein. "Insolvency Exercise, Risk-Based Capital and Prompt Corrective Action in Property-Liability Insurance." *Journal of Banking and Finance* 1995, pp. 511–527.

Dalta, S., M. Iskandar-Dalton, and A. Patel. "The Pricing of Initial Public Offers of Corporate Straight Debt." *Journal of Finance*, March 1997, pp. 379–396.

"Debt Dogs Japan's Banks Despite Write-Offs." *The Banker*, February 1997, p. 4.

Department of the Treasury. "Modernizing the Financial System: Recommendations for Safer, More Competitive Banks." Washington, DC: Department of Treasury, February 1991.

Dunaief, D. "Rate Risks Spur Banks to Cut Exposure." *The American Banker*, June 4, 1996, p. 3A.

The Economist, March 20, 1993, p. 86; January 21, 1995, p. 78; April 6, 1995, p. 110; October 26, 1996, p. 7; February 7, 1998, p. 110.

Edwards, F. R. "Derivatives Can Be Hazardous to Your Health." Working Paper, London School of Economics, December 1994.

EIU Country Risk Service. *The Economist*, March 22, 1997, p. 130.

Elstein, A. "Afraid of Derivatives? Not These Three Little Banks." *The American Banker*, November 7, 1996, p. 20.

———. "Risk Management: Oversupply of Interest Swaps Slows Growth in Trade." *The American Banker*, November 7, 1996, p. 20.

———. "Banks Joining Parade of Buyers of Asset-Backed Paper from Third World." *The American Banker*, November 13, 1996, p. 32.

Elton, E. J., and M. J. Gruber. *Modern Portfolio Theory and Investment Analysis*, 5th ed. New York: John Wiley, 1995, chapter 2.

Feder, B. J. "A Risky Business Gets Even Riskier: Big Losses and Bad Accounting Leave 'Subprime' Lenders Reeling." The *New York Times*, February 12, 1997, p. 1.

Federal Deposit Insurance Corporation. *Failed Bank Cost Analysis, 1985–1995*.

Federal Reserve Board of Governors. "Revisions to Risk-Based Capital Standards to Account for Concentration of Credit Risk and Risks of Non-Traditional Activities." Washington, DC: FDICIA, March 26, 1993, Section 305.

———. "Risk-Based Capital and Interest Rate Risk." Press release, July 30, 1992.

———. "Risk-Based Capital Standards: Interest Rate Risk, Final Ruling." Federal Reserve Document R-0802, August 2, 1995.

Federal Reserve Board. Statistical Releases, "Flow of Funds Accounts." Washington, DC: Federal Reserve Board, March 1998.

Federal Reserve Bulletin, June 1978, p. A39; December 1982; February 1993; November 1997, p. A15, Table 1.26, Table 4.23, Table A12; January 1997; December 1997, p. 74, 85, 90, A33, Table 1.26, Table 1.53, Table 1.54, Table 1.55, Table 1.56; December 1997, p. 77; January 1998, Table 3.21.

Felgren, S. D. "Banks as Insurance Agencies: Local Constraints and Competitive Advances." *New England Economic Review*, Federal Reserve Bank of Boston, September–October 1985, pp. 34–39.

Finnerty, J. D. "Credit Derivatives, Infrastructure Finance, and Emerging Market Risk." *The Financier, ACMT*, February 1996, pp. 64–75.

Flannery, M., and J. Houston. "Market Responses to Federal Examinations of U.S. Bank Holding Companies," Graduate School of Business Administration, University of Florida, October 1993.

Frank, S. E. "J. P. Morgan Plans to Fire 700 Staffers Amid Surging Costs, Crimpled Earnings." The *Wall Street Journal*, February 24, 1998, p. A3.

Friedman, M., and A. J. Schwartz. *A Monetary History of the United States, 1867–1960*. Princeton, NJ: Princeton University Press, 1963.

Fuerbringer, J. "Many Players, Many Losers: How and Why Asian Currencies Tumbled So Quickly." The *New York Times*, December 10, 1997, p. D1.

Gande, A., M. Puri, A. Saunders, and I. Walter. "Bank Underwriting of Debt Securities: Modern Evidence." *Review of Financial Studies, 1997.*

General Accounting Office. "Bank Powers: Issues Relating to Banks Selling Insurance," GAO/GGO 90-113. Washington, DC: Government Printing Office, 1990.

———. "U.S. Credit Card Industry: Competitive Developments Need to Be Closely Monitored," GAO/GGD-94-23, Washington, DC: Government Printing Office, 1994, p. 57.

———. *Securities Investor Protection*, GAO/GGD-92-109. Washington, DC: Government Printing Office, September 1992.

———. *Interstate Banking*, GAO/GGD, 95-35. Washington, DC: Government Printing Office, December 1994, p. 101.

———. *Report on Financial Derivatives*, Washington, DC: Government Printing Office, November 1996.

Gilpin, K. N. "Piggy Banks with Muscles: As Credit Unions Boom, Financial Rivals Cry Foul." The *New York Times*, February 26, 1997, p. D1.

Glassman, C. A. "Information on Six Large Finance Companies." *The Journal of Lending & Credit Risk Management*, December 1996.

"Glass-Steagall Revisited: The Impact on Banks, Capital Markets, and the Small Investor." *The Banking Law Journal* 97 (1980), pp. 811–840.

"Going Metric." *Financial Regulation Report*, London: Financial Times Newsletters, May 1997.

Goodman, L. S., P. Fischer, and C. Anderson. "The Impact of Risk-Based Capital Requirements on Asset Allocation for Life Insurance Companies." *Insurance Executive Review*, Fall 1992, pp. 14–21.

Gorton, G., and R. Rosen. "Banks and Derivatives." Working Paper, University of Pennsylvania Wharton School, February 1995.

Greenspan, A. "Remarks." Boston College Conference on Financial Markets and the Economy, Boston, September 19, 1994.

Haraf, W. S. "The Collapse of Drexel Burnham Lambert: Lessons for Bank Regulators." *Regulation*, Winter 1991, pp. 22–25.

Hassan, M. K., and W. H. Sackley. "Determinants of Thrift Institution Off-Balance-Sheet Activities: An Empirical Investigation." Working Paper 70148, Department of Finance, University of New Orleans.

Hawawini, G. "Controlling the Interest Rate Risk of Bonds: An Introduction to Duration Analysis and Immunization Strategies." *Finanzmarket and Portfolio Management* 1 (1986–1987), pp. 8–18.

Herring, R. J. "Innovations to Enhance Liquidity: The Implications for Systemic Risk." University of Pennsylvania, Wharton School, October 1992.

Holifield, S., M. Madaris, and W. H. Sackley. "Regulatory Risk and Hedging Accounting Standards in Financial Institutions." Working Paper, University of Southern Mississippi, April 1994.

Houston, J., and M. Ryngaert. "The Overall Gains from Large Bank Mergers." *Journal of Banking and Finance* 18 (1994), pp. 1155–1176.

———. "Equity Issuance and Adverse Selection: A Direct Test Using Conditional Stock Offers." *Journal of Finance* 52 (1997), pp. 197–219.

Humphrey, D. B. "Future Directions in Payment Risk Reduction." *Journal of Cash Management*, 1988.

"In Hong Kong, Runs on Banks and Cakes." The *New York Times*, December 19, 1997.

Institute of International Bankers. *1994 Global Survey of Regulatory and Market Developments in Banking, Securities and Insurance*, New York: Institute of International Bankers, September 1994, p. 17.

Institutional Investor, September 1997, p 114.

"Insurer Topics: Employee Recruiting and Training; Insurers Are Past the Point of No Return; Facing Volatility in Interest Rates and Squeezed Profit Margins, Companies Must Take a New Approach to Investment." *Business Insurance*, September 16, 1996.

Investment Company Institute. *Perspective*. Washington, DC: Investment Company Institute, March 1997.

Jack, A. "The End of a European Banking Dream: Credit Lyonnais Is Preparing to Sell Much of Its Network Outside France." *Financial Times*, January 16, 1997, p. 34.

"Japan Banks That Ventured Abroad Come Back Home." *International Herald Tribune*, December 10, 1997, p. 20.

"Japan: There's Even Further to Fall." *The Banker*, September 1996.

John, K., T. John, and L. W. Senbet. "Risk Shifting Incentives of Depository Institutions: A New Perspective on Federal Deposit Insurance Reform." *Journal of Banking and Finance* 36 (1991), pp. 335–367.

Jones, D. S., and K. K. King. "The Implementation of Prompt Corrective Action: An Assessment." *Journal of Banking and Finance*, 1995.

J. P. Morgan. *Introduction to CreditMetrics*. New York: J. P. Morgan Securities, April 1997.

J. P. Morgan. *Introduction to RiskMetrics*. New York: J. P. Morgan Securities, October 1994.

Kane, E. J. "What Is the Value-Added Large U.S. Banks Find in Offering Mutual Funds?" Working Paper, Boston College, November 1994.

———. "Accelerating Inflation, Technological Innovation, and the Decreasing Effectiveness of Banking Regulation." *Journal of Finance* 36 (1981), pp. 335–367.

———, and R. Hendershott. "The Federal Deposit Insurance Fund That Didn't Put a Bite on U.S. Taxpayers." *Journal of Banking and Finance* 20, no. 5 (1996), pp. 1305–1327.

Kaufman, G. G. "Bank Contagion: Theory and Evidence." *Journal of Financial Intermediation*, 1996.

———. "Measuring and Managing Interest Rate Risk: A Primer." *Economic Perspectives*, Federal Reserve Bank of Chicago, 1984, pp. 16–29.

KMV Corporation. *Credit Monitor*. San Francisco: KMV Corporation, 1994.

Kolor, J. "Home Banking Crossroads: The Web, the PC, or Both?" *Bank Technology*, September 1996, p. 1.

Krozner, R. "The Evolution of Universal Banking and Its Regulation in Twentieth Century America." In A. Saunders and I. Walter, eds. *Universal Banking Financial System Design Reconsidered*. Burr Ridge, IL: Irwin, 1996.

"Largest Mutual Funds," Associated Press Wire Release. New York: Associated Press, December 28, 1997.

Lee, W. "The Value of Risk Reduction to Investors." Research Paper 9312, Federal Reserve Bank of New York, 1993.

Levonian, M. "Interstate Banking and Risk." *Weekly Letter*, Federal Reserve Bank of San Francisco, 1994, pp. 94–126.

Loan Pricing Corporation. *Goldsheets*, November 10, 1997, p. 23.

Loderer, C. F., D. P. Sheehan, and G. B. Kadler. "The Pricing of Equity Offerings." *Journal of Financial Economics*, 1991, pp. 35–57.

McClatchey, C. A., and G. V. Karels. "Deposit Insurance and Risk-Taking Behavior in the Credit Union Industry." Working paper.

McGough, R. "Mutual Funds Rake in a Record $29.39 Billion." *The Wall Street Journal*, February 28, 1997, p. C1.

Meier, K. J. *The Political Economy of Regulation: The Case of Insurance*. Albany, NY: State University of New York Press, 1988.

Merton, R. C. "On the Pricing of Corporate Debt: The Risk Structure of Interest Rates." *Journal of Finance* 29 (1974), pp. 449–470.

Mester, L. "Efficient Production of Financial Services; Scale and Scope Economics." *Economic Review*, Federal Reserve Bank of Philadelphia, January–February 1987, pp. 15–25.

Mester, L., and A. Saunders. "When Does the Prime Rate Change?" *Journal of Banking and Finance* 19 (1995), pp. 743–764.

Morgan, D. P. "The Credit Effects of Monetary Policy: Evidence Using Loan Commitments." *Journal of Money, Credit, and Banking*, February 1998, pp. 102–118.

Morrison, J. "News and Trends: Derivatives Showed Gains in All Sectors, ISDA Surveys Says." *The Bond Buyer*, July 16, 1996, p. 30.

Munter, P. H., D. K. Clancy, and C. T. Moores. "Accounting for Financial Futures: A Question of Risk Reduction." *Advances in Accounting* 3 (1986), pp. 51–70.

Muscarella, C., and M. R. Vetsuypens. "A Simple Test of Baron's Model of IPO Underpricing." *Journal of Financial Economics* 24 (1989), pp. 125–136.

Nabar, P., S. Park, and A. Saunders. "Prime Rate Changes: Is There an Advantage in Being First?" *Journal of Business* 66 (1993), pp. 69–92.

National Association of Insurance Commissioners. Investments of Insurers Model Act, draft. Washington, DC: NAIC, August 12, 1994.

"NationsBank: An Excess of Zeal." *Business Week*, November 28, 1994, pp. 104–106.

The *New York Times*, September 16, 1992, p. D2; November 29, 1994, p. D1; January 21, 1995, p. 78; February 1, 1995, p. 1, p. C1; July 5, 1996, p. D1; February 6, 1997, p. D1; December 19, 1997, p. D3; January 2, 1998, p. D5.

Office of Economic Analysis. *Focus Report*. Washington, DC: U.S. Securities and Exchange Commission, 1997.

Padley, K. "Public's Confidence in Bank System Tested." *Investor's Daily*, January 8, 1991, p. 1.

Palia, D. "Recent Evidence on Bank Mergers." *Financial Markets, Instruments, and Institutions* 3, no. 5 (1994), pp. 36–59.

"Pitcairn Cuts Govies." *Bondweek*, May 26,1997, p. 8.

Powell, B. "The Globe Shudders: The Asian Contagion Spreads, Sending the World's Markets on a Wild Ride." *Newsweek*, November 10, 1997, p. 32.

"A Question of Collateral." *Euromoney*, November 1995, pp. 46–49.

Raghavan, A., and S. Lipin. "Morgan Stanley Group and Dean Witter Plan an $8.8 Billion Merger: They Face Challenge Melding Elite Institutional Firm with Large Retail Broker. The *Wall Street Journal*, February 5, 1997, p. A1.

Rock, K. "Why New Issues Are Underpriced." *Journal of Financial Economics* 15 (1986), pp. 187–212.

Ross, S., R. Westerfield, and J. Jaffe. *Corporate Finance*, 4th edition. Burr Ridge, IL: Irwin/McGraw-Hill, 1996.

Rossi, C. "The Viability of the Thrift Industry." Washington, DC: Office of Thrift Supervision, December 1992.

Roy, E. "Federated Cuts Duration Ahead of FOMC." *The Bond Buyer*, November 13, 1996, p. 6.

Salomon Brothers. *Bank Annual: 1996 Edition*.

———. *Emerging Market Research*, November 14, 1996.

Sandor, R. L. "U.S. Catastrophes." New York: Centre Financial Products, 1949–1994.

Saunders, A. "Why Are So Many Stock Issues Underpriced?" *Business Review*, Federal Reserve Bank of Philadelphia, March–April 1990, pp. 3–12.

Saunders, A., and I. Walter. *Universal Banking in the U.S.?* New York: Oxford University Press, 1994.

———. *Financial System Design: Universal Banking Considered*. Burr Ridge, IL: Irwin Professional Publishing, 1996.

Saunders, A., and B. Wilson. "Informed and Uninformed Depositor Runs and Panics." *Journal of Financial Intermediation*, 1996.

———. "Bank Capital Structure: An Analysis of the Charter Value Hypothesis." Working paper, New York: Salomon Center–New York University, December 1996.

Schmeltzer, J. "Jayhawk Sets Its Sights on Market for Vanity Loans." The *Chicago Tribune*, March 10, 1997, p. 5, Zone: C.

Sczudio, R. S. "NAFTA: Opportunities Abound for U.S. and Canadian Financial Institutions." *Bankers Magazine*, July–August 1993, pp. 28–32.

"SEC Official Sees Small-Market Fund Liquidity Risk." *The Reuters Business Report*, November 12, 1996.

Security Trends, October 19, 1992.

Seiberg, J. "Risk-Management Models Kept Even Keel in Topsy-Turvy Week." *The American Banker*, October 31, 1997, p. 3.

———. "Reliance on Sweep Accounts May Prompt Fed to Revise Requirement Rules." *The American Banker*, January 2, 1997, p. 1.

Sesit, M. R., and M. Murray. "Chase Manhattan Pounded in Emerging Markets." The *Wall Street Journal*, November 3, 1997, p. A4.

Shirouzu, N., S. Frank, and S. McGee. "Sumitomo Puts Its Copper Losses at $2.6 Billions, Will Sue Ex-Trader." The *Wall Street Journal*, September 20, 1996, p. C1.

Silber, W. L. "Municipal Revenue Bond Costs and Bank Under-writing: A Survey of the Evidence." Monograph Series in Finance and Economics, Salomon Center for the Study of Financial Institutions, New York University, 1979.

Spong, K., and J. D. Shoenhair. "Performance of Banks Acquired on an Interstate Basis." *Financial Industry Perspectives*, Federal Reserve Bank of Kansas City, December 1992, pp. 15–23.

Standard and Poor's. *Industry Survey: Insurance*. New York: Standard and Poor's, 1994, pp. 1–3.

Stoebe, R. "Macrohedging Bank Investment Portfolios." *Bankers Magazine*, November–December 1994, pp. 45–48.

Swary, I. "Stock Market Reaction to Regulatory Action in the Continental Illinois Crisis." *Journal of Business* 59 (1986), pp. 451–473.

"Sweeps of Retail Transaction Deposits." *Federal Reserve Bulletin*, August 1996, p. 715.

Travlos, N. "Corporate Takeover Bids, Methods of Payment, and Bidding Firm Stock Returns." *Journal of Finance* 42 (1987), pp. 943–963.

Treasury Bulletin, December 1997, pp. 98–102.

U.S. Treasury. "Modernizing the Financial System." Washington, DC: U.S. Treasury Department, 1991.

———. *Modernizing the Financial System: Recommendations for Safer, More Competitive Banks*. Washington, DC: U.S. Treasury Department, February 1991.

Wagster, J. "Impact of the Basle Accord on International Banks." *Journal of Finance*, September 1996, pp. 1321–1346.

Wagster, J., J. Kolari, and K. Cooper. "Market Reaction to National Discretion in Implementing the Basle Accord." *Journal of Financial Research*, Fall 1996, pp. 339–357.

Wall, L., and D. R. Peterson. "The Effect of Continental Illinois' Failure on the Performance of Other Banks." *Journal of Monetary Economics*, 1990, pp. 77–99.

The *Wall Street Journal*, January 15, 1997, p. A4; October 27, 1997, pp. C14, C15, C19, C24; January 21, 1998, p. C24; February 27, 1998, p. C25.

Weber, B. "A Note on the Impact of Financial Technology: Money and Electronic Money." Stern School of Business, New York University, September 1997.

Weinberger, A. "Insurance Strategies." Salomon Brothers, August 2, 1993.

Wheelock, D. C. "A Changing Relationship Between Bank Size and Profitability." *Monetary Trends*, Federal Reserve Bank of St. Louis, September 1996, p. 1.

White, L. J. *The S and L Debacle*. New York: Oxford University Press, 1991, p. 89.

Wilke, J. R. "Banks' Profits Climbed to Record in Third Quarter." The *Wall Street Journal*, December 12, 1997, A2.

Wirth, G., and E. Copulsky. "No Signs of Slowing." *Investment Dealers' Digest*, October 6, 1997, p. 14.

Wulff, M. "Automated Loan Machines Migrate to the Net." *Financial NetNews*, October 7, 1996, p. 1.

Wyatt, E. "A Low-Key Fund Group Nears a Limelight Level: Money Markets Approach $1 Trillion." The *New York Times*, February 2, 1997, p. F4.

Index

The Regulators of Financial Institutions

Federal Deposit Insurance Corporation (FDIC): The FDIC insures the deposits of its member commercial banks and savings institutions. To do so, it levies insurance premiums on member institutions, manages the deposit insurance fund, and conducts bank examinations. When an insured bank is closed, the FDIC acts as the receiver and liquidator. The FDIC oversees the Bank Insurance Fund (BIF) for commercial and savings banks and the Savings Association Insurance Fund (SAIF) for savings and loans.

Office of the Comptroller of the Currency (OCC): The OCC determines the issuance of charters and the closures of national banks. It examines national banks and has the power to approve or disapprove their merger applications.

Federal Reserve System (FRS): In addition to being concerned with the conduct of monetary policy, the FRS, as this country's central bank, also has regulatory power over some banks and (when relevant) their holding company parents. The FRS regulates and examines both banks and bank holding companies. All nationally chartered banks are members of the FRS.

State Regulators: State-chartered commercial banks, savings institutions, and credit unions are regulated by state agencies.

Office of Thrift Supervision (OTS): The OTS charters and examines all federal savings and loans. It also supervises the holding companies of savings and loans.

National Credit Union Administration (NCUA): The NCUA regulates federally chartered credit unions. It oversees the National Credit Union Insurance Fund (NCUIF) and accordingly, examines credit unions covered by this fund.

State Insurance Commissioners: These commissioners charter, supervise, and examine life insurance companies and property-casualty insurance companies in their home states. States also promote life insurance and property-casualty guaranty funds that require surviving within-state insurance companies to compensate the policyholders of an insurer after a failure has occurred.

National Association of Insurance Commissioners (NAIC): NAIC is a national organization consisting of state insurance commissioners. State insurance commissions supervise and examine insurance companies using a coordinated examination system developed by the NAIC. The association also provides state property-casualty commissioners with the Insurance Regulatory Information System (IRIS) to identify insurers with loss, combined, and other ratios operating outside normal ranges.

Securities and Exchange Commission (SEC): The SEC is the primary regulator of securities firms, investment banks, and mutual funds. Among other things, the SEC sets rules governing securities firms' underwriting and trading activities. Mutual funds are required to file a registration statement with the SEC, which in turn sets rules and procedures regarding the fund's prospectus that is sent to investors. The SEC also requires mutual funds to furnish full and accurate information on all financial and corporate matters to prospective fund purchasers.

New York Stock Exchange (NYSE) and National Association of Securities Dealers (NASD): These organizations regulate the day-to-day trading practices on their exchanges (the New York Stock Exchange and the National Association of Securities Dealers Automated Quotation, or NASDAQ) by monitoring trading abuses and securities firms' capital. The NASD also supervises mutual fund share distributions.

Securities Investor Protection Corporation (SIPC): The SIPC protects investors against losses of up to $100,000 on securities firm failures due to other than poor investment choices by management. The fund is financed by premium contributions from member firms.